SEVENTEENTH EDITION

Introduction to Finance

Markets, Investments, and Financial Management

Ronald W. Melicher

Professor Emeritus of Finance
University of Colorado at Boulder

and

Edgar A. Norton

Professor of Finance
Illinois State University

WILEY

VP AND EDITORIAL DIRECTOR	Mike McDonald
EXECUTIVE EDITOR	Lise Johnson
EDITORIAL MANAGER	Judy Howarth
CONTENT MANAGEMENT DIRECTOR	Lisa Wojcik
CONTENT MANAGER	Nichole Urban
SENIOR CONTENT SPECIALIST	Nicole Repasky
PRODUCTION EDITOR	Meghana Antony
COVER PHOTO CREDIT	© colin wilson/Getty Images

This book was set in 10/12 TimesLTStd-Roman by SPi Global, Chennai and printed and bound by Quad/Graphics.

Founded in 1807, John Wiley & Sons, Inc. has been a valued source of knowledge and understanding for more than 200 years, helping people around the world meet their needs and fulfill their aspirations. Our company is built on a foundation of principles that include responsibility to the communities we serve and where we live and work. In 2008, we launched a Corporate Citizenship Initiative, a global effort to address the environmental, social, economic, and ethical challenges we face in our business. Among the issues we are addressing are carbon impact, paper specifications and procurement, ethical conduct within our business and among our vendors, and community and charitable support. For more information, please visit our website: www.wiley.com/go/citizenship.

ISBN: 978-1-119-56117-0 (PBK)
ISBN: 978-1-119-60524-9 (EVALC)

LCCN: 2019032259

The inside back cover will contain printing identification and country of origin if omitted from this page. In addition, if the ISBN on the back cover differs from the ISBN on this page, the one on the back cover is correct.

SKY10027994_070721

To my wife, Sharon, and our children, Michelle, Sean, and Thor

Ronald W. Melicher

To my best friend and wife, Becky; our son Matthew and his wife, Angie; our daughter Amy and her husband, Jake

Edgar A. Norton

Preface

The seventeenth edition of *Introduction to Finance: Markets, Investments, and Financial Management* builds upon the successes of its earlier editions while maintaining fresh and up-to-date coverage of the field of finance. This edition introduces several new electronic features to assist with student access to the textbook and with learning.

Our text is designed to present a more-balanced first course in finance, one that offers students perspectives on financial markets, investing, and financial management. We use a successful pedagogy that reviews, first, markets and institutions; then, the world of investments; and finally, the concepts and applications of business financial management.

Unlike other textbooks with a singular "corporate finance" focus, our text offers a balanced first course in finance. Eighteen chapters cover the three major financial areas involving the financial system, investments, and business finance. For the student who does not plan to take additional courses in finance, this book provides a valuable overview of the discipline's major concepts. For the student who wants to take additional courses in finance, the overview presented provides a solid foundation upon which future courses can build.

Introduction to Finance is meant to be used in a course whose purpose is to survey the foundations of the finance discipline. As such, it is designed to meet the needs of students in various programs. Specifically, *Introduction to Finance* can be used in any of the following four ways:

1. As the first course in finance at a college or university where the department wants to expose students to a broad foundational survey of the discipline.

2. As the first and only course in finance for nonfinance business students.

3. As an appropriate text to use at a school that seeks to provide liberal arts majors with a business minor or business concentration. The writing level is appropriate to provide students with a good foundation in the basics of our discipline.

4. As a "lower division" service course whose goal is to attract freshmen and sophomores to business and to attract them to become finance majors.

The philosophy behind the book is threefold. First, we believe that a basic understanding of the complex world of finance should begin with a survey course that covers an introduction to financial markets, investments, and financial management or business finance. Students can gain an integrated perspective of the interrelationships among these three areas. They will appreciate how businesses and individuals are affected by markets and institutions, as well as of how markets and institutions can be used to meet the goals of individuals or firms. Given the events in the financial markets and the economy in 2007–2009 and the financial implications of the United Kingdom's 2016 decision to withdraw from the European Union (known as "Brexit"), this integrated perspective adds value to student learning and an understanding of the field.

Second, we wrote the book as an introductory survey of finance with a readable and user-friendly focus in mind. We seek to convey basic knowledge, concepts, and terms that will serve the nonfinance major into the future and that will form a foundation upon which the finance major can build. Some finer points, discussions of theory, and complicated topics are reserved for "Learning Extensions" in selected chapters. We aim to make students using our text financially literate and cognizant of the richness of finance. The book provides a good foundation for students to build upon in later courses in financial management, investments, or financial markets.

Third, we focus on the practice of finance in the settings of markets, investments, and financial management. We focus on the descriptive in each of these fields. We don't want students to be unable to see the forest of finance because the trees of quantitative methods obscure their view or scare them away. When we do introduce equations and mathematical concepts that are applicable to finance, we will show step-by-step solutions.

By learning about markets (including gaining knowledge about institutions), investments, and management as the three major strands of finance, students will finish their course with a greater understanding of how these three fields interrelate. Financial markets will be seen as the arena to which businesses and financial institutions go to raise funds, and as the mechanism through which individuals can invest their savings to meet their future goals. The topic of investments is important in facilitating the savings–investment process. Understanding the trade-off of risk and return, as well as the valuation of bonds and stocks, is essential to investors and businesses raising financial capital. Understanding how securities markets work is equally important. Financial management uses information it obtains from securities and other financial markets to efficiently and profitably manage assets and to raise needed funds in a cost-efficient manner.

A broad exposure to the discipline of finance will meet the needs of nonmajors who should know the basics of finance so they can read the *The Wall Street Journal*, visit business-related Internet sites, and analyze other business information sources intelligently. It will help the nonfinance major work as a member of a cross-functional work team, a team that will include finance professionals. In addition, this overview of finance will start the finance major off on the right foot. Rather than receiving a compartmentalized idea of finance—often viewed through the corporate finance lens that many texts use—the finance major will receive a practical introduction to the different disciplines of finance, and will better appreciate the relationships among them.

Part 1 of the book contains six chapters on the financial system, with primary emphasis on financial markets and the tools and skills necessary to better understand how such markets work. We begin with an overview of the three main subfields of finance, identify the "six principles of finance," and discuss career opportunities. The principles of finance are the following:

1. Money has a time value.

2. Higher returns are expected for taking on more risk.

3. Diversifying one's investments can reduce risk.

4. Financial markets are efficient in pricing securities.

5. The objectives of managers and stockholders may differ.

6. Reputation matters.

We discuss finance and the role and functions of the financial system to a nation's economy. The role of banks, other financial intermediaries, and the Federal Reserve are reviewed, as are their functions in the financial system. Part 1 introduces the international role of finance and how modern economies are affected by exchange rates, trade, and the flow of global funds.

Following this introduction to the financial system, Part 2 focuses on investments. We review the role of savings in an economy and the ways in which funds flow to and from different sectors. Interest rates are introduced, and the discussion centers on making the student aware of the different influences on interest rate levels and why the rates change over time. Because interest rates measure the cost of moving money across time, this section reviews basic time-value-of-money concepts with many worked-out examples, including the keystrokes that students can use when working with financial calculators.

Next, after reviewing the characteristics of bonds and stocks, students will learn to apply time-value-of-money concepts to find the prices of these securities. Continuing our overview of investments, we discuss investment banking basics and the operations of securities markets, as well as the fundamentals of investment risks and returns, to conclude Part 2. Advanced classes may want to review the financial derivatives basics, which are explained in a Learning Extension of Chapter 11's discussion of securities and markets.

The raising of funds by businesses in the institutional and market environments is covered in Parts 1 and 2. Next, in Part 3, the final six chapters of the text introduce students to financial management. The discussion begins with the different ways in which to organize a business, and the financial implications of each organizational form. We introduce accounting concepts, such as the balance sheet, income statement, and statement of cash flows, with simple examples. We discuss financial ratios, which assist in the process of analyzing a firm's strengths and weaknesses. We review their use as a means of helping managers plan ahead for future asset and financing needs. Strategies for managing a firm's current assets and current liabilities are examined, as are the funding sources firms use to tap the financial markets for short-term financing. Finally, we introduce students to capital budgeting basics and capital structure concepts.

NEW AND IMPROVED

Many new pedagogical features are included in the textbook, including the following:

- An enhanced e-book format for electronic access to the textbook and related learning material. A paperback version is available as well for those preferring a print copy.

- Coordinated chapter learning objectives, chapter summaries, and end-of-chapter review questions. Each chapter learning objective is numbered; the expanded chapter summaries review each individual learning objective and each review question is keyed to a specific learning objective number.

- Every chapter contains 3 or 4 Discussion Questions that can be used in class, assigned to students, or used by the instructor on learning management systems such as Blackboard, Moodle, Sakai, and others to form the basis of graded or ungraded class participation and critical thinking.

- The enhanced e-book version presents, at the end of each section (corresponding to each learning objective) several multiple choice questions for students to use as a review of chapter concepts.

- Key terms, new to the seventeenth edition, are introduced and discussed in several chapters.

- Some of the tables, charts, and graphics include interactive features that allow students to sort, categorize, or focus on a single graph feature at a time as it changes values over time.

- Excel templates have been updated and revised to reflect the book's content.

- Existing test bank items were re-examined and new questions added to reflect the many content changes and to better test student knowledge.

The content of *Introduction to Finance* has been updated to incorporate many of the economic and financial events of the past few years. The financial crisis of 2007–2008 and the subsequent recession and recovery—along with the behavior of the Federal Reserve and securities markets—provide a means to highlight causes, effects, and the integration of finance into our everyday lives, as well as the implications for markets, investments, and business finance. A *financial crisis* colored label, denoting a "Focus Point," is placed next to relevant text material.

We continue with our innovation found in previous editions, featuring a real firm (Walgreens Boots Alliance, the retail drugstore chain) in many of the chapters on investments and financial management as a means of presenting and analyzing data.

In addition to these broad improvements, all chapters have been updated and revised to reflect recent events and data. Specific notable changes in this seventeenth edition include the following:

Chapter 1, The Financial Environment, provides an overview of the financial system and environment within the framework of capitalism and democracy. The U.S. operates in a mixed market capitalistic economic system which combines elements of a free market system with elements of a planned economic system administered by the federal government. The U.S. is a representative democracy where citizens elect representatives from amongst their peers who vote on government economic goals and actions. Understanding economic and financial developments during the 2007–2008 financial crisis and the 2008–2009 Great Recession will hopefully avoid repeating similar economic problems in the future.

Chapter 2, Money and the Monetary System, discusses the process of moving savings into investments and provides an overview of the monetary system. While physical money (coin and paper currency) in the United States continues to be our focus, we provide new materials on the use of electronic money in the form of digital currency, virtual currency, and cryptocurrency, with bitcoin being a type of cryptocurrency. The relationship between money supply and economic activity is discussed in light of changing monetary policies.

Chapter 3, Banks and Other Financial Institutions, covers the types and roles of financial institutions. During the 2007–2009 period, falling housing prices, mortgage loan defaults, and declining values on mortgage-backed securities that resulted in many financial institutions not having adequate equity capital to continue to operate, and, thus, needing to merge or be "bailed out." The ability of banks to maintain sound balance sheets, including adequate capital ratios, continues to be of concern.

Chapter 4, Federal Reserve System, describes the current structure and operations of the Federal Reserve. The Fed's near zero interest rate targets and its use of quantitative easing efforts in response to the 2007–2009 financial crisis and economic downturn is covered. We also present materials on the Fed's ending of its easy money policies in late 2015 when it increased its target for the federal funds rate in December 2015 and followed with several more increases by the end of 2018. Jerome Powell, who was appointed chair of the Fed's board of governors in April 2018, is faced with the difficult task of simultaneously maintaining economic growth and raising interest rates to more normal historical levels.

Chapter 5, Policy Makers and the Money Supply, describes how the four policy maker groups (Federal Reserve System, the President, Congress, and the U.S. Treasury) operate within the context of democracy and capitalism. These policy makers are responsible for carrying out the national economic policy objectives of economic growth, high employment, and price stability. We review the U.S. government's response to the perfect financial storm involving the financial crisis and the subsequent Great Recession. We discuss the impact of the Tax Cuts and Jobs Act of 2017, which reduced tax rates for corporations and individuals, on the federal budget. An annual deficit of $1 trillion or more is expected in fiscal 2019.

Chapter 6, International Finance and Trade, covers the evolution of the international monetary system and efforts by European countries to achieve unification. The status of Brexit, the United Kingdom's plan to withdraw from the European Union still was not approved as of early 2019. We discuss the use of hedging, forward contracts, and forward rates in the section that covers managing currency exchange risk. The possible use of trade tariffs on imports to bring export and import amounts more in balance is discussed. Of course, imposing tariffs could result in retaliatory trade tariffs by a trading partner and a possible trade war. Countries with large trade deficits might also try to negotiate more favorable trade agreements as a way of improving exports relative to imports.

Chapter 7, Savings and Investment Process, discusses the relationship between gross domestic product and capital formation. The U.S. practices democratic capitalism which is a country or state organized as a democracy that uses or adopts a capitalistic economic system. Capital formation involves the creation of capital goods including buildings, equipment, and business inventories. Capital goods, in turn, are used to make more goods and provide more services which leads to higher gross domestic product. The savings–investment or capital formation process begins with the creation of savings that are, in turn, invested to produce capital goods. We cover the major sources of income and outlays involved in the annual federal budget. Recent data on personal and corporate savings are presented and discussed. Capital market securities are described and characteristics of mortgage markets are discussed.

Chapter 8, Interest Rates, discusses the supply and demand for loanable funds and the components of market interest rates. We introduce the concept of a negative interest rate which occurs when a bank or government charges depositors or investors to keep their money with the bank or to hold government debt securities. Negative interest rates have been used as a monetary policy tool by several central banks who have charged member banks interest on their excess reserves held at the central banks. Yield curves currently are flat, that is the short-term interest rates and longer-term interest rates on government securities are nearly the same. While the Fed has forced up short-term rates, longer-term rates have remained relatively low. Recent default risk premium levels are also presented and discussed.

Chapter 9, Time Value of Money, conveys the importance of compounding (earning interest on interest) in building wealth over time. We continue to present examples of how to perform time value calculations using formulas, interest factor tables, step-by-step financial calculator keystrokes, and Excel spreadsheets. We introduce the concept of an inflation-adjusted interest rate which is an interest rate earned after adjusting for the change in purchasing power. In instances where the actual inflation rate exceeds the expected default risk-free rate (a real rate plus an expected inflation rate), the result would be a negative inflation-adjusted rate due to the loss of purchasing power. We also provide coverage of the cost of consumer credit.

Chapter 10, Bond and Stocks: Characteristics and Valuations, uses the "annual percentage rate" (APR) approach as opposed to the "effective interest rate" (EAR) approach in the bond valuation section. The chapter contains updated data and improved discussions of bonds and stocks. We have revised the discussion of the risks facing investors in the low interest rate environment sustained by the Fed since the Great Recession. Spreadsheet examples show how to apply time value concepts to calculate bond prices and stock prices.

Chapter 11, Securities and Markets, incorporates changes in securities trading, including high-frequency trading. We updated discussions of IPO and post-IPO stock market performance of firms in recent years. This chapter's Learning Extension on futures and options has been revised to reflect reviewer suggestions.

Chapter 12, Financial Returns and Risk Concepts, is one of the more mathematical chapters; it shows how to do calculations with step-by-step calculator keystrokes and spreadsheet functions. Its content is updated, especially evidence regarding the difficulty in "beating the market" by active investors.

Chapter 13, Business Organization and Financial Data, features data from the Walgreens Boots Alliance's financial statements. We maintain that a firm's goal is to maximize shareholder wealth, and we discuss "sustainability" in light of this goal. The Learning Extension is updated to reflect tax rate and other changes due to the Tax Cut and Jobs Act of 2017.

Chapter 14, Financial Analysis and Long-Term Financial Planning, uses updated data from Walgreens and one of its competitors, CVS, in a practical example of financial ratio analysis using industry averages.

Chapter 15, Managing Working Capital, expands the discussion of managing cash in a difficult business environment with low interest rates. We discuss how the Tax Cut and Jobs Act of 2017 should encourage firms to bring overseas cash into the United States.

Chapter 16, Short-Term Business Financing, contains information on real firms' working capital financing strategies and on the implications of the financial crisis on a firm's ability to obtain short-term financing, including the role of "supply chain financing" by some banks and suppliers. We include a section on the American Energy and Infrastructure Jobs Act of 2012 (JOBS Act of 2012), a tool to help small firms obtain financing, including the use of "crowdfunding."

Chapter 17, Capital Budgeting Analysis, relates the cash flow estimation process for a project to the firm's statement of cash flows found in Chapter 13 and reviews standard capital budgeting analysis tools, such as net present value (NPV), internal rate of return (IRR), profitability index (PI), and modified internal rate of return (MIRR).

Chapter 18, Capital Structure and the Cost of Capital, contains updated discussions of trends in the use of debt by corporations and the use of debt financing in the low interest rate environment that has existed since the Great Recession. We include information of how managers compute capital costs from KPMG and the Cost of Capital Survey issued by the Association of Finance Professionals.

LEARNING AND TEACHING AIDS

The seventeenth edition of *Introduction to Finance* offers the following aids for students and instructors:

Chapter Openers: Each chapter begins with the following:

- Chapter Learning Objectives, which students can use to review the chapter's main points and which instructors can use as a basis for in-class lecture or discussion;

- Where We Have Been statements that remind students of what was covered in the previous chapters;

- Where We Are Going, which are previews of chapters to come;

- How This Chapter Applies To Me that explain how the content of the chapter, no matter how technical or business specific, has applications to the individual student.

Applying Finance To: These boxes show how the topic of each chapter relates to the finance fields of institutions and markets, investments, and financial management.

Learning Activities: We direct the student to relevant websites at different points in each chapter.

Margin Definitions: Margin definitions of key terms are provided to assist students in learning the language of finance.

Focus Icons: Icons are placed by relevant text to indicate discussions of finance principles, implications of the recent financial crisis, financial or business ethical issues, and global or international discussions.

Spreadsheet Illustrations: We show how to use spread-sheets to solve problems, and to teach students about the power of spreadsheet functions and analysis.

Boxed Features: Throughout the book, boxes are used to focus on current topics or applications of interest. They are designed to illustrate concepts and practices in the dynamic field of finance.

- Small Business Practice boxes highlight aspects of the chapter topics relating directly to small businesses and entrepreneurship.

- Career Opportunities in Finance boxes provide information about various careers in finance and appear in many chapters.

- Personal Financial Planning boxes provide insight into how the chapter's content can be applied to an individual's finances.

Learning Extensions: Chapter appendixes, called Learning Extensions, are included in many chapters. Learning Extensions provide additional in-depth coverage of topics related to their respective chapters, and many challenge students to use their mathematical skills.

End-of-Chapter Materials: Each chapter provides the following:

- Review Questions, keyed to specific chapter learning objectives that review chapter material

- Exercises and/or problems for students to work or solve, and to exercise their mathematical skills

- Problems that are more difficult and that should be solved by using spreadsheets. Downloadable templates are available for each problem.

Companion Website: The instructor's text website at www.wiley.com/go/Melicher/Introduction contains a myriad of resources and links to aid learning and teaching.

Instructor's Manual: The Instructor's Manual, written by the book's authors, is available to adopters of this text. It features detailed chapter outlines, lecture tips, and answers to end-of-chapter review questions and problems.

Test Bank: A comprehensive test bank, prepared by Ronny Richardson of Kennesaw State University, is available for use by instructors in both print and computerized versions.

Powerpoint Presentations: Created by the authors, a PowerPoint presentation is provided for each chapter of the text. Slides include outline notes on the chapter, additional presentation topics, and figures and tables from the text.

Image Gallery: A complete set of images is provided for each chapter of the text for instructor's to use to create teaching materials.

Spreadsheet Templates: Excel-compatible templates are available on the instructor's website for distribution to students. Students can use the financial analysis tools worksheets and templates to help apply what they've learned in the text and solve some of the end-of-chapter problems and challenge problems.

ACKNOWLEDGMENTS

We would like to thank the Wiley Publishing team of Executive Editor, Lise Johnson, Production Editor, Meghana Antony, Editorial Manager, Judy Howarth, and Editorial Assistant, Cecilia Morales for their role in preparing and publishing the seventeenth edition of *Introduction to Finance*.

In addition, we are especially grateful to the reviewers for their comments and constructive criticisms of this and previous editions:

Saul W. Adelman, Miami University, Ohio
Tim Alzheimer, Montana State University
Allan Blair, Palm Beach Atlantic College
Stewart Bonem, Cincinnati State Technical and Community College
Linda K. Brown, St. Ambrose University
Joseph M. Byers, Community College of Allegheny County, South Campus
Robert L. Chapman, Orlando College
William Chittenden, Texas State University
Sara J. Conroy, Community College of Allegheny County
Will Crittendon, Bronx Community College
David R. Durst, University of Akron
Sharon H. Garrison, Florida Atlantic University
Asim Ghosh, Saint Joseph's University
Stephen S. Gray, Western Illinois University
Lester Hadsell, University of Albany
Irene M. Hammerbacher, Iona College
Kim Hansen, Mid-State Technical College
Jeff Hines, Davenport College
Jeff Jewell, Lipscomb University
Lisa Johnson, Centura College
Ed Krohn, Miami Dade Community College
Jessica Lancaster, McCann School of Business and Technology
P. John Limberopoulos, University of Colorado Boulder
Leslie Mathis, University of Memphis
Michael B. McDonald, Fairfield University
John K. Mullen, Clarkson University
Michael Murray, Winona State University
Napoleon Overton, University of Memphis
Michael Owen, Montana State University
Marco Pagani, San Jose State University
Jason Powers, Strayer University
Barbara L. Purvis, Centura College

Alan Questell, Richmond Community College
Ernest Scarbrough, Arizona State University
Raymond Shovlain, St. Ambrose University
Amir Tavakkol, Kansas State University
Jim Washam, Arkansas State University
Howard Whitney, Franklin University
Lawrence Wolken, Texas A&M University
K. Matthew Wong, St. John's University
David Zalewski, Providence College

Likewise, we appreciate the comments from students and teachers, who have used previous editions, and the assistance from the dozens of reviewers, who have commented about the early editions. Special recognition goes to Carl Dauten, who coauthored the first four editions, and Merle Welshans, who was a coauthor on the first nine editions of the book. Finally, and perhaps most importantly, we wish to thank our families for their understanding and support during the writing of the seventeenth edition.

RONALD W. MELICHER,
Boulder, Colorado

EDGAR A. NORTON,
Normal, Illinois

Author Bios

Ron Melicher is professor emeritus of finance and previously served three different terms as chair of the Finance Division, Leeds School of Business, University of Colorado, Boulder. He is a past president of the Financial Management Association. Ron earned undergraduate, M.B.A., and doctoral degrees from Washington University in St. Louis, Missouri. While at the University of Colorado, he received several distinguished teaching awards and was designated a university-wide President's Teaching Scholar. Ron has taught corporate finance and financial strategy and valuation in M.B.A. and Executive M.B.A. programs in addition to entrepreneurial finance and investment banking to undergraduate students. He also has taught financial management materials in executive education courses and in in-house corporate programs. His research has been published in major finance journals, including the *Journal of Finance, Journal of Financial and Quantitative Analysis,* and *Financial Management.* He is also the coauthor of *Entrepreneurial Finance,* sixth edition (Cengage Learning, 2018).

Edgar A. Norton is professor of finance and director of the Institute for Financial Planning and Analysis in the College of Business at Illinois State University. He holds a double major in computer science and economics from Rensselaer Polytechnic Institute and received his M.S. and Ph.D. from the University of Illinois at Urbana–Champaign. A Chartered Financial Analyst (CFA), he regularly receives certificates of achievement in the field of investments. He has consulted with COUNTRY Financial, Maersk, and the CFA Institute; does pro bono financial planning; and is a past president of the Midwest Finance Association. His research has appeared in numerous journals, such as *Financial Review, Journal of Business Venturing,* and *Journal of Business Ethics.* He has coauthored four textbooks, including *Introduction to Finance.*

Brief Contents

Contents

4 Federal Reserve System

82

PART 2   Investments

7   Savings and Investment Process   173

8   Interest Rates   197

9 Time Value of Money   **225**

10 Bonds and Stocks: Characteristics and Valuations   262

---

11   Securities and Markets   308

12 Financial Return and Risk Concepts   352

16   Short-Term Business Financing   503

Institutions and Markets

Ask someone what he or she thinks "finance" is about. You'll probably get a variety of responses: "It deals with money." "It is what my bank does." "The New York Stock Exchange has something to do with it." "It's how businesses and people get the money they need – you know, borrowing and stuff like that." And they'll all be correct!

Finance is a broad field. It involves national and international systems of banking and the financing of business. It also deals with the process you go through to get a car loan and what a business does when planning for its future needs.

It is important to understand that while U.S. capitalism and the financial system are quite complex, the economic system generally operates very efficiently and has produced over time economic growth and higher living standards. However, on occasion, imbalances can result in economic, real estate, and stock market "bubbles" that, when they burst, cause havoc on the workings of the financial system. The decade of the 2000s began with the bursting of the "tech" or technology bubble and the "dot.com" bubble. Then, in mid-2006, the real estate bubble, in the form of excessive housing prices, burst. This was followed by peaking stock prices in 2007 that were, in turn, followed by a steep decline that continued into early 2009. Economic activity began slowing in 2007 and deteriorated into an economic recession beginning in December, 2007, which was accompanied by double-digit unemployment rates. The result was the 2007–2009 "perfect financial storm" that produced the most distress on the U.S. financial system since the Great Depression years of the 1930s. More recently the United States has experienced ten plus years of economic growth. Of course, new economic and financial crisis probably will continue to occur in the future.

Within the general field of finance, there are three areas of study – financial institutions and markets, investments, and financial management. Financial institutions collect funds from savers and lend them to, or invest them in, businesses or people that need cash. Examples of financial institutions are commercial banks, investment banks, insurance companies, and mutual funds. Financial institutions operate as part of the financial system. The financial system is the environment of finance. It includes the laws and regulations that affect financial transactions. The financial system encompasses the Federal Reserve System, which controls the supply of money in the U.S. economy. It also consists of the mechanisms that have been constructed to facilitate the flow of money and financial securities among countries. Financial markets represent ways for bringing those who have money to invest together with those who need funds. Financial markets, which include markets for mortgages, securities, and currencies, are necessary for a financial system to operate efficiently. Part 1 of this book examines the financial system, and the role of financial institutions and financial markets in it.

Securities markets play an important role in helping businesses and governments raise new funds. Securities markets also facilitate the transfer of securities between investors. A securities market can be a central location for the trading of financial claims, such as the New York Stock Exchange. It may also take the form of a communications network, as with the over-the-counter market, which is another means by which stocks and bonds can be traded.

When people invest funds, lend or borrow money, or buy or sell shares of a company's stock, they are participating in the financial markets. Part 2 of this book examines the role of securities markets and the process of investing in bonds and stocks.

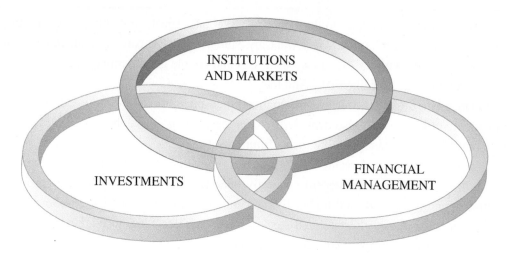

The third area of the field of finance is financial management. Financial management studies how a business should manage its assets, liabilities, and equity to produce a good or service. Whether or not a firm off ers a new product or expands production, or how to invest excess cash, are examples of decisions that financial managers are involved with. Financial managers are constantly working with financial institutions and watching financial market trends as they make investment and financing decisions. Part 3 discusses how financial concepts can help managers better manage their firms.

The three areas of finance interact with, and overlap, one another. Financial institutions operate in the environment of the financial markets and work to meet the financial needs of individuals and businesses. Financial managers do analyses and make decisions based on information they obtain from the financial markets. They also work with financial institutions when they need to raise funds and when they have excess funds to invest. Participants investing in the financial markets use information from financial institutions and firms to evaluate different investments in securities such as stocks, bonds, and certificates of deposit. A person working in one field must be knowledgeable about all three. Thus, this book is designed to provide you with a survey of all three areas of finance.

Part 1, Institutions and Markets, presents an overview of the financial system and its important components: policy makers, monetary system, financial institutions, and financial markets. Financial institutions operate within the financial system to facilitate the work of the financial markets. For example, you can put your savings in a bank and earn interest. But your money just doesn't sit in the bank. The bank takes your deposit and the money from other depositors and lends it to Kathy, who needs a short-term loan for her business; to Ian for a college loan; and to Roger and Jayden, who borrow the money to help buy a house. Banks bring together savers and those who need money, such as Kathy, Ian, Roger, and Jayden. The interest rate the depositors earn and the interest rate that borrowers pay are determined by national and even international economic forces. Just what the bank does with depositors' money and how it reviews loan applications is determined to some extent by bank regulators and financial market participants, such as the Federal Reserve Board. Decisions by the president and Congress relating to fiscal policies and regulatory laws may also directly influence financial institutions and markets and alter the financial system.

Chapter 1 provides an overview of the financial environment. Chapter 2 covers the role and functions of money, money market securities, and the interaction of money supply and economic activity in the monetary system. Depository institutions, such as banks and savings and loan associations, as well as other financial institutions involved in the financial inter-mediation process are the topics of Chapter 3. The Federal Reserve System, the U.S. central bank that controls the money supply, is discussed in Chapter 4. Chapter 5 places the previous chapters in perspective, discussing the role of the Federal Reserve and the banking system in helping meet national economic goals for the United States, such as economic growth, high levels of employment, and stable prices. Part 1 concludes with a discussion of the international monetary system, currency exchange markets and rates, and international trade in Chapter 6.

The Financial Environment

CHAPTER 1

LEARNING OBJECTIVES

After studying this chapter, you should be able to do the following:

LO 1.1 Define *finance* and describe the three areas of finance.

LO 1.2 Explain why finance should be studied.

LO 1.3 Describe and discuss the six principles of finance.

LO 1.4 Identify the four components of the financial system and describe their roles.

LO 1.5 Describe financial markets characteristics and the four types of financial markets.

LO 1.6 Identify several major career opportunities in finance.

LO 1.7 Describe this textbook's plan of study.

Where we have been. . . As we progress through this book, we will start each chapter with a brief review of previously covered materials. This will provide you with a reference base for understanding the transition from topic to topic. After completing the text, you will be at the beginning of what we hope is a successful business career.

Where we are going. . . The financial environment within which we live and work is composed of a financial system, institutions, and markets. Part 1 of this text focuses on developing an understanding of the financial institutions and markets that operate to make the financial system work efficiently. Chapter 2 describes the U.S. monetary system, including how it is intertwined with the capital formation process and how it has evolved. Current types of money are described, and we discuss why it is important to control the growth of the money supply. In following chapters, we turn our attention to understanding how financial institutions, policy makers, and international developments influence how the financial system functions.

How this chapter applies to me. . . While it is impossible to predict what life has in store for each of us in terms of health, family, and career, everyone can be a productive member of society. Nearly all of us will take part in making social, political, and economic decisions. A basic understanding of the financial environment that encompasses economic and financial systems will help you in making informed economic choices.

Let us begin with the following quote by George Santayana, a U.S. philosopher and poet:

> *Those who cannot remember the past are condemned to repeat it.*[1]

While this quotation refers to the need to know something about history so that individuals can avoid repeating bad social, political, and economic decisions, it is equally important to the field of finance. It is the responsibility of all individuals to be able to make informed public choices involving the financial environment. By understanding the financial environment and studying the financial system, institutions and markets, investments, and financial management, individuals will be able to make informed economic and financial choices that will lead to better financial health and success. After studying the materials in this book, you will be better informed in making choices that affect the economy and the financial system, as well as be better prepared for a business career – possibly even one in the field of finance.

---

[1] George Santayana, *Reason in Common Sense, The Life of Reason*, Vol. 1 (Charles Scribner's Sons, 1905), p. 284.

1.1 WHAT IS FINANCE?

capitalism economic system with private ownership of assets, production of goods and services for profit, a price mechanism for allocating resources, and financial markets

Capitalism is an economic system based on private ownership of physical and financial assets, the production of goods and services for profit, a mechanism for setting prices for allocating resources, and financial markets. Private people invest their assets or wealth in the production of goods and services and selling this "supply" at a price that will produce profits. "Demand" is the price others are willing to pay for these goods and services. When demand exceeds supply, prices rise, and vice versa. When the selling prices exceed the total costs of producing and selling the goods or services, a profit is earned. The profit, in turn, can be used to invest in more plant and equipment and to hire more employees (or pay existing employees more for additional work).

In free market or *laissez-faire* capitalistic systems there is no role for government. Rather, it is argued that competition among producers of comparable goods and services will lead to lower prices and innovation. The price mechanism is also expected to allocate physical capital and wage labor resources among competing alternatives. However, capitalism without competition could result in excessive prices and limited supply if there is a single supplier, or monopolist, in a market.

Hybrid or mixed market capitalistic systems combine elements of planned economic systems that are administered by national governments with elements of free market economic systems. The United States of America is a mixed market capitalistic system. The U.S. federal government establishes economic goals and attempts to achieve those goals through fiscal and monetary policy actions. The government also regulates business activities, financial institutions, and financial markets, as well as establishes social programs for the public good.[2]

finance study of how individuals, institutions, governments, and businesses acquire, spend, and manage financial resources

We describe, define, and examine *finance* in this textbook within the framework of the U.S. capitalistic economic system. We begin by defining *finance* and describing the financial environment and the three areas of finance.

Almost every day we hear news reports about economic conditions, unemployment, price changes, interest rates, stock prices, government expenditures and taxes, and monetary policy. Many of us are often overwhelmed trying to understand and interpret developments and interactions among these topics. We begin this textbook by defining *finance* and describing the financial environment and the three areas of finance.

financial environment financial system, institutions, markets, businesses, individuals, and global interactions that help the economy operate efficiently

Finance is the study of how individuals, institutions, governments, and businesses acquire, spend, and manage money and other financial assets. Understanding finance is important to all students regardless of the discipline or area of study, because nearly all business and economic decisions have financial implications. The decision to spend or consume now (for new clothes or dinner at a fancy restaurant) rather than save or invest (for spending or consuming more in the future) is an everyday decision that we all face.

financial institutions intermediaries that help the financial system operate efficiently and transfer funds from savers to individuals, businesses, and governments that seek to spend or invest the funds

The **financial environment** encompasses the financial system, institutions or intermediaries (we will use these terms interchangeably throughout this text), financial markets, business firms, individuals, and global interactions that contribute to an efficiently operating economy. Figure 1.1 depicts the three areas of finance – institutions and markets, investments, and financial management – within the financial environment. Note that while we identify three distinct finance areas, these areas do not operate in isolation but rather interact or intersect with each other. Our focus in this book is to provide the reader with exposure to all three areas, as well as to show how they are integrated. Of course, students pursuing a major or area of emphasis in finance will take multiple courses in one or more of these areas.

financial markets locations or electronic forums that facilitate the flow of funds among investors, businesses, and governments

Financial institutions are organizations or intermediaries that help the financial system operate efficiently and transfer funds from savers and investors to individuals, businesses, and governments that seek to spend or invest the funds in physical assets (inventories, buildings, and equipment). **Financial markets** are physical locations or electronic forums that facilitate the flow of funds among investors, businesses, and governments. The **investments** area involves the sale or marketing of securities, the analysis of securities, and the management of investment risk through portfolio diversification.

Investments involves the sale or marketing of securities, the analysis of securities, and the management of investment risk through portfolio diversification

---

[2] For an extensive coverage of the history of the U.S. economic system, see: Alan Greenspan and Adrian Wooldridge, *Capitalism in America* (New York: Penguin Press, 2018).

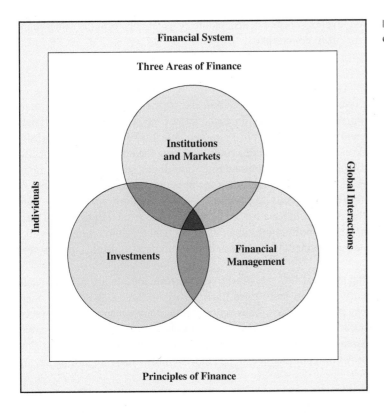

FIGURE 1.1 Graphic illustration of the financial environment

Financial management involves financial planning, asset management, and fund-raising decisions to enhance the value of businesses.

financial management involves financial planning, asset management, and fund-raising decisions to enhance the value of businesses

Finance has its origins in economics and accounting. Economists use a supply-and-demand framework to explain how the prices and quantities of goods and services are determined in a free-market economic system. Accountants provide the record-keeping mechanism for showing ownership of the financial instruments used in the flow of financial funds between savers and borrowers. Accountants also record revenues, expenses, and profitability of organizations that produce and exchange goods and services.

Efficient methods of production and specialization of labor can exist only if there is an effective means of paying for raw materials and final products. Businesses can obtain the money needed to buy capital goods, such as machinery and equipment, only if a mechanism has been established for making savings available for investment. Similarly, federal and other governmental units, such as state and local governments and tax districts, can carry out their wide range of activities only if efficient means exist for raising money, for making payments, and for borrowing.

Financial institutions, financial markets, and investment and financial management are crucial elements of the financial environment and well-developed financial systems. Financial institutions are intermediaries, such as banks, insurance companies, and investment companies that engage in financial activities to aid the flow of funds from savers to borrowers or investors.

Financial markets provide the mechanism for allocating financial resources or funds from savers to borrowers. Individuals make decisions as investors and financial managers. Investors include savers and lenders as well as equity investors.

While we focus on financial managers in this book, we recognize that individuals also must be continuously involved in managing their personal finances. Investment management involves making decisions relating to issuing and investing in stocks and bonds. Financial management in business involves making decisions relating to the efficient use of financial resources in the production and sale of goods and services. The goal of the financial manager in a profit-seeking organization should be to maximize the owners' wealth. This is accomplished through effective financial planning and analysis, asset management, and the acquisition of financial capital. Financial managers in not-for-profit organizations aim to provide a desired level of services at acceptable costs and perform the same financial management functions as their for-profit counterparts.

1.1.1 TWO THEMES

As we progress through this book, we offer two themes within the financial institutions and markets, investments, and financial management topic areas. In each chapter we provide boxed materials relating to *small business practice* and *personal financial planning*. Successful businesses typically progress through a series of life-cycle stages – from the idea stage to exiting the business. More specifically, the successful business typically moves through five stages: development, start-up, survival, rapid growth, and maturity. Individuals who choose to become small business owners do so for a number of different reasons. Some small business owners focus on salary-replacement opportunities, where they seek income levels comparable to what they could have earned by working for much larger firms. Other individuals pursue lifestyle small business opportunities, where they get paid for doing things they like to do. Entrepreneurs seek to own and run businesses that stress high growth rates in sales, profits, and cash flows.

entrepreneurial finance study of how growth-driven, performance-focused, early-stage firms raise financial capital and manage operations and assets

Entrepreneurial finance is the study of how growth-driven, performance-focused, early-stage firms (from development through early rapid growth) raise financial capital and manage their operations and assets. Our small business practice boxes focus on operational and financial issues faced by early stage firms. **Personal finance** is the study of how individuals prepare for financial emergencies, protect against premature death and the loss of property, and accumulate wealth over time. Our personal financial planning boxes focus on planning decisions made by individuals, regarding saving and investing their financial resources.

personal finance study of how individuals prepare for financial emergencies, protect against premature death and property losses, and accumulate wealth

LEARNING ACTIVITY

Go to the Small Business Administration website, https://www.sba.gov, and explore what is involved in deciding whether to start a new business.

1.2 WHY STUDY FINANCE?

The initial two decades of the twenty-first century have been an economically volatile time in the United States and worldwide. Whereas the 1990s decade was a period of economic growth and prosperity, the early part of the twenty-first century has been characterized by economic and financial markets volatility, along with many individuals just "treading water" in trying to maintain the standards of living they had previously achieved.

A "price bubble" for technology stocks, including so-called "dot.com" start-ups, burst in the United States in 2000. An economic downturn followed and was exacerbated by the terrorist attack on September 11, 2001. Economic recovery occurred over several years until the housing price bubble burst in 2006 and housing values declined sharply. Securities tied to housing prices also declined sharply, causing concerns that "overborrowed" financial institutions might fail because they held insufficient equity capital resources to cover the decline in values of the home mortgages and housing-related debt securities they held. This led to the 2007–2008 financial crisis. A major economic recession (sometimes called the Great Recession) began in late 2007 and continued through mid-2009 and turned out to be the deepest and longest recession since the Great Depression of the 1930s. Unemployment rates in the United States reached 10% in 2009. As the economy continued to recover, unemployment rates dropped to 7% in 2012, 5% in 2015, and were under 4% in 2018.

The health of economies and financial institutions and markets are linked throughout the world. European and other major foreign financial institutions were caught in the 2007–2008 financial crisis and most foreign economies suffered economic downturns near the end of the 2000s decade. Since then, European and many other economies have been slow to recover and some continued to suffer no or low economic growth in 2018. Even China, which had been growing its economy at a double-digit rate during the first decade of the 2000s, has been characterized by slowing economic activity in recent years. This has worldwide implications since many developed and developing (emerging market) economies are tied to demand for natural resources and other products manufactured by Chinese firms. Even as China attempts to move from an exports-based economy to a consumer-based economy, their

SMALL BUSINESS PRACTICE

IMPORTANCE OF SMALL FIRMS IN THE U.S. ECONOMY

As the U.S. economy moved from the industrial age to the information age, dramatic changes occurred in the importance of small businesses. While large firms with 500 or more employees continued to downsize and restructure throughout the 1990s and into the twenty-first century, small firms provided the impetus for economic growth.

During the mid-1970s through the 1980s period, firms with fewer than 500 employees provided over one-half of total employment and nearly two-thirds of the net new jobs in the United States. Small firms provided most of the net new jobs during the 1990s. And, while the decade of the 2000s involved a housing price collapse, a major financial crisis, and economic recession, small firms continued to be the primary supplier of new jobs.

Why have small firms been so successful in creating new jobs? A Small Business Administration white paper suggests two reasons. First, small firms play a crucial role in technological change and productivity growth. Market economies change rapidly, and small firms are able to adjust quickly. Second, small firms provide the mechanism and incentive for millions of individuals to pursue the opportunity for economic success.

Others may argue that it is the entrepreneurial spirit and activity that account for the importance of small firms in the U.S. economy. Whatever the reasons, the ongoing growth of small businesses continues to be an important stimulus to the economy in the early years of the twenty-first century. For current statistics, visit the Small Business Administration, Office of Advocacy website at https://www.sba.gov/advo.

---

economic slowdown has made it difficult for many U.S. and other foreign companies to grow their sales in China.

We believe the analysis and understanding of past developments in economic activity and financial markets are useful to governments, businesses, and individuals in planning their futures. By learning from the past, we may be able to avoid, or mediate, similar pitfalls in the future.

There are several reasons to study finance. Knowledge of the basics of finance covered in this text should help you make informed economic decisions, personal and business investment decisions, and career decisions.

1. *To make informed economic decisions.* As we will see, the operation of the financial system and the performance of the economy are influenced by policy makers. Individuals elect many of these policy makers in the United States, such as the president and members of Congress. Since these elected officials have the power to alter the financial system by creating laws, and since their decisions can influence economic activity, it is important that individuals be informed when making political and economic choices. Do you want a balanced budget, lower taxes, free international trade, low inflation, and full employment? Whatever your financial and economic goals may be, you need to be an informed participant if you wish to make a difference. Every individual should attain a basic understanding of finance as it applies to the financial system. Part 1 of this book focuses on understanding the roles of financial institutions and markets and how the financial system works.

2. *To make informed personal and business investment decisions.* An understanding of finance should help you better understand how the institution, government unit, or business that you work for finances its operations. At a personal level, the understanding of investments will enable you to better manage your financial resources and provide the basis for making sound decisions for accumulating wealth over time. Thus, in addition to understanding finance basics relating to the financial system and the economy, you also need to develop an understanding of the factors that influence interest rates and security prices. Part 2 of this book focuses on understanding the characteristics of stocks and bonds and how they are valued, on securities markets and how to make risk versus return investment decisions.

3. *To make informed career decisions based on a basic understanding of business finance.* Even if your business interest is in a nonfinance career or professional activity, you likely will need to interact with finance professionals both within and outside your firm or organization. Doing so will require a basic knowledge of the concepts, tools, and applications of financial management. Part 3 of this book focuses on providing you with an understanding of how finance is applied within a firm by focusing on decision-making by financial managers.

Of course, you may be interested in pursuing a career in finance or at least want to know what people who work in finance actually do. Throughout this text, you will find discussions of career opportunities in finance, as well as a boxed feature entitled Career Opportunities in Finance.

DISCUSSION QUESTION 1

Are individuals in the United States "better off" economically now than they were at the beginning of the twenty-first century? Why?

1.3 SIX PRINCIPLES OF FINANCE

FINANCE Finance is founded on six important principles. The first five relate to the economic behavior of individuals, and the sixth focuses on ethical behavior. Knowing about these principles will help us understand how managers, investors, and others incorporate time and risk into their decisions, as well as why the desire to earn excess returns leads to information-efficient financial markets in which prices reflect available information. Unfortunately, sometimes greed associated with the desire to earn excess returns causes individuals to risk losing their reputations by engaging in questionable ethical behavior and even unethical behavior in the form of fraud or other illegal activities. The bottom line is "Reputation matters!" The following are the six principles that serve as the foundation of finance:

- Money has a time value.

- Higher returns are expected for taking on more risk.

- Diversification of investments can reduce risk.

- Financial markets are efficient in pricing securities.

- Manager and stockholder objectives may differ.

- Reputation matters.

1.3.1 TIME VALUE OF MONEY

Let's look at these principles one by one. Money in hand today is worth more than the promise of receiving the same amount in the future. The "time value" of money exists because a sum of money today could be invested and grow over time. For example, assume that you have $1,000 today and that it could earn $60 (6%) interest over the next year. Thus, $1,000 today would be worth $1,060 at the end of one year (i.e. $1,000 plus $60). As a result, a dollar today is worth more than a dollar received a year from now. The time-value-of-money principle helps us to understand the economic behavior of individuals and the economic decisions of the institutions and businesses that they run. This finance principle pillar is apparent in many of our day-to-day activities, and knowledge of it will help us better understand the implications of time-varying money decisions. We explore the details of the time value of money in Chapter 9, but this first principle of finance will be apparent throughout this book.

1.3.2 RISK VERSUS RETURN

A trade-off exists between risk and expected return in all types of investments – both assets and securities. Risk is the uncertainty about the outcome or payoff of an investment in the future. For example, you might invest $1,000 in a business venture today. After one year, the firm might be bankrupt and you would lose your total investment. On the other hand, after one year your investment might be worth $2,400. This variability in possible outcomes is your risk. Instead, you might invest your $1,000 in a U.S. government security, where after one year the value may be $950 or $1,100. Rational investors would consider the business venture investment to be riskier and would choose this investment only if they feel the expected return is high enough to justify the greater risk. Investors make these trade-off decisions every day.

Business managers make similar trade-off decisions when they choose between different projects in which they could invest. Understanding the risk/return trade-off principle also helps us understand how individuals make economic decisions. While we specifically explore the trade-off between risk and expected return in greater detail in Part 2, this second principle of finance is involved in many financial decisions throughout this text.

1.3.3 DIVERSIFICATION OF RISK

While higher returns are expected for taking on more risk, all investment risk is not the same. In fact, some risk can be removed or *diversified* by investing in several different assets or securities. Let's return to the example involving a $1,000 investment in a business venture, where after one year the investment could provide a return of either zero dollars or $2,400. Now let's assume that there also is an opportunity to invest $1,000 in a second, unrelated business venture in which the outcomes would be zero dollars or $2,400. Let's further assume that we will put one-half of our $1,000 investment funds in each investment opportunity such that the individual outcomes for each $500 investment would be zero dollars or $1,200.

While it is possible that both investments could lose everything (i.e. return zero dollars) or return $1,200 each (a total of $2,400), it is also possible that one investment would go broke and the other would return $1,200. So, four outcomes are now possible:

Possible outcomes	Combined investment	Possible returns		Combined return
Outcome 1:	$500 + $500	$0 + $0	=	$0
Outcome 2:	$500 + $500	$0 + $1,200	=	$1,200
Outcome 3:	$500 + $500	$1,200 + $0	=	$1,200
Outcome 4:	$500 + $500	$1,200 + $1,200	=	$2,400

If each outcome has an equal, one-fourth (25%), chance of occurring, most of us would prefer this diversified investment. While it is true that our combined investment of $1,000 ($500 in each investment) at the extremes could still return zero dollars or $2,400, it is also true that we have a 50% chance of getting $1,200 back for our $1,000 investment. As a result, most of us would prefer investing in the combined or diversified investment rather than in either of the two investments separately. We will explore the benefits of investment diversification in Part 2 of this text.

1.3.4 FINANCIAL MARKETS ARE EFFICIENT

A fourth finance-related aspect of economic behavior is that individuals seek to find undervalued and overvalued investment opportunities involving both real and financial assets. It is human nature, economically speaking, to search for investment opportunities that will provide returns higher than those expected for undertaking a specified level of risk. This attempt by many to earn excess returns, or to "beat the market," leads to information-efficient financial markets. However, at the same time, it becomes almost impossible to consistently earn returns higher than those expected in a risk/return trade-off framework. Rather than looking at this third pillar of finance as a negative consequence of human economic behavior, we prefer to couch it positively in that it leads to information-efficient financial markets.

A financial market is said to be information efficient if at any point the prices of securities reflect all information available to the public. When new information becomes available, prices quickly change to reflect that information. For example, let's assume that a firm's stock is currently trading at $20 per share. If the market is efficient, both potential buyers and sellers of the stock know that $20 per share is a fair price. Trades should be at $20, or near to it, if the demand (potential buyers) and supply (potential sellers) are in reasonable balance. Now, let's assume that the firm announces the production of a new product that is expected to substantially increase sales and profits. Investors might react by bidding up the price to, say, $25 per share to reflect this new information. Assuming this new information is assessed properly, the new fair price becomes $25 per share. This informational efficiency of financial markets exists because a large number of professionals are continually searching for mispriced securities. Of course, as soon as new information is discovered, it is immediately reflected in the price of the associated security. Information-efficient financial markets play an important role in the marketing and transferring of financial assets between investors by providing liquidity and fair prices. The importance of information-efficient financial markets is examined throughout this text and specifically in Chapter 12.

1.3.5 MANAGEMENT VERSUS OWNER OBJECTIVES

A fifth principle of finance relates to the fact that management objectives may differ from owner objectives. Owners, or equity investors, want to maximize the returns on their investments but often hire professional managers to run their firms. However, managers may seek to emphasize the size of firm sales or assets, have company jets or helicopters available for their travel, and receive company-paid country club memberships. Owner returns may suffer as a result of manager objectives. To bring manager objectives in line with owner objectives, it often is necessary to tie manager compensation to measures of performance beneficial to owners. Managers are often given a portion of the ownership positions in privately held firms and are provided stock options and bonuses tied to stock price performance in publicly traded firms.

The possible conflict between managers and owners is sometimes called the *principal-agent problem*. We will explore this problem in greater detail and describe how owners provide incentives to managers to manage in the best interests of equity investors, or owners, in Chapter 13.

1.3.6 REPUTATION MATTERS

ETHICAL The sixth principle of finance is "Reputation matters!" An individual's reputation reflects his or her ethical standards or behavior. Ethical behavior is how an individual or organization treats others legally, fairly, and honestly. Of course, the ethical behavior of organizations reflects the ethical behaviors of their directors, officers, and managers. For institutions or businesses to be successful, they must have the trust and confidence of their customers, employees, and owners, as well as that of the community and society they operate in. All would agree that firms have an ethical responsibility to provide safe products and services, to have safe working conditions for employees, and not to pollute or destroy the environment. Laws and regulations exist to ensure minimum levels of protection and maintain the difference between unethical and ethical behavior. Examples of high ethical behavior include when firms establish product safety and working-condition standards well above the legal or regulatory standards.

Unfortunately, and possibly due in part to the greed for excess returns (such as higher salaries, bonuses, more valuable stock options, personal perquisites, etc.), directors, officers, managers, and other individuals sometimes are guilty of unethical behavior for engaging in fraudulent or other illegal activities. Reputations are destroyed, criminal activities are prosecuted, and involved individuals may receive jail sentences. The unethical behavior of directors, officers, and managers also may lead to a loss of reputation and even destruction of the institutions and businesses for which they work.

Many examples of fraudulent and illegal unethical behavior have been cited in the financial press over the past few decades, and most seem to be tied to greed for personal gain. In such cases, confidential information was used for personal benefit, illegal payments were made to gain business, accounting fraud was committed, business assets were converted to personal use, and so forth. In the early 1980s, a number of savings and loan association managers were found to have engaged in fraudulent and unethical practices, and some managers were prosecuted and sent to prison while their institutions were dissolved or merged with other institutions.

In the late 1980s and early 1990s, fraudulent activities and unethical behavior by investment banking firms resulted in several high-profile financial wheeler-dealers going to prison. This led to the collapse of Drexel Burnham Lambert and the near collapse of Salomon Brothers. By the early part of the twenty-first century, such major firms as Enron, its auditor Arthur Andersen, and WorldCom ceased to exist because of fraudulent and unethical behavior on the part of their managers and officers. In addition, key officials of Tyco and Adelphia were charged with illegal actions and fraud.

ethical behavior how an individual or organization treats others legally, fairly, and honestly

In 2009, Bernie Madoff was convicted and sent to prison for operating a "Ponzi scheme" that resulted in investor losses of billions of dollars. Returns in a Ponzi scheme are fictitious and not earned. Early investors receive their "returns" from the contributions of subsequent investors. Ultimately, the scheme collapses when there are no substantial new investors and when existing investors want to sell their investments. In 2015, Volkswagen Corporation executives were questioned about rigging pollution controls on diesel engine automobiles to deceive government emissions tests. Criminal and civil penalties were agreed to by Volkswagen in 2017 and the former CEO was indicted in 2018.

While the financial press chooses to highlight examples of unethical behavior, most individuals exhibit sound ethical behavior in their personal and business dealings and practices. In fact, the sixth principle of finance depends on most individuals practicing high-quality ethical behavior and believing that reputation matters. To be successful, an organization or business must have the trust and confidence of its various constituencies, including customers, employees, owners, and the community. High-quality ethical behavior involves treating others fairly and honestly and goes beyond just meeting legal and regulatory requirements. High reputation value reflects high-quality ethical behavior, so employing high ethical standards is the right thing to do. Many organizations and businesses have developed and follow their own code of ethics. The importance of practicing sound ethical behavior is discussed throughout this text.

DISCUSSION QUESTION 2

Would you purchase an automobile from a manufacturer that may have been modifying computer software on its vehicles in order to pass government regulations?

1.4 OVERVIEW OF THE FINANCIAL SYSTEM

A democracy is a system of government where limited authority and power are granted by law to its people, who participate in the government's decision-making through the process of voting. A direct democracy exists when the people of a country or entity, as a whole, form a government and individually vote on government goals, actions, and other issues.

> **democracy** system of government where limited authority and power are granted by law to its people who participate by voting on government goals and actions

In a representative democracy the people elect representatives to vote and represent the views of the people who elected them when the representatives engage in government issues. The United States of America is a representative democracy where U.S. citizens elect representatives from among their peers to participate in formulating government policies and plans and addressing government issues.

The highest rule of law in the United States was established when the U.S. Constitution was created and ratified. The first three articles of the Constitution focused on the separation of powers by dividing the federal government into legislative (Congress), executive (the President), and judicial (Supreme Court and other federal courts) branches. The intent was to provide "checks and balances" among the three branches to achieve a dispersion of government powers. Legislative powers include creating law, levying and collecting taxes, and printing money. While legislation proposed by Congress can be vetoed by the President, Congress can override the veto. In the event Congress passes an unconstitutional law, the Supreme Court can invalidate such a law.

The U.S. government system of representative democracy provides the framework for viewing and describing the U.S. financial system in this textbook. The financial system is a complex mix of financial intermediaries, markets, instruments, policy makers, and regulations that interact to expedite the flow of financial capital from savings into investment. We present a brief overview of the financial system in Chapter 1 and then follow with more-detailed coverage in the remaining chapters of Part 1.

> **financial system** interaction of intermediaries, markets, instruments, policy makers, and regulations to aid the flow from savings to investments

1.4.1 CHARACTERISTICS AND REQUIREMENTS

Figure 1.2 provides a graphical review of the four major components of the U.S. financial system. First, an effective financial system must have several sets of *policy makers* who pass laws and make decisions relating to fiscal and monetary policies. These policy makers include the president, Congress, and the U.S. Department of Treasury, plus the Federal Reserve Board, which oversees the Federal Reserve System. Since the United States operates within a global economy, political and economic actions of

FIGURE 1.2 Graphical view of the major components of the U.S. financial system

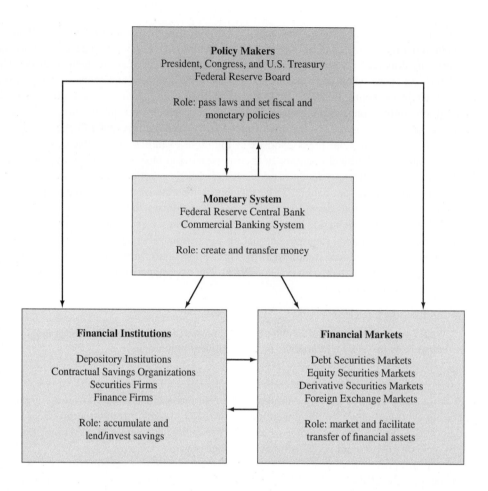

foreign policy makers influence, although indirectly, the U.S. financial system and its operations. Major economic goals are identified and policy-maker actions designed to achieve those goals are discussed in Chapter 5.

Second, an effective financial system needs an efficient *monetary system* that is composed of a central bank and a banking system that is able to create and transfer a stable medium of exchange called money. In the United States, the dollar is the medium of exchange, the central bank is the Federal Reserve System, and the banking system is commonly referred to as the commercial banking system. Characteristics of money and the monetary system are discussed in Chapter 2, and the Federal Reserve System is covered in Chapter 4.

Third, an effective financial system also must have *financial institutions*, or intermediaries, that support capital formation either by channeling savings into investment in real assets or by fostering direct financial investments by individuals in financial institutions and businesses.

Four types of financial intermediaries are listed in Figure 1.2. Depository institutions, contractual savings organizations, securities firms, and finance firms are discussed in Chapter 3. The process of accumulating and then lending and investing savings is referred to as the savings-investment process. We cover the types of financial asset instruments and securities used in the United States throughout the text and discuss how the savings-investment process works in Chapter 7.

Fourth, an effective financial system must also have *financial markets* that facilitate the transfer of financial assets among individuals, institutions, businesses, and governments. Figure 1.2 identifies three types of financial markets – debt securities markets, equity securities markets, and derivative securities markets. We briefly discuss these markets later in this chapter and then provide more-detailed coverage of the various securities markets throughout the text. Foreign exchange markets are discussed in Chapter 6.

1.4.2 FINANCIAL SYSTEM COMPONENTS AND FINANCIAL FUNCTIONS

As previously noted, the role of policy makers is to pass laws and to set both fiscal and monetary policy. Here we focus on the monetary system, financial institutions, and financial markets components by expressing their roles as financial functions that are necessary in an effective financial system. Figure 1.3 indicates that the role of monetary system is creating and transferring money. Financial institutions carry out their role by efficiently accumulating savings and then lending or investing these savings. Financial institutions play an important role in the savings-investment process both through financial intermediation activities and by facilitating direct investments by individuals. Financial markets, along with certain securities firms, are responsible for marketing and transferring financial assets or claims.

1.4.3 CREATING MONEY

Since money is something that is accepted as payment for goods, services, and debts, its value lies in its purchasing power. Money is the most generalized claim to wealth, since it can be exchanged for almost anything else. Most transactions in today's economy involve money, and most would not take place if money were not available.

One of the most significant functions of the monetary system within the financial system is creating money, which serves as a medium of exchange. In the United States, the Federal Reserve System is primarily responsible for the amount of money that is created, although most of the money is actually created by depository institutions. A sufficient amount of money is essential if economic activity is to take place at an efficient rate. Having too little money constrains economic growth. Having too much money often results in increases in the prices of goods and services.

1.4.4 TRANSFERRING MONEY

Individuals and businesses hold money for purchases or payments they expect to make in the near future. One way to hold money is in checkable deposits at depository institutions. When money is held in this form, payments can be made easily by check. The check is an order to the depository institution to transfer money to the party who received the check. This is a great convenience, since checks can be written for the exact amount of payments, be safely sent in the mail, and provide a record of payment. Institutions can also transfer funds between accounts electronically, making payments without paper checks.

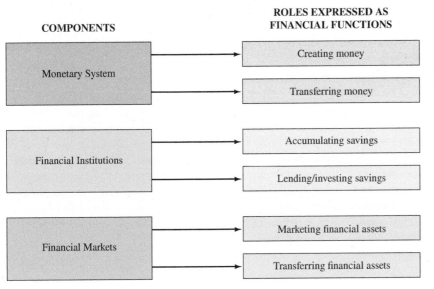

COMPONENTS

ROLES EXPRESSED AS FINANCIAL FUNCTIONS

Monetary System → Creating money

Transferring money

Financial Institutions → Accumulating savings

Lending/investing savings

Financial Markets → Marketing financial assets

Transferring financial assets

FIGURE 1.3 Three financial system components and the financial functions used to carry out their roles

Funds transfers can be made by telephone, at automated teller machines (ATMs) connected to a bank's computer, and via the Internet.

1.4.5 ACCUMULATING SAVINGS

A function performed by financial institutions is the accumulation or gathering of individual savings. Most individuals, businesses, and organizations do not want to take the risks involved in having cash on hand. Even if cash amounts are relatively small, these are put into a depository institution for safe-keeping. When all the deposits are accumulated in one place, they can be used for loans and investments in amounts much larger than any individual depositor could supply. Depository institutions regularly conduct advertising campaigns and other promotional activities to attract deposits.

1.4.6 LENDING AND INVESTING SAVINGS

Another basic function of financial institutions is lending and investing. The money that has been put into these intermediaries may be lent to businesses, farmers, consumers, institutions, and governmental units. It may be lent for varying periods and for different purposes, such as to buy equipment or to pay current bills. Some financial institutions make almost all types of loans. Others specialize in only one or two types of lending. Still other financial institutions invest all or part of their accumulated savings in the stock of a business or in debt obligations of businesses or other institutions.

1.4.7 MARKETING FINANCIAL ASSETS

New financial instruments and securities are created and sold in the primary securities market. For example, a business may want to sell shares of ownership, called stock, to the general public. It can do so directly, but the process of finding individuals interested in investing funds in the business is likely to be difficult, costly, and time consuming. One particular financial intermediary – an investment banking firm – can handle the sale of shares of ownership. The function of the investment banking firm is essentially one of merchandising. Brokerage firms market existing, or "seasoned," instruments and securities.

1.4.8 TRANSFERRING FINANCIAL ASSETS

Several types of financial institutions facilitate or assist in the processes of lending and selling securities. Brokerage firms market and facilitate the transferring of existing, or seasoned, instruments and securities. Also, if shares of stock are to be sold to the general public, it is desirable to have a ready

---

PERSONAL FINANCIAL PLANNING

People Are the Financial System

The main participant in the financial system is not the large institution or corporation . . . it's you and others like you. Households, families, and individuals provide up to 80% of the savings flows in the U.S. economy in any year. There are three main sources of savings: personal savings, business savings (that is, retained earnings), and government surpluses. Personal savings far outweigh the other two sources combined as a source of savings flows in the United States.

Another way to look at this is to consider this question: where do financial institutions get the funds they invest and loan? Banks get their funds mainly from individuals' checking and savings accounts and certificates of deposit (CDs). Pension funds obtain their cash from the savings of working people. Insurance firms accumulate funds to invest from policyholders' payments of premiums for their life, health, car, and home insurance. Mutual funds obtain investable cash by selling their shares to investors like you who want to accumulate savings and returns on savings to fund a future goal such as retirement, a new car, a house down payment, or children's college expenses.

market in which such stocks can be resold when the investor desires. Organized stock exchanges and the over-the-counter market provide active secondary markets for existing securities. The ability to buy and sell securities both quickly and at fair-market values is important in an efficient financial system.

DISCUSSION QUESTION 3

How "effective" have the president and Congress been as "policy makers" in passing laws and setting fiscal policy for the benefit of the people during the past few years?

LEARNING ACTIVITY

Go to the Bloomberg Businessweek website, https://www.bloomberg.com/businessweek, and identify a major business development relating to the financial environment.

Financial markets facilitate the raising of financial capital by government entities and business firms. Government entities can issue or sell debt securities to finance the building of roads and bridges or to provide added services to the people. Business firms can issue debt securities, and corporations can sell equity securities or stocks to raise funds to invest in and grow their businesses. Financial markets also facilitate the transfer of previously issued debt and equity securities from existing to new investors.

1.5 FINANCIAL MARKETS: CHARACTERISTICS AND TYPES

1.5.1 MONEY AND CAPITAL MARKETS

Money markets are where debt securities with maturities of one year or less are issued and traded. These markets are generally characterized by high liquidity whereby *money market securities* can be easily sold or traded with little loss of value. These short-lived securities generally have low returns and low risk. Money market securities will be discussed in Chapter 2.

> **money markets** where debt securities of one year or less are issued or traded

    Capital markets are where debt instruments or securities with maturities longer than one year and corporate stocks or equity securities are issued and traded. *Capital market securities* are generally issued to finance the purchase of homes by individuals, buildings and equipment by businesses, and for provision of infrastructure (roads, bridges, buildings, etc.) by governments. Business firms and governments issue long-term debt securities, called bonds, to finance their assets and operations. *Mortgages* are issued to finance homes and buildings. Corporations also issue stocks to meet their financing needs. We will cover capital market securities in Part 2.

> **capital markets** where debt securities with maturities longer than one year and corporate stocks are issued or traded

1.5.2 PRIMARY AND SECONDARY MARKETS

There are primary and secondary markets for debt (bonds and mortgages) and equity securities. The initial offering, or origination, of debt and equity securities takes place in a **primary market**. Proceeds from the sale of new securities after issuing costs go to the issuing business or government issuer. The primary market is the only "market" where the security issuer directly benefits (receives funds) from the sale of its securities. Mortgage loans provide financing for the purchase of homes and other real property.

> **primary market** where the initial offering or origination of debt and equity securities takes place

    Secondary markets are physical locations or electronic forums where debt (bonds and mortgages) and equity securities are traded. Secondary markets for securities facilitate the transfer of previously issued securities from existing investors to new investors. Security transactions or transfers typically take place on organized security exchanges or in the electronic over-the-counter market. Individuals and other investors can actively buy and sell existing securities in the secondary market. While these secondary market investors may make gains or losses on their securities investments, the issuer of the securities does not benefit (nor does it lose) from these activities. The secondary market for securities is typically divided into short-term (money) and long-term (capital) market categories. We discuss primary and secondary securities markets in detail in Chapter 11. There also is an active secondary market for real estate mortgages. We will discuss the basics of secondary markets for mortgages in Chapter 7.

> **secondary markets** where the transfer of existing debt (bonds and mortgages) and equity securities between investors occurs

1.5.3 MAJOR TYPES OF FINANCIAL MARKETS

debt securities obligations to repay borrowed funds

debt securities markets where money market securities, bonds, and mortgages are originated and traded

bond markets where debt securities with longer-term maturities are originated and traded

mortgage markets where loans to purchase real estate are originated and traded

equity securities ownership shares, called common stocks, in corporations

equity securities markets where corporate ownership shares are initially sold and traded

derivative securities markets where financial contracts that derive their values from underlying debt and equity securities are originated and traded

foreign exchange markets electronic markets in which banks and institutional traders buy and sell various currencies on behalf of businesses and other clients

There are four main types of financial markets – debt securities markets, equity securities markets, derivative securities markets, and foreign exchange markets. Debt securities are obligations to repay borrowed funds. Debt securities markets are markets where money market securities, bonds (corporate, financial institution, and government), and mortgages are originated and traded. Bond markets are where debt securities with longer-term maturities are originated and traded. Government entities (federal, state, and local), financial institutions, and business firms can issue bonds. While bonds and bond markets are discussed throughout this text, there is a specific focus on them in Chapter 10. Mortgage markets are where loans to purchase real estate (buildings and houses) are originated and traded. Mortgage markets are discussed in Chapter 7.

Equity securities, also called common stocks, are ownership shares in corporations. Equity securities markets are markets where ownership shares in corporations are initially sold and traded. Corporations can raise funds either through a *private placement*, which involves issuing new common stocks directly to specific investors, or through a *public offering*, which involves selling new common stocks to the general public. Financial institutions can also raise equity capital by selling common stocks in their firms. Equity securities and markets are discussed in detail in Chapter 11.

In addition to money and capital markets, there are derivative securities markets, which are markets for financial contracts or instruments that derive their values from underlying debt and equity securities. A familiar form of *derivative security* is the opportunity to buy or sell a corporation's equity securities for a specified price and within a certain amount of time. Derivative securities may be used to speculate on the future price direction of the underlying financial assets or to reduce price risk associated with holding the underlying financial assets. Organized exchanges handle standardized derivative security contracts, while negotiated contracts are handled in electronic markets often involving commercial banks or other financial institutions. We discuss derivative securities in the Learning Extension to Chapter 11.

Foreign exchange markets (also called FOREX markets) are electronic markets in which banks and institutional traders buy and sell various currencies on behalf of businesses and other clients. In the global economy, consumers may want to purchase goods produced or services provided in other countries. Likewise, an investor residing in one country may wish to hold securities issued in another country. For example, a U.S. consumer may wish to purchase a product in a foreign country. If the product is priced in the foreign country's currency, it may be necessary to exchange U.S. dollars for the foreign currency in order to complete the transaction. Businesses that sell their products in foreign countries usually receive payment in the foreign currencies. However, because the relative values of currencies may change, firms often use the currency exchange markets to reduce the risk of holding too much of certain currencies. We discuss currency exchange rates and foreign exchange markets in Chapter 6.

1.6 CAREERS IN FINANCE

Career opportunities in finance are available in business financial management, depository financial institutions, contractual savings and real property organizations, and securities markets and investment firms. While you may aspire to own your own business or to be a chief executive officer (CEO) or chief financial officer (CFO) in a major corporation, most of us must begin our careers in an entry-level position. Following are some of the ways to get started in a finance career.

1. ***Business financial management*** Larger businesses or corporations divide their finance activities into treasury and control functions, whereas smaller firms often combine these functions. The treasurer is responsible for managing the firm's cash, acquiring and managing the firm's assets, and selling stocks and bonds to raise the financial capital necessary to conduct business. The controller is responsible for cost accounting, financial accounting, and tax record-keeping activities. Entry-level career opportunities include the following:
   - *Cash management analyst*: involves monitoring and managing the firm's day-to-day cash inflows and outflows

- *Capital expenditures analyst*: involves estimating cash flows and evaluating asset investment opportunities
- *Credit analyst*: involves evaluating credit applications and collecting amounts owed by credit customers
- *Financial analyst*: involves evaluating financial performance and preparing financial plans
- *Cost analyst*: involves comparing actual operations against budgeted operations
- *Tax analyst*: involves preparing financial statements for tax purposes.

2. **Depository financial institutions** Banks and other depository institutions offer the opportunity to start a finance career in consumer or commercial lending. Banks also hold and manage trust funds for individuals and other organizations. Entry-level career opportunities include the following:
   - *Loan analyst*: involves evaluating consumer and/or commercial loan applications
   - *Bank teller*: involves assisting customers with their day-to-day checking and banking transactions
   - *Investments research analyst*: involves conducting research on investment opportunities for a bank trust department.

3. **Contractual savings and real property organizations** Insurance companies, pension funds, and real estate firms also provide opportunities for starting a career in finance. These institutions need a variety of employees willing to blend marketing or selling efforts with financial expertise. Entry-level career opportunities include the following:
   - *Insurance agent (broker)*: involves selling insurance to individuals and businesses and participating in the processing of claims
   - *Research analyst*: involves analyzing the investment potential of real property and securities for pension fund holdings
   - *Real estate agent (broker)*: involves marketing and selling or leasing residential or commercial property
   - *Mortgage analyst*: involves analyzing real estate loan applications and assisting in the arranging of mortgage financing.

4. **Securities markets and investment firms** Securities firms and various investment-related businesses provide opportunities to start a finance career in the investments area. Opportunities include buying and selling seasoned securities, analyzing securities for investment potential, marketing new securities issues, and even helping individuals plan and manage their personal financial resources. Entry-level career opportunities include the following:
   - *Stockbroker (account executive)*: involves assisting clients in purchasing stocks and bonds and building investment wealth
   - *Security analyst*: involves analyzing and making recommendations on the investment potential of specific securities
   - *Investment banking analyst*: involves conducting financial analysis and valuation of new securities being issued
   - *Financial planner assistant*: involves analyzing individual client insurance needs and investment plans to meet retirement goals.

While we have focused on entry-level careers in profit-motivated businesses and financial organizations, careers in finance are also available in government or not-for-profit organizations. Finance opportunities at the federal or state government levels include managing cash funds, making asset expenditure decisions, and issuing debt securities to raise funds. Hospitals and other not-for-profit organizations also need expert financial managers to manage assets, control costs, and obtain funds. Financial and other analysts are hired both by government units and not-for-profit organizations to perform these tasks.

All of these entry-level finance job opportunities also can be found in the international setting. For example, many businesses engaged in producing and marketing products and services in foreign markets often offer employees opportunities for international job assignments. Large U.S. banks also offer international job experiences through their foreign banking operations. Furthermore, since

CAREER OPPORTUNITIES IN FINANCE

YOU ARE LIKELY TO HAVE MORE THAN ONE BUSINESS CAREER

Students are advised today to prepare for several business careers during their working lifetimes. Corporate America continues to restructure and reinvent itself. At the same time, new industries associated with the information age are developing, and old industries are dropping by the wayside. These developments make it even more likely that each of you will have the opportunity for multiple business careers.

Graduates of Harvard University are periodically surveyed concerning their work experiences and careers. Responses to one survey of individuals 25 years after graduation found that over one-half had worked for four or more employers while one-fourth had been fired (or, in kinder terms, "involuntarily terminated"). Over half of the men and women respondents had had at least two substantially different careers, and in many instances significant retraining was required.

Remember as you read this book that even if you don't currently plan on a career in finance, learning about finance might become very important to you later in your working lifetime. And, no matter where your business career takes you, you will always need to know and understand your personal finances.

worldwide securities markets exist, securities analysts and financial planners often must analyze and visit foreign-based firms.

Several detailed Career Opportunities in Finance boxes are presented in selected chapters. We hope these materials provide you with a better understanding of some of the many career opportunities that exist in the finance field. We are also sure that new finance job opportunities will occur in the future as the field continues to develop and change. It is now time to begin learning about finance!

LEARNING ACTIVITY

1. Go to *The Wall Street Journal* website section at https://guides.wsj.com/careers, and find information related to job hunting and career development.
2. The Monster.com website, https://www.monster.com, provides information on current finance. Search for "finance" jobs and list some of the entry-level finance positions that are currently available.

1.7 THE PLAN OF STUDY

The subject matter of this book includes the entire scope of the financial environment from the perspective of the financial system and the three areas of finance – institutions and markets, investments, and financial management. You will learn about the markets in which funds are traded and the institutions that participate in and assist these flows of funds. You will learn about the investments area of finance, including the characteristics of debt and equity securities that are issued, the markets where securities are traded, and investment risk/return concepts. You will study the financial management principles and concepts that guide financial managers to make sound financial planning, asset acquisition, and financing decisions. International finance applications also are integrated throughout the text.

Part 1 focuses on the financial institutions, markets, and other participants that make the U.S. financial system operate effectively both domestically and within the global economy. Chapter 2 introduces the role of money within the overall financial system and its monetary system component. Chapter 3 focuses on the financial intermediation roles of depository and other financial institutions, as well as how they operate within the financial system. Chapter 4 discusses the Federal Reserve System. Chapter 5 discusses economic objectives, the role and actions of policy makers, and how money and credit are provided to meet the needs of the economy. We conclude Part 1 with a chapter on international finance and trade because of its importance in understanding market economies worldwide.

Part 2 is concerned with the investments area of finance. Chapter 7 discusses the savings and investment process and its major role in the U.S. market economy. This is followed by Chapter 8, which describes the structure of interest rates. Time-value-of-money concepts are covered in Chapter 9, and the characteristics and valuations of bonds and stocks are presented in Chapter 10. Chapter 11 discusses the characteristics and workings of the securities market. Part 2 concludes with Chapter 12, which describes financial return and risk concepts for a single asset or security, and for portfolios of securities.

Part 3 focuses on the financial management of businesses. We begin Chapter 13 with an introduction and overview of the types of business organizations, and follow with a review of basic financial statements and financial data important to the financial manager. Chapter 14 discusses the need for, and the way in which to conduct, financial analysis of past performance and concludes with a section on financial planning for the future. Chapter 15 covers the management of working capital, while Chapter 16 focuses on sources of short-term business financing. We then turn our attention in Chapter 17 to the process and methods for conducting capital budgeting analysis. We conclude Part 3 with Chapter 18, which provides a discussion of capital structure and cost of capital concepts.

Of course, as we illustrated in Figure 1.1, the three areas of finance are not independent but, rather, are continually interacting or overlapping. For example, financial institutions provide an important financial intermediation role by getting individual savings into the hands of businesses so that financial managers can efficiently use and invest those funds. Financial managers also rely heavily on the investments area of finance when carrying out their financial management activities. Corporations often need to raise funds in the primary securities markets, and secondary securities markets, in turn, provide investors with the liquidity of being able to buy and sell previously issued securities. Our approach in this book is to provide survey exposure to all three areas of finance.

• **Institutions and Markets** Financial institutions and financial markets are necessary components of an efficient financial system. Institutions perform an important financial intermediation role by gathering the savings of individuals and then lending the pooled savings to businesses that want to make investments.

• **Investments** Securities markets are also important components of an efficient financial system. The primary securities market facilitates raising funds by issuing new debt and equity securities. The secondary market for securities facilitates the transfer of ownership of existing securities among investors.

• **Financial Management** Business firms continually interact with financial institutions as they carry out their day-to-day operations. Businesses also often seek to raise additional funds to finance investment in inventories, equipment, and buildings needed to support growth in sales. Bank loans and mortgage loans are important financing sources, along with the proceeds from the issuance of new debt and equity securities.

SUMMARY

LO 1.1 Finance is the study of how businesses and others acquire, spend, and manage money and other financial resources. More specifically, finance is composed of three areas – financial institutions and markets, investments, and financial management. However, these three areas are not independent of one another but rather intersect or overlap. This book's survey approach to the study of finance covers all three areas.

LO 1.2 You should study finance so that you can make informed economic, personal and business investment, and career decisions.

LO 1.3 There are six principles of finance: (1) money has a time value, (2) higher returns are expected for taking on more risk, (3) diversification of investments can reduce risk, (4) financial markets are efficient in pricing securities, (5) manager and stockholder objectives may differ, and (6) reputation matters.

LO 1.4 An effective financial system has four major components – policy makers, a monetary system, financial institutions, and financial markets – to facilitate the flow of financial capital from savings into investments. Policy makers pass laws and set fiscal and monetary policies designed to manage the economy. A monetary system creates and transfers money. Financial institutions accumulate and lend/invest individual savings. Financial markets are needed to market and transfer securities and other financial assets.

LO 1.5 Financial markets can be classified as either money or capital markets, or as primary or secondary markets. There are four major types of financial markets – debt securities markets, equity securities markets, derivative securities markets, and foreign exchange markets.

LO 1.6 Career opportunities in finance are available in financial management, depository financial institutions, contractual savings and real property organizations, and securities markets and investment firms.

LO 1.7   The plan of study in this book consists of three parts. Part 1 focuses on the financial institutions, markets, and other participants that make the U.S. financial system operate effectively. Part 2 covers the investments area of finance. Part 3 focuses on the financial management of businesses.

KEY TERMS

bond markets	derivative securities	financial environment	investments
capitalism	markets	financial institutions	money markets
capital markets	entrepreneurial finance	financial management	mortgage markets
debt securities	equity securities	financial markets	personal finance
debt securities markets	equity securities markets	financial system	primary market
democracy	ethical behavior	foreign exchange	secondary market
	finance	markets	

REVIEW QUESTIONS

1. **(LO 1.1)** What is finance?

2. **(LO 1.1)** What is meant by the term financial environment?

3. **(LO 1.1)** What are the three areas of finance?

4. **(LO 1.1)** Briefly describe the terms *entrepreneurial finance* and *personal finance*.

5. **(LO 1.2)** Briefly describe how the financial environment has changed during the past few years.

6. **(LO 1.2)** Identify and briefly describe several reasons for studying finance.

7. **(LO 1.3)** What are the six principles of finance?

8. **(LO 1.3)** Describe what is meant by *ethical behavior*.

9. **(LO 1.4)** What are the four major components of an effective financial system?

10. **(LO 1.4)** Identify and briefly describe the financial functions in the financial system.

11. **(LO 1.5)** Briefly describe the differences between money and capital markets.

12. **(LO 1.5)** What are the differences between primary and secondary markets?

13. **(LO 1.5)** How do debt securities and equity securities differ?

14. **(LO 1.5)** Identify the four types of major financial markets.

15. **(LO 1.6)** Indicate some of the career opportunities in finance available to business graduates today.

EXERCISES

1. Match the following dates with the associated events.

Year	Event
a. 2000	1. Great recession
b. 2001	2. U.S. terrorist attack
c. 2006	3. Financial crisis
d. 2007–2008	4. Technology stock bubble
e. 2008–2009	5. Housing price bubble

2. The U.S. financial system is composed of (1) policy makers, (2) a monetary system, (3) financial institutions, and (4) financial markets. Indicate which of these components is associated with each of the following roles.
   a. Accumulate and lend or invest savings
   b. Create and transfer money
   c. Pass laws and set fiscal and monetary policies
   d. Market and facilitate transfer of financial assets

3. Financial markets may be categorized as (1) debt securities markets, (2) equity securities markets, (3) derivative securities markets, and (4) foreign exchange markets. Indicate in which of these markets the following securities trade.
   a. Mortgages
   b. Bonds
   c. Common stocks
   d. Currencies

4. In business, ethical dilemmas or situations occur frequently. Laws and regulations exist to define what unethical behavior is. However, the practicing of high-quality ethical behavior often goes beyond just meeting laws and regulations. Indicate how you would respond to the following situations.
   a. Your boss has just told you that tomorrow the Federal Drug Administration will announce its approval of your firm's marketing of a

new breakthrough drug. As a result of this information, you are considering purchasing shares of stock in your firm this afternoon. What would you do?

b. In the past, your firm has been in compliance with regulatory standards relating to product safety. However, you have heard through the company grapevine that recently some of your firm's products have failed, resulting in injuries to customers. You are considering quitting your job due to personal moral concerns. What would you do?

5. Obtain several recent issues of *The Wall Street Journal* or *Bloomberg Businessweek*. Identify, read, and be prepared to discuss at least one article relating to one of the six principles of finance.

6. Obtain several recent issues of *The Wall Street Journal* or *Bloomberg Businessweek*. Identify, read, and be prepared to discuss at least one article relating to one of the four types of financial markets identified in Chapter 1.

7. Obtain several recent issues of *The Wall Street Journal* or *Bloomberg Businessweek*. Identify, read, and be prepared to discuss at least one article relating specifically to recent changes in the financial environment.

8. Go to the U.S. Small Business Administration (SBA) website, https://www.sba.gov, and search for sources of information on starting a new business. Identify and prepare a written summary of the *start-up basics* described on the SBA site.

LEARNING OBJECTIVES

After studying this chapter, you should be able to do the following:

LO 2.1 Discuss the developments that led to the 2007–2008 financial crisis.	**LO 2.6** Describe the major types of money market securities.
LO 2.2 Describe three ways in which money is transferred from savers to businesses.	**LO 2.7** Explain the M1 and M2 definitions of the money supply.
LO 2.3 Identify the major components of the monetary system.	**LO 2.8** Explain possible relationships between money supply and economic activity.
LO 2.4 Describe the functions of money.	**LO 2.9** Describe developments in the international monetary system.
LO 2.5 Discuss how money developed in the United States.	

Where we have been. . . In Chapter 1, we provided a general overview of the financial environment including the three areas of finance: institutions and markets, investments, and financial management. We also hope that we provided you with a convincing argument as to why you should study finance, and an understanding of the career opportunities that are available in finance. Six principles of finance were described. You should also know what is required for a financial system to be effective and know the types of financial markets that are available to aid the transferring of financial assets.

Where we are going. . . As we progress through Part 1, we build on our understanding of the U.S. financial system. Chapter 3 focuses on understanding the importance of depository and other institutions in the financial system. We discuss how your savings are pooled with the savings of other individuals in financial institutions and then are made available to businesses, governments, and other individuals who may want to invest in inventories, invest in highways, or purchase homes. The remaining chapters in Part 1 focus on the Federal Reserve System, the role of policy makers, and how international developments influence the financial system.

How this chapter applies to me. . . Each of us needs money. While you may feel you need more or less money than your friend, money is necessary for each of us to conduct day-to-day activities. You may have to buy gas for your car or pay for public transportation to school or work. You may need money for lunch or supplies. You may even want to borrow money to purchase a house someday. After reading this chapter, you should have a clearer understanding of the functions and types of money available to you.

John Kenneth Galbraith, a U.S. economist, said the following about money:

> *Money is a singular thing. It ranks with love as man's greatest source of joy. And with death as his greatest source of anxiety. Over all history it has oppressed nearly all people in one of two ways: either it has been abundant and very unreliable, or reliable and very scarce.*[1]

Why should any "one thing" be so important? Money is what makes the financial system work. Money is a measure of wealth. Money can be used to purchase goods and services. Money is acceptable to repay debts. Creating and transferring money are integral parts of the capital formation process. However, too much money in an economy is associated with unsustainable economic growth

---

[1] John Kenneth Galbraith, *The Age of Uncertainty* (Boston: Houghton Mifflin, 1977), Print.

and rapidly rising prices. On the other hand, too little money in an economy is associated with poor economic performance and sometimes recession. Of course, the relationships between money supply and economic activity and money supply and rising prices also are impacted by a number of other factors as we will see later in this chapter, as well as in other chapters.

CRISIS A number of negative economic and financial trends and events all came together to contribute to the financial crisis of 2007–2008 and the Great Recession of 2008–2009. A rapid decline in housing prices began in 2006. This led to increased unemployment, first in housing-related activities and then more broadly. As a result, many homeowners were forced to default on their home mortgage loans. These developments occurred at a time when individuals, financial institutions, and business firms were heavily in debt. The result was a so-called "perfect financial storm" accompanied by a fear that the financial system might collapse.

> **2.1 THE 2007–2008 FINANCIAL CRISIS AND SUBSEQUENT RECOVERY**

While there continues to be some disagreement as to specific causes of the financial crisis, most economists and others trace the beginning of the crisis to the bursting of the U.S. housing bubble in mid-2006. For a period of time prior to mid-2006, housing prices were continually rising year over year with some areas of the United States experiencing annual double-digit housing price increases. The first part of the twenty-first century was a time when U.S. federal government policies encouraged home ownership. Lenders were willing to lend to financially "risky" borrowers seeking mortgage loans to make home purchases, and individual borrowers were willing to take on excessive amounts of mortgage debt, all in the belief that housing prices would continue to rise. Once housing prices began to decline, many homeowners had the equity in their homes "wiped out" and many mortgage loans became "underwater," which occurs when mortgage debt on the home exceeds the value of the home. This rapid decline in housing values was accompanied by a major loss of jobs in home construction and related industries.

Many home mortgage loans were combined into "pools" of loans, and then mortgage-backed securities were issued with the mortgage loan pools as backing, or collateral. Large amounts of mortgage-backed securities were held by banks and other financial institutions, and as home prices collapsed it became clear that these mortgage-backed securities had been previously overvalued and they also declined sharply in value. A "credit crunch" occurred when banks and other financial institutions found that they did not have adequate equity capital to cover their large mortgage loan and other debt commitments. As a result, financial institutions were forced to lay off many employees. Businesses found it difficult to borrow from banks and other financial institutions because of the credit crunch, causing even higher levels of unemployment.

During 2008, the federal government helped some financial institutions to merge, "bailed out" a number of institutions and businesses, and allowed other financial institutions to fail. The financial crisis and associated credit crunch were accompanied by the 2008–2009 economic downturn, which began in late 2007 and ended in mid-2009 with economic activity declining more than 4% and the unemployment rate reaching 10% during 2009. The 2008–2009 economic downturn is referred to as the Great Recession since it involved the largest economic downturn since the Great Depression of the 1930s.

Fiscal policy spending programs and easy monetary policy and financial debt acquisitions by the Federal Reserve helped the subsequent U.S. economic recovery which has lasted more than 10 years. By the end of 2018, the unemployment rate had declined to less than 4% and economic growth as measured by the gross domestic product was at 3%. Of course, there are likely to be more crises in the future, making it important that we understand the causes of, and possibly avoid repeating, past financial crises.

We will discuss more details relating to the financial crisis and the Great Recession at various points throughout the first two parts of this textbook. In this chapter we begin with a discussion of money and the monetary system. Many economists and others believe there is a link between the supply, or availability, of money and economic activity. The argument is that monetary policy makers can stimulate economic activity through increased monetary liquidity by making more money available (at lower borrowing costs) to businesses, investors, and others. It is presumed that the investment of these low-cost funds will result in more economic growth. However, there is a difference of opinion as to how direct the relationship is between the availability of money and economic activity. We will provide further discussion later in the chapter.

> **DISCUSSION QUESTION 1**
>
> **How were your family and you impacted by the 2007–2008 financial crisis?**

2.2 PROCESS OF MOVING SAVINGS INTO INVESTMENTS

surplus economic unit generates more money than it spends resulting in excess money to save or invest

deficit economic unit generates less money than that it spends resulting in a need for additional money

savings-investment process involves the direct or indirect transfer of individual savings to business firms in exchange for debt and equity securities of the firm

Financial institutions and markets move or transfer money from individuals and institutions with excess money to business firms and others who have needs for more money. We usually look at individuals in total, or in the aggregate, as an economic unit. Financial institutions, business firms, and governments (federal, state, and local) also are viewed as economic units. A surplus economic unit generates more money than it spends, and thus it has excess money to save or invest. A deficit economic unit spends more money than it brings in and must balance its money receipts with money expenditures by obtaining money from surplus units.

Individuals taken as a group have generally been a surplus economic unit in the past. Of course, while some individuals are saving, others are borrowing to cover the purchase of goods and services. Individuals desiring to purchase homes also borrow by taking out mortgage loans. Some business firms are savers when their revenues exceed their costs of operation and reinvest back into the businesses. Other businesses choose to borrow or sell stock to finance their operations and grow their businesses with the intent of providing higher returns to their investors. Private sector financial institutions also have responsibilities to provide returns to their investor-owners and sometimes borrow heavily to grow their institutions and, hopefully, provide higher returns. Sometimes, government entities (federal, state, and local) have tax revenues that exceed expenditures and, thus, are surplus economic units. However, when government entities spend more than they receive from tax revenues, they must borrow the money shortfall and, thus, are deficit economic units.

The ability of the U.S. financial system to operate effectively over time depends on each of the three overall economic units (individuals, business firms, and government entities) achieving a reasonable balance between their aggregate revenues and expenditures. When expenditures exceed revenues for extended periods of time, deficit economic units must build up large amounts of debts. A major factor in the severity of the 2007–2008 financial crisis and the 2008–2009 Great Recession was the massive amount of debt taken on by individuals, business firms, financial institutions, and government entities during the decade leading up to the crises. In an effort to survive the financial crisis and recover from the recession, government entities, through increased expenditures in the form of stimulus programs, increased their deficits and, in the case of the U.S. government, dramatically increased the size of the national debt.

Our primary focus is on the savings-investment process that involves the direct or indirect transfer of individual savings to business firms in exchange for their debt and stock securities. Figure 2.1 shows three ways whereby money is transferred from savers to a business firm. As illustrated in the top portion of the figure, savers can directly purchase the debt or equity (in the form of common stock issued by a corporation) securities of a business firm by exchanging money for the firm's securities. No financial institution is used in this type of savings-investment transaction since it involves only a saver and the business firm.

The use of indirect transfers is the more common way by which money is transferred from savers to investors. The middle part of Figure 2.1 shows how the transfer process usually takes place when savers purchase new securities issued by a business. From Chapter 1, you should recall that this indirect transfer involves use of the primary securities market. In this process, financial institutions operate to bring savers and security issuers together. Savers provide money to purchase the business firm's securities. However, rather than a direct transfer taking place, financial institutions, such as investment banks, may facilitate the savings-investment process by first purchasing the securities being issued by a corporation and then reselling the securities to savers. No additional securities are created in this type of indirect transfer.

The bottom part of Figure 2.1 illustrates the typical capital formation process involving a financial institution. Savers deposit or invest money with a financial institution, such as a bank, an insurance

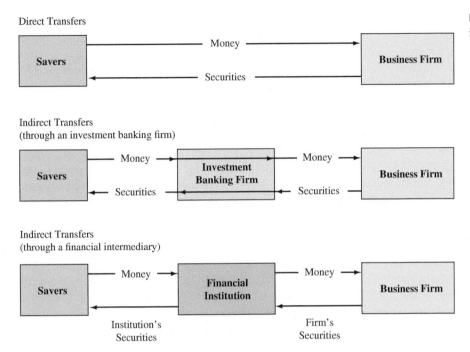

company, or a mutual fund. The financial institution issues its own securities to the saver. For example, a saver may give money in the form of currency to a bank in exchange for the bank's savings or time-deposit obligation. The bank, in turn, may lend money to a business firm in exchange for that firm's "I owe you" (IOU) in the form of a loan. As money passes from savers through a financial institution to a business firm, a debt instrument or security is created by the financial institution and by the business firm. This is the process of financial intermediation that we will discuss further in Chapter 3.

Of course, the savings-investment process could, alternatively, focus on the flow of money from savers to government entities that are operating at deficits caused by expenditures greater than tax revenues. The U.S. government and state and local governments can sell their debt securities directly to savers who might be individuals, business firms, or financial institutions. Indirect transfers also could take place with the aid of financial institutions to facilitate the movement of government entity debt securities to savers. A financial institution may operate as a conduit in the primary securities market. Alternatively, the financial institution may purchase the government entity's debt securities and, in turn, issue its own debt securities to individuals and other savers.

The savings-investment process could also focus on moving the savings of individuals and other savers to those individuals, businesses, institutions, and governments that want to finance real estate investments. Many individuals want to own their own homes and can do so only by taking on mortgage

SMALL BUSINESS PRACTICE

STARTING YOUR SMALL BUSINESS

Today, with modern telecommunication facilities and the Internet, many small businesses can be located wherever their owners want to live and work. At the same time, certain cities and geographical areas in the United States may be more conducive to helping small businesses succeed.

The Dun & Bradstreet Company (D&B) provides a wealth of information relating to the starting of a new business. D&B provides

information on how to establish, manage, and grow your small business. When considering whether to establish, or start, a business, it is important to ask, "Are you really ready to start?" It is also important to "plan your business," as well as "understand legal and tax issues." And, before "opening your doors," you might want to access the D&B website at https://www.dnb.com.

debt or home loans. Other organizations also may wish to invest in real property in the form of offices, manufacturing facilities, or other buildings. Doing so often requires the need to finance a part of the purchase price with a mortgage loan on the real property being purchased. While our focus in this text is primarily on the savings-investment process involving the raising of money or financial capital by business firms, the process for financing deficits by government entities will be discussed in Chapter 5, and the financing of residential and commercial property will be addressed in Chapter 7.

2.3 OVERVIEW OF THE MONETARY SYSTEM

The monetary system is responsible for carrying out the financial functions of creating and transferring money. Money is needed to conduct day-to-day activities, facilitate the capital investment process, and support economic growth. Businesses need money to invest in inventories, equipment, and buildings. Governments need money to construct roads, buildings, parks, and other infrastructure for the people. Individuals need money to purchase goods, services, and homes.

Figure 2.2 indicates the major participants in the U.S. monetary system. A central bank is needed to define and regulate the amount of the money supply in the financial system. A central bank also facilitates the transferring of money by processing and clearing checks, a form of money called deposit money. The central bank in the United States is called the Federal Reserve System (or Fed, for short). We will discuss the characteristics and operation of the Fed in Chapter 4 and cover its policy-making activities in Chapter 5.

An efficient banking system also is needed. Not all types of financial institutions are the same. For example, while insurance companies and investment companies can provide a financial intermediation function between savers and investors, only depository institutions as a group can create money. Depository institutions include commercial banks, savings and loan associations (S&Ls), savings banks, and credit unions. For purposes of presentation, it is common practice to refer to all depository institutions as "banks," and they all are part of the banking system. We discuss the characteristics of depository and other major financial institutions in Chapter 3.

FIGURE 2.2 The U.S. monetary system

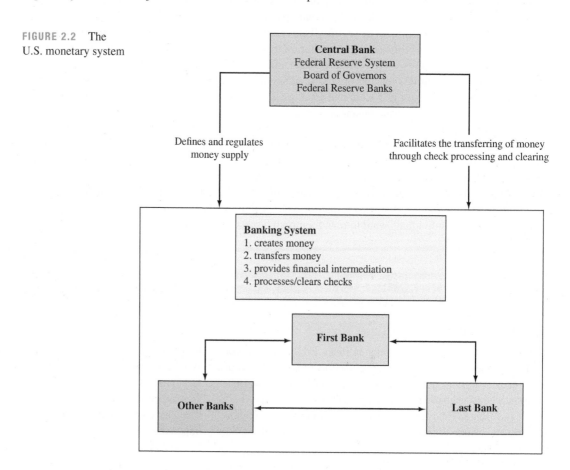

The banking system, as depicted in Figure 2.2, is composed of all the banks in the system. For illustration purposes, there is a "first bank" and a "last bank." The banking system creates money (technically, deposit money) and, along with the Fed, clears checks and transfers money within the overall financial system. Checks can be cleared either through other banks in the banking system or with the aid of the Fed. We will examine the check-clearing process in Chapters 3 and 4.

While an individual bank, such as First Bank, cannot create money, the banking system can. Let's assume that First Bank receives $1,000 from the ABC business firm and sets up a checking account (demand deposit) for the firm. The $1,000 received by First Bank is called "reserves" and represents money held by First Bank so that it can pay off checks written by ABC against its checking account balance. However, rather than holding the full $1,000 in reserves, First Bank will only hold a fraction (e.g. 20%, or $200) in reserves and will lend out the remaining $800 to the XYZ firm. As long as XYZ places the $800 loan proceeds in its checking account at a bank (e.g. Last Bank) somewhere in the banking system, the initial $1,000 demand deposit established for ABC has increased to $1,800 (the $1,000 for ABC plus the $800 for XYZ). As long as deposit money keeps coming back into the banking system, more deposit money is created. In practice, the Fed specifies the percentage of reserves that banks must hold against demand deposits. We will explore the deposit money creation process in greater detail in Chapter 5 when we discuss the Fed's monetary policy-making activities.

2.4 CHARACTERISTICS AND FUNCTIONS OF MONEY

Real assets include the direct ownership of land, buildings or homes, equipment, inventories, durable goods, and even precious metals. Financial assets are money, debt instruments, equity securities, and other financial contracts that are backed by real assets and the earning abilities of issuers. A loan to you to purchase an automobile usually provides for the lender to hold the auto title (ownership) until the loan is repaid. Long-term debt issued by a corporation may represent a claim against specific assets, such as buildings and equipment, or the general assets of the issuer. A mortgage loan to you will be backed by the house against which the loan is being made.

Money is a physical or electronic asset that is accepted as payment for goods and services, as well as for the repayment of debts. Money can sometimes be a real asset. For example, when the money value of a coin is determined by the number of grains of gold or silver in the coin, money is a real asset. Today the value of money is dependent on the creditworthiness and taxing capabilities of issuers, rather than the value of a precious metal, making money a financial asset.

Digital currency is an electronic money asset in digital form accepted for making payments for goods, services, and debts. Digital currency can either be centralized where a central authority or government entity controls the digital money supply, or be decentralized or unregulated where the digital money supply is determined by the currency's developers and users. Digital currency traditionally has been centralized where a government entity has control over the supply of money both physical and digital. In a centralized system, banks or other financial institutions operate as intermediaries in the electronic money transactions between buyers and providers. Transactions are recorded, stored, and records of ownership are maintained. For example, the U.S. Federal Reserve System controls the amount of physical money in the U.S. economy and the amount of digital currency in the form of bank or deposit money created by the U.S. banking system.

Virtual currency is unregulated digital money issued, and often controlled, by its decentralized developers and used to make electronic payments where transactions are recorded, stored, and maintained. In this view, virtual currency is a subset of digital currency. One type of subset of virtual currency that has been growing rapidly in recent years is called cryptocurrency.

Cryptocurrency is a decentralized and unregulated digital money that uses cryptography to record, maintain, and secure electronic payment transactions among participants in a network. Cryptography was initially developed to secure communications information by encrypting records to prevent enemies and others from viewing confidential communications. Today, cryptography uses mathematical algorithms and computer programming languages to record, maintain, and secure payment transactions. Cryptocurrency developers also typically construct algorithms to control how additional units of the currency are created through a process called "mining."

real assets include the direct ownership of land, buildings or homes, equipment, inventories, durable goods, and precious metals

financial assets money, debt securities and financial contracts, and equity securities that are backed by real assets and the earning power of the issuers

money physical or electronic asset accepted as payment for goods, services, and debts

digital currency electronic money accepted for making payments

virtual currency unregulated digital money issued, and often controlled, by its decentralized developers and used to make electronic payments

cryptocurrency decentralized and unregulated digital money that uses cryptography to record, maintain, and secure electronic payments

bitcoin specific type of cryptocurrency that uses a ledger system technology called blockchain to record, maintain, and secure payment transactions

Bitcoin is a cryptocurrency that uses a ledger system technology called blockchain for handling payment transactions that occur on a peer-to-peer network. The *blockchain* technology was initially developed in 2008 and permanently records, maintains, and secures payment transactions by making it virtually impossible to alter or change prior transactions. New transactions are grouped into "blocks" and are linked or "chained" to other blocks using cryptography to maintain an evergrowing payment transactions record. Bitcoin was introduced in 2009 and is considered to be the first decentralized cryptocurrency to use mathematical algorithms. Since then, more than a thousand other cryptocurrencies have been developed and introduced to the public.

Only time will tell if cryptocurrencies are accepted as "money." It is argued that decentralized and unregulated ledger-based peer-to-peer payment networks can offer instantaneous transactions and borderless currencies. However, the lack of both financial institution participation in transactions and central authority regulation has resulted in cryptocurrencies being used to launder "dirty" money from illegal drug sales, credit card thefts, and Ponzi schemes. In addition, large amounts of cryptocurrency coins have been stolen or "disappeared," and government agencies are examining whether "initial coin offerings" need to be properly registered. Also, the very wide and wild swings in the prices of cryptocurrencies that have taken place over time make it questionable whether they provide a reasonable store of value.

Money must perform three basic functions, serving as a medium of exchange, a standard of value, and a store of value. Money was first developed to serve as a **medium of exchange**, which means that money must be accepted and used to facilitate the exchange of goods and services. Primitive economies consisted largely of self-sufficient units, or groups, that lived by means of hunting, fishing, and simple agriculture. There was little need or occasion to exchange goods or services. As economies developed, however, the process of exchange became important. Some individuals specialized, to a degree at least, in herding sheep, raising grain, or shaping gold as metal smiths. To aid in the exchanging of goods for goods, called **barter**, tables of relative values were developed from experience. For example, a table might show the number of furs, measures of grain, or amount of cloth agreed to equal one cow. This arrangement eased exchanges, but the process still had many serious drawbacks. For example, if a person had a cow and wanted to trade it for some nuts and furs, he or she would need to find someone who had an excess of both these items to trade. The need for a simpler means of exchange led to the development of money, with its relatively low storage and transfer costs, to be used as a medium of exchange.

medium of exchange money must be accepted and used to facilitate the exchange of goods and services

barter exchange of goods or services without using money

As early societies evolved, they began using physical money that took the form of "*commodity*" money where the money value was determined by the commodity from which the money was made. Examples of commodity money included barley, cowry shells, and gold and silver coins.[2]

Money also must serve as a **standard of value** where prices and debts are expressed in terms of the money's monetary unit. For example, in the United States, prices and debts are usually expressed in terms of dollars without stating whether the purchase will be cash or credit. Of course, if money is to perform its function as a standard of value, it is essential that the value of the monetary unit be relatively stable over time.

standard of value occurs when prices and debts are stated in terms of the money's monetary unit

store of value exists when the price or value of money remains relatively stable over time

Money also may be held as a **store of value** when the price or value of money remains relatively stable over time. That is, money may be spent immediately after it is received or after it has been held for some time. While money is held, it is a liquid asset and provides its owner with flexibility, but the owner pays for this flexibility by giving up the potential return that could be earned through investment or the satisfaction that could be gained from spending it for goods and services. **Purchasing power** is the amount of goods and services that can be purchased with a unit of money. Money can perform its function as a store of value only if its purchasing power is relatively stable over time. Under this condition, the spending decision is separated from the income decision. Once income is received, the holder of the income can choose to spend it or save it. If the decision is to save, then that money can be made available through the savings-investment process to those who may want to invest now. Purchasing power is reduced by **inflation**, which is a rise, or increase, in the prices of goods and services that is not offset by increases in their quality.

purchasing power amount of goods and services that can be purchased with a unit of money

inflation an increase in the prices of goods and services that is not offset by increases in their quality

---

[2] For an interesting discussion of the historical development of money, see Yuval Noah Harari, *Sapiens* (New York: Harper Perennial, 2015), ch. 10.

Any asset other than money can also serve as a store of value as long as that asset can be converted into money quickly and without significant loss of value. We refer to this quality – the ease with which an asset can be exchanged for money or other assets – as liquidity. Money is perfectly liquid since it is a generally accepted medium of exchange. Other assets, such as savings deposits held at depository institutions, approach the liquidity of money. The existence of such liquid assets reduces the need for holding money itself as a store of value.

liquidity how easily and with little loss of value an asset can be exchanged for money or other assets

While money is the fundamental measure of wealth, an individual's net worth usually consists of more than just money. Individual net worth is the sum of an individual's money, real assets, and financial assets, or claims against others less the individual's debt obligations. Recall that real assets include the automobile that you own, your house (if you have one) and its contents, clothes, and even jewelry or precious stones. You may also own shares of stock in a mutual fund. While this is a financial asset, it is still part of your net worth. However, you may have borrowed from a bank to purchase your automobile, and you probably have a mortgage loan on the house you purchased. These are financial claims held by others against some of your real property. You must subtract debt obligations, or financial claims against you or your real property, in order to determine your individual net worth. There are probably more than 8 million millionaires in the world with about one-third of them being in the United States. If you wish to join this group someday, you will have to accumulate a net worth in excess of $1 million. Good luck!

individual net worth sum of an individual's money, real assets, and financial assets less the individual's debt obligations

---

The two basic components of money supply in the United States are physical (coin and currency) money and deposit money. A review of the development of money in the United States will help us understand the characteristics of money today, as well as how well U.S. money performs the three functions of money.

2.5 DEVELOP-MENT OF MONEY IN THE UNITED STATES

2.5.1 PHYSICAL MONEY (COIN AND PAPER CURRENCY)

The first function of "successful" money is that it serves as a medium of exchange. Physical money is the coin and paper currency used to purchase goods and services and to settle debts. We will first examine how U.S. coins have changed in terms of their precious metal (gold and silver) content over time. Then, we will examine how U.S. paper currency has changed in terms of both its physical characteristics and "backing" with precious metals.

2.5.1.1 U.S. Coins

While barter was undoubtedly important in early American history, the government moved swiftly toward a monetary system based on precious metals that would serve as an efficient medium of exchange. During much of the seventeenth and eighteenth centuries, the American colonies relied primarily on the Spanish dollar to conduct business transactions.[3] In 1785, the word *dollar* was adopted by the U.S. Congress as the standard monetary unit, or standard of value. The first monetary act in the United States, passed in 1792, provided for a bimetallic standard based on both gold and silver. The dollar was defined in both grains of pure silver and grains of pure gold. All gold and silver coins were to be full-bodied money because their metal content was worth the same as their face values. For example, one silver dollar was to contain one dollar's worth of silver, a ten-dollar gold coin was to contain ten dollars' worth of gold, and so on.

bimetallic standard monetary standard based on two metals, usually silver and gold

full-bodied money coins that contain the same value in metal as their face value

A law enacted in 1837 modified the weight for the silver dollar to 412.5 grains of silver with .900 fineness. Copper of .100 fineness was used to make the coins last longer. The result was that each dollar contained .77344 ounce of pure silver. Since the value of the silver content was to be $1, silver was valued at $1.29 per ounce ($1/.77344).

Figure 2.3 shows examples of full-bodied and token U.S. coins. The top portion shows the front side (obverse) of the peace-type dollar and the Franklin half-dollar. The peace-type dollar was produced from 1921 to 1935. The Franklin half-dollar, produced from 1948 to 1963, contained .36169 ounce

---

[3] The Spanish dollar often was cut into eight pieces or "bits" to make change. Sometimes the U.S. quarter dollar is referred to as "two bits." This term originated from cutting the Spanish dollar into "pieces of eight."

FIGURE 2.3 Examples of full-bodied and token (copper–nickel clad) U.S. coins

Two Full-Bodied Coins

[Face value and silver metal content were equal when coin was issued]

Peace-Type Dollar
(issued 1921–1935)
[contains .77344
ounces of silver]

Franklin Half Dollar
(issued 1948–1963)
[contains .36169
ounces of silver]

Two Token Coins

[Face value much greater than metal (no silver) content]

Eisenhower Dollar
(issued 1971–1978)
[contains only
copper and nickel]

Kennedy Half-Dollar
(issued 1971–present)
[contains only
copper and nickel]

of pure silver. Since silver prices had been gradually rising, the Franklin half-dollar was full-bodied money at a silver price of $1.38 ($.50/.36169). Depending on the prevailing market price of silver, a silver coin such as the half-dollar could be less than, greater than, or exactly full-bodied.

The store of value of full-bodied money was reflected in the then-current value of its precious metal content, and as long as the price of precious metals moved in unison with the prices of goods and services, this money's store of value reflected the store of purchasing power.

Rapidly rising silver prices in the 1960s, however, made silver coins worth more as melted-down bullion than their face values. As a result, the U.S. government "debased" its full-bodied money by replacing silver content with copper and nickel. Coins with face values higher than the value of their metal content are called **token coins**. The bottom portion of Figure 2.3 shows two copper–nickel clad (token) U.S. coins. The Eisenhower dollar was minted from 1971 to 1978. Kennedy half-dollars were full-bodied coins in 1964, were changed to silver-clad (reduced silver content) coins from 1965 to 1970, and have been copper–nickel clad coins since 1971.

The production of gold coins began in 1795 with the $5 and $10 coins. The issuance of full-bodied gold dollars was authorized in 1849, and production continued through 1889. For several decades, the value of a U.S. dollar was expressed both in terms of silver and gold. All gold coin production was stopped in 1933, and in 1934 U.S. citizens were prohibited from holding monetary gold in the United States. This restriction was extended in 1961 to gold held abroad by U.S. citizens. All restrictions on holding gold in money form were removed in 1975.

token coins coins containing metal of less value than their stated value

2.5.1.2 Paper Currency

The evolution and use of paper currency in the United States have been characterized by a very erratic history. While some paper money was issued by individual colonies, the first effort of a government to issue paper money occurred when the Continental Congress authorized the issuance of notes called Continentals to finance the Revolutionary War. While these notes were denominated in dollars, they had no backing in either silver or gold. Rather, they were backed only by possible future tax revenues to be gathered when the colonies became independent. As you might guess, the Continentals soon became worthless. This led to a long period of distrust of paper money. After a brief experience with two national banks, American banking went through a period of no federal regulation and nonuniformity in operating laws. State-chartered banks issued their own paper currency almost at will and in many cases with no or little backing of their notes with gold or silver deposits.[4]

Paper money may be either representative full-bodied money or fiat money. **Representative full-bodied money** is paper money that is backed by an amount of precious metal equal in value to the face amount of the paper money. The U.S. government has issued two types of representative full-bodied money. Gold certificates were issued from 1865 through 1928. Since they could be redeemed for gold with a value equal to the paper currency's face amount, they were "as good as gold." However, since most gold certificates were issued in large denominations, they were not intended to be used in general circulation but rather to settle institutional gold accounts. The issuance of silver certificates was authorized beginning in 1878. A switch to "small-size" silver certificates occurred in 1929, and they continued to be issued and used through 1963.

> **representative full-bodied money** paper money fully backed by a precious metal

Figure 2.4 shows examples of full-bodied and fiat U.S. paper currency. The top portion shows a silver certificate. These certificates could be exchanged for silver dollars or silver bullion when presented to the U.S. Treasury. Of course, like full-bodied silver coins, these silver certificates became worth more in terms of the bullion value of silver relative to their face values as silver prices began climbing in the 1960s. As a result, redemption of silver certificates in silver dollars was halted in 1964 by the U.S. government, and in 1968 redemption in silver bullion also was stopped.

Today, almost all paper money in circulation is in the form of Federal Reserve Notes, which were authorized under the *Federal Reserve Act of 1913*. The bottom portion of Figure 2.4 shows a Federal Reserve Note. These notes, which are not backed by either gold or silver, are called **fiat money** because the government decreed the notes to be "legal tender" for purposes of making payments and discharging public and private debts. Of course, the copper – nickel clad, or token, coins of today are also fiat money because their metal content values are less than their face values.

> **fiat money** paper money proclaimed to be legal tender by the government for making payments and discharging public and private debts

The reliance on the use of fiat money can be problematic. First, fiat money generally becomes worthless if the issuing government fails. As an example, Confederate currency was issued during the U.S. Civil War. However, when the Confederacy lost the war, this fiat money became worthless. Second, since there is no required backing in gold or silver, it is relatively easy to issue more and more fiat money. Issuing too much money can, in turn, lead to rising prices and a lack of confidence in the government. An effective monetary system with a strong central bank and prudent policy makers are needed when a financial system relies on fiat money to carry out its transactions.

Several major changes in Federal Reserve Notes have taken place over time. In 1929, the size of the notes was reduced about 30%, from large notes (7.42 inches by 3.13 inches) to small notes (6.14 inches by 2.61 inches). This change made production less expensive and made it easier to handle and less costly to store and transfer paper money. Figure 2.5 shows the old and current design of the $20 U.S. Federal Reserve Note. The "small portrait" $20 note is shown in the top portion of the figure.

ETHICAL When it comes to money, how individuals "behave" ranges from exhibiting high ethical standards down to deceit, fraud, and counterfeiting. How you acquire and deal with money affects your reputation. Individuals who work hard, follow the law, and treat other individuals they are involved with in money transactions fairly and honestly are able to find success, accumulate wealth, and build high-quality reputations. However, probably almost from the origins of money creation, there have been individuals driven by greed who have engaged in counterfeiting activities to illegally obtain money rather

---

[4] By 1865, it was estimated that about one-third of the circulating paper currency was counterfeit. As a result, the U.S. Treasury established the U.S. Secret Service to control counterfeiting activities.

Representative Full-Bodied Paper Currency
[Face value and silver metal "backing" were equal when the bill was issued]

Silver Certificate (small size issued 1929–1963)
[exchangeable for silver dollars or silver bullion equal to face amount]

Fiat Paper Currency
[No "backing" with silver (or other precious metal) deposits]

Federal Reserve Note (small size issued 1929–present)
[U.S. government states on each note: "This note is legal tender for all debts, public and private"]

than work for it. It is difficult for most of us to understand such extreme unethical behavior, which typically results in getting caught, serving prison time, and destroying reputations of those involved.

Unfortunately, attempts to counterfeit U.S. currencies represent a big illegal business for some individuals and organizations. Furthermore, the ability to counterfeit currency has been aided in recent years by the introduction of high-quality color copiers. To thwart counterfeiting efforts, the U.S. Treasury Department's Bureau of Engraving and Printing has developed new currency designs in recent years. A new series of notes that made use of microprinting and an embedded security strip was introduced in 1990 to improve security and to make counterfeiting more difficult. A more complete design change began with the $100 "large-portrait" bill in 1996. Large-portrait $50 bills were introduced in 1997, and $20 bills were placed in circulation in 1998. New $5 and $10 bills were introduced in 2000 so that today only the $1 bill continues to use the small-portrait format.

Further currency design changes were implemented in 2003. The bottom portion of Figure 2.5 shows the most recent large-portrait $20 bill, which still features Andrew Jackson. In the 1998 version, the larger portrait was for the first time placed off-center to allow the inclusion of a watermark that is visible from both sides when held up against a light. The bill contains a vertically embedded security thread, which glows red when exposed to ultraviolet light, at the far left of the portrait. Color-shifting ink, fine line printing, and microprinting were added. In the 2003 version, U.S. currency began taking on added colors. Peach and light blue hues were added to the previous green-and-black bills. Other

Old Design $20 Bill
[Relatively easy to copy and counterfeit]

FIGURE 2.5   Old and current designs of the $20 U.S. Federal Reserve Note

Old Design $20 Federal Reserve Note (small size issued 1929–1997)

Current Design $20 Bill
[More difficult to copy and counterfeit]

Current Design $20 Federal Reserve Note (issued beginning in 2003)

changes included removing the circle around Andrew Jackson's head and adding a faded bald eagle to the left of the portrait and the words "Twenty USA" and "USA Twenty" to the right of the portrait.

These anti-counterfeiting efforts, while very costly, are essential to maintaining the public's trust and confidence in fiat money. Of course, it is important to remember that even though the appearance of U.S. paper money may be changing, the government honors all previously issued U.S. paper currency at full face value. There is no requirement or time limit for exchanging old notes for new ones. Old notes continue to remain in circulation until depository institutions return them to the Fed to be retired.

LEARNING ACTIVITY

Go to the U.S. Treasury website, https://www.treas.gov. Go to "Services," and click on "Coins and currency." Then click on "Bureau of Engraving and Printing." Find recent information on redesigned currency.

2.5.2 CREDIT MONEY AND DEPOSIT MONEY

Credit money is money backed by the creditworthiness and taxing capabilities of the issuer. Recall that paper currency issued in the United States is called fiat money because the government proclaimed the currency to be legal tender for purposes of making payments and discharging public and private debts. Fiat money is a form of credit money.

credit money money backed by the creditworthiness and taxing capabilities of the issuer

Local Currency: Another Form of Savings and Spending Power

The monetary system has evolved from barter of goods and services to today's credit money. Money is a means to facilitate exchange. Rather than carpenter Jim trading a chair for new shirts sewn by seamstress Jane, Jim and Jane use Federal Reserve Notes to buy chairs and shirts from each other.

Some areas of the United States have two monetary systems. More than two dozen cities and towns have printed their own versions of money used for transactions within a locality. One reason communities do so is to keep money in the community. For example, local currency has circulated in Ithaca, New York; Madison, Wisconsin; Takoma Park, Maryland; Detroit, Michigan; Austin, Texas; Santa Barbara, California; and Corvallis, Oregon. Such currency is legal, but it must be printed in a size that is smaller than the U.S. $1 bill.

Ithaca's local currency is denominated in Ithaca Hours; each Hour is worth about $10, the area's average hourly wage.

Denominations range from one-tenth of an Hour up to two Hours. Since it started in 1991, Hours have been earned and spent by thousands of residents and accepted by over 500 businesses. However, there has been a decline in the use of Hours in recent years due, in part, to a shift to using debit and credit cards instead of making cash transactions.

The idea of local currency in the United States is not new; it has a long history. You may have experience with traveler's checks; they also are a form of private currency. One purchases traveler's checks with cash, and the checks can then be used as currency because they represent this cash. The recognizable name and good credit of the issuer (e.g. American Express or Thomas Cook), rather than that of the individual making the payment, guarantees the value of the checks. Since lost or stolen traveler's checks can be reported, payment stopped, and new checks issued in their place, they provide users with a level of safety not available with cash.

---

deposit money electronic money backed by the creditworthiness of the depository institution that issued the deposit

The use of physical (coin and currency) money to complete transactions can be costly and inefficient if large amounts and/or long distances are involved. As a result of these constraints on the use of physical money, along with concerns over confidence in the banking system, a special type of credit money called deposit money has grown readily in importance in the U.S. monetary system. Deposit money is electronic money backed by the creditworthiness of the depository institution that issued the deposit. While deposit money is a form of credit money, it is not fiat money in that it has not been proclaimed to be legal tender by the government for payment of debts.

Deposit money takes the form of demand deposits held at commercial banks, or other checkable deposits held at S&Ls, savings banks, and credit unions. A demand deposit gets its name from the fact that the owner of a deposit account "demands" that all or a portion of the amount in his or her demand deposit account be transferred to another individual or organization. Checks or drafts have traditionally been used to transfer demand deposit or other checkable deposit amounts. Let's return to our example in which the ABC business firm deposits $1,000 at First Bank to set up a $1,000 demand deposit account in ABC's name. ABC then writes a $1,000 check against its deposit account and sends the check to an equipment manufacturer as payment for purchase of equipment. The equipment manufacturer deposits the check in its own demand deposit account in a bank (e.g. Last Bank). The check then must be processed and cleared through the banking system, either with or without the assistance of the Fed. That is, it must be returned to First Bank, which will pay the check amount to Last Bank and deduct $1,000 from the business firm's demand deposit account at First Bank. To aid and speed the clearing process, copies of checks can be sent electronically rather than having to wait for actual paper checks to be delivered.

The use of electronic ways to transfer funds held in demand and other checkable deposit accounts continues to increase and replace the use of more costly and time-consuming paper checks. Automatic transfer service (ATS) accounts are used to make direct deposits to and payments from checkable deposit accounts. Employers often have their employees' wages deposited directly in their employees' checking accounts, rather than issuing payroll checks. Electronic funds transfers for payment of utility bills, mortgage loans, credit card balances, and so forth, are increasingly common.

automatic transfer service (ATS) accounts provide for direct deposits to, and payments from, checkable deposit accounts

debit cards provide for immediate direct transfer of deposit amounts

Debit cards provide for the immediate direct transfer of deposit amounts. For example, when a debit card is used to purchase merchandise at a retailer's point-of-sale (POS) cash register or from their Internet sites, the card holder's bank transfers the designated amount from the purchaser's demand account to the retailer's account. Debit cards also are used to make cash withdrawals from automated teller machines (ATMs). When cash is dispersed, the user's demand deposit account's balance is immediately reduced by the amount of cash withdrawn.

A number of firms have recently introduced digital and mobile payments systems designed to provide more efficient online and POS experiences. Examples are Apple Pay, PayPal, and Square. Fewer physical money transactions will be needed in the future and the United States will move toward a cash-free monetary system.

> **DISCUSSION QUESTION 2**
>
> U.S. paper currency in the form of Federal Reserve Notes is no longer backed by silver or gold. Are you concerned?

2.6 MONEY MARKET SECURITIES

As noted in Chapter 1, *Money markets* are the markets where debt securities with maturities of one year or less are originated (primary markets) or traded (secondary markets). **Money market securities** are debt instruments or securities with maturities of one year or less. In general, money market securities have low default risk and high liquidity. That is, issuers are expected to meet their debt obligations when due, and short maturities and secondary markets for many of these securities allow them to be sold with little loss of value.

> **money market securities** debt securities with maturities of one year or less

Figure 2.6 identifies characteristics of major money market securities. A **Treasury bill** is a short-term debt obligation issued by the U.S. federal government to meet its short-term borrowing needs when imbalances exist between tax revenues and government expenditures. Treasury bills are generally issued with maturities between three months (technically, 90 days) and one year. Investors buy Treasury bills for safety and liquidity reasons. First, it is extremely unlikely that the federal government will default on its debt obligations. Second, there is an active secondary money market for Treasury bills, so investors can easily sell them at any time before maturity if cash needs arise.

> **treasury bills** short-term debt obligation issued by the U.S. federal government

Businesses often find it necessary to borrow in the short term to meet temporary imbalances between when cash is received from sales and when bills must be paid. **Commercial paper** is a short-term unsecured promissory note issued by a high credit – quality corporation. Maturities on commercial paper are generally one to three months in length. However, since there is an active secondary money market for commercial paper, purchasers can easily sell their commercial paper holdings at any time to meet their cash needs.

> **commercial paper** short-term unsecured promissory note issued by a high credit – quality corporation

A **negotiable certificate of deposit (negotiable CD)** is a short-term debt instrument issued by depository institutions to individual or institutional depositors. Negotiable certificates of deposit are issued by commercial banks in denominations of $100,000 or more with typical maturities ranging from one month to one year. Negotiable CDs are money market securities with an active secondary

> **negotiable certificate of deposit (negotiable CD)** short-term debt instrument issued by depository institutions that can be traded in the secondary money markets

> **FIGURE 2.6** Major money market securities

Type	Typical maturities	Issuers	Investors	Secondary market
Treasury bills	91 days to 1 year	U.S. government	Individuals, business firms, and institutions	High activity
Commercial paper	1 day to 9 months	Business firms and institutions	Business firms and institutions	Moderate activity
Negotiable certificates of deposit (negotiable CDs)	Up to 1 year	Depository institutions	Business firms	Low activity
Banker's acceptances	Up to 6 months	Banks	Business firms	High activity
Repurchase agreements	Up to 1 year	Business firms and institutions	Business firms and institutions	No market
Federal funds	1 day to 1 week	Depository institutions	Depository institutions	No market

market that allows short-term investors to easily match their cash or liquidity needs when they arise. It is important, of course, to recognize that negotiable CDs differ from smaller-denomination CD time deposits offered by depository institutions to individual depositors. Small-deposit CDs are nonnegotiable and must be redeemed with the issuer, and thus no secondary securities market exists for them. In fact, owners of nonnegotiable CDs redeemed before maturity usually are charged an interest deduction penalty.

banker's acceptance promise of future payment issued by an importing firm and guaranteed by a bank

A **banker's acceptance** is a promise of future payment issued by a firm and guaranteed by a bank. Banker's acceptances are used to finance international trade and, typically, have maturities from one to six months. For example, a U.S. exporter that is sending goods to an importer in a foreign country may not know the credit quality of the importer. To facilitate the transaction, a bank may be asked to guarantee payment of the "draft" or bill for the goods, which will be due at a future date. The "accepted" draft is sent to the exporter. The importer pays the amount of the draft, plus a fee for the guarantee, to the bank when due.

The bank, in turn, pays the exporter or whoever is holding the draft at the time of maturity. Exporters often sell their banker's acceptances at a discount to obtain cash prior to the due date. There is a very active secondary market for banker's acceptances, with other business firms often buying banker's acceptances as a source of low default risk, high-liquidity short-term investments. We will discuss the process of conducting international trade in greater detail in Chapter 6.

repurchase agreement short-term debt security where the seller agrees to repurchase the security at a specified price and date

A **repurchase agreement** is a short-term debt security sold by a business firm or financial institution to another business or institution, where the seller agrees to repurchase the security at a specified price and date. Repurchase agreements may be as short as one day or involve several months. Most repurchase agreements utilize Treasury bills but may also include commercial paper or negotiable certificates of deposit.

Brokers and dealers, through an electronic network, facilitate the bringing together of organizations with excess funds and those in need of funds. Since cash receipts relative to cash expenditures can change almost daily for business firms, a firm might be a seller of a repurchase agreement at one time and a buyer of a repurchase agreement at another time. No secondary market exists for repurchase agreements.

federal funds very short-term loans between depository institutions with excess funds and those with a need for funds

Federal funds are very short-term loans, usually with maturities of one day to one week made between depository institutions. For example, a commercial bank with excess funds may make a short-term loan to another depository institution with a shortage of funds. The interest rate on federal funds is determined by supply and demand for very short-term loans by banks. The Federal Reserve, as we will see in Chapters 4 and 5, can directly influence the federal funds rate as it carries out monetary policy.

Federal funds brokers bring together banks who want to purchase federal funds with those who want to sell funds. Transactions typically start at $5 million, with the interbank loan volume being in the billions of dollars. There is no secondary market for federal funds due to their extremely short maturities. A one day or overnight loan is highly liquid. While there is some credit risk concerning the ability of the borrowing depository institution to repay the loan, very short maturities also mitigate such risk.

2.7 MEASURES OF THE U.S. MONEY SUPPLY

Now that we have a basic understanding how money developed in the United States, it is time to examine how the money supply or "stock" is measured today. Since we are trying to "count" the money supply in the financial system as of a point in time, this can also be viewed as the amount of money stock on a particular date. We will start with a narrow definition of the money supply referred to as M1 and then consider M2, which is a broader definition.

2.7.1 M1 MONEY SUPPLY

M1 money supply consists of currency, traveler's checks, demand deposits, and other checkable deposits

As noted, the basic function of money is that it must be acceptable as a medium of exchange. The M1 definition of the money supply includes only types of money that meet this basic function. More specifically, the **M1 money supply** consists of currency, traveler's checks, demand deposits, and other checkable deposits at depository institutions. For December, 2018, the Fed reported the not-seasonally adjusted M1 and its four components, as listed on the next page (see: https://www.federalreserve.gov/releases/h6/current).

MI Component	$Billions	Percentage
Currency	1,626.1	42.6
Traveler's checks	1.7	.0
Demand deposits	1,553.4	40.7
Other checkable deposits	637.7	16.7
Total M1	**3,818.9**	**100.0**

All four components are types of credit money. Currency is U.S. physical money in the form of coins and paper currency. The coins are token money, and the paper currency is fiat money in the form of Federal Reserve Notes. However, U.S. currency (both coins and paper money) is readily accepted for making payments and retiring debts and, thus, serves as an important medium of exchange. Currency comprises nearly 43% of the M1 money supply. Traveler's checks, offered by banks and other organizations, promise to pay on demand the face amounts of the checks with their acceptance based on the creditworthiness of the issuer. Since traveler's checks are a widely accepted medium of exchange, they qualify as a component of the M1 money supply. Even so, their relative importance is small, as indicated by the fact that they represent substantially less than 1% of the M1 total.

As noted, demand deposits (checking accounts) at commercial banks, and other checkable deposits at savings and loan associations (S&Ls), savings banks, and credit unions, also are considered to be credit money, since these deposits are backed solely by the creditworthiness of the issuing institutions when checks are presented for collection. Demand deposits at commercial banks account for over 40% of the money supply. Other checkable deposits represent over 16% of M1 and include ATS accounts and negotiable order of withdrawal (NOW) accounts at depository institutions; credit union share draft accounts; and demand deposits at S&Ls, credit unions, and savings banks.

Taken together, demand deposit and other checkable deposit accounts comprise a little less than half of the M1 money supply. This high percentage shows the importance of the banking system and its money-creating function within the monetary system and in terms of the broader U.S. financial system.

Before moving to a broader definition of the money supply, we should point out some of the adjustments or exclusions that take place when estimating the M1 money supply, or stock. M1 measures transaction balances. These are sums of money that can be spent without first converting them to some other asset and that are held for anticipated or unanticipated purchases or payments in the immediate future. Essentially, only those amounts that represent the purchasing power of units in the U.S. economy other than the federal government are counted. Specifically excluded from M1 is currency in the vaults of depository institutions or held by the Fed and the U.S. Treasury. Demand deposits owed to depository institutions, the federal government, and foreign banks and governments also are excluded. Adjustment is also made to avoid double-counting checks being processed. The vault cash and deposits belonging to depository institutions do not represent purchasing power and, therefore, are not money. However, they serve as reserves, an important element of our financial system that will be discussed in the next several chapters.

2.7.2 M2 MONEY SUPPLY

The Fed's second definition of the money stock, M2, is a broader measure than M1 because it emphasizes money as a store of value in addition to its function as a medium of exchange. In general terms, the **M2 money supply** includes M1 plus highly liquid financial assets, including savings accounts, small time deposits, and retail money market mutual funds. Most of the financial assets added to M2 provide their owners with a higher rate of return than would M1 components. More specifically, M2 adds to M1 savings deposits (including money market deposit accounts), small-denomination time deposits (under $100,000) less individual retirement account (IRA) and Keogh account balances at depository institutions, plus balances in retail money market mutual funds (MMMFs) less IRA and Keogh balances at money market mutual funds.

M2 money supply M1 plus highly liquid financial assets, including savings accounts, small time deposits, and retail money market mutual funds

As of December, 2018, the Fed reported M2 at $14,538.8 billion, which is about four times the size of M1. Some of the owners of the assets included in M2 hold them as long-term savings instruments. Other individuals and firms hold these M2-specific assets even though they plan to spend the funds within a few days, because the assets are very liquid. M1, thus, understates purchasing power by the amount of these M2 balances held for transaction purposes.

The components of M2 illustrate the difficulties the Fed has faced in drawing the boundaries of these definitions. For example, money market deposit accounts (MMDAs) provide check-writing privileges and can, therefore, be used for transaction purposes. Some analysts argue on this basis that MMDA balances should be a part of M1. The Fed has included MMDA balances in M2, but not in M1, because MMDAs are different from traditional money components and because MMDAs seem to be used more as savings instruments than as transaction balances. On the other hand, it can be argued that small time deposits should be excluded from M2 because they are not, in practice, very liquid. Small time-deposit holders, who wish to cash them in before maturity, are penalized by having to forfeit some of the interest they have earned. However, small time deposits are included because they are considered to be close substitutes for some of the other savings instruments included in M2. Savings deposits, including MMDAs, at depository institutions are greater than the M1 total.

money market mutual funds (MMMFs) issue shares to customers and invest the proceeds in highly liquid, very short maturity, interest-bearing debt instruments

Money market mutual funds (MMMFs) issue shares to customers and invest the proceeds in highly liquid, very short maturity, interest-bearing debt instruments called *money market investments*. MMMFs get their name from the type of investments they make. The nature of their investments, coupled with payment of interest daily, keeps MMMF shares valued at $1. Many MMMFs allow shareholders to write checks against their accounts. When checks are cleared and presented to the MMMF for payment, the number of shares owned by the shareholder is reduced accordingly. This process, of course, is very similar to writing checks against checkable deposits held at depository institutions. However, rather than including retail MMMF balances in M1, the Fed decided that consumers use the accounts more as a store of purchasing power and less as a medium of exchange.

2.7.3 EXCLUSIONS FROM THE MONEY SUPPLY

The Fed excludes certain stores of value and borrowings from its money supply definitions. For example, stock and bond mutual funds held by individuals represent stores of value, and some even permit limited check writing against these accounts. However, because the value of shares in these funds often fluctuates widely and individuals may hold these security investments for a long time, the Fed does not consider these to be part of the money supply.

credit cards provide predetermined credit limits to consumers when the cards are issued

Credit cards provide predetermined credit limits to consumers at the time the cards are issued. No checkable or other deposits are established at the time of issue. Thus, neither credit card limits nor outstanding balances are part of the money supply. Rather, credit cards just allow their holders to borrow up to a predetermined limit. However, the use of credit cards can affect the rate of turnover of the money supply and may contribute to money supply expansion. If credit card borrowing stimulates the demand for goods and services, a given money supply can support a higher level of economic activity. We will explore the relationship between money supply and economic activity in the next section. Also, when you use your credit card to purchase a product for, say, $50 at a retailer, the bank that issued the credit card lends you $50 and increases the retailer's demand deposit account by $50. As your credit card balance increases as you purchase goods and services on credit, the checkable deposit accounts of those who sold the goods and services also increase. Of course, users of credit cards must eventually pay off their debts.

LEARNING ACTIVITY

1. Go to the Federal Reserve Bank of St. Louis website, https://www.stlouisfed.org, access the Federal Reserve Economic Database (FRED) and find information on the current money supply. Determine the current size of M1 and its four components, along with the size of M2.
2. Go to the Federal Reserve Bank of San Francisco's website, https://www.frbsf.org. Go to the "Cash" tab and find information on consumer use of cash, debit cards, and credit cards.

Many economists believe that money supply matters when they try to manage economic activity. They have observed that economic activity, money supply, and the price levels of goods and services generally move together over time. However, economists disagree as to how these relationships are to be explained.

The output of goods and services in the economy is referred to as the gross domestic product (GDP). Since we typically measure output in current dollars, we are measuring "nominal" GDP. Some economists, called *monetarists*, believe that the amount of money in circulation determines the level of GDP or economic activity. If we divide GDP by the money supply (MS), we get the number of times the money supply turns over to produce GDP. Economists refer to the turnover of money as the velocity of money (VM). More specifically, the velocity of money measures the rate of circulation of the money supply. For example, if the annual GDP is $15 million and the MS is $5 million, the VM is three times (i.e. $15 million/$5 million). In alternative form, we can say that

$$MS \times VM = GDP \qquad (2.1)$$

For our example, we have

$$\$5 \text{ million} \times 3 = \$15 \text{ million}$$

Economists also express nominal GDP as being equal to real output (RO) times the price level (PL) of goods and services, or,

$$RO \times PL = GDP \qquad (2.2)$$

For example, if the real output in the economy is 150,000 products and the average price is $100, the GDP is $15 million (i.e. 150,000 × $100). Putting these two equations together, we have,

$$MS \times VM = RO \times PL \qquad (2.3)$$

An increase in the money supply and/or velocity causes nominal GDP to increase. And, for nominal GDP to increase, real output and/or price levels must increase. For example, let's assume the money supply increases by 10%, or $500,000, to $5.5 million while the velocity stays at three times. Nominal GDP will increase to,

$$\$5.5 \text{ million} \times 3 = \$16.5 \text{ million}$$

Since GDP equals RO × PL, some change in real output or price level (or a combination of the two) needs to take place. One possibility is for real output to increase by 15,000 products or units to 165,000 with no change in prices. GDP then would be

$$165,000 \text{ units} \times \$100 = \$16.5 \text{ million}$$

Monetarists also believe that when the money supply exceeds the amount of money demanded, the public will spend more rapidly, causing real economic activity or prices to rise. A too rapid rate of growth in the money supply will, ultimately, result in rising prices or inflation, because excess money will be used to bid up the prices of existing goods. Recall that inflation is an increase in the prices of goods and services that is not offset by increases in their quality. Because of the difficulty in measuring changes in quality, a more operational definition of inflation is a continuing rise in prices. For example, instead of the $1.5 million increase in GDP from $15 million to $16.5 million being due to a 10% increase in the money supply, the increase might have been due solely to inflation. Let's assume that the quantity of products sold remains at the original 150,000-unit level but that the average price increases by 10% to $110. GDP would be calculated as

$$150,000 \text{ units} \times \$110 = \$16.5 \text{ million}$$

Of course, there could be almost unlimited combinations of real outputs and price levels, including reducing one of the variables that could produce the same new GDP.

gross domestic product (GDP) a measure of the output of goods and services in an economy

velocity of money the rate of circulation of the money supply

Other economists, called Keynesians in honor of John Maynard Keynes, believe that a change in the money supply has a less-direct relationship with GDP. They argue that a change in money supply first causes a change in interest rate levels, which, in turn, alters the demand for goods and services. For example, an increase in the money supply might cause interest rates to fall (at least initially) because more money is being supplied than is being demanded. Lower interest rates, in turn, will lead to an increase in consumption and/or investment spending, causing the GDP to grow.[5] In contrast, a decrease in the money supply will likely cause interest rates to rise. As a result, the GDP will grow more slowly or even decline, depending on how the higher interest rates affect consumption and spending decisions.

As you might guess, it is not possible to say that one group of economists (monetarists or Keynesians) is right and the other is wrong. The ability to identify relationships among GDP, money supply, and price levels has been complicated by the fact that the VM has increased and the various measures of the money supply have grown at different rates. M1 velocity has increased as credit card usage has replaced the more traditional use of currency and deposit money when purchasing goods and services. The velocity of M1 money also has increased as the public has made more use of money market mutual funds and other liquid accounts that serve as stores of value relative to their usage of traditional deposit money in demand and other checkable accounts.

Recent developments have made it difficult to interpret the near-term impact of changes in the money supply. Decreasing regulation and increasing competition among financial institutions have led to changes in the types of deposit money that individuals use for medium of exchange purposes. Likewise, there are ongoing changes in how individuals use "near cash" accounts for store of value purposes. Thus, recent changes in growth rates for different definitions of the money supply reflect in part changes in how individuals pay bills and store purchasing power. This is one reason why the Fed simultaneously keeps track of more than one measure of the money supply.

Some economists believe that there is a "psychological" factor that impacts the relationship between money supply and economic activity. The action of increasing the money supply does not automatically result in higher GDP. Businesses and individuals may choose not to borrow low-cost funds due to perceived uncertainty about future economic conditions. Some view the practice of increasing the money supply and liquidity akin to "trying to push on a string" in terms of increased economic activity. If businesses and individuals choose not to increase their investments and expenditures, the link between money supply and GDP may be difficult to observe.

As a result of the economic downturn in 2001 and the September 11, 2001, terrorist attacks, the Federal Reserve moved to maintain financial liquidity through continued increases in M1 and M2 and by lowering federal funds rates to historically low levels. Continued monetary easing occurred during the latter half of the decade of the 2000s in response to the 2007–2008 financial crisis and the 2008–2009 Great Recession. We will explore how the Fed administers monetary policy in our dynamic and complex financial system in Chapters 4 and 5.

DISCUSSION QUESTION 3

Some economists believe that an increase in the money supply will lead to inflation. Do you agree?

LEARNING ACTIVITY

Go to the Federal Reserve Bank of St. Louis website, https://www.stlouisfed.org, and access the FRED database. Find the current size of the M1 money supply and the annual GDP, and then calculate the VM.

2.9 INTERNATIONAL MONETARY SYSTEM

GLOBAL The international monetary system was historically tied to the gold standard. An international gold standard was used to conduct most international trade during the latter part of the 1800s and the early part of the 1900s. However, a breakdown in the gold standard occurred during World War I, and less-formal exchange systems continued during the worldwide depression of the 1930s and during World War II.

---

[5] If the increase in money supply leads to price level increases (inflation), nominal interest rates that include inflation expectations might actually increase. We will cover the determinants of market interest rates in Chapter 8.

In 1944, many of the world's economic powers met at Bretton Woods, New Hampshire. They agreed to an international monetary system tied to the U.S. dollar or gold via fixed or pegged exchange rates. One ounce of gold was set equal to $35. Each participating country then had its currency pegged to either gold or the U.S. dollar. This system of fixed exchange rates became known as the Bretton Woods system and was maintained until March 1973 when major currencies were allowed to float against each other. The result was a flexible, or floating, exchange rate system. While free market forces are allowed to operate today, central monetary authorities attempt to intervene in exchange markets when they believe that exchange rates between two currencies are harming world trade and the global economy. This actually makes the current international monetary system a managed floating exchange rate system.

Virtually all international transactions now involve the exchange of currencies or checkable deposits denominated in various currencies. Exchanges occur either for goods and services, for financial claims, or for other currencies. A **currency exchange rate** reflects the value of one currency relative to another. The relationship between currencies depends on both the supply and the demand for each currency relative to the other. The supply of a currency in international markets depends largely on the imports of the issuing country; that is, how much of its currency the country spends in world markets. Demand for a currency depends on the amount of exports that currency will buy from the issuing country. Demand also depends on the confidence of market participants in the restraint and stability of the monetary authority issuing the currency. If demand for a particular currency falls relative to its supply, then the exchange rate falls and the international purchasing power of that nation's money supply drops. Domestic inflation, political instability, or an excess of imports over exports can cause one currency to decline relative to another currency. If a currency is widely accepted, the demand for it may be increased by the desire of people worldwide to hold it as an international medium of exchange. Such is the case of the U.S. dollar, which is widely held internationally because of its general acceptance and the ability to hold its value. International finance is discussed in detail in Chapter 6.

> **currency exchange rate** value of one currency relative to another

A major international development occurred when 11 countries of the 15-member European Union, which met necessary economic and financial qualifications, agreed to give up their individual currencies and adopt a unified currency called the **euro** beginning on January 1, 1999. For example, the French gave up the franc, the Germans the mark, and the Italians the lira. Greece qualified in 2000 and was admitted as the twelfth euro-member country in 2001. Official implementation of the euro began on January 1, 2002. It is interesting to note that all members of the European Union do not currently use the euro, either because they have chosen to keep their own national currencies or because they do not qualify for adoption due to fiscal deficit and other constraints. The creation of the euro was accompanied by the formation of the European Central Bank, which replaces the central banks of each of the participating countries.

> **euro** a single currency that has replaced the individual currencies of a group of European countries

Although our focus is on the U.S. monetary system, we operate in a global economy. Thus, we must interact with other monetary systems, and a change in either the European Union or Japanese monetary systems will directly affect the U.S. monetary system. For example, when the European Central Bank increases interest rates in the European Union, the value of the U.S. dollar weakens relative to the euro. This increases the cost of products imported into the United States unless the Federal Reserve takes countering actions.

A growing international interest in the use of digital currencies is worth watching. As previously defined, digital currency is electronic money accepted for making payments. Digital currency serves as a medium of exchange and may be centralized or decentralized. Centralized digital currency is backed by the creditworthiness and taxing ability of a government issuer along with a central banking authority that controls the supply of the currency. For example, electronic money in the United States is denominated in dollars backed by the creditworthiness and taxing power of the government with the Fed controlling the money supply. Electronic money in European and other developed countries also takes the form of centralized digital currency.

Decentralized digital currency is unregulated digital money issued and generally controlled by its decentralized developers. Cryptocurrency is a special type of decentralized digital currency that uses cryptography to record and secure electronic payment transactions. Bitcoin is the most recognized example of the many types of cryptocurrency that have been developed in recent years. At this time, the acceptance and use of cryptocurrencies remains to be seen. However, the inability to regulate and control the amount of decentralized digital currencies remains a concern to central banking authorities and governments who are trying to manage money supplies throughout the world.

- **Institutions and Markets** The monetary system is composed of a central bank, the Federal Reserve System, and a banking system. In order for the monetary and financial systems to work, money must be accepted as the medium of exchange by each of us. Commercial banks, in the aggregate, help create and transfer money and, thus, help the monetary system operate efficiently. Other financial institutions also help in the savings-investment process, when individual savings are pooled and lent or invested in business firms.

   Occasionally the savings of some individuals are directed to other individuals who want to purchase homes using mortgage loans. Individual, institutional, and business savings also may be directed to help government entities to finance deficits caused by tax revenues being exceeded by expenditures.

- **Investments** Money is the fundamental store of wealth. While we often think of money in terms of coin and currency, the money supply also includes demand and other checkable deposits. Some definitions of the money supply also include savings accounts, time deposits, and money market mutual funds. An individual's net worth consists of real assets, such as automobiles and houses, mutual fund shares held, and holdings of the various types of money, less any debts.

Money markets are where debt securities with maturities of one year or less are originated and sometimes traded. Major money market securities include Treasury bills, commercial paper, negotiable certificates of deposit, banker's acceptances, repurchase agreements, and federal funds.

- **Financial Management** Business firms rely on financial institutions to help them raise funds from the savings of individuals. Businesses need money to conduct their day-to-day operations and need an efficient monetary system for collecting funds from customers and for paying their own bills in a timely fashion. Some businesses make use of money market securities for short-term investment purposes when they have surplus funds. Other businesses borrow in the money markets to help finance their short-term debt needs. Some business firms issue, while others invest in, commercial paper and repurchase agreements. Other business firms may hold their money market investments in Treasury bills or negotiable certificates of deposit. While money market securities are originated in primary markets, some trade actively in secondary markets.

SUMMARY

LO 2.1 Several developments led to the 2007–2008 financial crisis. A rapid decline in housing prices led to increased unemployment, first in housing-related activities and then more broadly. As a result, many homeowners were forced to default on their home mortgage loans. The financial crisis was made worse because the downturn occurred at a time when individuals, financial institutions, and businesses were heavily in debt.

LO 2.2 Money is transferred from savers to businesses in three ways. Direct transfers occur when savers purchase a business firm's securities from the business firm that issued the securities. Indirect transfers can involve an investment banking firm that uses money from savers to purchase a business firm's securities and then distribute the securities to savers. Indirect transfers also may be carried out through a financial intermediary. For example, a financial institution may issue its own securities to obtain money from savers, and then use the money to purchase a business firm's securities.

LO 2.3 The major components of the monetary system include a central bank (the Fed) and a banking system. The Fed defines and regulates the money supply, as well as facilitates the transferring of money through check processing and clearing. An efficient banking system, creates money, transfers money, provides financial intermediation, and processes/clears checks.

LO 2.4 Money is a physical or electronic asset accepted as a means of payment for goods, services, and debts. The functions of money include serving as a medium of exchange, a standard of value, and a store of value.

LO 2.5 Physical money (coin and currency) in the United States developed from full backing in gold or silver to token coins or fiat money. Coins were initially full-bodied money because they contained the same value in metal as their face value. Today, we have token coins because their face values are higher than the value of their metal content. Paper money was originally representative full-bodied money because the money was backed by an amount of precious metal equal in value to the face amount of the currency. Today, paper money is not backed by precious metals and is referred to as fiat money because currency is declared legal tender for purposes of making payments and discharging debts.

LO 2.6 The major types of money market securities are Treasury bills (short-term debt obligation issued by the government), commercial paper (short-term unsecured promissory note issued by high-quality corporations), negotiable certificate of deposit (short-term debt instrument issued by depository institutions), banker's acceptance (promise of future payment issued by a firm and guaranteed by a commercial bank), repurchase agreement (short-term debt security where the seller agrees to repurchase the security at a specified price and date), and federal funds (short-term loans typically for one day to one week made between depository institutions.

LO 2.7 The M1 money supply consists of currency, traveler's checks, demand deposits, and other checkable deposits at depository institutions. The M2 money supply definition consists of M1 plus highly liquid financial assets, including savings accounts, small time deposits, and retail money market mutual funds.

LO 2.8 The output of goods and services in the economy is known as the GDP. The money supply times the VM equals GDP. A net increase in the changes in the money supply and the VM will lead to a higher GDP.

Economists also express GDP as being equal to real output times the price level. Thus, a larger GDP due to an increase in the money supply with no change in the VM also means that a net increase in changes in real output and price level must occur. Monetarists contend that there is a direct link between the money supply and GDP via the VM. Keynesians believe the link is less direct because changes in money supply first affect interest rates, which, in turn, influence GDP through changes in consumption and investment. Evidence does not indicate that one group is right and the other is wrong.

LO 2.9 The international monetary system was historically tied to the gold standard. In 1944, the exchange rates between the currencies of most industrialized countries were fixed relative to the U.S. dollar or gold. By early 1973, major currencies were allowed to float against each other, resulting in a flexible, or floating, exchange rate system. Another major international monetary system development occurred when an initial 11 European Union countries agreed to give up their individual currencies for a unified currency called the euro, beginning January 1, 1999, with monetary policy being administered by the European Central Bank.

KEY TERMS

automatic transfer service (ATS) accounts	deposit money	M2 money supply	repurchase agreement
banker's acceptance	digital currency	medium of exchange	savings-investment process
barter	euro	money	standard of value
bimetallic standard	federal funds	money market mutual funds (MMMFs)	store of value
bitcoin	fiat money	money market securities	surplus economic unit
commercial paper	financial assets	negotiable certificate of deposit (negotiable CD)	token coins
credit cards	full-bodied money	purchasing power	Treasury bill
credit money	gross domestic product (GDP)	real assets	velocity of money
cryptocurrency	individual net worth	representative full-bodied money	virtual currency
currency exchange rate	inflation		
debit cards	liquidity		
deficit economic unit	M1 money supply		

REVIEW QUESTIONS

1. (LO 2.1) Briefly discuss the developments that led to the 2007–2008 financial crisis.

2. (LO 2.2) How do surplus economic units and deficit economic units differ?

3. (LO 2.2) Describe the three basic ways whereby money is transferred from savers to business firms.

4. (LO 2.2) Identify economic units in addition to business firms who might need funds from savers.

5. (LO 2.3) Identify the major participants in the U.S. monetary system.

6. (LO 2.4) Indicate how real assets and financial assets differ.

7. (LO 2.4) Define money and indicate the basic functions of money.

8. (LO 2.4) Describe how an individual's net worth is determined.

9. (LO 2.5) Briefly describe the development of money, from barter to the use of precious metals.

10. (LO 2.5) What is the difference between full-bodied money and token coins?

11. (LO 2.5) Describe how representative full-bodied money and fiat money differ.

12. (LO 2.5) What is deposit money and how it is "backed"?

13. (LO 2.5) What are ATS accounts?

14. (LO 2.5) What are debit cards and how are they used?

15. (LO 2.6) Define money market securities and briefly describe the major types of these securities.

16. (LO 2.7) Describe the M1 definition of the money supply and indicate the relative significance of the M1 components.

17. (LO 2.7) How does M2 differ from M1? What are money market mutual funds?

18. (LO 2.8) Briefly describe the monetarists' view of the relationship between money supply and economic activity.

19. (LO 2.8) How do Keynesians view the relationship between money supply and economic activity?

20. (LO 2.9) Briefly describe the development of the international monetary system.

EXERCISES

1. Match the following money market securities with their issuers.

Securities	Issuers
a. Treasury bills	1. Depository institutions
b. Negotiable CDs	2. U.S. government
c. Commercial paper	3. Banks
d. Banker's acceptances	4. Business firms and institutions

2. Match the following money market securities with the level of secondary market activity.

a. Treasury bills	1. no activity
b. Commercial paper	2. low activity
c. Federal funds	3. moderate activity
d. Negotiable CDs	4. high activity

3. Go to the website of the Federal Reserve Bank of St. Louis at https://www.stlouisfed.org. Go to "Research and Data" and access the Federal Reserve Economic Database (FRED). Compare the present size of M1 and M2 money stock measures with the data presented in the Measures of the U.S. Money Supply section of this chapter. Also find the current sizes of these M1 components: currency, travelers' checks, demand deposits, and other checkable deposits. Express each component as a percentage of M1 and compare your percentages with those presented in the chapter.

4. Find several recent issues of *Bloomberg Businessweek*. Identify articles relating to developments in the U.S. monetary system. Also search for possible developments occurring in foreign monetary systems.

5. We are faced with ethics decisions involving money almost every day. For example, we all probably have seen money in the form of coin or currency lying on the ground or floor somewhere. We also may have at some time discovered a lost wallet. Should it matter if the amount of money is small or large? Should it matter if no one else is around or there is no evidence of who lost the money? Sometimes we hear the finders-keepers argument being used to rationalize an individual's decision. How would you react to the following scenarios?

    a. You are walking down a street and find a dollar bill lying on the ground. No one else is close by. You consider picking up the dollar, acknowledging your good luck, and putting it in your pocket. What would you do?

    b. While you are shopping in a grocery store you see a wallet lying on the floor. You don't know who dropped the wallet. You consider holding on to the wallet until you get home and then search for the owner's identification so that you might contact the owner with information that you have the wallet. Alternatively, you could just give the wallet to the store manager. What would you do?

1. Determine the size of the M1 money supply using the following information.

Currency plus Traveler's checks	$25 million
Negotiable CDs	$10 million
Demand deposits	$13 million
Other checkable deposits	$12 million

2. Determine the size of the M1 money supply using the following information.

Currency	$700 billion
Money market mutual funds	$2,000 billion
Demand deposits	$300 billion
Other checkable deposits	$300 billion
Traveler's checks	$10 billion

3. Determine the size of the demand deposits component of the M1 money supply using the following information.

Currency	$350 million
Traveler's checks	$10 million
Other checkable deposits	$200 million
Small time deposits	$100 million
M1 money supply	$800 million

4. Following are components of the M1 money supply at the end of last year. What will be the size of the M1 money supply at the end of next year if currency grows by 10%, demand deposits grow by 5%, other checkable deposits grow by 8%, and the amount of traveler's checks stays the same?

Currency	$700 billion
Demand deposits	$300 billion
Other checkable deposits	$300 billion
Traveler's checks	$10 billion

5. The following information is available to you: travelers' checks = $1 million, coin and paper currency = $30 million, repurchase agreements and Eurodollars = $15 million, demand deposits = $25 million, retail money market mutual funds = $60 million, savings accounts at depository institutions = $40 million, checkable deposits at depository institutions = $35 million, large-denomination time deposits = $50 million, institutional money market mutual funds = $65 million, and small-denomination time deposits = $45 million. Using Fed definitions, determine the dollar sizes of the
   a. M1 money supply
   b. M2 money supply

6. A country's GDP is $20 billion, and its money supply (MS) is $5 billion.
   a. What is the country's VM?
   b. If the MS stays at the same level next year while the velocity of money "turns over" 4.5 times, what would be the level of GDP?
   c. Assume that the VM will turn over four times next year. If the country wants a GDP of $22 billion at the end of next year, what will have to be the size of the money supply? What percentage increase in the MS will be necessary to achieve the target GDP?

7. Assume that the real output (RO) for a country is expected to be 2.4 million products.
   a. If the price level (PL) is $250 per product, what will be the amount of the GDP?
   b. Now assume that the GDP is projected to be $8 million next year. What will the PL of the products need to be to reach the GDP target?
   c. Now assume that the RO of 2.4 million products is composed of equal amounts of two types of products. The first product sells for $100 each, and the second product sells for $500 each. What will be the size of the GDP?

8. Assume that a country estimates its M1 money supply at $20 million. A broader measure of the money supply, M2, is $50 million. The country's GDP is $100 million. Production or real output for the country is 500,000 units or products.
   a. Determine the VM based on the M1 money supply.
   b. Determine the VM based on the M2 money supply.
   c. Determine the average price for the real output.

9. Using the data in Problem 7 along with the monetarists' view of the relationship between money supply and GDP, answer the following:
   a. If the M1 money supply increases by 10% and the M1 VM does not change, what is the expected value of the GDP for next year?
   b. Based on the information from (a), if real output does not change next year, what is the expected average price for the products? What percentage change, if any, would take place in the price level?
   c. If the M2 money supply decreases by 10% and the M2 VM does not change, what is the expected value of GDP next year?
   d. Based on information from (c), if the price level does not change next year, what is the expected real output in units or products?

10. The following information was gathered for the XYZ economy: VM = 3.8 times, average price level = $85, and real output = 10,000 units.
    a. What is the nominal GDP for the XYZ economy?
    b. What is the size of the money supply for the XYZ economy?
    c. If real output increases by 10% next year, but the price level and VM do not change, what money supply amount will be needed to support this real growth in economic activity?
    d. What will be the money supply needed to support economic activity next year if real output increases to 12,000 units, the average price increases to $90, and velocity increases by four times?

11. The One Product economy, which produces and sells only personal computers (PCs), expects that it can sell 500 more, or 12,500 PCs, next year. Nominal GDP was $20 million this year, and the money supply was $7 million. The central bank for the One Product economy plans to increase the money supply by 10% next year.
    a. What was the average selling price for the personal computers this year?
    b. What is the expected average selling price next year for personal computers if the VM remains at this year's turnover rate? What percentage change in price level is expected to occur?
    c. If the objective is to keep the price level the same next year (i.e. no inflation), what percentage increase in the money supply should the central bank plan for?
    d. How would your answer in (c) change if the VM is expected to be three times next year? What is it now?

12. **Challenge Problem** The following problem requires a basic knowledge about probabilities and the calculation of expected values. The problem is more easily solved using Excel spreadsheet software.

Scenario	A	B	C	D	E	Metric
Probability	.10	.20	.40	.20	.10	Percent
VM	1.75	2.5	3.0	3.5	4.25	Turnover
Real output	375	450	500	550	625	Units in thousands
Price level	75	90	100	110	125	Dollars

a. Calculate the dollar amount of the money supply under each scenario or outcome.
b. Calculate the expected value of the money supply, taking into consideration each scenario and its probability of occurrence.
c. Scenario C is the most likely scenario given that its probability of occurrence is 40%. Show how the amount of the money supply would change holding real output at 500,000 units and the price level at $100 for each of the VM turnover rates (you have previously calculated the money supply under Scenario C for a turnover of three times).
d. Repeat the Scenario C exercise in (c) but now hold the VM at three times and price level at $100 and allow real output to change.
e. Repeat the Scenario C exercise in (c) but now hold the VM at three times and real output at 500,000 units and allow the price level to change.

Banks and Other Financial Institutions

CHAPTER 3

LEARNING OBJECTIVES

After studying this chapter, you should be able to do the following:

LO 3.1   Describe how financial institutions were impacted by the financial crisis.

LO 3.2   Identify the major financial institutions and their roles in the financial system.

LO 3.3   Describe how commercial banking and investment banking differ, and identify the functions of banks and the banking system.

LO 3.4   Discuss the historical development of the U.S. banking system.

LO 3.5   Discuss general regulation of the banking system and how depositors' funds are protected.

LO 3.6   Describe the structure of banks in terms of bank charters, branch banking, and bank holding companies.

LO 3.7   Describe the bank balance sheet and the major account categories that it contains.

LO 3.8   Describe bank management practices in terms of bank liquidity and bank solvency, and explain why and how bank capital is managed.

LO 3.9   Describe characteristics of several foreign banking systems.

Where we have been. . . In Chapter 2, we presented an overview of the U.S. monetary system. We discussed how the monetary system is intertwined with the savings-investment process, and we identified the major participants in the monetary system. Money has three functions, which are a medium of exchange, a standard of value, and a store of value. An understanding of how money developed in the United States over time, as well as knowing current definitions of the U.S. money supply, will be useful as we move through Part 1. Having an understanding of the relationship between the money supply and the economy will help us understand how the actions of policy makers influence economic activity and the financial system itself.

Where we are Going. . . As we move through Part 1, we continue to build on our understanding of the U.S. financial system. Chapter 4 focuses on the Federal Reserve System. We will describe the structure of the Fed and discuss the Fed's functions. The Fed directs monetary policy by setting reserve requirements and interest rates on loans to depository institutions and through buying and selling U.S. government securities. We will also discuss the Fed's supervisory and regulatory responsibilities. The last two chapters in Part 1 focus on the role of the policy makers (those responsible for carrying out fiscal policy, monetary policy, and debt management) and on how international developments influence the financial system.

How this chapter applies to me. . . You probably have a checking account at a depository institution. You may also have a savings account or own some shares in a mutual fund. You may even have a loan on an automobile or a home mortgage. Each of these activities requires an interaction with a financial institution. After reading this chapter you should have a better understanding of what depository and other financial institutions do in carrying out the savings-investment process and how banks operate and are managed.

Webster's New English Dictionary defines *bank* as,

an establishment for the deposit, custody, and issue of money, for making loans and discounts, and for making easier the exchange of funds by checks, notes, etc.

Webster also defines *bank* as,

the funds of a gambling establishment; the fund or pool by the banker or dealer in some gambling games.

Most of us associate the first definition with our perception of banks and banking in the United States. However, there have been examples throughout history and even recently where the second definition seems to fit. For example, isolated fraudulent behavior on the part of some commercial bank and savings and loan association (S&L) officers has resulted in criminal indictments and even in prison sentences. Overall, of course, banks and other financial institutions have performed admirably well in getting savings to investors and contributing to an efficient financial system.

3.1 FINANCIAL INSTITUTION PROBLEMS DURING THE 2007–2008 FINANCIAL CRISIS

mortgage loan backed by real property in the form of buildings and houses

mortgage-backed security debt security created by pooling together a group of mortgage loans

CRISIS Homeowners typically finance a portion of the purchase of their houses with mortgage loans. A mortgage is a loan backed by real property in the form of buildings and houses. During the first decade of the twenty-first century, banks and other mortgage lenders participated in "pooling" together loans they originated into securities. Other financial intermediaries also "repackaged" mortgage loans into mortgaged-backed securities. A mortgage-backed security is a debt security created by pooling together a group of mortgage loans whose periodic payments belong to the holders of the security. The value of mortgage-backed securities depend on the value of the homes against which the underlying mortgages are issued.

As previously noted, housing prices peaked in 2006 and home values then began a sharp decline leading to the 2007–2008 financial crisis. Housing-related jobs were lost and unemployment increased, resulting in increasing mortgage loan defaults by homeowners. Falling house prices and rising mortgage loan defaults, in turn, caused the value of mortgage loans, and associated mortgage-backed securities, on those houses to also drop. In many instances, the value of houses declined to levels below the amounts of the underlying mortgages, wiping out all equity the homeowners had in the houses. When mortgage loans exceed the value of the underlying houses, the mortgage loans are said to be "underwater."

Many banks and other financial institutions that held mortgage loans and mortgage-backed securities as assets suffered liquidity and solvency problems when the values of these loans and securities fell to such low levels that there was concern whether the financial institutions could meet their liability obligations when they came due. This situation was made worse by increasing unemployment throughout the United States, resulting in a contraction in economic activity that culminated in the Great Recession of 2008–2009.

In March 2008, Bear Sterns, a major financial institution, was on the verge of failing due to the collapse of the values of mortgage-backed securities and had to be acquired by the JPMorgan Chase & Co. with the help of the Federal Reserve and the U.S. Treasury. By September 2008, the financial crisis was at its peak. Lehman Brothers, a major investment bank, was allowed to fail, and Merrill Lynch was sold to Bank of America.

Shortly after the Lehman bankruptcy and the Merrill sale, American International Group (AIG), the largest insurance firm in the United States, was "bailed out" by the Federal Reserve with the U.S. government receiving an ownership interest in AIG. Like Merrill, the Federal National Mortgage Association (Fannie Mae), and the Federal Home Mortgage Association (Freddie Mac), AIG was considered "too large to fail" due to its potential impact on the global financial markets.

In late September 2008, Washington Mutual, the largest S&L in the United States, failed with most of its assets being purchased by JPMorgan Chase. Wachovia Bank, then the fourth largest commercial bank in the United States, was also on the brink of bankruptcy before finally agreeing to be purchased by Wells Fargo Bank. Citigroup and Bank of America, the first and second largest U.S. banks, respectively, also were suffering financial difficulties.

The U.S. government responded with the passage of the Economic Stabilization Act of 2008 in early October 2008. A primary focus of the legislation was to allow the U.S. Treasury to purchase up to $700 billion of "troubled" or "toxic" assets held by financial institutions. This became known as the Troubled Asset Relief Program (TARP). However, much of the TARP funds were actually used to invest capital in banks with little equity on their balance sheets, as well as to rescue large nonfinancial business firms, specifically General Motors and Chrysler, who were on the verge of failing. In an effort to stimulate economic activity, the U.S. government also passed the $787 billion American Recovery and Reinvestment Act of 2009 in February 2009. Funds were to be used to provide tax relief, appropriations, and direct spending. In Chapter 5, we will discuss the legislative and other actions by the U.S. government and the Federal Reserve to counter the perfect financial storm.

3.2 TYPES AND ROLES OF FINANCIAL INSTITUTIONS

The current system of financial institutions or intermediaries in the United States, like the monetary system, evolved to meet the needs of the country's citizens and to facilitate the savings-investment process. Individuals may save and grow their savings with the assistance of financial institutions. While individuals can invest directly in the securities of business firms and government units, most individuals invest indirectly through financial institutions that do the lending and investing for them. Financial intermediation is the process by which individual savings are accumulated in depository institutions and, in turn, lent or invested.

Figure 3.1 shows the major types of financial intermediaries grouped into four categories – depository institutions, contractual savings organizations, securities firms, and finance companies. Depository institutions accept deposits or savings from individuals and then lend these pooled savings to businesses, governments, and individuals. Depository institutions include commercial banks, savings and loan associations (S&Ls), savings banks, and credit unions. Contractual savings organizations collect premiums on insurance policies and employee/employer contributions from pension fund participants and provide retirement benefits and insurance against major financial losses. Insurance companies and pension funds are the two important forms of contractual savings organizations.

Securities firms accept and invest individual savings and also facilitate the sale and transfer of securities between investors. In addition to pooling individual savings and investments, securities firms receive funds from other financial intermediaries. Investment companies (mutual funds), investment banking firms, and brokerage firms are the primary types of securities firms that we will cover. Finance firms provide loans directly to consumers and businesses, as well as help borrowers obtain mortgage loans on real property. Our emphasis will be on finance companies and mortgage banking firms when discussing finance firms.

Few of today's financial intermediaries existed during the American colonial period. Only commercial banks and insurance companies (life and property) can be traced back prior to 1800. Savings banks and S&Ls began developing during the early 1800s. Investment banking firms (and

financial intermediation process by which savings are accumulated in financial institutions and then lent or invested

depository institutions accept deposits from individuals and then lend pooled deposits to businesses, governments, and individuals

contractual savings organizations collect premiums and contributions from participants and provide retirement benefits and insurance against major financial losses

securities firms accept and invest individual savings and also facilitate the sale and transfer of securities between investors

finance firms provide loans directly to consumers and businesses and help borrowers obtain mortgage loans on real property

Financial institutions categories	Primary sources of funds
Depository institutions	
Commercial banks	Individual savings
Savings and loan associations	Individual savings
Savings banks	Individual savings
Credit unions	Individual savings
Contractual savings organizations	
Insurance companies	Premiums paid on policies
Pension funds	Employee/employer contributions
Securities firms	
Investment companies (mutual funds)	Individual savings (investments)
Investment banking firms	Other financial institutions
Brokerage firms	Other financial institutions
Finance firms	
Finance companies	Other financial institutions
Mortgage banking firms	Other financial institutions

FIGURE 3.1 Types of financial institutions

organized securities exchanges) also can be traced back to the first half of the 1800s. No new major financial intermediaries evolved during the last half of the nineteenth century. Credit unions, pension funds, mutual funds, and finance companies began during the early part of the 1900s. Thus, throughout much of the 1900s and into the twenty-first century, emphasis has been on redefining and restructuring existing financial intermediaries rather than introducing new ones.

3.2.1 DEPOSITORY INSTITUTIONS

commercial banks depository institutions that accept deposits, issue check-writing accounts, and make loans

When we refer to banks and the banking system in the United States, we primarily think in terms of commercial banking. **Commercial banks** are depository institutions that accept deposits, issue check-writing accounts, and make loans to businesses and individuals. Depository institutions also include three thrift institutions in addition to commercial banks. **Thrift institutions** are noncommercial bank depository institutions referred to as savings and loan associations (S&Ls), savings banks, and credit unions that accumulate individual savings and lend primarily to other individuals. S&Ls engage in some lending to businesses but focus primarily on loans to individuals. Savings banks and credit unions focus on providing consumer and home mortgage loans to individuals seeking to purchase items such as automobiles and houses.

thrift institutions noncommercial bank depository institutions that accumulate individual savings and primarily make consumer and mortgage loans

Savings banks made their appearance in 1812, emphasizing individual thrift savings and safety of principal. **Savings banks** accept the savings of individuals and lend pooled savings to individuals, primarily in the form of mortgage loans. Very often the trustees of these banks were prominent local citizens, serving without pay, who regarded their service as an important civic duty. Today, savings banks operate almost entirely in New England, New York, and New Jersey, with most of their assets continuing to be invested in mortgage loans.

savings banks accept the savings of individuals and lend pooled savings to individuals primarily in the form of mortgage loans

Savings and loan associations (S&Ls), known also as either savings and loans or S&Ls, came on the scene in 1831. The basic mission of these institutions, which were first known as building societies and then as building and loan associations, was to provide home mortgage financing. In distinguishing between savings banks and S&Ls, it might be said that, originally, the savings banks' emphasis was on thrift and the safety of savings, while the emphasis of the S&Ls was on home financing. Today, S&Ls accept individual savings and lend pooled savings to businesses and to individuals, primarily in the form of mortgage loans. In contrast with the limited geographic expansion of savings banking, savings and loan activity spread throughout the United States.

savings and loan associations (S&Ls) accept individual savings and lend pooled savings to individuals, primarily in the form of mortgage loans, and businesses

Credit unions came on the American scene much later than the other thrift institutions. **Credit unions** are cooperative, nonprofit organizations that exist primarily to provide member depositors with consumer credit, including the financing of automobiles and the purchase of homes. Credit unions are made up of individuals who possess common bonds of association, such as occupation, residence, or church affiliation. These institutions derive their funds almost entirely from the savings of their members. The first official credit union was formed in the United States in 1909, but it was not until the 1920s that credit unions became important as a special form of depository institution.

credit unions cooperative, nonprofit organizations that exist primarily to provide member depositors with consumer credit

Figure 3.2 illustrates graphically the process of getting funds from individual savers and investors into the hands of *business firms* that want to make investments to maintain and grow their firms. Individuals make deposits in commercial banks that, in turn, make loans to and purchase debt securities from business firms. Since thrift institutions focus primarily on gathering the savings of individuals and, in turn, lending those funds to individuals, they are not depicted on Figure 3.2.

3.2.2 CONTRACTUAL SAVINGS ORGANIZATIONS

Contractual savings organizations in the form of insurance companies and pension funds play important roles by collecting premiums and contributions and using these pooled funds to purchase the debt and equity securities of business firms, as depicted in Figure 3.2. Of course, contractual savings organizations also actively purchase the debt securities issued by governmental units. **Insurance companies** provide financial protection to individuals and businesses for life, property, liability, and health uncertainties. Policyholders pay premiums to insurance companies that invest these funds until the insured claims must be paid. Life insurance provides economic security for dependents in the event of premature death of the insured individual. Health insurance provides protection against possible catastrophic

insurance companies provide financial protection to individuals and businesses for life, property, liability, and health uncertainties

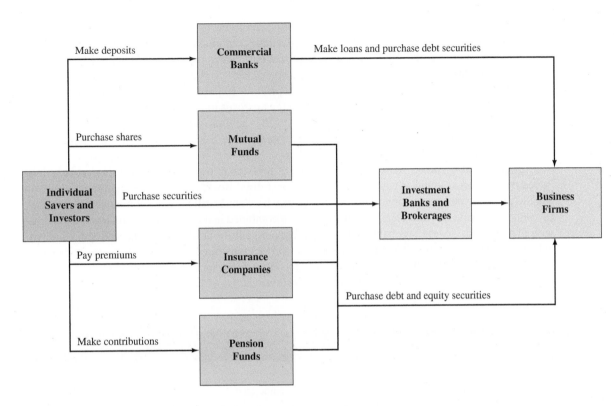

FIGURE 3.2
Role of financial
institutions in
directing savings
to business firms

medical expenses in the event the insured individual becomes ill or is in an accident. Property insurance protects a policyholder against possible financial loss from fire, theft, and other insured perils. Liability insurance protects a policyholder against possible financial loss from a claim of negligence charged by another individual.

Pension funds receive contributions from employees and/or their employers and invest the proceeds on behalf of the employees. The purpose of a pension plan is to provide income during an individual's retirement years. Pension funds are either private pension plans or government-sponsored plans. Many business organizations provide private pension plans for their employees. A private pension plan may be either insured or noninsured. A contractual plan with a life insurance company is an insured plan. An uninsured plan uses a trustee, often a commercial bank or trust company, to manage, invest, and distribute benefits as established in the trust arrangement. Government-sponsored plans may involve either the federal government or state and local governments. Social Security is the largest federal pension plan. The Social Security plan is funded by currently working individuals paying Social Security taxes. Social Security is designed to provide only minimum retirement benefits, so most individuals will need to accumulate additional funds before retirement. The federal government also provides pension plans for its employees, known as civil servants, as well as for military employees. State and local government pension plans typically are established to cover teachers, police and fire employees, and other civil servants.

pension funds receive contributions from employees and/or their employers and invest the proceeds on behalf of the employees for use during their retirement years

3.2.3 SECURITIES FIRMS

Securities firms perform several financial functions. Some securities firms are active in the savings-investment process, while others concentrate primarily on marketing new securities and facilitating the transfer of existing securities between investors. **Investment companies** sell shares in their firms to individuals and others and invest the pooled proceeds in corporate and government securities. An investment company may be either a closed-end fund or an open-end fund. A closed-end fund issues a fixed number of its shares to investors and invests the pooled funds in securities. Shares in a closed-end fund are bought and sold in secondary securities markets once they have been initially issued.

investment companies sell shares in their firms to individuals and others and invest the pooled proceeds in corporate and government securities

mutual funds open-end investment companies that can issue an unlimited number of their shares to their investors and use the pooled proceeds to purchase corporate and government securities

investment banking firms sell or market new securities issued by businesses to individual and institutional investors

brokerage firms assist individuals to purchase new or existing securities issues or to sell previously purchased securities

Open-end funds, typically called mutual funds, can issue an unlimited number of their shares to their investors and use the pooled proceeds to purchase corporate and government securities. However, unlike with closed-end funds, investors purchase new shares or redeem old shares directly with their mutual fund rather than buying and selling the shares in a secondary securities market. Figure 3.2, which focuses on getting funds to business firms, depicts the important role that mutual funds play by selling shares to individual investors and then using the proceeds to purchase debt and equity securities issued by business firms. Mutual funds grow by investing the funds of their existing investors in securities that will pay or distribute cash and will appreciate in value. Successful mutual funds attract more investor funds and, in turn, invest in more securities.

Investment banking firms, also referred to as investment banks, sell or market new securities issued by businesses to individual and institutional investors. Brokerage firms assist individuals who want to purchase new or existing securities issues or who want to sell previously purchased securities. Investment banking and brokerage activities are often combined in the same firms. However, in contrast with mutual funds, investment banking firms and brokerage firms do not gather the savings of individuals but rather market or sell securities issued by corporations directly to individuals, as depicted in Figure 3.2. Investment banking and brokerage firms obtain financial capital to carry out their activities from their own resources or from other financial institutions.

SMALL BUSINESS PRACTICE

TYPES OF CREDIT USED BY SMALL BUSINESSES

At various times the Fed conducts national surveys of small business finances. These are nationally representative surveys of small businesses designed to gather data on bank and nonbank participants in the supplying of credit to small businesses.

Data are gathered on six types of loans – credit lines used, mortgage loans, equipment loans, vehicle loans, capital leases, and other loans. Data on trade credit and credit card debt are not gathered. Bank credit lines used is the single most important source of the six types of credit used by small businesses. Lines of credit are bank loans against which small businesses can "draw down" or borrow against.

3.2.4 FINANCE FIRMS

finance companies provide loans directly to consumers and businesses or aid individuals in obtaining financing of durable goods and homes

Finance firms, while an important type of financial institution, are not included in Figure 3.2 because they focus largely on providing loans to individuals for meeting credit needs and purchasing durable goods and homes. Finance companies provide loans directly to consumers and businesses or aid individuals in obtaining financing. Sales and consumer finance companies lend to individuals. *Sales finance companies* finance installment loan purchases of automobiles and other durable goods, such as washers, dryers, and refrigerators. *Consumer finance companies* provide small loans to individuals and households. *Commercial finance companies* provide loans to businesses that are unable to obtain financing from commercial banks. However, commercial finance companies are not included in Figure 3.2 because they do not accumulate the savings of individuals but rather get funds for making loans to businesses from other financial institutions.

mortgage banking firms originate mortgage loans on homes and other real property by bringing together borrowers and institutional investors

Mortgage banking firms, or mortgage companies, help individuals obtain mortgage loans by bringing together borrowers and institutional investors. A *mortgage loan* is a loan on real property, such as a house, whereby the borrower pledges the property as collateral to guarantee that the loan will be repaid. The primary mortgage market, where home and other real property loans are "originated," is very important to the success of the financial system. Traditionally, once a mortgage loan was originated, it was held by the lender until maturity or until the loan was prepaid. However, as individual mortgage loans became more standardized, there have arisen secondary mortgage markets, in which existing real property mortgages are bought and sold.

DISCUSSION QUESTION 1

Assume you want to open both a check-writing account and a savings account. Would you prefer holding the accounts in a commercial bank, savings and loan association, or a credit union? Why?

LEARNING ACTIVITY

1. Go to the Citibank website, https://www.citibank.com. Find information on the savings alternatives and interest rates currently being paid.
2. Go to the Small Business Administration's website, https://www.sba.gov. Find information about small business lending in the United States and write a brief summary.

We now turn our attention to the development of a basic understanding of the current U.S. banking system. First, we describe the traditional differences between commercial banking and investment banking and their combination to provide universal banking. Then we cover the functions of banks and the banking system.

3.3 OVERVIEW OF THE BANKING SYSTEM

3.3.1 COMMERCIAL, INVESTMENT, AND UNIVERSAL BANKING

When we refer to banks and the banking system in the United States, we primarily think in terms of commercial banking. As previously noted, a *commercial bank* accepts deposits, issues check-writing accounts to facilitate purchases and paying bills, and makes loans to individuals and businesses. This definition of a bank is consistent with the Webster's dictionary definition cited at the beginning of the chapter. In contrast, an **investment bank** helps businesses sell their new debt and equity securities to raise financial capital.

investment bank a bank that helps businesses sell their new debt and equity securities to raise financial capital

Figure 3.3 depicts these two types of indirect transfers from savers to a business firm. You should be able to recall a similarity between this figure and Figure 2.2 in Chapter 2, which also included direct transfers between individuals and business firms whereby no financial institution performs an intermediary role by bringing individual investors together with business firms desiring to sell securities. Direct investments are relatively rare occurrences. The top portion of Figure 3.3 shows the traditional role of the commercial bank as a financial institution that accepts the deposits of savers in exchange for the bank's securities (e.g. certificates of deposit, or CDs). The bank then lends money to the business firm in exchange for the firm's promise (e.g. a note) to repay the loan. The bottom portion of Figure 3.3 shows that the investment bank markets the business firm's securities (e.g. a bond) to savers. This can be done either by first purchasing the securities from the firm and then reselling the securities (a practice called "underwriting," as we will see in Chapter 11) or by just marketing the securities on behalf of the issuing firm to savers.

In the midst of the Great Depression, Congress passed the *Banking Act of 1933*. This legislation, commonly known as the **Glass–Steagall Act of 1933** recognizing those individuals responsible for

Glass–Steagall Act of 1933 the act provided for separation of commercial banking and investment banking activities in the United States

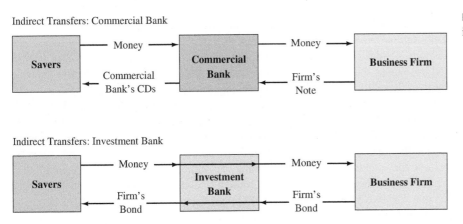

Indirect Transfers: Commercial Bank

Indirect Transfers: Investment Bank

FIGURE 3.3 Commercial banking and investment banking intermediation activities

introducing and supporting the act, provided for the separation of commercial banking and investment banking in the United States. Many banks failed during the late 1920s and early 1930s, and efforts were undertaken to assess why banks failed. Some politicians, regulators, and others thought that many of the bank failures had been caused, in part, by investment banking activities involving underwriting and the holding of equity securities. The result was passage of the Glass–Steagall Act.

Gramm–Leach–Bliley Act of 1999 the act repealed the separation of commercial banking and investment banking provided for in the Glass–Steagall Act

After more than six decades, the Glass–Steagall Act was repealed with the passage of the **Gramm–Leach–Bliley Act of 1999**. When Glass–Steagall was enacted, many officials and individuals believed that government regulation was the answer to avoiding banking excesses and mismanagement. An underlying belief was that competition and free markets represent the best way to manage banking risks and create stability in the financial system. Commercial banks were no longer prohibited from engaging in investment banking and insurance underwriting. Likewise, insurance companies and investment banking firms could engage in commercial banking. Universal banking was permitted in the United States, as in various other countries. A **universal bank** is a bank that engages in both commercial banking and investment banking. Germany also has universal banking, and the United Kingdom does not legally separate commercial banking from investment banking.

universal bank bank that engages in both commercial banking and investment banking activities

However, as a result of the 2007–2008 financial crisis and the 2008–2009 Great Recession, government officials and others promoted the need to move toward more re-regulation of financial institutions to help restore financial stability in the United States. The result was the passage of the Dodd–Frank Wall Street Reform and Consumer Protection Act in 2010, which we will discuss later in this chapter.

3.3.2 FUNCTIONS OF BANKS AND THE BANKING SYSTEM

Depository institutions accept deposits, make loans, and issue checkable deposit accounts. Like commercial banks, savings and loan associations (also called savings and loans or S&Ls), savings banks, and credit unions perform these activities. The U.S. **banking system** includes commercial banks, savings and loans, savings banks, and credit unions. It is common practice today to refer to all depository institutions as banks. Banks and the banking system perform five functions:

banking system commercial banks, savings and loans, savings banks, and credit unions that operate in the U.S. financial system

1. Accepting deposits
2. Granting loans
3. Issuing checkable deposit accounts
4. Clearing checks
5. Creating deposit money.

To the extent that commercial banks also perform investment banking operations (i.e. universal banks), they perform an additional function:

6. Raising financial capital for businesses

In accepting deposits, banks provide a safe place for the public to keep money for future use. Individuals and businesses seldom wish to spend their money as it becomes available; without depository facilities such funds may lie idle. The banking system puts the accumulated deposits to use through loans to persons and businesses that have an immediate use for them. This, of course, is the financial intermediation activity of depository institutions in the savings-investment process.

Banks play an important role in the payments process or mechanism in place in the U.S. financial system by creating electronic deposit money. By writing checks against demand and other checkable deposits, it is easier for individuals and businesses to make purchases and to pay bills or debts. Of course, it is not enough just to permit check writing; there must also be an efficient mechanism for processing the checks so they can be presented to the bank that authorized the check for payment.

Let's take a brief look at how checks were traditionally "cleared" or processed in the United States. Let's assume that you owe $100 for the purchase of a product on credit from the ABC firm. You write a $100 check against your checkable deposit account, held at First Bank, payable to ABC and mail the check to ABC. An ABC employee opens the envelope containing your check and deposits the check in the ABC's deposit account held at Last Bank.

The traditional ways to clear a check through the U.S. banking system are as follows:

- Bank to bank

- Through a bank clearinghouse

- Through a Federal Reserve Bank.

Figure 3.4 shows these three ways of processing or collecting a check. Last Bank could present your check directly to First Bank for payment. First Bank pays the check and deducts the amount of the check from your checkable deposit account. Since First Bank authorized or issued the deposit money, confidence in its creditworthiness is important in making the clearing process work.

However, since direct check presentation is both costly and time-consuming, most banks use bank clearinghouses. This is particularly useful when the two banks are in different cities. In our example, the bank clearinghouse would receive the check from Last Bank, credit the bank's account at the clearinghouse, and subtract the amount of your check from First Bank's account at the clearinghouse. At the end of each day, all of a bank's transactions handled through the clearinghouse are "netted out," with the result being an increase or decrease in the bank's account with the clearinghouse. Of course, when presented with your check, First Bank will reduce your checkable deposit account accordingly.

Sometimes banks work closely with and hold deposit accounts at other banks known as "correspondent" banks in distant cities. For example, Last Bank may hold a deposit account at one of its correspondent banks called Middle Bank, which is in the same city as First Bank. In this case, when Last Bank receives your check from ABC, it is deposited in Last Bank's account at Middle Bank. Middle Bank, in turn, either presents your check directly to First Bank or uses the bank clearinghouse in its and First Bank's city.

Most depository institutions with large checkable deposit accounts are required to hold accounts with the Federal Reserve. Actually, the funds are held with the Federal Reserve Bank responsible for

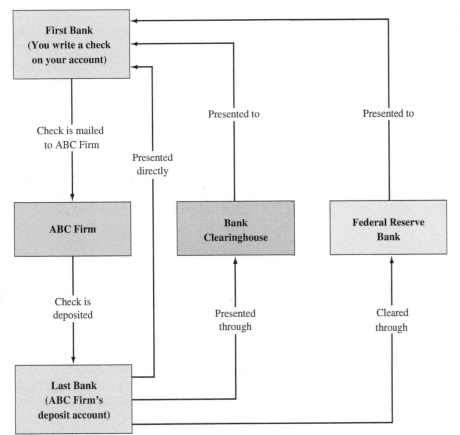

FIGURE 3.4 Traditional methods for processing checks through the banking system

their city or area, as we will see in the next chapter. If Last Bank wants to use the Federal Reserve for check-clearing purposes, it will first deposit your check with its Federal Reserve Bank, where Last Bank's account will be increased. The Fed Bank will also reduce First Bank's account held at the Federal Reserve even if it is held at a different Federal Reserve Bank. The check then is returned to First Bank so that your checkable account balance can be reduced by the $100.

When paper checks were physically transferred and cleared through the financial system, the process was time-consuming and expensive. Once photos of checks became legally acceptable in lieu of actual paper checks, and they could be transferred electronically, the check clearing process became much more efficient. The acceptance of photo copies of checks also facilitated the development of online banking. For example, a check received in the mail can be photo copied with a smart phone camera and then the photo sent electronically for deposit in one's checking account. We examine the Fed's check-clearing process in greater detail in Chapter 4.

Today, automated clearinghouses (ACHs) provide clearing or settlement services in addition to the clearing of checks. An ACH is a computer-based system for processing the exchange of electronic credit and debit transactions between financial institution participants. Examples of credit transactions include payroll and direct deposit payments. Examples of debit transactions include consumer payments for utility bills and mortgage loans. Transactions are gathered in batches by individual financial institutions and are then sent to the ACH, which determines net settlements between participants.

The banking system has the unique ability to create electronic deposit money and thus expand the money supply. The ability to create more and more deposit money would be almost limitless as long as the deposit money keeps coming back into the banking system, unless banks are required to hold a portion of their checkable deposits in the form of reserves. We examine deposit, reserves, and other accounts later in this chapter. Chapter 4 will cover how the Fed can regulate the money supply by setting reserve requirements that banks must hold against their checkable deposits. Chapter 5 will explore how reserve requirements and other Fed tools can be used to set monetary policy.

3.4 HISTORICAL DEVELOPMENT OF THE U.S. BANKING SYSTEM

Before we examine the current structure of the banking industry, we will review a little U.S. banking history. We know you are about to ask, "Why should I learn anything about the history of banking?" First, a basic understanding of how the banking system evolved should help us better understand how and why the system operates the way it does today. Second, to paraphrase the quotation at the beginning of Chapter 1, "Those who don't study history are doomed to repeat its mistakes."

3.4.1 BEFORE THE CIVIL WAR

Until the Civil War, banking in the United States developed under confusing and difficult circumstances. The population lived for the most part on farms. Families were self-sufficient, and transportation and communications were poor. The friction between those who supported a strong central government and those who did not existed in the early years of U.S. history, as it does today. The country had little experience in money and financial management, and much controversy raged over the power to charter and regulate banks.

3.4.1.1 Early Chartered Banks

During the colonial period, small unincorporated banks were established to ease the shortage of financial capital for businesses. Their operations consisted largely of issuing their own paper money. Outside of the larger towns, deposit banking was of minor significance. It was not until 1782 that the first incorporated bank, the Bank of North America, was created. It was established in Philadelphia by Robert Morris to assist in financing Revolutionary War expenditures. This bank set a good example for successful banking: its notes served as a circulating medium of exchange, it lent liberally to the U.S. government, and it redeemed its own notes in metallic coins upon demand. Two years later, the Bank of Massachusetts and the Bank of New York were established. These three incorporated banks were the only such banks until 1790.

3.4.1.2 First Bank of the United States

Alexander Hamilton was the first secretary of the Treasury of the United States. For several years he had harbored the idea of a federally chartered bank that would adequately support the rapidly growing economy and would give financial assistance to the government during its crises. His recommendations were submitted to the House of Representatives of the United States in 1790, and in 1791 a 20-year charter was issued to the First Bank of the United States. This bank served the nation effectively by issuing notes, transferring funds from region to region, and curbing the excessive note issues of state banks by periodically presenting such notes to the issuing banks for redemption. However, strong opposition existed to the renewal of its charter, and it ceased operations in 1811. The antagonism of state banking interests was an important cause of the demise of the First Bank.

Following the expiration of the charter of the First Bank, the number of state banks increased rapidly, as did the volume of their note issues. Abuses of banking privileges were extensive. The capital of many banks was largely fictitious, and a flood of irredeemable notes was issued to the public.

3.4.1.3 Second Bank of the United States

The Second Bank of the United States was chartered primarily to restore order to the chaotic banking situation that had developed after the First Bank of the United States ceased operations in 1811. Like the First Bank, it received a 20-year federal charter. The Second Bank began operations in 1816 and ably served individuals, businesses, and the government. It accepted deposits, made loans, and issued notes. Furthermore, it restrained the note-issuing practices of state banks by periodically presenting their notes for redemption. The Second Bank also served as the fiscal agent for the government. It received all deposits of government funds and reported regularly on all government receipts and expenditures.

In 1833, President Andrew Jackson and many of his associates began such a vigorous campaign against the Second Bank that it became apparent its charter would not be renewed when it expired in 1836. Jackson claimed that the bank was being run to benefit private interests and was operated in such a way as to weaken government policies. Like the First Bank, it became a victim of political pressure. Not until 1863 was another bank in the United States to receive a federal charter.

3.4.1.4 State Banks from 1836 to the Civil War

When the Second Bank's charter expired, the excesses that had plagued the period between 1811 and 1816 began again. This period is characterized as one of "wildcat" banking.[1] Although many state

---

PERSONAL FINANCIAL PLANNING

Saving with a Credit Union

Banks' fondness for charging fees can make banking expensive for individuals who do not shop around for the bank that best and most inexpensively meets their needs. For individuals, the best place to bank may not be a bank, but rather a credit union. Credit union members, who have some kind of common affiliation, such as an employer or religious organization membership, run these. Credit unions are tax-exempt depository institutions. Although they do not pay any taxes, any interest or dividends received by their members is taxable.

While both commercial banks and credit unions accept the savings deposits of individuals, their lending objectives differ. Commercial banks provide loans to both businesses and individuals, whereas credit unions emphasize consumer loans.

Credit unions often pay slightly higher interest rates than their commercial bank counterparts on interest-bearing checking accounts, savings accounts, and CDs. At the same time, credit union members often receive lower credit card and new car loan interest rates than what they would have to pay at a commercial bank. However, interest rates on home equity loans tend to be about the same at credit unions and commercial banks. Of course, in order to compare and take advantage of possible differences in savings and borrowing rates between a commercial bank and a credit union, you must first become a member of a credit union.

---

[1] This nickname was used to refer to banks located in wilderness areas that were more accessible to wildcats than people. This made it difficult for anyone to redeem these banks' notes.

banks operated on a conservative and very sound basis, the majority engaged in risky banking practices through excessive note issues, lack of adequate bank capital, and insufficient reserves against their notes and deposits.

Because the notes of even well-established banks were often of inferior quality, it was easy for skillful counterfeiters to increase the denomination of notes. Also, because of the poor communications that existed between various sections of the country, it was often quite difficult for a banker to be certain whether notes presented for payment were real. Skillfully prepared counterfeit notes frequently circulated with greater freedom than did the legitimate notes of weak and little-known banks.

In spite of the many abuses of state banks during this period, New York, Massachusetts, and Louisiana originated sound banking legislation, much of which provided the basis for the establishment of the National Banking System in 1863.

3.4.2 ENTRY OF THRIFT INSTITUTIONS

The chaotic banking conditions of the early 1800s left individuals with few safe institutions in which they could place their savings. The lack of safe depository institutions, in turn, inhibited the effective development of home financing. The rapidly growing population depended, to a large extent, on individual financial arrangements to meet its need for housing. The accumulated savings of most individual home buyers, then as now, were simply not enough to buy a house. In response to this problem, two new forms of depository institutions, known as *thrift institutions*, came into being: savings banks and savings and loan associations. Credit unions developed later.

3.5 REGULATION OF THE BANKING SYSTEM

The purpose of this section is to provide a brief review of major legislation that has shaped the development of the U.S. banking system. We separate our discussion into general banking legislation, the savings and loan crisis, and legislation enacted to protect depositors' funds.

3.5.1 GENERAL BANKING LEGISLATION

A variety of laws have been passed in the United States to regulate the banking system. Early laws focused on establishing, first, a system of federally chartered banks and then a system of central banks. More-recent legislation has focused on deregulating banking activities and improving the effectiveness of monetary policy.

3.5.1.1 National Banking Act of 1864

In 1864, the *National Banking Act* made it possible for banks to receive federal charters. This legislation provided the basis for the present national banking laws. As in the cases of the First and Second Banks of the United States, the reasons for federal interest in the banking system were to provide for a sound banking system and to curb the excess of the state banks. An important additional purpose of the National Banking Act was to provide financing for the Civil War. Secretary of the Treasury Salmon P. Chase and others believed that government bonds could be sold to the nationally chartered banks, which could, in turn, issue their own notes based in part on the government bonds they had purchased.

Through the National Banking Act, various steps were taken to promote safe banking practices. Among other things, minimum capital requirements were established for banks with federal charters, loans were regulated with respect to safety and liquidity, a system of supervision and examination was instituted, and minimum reserve requirements against notes and deposits were established. In general, while these reform measures were constructive, they also were viewed by some as being too restrictive. For example, loans against real estate were not allowed. Much of the criticism of the national banking system, in fact, was caused by the inflexibility of its rules.

3.5.1.2 Federal Reserve Act of 1913

The *Federal Reserve Act of 1913* established a central banking system in the United States. The Federal Reserve System was designed to eliminate many of the weaknesses that had persisted under the

National Banking Act and to increase the effectiveness of commercial banking in general. It included not only strong central domination of banking practices but also many services for commercial banks. The structure and functions of the Federal Reserve System are described in Chapter 4. Implementation and management of monetary policy are discussed in Chapter 5.

3.5.1.3 Glass–Steagall Act of 1933

As previously noted, the Banking Act of 1933, referred to as the Glass–Steagall Act of 1933, was passed during the Great Depression. This act provided for the separation of commercial banking activities and investment banking activities in the United States. Some politicians, regulators, and others thought that many bank failures during the late 1920s and early 1930s were caused by high-risk investment banking activities involving securities underwriting and the holding of equity securities. As a result, the Glass–Steagall Act was passed.

3.5.1.4 Depository Institutions Deregulation and Monetary Control Act of 1980

In 1980 President Jimmy Carter signed into law the *Depository Institutions Deregulation and Monetary Control Act*, which for ease of reference is often just called the Monetary Control Act. This act represented a major step toward deregulating banking in the United States and improving the effectiveness of monetary policy. The two main provisions of the act are deregulation and monetary control.

3.5.1.4.1 Depository Institutions Deregulation The Depository Institutions Deregulation part of the Monetary Control Act was designed to reduce or eliminate interest rate limitations imposed on the banking system, increase the various sources of funds, and expand the uses of the funds of S&Ls. One significant change affected the Fed's Regulation Q, which established interest rate ceilings on time and savings deposits. Most provisions of Regulation Q were phased out by early 1986. Furthermore, state-imposed interest rate ceilings were substantially modified, and state restrictions on deposit interest rates for insured institutions were eliminated.

To enable depository institutions to compete effectively for funds that were flowing in large amounts to money market mutual funds (MMMFs), negotiable orders of withdrawal (NOW) accounts were authorized. While NOW accounts carried interest rates that are more competitive with MMMF accounts, they still fell under Regulation Q restrictions. Credit unions were permitted to issue draft accounts that for all intents and purposes were the same as NOW accounts. Federal deposit insurance, which we discuss in greater detail later, was increased from $40,000 to $100,000 for each account. This large increase in deposit protection, although politically popular at the time, is now described as an undue expansion of protection. The U.S. Treasury stated that it undermined market discipline and enabled depository institutions to make high-risk loans for which the taxpayers in the long run have become liable. To enhance competition among depository institutions, Title IV of the Monetary Control Act amended the Home Owners' Loan Act of 1933. Federally chartered S&Ls were permitted to invest up to one-fifth of their assets in corporate debt securities, commercial paper, and consumer loans. Prior residential mortgage loan restrictions related to geographical areas and first mortgage lending requirements were removed. Greater authority was also permitted for granting real estate development and construction loans by federally chartered S&Ls. In addition, federal savings banks were allowed to make a small number of commercial loans and accept some checkable deposits.

3.5.1.4.2 Monetary Control The Monetary Control Act was designed to extend the Fed's control to thrift institutions and to commercial banks that are not members of the system. This was accomplished by extending both reserve requirements and general controls to these institutions. Because the Fed had more stringent regulations than many state regulatory agencies, many commercial banks had given up their membership in the system to become state-chartered, nonmember banks. The Monetary Control Act, therefore, has had the effect of halting the declining system membership by transferring much regulatory control from the state to the federal level.

In the past, reserve requirements imposed by the Fed applied only to member banks. The requirements were based on a complicated formula involving size, location, and type of charter. These differential reserve requirements have now been eliminated. Even foreign banks and offices operating in this country have been included in these simplified reserve requirements. Along with the broadening of control by the Fed, there has also been a broadening of privileges to those institutions brought under its control. All depository institutions may now borrow from the Fed on the same basis, and the fee schedule for services rendered by the Fed applies to all regulated depository institutions.

3.5.1.5 Garn–St. Germain Depository Institutions Act of 1982

There had been high hopes that the Monetary Control Act would have a quick and beneficial effect on the banking system as well as on the effectiveness of monetary control by the Fed. However, this was not the case. Of special significance was the dramatic increase in interest rates in late 1980 and 1981. S&Ls and savings banks were faced with heavy increases in their cost of funds as depositors shifted from low-interest passbook savings to higher-yielding NOW accounts and savings certificates. Furthermore, since the interest rates on NOW accounts were restricted by Regulation Q, money market mutual funds had a clear competitive advantage in attracting funds. Rapidly increasing federal deficits and troubles in the automobile and housing industries added to the demand for legislation to address these problems. The *Garn–St. Germain Act of 1982* resulted.

Although the Garn–St. Germain Act had many provisions, its principal focus was to assist the savings and loan industry, which had deteriorated to dangerous levels. Depository institutions in general were authorized, among other things, to issue a new money market deposit account with no regulated interest rate ceiling. S&Ls were authorized to make nonresidential real estate loans, commercial loans, and variable-rate mortgages.

3.5.1.6 Gramm-Leach–Bliley Act of 1999

This legislation is also known as the *Financial Services Modernization Act of 1999*. As previously noted, after more than 60 years, the Glass–Steagall Act was repealed and replaced by the Gramm–Leach–Bliley Act of 1999, which allowed commercial banks to again participate in investment banking activities and insurance underwriting. As a result, U.S. banks were allowed to be "universal" banks according to policies similar to those in place in the United Kingdom and Germany. In a broader context, commercial banks, investment banks, securities firms, and insurance companies were allowed to combine or merge. These consolidations allowed bank holding companies to take on more risk by engaging in nonbanking speculative investment practices including proprietary trading accounts, investments in commodities and derivative securities, and through owning hedge and private equity funds. At the time the Act was passed, many politicians and economists believed that deregulation of financial institutions would lead to greater competition, with consumers benefiting from more financial product choices and lower costs.

3.5.1.7 Dodd–Frank Wall Street Reform and Consumer Protection Act of 2010

The 2007–2008 financial crisis and the 2008–2009 Great Recession led politicians, regulators, and others to call for major changes in the regulation of financial institutions. The result was passage of the **Dodd–Frank Wall Street Reform and Consumer Protection Act of 2010**, commonly referred to as the Dodd–Frank Act, which was designed to promote financial stability by improving accountability and transparency in the financial system. Other components of the act included prohibiting banks from priority trading and investing in hedge funds and private equity funds, ending the "too big to fail" argument, ending bailouts of financial institutions and other business organizations, and protecting consumers from abusive financial services practices. Unfortunately, the effort to make the Act comprehensive resulted in a 2300-page document that became very difficult to implement.

The Dodd–Frank Act called for the creation of new agencies and the consolidation of existing regulatory agencies. An oversight counsel was created to evaluate systemic risk involving financial institutions. **Financial systemic risk** is the possibility that the collapse of one or a group of financial institutions could lead to the collapse of an entire financial system or market. The Act also provided increased regulation of financial markets including regulation of derivative securities. A new consumer protection agency and uniform standards for consumer financial products were also established.

Section 619 of the Dodd–Frank Act, often referred to as the *Volker Rule*, prohibits banks from engaging in certain high-risk activities that are not traditional banking functions. Specifically, banks

Dodd–Frank Wall Street Reform and Consumer Protection Act of 2010 promotes stability in the financial system by improving accountability and transparency and provides increased consumer protection

financial systemic risk possibility that the collapse of one or several financial institutions could lead to the collapse of an entire financial system or market

were prohibited from proprietary trading using bank funds and from investing in hedge funds and private equity funds.

After several years of trying to implement the Act, smaller banks, often called community banks, complained that the increased regulations and reporting were onerous. Banks and their constituencies also complained about the restrictiveness of the Volker Rule. In response, the *Economic Growth, Regulatory Relief and Consumer Protection Act of 2018* was passed. In the future, only banks with $250 billion or more in assets (about a dozen banks) will be considered "systemically important financial institutions" that must meet higher regulatory scrutiny and stricter regulatory oversight.

Smaller banks will have reduced regulatory restrictions. The Volker Rule was not changed.

DISCUSSION QUESTION 2

Given recent bank legislation, do you believe banks are overregulated?

3.5.2 THE SAVINGS AND LOAN 1980s–1990s CRISIS

During the last half of the 1980s and the first half of the 1990s, well over 2000 savings and loan associations were closed or merged into other organizations. Why did this happen? The bottom line is that S&Ls failed because of mismanagement and greed that led to fraudulent activities on the part of some of the institutions' officers.

The S&L business has historically been a difficult one. S&Ls borrow in the short term by accepting the deposits of savers and paying interest on the savings. S&Ls, in turn, provide long-term mortgage loans to help finance homes. As long as short- and long-term interest rates remain relatively the same, S&Ls are concerned primarily with illiquidity due to lending long term but borrowing short term. In situations when many depositors want their money back, S&Ls may be forced to liquidate their mortgage loans, even at unfavorable prices. When short-term interest rates rise as they did in the late 1980s, S&Ls may find themselves paying higher interest rates to depositors than they are earning on their mortgage loans. Unfortunately, S&L managements did not handle the illiquidity and rising short-term interest rate developments very well.

To make matters worse, S&L managements were ill prepared for the consequences of deregulation. Authorization in the early 1980s to invest funds in a wide range of higher-yielding investments permitted many savings and loan associations to run wild by supporting speculative office buildings and other commercial ventures. This resulted not only in overbuilding at inflated costs, but as the promoters were unable to honor the terms of their loan contracts many S&Ls became insolvent. Deregulation also permitted S&Ls to invest in "junk" bonds, which are low-quality, high-risk bonds issued by businesses. Many of the issuers defaulted on these bonds, resulting in even greater pressures on S&L operations.

ETHICAL Mismanagement was a major reason for the collapse of much of the S&L industry. This problem was exacerbated by the fact that greed also led to fraudulent behavior on the part of some S&L officers and managers. Depositors' funds were used to pay exorbitant salaries, purchase expensive automobiles and yachts for personal use, and so forth. Top officers borrowed excessively from their own S&Ls and, in at least one instance, S&L presidents of two associations made loans to each other using depositors' funds.

There is no evidence to suggest that the S&L industry was run by unethical individuals prior to the 1980s. Apparently, deregulation provided the opportunity for unscrupulous individuals from outside the industry to pursue personal greed by becoming officers and managers of S&Ls. Of course, the opportunity for greed associated with deregulation also resulted in some existing S&L officers behaving unethically and even committing fraud. Individuals who acted illegally were prosecuted, some served prison terms, and reputations were lost. Failure to treat depositors and other constituents honestly and fairly resulted in loss of confidence and trust and surely contributed to the demise of many S&Ls.

The Federal Savings and Loan Insurance Corporation (FSLIC) had insured the deposits of most S&L depositors since the early 1930s. However, because of the number and size of the S&L failures, the FSLIC was bankrupt by early 1988. As a result, the *Financial Institutions Reform, Recovery, and*

Enforcement Act (FIRREA) was passed in 1989. FIRREA provided for the termination of the FSLIC and the formation of the Savings Association Insurance Fund (SAIF). Also, the Office of Thrift Supervision (OTS) took over the regulation of S&Ls from the Federal Home Loan Bank Board (FHLBB). The Act also required S&Ls to commit more of their assets to home loans, restricted S&Ls from holding junk bonds, and allowed commercial banks to purchase S&Ls.

Congress created the Resolution Trust Corporation (RTC) in 1988 to take over and dispose of the assets of failed associations by finding acquirers or through liquidations. For some failed S&Ls, deposit transfers were made to sound organizations for a fee without requiring the assumption of any of the defunct S&Ls' poor-quality assets. Some risky assets of failed S&Ls, such as junk bonds, were purchased at deep discount prices by the RTC and later resold. Assets of failed S&Ls that acquiring firms did not want were disposed of by the RTC. Congress shut down the RTC in 1995.

Commercial banks have suffered some of the same difficulties as the S&Ls. However, losses from international loans, agricultural loans, and loans to the petroleum industry have been more significant for commercial banks – many banks had to be merged with other banks. Savings banks and credit unions experienced some difficulties as well but to a lesser extent.

3.5.3 PROTECTION OF DEPOSITORS' FUNDS

As a result of bank "runs," caused by many depositors trying to retrieve their deposited funds at the same time during the late 1920s and early 1930s, insurance protection laws for deposits at depository institutions were passed to restore the confidence of depositors. The Federal Deposit Insurance Corporation (FDIC) was created in 1933 to protect deposits in banks. This was followed by federal legislation that created the Federal Savings and Loan Insurance Corporation (FSLIC) and the National Credit Union Share Insurance Fund (NCUSIF) to protect deposits in S&Ls and credit unions, respectively. Of course, as previously noted, the S&L crisis of the 1980s led to insolvency of the FSLIC and its replacement with SAIF, which is now the insuring agency for S&Ls. Over the years, the limitation on deposit account insurance was increased until by 1980 it was set at $100,000 per account. Today, deposit account insurance is $250,000 per account.

The pool of funds available to the FDIC for covering insured depositors is called the *Bank Insurance Fund*, which collects annual insurance premiums from commercial banks. Prior to 1991, all banks paid the same premium rate on their deposits. Thus, riskier banks were being subsidized by safer banks. The *Federal Deposit Insurance Corporation Improvement Act of 1991 (FDICIA)* was enacted, in part, to address this problem. The FDICIA provided for differences in deposit premiums based on the relative riskiness of banks.

One of the special problems of insuring bank losses has been the practice and assumption that some banks are "too big to fail"; too big in the sense that the problems created by losses may extend far beyond the failed bank. It is on the basis that depositors have typically received 100% coverage of their funds even though coverage of only the first $250,000 deposited is guaranteed by law. This practice tended to reduce the incentive for large depositors to exercise market discipline and created an incentive for large deposits to be shifted to "too big to fail" banks. Congress addressed this issue with the FDICIA, which generally requires that failed banks be handled in such a way to provide the lowest cost to the FDIC. Limited exceptions, however, were provided if very serious adverse effects on economic conditions could be expected as a result of failure of big banks.

There is little doubt that deposit insurance will continue to exist. It is also obvious that changes will have to be made if we are to avoid future burdens on taxpayers resulting from deposit insurance programs. Suggestions for solving these problems include eliminating all deposit insurance, reducing insurable deposits limits to protect only the small deposits, levying higher premiums on depository institutions for the insurance, and having more strict regulatory and supervisory control.

LEARNING ACTIVITY

Go to the Federal Reserve Board of Governors' website, https://www.federalreserve.gov, and find information on regulation and operations of the banking system.

Bank structure is characterized by how a bank is established, the extent to which branching takes place, and whether a holding company organizational structure is used. We will address each of these structural characteristics in terms of commercial banks and comment on how the other three depository institutions are structured.

3.6 STRUCTURE OF BANKS

3.6.1 BANK CHARTERS

To start and operate a bank or other depository institution, a charter must be obtained that spells out the powers of the institution. Commercial banks may obtain charters either from the federal government or from a state government, making the United States a **dual banking system**. While there are many similarities between federal and state charters, federally chartered banks must include *national* (or N.A.) in their titles while state-chartered banks cannot use that word. Federally chartered banks also must be members of the Federal Reserve System and the FDIC. State-chartered banks are not required to join either the Fed or the FDIC, although today almost all banks are covered by federal deposit insurance.

dual banking system allows most depository institutions to obtain charters either from the federal government or a state government

There are about 5000 commercial banks insured by the FDIC. Less that 1000 of these banks hold national charters and the remainder are state chartered. Approximately 20% of the state banks are members of the Fed. For some time, concern was expressed that the Fed might not be able to administer monetary policy effectively if it could not regulate nonmember state banks. This concern disappeared at the beginning of the 1980s when reserve requirements set by the Fed for member banks were extended to state nonmember banks.

Savings and loan associations and credit unions also can obtain federal or state charters. Savings banks are state chartered. Savings institutions can be FDIC-insured. Approximately one-half of these savings institutions hold federal charters and one-half have state charters. Credit unions are not insured by the FDIC. While S&Ls, credit unions, and savings banks are important components of the banking system, we will continue to focus on commercial banks because of their dominant role in the banking system.

3.6.2 DEGREE OF BRANCH BANKING

Commercial banks wanting to operate branches away from their home offices are restricted by state laws as to the number of offices they are permitted, as well as to where the offices may be located. **Unit banking** means that a bank can have only one full-service office. Back in the 1960s, about one-third of the states were unit-banking states. Today there are no unit-banking states. Colorado was the last unit-banking state before it began permitting some form of limited branching in 1991.

unit banking exists when a bank can have only one full-service office

In addition to unit banking, there are limited banking and statewide banking. States with **limited branch banking** permit banks under their jurisdiction to locate offices within a geographically defined (e.g. within a county) distance of their main office. **Statewide branch banking** means, as the name implies, that banks can operate offices throughout the state. Back in the 1960s, about one-third of the states permitted limited branching and about one-third permitted statewide branching. Today, statewide branching is permitted in most states.

limited branch banking allows additional banking offices within a geographically defined distance of a bank's main office

statewide branch banking allows banks to operate offices throughout a state

One of the particular merits of branch banking is that these systems are less likely to fail compared to independent unit banks. In a branch banking system, a wide diversification of investments can be made. Therefore, the temporary reverses of a single community are not as likely to cause the complete failure of an entire banking chain. This is true primarily of those branch systems that operate over wide geographical areas rather than in a single metropolitan area.

An independent bank cannot rely on other banks to offset local economic problems. It is on this point that branch banking operations appear to have their strongest support. The record of bank failures in the United States is one of which the banking system as a whole cannot be proud. However, opponents of branch banking have pointed out that the failure of a system of banks, although less frequent, is far more serious.

There are also conflicting viewpoints on the pros and cons of branch banking among bank customers. The placement of branches in or near shopping centers, airports, and other centers of activity is convenient for consumers. The ability to make deposits or to withdraw funds at a branch is a special advantage for the elderly. Businesses may satisfy very large borrowing requirements by dealing with a bank that has been able to grow to a substantial size through its branch operations.

3.6.3 BANK HOLDING COMPANIES

one-bank holding companies (OBHCs) permit a firm to own and control only one bank

multibank holding companies (MBHCs) permit a firm to own and control two or more banks

Bank Holding Company Act of 1956 defined bank holding companies, established control over MBHC expansions, and required divestment of MBHC existing nonbanking activities

A bank may be independently owned by investors, or it may be owned by a holding company. As the name suggests, a holding company owns and controls other organizations or firms. One-bank holding companies (OBHCs) own only one bank. Multibank holding companies (MBHCs) own and control two or more banks. Both OBHCs and MBHCs may also own other businesses permitted by law. The policies of banks controlled by a holding company are determined by the parent company and coordinated for the purposes of that organization. The holding company itself may or may not engage in direct banking activities. The banks controlled by the holding company may operate branches.

There was little control over bank holding companies until the Depression years of the early 1930s. Bank holding companies did not come under the jurisdiction of either state or federal control unless they also engaged directly in banking operations themselves. The Banking Act of 1933 and the Securities Acts of 1933 and 1934 imposed limited control on bank holding companies, but it remained for the Bank Holding Company Act of 1956 to establish clear authority over these operations.

The Bank Holding Company Act of 1956 defined bank holding companies, established control of how they could expand in the future, and required divestment of existing nonbanking interests. The Act defined a bank holding company as one that directly or indirectly owns, controls, or holds the power to vote 25% or more of the voting shares of each of two or more banks. Federal Reserve Board approval was required in order to establish a new bank holding company, and a bank holding company headquartered in one state could not acquire a bank located in another state. The Act of 1956 regulated MBHCs, but not OBHCs. MBHCs were not permitted to engage in nonfinancial activities, and financial activities were restricted primarily to direct banking activities. As a result, during the 1960s, while the MBHCs were heavily restricted in terms of their nonbanking activities, the OBHCs diversified widely into nonfinancial areas, including manufacturing, retailing, and transportation.

The Bank Holding Company Amendments of 1970 allowed bank holding companies to acquire companies with activities closely related to banking, such as credit card operations, insurance, and data processing services. The 1970 amendments also brought the OBHCs under the provisions of the 1956 Act. Thus, while the MBHCs were granted more flexibility in terms of banking-related activities, the OBHCs had to divest their nonfinancial holdings.

The interstate restrictions of the 1956 Act were repealed by the Riegle–Neal Interstate Banking and Branching Efficiency Act of 1994. In addition, the Gramm–Leach–Bliley Act of 1999 repealed the 1956 Act's restriction that bank holding companies could not own other financial institutions (such as investment banks, securities firms, and insurance companies). However, bank holding companies continue to be prohibited from owning nonfinancial companies. Today, bank holding companies control over three-fourths of the banks in the United States and most of the banking assets.

The liberalization of regulations relating to interstate banking is as significant as the liberalization of branch banking within states. All states currently permit the acquisition of banks by out-of-state bank holding companies. In contrast, only one state permitted interstate banking before 1982. However, while some state laws still limit entry to banking organizations from nearby states, called regional reciprocal, states are increasingly permitting entry on a nationwide basis, known as national reciprocal or open entry. Today, nationwide banking systems are common in the United States.

3.7 THE BANK BALANCE SHEET

A balance sheet indicates an organization's financial position at a particular point. In other words, the balance sheet represents a "snapshot" of its assets, liabilities, and stockholders' equity. Assets are the financial and physical items owned by the bank. Liabilities are the financial debts and obligations owed by the bank. Stockholders' equity is the financial equity capital supplied by the bank's owners. Since the term *balance sheet* is used, total assets must equal the sum of the bank's liabilities and its stockholders' equity. Figure 3.5 shows a representative composite balance sheet for commercial banks. Here

	Percent of total assets		Percent of total liabilities and stockholders' equity
Assets		**Liabilities and stockholders' equity**	
Cash & balances due from **depository institutions**	7%	**Deposits**	68%

Vault cash and cash items in
    process of collection
  Balances due from depository
    institutions
  Balances due from Federal
    Reserve Banks
		Transaction accounts
		  Demand deposits
		  NOW accounts
		  Nontransactional accounts
		  Time deposits
		  Savings deposits
		  Foreign deposits	

Securities	18	**Other liabilities**	24

U.S. government securities
  State and local government
    securities
  Other debt securities
  Equity securities
		Federal funds purchased
		  Other borrowed money &
		    liabilities	

		Stockholders' equity	8

Loans	59	Preferred stock
		  Common stock
		  Capital surplus
		  Retained earnings	

Loans secured by real estate
  Loans to depository institutions
  Commercial and industrial loans
  Loans to individuals
  Other loans
		Total liabilities & stockholders' equity	100%

Other assets	16		

Bank premises and fixed assets
  Assets held in trading accounts
  All other assets			

Total assets	100%		

FIGURE 3.5
Representative composite balance sheet for commercial banks

we continue to focus on commercial banks because of their dominant role in the banking system, and while the balance sheets of the three other types of depository institutions differ somewhat in terms of weights for individual accounts, the account categories are similar.

3.7.1 ASSETS

The principal assets of banks and other depository institutions are cash assets, securities owned, loans, and bank fixed assets.

3.7.1.1 Cash and Balances Due from Depository Institutions

"Cash and balances due from depository institutions" account for less than 10% of commercial bank assets. "Currency plus cash items in the process of collection" is the most important component and represents about one-half of the total for this account. "Balances due from depository institutions" is a very large component, with "balances due from Federal Reserve Banks" being a relatively small portion of this account.

A certain minimum of vault cash is needed to meet the day-to-day currency requirements of customers. The amount of cash required may be small compared to total resources because the typical day's operation will result in approximately the same amount of cash deposits as cash withdrawals. A margin of safety, however, is required to take care of those periods when, for one reason or another, withdrawals greatly exceed deposits.

The appropriate amount of cash a bank should carry depends largely on the character of its operations. For example, a bank that has some very large accounts might be expected to have a larger volume of unanticipated withdrawals (and deposits) than a bank that has only small individual accounts. An unpredictable volume of day-to-day withdrawals requires, of course, a larger cash reserve.

"Balances due from depository institutions" reflect, in large part, the keeping of substantial deposits with correspondent banks. Correspondent banks typically are located in large cities, and these relationships can help speed the check-clearing process, as discussed earlier in the chapter.

"Balances due from Federal Reserve Banks" reflect reserves held at Federal Reserve Banks. Bank and other depository institutions are required to keep a percentage of their deposits as reserves either with the Reserve Bank in their districts or in the form of vault cash. As noted, the Monetary Control Act requires uniform reserve amounts for all depository institutions to enhance monetary control and competitive fairness. As withdrawals are made and total deposit balances decrease, the amount of the required reserves also decreases. The vault cash reserves that have been freed may then be used to help meet withdrawal demands.

3.7.1.2 Securities

Securities are the second major group of bank assets and account for about one-fifth of total assets. Securities issued by the U.S. Treasury and by U.S. government corporations and agencies account for about three-fourths of the total securities held by banks. Commercial banks also hold debt securities issued by state and local governments, as well as other types of debt instruments. Equity securities include investments in mutual funds and other equity securities, such as the holding of capital stock in a Federal Reserve Bank. Member banks of the Fed must hold shares of stock in the Federal Reserve Bank in their district.

3.7.1.3 Loans

secured loan loan backed by collateral

Loans account for about three-fifths of bank assets, making this the most important account category. Loans secured by real estate comprise about two-fifths of total bank loans and also represent one-fourth of total bank assets. In a **secured loan**, specific property is pledged as collateral for the loan. In the event the borrower fails to repay the loan, the lending institution will take the assets pledged as collateral for the loan. In all cases, the borrower is required to sign a note specifying the details of the indebtedness, but unless specific assets are pledged for the loan, it is classified as unsecured.

unsecured loan loan that is a general claim against the borrower's assets

prime rate interest rate on short-term unsecured loans to highest-quality business customers

The second most important loan category is composed of commercial and industrial loans, which represent a little more than one-fourth of all bank loans. These are loans made to businesses, and they may be secured or unsecured. An **unsecured loan** represents a general claim against the assets of the borrower. The interest rate charged by banks for short-term unsecured loans to their highest-quality business customers is referred to as the **prime rate**. This represents, in theory, the lowest business loan rate available at a particular point and is sometimes called the floor rate.[2] Less-qualified business borrowers will be charged a higher rate; for example, prime plus two percentage points. If the prime rate is 5%, then the financially weaker business borrower would be charged 7% (5% prime plus 2 percentage points more).

Since the peak in bank prime rates at around 20% during the early 1980s, rates have been in a general decline. A secondary peak occurred in 2006 at 8.25%. However, as the 2007–2008 financial crisis and the 2008–2009 Great Recession unfolded, the prime rate declined to 3.25% by 2009. Monetary easing efforts by the Fed contributed to the prime rate staying at the 3.25% level through late 2015. In December 2015, the Fed started to move away from monetary easing by increasing its target for the federal funds rate by .25% to a range of .25–.50%, and the bank prime rate was increased to 3.5%. Since then, the Fed has continued to increase its federal funds target rate. At the end of 2018, the target rate range was 2.25–2.50%, and the bank prime rate was 5.5%.

A loan customarily includes a specified rate of interest, such as the prevailing prime rate or prime plus some percentage point amount. For short-term loans, the interest often is paid along with the principal amount of the loan when the loan contract matures. In some instances, a discount loan or note is offered. With a discount loan, the interest is deducted from the stated amount of the note at the time the money is lent. The borrower receives less than the face value of the note, but repays the full amount of the note when it matures.

---

[2] We say that, "in theory," the prime rate is the lowest borrowing rate for unsecured loans because almost everything is negotiable. In fact, there have been many instances in which large corporate borrowers have negotiated bank loans at interest rates below the prevailing prime rate.

A given discount rate results in a higher cost of borrowing than an interest loan made for the same rate. This is true, because under the discount arrangement actual money received by the borrower is less, although the amount paid for its use is the same. For example, if $10,000 is borrowed on a loan basis at an interest rate of 5% for one year, at maturity $10,000 plus $500 interest must be repaid. In general terms, the annual percent cost of borrowing for a one-year loan with interest paid annually is determined as follows:

Standard loan:

$$\text{Percent annual rate} = \frac{\text{Interest paid}}{\text{Amount borrowed}} \times 100 \quad\quad (3.1)$$

For our example, we have,

$$\text{Percent annual rate} = \frac{\$500}{\$10,000} \times 100 = .05 \times 100 = 5.0\%$$

In contrast, if the $10,000 is borrowed on a discount basis and the rate is 5%, a deduction of $500 from the face value of the note is made and the borrower receives only $9500. At the end of the year, the borrower repays the face amount of the note, $10,000. In general terms, the percent annual rate on a one-year discount loan is calculated as follows:

Discount loan:

$$\text{Percent annual rate} = \frac{\text{Discount amount}}{\text{Amount borrowed} - \text{Discount amount}} \times 100 \quad\quad (3.2)$$

For our example, we have,

$$\text{Percent annual rate} = \frac{\$500}{\$10,000 - \$500} \times 100 = \frac{\$500}{\$9500} \times 100 = .0526 \times 100 = 5.26\%$$

In the first case, the borrower has paid $500 for the use of $10,000; in the second case, $500 has been paid for the use of only $9500. The effective rate of interest, therefore, on the discount basis is approximately 5.26% compared with the even 5% paid when the $10,000 was borrowed on a standard loan basis.

Loans to individuals also are an important category for commercial bank lending. Loans to individuals constitute about one-fifth of all bank loans. Credit cards and related loan plans comprise a little less than half of all bank loans to individuals.

3.7.1.4 Other Bank Assets

Other bank assets represent about 16% of total bank assets. They include bank premises and fixed assets, assets held in trading accounts, and all other assets, including other real estate owned and intangible assets.

As noted, about three-fifths of the assets of commercial banks are in the form of loans, with about one-fourth of assets being held in the form of real estate loans. In contrast, S&Ls and savings banks have about three-quarters of their assets in the form of real estate mortgages and mortgage-backed securities. The assets of credit unions are largely consumer loans with a small percentage in government securities. Some credit unions also make home mortgage loans, although such mortgage financing typically constitutes a small percentage of their total assets.

3.7.2 LIABILITIES AND STOCKHOLDERS' EQUITY

There are two major sources from which banks and other depository institutions acquire their capital funds and liabilities. Common equity capital comes from the initial investment and retained earnings of the owners of the institutions. Liabilities represent the funds owed to depositors and others from whom

CAREER OPPORTUNITIES IN FINANCE

FINANCIAL INSTITUTIONS

Opportunities

Financial institutions, such as banks, S&Ls, and credit unions, assist businesses and individuals with the flow of funds between borrowers. Financial intermediary jobs provide the chance to work with individuals, small businesses, and large corporations on a variety of financial matters, and therefore, provide invaluable business world experience. In addition, individuals interested in finance may find numerous entry-level jobs with strong advancement opportunities.

Jobs

Loan analyst
Loan officer
Financial economist

Responsibilities

A *loan analyst* evaluates loan applicants in terms of their creditworthiness and ability to repay. Since these types of loans are usually for one or more years, the loan analyst must monitor and reevaluate outstanding loans on a periodic basis.

A *loan officer* is responsible for generating new loan business and managing existing loans. As such, a loan officer must have the ability to address the needs of existing clients while at the same time identify and actively pursue new clients.

A *financial economist* analyzes business conditions over time and prepares forecasts of economic activity and employment trends. This information is crucial for lending institutions so that they do not make unwise loans.

Education

The level of education needed varies among different jobs. However, all of these jobs require a solid background in economics and finance, as well as experience with computers, statistics, and communication.

---

the bank has borrowed. The most important liability of a depository institution consists of its deposits of various kinds, but the other liabilities should be understood also.

3.7.2.1 Deposits

As can be seen in Figure 3.5, deposits represent about two-thirds of commercial bank liabilities and owners' capital. Deposits are separated into transactional accounts, which include demand (checking account) deposits and NOW accounts, and nontransactional accounts. Transactional accounts constitute about one-fifth of total deposits, and demand deposits represent over three-fourths of transactional account deposits. Nontransactional accounts comprise three-fifths of total deposits. The remaining components are nondomestic or foreign deposits. Nontransactional accounts are in the form of time and savings deposits, each being about one-half of the total. Money market deposit accounts (MMDAs) represent the largest component of savings accounts.

certificates of deposit (CDs) time deposits with a stated maturity

Most time deposits are **certificates of deposit (CDs)** that have a stated maturity and either pay a fixed rate of interest or are sold at a discount. Although records reveal that commercial banks issued CDs as early as 1900, a major innovation in the early 1960s resulted in a tremendous growth in their importance. Large-denomination CDs for deposits of $100,000 or more were issued in negotiable form, which meant they could be bought and sold. *Negotiable certificates of deposit (negotiable CDs)* were discussed in Chapter 2. The vastly increased use of negotiable CDs in the 1960s caused a secondary market for them to develop. Today, negotiable CDs issued by banks and other depository institutions are purchased and sold in the money markets as readily as most forms of debt obligations.

3.7.2.2 Other Liabilities

The second category of liabilities is represented by items that, when combined, have a smaller dollar significance than that of deposits. Included are federal funds purchased or borrowed from other banks. As discussed in Chapter 2, *federal funds* are very short-term (usually overnight) loans from banks with excess reserves to banks that need to borrow funds to meet minimum reserve requirements. Other borrowed money and liabilities include longer-term notes and debt issues, as well as taxes, interest, and wages owed.

3.7.2.3 Stockholders' Equity

Stockholders' equity includes preferred stock and common equity capital. Common equity includes common stock, capital surplus, and retained earnings. Characteristics of preferred stock and common stock are discussed in Chapter 10. At the time a bank is formed, stock is purchased by the owners of the bank or by the public.[3] From time to time, additional stock may be sold to accommodate bank expansion. A bank's common stock account reflects the number of shares of stock outstanding times a "par," or stated value, per share. The capital surplus account is used to record separately the difference between the sales price of the stock and the stock's par value. If shares of previously issued common stock are repurchased by a bank, an account called Treasury Stock is used to record the cost of the shares repurchased, and serves to reduce the prepurchase amount of common equity capital.

For banks that don't issue preferred stock, the common equity is the same as the stockholders' equity.

LEARNING ACTIVITY

1. **Go to the St. Louis Federal Reserve Bank's website for financial and economic data (referred to as FRED), https://www.stlouisfed.org, and find current information on the prime rate charged by commercial banks.**
2. **Go to the Chase Corporation website, https://www.chase.com. Find information on types of personal loans and their costs.**

3.8 BANK MANAGEMENT

Banks are managed to make profits and increase the wealth of their owners. However, bank management must also consider the interests of depositors and bank regulators. Profitability often can be increased when bank managers take on more risk at the expense of bank safety. The lower the level of bank safety is, the greater the likelihood of bank failure will be. Bank managers must trade off higher profitability objectives against the desire of depositors to maintain the safety of their deposits. Bank regulators try to ensure that bank managers are prudent in their trade-off decisions between profitability and risk or safety.

Banks can fail either because of inadequate liquidity or by becoming insolvent. **Bank liquidity** reflects the ability to meet depositor withdrawals and to pay off other liabilities when they come due. The inability to meet withdrawal and debt repayments results in bank failure. **Bank solvency** reflects the ability to keep the value of a bank's assets greater than its liabilities. When the value of a bank's liabilities exceeds its assets, the bank is insolvent and, thus, has "failed." However, from a technical standpoint, failure does not take place until depositors or creditors are not paid and consequently take legal action. Figure 3.6 illustrates the trade-off involving profitability and bank safety, or risk. Bank managers manage their bank's riskiness in terms of bank liquidity and bank solvency. We will first discuss bank liquidity management and then cover the issue of bank solvency in terms of capital adequacy management.

bank liquidity ability to meet depositor withdrawals and to pay off other liabilities when due

bank solvency ability to keep the value of a bank's assets greater than its liabilities

3.8.1 LIQUIDITY MANAGEMENT

Liquidity management is the management of a bank's **liquidity risk**, which is the likelihood that the bank will be unable to meet its depositor withdrawal demands and/or other liabilities when they are due. Figure 3.6 shows that lower liquidity risk is associated with higher bank safety and generally lower bank profits. The opposite is the case when bank managers choose to take on greater liquidity risk to improve profits. In deciding on how much liquidity risk is appropriate, bank managers make asset management and liability management decisions.

liquidity risk likelihood that a bank will be unable to meet depositor withdrawal demands and other liabilities when due

3.8.1.1 Asset Management

A bank needs cash assets to meet depositor withdrawal requests when demanded. However, cash assets do not earn interest for the bank. Thus, the more cash assets are held, the lower the profitability, and

---

[3] In the case of credit unions, the members buy shares.

FIGURE 3.6 Trade-off of profitability objective against bank liquidity and bank solvency

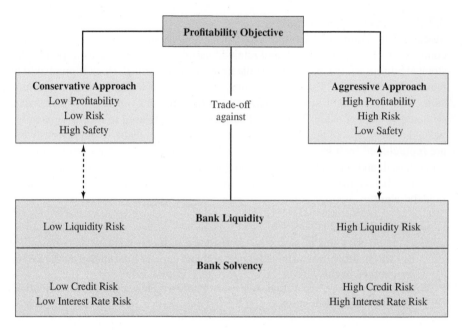

vice versa. In contrast, banks earn higher interest on loans and on longer-maturity securities investments. However, these types of assets are not easily converted into cash assets, and if converted the conversion costs can be quite high. For example, if a loan is sold to another investor, the loan may have to be heavily discounted, that is, sold well below its face value.

Let's now return to the aggregate bank balance sheet depicted in Figure 3.5. The cash assets of the firm included under the heading "cash and balances due from depository institutions" are considered to be the bank's **primary reserves** to meet liquidity requirements. Vault cash and deposits held at other depository institutions and at Federal Reserve Banks are immediately available. Cash items in process of collection, while not immediate cash, are being converted into cash on an ongoing basis. However, primary reserves do not earn interest, and thus, bank managers want to minimize the amount of primary reserves they hold. Notice that commercial banks hold primary reserves that amount to about 7% of total bank assets.

To supplement their primary reserves, banks also hold secondary reserves to help meet depositor withdrawal demands and other liabilities as they come due. Secondary reserves are short-term securities held by banks that are quickly converted into cash at little cost to the banks. For example, the holding of U.S. Treasury bills is an important source of secondary reserves for most banks. Banks would prefer to hold secondary reserves over primary reserves because interest is earned on secondary reserves. On the other hand, secondary reserves are less liquid than cash assets and thus provide a little more liquidity risk than do primary reserves. In Figure 3.5, both short- and long-term securities are grouped together under the heading "securities." As a consequence, we cannot readily estimate the average amount of secondary reserves held by banks.

Let's not lose sight of the fact that banks are in business to make profits for bank owners. Banks accept deposits from savers and, in turn, make loans to businesses and individuals. Figure 3.5 shows that nearly three-fifths of bank assets are in the form of loans. Bank loans are generally less liquid and have higher risks of default than other bank assets. As a consequence, bank loans offer higher potential profit than do other securities. Thus, after setting primary reserve and secondary reserve targets, banks concentrate on meeting loan demand by individuals and businesses. Credit (default) risk is the likelihood that borrowers will not make interest and principal payments. Higher interest rates can be charged to riskier borrowers, but such customers are also more likely to default on their loans. Bank managers must trade off the size of their loan portfolios against the amount of credit risk they are willing to assume. The acceptance of higher credit risk also increases the likelihood of insolvency.

primary reserves vault cash and deposits held at other depository institutions and at Federal Reserve Banks

secondary reserves short-term securities held by banks that can be quickly converted into cash at little cost

credit risk (default risk) the chance of nonpayment or delayed payment of interest or principal

After primary reserve and secondary reserve targets have been set, loan demand met, and bank fixed asset decisions have been made, remaining funds are invested in longer-maturity securities. Included would be U.S. government notes and bonds, state and local government debt securities, and other securities. These are riskier than the short-term securities held as secondary reserves and, thus, offer higher potential profitability that is second only to the potential profitability of bank loans.

3.8.1.2 Liability Management

A bank's liabilities can be managed to help the bank maintain a desired level of liquidity. This is possible because certain types of bank liabilities are very sensitive to changes in interest rates. Included would be negotiable CDs, commercial paper, and federal funds. For example, if a bank needs cash to meet unexpected depositor withdrawals, it could immediately attract more liabilities by raising short-term interest rates it will pay on negotiable CDs or by issuing commercial paper at acceptable interest rates being demanded in the marketplace. Likewise, the bank could borrow federal funds from other banks that have excess reserves, as long as it is willing to pay that day's interest rate. You should recall that federal funds are overnight loans, and thus the bank may have to reborrow each day for several days to offset liquidity pressures.

Time and savings deposits generally are less sensitive to immediate changes in interest rates and, thus, receive less focus from a liability management standpoint. Longer-term debt and bank equity capital do not work well in terms of liquidity management because of the time it takes for debt and equity securities to be issued or sold.

Liability management is meant to supplement asset management in managing bank liquidity. In banks incurring severe liquidity problems, bank managers may find that they are unable to even sell their negotiable CDs or commercial paper. Furthermore, if banks pay higher and higher interest rates to sell negotiable CDs, they must find assets to invest in that will provide returns higher than the cost of funds. Otherwise, profitability will suffer.

> **DISCUSSION QUESTION 3**
>
> **In your opinion, should bank managers be allowed to seek high profitability by taking on high risk and low safety?**

3.8.2 CAPITAL MANAGEMENT

Adequate capital is necessary to ensure that banks remain solvent, meet depositor demands, and pay their debts as they come due. A bank is considered solvent as long as its assets are worth more than its liabilities. Let's return to Figure 3.5. Since we know that total assets must equal total liabilities plus stockholders' equity, the difference between total assets and total liabilities reflects the degree of solvency.

What can cause a bank to become insolvent? One reason is that excessive credit risk could result in nonrepayment of loans. For example, if businesses default on the loans they owe to a bank, that bank's assets will decline by the amount of the defaults. If a bank's assets decline enough relative to its liabilities, the bank could become insolvent. In addition to credit risk reasons, a bank may become insolvent because of **interest rate risk**, which is the risk associated with changing market interest rates on the value of underlying debt instruments.[4] For example, let's assume that a bank purchases $100 million of long-term U.S. government bonds when interest rates are 6%. If interest rates rise, the value of the bonds held as assets will decline. If the decline in the bond value causes the bank's assets to be less than its liabilities, the bank would be insolvent.

Adequate bank capital represents an important cushion against both credit risk and interest rate risk as they affect bank solvency. Bank regulators set minimum capital ratio requirements for the banks

interest rate risk possible price fluctuations in fixed rate debt instruments associated with changes in market interest rates

---

[4] There is an inverse relationship between the price or value of debt instruments and interest rates. When market interest rates increase, debt instruments go down in value, and vice versa.

and other depository institutions that they regulate. A basic common equity capital ratio is defined as a bank's common equity divided by total assets.

$$\text{Common equity capital ratio} = \frac{\text{Common equity}}{\text{Total assets}} \times 100 \qquad (3.3)$$

The common equity capital ratio for a bank with common equity of $3 million and total assets of $50 million would be

$$\text{Common equity capital ratio} = \$3 \text{ million}/\$50 \text{ million} = 6\%$$

Other capital ratios are now in use by bank regulators. Adjustments often are made to exclude intangible assets such as goodwill, which is created in mergers and acquisitions. A broader view of capital also is often used. In addition to noncumulative preferred stock, banks sometimes issue trust-preferred securities, and provide for loan-loss reserves in the event that loans have to be written off. Trust-preferred securities have both debt and equity characteristics in that an issuing bank creates a trust, issues debt to the trust, and then sells preferred stock to investors. Tier 1 capital is composed of common equity, noncumulative preferred stock, and trust-preferred securities, minus intangible assets. Tier 2 capital is a bank's loan-loss reserve amount plus other qualifying securities (e.g. subordinated debt and perpetual preferred stock) plus net unrealized gains on marketable securities. Total capital is the sum of tier 1 and tier 2 capital.

The central banks and other national supervisory authorities of major industrialized countries met in Basel, Switzerland, in mid-1988 (*Basel I Accord*), in 2003 (*Basel II Accord*), and again in 2010 (*Basel III Accord*). The objectives were to improve risk measurement and management of large internationally involved banks, and to improve the transparency of bank riskiness to customers and other constituencies. As a result, the Bank for International Settlements (BIS) established capital adequacy requirements for banks with international operations, based on the use of risk-weighted assets. The weightings were established as follows:

Bank assets	Risk-weight (%)
Cash and equivalents	0%
Government securities	0
Interbank loans	20
Mortgage loans	50
Ordinary loans	100
Standby letters of credit	100

Two capital ratios (tier 1 and total capital) are calculated using risk-adjusted assets. They are defined as follows:

$$\text{Tier 1 ratio} = \frac{\text{Tier 1 capital}}{\text{Risk-adjusted assets}} \times 100 \qquad (3.4)$$

$$\text{Total capital ratio} = \frac{\text{Tier 1 + Tier 2 capital}}{\text{Risk-adjusted assets}} \times 100 \qquad (3.5)$$

Let's assume that a bank has common equity of $3.0 million, no noncumulative preferred stock, trust-preferred securities of $.5 million, and a $1 million loan-loss reserve account. Intangible assets (goodwill) amount to $1.5 million. In terms of other assets: cash and equivalents = $1 million; government securities = $2 million; interbank loans = $5 million; mortgage loans = $20 million; ordinary loans = $18 million; and standby letters of credit = $2 million.

Tier 1 capital = \$3 million in common equity + \$.5 million in trust-preferred securities − \$1.5 million in intangible assets, or \$2 million. Total capital = tier 1 capital of \$2.0 million + \$1.0 million in loan-loss reserves, or \$3.0 million. Risk-adjusted assets are given as follows:

Cash and equivalents	=	\$1 million	×	.00	=	\$0 million
Government securities	=	\$2 million	×	.00	=	\$0 million
Interbank loans	=	\$5 million	×	.20	=	\$1 million
Mortgage loans	=	\$20 million	×	.50	=	\$10 million
Ordinary loans	=	\$18 million	×	1.00	=	\$18 million
Standby letters of credit	=	\$2 million	×	1.00	=	\$2 million
Risk-adjusted assets	=					\$31 million

The tier 1 and total capital ratios are calculated as follows:

$$\text{Tier 1 ratio} = \frac{\$2.0 \text{ million}}{\$31 \text{ million}} \times 100 = .0645 \times 100 = 6.45\%$$

$$\text{Total capital ratio} = \frac{\$3.0 \text{ million}}{\$31 \text{ million}} \times 100 = .0968 \times 100 = 9.68\%$$

To be considered "adequately capitalized," a bank needs to have a 6% tier 1 capital ratio and an 8% total capital (tier 1 plus tier 2) ratio. The bank in our example surpassed both capital adequacy hurdles with a tier 1 ratio of 6.45% and a total capital ratio of 9.68%.

There is a strong incentive for bank managers to meet minimum capital ratio requirements. Banks that are classified as being undercapitalized by the FDIC must submit plans to the FDIC indicating how they intend to become adequately capitalized. Significantly undercapitalized banks may be required to replace their managers and even their board of directors, as well as restructure their balance sheets. Critically undercapitalized banks must restructure and may even be seized by the FDIC.

The 2007–2008 financial crisis impacted many countries throughout the world causing great concern that the international financial system might collapse. Underperforming mortgages and mortgage-related securities soon became referred to as "troubled" or "toxic assets." Banks and other holders of these securities were forced to "write down" the values of these assets to reflect their new market values. This, in turn, reduced their bank capital ratios to unacceptable levels.

As a result, global banking regulators passed Basel III in late 2010 requiring banks throughout the world to keep much larger capital reserves to protect against possible losses. Also, passage of the Dodd–Frank Act in 2010 impacts how risk-adjustments to bank assets are to be made for use in ratio calculations. While further rule changes are likely, regulators continue to focus on reducing the likelihood of bank failures in the United States and throughout the world by implementing higher capital minimum requirements on banks.

3.9 INTERNATIONAL BANKING AND FOREIGN SYSTEMS

GLOBAL Banks with headquarters in one country may open offices or branches in other countries. When banks operate in more than one country, we call this international banking. European banks dominated international banking until the 1960s, when world trade began expanding rapidly and multinational corporations increased in number and size. As a response to these and other developments involving international trade, American banks began opening offices in foreign countries and establishing correspondent banking arrangements with foreign banks. In essence, as U.S. corporations began expanding their operations in other countries, the American banks with which they were working followed them. Likewise, the growing importance of the U.S. dollar in international transactions and the movement by foreign corporations to invest in the United States resulted in foreign banks opening offices in the United States. Today, U.S. banks are actively involved throughout the world with major operations in Europe, Asia, and Latin America, and foreign banks have opened hundreds of offices in the United States.

international banking
when banks operate in more than one country

Banking in the United States has traditionally been highly regulated to protect depositor funds and to maintain citizen confidence in the U.S. banking system. European and most other countries generally have adopted less-restrictive approaches to bank regulation. This led to a competitive disadvantage for U.S. domestic banks relative to foreign-owned banks. The result was the passage of the *International Banking Act (IBA)* of 1978, which was intended to provide a "level playing field" for all banks. Some of the provisions included restricting foreign banks in terms of their U.S. interstate banking activities and giving authority to the Fed to impose reserve requirements on foreign banks. Rules against nonbanking operations for U.S. banks were extended to foreign banks operating in the United States. Congress strengthened regulations relating to foreign banks by enacting the *Foreign Bank Supervision Enhancement Act* in 1991. This act requires that the Fed give its approval before foreign banks can open offices in the United States and that the Fed examine U.S. offices of foreign banks each year.

While most countries have central banking systems that operate much like the U.S. Federal Reserve System, some countries allow their banks to engage in both commercial banking and investment banking. This is called *universal banking*. As noted earlier in the chapter, Germany is a universal banking country. Its largest banks participate in both types of banking. The United Kingdom does not restrict its banks from engaging in both commercial banking and investment banking. However, British banks traditionally have been either "clearing banks," which are similar to U.S. commercial banks, or "merchant banks," which are similar to U.S. investment banks. In recent years, some British clearing banks have formed subsidiaries to perform a wide range of investment banking activities. Likewise, merchant banks are expanding beyond investment banking. As a result, banking consolidations are taking place and the United Kingdom is moving more toward universal banking. Commercial banking and investment banking are separated in Japan.

As previously noted, bank holding companies in the United States are prohibited from owning nonfinancial firms. In contrast, German banks are allowed to own shares of stock in German firms and also are permitted to vote those shares. Japanese banks also are allowed to own common stock in their business customer firms, as well as to engage in various cross holdings of stock involving other Japanese firms and banks. U.K. banks are not actively involved with the firms that they conduct business with. While stock ownership in business firms by banks is not restricted in the United Kingdom, British banks are generally risk averse to ownership of common stock.

APPLYING FINANCE TO. . .

• **Institutions and Markets** Commercial banks, insurance companies, pension funds, and mutual funds play important roles in getting the savings of individuals into the hands of business firms so that investments can be made to maintain and grow the businesses. Thrift institutions (savings and loans, savings banks, and credit unions) along with commercial banks comprise the banking system and help with the financial functions of creating money and transferring money, which is conducted largely through a highly efficient check processing or clearing system. In contrast with commercial banks, while thrift institutions also accept the savings of individuals, they focus on lending to individuals who want to purchase durable goods and homes.

• **Investments** Bank loans to businesses and other debt obligations, such as small CDs, originate in the primary debt obligations market. However, since they are specific arrangements with business borrowers and depositors, these debt obligations do not trade in a secondary debt obligations market. Rather, business loans and small CDs are usually held to maturity, and loans are repaid and depositors redeem their CDs. Investment banking firms and brokerage houses help businesses market their new debt and equity securities issues so funds can be raised in addition to those provided by banks.

• **Financial Management** Financial managers borrow from commercial banks and depend on the banking system to help support day-to-day operating activities involving producing and selling their products and services. Materials must be purchased from suppliers and are usually paid for by writing checks. Sales made to consumers also are often paid by check. Business firms depend on the banking system having a highly efficient check clearing system so that cash outflows and inflows can be reasonably balanced. Financial managers also rely on mutual funds, insurance companies, and pension funds to buy their new security issues.

LO 3.1 Beginning in 2006, declining housing prices led to higher unemployment rates and defaults on mortgage loans by homeowners. Many banks and other financial institutions that held mortgage loans and mortgage-backed securities as assets suffered liquidity and solvency problems when the values of these loans and securities fell to such low levels that there was concern whether the financial institutions could meet their liability obligations.

LO 3.2 The four categories of financial institutions are depository institutions, contractual savings organizations, securities firms, and finance firms. Individual savers and investors make deposits in commercial banks, purchase shares in mutual funds, purchase securities through investment banks and brokerages, pay premiums to insurance companies, and make contributions to pension funds. Commercial banks, in turn, make loans to, and purchase debt securities from, business firms. Investment banks and brokerage firms purchase securities on behalf of individuals from business firms. Mutual funds, insurance companies, and pension funds purchase debt and equity securities from business firms.

LO 3.3 A commercial bank accepts deposits, issues check-writing accounts to facilitate purchases and paying bills, and makes loans to individuals and businesses. An investment bank helps businesses sell their new debt and equity securities to raise financial capital. A universal bank, which is currently permitted in the United States, can engage in both commercial banking and investment banking activities. Banks and the banking system perform five functions: (1) accepting deposits, (2) granting loans, (3) issuing checkable deposit accounts, (4) clearing checks, and (5) creating deposit money. For banks that also offer investment banking activities, an additional function, (6) raising financial capital for businesses, would be added.

LO 3.4 Banking prior to the Civil War was controversial in terms of whether the central government or individual states should have the power to charter and regulate banks. The First Bank of the United States received a 20-year charter in 1791. In 1816, a 20-year charter was granted to the Second Bank of the United States. The next federally chartered bank did not occur until 1863. During the period prior to the Civil War, many state-chartered banks engaged in highly risky banking practices.

LO 3.5 The National Banking Act of 1864 permitted banks to receive federal charters and provides the basis for the present national banking laws. The Federal Reserve Act of 1913 established the central banking system in the United States. Separation of commercial banking and investment banking activities was provided for in the Glass–Steagall Act of 1933. The Glass–Steagall Act was not repealed until the Gramm–Leach–Bliley Act of 1999 was passed. As a result of the 2007–2008 financial crisis and the 2008–2009 Great Recession, Congress passed the Dodd–Frank Wall Street Reform and Consumer Protection Act of 2010. The Federal Deposit Insurance Corporation (FDIC) provides for deposit insurance up to $250,000 per account.

LO 3.6 Banks may obtain either state or federal charters, which makes the United States a dual banking system. Individual states have the authority to decide whether banks can operate branches in their states. Today, most states permit statewide branching, although a few states still have limited branch banking laws that restrict branching to a specified geographical area, such as a county. Banks may be independently owned or owned by either a one-bank holding company (OBHC) or a multibank holding company (MBHC).

LO 3.7 A bank's balance sheet is composed of assets that equal its liabilities and stockholders' equity. Bank assets are primarily in the form of cash and balances due from depository institutions, securities, loans, and fixed assets. Most assets are held in the form of loans. A bank's liabilities are primarily in the form of deposits that may take the form of transaction accounts, such as demand deposits, or nontransactional accounts, which are time and savings deposits. A bank's common equity equals the stockholders' equity unless preferred stock has been issued by the bank. Common equity includes the proceeds from the sale of common stock plus the bank's retained earnings accumulated over time.

LO 3.8 Bank management involves the trade-off of potential profitability against bank safety. Banks can fail because of inadequate bank liquidity or because of bank insolvency.

Bank liquidity is the ability to meet depositor withdrawals and to pay debts as they come due. Bank solvency reflects the ability to maintain the value of the bank's assets above the value of its liabilities. Liquidity management is practiced in terms of both asset management and liability management. Capital management focuses on maintaining adequate stockholders' equity relative to assets to protect the bank against insolvency and liquidity risk.

LO 3.9 International banking is when banks operate in more than one country. While most developed countries have central banking systems, some countries allow universal banking while others restrict commercial banking and investment banking activities. Germany is a universal banking country. The United Kingdom is moving toward universal banking, while Japan separates the two banking activities.

KEY TERMS

Bank Holding Company Act of 1956	Dodd–Frank Wall Street Reform and Consumer Protection Act of 2010	investment bank	primary reserves
banking system		investment banking firms	prime rate
bank liquidity	dual banking system	investment companies	savings and loan
bank solvency	finance companies	limited branch banking	associations (S&Ls)
brokerage firms	financial intermediation	liquidity risk	savings banks
certificates of deposit (CDs)	financial systemic risk	mortgage	secondary reserves
commercial banks	Glass–Steagall Act of 1933	mortgage-backed security	secured loan
contractual savings organizations	Gramm–Leach–Bliley Act of 1999	mortgage banking firms	securities firms
credit (default) risk	insurance companies	multibank holding companies (MBHCs)	statewide branch banking
credit unions	interest rate risk	mutual funds	thrift institutions
depository institutions	international banking	one-bank holding companies (OBHCs)	unit banking
		pension funds	universal bank
			unsecured loan

REVIEW QUESTIONS

1. **(LO 3.1)** Discuss how and why banks suffered financial difficulties during the financial crisis.

2. **(LO 3.2)** Describe the major financial institutions engaged in getting the savings of individuals into business firms that want to make investments to maintain and grow their firms.

3. **(LO 3.3)** Compare commercial banking with investment banking. What is universal banking?

4. **(LO 3.3)** Describe the functions of banks and the banking system.

5. **(LO 3.3)** Describe the three basic ways for processing or collecting a check in the United States.

6. **(LO 3.4)** How did the First Bank of the United States serve the nation? Also briefly describe why the Second Bank of the United States was chartered.

7. **(LO 3.4)** Briefly describe why and when thrift institutions were founded.

8. **(LO 3.5)** Why was it considered necessary to create the Federal Reserve System when we already had the benefits of the National Banking Act?

9. **(LO 3.5)** Comment on the objectives of the Depository Institutions Deregulation and Monetary Control Act of 1980.

10. **(LO 3.5)** Why was the Garn–St. Germain Depository Institutions Act of 1982 thought to be necessary?

11. **(LO 3.5)** Why was the Dodd–Frank Wall Street Reform and Consumer Protection Act of 2010 passed?

12. **(LO 3.5)** Describe the reasons for the savings and loan crisis that occurred during the late 1980s.

13. **(LO 3.5)** Briefly describe the purpose of the Financial Institutions Reform, Recovery, and Enforcement Act (FIRREA) of 1989. Also, indicate the purpose of the Resolution Trust Corporation (RTC).

14. **(LO 3.5)** How are depositors' funds protected today in the United States?

15. **(LO 3.6)** Describe the structure of banks in terms of bank charters, branch banking, and bank holding companies.

16. **(LO 3.7)** What are the major asset categories for banks? Identify the most important category. What

are a bank's major liabilities and stockholders' equity, and which category is the largest in size?

17. **(LO 3.8)** What is meant by bank liquidity and bank solvency?

18. **(LO 3.8)** Describe how assets are managed in terms of a bank's liquidity risk. Also, briefly describe how liquidity management is used to help manage liquidity risk.

19. **(LO 3.8)** Describe what is meant by liquidity risk, credit risk, and interest rate risk.

20. **(LO 3.8)** Define and describe the following terms: common equity capital ratio, tier 1 ratio, and total capital ratio. How are these used by bank regulators?

21. **(LO 3.8)** What are the Basel Capital Accords, and what is their purpose?

22. **(LO 3.9)** Define international banking. Describe how some foreign banking systems differ from the U.S. banking system.

EXERCISES

1. Go to https://www.stlouisfed.org and identify sources and uses of funds for commercial banks.

2. You are the treasurer of a mid-size industrial manufacturer. Your firm's cash balances vary between $300,000 and $1,000,000. During the last three board meetings, a board member has asked how you protect this cash while it is being lodged in banks or other temporary facilities. Your problem is to satisfy the board member, obtain some income from the cash or cash equivalent balances, and have funds available for immediate payout if required. What course of action do you follow?

3. You and three other staff members of the U.S. Office of Comptroller of the Currency have been assigned identical projects. You are to review the articles that have been written, the speeches made, and in general the suggestions that have been offered to revamp the structure of the FDIC to render it more stable and financially able to withstand adverse events. Based on the few suggestions offered in this chapter and your own ideas, what is your conclusion?

4. You are the mayor of a community of 12,000 people. You are active in virtually all of the civic activities of the town and as such your opinion is solicited on political, economic, sociological, and other factors. You have been asked by one of the civic groups to comment on the implications for the community of a prospective purchase of the largest local commercial bank by an out-of-state bank holding company. What is your response?

5. Banks provide checking account services, accept savings deposits, and lend to borrowers. In other words, they are in the money business. We all have heard stories of banks or their partner firms "misplacing" or "losing" bags of money. Lending rates are also subject to change periodically. Both of these situations can produce ethical dilemmas or decisions. How would you react to the following scenarios?

   a. You are walking down the street and see a large money bag with "First National Bank" printed on it. The bag is sitting on the sidewalk in front of a local office of First National Bank. You are considering whether to pick up the bag, check its contents, and then try to find the owner. Alternatively, you could pick up the money bag and take it to the local police station, or return it directly to the bank itself. What would you do?

   b. You are a loan officer of First National Bank. The owner of a small business has come into the bank today and is requesting an immediate $100,000 loan for which she has appropriate collateral. You also know that the bank is going to reduce its lending interest rate to small businesses next week. You could make the loan now or inform the small business owner that she could get a lower rate if the loan request is delayed. What would you do?

PROBLEMS

1. The following three one-year "discount" loans are available to you:

   Loan A: $120,000 at a 7% discount rate
   Loan B: $110,000 at a 6% discount rate
   Loan C: $130,000 at a 6.5% discount rate

   a. Determine the dollar amount of interest you would pay on each loan and indicate the amount of net proceeds each loan would provide. Which loan would provide you with the most upfront money when the loan takes place?

   b. Calculate the percent interest rate or effective cost of each loan. Which one has the lowest cost?

2. Assume that you can borrow $175,000 for one year from a local commercial bank.

a. The bank loan officer offers you the loan if you agree to pay $16,000 in interest plus repay the $175,000 at the end of one year. What is the percent interest rate or effective cost?

b. As an alternative you could get a one-year $175,000 discount loan at 9% interest. What is the percent interest rate or effective cost?

c. Which one of the two loans would you prefer?

d. At what discount loan interest rate would you be indifferent between the two loans?

3. ABE Bank has the following asset categories:

Cash	$1 million
Securities	$4 million
Loans	?
Other assets	$2 million
Total assets	?

a. What would be the bank's total assets if loans were twice the size of the amount of securities?

b. If total assets were $12 million, what would be the amount of the loans?

c. If total assets were $11 million, and $1 million of securities were sold with the proceeds placed in the cash account, what would be the amount of the loans?

4. ATM Bank has the following liabilities and equity categories:

Deposits	$9 million
Other liabilities	$4 million
Stockholders' equity	?
Total liabilities and stockholders' equity	?

a. What would be the bank's total liabilities and stockholders' equity if stockholders' equity were one-half the size of other liabilities?

b. If total liabilities and stockholders' equity capital were $15.5 million, what would be the amount of the stockholders' equity?

c. If total liabilities and stockholders' equity were $14 million, and $1 million of deposits were withdrawn from the bank, what would be the amount of the stockholders' equity?

5. Following are selected balance sheet accounts for Third State Bank: vault cash = $2 million, U.S. government securities = $5 million, demand deposits = $13 million, nontransactional accounts = $20 million, cash items in process of collection = $4 million, loans to individuals = $7 million, loans secured by real estate = $9 million, federal funds purchased = $4 million, and bank premises = $11 million.

a. From these accounts, select only the asset accounts and calculate the bank's total assets.

b. Calculate the total liabilities for Third State Bank.

c. Based on the totals for assets and liabilities, determine the amount in the stockholders' equity account.

6. A bank's assets consist of the following:

Cash	$1.5 million
Loans	$10 million
Securities	$4.5 million
Fixed assets	$2 million

In addition, the bank's common equity is $1.5 million.

a. Calculate the common equity capital ratio.

b. If $2 million in bad loans were removed from the bank's assets, show how the common equity capital ratio would change.

7. Rearrange the following accounts to construct a bank balance sheet for Second National Bank. What are the total amounts that make the bank's balance sheet balance?

Demand deposits: $20 million	Government securities owned: $7 million
Cash assets: $5 million	Bank fixed assets: $14 million
Loans secured by real estate: $30 million	Time and savings deposits: $40 million
Commercial and industrial loans: $18 million	Federal funds purchased: $6 million
Stockholders' equity: $6 million	Other long-term liabilities: $2 million

8. Use the data from Problem 7 for Second National Bank and calculate the common equity capital ratio assuming that stockholders' equity was equal to common equity (i.e. there was no preferred stock).

9. Tenth National Bank has common stock of $2 million, retained earnings of $5 million, loan-loss reserves of $3 million, and subordinated notes outstanding in the amount of $4 million. Total bank assets are $105 million. Calculate the common equity capital ratio.

10. Let's assume that you have been asked to calculate risk-based capital ratios for a bank with the following accounts:

Cash = $5 million
Government securities = $7 million
Mortgage loans = $30 million
Other loans = $50 million
Fixed assets = $10 million
Intangible assets = $4 million
Loan-loss reserves = $5 million
Common equity = $5 million
Trust-preferred securities = $3 million

Cash assets and government securities are not considered risky. Loans secured by real estate have a 50% weighting factor. All other loans have a 100% weighting factor in terms of riskiness.

a. Calculate the common equity capital ratio.

b. Calculate the tier 1 ratio using risk-adjusted assets.

c. Calculate the total capital (tier 1 plus tier 2) ratio using risk-adjusted assets.

11. **Challenge Problem** This problem focuses on bank capital management and various capital ratio measures. Following are recent balance sheet accounts for Prime First National Bank.

Cash assets	$ 17 million	Demand deposits	$ 50 million
Loans secured by real estate	40	Time and savings deposits	66
Commercial loans	45	Federal funds purchased	15
Government securities owned	16	Trust-preferred securities	2
Goodwill	5	Common equity	5
Bank fixed assets	15	Total liabilities and	
Total assets	$138 million	stockholders' equity	$138 million

Note: The bank has loan-loss reserves of $10 million. The real estate and commercial loans shown on the balance sheet are net of the loan-loss reserves.

a. Calculate the common equity capital ratio. How could the bank increase its equity capital ratio?

b. Risk-adjusted assets are estimated using the following weightings process: cash and government securities = .00, real estate loans = .50, and commercial and other loans = 1.00.

Calculate the risk-adjusted assets amount for the bank.

c. Calculate the tier 1 ratio based on the information provided and the risk-adjusted assets estimate from Part b.

d. Calculate the total capital (tier 1 plus tier 2) ratio based on the information provided and the risk-adjusted assets estimate from Part b.

e. What actions could the bank management team take to improve the bank's tier 1 and total capital ratios?

CHAPTER 4

Federal Reserve System

LEARNING OBJECTIVES

After studying this chapter, you should be able to do the following:

LO 4.1 Discuss how the Federal Reserve System (Fed) responded to the recent financial crisis and Great Recession.

LO 4.2 Identify three weaknesses of the national banking system that existed before the Federal Reserve System was created.

LO 4.3 Describe the Federal Reserve System and identify the five major components into which it is organized.

LO 4.4 Identify and describe the policy instruments used by the Fed to carry out monetary policy.

LO 4.5 Discuss the Fed's supervisory and regulatory functions.

LO 4.6 Identify important Fed service functions.

LO 4.7 Identify specific examples of foreign countries that use central banking systems to regulate money supply and implement monetary policy.

Where we have been. . . In Chapter 3 we discussed the types and roles of financial institutions that have evolved in the United States to meet the needs of individuals and businesses and help the financial system operate efficiently. We also described the traditional differences between commercial banking and investment banking, followed by coverage of the functions of banks (all depository institutions) and the banking system. By now you also should have an understanding of the structure and chartering of commercial banks, the availability of branch banking, and the use of bank holding companies. You also should now have a basic understanding of the bank balance sheet and how the bank management process is carried out in terms of liquidity and capital management. Selected information also was provided on international banking and several foreign banking systems.

Where we are going. . . The last two chapters in Part 1 address the role of policy makers in the financial system and how international trade and finance influence the U.S. financial system. In Chapter 5 you will have the opportunity to review economic objectives that direct policy-making activities. We then briefly review fiscal policy and how it is administered through taxation and expenditure plans. This is followed by a discussion of the policy instruments employed by the U.S. Treasury and how the Treasury carries out its debt management activities. You will then see how the money supply is changed by the banking system, as well as develop an understanding of the factors that affect bank reserves. The monetary base and the money multiplier also will be described and discussed. Chapter 6 focuses on how currency exchange rates are determined and how international trade is financed.

How this chapter applies to me. . . Actions taken by the Fed impact your ability to borrow money and the cost of, or interest rate on, that money. When the Fed is taking an easy monetary stance, money becomes more easily available, which in turn leads to a lower cost. Such an action, in turn, will likely result in lower interest rates on your credit card, your new automobile loan, and possibly your interest rate on a new mortgage loan. Actions by the Fed also influence economic activity and the type and kind of job opportunities that may be available to you. For example, a tightening of monetary policy in an effort to control inflation may lead to an economic slowdown.

While many individuals know that the Federal Reserve System is the central bank of the United States, what the Fed does and how it operates are less clear. Stephen H. Axilrod comments,

There must be almost as many images of the Fed as an institution and of the wellsprings of its actions as there are viewers. Mine, born of a particular experience, is a generally benign one. It is of an unbiased, honest, straightforward institution that quite seriously and carefully carries out its congressionally given mandates. . . .. It is of course through the window of monetary policy that the public chiefly sees and judges the Fed.[1]

This chapter focuses on understanding the structure and functions of the Fed. Chapter 5 describes how the Fed administers monetary policy in cooperation with fiscal policy and Treasury operations to carry out the nation's economic objectives.

4.1 U.S. CENTRAL BANK RESPONSE TO THE FINANCIAL CRISIS AND GREAT RECESSION

CRISIS As previously noted, the 2007–2008 financial crisis and the 2008–2009 Great Recession combined to create a "perfect financial storm." Many government officials, politicians, financial institution executives, and business professionals felt during the midst of the financial storm that both the U.S. and world financial systems were on the verge of collapse in 2008. The Federal Reserve System (Fed), the central bank of the United States, is responsible for setting monetary policy and regulating the banking system. Direct actions and involvement by the Fed were critical in government and related institutional efforts to avoid financial collapse.

The federal government has historically played an active role in encouraging home ownership by supporting liquid markets for home mortgages. If banks and other lenders originate home mortgages and then "hold" the mortgages, new mortgage funds are not readily available. However, when banks and other lenders are able to sell their mortgages in a secondary mortgage market to other investors, the proceeds from the sales can be used to make new mortgage loans. In 1938, the president and Congress created the Federal National Mortgage Association (Fannie Mae) to support the financial markets by purchasing home mortgages from banks and, thus, freeing-up funds that could be lent to other borrowers. Fannie Mae was converted to a government-sponsored enterprise (GSE), or "privatized," in 1968 by making it a public, investor-owned company. The Government National Mortgage Association (Ginnie Mae) was created in 1968 as a government-owned corporation. Ginnie Mae issues its own debt securities to obtain funds that are invested in mortgages made to low to moderate income home purchasers. The Federal Home Loan Mortgage Corporation (Freddie Mac) was formed in 1970, also as a government-owned corporation to aid the mortgage markets by purchasing and holding mortgage loans. In 1989, Freddie Mac also became a GSE when it became a public, investor-owned company.

Ginnie Mae and Fannie Mae issue mortgage-backed securities to fund their mortgage purchases and holdings. Ginnie Mae purchases Federal Housing Administration (FHA) and Department of Veterans Affairs (VA) federally insured mortgages and packages them into mortgage-backed securities that are sold to investors. Ginnie Mae guarantees the payment of interest and principal on the mortgages held in the pool. Fannie Mae purchases individual mortgages or mortgage pools from financial institutions and packages or repackages them into mortgage-backed securities as ways to aid development of the secondary mortgage markets. Freddie Mac purchases and holds mortgage loans.

As housing prices continued to increase, these mortgage-support activities by Ginnie Mae, Fannie Mae, and Freddie Mac aided the government's goal of increased home ownership. However, after the housing price bubble burst in mid-2006 and housing-related jobs declined sharply, mortgage borrowers found it more difficult to meet interest and principal payments, causing the values of mortgage-backed securities to decline sharply. To make the housing-related developments worse, Fannie Mae and Freddie Mac held large amounts of low quality, subprime mortgages that had higher likelihoods of loan defaults. As default rates on these mortgage loans increased, both Fannie and Freddie suffered cash and liquidity crises. To avoid a meltdown, the Federal Reserve provided rescue funds in July 2008, and the U.S. government assumed control of both firms in September 2008.

The Federal Reserve, sometimes with the aid of the U.S. Treasury, helped a number of financial institutions on the verge of failing, due to the collapse in value of mortgage-backed securities, to merge

Federal Reserve System (Fed) U.S. central bank that sets monetary policy and regulates banking system

Federal National Mortgage Association (Fannie Mae) created to support the financial markets by purchasing home mortgages from banks so that the proceeds could be lent to other borrowers

Government National Mortgage Association (Ginnie Mae) created to issue its own debt securities to obtain funds that are invested in mortgages made to low to moderate income home purchasers

Federal Home Loan Mortgage Corporation (Freddie Mac) formed to support mortgage markets by purchasing and holding mortgage loans

---

[1] Stephen H. Axilrod, *Inside the Fed*, (Cambridge: The MIT Press, 2009), p. 159.

with other firms. Examples included the Fed's efforts in aiding the March 2008 acquisition of Bear Stearns by the JPMorgan Chase bank and the sale of Merrill Lynch to Bank of America during the latter part of 2008. However, Lehman Brothers, a major investment bank, was allowed to fail in September 2008. Shortly after the Lehman bankruptcy and the Merrill sale, American International Group (AIG), the largest insurance firm in the United States, was "bailed out" by the Federal Reserve with the U.S. government receiving an ownership interest in the company. Like Merrill, Fannie, and Freddie, AIG was considered "too large to fail," due to the potential impact of this on the global financial markets.

In addition to direct intervention, the Fed also engaged in quantitative easing actions to help avoid a financial system collapse in 2008, and to stimulate economic growth after the 2008–2009 recession. We will discuss the Fed's quantitative easing actions later in the chapter.

DISCUSSION QUESTION 1

Do you support the Fed's decision to bail out selected financial institutions that were suffering financial distress in 2008?

4.2 THE U.S. BANKING SYSTEM PRIOR TO THE FED

In Chapter 1, when we discussed the characteristics of an effective financial system, we said that one basic requirement was a monetary system that efficiently carried out the financial functions of creating and transferring money. While we have an efficient monetary system today, this was not always the case. To understand the importance of the Federal Reserve System, it is useful to review briefly the weaknesses of the banking system that gave rise to the establishment of the Fed. The National Banking Acts passed in 1863 and 1864 provided for a national banking system. Banks could receive national charters, capital and reserve requirements on deposits and banknotes were established, and banknotes could be issued only against U.S. government securities owned by the banks but held with the U.S. Treasury Department. These banknotes, backed by government securities, were supposed to provide citizens with a safe and stable national currency. Improved bank supervision also was provided for with the establishment of the Office of the Comptroller of the Currency under the control of the U.S. Treasury.

4.2.1 WEAKNESSES OF THE NATIONAL BANKING SYSTEM

Although the national banking system overcame many of the weaknesses of the prior systems involving state banks, it lacked the ability to carry out other central banking system activities that are essential to a well-operating financial system. Three essential requirements include (1) an efficient national payments system, (2) an elastic or flexible money supply that can respond to changes in the demand for money, and (3) a lending/borrowing mechanism to help alleviate liquidity problems when they arise. The first two requirements relate directly to the transferring and creating money functions. The third requirement relates to the need to maintain adequate bank liquidity. Recall from Chapter 3 that we referred to bank liquidity as the ability to meet depositor withdrawals and to pay other liabilities as they come due. All three of these required elements were deficient until the Federal Reserve System was established.

The payments system under the National Banking Acts was based on an extensive network of banks with correspondent banking relationships. It was costly to transfer funds from region to region, and the check clearing and collection process sometimes was quite long. Checks written on little-known banks located in out-of-the-way places often were discounted or were redeemed at less than face value. For example, let's assume that a check written on an account at a little-known bank in the western region of the United States was sent to pay a bill owed to a firm in the eastern region. When the firm presented the check to its local bank, the bank might record an amount less than the check's face value in the firm's checking account. The amount of the discount was to cover the cost of getting the check cleared and presented for collection to the bank located in the western region. Today, checks are processed or cleared quickly and with little cost throughout the U.S. banking system. Recall from Chapter 3 that the current U.S. payments system allows checks to be processed either directly or indirectly. The indirect clearing process can involve the use of bank clearinghouses as discussed in Chapter 3 or a Federal Reserve Bank. The role of the Fed in processing checks is discussed in this chapter.

A second weakness of the banking system under the National Banking Acts was that the money supply could not be easily expanded or contracted to meet changing seasonal needs and/or changes in economic activity. As noted, banknotes could be issued only to the extent that they were backed by U.S. government securities. Note issues were limited to 90% of the par value, as stated on the face of the bond, or the market value of the bonds, whichever was lower. When bonds sold at prices considerably above their par value, the advantage of purchasing bonds as a basis to issue notes was eliminated.[2]

For example, if a $1,000 par value bond was available for purchase at a price of $1,100, the banks would not be inclined to make such a purchase since a maximum of $900 in notes could be issued against the bond, in this case 90% of par value. The interest that the bank could earn from the use of the $900 in notes would not be great enough to offset the high price of the bond. When government bonds sold at par or at a discount, on the other hand, the potential earning power of the note issues would be quite attractive and banks would be encouraged to purchase bonds for note issue purposes. The volume of national bank notes, thus the money supply, therefore depended on the government bond market rather than on the seasonal, or cyclical, needs of the nation for currency.

A third weakness of the national banking system involved the arrangement for holding reserves and the lack of a central authority that could lend to banks experiencing temporary liquidity problems. A large part of the reserve balances of banks was held as deposits with large city banks, in particular with large New York City banks. Banks outside of the large cities were permitted to keep part of their reserves with their correspondent large city banks. Certain percentages of deposits had to be retained in their own vaults. These were the only alternatives for holding reserve balances. During periods of economic stress, the position of these large city banks was precarious because they had to meet the demand for deposit withdrawals by their own customers as well as by the smaller banks. The frequent inability of the large banks to meet such deposit withdrawal demands resulted in extreme hardship for the smaller banks whose reserves they held. A mechanism for providing loans to banks to help them weather short-term liquidity problems is crucial to a well-functioning banking system.

4.2.2 THE MOVEMENT TO CENTRAL BANKING

A **central bank** is a government-established organization responsible for supervising and regulating the banking system and for creating and regulating the money supply. While central bank activities may differ somewhat from country to country, central banks typically play an important role in a country's payments system. It is also common for a central bank to lend money to its member banks, hold its own reserves, and be responsible for creating money.

> **Central bank** federal government agency that facilitates the operation of the financial system and regulates the money supply

Even though the shortcomings of the national banking system in terms of the payments system, inflexible money supply, and illiquidity were known, opposition to a strong central banking system still existed in the United States during the late 1800s. The vast western frontiers and the local independence of the southern areas during this period created distrust of centralized financial control. This distrust deepened when many of the predatory practices of large corporate combinations were being made public by legislative commissions and investigations around the turn of the century.

The United States was one of the last major industrial nations to adopt a permanent system of central banking. However, many financial and political leaders had long recognized the advantages of such a system. These supporters of central banking were given a big boost by the financial panic of 1907. The central banking system adopted by the United States under the Federal Reserve Act of 1913 was, in fact, a compromise between the system of independently owned banks in this country and the single central bank systems of such countries as Canada, Great Britain, and Germany. This compromise took the form of a series of central banks, each representing a specific region of the United States. The assumption was that each central bank would be more responsive to the particular financial problems of its region.

---

[2] A bond's price will differ from its stated or face value if the interest rate required in the marketplace is different from the interest rate stated on the bond certificate. Bond valuation calculations are discussed in Chapter 10.

4.3 STRUCTURE OF THE FEDERAL RESERVE SYSTEM

The Federal Reserve System is the central bank of the United States and is responsible for setting monetary policy and regulating the banking system. It is important to understand that the Fed did not replace the system that existed under the National Banking Acts of 1863 and 1864 but, rather, it was superimposed on the national banking system created by these acts. Certain provisions of the National Banking Acts, however, were modified to permit greater flexibility of operations.

The Fed system consists of five components:

Member banks

Federal Reserve District Banks

Board of Governors

Federal Open Market Committee

Advisory committees.

These five components are depicted in Figure 4.1.

4.3.1 MEMBER BANKS

The Federal Reserve Act provided that all national banks were to become members of the Fed. In addition, state-chartered banks were permitted to join the system if they could show evidence of a

FIGURE 4.1   Organization of the Federal Reserve System

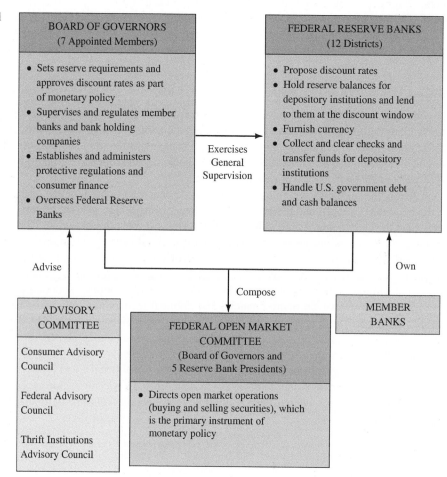

SMALL BUSINESS PRACTICE

COMMERCIAL BANKS AS PROVIDERS OF SMALL BUSINESS CREDIT

The 1980s and 1990s were difficult for the banking industry in the United States. Many savings and loan associations (S&Ls) failed, and there were many mergers involving S&Ls and commercial banks. Furthermore, many of the consolidations involved small commercial banks that traditionally tended to specialize in small business lending. As a result, concern has been expressed about where, or even whether, small businesses are able to obtain loans and other forms of business credit.

In contrast, the first part of the decade of the 2000s was characterized by Fed monetary policy that emphasized liquidity and low interest rates in an effort to stimulate economic recovery after the dot-com and the tech bubbles burst at the beginning of the decade and in reaction to the September 11, 2001, terrorist attack. Even after the U.S. economy began recovering, the Fed maintained an easy monetary policy. Then came the real estate price bubble burst, followed by the 2007–2008 financial crisis and 2008–2009 Great Recession. During the crisis, the availability of bank loans for small businesses virtually dried up. There now is an ongoing effort to encourage banks to increase the availability of loan funds to small businesses.

---

satisfactory financial condition. The Federal Reserve Act also required that all member banks purchase capital stock of the Reserve Bank of their district up to a maximum of 6% of their paid-in capital and surplus. In practice, however, member banks have had to pay only 3%; the remainder is subject to call at the discretion of the Fed. Member banks are limited to a maximum of 6% dividends on the stock of the Reserve Bank that they hold. The Reserve Banks, therefore, are private institutions owned by the many member banks of the Fed.

State-chartered banks are permitted to withdraw from membership with the Fed six months after written notice has been submitted to the Reserve Bank of their district. In such cases, the stock originally purchased by the withdrawing member is canceled and a refund is made for all money paid in.

About one-third of the nation's 5,000 commercial banks are members of the Fed. This includes all commercial banks with national charters plus, roughly, one-fifth of the state-chartered banks. These member banks hold approximately three-fourths of the deposits and total assets of all commercial banks. Even these figures understate the importance of the Federal Reserve in the nation's financial system. As indicated in Chapter 3, the Monetary Control Act of 1980 generally eliminated distinctions between banks that are members of the Fed and other depository institutions by applying comparable reserve and reporting requirements to all these institutions.

4.3.2 FEDERAL RESERVE DISTRICT BANKS

The Federal Reserve Act of 1913 provided for the establishment of 12 Federal Reserve districts. Each district is served by a Federal Reserve Bank. Figure 4.1 indicates that district banks have a wide range of responsibilities, including holding reserve balances for depository institutions and lending to them at the prevailing discount (interest) rate. The district banks also issue new currency and withdraw damaged currency from circulation, as well as collect and clear checks and transfer funds for depository institutions. The boundaries of the districts and the cities where district banks are located are shown in Figure 4.2.

4.3.2.1 Directors and Officers

Each Reserve Bank has corporate officers and a board of directors. The selection of officers and directors is unlike that of other corporations. Each Reserve Bank has on its board nine directors, who must be residents of the district in which they serve. The directors serve terms of three years, with appointments staggered so that three directors are appointed each year. To ensure that the various economic elements of the Federal Reserve districts are represented, the nine members of the board of directors are divided into three groups: *Class A*, *Class B*, and *Class C*.

Both Class A and Class B directors are elected by the member banks of the Federal Reserve district. The Class A directors represent member banks of the district, and the Class B directors represent

FIGURE 4.2 The Federal Reserve System

Source: Board of Governors of the Federal Reserve System.

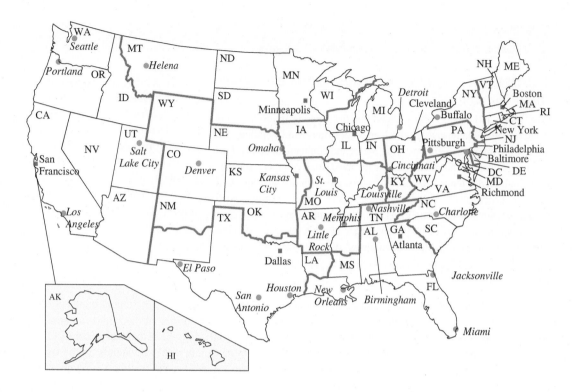

○ Board of Governors of the Federal Reserve System
■ Federal Reserve Bank cities
● Federal Reserve Branch cities

nonbanking interests. These nonbanking interests are commerce, agriculture, and industry. The Class C directors are appointed by the Board of Governors (BOG) of the Federal Reserve System. These persons may not be stockholders, directors, or employees of existing banks.

The majority of the directors of the Reserve Banks are elected by the member banks of each district. However, the three nonbanking members of each board appointed by the BOG of the Federal Reserve System are in a more strategic position than the other board members. One member appointed by the BOG is designated chairperson of the board of directors and Federal Reserve agent, and a second member is appointed deputy chairperson. The Federal Reserve agent is the Board of Governor's representative at each Reserve Bank. He or she is responsible for maintaining the collateral that backs the Federal Reserve notes issued by each Reserve Bank.

Each Reserve Bank also has a president and first vice president, who are appointed by its board of directors and approved by the BOG. A Reserve Bank may have several additional vice presidents. The president is responsible for executing policies established by the board of directors and for the general administration of Reserve Bank affairs. All other officers and personnel of the Reserve Bank are subject to the authority of the president.

4.3.2.2 Federal Reserve Branch Banks

In addition to the 12 Reserve Banks, 25 branch banks have been established. These branch banks are for the most part in geographical areas not conveniently served by the Reserve Banks themselves. For this reason, the geographically large western Federal Reserve districts have most of the Reserve Branch Banks. The San Francisco district has four, the Dallas district has three, and the Atlanta district has five branch banks. The New York Federal Reserve district, on the other hand, has only one branch bank, while the Boston district has no branches. The cities in which Reserve Banks and their branches are located are also shown in Figure 4.2.

4.3.3 BOARD OF GOVERNORS

The **Fed Board of Governors**, or formally the Board of Governors, of the Federal Reserve System, is composed of seven members and is responsible for setting monetary policy. Each member is appointed for a term of 14 years. The purpose of the 14-year term undoubtedly was to reduce political pressure on the BOG. Board members can be of any political party, and there is no specific provision concerning the qualifications a member must have. All members are appointed by the president of the United States with the advice and consent of the Senate. One member is designated as the chairperson and another as the vice chairperson.

Fed board of governors seven-member board of the Federal Reserve that sets monetary policy

The appointive power of the president and the ability of Congress to alter its structure make the BOG a dependent political structure. However, it enjoys much independence in its operations. The BOG of the Federal Reserve System is, in fact, one of the most powerful monetary organizations in the world. The chair of the board plays an especially influential role in policy formulation. Because the board attempts to achieve its goals without political considerations, disagreement between the administration in power and the board is common. From time to time, pressures from Congress or the president have undoubtedly influenced the board's decisions, but its semi-independence generally prevails.

Figure 4.1 illustrates how the BOG establishes monetary policy. The Fed BOG sets reserve requirements and reviews and approves the discount rate actions of the 12 district banks. The Fed BOG also operates through the Federal Open Market Committee to control the money supply as a means of meeting monetary policy objectives. We will explore these monetary policy instruments in more detail later in the chapter.

In addition to setting the nation's monetary policy, the board directs and coordinates the activities of the 12 Reserve Banks under its jurisdiction. The board is responsible for approving the applications of state-chartered banks applying for membership in the system and for recommending the removal of officers and directors of member banks when they break rules established by the Fed and other regulatory authorities. In addition, the board implements many of the credit control devices that have come into existence since the mid-1960s, such as the *Truth in Lending Act*, the *Equal Credit Opportunity Act*, and the *Home Mortgage Disclosure Act*.

The BOG staff conducts economic research, compiles economic data, and prepares publications that provide consumer and regulatory information. The board and all 12 of the Reserve Banks engage in intensive research in monetary matters.

4.3.4 FEDERAL OPEN MARKET COMMITTEE

As early as 1922, efforts were made to coordinate the timing of purchases and sales of securities by the Federal Reserve Banks to achieve desirable national monetary policy objectives. The Federal Open Market Committee (FOMC), with the additional powers granted to it by the *Banking Act of 1935*, has full control over all open-market operations of the Reserve Banks. As noted in Figure 4.1, this committee consists of the seven members of the Fed BOG plus five presidents (one of whom must be from New York) of Reserve Banks. The FOMC conducts open-market operations through the process of buying and selling U.S. government and other securities. These activities represent the primary method for carrying out monetary policies.

4.3.5 ADVISORY COMMITTEES

Figure 4.1 indicates that the Federal Reserve System has three major advisory committees. The Federal Advisory Council provides advice and general information on banking-related issues to the BOG. Each of the 12 Federal Reserve districts elects one member to serve on the council. The membership of the Consumer Advisory Council is composed of representatives from depository institutions and their customers and, as the committee title suggests, provides advice relating to consumer issues. The Thrift Institutions Advisory Council consists of members from S&Ls, savings banks, and credit unions and provides advice on issues that directly affect thrift institutions.

4.3.6 ROLE OF THE CHAIR OF THE FED BOARD OF GOVERNORS

Special authority attaches to the chairperson of any board. The chair of the BOG of the Federal Reserve System is no exception. The holder of that position is generally recognized as the most powerful influence on monetary policy in the nation. As for any chairperson, the chair's power derives in large measure from the personality, experience, and leadership of the individual.

ETHICAL High moral and ethical standards are a must for the chairperson of the Fed BOG. A successful chair must have the confidence and trust of the president and Congress, bank officers, business leaders, foreign officials, and the general public. While the Fed has tried in recent years to make its activities and intentions more transparent, the impact of Fed actions are not often felt until many months afterward. Constituents must trust the chair will do what is right for the economy and society. Unethical behavior on the part of a Fed BOG chair would not be tolerated. High-quality reputation matters!

While there have been a total of 16 Fed chairs, we focus on the eight most recent chairs beginning with the early 1950s. The chairs, along with the period served, are, as follows:

1. William McChesney Martin Jr. (1951–1970)

2. Arthur Burns (1970–1978)

3. G. William Miller (1978–1979)

4. Paul Volcker (1979–1987)

5. Alan Greenspan (1987–2006)

6. Ben Bernanke (2006–2014)

7. Janet Yellen (2014–2018)

8. Jerome Powell (2018–present).

William Martin's tenure as chair has been the longest in Fed history. He focused on maintaining the Fed's independence from Congress and the president. The 1970s were a particularly difficult decade from an economic standpoint in the United States. Inflation was increasing at a rapid rate. Oil price shocks occurred in 1973–1974 and again in 1978–1979. Wage and price controls were tried with no success. Arthur Burns served as chair throughout most the 1970s until his term expired in 1978. President Jimmy Carter nominated William Miller as chair, but he served only one year. By 1979, public confidence in Carter was very low. Reactions in the financial markets in New York City also suggested concern over whether the president could control inflation.

In July 1979, Paul Volcker's name had surfaced as a possible chair of the Fed who could ably fight inflation in the United States. Volcker was an economist who had served as president of the New York Federal Reserve Bank and was well known on Wall Street. Volcker also had served in government positions in the Kennedy, Johnson, and Nixon administrations, and he had worked as well as in commercial banking with Chase Manhattan.

While Volcker had impressive credentials, some of the comments gathered by the Carter administration included, "rigidly conservative . . . very right-wing . . . arbitrary and arrogant . . . not a team player."[3] While the Fed is legally independent from the White House, it is normal for the Fed chair to work with a president's economic advisors in a joint effort to reach certain economic objectives. Of course, there are times when it might be in the best interest of the people if the Fed pursues its own direction in applying monetary policy to achieve objectives such as lower inflation.

History shows that under the guidance of Paul Volcker, a restrictive Fed policy brought down the double-digit inflation of the 1970s and the early 1980s. Volcker dominated the board during his tenure, and the FOMC consistently responded to his leadership. When Volcker resigned as chairman in June 1987, the financial markets reacted negatively. The U.S. dollar fell relative to other currencies, and

---

[3] William Greider, *Secrets of the Temple: How the Federal Reserve Runs the Country* (New York: Simon and Schuster, 1987), p. 35.

U.S. government and corporate bond prices fell. Why? In a word – uncertainty; that is, uncertainty about the future direction of monetary policy. Volcker was a known inflation fighter. In contrast, the policies of the incoming Fed chair, Alan Greenspan, were unknown.

Greenspan was viewed as a conservative economist. He served as an economics advisor to President Gerald Ford and as a business consultant. Greenspan's first big test was the stock market crash of October 1987. He responded by immediately pumping liquidity into the banking system. The result was avoidance of monetary contraction and asset devaluation of the kind that followed the stock market crash of 1929. A reversal of policy occurred in mid-1988 when interest rates were raised to fight increasing inflation. A relatively mild recession occurred during 1990–1991. However, inflation has been kept below the 3% level since then. During Greenspan's service as chair of the Fed BOG, there was real economic growth in the U.S. economy, interest rates declined to historic lows, and stock prices reached all-time highs. A 1996 survey of more than two hundred chief executive officers of the largest U.S. corporations gave overwhelming support for the "good job" that Greenspan was doing. Since then, the business and financial sectors of the United States have maintained their strong support of Greenspan's Fed leadership. In 2004, Greenspan was nominated by President George W. Bush and confirmed by the U.S. Senate for a fifth and final four-year term as chair of the Fed. A Fed policy of high monetary liquidity and low interest rates was established during the early part of the decade of the 2000s in response to an economic downturn that was exacerbated by the September 11, 2001, terrorist attack. This easy money policy was continued through Greenspan's tenure, which lasted through January 2006.

Ben Bernanke became chair of the Fed BOG in February 2006. It was only a few months before the housing price bubble burst and the economy started slowing down. Bernanke was responsible for overseeing easy monetary policies that helped guide the United States through the "perfect financial storm" involving the 2007–2008 financial crisis, which had placed the U.S. economic system on the verge of collapse, and the subsequent 2008–2009 Great Recession.[4] The Fed reacted by bringing down its target interest rate for federal funds to virtually zero, and the Fed greatly increased its holdings of Treasury and other securities. At the time Ben Bernanke stepped down as the Fed Chair in early 2014, the economy was growing, unemployment was decreasing, and inflation remained low.

Janet Yellen assumed office in February 2014. Prior to becoming chair of the Fed BOG, she served as vice chair from October 2010 until she was appointed Fed BOG chair. Yellen is viewed as being a Keynesian economist who favors the use of monetary policy to manage economic activity over the business cycle. She inherited from Ben Bernanke the Fed's easy monetary policy developed to address the 2007–2009 financial and economic crises. She also participated in the subsequent continuing quantitative easing efforts during her role as vice chair. However, after seven years of easy money policies, the Fed moved in December 2015 to start increasing interest rates by raising its target interest rate on federal funds by .25% from an existing near zero rate. There were several additional increases in target federal funds rates prior to Janet Yellen stepping down as the Fed BOG chair on February 3, 2018. During her four-year term, the economy continued to grow, unemployment rates continued to decline, and inflation remained low.

Jerome Powell became the chair of the Fed BOG on February 5, 2018. Unlike most of his predecessors who were economists, Powell earned a law degree and had a diverse business career including working in investment banking and for several investment firms. He also worked in the U.S. Department of the Treasury. During his brief tenure as the Fed BOG chair, Powell has continued to periodically raise the target rates on federal funds, and he oversaw a policy to reduce the size of the Fed's balance sheet, which had increased fourfold as part of the Fed's quantitative easing effort. Time will tell whether Powell will succeed in establishing a balance between attempting to "normalize" monetary policy and the need for reasonably easy money to avoid an economic downturn.

---

[4] For an interesting personal experience perspective of working with the Fed chairs, see Stephen H. Axilrod, *Inside the Fed* (Cambridge: The MIT Press, 2009).

DISCUSSION QUESTION 2

How would you evaluate the performance of Janet Yellen as chair of the Fed BOG?

LEARNING ACTIVITY

Each of the 12 Federal Reserve Banks has its own website and tries to specialize in specific types of information. Go to the Federal Reserve Bank of San Francisco's website, https://www.frbsf.org, and the Federal Reserve Bank of Minneapolis's website, https://www.minneapolisfed.org, and identify the types of consumer and economic information they provide.

4.4 MONETARY POLICY FUNCTIONS AND INSTRUMENTS

monetary policy formulated by the Fed to regulate money supply growth

dynamic actions Fed actions that stimulate or repress economic activity or the level of prices

defensive activities Fed activities that offset unexpected monetary developments and contribute to the smooth, everyday functioning of the economy

accommodative function Fed efforts to meet credit needs of individuals and institutions, clearing checks, and supporting depository institutions

4.4.1 OVERVIEW OF RESPONSIBILITIES

The primary responsibility of the Fed is to formulate monetary policy, which involves regulating the growth of the supply of money and, therefore, regulating its cost and availability. By exercising its influence on the monetary system of the United States, the Fed performs a unique and important function: promoting economic stability. It is notable that the system's broad powers to affect economic stabilization and monetary control were not present when the Fed came into existence in 1913. At that time, the system was meant to do the following: help the money supply contract and expand as dictated by economic conditions, serve as bankers' banks in times of economic crisis, provide a more effective check-clearance system, and establish a more effective regulatory system. Many of these responsibilities initially fell to the 12 Reserve Banks, but as the scope of responsibility for the monetary system was broadened, power was concentrated with the BOG. Today the responsibilities of the Fed may be described as relating to monetary policy, supervision and regulation, and services provided for depository institutions and the government.

Public discussions of Fed operations are almost always directed toward dynamic actions that stimulate or repress economic activity or the level of prices. However, we should recognize that this area is but a minor part of the continuous operation of the Federal Reserve System. Far more significant in terms of time and effort are the defensive and accommodative responsibilities. Defensive activities are those that contribute to the smooth, everyday functioning of the economy. Unexpected developments and shocks occur continually in the economy; unless these events are countered by appropriate monetary actions, disturbances may develop. Large, unexpected shifts of capital out of or into the country and very large financing efforts by big corporations may significantly alter the reserve positions of the banks. Similarly, buyouts and acquisitions of one corporation by another, supported by bank financing, also affect reserve positions. In our competitive market system, unexpected developments contribute to the vitality of our economy. Monetary policy, however, has a special responsibility to absorb these events smoothly and prevent many of their traumatic short-term effects. The accommodative function of the nation's monetary system is the one with which we are the most familiar. Meeting the credit needs of individuals and institutions, clearing checks, and supporting depository institutions represent accommodative activities.

The basic policy instruments of the Fed that allow it to increase or decrease the money supply are, as follows:

- Changing reserve requirements

- Changing the lending rate (discount rate/primary credit rate)

- Conducting open-market operations.

In recent years, the Fed has also engaged in a nontraditional monetary policy:

- Quantitative easing

We will first cover the traditional policy instruments and then discuss the use of quantitative easing.

The Fed sets reserve requirements for depository institutions (i.e. banks), sets the interest rate at which to lend to banks, and executes open-market operations. By setting reserve requirements, the Fed establishes the maximum amount of deposits the banking system can support with a given level of reserves. The amount of reserves can be affected directly through open-market operations, thereby causing a contraction or expansion of deposits by the banking system. Discount or interest rate policy on loans to banks also affects the availability of reserves to banks and influences the way they adjust to changes in their reserve positions. Thus the Fed has a set of tools that, together, enables it to influence the size of the money supply to attain the Fed's broader economic objectives.

4.4.2 RESERVE REQUIREMENTS

The banking system of the United States is a **fractional reserve system** because banks are required by the Fed to hold reserves equal to a specified percentage of their deposits. **Bank reserves** are defined as vault cash and deposits held at the Reserve Banks. **Required reserves** are the minimum amount of bank reserves that must be held by banks. The **required reserves ratio** is the percentage of deposits that must be held as reserves. If a depository institution has reserves in excess of the required amount, it may lend them out. This is how institutions earn a return, and it is also a way in which the money supply is expanded. In our system of fractional reserves, control of the volume of checkable deposits depends primarily on reserve management. In Chapter 5, the mechanics of money supply expansion and contraction are explained in detail.

The banking system has **excess reserves** when bank reserves are greater than required reserves. The closer to the required minimum the banking system maintains its reserves, the tighter the control the Fed has over the money creation process through its other instruments. If the banking system has close to the minimum of reserves (i.e. if excess reserves are near zero), then a reduction of reserves forces the system to tighten credit. If substantial excess reserves exist, the pressure of reduced reserves is not felt so strongly. When reserves are added to the banking system, depositories may expand their lending but are not forced to do so. However, since depositories earn low interest rates on reserves, profit maximizing motivates them to lend out excess reserves to the fullest extent consistent with their liquidity requirements. When interest rates are high, this motivation is especially strong.

The ability to change reserve requirements is a powerful tool the Fed uses infrequently. For a number of reasons, the Fed prefers to use open-market operations to change reserves rather than change reserve requirements. If reserve requirements are changed, the maximum amount of deposits that can be supported by a given level of reserves changes. It is possible to contract total deposits and the money supply by raising reserve requirements while holding the dollar amount of reserves constant. Lowering reserve requirements provides the basis for expanding money and credit.

It has been argued that "changing reserve requirements" is too powerful a tool and that its use as a policy instrument would destabilize the banking system. The institutional arrangements through which the banking system adjusts to changing levels of reserves might not respond as efficiently to changing reserve requirements. Another advantage of open-market operations is that they can be conducted quietly, while changing reserve requirements requires a public announcement. The Fed feels that some of its actions would be opposed if public attention were directed toward them.

Changing reserve requirements has been used as a policy instrument on occasion. In the late 1930s, the nation's banks were in an overly liquid position because of excess reserves. Banks had large amounts of loanable funds that businesses did not wish, or could not qualify, to borrow because of the continuing depression. The reserves were so huge that the Fed could no longer resolve the situation through its other policy instruments. Therefore, it increased reserve requirements substantially to absorb excess reserves in the banking system.

Reserve requirements were lowered during World War II in order to ensure adequate credit to finance the war effort. But they were raised again in the postwar period to absorb excess reserves. In the 1950s and early 1960s, reserve requirements were lowered on several occasions during recessions. In each case, the lowering made available excess reserves to encourage bank lending, ease credit, and stimulate the economy. By using this policy tool, the Fed was publicly announcing its intention to ease credit, in hopes of instilling confidence in the economy.

In the late 1960s and 1970s, reserve requirements were selectively altered to restrain credit, because the banking system was experimenting with new ways to get around Fed controls. Banks were using more negotiable certificates of deposit, Eurodollar borrowings, and other sources of reserve funds.

fractional reserve system reserves must be held equal to a certain percentage of bank deposits

bank reserves vault cash and deposits held at Federal Reserve Banks

required reserves the minimum amount of total reserves that a depository institution must hold

required reserves ratio percentage of deposits that must be held as reserves

excess reserves the amount by which total reserves are greater than required reserves

This prompted the Fed to impose restraint on the banks by manipulating the reserve requirements on specific liabilities.

The evolution of the banking system eventually led Congress to pass the *Depository Institutions Deregulation and Monetary Control Act (DIDMCA) of 1980*, which made significant changes in reserve requirements throughout the financial system. Up to this time the Fed had control over the reserve requirements of its members only. Nonmember banks were subject to reserve requirements established by their own states, and there was considerable variation among states. As checks written on member banks were deposited in nonmember banks and vice versa, funds moved among banks whose deposits were subject to different reserve requirements. This reduced the Fed's control over the money supply.

The 1980 act applies uniform reserve requirements to all banks with certain types of accounts. For banks that were members of the Fed, these requirements are, in general, lower now than they were prior to the act. In general, for approximately the first $50 million of transaction account deposits at a depository institution, the reserve requirement is 3%. For deposits over approximately $50 million, the reserve requirement is 10%, which was reduced from 12% in April 1992. The "break point" between the 3% and the 10% rates is subject to change each year based on the percentage change in transaction accounts held by all depository institutions. In general, transaction accounts include deposits against which the account holder is permitted to make withdrawals to make payments to third parties or others. Accounts that restrict the amount of withdrawals per month are considered to be savings accounts rather than transaction accounts.

Banks and other depository institutions with large transaction account balances, thus, are required to hold a proportionately higher percentage of reserves. Let's illustrate this point under the assumption that the reserve requirement will be 3% on the first $50 million of transaction account balances and 10% on amounts over $50 million. Assume that First Bank has $50 million in transaction accounts while Second Bank has $100 million. What are the dollar amounts of required reserves for each bank? What percentage of required reserves to total transaction deposits must be held by each bank? Following are the calculations:

Bank	Account amount	Reserve percentage	Reserve requirement amount
First Bank	$50 million	3%	$1.5 million
	0	10%	0
Total	**$50 million**		**$1.5 million**
Percent	($1.5 million/$50 million) =		3.0%
Second Bank	$50 million	3%	$1.5 million
	50	10%	5.0
Total	**$100 million**		**$6.5 million**
Percent	($6.5 million/$100 million) =		6.5%

Notice that while First Bank was required to hold reserves of only 3% against its $50 million in transaction account balances, Second Bank had to hold reserves of 6.5% of its $100 million in transaction accounts. Depository institutions with even larger transaction account balances will have to hold proportionately higher reserves. As a result, their percentage of reserves to total transactions accounts will be closer to 10%.

A change in reserve requirement percentages on large transaction account balances has the most impact. For example, if the reserve requirement for transaction balances greater than $50 million is increased from 10% to 12%, Second Bank would have reserve requirements of $7.5 million – or 7.5% of its $100 million in transaction accounts. The required reserves on the second $50 million increase to $6 million, which is the result of multiplying $50 million times 12%. Adding the $1.5 million on the first $50 million in transaction accounts and the $6 million on the second $50 million results in total required reserves of $7.5 million, which is 7.5% of the total transaction accounts of $100 million. Thus, it should be evident that even a small change in reserve requirements is likely to have a major impact on the money supply and economic activity.

4.4.3 FED LENDING RATE POLICY

The Fed serves as a lender to depository institutions. Banks can go to the Fed's "discount window" and borrow funds to meet reserve requirements, depositor withdrawal demands, and even business loan demands. The **Fed discount rate** is the interest rate that a bank or other depository institution must pay to borrow from its regional Federal Reserve Bank. The Federal Reserve Banks currently offer three discount window programs referred to as primary credit, secondary credit, and seasonal credit. The **primary credit rate** is the Fed's main discount window program and, in practice, its rate is used interchangeably with the term "discount rate." While each Fed Bank sets its own discount rate, the rates have been similar across all 12 Reserve Banks in recent years. The Fed sets the interest rate on these loans to banks and, thus, can influence the money supply by raising or lowering the cost of borrowing from the Fed. Higher interest rates will discourage banks from borrowing, while lower rates will encourage borrowing. Increased borrowing will allow banks to expand their assets and deposit holdings, and vice versa.

> **Fed discount rate** interest rate that a bank must pay to borrow from its regional Federal Reserve Bank
>
> **primary credit rate** interest rate used in practice to reflect the discount rate charged by Reserve Banks for loans to depository institutions

Loans to depository institutions by the Reserve Banks may take two forms. One option allows the borrowing institution to receive an advance, or loan, secured by its own promissory note together with "eligible paper" it owns. In the second option, the borrower may discount – or sell to the Reserve Bank – its eligible paper, which includes securities of the U.S. government and federal agencies, promissory notes, mortgages of acceptable quality, and bankers' acceptances. This discounting process underlies the use of the terms "discount window" and "discount rate policy."

The Fed's lending rate policy was originally intended to work in the following fashion. If the Fed wanted to cool an inflationary boom, it would raise the discount rate. An increase in the discount rate would lead to a general increase in interest rates for loans, decreasing the demand for short-term borrowing for additions to inventory and accounts receivable. This, in turn, would lead to postponing the building of new production facilities and, therefore, to a decreased demand for capital goods. As a consequence, the rate of increase in income would slow down. In time, income would decrease and with it the demand for consumer goods. Holders of inventories financed by borrowed funds would liquidate their stocks in an already weak market. The resulting drop in prices would tend to stimulate the demand for, and reduce the supply of, goods. Thus economic balance would be restored. A reduction in the discount rate was expected to have the opposite effect.

Fed lending rate policy is no longer a major instrument of monetary policy and, in fact, is now regarded more as an adjustment or fine-tuning mechanism. As an adjustment mechanism, the discount arrangement does provide some protection to depository institutions in that other aggressive control actions may be temporarily moderated by the ability of banks to borrow. For example, the Fed may take a strong restrictive position through open-market operations. Individual banks may counter the pressure by borrowing from their Reserve Banks. The Reserve Banks are willing to tolerate what appears to be an avoidance of their efforts while banks are adjusting to the pressure being exerted. Failure to reduce their level of borrowing can always be countered by additional Fed open-market actions.

Figure 4.3 shows year-end Fed discount rates charged by Federal Reserve Banks to depository institutions to borrow at the discount window beginning in 1980 and continuing through 2018. Interest rates for *adjustment credit* are plotted through 2002 and reflect the rate on short-term loans made available to depository institutions that had temporary needs for funds not available through "reasonable" alternative sources. Beginning in 2003, the discount window interest rate reflects the primary credit rate. Primary credit is available ordinarily for overnight loans to depository institutions in generally sound financial condition.

In response to the financial crisis and the beginning of the Great Recession, the primary credit rate was lowered to 1.25% by the end of 2008 and reduced further to .50% in 2009. In 2010, the primary credit rate was increased to .75% and was held at that level through most of 2015 in support of the Fed's easy money policy and quantitative easing efforts. The rate was increased to .87% as the Fed began reversing its previous quantitative easing efforts. The primary credit rate continued to be periodically increased until it reached 3% by the end of 2018.

For comparative purposes, year-end bank prime rates, discussed in Chapter 3, are also plotted in Figure 4.3. Recall that the prime rate is the interest rate charged by banks for short-term loans to their

FIGURE 4.3 Fed lending rate versus bank prime rate changes, 1980–2018

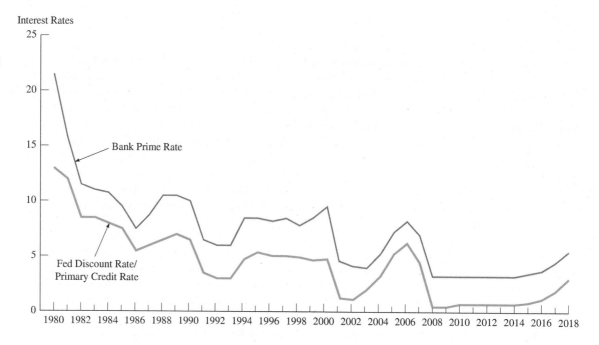

highest quality business customers. The Fed discount rate and the bank prime rate generally "track" each other over time. Both interest rate series were at very high historical levels at the start of the 1980s when inflation also was rampant in the United States. The downward trend in the prime rate has generally continued as inflation rates have also declined. In response to the financial crisis and the Great Recession, the prime rate was reduced to 3.25% by the end of 2008 and remained at that level through most of 2015. In December 2015, the bank prime rate was increased by .25% to 3.50% in response to the Fed increasing the primary credit rate. Several subsequent increases in the prime rate occurred with its level being 5.50% at the end of 2018.

Notice that the Fed's lending rate to depository institutions was consistently lower than the bank prime lending rate throughout the time period shown in Figure 4.3. Of course, in order to make profits, banks must be able to borrow from depositors, and sometimes from the Fed, at rates lower than the rates the banks lend at. The determinants of interest rates will be discussed in detail in Chapter 8.

4.4.4 OPEN-MARKET OPERATIONS

open-market operations buying and selling of securities by the Federal Reserve to alter the supply of money

The most-used instrument of monetary policy is open-market operations; that is the buying and selling of securities in the "open market" by the Fed through its FOMC to alter bank reserves. The Fed can purchase securities to put additional reserves at the disposal of the banking system or sell securities to reduce bank reserves. You might ask, "Where does the Fed get securities to sell?" A brief look at the Fed's balance sheet will help provide an answer.

The Fed's assets are primarily held in the form of U.S. Treasury, government agency, and mortgage-backed securities, which in recent years represent over 90% of total assets. Coins and cash in the process of collection are about 2% of total assets. The remainder is assets that include gold certificates and Fed premises. Federal Reserve notes (recall our discussion of fiat money in Chapter 2) represent nearly 90% of the Fed's total liabilities and capital. Deposits in the form of depository institution reserves held at the Reserve Banks are about 7% of the total. Other liabilities, particularly U.S. Treasury deposits and capital in the form of stock purchased by member banks and surplus earned from operations, make up the remaining total liabilities and capital.

The original Federal Reserve Act did not provide for open-market operations. However, to maintain stability in the money supply, this policy instrument developed out of Reserve Bank experiences during the early years of Fed operations. Unfortunately, these early efforts were not well coordinated.

Reserve Banks bought government securities with funds at their disposal to earn money for meeting expenses and to make a profit and pay dividends on the stock held by member banks. All 12 Reserve Banks usually bought and sold the securities in the New York market. At times, their combined sales were so large that they upset the market. Furthermore, the funds used to buy the bonds ended up in New York member banks and enabled them to reduce their borrowing at the Reserve Bank of New York. This made it difficult for the Reserve Bank of New York to maintain effective credit control in its area. As a result, an open-market committee was set up to coordinate buying and selling of government bonds. The FOMC was legally established in 1933. In 1935 its present composition was established: the Federal Reserve BOG plus five of the presidents of the 12 Reserve Banks, who serve on a rotating basis.

Open-market operations have become the most important and effective means of monetary and credit control. These operations can take funds out of the market and, thus, raise short-term interest rates and help restrain inflationary pressures, or they can provide for easy money conditions and lowered short-term interest rates. Of course, such monetary ease will not necessarily start business on the recovery road after a recession. When used with discount rate policy, open-market operations are basically an effective way of restricting credit or making it more easily available.

Open-market operations differ from discount operations in that they increase or decrease bank reserves at the initiative of the Fed, not of individual banking institutions. The process, in simplified form, works as follows. If the FOMC wants to buy government securities, it contacts dealers to ask for offers and then accepts the best offers that meet its needs. The dealers receive wire transfers of credit for the securities from the Reserve Banks. These credits are deposited with member banks. The member banks, in turn, receive credit for these deposits with their Reserve Banks, thus adding new bank reserves that form the basis for additional credit expansion. The Fed usually restricts its purchases to U.S. government securities primarily because of their liquidity and safety.

If the Fed wants to reduce bank reserves, it sells government securities to the dealers. The dealers pay for them by a wire transfer from a depository to a Reserve Bank. The Reserve Bank then deducts the amount from the reserves of the depository institution.

Open-market operations do not always lead to an immediate change in the volume of deposits. This is especially true when bonds are sold to restrict deposit growth. As bonds are sold by the Reserve Banks, some banks lose reserves and are forced to borrow from their Reserve Bank. Since they are under pressure from the Fed to repay the loans, they use funds from maturing loans to repay the Reserve Bank. Thus, credit can be gradually restricted as a result of the adjustments banks must make to open-market operations.

4.4.5 QUANTITATIVE EASING

Quantitative easing (QE) is a nontraditional monetary policy approach to stimulate economic activity when conventional monetary policy methods are ineffective. The Fed engages in purchasing financial assets from banks and other financial institutions with newly created money, resulting in larger bank excess reserves and increased money supply and liquidity. In response to the financial crisis and the Great Recession that was followed by relatively slow economic growth, the Fed engaged in three rounds (QE1, QE2, and QE3) of quantitative easing. QE1 was initiated in late 2008 when the Fed began buying large amounts of mortgage-backed securities and Treasury securities from banks. These actions helped avoid a financial system collapse and contributed to the recovery from the Great Recession. However, slowing economic activity in 2010 led to the Fed announcing QE2, which provided for the purchase of an additional $600 billion of Treasury securities. In an effort to provide further monetary liquidity to encourage economic growth, QE3 was initiated in September 2012 when the Fed stated it planned to purchase $40 billion in mortgage-backed securities per month. This QE program ended in late 2014. In October, 2017, the Fed began unwinding its prior quantitative easing efforts by selling some of the Treasury and mortgage-backed securities it held as assets. Total assets at the end of 2018 were about $4 trillion.

quantitative easing (QE) a nontraditional monetary policy approach to stimulate economic activity

| DISCUSSION QUESTION 3
| **Did the Fed maintain an easy monetary policy for too many years after the Great Recession?**

4.4.6 IMPLEMENTATION OF MONETARY POLICY

federal funds rate interest rate on overnight loans from banks with excess reserves to banks that have deficit reserves

Monetary policy has traditionally focused either on trying to control the rate of change or growth in the money supply (such as M1) or by targeting a level for a specific type of interest rate. One interest rate that the Fed's FOMC could focus on is the **federal funds rate**, which is the rate on overnight loans from banks with excess reserves to banks that have deficit reserves. Open-market purchases of securities add to bank reserves and increase the money supply. Sales of securities lower reserves and the money supply. However, when the target is the money supply, interest rates may fluctuate widely, because the demand for money may change relative to a specific money supply target. Furthermore, a focus on the money supply might not produce the desired impact on gross domestic product because of changes in the velocity of money, as we saw in Chapter 2.

In recent years, the Fed, through its FOMC, has chosen to focus on setting target interest rate levels for the federal funds rate as the primary means of carrying out monetary policy. Evidence indicates that observed federal funds rates track closely with the Fed's target federal funds rates over time. Banks with excess reserves lend to banks that need to borrow funds to meet reserve requirements. Interest rates, such as the federal funds rate, reflect the intersection of the demand for reserves and the supply of reserves. Open-market purchases of securities cause the federal funds rate to fall, whereas sales of securities cause the rate to rise. Of course, while the FOMC can set targets for federal funds rates, actual federal funds rates are determined in the market by banks with excess reserves and banks that need to borrow reserves to meet their minimum reserve requirement.

The Fed uses its open-market operations to provide liquidity to the banking system in times of emergency and distress. For example, the stock market crash on October 19, 1987, caused concern about a possible economic collapse. The Fed, through FOMC open-market purchases, moved quickly to increase the money supply. The terrorist attacks on September 11, 2001, caused widespread concern about the near-term ability of stock and other financial markets to function properly with a related possibility of economic collapse. The FOMC moved quickly to provide liquidity to the banking system, and to encourage renewed confidence in the financial system by reducing the target rate for federal funds on September 17, 2001, from 3.5% to 3.0%.

In 2001, the FOMC further lowered its target for the federal funds rate to 2.5% on October 2, to 2.0% on November 2, and finally to 1.75% on December 11. A target rate reduction to 1.25% occurred on November 6, 2002, and this was followed by a further reduction in the target rate to 1.0% on June 25, 2003. As the U.S. economy began growing, concern shifted to the possibility of renewed inflation, causing the Fed to begin increasing the target for the federal funds rate in 2004.

Although the target for the federal funds rate was 5.25% at the end of 2006, target rates were reduced quickly as the 2007–2008 financial crisis developed and the 2008–2009 Great Recession began. In December 2008, the FOMC established a near-zero target federal funds rate range, between 0.00 and 0.25%. This 0.00–0.25% target was subsequently maintained until December 2015 when the target federal funds rate range was increased to 0.25–0.50 as the initial step toward monetary policy normalization. Since then, there have been eight more .25% target rate increases (one in 2016, three in 2017, and four in 2018), with the December, 2018 target federal funds rate being set with a range of 2.25–2.50%.

As a result of the severity of the 2007–2008 financial crisis and the beginning of the Great Recession, the Fed took unusual steps to avoid a possible financial collapse. In addition to setting target federal rates at near zero levels in December 2008, the Fed engaged in a nontraditional monetary activity called quantitative easing, or QE, in late 2008. As discussed in the previous section, the Fed aggressively purchased U.S. Treasury, government agency, and mortgage-backed securities from banks and other financial institutions so as to provide even more monetary liquidity in the financial system. Round two of quantitative easing was implemented in 2010 and round three in 2012 in an effort to encourage economic growth through further monetary liquidity.

In mid-2008, the Fed's balance sheet showed assets, primarily in the form of U.S. government securities, of nearly $1 trillion. Under the three QE programs, large amounts of Treasury and mortgage-backed securities were purchased by the Fed. The Fed's asset holdings reached $4.5 trillion in late 2014 when QE3 was ended. In October 2017, the Fed announced that it was starting to unwind QE by reducing or "tapering" assets at a target amount of $50 billion per month. Funds from maturing securities would not be reinvested and Treasury and mortgage-backed securities would be sold. By the end of 2018, the Fed's total assets were down to about $4 trillion.

In early 2019, some economists and others expressed concern that economic growth was slowing in the United States and worldwide. They urged Fed Chair Powell to postpone planned increases in the federal funds target rates and hold off on further QE unwinding efforts. Time will tell whether the Fed can achieve monetary policy "normalization" while avoiding an economic downturn.

| **LEARNING ACTIVITY**
| Go to the St. Louis Federal Reserve Bank's website, https://www.stlouisfed.org, and find the current Fed discount rate (primary credit rate) charged by Federal Reserve Banks on loans to depository institutions. Describe recent changes or trends in the discount or primary credit rate.

A strong and stable banking system is vital to the growth and the stability of the entire economy. The supervision of commercial banks and other depository institutions is primarily concerned with the safety and soundness of individual institutions. It involves oversight to ensure that depository institutions are operated carefully. Depository institution regulation relates to the issuance of specific rules or regulations that govern the structure and conduct of operations.

> **4.5 FED SUPERVISORY AND REGULATORY FUNCTIONS**

4.5.1 SPECIFIC SUPERVISORY RESPONSIBILITIES

On-site examination of commercial banks is one of the Fed's most important responsibilities. This function is shared with the federal Office of the Comptroller of the Currency (OCC), the Federal Deposit Insurance Corporation (FDIC), and state regulatory agencies. Although the Federal Reserve is authorized to examine all member banks, in practice it limits itself to state-chartered member banks and all bank holding companies. It cooperates with state examining agencies to avoid overlapping examining authority. The OCC directs its attention to nationally chartered banks, and the FDIC supervises insured nonmember commercial banks.

In addition to these three federal banking supervisory agencies, two federal agencies are primarily responsible for supervising and regulating depository institutions that are not commercial banks. The National Credit Union Administration (NCUA) supervises and regulates credit unions, and the Office of Thrift Supervision (OTS) oversees S&Ls and other savings institutions. The examination generally entails (1) an appraisal of the soundness of the institution's assets; (2) an evaluation of internal operations, policies, and management; (3) an analysis of key financial factors, such as capital and earnings; (4) a review for compliance with all banking laws and regulations; and (5) an overall determination of the institution's financial condition.

The Federal Reserve conducts on-site inspections of parent bank holding companies and their nonbank subsidiaries. These inspections include a review of nonbank assets and funding activities to ensure compliance with the Bank Holding Company Act.

The Federal Reserve has broad powers to regulate the overseas activities of member banks and bank holding companies. Its aim is to allow U.S. banks to be fully competitive with institutions of host countries in financing U.S. trade and investment overseas. Along with the OCC and the FDIC, the Federal Reserve also has broad oversight authority to supervise all federal and state-licensed branches and agencies of foreign banks operating in the United States.

4.5.2 SPECIFIC REGULATORY RESPONSIBILITIES

The Federal Reserve has legal responsibility for the administration of the Bank Holding Company Act of 1956, the Bank Merger Act of 1960, and the Change in Bank Control Act of 1978. Under these acts, the Fed approves or denies the acquisitions of banks and other closely related nonbanking activities by bank holding companies. Furthermore, it permits or rejects changes of control and mergers of banks and bank holding companies.

The Federal Reserve is responsible for writing rules or enforcing a number of major laws that offer consumers protection in their financial dealings. In 1968 Congress passed the **Consumer Credit Protection Act**, which requires the clear explanation of consumer credit costs and garnishment procedures (taking wages or property by legal means) and prohibits overly high-priced credit transactions.

Consumer Credit Protection Act 1968 act requiring clear explanation of consumer credit costs and prohibiting overly high-priced credit transactions

FIGURE 4.4 Consumer protection responsibilities of the Federal Reserve System

Source: The Federal Reserve System Purposes & Functions, 9th ed. (Board of Governors of the Federal Reserve System, Washington, D.C., 2005), ch. 6.

- The Truth in Lending section of the *Consumer Credit Protection Act* requires disclosure of the finance charge and the annual percentage rate of credit along with certain other costs and terms to permit consumers to compare the prices of credit from different sources. This act also limits liability on lost or stolen credit cards.
- The *Fair Credit Billing Act* sets up a procedure for the prompt correction of errors on a revolving charge account and prevents damage to credit ratings while a dispute is being settled.
- The *Equal Credit Opportunity Act* prohibits discrimination in the granting of credit on the basis of sex, marital status, race, color, religion, national origin, age, or receipt of public assistance.
- The *Fair Credit Reporting Act* sets up a procedure for correcting mistakes on credit records and requires that records be used only for legitimate business purposes.
- The *Consumer Leasing Act* requires disclosure of information to help consumers compare the cost and terms of one lease of consumer goods with another and to compare the cost of leasing versus buying on credit or for cash.
- The *Real Estate Settlement Procedures Act* requires disclosure of information about the services and costs involved at the time of settlement when property is transferred from seller to buyer.
- The *Electronic Fund Transfer Act* provides a basic framework regarding the rights, liabilities, and responsibilities of consumers who use electronic transfer services and of the financial institutions that offer them.
- The *Federal Trade Commission Improvement Act* authorizes the Federal Reserve BOG to identify unfair or deceptive acts or practices on the part of banks and to issue regulations to prohibit them.

Regulation Z enacts Truth in Lending section of the Consumer Credit Protection Act with intent to make consumers able to compare costs of alternate forms of credit

Regulation Z, which was drafted by a Federal Reserve task force, enacts the Truth in Lending section of the act. The purpose of the law and Regulation Z is to make consumers aware of, and able to compare, the costs of alternate forms of credit. Regulation Z applies to consumer finance companies, credit unions, sales finance companies, banks, S&Ls, residential mortgage brokers, credit card issuers, department stores, automobile dealers, hospitals, doctors, dentists, and any other individuals or organizations that extend or arrange credit for consumers.

The law requires a breakdown of the total finance charge and the annual percentage rate of charge. The finance charge includes all loan costs, including not only interest or discount but service charges, loan fees, finder fees, insurance premiums, and points (an additional loan charge). Fees for such items as taxes not included in the purchase price, licenses, certificates of title, and the like may be excluded from the finance charge if they are itemized and explained separately. Figure 4.4 lists the Truth in Lending and other consumer protection acts that fall under Fed jurisdiction.

In addition to consumer protection laws, the Federal Reserve, through the Community Reinvestment Act of 1977, encourages depository institutions to help meet the credit needs of their communities for housing and other purposes, while maintaining safe and sound operations. This is particularly true in neighborhoods of families with low or moderate income.

PERSONAL FINANCIAL PLANNING

The Fed and the Consumer

The Fed affects personal finance in several ways. First, the Fed controls the money supply. Actions that severely restrict the supply of money may lead to an economic recession. Too rapid a growth in the money supply may result in inflation and a decrease in purchasing power. Should the Fed act to slow down or reduce the growth rate of the money supply, there will be growing constraints on the ability of banks to lend as their excess reserves decline. This may result in higher loan rates, as loanable funds become scarcer. This could help bank savers, however, as banks and other depository institutions may raise the interest they pay on saving accounts and CDs to attract more funds that they will later lend to others.

The Fed acts in other ways to maintain people's trust and confidence in the banking system. As this chapter discusses, the Fed has supervisory power over many banks to ensure they have adequate capital and reserves and are following regulations. The Fed's Regulation Z requires lenders to tell borrowers the annual percentage rate on the loans they receive. The Fed clears checks by transporting them between banking centers and by debiting and crediting bank balances with the Fed.

The Reserve Banks provide a wide range of important services to depository institutions and to the U.S. government. The most important of these services is the payments mechanism, a system whereby billions of dollars are transferred each day. Other services include electronic fund transfers, net settlement facilities, safekeeping and transfer of securities, and serving as fiscal agent for the United States.

4.6 FED SERVICE FUNCTIONS

4.6.1 THE PAYMENTS MECHANISM

An efficient payments mechanism is necessary for the monetary system to carry out the financial function of transferring money, which in turn is a requirement for an effective financial system. For a review of how checks have traditionally been processed through the banking system, refer to Figure 3.4 in Chapter 3. Recall that banks can clear checks either directly with one another or indirectly through bank clearinghouses. Checks also can be processed or cleared through the Federal Reserve Banks. Electronic processing of checks, rather than transporting the actual paper checks, has made the clearing process much more efficient. The payments mechanism administered by the Fed also includes providing currency and coin and electronic funds transfers.

Electronic forms of payment are replacing the check as a payment method. Included alternatives are credit cards, debit cards, and online account transfers. Business firms, such as PayPal, Square, and Apple Pay, also provide mobile payment and point-of-sale systems that further reduce the need for traditional checks.

4.6.1.1 Coin and Currency

Even though the movement toward a cashless society continues, the United States remains highly dependent on currency and coin to conduct transactions. The Fed is responsible for ensuring that the economy has an adequate supply of cash to meet the public's demand. Currency and coin are put into or retired from circulation by the Reserve Banks, which use depository institutions for this purpose. Virtually all currency in circulation is in the form of Federal Reserve notes. These notes are printed by the Bureau of Engraving and Printing of the U.S. Treasury.

4.6.1.2 Check Clearance and Collection

One of the Fed's important contributions to the smooth flow of financial interchange is to facilitate the clearance and collection of checks of the depository institutions of the nation. Each Reserve Bank serves as a clearinghouse for all depository institutions in its district, provided that they agree to pay the face value on checks forwarded to them for payment. Today, nearly all the checks processed for collection by Federal Reserve Banks are received as electronic check images.

Let's illustrate how the check-clearing process traditionally took place through Reserve Banks. Assume that the owner of a business in Sacramento, California, places an order for merchandise with a distributor in San Francisco. The order is accompanied by a check drawn on the owner's bank in Sacramento. The distributor deposits the check with its bank in San Francisco, at which time the distributor receives a corresponding credit to its account with the bank. The distributor's bank will send the check to the Reserve Bank of its district, also located in San Francisco. The Reserve Bank will forward the check to the bank in Sacramento on which the check was drawn. The adjustment of accounts is accomplished at the Reserve Bank through an alternate debit and credit to the account of each bank involved in the transaction. The San Francisco bank, which has honored the check of its customer, will receive an increase in its reserves with the Reserve Bank, while the bank in Sacramento will have its reserves decreased by a corresponding amount. The bank in Sacramento will then reduce the account of the business on which the check was written. Notice that the exchange takes place without any transfer of currency.

4.6.1.3 Check Clearance Among Federal Reserve Districts

If an order was also placed by the Sacramento firm with a distributor of goods in Chicago, the check would be subject to an additional step in being cleared through the Fed. The Chicago distributor, like the San Francisco distributor, deposits the check with the bank of its choice and, in turn, receives an increase in its account. The Chicago bank deposits the check for collection with the Reserve Bank of Chicago, which forwards the check to the Reserve Bank of San Francisco. The Reserve Bank of San Francisco, of course, then presents the check for payment to the bank on which it was drawn. Thus, there are two routes of check clearance: the *intradistrict settlement*, in which the transaction takes place entirely within a single Federal Reserve district, and the *interdistrict settlement*, in which there are relationships between banks of two Federal Reserve districts.

As described, Reserve Banks are able to minimize the actual flow of funds by increasing or decreasing reserves of the participating depository institutions. In the same way, the Interdistrict Settlement Fund eliminates the flow of funds between the Reserve Banks needed to make interdistrict settlements. The Interdistrict Settlement Fund in Washington, D.C., has a substantial deposit from each of the Reserve Banks. These deposit credits are alternately increased or decreased, depending on the clearance balance of the day's activities on the part of each Reserve Bank. At a certain hour each day, each Reserve Bank informs the Interdistrict Settlement Fund by direct wire of the amount of checks it received the previous day that were drawn upon depository institutions in other Federal Reserve districts. The deposit of each Reserve Bank with the Interdistrict Settlement Fund is increased or decreased according to the balance of the day's check-clearance activities.

4.6.1.4 Check Clearance Through Federal Reserve Branch Banks

Branch banks of the Reserve Banks enter into the clearance process in a very important way. If a check is deposited with a depository located closer to a Reserve Branch Bank than to a Reserve Bank, the branch bank, in effect, takes the place of the Reserve Bank. The Federal Reserve facilitates the check-clearing services of the Reserve Banks and their branches by maintaining a small group of regional check-processing centers.

4.6.1.5 Check Routing

In the past, a many employees at the 12 Reserve Banks were engaged in check clearing. Fundamental to the clearance process was the need to read the system of symbols and numerals shown in Figure 4.5. Although these symbols are slightly different from conventional numbers, they are easily read and are referred to as the magnetic ink character recognition (MICR) line. Information about the clearance process is printed on the lower part of the check. In addition to the clearance symbol, banks include a symbol for each customer's account. Banks also continue to include the older check routing symbol in the upper right-hand corner of their checks. Today, banks can keep an image of a check and process payment electronically through automated clearing houses (ACHs). Banks now also have several ways to clear checks.

4.6.2 TRANSFER OF CREDIT

The Fed provides for the transfer of hundreds of millions of dollars in depository balances around the country daily. The communication system called Fedwire may be used by depository institutions to transfer funds for their own accounts, to move balances at correspondent banks, and to send funds to another institution on behalf of customers.

4.6.3 OTHER SERVICE ACTIVITIES

A large portion of Fed employees hold jobs directly related to the Fed's role as *fiscal agent* for the U.S. government. The services include holding the Treasury's checking accounts; assisting in the collection of taxes; transferring money from one region to another; and selling, redeeming, and paying interest on federal securities. The federal government makes most of its payments to the public from funds on deposit at the Reserve Banks. The Fed also acts as fiscal agent for foreign central banks and international organizations such as the International Monetary Fund.

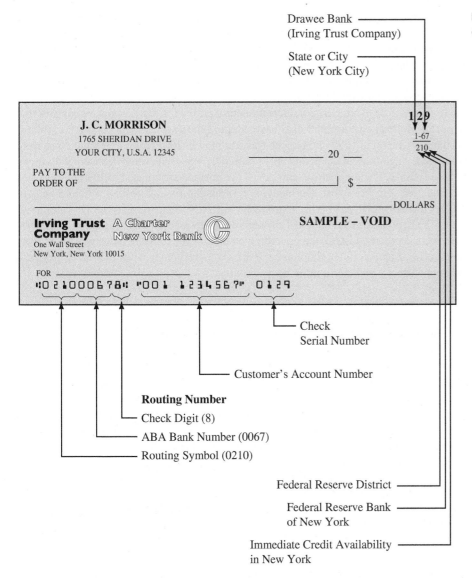

Drawee Bank
(Irving Trust Company)

State or City
(New York City)

FIGURE 4.5   Traditional use
of check routing symbols

Check
Serial Number

Customer's Account Number

Routing Number

Check Digit (8)

ABA Bank Number (0067)

Routing Symbol (0210)

Federal Reserve District

Federal Reserve Bank
of New York

Immediate Credit Availability
in New York

GLOBAL Central banks in other developed countries, like the U.S. Fed, are responsible for regulating the country's money supply, safeguarding the country's currency, and carrying out the country's monetary policy. Most other countries have a single central bank with branches that differ from the Fed's 12 Reserve Banks. Of course, the Fed BOG has effectively centralized control of U.S. monetary policy.

Empirical evidence shows a link between central bank independence from government intervention and inflation and economic growth rates. In countries where central banks are relatively independent from their governments, there have generally been lower inflation rates and higher economic growth rates than in countries where central banks are closely tied to their governments.

Three economically important foreign central banks are those of the United Kingdom, Japan, and the European Monetary Union. The central bank in the United Kingdom is the *Bank of England (BOE)*. It was created well before the formation of the Federal Reserve System in 1913. The BOE is managed by a governor and five additional officers, all of whom are appointed for five-year terms. The BOE governor reports to the chancellor, who has final responsibility for setting monetary policy. In contrast with the United States, commercial banks in Great Britain are not required to hold reserves at the Bank of England. Also, recall from Chapter 3 that Great Britain does not legally separate commercial banking and investment banking activities.

4.7 CENTRAL BANKS IN OTHER COUNTRIES

The central bank of Japan, called the *Bank of Japan (BOJ)*, was created in 1947. The top official of the BOJ is the governor, who heads the Policy Board, which is the central decision-making authority. The governor and some members of the board are appointed by the Japanese equivalent of the U.S. Congress, and other board members are appointed by the finance minister. Japanese commercial banks, like their U.S. counterparts, are required to hold reserves on deposit with the BOJ, and banks can borrow at an official discount rate from the BOJ.

European Central Bank (ECB) conducts monetary policy for the European countries that adopted the euro as their common currency

The **European Central Bank (ECB)** conducts monetary policy for the European countries that belong to the European Monetary Union and also have adopted the euro as their common currency. Eleven European countries joined in 1999 and Greece was admitted in 2001. Euro notes and coins were officially introduced at the beginning of 2002, and all 12 individual national currencies were withdrawn as legal tender by July 1, 2002. The number of "eurozone" members has increased to 19 countries. The ECB, which is headquartered in Frankfurt, Germany, is responsible for controlling inflation and for managing the value of the euro relative to other currencies. The ECB structure is somewhat similar to the U.S. Fed's in that the national central banks of the euro countries operate much like the 12 Federal Reserve District Banks. Like the Fed BOG, the governing council of the ECB includes governors from some of the national central banks. Each national central bank is responsible for managing payment systems and furnishing currency and credit in its home country.

LEARNING ACTIVITY

Go to the European Central Bank's website, https://www.ecb.int, and find information on how that bank is structured and how it operates.

APPLYING FINANCE TO. . .

- **Institutions and Markets** Depository institutions, commercial banks, S&Ls, savings banks, and credit unions comprise the banking system. The Fed is the U.S. central bank, which supervises and regulates the banking system. The Fed, along with depository institutions, creates and transfers money. Monetary policy actions of the Fed affect the primary financial markets for debt obligations, influencing the availability of bank loans and the interest rates that must be paid on those loans.

- **Investments** Securities markets, both primary and secondary, are also affected by Fed actions. An increase in reserve requirements will restrict the amount of individual savings that would be available to make loans. Other Fed actions may cause banks to raise loan interest rates, and cause the economy to slow down and security prices to decline. When the Fed raises the discount rate, banks react to protect their profit margins by raising their lending rates to individuals and businesses.

- **Financial Management** Financial management activities are directly affected by Fed monetary policy actions. A tightening of monetary policy makes it more difficult and costly for businesses to borrow funds. To the extent that economic activity also declines, it is more difficult for financial managers to sell new stocks and bonds in the primary securities markets. Of course, an easing of monetary policy will make it easier for financial managers to raise financial capital and they will be able to do so at lower interest rates.

SUMMARY

LO 4.1 The Federal Reserve System (Fed) responded to the recent financial crisis and Great Recession by providing rescue funds to some financial institutions and by helping other financially weak institutions merge with stronger institutions. These actions were necessary to keep many financial institutions from failing due to liquidity crises caused by precipitous declines in the values of the home mortgage loans and mortgage-backed securities that they held because of mortgage loan defaults.

LO 4.2 The national banking system that existed before the Federal Reserve System was created lacked an efficient national payments system for transferring money, a flexible money supply that can respond to changes in the demand for money, and a lending/borrowing mechanism to help alleviate liquidity problems when they arise.

LO 4.3 The Federal Reserve System is the central bank of the United States and is responsible for setting monetary policy and regulating the banking system. The Fed is organized into five major components: (1) member banks, (2) Federal Reserve District Banks, (3) Board of Governors, (4) Federal Open Market Committee, and (5) advisory committees.

LO 4.4   The policy instruments used by the Fed to carry out monetary policy are changing reserve requirements, changing the lending (discount/primary credit) rate, and conducting open-market operations. In recent years, the Fed has also engaged in a nontraditional monetary policy called quantitative easing. Banks are required by the Fed to hold reserves equal to a specified percentage of their deposits. An increase in the required reserves ratio reduces bank reserves, and vice versa. The Fed lending rate is the interest rate that a bank must pay to borrow from its regional Reserve Bank. Higher lending rates will discourage money supply expansion, and vice versa. Open-market operations involves the buying and selling of securities in the open market by the Fed through its FOMC to alter bank reserves. The purchasing of securities increases bank reserves, and vice versa. Quantitative easing involves the purchasing of securities from banks and other financial institutions to increase the money supply and liquidity.

LO 4.5   The Fed is authorized to supervise and examine member bank assets, operations, financial conditions, and compliance with banking laws and regulations. In practice, the Fed focuses on examination of state-chartered member banks and all bank holding companies. Nationally chartered banks are examined by the Office of the Comptroller of the Currency. The Fed has legal responsibility for administering several banking laws and is responsible for enforcing laws, such as the Consumer Credit Protection Act of 1968, that help consumers understand the costs of alternative forms of credit.

LO 4.6   Reserve Banks provide a range of services to depository institutions and to the U.S. government. The most important service is the payments mechanism for transferring money throughout the banking system. Other services include electronic funds transfers, safekeeping and transfer of securities, and serving as fiscal agent for the U.S. government.

LO 4.7   Foreign countries that use central banking systems, like the Fed in the United States, to regulate money supply and set monetary policy include the United Kingdom (Bank of England), Japan (Bank of Japan), and euro-member countries (European Central Bank). There is some similarity between the Fed operating with 12 Federal Reserve Banks that represent different districts in the United States and the European Central Bank operating with central banks from each euro-zone member.

KEY TERMS

accommodative function
bank reserves
central bank
Consumer Credit
   Protection Act
defensive activities
dynamic actions
European Central
   Bank (ECB)

excess reserves
Fed Board of
   Governors
Fed discount rate
federal funds rate
Federal Home
   Loan Mortgage
   Corporation
   (Freddie Mac)

Federal National Mort-
   gage Association
   (Fannie Mae)
Federal Reserve
   System (Fed)
fractional reserve system
Government National
   Mortgage Association
   (Ginnie Mae)

monetary policy
open-market operations
primary credit rate
quantitative easing (QE)
Regulation Z
required reserves
required reserves ratio

REVIEW QUESTIONS

1. **(LO 4.1)** Identify some of the institutional participants in the mortgage markets.

2. **(LO 4.1)** What actions did the Fed take to help avoid a financial system collapse in 2008–2009?

3. **(LO 4.2)** Describe the weaknesses of the national banking system that was in place prior to passage of the Federal Reserve Act of 1913.

4. **(LO 4.2)** What functions and activities do central banks usually perform?

5. **(LO 4.3)** Describe the organizational structure of the Federal Reserve System in terms of its five major components.

6. **(LO 4.3)** Explain how the banking interests of large, medium, and small businesses are represented on the board of directors of each Reserve Bank.

7. **(LO 4.3)** What is a Reserve Branch Bank? How many such branches exist, and where are most of them located?

8. **(LO 4.3)** How are members of the BOG of the Federal Reserve System appointed? To what extent are they subject to political pressures?

9. **(LO 4.3)** Discuss the structure, functions, and importance of the FOMC.

10. **(LO 4.3)** Identify the eight individuals who served as chairs of the Fed BOG since the early 1950s. Indicate each individual's approximate time and length of service as chair.

11. **(LO 4.4)** Distinguish among the dynamic, defensive, and accommodative responsibilities of the Fed.

12. **(LO 4.4)** Identify and briefly describe the three traditional instruments that may be used by the Fed to set monetary policy.

13. **(LO 4.4)** Describe what is meant by quantitative easing by the Fed.

14. **(LO 4.4)** Reserve Banks have at times been described as bankers' banks because of their lending powers. What is meant by this statement?

15. **(LO 4.4)** Describe the two "targets" that the Fed can use when establishing monetary policy. Which target has the Fed focused on in recent years?

16. **(LO 4.5)** Explain the usual procedures for examining national banks. How does this process differ from the examination of member banks of the Federal Reserve System holding state charters?

17. **(LO 4.5)** What federal agencies are responsible for supervising and regulating depository institutions that are not commercial banks?

18. **(LO 4.5)** Describe the objectives of the Consumer Credit Protection Act of 1968. What is the Truth in Lending section of the act? What is Regulation Z?

19. **(LO 4.6)** Explain the process by which the Federal Reserve Banks provide the economy with currency and coin.

20. **(LO 4.6)** Describe how a check drawn on a commercial bank but deposited for collection in another bank in a distant city might be cleared through the facilities of the Federal Reserve System.

21. **(LO 4.6)** What is the special role of the Federal Reserve Inter-district Settlement Fund in the check-clearance process?

22. **(LO 4.6)** In what way do the Reserve Banks serve as fiscal agents for the U.S. government?

23. **(LO 4.7)** Briefly describe and compare the central banks in the United Kingdom, Japan, and Economic Monetary Union.

EXERCISES

1. You are a resident of Seattle, Washington, and maintain a checking account with a bank in that city. You have just written a check on that bank to pay your tuition. Describe the process by which the banking system enables your college to collect the funds from your bank.

2. As the executive of a bank or thrift institution you are faced with an intense seasonal demand for loans. Assuming that your loanable funds are inadequate to take care of the demand, how might your Reserve Bank help you with this problem?

3. The Federal Reserve BOG has decided to ease monetary conditions to counter early signs of an economic downturn. Because price inflation has been a burden in recent years, the Board is eager to avoid any action that the public might interpret as a return to inflationary conditions. How might the Board use its various powers to accomplish the objective of monetary ease without drawing unfavorable publicity to its actions?

4. An economic contraction (recession) is now well under way, and the Fed plans to use all facilities at its command to halt the decline. Describe the measures that it may take.

5. You have recently retired and are intent on extensive travel to many of the exotic lands you have only read about. You will be receiving not only a pension check and Social Security check but also dividends and interest from several corporations. You are concerned about the deposit of these checks during your several months of absence, and you have asked your banker if there is an arrangement available to solve this problem. What alternative might the banker suggest?

6. The prime rate, and other interest rates, offered by banks often change in the same direction as a change in the Fed's target for the federal funds rate. As an employee of a Federal Reserve District Bank you have been told that your district bank will be increasing its discount rate early next week. Expectations are that an increase in the discount rate will

lead to an increase in the federal funds rate, which will lead to an increase in the prime rate and other bank lending rates. You have been thinking about buying a new automobile for the past couple of months. Given this information of a planned discount rate increase, you are considering buying your new automobile before the end of the week. What are the ethical issues, if any, involved in this scenario? What would you do?

PROBLEMS

1. A new bank has vault cash of $1 million and $5 million in deposits held at its Federal Reserve District Bank.
   a. If the required reserves ratio is 8%, what dollar amount of deposits can the bank have?
   b. If the bank holds $65 million in deposits and currently holds bank reserves such that excess reserves are zero, what required reserves ratio is implied?

2. Assume a bank has $5 million in deposits and $1 million in vault cash. If the bank holds $1 million in excess reserves and the required reserves ratio is 8%, what level of deposits are being held?

3. A bank has $110 million in deposits and holds $10 million in vault cash.
   a. If the required reserves ratio is 10%, what dollar amount of reserves must be held at the Federal Reserve Bank?
   b. How would your answer in part (a) change if the required reserves ratio was increased to 12%?

4. A bank has $10 million in vault cash and $110 million in deposits. If total bank reserves were $15 million with $2 million considered to be excess reserves, what required reserves ratio is implied?

5. The Friendly National Bank holds $50 million in reserves at its Federal Reserve District Bank. The required reserves ratio is 12%.
   a. If the bank has $600 million in deposits, what amount of vault cash would be needed for the bank to be in compliance with the required reserves ratio?
   b. If the bank holds $10 million in vault cash, determine the required reserves ratio that would be needed for the bank to avoid a reserves deficit.
   c. If the Friendly National Bank experiences a required reserves deficit, what actions can it take to be in compliance with the existing required reserves ratio?

6. Assume that banks must hold a 2% reserve percentage against transaction account balances up to and including $40 million. For transaction accounts above $40 million, the required reserve percentage is 8%. Also assume that Dell National Bank has transaction account balances of $200 million.
   a. Calculate the dollar amount of required reserves that Dell National Bank must hold.
   b. What percentage of Dell's total transaction account balance must be held in the form of required reserves?

7. Assume that the Fed decides to increase the required reserve percentage on transaction accounts above $40 million from 8% to 10%. All other information remains the same as given in Problem 6, including the transaction account balances held by Dell National Bank.
   a. What would be the dollar amount of required reserves?
   b. What percentage of total transaction account balances held by Dell would be held as required reserves?

8. Show how your answers in Problem 6 would change if the Fed lowered the cut-off between the 2% rate and the 8% rate from $40 million in transaction account balances down to $20 million.

9. **Challenge Problem** You have been asked to assess the impact of possible changes in reserve requirement components on the dollar amount of reserves required. Assume the reserve percentages are set at 2% on the first $50 million of transaction account amounts, 4% on the second $50 million, and 10% on transaction amounts over $100 million. First National Bank has transaction account balances of $100 million, while Second National Bank's transaction balances are $150 million and Third National Bank's transaction balances are $250 million.

a. Determine the dollar amounts of required reserves for each of the three banks.

b. Calculate the percentage of reserves to total transactions accounts for each of the three banks.

c. The central bank wants to slow the economy by raising the reserve requirements for member banks. To do so, the reserve percentages will be increased to 12% on transaction balances above $100 million. Simultaneously, the 2% rate will apply on the first $25 million. Calculate the reserve requirement amount for each of the three banks after these changes have taken place.

d. Show the dollar amount of changes in reserve requirement amounts for each bank.

Calculate the percentage of reserve requirement amounts to transaction account balances for each bank.

e. Which of the two reserve requirement changes discussed in (c) causes the greatest impact on the dollar amount of reserves for all three of the banks?

f. Now assume that you could either (1) lower the transactions account amount for the lowest category from $50 million down to $25 million or (2) increase the reserve percentage from 10% to 12% on transactions account amounts over $200 million. Which choice would you recommend if you were trying to achieve a moderate slowing of economic activity?

Policy Makers and the Money Supply

CHAPTER 5

LEARNING OBJECTIVES

After studying this chapter, you should be able to do the following:

LO 5.1 Describe the U.S. national economic policy objectives and possible conflicts among these objectives.

LO 5.2 Identify the major policy makers and describe their primary responsibilities.

LO 5.3 Discuss how the U.S. government influences the economy and how the government reacted to the 2007–2009 perfect financial storm.

LO 5.4 Describe the U.S. Treasury's cash and general management responsibilities.

LO 5.5 Describe the U.S. Treasury's deficit financing and debt management responsibilities.

LO 5.6 Discuss how expansion of the money supply takes place in the U.S. banking system.

LO 5.7 Summarize the factors or transactions that affect bank reserves.

LO 5.8 Explain the terms monetary base, money multiplier, and the velocity of money and their relationships to the money supply.

Where we have been. . . In Chapter 4, we discussed the role of the Federal Reserve System as the central bank in the U.S. banking system. Money must be easily transferred, checks must be processed and cleared, banks must be regulated and supervised, and the money supply must be controlled. The Fed either assists or directly performs all of the activities that are necessary for a well-functioning financial system. You also learned about the characteristics and requirements of Federal Reserve membership and the composition of the Fed Board of Governors. You were introduced to the Fed's monetary policy functions – its open-market operations, the administration of reserve requirements, and the setting of interest rates on loans to depository institutions. Fed supervisory and regulatory functions were also discussed.

Where we are going. . . The last chapter in Part 1 focuses on how currency exchange rates are determined and how international trade is financed. We begin by discussing what is meant by currency exchange rates and foreign exchange markets. This is followed by a discussion of factors that determine exchange rate relationships and changes in those relationships over time. You will then learn how the financing of international trade takes place, including how exporters finance with a draft or bill of exchange. Financing by the importer and the use of a commercial letter of credit and a trust receipt are also covered. The last section will introduce you to developments in international transactions as measured by balance-of-payments accounts. In Part 2 our focus will be on investments, including the securities and other financial markets needed to market and transfer financial assets.

How this chapter applies to me. . . The opportunity to vote gives you a way of influencing economic and political developments in this country. The president and members of Congress are policy makers elected by the people. After reading this chapter, you should have a better understanding of the national economic policy objectives in the United States and how government officials and the Fed influence the economy. You then will be in a more knowledgeable position to make informed economic decisions about activities that may influence your life and career.

Government and private policy makers often are maligned in the press and sometimes even by themselves. For example, President Ronald Reagan in 1986 said,

The government's view of the economy could be summed up in a few short phrases: If it moves, tax it. If it keeps moving, regulate it. And if it stops moving, subsidize it.[1]

While this statement is somewhat humorous to most of us, it also serves to start us thinking about what should be the country's broad-based economic objectives and what mechanisms are needed for achieving these objectives. We need a system of checks and balances to ensure that policy makers will operate in the best interests of the people of the United States. The president and Congress pass laws and set fiscal policy, while the Fed sets monetary policy and attempts to regulate the supply of money and the availability of credit.

5.1 NATIONAL ECONOMIC POLICY OBJECTIVES

Ernest Hemingway said,

The first panacea for a mismanaged nation is inflation of the currency; the second is war. Both bring a temporary prosperity; both bring a permanent ruin. Both are the refuge of political and economic opportunists.[2]

Most of us would agree with Hemingway that currency inflation and war are not acceptable economic objectives. While people with differing views debate the proper role of government, there is broad agreement that decisions by government policy makers to levy taxes and make expenditures significantly affect the lives of each of us. In addition to the checks and balances offered by two political parties, the Fed is expected to operate independently of the government but also in the best interests of the country and its people. There is also a strong tradition in the United States that national economic objectives should be pursued with minimum interference to the economic freedom of individuals.

The *Employment Act of 1946* and the *Full Employment and Balanced Growth Act of 1978*, which is typically referred to as the *Humphrey-Hawkins Act*, spell out the role of the U.S. government in carrying out the economic goals of economic growth and stable prices. Most of us also would agree that economic growth is good if it leads to improved living standards for the people. However, for this to occur, economic growth must be accompanied by stable prices and high and stable employment levels. The relationship between the money supply and demand affects the level of prices and economic activity in our market economy. Therefore, the process by which the money supply is increased and decreased is a very important factor to the success of the economy. Since we live in a global environment, our economic well-being also depends on achieving a reasonable balance in international trade and other transactions. To summarize, our country's economic policy actions are directed toward these three national economic policy goals:

- Economic growth

- High employment

- Price stability

Accompanying these economic goals is also a desire for stability in interest rates, financial markets, and foreign exchange markets.

5.1.1 ECONOMIC GROWTH

The standard of living of U.S. citizens has increased dramatically during the history of the United States as a result of the growth of the economy and its productivity. Of course, growth means more than merely increasing total output. It requires that output increase faster than the population so that the average output per person expands. Growth is a function of two components: an increasing stock of productive resources – the labor force and stock of capital – and improved technology and skills.

---

[1] Address, White House Conference on Small Business, August 15, 1986.
[2] "Notes on the Next War: A Serious Topical Letter," *Esquire*, September, 1935.

The output of goods and services in an economy is referred to as the gross domestic product (GDP). The United States began the 1980s with a double-dip recession, or economic downturn, in "real" terms (i.e., after price changes have been factored out). A mild economic decline occurred in 1980, followed by a deeper decline that lasted from mid-1981 through most of 1982. The GDP then grew in real terms throughout the remainder of the 1980s, before a mild downturn began in mid-1990 and lasted through the first quarter of 1991. Although some industries underwent substantial downsizing and restructuring, the economy continued to grow in real terms throughout the 1990s. As we moved into the twenty-first century, economic growth slowed both domestically and worldwide, resulting in a U.S. recession in 2001. Economic recovery began in 2002 and economic growth continued for a number of years until the United States entered into the Great Recession of 2008–2009. Since then, economic growth through 2018 has averaged about 2 to 3% annually.

gross domestic product (GDP) measures the output of goods and services in an economy

5.1.2 HIGH EMPLOYMENT

Unemployment represents a loss of potential output and imposes costs on the entire economy. The economic and psychological costs are especially hard on the unemployed. While there is some disagreement over what we should consider full employment, it is a stated objective of the U.S. government to promote stability of employment and production at levels close to the national potential. This aim seeks to avoid large changes in economic activity, minimizing the hardships that accompany loss of jobs and output.

The U.S. unemployment rate reached double-digit levels during the early 1980s with a peak at about 11% near the end of 1982. As the economy began expanding, unemployment levels declined throughout the remainder of the 1980s until the rate fell below 5.5%. The recession that began in mid-1990, along with other job dislocations associated with corporate downsizing and restructuring, resulted in an unemployment rate exceeding 7.5% in 1992. The remainder of the 1990s was characterized by a steady decline in the unemployment rate to a level below 4.5%. As the country entered the twenty-first century, economic activity slowed and the unemployment level began rising. With an economic recovery beginning in 2002, employment opportunities improved for a period of years. However, the economy began slowing in 2007 and entered into a steep decline in 2008, causing the unemployment rate to reach the 10% level. Even with economic recovery beginning during the second-half of 2009, the unemployment rate remained near the double-digit level at the end of 2010. By the end of 2015, the unemployment rate had fallen to about the 5% level, and was under 4% by the end of 2018.

5.1.3 PRICE STABILITY

The importance of stable prices is well accepted but sometimes has been difficult to achieve. Consistently stable prices help create an environment in which the other economic goals are more easily reached. Inflation, which we initially defined in Chapter 2, occurs when a rise or increase in the prices of goods and services is not offset by increases in the quality of those goods and services. Inflation discourages investment by increasing the uncertainty about future returns. Therefore, high inflation rates are not considered acceptable as a price to pay for high levels of employment. Today, the Fed has an annual inflation target rate of 2%.

inflation an increase in the price of goods or services that is not offset by an increase in quality

Inflation was at double-digit levels during the early 1980s, and this was reflected in record-high interest rates. However, as the economy turned down in the 1981–1982 recession, inflation rates also started down and continued down until inflation fell below 3%. After a brief rise at the beginning of the 1990s, inflation steadily declined to 2% and continued at very low levels in the early years of the twenty-first century. The Fed began increasing its federal funds rate target in 2004 because of concern about possible increasing inflation. After the housing bubble collapse in mid-2006, the Fed began lowering its federal funds rate target. Then, in response to the financial crisis and the start of the Great Recession, the Fed reduced its target for the federal funds rate to a near zero level beginning in late 2008. Inflation rates remained below the 2% Fed target level in 2018 and early 2019.

5.1.4 DOMESTIC AND INTERNATIONAL IMPLICATIONS

The three national economic policy objectives are sometimes in conflict with each other. For example, while economic growth generally leads to higher employment, a too rapid growth rate is likely to lead to higher inflation. Greater demand relative to supply for workers and materials could cause prices to rise. On the other hand, a very slow growth rate, or even economic contraction will lead to higher unemployment rates and little pressure on prices. Thus, policy makers must attempt to balance these economic goals as they establish economic policy.

Actions taken with respect to a country's own national affairs also influence the economies of other nations. Thus, it is important for economic policy makers to maintain a worldview rather than just a narrow nationalistic approach. Nations that export more goods and services than they import have a net trade surplus, and vice versa. When funds received from the sale (export) of goods and services to other countries are less than the payments made for the purchase (import) of goods and services from other countries, these trade deficits must be made up by positive net financial transactions and foreign exchange operations with the rest of the world. We discuss balance of payments components and implications in Chapter 6.

5.2 FOUR POLICY MAKER GROUPS	Recall from Chapter 1 that "*capitalism*" is an economic system with private ownership of assets, the production of goods and services for profit, a price mechanism for allocating resources, and efficient financial markets. We also noted that the U.S. was a mixed market capitalistic system where elements of a planned economic system administered by a central government is combined with elements of a free market economic system. The U.S. government establishes economic goals and attempts to achieve those goals through fiscal and monetary policy actions. The government also regulates business activities, financial institutions, and financial markets. It also establishes social programs for the public good.

A "*democracy*," also discussed in Chapter 1, is a system of government where limited authority and power are granted by law to its people who participate by voting on government goals and objectives. The U.S. is a representative democracy where citizens elect representatives from amongst their peers who, in turn, help formulate government economic and other goals.

Four groups of policy makers are actively involved in achieving the nation's economic policy objectives:

- Federal Reserve System
- The president
- Congress
- U.S. Treasury

Citizens elect the members of Congress and the president to represent them in formulating fiscal policy. The Fed was created as an independent organization that establishes monetary policy without needing approval from the executive and legislative branches of government. The Treasury advises the executive and legislative branches on fiscal policy matters and is responsible for managing the national debt. Figure 5.1 illustrates how these groups use monetary and fiscal policies, supported by debt management practices, to carry out the three economic objectives of economic growth, high employment, and stable prices.

FIGURE 5.1 Policy makers and economic policy objectives

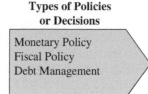

Policy Makers	**Types of Policies or Decisions**	**Economic Objectives**
Federal Reserve System The President Congress U.S. Treasury	Monetary Policy Fiscal Policy Debt Management	Economic Growth High Employment Price Stability

As discussed in Chapter 4, the Fed establishes monetary policy, including managing the supply and cost of money. We will see later in this chapter how the money supply is actually changed. **Fiscal policy** involves setting the annual federal budget, and it reflects government influence on economic activity through taxation and expenditure plans. Fiscal policy is carried out by the president and Congress. The U.S. Treasury supports economic policy objectives through its debt management practices.

fiscal policy government influence on economic activity through taxation and expenditure plans

5.2.1 ETHICAL BEHAVIOR IN GOVERNMENT

ETHICAL Since World War II, 13 individuals served as president of the United States. The 1990s were under the direction of George H. W. Bush and William (Bill) Clinton. George W. Bush, Barack Obama, and Donald Trump led the U.S. during the first two decades of the twenty-first century.

One would expect that the leader of the United States should and would exhibit a very high level of moral and ethical behavior. We expect the people of our nation to practice sound ethical behavior by treating others fairly and honestly. Certainly, the president has the opportunity to lead by example. Two recent presidents, Richard Nixon (who served as president during 1969–1974) and Bill Clinton (who served as president during 1993–2001), were each accused of unethical behavior while president. Nixon resigned on August 9, 1974, just before he was impeached because of the Watergate scandal involving office break-ins. In 1998, Clinton became the second president to be impeached by the House of Representatives. Clinton's handling of personal indiscretions with a White House intern led to his trial in the Senate. He was found not guilty and completed his second term.[3]

Unethical behavior in government has not been limited to presidents. There also have been numerous accounts of unethical behavior on the part of members of Congress. Some individuals have been impeached and others have been sent to prison. With this said, the vast majority of members of Congress and past presidents have practiced high ethical behavior, including fair and honest treatment of their constituents. The other good news is that the U.S. government and society have overcome the isolated unethical behavior of a few leaders.

5.2.2 POLICY MAKERS IN THE EUROPEAN ECONOMIC UNION

GLOBAL As in the United States, European governments use monetary and fiscal policies to try to achieve similar economic goals, such as economic growth and price stability. In December 1991, the members of the *European Union (EU)* signed the *Maastricht Treaty* in Maastricht, Netherlands. The objective was to converge their economies, fix member country exchange rates, and introduce the euro as a common currency at the beginning of 1999. Monetary and fiscal policy actions of each country were to focus on maintaining price stability, keeping government budget deficits below 3% of gross domestic product (GDP) and total government debt below 60% of GDP, and maintaining stability in relative currency exchange rates. Of the 15 EU countries, 12 members formed the *European Monetary Union (EMU)*, ratified the Maastricht Treaty, and qualified to adopt the euro as their common currency with conversion officially taking place in 2002. Since then, EU membership has grown to 28 countries, with 19 of these countries joining the EMU and adopting the euro as their common currency. The people of the U.K. voted in a 2016 referendum to withdraw from the EU. However, as of early 2019 no withdrawal agreement had been approved.

It is striking that initially 12 and now 19 countries with widely different past applications of monetary and fiscal policies could agree on similar economic and financial objectives. While each country continues to formulate its own fiscal policies today, the *European Central Bank (ECB)* focuses on maintaining price stability across the 19 eurozone countries. The sheer size of the EMU also means that European policy makers and U.S. policy makers must work closely together in trying to achieve the worldwide goals of economic growth and price stability.

---

[3] For a further discussion of past U.S. presidents, see Frank Freidel and Hugh S. Sidey, *The Presidents of the United States of America* (Willard, OH: R.R. Donnelley and Sons, 1996).

DISCUSSION QUESTION 1

How successful have U.S. policy makers been in achieving high employment and low inflation in recent years?

5.3 GOVERNMENT INFLUENCE ON THE ECONOMY

federal budget annual revenue and expenditure plans that reflect fiscal policy objectives concerning government influence on economic activity

budget surplus occurs when tax revenues (receipts) are more than expenditures (outlays)

budget deficit occurs when tax revenues (receipts) are less than expenditures (outlays)

The federal government plays a dual role in the economy. It provides social and economic services to the public that cannot be provided as efficiently by the private sector. The federal government is also responsible for guiding or regulating the economy. Actions by the four policy maker groups need to be coordinated to achieve the desired national economic objectives. The president and the Council of Economic Advisors (CEA) prepare an annual **federal budget** containing revenue and expenditure plans that reflect fiscal policy objectives concerning government influence on economic activity. Congress reviews, makes changes, and passes legislation relating to budget expenditures. A **budget surplus** occurs when tax revenues (receipts) are more than expenditures (outlays). When revenues are less than expenditures, there is a **budget deficit**. The Treasury must borrow funds by selling government (Treasury) securities to cover a deficit.

A government raises funds to pay for its activities in three ways:

- Levies taxes

- Borrows

- Prints money for its own use

Because the last option has tempted some governments, with disastrous results, Congress delegated the power to create money and manage the money supply to the Fed. Our federal government collects taxes to pay for most of its spending, and it borrows, competing for funds in the financial system, to finance its deficits.

To illustrate the complex nature of the government's influence on the economy, consider the many effects of a federal deficit. To finance it, the government competes with other borrowers in the financial system. This absorbs savings, and it may raise interest rates. Private investment may be reduced if it becomes more difficult for firms to borrow the funds needed. On the other hand, a deficit stimulates economic activity. The government is either spending more or collecting less in taxes, or both, leaving more income for consumers to spend. The larger the deficit, the more total spending, or aggregate demand, there will be. In some circumstances, this stimulation of the economy generates enough extra income and savings to finance both the deficit and additional investment by firms.

monetizing the debt Fed buys government securities to help finance a budget deficit and to add to bank reserves and increase the money supply

During periods of war-related budget deficits (e.g., World Wars I and II), the Fed engaged in an activity known as **monetizing the debt** whereby the Fed buys government securities to help finance the deficit and to provide additional bank reserves and increase the money supply. The Fed does not practice this activity today since it would be counter to current monetary policy and would also have a significant impact on the financial markets. The competition for funds would make it more difficult for some borrowers to meet their financing needs.

Fiscal policy is developed and implemented by the president (with the assistance of the CEA) and Congress. The president and the CEA prepare annual budgets reflecting their tax and expenditure plans. Congress reviews, modifies, and passes legislation authorizing the implementation of budget plans. When plans call for expenditures to exceed tax revenues, the resulting budget deficit is designed to stimulate economic activity.

The Treasury is responsible for collecting taxes and disbursing funds, and for debt management, which includes financing current deficits and refinancing the outstanding national debt. As discussed in Chapter 4, the Fed contributes to the attainment of the nation's economic goals by formulating monetary policy. It uses its powers to regulate the growth of the money supply and, thus, influence interest rates and the availability of loans.

The principal responsibilities of these policy makers have not always been the same. When the Fed was established in 1913, most of the power to regulate money and credit was placed in its hands. However, as the public debt grew during World War I, the Great Depression of the 1930s, and World War II, the Treasury became vitally interested in credit conditions. Policies that affect interest rates and the size of the money supply affect the Treasury directly, since it is the largest borrower in the nation. Therefore, the U.S. Treasury took over primary responsibility for managing the federal debt. In managing the large public debt and various trust funds placed under its jurisdiction, the Treasury has the power to influence the money market materially. The Fed came back into its own in the 1950s and is now the chief architect of monetary policy.

It should not be surprising that the policy instruments of the various policy makers at times put them at cross purposes. A long-standing debate continues over the balance between full employment and price stability. A particular policy that leads toward one may make the other more difficult to achieve, yet each objective has its supporters. As with all governmental policy, economic objectives are necessarily subject to compromise and trade-offs.

5.3.1 GOVERNMENT REACTION TO THE PERFECT FINANCIAL STORM

CRISIS As we briefly discussed in earlier chapters, a "perfect financial storm" developed in the midst of the 2007–2008 financial crisis and 2008–2009 Great Recession. In 2008, the U.S. economy was on the verge of financial collapse. The housing price "bubble" burst in 2006 and home prices began a sharp and prolonged decline. Stock market prices peaked in 2007 and fell sharply until mid-2009. The economy began slowing in 2007, with economic contraction beginning in early 2008. The resulting 2008–2009 recession turned out to be the steepest U.S. recession since the Great Depression of the 1930s. Individuals were defaulting on their home mortgages in increasing numbers due to falling home prices and increasing unemployment. Business firms and financial institutions, who had borrowed heavily during years of easy money and low interest rates, were faced with their own financial difficulties as economic activity slowed markedly. Many of the debt securities issued and backed by home mortgage loans, called mortgage-backed securities, became difficult to value and quickly became known as "troubled" or "toxic" assets.

Many major financial institutions and business corporations were on the verge of collapse or failure. Some of the very largest financial institutions were deemed as being "too big to fail" because their failure would cause cascading negative repercussions throughout the United States and many foreign economies. As discussed in Chapter 4, the Federal Reserve moved to increase liquidity in the monetary system and reduced its target federal funds rate to below the 0.25% level. The Fed also worked with the U.S. Treasury to help facilitate the merging of financially weak institutions with those that were financially stronger. For example, in March 2008, the Fed and Treasury assisted in the acquisition of Bear Sterns by JPMorgan Chase & Co.

The Federal National Mortgage Association (Fannie Mae) and the Federal Home Mortgage Association (Freddie Mac), briefly discussed in Chapter 4 as being major participants in the secondary mortgage markets, were on the verge of financial insolvency and possible collapse in mid-2008. Fannie Mae was actively creating and packaging mortgage-backed securities, many of which became troubled assets as home owners began defaulting on the underlying mortgages. Freddie Mac purchased home mortgages, including lower-quality subprime mortgages, attempting to support the mortgage markets and home ownership. In an attempt to avoid a meltdown, the Fed provided rescue funds in July 2008 and the U.S. government assumed control of both Fannie Mae and Freddie Mac in September 2008.

In addition to the efforts of the Fed and the Treasury, the U.S. Congress and the president responded with the passage of the *Economic Stabilization Act of 2008* in early October of that year. A primary focus of this legislation, which became known as the *Troubled Asset Relief Program (TARP)*, was to allow the U.S. Treasury to purchase up to $700 billion of troubled or toxic assets held by financial institutions. Then, in an effort to stimulate economic activity, Congress and the president passed the $787 billion *American Recovery and Reinvestment Act of 2009* in February 2009, with the funds to be used to provide tax relief, appropriations, and direct spending. In part, as a result of these actions, economic activity in the United States began recovering in the second half of 2009.

As it turned out, the U.S. Treasury purchase of troubled bank-held assets developed slowly. In fact, passage of the *Dodd-Frank Wall Street Reform and Consumer Protection Act of 2010* amended the *Emergency Economic Stabilization Act of 2008*. Title XIII, known as the "Pay It Back Act," reduced the availability of TARP funds from $700 billion to $475 billion and mandated that any unused funds could not be used in new programs.

SMALL BUSINESS PRACTICE

GOVERNMENT FINANCING ASSISTANCE FOR SMALL BUSINESSES

Small businesses can seek financing help from both the federal and state or from local levels. The Small Business Administration (SBA) was created in 1953 by the federal government. The SBA provides financial assistance to small firms that are unable to obtain loans from private lenders at reasonable terms and interest costs. We discuss the SBA in greater detail in Chapter 16.

Small business investment companies (SBICs) are chartered and regulated by the SBA. SBICs help finance small businesses by making both equity investments and loans. SBICs get their funds (to be lent or invested in small businesses) from privately invested capital and long-term bonds purchased or guaranteed by the SBA. These bonds typically have ten-year maturities. A small business is currently defined as a firm with less than $6 million in net worth or net income of less than $2 million.

At the state and local level, there also are possible sources of financing help for small businesses. For example, most states have Small Business Development Centers (SBDCs) that can help small businesses find sources of financing. Small businesses also may find sources of financing help by contacting their state's Department of Economic Development or Department of Commerce.

These fiscal stimulus packages and modifications, along with the three quantitative easing efforts by the Fed in 2008, 2010, and 2012, helped the U.S. economy grow, on average, at 2–3% annually through 2018. The unemployment rate also declined from near a double-digit level at the end of 2010 to below 4% at the end of 2018.

5.4 TREASURY CASH AND GENERAL MANAGEMENT RESPONSIBILITIES

The U.S. Treasury promotes economic growth, overseas the production of coins and currency, and is responsible for collecting taxes, paying bills, and managing its cash balances so that its day-to-day operations have a stable impact on bank reserves and the money supply. The Treasury is also responsible for borrowing funds to finance budget deficits and for managing the national debt. The Treasury played an important role during the 2007–2009 perfect financial storm by helping financial institutions merge and through administering government legislation designed to prevent financial institutions and some business firms from failing. We will cover deficit financing and debt management by the Treasury in the next section.

The magnitude of Treasury operations dictates that it must play as defensive or neutral a role as possible in its influence on the supply of money and credit. While the power to regulate the money supply has been placed primarily in the hands of the Fed, close cooperation between the Treasury and the Fed must exist if Treasury operations are not to disrupt the money supply.

Consider the impact on monetary affairs of a massive withdrawal of taxes from the banking system without offsetting actions. The decrease in bank deposits would result in a temporary breakdown of the system's ability to serve the credit needs of the public. Yet, the federal government periodically claims taxes without significant impact on lending institutions. In like manner, borrowing by the government or the refunding of maturing obligations could be traumatic in their effect on money and credit, but such is not the case. In short, the Fed efficiently manages these dynamic aspects of money and credit, while the Treasury largely limits its actions to taxing, borrowing, paying bills, and refunding maturing obligations. The Treasury carries out these functions with as little interference with the conduct of monetary affairs as possible. This is no small challenge.

5.4.1 MANAGING THE TREASURY'S CASH BALANCES

Treasury operations involve spending over $3 trillion a year. It is necessary to maintain a large cash balance, since Treasury receipts and payments do not occur on a regular basis throughout the year. This makes it critical for the Treasury to handle its cash balances in such a way that it will not create undesirable periods of credit ease or tightness. To affect bank reserves as little as possible, the Treasury has developed detailed procedures for handling its cash balances.

5.4.1.1 Treasury Tax and Loan Accounts

The Treasury's primary checkable deposit accounts for day-to-day operations are kept at Reserve Banks. Most cash flows into the Treasury through Treasury Tax and Loan Accounts of banks, S&Ls, and credit unions (referred to here as *banks*, for short). Employers deposit the income taxes, Social Security, and railroad retirement taxes they withheld in their Treasury Tax and Loan Accounts. They have the option of depositing these government receipts with either Reserve Banks or one of the other banks. Most employers make their payments to the latter.

The Treasury may also pay income and eligible profits taxes into Tax and Loan Accounts. Many excise taxes may also be paid either to a Reserve Bank or to a qualified bank with a Tax and Loan Account. The proceeds from a large portion of the sales of new government securities also flow into Tax and Loan Accounts. If the Treasury feels its balances at the Reserve Banks are too large, it can transfer funds to its accounts at the banks.

5.4.1.2 Treasury Receipts and Outlays

The Treasury tries to handle its cash receipts, outlays, and balances to avoid large changes in bank reserves. To do this, the Treasury tries to keep balances in its accounts at the Reserve Banks relatively stable. Almost all Treasury disbursements are made by checks drawn against its deposits at the Reserve Banks. Most Treasury receipts are deposited in Tax and Loan Accounts at the various banks, but some are deposited directly in the Treasury accounts at the Reserve Banks. The Treasury adjusts its withdrawals to keep its balances at the Reserve Banks as stable as possible. This means that the funds shifted from banks and the funds deposited directly in Reserve Banks must closely correspond to the volume of Treasury checks that are likely to be presented to the Reserve Banks.

If the Treasury accounts at the Reserve Banks are kept at a stable level, bank reserves are not changed. This is possible only if accurate forecasts are made of the daily receipts and spending from the Treasury account so that funds from the Tax and Loan Accounts may be shifted in the right amounts at the right time. If the forecasts were not worked out with a reasonable degree of success, Treasury operations would cause bank reserves to change a great deal over short periods. Despite these precautions, the Treasury's account frequently does fluctuate by as much as several billion dollars from day to day. The Fed closely monitors the Treasury account and takes any changes into consideration in conducting daily open-market operations to minimize the effect on bank reserves.

5.4.2 POWERS RELATING TO THE FEDERAL BUDGET AND TO SURPLUSES OR DEFICITS

The government may also influence monetary and credit conditions indirectly through taxation and expenditure programs, especially by having a significant cash deficit or surplus. Budget-making decisions rest with Congress and are usually based on the needs of the government and on political considerations, without giving much weight to monetary and credit effects. Because of the magnitude of the federal budget, government income and spending may be one of the most important factors in determining credit conditions.

5.4.2.1 General Economic Effects of Fiscal Policy

Economic activity depends largely on **aggregate demand**, which is the total demand for final goods and services in the economy at a point in time. An increase in aggregate demand will, generally, cause an increase in production and employment but may also cause prices to rise. If the economy is already close to full employment, increases in aggregate demand will likely increase prices more than output. Similarly, decreases in aggregate demand will result in lower employment and reduced prices.

aggregate demand total demand for final goods and services in the economy at a point in time

Fiscal policy significantly affects aggregate demand and economic activity. Not only is government spending itself a large component of aggregate demand, but also, any change in government spending has a multiplied effect on aggregate demand. An increase in government spending increases employment and incomes and, thus, also increases consumer spending. In a downturn, not only does spending decrease, but tax receipts of all types – including those for Social Security – also decrease when fewer people are at work, because these taxes are based on payrolls. Changes in taxes also directly affect both disposable income and aggregate demand through consumer spending.

automatic stabilizers
continuing federal programs that stabilize economic activity

Various federal government programs act to stabilize disposable income and economic activity in general. Some act on a continuing basis as automatic stabilizers. Other government fiscal actions, such as actions taken to continue federal programs that stabilize economic activity, are discretionary and depend on specific congressional actions. Automatic stabilizers include the following:

- Unemployment insurance program

- Welfare payments

- Pay-as-you-go progressive income tax

transfer payments
government payments for which no current services are given in return

The unemployment insurance program is funded largely by the states. Under this program, payments are made to workers who lose their jobs, providing part of their former incomes. Another stabilizer is welfare payments under federal and state aid programs. Both unemployment and welfare benefits are examples of transfer payments, or government income payments for which no current productive service is rendered.

Another important automatic stabilizer is the pay-as-you-go progressive income tax. Pay-as-you-go refers to the requirement that tax liabilities of individuals and institutions be paid on a continuing basis throughout the year. The progressive nature of our income tax means that as income increases to various levels the tax rate increases also. In other words, as incomes increase, taxes increase at a faster rate. The reverse is also true: at certain stages of decreased income, the tax liability decreases more quickly. The result is, generally, immediate since, for most wages subject to withholding taxes, tax revenues change almost as soon as incomes change.

These programs are a regular part of our economy. In times of severe economic fluctuations, Congress can help stabilize disposable income. Income tax rates have been raised to lower disposable income and to restrain inflationary pressures; they have been lowered during recessions to increase disposable income and spending. Government spending can also be increased during recessions to increase disposable income. Likewise, it could be cut during prosperity to reduce disposable income, but for political reasons attempts to do this have not been successful.

When a recession is so severe that built-in stabilizers or formulas are not adequate to promote recovery, there is seldom complete agreement on the course of action to take. A decision to change the level of government spending and/or the tax rates must be made. Increased spending or a comparable tax cut would cost the same number of dollars initially, but the economic effects would not be the same. When income taxes are cut, disposable income is increased almost immediately under our system of tax withholding. This provides additional income for all sectors of the economy and an increase in demand for many types of goods.

Congress may decide to increase government spending, but the effects of increased government spending occur more slowly than those of a tax cut, since it takes time to get programs started and put into full operation. The increased income arises first in those sectors of the economy where the money is spent. Thus, the initial effect is on specific areas of the economy rather than on the economy as a whole.

The secondary effects of spending that result from a tax cut or from increased government spending depend on how and what proportion the recipients spend. To the extent that they spend it on current consumption, aggregate demand is further increased in the short run. The goods on which recipients spend the income determine the sectors of the economy that receive a boost. If they invest the added income and later use it to purchase capital goods, spending is also increased.

In this case, however, there is a time lag, and different sectors of the economy are affected. If the money is saved, thus added to idle funds available for investment, there is no secondary effect on spending.

The effects must also be considered if economic activity is to be restrained by a decrease in government spending or by a tax increase. A decrease in spending by the government will cut consumer spending by at least that amount; the secondary effects may cut it further. A tax increase may not cut spending by a like amount, since some taxpayers may maintain their level of spending by reducing current saving or by using accrued savings. A tax increase could, however, cut total spending more if it should happen to discourage specific types of spending, such as on home building or on credit purchases of consumer durable goods. This could lead to a spending cut that is substantially greater than the amount of money taken by the higher taxes.

5.4.2.2 Effects of Tax Policy

The **tax policy** and tax program of the federal government have a direct effect on monetary and credit conditions that may work in several ways. The level of taxes in relation to national income may affect the volume of saving and, thus, the funds available for investment without credit expansion. The tax structure also determines whether saving is done largely by upper-income groups, middle-income groups, or all groups. This can affect the amount of funds available for different types of investment. Persons in middle-income groups may be more conservative than those with more wealth. They tend to favor bonds or mortgages over equity investments. Persons in high tax brackets, on the other hand, tend to invest in securities of state and local governments because income from these investments is not subject to federal income taxes. They also may invest for capital gains, since taxes on the gains may be deferred until the asset is sold.

tax policy setting the level and structure of taxes to affect the economy

Changes in corporate tax rates also may affect the amount of funds available for short-term investment in government bonds and the balances kept in bank accounts. The larger the tax payments, the less a corporation has available for current spending. Also, if tax rates are raised with little warning, a corporation may be forced to use funds it had been holding for future use. Businesses that are short of funds may be forced to borrow to meet their taxes. In either case, a smaller amount of credit is available for other uses.

5.4.3 FINANCIAL CRISIS RELATED ACTIVITIES

CRISIS The U.S. Treasury, under the leadership of Treasury Secretary Henry Paulson, played an important role in helping the United States survive the 2007–2008 financial crisis and the subsequent recession. The Treasury, sometimes working closely with the Fed, helped bring about the acquisition of Bear Sterns by JPMorgan Chase & Co. in March 2008. Under the leadership of Henry Paulson, the Treasury was actively involved in assisting financial institutions on the brink of collapse to find help through mergers with financially stronger institutions. In September 2008, Bank of America acquired Merrill Lynch. However, during the same month, Lehman Brothers declared bankruptcy when no viable financial alternatives surfaced. Shortly thereafter, American International Group (AIG) was "bailed out" by the Federal Reserve and Treasury efforts, with the U.S. government receiving an ownership interest in AIG.

The *Economic Stabilization Act of 2008* provided the Treasury with funds to purchase troubled or toxic assets held by financial institutions. However, much of the *Troubled Asset Relief Program (TARP)* funds were used to invest capital in banks with little equity on their balance sheets, as well as to rescue large "too big to fail" financial institutions and even large nonfinancial business firms – such as General Motors and Chrysler – that were on the verge of failing.

> **LEARNING ACTIVITY**
>
> Go to the U.S. Treasury's website, https://www.treasury.gov, and identify the mission and goals of the U.S. Department of the Treasury. Write a brief summary.

5.5 TREASURY DEFICIT FINANCING AND DEBT MANAGEMENT RESPONSIBILITIES

deficit financing borrowing of funds by selling Treasury securities to meet revenue shortfalls relative to expenditures

crowding out occurs when there is a lack of funds for private borrowing due to the sale of Treasury securities to cover budget deficits

The U.S. government collects taxes (receipts) and makes expenditures (outlays) for national defense, social programs, and so forth. When receipts total more than outlays over a time period, such as a year, a budget surplus occurs. A budget deficit exists when outlays are greater than receipts. Deficit financing involves the U.S Treasury borrowing funds by selling government (Treasury) securities to cover revenue shortfalls relative to expenditures. Large budget deficits can result in government competition for private investment funds. Crowding out occurs when there is a lack of funds for private borrowing due to the sale of Treasury securities to cover large budget deficits. When deficit financing is so large that the private sector cannot or will not absorb the Treasury obligations offered, the Fed may purchase a significant portion of the issues.

Annual government expenditures have exceeded annual tax receipts each fiscal year (October 1 through September 30) since the end of the 1960s, with the exception of the four-year period 1998–2001. For fiscal year 2001, receipts totaled $1,991,082 million and outlays were $1,862,846 million resulting in a surplus of $128,236 million, or $128.2 billion. In the effort to recover from the financial crisis and the Great Recession, the fiscal 2009 budget deficit peaked at more than $1.4 trillion, and annual deficits remained above the $1.0 trillion level in fiscal years 2010, 2011, and 2012. Deficits declined to under $700 billion in fiscal 2013 and to less than $500 billion in fiscal years 2014 and 2015. For fiscal year 2018, receipts totaled $3,328,745 million compared to outlays of $4,107,741 million for a deficit of $778,996 million, or $779.0 billion.[4]

The Tax Cuts and Jobs Act of 2017 became law in December 2017 with implementation beginning in 2018. Passage of the Act was expected to enhance economic growth and provide U.S. corporations with tax rates comparable to business tax rates in other developed countries. The Act provides for small reductions in income tax rates for most individual tax brackets. Personal exemptions are suspended while the standard deduction is roughly doubled. However, these changes are temporary and are scheduled to expire in 2025. In contrast, tax rate reductions for corporations are permanent. Instead of a graduated tax rate from 15% to 35% on taxable income, the Act provides for a flat corporate tax rate of 21%.

As a result of this Act, a budget deficit of about $1 trillion is projected for fiscal 2019, and annual deficits of this magnitude are expected over the next several years. Specific sources of federal government receipts and specific types of outlays will be discussed in Chapter 7.

national debt total debt owed by the government

The U.S. national debt is the total debt owed by the government and consists of debt held by the public and intergovernmental holdings. The cumulative amount of historical annual deficits and surpluses resulted in a national debt of about $5.8 trillion at the end of fiscal 2001. Since then, the cumulative impact of large annual deficits caused the national debt to increase to $18.1 trillion in fiscal 2015, and $21.5 trillion at the end of fiscal 2018.[5] This nearly $16 trillion increase in the national debt over a 17-year period has kept the Treasury busy issuing more and more government securities to finance the underlying annual deficits. The ownership of the U.S. public debt, as well as the maturities of the debt, will be discussed in Chapter 8.

debt management involves funding budget deficits and refinancing maturing Treasury securities used to fund the national debt.

Debt management involves funding budget deficits and refinancing maturing Treasury securities previously issued to fund the national debt. The Treasury has formulated three debt management goals:

- Fund deficits and refinance maturing debt at the lowest cost to taxpayers over time.

- Manage Treasury's cash flows in an uncertain environment.

- Manage the risk profile of outstanding debt.

The Treasury carries out its debt management policy by operating in a "regular and predictable" manner to minimize disruption in the financial markets and to support fiscal and monetary policies formulated by the other policy-making groups. Treasury security auctions are scheduled and announced well in advance of the actual auctions to allow investors to plan their security purchases.[6]

---

[4] Historical budget results are available at www.whitehouse.gov/omb/budget/.
[5] Historical data about the levels of the national debt are available at www.treasurydirect.gov/.
[6] Debt management goals are stated in, "The Meaning and Implications of 'Regular and Predictable' (R&P) as a Tenet of Debt Management," (August, 2015), https://www.treasury.gov.

The last surplus federal budget occurred in fiscal 2001. Since then, the Treasury has been actively involved in deficit financing each year. As discussed earlier, the national debt increased from less than $6 trillion at the end of fiscal 2001 to $21.5 trillion by the end of fiscal 2018, meaning that the Treasury had to finance nearly $16 trillion in new national debt since fiscal 2001. At the same time, the Treasury had to refinance trillions of dollars of maturing government securities that were previously issued to fund prior levels of the national debt. The Treasury set a formidable goal of conducting these new financing needs and the refunding of existing Treasury securities while attempting to minimize the interest costs on the national debt.

The Treasury's second debt management goal involves efficiently managing the Treasury's cash flows associated with its financing and refunding activities in an uncertain environment. Debt management operations have to be conducted within an environment where there are uncertainties relating to the size of net financing needs, auction market demand conditions, financial market liquidity, economic conditions, and Fed monetary policy actions.

Market interest rates on Treasury securities fluctuate, or change over time, with changes in economic conditions and expectations, and with the Fed's monetary policies. The Treasury could adjust the size and timing of its auctions to attempt to mitigate this economic/monetary policy risk. Market interest rates, at a point in time, are generally lower for shorter-maturity Treasury securities and higher for longer-maturity Treasury securities. In essence, the longer the maturity of a debt security, the greater the uncertainty the investor will feel concerning future economic and financial market conditions at maturity. As a consequence, investors require a higher expected return for investing in longer-maturity debt securities. This is sometimes referred to as term structure, or maturity risk. Furthermore, the values of longer-maturity debt securities will change more (relative to shorter-maturity securities) given changes in market interest rates. We explore the term, or maturity structure, of interest rates in Chapter 8 and the impact on bond values given changes in market interest rates in Chapter 10.

The Treasury must continually make the trade-off decision of whether to issue shorter-maturity Treasury securities at generally lower interest rates and accept more frequent refunding of these securities at times when the then-existing market interest rates may be at higher levels due to changing economic conditions and Fed actions. The alternative would be to issue longer-term Treasury securities at relatively higher interest rates in exchange for not having to refund these securities until much further in the future.

The Treasury has benefitted in its efforts to manage its financing budget deficits and the national debt in recent years due to the unusually low interest rates that are the result of, in part, the Fed's easy money and quantitative easing efforts initiated in late 2008. However, as interest rates move back to more "normal" levels, and given the current size of the national debt, concern is being expressed about how very large annual interest payments on the national debt will impact on economic activity and the financial markets.

PERSONAL FINANCIAL PLANNING

How Does the Fed Affect Me?

Suppose you hear on the radio that the Fed has moved to cut interest rates. Such a rate cut does not affect just banks or large corporate borrowers; it can have an impact on individuals, too. So how might a rate cut affect you?

If you have savings at a depository institution, the effect may be negative. Attempts to lower interest rates in the economy may lead to lower interest rates on your checking account, your savings account, or the next CD you invest in.

Of course, there is a potential benefit on the borrowing side. An attempt to lower rates can lead to lower loan rates for a car loan, student loan, home equity loan, or a home mortgage. If someone has a variable or adjustable rate mortgage, his or her interest payments may fall as rates decline. Some interest rates on credit card balances are linked to a market interest rate, so as market interest rates fall, the interest rates on credit card balances will fall, too.

Lower interest rates can help investors in stocks and bonds, too. As we will see in Chapter 10, an economic environment with lower interest rates can lead to increases in stock and bond prices, thus increasing the value of an investor's stock and bond holdings.

DISCUSSION QUESTION 2

How will the U.S. government be able to repay the amount of national debt that is currently outstanding?

LEARNING ACTIVITY

Go to the U.S. Treasury's Bureau of Fiscal Service website at https://www.treasurydirect.gov/. Go to "Reports" and then to "Historical Debt Outstanding." Find information on the changing size of the national debt during the past five years. Write a brief summary of what has happened.

5.6 CHANGING THE MONEY SUPPLY

As we saw in Chapter 2, the M1 money supply consists of currency (including coins), demand deposits, other checkable deposits, and traveler's checks. Currency and coins are called fiat money because the U.S. government proclaims they are legal tender for making payments and discharging debts. This physical money is backed only by the credit worthiness of the government and by its taxing capabilities. Currency and coins represent about 43% of the M1 money supply.

Demand deposits and other checkable deposits at commercial banks, S&Ls, savings banks, and credit unions comprise about 57% of the M1 money supply and are collectively termed *checkable deposits*. To simplify further discussion of money supply expansion and contraction, we will refer to checkable deposits simply as *deposits* in the *banking system*, which includes all of the depository institutions. The word *bank* also is used generically to refer to a depository institution.

The banking system of the United States can change the volume of deposits as the need for funds by individuals, businesses, and governments change. This ability to alter the size of the money supply is based on the use of a **fractional reserve system**. In the U.S. fractional reserve system, banks and other depository institutions must hold funds in reserve equal to a certain percentage of their deposit liabilities. Vault cash and funds held at regional Reserve Banks comprise bank reserves. To understand the deposit expansion and contraction process, one must study the operations of banks as units in a banking system and the relationship of bank loans to deposits and to bank reserves.

In analyzing deposit expansion, it is helpful to distinguish between primary deposits and derivative deposits. For example, the deposit of a check drawn on the Fed is a **primary deposit** because it adds new reserves to the bank where deposited and to the banking system. A **derivative deposit** occurs when reserves created from a primary deposit are made available to borrowers through bank loans. Borrowers then deposit the loans so they can write checks against the funds. When a check is written and deposited in another bank, there is no change in total reserves of the banking system. The increase in reserves at the bank where the check is deposited is offset by a decrease in reserves at the bank on which the check is drawn. Banks must keep reserves against both primary and derivative deposits.

fractional reserve system banking system where depository institutions must hold funds in reserve equal to a certain percentage of their deposit liabilities

primary deposit deposit that adds new reserves to a bank

derivative deposit deposit of funds that were borrowed from the reserves of primary deposits

5.6.1 CHECKABLE DEPOSIT EXPANSION

When reserves were first required by law, the purpose was to assure depositors that banks had the ability to handle withdrawals of cash. This was before the establishment of the Federal Reserve System that made it possible for a healthy bank to obtain additional funds in time of need. Depositor confidence is now based on deposit insurance and more complete and competent bank examinations by governmental agencies. Today, the basic function of reserve requirements is to provide a means for regulating deposit expansion and contraction.

Deposit creation takes place as a result of the operations of the whole system of banks, but it arises out of the independent transactions of individual banks. To explain the process, therefore, we will consider the loan activities of a single bank. First, we will focus on the bank itself; then we will examine its relationship to a system of banks. This approach is somewhat artificial since a bank practically never acts independently of the actions of other banks, but it has been adopted to clarify the process. Furthermore, it helps explain the belief of some bankers that they cannot create deposits, since they only lend funds placed on deposit in their banks by their depositors. This analysis shows how a system of banks, in which each bank is carrying on its local activities, can do what an individual banker cannot do.

For illustration, let us assume that a bank receives a primary deposit of $10,000 and that it must keep reserves of 20% against deposits. The $10,000 becomes a cash asset to the bank as well as a $10,000 liability, since it must stand ready to honor a withdrawal of the money. The bank statement, ignoring all other items, would then show the following:

Assets		Liabilities	
Reserves	$10,000	Deposits	$10,000

Against this new deposit of $10,000, the bank must keep required reserves of 20%, or $2,000. Therefore, it has $8,000 of excess reserves available. Excess reserves are reserves above the level of required reserves.

It may appear that the banker could proceed to make loans for $40,000, since all that is needed is a 20% reserve against the resulting checkable deposits. If this were attempted, however, the banker would soon be in a difficult situation. Since bank loans are usually obtained just before a demand for funds, checks would very likely be written against the deposit accounts almost at once. Many of these checks would be deposited in other banks, and the bank would be faced with a demand for cash as checks were presented for collection. This demand could reach the full $40,000. Since the bank has only $8,000 to meet it, it could not follow such a course and remain in business.

The amount that the banker can safely lend is the $8,000 of excess reserves. If more is lent, the banker runs the risk of not being able to make payments on checks. After an $8,000 loan, the books show the following:

Assets		Liabilities	
Reserves	$10,000	Deposits	$18,000
Loans	$ 8,000		

If a check were written for the full amount of the derivative deposit ($8,000) and sent to a bank in another city for deposit, the lending bank would lose all of its excess reserves. This may be seen from its books, which would appear as follows:

Assets		Liabilities	
Reserves	$2,000	Deposits	$10,000
Loans	$8,000		

In practice, a bank may be able to lend somewhat more than the $8,000 in this example, because banks frequently require customers to keep an average deposit balance of about 15 to 20% of the loan. The whole of the additional $1,500 to $2,000 cannot be lent safely, because an average balance of $1,500 to $2,000 does not prevent the full amount of the loan from being used for a period of time. With an average balance in each derivative deposit account, however, not all accounts will be drawn to zero at the same time. Therefore, some additional funds will be available for loans.

It may be argued that a banker will feel sure that some checks written against the bank will be redeposited in the same bank and, therefore, larger sums can be lent. However, because any bank is only one of thousands, the banker cannot usually count on such redepositing of funds. Banks cannot run the risk of being caught short of reserves. Thus, when an individual bank receives a new primary deposit, it cannot lend the full amount of that deposit but only the amount available as excess reserves. From the point of view of an individual bank, therefore, deposit creation appears impossible. Because a part of every new deposit cannot be lent out due to reserve requirements, the volume of additional loans is less than new primary deposits.

It is important to recognize that *what cannot be done by an individual bank can be done by the banking system*. This occurs when many banks are expanding loans and derivative deposits at the same time. To illustrate this point, assume that we have an economy with just two banks, A and B. This example can be realistic if we assume, further, that Bank A represents one bank in the system and Bank B represents all other banks combined. Bank A, as in our previous example, receives a new primary deposit of $10,000 and is required to keep reserves of 20% against deposits. Therefore, its books would appear as follows:

Bank A			
Assets		**Liabilities**	
Reserves	$10,000	Deposits	$10,000

A loan for $8,000 is made and credited as follows:

Bank A			
Assets		**Liabilities**	
Reserves	$10,000	Deposits	$18,000
Loans	$ 8,000		

Assume that a check is drawn against this primary deposit almost immediately and deposited in Bank B. The books of the two banks would then show the following:

Bank A			
Assets		**Liabilities**	
Reserves	$2,000	Deposits	$10,000
Loans	$8,000		

Bank B			
Assets		**Liabilities**	
Reserves	$8,000	Deposits	$8,000

The derivative deposit arising out of a loan from Bank A has now been transferred by check to Bank B, where it is received as a primary deposit. Bank B must now set aside 20% as required reserves and may lend or reinvest the remainder. Its books after such a loan (equal to its excess reserves) would appear as follows:

Bank B			
Assets		**Liabilities**	
Reserves	$8,000	Deposits	$14,400
Loans	$6,400		

Assume a check is drawn against the derivative deposit of $6,400 that was created due to the loan by Bank B. This reduces its reserves and deposits as follows:

Bank B			
Assets		**Liabilities**	
Reserves	$1,600	Deposits	$8,000
Loans	$6,400		

The check for $6,400 will most likely be deposited in a bank, in our example in Bank A or Bank B itself, since we have assumed that only two banks exist. In the U.S. banking system, it may be deposited in one of the thousands of banks or other depository institutions.

Deposit expansion as when a bank makes a loan can take place in the same way when it buys securities. Assume, as we did in the case of a bank loan, the following situation:

Bank A			
Assets		**Liabilities**	
Reserves	$10,000	Deposits	$10,000

Securities costing $8,000 are purchased and the proceeds credited to the account of the seller, giving the following situation:

Bank A			
Assets		**Liabilities**	
Reserves	$10,000	Deposits	$18,000
Loans	$ 8,000		

Assume that a check is drawn against the seller's deposit and is deposited in Bank B. The books of the two banks would then show as follows:

Bank A			
Assets		**Liabilities**	
Reserves	$2,000	Deposits	$18,000
Loans	$8,000		

Bank B			
Assets		**Liabilities**	
Reserves	$8,000	Deposits	$8,000

As in the case of a loan shown earlier, the derivative deposit has been transferred to Bank B, where it is received as a primary deposit.

At each stage in the process, 20% of the new primary deposit becomes required reserves, and 80% becomes excess reserves that can be lent out. In time, the whole of the original $10,000 primary deposit will have become required reserves, and $50,000 of deposits will have been credited to deposit accounts, of which $40,000 will have been lent out.

Table 5.1 further illustrates the deposit expansion process for a 20% reserve ratio. A primary deposit of $1,000 is injected into the banking system, making excess reserves of $800 available for loans and investments. Eventually, $5,000 in checkable deposits will be created.

Multiple expansions in the money supply created by the banking system through its expansion of checkable deposits also can be expressed in formula form as follows:

$$\text{Change in checkable deposits} = \frac{\text{Increase in excess reserves}}{\text{Required reserves ratio}} \qquad (5.1)$$

We define the terms *excess reserves* and the *required reserves ratio* in the next section. For our purposes, the maximum increase in the amount of checkable deposits is determined by dividing a new inflow of reserves into the banking system by the percentage of checkable deposits that must be held in reserves.

In the example presented in Table 5.1, the maximum expansion in the checkable deposits component of the money supply, which is the same as the final-stage figure shown for checkable deposit liabilities, would be, as follows:

$$\text{Change in checkable deposits} = \$1,000 \div 0.20 = \$5,000$$

The maximum increase in deposits (and money supply) that can result from a specific increase in excess reserves is referred to as a *money multiplier*. In our very basic example, the money multiplier (m) is equal to one divided by the required reserves ratio, or $m = 1 \div 0.20 = 5$. However, in the complex U.S. economy there are several factors or "leakages" that reduce the ability to reach the maximum expansion in the money supply depicted in this simplified example. We will discuss a more realistic money multiplier ratio in the last section of this chapter.

TABLE 5.1 Multiple Expansion of Deposits – 20% Reserve Ratio

| | Assets | | | | Liabilities |
| | Reserves | | | Loans and Investments | Checkable Deposits |
	Total	Required	Excess		
Initial					
Reserves	$1,000	$200	$800	$0	$1,000
Stage 1	1,000	360	640	800	1,800
Stage 2	1,000	488	512	1,440	2,440
Stage 3	1,000	590	410	1,952	2,952
Stage 4	1,000	672	328	2,362	3,362
Stage 5	1,000	738	262	2,690	3,690
Stage 6	1,000	790	210	2,952	3,952
Stage 7	1,000	832	168	3,162	4,162
Stage 8	1,000	866	134	3,330	4,330
Stage 9	1,000	893	107	3,464	4,464
Stage 10	1,000	914	86	3,571	4,571
.	.	.	.	.	.
.					.
.	.	.	.	.	.
Final					
Stage	$1,000	$1,000	$ 0	$4,000	$5,000

5.6.2 OFFSETTING OR LIMITING FACTORS

Deposit creation can go on only to the extent that the activities described actually take place. If for any reason the proceeds of a loan are withdrawn from the banking system, no new deposit arises to continue the process. A new deposit of $10,000 permits loans of $8,000 under a 20% required reserve, but if this $8,000 were used in currency transactions without being deposited in a bank, no deposit could be created. The custom of doing business by means of checks makes deposit creation possible.

In the examples above, no allowance was made for either cash leakage or currency withdrawal from the system. In actual practice, as the volume of business in the economy increases, some additional cash is withdrawn for hand-to-hand circulation and to meet the needs of business for petty cash.

Money may also be withdrawn from the banking system to meet the demand for payments to foreign countries, or foreign banks may withdraw some of the money they are holding on deposit in U.S. banks. The U.S. Treasury may withdraw funds it has on deposit in banks. All of these factors reduce the multiplying capacity of primary deposits.

Furthermore, this process can go on only if excess reserves are actually being lent by the banks. This means that banks must be willing to lend the full amount of their excess reserves and that acceptable borrowers who have a demand for loans must be available.

The nonbank public's decisions to switch funds between checkable deposits and time or savings deposits also will influence the ability to expand the money supply and credit. This is explored later in the chapter.

5.6.3 CONTRACTION OF DEPOSITS

When the need for funds by business decreases, deposit expansion can work in reverse. Expansion takes place as long as excess reserves exist and the demand for new bank loans exceeds the repayment of old loans. Deposit contraction takes place when old loans are being repaid faster than new loans are being granted and banks are not immediately investing these excess funds.

The opposite takes place when the public demands additional currency. Let us assume that a customer of Bank A needs additional currency and cashes a check for $100. The deposits of the bank are reduced by $100, and this reduces required reserves by $20. If the bank has no excess reserves, it must take steps to get an additional $80 of reserves by borrowing from its Reserve Bank, demanding payment for a loan or not renewing one that comes due or selling securities. When the check is cashed, the reserves of the bank are also reduced by $100. If the bank has to replenish its supply of currency from its Reserve Bank, its reserve deposits are reduced by $100. These transactions may be summarized thus:

1. Deposits in Bank A are reduced by $100 ($20 in required reserves and $80 in excess reserves).

2. Bank A's deposit at its Reserve Bank is reduced by $100.

3. The amount of Federal Reserve notes in circulation is increased by $100.

Changes in the components of the money supply traditionally have occurred during holiday periods, with the most pronounced change taking place during the year-end holiday season. These changes are beyond the immediate control of the Fed, which must anticipate and respond to them to carry out possible money supply growth targets. Generally, there has been an increase in currency outstanding between November and December and a subsequent partial reversal during January. An increase in circulating currency prior to the Christmas holidays requires adjustment by the Fed to control the money supply. As large amounts of cash are withdrawn from depository institutions, deposit contraction might occur unless the Fed moves to offset it by purchasing government or other securities in the open market.

Also there traditionally has been an increase in demand deposits between November and December and a subsequent decline in demand deposits during the early part of the next year. This also seems to reflect the public's surge in spending during the Christmas holiday season and the payment for many of the purchases early in the next year by writing checks on demand deposit accounts. The Fed, in its effort to control bank reserves and the money supply, also must take corrective actions to temper the impact of these seasonal swings in currency and checking account balances. Of course, the increasing use of credit cards and debit cards continues to alter the use of currency and the writing of checks.

5.7.2 FEDERAL RESERVE SYSTEM TRANSACTIONS

Transactions between banks and the Fed and changes in reserve requirements by the Fed also affect either the level of total reserves or the degree to which deposits can be expanded with a given volume of reserves. Such transactions are initiated by the Fed when it buys or sells securities, by a depository institution when it borrows from its Reserve Bank, or by a change in Federal Reserve float. These are examined here in turn, and then the effect of a change in reserve requirements is described. Finally, we will look at Treasury transactions, which can also affect reserves in the banking system.

5.7.2.1 Open-Market Operations

When the Fed, through its open-market operations, purchases securities such as government bonds it adds to bank reserves. The Fed pays for the bonds with a check. The seller deposits the check in an account and receives a deposit account credit. The bank presents the check to the Reserve Bank for payment and receives a credit to its account. When the Fed buys a $1,000 government bond, the check for which is deposited in Bank A, the transactions may be summarized, as follows:

1. Bank A's deposit at its Reserve Bank is increased by $1,000. The Reserve Bank has a new asset – a bond worth $1,000.

2. Deposits in Bank A are increased by $1,000 ($200 in required reserves and $800 in excess reserves).

The opposite takes place when the Fed sells securities in the market.

In contrast to the other actions that affect reserves in the banking system, open-market operations are entirely conducted by the Fed. For this reason, they are the most important policy tool the Fed has to control reserves and the money supply. Open-market operations are conducted virtually every business day, both to smooth out ups and downs caused by other transactions and to implement changes in the money supply called for by the Federal Open Market Committee.

5.7.2.2 Depository Institution Transactions

When a bank borrows from its Reserve Bank, it is borrowing reserves, so reserves are increased by the amount of the loan. Similarly, when a loan to the Reserve Bank is repaid, reserves are reduced by that amount. The transactions when Bank A borrows $1,000 from its Reserve Bank may be summarized as follows:

1. Bank A's deposit at its Reserve Bank is increased by $1,000. The assets of the Reserve Bank are increased by $1,000 by the note from Bank A.

2. Bank A's excess reserves have been increased by $1,000. It also has a new $1,000 liability, its note to the Reserve Bank.

This process is reversed when a debt to the Reserve Bank is repaid.

5.7.2.3 Federal Reserve Float

Federal Reserve float
temporary increase in bank reserves from checks credited to the reserve accounts of depositing banks but not yet debited to the reserve accounts of those banks from which the checks were drawn

Changes in Federal Reserve float also affect bank reserves. *Float* arises out of the process of collecting checks handled by Reserve Banks. **Federal Reserve float** is the temporary increase in bank reserves that results when checks are credited to the reserve account of the depositing bank before they are debited from the account of the banks on which they are drawn. Checks drawn on nearby banks are credited almost immediately to the account of the bank in which they were deposited and debited to the account of the bank on which the check was drawn. Under Fed regulations, all checks are credited one or two days later to the account of the bank in which the check was deposited. It may take longer for the check to go through the collection process and be debited to the account of the bank upon which it is drawn. When this happens, bank reserves are increased, and this increase is called *float*. The process by which a $1,000 check drawn on Bank B is deposited in Bank A and credited to its account before it is debited to the account of Bank B may be summarized, as follows:

1. Bank A transfers $1,000 from its Cash Items in the Process of Collection to its account at the Reserve Bank. Its reserves are increased by $1,000.

2. The Reserve Bank takes $1,000 from its Deferred Availability Account and transfers it to Bank A's account.

Thus, total reserves of banks are increased temporarily by $1,000. They are reduced when Bank B's account at its Reserve Bank is reduced by $1,000 a day or two later.

Changes in reserve requirements change the amount of deposit expansion that is possible with a given level of reserves. With a reserve ratio of 20%, excess reserves of $800 can be expanded to $4,000 of additional loans and deposits. If the reserve ratio is reduced to 10%, it is possible to expand $800 of excess reserves to $8,000 of additional loans and deposits. When the reserve ratio is lowered, additional expansion also takes place because part of the required reserves becomes excess reserves. This process is reversed when the reserve ratio is raised.

Bank reserves are also affected by changes in the level of deposits of foreign central banks and governments at the Reserve Banks. These deposits are maintained with the Reserve Banks at times as part of the monetary reserves of a foreign country and may also be used to settle international balances. A decrease in such foreign deposits with the Reserve Banks increases bank reserves; an increase in them decreases bank reserves.

5.7.2.4 Treasury Transactions

The transactions of the Treasury also affect bank reserves. They are increased by spending and making payments, and decreased when the Treasury increases the size of its accounts at the Reserve Banks. The Treasury makes almost all of its payments out of its accounts at the Reserve Banks, and such spending adds to bank reserves. For example, the recipient of a check from the Treasury deposits it in a bank. The bank sends it to the Reserve Bank for collection and receives a credit to its account. The Reserve

Bank debits the account of the Treasury. When a Treasury check for $1,000 is deposited in Bank A and required reserves are 20%, the transactions may be summarized as follows:

1. The deposits of Bank A are increased by $1,000, its required reserves by $200, and excess reserves by $800.

2. Bank A's reserves at the Reserve Bank are increased by $1,000.

3. The deposit account of the Treasury at the Reserve Bank is reduced by $1,000.

Treasury funds from tax collections or the sale of bonds are generally deposited in its accounts in banks. When the Treasury needs payment funds from its accounts at the Reserve Banks, it transfers funds from commercial banks to its accounts at the Reserve Banks. This process reduces bank reserves. When $1,000 is transferred from the account in Bank A and required reserves are 20%, transactions may be summarized as follows:

1. The Treasury deposit in Bank A is reduced by $1,000, required reserves by $200, and excess reserves by $800.

2. The Treasury account at the Reserve Bank is increased by $1,000, and the account of Bank A is reduced by $1,000.

The Treasury is the largest depositor at the Fed. The volume of transfers between the account of the Treasury and the reserve accounts of banks is large enough to cause significant changes in reserves in the banking system. For this reason, the Fed closely monitors the Treasury's account and often uses open-market operations to minimize its effect on bank reserves. This is accomplished by purchasing securities to provide reserves to the banking system when the Treasury's account increases and by selling securities when the account of the Treasury falls to a low level.

The effect on bank reserves is the same for changes in Treasury cash holdings as it is for changes in Treasury accounts at the Reserve Banks. Reserves are increased when the Treasury decreases its cash holdings, and reserves are decreased when it increases such holdings.

DISCUSSION QUESTION 3

Is monetary policy or fiscal policy more important in achieving the U.S. national policy objectives?

5.8 THE MONETARY BASE AND THE MONEY MULTIPLIER

Earlier in this chapter we examined the deposit multiplying capacity of the banking system. Recall that, in the example shown in Table 5.1, excess reserves of $1,000 were introduced into a banking system having a 20% required reserves ratio, resulting in a deposit expansion of $5,000. This can also be viewed as a money multiplier of 5.

In our complex financial system, the money multiplier is not quite so straightforward. It will be useful to focus on the relationship between the monetary base and the money supply to better understand the complexity of the money multiplier. The monetary base is defined as banking system reserves plus currency held by the public. More specifically, the monetary base consists of reserve deposits held in Reserve Banks, vault cash or currency held by depository institutions, and currency held by the nonbank public. The money multiplier is the number of times the monetary base can be expanded or magnified to produce a given money supply level. Conceptually, the M1 definition of the money supply is the monetary base (MB) multiplied by the money multiplier (m). In equation form we have, as follows:

$$M1 = MB \times m \tag{5.2}$$

monetary base banking system reserves plus currency held by the public

money multiplier number of times the monetary base can be expanded to produce a given money supply level

The size and stability of the money multiplier are important because the Fed can control the monetary base but it cannot directly control the size of the money supply. Changes in the money supply are caused by changes in the monetary base, in the money multiplier, or in both. The Fed can change the size of the monetary base through open-market operations or changes in the reserve ratio. The money multiplier is not constant. It can and does fluctuate over time, depending on actions taken by the Fed, as well as by the nonbank public and the U.S. Treasury.

At the end of December 2018, the money multiplier was approximately 1.12, as determined by dividing the not seasonally adjusted $3,818.9 billion M1 money stock by the $3,420.1 billion monetary base.[7] Taking into account the actions of the nonbank public and the Treasury, the formula for the money multiplier in today's financial system can be expressed as,[8]

$$m = \frac{(1+k)}{\left[r(1+t+g)+k\right]} \tag{5.3}$$

where

r = the ratio of reserves to total deposits (checkable, noncheckable time and savings, and government)

k = the ratio of currency held by the nonbank public to checkable deposits

t = the ratio of noncheckable deposits to checkable deposits

g = the ratio of government deposits to checkable deposits

Let's illustrate how the size of the money multiplier is determined by returning to our previous example of a 20% reserve ratio. Recall that in a more simple financial system, the money multiplier would be determined as $1 \div r$ or $1 \div 0.20$, which equals 5. However, in our complex system we also need to consider leakages into currency held by the nonbank public, noncheckable time and savings deposits, and government deposits. Let's further assume that the reserve ratio applies to total deposits, a k of 40%, a t of 15%, and a g of 10%. The money multiplier then would be estimated, as follows:

$$m = \frac{(1+.40)}{\left[.20(1+.15+.10)+.40\right]} = \frac{1.40}{.65} = 2.15$$

Of course, if a change occurred in any of the components, the money multiplier would adjust accordingly, as would the size of the money supply.

In Chapter 2 we briefly discussed the link between the money supply and economic activity. You should be able to recall that the money supply (M1) is linked to the gross domestic product (GDP) via the velocity, or turnover, of money. More specifically, the velocity of money measures the rate of circulation of the money supply. It is expressed as the average number of times each dollar is spent on purchases of goods and services, and is calculated as nominal GDP (GDP in current dollars) divided by M1. Changes in the growth rates for money supply (M1g) and money velocity (M1Vg) affect the growth rate in real economic activity (RGDPg), and the rate of inflation (Ig) and can be expressed in equation form as follows:

$$M1_g + M1V_g = RGDP_g + I_g \tag{5.4}$$

For example, if the velocity of money remains relatively constant, then a link between money supply and the nominal GDP should be observable. Likewise, after nominal GDP is adjusted for inflation, the resulting real GDP growth can be examined relative to M1 growth rates. Changes in money supply have been found, in the past, to lead to changes in economic activity. However, a relationship between money supply and economic activity has been questioned during the recent perfect financial storm. In an effort to thwart a possible collapse of the financial system, recall that the Fed moved to force

velocity of money average number of times each dollar is spent on purchases of goods and services

---

[7] Federal Reserve Bank of St. Louis, Federal Reserve Economic Database (FRED), https://stlouisfed.org. As the 2007–2008 financial crisis worsened, the money multiplier ratio dropped below 1.0 in late 2008 and continued low for several years thereafter. A very low multiplier reflected the high liquidity in the banking system brought about by the Fed's easy money and quantitative easing policies.
[8] The reader interested in understanding how the money multiplier is derived will find a discussion in most financial institutions and markets textbooks.

short-term interest rates to near zero and provided massive amounts of money liquidity. Furthermore, the Fed introduced the use of a nontraditional monetary tool called quantitative easing to further support the economic recovery efforts after the 2007–2008 financial crisis and the 2008–2009 Great Recession. These efforts have distorted the traditional money multiplier and velocity of money relationships.

The Fed signaled a change from its very easy money policy when the target for the federal funds rate which was set in late 2008 at 0.00-0.25%, was increased to 0.25-0.50% in December 2015. This increase was followed by 8 additional 0.25% increases (one in 2016, three in 2017, and four in 2018). Of course, economic activity also is affected by government actions concerning government spending, taxation, and the management of the public debt. Thus, it is important that monetary and fiscal policy work together to achieve the United States' national economic policy objectives.

LEARNING ACTIVITY

Go to the St. Louis Federal Reserve Bank's website, https://www.stlouisfed.org, and access the Federal Reserve Economic Database (FRED). Find monetary base, money supply, and gross domestic product data. Calculate the money multiplier and the velocity of money.

APPLYING FINANCE TO. . .

• **Institutions and Markets**   Policy makers pass laws and implement fiscal and monetary policies. A change in law, as noted in Chapter 3, allows U.S. commercial banks again to engage in both commercial banking and investment banking activities and become universal banks. Policy makers influence and change the types of financial institutions and their operations. The operations of depository institutions are directly influenced by monetary policy decisions relating to reserve requirements and Fed discount rates. The ability of financial institutions to carry out the savings-investment process also is affected by the actions of policy makers.

• **Investments**   The prices of securities, typically, reflect economic activity and the level of interest rates. Real growth in the economy, accompanied by high employment and low interest rates, makes for attractive investment opportunities. Individual and institutional investors usually find the values of their investments rising during periods of economic prosperity. However, there are times when policy makers fear that the loss of purchasing power associated with high inflation outweighs the value of economic expansion. During these times, securities prices suffer.

• **Financial Management**   The operations of businesses are directly affected by policy makers. Fiscal and monetary policies that constrain economic growth make it difficult for businesses to operate and make profits. Financial managers must periodically raise financial capital in the securities markets. Actions by policy makers to constrain the money supply and to make borrowing more costly will give financial managers many sleepless nights. On the other hand, expansive monetary policy accompanied by low inflation usually is conducive to business growth, lower interest rates, and higher stock prices – making it easier for financial managers to obtain, at reasonable costs, the financial capital needed to grow their businesses.

SUMMARY

LO 5.1   The three major U.S. national economic policy objectives are economic growth, high employment, and price stability. On occasion, conflicts among these objectives can develop. For example, too rapid economic growth could result in materials and/or labor shortages that, in turn, could lead to price instability associated with inflation.

LO 5.2   There are four major policy maker groups: Federal Reserve System, the president, Congress, and the U.S. Treasury. The Fed is responsible for formulating monetary policy and the president and Congress determine fiscal policy. Debt management practices are established by the Treasury.

LO 5.3   The federal government provides social and economic services to the public that cannot be provided as efficiently by the private sector, and it is also responsible for guiding or regulating the economy. The president and the Council of Economic Advisors prepare annual budgets and formulate fiscal policy. Congress reviews, makes changes, and passes legislation relating to budget expenditures. Funds are raised by the government by levying taxes, and when necessary, the Treasury borrows to cover budget deficits. Government reaction to the 2007–2009 perfect financial storm included the Fed providing rescue funds to institutions to help avoid bankruptcy and the Fed working with the Treasury to merge financially weak financial institutions with stronger institutions. Congress and the president passed legislation to stabilize and grow economic activity.

LO 5.4 The U.S. Treasury's cash and general management responsibilities include collecting taxes, paying bills, and managing its cash balances so that its day-to-day operations have a stable impact on bank reserves and the money supply. During financial crises and economic downturns, the Treasury may be called upon to help financial institutions merge, and to administer government legislation intended to keep financial institutions from failing.

LO 5.5 The Treasury is responsible for financing budget deficits and for financing and managing the national debt. The Treasury's debt management goals include funding deficits and refinancing maturing debt at the lowest interest cost to taxpayers; managing the Treasury's cash flows in uncertain economic, financial market, and Fed policies environment; and managing risk associated with interest rate costs and the maturities of outstanding debt. The Treasury carries out its debt management policy by operating in a "regular and predictable" manner to minimize disruption in the financial markets and to support fiscal and monetary policies.

LO 5.6 The U.S. banking system is a fractional reserve system where depository institutions must hold funds at their regional Reserve Banks equal to a certain percentage of their deposit liabilities. Since an individual depository institution is required to hold only a portion of its deposits as reserves, the remaining funds from a new deposit can be lent to borrowers who, in turn, may deposit the funds they receive in the same or another bank in the banking system, and so forth. An estimate of the potential change in checkable deposits, a component of the M1 money supply, can be made by dividing the amount of an increase (or decrease) in excess reserves by the required reserves ratio.

LO 5.7 The factors or transactions that affect bank reserves include changes in the demand for currency by the nonbank public; Fed transactions, such as changes in the required reserves ratio, open-market operations, and changes in bank borrowings; and U.S. Treasury actions involving changes in Treasury spending from its accounts held at Reserve Banks and changes in its cash holdings.

LO 5.8 The monetary base consists of banking system reserves plus currency held by the public, while the money multiplier is the number of times the monetary base can be expanded to produce a money supply level. Multiplying the monetary base times the money multiplier produces the amount of the M1 money supply. The velocity of money is the average number of times each dollar is spent on purchases of goods and services. By dividing nominal gross domestic product by M1 produces a measure of the velocity of money.

KEY TERMS

aggregate demand	deficit financing	fractional reserve system	national debt
automatic stabilizers	deficit reserves	gross domestic	primary deposit
bank reserves	derivative deposit	product (GDP)	required reserves
budget deficit	excess reserves	inflation	required reserves ratio
budget surplus	federal budget	monetary base	tax policy
crowding out	Federal Reserve float	monetizing the debt	transfer payments
debt management	fiscal policy	money multiplier	velocity of money

REVIEW QUESTIONS

1. **(LO 5.1)** List and describe briefly the economic policy objectives of the nation.

2. **(LO 5.2)** Describe the relationship among policy makers, the types of policies, and their economic objectives.

3. **(LO 5.3)** Discuss how the U.S. government influences the economy and how the government responded to the 2007–2009 perfect financial storm.

4. **(LO 5.4)** Describe the effects of tax policy on monetary and credit conditions.

5. **(LO 5.5)** Federal government deficit financing may have a very great influence on monetary and credit conditions. Explain.

6. **(LO 5.5)** Discuss the various objectives of debt management.

7. **(LO 5.6)** Explain how Federal Reserve notes are supported or backed in our financial system.

8. **(LO 5.6)** Why are the expansion and contraction of deposits by the banking system possible in our financial system?

9. **(LO 5.6)** Trace the effect on its accounts of a loan made by a bank that has excess reserves available from new deposits.

10. **(LO 5.6)** Explain how deposit expansion takes place in a banking system consisting of two banks.

11. **(LO 5.6)** Explain the potential for deposit expansion when required reserves average 10% and $2,000 in excess reserves are deposited in the banking system.

12. **(LO 5.7)** Trace the effect on bank reserves of a change in the amount of cash held by the public.

13. **(LO 5.7)** Describe the effect on bank reserves when the Federal Reserve sells U.S. government securities to a bank.

14. **(LO 5.7)** Summarize the factors that can lead to a change in bank reserves.

15. **(LO 5.8)** What is the difference between the monetary base and total bank reserves?

16. **(LO 5.8)** Briefly describe what is meant by the money multiplier and indicate the factors that affect its magnitude or size.

17. **(LO 5.8)** Define the velocity of money, and explain why it is important to anticipate changes in money velocity.

18. **(LO 5.8)** Why does it seem to be important to regulate and control the supply of money?

EXERCISES

1. Go to the St. Louis Federal Reserve Bank's website at https://www.stlouisfed.org, and access current economic data.
   a. Find M1 and the monetary base, and then estimate the money multiplier.
   b. Determine the nominal gross national product (GNP in current dollars). Estimate the velocity of money using M1 from (a) and nominal GNP.
   c. Indicate how the money multiplier and the velocity of money have changed between two recent years.

2. Important policy objectives of the federal government include economic growth, high employment, and price stability. The achievement of these objectives is the responsibility of monetary policy, fiscal policy, and debt management carried out by the Federal Reserve System, the president, Congress, and the U.S. Treasury. Describe the responsibilities of the various policy makers in trying to achieve the three economic policy objectives.

3. An economic recession has developed, and the Federal Reserve Board has taken several actions to retard further declines in economic activity. The U.S. Treasury now wishes to take steps to assist the Fed in this effort. Describe the actions the Treasury might take.

4. The president and members of Congress are elected by the people and are expected to behave ethically. Let's assume that you are a recently elected member of Congress. A special-interest lobbying group is offering to contribute funds to your next election campaign in the hope that you will support legislation being proposed by others that will help the group achieve its stated objectives. What would you do?

PROBLEMS

1. Assume that Bank One receives a primary deposit of $1 million. The bank must keep reserves of 20% against its deposits. Prepare a simple balance sheet of assets and liabilities for Bank One immediately after the deposit is received.

2. Assume that Bank A receives a primary deposit of $100,000 and that it must keep reserves of 10% against deposits.
   a. Prepare a simple balance sheet of assets and liabilities for the bank immediately after the deposit is received.
   b. Assume Bank A makes a loan in the amount that can be "safely lent." Show what the bank's balance sheet of assets and liabilities would look like immediately after the loan.
   c. Now assume that a check in the amount of the "derivative deposit" created in (b) was written and sent to another bank. Show what Bank A's (the lending bank's) balance sheet of assets and liabilities would look like after the check is written.

3. Rework Problem 5.2 assuming Bank A has reserve requirements that are 15% of deposits.

4. Assume that there are two banks, A and Z, in the banking system. Bank A receives a primary

deposit of $600,000, and it must keep reserves of 12% against deposits. Bank A makes a loan in the amount that can be safely lent.

a. Show what Bank A's balance sheet of assets and liabilities would look like immediately after the loan.

b. Assume that a check is drawn against the primary deposit made in Bank A and is deposited in Bank Z. Show what the balance sheet of assets and liabilities would look like for each of the two banks after the transaction has taken place.

c. Now assume that Bank Z makes a loan in the amount that can be safely lent against the funds deposited in its bank from the transaction described in (b). Show what Bank Z's balance sheet of assets and liabilities would look like after the loan.

5. The SIMPLEX financial system is characterized by a required reserves ratio of 11%; initial excess reserves are $1 million, and there are no currency or other leakages.

a. What would be the maximum amount of checkable deposits after deposit expansion, and what would be the money multiplier?

b. How would your answer in (a) change if the reserve requirement had been 9%?

6. Assume a financial system has a monetary base of $25 million. The required reserves ratio is 10%, and there are no leakages in the system.

a. What is the size of the money multiplier?

b. What will be the system's money supply?

7. Rework Problem 5.6 assuming the reserve ratio is 14%?

8. The BASIC financial system has a required reserves ratio of 15%; initial excess reserves are $5 million, cash held by the public is $1 million and is expected to stay at that level, and there are no other leakages or adjustments in the system.

a. What would be the money multiplier and the maximum amount of checkable deposits?

b. What would be the money supply amount in this system after deposit expansion?

9. Rework Problem 5.8, assuming that the cash held by the public drops to $500,000 with an equal amount becoming excess reserves and the required reserves ratio drops to 12%.

10. The COMPLEX financial system has these relationships: the ratio of reserves to total deposits is 12%, and the ratio of noncheckable deposits to checkable deposits is 40%. In addition, currency held by the nonbank public amounts to 15% of checkable deposits. The ratio of government deposits to checkable deposits is 8%, and the monetary base is $300 million.

a. Determine the size of the M1 money multiplier and the size of the money supply.

b. If the ratio of currency in circulation to checkable deposits were to drop to 13% while the other ratios remained the same, what would be the impact on the money supply?

c. If the ratio of government deposits to checkable deposits increases to 10% while the other ratios remained the same, what would be the impact on the money supply?

d. What would happen to the money supply if the reserve requirement increased to 14% while noncheckable deposits to checkable deposits fell to 35%? Assume the other ratios remain as originally stated.

11. **Challenge Problem** ABBIX has a complex financial system with the following relationships: the ratio of required reserves to total deposits is 15%, and the ratio of noncheckable deposits to checkable deposits is 40%. In addition, currency held by the nonbank public amounts to 20% of checkable deposits. The ratio of government deposits to checkable deposits is 8%. Initial excess reserves are $900 million.

a. Determine the M1 multiplier and the maximum dollar amount of checkable deposits.

b. Determine the size of the M1 money supply.

c. What will happen to ABBIX's money multiplier if the reserve requirement decreases to 10% while the ratio of noncheckable deposits to checkable deposits falls to 30%? Assume the other ratios remain as originally stated.

d. Based on the information in (c), estimate the maximum dollar amount of checkable deposits, as well as the size of the M1 money supply.

e. Assume that ABBIX has a target M1 money supply of $2.8 billion. The only variable that you have direct control over is the required reserves ratio. What would the required reserves ratio have to be to reach the target M1 money supply amount? Assume the other original ratio relationships hold.

f. Now assume that currency held by the nonbank public drops to 15% of checkable deposits and that ABBIX's target money supply is changed to $3.0 billion. What would the required reserves ratio have to be to reach the new target M1 money supply amount? Assume the other original ratio relationships hold.

International Finance and Trade

LEARNING OBJECTIVES

After studying this chapter, you should be able to do the following:

LO 6.1 Explain how the international monetary system evolved and how it operates today.

LO 6.2 Describe the efforts undertaken to achieve economic unification of Europe.

LO 6.3 Describe how currency exchange markets operate and explain how currency exchange rates are quoted.

LO 6.4 Describe the factors that affect currency exchange rates.

LO 6.5 Identify factors to consider when conducting business internationally.

LO 6.6 Describe how international banking systems facilitate financing of sales by exporters and purchases by importers.

LO 6.7 Identify recent developments in U.S. international transactions.

Where we have been. . . In Chapter 5, you learned how the Fed operates in conjunction with governmental policy makers (the president, Congress, and the U.S. Treasury) in the common effort of trying to achieve the goals of economic growth, high employment levels, and stable prices. You now understand policy instruments of the Treasury and how the national debt is managed. You also learned how the money supply is expanded and contracted and the importance of the monetary base and money multiplier in setting monetary policy.

Where we are going. . . In Part 2, we focus on developing a better understanding of the area of investments, including how securities are valued and how securities markets operate. Chapter 7 examines how savings are directed into various investments, and Chapter 8 discusses how interest rates, or the "price" of money, are determined in the financial markets. Chapter 9 introduces "time" as a factor when determining rates of return on investments. In the remaining chapters you will learn about the characteristics of bonds and stocks and how they are priced or valued, how securities markets work, and the need to consider risk versus return trade-offs when investing in securities.

How this chapter applies to me. . . You live in a global environment. You likely have already purchased products grown or manufactured in foreign countries and sold in the United States. For example, you may purchase fresh fruit during the winter that was grown in and shipped from South America. Or, you may have purchased a Swiss-made watch from a retail store in the United States. You may also have had to convert U.S. dollars into a foreign currency such as euros for a direct product purchase from a manufacturer in Germany. You may have traveled internationally and needed to exchange your dollars for that country's currency. You may even live and work outside the United States in the future. Thus, a basic understanding of international trade and factors that affect currency exchange rates will be useful knowledge to have.

It is important to have an "open view" of other countries from the perspective of what they do and why they do it. Maria Mitchell, a U.S. astronomer, probably summed it up best when she stated,

> *I have never been in any country where they did not do something better than we do it, think some thoughts better than we think, catch some inspiration from heights above their own.*[1]

---

[1] Maria Mitchell, *Life, Letters, and Journals*, 1896.

Interactions among countries are quite complex. Philosophical, cultural, economic, and religious differences exist. These differences jointly establish the basis for international relations and help us understand the practice of internationalism by specific countries. Differences in philosophies, cultures, economic models, and religion also often provide the basis for establishing a nation's foreign policy. At the same time, virtually everyone would agree that it is in the best interests of worldwide economic growth and productivity for countries to work together in facilitating international trade and the flow of financial capital. While this chapter focuses on the economics of international trade and finance, we recognize the importance of being willing to try to understand the basis for differences among countries in terms of philosophies, cultures, economic models, and religions.

6.1 INTER-NATIONAL MONETARY SYSTEM

GLOBAL In the first five chapters of Part 1, we focused on covering the role of the U.S. financial system, monetary system, and monetary policy. When viewed in a global context, responsibilities become more complex. The global or **international monetary system** is a system of institutions and mechanisms to foster world trade, manage the flow of financial capital, and determine currency exchange rates. We begin with a brief discussion of the historical development of international trade and finance. Then we turn our attention to how the international monetary system has changed or evolved over the past couple of centuries.

international monetary system system of institutions and mechanisms to foster international trade, manage the flow of financial capital, and determine currency exchange rates

6.1.1 DEVELOPMENT OF INTERNATIONAL FINANCE

International finance probably began about 5,000 years ago when Babylonian cities rose to importance as centers of trade between the Mediterranean Sea and civilizations in the East. Gold was used for transactions and as a store of value, probably beginning around 3000 B.C., when the pharaohs ruled Egypt. Centers of international finance shifted to the Greek city of Athens around 500 B.C. and to the Roman Empire and Rome around 100 B.C.[2] It appears that whenever international trade developed, financial institutions came into existence and international bankers followed.

Instruments and documents similar to those in use today were designed to control movement of cargo, insure against losses, satisfy government requirements, and transfer funds. Financial centers shifted to the northern European cities during the 1500s, and in more recent years to London, New York, and Tokyo. Today, international trade takes place and international claims are settled around the clock. It is no longer necessary to have a physical center, such as a city, in which to carry out international financial operations.

6.1.2 HOW THE INTERNATIONAL MONETARY SYSTEM EVOLVED

6.1.2.1 Before World War I

Prior to the start of World War I in 1914, the international monetary system operated mostly under a **gold standard** whereby the currencies of major countries were convertible into gold at fixed exchange rates. For example, 1 ounce of gold might be worth 20 U.S. dollars, or $1 would be worth one-twentieth (or 0.05) of an ounce of gold. At the same time, 1 ounce of gold might be worth 5 French francs (FF), or FF1 would be worth one-fifth (or 0.20) of an ounce of gold. Since $20 could be converted into one ounce of gold that could then be used to purchase 5 FF, or 20 U.S. dollars, the exchange rate between the dollar and franc would be 20 to 5, or 4 to 1. Alternatively, $0.20 \div 0.05$ equals 4 to 1.

gold standard standard by which currencies of major countries are convertible into gold at fixed exchange rates

Recall from Chapter 2 that the American colonies relied primarily on the Spanish dollar to conduct business transactions prior to the 1800s. In 1792, the first U.S. monetary act was enacted and provided for a *bimetallic standard* based on both gold and silver. A standard based solely on gold was not adopted until 1879. In those days, coins were *full-bodied money* in that their metal content was worth the same as their face values. Paper money then was *representative full-bodied money*, because the paper money was backed by an amount of precious metal equal to the money's face value.

During the 1800s most other developed countries also had their own currencies tied to gold, silver, or both. By the end of the 1800s most countries had adopted just the gold standard. However,

---

[2] For a more detailed look at the early development of international finance, see Robert D. Fraser, International Banking and Finance, 6th ed. (Washington, DC: R&H Publishers, 1984), ch. 2.

coinciding with the start of World War I, most countries went off the gold standard. For example, the Federal Reserve Act of 1913 provided for the issuance of Federal Reserve Notes, called *fiat money* because they were not backed by either gold or silver. Recall from Chapter 2 that the government decreed the notes to be "legal tender" for purposes of making payments and discharging public and private debts. Fiat money has value that is based solely on confidence in the U.S. government's being able to achieve economic growth and maintain price stability. Most foreign governments also moved to monetary systems based on fiat money.

A major criticism of the gold standard was that as the volume of world trade increased over the years, the supply of "new" gold would fail to keep pace. Thus, without some form of supplementary international money, the result would be international deflation. A second criticism of the gold standard was a lack of an international organization to monitor and report whether countries were deviating from the standard when it was in their own best interests.

6.1.2.2 World War I through World War II: 1915–1944
During the interwar period from 1915 through 1944, which encompassed most of World War I, the period in between, and World War II, an attempt was made to go back onto the gold standard. Many nations returned to the gold standard during the 1920s only to go off it again in the early 1930s because of financial crises associated with the Great Depression. A series of bank failures and continued outflow of gold caused the United States to abandon the gold standard in 1933.

6.1.2.3 Bretton Woods Fixed Exchange Rate System: 1945–1972
In mid-1944, authorities from all major nations met in Bretton Woods, New Hampshire, to formulate a post–World War II international monetary system. The **International Monetary Fund (IMF)** was created to promote world trade through monitoring and maintaining fixed exchange rates and by making loans to countries facing balance of trade and payments problems. The International Bank for Reconstruction and Development, or **World Bank**, also was created to help economic growth in developing countries.

The most significant development of the conference was the exchange rate agreement commonly called the *Bretton Woods system*, in which individual currencies would be tied to gold through the U.S. dollar via fixed, or pegged, exchange rates. One ounce of gold was set equal to $35. Each participating country's currency was then set at a "par," or fixed value, in relation to the U.S. dollar. For example, one French franc might be one-seventh of a U.S. dollar, or $0.1429. Thus, a franc would "indirectly" be worth $5 in gold (i.e., $35 ÷ 7). In essence, one franc could be exchanged for $0.1429, which could be exchanged for $5 in gold (0.1429 × $35).

Countries adopting the Bretton Woods system could hold their reserves either in gold or U.S. dollars, because the dollar was the only currency on the gold standard. This eliminated one of the criticisms associated with all currencies being on a gold standard system in that world economic growth was restricted to the rate of increase in new gold production, since gold was the only monetary reserve. Since the Bretton Woods system allowed for the holding of both gold and U.S. dollars as foreign exchange reserves, this new monetary system allowed for less restrictive world economic growth. The negative side of the Bretton Woods system was that the U.S. government had to produce balance-of-payments deficits so that foreign exchange reserves would grow.

Unfortunately, by the 1960s the value of the U.S. gold stock was less than the amount of foreign holdings of dollars. This, of course, caused concern about the viability of the Bretton Woods system. To help keep the system operating, in 1970 the International Monetary Fund (IMF) created a new reserve asset called **special drawing rights (SDRs)**, a basket, or portfolio, of currencies that could be used to make international payments. At first the SDR was made up of a weighted average of 16 currencies. At the beginning of the 1980s, the SDR basket was reduced to include only five major currencies. The current SDR basket includes the U.S. dollar (41.9% weight), euro (37.4% weight), Japanese yen (9.4% weight), and British pound (11.3% weight).

Attempts were made to save the Bretton Woods system in 1971 when representatives of major central banks met at the Smithsonian Institution in Washington, D.C., and raised the price of gold to $38 per ounce. In early 1973, the price of gold was further increased to $42 per ounce. However, the end of fixed exchange rates was at hand.

International Monetary Fund (IMF) created to promote world trade through monitoring and maintaining fixed exchange rates and by making loans to countries facing balance of trade and payments problems

World Bank created to help economic growth in developing countries (also called the International Bank for Reconstruction and Development)

Bretton Woods system system in which individual currencies would be tied to gold through the U.S. dollar via fixed, or pegged, exchange rates

special drawing rights (SDRs) reserve assets created by the IMF and consisting of a basket of currencies that could be used to make international payments

6.1.2.4   Flexible Exchange Rate System: 1973–Present

Beginning in March 1973 major currencies were allowed to "float" against one another. By the mid-1970s gold was abandoned as a reserve asset, and IMF members accepted a system of **flexible exchange rates** in which currency exchange rates are determined by supply and demand. A primary objection to flexible exchange rates is the possibility of wide swings in response to changes in supply and demand, with a resulting uncertainty in world trade. Evidence indicates that exchange rates indeed have been much more volatile since the collapse of the Bretton Woods system compared to when the system was in place.

flexible exchange rates system in which currency exchange rates are determined by supply and demand

Today, many countries, including Australia, Japan, Canada, the United States, and the United Kingdom, allow their currencies to float against others. The European Monetary Union also allows the euro to float freely. In contrast, India, China, and Russia employ semifloating or managed floating systems involving active government intervention. Most countries in Africa currently peg their currencies to the euro. Thus, the current exchange rate system is a composite of flexible or floating exchange rates, managed floating exchange rates, and pegged exchange rates.

> **LEARNING ACTIVITY**
>
> Go to the International Monetary Fund website, https://www.imf.org, and find information about "special drawing rights" and how they are used as reserve assets.

6.2 EUROPEAN UNIFICATION

6.2.1   EUROPEAN UNION

GLOBAL The **European Union (EU)** was established to promote trade and economic development among European countries. Economic integration was to be achieved by eliminating barriers that previously restricted the flow of labor, goods, and financial capital among countries. The European Union's history can be traced back to the early 1950s. Six European countries signed the Treaty of Rome that established the *European Economic Community (EEC)* in 1957. The EEC became the *European Community (EC)* in 1978.

European Union (EU) organization established to promote trade and economic development among European countries

In late 1991, members of the European Community met in Maastricht, Netherlands, to draft a treaty. The resulting *Treaty on European Union*, referred to as the *Maastricht Treaty*, was signed in 1992 by the following 12 members: Belgium, Denmark, France, Germany, Greece, Ireland, Italy, Luxembourg, Netherlands, Portugal, Spain, and the United Kingdom. The *Maastricht Treaty* created the European Union and provided for the economic convergence, fixing of member country exchange rates, and planned introduction of the euro as the common currency. Austria, Finland, and Sweden joined the EU in 1995, bringing the membership, then, to 15 countries. Ten additional countries (Cyprus, Czech Republic, Estonia, Hungary, Latvia, Lithuania, Malta, Poland, Slovakia, and Slovenia) joined the EU in 2004. Bulgaria and Romania were added in 2007, and Croatia became a member in 2013, bringing the total then to 28 EU member states.

Brexit the plan for the withdrawal of the United Kingdom from the European Union

In June 2016, a referendum was held on whether the United Kingdom should withdrawal from the EU. Fifty-two percent of those who voted supported withdrawal. "**Brexit**," a combination of "Britain" and "exit," is the plan for the United Kingdom to withdraw from the European Union. At the end of March 2017, the withdrawal process was initiated and it was stipulated that the withdrawal agreement would be completed by the end of March 2019. As of early 2019, an agreement still had not been reached causing the future status of Brexit to remain uncertain.

6.2.2   EUROZONE MEMBERS

European Monetary Union (EMU) subset of European Union countries called eurozone members that have adopted the euro

The **European Monetary Union (EMU)** began as a 12-member subset of the 1995 15-member EU. Technically, by the end of 1998, 11 countries had met the economic and financial requirements to convert to the euro. Greece was able to qualify in 2000 making it the twelfth member. EU members Denmark, Sweden, and the United Kingdom chose not to join the EMU. By ratifying the Maastricht Treaty, the EMU agreed to have overall monetary policy set by the *European Central Bank (ECB)* and adopted the euro as its common currency. It is common practice today to refer to the subset of EU members that have adopted the euro as their common currency as eurozone members. Slovenia became a eurozone member in 2007, Cyprus and Malta joined in 2008, Slovakia joined in 2009 and Estonia became a member in 2011. Latvia was admitted as a eurozone member in 2014 and Lithuania joined in 2015 bringing total eurozone membership to 19 country states.

eurozone members
European Monetary Union members that have adopted the euro as their common currency

6.2.3 THE EURO

On January 1, 1999, the euro became the official currency of 11 EMU members. Greece qualified to adopt the euro in 2000 and was admitted in 2001. Euro coins and currency were introduced on January 1, 2002, and began replacing (phasing out) the national currencies of the 12 Eurozone members. Only the euro coins and currency were legal tender by July 2002.

euro official coins and paper currency of the eurozone member countries

Designing the euro paper currency was a difficult task. It could not include images (e.g., the Eiffel Tower) that could be associated with a single country. Likewise, portraits of individuals (e.g., royalty, military leaders) could not be used. Ultimately, the euro was designed to include "gates" and "windows" for the front of the bills "to symbolize the future"; "bridges" were chosen for the back of the bills. The paper currency uses multicolored ink, watermarks, and three-dimensional holographic images to thwart counterfeiting efforts. Seven denominations, from 5 to 500 euros were issued.

6.2.4 EUROPEAN UNION FINANCIAL CRISES

CRISIS The European Union suffered many of the economic problems that the United States went through in the 2007–2008 financial crisis involving the fear of a worldwide financial system collapse. However, while the United States was able to recover from its 2008–2009 Great Recession, the economies of many European Union countries continue to face economic development uncertainties and high levels of unemployment. Tax receipts often have been less than government expenditures in many of the EU countries, causing national debts to grow rapidly and resulting in some countries having difficulty paying interest due on their debts.

Some EU countries have been forced into austerity government expenditure plans at a time of no economic growth and high unemployment, in some instances causing social unrest. Greece continues to experience the need to make difficult economic trade-offs, and concerns exist as to whether the country will remain a eurozone member. Concern also has been expressed about the economic and financial viability of Spain, Portugal, and Italy.

SMALL BUSINESS PRACTICE

FINDING FOREIGN CUSTOMERS

To conduct business in a foreign country, a domestic firm must either export to that country or produce goods or offer services in that country. Exporting may take place indirectly or directly. Indirect exporting by U.S. companies involves U.S.–based exporters. These exporters may sell for manufacturers, buy for overseas customers, buy and sell for their own account, and/or buy on behalf of middle-persons or wholesalers.

Exporters that sell for manufacturers usually are manufacturers' export agents or export management companies. A manufacturer's export agent usually represents several noncompeting domestic manufacturers. An export management company acts as an export department for a number of noncompeting domestic firms. Exporters that purchase for overseas customers are called export commission agents since they are paid a commission by foreign purchasers to buy on their behalf.

Small businesses usually find it necessary to use indirect exporting. Direct exporting uses manufacturers' agents, distributors, and

retailers located in the countries where they are conducting business. Only large domestic firms are able to engage in direct exporting.

Various forms of government assistance are available to help businesses in their exporting efforts. Many states have government "trade export" departments that assist firms in their export activities. At the federal level, the Export-Import Bank of the United States was founded in 1934 to aid domestic businesses in finding foreign customers and markets for their products. Export credit insurance also is available to help exporters. The Foreign Credit Insurance Association (FCIA) provides credit insurance policies to U.S. exporters to protect against nonpayment by foreign customers.

In some instances, "countertrading" is used to foster sales to foreign customers. Under such an arrangement, a U.S. exporter sells its goods to a foreign producer in exchange for goods produced by that foreign company. Simple kinds of countertrading take the form of a barter arrangement between a domestic firm and a foreign firm.

The European Central Bank, as well as the central banks of EU members not part of the euro-zone, have engaged in easy money policies to attempt to stimulate economic growth and to reduce unemployment rates. The ECB, like the Fed, has engaged in quantitative easing programs, including buying bonds issued by eurozone countries having financial troubles in order to help stabilize the costs of government debt financing. Recall that the Fed targeted the short-term federal funds rate at 0.00 to 0.25% from late 2008 until late 2015 when there was a 0.25 percent increase. As the U.S. economy continued to grow, eight more 0.25 percent increases were implemented during the 2016–2018 period producing a target rate of 2.25–2.50 percent for federal funds at the end of 2018. In contrast, as noted above, many eurozone countries have suffered from little, if any, economic growth and high unemployment rates. This has caused the ECB to continue to target short-term interest rates near zero and has even experimented with negative interest rate policies. In a negative interest rate situation, the purchaser of a government security pays the government more than the interest received on the security for the "right" to hold the security.

Concern has been expressed that the EU may face new economic problems and possibly a new financial crisis because of the United Kingdom's June, 2016 referendum vote to leave the EU. The United Kingdom, consisting of England, Northern Ireland, Scotland, and Wales, has major trade and financial arrangements with countries remaining in the EU that could be disrupted by its decision to leave the EU. However, as of early 2019 it remained unclear as to whether Brexit would be implemented. There also is concern about what would happen if other EU-member countries tried to leave the EU. It will be interesting to follow how the EU responds and adapts to these new economic and financial challenges.

DISCUSSION QUESTION 1

Has the decision by the eurozone countries to give up their individual national currencies and adopt the euro as a common currency produced economic benefits?

LEARNING ACTIVITY

Go to the European Central Bank website, https://www.ecb.int, and find information about the history of the euro.

6.3 CURRENCY EXCHANGE MARKETS AND RATES

6.3.1 CURRENCY EXCHANGE MARKETS

GLOBAL We ordinarily think of a market as a specific place or institution, but this is not always so. **Currency exchange markets**, also called **foreign exchange markets**, are electronic markets where banks and institutional traders buy and sell various currencies on behalf of businesses, other clients, and themselves. The major financial centers of the world are connected electronically so that when an individual or firm engaged in a foreign transaction deals with a local bank, that individual or firm is, in effect, dealing with the exchange markets of the world. Transactions throughout the world may be completed in only a few minutes by virtue of the effective communications network serving the various financial institutions, including central banks of every nation.

6.3.2 EXCHANGE RATE QUOTATIONS

A **currency exchange rate** indicates the value of one currency relative to another currency. Table 6.1 shows the currency exchange rates for a variety of foreign currencies relative to the U.S. dollar during late January, 2019. Currency exchange rates are stated in two basic ways. The **direct quotation method** indicates the value of one unit of a foreign currency in terms of a home country's currency. For illustration purposes, let's focus on the U.S. dollar as the domestic or home country's currency relative to the European euro. Notice in Table 6.1 that the "U.S. dollar equivalent" of one euro was $1.1448; or, stated differently, it took $1.1448 to buy one euro. The

currency exchange markets (foreign exchange markets) electronic markets where banks and institutional traders buy and sell currencies on behalf of businesses, other clients, and themselves

foreign exchange markets same as currency exchange markets

currency exchange rate value of one currency relative to another currency

direct quotation method indicates the amount of a home country's currency needed to purchase one unit of a foreign currency

TABLE 6.1   Selected Foreign Exchange Rates, Late January 2019

Country	Currency	Foreign currency in U.S. Dollars (Direct Method)	Foreign currency per U.S. Dollar (Indirect Method)
Australia	dollar	$0.7156	1.3974
Brazil	real	0.2714	3.6850
Canada	dollar	0.7537	1.3268
China	yuan	0.1489	6.7159
European	euro	1.1448	0.8735
Hong Kong	dollar	0.1275	7.8431
India	rupee	0.01409	70.9723
Japan	yen	0.009171	109.0394
Mexico	peso	0.0523	19.1205
Russia	ruble	0.01530	65.3595
Singapore	dollar	0.7396	1.3521
South Africa	rand	0.0755	13.2450
Switzerland	franc	1.0054	0.9946
United Kingdom	pound	1.3115	0.7625

Sources: https://www.money.cnn.com and https://www.reuters.com.

indirect quotation method indicates the number of units of a foreign currency needed to purchase one unit of the home country's currency. By, again, turning to Table 6.1, we see that it takes 0.8735 euros to purchase one U.S. dollar.

Table 6.1 also shows the value of other major currencies in U.S. dollar terms in late January, 2019. An Australia dollar was worth $0.7156, a United Kingdom (British) pound had a value $1.3115, a Swiss franc equaled $1.0054, and a Japanese yen was worth $0.009171. The corresponding indirect quotations in units relative to one U.S. dollar were, as follows: Australia dollar = 1.3974, United Kingdom pound = 0.7625, Swiss franc = 0.9946, and Japanese yen = 109.0394. It should be apparent that it is easy to find the other quotation if we know either the direct quotation or the indirect quotation. For example, the indirect quotation can be calculated, as follows:

$$\text{Indirect Quotation (foreign currency units)} = \frac{1}{\text{Direct quotation (home currency value)}} \qquad (6.1)$$

For illustration purposes, let's use the euro versus U.S. dollar relationships previously noted. A euro was worth $1.1448 and represents a direct quotation, whereas the United States is the home country. To find the indirect quotation, we would calculate,

$$\text{Indirect Quotation} = \frac{1}{\$1.1448} = .8735 \text{ euros}$$

Of course, if we knew that the indirect quotation for the euro relative to the dollar was 0.8735 euros per U.S. dollar, we could divide that value into one to get the direct quotation value: $1 \div 0.8735 = 1.1448$ or $1.1448.

Table 6.2 shows the "crossrates" among several major currencies—the U.S. dollar, the British pound, the yen, and the euro. It is possible to calculate the exchange rate between the yen and the euro by first knowing each of their values relative to the U.S. dollar. For example, a yen was worth 0.009171 and a euro $1.1448 in late January 2019. Dividing 0.009171 by 1.1448 gives a value of one yen, in euros, as 0.008011 euros. Since Table 6.2 shows the crossrates between the yen and the euro,

indirect quotation method indicates the number of units of a foreign currency needed to purchase one unit of the home country's currency

TABLE 6.2   Selected Foreign Exchange Crossrates, Late January 2019

Currency	U.S. dollar	euro	yen	British pound
U.S. dollar	1.0	0.8735	109.0394	0.7625
euro	1.1448	1.0	124.8283	0.8729
yen	0.009171	0.008011	1.0	0.006993
British pound	1.3115	1.1456	143.0051	1.0

Sources: https://www.money.cnn.com and https://www.reuters.com.

we can read the value of one yen in terms of euros as 0.008011 euros. Of course, if we wanted to know the value of a Brazilian real in euros, we would have to return to Table 6.1 and make the calculation directly. In late January 2019, the U.S. dollar value of a Brazilian real was $.2714 and the value of a euro was $1.1448. Dividing 0.2714 by 1.1448 indicates that one real was worth 0.2371 euros.

It is worth noting that electronic and newspaper exchange rate quotes are for large unit transfers within the currency exchange markets. Consequently, individuals buying foreign currencies would not get exactly the same ratio. The currency exchange prices for an individual always favor the seller, who makes a margin of profit.

The balance in the foreign account of a U.S. bank is subject to constant drain as the bank sells foreign currency claims to individuals who import goods or obtain services from other countries. These banks may reestablish a given deposit level in their correspondent banks either through selling dollar claims in the foreign countries concerned or by buying claims from another dealer in the foreign exchange.

6.3.3   CURRENCY EXCHANGE RATE APPRECIATION AND DEPRECIATION

spot exchange rate rate being quoted for current delivery of the currency

currency appreciation occurs when there is an increase in a currency's value

currency depreciation occurs when there is a decrease in a currency's value

Each currency exchange rate shown in Table 6.1 is said to be a spot exchange rate, or the current rate being quoted for delivery of the currency "on the spot." Actually, it is common practice to have up to two days for delivery after the trade date. Spot rates at different points in time can be compared. Currency appreciation occurs when there is an increase in a currency's value. A decrease in a currency's value is called currency depreciation. If we denote the most recent spot rate as SR_t, the earlier spot rate as SR_{t-1}, and the percentage change in a foreign currency as %FC Change, we have the following:

$$\%FC \text{ Change} = \frac{SR_t - SR_{t-1}}{SR_{t-1}} \qquad (6.2)$$

The value of a euro in U.S. dollars has ranged between about $1.07 and $1.15 in recent years. For illustrative purposes, let's use an example where the spot rate for a euro increased from a $1.09 value a year ago to a current spot rate of $1.12. The percentage change in the foreign currency (euro) would be,

$$\%FC \text{ (euro) Change} = \frac{\$1.12 - \$1.09}{\$1.09} = \frac{\$0.03}{\$1.09} = 2.75\%$$

In other words, the euro would have appreciated by 2.75% relative to the U.S. dollar.

If, instead, the value of a euro declined from $1.09 to $1.07 the percentage change in the euro would be calculated as,

$$\%FC \text{ (euro) Change} = \frac{\$1.07 - \$1.09}{\$1.09} = \frac{-\$0.02}{\$1.09} = -1.83\%$$

Thus, the euro depreciated by 1.83% relative to the U.S. dollar.

LEARNING ACTIVITY

1. Go to the CNNMoney website, https://www.money.cnn.com. Access "markets" and then "currencies" and find current currency exchange rates for the U.S. dollar relative to the Australian dollar, British pound, and Canadian dollar. Find either the direct or indirect exchange rate and calculate the other one.
2. Go to the Reuters website, https://www.reuters.com, and find current currency exchange rates for the U.S. dollar relative to the Japanese yen, European euro, and the Swiss franc. Find either the direct or indirect exchange rate and calculate the other one.

Currency exchange rates are affected by changes in supply and demand relationships, relative inflation rates, relative interest rates, and political risk and/or economic risk. Banks and institutional investors that are engaged in foreign currency transactions bring differences in the supply and demand for currencies into "balance" through the process of adjusting exchange rates up or down.

6.4 FACTORS THAT AFFECT CURRENCY EXCHANGE RATES

6.4.1 BASIC SUPPLY AND DEMAND RELATIONSHIPS

The supply and demand relationship involving two currencies is said to be in "equilibrium" at the current or spot exchange rate. Thus, the equilibrium exchange rate is the currency exchange rate that exists when the supply and demand for a currency are in balance. Demand for a foreign currency derives from the demand for the goods, services, and financial assets of a country (or group of countries, such as the eurozone members). For example, U.S. consumers and investors demand a variety of eurozone member goods, services, and financial assets, most of which must be paid for in euros. The supply of European euros comes from eurozone member demand for U.S. goods, services, and financial assets. A change in the relative demand for euros versus U.S. dollars will cause the spot exchange rate to change. Currency exchange rates also depend on relative inflation rates, relative interest rates, and political and economic risks.

Figure 6.1 illustrates how exchange rates are determined in a currency exchange market by banks that provide foreign exchange services. Graph A depicts a supply and demand relationship between

equilibrium exchange rate currency exchange rate where the supply and demand for a currency are in balance

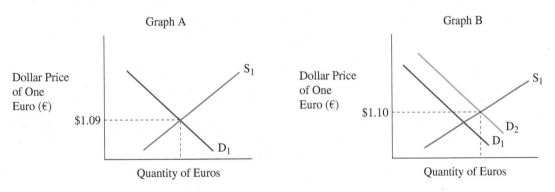

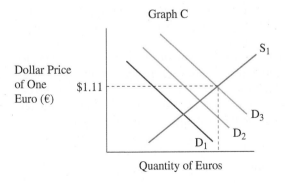

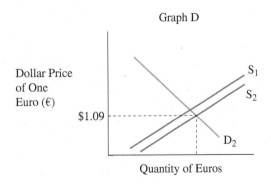

FIGURE 6.1   Exchange rate determination in the currency exchange market

the U.S. dollar and the European euro (€). The demand curve is downward sloping, indicating that the U.S. demand for goods and services from eurozone countries would increase as the dollar value of the euro declines. The upward sloping supply curve reflects the demand for U.S. dollars, or the supply of euros for sale, and indicates the willingness to supply larger quantities of euros as the dollar value of euros increase. The market, in our example, is in balance, or in "equilibrium," when one euro is worth $1.09. This price reflects the market-clearing price that equates the demand (D_1) for euros relative to the supply (S_1) of euros.

Now, assume Americans increase their demand for goods and services from eurozone member countries such as Germany and France. These goods and services would be priced in euros. Americans will need to exchange their dollars for euros to pay for their purchases. The consequence is an increase or shift in demand for euros from D_1 to D_2, as depicted in Graph B of Figure 6.1. The supply of euros reflects demand by eurozone member countries for U.S. goods and services, and as long as there is no change, S_1 will remain unchanged. As a consequence of this scenario, the increased demand for euros results in a new higher equilibrium price of $1.10.

A further increase in the demand for the goods and services provided by eurozone member countries could cause the dollar price or value of one euro to increase even more. Graph C in Figure 6.1 depicts such an increase as a shift from D_2 to D_3. Again, with no change in the supply of euros, the new market-clearing price of a euro might be $1.11. Of course, as the euro's dollar value increases, the prices of eurozone member goods also increase. At some point, as eurozone member goods become more costly, U.S. demand for these foreign goods will decline. Graph D depicts this cutback in U.S. demand for euros as a shift downward from D_3 in Graph C to D_2. In a similar fashion, the higher dollar value of the euro in Graph C makes U.S. goods and services less costly to eurozone members, and thus the supply of euros might increase or shift from S_1 to S_2. The net result could be a new equilibrium exchange rate in which the dollar price of a euro is $1.09.

A change in the demand for one country's financial assets relative to another country's financial assets also will cause the currency exchange rate between the two countries to change to a new equilibrium price. For example, a nation with a relatively strong stock market will attract investors who seek out the highest returns on their investment funds, much as a nation with a higher relative economic growth rate attracts capital investments. For example, if the stock market in the United States is expected to perform poorly relative to the stock markets in eurozone member countries, investors will switch or move their debt investments denominated in U.S. dollars into euro-denominated debt investments. This increased demand for euros relative to U.S. dollars will cause the euro's dollar value to increase.

6.4.2 INFLATION, INTEREST RATES, AND OTHER FACTORS

In addition to changes in supply and demand relationships, currency exchange rates are also affected by changes in relative inflation rates, relative interest rates, and political and economic risks. Let's first turn our attention to what happens if differences occur in expected inflation rates between two countries. A nation with a relatively lower expected inflation rate will have a relatively stronger currency. For example, if inflation becomes lower in the United States relative to eurozone member countries, eurozone member products of comparable quality will become increasingly more expensive. Americans will find it less expensive to buy American products and so will eurozone members. The result will be fewer eurozone member imports into the United States and greater U.S. exports to eurozone member countries, causing an appreciation of the dollar relative to the euro.

purchasing power parity (PPP) currency of a country with a relatively lower inflation rate will appreciate relative to the currency of a country with a relatively higher inflation rate

Purchasing power parity (PPP) theory states that a country with a relatively lower expected inflation rate will have its currency appreciate relative to a country (or group of countries using a single currency) with a relatively higher expected inflation rate. A simplified PPP relationship can be viewed as the percentage change in a foreign currency (% FC Change) being approximately equal to the difference in inflation rates expected for the two involved countries. This can be expressed as,

$$\text{Expected \% FC Change} \approx \text{InfR}_{hc} - \text{InfR}_{fc}$$

InfR$_{hc}$ is the expected inflation rate for the home country and the InfR$_{fc}$ is the expected inflation rate for the foreign country. For example, if the U.S. (home country) inflation rate is expected to be 3% next year and the eurozone member (foreign country) inflation rate is expected to be 2%, we would expect the euro to appreciate (and the U.S. dollar to depreciate) over the next year. Using the above relationship,

$$\text{Expected \% FC Change} \approx 3\% - 2\% = 1\%$$

Thus, the euro would be expected to appreciate relative to the U.S. dollar by 1% over the next year.

It is more technically accurate to express the expected percentage change in the FC using the relative inflation rates between the two countries, as follows:

$$\text{Expected \% FC Change} = \frac{1 + \text{InfR}_{hc}}{1 + \text{InfR}_{fc}} = 1 \tag{6.3}$$

The value "1" is subtracted from the relative inflation ratio to show the expected FC change as a percentage.

Returning to our example of an expected inflation rate over the next year of 3% for the U.S. dollar and 2% for the euro, the expected percentage change in the foreign currency (euro) is,

$$\text{Expected \% FC Change} = \frac{1.03}{1.02} - 1$$
$$\text{Expected \% FC Change} = 1.0098 - 1 = 0.0098, \text{or } 0.98\%$$

Thus, based on relative expected inflation rates, PPP theory suggests that the euro will appreciate by .98% over the next year.

Some economists use relative interest rates, instead of relative inflation rates, between countries to estimate expected changes in currency exchange rates. Irving Fisher contended that the nominal (quoted) interest rate and the inflation rate are related, and that the nominal interest rate consisted of a real rate of interest and an expected inflation premium or rate.[3] The **international Fisher effect (IFE)** theory states that a country with a relatively lower nominal interest rate (due to a lower expected inflation rate) will have its currency appreciate relative to a country with a relatively higher interest rate.

We can modify equation (6.3) to include relative interest rates instead of expected inflation rates as follows:

$$\text{Expected \% FC Change} = \frac{1 + \text{IntR}_{hc}}{1 + \text{IntR}_{fc}} - 1 \tag{6.4}$$

IntR$_{hc}$ is the nominal interest rate for the home country and the IntR$_{fc}$ is the nominal interest rate for the foreign country.

For example, if U.S banks are offering a 5% interest rate on one-year deposits and euro member banks are offering a 4% interest rate on comparable one-year deposits, we can estimate the expected percent change in the euro, as follows:

$$\text{Expected \% FC Change} = \frac{1.05}{1.04} - 1$$
$$\text{Expected \% FC Change} = 1.0096 - 1 = 0.0096, \text{or } 0.96\%$$

Thus, based on relative one-year bank deposit interest rates, IFE theory suggests that the euro is expected to appreciate by 0.96% over the next year.

Political risk is the risk associated with the possibility that a national government might confiscate or expropriate assets held by foreigners. A nation with relatively lower political risk will generally

international Fisher effect (IFE) currency of a country with a relatively lower nominal interest rate (due to a lower expected inflation rate) will have its currency appreciate relative to a country with a relatively higher interest rate

political risk risk associated with the possibility that a national government might confiscate or expropriate assets held by foreigners

---

[3] We will cover the factors that determine market interest rates in detail in Chapter 8.

economic risk risk associated with possible slow or negative economic growth, as well as variability in economic growth

have a relatively stronger currency. Economic risk is the risk associated with the possibility of slow or negative economic growth, as well as variability in economic growth. A nation that has a relatively higher economic growth rate, along with growth stability, will generally have a stronger currency. Furthermore, a nation with a relatively stronger economic growth rate will attract more capital inflows relative to a nation growing more slowly. For example, a stronger U.S. economy relative to the eurozone member economy will cause investors in both countries to switch from euro investments to dollar investments.

6.4.3 ARBITRAGE

arbitrage simultaneous, or nearly simultaneous, purchasing of commodities, securities, or currencies in one market and selling them in another where the price is higher

Arbitrage is the simultaneous, or nearly simultaneous, purchasing of commodities, securities, or currencies in one market and selling them in another where the price is higher. In international exchange, variations in quotations among countries at any time are quickly brought into alignment through the arbitrage activities of international financiers. For example, if the exchange rate for a euro was reported in New York at €1 = $1.14 and in Brussels, Belgium, at €1 = $1.13, alert international arbitrageurs simultaneously would sell claims to euros in New York at the rate of $1.14 and would have Brussels correspondents sell claims on U.S. dollars in Brussels at the rate of $1.13 for each euro. Such arbitrage would be profitable only when dealing in large sums. Under these circumstances, if an arbitrageur sold a claim on €100 million in New York, $114 million would be received. The corresponding sale of claims on American dollars in Brussels would be at the rate of €100 million for $113 million. Hence, a profit of $1 million would be realized on the transaction. A quotation differential of as little as one-sixteenth of one cent may be sufficient to encourage arbitrage activities.

The ultimate effect of large-scale arbitrage activities on exchange rates is the elimination of the variation between the two markets. The sale of large amounts of claims to American dollars in Brussels would drive up the price for euros, and in New York the sale of claims to euros would force the exchange rate down.

DISCUSSION QUESTION 2

Do you expect the U.S. dollar will appreciate or depreciate against the euro during the next year? Why?

LEARNING ACTIVITY

Go to the CNNMoney website, https://www.money.cnn.com. Access "markets," and then "currencies" and find current currency exchange rates for the European euro relative to the United Kingdom (British) pound, and the Japanese yen. Find both direct and indirect currency exchange quotations.

PERSONAL FINANCIAL PLANNING

Investing Overseas

People living in the United States are affected by international finance in at least two ways. First, the growth or recession of overseas economies affects jobs in the United States. If foreign economies grow more slowly or go into recession, there will be less export demand for U.S. goods and services. Thus, a worker's personal financial status can be imperiled by a layoff or reduced working hours.

The second effect on individuals is perhaps less clear to see—the effect of foreign investors on U.S. financial markets and interest rates. Stock and bond prices are affected, as are any other price, by supply and demand. Foreign inflows of capital into U.S. financial markets can help raise U.S. stock and bond prices, giving U.S. investors better returns on their own investment. Of course, money can flow out, too. If foreign investors sell their U.S. security holdings, this can lead to lower security prices and lower, even negative, returns to U.S. investors.

Pessimism about the strength of the U.S. dollar can even lead to higher U.S. interest rates on everything from Treasury bills to home mortgages. Here's how this can happen, using a Japanese

investor as an example. A Japanese investor will compare U.S. and Japanese interest rates before deciding to, say, buy Japanese government debt or U.S. Treasury bonds. But, in addition to looking at U.S. interest rates, the Japanese investor will also consider the expected change in the U.S. dollar exchange rate with the Japanese yen. If the U.S. dollar is expected to weaken against the yen, this means the Japanese investor's U.S. dollar investment may lose value by the time it is converted back to yen at maturity. To be attractive, U.S. interest rates will have to be higher to compensate the Japanese investor for the falling dollar.

Suppose interest rates in Japan are 1% and economists predict the U.S. dollar will fall in value against the yen by 3% in the next year. That means Japanese investors will not find U.S. bonds attractive unless their interest rate is at least 1% (the Japanese interest rate) plus 3% (the expected loss in the value of the U.S. dollar), or 4%. If the dollar is expected to fall by 5%, U.S. interest rates will have to be 6% (1% + 5%) to attract Japanese investors. A falling or weaker dollar puts upward pressure on interest rates throughout the U.S. economy.

A **multinational corporation** is a firm that engages in international business activities such as selling goods and services in foreign countries or purchasing goods and services from providers in foreign countries. U.S. firms conducting business internationally are concerned about the value of the U.S. dollar relative to the values of other currencies. A higher U.S. dollar relative to, say, the euro makes U.S. products and services more costly than their eurozone competitors in eurozone member countries. Thus, a higher U.S. dollar is likely to result in lower export levels and higher import levels.

Firms that have foreign sales must be concerned with the stability of the governments and changing values of currency in the countries in which they do business. They must also pay attention to commodity price changes and other uncertainties related to monetary systems. Multinational corporations may also be faced with ethical situations that must be addressed. While our focus here is on business corporations, individuals and institutional investors engaged in international business activities also face many of the same trade and currency-related issues.

6.5 CONDUCTING BUSINESS INTER-NATIONALLY

multinational corporation
a firm that engages in international business activities such as selling or purchasing goods and services involving foreign countries

6.5.1   EXCHANGE RATE DEVELOPMENTS FOR THE U.S. DOLLAR

The dollar continues to be an important currency for international commercial and financial transactions. Because of this, both the United States and the rest of the world benefit from a strong and stable U.S. dollar. Its strength and stability depend directly on the ability of the United States to pursue non-inflationary economic policies. In the late 1960s and the 1970s, the United States failed to meet this objective. Continuing high inflation led to a dollar crisis in 1978, which threatened the stability of international financial markets.

Figure 6.2 shows the strength of the U.S. dollar relative to an index of major currencies (Canada, European eurozone countries, Japan, Sweden, Switzerland, and the United Kingdom) for the 1984 through 2018 period. As inflation was brought under control in the early 1980s and economic growth accelerated after the 1981–1982 recession, the dollar rose against other major currencies until it reached record highs in 1985. As discussed, relatively higher economic growth and relatively lower inflation rates lead to a relatively stronger currency. These economic developments, coupled with a favorable political climate, caused the value of the dollar to rise sharply.

However, the renewed strength of the dollar contributed to a worsening of the trade imbalance, because import prices were effectively reduced while exported U.S. goods became less cost competitive. Beginning in 1985, United States economic growth slowed relative to economic growth in other developed countries. Also, the belief that the U.S. government wanted the dollar to decline on a relative basis so as to reduce the trade deficit contributed to a decline in the desirability of holding dollars. This resulted in a major shift toward holding more foreign assets and fewer U.S. assets. As a consequence, the dollar's value declined by 1987 to levels below those in place when flexible exchange rates were reestablished in 1973. Between 1987 and 2000, the value of the dollar in international exchange fluctuated within a fairly narrow range compared to the 1980–1987 period.

CRISIS The U.S. dollar appreciated relative to other currencies in 2000 and 2001. Stock prices peaked in 2000 and then began declining rapidly as the "Internet/tech" bubble burst. Declining stock

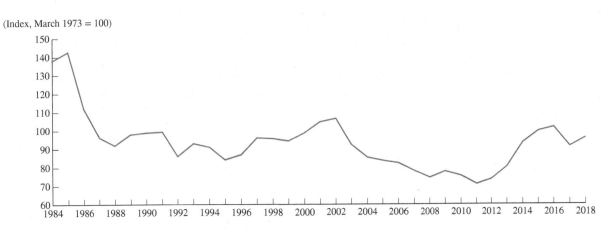

(Index, March 1973 = 100)

FIGURE 6.2
U.S. dollar value relative to an index of major currencies

prices were followed by a recession in 2001 and the terrorist attack on September 11, 2001. After first raising interest rates, the Federal Reserve moved quickly to reduce interest rates and to provide liquidity in the financial markets. The Fed then continued its high liquidity, low interest rate environment throughout the remainder of the decade. This financial markets environment was accompanied by large amounts of borrowing by business firms, financial institutions, and individuals.

Housing prices peaked in 2006, stock prices peaked in 2007, the financial crisis developed in 2007–2008, and the U.S. economy entered the Great Recession in 2008–2009. Debt-heavy individuals began defaulting on their home mortgages, financial institutions were finding it difficult to remain solvent, and business firms were failing during this "perfect financial storm." These economic developments were accompanied by a rapid decline of the U.S. dollar against an index of major currencies beginning in 2002. Figure 6.2 shows this decline generally continuing until it reached a bottom in 2011. Since then, the U.S. dollar peaked in 2016 before declining to below the 100 index level in 2017 and 2018.

In contrast, a stronger dollar leads to concern about the deficit in the U.S. trade balance, but at the same time it offers hope of lower inflation. A stronger dollar results in more imports of foreign merchandise since it requires fewer dollars for purchases. Just as a U.S. tourist abroad finds it cheaper to travel when the dollar is strong, importers find prices lower when their dollars increase in relative strength. When the dollar weakens, inflation may follow, countered by a reduced balance of trade deficit. We discuss balance of trade and balance of payments implications in the last section of this chapter.

6.5.2 MANAGING CURRENCY EXCHANGE RISK

currency exchange rate risk the price risk associated with fluctuating exchange rates over time

Currency exchange rate risk is the price risk associated with fluctuating exchange rates over time. For example, a business transaction (involving, say, the purchase of goods from a foreign manufacturer) conducted at today's U.S. dollar to euro exchange rate with payment being due immediately would not be subjected to a currency exchange rate risk. However, when the date of the transaction precedes the payment date, the U.S. dollar to euro exchange rate relationship could change, causing the final results of the transaction to be more costly (or less costly).

While multinational corporations, as well as individuals and institutional investors, may engage in foreign exchange speculation as opportunities arise, risk reduction is their primary goal. Among the possible actions of foreign exchange specialists are hedging, adjusting accounts receivable and payable procedures, cash management, and borrowing and lending activities. Existing or anticipated variations in the value of foreign currencies guide all these actions.

hedging action taken to reduce risk or insure against a possible negative outcome

Hedging is an action taken to reduce risk or insure against a possible negative outcome. A multinational corporation may want to lock in an exchange rate at which a currency can be obtained at in the future. For example, a multinational corporation with a claim for payment within 90 days may anticipate a possible decline in the currency value of the customer's country. The seller can hedge by entering into a financial contract for the delivery of that currency at the existing exchange rate on the day of the contract. To accomplish the hedge, the multinational corporation might enter into a **forward contract** that specifies the currencies to be exchanged, an exchange rate, and a future date when the transaction will be completed. The exchange rate specified in the forward contract is called the **forward rate**. The terms of the forward contract are established between the multinational corporation and a bank or other institutional foreign exchange dealer. Other financial instruments available for currency hedging activities include currency futures contracts and currency options contracts.[4]

forward contract specifies the currencies to be exchanged, an exchange rate, and a future date when the transaction will be completed

forward rate exchange rate specified in the forward contract

Large multinational corporations enjoy special opportunities for risk reduction and speculation since they can move cash balances from one country to another as monetary conditions warrant. For example, if a decline in the value of a particular currency is expected, cash in the branch in that country may be moved back to the United States, or a firm may borrow funds in a foreign market and move them immediately to the United States (or to another country) with the expectation of repaying the loan at a reduced exchange rate. This is speculation rather than a risk-reduction activity. An expected decline

---

[4] We discuss the use of forward contracts in the Learning Extension at the end of this chapter. Futures and options contracts are covered in the Learning Extension at the end of Chapter 11.

in a currency may lead to an attempt to accelerate collection of accounts receivable, with funds transferred quickly to another country. Payments on accounts payable may be delayed in the expectation of a decline in exchange rates. If, on the other hand, a foreign currency is expected to increase in relative value, the preceding actions would be reversed.

Career opportunities have developed with the increasing importance of multinational financial management. Some corporations maintain special departments to study foreign business activities and their prospective profitability; for example, to analyze governmental attitudes, tax rates, and duties, as well as to determine how foreign operations are to be financed. In addition, to protect bank balances and other investments, almost constant attention must be given to day-to-day exchange rate changes.

6.5.3 ETHICAL CONSIDERATIONS

ETHICAL The concept of acceptable ethical behavior differs across cultures and countries. In some primarily developing countries, it seems to be acceptable practice for government officials and others to request "side" payments and even bribes as a means for foreign companies being able to do business in these countries. This is morally wrong. In addition, the Foreign Corrupt Practices Act (FCPA) prohibits U.S. firms from bribing foreign officials. For violators of the FCPA, the U.S. Justice Department may impose monetary penalties, and criminal proceedings may be brought against violators. Government actions may result in lost reputations and firm values.

For example, Titan Corporation had its proposed 2004 sale to Lockheed Martin Corporation implode because it could not promptly resolve a bribery investigation brought by the Justice Department. Another example was the 2004 indictment of two former HealthSouth Corporation executives for conspiracy in a bribery scheme involving a Saudi Arabian hospital. An attempt was made to conceal the bribery by setting up a bogus consulting contract for the director general of the Saudi foundation that owned the hospital. The former HealthSouth executives were indicted after a Justice Department investigation alleged that they had violated the *U.S. Travel Act* by using interstate commerce when making the bribes and the FCPA by falsely reflecting the bogus bribe payments as legitimate consulting expenses on HealthSouth's financial statements.

When conducting business activities in certain foreign countries, business executives also are sometimes faced with extortion demands by organized criminals. Most of us would agree that extortion payments are morally wrong. Paying organized criminals is not different from paying corrupt government officials.

GLOBAL One of the substantial financial burdens of any industrial firm is the process of manufacture itself. When a U.S. manufacturer exports goods to distant places such as India or Australia, funds are tied up not only for the period of manufacture but also for a lengthy period of transportation. To reduce costs, manufacturers may require the foreign importer to pay for the goods as soon as they are on the way to their destination. In this way, a substantial financial burden is transferred to the importer.

| **6.6 FINANCING INTERNATIONAL TRADE** |

6.6.1 FINANCING BY THE EXPORTER

If the exporter has confidence in foreign customers and is in a financial position to sell to them on an open-book account, then sales arrangements should operate very much as in domestic trade, subject, of course, to the complex nature of any international transaction.

6.6.1.1 Sight and Time Drafts

As an alternative to shipping merchandise on open-account financing, the exporter may use a collection draft. A **draft** or **bill of exchange** is an unconditional written order, signed by the party drawing it, requiring the party to whom it is addressed to pay a certain sum of money to order or to bearer. A draft may require immediate payment by the importer upon its presentation – on demand – or it may require only acceptance on the part of the importer, providing for payment at a specified future time. An instrument requiring immediate payment is classified as a **sight draft**; one requiring payment later is a

draft (bill of exchange) an unconditional order for the payment of money from one person to another

sight draft draft requiring immediate payment

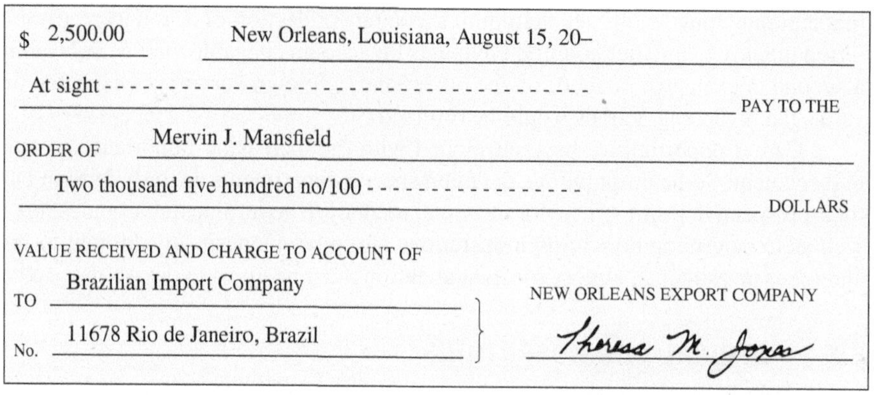

$ 2,500.00	New Orleans, Louisiana, August 15, 20–

At sight - PAY TO THE

ORDER OF   Mervin J. Mansfield

Two thousand five hundred no/100 - - - - - - - - - - - - - - - - DOLLARS

VALUE RECEIVED AND CHARGE TO ACCOUNT OF

TO   Brazilian Import Company   NEW ORLEANS EXPORT COMPANY

No.   11678 Rio de Janeiro, Brazil   *Theresa M. Jones*

FIGURE 6.3 Sight draft or bill of exchange

time draft draft that is payable at a specified future date

documentary draft draft that is accompanied by an order bill of lading and other documents

order bill of lading document given by a transportation company that lists goods to be transported and terms of the shipping agreement

clean draft a draft that is not accompanied by any special documents

time draft. A draft may require remittance, or payment, in the currency of the country of the exporter or of the importer, depending on the transaction's terms. An example of a sight draft form is shown in Figure 6.3.

Drafts may be either documentary or clean. A **documentary draft** is accompanied by an order bill of lading along with other papers such as insurance receipts, certificates of sanitation, and consular invoices. The **order bill of lading** (see Figure 6.4) represents the written acceptance of goods for shipment by a transportation company and the terms under which the goods are to be transported to their destination. In addition, the order bill of lading carries title to the merchandise being shipped, and only its holder may claim the merchandise from the transportation company. The documentary sight draft is generally referred to as a D/P draft (documentary payments draft), and the documentary time draft is referred to as a D/A draft (documentary acceptance draft).

A **clean draft** is one that is not accompanied by any special documents and is generally used when the exporter has confidence in the importer's ability to meet the draft when presented. Once the merchandise is shipped to the importer, it is delivered by the transportation company, regardless of any actions by the importer in terms of the draft.

6.6.1.2 Bank Assistance in the Collection of Drafts

An importer will generally try to avoid paying for a purchase before the goods are actually shipped, because several days or perhaps weeks may elapse before the goods arrive. But the exporter is often unwilling to send the draft and documents directly to the importer. Therefore, the exporter usually works through a commercial bank.

A New York exporter dealing with an importer in Portugal with whom there has been little experience may ship goods on the basis of a documentary draft that has been deposited for collection with the local bank. That bank, following the specific instructions regarding the manner of collection, forwards the draft and the accompanying documents to its correspondent bank in Lisbon. The correspondent bank holds the documents until payment is made in the case of a sight draft, or until acceptance is obtained if a time draft is used. When collection is made on a sight draft, it is remitted to the exporter.

6.6.1.3 Financing Through the Exporter's Bank

It is important to recognize that throughout the preceding transaction the banking system only provided a service to the exporter and in no way financed the transaction itself. The exporter's bank, however, may offer financing assistance by allowing the exporter to borrow against the security of a documentary draft. Such loans have the financial strength of both the exporter and the importer to support them, since documents for taking possession of the merchandise are released only after the importer has accepted the draft.

The amount that the exporter can borrow is less than the face amount of the draft and depends mainly on the credit standing of both the exporter and the importer. When the exporter is financially strong enough to offer suitable protection to the bank, a substantial percentage of the draft may be advanced even though the importer may not be known to the exporter's bank. In other cases, the advance may be based on the importer's financial strength.

FIGURE 6.4 Order bill of lading

UNITED STATES LINES CO.

(SPACES IMMEDIATELY BELOW FOR SHIPPERS MEMORANDA– NOT PART OF BILL OF LADING)

FORWARDING AGENT – REFERENCES	EXPORT DEC. No.
John Doe Shipping Co., #E6776 F.M.B. #9786	X67-90687

DELIVERING CARRIER TO STEAMER:	CAR NUMBER – REFERENCE
Penn Central Company	876528

BILL OF LADING
(SHORT FORM)

(NOT NEGOTIABLE UNLESS CONSIGNED "TO ORDER")

SHIP American Banker — FLAG AM. — PIER 61 N.R. — PORT OF LOADING NEW YORK

PORT OF DISCHARGE FROM SHIP (Where goods are to be delivered to consignee or On-carrier) Liverpool

THROUGH BILL OF LADING

If goods to be transhipped beyond Port of Discharge, show destination Here ⟶ To

SHIPPER Midwest Printing Company

CONSIGNED TO: ORDER OF M.T. Wilson & Co.

ADDRESS ARRIVAL NOTICE TO Same at 15 Dock St., Liverpool, E.C. 3

PARTICULARS FURNISHED BY SHIPPER OF GOODS

MARKS AND NUMBERS	NO. OF PKGS.	DESCRIPTION OF PACKAGES AND GOODS	MEASUREMENT	GROSS WEIGHT IN POUNDS
M. T. W. & Co. Liverpool	56	Books		10,145

SPECIMEN

FREIGHT PAYABLE IN NEW YORK

(10,145) @ ____ PER 2240 LBS........$			
____ @ ____ PER 100 LBS..........$			
____ FT. @ ____ PER 40 CU. FT.......$			
545 FT. @ $1.05 PER CU. FT............$	572	25	
$			
$			
$			
$			
TOTAL................$			

(TERMS OF THIS BILL OF LADING CONTINUED FROM REVERSE SIDE HEREOF)

IN WITNESS WHEREOF, THE MASTER OR AGENT OF SAID VESSEL HAS SIGNED........3

BILLS OF LADING, ALL OF THE SAME TENOR AND DATE, ONE OF WHICH BEING ACCOMPLISHED, THE OTHERS TO STAND VOID.

UNITED STATES LINES COMPANY

BY J.H. FOR THE MASTER

ISSUED AT NEW YORK, N.Y.

B/L No. M-105

January 12 20--
MO. DAY YEAR

The character of the goods shipped also has an important bearing on the amount lent, since the goods offer collateral security for the advance. Goods that are not breakable or perishable are better as collateral; goods for which there is a ready market are preferable to those with a very limited market.

6.6.2 FINANCING BY THE IMPORTER

Like the exporter, the importer may also arrange payment for goods without access to bank credit. When an order is placed, payment in full may be made or a partial payment offered. The partial payment gives some protection to both the exporter and the importer. It protects the exporter against rejection of the goods for no reason, and it gives the importer some bargaining power in the event the merchandise is damaged in shipment or does not meet specifications. When the importer is required to make full payment with an order but wants some protection in the transaction, payment is sent to a bank in the exporter's country. The bank is instructed not to release payment until certain documents are presented to the bank to prove shipment of the goods according to the terms of the transaction. The bank, of course, charges a fee for this service.

6.6.2.1 Financing Through the Importer's Bank

In foreign trade, because of language barriers and the difficulty in obtaining credit information about companies in foreign countries, the use of the banker's acceptance is common. The "*banker's acceptance*," which was first described in Chapter 2, is a draft drawn on and accepted by a bank rather than the importing firm. An example of a banker's acceptance is shown in Figure 6.5. The importer must, of course, make arrangements with the bank in advance.

The exporter, too, must know before shipment is made whether or not the bank in question has agreed to accept the draft. This arrangement is facilitated by the use of a **commercial letter of credit**, a bank's written statement to an individual or firm guaranteeing acceptance and payment of a draft up to a specified sum if the draft is presented according to the terms of the letter (see Figure 6.6).

commercial letter of credit a bank's written statement to an individual or firm guaranteeing acceptance and payment of a draft up to a specified sum if the draft is presented according to the terms of the letter

6.6.2.2 Importer Bank Financing – An Example

The issue of a commercial letter of credit and its use in international finance are shown in this example. The owner of a small, exclusive shop in Chicago wishes to import expensive perfumes from Paris. Although the shop is well-known locally, its financial reputation is not known widely enough to permit it to purchase from foreign exporters on the basis of an open-book account or drafts drawn on the firm. Under these circumstances, the firm would substitute the bank's credit for its own through the use of a letter of credit. Upon application by the firm, the bank issues the letter if it is entirely satisfied that its customer is in a satisfactory financial condition.

The letter of credit is addressed to the French exporter of perfumes. The exporter, upon receipt of the commercial letter of credit, would not be concerned about making the shipment. Although the exporter may not have heard of the Chicago firm, the bank issuing the commercial letter of credit may be known to the exporter or to his bank. (International bank directories provide bank credit information.) The French exporter then ships the perfumes and at the same time draws a draft in the appropriate amount on the bank that issued the letter of credit. The draft and the other papers required by the commercial letter of credit are presented to the exporter's bank. The bank sends the draft and the accompanying documents to its New York correspondent, who forwards them to the importer's bank in Chicago. The importer's bank thoroughly inspects the papers that accompany the draft to make sure that all provisions of the letter of credit have been met. If the bank is satisfied, the draft is accepted and the appropriate bank officials sign it. The accepted draft, now a banker's acceptance, may be held until maturity by the accepting bank or returned to the exporter on request. If the acceptance is returned to the exporter, it may be held until maturity and sent to the accepting

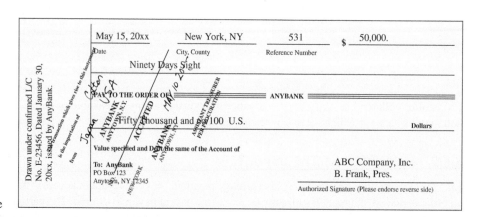

FIGURE 6.5 Banker's acceptance

Irrevocable Commercial Letter Of Credit

AnyBank
P.O. Box 123
Anytown, New York 12345

AnyBank

Cable Address: AnyBank

Letter Of Credit Division

May 2, 20--

$50,000.

Drafts drawn hereunder must be marked
"Drawn under AnyBank Anytown
L/C Ref. E-23456 "and indicate the date hereof

ABC Company, Inc.

B. Frank, President

SPECIMEN

Gentlemen:
We hereby authorize you to draw on AnyBank, Anytown

by order of J. R. Doe & Company, New York, N.Y.

and for account of J. R. Doe & Company

up to an aggregate amount of Fifty Thousand Dollars U.S. Currency

available by your drafts at 90 days sight, for full invoice value, in duplicate
accompanied by Commercial Invoice in triplicate . . .
Consular Invoice in duplicate . . .
Full set of onboard Bills of Lading to order of AnyBank,
Anytown, marked Notify J. R. Doe & Company, New York, N.Y., and bearing
a separate onboard endorsement signed by the Master and also marked
freight collect at port of destination . . . .

Relating to shipment of Cotton.

. . . Any charges for negotiation of the draft(s) are for your account.
. . . Marine and war risk insurance covered by buyers.

Drafts must be drawn and negotiated not later than October 2, 20--

The amounts thereof must be endorsed on this Letter Of Credit.
We hereby agree with the drawers, endorsers, and bonafide holders of all drafts drawn under and in compliance with the terms of this credit, that such drafts will be duly honored upon presentation to the drawee.
This letter of credit is subject to the Uniform Customs and Practice for Documentary Credits (1974 Revision) International Chamber Of Commerce Publication No. 290.

Yours very truly,

D.E. Price

D. E. Price
Vice President
Authorized Signature

FIGURE 6.6 Irrevocable commercial letter of credit

bank for settlement or it may be sold to other investors. An active market for bankers' acceptances exists in the world's money centers.

After having accepted the draft, the Chicago bank notifies its customer that it has the shipping documents and that arrangements should be made to take them over. As the shop sells the perfume, it builds up its bank account with daily deposits until it is sufficient to retire the acceptance. The bank can then meet its obligation on the acceptance without having advanced its other funds at any time.

In releasing shipping documents to a customer, some banks prefer to establish an agency arrangement between the firm and the bank whereby the bank retains title to the merchandise. The instrument that provides for this is called a **trust receipt**. Should the business fail, the bank would not be in the position of an ordinary creditor trying to establish its claim on the business assets. Rather, it could repossess, or take back, the goods and place them with another agent for sale since title had never been transferred to the customer. As the merchandise is sold under a trust receipt arrangement, generally, the business must deposit the proceeds with the bank until the total amount of the acceptance is reached.

trust receipt an instrument through which a bank retains title to goods until they are paid for

In summary, the banker's acceptance and the commercial letter of credit involve four principal parties: the importer, the importer's bank, the exporter, and the exporter's bank. Each benefits to a substantial degree through this arrangement. The importer benefits by securing adequate credit. The importer's bank benefits because it receives a fee for issuing the commercial letter of credit and for the other services provided in connection with it. The exporter benefits by being assured that payment will be made for the shipment of merchandise. Thus, a sale is made that might otherwise have been rejected because of lack of guaranteed payment. Finally, the exporter's bank benefits if it discounts the acceptance, since it receives a high-grade credit instrument with a definite, short-term maturity. Acceptances held by commercial banks provide a low, but certain, yield, and banks can liquidate them quickly if funds are needed for other purposes.

6.6.3 BANKER'S ACCEPTANCE

banker's acceptance a promise of future payment issued by a firm and guaranteed by a bank

The Board of Governors of the Federal Reserve System authorizes member banks to accept drafts that arise in the course of certain types of international transactions. These include the import and export of goods, the shipment of goods between foreign countries, and the storage of highly marketable staple goods in any foreign country. A **banker's acceptance** is a promise of future payment issued by a firm and guaranteed by a bank. The maturity of a banker's acceptance arising out of international transactions may not exceed six months. This authority to engage in banker's acceptance financing is intended to encourage banks to participate in financing international trade and to strengthen the U.S. dollar abroad.

Bankers' acceptances are used to finance international transactions on a wide variety of items, including coffee, wool, rubber, cocoa, metals and ores, crude oil, jute, and automobiles. Because of the growth of international trade in general and the increasing competition in foreign markets, banker's acceptances have become increasingly important. Exporters have had to offer more liberal terms on their sales to compete effectively. The banker's acceptance permits them to do so without undue risk.

The cost of financing an international transaction with the banker's acceptance involves not only the interest cost involved in the exporter's discounting the acceptance but also the commission charge of the importer's accepting bank. Foreign central banks and commercial banks regard banker's acceptances as attractive short-term funds commitments. In recent years, foreign banks have held more than one-half of all dollar-denominated banker's acceptances, with most of the remainder held by domestic banks. Nonfinancial corporations have played only a small role as investors in acceptances. Relatively few firms deal in banker's acceptances. These dealers arrange nearly simultaneous exchanges of purchases and sales.

6.6.4 OTHER AIDS TO INTERNATIONAL TRADE

6.6.4.1 The Export-Import Bank

Export Import bank bank established to aid in financing and facilitating trade between the United States and other countries

The **Export-Import Bank** was authorized in 1934 and became an independent agency of the government in 1945. The bank's purpose is to help finance and facilitate exports and imports between the United States and other countries. It is the only U.S. agency engaged solely in financing foreign trade.

The Export-Import Bank is a government-owned corporation with capital of $1 billion in nonvoting stock paid in by the U.S. Treasury. It may borrow from the Treasury on a revolving basis and sell short-term discount promissory notes. It pays interest on these loans and dividends on the capital stock. In performing its function, the bank makes long-term loans to private enterprises and governments abroad to finance the purchase of U.S. equipment, goods, and services. The Export-Import Bank also aids substantially in the economic development of foreign countries by giving emergency credits to assist them in maintaining their level of U.S. imports during temporary balance-of-payments difficulties. In addition, the bank finances or guarantees the payment of medium-term commercial export credit extended by exporters and, in partnership with private insurance companies, offers short- and medium-term credit insurance. It lends and guarantees only where repayment is reasonably assured and avoids competition with sources of private capital.

6.6.4.2 Traveler's Letter of Credit

A firm's buyer who is traveling abroad may not know in advance from which individuals or firms purchases will be made – for example, an art buyer touring several countries. The buyer could carry U.S. currency, but this involves possible physical loss of the money and sometimes a substantial discount for its conversion into the local currency. A traveler's letter of credit is a convenient and safer method for travelers who need large amounts of foreign currency.

The **traveler's letter of credit** is issued by a bank in one country and addressed to a list of foreign banks. These banks are usually correspondents of the issuing bank and have agreed to purchase sight drafts presented to them by persons with appropriate letters of credit. When a bank issues a letter of credit, it sends a copy of the signature of the person to whom the letter is issued to each of its foreign correspondent banks. When someone presents a draft for payment in foreign currency to one of these correspondent banks, his or her signature is compared with the signature the bank already has. The bank may also ask the individual for supplementary identification.

As with a commercial letter of credit, a maximum total draft amount is stated in a traveler's letter of credit. So that an individual with such a letter does not exceed authorized withdrawals, each bank to which the letter is presented enters on it the amount of the draft it has honored.

> **traveler's letter of credit** issued by a bank to banks in other countries authorizing them to cash checks or purchase drafts presented by the bearer

6.6.4.3 Traveler's Checks

Traveler's checks, which are offered by banks and other financial intermediaries in the United States, are generally issued in several different denominations. These checks, generally purchased by an individual before leaving for a foreign country, promise to pay on demand the even amounts indicated on the face of the checks. Each check must be signed by the purchaser twice, once when it is bought and again in the presence of a representative of the business, hotel, or financial institution where it is presented for payment. This allows the person cashing a traveler's check to determine whether the signature is authentic.

The use of traveler's checks is widespread and offers several advantages to the traveler, including protection in the event of loss and almost certain acceptance when they are presented for payment. Traveler's checks are usually sold for their face amount plus a charge of 1%. They can now be purchased in the United States in major foreign currency denominations – for example, British pounds. This eliminates a traveler's exposure to varying exchange rates and the extra amount that is often charged (in the form of a less favorable exchange rate than the official rate) when U.S. dollar checks are cashed in a foreign country.

> **DISCUSSION QUESTION 3**
>
> **What are the risks associated with buying a product directly from a foreign manufacturer?**

GLOBAL Just as monetary policy plays an important role in the nation's stability, growth, interest rates, and price levels, it also helps keep international financial relationships in balance. Since the dollar is widely held as a medium of international exchange, U.S. monetary policy has especially significant effects on the world economy. No nation is a world unto itself, nor can a nation pursue whatever policies it desires without regard to other nations. Policy makers of all economies must recognize the interdependence of their actions in attempting to maintain a balance in international transactions that is sometimes referred to as international financial equilibrium.

Briefly, the nations of the world attempt to achieve international financial equilibrium by maintaining a balance in their exchange of goods and services. In general, international trade benefits all countries involved. Consumers benefit by getting lower-cost goods, since the goods come from the country where they are produced most efficiently. Producers benefit by expanding their markets. The national incomes of countries benefit from selling goods to foreigners. Likewise, a portion of the products sought by individuals can be met through possibly less-costly imports. However, individuals, firms, and governments make decisions to import and export, and problems arise if they are out of balance over time.

> **6.7 DEVELOP-MENTS IN U.S. INTERNATIONAL TRANSACTIONS**

trade tariff tax on imports of goods and services

When one country consistently imports more goods and services from another country or countries than it exports to them, certain actions may be undertaken to attempt to bring the total amounts of exports and imports into balance. A "trade tariff" is a tax on imports of goods and services. Imports are restricted due to increased prices for foreign products and services relative to domestic alternatives. While the use of trade tariffs may seem to be a sound way of balancing the amounts of imports and exports, the country that is having its exports taxed might retaliate by imposing its own trade tariffs on its imports. The result might be an overall decrease in trade between the involved countries.

Another alternative is to try to negotiate, or re-negotiate, trade arrangements or agreements between countries that trade with each other so as to bring total exports and imports into acceptable balances. Bilateral or multi-lateral trade agreements might include protecting domestic production, the opening of new markets to participants, and intellectual property protections.

6.7.1 INTERNATIONAL BUSINESS ISSUES

Exports are sales to foreigners; they are a source of income to domestic producers. Imports divert spending to foreign producers and, therefore, represent a loss of potential income to domestic producers. When the two are in balance there is no net effect on total income in the economy. However, an increase in exports over imports tends to expand the economy just as an increase in investment or government spending does. An excess of imports tends to contract the economy.

As in the domestic economy, goods and services are not exchanged directly in international trade; payment flows through monetary or financial transactions. Methods of making payments and financing international trade were discussed previously. Other short- and long-term lending and investment is conducted across national boundaries on a large scale. In addition, government grants for both military and civilian purposes and private gifts and grants are sources of international financial flows. These flows can have an important impact on domestic economies and may affect monetary policy.

Since producers, consumers, and investors in different countries use different currencies, the international financial system requires a mechanism for establishing the relative values, or exchange rates, among currencies and for handling their actual exchange. Under the system of *flexible exchange rates* that began in 1973, rates are determined in the actual process of exchange: by supply and demand in the foreign exchange market. This system reduces the impact of international financial transactions on domestic money supplies. Still, changes in exchange rates do affect imports and exports and can, thus, affect domestic production, incomes, and prices. International financial markets strongly influence domestic interest rates, and vice versa, so that domestic monetary policy still involves international considerations.

Domestic economies are linked to one another in a worldwide economic and financial system, and the United States has played a leading role in the development of the system. We next turn our attention to international transaction details.

6.7.2 BALANCE-OF-PAYMENTS ACCOUNTS

balance of payments record of the transactions between one country and all other countries over a specific period

balance of trade net value of a country's exports of goods and services compared to its imports

merchandise trade balance net difference between a country's import and export of goods

The balance of payments is a record of the transactions between one country and all other countries over a specific period, such as a year. The U.S. balance of payments involves all of its international transactions, including foreign investment, private and government grants, U.S. military spending overseas, and many other items besides the buying and selling of goods and services. The most important component of the balance of payments is the balance of trade, which is the net balance of exports and imports of goods and services. A more narrow view considers only the import and export of goods and is termed the merchandise trade balance. The merchandise trade balance was positive for the U.S. during the 1950s and 1960s. However, imports of goods have consistently exceeded exports since the latter part of the 1970s.

The following are exports, imports, and balance on goods amounts in billions of dollars for selected years at the beginning of each decade starting with 1980 and ending with 2010, plus data for 2017.

Year	Exports	Imports	Balance on Goods
1980	$224.3	−$249.8	−$25.5
1990	387.4	−498.4	−111.0
2000	772.0	−1,224.4	−452.4
2010	1,288.7	−1,934.6	−645.9
2017	1,553.4	2,360.9	−807.5

Source: *Economic Report of the President* and https://www.bea.gov.

It can be seen that exports of goods increased nearly six times, from $224.3 billion in 1980 to $1,288.7 billion in 2010. However, over the same period, imports of goods increased nearly eight times, from $249.8 billion in 1980 to $1,934.6 billion in 2010, and the balance on goods grew from −$25.5 billion in 1980 to −$645.9 billion in 2010. And, by 2017, the importing over exporting of goods continued to grow, resulting in a net balance of −$807.5 billion.

Factors that impact international trade balances include the exchange value of the U.S. dollar relative to other currencies, relative inflation rates, and economic growth. A relatively stronger U.S. economy means that more will be spent on imports, while the weaker foreign economy means that less will be spent on U.S. exports. A relatively weaker real exchange rate, where the nominal exchange rate is adjusted for inflation differences, makes for a weaker U.S. dollar, which lowers the dollar cost of U.S. goods relative to foreign goods.

Table 6.3 shows the U.S. balance of payments statement (also referred to as U.S. international transactions) for 2017. Balances are shown for the current account, capital account, and financial

TABLE 6.3   U.S. Balance of Payments or International Transactions in 2017 ($ Billions)

	Amount
Current Account	
Goods and services	
Exports	$2,351.1
Imports	$2,903.3
Balance on goods and services (exports less imports)	−552.2
Primary income, net	221.7
Secondary income (current transfers), net	−118.6
Balance on current account	−449.1
Capital Account	
Capital transfer receipts and other credits	24.7
Capital transfer payments and other debits	0.0
Balance on capital account (receipts less payments), net	24.7
Financial Account	
U.S. acquisition of financial assets, net	1,182.7
U.S. incurrence of liabilities, net	1537.7
Financial derivatives, net	23.1
Balance on financial account (assets less liabilities plus derivatives)	−331.9
Balances	
Net borrowing from current account plus capital account balances	−424.4
Net borrowing from financial account balances	−331.9
Statistical discrepancy (net financial balances less net current & capital balances)	92.5

Note: the statistical discrepancy is the difference between the total of the current account plus capital account balances relative to the financial account balances.

Source: https://www.bea.gov/.

current account summary of the flow of funds between one country and all other countries involving the sale and purchase of goods and services plus funds from income-generating financial assets during a specified period

capital account summary of the flow of funds between one country and all other countries involving the transfer of financial assets across country borders during a specified time period

financial account summary of the flow of funds between one country and all other countries involving foreign investments in fixed assets and financial assets during a specified time period

account. Positive numbers reflect inflows of funds while negative numbers reflect outflows of funds. The current account is a summary of the flow of funds between one country and all other countries involving the sale and purchase of goods and services plus funds from income-generating financial assets during a specified period. The balance of goods and services was –$552.2 billion for 2017. We reported above that the balance on goods for 2017 was –$807.5 billion. Because the U.S. exports more services than it imports, exports less imports for both goods and services was only –$552.2 billion. By adding net primary income (interest, dividends, debt repayments, etc. from foreign investments in securities) of $221.7 billion and net secondary income (U.S. government and private transfers, including government grants and pensions and insurance-related transfers) of –$118.6 billion, results in a net current account of –$449.1 billion.

The capital account is a summary of the flow of funds between one country and all other countries involving the transfer of financial assets across country borders during a specified time period. Included are transfers of patent values and financial assets by individuals who move to another country. As currently defined, the capital account balance has a minor impact on the balance of payments. Table 6.3 shows that for 2017 capital transfer receipts were $24.7 billion and since capital transfer payments were near zero, the balance on capital account was $24.7 billion. Adding the balance on the current account and the balance on the capital account resulted in a net borrowing from current account and capital account transactions of –$424.4 billion.

The financial account is a summary of the flow of funds between one country and all other countries involving foreign investments in fixed assets and financial assets during a specified time period. Included are business direct foreign investment (e.g., construction of fixed assets and acquisitions of foreign companies), portfolio investments (stock and bond investments in foreign companies), and other capital investments (e.g., short-term foreign securities). Table 6.3, under the financial account heading, shows the net U.S. acquisition of financial assets (excluding financial derivatives), net U.S. incurrence of liabilities (excluding financial derivatives), and the net impact of financial derivatives. The net impact of these three accounts (acquisition of financial assets less incurrence of liabilities plus financial derivatives) resulted in a net borrowing from financial account transactions of –$331.9 billion.

Due to the difficulty in accurately measuring the flow of funds between countries, a statistical discrepancy account is used to balance cumulative differences across the current, capital, and financial accounts. For 2017, the difference between the –$331.9 billion on the financial account transactions and the –$424.4 billion on the current account and capital account transactions resulted in a statistical discrepancy of $92.5 billion.

When U.S. imports exceed exports of goods and services, a negative current account balance in the balance of payments statement occurs. To offset current account deficits, direct investments (business fixed assets and acquisitions), and portfolio investments (corporate stocks and bonds and government debt securities) by foreign businesses and governments need to be greater than the direct and portfolio investments of their U.S. counterparts. The Fed may also adjust its holdings of foreign exchange reserves when needed.

The United States has experienced a growing negative balance of trade (imports exceed exports) for many years. The current U.S. government administration has recently proposed using tariffs on imports from selected countries to protect domestic producers and to attempt to bring import and export amounts more into balance. In 2018, a new trade agreement involving the United States, Mexico, and Canada was drafted and signed. This agreement, which still needs to be ratified, is an effort to bring imports and exports more in balance across the three countries. In early 2019, the U.S. and China continue to engage in trade talks involving the dumping of below-cost products in U.S. markets, the opening of new markets in China to U.S. producers, and the need for improved intellectual property protections. While both countries have threatened the use of trade tariffs, it is hoped that such actions can be avoided. Trade discussions between the European Union countries and the U.S. also are ongoing.

- **Institutions and Markets** Commercial banks play an important role in financing international trade. Banks provide commercial letters of credit that guarantee acceptance and payment of drafts. Banker's acceptances, which are promises of future payment issued by a firm and guaranteed by a bank, also are important financial instruments that facilitate international trade. Banks throughout the world also are important participants in the electronic currency exchange markets. Traveler's letters of credit and traveler's checks are provided by financial institutions to help travelers purchase products and cover living expenses while in foreign countries.

- **Investments** Individuals and businesses interested in investing in securities issued by foreign corporations may need to use the currency exchange markets to convert U.S. dollars into the currencies of the countries where those corporations are located. Individuals traveling internationally also will need to convert their U.S. dollars into the local currencies through the aid of financial institutions. Investors may also speculate on the relative future movements of currencies through the use of spot and forward markets.

- **Financial Management** Financial managers use currency exchange markets to hedge against currency exchange risk associated with possible changes in the exchange rates between currencies. Financial managers may hedge in the forward markets or seek the aid of banks to sell unneeded currencies or to purchase currencies needed to conduct business operations. Financial managers also rely on banks and other financial institutions to aid them in their international transactions, both as importers and as exporters.

LO 6.1 The international monetary system evolved from a gold standard system to today's system of flexible exchange rates.

LO 6.2 The developments toward European economic unification began through the creation of the European Union (EU) which consisted of 28 member countries at the end of 2018. However, the future economic and financial viability of the EU will be tested by the United Kingdom's ongoing Brexit efforts to withdraw from the EU. Nineteen of the EU countries, known as eurozone members, have adopted the euro as their common currency and the European Central Bank as their central monetary policy-making authority.

LO 6.3 Currency exchange markets are electronic markets where banks and institutional traders buy and sell currencies on behalf of businesses and others, and for their own accounts. A currency exchange rate indicates the value of one currency relative to another currency.

LO 6.4 Currency exchange rates are determined by supply and demand relationships, relative inflation rates, relative interest rates, and political and economic risks.

LO 6.5 Firms that engage in international business activities, such as selling goods and services in foreign countries or purchasing goods and services from providers in foreign countries, are concerned with currency exchange rate risk, which is the risk of fluctuating currency exchange rates over time. Changes in relative exchange rates can alter the costs of exporting relative to those of importing goods and services, and can affect the profitability of international business transactions that have settlement dates in the future. Businesses have the opportunity of "hedging" against negative movements in relative exchange rates by entering into forward exchange rate contracts.

LO 6.6 Firms engaged in international business activities often have limited knowledge of the credit worthiness of their foreign counterparts, and vice versa. The world banking systems facilitate financing of sales by exporters and purchasers by importers through legal documents such as a draft (sight or time) or bill of exchange and an order bill of lading. Bank guarantees of payments take the form of a banker's acceptance or a commercial letter of credit.

LO 6.7 U.S. imports continue to exceed exports of goods and services each year. This is the primary reason for a negative current account balance in the balance of payments or international transactions statement. To offset current account deficits, direct investments (business fixed assets and acquisitions) and portfolio investments (corporate stocks and bonds and government debt securities) by foreign businesses and governments need to be greater than the comparable investments of their U.S. counterparts. The Fed may also adjust its holdings of foreign exchange reserves when needed.

KEY TERMS

arbitrage
balance of payments
balance of trade
banker's acceptance
Bretton Woods system
Brexit
capital account
clean draft
commercial letter
  of credit
currency appreciation
currency depreciation
currency exchange
  markets
currency exchange rate

currency exchange
  rate risk
current account
direct quotation method
documentary draft
draft or bill of exchange
economic risk
equilibrium exchange rate
euro
European Monetary
  Union (EMU)
European Union (EU)
eurozone members
Export-Import Bank
financial account

flexible exchange rates
foreign exchange markets
forward contract
forward rate
gold standard
hedging
indirect quotation method
international Fisher
  effect (IFE)
International Monetary
  Fund (IMF)
International
  monetary system
merchandise trade
  balance

multinational corporation
order bill of lading
political risk
purchasing power
  parity (PPP)
sight draft
special drawing
  rights (SDRs)
spot exchange rate
time draft
trade tariff
traveler's letter of credit
trust receipt
World Bank

REVIEW QUESTIONS

1. **(LO 6.1)** What is the purpose of an international monetary system?

2. **(LO 6.1)** What is meant by the statement that the international monetary system has operated mostly under a "gold standard"? What are the major criticisms associated with being on a gold standard?

3. **(LO 6.1)** Describe the Bretton Woods system for setting currency exchange rates. What are "special drawing rights" and how are they used to foster world trade?

4. **(LO 6.1)** What is an international monetary system based on "flexible exchange rates"?

5. **(LO 6.1)** Describe the international monetary system currently in use.

6. **(LO 6.2)** What is the European Union (EU)? How did it develop? Who are the current members of the EU?

7. **(LO 6.2)** What is meant by the term eurozone members? What countries are eurozone members?

8. **(LO 6.2)** What is the euro? Identify some of its distinguishing characteristics.

9. **(LO 6.2)** What types of financial crises have some countries in the European Union faced in recent years?

10. **(LO 6.3)** What are currency or foreign exchange markets? How are exchange rates quoted?

11. **(LO 6.4)** Explain the role of supply and demand in establishing exchange rates between countries. What other factors affect currency exchange rates?

12. **(LO 6.5)** How has the value of the U.S. dollar changed relative to other major currencies in recent

years? What is "hedging" and how are forward contracts used to manage foreign exchange risk?

13. **(LO 6.6)** What are sight and time drafts? Indicate how they differ.

14. **(LO 6.6)** Describe the various ways by which an exporter may finance an international shipment of goods. How may commercial banks assist the exporter in collecting drafts?

15. **(LO 6.6)** How do importers protect themselves against improper delivery of goods when they are required to make payment as they place an order?

16. **(LO 6.6)** Describe the process by which an importing firm may substitute the credit of its bank for its own credit in financing international transactions.

17. **(LO 6.6)** How may a bank protect itself after having issued a commercial letter of credit on behalf of a customer?

18. **(LO 6.6)** Describe the costs involved in connection with financing exports through banker's acceptances.

19. **(LO 6.6)** Describe the ultimate sources of funds for export financing with banker's acceptances. How are acceptances acquired for investment by these sources?

20. **(LO 6.6)** Explain the role played in international trade by the Export-Import Bank. Do you consider this bank to be in competition with private lending institutions?

21. **(LO 6.6)** Commercial letters of credit, traveler's letters of credit, and traveler's checks all play an important role in international finance. Distinguish among these three types of instruments.

22. **(LO 6.7)** Briefly indicate the problems facing the United States in its attempt to maintain international financial equilibrium.

23. **(LO 6.7)** The current account is an important component of the U.S. balance of payments. Describe the current account and indicate its major components.

24. **(LO 6.7)** Discuss the meaning of the financial account and identify its major components.

EXERCISES

1. You are the owner of a business that has offices and production facilities in several foreign countries. Your product is sold in all these countries, and you maintain bank accounts in the cities in which you have offices. At present, you have short-term notes outstanding at most of the banks with which you maintain deposits. This borrowing is to support seasonal production activity. One of the countries in which you have offices is now strongly rumored to be on the point of devaluation, or lowering, of its currency relative to that of the rest of the world. What actions might this rumor cause you to take?

2. Explain the concept of "balance" as it relates to a nation's balance of payments.

3. As an exporter of relatively expensive electronic equipment you have a substantial investment in the merchandise that you ship. Your foreign importers are typically small or medium-size firms without a long history of operations. Although your terms of sales require payment upon receipt of the merchandise, you are concerned about the possible problem of nonpayment and the need to reclaim merchandise that you have shipped. How might the banking system assist and protect you in this situation?

4. As an importer of merchandise you depend on the sale of the merchandise for funds to make payment. Although customary terms of sale are 90 days for this type of merchandise, you are not well-known to foreign suppliers because of your recent entry into business. Furthermore, your suppliers require almost immediate payment to meet their own expenses of operations. How might the banking systems of the exporter and importer accommodate your situation?

5. As a speculator in the financial markets you notice that for the last few minutes Swiss francs are being quoted in New York at a price of $0.5849 and in Frankfurt at $0.5851.
   a. Assuming that you have access to international trading facilities, what action might you take?
   b. What would be the effect of your actions and those of other speculators on these exchange rates?

6. You manage the cash for a large multinational industrial enterprise. As a result of credit sales on 90-day payment terms, you have a large claim against a customer in Mexico City. You have heard rumors of the possible devaluation of the Mexican peso. What actions, if any, can you take to protect your firm against the consequences of a prospective devaluation?

7. Assume, as the loan officer of a commercial bank, that one of your customers has asked for a commercial letter of credit to enable his firm to import a supply of well-known French wines. This customer has a long record of commercial success, yet has large outstanding debts to other creditors. In what way might you accommodate the customer and at the same time protect your bank?

8. For the entire year, the nation's balance of trade with other nations has been in a substantial deficit position, yet, as always, the overall balance of payments will be in "balance." Describe the various factors that accomplish this overall balance, in spite of the deficit in the balance of trade.

9. Assume you are the international vice president of a small U.S.-based manufacturing corporation. You are trying to expand your business in several developing countries. You are also aware that some business practices are considered to be "acceptable" in these countries but not necessarily in the United States. How would you react to the following situations?
   a. You met yesterday with a government official from one of the countries in which you would like to make sales. He said that he could speed up the process for acquiring the necessary licenses for conducting business in his country if you would pay him for his time and effort. What would you do?
   b. You are trying to make a major sale of your firm's products to the government of a foreign country. You have identified the key decision maker. You are considering offering the official a monetary payment if she would recommend buying your firm's products. What would you do?
   c. Your firm has a local office in a developing country where you are trying to increase business opportunities. Representatives from a local crime syndicate have approached you and have offered to provide "local security" in exchange for a monthly payment to them. What would you do?

PROBLEMS

1. Exchange rate relationships between the U.S. dollar and the euro have been quite volatile. When the euro began trading at the beginning of 1999, it was valued at 1.17 U.S. dollars. By late-2000, a euro was worth only $.83 and peaked at $1.60 in mid-2008. Calculate the percentage changes in the value of a euro from its initial value to its late-2000 value and to its high mid-2008 value.

2. Over a two-year period, the U.S. dollar equivalent of a euro increased from $1.3310 to $1.4116. Using the indirect quotation method, determine the currency per U.S. dollar for each of these dates.

3. Over a two-year period, the U.S. dollar equivalent of a euro increased from $1.3310 to $1.4116. Determine the percentage change of the euro between these two dates.

4. A few years ago, the U.S. dollar equivalent of a foreign currency was $1.2167. Today, the U.S. dollar equivalent of a foreign currency is $1.3310. Using the indirect quotation method, determine the currency per U.S. dollar for each of these dates.

5. A few years ago the U.S. dollar equivalent of a foreign currency was $1.2167. Today, the U.S. dollar equivalent of a foreign currency is $1.3310. Determine the percentage change of the foreign currency between these two dates.

6. If the U.S dollar value of a British pound is $1.95 and a euro is $1.55, calculate the implied value of a euro in terms of a British pound.

7. Assume a U.S. dollar is worth 10.38 Mexican pesos and 0.64 euros. Calculate the implied value of a Mexican peso in terms of a euro.

8. Assume that five years ago a euro was trading at a direct method quotation of $.8767. Also assume that this year the indirect method quotation was .8219 euros per U.S. dollar.
   a. Calculate the euro "currency per U.S. dollar" five years ago.
   b. Calculate the "U.S. dollar equivalent" of a euro this year.
   c. Determine the percentage change (appreciation or depreciation) of the U.S. dollar value of one euro between five years ago and this year.
   d. Determine the percentage change (appreciation or depreciation) of the euro currency per U.S. dollar between five years ago and this year.

9. Assume that last year the Australian dollar was trading at $.5527, the Mexican peso at $.1102, and the United Kingdom (British) pound was worth $1.4233. By this year, the U.S. dollar value of an

Australian dollar was $.7056, the Mexican peso was $.0867, and the British pound was $1.8203. Calculate the percentage appreciation or depreciation of each of these three currencies between last year and this year.

10. Assume that the Danish krone (DK) has a current U.S. dollar ($US) value of $0.18.
    a. Determine the number of DK that can be purchased with one U.S. dollar.
    b. Calculate the percentage change (appreciation or depreciation) in the Danish krone if it falls to $0.16.
    c. Calculate the percentage change (appreciation or depreciation) in the U.S. dollar if the DK falls to $0.16.

11. Assume the U.S. dollar value of the Australian dollar is $0.73 while the U.S. dollar value of the Hong Kong dollar is $0.13.
    a. Determine the number of Australian dollars that can be purchased with one U.S. dollar.
    b. Determine the number of Hong Kong dollars that can be purchased with one U.S. dollar.
    c. In U.S. dollar terms, determine how many Hong Kong dollars can be purchased with one Australian dollar.

12. Assume one U.S. dollar can currently purchase 1.316 Swiss francs. However, it has been predicted that one U.S. dollar soon will be exchangeable for 1.450 Swiss francs.
    a. Calculate the percentage change in the U.S. dollar if the exchange rate change occurs.
    b. Determine the dollar value of one Swiss franc at both of the above exchange rates.
    c. Calculate the percentage change in the dollar value of one Swiss franc based on the preceding exchange rates.

13. Assume inflation is expected to be 3% in the United States next year compared with 6% in Australia. If the U.S. dollar value of an Australian dollar is currently $0.500, what is the expected exchange rate one year from now based on purchasing power parity theory?

14. Assume inflation is expected to be 8% in New Zealand next year compared with 4% in France. If the New Zealand dollar value of a euro is $0.400, what is the expected exchange rate one year from now based on purchasing power parity theory?

15. Assume the interest rate on a one-year U.S. government debt security is currently 9.5% compared with a 7.5% on a foreign country's comparable maturity debt security. If the U.S. dollar value of the foreign country's currency is

$1.50, what is the expected exchange rate one year from now based on international Fisher effect theory?

16. Assume the interest rate in Australia on one-year government debt securities is 10% and the interest rate on Japanese one-year debt is 5%. Assume the current Australian dollar value of the Japanese yen is $0.0200. Using international Fisher effect theory parity, estimate the expected value of the Japanese yen in terms of Australian dollars one year from now.

17. **Challenge Problem** Following are currency exchange "crossrates" between pairs of major currencies. Currency crossrates include both direct and indirect methods for expressing relative exchange rates.

	U.S. Dollar	UK Pound	Swiss Franc	Japanese Yen	European Euro
European Monetary Union	1.1406	?	0.6783	0.0087	–
Japan	130.66	185.98	77.705	–	114.60
Switzerland	1.6817	2.3936	–	0.0129	?
United Kingdom	?	–	0.4178	?	0.6162
United States	–	1.4231	?	0.0077	0.8767

a. Fill in the missing exchange rates in the crossrates table.

b. If the inflation rate is expected to be 3% in the European Monetary Union and 4% in the United States next year, estimate the forward rate of one euro in U.S. dollars one year from now.

c. If the one-year government interest rate is 6% in Japan and 4% in the United Kingdom, estimate the amount of yen that will be needed to purchase one British pound one year from now.

d. Based solely on purchasing power parity theory, calculate the expected one-year inflation rate in the United States if the Swiss inflation rate is expected to be 3.5% next year and the one-year forward rate of a Swiss franc is $.6100.

e. Assume the U.S. dollar is expected to depreciate by 15% relative to the euro at the end of one year from now and the interest rate on one-year government securities in the European Monetary Union is 5.5%. What would be the current U.S. one-year government security interest rate, based solely on the use of international Fisher effect theory to forecast forward currency exchange rates?

Learning Extension 6

Forward Contracts in International Finance

LO 6.8   Explain how forward contracts can be used in global business and investing.

<table>
<tr><td>

6.8 EXCHANGE RATE RISKS IN GLOBAL BUSINESS

</td><td>

One risk that is faced by all international businesses is currency exchange rate risk, which is the risk that exchange rates may change between the time a transaction is negotiated and when the contract is due. Here are four situations that involve uncertain cash flows or returns because of fluctuating exchange rates.

</td></tr>
</table>

1. A U.S. company has to pay a supplier in Japan in 60 days, in yen. It wants to hold onto the cash as long as possible but the firm's treasurer is concerned about changing exchange rates between now and when the bill comes due.

2. A U.S. manufacturer shipped goods to Europe. It expects to receive payments, in euros, in 90 days at which time the U.S. firm will convert them to dollars. Can it "lock in" an exchange rate today?

3. A speculator believes the market's expectations about future exchange rates, as reflected in today's forward rate, are incorrect. How can they take advantage of the situation and profit – if indeed the speculator's expectations are correct?

4. A U.S. corporate treasurer is deciding whether to invest extra funds for the next few month in the United States or to invest them overseas where interest rates are higher – but where there is also the risk of changing exchange rates.

International businesses, individuals, or institutional investors involved in paying, receiving, or investing face risks from fluctuating exchange rates if the transaction involves a currency besides the "home" currency. As with most risks, the situation may work in our favor – or against us. A U.S.-based firm may receive more U.S. dollars than expected or pay fewer U.S. dollars than expected due to favorable exchange rate changes. Or exchange rates may move to decrease U.S. dollar receipts or increase our costs.

Suppose $1 can purchase 120 Japanese yen. Today, an item that costs 2.4 million yen will cost, in U.S. dollar terms,

$$2.4 \text{ million yen} \times (\$1/120 \text{ yen}) = \$20{,}000$$

But as we've seen in Chapter 6, international trade can take place over several months. Goods are ordered, manufactured, transported, shipped, and received by the customer, then inspected by the customer and accepted if everything is in proper order. During this time-consuming process, the exchange rate may change. Let's say this process takes place over 60 days. During these 60 days, suppose the dollar weakens and buys fewer yen (say, $1 will now purchase 100 yen) so that 2.4 million yen item will now cost a U.S. firm,

$$2.4 \text{ million yen} \times (\$1/100 \text{ yen}) = \$24{,}000$$

More dollars will be needed to buy the item. The yen price hasn't changed – it is still 2.4 million yen – but more dollars are needed to purchase the item since the dollar is weaker and the yen is stronger.

On the other hand, suppose over this 60-day time frame the dollar strengthens against the yen. Now, 60 days after placing the order, one dollar can purchase more yen (say, $1 can buy 150 yen), so the 2.4 million yen product will now cost a U.S. firm,

$$2.4 \text{ million yen} \times (\$1/150 \text{ yen}) = \$16,000$$

Fewer dollars will be needed to buy the item. The yen price hasn't changed – it is still 2.4 million yen – but fewer dollars are needed to purchase the item as the dollar strengthened and the yen weakened. So, if you are doing business in the United States and you wish to purchase that Japanese item – you'd like very much to place your order and then have the U.S. dollar strengthen against the yen!

The problem is that it is difficult to predict exchange rate changes. Changing trade balances, expectations of changes in inflation and interest rates between countries, political discussions, and one economy unexpectedly growing more quickly than the other can all affect the current, or spot, price of one currency in terms of the other, as well as the price of one currency in terms of another at a given date in the future – namely, the forward rate.

We learned in this chapter that the *forward rate* is the negotiated exchange rate for the purchase or sale of currency when the delivery will take place at an agreed-upon future date. Usually such agreements are made with banks that are willing to buy currency that you wish to sell or they are willing to sell the currency you wish to purchase.[5] Forward rates can be used to mitigate or reduce currency exchange rate risk and to try to profit from expected currency exchange rate changes.

HEDGING CASH FLOWS

In the case of our U.S. firm purchasing the 2.4 million yen item, the U.S. firm will seek out a partner who is willing to sell yen in exchange for dollars in 60 days. By agreeing on a specific exchange rate for a specific date, the forward contract will "lock in" the exchange rate and remove exchange rate risk from the transaction. If an Asian bank and the U.S. firm agree to exchange U.S. dollars for yen in 60 days at 125 yen to the dollar, the U.S. firm now knows its dollar cost: the Japanese product will cost,

$$2.4 \text{ million yen} \times (\$1/125 \text{ yen}) = \$19,200$$

Note that there are four requirements the U.S. firm must determine before entering this contract:

1. *Does the firm want to buy or sell currency?* In this example, the U.S. firm wants to buy Japanese yen.

2. *How much does it wish to buy or sell?* In this example, the cost of the item is 2.4 million Japanese yen, so the firm wants to buy 2.4 million Japanese yen.

3. *What is the time frame?* In this example, the U.S. firm is entering into an agreement today but will not buy the yen for 60 days.

4. *What is the forward rate?* In this example, the forward rate is agreed to be 125 yen per dollar.

In 60 days, the firm will give the bank $19,200 in order to purchase 2.4 million yen at the forward rate of 125 yen per dollar. The firm will then use the yen to complete its transaction for purchasing the Japanese product. By locking in a known exchange rate, the U.S. firm eliminates the exchange rate risk for this transaction. This is an example of using forward rates to *hedge* (the concept of hedging was introduced earlier in the chapter) or reduce the risk of changing prices – in this case, of price of

---

[5] We use forward rate to describe currency transactions to be settled on a specific date in the future that are negotiated outside of an exchange. In Chapter 11, we will review future contracts, which are similar to forward contracts except that they are traded on exchanges and are standardized. For example, the Japanese yen futures contract traded on the Chicago Mercantile Exchange is for 12,500,000 yen. As a negotiated agreement, a forward contract is more flexible and can accommodate the desired quantity to be exchanged and specific transaction dates. Also discussed in Chapter 11 are options contracts – exchange-traded contracts with a specified contract price (called a strike or exercise price) for future delivery of a specified quantity. For example, the Japanese yen options contract traded on the Chicago Merc is a contract for 12,500,000 yen.

one currency in terms of another. By locking in the exchange rate today, the U.S. firm is insuring itself against adverse moves (in this case, a weaker dollar) in the exchange rate over the next 60 days.

SPECULATING OR TAKING EDUCATED GUESSES ON EXCHANGE RATE MOVEMENTS

As another example, forward agreements can be used by speculators to try to profit from future exchange rate movements. For example, suppose Kristen, a speculator, believes that in two months the spot rate between the U.S. dollar and the euro (€) will be $1.20 per euro. Right now, the two-month forward rate is $1.25 per euro ($1.25/€), reflecting the market's expectation that the euro will be stronger than Kristen believes to be true. What can a speculator like Kristen do to take advantage of her expectations?

The way to make money speculating – in any asset, even in currencies – is to buy low and sell high. Right now, the forward rate for euros is higher ($1.25/€) than the speculator believes is appropriate. So the speculator will want to enter a forward contract to sell euros at $1.25/€ (that is, sell high). In two months, if Kristen's prediction of a $1.20/€ spot exchange rate is indeed correct, she will convert dollars to euros at $1.20/€ (buy at the lower price) and then fulfill the forward contract by selling these euros at the agreed-upon forward rate of $1.25/€. By buying euros at $1.20 and selling them at $1.25 she will gain a profit of $0.05 per euro.

For example, today she will enter a two-month forward contract to sell, say, €100,000 at $1.25/€. In two months, if her predictions are correct, she will buy €100,000 at her predicted spot rate of $1.20/€, costing her $120,000. Next, the forward contract is executed by selling the €100,000 at $1.25/€. She will receive $125,000 from selling the euros. This gives her a profit of $5,000 ($125,000 – $120,000).

Note there are four requirements for our speculator to determine before entering this contract:

1. *Is the speculator wanting to buy or sell currency?* In this example, the U.S. speculator wants to sell as the forward rate is higher than her predictions for the spot rate.

2. *How much does the speculator wish to buy or sell?* In this example, this number is determined by the speculator and how much money she wishes to put at risk.

3. *What is the time frame?* In this example, the time frame is two months. The speculator wants to take advantage of an expected difference between what she expects the spot rate to be two months from today and today's two-month forward rate.

4. *What is the forward rate?* In this example, the forward rate is agreed to be 1.25 dollars per euro.

This is a risky investment. If, for example, our speculator's expectations were incorrect and in two months the spot rate was $1.27/€ rather than $1.20/€, she would lose $2,000. That is, two months from today, to fulfill the forward contract, she would have to use $127,000 to purchase €100,000; she would then fulfill the forward contract, as she is obligated to sell €100,000 at the forward rate of $1.25/€. Fulfilling her obligation, she will receive $125,000 from the sale, which represents a loss of $2,000 on the transaction.

Let's change this example to show what would happen if the expected spot rate were *higher* than today's forward rate. The two-month forward rate is $1.25/€ but now the speculator believes in two months the spot rate will be $1.30/€. What transactions should the speculator do to profit from the difference between today's forward rate and what she expects the spot rate to be two months from now?

To buy low and sell high, the speculator will want to buy euros two months from today at today's forward rate of $1.25 per euro and sell them at the predicted spot rate of $1.30 per euro. For example, she could convert $125,000 to €100,000 in two months at today's $1.25/€ forward rate. Then she will sell the euros at the spot rate of (if her prediction is correct) $1.30/€. By buying at $1.25 and selling at $1.30 she will make a profit of $0.05 per euro. In this case, she will make a profit of $5,000.

WHERE TO INVEST?

A corporate treasurer needs to decide whether to invest funds in the United States or overseas. Forward exchange rates can be used to lock in a future exchange rate from an overseas investment. Let's suppose the current exchange rate between the U.S. dollar and the euro is €0.90/$ (or $1.111/€). Assume that the one-year interest rate in the United States is 5% and the one-year interest rate in Europe is 7%. One other piece of information we need is the one-year forward rate: let's say it is €0.87/$ (or $1.1494/€). The treasurer has $100,000 to invest – where should he invest it?

Alternative 1: If he invests the funds in the United States, after one year he will have $100,000 × 1.05 = $105,000.

Alternative 2: If he converts the funds to euros and invests in Europe, after one year he will have €96,300. That is, converting $100,000 to euros today (spot rate is €0.90/$) results in $100,000 × €0.90/$ = €90,000. After being invested at 7% for one year, they will grow to €90,000 × 1.07 = €96,300.

Is it better to have $105,000 or €96,300 after one year? That depends on the exchange rate at which the euros can be converted back to U.S. dollars. If the treasurer entered into a forward contract today to sell the €96,300 one year from today, the treasurer would be able convert the euros at the agreed-upon forward rate of €0.87/$ (or $1.1494/€, as 1/0.87 = 1.1494):

$$€96,300 \times \$1.1494/€ = \$110,687.22.^{[6]}$$

In this case, the treasurer will want to invest in Europe and lock in the one-year forward exchange rate. The combined effect of the exchange rates and European interest rate ($110,687.22) results in a larger sum than investing at the U.S. interest rate ($105,000).

Note the four requirements are met in this example:

1. *Is the investor wanting to buy or sell currency?* In this example, the treasurer wants to *sell* euros in the forward market. He will buy euros at today's spot rate, invest them for a year, and then *sell* them for dollars at the forward rate to convert the euros back to dollars.

2. *How much does the investor wish to buy or sell?* In this example, this number is determined by the treasurer and how much money the firm has to invest.

3. *What is the time frame?* In this example, the treasurer has excess funds to invest for the next year.

4. *What is the forward rate?* In this example, the forward rate is €0.87/$ (or $1.1494/€).

What if today's one-year forward rate was €0.93/$ (or $1.07527/€)? In this case, the treasurer would decide to keep the funds invested in the United States. We know that after one year his $100,000 will grow to $105,000 if he does so. If he invests in Europe, the $100,000 is converted to €90,000 at today's spot rate and invested at 7%. After one year, the treasurer will have €96,300. Thus far, this is the same as the prior example – but now we apply the forward rate of €0.93/$ (or $1.07527/€).

Converting the euros back to dollars, the treasurer will have €96,300 × $1.07527/€ = $103,548.50. In this case, the decision to invest at the United States interest rate of 5% results in a greater amount, $105,000, after one year than investing in Europe even though Europe has the higher interest rate. Forward rates matter!

SUMMARY

(LO 6.8) International business transactions can take weeks, if not months, to close. Products must be shipped vast distances, possibly with several carriers. Delivered goods must be inspected and any damage or incorrect shipments settled. In sum, a transaction today may not result in a dollar cash flow stream until some future time.

To reduce the risk of exchange rate fluctuations during this time, firms can enter into forward contracts with a bank to lock in a transaction today for a specific amount of currency at a specific date in the future. Firms will have greater certainty with respect to its cash receipts, or payments, in terms of its home currency once the exchange rate is negotiated in a forward contract.

We learned that forward rates can play a role with speculators. Those who invest in currencies can use forwards to speculate that their expectations of future spot

---

[6] A confusing point to some students is choosing which number to multiply by – should we multiply the €96,300 by €0.87/$ or $1.1494/€? Here, since we want to compare dollars invested in the U.S. with dollars after investing overseas, we want our final answer to be in dollar units. Therefore, we want to calculate €96,300 × $1.1494/€ = $110,687.22. Why? We have euros in the numerator of €96,300 and euros in the denominator of $1.1494/€; they will cancel out leaving the units of the final answer to be U.S. dollars.

If we erroneously multiply €96,300 by €0.87/$, we have a final answer with units of €2/$. Since those units do not make economic sense, we know that the correct calculation is €96,300 × $1.1494/€ = $110,687.22.

rates are more accurate than the current forward rate. Investors decide where to invest excess funds by considering both interest rates in different countries but also forward exchange rates to lock in the future conversion of the foreign currency back into the home currency.

Any forward rate situation will require the answer to these four questions:

1. *Is the person entering into the forward contract wanting to buy or sell the foreign currency?*

2. *How much does the person wish to buy or sell?*

3. *What is the time frame?*

4. *What is the forward rate?*

REVIEW QUESTIONS

1. What risks does a company face due to changing exchange rates?

2. What are the four requirements that need to be determined when entering into a forward contract?

3. Why is hedging similar to buying insurance?

4. If your belief about future exchange rates differ from those quoted as forward rates, how can you attempt to profit from this difference in expectations?

5. Explain the process for using forward contracts when comparing home currency investments and overseas investments over a given time period.

6. The current U.S. one-month interest rate is 5% compared to 7% in Europe. Today's spot rate between the euro and dollar is $1.18/€, and today's one-month forward rate is $1.25/€. The United States is the home country. You have $1,000 to invest. What steps should you take today and one month from today to be able to invest overseas and convert funds back to dollars? Compare the rate of return you would get investing in the United States to your covered investment in Europe.

7. The current U.S. one-month forward rate is $1.25/€. You are an American speculator with $40,000. You are sure the spot rate will be $1.32/€ one month from today. What steps should you take

today and one month from today to make a profit buying and selling euros using your $40,000 and a forward contract?

8. A U.S.-based multinational corporation (MNC) purchased equipment from a British firm today and must pay them £1,000,000 one month from today. The MNC is certain the spot rate will be $1.10/£ one month from today. The current forward rate is $1.05/£. Should the MNC wait one month to buy the pounds using a forward contract? Explain what steps you would take today and one month from today. Why did you choose this course of action? What is the cost of the equipment in terms of dollars?

9. A U.S.-based multinational corporation (MNC) sold some equipment to a British firm today and will receive £1,000,000 from the British firm one month from today. Today's spot rate is $1.12/£. The MNC is certain the spot rate will be $1.10/£ one month from today. The current forward rate is $1.05/£. Should the MNC wait one month and sell the £1,000,000 in the spot market (that is, convert the pounds to dollars) or enter a forward contract to sell (that is, convert) the pounds? Explain what steps you would take today and one month from today. Why did you choose this course of action? How many dollars did the MNC receive for this piece of equipment?

Investments

The field of finance is composed of three areas—institutions and markets, investments, and financial management. Part 2 focuses on the investments area of finance. Investments involve the sale or marketing of securities, the analysis and valuation of securities and other financial claims, and the management of investment risk through holding diversified portfolios. Money flows into the financial markets from the savings of households and the earnings retained by businesses. Funds flow into financial institutions, such as banks and life insurance companies, which, in turn, invest the funds in various securities, such as stocks and bonds as well as other financial claims. Financial claims are anything that has a debt or equity claim on income or property, such as a car loan, a mortgage, or an equity investment in a small partnership. Financial institutions facilitate the work of the financial markets by directing funds from savers to those individuals, firms, or governments who need funds to finance current operations or growth.

Part 1 dealt with the operations of the financial markets in general within the context of the financial system. The combined financial crisis and Great Recession of 2007–2009, sometimes referred to as the "perfect financial storm," tested the workings of the U.S. financial system to an extent not seen since the 1930s depression. Although some evidence suggested that the U.S. financial system was on the verge of collapse in late 2008, efforts on the part of policy makers, business leaders, and individuals set the stage for economic recovery and a return to financial stability. Since the end of the 2008–2009 recession, the U.S. economy has been growing for more than a decade and interest rates have remained relatively low.

Part 2 introduces many of the important concepts and tools that financial institutions and investors use in the financial markets. For example, no one would want to invest (except perhaps altruistically) $100 now and expect to receive only their $100 back after one year. Because they give up the use of their money for some time, investors expect a return on their investments. Thus, we say that money has a "time value." Having one dollar today is of greater value to us than the promise of receiving one dollar sometime in the future.

How much can we expect to receive for our $100 investment? The answer is determined in the financial markets. As with any other market, the financial markets consider demand and supply forces to determine the "price" of money; namely, the interest rate, or the expected return on an investment. The amount of interest received on a certificate of deposit or a bond, or the expected return on a common stock investment, all depend on the workings of the financial markets and the marketplace's evaluation of the investment opportunity.

It is through the investing process that institutions, firms, and individual investors come together. Firms and governments go to the financial markets seeking investors and institutions to which they can sell financial securities. Investors and institutions participate in the financial markets, seeking profitable investments to help meet their goals. For an investor, the goal may be a comfortable retirement, or accumulating funds to purchase a car or house. For

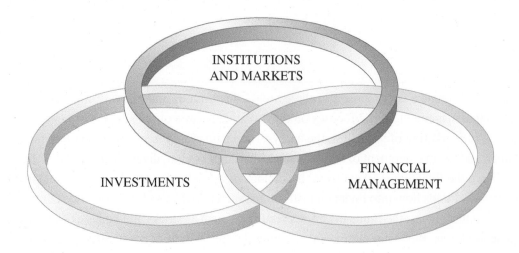

financial institutions, the higher the returns they earn on prudent investments, the greater will be their profits and the stronger their competitive position. A financial institution that prudently earns higher returns in the financial markets will be able to offer current and potential customers higher interest rates on their deposits than a competitor whose financial market returns are lower.

Part 2 also introduces us to the process of investing and to the tools that can be used to evaluate financial market securities. Chapter 7 examines the work of financial markets to direct savings into various investments. Chapter 8 discusses influences that affect the financial market's determination of the price of money, or the interest rate or expected return on an investment. Chapter 9 examines the effect of interest rates more closely by introducing the concept of time value of money. This chapter shows us how we can compare different dollar amounts of cash over time to determine whether an investment is attractive or not. Chapter 10 introduces us to bonds and stocks. We review their characteristics and we use the time value concepts from Chapter 9 in a pragmatic manner to see how we can estimate their value. We also learn in Chapter 10 how to read and interpret information about bonds and stocks from the financial pages of papers such as *The Wall Street Journal*.

Chapter 11 delves deeper into the workings of the securities markets. It focuses on the processes that institutions and firms use to issue securities, and the process that investors use when buying or selling securities. Chapter 12 completes our overview of investing in the securities markets by examining the trade-off between risk and expected return—to have an incentive to invest in higher-risk securities, investors must have higher returns. Chapter 12 introduces us to the tools that investors and securities market participants use to evaluate and control investment risk.

Savings and Investment Process

LEARNING OBJECTIVES

After studying this chapter, you should be able to do the following:

LO 7.1 Identify and describe the major components of the gross domestic product (GDP).

LO 7.2 Describe the principal sources of federal government revenues and expenditures.

LO 7.3 Explain how savings are created and describe the major sources of savings in the United States.

LO 7.4 Identify and describe the factors that affect savings.

LO 7.5 Describe major capital market securities that facilitate the savings and investment process.

LO 7.6 Describe the types of mortgage loans available to individuals and how the mortgage markets facilitate home ownership.

LO 7.7 Discuss the role of individuals in the 2007–2008 financial crisis.

Where we have been. . . Part 1 of this book introduced you to how the U.S. financial system works. In Chapter 1 you learned about the role of finance and were able to answer the question, what is finance? Chapter 2 provided you with information about the development of the U.S. monetary system, and Chapter 3 covered the importance of commercial banks and other financial institutions in helping the financial system operate smoothly. In Chapter 4 you learned about the Federal Reserve System and its monetary policy functions and instruments. After reading Chapter 5, you should have a better understanding of who the U.S. policy makers are and how they carry out monetary policy, fiscal policy, and debt management to achieve the nation's economic objectives. Chapter 6 covered how the international monetary system developed, factors that affect currency exchange rates, and the financing of international trade.

Where we are going. . . Part 2 focuses on the area of finance called investments. In Chapter 8 you will be introduced to the structure of interest rates. You will learn about the supply and demand for loanable funds and the determinants of nominal or market interest rates. Characteristics of U.S. Treasury debt obligations, which are considered to be free of default risk, will be discussed. Our attention then turns to the term or maturity structure of interest rates. Next we cover inflation premiums and price movements. The last section of the chapter examines default risk premiums. The remainder of Part 2 includes Chapter 9 on the time value of money, Chapter 10 on the characteristics and valuations of bonds and stocks, Chapter 11 on securities markets, and Chapter 12 on financial return and risk concepts.

How this chapter applies to me. . . Every day you are faced with deciding whether to "consume more" or to "save." For example, after buying dinner at a restaurant you may still have a few dollars left in the form of extra income, possibly from a part-time job while you are in college. What will you do with the money? You might buy a new CD or take a friend to the movie theater. Alternatively, you might decide to place the money in a savings account at a bank. The process of intermediation then moves your discretionary money from savings into investment. Of course, saving is not costless. Each time you make a decision to save, you are foregoing current consumption. This action on your part not to immediately consume all of your income helps the economy grow.

Our parents and other "experts" have likely provided similar advice to each of us about the importance of saving for a "rainy day." Of course, they were telling us not to consume all of our current income but rather to put some aside for an unexpected financial need—that is, a "rainy day." Such an action of saving not only provides protection against unanticipated future expenditures for the individual, but also allows investment. You are probably not a saver at this stage in your life. We say this because most individuals are spenders of their parents' earnings and savings during their formative years, from birth through college. At the time of college graduation, most individuals have little or no savings but possess "earning power." As earnings exceed expenditures, individuals have the opportunity to save in a variety of ways, ranging from short-term money market investments (considered to be cash) to long-term real estate investments in the form of home ownership.

As you move through your life cycle, you likely will have the opportunity to invest in stocks and bonds. Likewise, having an understanding of the types of financial assets that are used by businesses to finance and grow their businesses will be of value to those of you who pursue business careers.

7.1 GROSS DOMESTIC PRODUCT AND CAPITAL FORMATION

democracy system of government where limited authority and power are granted by law to its people who participate by voting on government goals and actions

capitalism economic system with private ownership of assets, production of goods and services for profit, a price mechanism for allocating resources, and financial markets

democratic capitalism country or state organized as a democracy that uses or adopts a capitalistic economic system

autocratic capitalism country or state organized as an autocratic political system that uses elements of a markets-based economic system

gross domestic product (GDP) measure of the output of goods and services in an economy

The United States of America operates as a *democracy*. Recall from Chapter 1 that a democracy is a system of government where limited authority and power are granted by law to its people, who participate in the government's decision-making through the process of voting. Actually, the United States is a representative democracy where U.S. citizens elect representatives from amongst their peers to participate in formulating government goals, policies, and actions.

The United States also is based on *capitalism*. Recall from Chapter 1 that capitalism is an economic system based on private ownership of physical and financial assets, the production of goods and services for profit, a mechanism for setting prices for allocating resources, and financial markets. Private people invest their assets or wealth in the production of goods and services and hopefully selling them at prices that will produce profits. When selling prices exceed the total costs of producing and selling the goods and services, profits are earned. Profits, in turn, can be used to invest in more plant, equipment, and business inventories, as well as to increase existing employee salaries and to possibly hire additional employees.

The United States of America is actually a mixed market capitalistic system that combines elements of a planned economic system that are administered by a national government with elements of a free market economic system. The U.S. federal government establishes economic goals and attempts to achieve those goals through fiscal and monetary policy actions. The government also regulates business activities, financial institutions, and financial markets, as well as establishes social programs (such as Social Security and Medicare benefits) for the public good.

The result of combining democracy and capitalism is termed democratic capitalism which refers to a country or state organized as a democracy that uses or adopts a capitalistic economic system. The United States is a country that practices democratic capitalism. Other economically developed countries that practice democratic capitalism include France, Germany, and Japan. Countries that are still developing economically, such as Brazil and India, also practice democratic capitalism.

Countries or states that are based on socialism or communism are referred to as being autocratic political systems. Some of these political entities have chosen to move from centrally planned economies to market-based economies that utilize some aspects of economic capitalism. The combination of both systems is called autocratic capitalism which refers to a country or state organized as an autocratic political system that uses elements of a markets-based economic system. For example, China, Russia, and Turkey represent forms of autocratic capitalism.

Countries that practice democratic capitalism or autocratic capitalism generally focus on their production of goods and services as a measure of economic progress. The most widely used metric is gross domestic product (GDP) which is a measure of the output of goods and services in an economy achieved over a specified period, such as one year. As the GDP for a country increases or grows over time, standards of living of the country's people should also increase.

Recall from Chapter 5 our discussion of the national economic policy objectives of economic growth, high employment, and price stability. Economic growth and employment are reflected in the output of goods and services by a nation, as well as the nation's ability to construct or build buildings, roads, inventories, and other infrastructure.

Capital formation involves the creation of capital goods including the construction of residential and commercial buildings, the manufacture of equipment and machinery, and the production of business inventories. Capital goods, in turn, are used to make more goods and provide more services which leads to higher GDP levels. The capital formation process begins with the creation of savings followed by the investment of those savings. More capital goods, in turn, may be used to manufacture more goods and provide more services.

capital formation creation of capital goods including residential and commercial buildings, equipment and machinery, and business inventories

7.1.1 GDP COMPONENTS

Gross domestic product is composed of consumption and investment components, as well as the net export of goods and services. More specifically, GDP consists of four components:

1. Personal consumption expenditures

2. Government expenditures, including gross investment

3. Gross private domestic investment

4. Net exports of goods and services

Personal consumption expenditures (PCE) indicate expenditures by individuals for durable goods, nondurable goods, and services. We all like to eat, buy clothes, have roofs over our heads, enjoy the comforts of heating and cooling, benefit from interior lighting, own automobiles and televisions, receive education, travel, and get haircuts and other services. The fact is we consume throughout our lives. Depending on where we are in our life cycles, we typically meet our consumption desires by spending our parents' earnings and savings during our formative years from birth through college graduation, generating our own earnings during our working lives, and spending our own savings during our retirement years.

personal consumption expenditures (PCE) expenditures by individuals for durable goods, nondurable goods, and services

Government expenditures (GE) include expenditures for goods and services plus gross investments by both the federal and the state and local governments. The federal government spends over one-half of its total expenditures on direct payments to individuals in the form of health, Social Security, and income security support. This should not be a surprise, since some would argue that the elected representatives of the people run the U.S. government for the benefit of the people.

government expenditures (GE) expenditures for goods and services plus gross investments by federal, state, and local governments

Gross private domestic investment (GPDI) measures fixed investment in residential and nonresidential structures, producers' durable equipment, and changes in business inventories. The final component of GDP is the net exports (NE) of goods and services, or exports minus imports.

In equation form, we have,

$$GDP = PCE + GE + GDPI + NE \qquad (7.1)$$

gross private domestic investment (GPDI) measures fixed investment in residential and nonresidential structures, producers' durable equipment, and changes in business inventories

net exports (NE) exports of goods and services minus imports

Consumption is reflected by the sum of personal consumption expenditures and government purchases of goods and services. Savings used for capital formation produce the gross private domestic investment. In addition, if the exports of goods and services exceed imports, GDP will be higher.

Table 7.1 contains a breakdown of these four GDP components for the United States in 2006, 2009, 2015, and 2018. For 2018, the gross domestic product was $20.5 trillion, relative to $18.2 trillion for 2015. GDP was $13.3 trillion GDP in 2006 and $14.3 trillion for 2009. However, the rate of GDP increase over the decade of the 2000s slowed during the latter part, which coincided with the 2007–2008 financial crisis and the 2008–2009 Great Recession.

Personal consumption expenditures of nearly $14.0 trillion in 2018 accounted for about 68% of GDP. The size of this percentage relationship shows the importance of the individual in sustaining and improving the standard of living as reflected in GDP growth over time. In dollar terms, personal consumption expenditures for both durable and nondurable goods declined from the 2006 to 2009 levels, as the economy began slowing in 2007 and then entered the 2008–2009 Great Recession. However, increases in individual expenditures for services in 2009 more than offset the declines in durable and nondurable goods.

Capital formation measured in terms of gross private domestic investment dropped sharply from $2.2 trillion in 2006 to $1.6 trillion in 2009, before beginning a recovery that has lasted into early 2019.

Table 7.1 Gross Domestic Product and Its Major Components ($ Billions)

	2006	2009	2015	2018
Total gross domestic product	**$13,253.9**	**$14,258.7**	**$18,164.8**	**$20,500.6**
Personal consumption expenditures	**9,270.8**	**10,092.6**	**12,444.7**	**13,951.6**
Durable goods	1,071.3	1,034.4	1,346.9	1,461.5
Nondurable goods	2,716.0	2,223.3	2,664.6	2,880.7
Services	5,483.6	6,835.0	8,433.1	9,609.4
Gross private domestic investment	**2,218.4**	**1,622.9**	**3,030.6**	**3,652.2**
Fixed investment	2,165.0	1,747.9	2,943.7	3,595.6
Nonresidential	1,397.9	1,386.6	2,309.5	2,800.4
Structures	411.6	480.7	489.5	637.1
Equipment and intellectual prop.	986.2	906.0	1,819.9	2,163.3
Residential structures	767.1	361.3	634.2	795.3
Change in private inventories	53.4	−125.0	86.9	56.5
Net exports of goods and services	**−761.8**	**−390.1**	**−514.3**	**−625.6**
Exports	1,466.2	1,560.0	2,216.6	2,530.9
Imports	2,228.0	1,950.1	2,730.9	3,156.5
Government consumption expenditures and gross investment	**2,526.4**	**2,933.3**	**3,203.9**	**3,522.5**
Federal	926.4	1,144.9	1,235.2	1,319.9
State and local	1,600.0	1,788.4	1,968.7	2,202.6

Note: Some numbers may not sum exactly to total numbers shown because of rounding.
Source: U.S. Department of Commerce, Bureau of Economic Analysis, https://www.bea.gov.

Fixed investment declined sharply between 2006 and 2009, largely due to a dramatic decline in residential structures and as a reflection of the housing price bubble that burst in 2006, resulting in a steep decline in home prices that continued through 2009. The change in private inventories for 2009 was −$125 billion, reflecting the severity of the financial crisis of 2007–2008 and the 2008–2009 recession.

Government expenditures, in the form of consumption and gross investment, amounted to $3.5 trillion in 2018. Continued increases occurred in both federal and state and local government expenditures over the four annual periods shown in Table 7.1.

7.1.2 IMPLICATIONS OF INTERNATIONAL PAYMENT IMBALANCES

GLOBAL Table 7.1 shows that imports of goods and services exceeded exports by about $761.8 billion in 2006, $390.1 billion in 2009, $514.3 billion in 2015, and $625.6 billion in 2018. Dollar amounts of exports increased across the four annual periods depicted in Table 7.1. In contrast, the dollar amount of imports fell between 2006 and 2009. This development reflects the impact of the 2007–2008 financial crisis and the 2008–2009 recession, as well as the weakening of the U.S. dollar relative to other major currencies as the decade of the 2000s came to a close. However, imports increased rapidly in 2015 and 2018 reflecting recent economic recovery and the strengthening of the U.S. dollar.

Recall from our discussion in Chapter 6 that the *current account* records a summary of the flow of funds between one country and all other countries involving the sale and purchase of goods and services plus funds from income-generating financial assets during a specified period, such as a year. Also recall that the *capital account* is a summary of the flow of funds between one country and all other countries involving the transfer of financial assets across country borders during a specified time period. Included are transfers of patent values and financial assets by individuals who move to another country. However, as currently defined, the capital account balance has a minor impact on the balance of payments.

The *financial account* is a summary of the flow of funds between one country and all other countries involving foreign investments in fixed assets and financial assets during a specified time period. To offset current account deficits, direct investments (business fixed assets and acquisitions) and portfolio investments (corporate stocks and bonds and government debt securities) by foreign businesses and governments need to be greater than the direct and portfolio investments of their U.S. counterparts.

When a deficit in the current account is not fully offset by increases in the capital account and net increases in the financial account, the Fed must either reduce its reserve assets or borrow from foreign central banks. *Reserves* are in the form of gold, foreign exchanges (currencies), special drawing rights (SDRs), and reserves credit in the International Monetary Fund (IMF). Foreign exchanges (currencies) accounts represent the vast majority of all international reserve assets with the U.S. dollar forming the largest component of these currency assets.

SMALL BUSINESS PRACTICE

TYPICAL LIFE CYCLE PATTERNS FOR THE SMALL VENTURE FIRM

A successful entrepreneurial firm will typically progress through several stages of financing. The first stage is called the "seed" or *development* stage. Here a firm works on an idea, develops a concept or prototype product, and may conduct some preliminary market research. If the firm is successful in producing a product or delivering a service, it moves into the *start-up* stage. Financing will be needed for "working capital" investments in inventories and to extend trade credit to customers. A manufacturing start-up also will need to invest in plant and equipment.

A third stage can be viewed as the *breakeven* stage, the time when the firm is now starting to generate enough revenues to cover its operating costs. A fourth stage represents the *recovery of investment* stage. If the firm continues to be successful, the fifth stage results in the

maximum generation of profits. This occurs because cash flows from operations far exceed new capital expenditure requirements as well as additional investment in working capital. A sixth stage may be viewed as *maturity* or *stability*.

Timmons and Spinelli report that it takes an average of two and one-half years for a firm to break even from an operating standpoint, and over six years on average to recover initial equity investments.* Of course, some firms will recover initial investment more rapidly, while others will fail or not progress beyond the start-up stage. Ultimately, a plan is needed for how the successful entrepreneur will "exit" or leave the business. For example, the firm could be sold or merged with another firm.

*Jeffry A. Timmons and Stephen Spinelli, *New Venture Creation*, 7th Edition (New York: McGraw-Hill/Irwin, 2007), pp. 390–391.

LEARNING ACTIVITY

Go to the website of the U.S. Department of Commerce, Bureau of Economic Analysis, https://www.bea.gov, and find the current size of the U.S. gross domestic product (GDP) and its major components.

7.2 FEDERAL GOVERNMENT RECEIPTS AND EXPENDITURES

7.2.1 THE BUDGET

As noted in Chapter 1, the U.S. Constitution provided for a separation of government powers by dividing the federal government into legislative (Congress), executive (the president), and judicial (Supreme Court and other federal courts) branches. Legislative powers include creating law, levying and collecting taxes, and printing money. While legislation proposed by Congress can be vetoed by the president, Congress can override the veto. However, a check and balance exists since the Supreme Court has the power to invalidate unconstitutional laws passed by Congress.

In February of each year, the president submits to the U.S. Congress a proposed federal budget for the upcoming fiscal year that begins on October 1 of the current year and ends on September 30 of the following year. In Chapter 5, we defined the terms federal budget, budget surplus, and budget deficit. Let's review them here. The *federal budget* is the annual revenue and expenditure plans that reflect fiscal policy objectives concerning government influence on economic activity. We can also say that the federal budget sets out the annual receipts and expenditures, and any surplus or deficit for the federal government. A *budget surplus* occurs when tax revenues (receipts) are more than expenditures (outlays). A *budget deficit* occurs when tax revenues (receipts) are less than expenditures (outlays). Congress reviews the proposed budget, makes changes, and passes specific spending and revenue bills to implement this next fiscal budget.

Annual federal government spending may be either mandatory or discretionary. Mandatory spending is government spending on entitlement programs that must be funded according to existing law. The two largest entitlement programs that require mandatory spending are Social Security and Medicare. Discretionary spending is government spending provided through passage of appropriations bills that set aside funds for specific federal agencies and programs.

Actual results for federal budget operations are known only after revenues and expenditures have been recorded for a fiscal year. Thus, there is a lag between when a federal budget is implemented and results are measured. The Internal Revenue Service (IRS) of the Department of the Treasury provides useful summary information on the major sources of revenues and the major programs being funded. For fiscal 2017, federal income was $3.316 trillion and outlays were $3.982 trillion, resulting in a budget deficit of about $666 billion. Figure 7.1 provides a graphical illustration of the percentage breakdown of revenues (income) and expenditures (outlays) for fiscal year 2017, which is the most current data provided by the IRS. The major income sources are personal income taxes (40%) and social insurance receipts (Social Security, Medicare, and unemployment and other retirement taxes), which accounted for 29% of revenues. Corporate taxes accounted for 7% of income, and excise, customs, estate, gift, and miscellaneous taxes contributed 7% of income. The remaining income of 17% came from borrowing to cover the deficit.

mandatory spending
government spending on entitlement programs that must be funded according to existing law

discretionary spending
government spending provided by passage of appropriations bills that set aside funds for specific federal agencies and programs

WHERE IT COMES FROM (INCOME)...

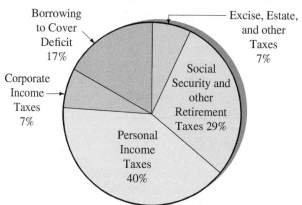

WHERE IT GOES (OUTLAYS)...

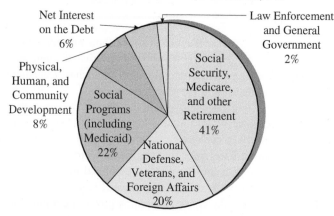

FIGURE 7.1 The federal government dollar, fiscal year 2017

Note: numbers may not total to 100% due to rounding.

Source: U.S. Department of the Treasury, Internal Revenue Service, https://www.irs.gov/.

The primary expenditures for fiscal year 2017 were in the form of Social Security, Medicare, and other retirement outlays that accounted for 41% of the total outlays. Outlays for national defense, veterans, and foreign affairs activities amounted to 20%. Social programs (Medicaid, food stamps, temporary assistance for needy families, supplemental security income, etc.) accounted for an additional 22% of fiscal 2017 expenditures. The remaining outlays were for physical, human, and community development (8%), net interest on the debt (6%), and law enforcement and general government activities (2%).

Local governments depend heavily on property taxes for their revenues, while state governments depend largely on sales taxes and special taxes, such as those on motor fuel, liquor, and tobacco products. In contrast, the federal government relies primarily on individual income taxes, social insurance taxes, and corporate income taxes for its revenues.

7.2.2 FISCAL POLICY MAKERS

ETHICAL In Chapter 5 we noted that Congress and the president determine the nation's fiscal policy. These individuals are elected by the people under the belief that they are to serve the people. Decisions relating to taxing and spending, and the resulting impact on whether federal budgets will be surpluses or deficits, are important to voters. Voters also expect their elected politicians to behave ethically by acting honestly and fairly with their constituencies.

For the most part, our elected federal politicians seemed to have acted ethically and with integrity. However, there have been some examples of unethical and illegal behavior. *Impeachment* is a formal legislative process in which charges of "high crimes and misdemeanors" are brought against high-level officials. The House of Representatives votes on whether to impeach an official; if it does impeach, a trial is held in the Senate. In the United States, only two presidents out of 45 have been impeached. They were Andrew Johnson, the 17th president, and William Clinton, the 42nd president. Both were acquitted. Former President Richard Nixon resigned before being impeached.

Occasionally, members of Congress have engaged in illegal activities. Some have been convicted in criminal court. Since the mid-1970s, more than a dozen members have received prison sentences for such activities as accepting bribes, taking part in kickback schemes, extortion, illegal sex offenses, and mail fraud. While the activities of these individuals have tainted Congress, by far most members behave ethically, both personally and professionally, when representing the people who elected them.

7.2.3 DEBT FINANCING

As defined in Chapter 5, the *national debt* is the total debt owned by the government and it reflects the cumulative amount of annual budget surpluses and deficits throughout the history of the United States. Annual budget deficits have occurred in most fiscal years since the end of the 1960s. Beginning in fiscal year 1970 and continuing until 1998, the federal government operated with an annual budget deficit. The government was willing to spend much more than it received in the form of taxes and other revenues for more than 25 consecutive fiscal years.

Surplus budgets lasted for only four fiscal years (1998–2001), with annual budget deficits again being the norm beginning in fiscal 2002. Deficits exceeded $1 trillion annually for fiscal years 2009 through 2012, as fiscal policy responded to the perfect financial storm created by the 2007–2008 financial crisis and the 2008–2009 Great Recession. Annual deficits have continued since then. On the one hand, fiscal policy can use a deficit budget to stimulate economic activity. On the other hand, recent large annual deficits have resulted in a rapidly growing national debt.

At the end of fiscal 2000, the national debt was $5.7 trillion. It increased to $21,5 trillion by the end of fiscal 2018, which was an increase of almost four times. By early calendar 2019, the national debt exceeded $22.0 trillion for the first time. The fiscal 2019 budget deficit is expected to exceed $1 trillion, in part due to the passage of the Tax Cuts and Jobs Act of 2017 that cut tax rates for corporations and individuals. When the size of the national debt was lower, Congress sets **federal statutory debt limits** that restrict the maximum amount of national debt that can be outstanding. This national debt limit is commonly referred to as the "national debt ceiling." However, it has been necessary to

federal statutory debt limits limits by Congress setting the maximum amount of national debt that can be outstanding

increase the limit several times in recent years due to continuing large annual federal government budget deficits.

Annual interest expense on the national debt increased from $362.0 billion in fiscal 2000 to $523.0 billion in fiscal 2018 even though market interest rates have been very low in recent years. Over 60% of the national debt is currently held by the public with the remainder being intragovernmental holdings.[1] In Chapter 8 we will identify and discuss those who are the major holders of the Treasury securities used to finance the national debt.

U.S. citizens and financial institutions hold or own a large portion of the U.S. national debt that is outstanding. Part of our debt is due to our role as a creditor nation from 1918 until 1985. Until World War I, the United States depended heavily on foreign investment, and it was not until 1985 that liabilities to foreign creditors again exceeded claims against foreign creditors. Our return to being a debtor nation was due in large measure to relatively high domestic interest rates, relative political stability in the world arena, and the development of an extremely unfavorable balance of trade. The nation's excess of imports relative to exports has continued to be very large since 1964. To the extent that foreign claims resulting from a surplus of imports are invested in federal obligations, foreign ownership of the federal debt increases.

It is notable that public borrowing is a relatively modern development. During the Middle Ages, governments borrowed from wealthy merchants and others on an individual basis. Often crown jewels were offered as collateral for such advances. Large public borrowing by governments, as by businesses, became possible only when monetary systems were refined, and efficient financial institutions developed that could facilitate the transfer of monetary savings.

DISCUSSION QUESTION 1

Are you concerned about the size of the national debt? Why, or why not?

7.3 ROLE AND MAJOR SOURCES OF SAVINGS

7.3.1 HISTORICAL SOURCES

As the size of U.S. businesses expanded, the importance of accumulating and converting large amounts of financial capital to business use increased. The corporate form of organization provided a convenient and flexible legal arrangement for bringing together available financial capital. These advantages of the corporation over sole proprietorship, or private ownership, and partnership are described in Chapter 13.

Developments in public transportation were often too costly and speculative for private promoters to undertake. The magnitude of early canal, turnpike, and railroad construction was such that the government undertook much of the financing of these projects. In fact, until the end of the nineteenth century, governmental units contributed more funding to these efforts than did private interests. Since this government financing was accomplished largely through bond issues rather than current revenues, the ultimate source of funds was the savings of individuals who bought the bonds.

7.3.1.1 Foreign Sources of Savings

Foreign investors purchased large amounts of the securities sold by government and private promoters to develop the United States. In particular, foreign capital played a decisive role in the development of the nation's early transportation system.

The huge role that foreign capital played in the economic development of the United States is found in the developing nations of today. These nations now face many of the financial problems that the United States experienced during its early years. Private savings in many of these countries are negligible because almost all current income must be used for immediate consumption. Individual nations and such international organizations as the World Bank supply large amounts of capital to the developing nations of the world to increase their productive capacity.

---

[1] For statistics relating to the national debt, see, U.S. Department of the Treasury, https://www.treasurydirect.gov/.

The flow of development capital not only stimulates economic expansion in these countries but also makes their capital much more efficient. For example, speedier transportation reduces the amount of goods in transit, thus releasing working capital for other purposes. In due time, as internal capital formation increases, it is hoped that the need for foreign capital will be eliminated and that these countries can then enjoy an independent capital formation process.

7.3.1.2 Domestic Supply of Savings

As capital formation began increasing at a faster and faster rate after the Civil War, the demand for funds also increased. Wealthy Americans and foreign investors could no longer provide funds at a rapid enough rate. Britain was investing heavily in India because of political commitments, and the other European countries were not large or wealthy enough to continue supplying funds in quantities adequate to sustain U.S. growth. The American family soon took over the function of providing savings for the capital formation process. Per capita income rose to a level at which American families could afford luxuries well beyond the subsistence level and they could also save part of what they had earned. Thus, the United States gradually developed to the stage where it could generate sufficient capital to finance its own expansion. Ultimately, the result was a change in the country's status from a debtor nation to a creditor nation.

7.3.2 CREATION OF SAVINGS

It is from individuals that most financial intermediaries accumulate capital. Individuals, as a group, consistently represent a savings surplus economic unit. Corporations also represent an important source of savings. However, their large demand for real asset investments, as is also the case for unincorporated business firms, generally results in a net need for external funds. While financial intermediaries can also save, their primary role in the U.S. financial system is to aid the savings-investment process. A third potentially important savings sector is governments (federal, and state and local). However, the U.S. government, in particular, has operated as a savings deficit unit in recent years due to budget deficits. Thus, the ability to provide adequate funds to meet investment needs primarily depends on the savings of individuals and corporations.

economic unit savings occur when an economic unit's income exceeds its expenses, taxes, and real asset investments

Economic unit savings occur when an economic unit's income exceeds its expenses, taxes, and real asset investments. Savings are held in the form of cash and other financial assets. A **savings surplus unit** is an economic unit that generates savings. These surplus savings are made available to savings deficit units. For example, business firms as a group are often unable to meet all their plant and equipment investment needs out of **undistributed profits** or earnings retained in the business, which are profits remaining after taxes and, in the case of corporations, after the cash dividends are paid to stockholders. A **savings deficit unit** is an economic unit with income less than its expenses, taxes, and real asset investments, making it necessary to acquire funds from a savings surplus unit.

savings surplus unit an economic unit that generates savings

undistributed profits proportion of after-tax profits retained by corporations

savings deficit unit an economic unit with income less than its expenses, taxes, and real asset investments

7.3.3 PERSONAL SAVINGS

An important savings sector in the economy is the savings of individuals called **personal saving**. In equation form, we have,

$$\text{Personal saving} = \text{personal income} - \text{personal current taxes} - \text{personal outlays} \qquad (7.2)$$

Personal income includes compensation of employees, personal income with capital consumption adjustment, personal interest and dividend income, and net government social benefits to individuals. Personal income less personal current taxes equals disposable personal income. Then, subtracting personal outlays (primarily personal consumption expenditures) equals personal saving. Technically, personal nonmortgage interest payments and personal transfer payments made to the government are also personal outlays.

personal saving savings of individuals equal to personal income less personal current taxes less personal outlays

Voluntary savings are savings in the form of financial assets held or set aside for use in the future. **Contractual savings** are savings accumulated on a regular schedule for a specified length of time by prior agreement. An example is the accumulation of reserves in insurance and pension funds.

voluntary savings savings held or set aside by choice for future use

contractual savings savings accumulated on a regular schedule by prior agreement

Contractual savings are not determined by current decisions. They are disciplined by previous commitments that the saver has some incentive to honor.

Individuals maintain savings for a number of reasons. They set aside a part of their current income to make mortgage payments on loans used to purchase homes. They also save to acquire costly durable consumer goods, such as cars and appliances. Savings are set aside by individuals to meet unforeseeable financial needs. These savings are not set aside for specific future consumption; instead, they represent emergency or rainy-day funds. Individuals may also save for such long-term, foreseeable spending as children's college education or for retirement. For short periods, people may save a portion of current income simply because desirable goods and services are not available for purchase.

personal saving rate
personal savings divided by disposable personal income

The **personal savings rate** is calculated as personal savings divided by disposable personal income. It represents the decision by individuals, as an economic unit, to save for future consumption by spending less on personal outlays relative to the disposable personal income they generate. Table 7.2 shows personal savings rates for selected years in the United States beginning in 1960. Personal savings rates were at double-digit levels in the 1960s and 1970s, and also in 1980. Saving a substantial portion of disposable personal income was considered to be important to individuals as a unit. Personal savings rates declined during the 1980s and 1990s, although they remained at relatively high, single-digit levels. Further declines in the personal savings rates occurred during the 2000s decade, with a drop to only 2.6% in 2005 before recovering to more than 5.0% in 2010 and 2015.

Table 7.3 shows personal savings amounts in the United States in 2006, 2009, 2015, and 2018. Personal income rose from $11.4 trillion in 2006 to $17.6 trillion in 2018. Disposable personal income also increased over the four time periods covered in Table 7.3. Individuals increased their personal outlays from about $9.7 trillion in 2006 to $14.5 trillion in 2018. Personal savings increased from the $331.4 billion level in 2006 to $1,043.4 in 2018.

Table 7.3 shows that the personal savings rate was 3.3% in 2006, increased to 6.1% in 2009, dropped to 5.1% in 2015, and then improved to 6.7% in 2018. Individuals as a unit seemed to have reacted to the 2007–2008 financial crisis and the 2008–2009 Great Recession by saving more of their disposable personal income.

Table 7.2 Historical Personal Savings Rates in the United States

Year	Personal savings rates (%)	Year	Personal savings rates (%)
1960	10.0%	1990	7.8%
1965	11.4	1995	6.4
1970	12.6	2000	4.2
1975	13.0	2005	2.6
1980	10.6	2010	5.6
1985	8.6	2015	5.1

Source: U.S. Department of Commerce, Bureau of Economic Analysis, https://www.bea.gov.

Table 7.3 Personal Savings in the United States ($ Billions)

	2006	2009	2015	2018
Personal income	$11,393.9	$12,094.8	$15,340.4	$17,581.4
Less: personal current taxes	1,375.1	1,152.3	1,945.4	2,050.4
Disposable personal income	10,036.9	10,942.5	13,395.0	15,531.0
Less: personal outlays	9,705.5	10,275.1	12,717.5	14,487.6
Personal savings	331.4	667.4	677.5	1,043.4
Savings rate (personal savings/disposable personal income)	3.3%	6.1%	5.1%	6.7%

Source: U.S. Department of Commerce, Bureau of Economic Analysis, https://www.bea.gov.

Individuals as a unit spent most of their disposable personal income and also borrowed heavily to finance purchases of homes and other durable goods during the middle of the 2000s decade. The federal government encouraged home ownership, and lenders contributed to the problem by offering subprime mortgage loans to home borrowers. We will discuss mortgage lending and changes in individual borrowing habits later in the chapter.

A number of media are available in which to maintain savings, ranging in liquidity from cash balances to stocks and bonds. Three factors usually influence a person's choice of medium: liquidity, degree of safety, and return. Various types of financial instruments and securities that individuals may hold are covered later in the chapter.

7.3.4 CORPORATE SAVINGS

Corporations generate revenues and incur operating expenses. When revenues exceed operating expenses, profits before taxes are generated. Corporations then pay taxes on their before-tax profits, resulting in profit after taxes. Corporations may also choose to pay dividends against their after-tax profits which leaves them with undistributed profits, or savings. A corporate savings rate called the **corporate retention rate** is calculated as undistributed profits divided by profits after taxes.

At the aggregate or unit level, corporate profits before taxes are usually recorded after adjustments for changes in inventory values and for capital consumption. More specifically, before-tax profits include an inventory valuation adjustment (IVA) and a capital consumption adjustment (CCAdj). Inventory values may increase or decrease in a given year and, thus, can affect corporate profits before taxes. **Capital consumption adjustment**, also called *depreciation*, is the estimate of the "using up" of plant and equipment assets for business purposes.

Since financial institution corporations have only a small impact, or corporate profitability and savings, it is common practice to concentrate on the impact of nonfinancial corporations as a unit when examining corporate savings. Table 7.4 shows nonfinancial corporate profits and savings in the United States for 2006, 2009, 2015, and 2017. Data for 2018 were not available at the time this table was prepared. Profits before taxes were only $718.1 billion in 2009, which was a substantial decline from the 2006 level. The post-2009 period has been one of continual economic growth resulting in a nearly three-fold increase in corporate before-tax profits between 2009 and 2017. A similar pattern occurred in terms of profits after taxes. About 30 percent of profits after taxes were being retained by nonfinancial corporations in recent years.

Corporate saving for short-term working capital purposes is by far the most important reason for accumulating financial assets. Seasonal business changes create an uneven demand for corporate operating assets, such as inventories and accounts receivable. Because of these seasonal changes, cash inflow is seldom in just the right amount and at the right time to accommodate the increased levels of

corporate retention rate calculated as undistributed profits divided by profits after taxes

capital consumption adjustment estimate of the "using up," or depreciation, of plant and equipment assets for business purposes

Table 7.4 Nonfinancial Corporate Savings in the United States ($ Billions)

	2006	**2009**	**2015**	**2017**
Profits before taxes (with IVA and CCAdj)	1,015.0	718.1	2,057.3	2,099.3
Less: tax liabilities	307.7	177.8	397.2	350.7
Profits after taxes	707.3	540.2	1,660.1	1,748.6
Less: dividends	471.1	351.4	1,164.9	1,215.3
Undistributed profits	236.2	188.9	495.2	533.3
Retention rate (undistributed profits/profits after taxes)	33.4%	35.0%	29.8%	30.5%
Addenda:				
Profits before taxes (without IVA and CCAdj)	1,180.1	752.5	2,134.2	2,181.9
Inventory valuation adjustment (IVA)	−35.7	6.7	52.8	−45.5
Capital consumption adjustment (CCAdj)	−129.4	−41.1	−129.8	−37.1

Where: IVA is an inventory valuation adjustment, and CCAdj is a capital consumption adjustment.
Note: 2018 data were not available at the time this table was prepared.
Source: U.S. Department of Commerce, Bureau of Economic Analysis, https://www.bea.gov.

operating assets. Quarterly corporate income tax liabilities also impose the necessity of accumulating financial assets.

The short-term accumulation of financial assets on the part of business corporations does not add to the level of long-term savings of the economy as a whole. However, these funds do enter the monetary stream and become available to users of short-term borrowed funds. As such, these short-term savings serve to meet a part of the demand for funds of consumers, government, and other businesses. A corporation, typically, holds this type of savings in the form of checkable deposits with commercial banks, short-term obligations of the federal government, commercial paper, and certificates of deposit issued by commercial banks. These financial assets meet the requirements of safety and liquidity.

Corporations also engage in the savings process to meet planned spending in the future. Reserves are often set up to provide all or part of the cost of construction, purchase of equipment, or major maintenance and repairs to existing facilities. Savings committed to these purposes are often invested in securities that have longer maturities and higher yields than those held for short-term business purposes. These securities include the debt obligations of both corporations and government and, to a limited extent, corporate stock.

> **DISCUSSION QUESTION 2**
>
> **What is a reasonable personal savings rate for individuals in the United States?**
>
> **LEARNING ACTIVITY**
>
> **Go to the website of the Bureau of Economic Analysis, https://www.bea.gov, and find current information on the size of disposable personal income and personal savings.**

7.4 FACTORS AFFECTING SAVINGS

Several factors influence the total amount of savings in any given period:

- Level of income
- Economic expectations
- Cyclical influences
- Life stage of the individual saver or corporation

The precise relationship between savings and consumption is the subject of much debate and continuing study, however, and we limit our observations here to broad generalizations.

7.4.1 LEVELS OF INCOME

Recall that personal saving is personal income less personal taxes less personal outlays (primarily consumption expenditures). Keeping this definition in mind, let us explore the effect of changes in income on the levels of savings of individuals. As income falls, the individual attempts to maintain his or her present standard of living as long as possible. In so doing, the proportion of his or her consumption spending increases and total savings diminish. As income is further reduced, the individual may be forced to curtail consumption spending, which results in a lower standard of living. Such reduction is reasonably limited, however, since the basic needs of the individual or family unit must be met. Not only will personal savings be eliminated when income is drastically reduced, but the individual may also engage in dissaving; that is, spending accumulated savings when consumption spending exceeds after-tax income.

As income increases, the individual will again be in a position to save. However, the saving will not necessarily begin immediately, as the individual may desire to buy the things that he or she could not afford during the low-income period. The amount of this need, notably for durable consumer goods, largely determines the rate of increase in savings during periods of income recovery.

On the whole, income levels are closely associated with levels of employment. Changes in business activity, in turn, influence employment levels. Downturns in the economy during 1980, 1981–1982, 1990, 2001, and 2008–2009 resulted in declines in employment levels and correspondingly lowered levels of

dissaving involves spending of accumulated savings when consumption spending exceeds after-tax income

income. Post–World War II unemployment highs of the early 1980s exceeded 10%. During the decade of the 1990s, unemployment averaged less than 5%, with deviations resulting in higher levels in the 1990 and 2001 recessions. The 2007–2008 financial crisis and the 2008–2009 Great Recession led to unemployment levels reaching 10%. However, the unemployment rate had declined to under 4% by the end of 2018.

7.4.2 ECONOMIC EXPECTATIONS

The anticipation of future events has a significant effect on savings. If individuals believe that their incomes will decrease in the near future, they may curtail their spending to establish a reserve for the expected period of low income. For example, a worker anticipating a protracted labor dispute may increase current savings as partial protection against the financial impact of a strike.

Expectations of a general increase in price levels may also have a strong influence on the liquidity that savers want to maintain. The prospect of price increases in consumer durable goods may cause an increase in their sales as individuals try to buy before prices increase. Savings are, thus, quickly converted to consumer spending. Corporate savings, too, may be reduced as a result of price increase expectations. In addition to committing funds to plant and office equipment before price increases take place, corporations typically increase their inventory positions. As for the individual, the prospect of an interruption in the supply of inventory because of a labor strike or other cause often results in a rapid stockpiling of raw materials and merchandise. The prospect of price decreases and of large production capacity has the opposite effect: the liquidity and financial assets of a business increase relative to its operating assets.

Unprecedented price increases during the inflationary 1970s led many individuals to develop a "buy it now because it will cost more later" philosophy. This resulted in a classic example of the impact that price increase expectations have on the spend-save decisions of individuals. Inflation peaked at double-digit levels at the beginning of the 1980s. However, after some upward pressure in the form of price increases at the end of the 1980s, inflation during the 1990s and the early years of the twenty-first century were generally in the 2 to 3% range. Inflation rates since the end of the great recession have been below the 2% inflation rate target being used by the Fed in setting monetary policy.

7.4.3 ECONOMIC CYCLES

Cyclical movements in the economy are the primary cause of changes in levels of income, and they affect not only the amounts but also the types of savings. Economic cycles may be viewed in terms of the two- to four-year traditional business cycle or in terms of much longer cycles that correspond with generations of people.

Let's begin with a discussion that concentrates on the traditional business cycle. In general, interest rates on securities with short maturities are lower than interest rates on long-term maturities.[2] However, when economic activity is peaking, short-term interest rates are higher than long-term interest rates. Generally, interest rates are high because inflation rates are high, and the Fed then raises short-term interest rates even further to slow economic activity and reduce inflation. As a recession deepens, short-term interest rates fall faster than long-term interest rates. Finally, when interest rates get low enough, businesses will find it attractive to borrow and grow. The savings rate usually goes down in a recessionary period and savers emphasize liquidity and safety when they do save. When the economy is growing, individuals usually save more and may hold their savings in riskier short-term securities.

Harry Dent Jr. examined much longer cycles based on *generation waves*, with the largest generation wave in the history of the United States being the baby boom wave.[3] In his view, a generation wave consists of birth wave, innovation wave, spending wave, and organization wave components, or stages. These components correspond with birth, coming of age, adulthood, and maturity. For the baby

---

[2] We discuss the term, or maturity structure, of interest rates in detail in Chapter 8.
[3] Harry Dent, Jr., *The Great Boom Ahead*, (New York: Hyperion, 1993). Also see Harry Dent, Jr., *The Roaring 2000s*, (New York: Simon & Schuster, 1998).

boom (or Boomers) generation, the birth wave peaked in the early 1950s. The innovation wave peaked in the 1980s, a period of rapid introduction of new technologies, when the country began the movement from a production economy to an information economy. According to Dent, the spending wave, which peaked early in this century, has driven the economic successes of the 1990s. The last stage will peak when the last Boomers reach age 65 in roughly 2025. While a lot of economists are skeptical about broad-based generalizations made by Harry Dent and others, all will agree that the economic clout of a large number of individuals moving through their life cycles at about the same time can influence the economy and the securities markets. Newer waves include Generation X, Millennials, and Generation Z demographic groups.

7.4.4 LIFE STAGES OF THE INDIVIDUAL SAVER

The pattern of savings over an individual's life span follows a somewhat predictable pattern when viewed over the total population. A successful individual life cycle would have the following stages:

- Formative/education developing

- Career starting/family creating

- Wealth building

- Retirement enjoying

Individuals save very little during their formative and education-developing stage simply because little income is produced. They, typically, consume a portion of their parents' earnings and savings, which is substantial if they attend college. As they enter their career and family creating stage, they possess little savings but have large "earning power" potential. Their income increases. However, expenses also increase during these early family forming years. Saving and investing typically focus on purchasing a home and accruing life and disability insurance.

By the time an individual reaches his or her wealth building stage, two new factors result in increased savings. First, income is typically much higher than at any previous time. Second, the expense of raising and educating children has been reduced or eliminated. Thus, it is this group that typically saves the most. At the retirement-enjoying stage, the individual's income is sharply reduced. He or she may now begin the process of *dissaving*. Pension fund payments along with accumulated savings are drawn upon for current living expenses.

The level of savings of individuals is therefore a function of the age composition of the population as a whole. A population shift to a large proportion of individuals in the productive middle-age years would result in a greater savings potential. These views of the life stages of the individual saver are consistent with the generation-wave approach described by Harry Dent Jr. That is, if a large number of individuals are moving through their individual life cycles at approximately the same time, their combined efforts will have a major impact on the overall economy. On a collective basis, they spend at about the same time and are also likely to save at about the same time. Spending has kept the U.S. economy in almost continual growth since the early 1980s, and saving/investing in retirement plans and directly in mutual funds (which, in turn, buy bonds and stocks) helped the stock market reach historical highs during the 1990s. A substantial decline in stock prices preceded a downturn in economic activity at the beginning of the twenty-first century, which was then followed by economic expansion and increasing stock prices until the onset of the 2007–2008 financial crisis and the 2008–2009 Great Recession. Since then, economic recovery and increasing stock prices have prevailed.

7.4.5 LIFE STAGES OF THE CORPORATION AND OTHER BUSINESS FIRMS

As the financial savings of individuals are governed partly by age, so the financial savings generated by a business firm are a function of its life stage. The following are the life cycle stages of a successful business firm:

- Start-up stage

- Survival stage

• Rapid growth stage

• Maturity stage

Not all business firms proceed through all fixed life cycle stages. To the extent, however, that a firm experiences the typical pattern of starting up, surviving, vigorous growth, and ultimate maturity, its flow of financial savings may experience a predictable pattern.

While developing the business idea and in the starting the business stage, the firm is spending cash rather than building cash. The business firm, typically, continues to burn cash as it tries to find a successful operating niche. During the early part of the expansion years (rapid growth stage) of a successful business, the volume of physical assets, typically, increases rapidly. So rapid is this growth that the firm is unable to establish a strong position with respect to its financial assets. Indeed, it is during these years of the corporate life cycle that there is a large need for borrowed capital. At this time, the corporation is typically a heavy user of financial assets rather than a provider.

PERSONAL FINANCIAL PLANNING

Develop a Personal Financial Plan

Developing a personal financial plan is necessary to increase the chances of reaching your financial goals. Goals in business, life, and finances rarely are met by accident. With a bewildering array of investment choices and confusing tax laws, more and more people are turning to an investment professional for help and guidance. An important step in creating a personal financial plan is to develop a policy statement. A policy statement contains basic information to help guide future financial decisions. A policy statement will describe an investor's objective. An objective will have two components: a return goal (capital gain, income, or both) and information about the investor's risk tolerance. Investors who cannot handle the ups and downs of the stock market will not want to place as much of their savings in stocks as someone who is willing to take on the additional risk.

In addition to an objective, the policy statement needs to include information relating to the five sets of constraints faced by every investor:

1. Liquidity needs. Does the investor need to be able to sell assets and obtain cash quickly?

2. Time horizon. Over what time horizon can funds be invested? Two years? Ten? Thirty years or more?

3. Taxes. The investor's tax situation is an important consideration as investing goals should focus on after-tax returns. Capital gains and losses, income, IRA accounts, 401(k) retirement plans, and taxable versus nontaxable securities all lead to decision-making complications.

4. Legal and regulatory factors. Investment decisions are affected by rules and regulations. Even something as basic as investing money in a bank certificate of deposit often carries with it the warning, "substantial interest penalty upon early withdrawal."

5. Unique needs and preferences. This constraint can include wanting to exclude certain investments because of personal preference or social consciousness reasons. For example, an investor may not want to own stock or bonds issued by firms that produce or sell pornography, tobacco, or alcoholic beverages.

As the firm reaches the second part of its rapid growth stage, it begins building surplus or "free" cash flow and increasing the firm's value. Free cash is money available after funds have been reinvested in the firm to sustain its growth. As the enterprise matures and its growth rate slows down to one that is sustainable in the long-run, it reaches its peak of savings. Earnings and cash flows are high, and commitment of funds to increased operating assets is reduced. The maturity stage can last almost indefinitely, as long as the firm remains competitive in its industry. Of course, sometimes a firm's products or services are no longer competitive or needed by consumers, and the firm again starts consuming more cash than it brings in. Such firms will eventually cease to exist.

Financial markets play an important role in the marketing and transferring of financial assets and, thus, are an integral part of the savings and investment process. In Chapter 1 we defined *money markets* as markets where debt securities of one year or less are issued or traded. In Chapter 2 we discussed *money market securities*—which, as you recall, are debt instruments or securities with maturities of one year	**7.5 CAPITAL MARKET SECURITIES**

or less. The major securities that trade in the money markets are Treasury bills, negotiable certificates of deposit, commercial paper, banker's acceptances, repurchase agreements, and federal funds. Treasury bills and negotiable certificates of deposit are short-term investment vehicles available to individuals. These two short-term investments as well as commercial paper, banker's acceptances, and repurchase agreements are investments used by business firms. Federal funds are used by depository institutions with excess funds lending to depository institutions that have a need for funds.

In Chapter 1 we also defined *capital markets* as markets were debt securities with maturities longer than one year and corporate stocks are issued or traded. **Capital market securities** are corporate stocks and debt securities with maturities longer than one year. Capital markets are important to individuals seeking to finance home purchases, and they are very important to corporations who raise funds to finance their operations. Individuals and corporations with excess funds also invest in capital market securities.

Figure 7.2 identifies the basic securities that are issued and traded in capital securities markets. In Chapter 3 we initially defined a mortgage. We review the definition here as part of our discussion of capital market securities. A **mortgage** is a loan backed by real property in the form of buildings and houses. In the event the debt is not repaid, the lender can use proceeds from the sale of the real property to extinguish any remaining loan interest or principal balance. Individuals rely heavily on residential mortgages to assist them in owning their own homes. Businesses also often find it worthwhile to borrow against the real property they own.

Bonds are longer-term debt instruments issued by government units and business corporations. A **Treasury note/bond** is a debt instrument or security issued by the U.S. federal government with typical maturities ranging from two years up to 30 years. Treasury notes or bonds are sold to raise funds needed to reconcile longer-term imbalances between tax receipts and government expenditures. These securities have very low risks of default, and investors know that they are easily marketable in the secondary securities market. For example, if an investor initially purchases a 20-year Treasury bond and later identifies another investment opportunity, the bond can be easily sold in the secondary capital market. A **municipal bond** is a debt instrument or security issued by a state or local government. Maturities on state and local government bonds, are generally greater than one year and up to 40 years. However, municipal bonds issued to build airports or bridges may have their maturities set approximately equal to the expected lives of the assets being financed. Some investors find municipal bonds to be attractive investments because the interest paid on these securities is exempt from federal income taxes and because these bonds also can be sold in a secondary market.

Corporations issue financial instruments, or securities, called debt and equity to raise funds to acquire real assets to support the operations of their firms. Corporate debt instruments are bonds and equity securities are stocks. A **corporate bond** is a debt instrument issued by a corporation to raise longer-term funds. Corporate bonds are, typically, issued with maturities ranging from greater than one year up to 30 years and may be secured by the pledge of real property, plant, or equipment or they may be issued with only the backing of the general credit strength of the corporation. A share of **common stock** represents an ownership interest in a corporation. Corporations often issue new shares of their common stocks to raise funds for capital expenditures and investments in inventories. Active secondary

capital markets securities debt securities with maturities longer than one year and corporate stocks

mortgage loan backed by real property in the form of buildings and houses

treasury note/bond debt instrument issued by the U.S. federal government

municipal bond debt instrument issued by a state or local government

corporate bond debt instrument issued by a corporation to raise longer-term funds

common stock ownership interest in a corporation

Securities	Typical maturities	Issuers	Investors	Secondary market
Mortgages	5 to 30 years	Financial intermediaries	Individuals, business firms, and institutions	High activity
Treasury notes/bonds	2 to 30 years	U.S. government	Individuals, business firms, and institutions	High activity
Municipal bonds	2 to 40 years	State/local governments	Individuals, business firms, and institutions	Moderate activity
Corporate bonds	2 to 30 years	Corporations	Individuals, business firms, and institutions	Moderate activity
Corporate stocks	None	Corporations	Individuals, business firms, and institutions	High activity

FIGURE 7.2 Major capital market securities

markets exist for trading the common stocks of larger corporations after the stocks are initially issued. Corporations also can issue various classes of common stock, another type of stock called *preferred stock*, and even securities that are convertible into shares of common stock.[4]

Corporations also can use derivative securities to insure or hedge against various financial risks. A **derivative security** is a financial contract that derives its value from the value of another asset such as a bond or stock. The use of derivative securities is explored in the Learning Extension to Chapter 11.

derivative security financial contract that derives its value from a bond, stock, or other asset

LEARNING ACTIVITY

Go to the website of the Federal Reserve Board of Governors of the Federal Reserve System, https://www.federalreserve.gov, and identify current interest rates on U.S. Treasury bonds.

7.6 MORTGAGE MARKETS

An important element of the savings-investment process is the availability of financing to purchase homes. Since most individuals do not have the funds to purchase their home outright, they must rely on mortgage loans. **Mortgage markets** are markets in which mortgage loans are created to purchase buildings and houses and are originated in primary markets and traded in secondary markets. Mortgage debt is, typically, divided into farm loans, nonfarm loans, nonresidential loans that include commercial property, and residential property loans. Mortgage loans on residential property also are typically divided into multifamily loans and one- to four-family loans. Residential mortgages account for the largest portion of outstanding mortgage debt and, thus, receive emphasis in this text. Furthermore, because residential mortgage-related developments contributed to the recent financial crisis, we discuss mortgage markets fundamentals now.

mortgage markets where mortgage loans to purchase buildings and houses are originated and traded

Mortgage loans are federally insured or conventional mortgages. In the event a borrower defaults on a mortgage, federal insurance guarantees the loan repayment to the bank making the mortgage loan. The Federal Housing Administration (FHA) and the Veterans Administration (VA) provide insurance on FHA and VA mortgage loans. Lenders making conventional mortgage loans may assume the risk that the borrower may default or purchase private insurance to protect against borrower default.

7.6.1 TYPES OF MORTGAGES AND MORTGAGE-BACKED SECURITIES

The purchase of houses in the United States traditionally has been financed with fixed interest rate, long-term loans. A **fixed-rate mortgage** typically has a fixed interest rate and constant monthly payments over the life of the loan, which is typically 15 or 30 years. A loan that is repaid in equal payments over a specified time period is referred to as an *amortized* loan. We discuss amortized loans in Chapter 9. The traditional fixed-rate residential mortgage loan also required a sizeable down payment, typically 20% of the house purchase price, at the time the loan was made.

fixed-rate mortgage fixed interest rate with a constant periodic payment over the real estate loan's life

Holders of fixed-rate mortgages benefited by knowing that their monthly mortgage payment would not change over the loan's life, and thus they could plan and budget for the contractual monthly payment amounts. As a result, the *default rate*, or failure to make timely periodic payments, was low on fixed-rate mortgage loans. However, the benefits of fixed-rate mortgages were offset, in part, by the fact that only a portion of the U.S. population could qualify to purchase their own houses.

During the past couple of decades, a period of generally high fixed-rate mortgage loan interest rates and a time in which it was desired to extend housing ownership to more individuals in the United States, the use of adjustable-rate mortgages grew. An **adjustable-rate mortgage (ARM)** has an interest rate that changes or varies over time with market-determined interest rates based on a U.S. Treasury bill or other debt security. The interest rate on an ARM is often adjusted annually to reflect changes in U.S. Treasury bill rates (or other interest rate benchmark). Also, lenders typically offer ARMs with variable interest rates for one to five years with a provision to switch to a fixed rate over the remaining life of the ARM.

adjustable-rate mortgage (ARM) interest rate and periodic payments that vary with market interest rates over the real estate loan's life

Because ARMs, typically, offer lower initial interest rates and lower monthly payments, more individuals can qualify for home ownership. However, because of possible changing market-determined

---

[4] Various types of corporate bonds and stocks, as well as their characteristics, are discussed in Chapter 10. Primary and secondary markets for corporate bonds and stocks are covered in Chapter 11.

interest rates and potential changeovers to fixed interest rates, individuals who were able to make initially low monthly mortgage payments may find themselves unable to meet their mortgage payments if interest rates are adjusted upwards.

Mortgage loans are originated in the primary mortgage markets by mortgage brokers, mortgage companies, and depository financial institutions, which include banks, savings and loan associations, savings banks, and credit unions. Mortgage brokers and mortgage companies typically sell the mortgage loans they originated in the secondary mortgage markets. Commercial banks, which are the dominant type of depository institution that originate mortgage loans, either hold and collect the periodic payments by borrowers on the loans they originated or sell the loans in the secondary mortgage markets.

In some instances, banks and other mortgage lenders "pool" together loans they originated into securities. Other financial intermediaries "repackage" mortgage loans into securities. Securitization is the process of pooling and packaging mortgage loans into debt securities. A mortgage-backed security is a debt security created by pooling together a group of mortgage loans whose periodic payments belong to the holders of the security. Some mortgage-backed securities "pass through" the interest and principal payments to the owners of the securities. Payments on the underlying mortgages are made to the financial institution that created the mortgage-backed security. The institution, in turn, pays or passes through the payments to the investors or owners of the securities. In some mortgage-backed securities, the issuer separates or "strips" the interest and principal payment streams into separate securities. Cash flows from interest and principal payments are dependent on continued mortgage payments by the borrowers on the underlying mortgage loans. The uncertainty of mortgage payments is further increased when mortgages are prepaid during periods of declining interest rates.

7.6.2 CREDIT RATINGS AND SCORES

A credit rating indicates the expected likelihood that a borrower will miss interest or principal payments and possibly default on the debt obligation in the form of a loan, mortgage, or bond. Credit ratings are prepared by private organizations on individuals, financial institutions, business firms, and government entities.

A credit rating for an individual is typically expressed in terms of a credit score, which is a number that indicates an individual's creditworthiness or likelihood that a debt will be repaid according to the terms that were initially agreed to. Creditworthiness reflects an individual borrower's capacity to pay, his or her character, and the collateral or security to the lender. Some borrowers have the capacity to pay but may not be sufficiently trustworthy for certainty that they will pay. Credit scores are based on an individual's credit history, as reflected in credit report information (e.g., payments on credit cards, auto loans, mortgages) and public records (e.g., bankruptcies, tax liens).

While there are many different credit score systems in use, they each attempt to differentiate among high quality, moderate quality, and low-quality borrowers. For example, a credit scoring system may range from 500 to 1,000 points in 100-point increments. Mortgage loans issued to borrowers with credit scores above 700 might be viewed as prime mortgage loans. A prime mortgage is a home loan to a borrower with relatively high credit worthiness, indicating a relatively high likelihood that mortgage payments will be made when due. Of course, the higher the credit score, the higher the borrower's credit quality, with scores above 900 reflecting the highest credit quality classification.

Mortgage loan borrowers with credit scores of 700 or below, for example, might be considered to be subprime borrowers. A subprime mortgage is a home loan to a borrower with a relatively poor credit score, indicating a higher likelihood the borrower will miss mortgage payments when due. Making mortgage loans to subprime borrowers is a risky business in that an event such as an economic downturn in the form of a recession could result in a large percentage of subprime mortgage borrowers missing their mortgage payments and even defaulting on their home loans.

7.6.3 MAJOR PARTICIPANTS IN THE SECONDARY MORTGAGE MARKETS

As previously discussed, banks and other financial institutions originate mortgage loans and sometimes package mortgages to create mortgage-backed securities that often are sold in the

---

securitization process of pooling or packaging mortgage loans into debt securities

mortgage-backed security debt security created by pooling together a group of mortgage loans

credit rating indicates the expected likelihood that a borrower will pay a debt according to the terms agreed to

credit score a number that indicates the creditworthiness or likelihood that a borrower will make loan payments when due

prime mortgage home loan made to a borrower with a relatively high credit score indicating the likelihood that loan payments will be made as agreed to

subprime mortgage home loan made to a borrower with a relatively low credit score indicating the likelihood that loan payments might be missed when due

secondary mortgage markets. Also, recall that the federal government has played an active role in the development of secondary mortgage markets. The Federal National Mortgage Association (Fannie Mae) was created in 1938 to support the financial markets by purchasing home mortgages from banks so that the resulting funds could be lent to other borrowers. The Government National Mortgage Association (Ginnie Mae) was created in 1968. Ginnie Mae issues its own debt securities to obtain funds that are invested in mortgages made to low-to-moderate income home purchasers. The Federal Home Loan Mortgage Corporation (Freddie Mac) was formed in 1970 to purchase and hold mortgage loans. Freddie Mac acquired both prime mortgages and subprime mortgages over time.

Ginnie Mae and Fannie Mae issue mortgage-backed securities to fund their mortgage purchases and holdings. The securitization of mortgage loans by pooling and packaging the loans into mortgage-backed securities by Ginnie Mae and Fannie Mae aided in the development of the secondary mortgage markets.

As default rates on mortgage loans and mortgage-backed securities increased sharply after the housing price bubble burst, both Ginnie Mae and Freddie Mac suffered liquidity problems. In mid-2008, in an effort to avoid a financial meltdown, the Fed provided rescue funds for both Ginnie Mae and Freddie Mac, and the federal government took over control of both organizations.

DISCUSSION QUESTION 3

It is important to own a home? Why, or why not?

7.7.1 EARLY FACTORS

7.7 ROLE OF THE INDIVIDUAL IN THE 2007–2008 FINANCIAL CRISIS AND TODAY

CRISIS The "seeds" that culminated in the 2007–2008 financial crisis were sown at the beginning of the twenty-first century. Businesses emphasized cost cutting and improved operating efficiencies in the latter part of the 1980s. These efforts, coupled with a nearly decade-long economic growth in the 1990s left the United States awash with vast amounts of unused financial capital. The U.S. economy benefited further from large expenditures to, hopefully, minimize the so-called "Year 2000 (or Y2K)" problem associated with the fact that many computer programs used only two digits to indicate the year. For example, 1901 was coded as "01" and 1999 as "99." No one was sure what would happen when the first year of the new century was designated as "00." As a result, large precautionary expenditures were incurred to hopefully minimize potential problems.

The late 1990s saw the Internet "bubble" in the stock market—stock prices rose out of proportion from the ability of firms to generate earnings or cash flows. In particular, "high-flying" stocks included Internet or "tech" oriented stocks. Some forecast the end of long-standing business models and the genesis of new ways of doing business with the Internet and information as tools to gain profits. However, the movement from "brick and mortar" firms to "e-commerce" firms did not pave the way to a "new economic world," and the Internet/tech bubble burst.

Stock prices peaked in 2000 and began a rapid decline. The falling stock market, coupled with a slowing post-Y2K economy and a recession in 2001, encouraged the Federal Reserve System to lower interest rates to try to stimulate spending, borrowing, and economic growth. The terrorist attacks of September 11, 2001, added concern and uncertainty about the economy. To assist the economy, the Federal Reserve maintained liquidity of the financial sector and continued to lower interest rates. The Federal Reserve System was covered in Chapter 4, and we discussed the role of the Federal Reserve Board as a major policy maker group in Chapter 5.

Fiscal policy became stimulative, with increased government spending and the passage of tax cuts in 2002. Fiscal policy influences economic activity through taxation and expenditure plans, and it is carried out by the president and Congress with the support of the U.S. Treasury. We discussed the role of fiscal policy in Chapter 5. Overall, the setting of low interest rates, fiscal policy stimulation, and the resulting economic growth helped to create an environment conducive to excessive spending and borrowing.

7.7.2 A BORROWING-RELATED CULTURAL SHIFT

On the whole, U.S. consumers had in the past limited their use of debt, but over time the American psyche changed to wanting sooner, if not instant, gratification with respect to buying large-ticket items. Rather than saving and waiting to purchase expensive items, the use of credit cards rose. Borrowing now replaced "save now, buy later" as a spending philosophy. As we saw earlier in the chapter, the personal savings rate exceeded 10% in the 1960s and 1970s before declining to high single-rate levels in the 1980s and 1990s. During the first half of 2000s decade, the personal savings rate declined to a 2 to 3% level that coincided with increased subprime mortgage loans and other large amounts of borrowing. However, probably as a result of the onset of the 2007–2008 financial crisis and the 2008–2009 Great Recession, individuals increased their personal savings rate to more than 5% of their disposable income.

The cultural shift that allowed the public to "spend now, pay later"—rather than their parents' or grandparents' philosophy of "save now, spend later"—also affected household budgets. In addition to carrying a home mortgage and/or car loan or lease payments, individuals increased their use of high interest rate credit card debt. The growing use of debt during most of the decade of the 2000s resulted in a larger portion of U.S. household budgets being used to service debt—repaying both the principal and interest on borrowed funds.

U.S. government officials engaged in efforts during the 1990s and the decade of the 2000s to expand home ownership by encouraging lenders to make mortgage loans available to a broader spectrum of individuals. The typical, traditional home loan has been a 30-year, fixed interest rate amortized loan involving a constant monthly payment that would result in a zero loan balance at maturity. These traditional home loans also typically required a 20% down payment. In order to increase the number of individuals who could qualify for home ownership, alternative mortgage loan instruments were developed and in some instances credit standards were lowered.

As discussed earlier in this chapter, the traditional fixed-rate mortgage was often replaced by an adjustable-rate mortgage called an ARM. Mortgage lenders often offered initial below market interest rates on ARMs, as well as offering subprime mortgages to borrowers with relatively low credit scores, which suggested a likelihood that loan payments might be missed when due. Soon after the housing price bubble burst in mid-2006 and the economy began slowing in 2007, poorly qualified borrowers began defaulting on their mortgages. Developments in the mortgage markets were major contributors to the severity of the 2007–2008 financial crisis and contributed to the 2008–2009 Great Recession. Of course, while individuals were ultimately responsible for entering into very risky home mortgages, they were encouraged to do so by government officials, government-supported agencies, and mortgage originators and financial institution lenders.

7.7.3 SUBSEQUENT RECOVERY

Fiscal stimulus efforts and Fed easy money policies helped foster an ongoing decade-long period of economic recovery and growth that began in mid-2009. Unemployment rates declined from 10 percent in 2008 to below 4 percent by the end of 2018. GDP has grown and standards of living have increased. Recall that personal consumption expenditures by individuals is the largest component of GDP making it important to keep individuals employed and financially healthy.

Individuals, as an economic unit, are the largest providers of savings needed to make the savings-investment (or capital formation) process work. Savings are invested to create more capital goods such as buildings, equipment and machinery, and business inventories. Capital goods, in turn, are used to produce more goods and provide more services which leads to higher GDP levels.

Individuals have increased their savings rates in recent years and seem to be more prudent in their use of credit, And, while housing prices in some markets have surpassed their 2006 levels, a new housing price bubble seems unlikely at this time.

We know that economic growth won't continue forever. Whether individuals are now better prepared to meet credit and mortgage loan payments will be tested during the next economic downturn. Unfortunately, evidence suggests that many individuals have inadequate savings to cover economic and/or other emergencies if they were to occur.

- **Institutions and Markets**   Savings of individuals are accumulated in a number of ways by financial institutions that, in turn, make pooled savings available to businesses so that they can maintain and grow their operations. Savings are gathered by commercial banks and other depository institutions. Insurance companies collect premium payments and pension funds, gather contributions, and invest these funds until needed. Mutual funds also play a major role in attracting the savings of individuals and then investing the pooled funds in securities.

- **Investments**   Governments issue debt securities to finance their needs and corporations issue both debt and equity securities to maintain and grow their businesses. The savings of individuals are the primary source for raising financial capital by governments and corporations. Capital market securities were covered, with specific attention given to mortgage loans and mortgage markets. Financial institutions gather savings and make the savings available to governments and corporations in the primary securities markets. The process of determining interest rates for borrowing financial capital and pricing new stock issues will be covered as we progress through Part 2.

- **Financial Management**   Financial managers often must raise additional amounts of debt and equity funds to finance the plans for their firms. While they may depend somewhat on loans from banks, they may also need to attract financial capital by selling bonds or stocks either privately or publicly. A decision to raise funds must be accompanied with the willingness to pay the required interest rates established in the marketplace or selling stock at a market-determined price.

SUMMARY

LO 7.1   The gross domestic product (GDP) has four major components. 1) Personal consumption expenditures (PCE) indicate expenditures by individuals for durable goods, nondurable goods, and services. 2) Government expenditures (GE) include expenditures for goods and services plus gross investments by both the federal and the state and the local governments. 3) Gross private domestic investment (GPDI) measures fixed investment in residential and nonresidential structures, producers' durable equipment, and changes in business inventories. 4) The net exports (NE) of goods and services is calculated as exports minus imports.

LO 7.2   The principal sources of federal government revenues (income) are Social Security and other retirement taxes; personal income taxes; corporate income taxes; borrowing to cover the deficit; and excise, estate, and other taxes. Principal expenditures (outlays) are Social Security, Medicare, and other retirement benefits; national defense, veterans, and foreign affairs; social programs (including Medicaid); physical, human, and community development; net interest on the debt; and law enforcement and general government.

LO 7.3   An economic unit (individuals, corporations, or governments) creates savings when all of its income is not consumed resulting in the accumulation of cash and other financial assets. The major sources of savings are personal savings and corporate savings. Personal saving occurs when personal income is greater than personal current taxes and personal outlays. Corporate saving occurs when profits before taxes are greater than tax liabilities and dividends, resulting in undistributed profits.

LO 7.4   The factors that affect savings in a given period are levels of income, economic expectations, cyclical influences, and life stage of the individual saver or corporation. Individual savings depend on the life stage of the saver which could be formative/education developing, career starting/family creating, wealth building, or retirement enjoying. Corporate savings also depend on the life stage of the corporation which could be start-up stage, survival stage, rapid growth stage, or maturity stage.

LO 7.5   Capital market securities are corporate stocks and debt securities with maturities longer than one year. The major capital market securities that facilitate the savings and investment process include mortgages, Treasury notes/bonds, municipal bonds, corporate bonds, and corporate stocks. A mortgage is a loan backed by real property in the form of buildings and houses. The federal government issues Treasury securities, and state and local governments issue municipal bonds. As the label indicates, corporations issue corporate bonds and corporate stocks.

LO 7.6   Individuals may obtain either a fixed-rate mortgage loan or an adjustable-rate mortgage loan. A fixed-rate mortgage has a fixed interest rate with constant monthly payments over the life of the loan, which is, typically, 15 or 30 years. An adjustable-rate mortgage has an interest rate that changes or varies over time according to market-determined interest rates on a Treasury bill or other debt security. Banks and other financial institutions that originate mortgage loans do not necessarily hold these loans but, rather, can sell them in secondary mortgage markets, and in so doing can free up funds for making new mortgage loans.

LO 7.7   Individuals as a unit had personal savings rates that were at low, double-digit levels in the 1960s and 1970s before declining to the high single-digit levels in the 1980s and 1990s. However, a change seems to have occurred in the first half of the 2000–2010 period when personal savings rates dropped to the low, single-digit levels. Individuals acquired risky mortgage loans and increased their credit card and other debt. Resulting debt defaults contributed to severity of the 2007–2008 financial crisis. More recently, personal savings rates have returned to the upper, single-digit levels and individuals have been de-leveraging.

KEY TERMS

- adjustable-rate mortgage (ARM)
- autocratic capitalism
- capital consumption adjustment
- capital formation
- capitalism
- capital market securities
- common stock
- contractual savings
- corporate bond
- corporate retention rate
- credit rating
- credit score
- democracy
- democratic capitalism
- derivative security
- discretionary spending
- dissaving
- economic unit savings
- federal statutory debt limits
- fixed-rate mortgage
- government expenditures (GE)
- gross domestic product (GDP)
- gross private domestic investment (GPDI)
- mandatory spending
- mortgage
- mortgage-backed security
- mortgage markets
- municipal bond
- net exports (NE)
- personal consumption expenditures (PCE)
- personal saving
- personal savings rate
- prime mortgage
- savings deficit unit
- savings surplus unit
- securitization
- subprime mortgage
- Treasury note/bond
- undistributed profits
- voluntary savings

REVIEW QUESTIONS

1. **(LO 7.1)** Describe the terms autocratic capitalism and democratic capitalism and discuss the model followed by the U.S.

2. **(LO 7.1)** What is capital formation?

3. **(LO 7.1)** Describe the major components of the gross domestic product.

4. **(LO 7.2)** Identify the various sources of revenues in the federal budget.

5. **(LO 7.2)** Identify the major expense categories in the federal budget.

6. **(LO 7.2)** Describe whether the federal government has been operating with surplus or deficit budgets in recent years.

7. **(LO 7.3)** Briefly describe the historical role of savings in the United States.

8. **(LO 7.3)** Compare savings surplus and savings deficit units. Indicate which economic units are generally of one type or the other.

9. **(LO 7.3)** Define *personal saving*.

10. **(LO 7.3)** Differentiate between voluntary and contractual savings.

11. **(LO 7.3)** Describe the recent levels of savings rates in the United States.

12. **(LO 7.3)** How and why do corporations save?

13. **(LO 7.4)** Describe the principal factors that influence the level of savings by individuals.

14. **(LO 7.4)** How do economic cycle movements affect the media or types of savings by businesses?

15. **(LO 7.4)** What are the life cycle stages of individuals?

16. **(LO 7.4)** How does each life cycle stage relate to the amount and type of individual savings?

17. **(LO 7.4)** What are the life cycle stages of corporations and other business firms?

18. **(LO 7.4)** Explain how financial savings generated by a business is a function of its life cycle stage.

19. **(LO 7.5)** What are the two types of financial market securities?

20. **(LO 7.5)** Identify and briefly describe the major securities that are originated or traded in capital securities markets.

21. **(LO 7.6)** What is a mortgage? What is meant by the term *mortgage markets*?

22. **(LO 7.6)** Identify and briefly describe the two major types of residential real estate mortgages.

23. **(LO 7.6)** What is meant by the term *securitization*? What is a mortgage-backed security?

24. **(LO 7.6)** Briefly describe credit ratings and credit scores.

25. **(LO 7.6)** Identify and describe the roles of several major participants in the secondary mortgage markets.

26. **(LO 7.7)** What role did individuals play in the development of the 2007–2008 financial crisis?

EXERCISES

1. Go to the U.S. Department of Commerce, Bureau of Economic Analysis website at https://www.bea.gov and determine the following:
   a. The current personal savings rate in the United States.
   b. The amount of current corporate savings as reflected in the amount of undistributed profits.

2. Assume you are an elected member of Congress. A lobbying group has agreed to provide financial support for your re-election campaign next year. In return for the group's support, you have been asked to champion their self-interests in the form of a spending bill that is being considered by Congress. What would you do?

3. Match the following financial instruments and securities with their issuers.

Instruments/Securities	Issuers
a. corporate stocks	1. commercial banks
b. Treasury bonds	2. corporations
c. municipal bonds	3. U.S. government
d. negotiable certificates of deposit	4. state/local governments

4. Match the following financial instruments and securities with their typical maturities.

Instruments/Securities	Maturities
a. corporate stocks	1. 2 to 40 years
b. Treasury notes/bonds	2. no maturity
c. mortgages	3. 2 to 30 years
d. municipal bonds	4. 5 to 30 years

PROBLEMS

1. A very small country's gross domestic product is $12 million.
   a. If government expenditures amount to $7.5 million and gross private domestic investment is $5.5 million, what would be the amount of net exports of goods and services?

2. How would your answer change in Problem 1 if the gross domestic product had been $14 million?

3. Personal income amounted to $17 million last year. Personal current taxes amounted to $4 million and personal outlays for consumption expenditures, nonmortgage interest, and so forth were $12 million.
   a. What was the amount of disposable personal income last year?
   b. What was the amount of personal saving last year?
   c. Calculate personal saving as a percentage of disposable personal income.

4. Assume personal income was $28 million last year. Personal outlays were $20 million and personal current taxes were $5 million.

   a. What was the amount of disposable personal income last year?
   b. What was the amount of personal saving last year?
   c. Calculate personal saving as a percentage of disposable personal income.

5. The components of a nation's gross domestic product were identified and discussed in this chapter. Assume the following accounts and amounts were reported by a nation last year. Government expenditures (purchases of goods and services) were $5.5 billion, personal consumption expenditures were $40.5 billion, gross private domestic investment amounted to $20 billion, capital consumption allowances were $4 billion, personal savings were estimated at $2 billion, imports of goods and services amounted to $6.5 billion, and the exports of goods and services were $5 billion.
   a. Determine the nation's gross domestic product.
   b. How would your answer change if the dollar amounts of imports and exports were reversed?

6. Assume that some of the data provided in Problem 5 change next year. Specifically, government

expenditures increase by 10%, gross private domestic investment declines by 10%, and imports of goods and services drop to $6 billion. Assume the other information as given remains the same.

a. Determine the nation's gross domestic product for next year.

b. How would your answer change in (a) if personal consumption expenditures are only $35 billion next year and capital consumption allowances actually increase by 10%?

7. A nation's gross domestic product is $600 million. Its personal consumption expenditures are $350 million, and government expenditures are $100 million. Net exports of goods and services amount to $50 million.

a. Determine the nation's gross private domestic investment.

b. If imports exceed exports by $25 million, how would your answer to (a) change?

8. A nation's gross domestic product is stated in U.S. dollars at $40 million. The dollar value of one unit of the nation's currency (FC) is $0.25.

a. Determine the value of GDP in FCs.

b. How would your answer change if the dollar value of one FC increases to $0.30?

9. A country in Southeast Asia states its gross domestic product in terms of yen. Assume that last year its GDP was 50 billion yen when one U.S. dollar could be exchanged for 120 yen.

a. Determine the country's GDP in terms of U.S. dollars for last year.

b. Assume the GDP increases to 55 billion yen for this year, while the dollar value of one yen is now $0.01. Determine the country's GDP in terms of U.S. dollars for this year.

c. Show how your answer in (b) would change if one U.S. dollar could be exchanged for 110 yen.

10. **Challenge Problem** (*Note:* This exercise requires knowledge of probabilities and expected values.) Following are data relating to a nation's operations last year.

Capital consumption allowances	$150 million
Undistributed corporate profits	40 million
Personal consumption expenditures	450 million
Personal savings	50 million
Corporate inventory valuation adjustment	−5 million
Federal government deficit	−30 million
Government expenditures	10 million
State and local governments surplus	1 million
Net exports of goods and services	−2 million
Gross private domestic investment	200 million

a. Determine the nation's gross domestic product (GDP).

b. How would your answer change in (a) if exports of goods and services were $5 million and imports were 80% of exports?

c. Show how the GDP in (a) would change under the following three scenarios:
Scenario 1 (probability of 0.20): the GDP components would be 120% of their values in (a).
Scenario 2 (probability of 0.50): the GDP component values used in (a) would occur.
Scenario 3 (probability of 0.30): the GDP components would be 75% of their values in (a).

d. Determine the nation's gross savings last year.

e. Show how your answer in (d) would change if each account simultaneously increases by 10%.

f. Show how your answer in (d) would change if each account simultaneously decreases by 10%.

g. Show how your answer in (d) would have changed if capital consumption allowances had been 10% less and personal consumption expenditures had been $400 million.

Interest Rates

LEARNING OBJECTIVES

After studying this chapter, you should be able to do the following:

LO 8.1　Describe how interest rates change in response to shifts in the supply and demand for loan-able funds.

LO 8.2　Identify the major components of market interest rates.

LO 8.3　Describe the types of U.S. Treasury marketable securities and indicate who owns them.

LO 8.4　Define the term structure of interest rates and describe the three theories used to explain the term structure.

LO 8.5　Discuss historical and recent price movements in the United States and describe the various types of inflation.

LO 8.6　Describe default risk and default risk premiums and discuss how these premiums are observed and measured.

Where we have been. . . In Chapter 7 you learned about the savings and investment process as it takes place in the United States. The gross domestic product (GDP) and capital formation were discussed. GDP is composed of personal consumption expenditures, government purchases, gross private domestic investment, and the net export of goods and services. The historical role of savings and how financial assets and liabilities are created was covered. You should now also have a basic understanding of the federal government's source of receipts and where expenditures are allocated. You should also understand the major sources of savings, how the major financial institutions direct funds from savings into investment, and factors that affect savings.

Where we are going. . . Chapter 9 focuses on the time value of money. By saving and investing, money can "grow" over time through the compounding of interest. We first cover simple interest and then turn to compounding of current investments (determining future values) and discounting of future cash receipts (finding present values). You will also be introduced to annuities, which are investments that involve constant periodic payments or receipts of cash. Chapter 10 focuses on the characteristics and valuations of bonds and stocks. In Chapter 11 you will learn about the characteristics and operation of primary and secondary securities markets. Part 2 concludes with Chapter 12, which focuses on helping you learn and understand concepts relating to financial returns and risks associated with investing in stocks and bonds.

How this chapter applies to me. . . It is nearly impossible to get through the day without seeing some reference to interest rates on saving or borrowing money. You may see interest rates being offered on savings accounts by depository institutions, interest rates on new and used automobiles, and even the rate at which you could borrow for a loan to pay your tuition or to purchase a home. Your cost of borrowing will generally be higher when you are just starting your working career and your credit quality has not yet been established. Understanding the factors that determine the level of interest rates, hopefully, will help you make more informed decisions concerning when to spend, save, and borrow.

We all have been tempted by the advertisements for goods and services that suggest we should "buy now and pay for it later." These advertisements are hoping that we will decide that, to us, the value of "more" current consumption is worth the added interest that we will have to pay on the funds that we must borrow to finance this consumption.

Sometimes, individuals like to consume more now, even though they don't have the money to pay for this consumption. For example, you may see a pair of shoes in a store window "that you have to have right now." Maybe you don't currently have the money to pay for the shoes. Don't despair; if you have a credit card, the credit card issuer may lend you the money to pay for the shoes. In return, you will have to pay back the amount borrowed plus interest on the loan.

You might also be considering making a current investment in your future by borrowing money to go to college. In this case, you hope that your current education will lead to an increase in your future earning power, out of which you will have to repay your student loan. When you purchased your shoes on credit, you decided to consume now and pay later for this current consumption. When you decide to invest in your education, you expect that future earnings will be larger, making it easier to repay the student loan. Businesses also borrow to make investments in inventory, plant, and equipment that will earn profits sufficient to pay interest, repay the amount borrowed, and provide returns to equity investors. In this chapter we focus on the cost or price of borrowing funds. An understanding of interest rates—what causes them to change and how they relate to changes in the economy—is of fundamental importance in the world of finance.

8.1 SUPPLY AND DEMAND FOR LOANABLE FUNDS

loanable funds amount of money made available by lenders to borrowers

interest rate price of loanable funds in financial markets

equilibrium interest rate price that equates the demand for and supply of loanable funds

Loanable funds are the amount of money made available by lenders to borrowers. Lenders are willing to supply funds to borrowers as long as lenders can earn a satisfactory return on their loans (i.e., an amount greater than that which was lent). Borrowers will demand funds from lenders as long as borrowers can invest the funds so as to earn a satisfactory return above the cost of their loans. Actually, the supply and demand for loanable funds will take place as long as both lenders and borrowers have the expectation of satisfactory returns. Of course, returns received may differ from those expected because of inflation, failure to repay loans, and poor investments. Return experiences will, in turn, affect future supply-and-demand relationships for loanable funds.

The **interest rate** is the price of loanable funds in financial markets. The price that equates the demand for and supply of loanable funds in the financial markets is the **equilibrium interest rate**. Figure 8.1 depicts how interest rates are determined in the financial markets. Graph A shows the interest rate (r) that clears the market by bringing the demand (D_1) by borrowers for funds in equilibrium with the supply (S_1) by lenders of funds. For illustrative purposes, we have chosen a rate of 4% as the cost, or price, which makes savings equal to investment (i.e., where the supply and demand curves intersect).

Interest rates may move from an existing equilibrium level to a new equilibrium level as the result of an unanticipated change or "shock" that causes the demand for, or supply of, loanable funds to change or shift. For example, a new increase in the desire to invest in business assets because of an expected expanding economy might cause the demand for loanable funds to increase or shift upward. Graph B depicts a shift in the demand for loanable funds (i.e., from D_1 to D_2) but no change in the supply curve (S_1). Given this demand for a larger quantity of loanable funds, borrowers must pay higher interest rates to get savers to provide a greater supply of loanable funds. An upward movement along the S_1 supply curve occurs until a new equilibrium interest level is reached at, say, 5% compared with the previous 4% equilibrium interest rate.

Graph C depicts the result of an unanticipated increase in inflation, which leads lenders (suppliers) to require a higher rate of interest. Stated differently, the interest rate observed in the marketplace reflects the existing expected inflation rate over the life of the debt instrument. When there is an increase in the expected inflation rate, lenders will expect to be compensated for this higher inflation rate by a higher market interest rate. This is shown by the shift in supply curves from S_1 to S_2, which, for illustrative purposes, shows an increase in the equilibrium interest rate from 4% to 6%. Given the assumption of no shift or change in the demand curve, the new equilibrium price is reached by borrowers being willing to pay increasingly higher interest rates until the new equilibrium interest rate is reached.

At this point, we have not taken into consideration the fact that borrowers also may adjust or shift their demand for loanable funds because of the likelihood of more-costly loans. Graph D depicts the situation that borrowers may cut back on their demand for loanable funds from D_1 to D_3 as a result of an

FIGURE 8.1 Interest rate determination in the financial markets

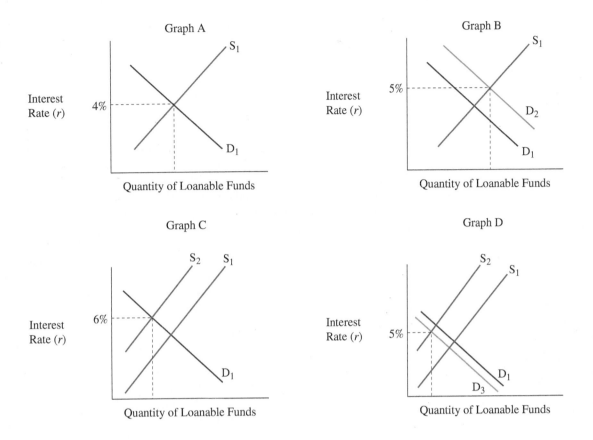

unanticipated increase in inflation. For example, this would occur if borrowers felt that their higher borrowing costs could not be passed on to their customers and, thus, the returns on their investments would be adversely affected by the higher inflation rates. Instead of the result of an unanticipated increase in inflation shock causing the interest rate to rise to 6% (Graph C), the new equilibrium rate where supply equals demand might be only 5%. In essence, the upward shift in the supply curve is offset in part by the downward shift in the demand curve.

8.1.1 HISTORICAL CHANGES IN U.S. INTEREST RATE LEVELS

Interest rates for loanable funds have varied throughout the history of the United States as the result of shifting supply and demand. Since just after the Civil War, there have been four periods of rising or relatively high long-term interest rates and four periods of falling or relatively low interest rates on long-term loans and investments.

Periods of increasing or high long-term interest rates were as follows:

- 1864–1873

- 1905–1920

- 1927–1933

- 1946–1982

The rapid economic expansion after the Civil War caused the first period of rising interest rates, from 1864 to 1873. The second period, from 1905 to 1920, was based on both large-scale prewar expansion and the inflation associated with World War I. The third period, from 1927 to 1933, was due to the economic boom from 1927 to 1929 and the unsettled conditions in the securities markets during the early part of the Great Depression, from 1929 to 1933. The rapid economic expansion following World War II led to the last period, from 1946 to 1982.

Periods of decreasing or low long-term interest rates were, as follows:

* 1873–1905

* 1920–1927

* 1933–1946

* 1982–present

The first period of falling interest rates was from 1873 to 1905. As the public debt was paid off and funds became widely available, the supply of funds grew more rapidly than the demand for them. Prices and interest rates fell, even though the economy was moving forward. The same general factors were at work in the second period, 1920 to 1927. The third period of low interest rates, from 1933 to 1946, resulted from the government's actions in fighting the Great Depression, and continued during World War II, when interest rates were pegged, or set.

Beginning in 1966, interest rates entered a period of unusual increases, leading to the highest rates in U.S. history. This increase in rates began as a result of the Vietnam War. It continued in the 1970s because of a policy of on-again, off-again price controls and increased demands for capital arising from ecological concerns and the energy crisis. Furthermore, several periods of poor crops coupled with sharp price increases for crude oil caused worldwide inflation. Interest rates peaked at the beginning of the 1980s, with short-term rates above 20% and long-term rates in the high teens. In summary, double-digit inflation, a somewhat tight monetary policy, and heavy borrowing demand by business contributed to these record levels.

The fourth period of declining long-term interest rates began in 1982, when rates peaked, and continues today. Inflation rates dropped dramatically from double-digit levels during the beginning of the 1980s to below 3% since the early 1990s. Low inflation rates, generally about 2%, have continued through 2018. The decline in inflation rates seems to have been a primary reason long-term interest rates have also trended downward.

Short-term interest rates generally move up and down with the business cycle. Therefore, they show many more periods of expansion and contraction. Both long-term and short-term interest rates tend to rise in prosperity periods during which the economy is expanding rapidly. A major exception was during World War II, when interest rates were pegged. During this period the money supply increased rapidly, laying the base for postwar inflation.

Today, both short-term and long-term interest rates continue to be at relatively low levels in the United States. This has been due, in part, to the Fed's efforts to avoid a financial meltdown during the 2007–2008 financial crisis and to support economic recovery from the 2008–2009 Great Recession. Recall from Chapter 4 that the Fed reacted by employing nontraditional monetary policy actions called quantitative easing. QE1 was implemented in 2008, QE2 began in 2010, and QE3 was initiated in 2012. In December 2015, the Fed initiated a change in monetary policy by raising its federal funds rate target from 0.00-0.25% to 0.25-0.50%. After eight additional quarter point increases, the target federal funds rate was 2.25–2.50% at the end of 2018.

8.1.2 LOANABLE FUNDS THEORY

Loanable funds theory holds that interest rates are a function of the supply of and demand for loanable funds

The **loanable funds theory** holds that interest rates are a function of the supply of and demand for loanable funds. This is a flow theory, in that it focuses on the relative supply and demand of loanable funds during a specified period. How the supply of and demand for loanable funds interact determines both the interest rate and the quantity of funds that flow through the financial markets during any period. If the supply of funds increases, holding demand constant, interest rates will tend to fall. Likewise, an increase in the demand for loans will tend to drive up interest rates. This is depicted in Graph B of Figure 8.1.

8.1.2.1 Sources of Loanable Funds

Current savings and the expansion of deposits by depository institutions represent two basic sources of loanable funds. The Fed, through its open-market operations, also provides a source of loanable funds when it purchases government securities.

SMALL BUSINESS PRACTICE

THE FAMILY BUSINESS OR VENTURE

Family businesses continue to be very popular in the United States. For publicly held firms, corporate goals may differ in part from the goals of managers. For closely held firms that are not family owned, the business goals and the personal goals of owner/managers are closely aligned. For family owned or family controlled firms, a third set of goals—family goals—also must be considered. When family goals are closely aligned with the business and manager goals, the business can benefit from family sharing and closeness. However, when family goals differ from business and/or manager goals, conflict and an argumentative environment may prevail. In such instances, family controlled businesses often fail or the family is forced to sell.

Jeffry Timmons lists several problems unique to family businesses or ventures.* First, problems of control, fairness, and equity often exist. For example, family members may have different ideas as to how the business should be run. Fairness and equity issues relate to the division of work and relative contributions to running the business. Second is the issue of credibility, whereby founding parents find it difficult to believe that their children can perform in a manner comparable to their own.

The third potential problem relates to family dynamics. Since it often is difficult to separate business operations from family life, tensions in one area often spill over into the other area. Fourth is the problem of deciding succession. If succession is to involve a next generation family member, the founder must disengage his or her ownership rights and delegate an increased level of responsibility to the new person in control. For succession to succeed, the founder must be willing to assume the role of advisor to the family member who was selected to run the firm in the future.

*Jeffry Timmons, *New Venture Creation*, 4th Edition (Boston: Irwin/McGraw-Hill, 1994). Also see Stephen Spineilli, Jr. and Robert J. Adams Jr., *New Venture Creation*, 10th Edition (New York: McGraw-Hill/Education, 2016), Chapter 17.

The supply of savings comes from all sectors of the economy, and most of it flows through U.S. financial institutions. Individuals may save part of their incomes, either as voluntary savings or through contractual savings programs—such as purchasing whole life or endowment insurance policies or repaying installment or mortgage loans. Governmental units and nonprofit institutions sometimes have funds in excess of current expenditures. Corporations may have savings available because they are not paying out all their earnings as dividends. Depreciation allowances that are not being used currently to buy new capital equipment to replace older equipment may also be available for lending.

Pension funds, both governmental and private, provide another source of saving. These funds, which are building up large reserves to meet future commitments, are available for investment.

Some savings are invested as ownership equity in businesses, either directly in single proprietorships or partnerships or by buying stock in corporations. This is, however, only a small part of total savings. The bulk of the total savings each year is available as loanable funds. Funds may be loaned directly; for example, when someone lends money to a friend to enable him or her to expand business operations. However, most savings are loaned through financial institutions, one of whose basic functions is the accumulation of savings.

The second basic source of loanable funds is that created by the banking system. Banks and other depository institutions not only channel savings to borrowers, but also create deposits, which are the most widely used form of money in the U.S. economy. This process was discussed in Chapter 5. Net additions to the money supply are a source of loanable funds; during periods when the money supply contracts, the flow of loanable funds can drop below the level of current savings.

In Chapter 4, we discussed the basic monetary policy instruments available to the Federal Reserve that allow it to increase or decrease the money supply and, thus, the availability of loanable funds. The primary way the Fed increases the money supply and loanable funds is through its open-market purchases of government securities. The Fed's quantitative easing initiatives are examples of its efforts to increase the money supply and loanable funds.

8.1.2.2 Factors Affecting the Supply of and Demand for Loanable Funds

Many factors can affect the supply of and demand for loanable funds. Following are several important factors.

8.1.2.2.1 Volume of Savings
The major factor that determines the volume of savings, corporate as well as individual, is the level of national income. When income is high, savings are high; when it is low, savings are low. The pattern of income taxes—both the level of the tax and the tax rates in various income brackets—also influences savings volume. Furthermore, the tax treatment of savings itself

influences the amount of income saved. For example, the tax deferral on (or postponement of) savings placed in individual retirement accounts (IRAs), increases the volume of savings.

The age of the population has an important effect on the volume of savings. As we discussed in Chapter 7, little saving is done during the formative and education-building stage or during the family creating stage. Therefore, an economy with a large share of young couples with children will have less total savings than one with more people in the older, wealth-building stage.

The volume of savings also depends on the factors that affect indirect savings. The more effectively the life insurance industry promotes the sale of whole life and endowment insurance policies, the larger the volume of savings. The higher the demand for private pension funds, which accumulate contributions during working years to make payments on retirement, the larger the volume of savings. The effect of interest rates on such savings is often just the opposite of the normal effect of price on supply. As interest rates decrease, more money must be paid for insurance for the same amount of coverage, because a smaller amount of interest will be earned from the reinvestment of premiums and earnings. Inversely, as interest rates rise, less money needs to be put into reserves to get the same objectives. The same is true of the amount of money that must be put into annuities and pension funds.

When savings result from the use of consumer credit, the effect of interest rates is delayed. For example, assume a car is bought with a three-year loan. Savings, in the form of repaying the loan, must go on for three years regardless of changes in interest rates. There may even be an opposite effect in the case of a mortgage because, if interest rates drop substantially, the loan can be refinanced. At the lower interest rate the same dollar payments provide a larger amount for repayment of principal; that is, for saving.

8.1.2.2.2 Expansion of Deposits by Depository Institutions

The amount of short-term credit available depends largely on the lending policies of commercial banks and other depository institutions, and on the policies of the Federal Reserve System. Lenders are influenced by such factors as present business conditions and future prospects. However, the Federal Reserve has great control over the ability of the banking system to create new deposits, as discussed in Chapter 4.

How much long-term credit of different types is available depends on the policies of the different suppliers of credit. Since depository institutions do not play a major role in this field, the money supply is not expanded directly to meet long-term credit demands. Indirectly, however, their policies and those of the Federal Reserve are very important: if the banking system expands the money supply to meet short-term needs, a larger proportion of the supply of loanable funds can be used for long-term credit.

8.1.2.2.3 Liquidity Attitudes

How lenders see the future has a significant effect on the supply of loanable funds, both long term and short term. Lenders may feel that the economic outlook is so uncertain that they are reluctant to lend their money. This liquidity preference can be so strong that large amounts of funds lie idle, as they did during the depression in the 1930s. Lenders may also prefer liquidity because they expect either interest rates to go up in the near future or opportunities for direct investment to be more favorable. Thus, liquidity attitudes may result in keeping some funds idle that would normally be available for lending.

8.1.2.2.4 Effect of Interest Rates on the Quantity of Loanable Funds Being Demanded

The demand for loanable funds comes from all sectors of the economy. Business borrows to finance current operations and to buy plant and equipment. Farmers borrow to meet short-term and long-term needs. Institutions, such as hospitals and schools, borrow primarily to finance new buildings and equipment. Individuals finance the purchase of homes with long-term loans, and purchase durable goods or cover emergencies with intermediate- and short-term loans. Governmental units borrow to finance public buildings, bridge the gap between expenditures and tax receipts, and meet budget deficits. The factors affecting the demand for loanable funds are different for each type of borrower. We have considered such factors in detail when analyzing the various types of credit. Therefore, this discussion covers only how interest rates affect the major types of borrowing.

Historically, one of the biggest borrowers has been the federal government, and Congress generally gives little consideration to interest rates in its spending programs. Minor changes in interest rates do not affect short-term business borrowing. However, historical evidence shows that large increases in short-term interest rates do lead to a decrease in the demand for bank loans and other forms of short-term business borrowing.

Changes in long-term interest rates also affect long-term business borrowing. Most corporations put off long-term borrowing when rates are up if they expect rates to go down in the near future.

While minor changes in interest rates generally have little effect on consumer borrowing, larger interest rate changes have strongly influenced consumer borrowing for durable goods and houses in the past. Lower mortgage loan rates, generally, result in greater demand for houses and lower car loan rates often are associated with increases in automobile purchases.

8.1.2.2.5 Actions of the Banking System, the Fed, and the Government While the effect of interest rates on loanable funds varies, both the supply of and the demand for loanable funds are affected by the actions of the banking system, the Fed, and the government. When depository institutions expand credit by increasing the total volume of short-term loans, the supply of loanable funds increases. When credit contracts, the supply of loanable funds decreases.

The actions of the Fed in setting discount rates, buying and selling securities in the open market, and changing reserve requirements also affect the supply of loanable funds. As previously noted, when the Fed purchases government securities the supply of loanable funds increases. When the Fed sells government securities the supply of loanable funds decreases. The selling of government securities by the Fed also can impact the demand for loanable funds since resulting higher interest rates may discourage borrowers.

Government borrowing has become a major influence on demand for funds and likely will remain so for the foreseeable future. Government surpluses or deficits make funds available in the market or take them out of the market in substantial amounts. Treasury debt management policies also affect the supply-and-demand relationships for short-term and long-term funds. The Treasury, through tax policies and other government programs, can affect the supply of funds. However, the Treasury's major influence is on the demand for funds, as it borrows heavily to finance federal deficits.

8.1.2.2.6 International Factors Affecting Interest Rates Interest rates in the United States are now no longer influenced only by domestic factors. The willingness of foreign institutions and governments to accumulate and hold U.S. government securities influences the interest rates the federal government pays in issuing new securities. This international influence adds to the need to balance the national budget and to reduce the amount of deficit financing. As production has shifted to many other countries, investment has also shifted. In short, the Treasury and the Federal Reserve must consider the influence of international movements of funds on domestic interest rates.

8.2 COMPONENTS OF MARKET INTEREST RATES

In addition to supply-and-demand relationships, interest rates are determined by a number of specific factors or components. The **market interest rate** is the interest rate observed in the marketplace for a debt instrument. A market, or *nominal*, interest rate contains at least two components—a real rate of interest and an inflation premium. The **real rate of interest** is the interest rate on a risk-free financial debt instrument when no inflation is expected. It is generally believed that investors must expect a minimum level of return in order to get them to invest in debt instruments instead of holding cash. The **inflation premium** is the additional expected return to compensate for anticipated inflation over the life of a debt instrument. In its simplest form, the observed market interest rate (r) can be expressed as,

$$r = RR + IP \tag{8.1}$$

where RR is the real rate of interest and IP is an inflation premium. For debt instruments that have no additional risk components, this interest rate is called the **risk-free interest rate**.

In practice, it is difficult to identify a debt instrument that trades in the market based only on a risk-free interest rate. In the next section we will discuss the possibility of using observed interest rates on U.S. Treasury securities as proxies for the risk-free interest rate. Most debt instruments will also have a default risk premium. Equation (8.1) can be expanded to include expected compensation for this additional risk:

$$r = RR + IP + DRP \tag{8.2}$$

where DRP is the default risk premium.

market interest rate interest rate observed in the marketplace for a debt instrument

real rate of interest interest rate on a risk-free debt instrument when no inflation is expected

inflation premium additional expected return to compensate for anticipated inflation over the life of a debt instrument

risk-free interest rate interest rate containing only a real rate of interest component and an inflation premium

default risk premium additional expected return to compensate for the possibility a borrower will fail to pay interest and/or principal when due

The **default risk premium** is the additional expected return to compensate for the possibility that the borrower will not pay interest and/or repay principal when due according to the debt instrument's contractual arrangements. The DRP reflects the application of the risk-return principle of finance presented in Chapter 1. In essence, "higher returns are expected for taking on more risk." This is a higher "expected" return because the issuer may default on some of the contractual returns. Of course, the actual "realized" return on a default risky debt investment could be substantially less than the expected return. At the extreme, the debt security investor could lose all of his or her investment. The DRP is discussed further in the last section of this chapter. The risk-return finance principle is extended to stock investments and to portfolios of securities in Chapter 12. Instead of a default risk premium, the concentration is on "stock risk premiums" and "market risk premiums."

Two additional premiums are added to equation (8.2) to explain market interest rates for debt instruments with varying maturities and liquidity. This expanded version can be expressed as,

$$r = \text{RR} + \text{IP} + \text{DRP} + \text{MRP} + \text{LP} \tag{8.3}$$

where MRP is the maturity risk premium and LP is the liquidity premium on a debt instrument.

maturity risk premium additional expected return to compensate for interest rate risk on debt instruments with longer maturities

interest rate risk risk of changes in the price or value of fixed-rate debt instruments resulting from changes in market interest rates

The **maturity risk premium** is the additional expected return to compensate interest rate risk on debt instruments with longer maturities. **Interest rate risk** is the risk of changes in the price or value of fixed-rate debt instruments resulting from changes in market interest rates. There is an inverse relationship in the marketplace between debt instrument values or prices and market interest rates. For example, if market interest rates rise from, say, 4% to 5% because of the expectation of higher inflation rates, the values of outstanding debt instruments will decline. Furthermore, the longer the remaining life until maturity, the greater the reductions in a fixed-rate debt instrument's value to a specific market interest rate increase. These concepts with numerical calculations are explored in Chapter 10.

liquidity premium additional expected return to compensate for debt instruments that cannot be easily converted to cash at prices close to their estimated fair market values

The **liquidity premium** is the additional expected return to compensate for debt instruments that cannot be easily converted to cash at prices close to their estimated fair market values. For example, a corporation's low-quality bond may be traded very infrequently. As a consequence, a bondholder who wishes to sell tomorrow may find it difficult to sell except at a very large discount in price. Possibly, this should be called an illiquidity premium since the premium is compensation for a lack of liquidity. However, it is common practice to use the term liquidity premium.

The factors that influence the market interest rate are discussed throughout the remainder of this chapter, beginning with the concept of a risk-free interest rate and a discussion of why U.S. Treasury securities are used as the best estimate of the risk-free rate. Other sections focus on the term or maturity structure of interest rates, inflation expectations and associated premiums, and default risk and liquidity premium considerations.

negative interest rate occurs when a financial institution or government charges an amount greater than the interest it pays to depositors or debt security holders

While it is common practice to focus on positive interest rates, the possibility of negative interest rates should be acknowledged. A "**negative interest rate**" occurs when a financial institution charges an amount or fee greater than the interest it pays to depositors or debt security holders. For example, a central bank might charge a fee greater than the interest it pays on money held by its member banks at the central bank. Likewise, a government might charge negative interest on the debt securities it issues. For example, a government might issue a zero interest rate debt security for $1,010 with the promise to pay back only $1,000 when the security matures.

Of course, one might ask why a depositor or government debt security investor would accept a negative interest rate? One argument might be that the depositor or investor is willing to pay for the security or safety of holding cash at the bank or investing in "default risk-free" government securities. In addition to minimizing default risk, financial institutions may have diversification investment policies that might be met in part by holding some government securities that pay negative interest rates.

Negative interest rate policies have been implemented by a number of central banks in recent years as a means of supporting their easy monetary policy efforts. In mid-2014, the European Central Bank imposed negative interest on bank excess reserves to discourage the holding of excess cash and to encourage lending to stimulate economic growth. The central banks of Sweden, Switzerland, and Denmark also have experimented with paying negative interest on excess reserves. While the U.S. Fed also explored the possibility of using negative interest rates on excess reserves, the idea never was adopted. In 2016, the Bank of Japan moved to a below zero interest rate policy in an effort to stimulate the Japanese economy.

As of early 2019, several European countries and Japan had negative-yielding government bonds that were outstanding. Negative interest rate bonds continue to grow as a share of global debt outstanding. Investors seem willing to pay some governments for the ability to hold the bonds these governments are issuing.

DISCUSSION QUESTION 1

How have you benefitted from the historically low interest rates in the United States in recent years?

U.S. Treasury debt instruments or securities are typically viewed as being free from default. Even with the large national debt, the U.S. government is not likely to renege on its obligations to pay interest and repay principal at maturity on its debt securities. While the probability of a U.S. government default is not absolutely zero, most analysts view default as being very unlikely. Thus, we view U.S. Treasury securities as being default risk free.

Treasury debt securities that can be traded in the marketplace, the majority of all outstanding U.S. debt, are said to be marketable securities. These securities have virtually no liquidity risk or premium for illiquidity. Short-term government securities do not have a maturity risk premium and, thus, are not exposed to interest rate risk. In contrast, longer-term Treasury securities have a market risk premium due to interest rate risk associated with possible changes in market interest rates. Thus, the closest approximation for the risk-free interest rate would be the interest rate on short-term government securities.

Economists have estimated that the annual real rate of interest in the United States and other countries has averaged about 1 to 2% in past years. One way of looking at the risk-free rate is to say that this is the minimum rate of interest necessary to get individuals and businesses to save. There must be an incentive to invest or save idle cash holdings. One such incentive is the expectation of some real rate of return above expected inflation levels. For illustrative purposes, let's assume 1% is the current expectation for a real rate of return. Let's also assume that the market interest rate is currently 3% for a one-year Treasury security.

Given these assumptions, we can turn to equation (8.3) to determine the average inflation expectations of holders or investors as follows:

$$3\% = RR + IP + DRP + MRP + LP$$
$$3\% = 1\% + IP + 0\% + 0\% + 0\%$$
$$IP = 3\% - 1\% - 0\% - 0\% - 0\% = 2\%$$

The default risk premium (DRP) is estimated to be zero, the market risk premium (MRP) also is estimated to be zero, and there is a zero liquidity premium (LP) on a one-year maturity Treasury security. Thus, investors expect a 2% inflation premium (IP) rate over the next year; and if they also want a real rate of return (RR) of 1%, the market interest rate (r) must be 3%.

Since there are no estimated default risk, market risk or liquidity premiums, the interest rate observed in the marketplace for a one-year Treasury security would be our best estimate of a risk-free interest rate. The impact of a maturity risk premium is introduced after discussion of the types of marketable securities issued by the Treasury.

8.3 DEFAULT RISK-FREE SECURITIES: U.S. TREASURY DEBT INSTRUMENTS

8.3.1 MARKETABLE SECURITIES

Marketable government securities, as the term implies, are Treasury securities that can be purchased and sold through customary market channels. Large commercial banks and securities dealers maintain markets for these government debt obligations. In addition, nearly all other securities firms and commercial banks, large or small, will help their customers purchase and sell federal obligations by routing orders to institutions that do maintain markets in them. The investments of institutional investors, and large personal investors in federal obligations, are centered almost exclusively in the marketable issues. Treasury auctions are held for the initial offering of bills, notes, and bonds, as well as for the sale of treasury inflation-protected securities and floating rate notes. Although the maturity of

marketable government securities Treasury securities that may be bought and sold through the customary market channels

an obligation is reduced as it remains in effect, the obligation continues to be called by its original descriptive title. Thus, a 20-year Treasury bond continues to be described in quotation sheets as a bond throughout its life.

8.3.1.1 Treasury Bills

Treasury bills government securities issued with maturities up to one year

Treasury bills are issued with maturities up to one year and, thus, are the shortest maturities of government securities. They are, typically, issued for 91 days, with some issues carrying maturities of 182 days. Treasury bills with a maturity of one year are also issued at auction every four weeks. Issues of Treasury bills are offered each week by the Treasury to refund the part of the total volume of bills that matures. In effect, the 91-day Treasury bills mature and are rolled over in 13 weeks. Each week, approximately 1/13th of the total volume of such bills is refunded.

When the flow of cash revenues into the Treasury is too small to meet expenditure requirements, additional bills are issued. During those periods of the year when revenues exceed expenditures, Treasury bills are allowed to mature without being refunded. Treasury bills, therefore, provide the Treasury with a convenient financial mechanism to adjust for the lack of a regular revenue flow into the Treasury. The volume of bills may also be increased or decreased in response to general surpluses or deficits in the federal budget from year to year.

Treasury bills are issued on a discount basis and mature at par. Each week the Treasury bills to be sold are awarded to the highest bidders. Dealers and other investors submit sealed binds. Upon being opened, these bids are arrayed from highest to lowest. Those bidders asking the least discount (offering the highest price) are placed high in the array. The bids are then accepted in the order of their position in the array until all bills are awarded. Bidders seeking a higher discount (offering a lower price) may fail to receive any bills that particular week. Investors interested in purchasing small volumes of Treasury bills ($10,000 to $500,000) may submit their orders on an average competitive price basis. The Treasury deducts these small orders from the total volume of bills to be sold. The remaining bills are allotted on the competitive basis described above. Then these small orders are executed at a discount equal to the average of the successful competitive bids for large orders.

Investors are not limited to purchasing Treasury bills on their original issue. Because Treasury bills are issued weekly, a wide range of maturities in the over-the-counter market is available. Bid and ask quotations are shown in terms of annual yield equivalents. The prices of the various issues obtained from a dealer would reflect a discount based on these yields. Because of their short maturities and their absence of risk, Treasury bills provide the lowest yield available on taxable domestic obligations. Although some business corporations and individuals invest in Treasury bills, by far the most important holders of these obligations are commercial banks.

8.3.1.2 Treasury Notes

Treasury notes government securities issued with maturities ranging from 2 to 10 years

Treasury notes are issued at specified interest rates for maturities ranging from 2 to 10 years. The Treasury currently issues 2-year, 3-year, 5-year, 7-year, and 10-year notes. These intermediate-term government securities are also held largely by commercial banks.

8.3.1.3 Treasury Bonds

Treasury bonds government securities issued with maturities ranging from 11 to 30 years

Treasury bonds have original maturities ranging from 11 to 30 years, with the current focus being on issuing bonds with 30-year maturities. These bonds bear interest at stated rates. Many issues of these bonds are callable, or paid off, by the government several years before their maturity. For example, a 30-year bond issued in 2018 may be described as having a maturity of 2043–2048. This issue may be called for redemption at par as early as 2043 but in no event later than 2048. Dealers maintain active markets for the purchase and sale of Treasury bonds and the other marketable securities of the government.

All marketable obligations of the federal government, with the exception of Treasury bills, are offered to the public through the Federal Reserve banks at prices and yields set in advance. Investors place their orders for new issues, and these orders are filled from the available supply of the new issue. If orders are larger than available supply, investors may be allotted only a part of the amount they requested.

Treasury bonds, because of at least initial long-term maturities, are subject to maturity or interest rate risk. Treasury notes with shorter maturities are affected to a lesser extent. For illustrative purposes, let's assume that the market interest rate on 30-year Treasury bonds is currently 4% and, given their marketability, there is no liquidity premium. Let's further assume that investors expect the inflation rate will average 2% over the next 30 years and they expect a real rate of return of 1% annually. By applying equation (8.3) we can find the maturity risk premium to be,

$$4\% = RR + IP + DRP + MRP + LP$$
$$4\% = 1\% + 2\% + 0\% + MRP + 0\%$$
$$MRP = 4\% - 1\% - 2\% - 0\% - 0\% = 1\%$$

Our interpretation is that the holders, or investors, require a 1% maturity risk premium to compensate them for the possibility of volatility in the price of their Treasury bonds over the next 30 years. If market-determined interest rates rise and investors are forced to sell before maturity, the bonds will be sold at a loss. Furthermore, even if these investors hold their bonds to maturity and redeem them with the government at the original purchase price, the investors would have lost the opportunity of the higher interest rates being paid in the marketplace. This is what is meant by interest rate risk. Of course, if market-determined interest rates decline after the bonds are purchased, bond prices will rise above the original purchase price.

8.3.2 DEALER SYSTEM

The **dealer system** for marketable U.S. government securities occupies a central position in the nation's financial markets. The smooth operation of the money markets depends on a closely linked network of dealers and brokers. Bank and nonbank dealers report their daily activity in U.S. government securities to the Federal Reserve Bank of New York. New dealers are added only when they can demonstrate a satisfactory level of responsibility and volume of activity. The dealers buy and sell securities for their own account, arrange transactions with both their customers and other dealers, and also purchase debt directly from the Treasury for resale to investors. Dealers do not typically charge commissions on their trades. Rather, they hope to sell securities at prices above the levels at which they were bought. The dealers' capacity to handle large Treasury financing has expanded enough in recent years to handle the substantial growth in the government securities market. In addition to the dealers' markets, new issues of federal government securities may be purchased directly at the Federal Reserve banks.

dealer system a small group of dealers in government securities with an effective marketing network throughout the United States

8.3.3 TAX STATUS OF FEDERAL OBLIGATIONS

Until March 1941, interest on all obligations of the federal government was exempt from all taxes. The interest on all federal obligations is now subject to federal income taxes and tax rates. The Public Debt Act of 1941 terminated the issuance of tax-free federal obligations. Since that time, all issues previously sold to the public have matured or have been called for redemption. Income from the obligations of the federal government is exempt from all state and local taxes. Federal obligations, however, are subject to federal and state inheritance, estate, or gift taxes.

8.3.4 OWNERSHIP OF PUBLIC DEBT SECURITIES

The U.S. national debt must be financed and refinanced through the issuance of government securities, both marketable and nonmarketable. **Nonmarketable government securities** are securities that cannot be transferred to other persons or institutions and can be redeemed only by being turned in to the U.S. government. The sheer size of the national debt, over $21.5 trillion at the end of fiscal year (September) 2018, makes the financing process a difficult one. In fact, the United States must rely on the willingness of foreign and international investors to hold a substantial portion of the outstanding, interest-bearing public debt securities issued to finance the national debt.

nonmarketable government securities securities that cannot be transferred between persons or institutions and must be redeemed with the U.S. government

The ownership of U.S. Treasury securities, by group or category, is shown in Table 8.1. Private investors, who owned approximately 51% of the total outstanding Treasury securities in 2008, increased their ownership to over 57% by 2011 and to nearly 62% by 2018. The percentage of Treasury securities held by U.S. government accounts (agencies and trust funds) and Federal Reserve banks dropped from

Table 8.1 Ownership of U.S. Treasury Securities (Percentage of Holdings)

	2008 (Sept)	2011 (Sept)	2015 (Sept)	2018 (June)
Federal Reserve and government accounts	49.4%	42.8%	41.3%	38.2%
Private investors				
Foreign and international investors	27.9	31.6	33.6	29.3
State and local governments	5.5	3.2	3.5	3.3
U.S. savings bonds	2.1	1.2	1.0	0.7
Depository institutions	1.2	2.0	2.8	3.2
Insurance companies	4.7	1.7	1.6	1.1
Mutual funds	4.1	4.7	6.0	8.6
Pension funds	3.8	5.9	2.8	4.2
Other miscellaneous groups of investors*	1.3	6.9	7.4	11.4
Total private investors	50.6%	57.2%	58.7%	61.8%
Total U.S. agencies and private investors	100.0%	100.0%	100.0%	100.0%
Dollar Amount of Public Debt ($ Trillions)	$9.5	$14.8	$18.2	$21.2

*Includes individuals, corporations and other businesses, dealers and brokers, government-sponsored agencies, bank personal trusts and estates, and other investors.

Sources: *Economic Report of the President* and Department of the Treasury, https://home.treasury.gov.

about 49% in 2008 down to about 38% in 2018. During the time period depicted in Table 8.1, foreign and international investors increased their holdings of total public debt from about 28% in 2008, to over 29% in 2018. This shows the continuing importance of foreign and international investors in financing the U.S. national debt. Except for the miscellaneous investor category, only mutual funds held as much as 8% of the outstanding amount of Treasury securities in 2018.

During the last half of the 1980s, the annual increase in foreign ownership was due primarily to the flow of Japanese capital to this country. Japanese investment in real estate and corporate securities has been well publicized. However, as the dollar declined relative to the Japanese yen and other major foreign currencies, investment in U.S. assets became less attractive after interest and other returns were converted back into the foreign currencies. In recent years, interest on the part of Europeans and Chinese has increased. The large trade surpluses China has had with the United States have resulted in the Chinese holding ever-increasing amounts of U.S. financial assets.

8.3.5 MATURITY DISTRIBUTION OF MARKETABLE DEBT SECURITIES

The various types of marketable securities of the federal government have already been described in this section. However, the terms of bills, notes, and bonds describe the general maturity ranges only at the time of issue. To determine the maturity distribution of all obligations, therefore, it is necessary to observe the remaining life of each issue, regardless of its class. The maturity distribution and average length of marketable interest-bearing public debt held by private investors are shown in Table 8.2. Notice that the average maturity was three years and 10 months in 2008 before increasing to about five years by 2011 and reached five years and 5 months in 2018.

The heavy concentration of debt in the very short maturity range (within one year) decreased from about 48% of the total amount outstanding in late 2008 when the United States was in the midst of the financial crisis and Great Recession. By 2011, the amount of privately held Treasury securities with maturities of less than one year was about 31.5% of the total, and it decreased to about 29.5% by 2018. A heavy concentration in very short-term maturities poses a special problem for the Treasury. This also is a problem for the securities markets, because the government is constantly selling additional securities to replace those that mature.

The heavy concentration of short-term maturities will not necessarily change by simply issuing a larger number of long-term obligations. Like all institutions that seek funds in the financial markets, the Treasury has to offer securities that will be readily accepted by the investing public. Furthermore,

Table 8.2   Maturity Distribution and Average Length of Marketable Interest-Bearing Public Debt Held by Private Investors (Percentage of Holdings)

Maturity Class	2008 (Sept)	2011 (Sept)	2015 (Sept)	2018 (Sept)
Within 1 year	47.8%	31.5%	28.1%	29.5%
1–5 years	28.1	38.8	42.0	40.2
5–10 years	14.3	19.4	20.1	19.0
10–20 years	6.7	3.9	1.8	0.9
20 years and over	3.1	6.4	8.0	10.4
Total	100.0%	100.0%	100.0%	100.0%
Average maturity of all marketable issues:	3 years, 10 months	5 years, 0 months	5 years, 1 month	5 years, 5 months

Sources: Economic Report of the President and Department of the Treasury, https://home.treasury.gov.

the magnitude of federal financing is such that radical changes in maturity distributions can upset the financial markets and the economy in general. The management of the federal debt has become an especially challenging financial problem, and much time and energy are spent in meeting the challenge.

If the Treasury refunds maturing issues with new short-term securities, the average maturity of the total debt is reduced. As time passes, longer-term issues are brought into shorter-dated categories. Net cash borrowing, which results from budgetary deficits, must take the form of maturities that are at least as long as the average of the marketable debt if the average maturity is not to be reduced. The average length of the marketable debt reached a low level of two years and five months in late 1975. Since that time, progress has been made in raising the average length of maturities to about five years by selling longer-term securities.

One of the new debt management techniques used to extend the average maturity of the marketable debt without disturbing the financial markets is *advance refunding*. This occurs when the Treasury offers owners of a given issue the opportunity to exchange their holdings well in advance of the holdings' regular maturity for new securities of longer maturity.

In summary, the Treasury is the largest and most active borrower in the financial markets. The Treasury is continuously in the process of borrowing and refinancing. Its financial actions are tremendous in contrast with all other forms of financing, including those of the largest business corporations. Yet, the financial system of the nation is well adapted to accommodate its needs smoothly. Indeed, the very existence of a public debt of this magnitude is predicated on the existence of a highly refined monetary and credit system.

DISCUSSION QUESTION 2

Do you believe that foreign and international investors will continue to hold large portions of the U.S. national debt in the future?

PERSONAL FINANCIAL PLANNING

Home Mortgages

Interest rates on home mortgages are affected by the influences discussed in this chapter. A typical 30-year fixed-rate mortgage incorporates the factors that affect a 30-year Treasury bond (real rate + inflation expectations + maturity risk premium + liquidity premium) in addition to these other influences, such as default risk premium (since the typical homeowner is a higher risk than the U.S. government) and security premium (this helps lower the mortgage interest rate, since, in case of default, the lender can take possession of the borrower's house and sell it to recoup the amount lent). Homeowners can play the short end of the term structure, too. Adjustable-rate or variable-rate mortgages rise and fall in line with a specified short-term interest rate, usually a Treasury security. The interest rate paid by the homeowner equals the short-term rate plus a premium, to reflect the homeowner's higher degree of default risk. The danger of buying a home with an adjustable-rate mortgage is that an inflation scare or some other reason may cause a rapid rise in short-term rates, whereas the rate on a fixed-rate loan does not fluctuate. Since short-term rates usually are less than long-term rates, an adjustable-rate mortgage is an attractive financing possibility for those willing to take the risk of fluctuating short-term rates or those who expect to own their home for only three to five years before they move out of it.

term structure of interest rates relationship between interest rates and the time to maturity for debt instruments of comparable quality

yield curve graphic presentation of the term structure of interest rates at a point in time

The **term structure of interest rates** indicates the relationship between interest rates or yields and the maturity of comparable quality debt instruments. This relationship is typically depicted through the graphic presentation of a **yield curve**. A properly constructed yield curve must first reflect securities of similar default risk. Second, the yield curve must represent a particular point in time, and the interest rates should reflect yields for the remaining time to maturity. That is, the yields should not only include stated interest rates but also consider that instruments and securities could be selling above or below their redemption values. (The process for calculating yields to maturity is shown in Chapter 9.) Third, the yield curve must show yields on a number of securities with differing lengths of time to maturity.

U.S. government securities provide the best basis for constructing yield curves because Treasury securities are considered to be risk free, as previously noted in terms of default risk. Table 8.3 contains interest rates for Treasury securities for various maturities at selected dates. In early 1980, the annual inflation rate was in double digits. As a result, interest rates were very high, even though the economy was in a mild recession. By the latter part of the 1980s, interest rates had dropped dramatically because of reduced inflation. Interest rates on one-year Treasury bills were at 6% in March 1991, compared with 14% in March 1980. Interest rates declined further as the economy began expanding from a mild recession at the beginning of the 1990s.

By November 1998, after the Fed first pushed up short-term interest rates in an effort to head off possible renewed inflation and then lowered rates in an effort to avoid a recession during the mid-1990s, interest rates were relatively flat across different maturities. The Fed lowered its discount rate many times during the first years of the twenty-first century due to concern about an economic downturn and the terrorist attack in New York City on September 11, 2001. By November 2001, one-year Treasury interest rates had dropped to about 2%. Short-term interest rates continued to fall and were at about 1% in November 2003. However, in an effort to keep inflation under control, the Fed forced short-term interest rates higher so that one-year rates reached about 5% in October 2006.

The Fed moved quickly in 2008 to help avoid a collapse in the financial system by first using its traditional open-market operations to increase monetary liquidity by purchasing government securities. Then, as previously noted, the Fed engaged in a new nontraditional monetary policy action termed quantitative easing (which became known as QE1) in late 2008 in response to the 2007–2008 financial crisis and the 2008–2009 Great Recession. As Table 8.3 shows, the yield on one-year Treasury securities declined to 0.4% by October 2008. By late 2008, the Fed had reduced its target for the federal funds rate to 0.00–.0.25%. Because of a relatively slow economic recovery from the Great Recession, QE2 was implemented by the Fed in late 2010. QE3 followed in late 2012. As a result of massive monetary easing efforts, the interest rates on Treasury securities were forced to historical lows as shown in Table 8.3. The rate on one-year Treasury bills was only 0.16% and even five-year Treasury securities were yielding only 0.72% at the end of December 2012. Interest rates on short-term Treasury securities increased in late 2015 in response to the Fed increasing its near-zero federal funds target interest rate, which had been in place since late – 2008, to 0.25–0.50%.

Figure 8.2 shows yield curves for March 1980, October 2006, October 2008, December 2012, and December 2018 reflecting the plotting of the corresponding data in Table 8.3. Because of high inflation rates and monetary policy attempting to constrain economic activity, the March 1980 yield

Table 8.3 Interest Rates for Treasury Securities by Term to Maturity at Selected Dates

Term to Maturity	March 1980	October 2006	October 2008	December 2012	December 2015	December 2018
6 months	15.0%	4.9%	0.2%	0.11%	0.50%	2.54%
1 year	14.0	5.0	0.4	0.16	0.65	2.66
5 years	13.5	4.7	2.3	0.72	1.70	2.68
10 years	12.8	4.7	3.4	1.78	2.24	2.83
20 years	12.5	4.9	4.2	2.54	2.61	2.98
30 years	12.3	4.9	4.2	2.95	2.97	3.10

Source: *Selected Interest Rates*, Board of Governors of the Federal Reserve System, https://www.federalreserve.gov.

FIGURE 8.2 Yield curves for treasury securities at selected dates

Source: Selected Interest Rates, Board of Governors of the Federal Reserve System, https://www.federalreserve.gov.

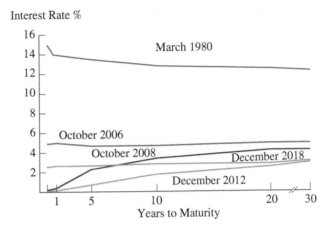

curve was both downward sloping and at very high overall interest rate levels. Although not plotted, the yield curve for November 2001 was upward sloping and much lower overall due to lower expected inflation rates and efforts by monetary policy to stimulate economic activity.

By October 2006, the yield curve was nearly flat across all maturities with a variation only between about 4.7% and 5.0%. This flattening of the yield curve was attributable primarily to the Fed's effort to raise short-term interest rates as a way of combating the possibility of increases in inflation rates. As the financial crisis of 2007–2008 developed and was followed by the 2008–2009 recession, short-term interest rates were forced to low levels, as depicted for October 2008. The yield curve for December 2012 shows interest rates on short-term Treasury securities at historically low levels due to the monetary easing policies of the Fed, including its quantitative easing efforts. The yield curve at the end of December 2018 was essentially flat reflecting the Fed's efforts to raise short-term interest rates that began at the end of 2015 and continued through 2018.

8.4.1 RELATIONSHIP BETWEEN YIELD CURVES AND THE ECONOMY

Historical evidence suggests that interest rates, generally, rise during periods of economic expansion and fall during economic contraction. Therefore, the term structure of interest rates, as depicted by yield curves, shifts upward or downward with changes in economic activity. Interest rate levels, generally, are lowest at the bottom of a recession and highest at the top of an expansion period. Furthermore, when the economy begins to recover from a recession, the yield curve typically slopes upward. The curve begins to flatten out during the latter stages of an expansion and, typically, starts sloping downward when economic activity peaks. As the economy turns downward, interest rates begin falling and the yield curve again goes through a flattening-out phase, to become upward sloping when economic activity again reaches a low point.

8.4.2 TERM STRUCTURE THEORIES

Three theories are commonly used to explain the term structure of interest rates. The **expectations theory** contends that the shape of a yield curve reflects investor expectations about future inflation rates. If the yield curve is flat, expectations are that the current short-term inflation rate will remain essentially unchanged over time. When the yield curve is downward sloping, investors expect inflation rates to be lower in the future. Recall from Figure 8.2 that the shape of the yield curve in March 1980 was downward sloping. Thus, investors believed that the double-digit inflation rates prevailing in 1980 were expected to decline in the future. In contrast, a relatively flat yield curve existed in November 1998, suggesting that investors expected the low inflation rates in late 1998 to remain at low levels in the future and that the economy would continue to grow at a moderate rate.

As the U.S. moved into the twenty-first century, the yield curve was generally upward sloping as economic growth continued after the 2001 recession. However, as the result of increases in short-term

expectations theory states that the shape of the yield curve indicates investor expectations about future inflation rates

interest rates, the yield curve became relatively flat by October 2006 causing some concern about the possibility of a slowdown in economic activity. This flat yield curve also preceded the 2007–2008 financial crisis and the 2008–2009 recession. By October 2008, the yield curve, while at then historically low interest rates for short maturities, was upward sloping, suggesting hope for future recovery. However, due to a slow economic recovery, further monetary easing activities resulted in the historically low yield curve depicted for the end of December 2012. By December 2018, increases in short-term interest rates resulted in a relatively flat yield curve causing new concerns about a possible future recession.

To differentiate yield curve shapes in terms of equations (8.1), (8.2), and (8.3), first recall that the liquidity and the default risk premiums are regarded as being zero for Treasury securities. Thus, equation (8.3) for Treasury securities becomes equation (8.1) plus a maturity risk premium (MRP). However, the expectations theory in its purest form also assumes the MRP to be zero. Given this assumption, we have reduced equation (8.3) back to equation (8.1) such that the yield curve reflects only the real rate (RR) of interest plus the expectation for an inflation premium (IP) over the life of the security.

Let's assume that the current rates of interest or yields are, as follows: one-year Treasury bills = 3%, two-year Treasury notes = 4%, and 10-year Treasury notes = 5%. Using a 1% real rate of return, we have the following relationships:

Maturity	r	=	RR	+	IP
1-year	3%	=	1%	+	2%
2-year	4%	=	1%	+	3%
10-year	5%	=	1%	+	4%

Thus, the inflation rate is expected to be 2% over the next year. However, the inflation rate is expected to average 3% per year over the next two years; or if inflation is 2% the first year, then the rate for the second year must be more than 3%. Working with simple averages, 3% average inflation times two years means that the total inflation will be 6%. Thus, 6% less 2% means that inflation in the second year must be 4%.

For years three through 10, inflation must exceed 4% annually to average 4% over the 10-year period. We can find the simple average by starting with the fact that inflation will be 40% (4% times 10 years) over the full 10-year period, and 40% less the 6% for the first two years means that cumulative inflation for the last eight years will be 34%. Then, dividing 34% by eight means that inflation will have to average 4.25% over years three through 10. In summary, we have the following:

Time Period	Average Inflation		Number of Years		Cumulative Inflation
Year 1	2%	×	1	=	2%
Year 2	4%	×	1	=	4%
Years 3–10	4.25%	×	8	=	34%
Total inflation					40%
Total years					10
Average inflation (40% ÷ 10 years)					4%

liquidity preference theory states that investors are willing to accept lower interest rates on short-term debt securities that provide greater liquidity and less interest rate risk

market segmentation theory states that interest rates may differ because securities of different maturities are not perfect substitutes for each other

These are only simple arithmetic averages. Technically, we have ignored the impact of the compounding of inflation rates over time. The concept of compounding is presented in Chapter 9, which focuses on the time value of money.

The liquidity preference theory holds that investors or debt instrument holders prefer to invest short term so that they have greater liquidity and less maturity or interest rate risk. Lenders also prefer to lend short term because of the risk of higher inflation rates and greater uncertainty about default risk in the future. Borrowers prefer to borrow long term so that they have more time to repay loans. The net result is a willingness to accept lower interest rates on short-term loans as a trade-off for greater liquidity and lower interest rate risk.

The market segmentation theory holds that securities of different maturities are not perfect substitutes for one another. For example, commercial banks concentrate on holding short-term government securities in an effort to match the short-term maturities of their demand and other deposit liabilities.

On the other hand, the nature of insurance company and pension fund liabilities allows these firms to concentrate holdings in long-term securities. Thus, supply-and-demand factors in each market segment affect the shape of the yield curve. Thus, in some time periods, interest rates on intermediate-term Treasury securities may be higher (or lower) than those for both short-term and long-term Treasuries.

> **LEARNING ACTIVITY**
>
> Go to the website of the Board of Governors of the Federal Reserve System, https://www.federalreserve.gov. Find current interest rates for different maturities of U.S. Treasury securities, and construct the current yield curve.

Actions or factors that change the value of the money unit or the supply of money and credit affect the whole economy. The change affects, first, the supply of loanable funds and interest rates and, later, both the demand for and the supply of goods in general. Inflation, as previously defined, is an increase in the price of goods or services that is not offset by an increase in quality. Recall that when investors expect higher inflation rates, they will require higher market interest rates so that a real rate of return will remain after the inflation. A clearer understanding of investor expectations about inflation premiums can be had by first reviewing past price movements, and then exploring possible types of inflation.

| 8.5 INFLATION PREMIUMS AND PRICE MOVEMENTS |

inflation an increase in the price of goods or services that is not offset by an increase in quality

8.5.1 HISTORICAL INTERNATIONAL PRICE MOVEMENTS

GLOBAL Changes in the money supply or in the amount of metal in the money unit have influenced prices since the earliest records of civilization. The money standard in ancient Babylon was in terms of silver and barley. The earliest available price records show that one shekel of silver was equal to 240 measures of grain. At the time of Hammurabi (about 1750 B.C.), a shekel in silver was worth between 150 and 180 measures of grain, while in the following century it declined to 90 measures. After Persia conquered Babylonia in 539 B.C., the value of the silver shekel was recorded as between 15 and 40 measures of grain.

Alexander the Great probably caused the greatest inflationary period in ancient history when he captured the large gold hoards of Persia and took them to Greece. Inflation was high for some years, but 20 years after Alexander's death, a period of deflation began that lasted for over 50 years.

The first recorded cases of deliberate currency debasement (lowering the value) occurred in the Greek city-states. The government would debase currency by calling in all coins and issuing new ones containing less of the precious metals. This must have been a convenient form of inflation, for there are many such cases in the records of Greek city-states.

8.5.1.1 Ancient Rome

During the Punic Wars, devaluation led to inflation as the heavy bronze coin was reduced in stages from one pound to one ounce. Similar inflation occurred in Roman history. Augustus brought so much precious metal from Egypt that prices rose and interest rates fell. From the time of Nero, debasements were frequent. The weight of gold coins was gradually reduced, and silver coins had baser metals added to them so that they were finally only 2% silver. Few attempts were made to arrest or reverse this process of debasement of coins as the populace adjusted to the process. When Aurelian tried to improve the coinage by adding to its precious metal content, he was resisted so strongly that armed rebellion broke out.

8.5.1.2 The Middle Ages Through Modern Times

During the Middle Ages, princes and kings debased the coinage to get more revenue. The rulers of France used this ploy more than others, and records show that profit from debasement was sometimes greater than the total of all other revenues.

An important example of inflation followed the arrival of Europeans in America. Gold and silver poured into Spain from Mexico and Peru. Since the riches were used to buy goods from other countries, they were distributed over the continent and to England. Prices rose in Spain and in most of Europe but not in proportion to the increase in gold and silver stocks. This was because trade increased and because many people hoarded the precious metals.

Paper money was not used generally until the end of the seventeenth century. The first outstanding example of inflation due to the issuing of an excessive amount of paper money was in France. In 1719, the government gave Scottish banker John Law a charter for a bank that could issue paper money. The note circulation of his bank amounted to almost 2,700 million livres (the monetary unit in use at that time in France), against which he had coin of only 21 million livres and bullion of 27 million livres. Prices went up rapidly, but they fell just as fast when Law's bank failed. Afterward, the money supply was again restricted.

The next outstanding periods of inflation were during the American Revolution (1775–1783) and French Revolution (1789–1799). For example, France's revolutionary government issued paper currency in huge quantities. This currency, called assignats, declined to 0.5% of its face value. Spectacular inflation also took place in Germany in 1923, when prices soared to astronomical heights. During World War II, runaway inflation took place in China and Hungary, as well as in other countries.

8.5.2 INFLATION IN THE UNITED STATES

Monetary factors have often affected price levels in the United States, especially during major wars.

8.5.2.1 Revolutionary War

The war that brought the United States into being was financed mainly by inflation. The Second Continental Congress had no real authority to levy taxes and, thus, found it difficult to raise money. As a result, the congress decided to issue notes for $2 million. It issued more and more notes until the total rose to over $240 million. The individual states issued $200 million more. Since the notes were crudely engraved, counterfeiting was common, adding to the total of circulating currency. Continental currency depreciated in value so rapidly that the expression "not worth a continental" became a part of the American language.

8.5.2.2 War of 1812

During the War of 1812, the government tried to avoid repeating the inflationary measures of the Revolutionary War. However, since the war was not popular in New England, it was impossible to finance it by taxation and borrowing. Paper currency was issued in a somewhat disguised form: bonds of small denomination bearing no interest and having no maturity date. The wholesale price index, based on 100 as the 1910–1914 average prices, rose from 131 in 1812 to 182 in 1814. Prices declined to about the prewar level by 1816 and continued downward as depression hit the economy.

8.5.2.3 Civil War

The Mexican War (1846–1848) did not involve the total economy to any extent and led to no inflationary price movements. The Civil War (1861–1865), however, was financed partly by issuing paper money. In the war's early stages, the U.S. Congress could not raise enough money by taxes and borrowing to finance all expenditures; therefore, it resorted to inflation by issuing U.S. notes with no backing, known as greenbacks. In all, $450 million was authorized. Even though this was but a fraction of the cost of the war, prices went up substantially. Wholesale prices on a base of 100 increased from 93 in 1860 to 185 in 1865. Attempts to retire the greenbacks at the end of the war led to deflation and depression in 1866. As a result, the law withdrawing greenbacks was repealed.

8.5.2.4 World War I

Although the U.S. government did not print money to finance World War I, it did practice other inflationary policies. About one-third of the cost of the war was raised by taxes and two-thirds of the cost by borrowing. The banking system provided much of this credit, which added to the money supply. People were even persuaded to use Liberty Bonds as collateral for bank loans to buy other bonds. The wholesale price index rose from 99 in 1914 to 226 in 1920. Then, as credit expansion was finally restricted in 1921, it dropped to 141 in 1922.

8.5.2.5 World War II and the Postwar Period

The government used fewer inflationary policies to finance World War II. Nevertheless, the banking system still took up large sums of bonds. By the end of the war, the debt of the federal government had increased by $207 billion. Bank holdings of government bonds had increased by almost $60 billion.

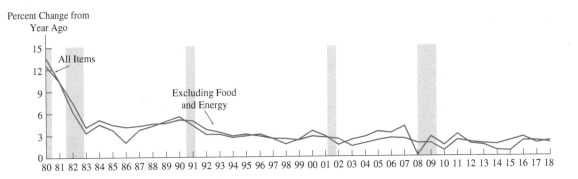

FIGURE 8.3 Changes in consumer price indexes, 1980–2018

Sources: Economic Report of the President, 2016 and Department of Labor, Bureau of Labor Statistics, https://www.bls.gov.

Prices went up by only about one-third during the war because they were held in check after the first year by price and wage controls. They then rose rapidly when the controls were lifted after the war. In 1948, wholesale prices had risen to 236 from a level of 110 in 1939.

Wholesale prices increased during the Korean War and again during the 1955–1957 expansion in economic activity as the economy recovered from the 1954 recession. Consumer goods prices continued to move upward during practically the entire postwar period, increasing gradually even in those years in which wholesale prices hardly changed.

8.5.2.6 Recent Decades

Figure 8.3 shows changes in the consumer price index (CPI) for all items, and a related consumer price measure when food and energy are excluded, beginning with 1980. Although not depicted, wholesale consumer goods prices increased substantially when the Vietnam War escalated after mid-1965. Prices continued upward after American participation in the Vietnam War was reduced in the early 1970s. After American participation in the war ended in 1974, prices rose at the most rapid levels since World War I. Inflation was worldwide in the middle 1970s; its effects were much worse in many other industrial countries than in the United States.

As the 1970s ended, economists realized the full impact of a philosophy based on a high inflation rate. Many economists thought high inflation could keep unemployment down permanently, even though history shows that it does not. The government's efforts to control interest rates by increasing the money supply created doubts that such policies would reduce inflation and high interest rates. By October 1979, the Federal Reserve System abandoned this failed approach to interest rate control and adopted a policy of monetary growth control. The result was twofold. First, there was a far greater volatility in interest rates as the Federal Reserve concentrated on monetary factors. Second, during the first three quarters of 1980, some monetary restraint was exercised. This monetary restraint depressed production and employment. The Federal Reserve System quickly backed off from this position of restraint, and by the end of 1980 a far greater level of monetary stimulus had driven interest rates to new peaks.

By this time, the prime rate had risen to 21.5% and three-month Treasury bills had doubled in yield from their midyear lows. These high interest rates had a profound negative effect on such interest-sensitive industries as housing and automobiles. The Fed reversed the rapid growth of money supply throughout 1981 and until late in 1982. Unemployment climbed as the effects of monetary restraint were imposed on the economy, but the back of inflation was broken. By the end of 1982, economic recovery was in place, along with an easing of monetary restraint.

Figure 8.3 shows that inflation stayed at moderate levels beginning in 1983 and continuing through most of the remainder of the 1980s until near the end of the decade. After peaking in 1990 above a 6% annual rate, changes in the CPI stayed at about 3% until 1997, when the inflation rate dropped even further. In early 1994, the Fed moved toward a tighter monetary policy in an effort to keep inflation from rising. As the country finished the 1990s and moved into the early twenty-first century, inflation rates remained at relatively low levels. For 2007, the rate of inflation using changes in the CPI for all items was 4.1%, reflecting record high oil prices. Using the alternative CPI measure, adjusted to exclude food and energy, the rate of inflation was 2.4% for 2007. Since 2007, changes in the all items CPI were generally under 2% (except for 2009 and 2011), and were less than 1% in 2014 and 2015, before returning to the 2 percent level in 2016 through 2018. Changes in the CPI measure that exclude food and energy have averaged a little more than 2% since 2014, with the differences between the two indexes primarily reflecting the wide fluctuations in oil prices that have occurred.

8.5.3 TYPES OF INFLATION

Inflation may be associated with a change in costs or a change in the money supply, or because of speculation or so-called administrative pressures.

8.5.3.1 Price Changes Initiated by a Change in Costs

The price level can sometimes increase without the original impulse coming from either the money supply or its velocity. If costs rise faster than productivity increases, as when wages go up, businesses with some control over prices will try to raise them to cover the higher costs. Such increases are likely to be effective when the demand for goods is strong compared to the supply. The need for more funds to meet production and distribution at higher prices usually causes the money supply and velocity to increase. This type of inflation is called **cost-push inflation**, as this rise in prices comes from the cost side, not from increases in the money supply. Prices may not go up, however, if the monetary authorities restrict credit expansion. In that case, only the most efficient businesses will have enough demand to operate profitably. As a result, some resources will be unemployed.

Cost-push inflation can occur only in industries in which labor negotiations are carried out industry-wide, and in which management has the ability to increase prices. Cost-push inflation is different from inflation caused by an increase in the money supply.

8.5.3.2 Price Changes Initiated by a Change in the Money Supply

Demand-pull inflation occurs when an excessive demand for goods and services is created during periods of economic expansion as a result of large increases in the money supply. While changes in the velocity, or turnover, of money can also impact price changes, we focus our discussion on changes in the supply of money.

An increase in the money supply occurs when the Fed purchases government securities through its open-market operations. If this happens when people and resources are not fully employed, the volume of trade goes up; prices are only slightly affected at first. As unused resources are brought into use, however, prices will go up. When resources, such as metals, become scarce, their prices rise. As any resource begins to be used up, the expectation of future price rises will itself force prices up, because attempts to buy before such price rises will increase demand above current needs. Since some costs will lag—such as interest costs and wages set by contract—profits will rise, increasing the demand for capital goods.

Once resources are fully employed, the full effect of the increased money supply will be felt on prices. Prices may rise out of proportion for a time as expectations of higher prices lead to faster spending and so raise the velocity of money. The expansion will continue until trade and prices are in balance at the new levels of the money supply. Velocity will probably drop somewhat from those levels during the period of rising prices, since the desire to buy goods before the price goes up has disappeared.

Even if the supply of money is increased when people and resources are fully employed, prices may not go up proportionately. Higher prices increase profits for a time, and so lead to a demand for more capital and labor. Thus, previously unemployed spouses, retired workers, and similar groups begin to enter the labor force. Businesses may use capital more fully by having two or three shifts use the same machines.

Demand-pull inflation traditionally exists during periods of economic expansion when the demand for goods and services exceeds the available supply of such goods and services. Demand-pull inflation may also be caused by changes in demand in particular industries. The demand for oil and natural gas, for example, may be greater than demand in general, so that prices rise in this industry before they rise generally. The first rise is likely to be in the price of basic materials themselves, leading to increased profits in the industries that produce them. Labor will press for wage increases to get its share of the total value of output, and thus labor costs also rise. Price increases in basic industries lead to price increases in the industries that use their products. Wage increases in one major industry are also likely to lead to demands for similar increases in other industries and among the nonorganized workers

cost-push inflation occurs when prices are raised to cover rising production costs, such as wages

demand-pull inflation occurs when an excessive demand for goods and services is created during periods of economic expansion as a result of large increases in the money supply in such industries. The process, once set into motion, can lead to general changes in prices, provided the monetary authorities do not restrict credit so as to prevent it.

Inflation associated with increases in the money supply also can occur because of monetization of the U.S. government debt. Recall from Chapter 5 that the Treasury finances government deficits by selling U.S. government securities to the public, financial institutions, foreign and international investors, and the Federal Reserve. When the Federal Reserve purchases U.S. government securities, reserves must be created to pay for the purchases. This, in turn, may lead to higher inflation because of an increase in money supply and bank reserves.

8.5.3.3 Speculation and Administrative Inflation

When an increased money supply causes inflation, it can lead to the additional price pressure called **speculative inflation**. Since prices have risen for some time, people believe that they will keep on rising. Inflation becomes self-generating for a time because, instead of higher prices resulting in lower demand, people may buy more to get goods before their prices go still higher, as happened in the late 1970s. This effect may be confined to certain areas, as it was to land prices in the 1920s Florida land boom, or to security prices in the 1928–1929 stock market boom. Such a price rise leads to an increase in velocity as speculators try to turn over their funds as rapidly as possible, and many others try to buy ahead of needs before there are further price rises.

Speculative inflation caused by the expectation that prices will continue to rise, resulting in increased buying to avoid even higher future prices

For three decades, until the early 1980s, price pressures and inflation were continual despite occasional policies of strict credit restraint. During this long period, in fact, prices continued upward in recession periods, though at a slower rate than in prosperity periods. The need to restrain price rises hampered the Fed's ability to promote growth and fight recessions. Prices and other economic developments during this period led many to feel that the economy had developed a long-run *inflationary bias*. However, the continued low inflation rates from the early 1990s to the present seem to have curtailed these beliefs.

Administrative inflation is the tendency of prices, aided by union-corporation contracts, to rise during economic expansion and to resist declines during recessions. Prices and wages tend to rise during periods of boom in a competitive economy. This tendency is reinforced by wage contracts that provide escalator clauses to keep wages in line with prices, and by wage increases that are sometimes greater than increases in productivity. Second, during recessions, prices tend to remain stable rather than decrease. This is because major unions have long-run contracts calling for annual wage increases no matter what economic conditions are at the time. The tendency of large corporations to rely on nonprice competition (advertising, and style, and color changes) and to reduce output rather than cut prices also keeps prices stable. Furthermore, if prices do decline drastically in a field, the government is likely to step in with programs to help take excess supplies off the market. There is little doubt that prices would decline in a severe and prolonged depression. Government takes action to counter resulting unemployment, however, before the economy reaches such a level. Thus, we no longer experience the downward price pressure of a depression.

administrative inflation the tendency of prices, aided by union-corporation contracts, to rise during economic expansion and to resist declines during recessions

Administrative inflation differs from demand-pull inflation that happens when demand exceeds the available supply of goods, either because demand is increasing faster than supply in the early stages of a recovery period or because demand from monetary expansion by the banking system or the government exceeds available supply. Traditional monetary policy is not wholly effective against administrative inflation. If money supplies are restricted enough, prices can be kept in line; this will lead to long-term unemployment and slow growth. It is also difficult for new firms and small, growing firms to get credit, since lending policies are likely to be conservative. If administrative inflation resurfaces, new tools may need to be developed to effectively deal with it.

DISCUSSION QUESTION 3

Given the current size and continued growth of the U.S. national debt, should Treasury securities be viewed as free from default risk?

LEARNING ACTIVITY

Go to the website of the Council of Economic Advisors, https://www.whitehouse.gov/cea/pubs.html, and access the Economic Report of the President. Next, access the statistical appendix tables and find current inflation rates based on the consumer price index for all items and for when food and energy prices are excluded.

8.6 DEFAULT RISK PREMIUMS

default risk risk that a borrower will not pay interest and/or principal on a debt instrument when due

FINANCE Investors are said to be "risk averse"; that is, they expect to be compensated with higher returns for taking on more risk in the form of greater uncertainty about return variability or outcome. This is the pillar of finance, known as the risk-return principle, or "higher returns are expected for taking on more risk" principle. Default risk is the risk that a borrower will not pay interest and/or repay the principal on a loan or other debt instrument according to the agreed contractual terms. The consequence may be a lower-than-expected interest rate or yield or even a complete loss of the amount originally lent. The *default risk premium* is an added market interest rate component that provides higher expected compensation for taking on default risk. The premium for default risk will increase as the probability of default increases.

To examine default risk premiums for debt securities, it is necessary to hold some of the other components of market interest rates constant. Referring to equation (8.3), we can develop a procedure for measuring that portion of a market interest rate (r) attributable to default risk. Recall that the market interest rate is a function of a real interest rate, an inflation premium, a default risk premium, a maturity risk premium, and a liquidity risk premium.

First, we constrain our analysis to the long-term capital markets by considering only long-term Treasury bonds and long-term corporate bonds. By focusing on long-term securities, the maturity risk will be the same for all the bonds and can be set at zero for analysis purposes. We have also said that the liquidity premium is zero for Treasury securities, because they can be readily sold without requiring a substantial price discount. Corporate securities are less liquid than Treasury securities. However, we can minimize any possible liquidity premiums by considering the bonds of large corporations. This also allows us to set the liquidity premium at zero for analysis purposes.

For the following example, assume that the real rate is 1%, inflation is expected to average 2%, the market interest rate is 3% for long-term Treasury bonds, and high-quality corporate bonds have a 5% market interest rate. Using equation (8.3), we have the following:

$$r = RR + IP + DRP + MRP + LP$$
$$5\% = 1\% + 2\% + DRP + 0\% + 0\%$$
$$DRP = 5\% - 1\% - 2\% - 0\% - 0\% = 2\%$$

Starting with the 5% corporate bond rate and subtracting the 1% real rate plus the 2% average annual inflation premium, results in a default risk premium of 2%. Another way of looking at the default risk premium (assuming zero maturity risk and liquidity premiums) is that it is the difference between the interest rates on the risky (corporate) and risk-free (Treasury) securities. In our example, we have,

$$DRP = 5\% - 3\% = 2\%$$

Thus, investors require a 2% premium to hold or invest in the corporate bond instead of the Treasury bond.

Another corporate bond with a higher default risk may carry an interest rate of, say, 7%. If the other assumptions used above are retained, the DRP would be,

$$7\% = 1\% + 2\% + DRP + 0\% + 0\%$$
$$DRP = 7\% - 1\% - 2\% - 0\% - 0\% = 4\%$$

Alternatively, we could find DRP as follows:

$$DRP = 7\% - 3\% = 4\%$$

Thus, to get investors to invest in these riskier corporate bonds, a default risk premium of four percentage points must be offered above the interest rate, or yield, on Treasury bonds.

The examination of actual default risk premiums in Table 8.4 shows long-term interest rates for Treasury bonds and two corporate bonds with different degrees of default risk. The characteristics of corporate bonds will be discussed in Chapter 10, but here it can be said that one way potential default risk is measured is through bond ratings. The highest rating assigned by Moody's, a major bond-rating

Table 8.4 Default Risk Premiums on Corporate Bonds at Selected Dates

	March 1980	Oct. 2006	Oct. 2008	Dec. 2012	Dec. 2015	Dec. 2018
Aaa-rated corporate bonds	13.0%	5.5%	5.2%	3.67%	3.97%	4.02%
Less: 20-year Treasury bonds	12.5	4.9	4.2	2.54	2.61	2.98
Equals: default risk premium on Aaa-rated bonds	0.5	0.6	1.0	1.13	1.36	1.04
Baa-rated corporate bonds	14.5	6.4	6.3	4.63	5.46	5.13
Less: 20-year Treasury bonds	12.5	4.9	4.2	2.54	2.61	2.98
Equals: default risk premium on Baa-rated bonds	2.0	1.5	2.1	2.09	2.85	2.15

Source: *Selected Interest Rates*, Board of Governors of the Federal Reserve System, https://www.federalreserve.gov, and https://fred.stlouisfed.org.

agency, is Aaa and indicates the lowest likelihood of default. Investors in these bonds require a small default risk premium over Treasury bonds. Baa-rated bonds have higher default risks but still are considered to be of reasonably high quality. **Investment grade bonds** have ratings of Baa or higher and meet financial institution (banks, pension funds, insurance companies, etc.) investment standards.

investment grade bonds ratings of Baa or higher that meet financial institution investment standards

In March 1980, the default risk premium on corporate Aaa-rated bonds over 20-year Treasuries was 0.5 percentage point (i.e., 13.0 − 12.5%). Although not shown, the default risk premium on Aaa-rated corporate bonds had increased to 1.7 percentage points in November 2001, reflecting an economic downturn and concerns about terrorism in the United States. The October 2006 risk premium for Aaa-rated bonds returned to a relatively low level at a 0.6 percentage point differential over 20-year Treasury bonds. By October 2008, when the United States was in the midst of the 2007–2008 financial crisis and the 2008–2009 recession, the risk premium for Aaa-rated bonds had increased to 1.0 percentage point. The Aaa-rated corporate bond risk premium was 1.13% in December 2012 and increased to 1.36% in December 2015 before returning to about the 1 percent level in December 2018.

The default risk premiums on Baa corporate bonds are generally better indicators of investor pessimism or optimism about economic expectations than are those on Aaa-rated bonds. More firms fail or suffer financial distress during periods of recession than during periods of economic expansion. Thus, investors tend to require higher premiums to compensate for default risk when the economy is in a recession or is expected to enter one. Notice in Table 8.4 that the risk premium on Baa-rated bonds was two percentage points in March 1980 (14.5 − 12.5%). Although not shown, the default risk premium on Baa-rated bonds was 2.5 percentage points in November 2001 and reflected concerns about the slowing of economic activity in the United States and continued uncertainty after the terrorist attack on September 11, 2001. As of October 2006, the risk premium on Baa-rated corporate debt was down to 1.5 percentage points over the interest rate on 20-year Treasury bonds.

The Baa-rated bond risk premium increased to 2.1 percentage points by October 2008, due to the financial difficulties in the United States. Baa-rated corporate bonds relative to 20-year Treasury bonds exhibited a 2.09% risk premium in December 2012 and a 2.85% premium in December 2015 before declining to 2.15 percentage points in December 2018. The relatively high default risk premium at the end of 2015 reflects concern about possibly slower economic growth. Being risk adverse, bond investors will require higher expected additional compensation when they believe the probability of default increases. Bond investors seemed relatively more optimistic about the economy in December 2018.

ETHICAL Sometimes corporations issue bonds with ratings lower than Baa. These are called **high-yield or junk bonds** because they have a substantial probability of default. While many institutional investors are restricted to investing in only investment grade (Baa-rated or higher) corporate debt, others are permitted to invest in high-yield, high-risk corporate debt. Recall the discussion in Chapter 2 about the savings and loan associations crisis that was caused in part by corporate defaults on high-yield or junk bonds that were held by S&Ls. Michael Milken, who was at Drexel Burnham Lambert at the time, was instrumental in getting those S&Ls and other institutions able to purchase junk bonds to

high-yield or junk bonds bonds that have a relatively high probability of default

do so. Some individuals would argue that the purchasers of junk bonds were sophisticated enough to make rational risk-return decisions; *caveat emptor*—let the buyer beware. Other individuals charged that unethical and illegal behavior on the part of the marketers of junk bonds contributed to the failure of many of the issuers of the bonds as well as the purchasers (particularly S&Ls) of the bonds. In 1989, Milken was sent to prison and Drexel Burnham Lambert went bankrupt.

| LEARNING ACTIVITY

Go to the website of the Federal Reserve Bank of St. Louis, https://www.stlouisfed.org, and access the FRED database. Find current interest rates for long-term Treasury bonds as well as Aaa-rated and Baa-rated corporate bonds, and indicate the size of default risk premiums.

APPLYING FINANCE TO. . .

• **Institutions and Markets**   Depository institutions make profits by achieving a spread between the interest rates they pay individuals on savings accounts and the interest rates they charge businesses and other individuals for loans. Interest rates are also important to financial institutions, such as insurance companies and pension funds, which accumulate premiums and contributions and invest these proceeds in government and corporate securities for the benefit of their policyholders and employees. The government depends on financial institutions holding or owning an important portion of the U.S. Treasury securities issued to finance the national debt.

• **Investments**   Interest rates are set in the financial markets based on the supply and demand for loanable funds. The cost, or price, of home mortgage loans depends on the supply and demand for such loans in the mortgage markets. Interest rates offered on Treasury debt securities reflect a real rate of interest and an expected inflation premium. Corporate bond borrowers must pay a default risk premium above the interest rate being offered on government debt securities. Corporate issuers of high-quality, investment grade bonds pay lower default risk premiums relative to issuers of lower-quality bonds. Observed interest rates may also reflect a maturity risk premium and/or a liquidity premium.

• **Financial Management**   The prevailing level of interest rates is particularly important to financial managers. When interest rates are high, businesses will find it less profitable to borrow from financial institutions or in the securities markets because investment in inventories, plant, and equipment will look less attractive. Likewise, when interest rates are relatively low, loans are generally readily available and stock prices are usually high. Thus, financial managers often find it attractive to grow their businesses during periods when funds to finance the expansion activities can be borrowed at relatively low interest rates, or when they can issue new shares of their common stocks at relatively high prices.

SUMMARY

LO 8.1   The interest rate is the price of loanable funds in financial markets, and the equilibrium interest rate is the price that equates the demand for and supply of loanable funds. Interest rates may move from an existing equilibrium level to a new equilibrium level as the result of a change in the supply of or demand for loanable funds. For example, if the quantity of loanable funds being demanded increases due to new business opportunities, suppliers of loanable funds will need to be offered a higher interest rate so that the supply of and demand for loanable funds will be brought back into balance.

LO 8.2   The major components of market interest rates include a real rate of interest plus possible premiums for inflation expectations, default risk, maturity risk, and lack of liquidity. A market interest rate that contains only a real rate of interest and an inflation expectation component is considered to be a risk-free interest rate. For many debt instruments, there is an additional expected return for assuming the risk that the borrower may not pay interest and/or principal when due. For debt instruments with longer maturities, an added return is usually expected by lenders and debt investors as compensation for interest rate risk. Bond investors also may require compensation for holding debt instruments that are not easily converted to cash at prices close to their estimated fair market values.

LO 8.3   Marketable government securities are securities than can be purchased and sold through customary market channels. There are three types of U.S. Treasury marketable securities. Treasury bills are issued with maturities up to one year. Treasury notes are usually issued with maturities of 2 to 10 years. Treasury bonds are issued with maturities greater than 10 years. A little less than 40% of the outstanding Treasury securities are currently held by the Federal Reserve and in government accounts. Foreign and international investors currently hold approximately 30% of the amount of outstanding Treasury securities.

LO 8.4   The term structure of interest rates indicates the relationship between interest rates, or yields, and the maturity of comparable quality debt instruments. This relationship is, typically, depicted through the graphic presentation of a yield curve. The three theories used to explain the term structure of interest rates are expectations theory, liquidity preference theory, and market segmentation theory.

LO 8.5   Inflation occurs when an increase in the price of goods or services is not offset by an increase in quality. Monetary factors have often affected price levels in the United States, especially during major wars. Since the end of the 1990s, inflation rates have remained at relatively low levels. The four types of inflation are cost-push inflation, which occurs when prices are raised to cover rising production costs such as wages; demand-pull inflation, which occurs when an excessive demand for goods and services is created during periods of economic expansion as a result of large increases in the money supply; speculative inflation; and administrative inflation.

LO 8.6   Because debt investors are risk adverse, they expect higher returns for taking on more risk or uncertainty. Default risk is the risk that a borrower will not pay interest and/or principal on a debt instrument when due. Differences between market interest rates on long-term risky corporate bonds that are liquid, and the rates on long-term Treasury bonds, indicate the then-prevailing default risk premiums. Bond investors expect higher default risk premiums on corporate bonds that have lower bond ratings.

KEY TERMS

administrative inflation
cost-push inflation
dealer system
default risk
default risk premium
demand-pull inflation
equilibrium interest rate
expectations theory
high-yield or junk bonds

inflation
inflation premium
interest rate
interest rate risk
investment grade bonds
liquidity preference theory
liquidity premium
loanable funds
loanable funds theory

marketable government
  securities
market interest rate
market segmentation
  theory
maturity risk premium
negative interest rate
nonmarketable
  government securities

real rate of interest
risk-free interest rate
speculative inflation
term structure of
  interest rates
Treasury bills
Treasury bonds
Treasury notes
yield curve

REVIEW QUESTIONS

1. **(LO 8.1)** What is the "interest rate," and how is it determined?

2. **(LO 8.1)** Describe how interest rates may adjust to an unanticipated increase in inflation.

3. **(LO 8.1)** Identify major periods of rising interest rates in U.S. history, and describe some of the underlying reasons for these interest rate movements.

4. **(LO 8.1)** How did the Fed contribute to the recent historically low interest rates?

5. **(LO 8.1)** How does the loanable funds theory explain the level of interest rates?

6. **(LO 8.1)** What are the main sources of loanable funds? Indicate and briefly discuss the factors that affect the supply of loanable funds.

7. **(LO 8.1)** Indicate the sources of demand for loanable funds, and discuss the factors that affect the demand for loanable funds.

8. **(LO 8.2)** What are the factors, in addition to supply-and-demand relationships, that determine market interest rates?

9. **(LO 8.3)** What are the types of marketable securities issued by the Treasury?

10. **(LO 8.3)** Explain the mechanics of issuing Treasury bills, indicating how the price of a new issue is determined.

11. **(LO 8.3)** Describe the dealer system for marketable U.S. government securities.

12. **(LO 8.3)** What is the tax status of income from federal securities?

13. **(LO 8.3)** Describe any significant changes in the ownership pattern of federal debt securities in recent years.

14. **(LO 8.3)** What have been the recent developments in the maturity distribution of marketable interest-bearing federal debt?

15. **(LO 8.3)** Describe the process of advance refunding of the federal debt.

16. **(LO 8.4)** What is the term structure of interest rates, and how is it expressed?

17. **(LO 8.4)** Identify and describe the three basic theories used to explain the term structure of interest rates.

18. **(LO 8.5)** Describe the process by which inflation took place historically before modern times.

19. **(LO 8.5)** Discuss the early periods of inflation based on the issue of paper money.

20. **(LO 8.5)** What was the basis for inflation during World Wars I and II?

21. **(LO 8.5)** Discuss the causes of the major periods of inflation in American history.

22. **(LO 8.5)** Explain the process by which price changes may be initiated by a general change in costs.

23. **(LO 8.5)** How can a change in the money supply lead to a change in the price level?

24. **(LO 8.5)** What is meant by the speculative type of inflation?

25. **(LO 8.6)** What is meant by default risk and a default risk premium?

26. **(LO 8.6)** How can a default risk premium change over time?

EXERCISES

1. Go to the Federal Reserve Bank of St. Louis website at https://www.stlouisfed.org, and find interest rates on U.S. Treasury securities and on corporate bonds with different bond ratings.
   a. Prepare a yield curve or term structure of interest rates.
   b. Identify existing default risk premiums between long-term Treasury bonds and corporate bonds.

2. As an economist for a major bank, you are asked to explain a substantial increase in the price level when neither the money supply nor the velocity of money has increased. How can this occur?

3. As an advisor to the U.S. Treasury, you have been asked to comment on a proposal for easing the burden of interest on the national debt. This proposal calls for the elimination of federal taxes on interest received from Treasury debt obligations. Comment on the proposal.

4. As one of several advisors to the secretary of the U.S. Treasury, you have been asked to submit a memo in connection with the average maturity of the securities of the federal government. The basic premise is that the average maturity is far too short. As a result, issues of debt are coming due with great frequency and need constant reissue. On the other hand, the economy shows signs of weakness. It is considered unwise to issue long-term obligations and absorb investment funds that might otherwise be invested in employment-producing construction and other private-sector support. Based on these conditions, what course of action do you recommend to the secretary of the U.S. Treasury?

5. Assume a condition in which the economy is strong, with relatively high employment. For one reason or another, the money supply is increasing at a high rate, with little evidence of money creation slowing down. Assuming the money supply continues to increase, describe the evolving effect on price levels.

6. Assume you are employed as an investment advisor. You are working with a retired individual who depends on her income from her investments to meet her day-to-day expenditures. She would like to find a way of increasing the current income from her investments. A new high-yield or junk bond issue has come to your attention. If you sell these high-yield bonds to a client, you will earn a higher-than-average fee. You wonder whether this would be a win-win investment for your retired client, who is seeking higher current income, and for you, who would benefit in terms of increased fees. What would you do?

1. Assume investors expect a 2.0% real rate of return over the next year. If inflation is expected to be 0.5%, what is the expected market interest rate for a one-year U.S. Treasury security?

2. A one-year U.S. Treasury security has a market interest rate of 2.25%. If the expected real rate of interest is 1.5%, what is the expected annual inflation rate?

3. A 20-year U.S. Treasury bond has a 3.50% interest rate, while a same maturity corporate bond has a 5.25% interest rate. Real interest rates and inflation rate expectations would be the same for the two bonds. If a default risk premium of 1.50 percentage points is estimated for the corporate bond, determine the liquidity premium for the corporate bond.

4. A 30-year U.S. Treasury bond has a 4.0% interest rate. In contrast, a 10-year Treasury note has an interest rate of 3.7%. If inflation is expected to average 1.5 percentage points over both the next 10 years and 30 years, determine the maturity risk premium for the 30-year bond over the 10-year note.

5. A 30-year U.S. Treasury bond has a 4.0% interest rate. In contrast, a 10-year Treasury note has an interest rate of 2.5%. A maturity risk premium is estimated to be 0.2 percentage points for the longer maturity bond. Investors expect inflation to average 1.5 percentage points over the next 10 years.
   a. Estimate the expected real rate of return on the 10-year U.S. Treasury note.
   b. If the real rate of return is expected to be the same for the 30-year bond as for the 10-year note, estimate the average annual inflation rate expected by investors over the life of the 30-year bond.

6. You are considering an investment in a one-year government debt security with a yield of 5% or a highly liquid corporate debt security with a yield of 6.5%. The expected inflation rate for the next year is expected to be 2.5%.
   a. What would be your real rate earned on either of the two investments?
   b. What would be the default risk premium on the corporate debt security?

7. Inflation is expected to be 3% over the next year. You desire an annual real rate of return of 2.5% on your investments.
   a. What market rate of interest would have to be offered on a one-year Treasury security for you to consider making an investment?

   b. A one-year corporate debt security is being offered at two percentage points over the one-year Treasury security rate that meets your requirement in (a). What would be the market interest rate on the corporate security?

8. Find the market interest rate for a debt security given the following information: real rate = 2%, liquidity premium = 2%, default risk premium = 4%, maturity risk premium = 3%, and inflation premium = 3%.

9. Find the default risk premium for a debt security given the following information: inflation premium = 3%, maturity risk premium = 2.5%, real rate = 3%, liquidity premium = 0%, and market interest rate = 10%.

10. Find the default risk premium for a debt security given the following information: inflation premium = 2.5%, maturity risk premium = 2.5%, real rate = 3%, liquidity premium = 1.5%, and market interest rate = 14%.

11. Assume that the interest rate on a one-year Treasury bill is 6% and the rate on a two-year Treasury note is 7%.
    a. If the expected real rate of interest is 3%, determine the inflation premium on the Treasury bill.
    b. If the maturity risk premium is expected to be zero, determine the inflation premium on the Treasury note.
    c. What is the expected inflation premium for the second year?

12. A Treasury note with a maturity of four years carries a market rate of interest of 10%. In contrast, an eight-year Treasury note has a yield of 8%.
    a. If inflation is expected to average 7% over the first four years, what is the expected real rate of interest?
    b. If the inflation rate is expected to be 5% for the first year, calculate the average annual rate of inflation for years 2 through 4.
    c. If the maturity risk premium is expected to be zero between the two Treasury securities, what will be the average annual inflation rate expected over years 5 through 8?

13. The interest rate on a 20-year Treasury bond is 9.25%. A comparable maturity, Aaa-rated corporate bond is yielding 10%. Another comparable maturity, but lower-quality corporate bond has a yield of 14%, which includes a liquidity premium of 1.5%.
    a. Determine the default risk premium on the Aaa-rated bond.
    b. Determine the default risk premium on the lower-quality corporate bond.

14. A 30-year corporate bond has a market interest rate of 12%. This bond is not very liquid and consequently requires a 2% liquidity premium. The bond is of low quality and thus has a default risk premium of 2.5%. The bond has a remaining life of 25 years, resulting in a maturity risk premium of 1.5%.

    a. Estimate the market interest rate on a 30-year Treasury bond.

    b. What would be the inflation premium on the Treasury bond if investors required a real rate of interest of 2.5%?

15. **Challenge Problem** Following are some selected interest rates.

Maturity or Term	Rate	Type of Security
1 year	4.0%	Corporate loan (high quality)
1 year	5.0%	Corporate loan (low quality)
1 year	3.5%	Treasury bill
5 years	5.0%	Treasury note
5 years	6.5%	Corporate bond (high quality)
5 years	8.0%	Corporate bond (low quality)
10 years	10.5%	Corporate bond (low quality)
10 years	8.5%	Corporate bond (high quality)
10 years	7.0%	Treasury bond
20 years	7.5%	Treasury bond

Maturity or Term	Rate	Type of Security
20 years	9.5%	Corporate bond (high quality)
20 years	12.0%	Corporate bond (low quality)

a. Plot a yield curve using interest rates for government default risk-free securities.

b. Plot a yield curve using corporate debt securities with low default risk (high quality) and a separate yield curve for low-quality corporate debt securities.

c. Measure the amount of default risk premiums, assuming constant inflation rate expectations and no maturity or liquidity risk premiums on any of the debt securities for both high-quality and low-quality corporate securities based on information from (a) and (b). Describe and discuss why differences might exist between high-quality and low-quality corporate debt securities.

d. Identify the average expected inflation rate at each maturity level in (a) if the real rate is expected to average 2% per year and if there are no maturity risk premiums expected on Treasury securities.

e. Using information from (d), calculate the average annual expected inflation rate over years 2 through 5. Also calculate the average annual expected inflation rates for years 6 through 10 and for years 11 through 20.

f. Based on the information from (e), reestimate the maturity risk premiums for high-quality and low-quality corporate debt securities. Describe what seems to be occurring over time and between differences in default risks.

Time Value of Money

LEARNING OBJECTIVES

After studying this chapter, you should be able to do the following:

LO 9.1 Explain what is meant by the "time value of money" and the concept of simple interest.

LO 9.2 Describe the process of compounding to determine future values.

LO 9.3 Describe the process of discounting to determine present values.

LO 9.4 Explain how to find interest rates and time requirements for problems involving compounding or discounting.

LO 9.5 Define an *annuity* and describe how to find the future value of an ordinary annuity.

LO 9.6 Explain how to calculate the present value of an ordinary annuity.

LO 9.7 Describe how to find interest rates and time requirements for problems involving ordinary annuities.

LO 9.8 Explain how to determine periodic ordinary annuity payments.

LO 9.9 Explain how to calculate future and present values when time intervals are less than one year, and describe how to estimate the cost of consumer credit.

Where we have been. . . In Chapter 8, you learned how interest rates are determined in the financial markets. The supply of and demand for loanable funds were discussed along with the determinants of market, or "nominal," interest rates. You should recall that the determinants are the real rate of interest, an inflation premium, and a default risk premium for risky debt. A maturity risk premium adjusts for differences in lives, or maturities, and there also may be a liquidity premium. You also learned about the characteristics of U.S. government debt securities and the term, or maturity structure, of interest rates. You now should know how inflation premiums and price movements affect interest rates, as well as why default risk premiums exist and how they are measured.

Where we are going. . . Chapter 10 focuses on the characteristics and valuations of bonds and stocks. You will learn about the long-term external financing sources available to and used by businesses. You will then explore the characteristics and features of both debt and equity capital. Next, the general principles of valuation, which build on the time value of money (covered in this chapter), and how bonds and stocks are valued will be covered. Calculating rates of return is the last topic in Chapter 10. In Chapter 11, you will focus on the characteristics and operation of primary and secondary securities markets. Chapter 12, the last chapter in Part 2, will focus on financial return and risk concepts.

How this chapter applies to me. . . You probably have experienced the need to save money to buy an automobile or to pay for your tuition. Your savings grow more rapidly when you can earn interest on previously earned interest in addition to interest on the starting amount of your savings. This is known as compounding and means that the longer you save the faster your savings will grow and the larger will be your down payment on your automobile purchase or the more money you will have for your tuition. An understanding of compounding also will be useful to you when investing in stocks and bonds and planning for eventual retirement.

Most of us would agree that if other things are equal,

More money is better than less money.

Most of us also would agree,

Money today is worth more than the same amount of money received in the future.

Of course, the value of an additional dollar is not necessarily the same for all individuals. For example, a person subsisting at the poverty level would likely find an added dollar to be worth more in "economic terms" than would an extra dollar to a millionaire or billionaire. It is probably safe to say that having an added dollar today has more "economic worth" to you or us than it would to Jeff Bezos, the founder, Chairman, CEO, and President of Amazon. At the same time, Jeff Bezos' personal desire or drive for accumulating more dollars is likely to be greater than your desire.

This chapter makes no attempt to consider the economic or psychological value of having more money to a specific individual. Rather, it concentrates on the principle of finance, initially presented in Chapter 1, stating that "money has a time value." The focus here is on how money can grow or increase over time, as well as how money has a lower worth today if one has to wait to receive the money sometime in the future. This occurs because one loses the opportunity of earning interest on the money by not being able to save or invest the money today.

Financial calculators or spreadsheet software programs will perform the calculations and procedures discussed in this chapter. However, the calculation procedures are first described in detail to enhance your understanding of the logic involved in the concepts of the time value of money. By learning to work the problems the "long way" using step-by-step calculations and following the steps given for financial calculators, spreadsheet programs, and tables-based calculations should make more sense. Students are encouraged to explore using multiple problem-solving methods.

9.1 BASIC TIME VALUE CONCEPTS

FINANCE In Chapter 1, we identified six principles of finance. These principles serve as the foundation of finance:

1. Money has a time value.

2. Higher returns are expected for taking on more risk.

3. Diversification of investments can reduce risk.

4. Financial markets are efficient in pricing securities.

5. Manager and stockholder objectives may differ.

6. Reputation matters.

time value of money math of finance whereby a financial return is earned over time by saving or investing money

The pricing and valuation of financial securities, including bonds, stocks, and real asset investments, are best understood in the context of the finance principles. The **time value of money** is the math of finance whereby a financial return (e.g., interest) is earned over time by saving or investing money.

In addition to investors requiring compensation or a financial return for lending or investing their financial capital, they also want to be compensated with higher expected returns for taking on more financial risk. For example, we explored in Chapter 8 the concept of default risk premiums for investing in corporate bonds relative to investing in Treasury bonds. Higher default risk premiums are required by investors in corporate bonds relative to government bonds, because there is a higher likelihood or probability that corporations will miss paying on time their interest and principal payment obligations. Risk-return trade-offs will be addressed in greater detail in future chapters. The ability to diversify away some investment risk through holding diversified portfolios of securities also is important to investors when making investment decisions.

The actions of individuals to seek out undervalued and overvalued investment opportunities contribute to making financial markets reasonably efficient – that is, current prices reflect the underlying intrinsic valuations of real and financial assets. We also know that management objectives may differ from owner objectives. Methods of getting managers to manage for the best interests of equity investors will be discussed in Part 3 of this textbook. The final principle is based on the belief that "reputation matters" and considers the ethical behavior of individuals and organizations as to legal, fair, and honest treatment of others.

We concentrate on the time value of money financial principle in this chapter. Money can increase, or grow, over time if we can save (invest) it and earn a return on our savings (investment). Let's begin with a savings account illustration. Assume you have $1,000 to save, or invest; this is your *principal*. The **present value** of a savings or an investment is its amount or value today. For our example, this is your $1,000.

present value value today of a savings amount or investment

A bank offers to accept your savings for one year and agrees to pay to you an 8% interest rate for use of your $1,000. This amounts to $80 in interest (0.08 × $1,000). The total payment by the bank at the end of one year is $1,080 ($1,000 principal plus $80 in interest). This $1,080 is referred to as the future value, or value after one year in this case. The **future value** of a savings amount or investment is its value at a specified time or date in the future. In general word terms, we have,

future value value of a savings amount or an investment at a specified time or date in the future

$$\text{Future value} = \text{Present value} + (\text{Present value} \times \text{Interest rate})$$

Or,

$$\text{Future value} = \text{Present value} \times (1 + \text{Interest rate})$$

In our example, we have,

$$\text{Future value} = \$1,000 + (\$1,000 \times 0.08)$$
$$= \$1,080$$

Or,

$$\text{Future value} = \$1,000 \times 1.08$$
$$= \$1,080$$

Let's now assume that your $1,000 investment remains on deposit for two years but the bank pays only simple interest, which is interest earned only on the investment's principal. In word terms, we have,

$$\text{Future value} = \text{Present value} \times \left[1 + (\text{Interest rate}) \times (\text{number of periods})\right]$$

For our example, this becomes,

$$\text{Future value} = \$1,000 \times \left[1 + (0.08 \times 2)\right]$$
$$= \$1,000 \times 1.16$$
$$= \$1,160$$

Another bank will pay you a 10% interest rate on your money. Thus, you would receive $100 in interest ($1,000 × 0.10), or a return at the end of one year of $1,100 ($1,000 × 1.10) from the second bank. While the $20 difference in return between the two banks ($1,100 versus $1,080) is not great, it has some importance to most people. For a two-year deposit that pays **simple interest** annually, the difference increases to $40. The second bank would return $1,200 ($1,000 × 1.20) to you, versus $1,160 from the first bank. If the funds were invested for ten years, we would accumulate $1,000 × [1 + (0.08 × 10)] or $1,800 at the first bank. At the second bank, we would have $1,000 × [1 + (0.10 × 10)] or $2,000; a $200 difference. This interest rate differential between the two banks will become even more important when we introduce the concept of compounding.

simple interest interest earned only on the investment's principal

Interest rates paid by banks and other depository institutions were very low during the 2008–2015 period reflecting the Fed's easy monetary policies during the 2007–2008 financial crisis, the 2008–2009 Great Recession, and the subsequent effort to foster economic recovery. During this period of near-zero short-term interest rates, depository institutions typically paid savers 0.1% or less interest on their savings accounts. Savers were willing to accept nearly zero interest rates in exchange for depository institutions providing safe keeping of their money. In December 2015 the Fed increased its target for the federal funds rate from 0.00–0.25% to 0.25–0.50%. Subsequent increases brought the target rate to 2.25–2.50% by the end of 2018. Today, some depository institutions are paying more than 2% interest on savings.

In Chapter 8, we noted that negative interest rates can occur if a central bank, or possibly even a private bank, charges depositors to keep their money at the bank. The U.S. Fed has in the past rejected the idea of using negative interest rates as a monetary policy tool. Also, there is no record of U.S. depository institutions charging negative interest rates on depositor accounts.

However, the European Central Bank, the central banks of several non-eurozone member European countries, and the Bank of Japan have charged negative interest rates on excess bank reserves. The easy monetary policies of these central banks also have led to some of their government-issued debt securities being offered at negative interest rates as we discussed in Chapter 8.

LEARNING ACTIVITY

Go to the Chase Bank website, https://www.chase.com. Under the "Savings Accounts and CDs" heading, go to "CDs" and identify the interest rates being paid on certificates of deposit (CDs) of various maturities and amounts.

9.2 COMPOUNDING TO DETERMINE FUTURE VALUES

compounding arithmetic process whereby an initial value increases or grows at a compound interest rate over time to reach a value in the future

compound interest involves earning interest on interest in addition to interest on the principal or initial investment

Compounding is an arithmetic process whereby an initial value increases or grows at a *compound interest* rate over time to reach a value in the future. **Compound interest** involves earning interest on interest in addition to interest on the principal or initial investment. To understand compounding, let's assume that you leave the investment with a bank for more than one year. For example, the first bank accepts your $1,000 deposit now, adds $80 at the end of one year, retains the $1,080 for the second year, and pays you interest at an 8% rate. The bank returns your initial deposit plus accumulated interest at the end of the second year. How much will you receive as a future value?

In word terms, we have the following calculation:

$$\text{Future value} = \text{Present value} \times \left[(1 + \text{Interest rate}) \times (1 + \text{Interest rate}) \right]$$

For our two-year investment example, we have,

$$\text{Future value} = \$1,000 \times (1.08) \times (1.08)$$
$$= \$1,000 \times 1.1664$$
$$= \$1,166.40$$
$$= \$1,166 \text{ (rounded)}$$

A time line also can be used to illustrate this two-year example as follows:

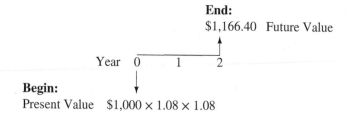

Thus, for a one-year investment, the return would be $1,080 ($1,000 × 1.08), which is the same as the return on a simple interest investment, as was previously shown. However, a two-year investment at an 8% compound interest rate will return $1,166.40, compared to $1,160 using an 8% simple interest rate.

The compounding concept also can be expressed in equation form as,

$$FV_n = PV(1 + r)^n \tag{9.1}$$

where FV is the future value, PV is the present value, r is the interest rate, and n is the number of periods in years. For our $1,000 deposit, 8%, two-year example, we have,

$$FV_2 = \$1,000(1 + 0.08)^2$$
$$= \$1,000(1.1164)$$
$$= \$1,166.40$$
$$= \$1,166 \text{ (rounded)}$$

If we extend the time period to ten years, the $1,000 deposit would grow to,

$$FV_{10} = \$1,000(1 + 0.08)^{10}$$
$$= \$1,000(2.1589)$$
$$= \$2,158.90$$
$$= \$2,159 \text{ (rounded)}$$

Now that we have set up an equation-based process for finding a future value when compounding is involved, we will demonstrate three other methods that could be used to find a future value. They include a financial calculator solution, a spreadsheet solution, and a table-based solution. We will use a similar format for solving other time value of money problems throughout the remainder of this chapter.

Texas Instruments (TI) and Hewlett Packard (HP) make two popular types of financial calculators. However, they are programmed differently.[1] Reference is made to the use of TI and HP calculators when discussing calculator solutions throughout the remainder of this chapter. Other available financial calculators are usually programmed like either the TI or HP calculators. What is important is that if you are going to use a financial calculator to solve time value of money problems, you must understand how your particular calculator works.

Most financial calculators are programmed to readily find future values. Typically, financial calculators will have a present value key (PV), a future value key (FV), a number of time periods key (N), an interest rate key (usually designated %i), and a compute key (usually designated as CPT). If you have a financial calculator, you can verify the future value result for the ten-year example.

First, clear any values stored in the calculator's memory. Next, enter 1000 and press the PV key (some financial calculators require that you enter the present value amount as a minus value because it is an investment, or outflow). Then, enter 8 and press the %i key (most financial calculators are programmed so that you enter whole numbers rather than decimals for the interest rate). Next, enter 10 for the number of time periods (usually years) and press the N key. Finally, press the CPT key followed by the FV key to calculate the future value of 2,158.93, which rounds to $2,159. Actually, financial calculators are programmed to calculate answers to 12 significant digits.

Financial Calculator Solution:

Inputs:	10	8	1000
	N	%i	PV
Press:	CPT	FV	
Solution:	2158.93		

Computer spreadsheet programs also are available for finding future values. Following is the same problem solved using *Microsoft's Excel* spreadsheet program. For presentation purposes, the solution for only the two-year version of the problem is shown. That is, how much would you accumulate after two years if you invested $1,000 at an 8% interest rate with annual compounding?

---

[1] For problems involving PVs and FVs, HP calculators require one of the values to be entered as a negative. In contrast, both PVs and FVs are entered as positive values in TI calculators, and the internal program makes one of the values negative for calculation purposes. Other TI and HP differences when entering data also are noted later in this chapter.

Spreadsheet Solution:

	A	B	C	D
1	Interest Rate	0.08		
2	Time Period	0	1	2
3	Cash Flow	1000		
4	Future Value (FV)		1080.00	1166.40
5				
6	Cash Flow fx Calc	-1000	0	0
7	Financial Function			
8	FV Solution			$1,166.40

We set up our spreadsheet with descriptive labels in cells A1 through A4. We then solve the compound interest problem by placing the interest rate in decimal form (0.08) in Cell B1. The time periods are placed on Row 2, beginning with period 0 (the current period) in Cell B2 and so forth. The cash flow of 1000 (an investment) is listed in cell B3. In this simple problem, we first replicate the basic "by hand" calculations in spreadsheet format and the future value calculations beginning in C4 and continuing to D4.

In Cell C4, we place the formula = B3*(1 + B1), which reflects compounding the $1,000 investment at 8% interest for one year. Cell D4 shows compounding of the investment at 8% for a second year and can be calculated as C4*(1 + B1), so compounding at an 8% interest rate results in a future value of $1,166.40 after two years. Of course, we could have made the FV calculation in one step as = B3*(1 + B1)^2, which also produces $1,166.40.

Excel and other spreadsheet programs have built-in "financial functions" so that spreadsheet solutions do not have to be calculated the "long way." The bottom portion of the spreadsheet solution example illustrates the use of the financial function for future value. Here we enter the cash flow in time period zero as −1000 to reflect an outflow and a present value. Click on the Excel financial wizard (*fx*) icon, then Financial, then FV, and then press OK to bring up the dialogue box where the FV components for the problem at hand are requested. The equation is FV(Rate, Nper, Pmt, PV, Type). The Rate is 0.08; Nper is the number of time periods (2 in the preceding example); Pmt is 0, since there are no periodic payments; PV is −1000; and Type is 0, reflecting that payments occur at the end of the period. Thus, we would have FV(0.08,2,0, −1000,0). Pressing OK results in a FV of $1,166.40, or $1,166 rounded. Of course, rather than inserting numbers, one could insert specific cell references in the FV function.

If the investment had been compounded for ten years, the FV function inputs would have been FV(0.08,10,0,−1000,0). Pressing OK would result in an answer of $2,158.92, or $2.159 rounded.

In addition, tables have been prepared to simplify the calculation effort if financial calculators or spreadsheet programs are not available. Equation 9.1 can be rewritten as,

$$FV_n = PV(FVIF_{r,n})$$ (9.2)

where the $(1 + r)^n$ part of equation 5.1 is replaced by a future value interest factor (FVIF) corresponding to a specific interest rate and a specified time period.

Table 9.1 shows FVIF values carried to three decimal places for a partial range of interest rates and time periods. (Table 1 in the Appendix is a more comprehensive FVIF table.) Let's use Table 9.1 to find the future value of $1,000 invested at an 8% compound interest rate for a ten-year period; notice that at the intersection of the 8% column and ten years, we find an FVIF of 2.159. Putting this information into equation 9.2 gives the following solution.

Table-based Solution:

$$FV_{10} = \$1,000(2.159)$$
$$= \$2,159$$

Further examination of Table 9.1 shows how a $1 investment grows or increases with various combinations of interest rates and time periods. For example, if another bank offers to pay you a 10%

Table 9.1   Future Value Interest Factor (FVIF) of $1

Year	5%	6%	7%	8%	9%	10%
1	1.050	1.060	1.070	1.080	1.090	1.100
2	1.102	1.124	1.145	1.166	1.188	1.210
3	1.158	1.191	1.225	1.260	1.295	1.331
4	1.216	1.262	1.311	1.360	1.412	1.464
5	1.276	1.338	1.403	1.469	1.539	1.611
6	1.340	1.419	1.501	1.587	1.677	1.772
7	1.407	1.504	1.606	1.714	1.828	1.949
8	1.477	1.594	1.718	1.851	1.993	2.144
9	1.551	1.689	1.838	1.999	2.172	2.358
10	1.629	1.791	1.967	2.159	2.367	2.594

interest rate compounded annually, notice that the FVIF at the intersection of 10% and ten years would be 2.594, making your $1,000 investment worth $2,594 ($1,000 × 2.594). Now the difference between the 8% and 10% rates is much more significant, at $435 ($2,594 − $2,159), than the $200 difference that occurred with simple compounding over ten years. Thus, we see the advantage of being able to compound at even slightly higher interest rates over a period of years.

The compounding or growth process also can be depicted in graphic form. Figure 9.1 shows graphic relationships among future values, interest rates, and time periods. For example, notice how $1 will grow differently over a ten-year period at 5% versus 10% interest rates. Of course, if no interest is being earned, then the initial $1 investment will remain at $1 no matter how long the investment is held. At a 10% interest rate, the initial $1 grows to $2.59 (rounded) after ten years. This compares with $1.63 (rounded) after ten years if the interest rate is only 5%. Notice that the future value grows at an increasing rate as the interest rate is increased and as the time period is lengthened.

In recent years, the benefits of compounding have been tempered by historically low interest rates. Recall that the Fed employed a policy of monetary easing through its open market operations and the nontraditional monetary policy tool of quantitative easing during the 2008–2015 period.

9.2.1 INFLATION OR PURCHASING POWER IMPLICATIONS

The compounding process described in the preceding section does not say anything about the purchasing power of the initial $1 investment at some point in the future. As seen, $1 growing at a

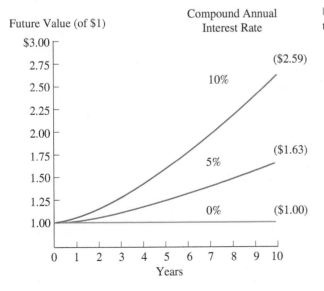

FIGURE 9.1   Future value, interest rate, and time period relationships

inflation-adjusted interest rate interest rate earned after adjusting for the change in purchasing power

10% interest rate would be worth $2.59 (rounded) at the end of ten years. With zero *inflation*, you could purchase $2.59 of the same quality of goods after ten years relative to what you could purchase now. An "**inflation-adjusted interest rate**" reflects the interest rate earned after adjusting for the change in purchasing power over the investment period. For example, if the stated, or *nominal*, interest rate is 10% and the inflation rate is 5%, then in terms of increased purchasing power, the "net" or differential compounding rate would be 5% (10% − 5%) and $1 would have an inflation-adjusted value of $1.63 after ten years. This translates into an increased purchasing power of $0.63 ($1.63 − $1.00).

Also note that if the compound inflation rate is equal to the compound interest rate, the purchasing power would not change. For example, if in Figure 9.1 both the inflation and interest rates were 5%, the purchasing power of $1 would remain the same over time. Thus, to make this concept operational, subtract the inflation rate from the stated interest rate and compound the remaining (differential) interest rate to determine the change in purchasing power over a stated time period. For example, if the interest rate is 10% and the inflation rate is 3%, the savings or investment should be compounded at a differential 7% rate. Turning to Table 9.1, we see that $1 invested at a 7% interest rate for ten years would grow to $1.967 ($1.97 rounded) in terms of purchasing power. Of course, the actual dollar value would be $2.594 ($2.59 rounded).

An inflation-adjusted interest rate can be negative. For example, this could occur if the actual inflation rate on a debt security exceeds the nominal or stated interest rate for the security. The result would be a decrease in the purchasing power for the debt security holder. Let's assume that a default risk-free debt security with no maturity and liquidity premiums is priced with a 4% annual interest rate (reflecting a 2% estimated real rate of interest and an expected 2% inflation premium). However, if the actual annual inflation rate is, say, 5%, the actual inflation-adjusted annual interest rate would be a negative 1% indicating a decrease in purchasing power.

GLOBAL Financial contracts (e.g., savings deposits and bank loans) in countries that have experienced high and volatile inflation rates sometimes have been linked to a consumer price or similar inflation index. Such actions are designed to reduce the exposure to inflation risk for both savers and lenders. Since the interest rate they receive on their savings deposits will vary with the rate of inflation, savers receive purchasing power protection. As inflation rises, so will the rate of interest individuals receive on their savings deposits such that purchasing power will be maintained.

Bank lenders are similarly protected against changing inflation rates, since the rates they charge on their loans will also vary with changes in inflation rates. At least in theory, banks will be able to maintain a profit spread between the interest rates they pay to savers and the higher interest rates they lend at to borrowers, because inflation affects both financial contracts. Of course, if the borrowers are business firms, they need to be able to pass on higher prices for their products and services to consumers to be able to maintain profit margins when interest rates are rising along with increases in inflation.

Inflation in the United States averaged about 2% annually during the first part of the twenty-first century. Some economists expressed concern that the Fed's emphasis beginning in late-2008 on near zero federal funds rate targets and its QE1, QE2, and QE3 quantitative easing efforts would result in much higher inflation rates in the future. However, the Fed increased its target federal funds rate to 0.25–0.50% in late 2015 and continued raising target rates until they reached 2.25–2.50% by late 2018. Annual inflation rates, in part due to Fed actions, have continued to average 2% or less through 2018.

DISCUSSION QUESTION 1

What do you expect the inflation rate to be over the next several years? Why?

9.3 DISCOUNTING TO DETERMINE PRESENT VALUES

Most financial management decisions involve present values rather than future values. For example, a financial manager who is considering purchasing an asset wants to know what the asset is worth now rather than at the end of some future time period. The reason that an asset has value is because it will produce a stream of future cash benefits. To determine its value now in time period zero, we have to discount, or reduce, the future cash benefits to their present value. **Discounting** is an arithmetic process whereby a future value decreases at a compound interest rate over time to reach a present value.

discounting arithmetic process whereby a future value decreases at a compound interest rate over time to reach a present value

Let's illustrate discounting with a simple example involving an investment. Assume that a bank or other borrower offers to pay you $1,000 at the end of one year in return for using $1,000 of your money now. If you are willing to accept a zero rate of return, you might make the investment. Most of us would not jump at an offer like this! Rather, we would require some return on our investment. To receive a return of, say, 8%, you would invest less than $1,000 now. The amount to be invested would be determined by dividing the $1,000 that is due at the end of one year by one plus the interest rate of 8%. This results in an investment amount of $925.93 ($1,000 ÷ 1.08), or $926 rounded. Alternatively, the $1,000 could have been multiplied by 1 ÷ 1.08, or 0.9259 (when carried to four decimal places) to get $925.90, or $926 rounded.

Let's now assume that you will not receive the $1,000 for two years and the compound interest rate is 8%. What dollar amount (present value) would you be willing to invest? In word terms, we have,

$$\text{Present value} = \text{Future value} \times \{[1 \div (1 + \text{Interest rate})] \times [1 \div (1 + \text{Interest rate})]\}$$

For our two-year investment example, we get,

$$\text{Present value} = \$1,000 \times (1 \div 1.08) \times (1 \div 1.08)$$
$$= \$1,000 \times (0.9259) \times (0.9259)$$
$$= \$1,000 \times 0.8573$$
$$= \$857.30$$

A time line also can be used to illustrate this two-year example as follows:

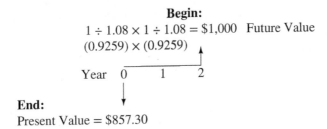

Begin:
$1 \div 1.08 \times 1 \div 1.08 = \$1,000$ Future Value
$(0.9259) \times (0.9259)$

Year   0   1   2

End:
Present Value = $857.30

Thus, for a one-year investment, the present value would be $925.90 ($1,000 × 1 ÷ 1.08, or 0.9259). A two-year investment would have a present value of only $857.30 ($1,000 × 0.9259 × 0.9259). The discounting concept can be expressed in equation form, as follows:

$$PV = FV_n \div (1 + r)^n$$

or

$$PV = FV_n[1 \div (1 + r)^n] \tag{9.3}$$

where the individual terms are the same as those defined for the future value equation. Notice that the future value equation has simply been rewritten to solve for the present value. For the $1,000, 8%, two-year example, we have,

$$PV = \$1,000[1 \div (1 + 0.08)^2]$$
$$= \$1,000(1 \div 1.1164)$$
$$= \$1,000(0.8573)$$
$$= \$857.30$$
$$= \$857 \text{ (rounded)}$$

If we extend the time period to ten years, the $1,000 future value would decrease to,

$$PV = \$1,000[1 \div (1 + 0.08)^{10}]$$
$$= \$1,000(1 \div 2.1589)$$
$$= \$1,000(0.4632)$$
$$= \$463.20$$
$$= \$463 \text{ (rounded)}$$

Most financial calculators are programmed to readily find present values. As noted, financial calculators, typically, have a present value (PV) key, a future value (FV) key, a number of time periods (N) key, an interest rate (%i) key, and a compute (CPT) key. If you have a financial calculator, you can verify the present value result for the ten-year example. First, clear the calculator. Then, enter 1000 (or −1000 for some calculators, to find a positive PV) and press the FV key, enter 8 and press the %i key, and enter 10 and press the N key. Finally, press the CPT key followed by the PV key to calculate the present value of 463.19, which rounds to $463.

Financial Calculator Solution:

Inputs:	10	8	1000
	N	%i	FV
Press:	CPT	PV	
Solution:	463.19		

Excel or another spreadsheet program also can be used to find present values. For a simple present value problem, we show the calculation by hand in spreadsheet format, as well as using the preprogrammed PV financial function. What would be the present value of receiving $1,000 two years from now if the annual discount rate is 8%?

Spreadsheet Solution:

	A	B	C	D
	D1		fx	
1	Interest Rate	0.08		
2	Time Period	0	1	2
3	Cash Flow	0	0	1000
4	Present Value	857.34	925.93	
5				
6	Cash Flow fx Calc	0	0	-1000
7	Financial Function			
8	PV Solution:	$857.34		

When making the calculation by hand, we enter 0.08 as the interest rate in Cell B1, then the time periods beginning with 0 in Cell B2 and so forth, and a cash flow of 1000 in Cell D3. In Cell C4 we insert the equation = D3/(1 + B1)^1 and get $925.93. Then, in Cell B4 we enter the equation = C4/(1 + B1)^1, with the result being $857.34. Of course, we could have solved for the present value in one step by entering in Cell B4 the equation = D3/(1 + B1)^2 and found 857.34 directly.

The bottom portion of the spreadsheet solution example illustrates the use of the Excel's financial function called present value (PV). In order to get a positive PV value, we enter −1000 as the cash flow in time period 2. Click on the Excel financial wizard (*fx*) icon, then Financial, then PV, and then OK to bring up the dialogue box where the PV components for the problem at hand are requested. The equation is PV(Rate, Nper, Pmt, FV, Type). The Rate is 0.08; Nper is the number of time periods, or two in this example; Pmt is zero, since there are no periodic payments; FV is −1000; and Type is 0, reflecting that payments occur at the end of the period. This equates to PV(0.08,2,0,−1000,0). Pressing OK results in a PV of $857.34, or $857 rounded. Because the PV function in Excel is programmed to give a negative number when there is a positive future value, much like the PV solutions on most calculators, we entered the FV as a negative number to get a positive PV. Of course, rather than inserting numbers, one could insert specific cell references in the PV function.

If the investment had been discounted for ten years, the PV function inputs would have been PV(0.08,10,0,−1000,0). Pressing OK would result in an answer of $463.19, or $463 rounded.

In addition, tables have been prepared to simplify the calculation effort if financial calculators or computer programs are not available. Equation 9.3 can be rewritten as,

$$PV = FV_n(PVIF_{r,n})$$ (9.4)

where the $1 \div (1 + r)^n$ part of equation 9.3 is replaced by a present value interest factor (PVIF) corresponding to a specific interest rate and a specified time period.

Table 9.2 shows PVIF values for a range of interest rates and time periods. (Table 2 in the Appendix is a more comprehensive PVIF table.) Let's use Table 9.2 to find the present value of $1,000 invested at an 8% compound interest rate for a ten-year period. Notice that at the intersection of the 8% column and ten years we find a PVIF of 0.463. Putting this information in equation 9.4 gives the following.

Table-based Solution:

$$PV = \$1,000(0.463)$$
$$= \$463$$

Further examination of Table 9.2 shows how a $1 investment decreases with various combinations of interest rates and time periods. For example, if another bank offers to pay interest at a 10% compound rate, the PVIF at the intersection of 10% and ten years would be 0.386, resulting in your $1,000 future value being worth an investment of $386 ($1,000 × 0.386). The difference between required investments at 8% and 10% interest rates needed to accumulate $1,000 at the end of ten years is $77 ($463 − $386). In essence, the present value of a future value decreases as the interest rate increases for a specified time period.

The discounting process also can be depicted in graphic form. Figure 9.2 shows graphic relationships among present values, interest rates, and time periods. For example, notice how a $1 future value will decrease differently over a ten-year period at 5% versus 10% interest rates.

Table 9.2   Present Value Interest Factor (PVIF) of $1

Year	5%	6%	7%	8%	9%	10%
1	0.952	0.943	0.935	0.926	0.917	0.909
2	0.907	0.890	0.873	0.857	0.842	0.826
3	0.864	0.840	0.816	0.794	0.772	0.751
4	0.823	0.792	0.763	0.735	0.708	0.683
5	0.784	0.747	0.713	0.681	0.650	0.621
6	0.746	0.705	0.666	0.630	0.596	0.564
7	0.711	0.665	0.623	0.583	0.547	0.513
8	0.677	0.627	0.582	0.540	0.502	0.467
9	0.645	0.592	0.544	0.500	0.460	0.424
10	0.614	0.558	0.508	0.463	0.422	0.386

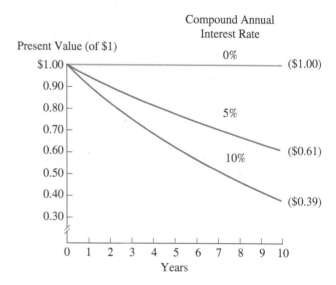

FIGURE 9.2   Present value, interest rate, and time period relationships

Of course, at a zero interest rate, the present value remains at $1 and is not affected by time. If no interest is being earned, the $1 future value will have a present value of $1 no matter how long the investment is held. At a 5% interest rate, the present value of $1 declines to $0.61 (rounded) if an investor has to wait ten years to receive the $1. This compares with a present value of $1 of only $0.39 (rounded) if the interest rate is 10% and the investor must wait ten years to receive $1. Notice that the present value decreases at an increasing rate as the interest rate is increased and as the time period is lengthened.

9.3.1 EQUATING PRESENT VALUES AND FUTURE VALUES

Notice that equations 9.1 and 9.3 are two ways of looking at the same process involving compound interest rates. That is, if we know the future value of an investment, we can find its present value, and vice versa. For example, an initial investment of $1,000 will grow to $1,116.40 at the end of two years if the interest rate is 8%. Note that to reduce the impact of rounding errors, we are carrying our calculations here to four decimal places:

$$\begin{aligned} FV_2 &= \$1,000(1 + 0.08)^2 \\ &= \$1,000(1.1664) \\ &= \$1,166.40 \end{aligned}$$

Now, what is the present value of a $1,166.40 future value if we must wait two years to receive the future value amount and if the interest rate is 8%? The solution would be,

$$\begin{aligned} PV &= \$1,166.40[1 \div (1 + 0.08)^2] \\ &= \$1,166.40(1 \div 1.1664) \\ &= \$1,166.40(0.8573) \\ &= \$1.000 \end{aligned}$$

Thus, an investor should be indifferent about receiving a $1,000 present value now or a $1,166 future value two years from now if the compound interest rate is 8%.

SMALL BUSINESS PRACTICE

CALCULATING RATES OF RETURN FOR VENTURE CAPITALISTS AND OTHER INVESTORS

Venture capitalists represent an important source of financing for small businesses. Venture capitalists, of course, are in the business of providing financial capital to small businesses with the expectation of earning a return on their investments commensurate with the risks associated with those investments. A typical "exit strategy" of venture capitalists is to maintain an investment in a firm for approximately five years and, if the investment is successful, then sell the firm to another company or take the firm public in an initial public offering (IPO).

A venture capitalist usually will invest in a small business by either taking a direct ownership position in the form of common stock or by accepting the firm's bond plus an "equity kicker," or the right to purchase a certain portion of the firm (e.g., 50%). For example, let's assume that a venture capitalist invests $5 million in a firm. In return,

the venture capitalist receives shares of stock representing 50% ownership in the firm. Let's assume that the firm can be sold for $40 million at the end of five years. What will be the rate of return that the venture capitalist will earn on the $5 million investment? The present value is $5 million and the future value is $20 million (i.e., $40 million times 0.5, or 50%). Since we know the time period is five years, we solve for the interest rate, r. Using a financial calculator results in a compound interest rate (%i) of 32.0%.

What would have been the venture capitalist's rate of return if the firm had been sold for $40 million at the end of six years instead of at the end of five years? Again, the present value is $5 million, the future value is $20 million, and the time period is six years. Solving for the interest rate yields 26.0%. Thus, if the sale of the firm is delayed by one year, the compound rate of return on the venture capitalist's investment drops six percentage points, from 32% down to 26%.

Recall the four variables from the future value (9.1 and 9.2) and present value (9.3 and 9.4) equations: PV = present value, FV = future value, r = interest rate, and n = number of periods. As long as we know the values for any three of these variables, we can solve for the fourth, or unknown, variable. This is accomplished by using a financial calculator, a financial function in a spreadsheet program, or tables.

> **9.4 FINDING INTEREST RATES AND TIME REQUIREMENTS**

9.4.1 SOLVING FOR INTEREST RATES

Assume that the present value of an investment is $1,000, the future value is $1,403 and the time period is five years. What compound interest rate would be earned on this investment?

This problem can be solved using a financial calculator. If a financial calculator is used, enter PV = 1000, FV = 1403, N = 5, and press CPT followed by the %i key to find an r of 7.01, or 7% rounded (some calculators may require either the PV entry or FV entry to be negative).

Financial Calculator Solution:

Inputs:	5	1000	1403
	N	PV	FV
Press:	CPT	%i	
Solution:	7.01		

A second way of solving for the interest rate is with a spreadsheet program using a financial function. Excel has a financial function called RATE that makes it possible to solve quickly for the interest rate. Click on the financial wizard (*fx*), then on Financial, then RATE. Entering the requested data and pressing OK gives the following solution.

Spreadsheet Solution:

$$= \text{RATE(Nper,Pmt,PV,FV,Type)}$$
$$= \text{RATE}(5,0,-1000,1403,0)$$
$$= 7.01\%$$

The number of periods (Nper) is 5, there are zero periodic payments (Pmt), the present value (PV) is entered as −1000, the future value (FV) is 1403, and the Type is zero, since cash flows occur at the end of a time period.

Table-based Solution:

The interest rate answer also can be found by setting up the problem using equation 9.2 and Table 9.1 as follows:

$$FV_5 = PV(FVIF_{r,5})$$

$$\$1,403 = \$1,000(FVIF_{r,5})$$

$$FVIF_{r,5} = 1.403$$

Since we know that the number of time periods is five, we can turn to Table 9.1 and read across the year-five row until we find FVIF of 1.403. Notice that this occurs under the 7% column, indicating that the interest rate, r, is 7%.

We also can work the problem using equation 9.4 and Table 9.2 as follows:

$$PV = FV_5(PVIF_{r,5})$$

$$\$1,000 = \$1,403(PVIF_{r,5})$$

$$PVIF_{r,5} = 0.713$$

Turning to Table 9.2, we read across the year-five row until we find the PVIF of 0.713. This occurs under the 7% column, indicating that the interest rate, r, is 7%.

9.4.2 SOLVING FOR TIME PERIODS

Now let's assume an investment has a present value of $1,000, a future value of $1,403, and an interest rate of 7%. What length of time does this investment involve?

This problem can be solved using a financial calculator and entering PV = 1000 (or −1000), FV = 1403, and %i = 7 and then pressing the CPT key followed by the N key to find an n of 5.01, or 5 years rounded.

Financial Calculator Solution:

Inputs:	7	1000	1403
	%i	PV	FV
Press:	CPT	N	
Solution:	5.01		

Spreadsheet Solution:

The number of time periods can also be determined by using the Excel financial function called NPER. Following the sequence described and, clicking on the NPER financial function, we have the following:

$$= NPER(Rate, Pmt, PV, FV, Type)$$

$$= NPER(.07, 0, -1000, 1403, 0)$$

$$= 5.00$$

The interest rate is 7%, there are no payments, the present value is −1000, the future value is 1403, and type is zero.

Table-based Solution:

The answer can also be found by using equation 9.2 and Table 9.1 as follows:

$$FV_n = PV(FVIF_{7\%,n})$$
$$\$1,403 = \$1,000(FVIF_{7\%,n})$$
$$FVIF_{7\%,n} = 1.403$$

Since we know the interest rate is 7%, we can turn to Table 9.1 and read down the 7% column until we find the FVIF of 1.403. Notice that this occurs in the year-five row, indicating that the time period, n, is five years.

We also can work the problem using equation 9.4 and Table 9.2 as follows:

$$PV = FV_n(PVIF_{7\%,n})$$
$$\$1,000 = \$1,403(PVIF_{7\%,n})$$
$$PVIF_{7\%,n} = .713$$

Turning to Table 9.2, we read down the 7% column until we find the PVIF of 0.713. This occurs at the year-five row, indicating that the time period, n is, five years.

9.4.3 RULE OF 72

Investors often ask, "How long will it take for my money to double in value at a particular interest rate?" Table 9.1 illustrates the process for answering this question. We pick a particular interest rate and read down the table until we find an FVIF of 2.000. For example, at an 8% interest rate, it will take almost exactly nine years (note the FVIF of 1.999) for an investment to double in value. At a 9% interest rate, the investment will double in about eight years (FVIF of 1.993). An investment will double in a little over seven years (FVIF of 1.949) if the interest rate is 10%.

A shortcut method referred to as the **Rule of 72** can be used to approximate the time required for an investment to double in value: divide the interest rate into the number 72. For example, if the interest rate is 8%, 72 divided by 8 indicates that the investment will double in value in nine years. Notice that this is the same conclusion drawn from Table 9.1. Likewise, at an interest rate of 10% it will take approximately 7.2 years (72 ÷ 10) for an investment to double in value. It is important to be aware that at very low or very high interest rates, the Rule of 72 does not approximate the compounding process as well, and thus a larger estimation error occurs in the time required for an investment to double in value.

Rule of 72 a shortcut method used to approximate the time required for an investment to double in value

DISCUSSION QUESTION 2

Let's assume that you want to become a millionaire before you retire. How do you plan build a net worth of one million dollars?

The previous discussion focused on cash payments, or receipts, that occurred only as lump sum present and future values. However, many finance problems involve equal payments or receipts over time, referred to as *annuities*. More specifically, an **annuity** is a series of equal payments, or receipts, that occur over a number of time periods.

An **ordinary annuity** exists when the equal payments (or receipts) occur at the end of each time period. An **annuity due** exists when equal periodic payments (or receipts) start at the end of time period zero, or in other words, at the beginning of each time period. We focus on problems involving ordinary annuities in this chapter.[2] For example, suppose you want to invest $1,000 per year for three years at an 8% interest rate. However, since you will not make your first payment until the end of the first year, this will be an ordinary annuity.

9.5 FUTURE VALUE OF AN ANNUITY

annuity a series of equal payments (or receipts) that occur over a number of time periods

ordinary annuity equal payments (or receipts) occur at the end of each time period

annuity due exists when equal periodic payments (or receipts) occur at the beginning of each time period

---

[2] Annuity due problems are discussed in the Learning Extension at the end of this chapter.

This problem also can be illustrated using a time line as follows:

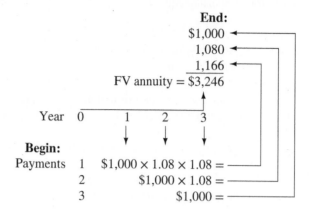

Notice that to calculate the future value of this ordinary annuity we must add the future values of the first payment ($1,166), the second payment ($1,080), and the third payment ($1,000). This results in a future value of $3,246. To summarize, since the first payment is made at the end of the first year, it is compounded for two years. The second payment is compounded for one year and the third payment earns zero interest since the payment is made at the end of the third year.

The future value of this annuity can also be determined by making the following computations:

$$\text{FV ordinary annuity} = \$1,000(1.08)^2 + \$1,000(1.08)^1 + \$1,000(1.08)^0$$
$$= \$1,000(1.166) + \$1,000(1.080) + \$1,000(1.000)$$
$$= \$1,000(3.246)$$
$$= \$3,246$$

While the computational process was relatively easy for the three-year ordinary annuity example, the required calculations become much more cumbersome as the time period is lengthened. As a result, the following equation was derived for finding the future value of an ordinary annuity (FVA):

$$\text{FVA}_n = \text{PMT}\{[(1+r)^n - 1] \div r\} \tag{9.5}$$

PMT is the periodic equal payment, r is the compound interest rate, and n is the total number of periods. Inserting the data from the preceding three-year annuity example results in the following answer:

$$\text{FVA}_3 = \$1,000\{[(1+0.08)^3 - 1] \div 0.08\}$$
$$= \$1,000[(1.2597 - 1) \div 0.08]$$
$$= \$1,000(3.246)$$
$$= \$3,246$$

Most financial calculators are programmed to readily find future values of annuities. In addition to the previously identified keys, financial calculators also will have a payments (PMT) key for purposes of working problems involving ordinary annuities. The result for the three-year ordinary annuity can be verified using a financial calculator.

First, clear the calculator. Next, enter −1000 (for both TI and HP calculators) and press the PMT key. Then, enter 8 and press the %i key, and enter 3 and press the N key. Finally, press the CPT key and then the FV key to calculate the FVA of 3246.40, which rounds to $3,246. Note that because this problem involves a periodic outflow of $1,000, most financial calculators require that the payment be entered as a negative number to solve for a positive FVA.

Financial Calculator Solution:

Inputs: 3   8   −1000

          [N]   [%i]   [PMT]

Press: [CPT]   [FV]

Solution: 3246.40

Spreadsheet programs also are available for finding future values of annuities. Following is a solution using an Excel spreadsheet and future value (FV). The difference here is that we have a constant periodic payment.

Spreadsheet Solution:

	A	B	C	D	E
1	Interest Rate	0.08			
2	Time Period	0	1	2	3
3	Cash Flow	0	-1000	-1000	-1000
4					
5	Financial Function				
6	FV Solution:				$3,246.40

We solve for the future value of the annuity as follows:

$$= FV(Rate, Nper, Pmt, PV, Type)$$
$$= FV(.08, 3, -1000, 0, 0)$$
$$= \$3,246.40$$

In addition, tables have been prepared to simplify the calculation effort if financial calculators or computer programs are not available. Equation 9.5 can be rewritten as,

$$FVA_n = PMT(FVIFA_{r,n}) \tag{9.6}$$

where the $[(1 + r)^n - 1] \div r$ part of equation 9.5 is replaced by a future value interest factor of an annuity (FVIFA) corresponding to a specific interest rate and a specified time period.

Table-based Solution:

Table 9.3 shows FVIFA values for a partial range of interest rates and time periods. (Table 3 in the Appendix is a more comprehensive FVIFA table.) Let's use Table 9.3 to find the future value of

Table 9.3 Future Value Interest Factor (FVIFA) for a $1 Ordinary Annuity

Year	5%	6%	7%	8%	9%	10%
1	1.000	1.000	1.000	1.000	1.000	1.000
2	2.050	2.060	2.070	2.080	2.090	2.100
3	3.152	3.184	3.215	3.246	3.278	3.310
4	4.310	4.375	4.440	4.506	4.573	4.641
5	5.526	5.637	5.751	5.867	5.985	6.105
6	6.802	6.975	7.153	7.336	7.523	7.716
7	8.142	8.394	8.654	8.923	9.200	9.487
8	9.549	9.897	10.260	10.637	11.028	11.436
9	11.027	11.491	11.978	12.488	13.021	13.579
10	12.578	13.181	13.816	14.487	15.193	15.937

an ordinary annuity involving annual payments of $1,000, an 8% interest rate, and a three-year time period. Notice that at the intersection of the 8% column and three years we find a FVIFA of 3.246. Putting this information into equation 9.6 gives,

$$FVA_3 = \$1,000(3.246)$$
$$= \$3,246$$

PERSONAL FINANCIAL PLANNING

So You Want to Be a Millionaire?

A million dollars can be acquired in a number of ways. Probably the easiest legal way is to inherit it. Those of us who won't benefit that way must save a portion of our disposable personal income and then live long enough to take advantage of compounding interest. For example, if you could invest $10,000 now (at the end of time period zero), the following combinations of annual compound interest rates and time periods would make you a millionaire.

Interest Rate (%)	Time (years)
5	94.4
10	48.3
15	33.0
20	25.3

Notice that at a 5% compound rate it would take more than 94 years to accumulate $1 million. This is probably not acceptable (or possible) for most of us. Even if we could compound our interest at a 20% annual rate, it would take a little more than 25 years to become a millionaire.

An alternative approach would be to create an investment annuity of $10,000 per year. Now let's show the time required to become a millionaire under the assumption of an ordinary annuity where the first investment will be made one year from now:

Interest Rate (%)	Time (years)
5	36.7
10	25.2
15	19.8
20	16.7

With this approach, the time required, particularly at higher interest rates, is more feasible. Compounding at 5% would still require making annual investments for nearly 37 years to accumulate $1 million. At 10%, it would take a little more than 25 years to attain that goal. Of course, the most critical factor, which might be easier said than done, is the ability to come up with $10,000 per year out of disposable personal income. Good luck!

Further examination of Table 9.3 shows how a $1 annuity grows, or increases, with various combinations of interest rates and time periods. For example, if $1,000 is invested at the end of each year (beginning with year one) for ten years at an 8% interest rate, the future value of the annuity would be $14,487 ($1,000 × 14.487). If the interest rate is 10% for ten years, the future value of the annuity would be $15,937 ($1,000 × 15.937). These results demonstrate the benefits of higher interest rates on the future values of annuities.

9.6 PRESENT VALUE OF AN ANNUITY

Many present value problems also involve cash flow annuities. Usually, these are ordinary annuities. Let's assume that we will receive $1,000 per year beginning one year from now for a period of three years at an 8% compound interest rate. How much would you be willing to pay now for this stream of future cash flows? Since we are concerned with the value now, this becomes a present value problem.

We can illustrate this problem using a time line as follows:

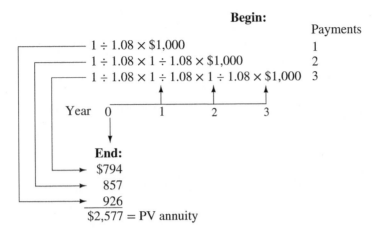

Begin:

Payments

$1 \div 1.08 \times \$1,000$ — 1

$1 \div 1.08 \times 1 \div 1.08 \times \$1,000$ — 2

$1 \div 1.08 \times 1 \div 1.08 \times 1 \div 1.08 \times \$1,000$ — 3

Year   0   1   2   3

End:

$794

857

926

$\overline{\$2,577}$ = PV annuity

Notice that to calculate the present value of this ordinary annuity we must sum the present values of the first payment ($926), the second payment ($857), and the third payment (794). This results in a present value of $2,577.

We also can find the present value of this annuity by making the following computations:

$$\text{PV ordinary annuity} = \{\$1,000[1 \div (1.08)^1]\} + \{\$1,000[1 \div (1.08)^2]\}$$
$$+ \{\$1,000[1 \div (1.08)^3]\}$$
$$= [\$1,000(0.926) + [\$1,000(0.857)]$$
$$+ [\$1,000(0.794)]$$
$$= \$1,000(2.577)$$
$$= \$2,577$$

While the computational process was relatively easy for the preceding three-year ordinary annuity example, the required calculations become much more cumbersome as the time period is lengthened. As a result, the following equation was derived for finding the present value of an ordinary annuity (PVA):

$$\text{PVA}_n = \text{PMT}\{[1 - (1 \div (1+r)^n)] \div r\} \tag{9.7}$$

The various inputs are the same as previously defined. Inserting the data from the preceding three-year annuity example results in the following answer:

$$\text{PVA}_3 = \$1,000\{[1 - (1 \div (1+0.08)^3)] \div 0.08\}$$
$$= \$1,000[(1 - 0.7938) \div 0.08]$$
$$= \$1,000(0.2062 \div 0.08)$$
$$= \$1,000(2.577)$$
$$= \$2,577$$

Most financial calculators are programmed to readily find present values of annuities. The result for the three-year present value of an ordinary annuity problem can be verified with a financial calculator. First, clear the calculator. Next, enter 1000 for a TI calculator (or −1000 for an HP calculator) and press the payments (PMT) key. Then, enter 8 and press the %i key, and enter 3 and press the N key. Finally, press the CPT key followed by the PV key to calculate the PVA of 2577.10, which rounds to $2,577.

Financial Calculator Solution:

Inputs: 3   8   1000

           N   %i   PMT

Press: CPT   FV

Solution: 2577.10

Spreadsheet programs also are available for finding present values of annuities. Following is an Excel spreadsheet solution.

Spreadsheet Solution:

	A	B	C	D	E
1	Interest Rate	0.08			
2	Time Period	0	1	2	3
3	Cash Flow	0	-1000	-1000	-1000
4					
5	Financial Function				
6	PV Solution:	$2,577.10			

Use the previously described present value (PV) financial function provided by Excel as follows:

$$= PV(Rate, Nper, Pmt, FV, Type)$$
$$= PV(0.8, 3, -1000, 0, 0)$$
$$= \$2,577.10$$

In addition, tables have been prepared to simplify the calculation effort if financial calculators or computer programs are not available. Equation 9.7 can be rewritten as:

$$PVA_n = PMT(PVIFA_{r,n}) \tag{9.8}$$

The $\{1 - [1 \div (1 + r)^n]\} \div r$ part of equation 9.7 is replaced by a present value interest factor of an annuity (PVIFA) corresponding to a specific interest rate and a specified time period.

Table-based Solution:

Table 9.4 shows PVIFA values for a partial range of interest rates and time periods. (Table 4 in the Appendix is a more comprehensive PVIFA table.) Let's use Table 9.4 to find the present value of an ordinary annuity involving annual payments of $1,000, an 8% interest rate, and a three-year time

Table 9.4   Present Value Interest Factor (PVIFA) for a $1 Ordinary Annuity

Year	5%	6%	7%	8%	9%	10%
1	0.952	0.943	0.935	0.926	0.917	0.909
2	1.859	1.833	1.808	1.783	1.759	1.736
3	2.273	2.673	2.624	2.577	2.531	2.487
4	3.546	3.465	3.387	3.312	3.240	3.170
5	4.329	4.212	4.100	3.993	3.890	3.791
6	5.076	4.917	4.767	4.623	4.486	4.355
7	5.786	5.582	5.389	5.206	5.033	4.868
8	6.463	6.210	5.971	5.747	5.535	5.335
9	7.108	6.802	6.515	6.247	5.995	5.759
10	7.722	7.360	7.024	6.710	6.418	6.145

period. Notice that at the intersection of the 8% interest rate column and three years we find a PVIFA of 2.577. Putting this information into equation 9.8 gives,

$$PVA_3 = \$1,000(2.577)$$
$$= \$2,577$$

Further examination of Table 9.4 shows how the present value of a $1 annuity decreases with various combinations of interest rates and time periods. For example, if $1,000 is paid at the end of each year (beginning with year one) for ten years at an 8% interest rate, the present value of the annuity would be $6,710 ($1,000 × 6.710). If the interest rate is 10% for ten years, the present value of the annuity would be $6,145 ($1,000 × 6.145). These results demonstrate the costs of higher interest rates on the present values of annuities.

How to find, or solve, for interest rates or time periods for problems involving a lump sum present value or future value was discussed previously in this chapter. That, originally, involved working with four variables: PV = present value, FV = future value, r = interest rate, and n = number of periods. A fifth variable is now added to reflect payments (PMT) involving ordinary annuities.

9.7 INTEREST RATES AND TIME REQUIREMENTS FOR ANNUITIES

9.7.1 SOLVING FOR INTEREST RATES

Assume that the future value of an ordinary annuity is $5,751, the annual payment is $1,000, and the time period is five years. What is the interest rate for this problem?

A financial calculator could be used to solve this problem if either the FV or PV of the ordinary annuity is known. If you have a financial calculator and you know the future value, enter FV = 5751, PMT = −1000 (for both TI and HP calculators), and N = 5. Press the CPT key followed by the %i key to find an r of 7%. (Note: Some financial calculators will give an error message if the 1000 PMT is entered as a positive number. If the present value of the ordinary annuity is known instead of the future value, the preceding procedure would be followed except that PV = 4100 would be entered instead of the future value amount.)

Financial Calculator Solution:

Inputs:	5	−1000	5751
	N	PMT	FV
Press:	CPT	%i	
Solution:	7.00		

Spreadsheet Solution:

Excel's RATE financial function also can be used to solve this interest rate of an ordinary annuity problem, much as the function was used elsewhere in this chapter for problems without periodic payments. The financial function solution would be the following:

$$= RATE(Nper, Pmt, PV, FV, Type)$$
$$= RATE(5, -1000, 0, 5751, 0)$$
$$= 7.00\%$$

Table-based Solution:

The answer can be found by setting up the problem using equation 9.6 and Table 9.3 as follows:

$$FVA_5 = PMT(FVIFA_{r,5})$$
$$\$5,751 = \$1,000(FVIFA_{r,5})$$
$$FVIFA_{r,5} = 5.751$$

Since we know that the number of time periods is five, we can turn to Table 9.3 and read across the year-five row until we find the FVIFA of 5.751. Notice that this occurs under the 7% column, indicating that the interest rate, r, is 7%.

Let's now assume that we know that the present value of the preceding ordinary annuity is $4,100. We could then find the interest rate for the problem using present value annuity tables as follows:

$$PVA_5 = PMT(PVIFA_{r,5})$$

$$\$4,100 = \$1,000(PVIFA_{r,5})$$

$$PVIFA_{r,5} = 4.100$$

Turning to Table 9.4, we read across the year-five row until we find the PVIFA of 4.100. This occurs under the 7% column, indicating that the interest rate, r, is 7%.

9.7.2 SOLVING FOR TIME PERIODS

Let's assume that the future value of an ordinary annuity is $5,751, the annual payment is $1,000, and the interest rate is 7%. How long would it take for your $1,000 annual investments to grow to $5,751?

We can solve this problem using a financial calculator. We know that the future value of the ordinary annuity is $5,751, so enter FV = 5751, PMT = –1000, %i = 7, and press the CPT key followed by the N key to find an n of five years. If we knew the present value of the annuity instead of the future value, we could work the problem by substituting the PV for the FV.

Financial Calculator Solution:

Inputs: 7   –1000   5751
             %i   PMT   FV
Press: CPT   N
Solution: 5.00

Spreadsheet Solution:

Excel's NPER financial function also can be used to solve for the number of periods in an annuity problem, much as we used the function earlier for problems without periodic payments. The financial function solution would be the following:

$$= NPER(Rate, Pmt, PV, FV, Type)$$

$$= NPER(7, -1000, 0, 5751, 0)$$

$$= 5.00$$

Table-based Solution:

The problem also can be set up by using equation 9.6 and Table 9.3 as follows:

$$FVA_n = PMT(FVIFA_{7\%,n})$$

$$\$5,751 = \$1,000(FVIFA_{7\%,n})$$

$$FVIFA_{7\%,n} = 5.751$$

Since we know the interest rate is 7%, we can turn to Table 9.3 and read down the 7% column until we find FVIFA of 5.751. Notice that this occurs in the year-five row, indicating that the time period, n, is five years.

If we knew the present value of the above ordinary annuity was \$4,100, we could also work the problem using equation 9.8 and Table 9.4 as follows:

$$PVA_n = PMT(PVIFA_{7\%,n})$$
$$\$4,100 = \$1,000(PVIFA_{7\%,n})$$
$$PVIFA_{7\%,n} = 4.100$$

Turning to Table 9.4, we read down the 7% column until we find PVIFA of 4.100. This occurs at the year-five row, indicating that the time period, n, is five years.

9.8.1 EXAMPLES INVOLVING ANNUAL PAYMENTS

It is necessary in many instances to determine the periodic equal payment required for an ordinary annuity. For example, you may wish to accumulate \$10,000 at the end of five years from now by making equal annual payments beginning one year from now. If you can invest at a compound 6% interest rate, what will be the amount of each of your annual payments?

This is a future value of an ordinary annuity problem. Using a financial calculator, the annual payment (PMT) would be found as follows:

Financial Calculator Solution:

Inputs:	6	5	10000
	%i	N	FV
Press:	CPT	PMT	
Solution:	1773.96		

Spreadsheet Solution:

Excel's PMT financial function also can be used to solve for the annual payment amount. The financial function solution would be,

$$= PMT(Rate, Nper, PV, FV, Type)$$
$$= PMT(.06, 5, 0, -10000, 0)$$
$$= \$1,773.96$$

Table-based Solution:

Equation 9.6 and Table 9.3 also can be used, as follows:

$$FVA_n = PMT(FVIFA_{r,n})$$
$$\$10,000 = PMT(FVIFA_{6\%,5})$$
$$\$10,000 = PMT(5.637)$$
$$PMT = \$1,773.99$$
$$= \$1,774 (rounded)$$

The FVIFA factor of 5.637 is taken from Table 9.3 at the intersection of the 6% column and the year-five row.

As another example, we might want to find the equal payment necessary to pay off, or *amortize*, a loan. An amortized loan is repaid in equal payments over a specified time period. Let's assume that a lender offers you a \$20,000, 10% interest rate, three-year loan that is to be fully amortized with three

amortized loan a loan repaid in equal payments over a specified time period

annual payments. The first payment will be due one year from the loan date, making the loan an ordinary annuity. How much will you have to pay each year?

This is a present value problem because the $20,000 is the value, or amount, of the loan now. The annual payment can be found with a financial calculator, a financial function in a spreadsheet program, or via a table-based approach using equation 9.8 and Table 9.4 as follows:

$$PVA_n = PMT(PVIFA_{10\%,3})$$
$$\$20,000 = PMT(2.487)$$
$$PMT = \$8,041.82$$
$$= \$8,042 \text{ (rounded)}$$

The PVIFA factor of 2.487 is taken from Table 9.4 at the intersection of the 10% column and the year-three row.

Table 9.5 illustrates the repayment process with a **loan amortization schedule**, which shows the breakdown of each payment between interest and principal, as well as the remaining balance after each payment. Since the interest rate is 10%, the first year interest will total $2,000 ($20,000 × 0.10). Subsequent interest payments are based on the remaining loan balances, which are smaller each year (also referred to as the *declining balance*). Since $6,042 ($8,042 − $2,000) of the first year's $8,042 payment is used to repay part of the principal, the second year's interest payment will only be $1,396 ($13,958 × 0.10). The third, and last, payment covers the final year's interest of $731 plus the remaining principal balance.

loan amortization schedule a schedule of the breakdown of each payment between interest and principal, as well as the remaining balance after each payment

9.8.2 REAL ESTATE MORTGAGE LOANS WITH MONTHLY PAYMENTS

CRISIS We discussed characteristics of home mortgages in Chapter 7. The traditional residential real mortgage loan has been a 30-year fixed interest rate mortgage loan requiring equal monthly payments that would pay off, or amortize, the loan over its life. Let's assume that you want to borrow $100,000 for 30 years, and the current interest rate is 6%. The mortgage requires you to make equal monthly payments so that the loan will be paid in full at maturity. What will be your monthly payment? We begin by first determining that you will have to make 360 (12 times 30 years) monthly payments. Since the annual interest rate is 6%, you will pay 0.50% (6% divided by 12) interest per month. With this information, we can calculate your monthly payment using a financial calculator as follows:

Financial Calculator Solution:

Inputs:	0.50	360	−100000
	%i	N	PV
Press:	CPT	PMT	
Solution:	599.55		

You would need to make a $599.55 monthly payment.

Of course, Excel's PMT financial function also can be used to solve for the monthly payment amount.

Table 9.5   Sample Loan Amortization Schedule

Year	Annual payment	Interest payment	Principal repayment	Loan balance
0	–	–	–	$20,000
1	$8,042	$2,000	$6,042	13,958
2	8,042	1,396	6,646	7,312
3	8,042	731	7,311*	0

*Because of rounding, the final principal repayment is off by $1.

Spreadsheet Solution:
The financial function solution would be,

$$= \text{PMT}(\text{Rate}, \text{Nper}, \text{PV}, \text{FV}, \text{Type})$$
$$= \text{PMT}(0.005, 360, -100000, 0, 0)$$
$$= 599.55$$

Unfortunately, due to rapidly rising housing prices during the decade prior to 2006, many home buyers needed increasingly larger loans to make their real property purchases. For example, a $200,000 fixed-rate mortgage loan would result in a much higher monthly payment compared to a $100,000 loan. Rework the above financial calculator and spread sheet solutions using a PV of −200000. The resulting doubled monthly payment of $1,199.10 means that fewer potential home buyers could qualify for these larger loans.

While the need for larger loans was increasing, many lenders – in part encouraged by government officials – also were willing to make subprime mortgage loans to individuals with poor credit scores or ratings in order to increase home ownership. These developments encouraged the increasing use of adjustable-rate mortgages (ARMs). Recall that an ARM, typically, has an interest rates tied to the bank prime rate or the Treasury bill rate, either of which normally is lower than long-term interest rates on fixed-rate mortgage loans, making it easier for borrowers with low credit scores and/or those wanting to borrow larger amounts to get mortgage loans.

Some lenders further offered initial below-market "teaser" rates, such as 1 or 2% for the first year or so on their ARM mortgage loans. Of course, when the "teaser" rate period ends, the ARM interest rate adjusts to the then-current market rate causing the possibility of a dramatic increase in monthly payments. Clearly, lenders lent (and individuals borrowed) mortgage loans characterized by high default risks.

During the second-half of 2016, average interest rates on home mortgage loans declined to about 3.4% making it easier for potential home buyers to qualify for mortgage loan financing. However, these lower borrowing costs were offset by lenders increasing the size of equity down payments on new mortgage loans, due to their recent experiences with loan default rates and "underwater" (where the mortgage loan amount is greater that the value of the home) mortgage loans. The average interest rate on 30-year fixed rate mortgage loans increased in 2017 and 2018 until the rate reached nearly 5% late 2018. Mortgage rates declined by about one-half percent during the early part of 2019.

LEARNING ACTIVITY
Go to the Citibank website, https://www.citibank.com, and identify the types of credit cards available to individuals, and the prevailing interest rates on the credit cards.

9.9.1 MORE FREQUENT THAN ANNUAL COMPOUNDING OR DISCOUNTING

In many situations, compounding or discounting may occur more often than annually. For example, recall from the beginning of this chapter the $1,000 that could be invested at one bank at an 8% annual interest rate for two years. Remember that the future value at the end of two years was as follows:

$$\text{FV}_2 = \$1,000(1.08)^2$$
$$= \$1,000(1.166)$$
$$= \$1,166.40$$

Now let's assume that another bank offers the same 8% interest rate but with semi-annual (twice a year) compounding. We can find the future value of this investment by modifying equation 5.1 as follows:

$$\text{FV}_n - \text{PV}(1 + r \div m)^{n \times m} \tag{9.9}$$

where m is the number of compounding periods per year. For this problem,

$$
\begin{aligned}
FV_2 &= \$1,000(1+0.08 \div 2)^{2 \times 2} \\
&= \$1,000(1.04)^4 \\
&= \$1,000(1.1699) \\
&= \$1,169.90
\end{aligned}
$$

Thus, by compounding semi-annually the future value would increase by $3.50.

The process for more frequent than annual compounding can be described, operationally, as follows. First, divide the annual interest rate of 8% by the number of times compounding is to take place during the year ($0.08 \div 2 = 0.04$). We also need to increase the total number of periods to reflect semi-annual compounding. To do this, multiply the number of years for the loan times the frequency of compounding within a year (two years $\times$ 2 = 4 periods).

Previously in this chapter, it was shown that a $1,000 investment at an 8% interest rate would grow to $2,158.92 or $2,159 (rounded) at the end of ten years. However, if semi-annual compounding had been available, the future value of the $1,000 investment would have been,

$$
\begin{aligned}
FV_{20} &= \$1,000(1.04)^{20} \\
&= \$1,000(2.1911) \\
&= \$2,191.10
\end{aligned}
$$

The following subsection shows how the financial calculator solution would be found.

Financial Calculator Solution:

Inputs:	20	4	1000
	N	%i	PV
Press:	CPT	FV	
Solution:	2191.12		

Spreadsheet Solution:

The Excel FV function inputs would be,

$$
\begin{aligned}
&= FV(0.04, 20, 0, -1000, 0) \\
&= \$2,191.12
\end{aligned}
$$

Table-based Solution:

The future value interest factor (FVIF) can also be found in Table 1 in the Appendix. When a three-decimal-place table is used, the factor is 2.191 with a future value of $2,191 (rounded). Notice that semi-annual compounding will result in $32 more than the $2,159 earned with annual compounding. It follows that more frequent compounding, such as quarterly or monthly, produces even higher earnings.

The process described also applies to discounting problems when discounting occurs more frequently than annually. The use of financial calculators and spreadsheet programs are more expedient as the frequency of compounding or discounting within a year increases.

DISCUSSION QUESTION 3

How can the high cost of consumer credit card debt be explained when interest rates on other types of consumer loans seem to be lower?

9.9.2 COST OF CONSUMER CREDIT

9.9.2.1 Unethical Lenders

ETHICAL History has shown many examples of individuals being charged exorbitant interest rates on loans. There is a word, *usury*, for this type of action. Usury is the act of lending money at an excessively high interest rate. Lenders who exhibited such unethical behavior were sometimes referred to as "loan sharks." Lenders, of course, are in the business of making a rate of return on the money that they have to lend. Without question, lenders deserve to earn a fair rate of return to compensate them for their time and for the risk that the borrower will not repay the interest and/or principal on time or in full.

In Chapter 8, we defined this added compensation as a risk premium above the prevailing risk-free rate. Good ethical behavior is consistent with treating borrowers honestly and fairly. However, because of the existence of unethical lenders, various laws have made usury illegal. While it is illegal to charge usurious rates of interest, some unscrupulous lenders still behave unethically when making loans to consumers. Congress passed the *Consumer Credit Protection Act of 1968*, which prohibits excessively high-priced credit transactions. Regulation Z enacts the Truth in Lending section of the Act, whereby the Federal Reserve has the responsibility of making consumers aware of the costs of alternative forms of credit. Lenders must disclose all loan costs (interest amounts, service charges, loan and finder fees, etc.), as well as the *annual percentage rate* of charge or interest. It is unfortunate, but a fact of life, that because of the unethical behavior of some lenders, laws must be enacted to protect consumers.

> **usury** the act of lending money at an excessively high interest rate

9.9.2.2 Annual Percentage Rate Versus Effective Annual Rate

Banks, finance companies, and other lenders are required by the Truth in Lending law to disclose their lending interest rates on credit extended to consumers. Such a rate is called a contract or stated rate or, more frequently, an annual percentage rate (APR). The method of calculating the APR on a loan is set by law. The APR is the interest rate, r, charged per period multiplied by the number of periods in a year, m:

$$APR = r \times m \tag{9.10}$$

> **annual percentage rate (APR)** determined by multiplying the interest rate charged per period by the number of periods in a year

Thus, a car loan that charges interest of 1% per month has an APR of 12% (i.e., 1% times 12 months). An unpaid credit card balance that incurs interest charges of 1.5% per month has an APR of 18% (1.5 times 12 months).

However, the APR misstates the true interest rate. The effective annual rate (EAR), sometimes called the *annual effective yield*, is the true opportunity cost measure of the interest rate, as it considers the effects of periodic compounding. For example, say an unpaid January balance of $100 on a credit card accumulates interest at the rate of 1.5% per month. The interest charge is added to the unpaid balance; if left unpaid, February's balance will be $101.50. If the bill remains unpaid through February, the 1.5% monthly charge is levied based on the total unpaid balance of $101.50. In other words, interest is assessed on previous months' unpaid interest charges. Thus, since interest compounds, the APR formula will *understate* the true or effective interest cost. This will always be true, except in the special case where the number of periods is one per year – that is, in annual compounding situations.

> **effective annual rate (EAR)** measures the true interest rate when compounding occurs more frequently than once a year

If the periodic interest charge, r, is known, the EAR is found by using equation 9.11:

$$EAR = (1 + r)^m - 1 \tag{9.11}$$

where m is the number of periods per year. If the APR is known instead, divide the APR by m and use the resulting number for r in equation 9.11.[3]

---

[3] Some financial calculators are preprogrammed with an "interest rate conversion" function, with which one can easily switch between an EAR (sometimes called EFF% for the "effective" rate) and the APR.

As an example of the effective annual rate concept, let's find the true annual interest cost of a credit card that advertises an 18% APR. Since credit card charges are, typically, assessed monthly, m (the number of periods per year) is 12. Thus, the monthly interest rate is,

$$r = \text{APR} \div m = 18\% \div 12 = 1.5\%$$

From equation 9.11, the EAR is,

$$(1 + 0.015)^{12} - 1 = 1.1956 - 1 = 0.1956, \text{ or } 19.56\%$$

The true interest charge on a credit card with an 18% APR is really 19.56%!

When the annual stated rate stays the same, more frequent interest compounding helps savers earn more interest over the course of a year. For example, is it better to put your money in an account offering (option 1) 8% interest per year, compounded quarterly, or (option 2) 8% interest per year, compounded monthly?

Compounding interest quarterly means that the bank is paying interest four times a year to its depositors. Option 1 involved four periods per year and a periodic interest rate, r, of 8% divided by 4, or 2%. Every dollar invested under option 1 will grow to $1.0824 [$1(1 + 0.02)^4$] after one year's time. Another way of expressing this is that the effective annual rate of 8% compounded quarterly is 8.24%.

Under option 2, the relevant time period is one month and the periodic interest rate is 8% ÷ 12, or 0.67%. Every dollar invested under option 2 will grow to $1.0830 [$1(1 + 0.0067)^{12}$]. Thus, the effective annual rate of 8% compounded monthly is 8.30%.

As option 2 gives the depositor more interest over the course of a year, depositors should choose it over option 1. This example illustrates that, for the same APR or stated rate, more frequent compounding increases the future value of an investor's funds more quickly.

LEARNING ACTIVITY

Go to the Board of Governors of the Federal Reserve website, https://www.federalreserve.gov. Access "Consumer Information" and describe some of the types of "consumer help" provided by the Federal Reserve.

APPLYING FINANCE TO. . .

• **Institutions and Markets** Depository institutions offer savings accounts and certificates of deposit (CDs) to individual savers. To entice individuals to save with them, these financial institutions often state annual percentage rates but compound the interest more frequently than once a year. The result is that the effective annual rate (EAR) is higher than the stated annual percentage rate (APR). Of course, since most financial institutions depend on the spread between their cost of obtaining funds and their lending rates, they must balance the effective annual rates at which they borrow and lend. Credit card loans typically provide for monthly compounding so that the EAR is higher than the APR.

• **Investments** Most financial decisions are based on the rate at which an investment is compounded or a future value is discounted. Savers are interested in growing, or compounding, their savings over time and know that the longer an investment can compound the more rapidly it will grow in value at a specified interest rate. Investors make plans, based on the compound rates of return they expect to earn on their investments, about when they can buy a home, when they can send their children to college, and when they can retire. The ability to compound interest more frequently than once a year means that investors can reach their goals sooner, or at lower interest rates.

• **Financial Management** Financial managers borrow from banks and issue debt to raise funds to maintain and grow their firms. While some business loans are simple interest loans, others take the form of fully amortized loans, whereby annuity payments are composed of a declining interest portion and a rising principal repayment portion over the life of the loan. Investors, of course, expect to earn compound rates of return on their debt and equity investments held for more than a year. Financial managers accordingly must invest funds in capital projects that will generate excess cash flows sufficient in amount to provide investors with their expected rates of return.

LO 9.1 The time value of money is the math of finance whereby a financial return is earned over time by saving or investing money. Simple interest is interest earned only on an investment's principal.

LO 9.2 Compounding is an arithmetic process whereby an initial value increases or grows at a compound interest rate over time to reach a value in the future. Compound interest involves earning interest on interest in addition to interest on the principal, or initial investment. Four approaches, or methods, are available for finding a future value when compounding is involved. They include an equation-based solution, a financial calculator solution, a spreadsheet solution, and a table-based solution.

LO 9.3 Discounting to determine present values is an arithmetic process whereby a future value decreases at a compound interest rate over time to reach a present value. Solving an equation, using a financial calculator, developing a spreadsheet program, and using pre-calculated tables are methods for finding present values.

LO 9.4 Four variables – present value, future value, interest rate, and number of periods – are included in the future value and present value equations. As long as the values for any three of these variables are known, we can solve for the fourth, or unknown, variable. For example, if the present value and future value amounts are known along with the number of periods, the interest rate can be found. Alternatively, if we knew the interest rate in addition to the present and future values, we could solve for the number of periods.

LO 9.5 An annuity is a series of equal payments (or receipts) that occur over a number of time periods. An ordinary annuity is when equal payments (or receipts) occur at the end of each time period. Necessary inputs include an interest rate, the number of periods, and a periodic payments variable. We then can solve for the future value of the ordinary annuity using one or more of the previously described solution methods.

LO 9.6 The present value of an ordinary annuity can be calculated using equations, financial calculators, spreadsheets, or tables. The necessary inputs are the amount of the periodic payments, an interest rate, and the number of periods. We then can solve for the present value of the ordinary annuity.

LO 9.7 The interest rate for an ordinary annuity can be found by entering the future value, the periodic payments amount, and the number of periods, and then solving for the interest rate. The number of time periods can be found in the same way, except the interest rate is one of the inputs and the number of periods is the unknown variable.

LO 9.8 The periodic payments amount for ordinary annuities can be determined using the same approach as previously described for finding the interest rate or number of periods. Amortized loans (such as real estate mortgage loans) are examples of ordinary annuities. After deciding the amount of the loan (present value), the interest rate on the loan, and the life of the loan, we can calculate the amount of each periodic payment necessary to pay off the loan in full at maturity.

LO 9.9 When more frequent than annual compounding (or discounting) occurs, the stated annual interest rate must be divided by the number of compounding periods within one year to get the rate per period, and the total number of periods calculated by multiplying the number of years by the number of compounding periods within a year. Then, future values (or present values) can be found using the same process employed when compounding occurred annually. The Truth in Lending law requires that the cost of consumer credit be stated as an annual percentage rate. However, when payments are made more frequently than annually, the effective annual rate measures the compounding impact on the cost of borrowing.

amortized loan
annual percentage rate (APR)
annuity
annuity due

compounding
compound interest
discounting
effective annual rate (EAR)

future value
inflation-adjusted interest rate
loan amortization schedule
ordinary annuity

present value
Rule of 72
simple interest
time value of money
usury

1. **(LO 9.1)** Identify the six principles of finance.

2. **(LO 9.1)** Briefly describe the time value of money.

3. **(LO 9.1)** Explain simple interest.

4. **(LO 9.2)** Describe the process of compounding and the meaning of compound interest.

5. **(LO 9.2)** Briefly describe how inflation, or purchasing power, impacts stated or nominal interest rates.

6. **(LO 9.3)** What is discounting? Give an illustration.

7. **(LO 9.3)** Briefly explain how present values and future values are related.

8. **(LO 9.4)** Describe the process for solving for the interest rate in present and future value problems.

9. **(LO 9.4)** Describe the process for solving for the time period in present and future value problems.

10. **(LO 9.4)** How can the Rule of 72 be used to determine how long it will take for an investment to double in value?

11. **(LO 9.5)** What is an ordinary annuity? What is an annuity due?

12. **(LO 9.6)** Describe how the present value of an annuity can be found.

13. **(LO 9.7)** Briefly describe how to solve for the interest rate or the time period in annuity problems.

14. **(LO 9.8)** Describe the process for determining the size of a constant periodic payment that is necessary to fully amortize a loan such as a home mortgage.

15. **(LO 9.9)** Describe compounding or discounting that is done more often than annually.

16. **(LO 9.9)** What is usury, and how does it relate to the cost of consumer credit?

17. **(LO 9.9)** Explain the difference between the annual percentage rate and the effective annual rate.

1. Go to the Federal Reserve website, https://www.federalreserve.gov. Go to "Economic Research and Data," and access "Consumer Credit." Find interest rates charged by commercial banks on new automobile loans, personal loans, and credit card plans.
   a. Compare the current or recent level of interest rates among the three types of loans.
   b. Compare trends in the cost of consumer credit provided by commercial banks over the past three years.

2. Go to the Federal Reserve website, https://www.federalreserve.gov. Go to "Economic Research and Data," and access "Consumer Credit." Determine current interest rates charged by finance companies versus commercial banks on new automobile loans. Also compare the cost of new automobile loans between finance companies and commercial banks over the past three years.

3. Assume that your partner and you are in the consumer lending business. A customer, talking with your partner, is discussing the possibility of obtaining a $10,000 loan for three months. The potential borrower seems distressed and says he needs the loan by tomorrow or several of his relatively new appliances will be repossessed by the manufacturers. You overhear your partner saying that that in order to process the loan within one day there will be a $1,000 processing fee so that $11,000 in principal will have to be repaid in order to have $10,000 to spend now. Furthermore, because the money is needed now and is for only three months the interest charge will be 6% per month. What would you do?

1. Find the future value one year from now of a $7,000 investment at a 3% annual compound interest rate. Also, calculate the future value if the investment is made for two years.

2. Find the future value of $10,000 invested now after five years if the annual interest rate is 8%.
   a. What would be the future value if the interest rate is a simple interest rate?
   b. What would be the future value if the interest rate is a compound interest rate?

3. Determine the future values if $5,000 is invested in each of the following situations:
   a. 5% for ten years
   b. 7% for seven years
   c. 9% for four years

4. You are planning to invest $2,500 today for three years at a nominal interest rate of 9% with annual compounding.
   a. What would be the future value of your investment?

b. Now assume that inflation is expected to be 3% per year over the same three-year period. What would be the investment's future value in terms of purchasing power?

c. What would be the investment's future value in terms of purchasing power if inflation occurs at a 9% annual rate?

5. Find the present value of $7,000 to be received one year from now, assuming a 3% annual discount interest rate. Also calculate the present value if the $7,000 is received after two years.

6. Determine the present values if $5,000 is received in the future (i.e., at the end of each indicated time period) in each of the following situations:
   a. 5% for ten years
   b. 7% for seven years
   c. 9% for four years

7. Determine the present value if $15,000 is to be received at the end of eight years and the discount rate is 9%. How would your answer change if you had to wait six years to receive the $15,000?

8. Determine the future value at the end of two years of an investment of $3,000 made now and an additional $3,000 made one year from now if the compound annual interest rate is 4%.

9. Assume you are planning to invest $5,000 each year for six years and will earn 10% per year. Determine the future value of this annuity if your first $5,000 is invested at the end of the first year.

10. Determine the present value now of an investment of $3,000 made one year from now and an additional $3,000 made two years from now if the annual discount rate is 4%.

11. What is the present value of a loan that calls for the payment of $500 per year for six years if the discount rate is 10% and the first payment will be made one year from now? How would your answer change if the $500 per year occurred for ten years?

12. Determine the annual payment on a $500,000, 12% business loan from a commercial bank that is to be amortized over a five-year period.

13. Determine the annual payment on a $15,000 loan that is to be amortized over a four-year period and carries a 10% interest rate. Also prepare a loan amortization schedule for this loan.

14. You are considering borrowing $150,000 to purchase a new home.
   a. Calculate the monthly payment needed to amortize an 8%, fixed-rate, 30-year mortgage loan.
   b. Calculate the monthly amortization payment if the loan in (a) was for 15 years.

15. Assume a bank loan requires an interest payment of $85 per year and a principal payment of $1,000 at the end of the loan's eight-year life.
   a. At what amount could this loan be sold for to another bank if loans of similar quality carried an 8.5% interest rate? That is, what would be the present value of this loan?
   b. Now, if interest rates on other similar-quality loans are 10%, what would be the present value of this loan?
   c. What would be the present value of the loan if the interest rate is 8% on similar-quality loans?

16. Use a financial calculator or computer software program to answer the following questions:
   a. What would be the future value of $15,555 invested now if it earns interest at 14.5% for seven years?
   b. What would be the future value of $19,378 invested now if the money remains deposited for eight years and the annual interest rate is 18%?

17. Use a financial calculator or computer software program to answer the following questions:
   a. What is the present value of $359,000 that is to be received at the end of 23 years if the discount rate is 11%?
   b. How would your answer change in (a) if the $359,000 is to be received at the end of 20 years?

18. Use a financial calculator or computer software program to answer the following questions:
   a. What would be the future value of $7,455 invested annually for nine years beginning one year from now if the annual interest rate is 19%?
   b. What would be the present value of a $9,532 annuity for which the first payment will be made beginning one year from now, payments will last for 27 years, and the annual interest rate is 13%?

19. Use a financial calculator or computer software program to answer the following questions.
   a. What would be the future value of $19,378 invested now if the money remains deposited for eight years, the annual interest rate is 18%, and interest on the investment is compounded semi-annually?
   b. How would your answer for (a) change if quarterly compounding were used?

20. Use a financial calculator or computer software program to answer the following questions.
   a. What is the present value of $359,000 that is to be received at the end of 23 years, the discount rate is 11%, and semi-annual discounting occurs?
   b. How would your answer for (a) change if monthly discounting were used?

21. What would be the present value of a $9,532 annuity for which the first payment will be made beginning one year from now, payments will last for 27 years, the annual interest rate is 13%, quarterly discounting occurs, and $2,383 is invested at the end of each quarter?

22. Answer the following questions.
    a. What is the annual percentage rate (APR) on a loan that charges interest of .75% per month?
    b. What is the effective annual rate (EAR) on the loan described in (a)?

23. You have recently seen a credit card advertisement stating that the annual percentage rate is 12%. If the credit card requires monthly payments, what is the effective annual rate of interest on the loan?

24. A credit card advertisement states that the annual percentage rate is 21%. If the credit card requires quarterly payments, what is the effective annual rate of interest on the loan?

25. **Challenge Problem** [Note: A computer spreadsheet software program or a financial calculator that can handle uneven cash flow streams will be needed to solve the following problems.] The following cash flow streams are expected to result from three investment opportunities.

Year	Investment Stable	Investment Declining	Investment Growing
1	$20,000	$35,000	$10,000
2	20,000	30,000	15,000
3	20,000	20,000	20,000
4	20,000	5,000	30,000
5	20,000	0	50,000

a. Find the present values at the end of time period zero for each of these three investments if the discount rate is 15%. Also, find the present values for each investment using 10% and 20% discount rates.

b. Find the future values of these three investments at the end of year five if the compound interest rate is 12.5%. Also, find the future values for each investment using 2.5% and 22.5% compound rates.

c. Find the present values of the three investments using a 15% annual discount rate but with quarterly discounting. Also, find the present values for both semi-annual and monthly discounting for a 15% stated annual rate.

d. Find the future values of the three investments using a 12.5% annual compound rate but with quarterly compounding. Also find the future values for both semi-annual and monthly compounding for a 12.5% stated annual rate.

e. Assume that the present value for each of the three investments is $75,000. What is the annual interest rate (%i) for each investment?

f. Show how your answers would change in (e) if quarterly discounting takes place.

g. Assume that the future value for each of the three investments is $150,000. What is the annual interest rate (%i) for each investment? [Note: (e) and (g) are independent of each other.]

h. Show how your answers would change in (g) if quarterly compounding takes place.

Learning Extension 9

Annuity Due Applications

LO 9.10 Understand and calculate annuity due problems involving future and present values.

FUTURE VALUE OF AN ANNUITY DUE

9.10 ANNUITY DUE PROBLEMS

In contrast with an ordinary annuity, an *annuity due* exists when the equal periodic payments occur at the beginning of each period. Let's return to the example used in the Future Value of an Annuity section in this chapter. Recall that the problem involved a three-year annuity, $1,000 annual payments, and an 8% interest rate. However, let's assume that the first payment now is made at the beginning of the first year, namely at time zero. This will allow the first $1,000 payment to earn interest for three years, the second payment to earn interest for two years, and the third payment to earn interest for one year.

The calculation process to find the future value of this annuity due problem can be demonstrated as follows:

$$\text{FV annuity due} = \$1,000(1.08)^3 + \$1,000(1.08)^2 + \$1,000(1.08)^1$$
$$= \$1,000(1.260) + \$1,000(1.166) + \$1,000(1.080)$$
$$= \$1,000(1.260 + 1.166 + 1.080)$$
$$= \$1,000(3.506)$$
$$= \$3,506$$

Notice that by making the first payment now, the future value of this annuity at the end of three years will be $3,506. This contrasts with a future value of $3,246 if payments are delayed by one year, as would be the case with an ordinary annuity.

Table-based Solution:

Equation 9.6 can be easily modified to handle annuity due problems as follows:

$$FVAD_n = PMT(FVIFA_{r,n})(1+r) \tag{LE9.1}$$

where FVAD is the future value of an annuity due and the $(1 + r)$ factor effectively compounds each payment by one more year to reflect the fact that payments start at the beginning of each period. In this problem, the annual payment is $1,000, the time period is three years, and the interest rate is 8%. Using equation LE9.1, the future value of this annuity due would be,

$$FVAD_3 = \$1,000(FVIFA_{8\%,3})(1 + 0.08)$$
$$= \$1,000(3.246)(1.08)$$
$$= \$1,000(3.506)$$
$$= \$3,506$$

The FVIFA of 3.246 comes from Table 9.3 at the intersection of the 8% interest rate column and the year-three row.

Annuity due problems also can be solved with financial calculators. In fact, most financial calculators have a DUE key (or a switch) for shifting payments from the end of time periods to the beginning of time periods. If you have a financial calculator, you can verify the future value of an annuity due result for the three-year annuity problem. First, clear the calculator. Next, enter −1000 (for both TI and HP calculators) and press the PMT key. Then enter 8 and press the %i key, and enter 3 and press the N key. Finally, instead of pressing the CPT key, press the DUE key followed by the FV key to find the future value of an annuity due of 3506.11, which rounds to $3,506.

Financial Calculator Solution:

Inputs: 3   8   −1000

              [N]   [%i]   [PMT]

Press: [DUE]   [FV]

Solution: 3506.11

Spreadsheet Solution:

The future value of an annuity due problem is solved by again using Excel's future value (FV) financial function, but adjusting for when the cash flows occur, as follows:

$$= \text{FV}(\text{Rate}, \text{Nper}, \text{Pmt}, \text{PV}, \text{Type})$$
$$= \text{FV}(.08, 3, -1000, 0, 1)$$
$$= \$3,506.11$$

Note that the "Type" value was given a "1" to indicate the beginning of period cash flows. Recall that previously we used a "0" value in "Type" to reflect cash flows occurring at the end of each time period.

PRESENT VALUE OF AN ANNUITY DUE

Occasionally, you will have to do present value annuity due problems. For example, leasing arrangements often require the person leasing equipment to make the first payment at the time the equipment is delivered. Let's illustrate by assuming that lease payments of $1,000 will be made at the beginning of each year for three years. If the appropriate interest rate is 8%, what is the present value of this annuity due leasing problem?

The calculation process to find the present value of this annuity due problem can be demonstrated as follows:

$$
\begin{aligned}
\text{PV annuity due} &= \$1,000[1 \div (1.08)^0] + \$1,000[1 \div (1.08)^1] + \$1,000[1 \div (1.08)^2] \\
&= \$1,000(1.000) + \$1,000(0.926) + \$1,000(0.857) \\
&= \$1,000(2.783) \\
&= \$2,783
\end{aligned}
$$

Notice that by making the first payment now, the present value of this annuity is $2,783. This contrasts with a present value of $2,577 if payments are delayed by one year, as would be the case with an ordinary annuity.

Table-based Solution:

Equation 9.8 can be easily modified to handle annuity due problems as follows:

$$\text{PVAD}_n = \text{PMT}(\text{PVIFA}_{r,n})(1 + r) \tag{LE9.2}$$

where PVAD is the present value of an annuity due and the $(1 + r)$ factor effectively compounds each payment by one more year to reflect the fact that payments start at the beginning of each period.

In the preceding problem, the annual payment is $1,000, the time period is three years, and the interest rate is 8%. Using equation LE9.2, the present value of this annuity due would be,

$$
\begin{aligned}
\text{PVAD}_3 &= \$1,000[(\text{PVIFA}_{8\%,3})(1 + 0.08)] \\
&= \$1,000[(2.577)(1.08)] \\
&= \$1,000(2.783) \\
&= \$2,783
\end{aligned}
$$

The PVIFA of 2.577 comes from Table 9.4 at the intersection of the 8% interest rate column and the year-three row. Present value annuity due problems also can be solved with computer software programs and financial calculators.

If you have a financial calculator, you can verify the present value of an annuity due result for the preceding three-year annuity problem. First, clear the calculator. Next, enter 1000 for TI calculators (or −1000 for HP calculators) and press the PMT key. Then enter 8 and press the %i key, and enter 3 and press the N key. Finally, instead of pressing the CPT key, press the DUE key followed by the PV key to find the present value of an annuity due of 2783.26, which rounds to $2,783.

Financial Calculator Solution:

Inputs:	3	8	1000
	N	%i	PMT
Press:	DUE	PV	
Solution:	2783.26		

Spreadsheet Solution:

The present value of an annuity due problem is solved by again using Excel's present value (PV) financial function, but adjusting for when the cash flows occur, as follows:

$$= PV(Rate, Nper, Pmt, FV, Type)$$
$$= PV(.08, 3, -1000, 0, 1)$$
$$= \$2,783.26$$

Note that the "Type" value was given a "1" to indicate beginning of period cash flows. Recall that previously we used a "0" value in "Type" to reflect cash flows occurring at the end of each time period.

INTEREST RATES AND TIME REQUIREMENTS FOR ANNUITY DUE PROBLEMS

Tables containing FVIFA and PVIFA factors are not readily available for annuity due problems. Thus, it is better to use a spreadsheet program or a financial calculator when trying to find the interest rate for an annuity due problem. Let's assume that the future value of an annuity due problem is $6,153, each payment is $1,000, and the time period is five years. What is the interest rate on this problem? If you have a financial calculator, enter FV = 6153, PMT = −1000, and N = 5. Press the DUE key and the %i key to find an r of 7%.

Financial Calculator Solution:

Inputs:	5	−1000	6153
	N	PMT	FV
Press:	DUE	%i	
Solution:	7.00		

Spreadsheet Solution:

Excel's RATE financial function also can be used to solve for the interest rate involving an annuity due problem. The process is very similar to the one used for an ordinary annuity problem, except that a "1" value in "Type" is entered to indicate that cash flows occur at the beginning of each time period. The financial function solution would be,

$$= RATE(Nper, Pmt, PV, FV, Type)$$
$$= RATE(5, -1000, 0, 6153, 1)$$
$$= 7.00\%$$

The *n* time periods involved in an annuity due problem also can be determined using either a computer software program or a financial calculator. For example, in the preceding problem, let's assume we know the interest rate is 7%, the future value is $6,153, and the payment is $1,000 (entered as −1000). What we don't know is the number of time periods required. We can solve for N as follows:

Financial Calculator Solution:

Inputs: 7 −1000 6153

%i PMT FV

Press: DUE N

Solution: 5.00

Spreadsheet Solution:
Excel's NPER financial function also can be used to solve for the number of periods in an annuity due problem. However, in contrast with an ordinary annuity, a value of "1" for "Type" must be entered to indicate that the cash flows occur at the beginning of the time periods. The financial function solution would be the following:

$$= \text{NPER}(\text{Rate}, \text{Pmt}, \text{PV}, \text{FV}, \text{Type})$$
$$= \text{NPER}(7, -1000, 0, 6153, 1)$$
$$= 5.00$$

Of course, the same process could be used for finding either interest rates or the number of time periods if the present value of the annuity due instead of the future value were known. This would be done by substituting the PV value for the FV value in financial calculator or spreadsheet calculations.

SUMMARY

LO 9.10 An annuity due exists when equal periodic payments (or receipts) occur at the beginning of each time period. As was the case for ordinary annuities (where periodic payments occur at the end of each time period), necessary inputs include an interest rate, the number of periods, and a periodic payments variable. We then can solve for the future value (or present value) of the annuity due by modifying the solution methods used for ordinary annuities.

QUESTIONS AND PROBLEMS

1. Assume you are planning to invest $100 each year for four years and will earn 10% per year. Determine the future value of this annuity due problem if your first $100 is invested now.

2. Assume you are planning to invest $5,000 each year for six years and will earn 10% per year. Determine the future value of this annuity due problem if your first $5,000 is invested now.

3. What is the present value of a five-year lease arrangement with an interest rate of 9% that requires annual payments of $10,000 per year with the first payment being due now?

4. Use a financial calculator to solve for the interest rate involved in the following future value of an annuity due problem. The future value is $57,000, the annual payment is $7,500, and the time period is six years.

5. **Challenge Problem** (Note: This problem requires access to a spreadsheet software package or a financial calculator that can handle uneven cash flows.) Following are the cash flows for three investments (originally presented in end-of-chapter problem 25) that actually occur at the beginning of each year rather than at the end of each year.

Year	Investment Stable	Investment Declining	Investment Growing
1	$20,000	$35,000	$10,000
2	20,000	30,000	15,000
3	20,000	20,000	20,000
4	20,000	5,000	30,000
5	20,000	0	50,000

a. Find the present values at the end of time period zero for each of these three investments if the discount rate is 15%.

b. Find the future values of these three investments at the end of year five if the compound interest rate is 12.5%.

c. Assume that the present value for each of the three investments is $75,000. What is the annual interest rate (%i) for each investment?

d. Assume that the future value for each of the three investments is $150,000. What is the annual interest rate (%i) for each investment? (Note: (c) and (d) are independent of each other.)

CHAPTER 10

Bonds and Stocks: Characteristics and Valuations

LEARNING OBJECTIVES

After studying this chapter, you should be able to do the following:

LO 10.1 Identify the major sources of external long-term financing for corporations.

LO 10.2 Describe the global market for bonds, the role of bond covenants, and bond ratings.

LO 10.3 Compare characteristics of corporate bonds with respect to bondholder security, time to maturity, and income return.

LO 10.4 Describe major characteristics of preferred stock and common stock.

LO 10.5 Describe the process for issuing dividends by a firm and differences between cash dividends, stock dividends, and share repurchases.

LO 10.6 Explain how financial securities are valued in general.

LO 10.7 Explain how bonds are valued.

LO 10.8 Explain how stocks are valued and the economic and industry influences that can affect stock prices.

Where we have been. . . The financial system is composed of a number of participants, such as banks, insurance companies, credit unions, and individuals, among others. Some borrow or lend funds; others seek to sell or purchase ownership rights, or common stock, in firms. We've seen how investors are willing to give up their money in the expectation of receiving a return that will exceed the inflation rate and will reward them for the risk of their investment. Time-value-of-money principles (present value, future value) help borrowers and lenders determine items such as how much to borrow, repayment schedules, and the return on an investment.

Where we are going. . . Bonds and stocks are traded in securities markets, which will be the topic of Chapter 11. We tie together the concepts of expected return, risk, and valuation in Chapter 12 when we discuss financial risk and return concepts. In Chapter 16, we will discuss additional sources of funds for business financing.

How this chapter applies to me. . . Time value of money is one of the most important concepts in finance. Here, we will see applications of time-value concepts to the investor and how an investor can evaluate a firm's prospects and estimate appropriate prices for its securities. Greater depth and detail will be presented in an investments course. Many investors lack the time or ability to analyze securities, so they will purchase a mutual fund, which is a professionally managed investment pool. As a financial manager, this chapter will introduce you to various types of capital market securities and their features, so you will know more about the financing choices facing firms.

Mark Twain made the following observation about financial markets:

October. That month is especially dangerous for investing in stocks. Other dangerous months include August, January, June, March, November, July, February, April, December, May, and September.[1]

---

[1] Mark Twain. *Pudd'nhead Wilson*, (Hartford, Conn: American Publishing Company, 1897). Print.

That pretty much covers them all! In this chapter we'll begin to learn about financial markets and the characteristics of stocks and bonds.

Borrowing money brings with it the obligation to repay the debt. Individuals and firms who do not repay their borrowing may find themselves unable to borrow again in the future and, worse yet, filing for bankruptcy. Prudent use of debt by issuers can help finance the purchase of capital, equipment, houses, and so forth. We'll learn more about the corporate decision to borrow in a future chapter. In this chapter, we'll begin to learn about the characteristics of bonds from an investor's perspective.

Investing in the stock market is, for many, the best means available for enjoying the benefits of corporate wealth creation. As firms grow in size, often profitability, market share, market value, and the value of the shares of stock grow, too. This helps investors meet their financial goals, such as preparing to pay for the college education of their child or their own retirement. In this chapter, we'll discuss common stock, preferred stock, and principles behind how to value equity.

In Chapter 2, we described **financial assets** as claims against the income or assets of individuals, businesses, and governments. Businesses obtain long-term external financial capital either by borrowing or by obtaining equity funds. Long-term borrowing can be privately negotiated or can be obtained by issuing debt obligations called bonds. Equity capital may be obtained by finding new partners with financial capital to invest or through the public markets by issuing shares. This chapter describes the characteristics of bonds and applies the time-value-of-money techniques from Chapter 9 to see how to value bonds. In the following chapter, we'll discuss the characteristics of stocks and tools used to value them.

financial assets claims against the income or assets of individuals, businesses, and governments

---

Businesses obtain long-term financing from internal funds, which are generated from profits, and from external funds, which are obtained from capital markets. Some firms will have little need for external funds. They may be able to generate sufficient internal funds to satisfy their need for capital, or they may require little investment in fixed assets (for example, firms operating in service industries). Other businesses, such as high-tech firms that experience rapid growth, cannot generate enough internal funds for their capital needs and may be forced to seek financing, often from the capital markets.

The proportion of internal to external financing varies over the business cycle. During periods of economic expansion, firms usually rely more on external funds because the funds needed for investment opportunities outstrip the firms' ability to finance them internally. During periods of economic contraction, the reverse is true. As profitable investment opportunities become fewer, the rate of investment is reduced and reliance on external capital markets decreases.

Long-term funds are obtained by issuing corporate bonds and stocks. In recent years, the total of new corporate security issues amounted to more than $2,600 billion in 2006 but declined to about $1,000 billion in in each year from 2008 to 2011 due to a steep recession and financial market anxiety. By 2017 new corporate security issues were about $2,000 billion.

Most of the funds raised annually from security issues come from corporate bond sales. In fact, corporate bonds accounted for about 94% of total new security issues from 1995 to 2018. Firms issue more bonds than equities for two basic reasons. First, as we will see in Chapter 18, borrowing is cheaper than raising equity financing. Second, bonds and other loans have a maturity date, when they expire or come due; at times, new bonds are sold to repay maturing ones. On the other hand, equity never matures. Firms can repurchase their outstanding stock, or the shares of one firm may be merged or acquired by another firm. For this reason, in Figure 10.1 the "net percent" line for common stocks mostly indicates negative numbers. This means, over the time period covered in the figure, corporations have been net repurchasers rather than net issuers of new equity.

Corporations raise about 90% of their publicly held long-term debt funds by selling their bonds through public issues in the United States. A second important method of raising long-term debt funds is through private sales or placements in the United States. Public security issues are offered for sale to all investors, must be approved by the Securities and Exchange Commission (SEC), and are accompanied by public disclosure of the firm's financial statements and other information. Private placements, on the other hand, are sold to specific qualified investors, do not go through SEC scrutiny, and do not require public disclosure of company information. Since private sales are "private," we do not have good data on these sales over time.

10.1 LONG-TERM EXTERNAL FINANCING SOURCES FOR BUSINESSES

FIGURE 10.1 Net percent of financing from bonds, new stock issues, and retained earnings, 1995–2018

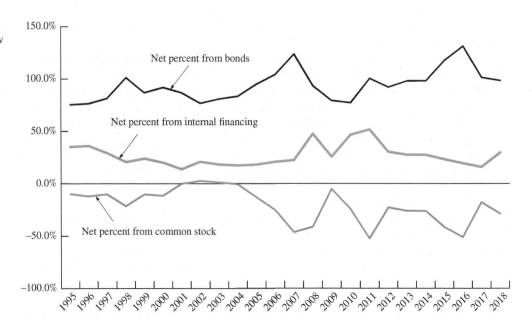

GLOBAL U.S. firms may borrow funds overseas. The percentage of funds raised overseas varies over this time frame, from over 19% in 2009 to 1.5% in 2010. There are four reasons why U.S. firms raise funds outside of the United States. First, if they have overseas plants or factories, it may make financial sense to raise funds in the country in which the plant is built. Second, financing costs, such as interest rates, are sometimes lower overseas, although the recent downtrend in overseas financing may be due to lower interest rates in the United States. Third, if securities are issued outside of the United States, the issuer avoids the costly and time-consuming SEC approval process. Fourth, the growing number of large bond offerings (issues of $1 billion or more at one time) causes issuers to seek access to the global capital markets to find buyers. Figure 10.1 shows the mix of external (bonds and stocks) financing and internal (retained profits) financing for U.S. corporations. Because of merger, acquisition, and stock buyback activity trends that began in the 1980s, external public equity has declined over time. To make up for the shortfall, publicly issued bonds have increased relative to retained earnings as a funding source. After the Great Recession, firms were more "tightfisted," seeking to retain more earnings and build up liquidity in the face of a weak economy and an uncertain regulatory environment. As the U.S. economy continued to slowly expand, the use of retained earnings and internal financing fell to pre-recession levels.

LEARNING ACTIVITY

Examine recent financing activity and data at the Federal Reserve Board and Securities Exchange Commission websites, https://www.federalreserve.gov and https://www.sec.gov.

10.2 BONDS

bond agreement or contract between investor (lender) and a debtor (borrower), typically a business firm or government body

par value (debt); face value principal amount that the issuer is obligated to repay at maturity

A **bond** is an agreement or contract between lenders and the borrowing organization; typically, a firm or government body. As such, the lenders or bondholders of a corporation have certain rights and privileges not enjoyed by the firm's owners (those holding shares of common stock). A debt holder may force the firm to abide by the terms of the debt contract even if the result is reorganization or bankruptcy of the firm. The periodic interest payments due to the holders of debt securities must be paid or else the creditors can force the firm into bankruptcy. Table 10.1 summarizes important characteristics of bonds, which we'll be reviewing in this section.

GLOBAL Except for rarely issued perpetuities,[2] all debt issues have maturity dates, the point when issuers are obligated to pay the bond's principal (**par value (debt); face value**) to bondholders. In the

[2] In this case, a perpetuity is a bond without a maturity date. Its owners and heirs receive interest payments on a regular basis as long as the firm exists. In general, a security that is a perpetuity pays a constant periodic cash flow as long as the issuer exists.

TABLE 10.1 Common Elements of Bonds

- **Represent borrowed funds**
- **Contractual agreement (indenture) between a borrower and lender**
- **Senior claim on assets and cash flow**
- **No voting rights**
- **Par value**
- **Having a bond rating improves the issue's marketability to investors**
- **Covenants**
- **Interest:** Tax deductible to the issuing firm.
  Usually fixed over the issue's life but can be variable if the indenture allows coupon rate to be affected by market interest rates and/or bond rating
- **Maturity:** Usually fixed; can be affected by convertibility, call and put provisions, sinking fund, and extendibility features in the indenture
- **Security:** Can have senior claim on specific assets pledged in case of default or can be unsecured (debenture or subordinated [junior claim] debenture)

United States, par value is usually $1,000 for corporate bonds. All but zero-coupon issues pay interest, called **coupon payments**. If a bond has an 8% coupon and a par value of $1,000, it pays annual interest of 8% of $1,000, or $0.08 \times \$1,000 = \$80$. A bond with a 10% coupon would pay interest of $100 per year. Eurobonds pay a single annual coupon interest payment. In the United States, bonds pay interest semi-annually; an 8% coupon will pay interest of $40 every six months during the life of the bond.

Bondholders have legal status as creditors, not owners, of the firm. As such, they have priority claims on the firm's cash flows and assets. This means that bondholders must receive their interest payments before the firm's owners receive their dividends. In the case of bankruptcy, the debt holders must receive the funds owed to them before funds are distributed to the firm's owners. Because of this first claim on a firm's cash flow and assets, debt is a less risky investment than equity.

Offsetting the advantages of owning debt is its lower return. The interest payments creditors receive usually are considerably less over a period of years than the returns received by equity holders. Also, as long as the corporation meets its contractual obligations, the creditors have little choice in its management and control except for those formal agreements and restrictions that are stated in the loan contract.

ETHICAL Long-term corporate debt securities fall into two categories: secured obligations and unsecured obligations. A single firm can have many types of debt contracts outstanding. Although ownership of many shares of stock may be evidenced by a single stock certificate, the bondholder has a separate security for each bond owned. Bonds can be registered bonds or bearer bonds. Bonds currently issued in the United States are **registered bonds** in that the issuer knows the bondholders' names and interest payments are sent directly to the bondholder. **Bearer bonds** have coupons that are "clipped" from the side of the bond certificate and presented, like a check, to a bank for payment. Thus, the bond issuer does not know who is receiving the interest payments. Bearer bonds are more prevalent outside of the United States. Regulations prevent their issuance in the United States, primarily because unscrupulous investors may evade income taxes on the clipped coupons.

Bonds can be sold in the public market, following registration with the SEC, and traded by investors. There is a "private" market, too; bonds can be sold in a private placement to qualified investors, typically institutional investors such as insurance companies and wealthy individuals. Other forms of debt capital exist in addition to bonds. Businesses can borrow from banks. A popular source of debt financing is commercial finance companies, which will be further discussed in Chapter 16.

coupon payments interest payments on a bond

registered bonds bonds issued in the United States; the issuer knows the names of the bondholders and the interest payments are sent directly to the bondholder

bearer bonds have coupons that are "clipped" and presented, like a check, to the bank for payment; the bond issuer does not know who is receiving the interest payments

10.2.1 WHO BUYS BONDS?

The U.S. Treasury has a Treasury Direct program to sell Treasury securities directly to individual investors, but the main buyers of Treasury bonds are large institutions, such as pension funds or insurance companies, which hold them for investment purposes. Others, such as investment banks, may purchase them and then resell them to smaller investors.

SMALL BUSINESS PRACTICE

FINANCING SOURCES FOR THE START-UP FIRM

So you want to start your own business? All businesses require some initial financial capital to carry out the firm's operations. A service business requires less financial capital than would a manufacturing business. Both need working capital in the form of inventories and possibly accounts receivable if sales are made on credit terms. In addition, a manufacturing business requires fixed assets to manufacture the products that are to be sold.

Now that you have decided to start a new business, where are you going to get the necessary financial capital? First, you can use your own assets. You may have some accumulated savings to use or have some financial assets in the form of stocks and bonds that can be sold. Second, you can turn to family and friends for financial support. You can borrow from family members and friends or you can offer them a partial ownership (equity) position in the firm.

A small business can sometimes get outside financing from business angels or venture capitalists. Angels are wealthy individuals who provide financial capital to small businesses, usually during their early development. Venture capitalists organize partnerships that specialize in providing debt and equity capital to small businesses in their development and early expansion stages. The partners in a venture capital pool typically include insurance companies, endowment funds, and other institutional investors.

After a firm begins operations, some financing may be obtained from customers and/or suppliers. Large customers may be willing to "lend" to you in the form of advance "partial payments" on products that have not yet been completed. Suppliers often will give small businesses credit, in some cases for several months, on purchases of materials and supplies. Bank financing is another source of possible outside financing for the small business once operations have begun. The federal government, through the Small Business Administration (SBA), provides an additional source of financing for small businesses. Many states and local communities also provide financing assistance to small businesses.

Similarly, corporate debt markets are oriented toward the large institutional investor who can purchase millions of dollars of bonds at a time. But several innovative firms, such as Ally Financial (formerly GMAC), IBM, United Parcel Service (UPS), Caterpillar, and GE Capital, initiated programs in recent years to sell $1,000 par value bonds directly to the retail, or individual, investor. Called Inter-Notes, medium-term notes, or direct access notes (depending on the issuer and the investment banker selling them), the programs target small investors who have only a few thousand dollars rather than millions to invest in bonds.

10.2.2 BOND COVENANTS

trust indenture an extensive document that details the various provisions and covenants of the loan arrangement

trustee represents the bondholders to ensure the bond issuer respects the indenture's provisions

covenants impose restrictions or extra duties on the firm

The **trust indenture** is an extensive document that details the various provisions and covenants of the loan arrangement. A **trustee** represents the bondholders to ensure the bond issuer respects the indenture's provisions. In essence, the indenture is a contract between the bondholders and the issuing firm. The indenture details the par value, maturity date, and coupon rate of the issue. A bond indenture may include **covenants**, which can impose restrictions or extra duties on the firm.

Examples of covenants include stipulations that the firm maintain a minimum level of net working capital,[3] keep pledged assets in good working order, and send audited financial statements to bondholders. Others include restrictions on the amount of the firm's debt, total annual dividend payments, the amount and type of additional covenants it may undertake, and asset sales.

ETHICAL These examples illustrate the purpose of covenants, which is to protect the bondholders' stake in the firm. Bonds have value, first, because of the firm's ability to pay coupon interest and, second, because of the value of the assets or collateral backing the bonds in case of default. Without proper covenant protection, the value of a bond can decline sharply if a firm's liquidity and assets depreciate or if its debt grows disproportionately to its equity. These provisions affect the issue's bond rating (discussed below) and the firm's financing costs, since bonds giving greater protection to the investor can be sold with lower coupon rates. The firm must decide if the restrictions and duties in the covenants are worth the access to lower-cost funds.

---

[3] This is a measure of a firm's ability to repay short-term bills as they come due. Net working capital will be discussed further in Chapters 15 and 16.

Covenants are important to bondholders. Holders of RJR Nabisco bonds owned high quality, A-rated bonds prior to the firm's takeover in 1988 by a leveraged buyout. After the buyout, large quantities of new debt were issued; RJR Nabisco's original bonds were given a lower rating and fell by 17% in value. Lawsuits by disgruntled bondholders against the takeover were unfruitful. The courts decided that the bondholders should have sought protection against such increases in the firm's debt load by seeking appropriate covenant language before investing, rather than running to the courts to correct their mistake. Covenants are the best way for bondholders to protect themselves against dubious management actions or decisions. For example, some bonds allow the investor to force the firm to redeem them if the credit rating falls below a certain level; others, such as Deutsche Telekom's $14.5 billion issue in 2000, increase the coupon rate (in this case by 50 basis points, or 0.50 percentage points) if the bond rating falls below an "A" rating. We'll discuss bond ratings in the next section.

10.2.3 BOND RATINGS

Most bond issuers purchase **bond ratings** from one or more agencies, such as Standard & Poor's (S&P), Moody's, or Fitch. For a one-time fee, the rater examines the credit quality of the firm (for example, its ability to pay the promised coupon interest), the indenture provisions, covenants, and the expected trends of firm and industry operations. From its analysis and discussions with management, the agency assigns a bond rating (as shown in Table 10.2) that indicates the likelihood of default (non-payment of coupon or par value, or violation of the bond indenture) on the bond issue.[4] In addition, the rating agency commits to continually reexamine the issue's risk. For example, should the financial position of the firm weaken or improve, S&P may place the issue on its *Credit Watch* list, with negative or positive implications. After that, S&P will downgrade, upgrade, or reaffirm the original rating.

> **bond ratings** assess both the collateral underlying the bonds as well as the ability of the issuer to make timely payments of interest and principal

ETHICAL Despite the initial cost and the issuer's concern of receiving a lower-than-expected rating, a bond rating makes it much easier to sell the bonds to the public. The rating acts as a signal to the market that an independent agency has examined the qualities of the issuer and the bond issue, and has determined that the credit risk of the bond issue justifies the published rating. An unrated bond issue will likely obtain a cool reception from investors. Investors may have good reason to wonder, "What is the firm trying to hide? If this was an attractive bond issue, the firm would have rated it." In addition, certain types of investors, such as pension funds and insurance companies, may face restrictions against purchasing unrated public debt.

A bond's security, or collateral provisions, (discussed below) affect its credit rating. Bonds with junior or unsecured claims receive lower bond ratings, leading investors to demand higher yields to compensate for the higher risk. Thus, bond issues of a single firm can have different bond ratings if their security provisions differ.

Viewing Table 10.2, investment-grade bonds are those with ratings of Baa3, BBB−, or better. They are called "investment grade" as, historically, investors (individuals and managed funds, such as bank trust department portfolios and pension funds) were allowed to invest in such bonds. Bonds below an investment-grade rating were deemed too risky for such conservative portfolios and were not allowed to be held.

Times and regulations change, however, and bonds that are below investment grade, meaning they have ratings of Ba1, BB+, or lower, have gained a spot in many investment portfolios. Known as **junk bonds** or (euphemistically) **high-yield bonds**, they have more risk but offer higher expected returns and have benefits in lowering unsystematic risk in diversified portfolios. Formerly, issuing companies would seek the highest bond rating possible for new issues for two reasons. First, having high-rated debt added prestige to the company; an AAA-rated firm was viewed as being managed well, financially stable, and strong. In addition, such bonds gave the appearance of being a safe investment and, as they had an investment-grade rating, they would find demand among investors such as trust

> **junk bonds (high-yield bonds)** bonds with ratings that are below investment grade; that is, rated Ba1, BB+, or lower

---

[4] In 2019, the minimum fee for a bond rating was about $100,000. Moody's and S&P set the fee at about 5 basis points (or 0.05%) of the issue size. See https://www.bloomberg.com/news/2011-11-15/credit-rating-fees-rise-faster-than-inflation-as-governments-fret-expenses.html and https://www.standardandpoors.com/en_US/delegate/getPDF?articleId=2148688&type=COMMENTS&subType=REGULAT ORY. For a review of S&P's rating process; G. Hessol, "Financial Management and Credit Ratings," *Midland Corporate Finance Journal* (Fall 1985), pp. 49–52. Moody's process is described at https://www.moodys.com/Pages/amr002001.aspx (accessed January 18, 2019).

TABLE 10.2 Examples of Bond Rating Categories

Moody's	Standard & Poors	Fitch	
Aaa	AAA	AAA	Best quality, least credit risk
Aa1	AA+	AA+	High quality, slightly more risk than a top-rated bond
Aa2	AA	AA	
Aa3	AA–	AA–	
A1	A+	A+	Upper-medium grade, possible future credit quality difficulties
A2	A	A	
A3	A–	A–	
Baa1	BBB+	BBB+	Medium-quality bonds
Baa2	BBB	BBB	
Baa3	BBB–	BBB–	
Ba1	BB+	BB+	Speculative issues, greater credit risk
Ba2	BB	BB	
Ba3	BB–	BB–	
B1	B+	B+	Very speculative, likelihood of future default
B2	B	B	
B3	B–	B–	
Caa	CCC	CCC	Highly speculative, in default or high likelihood of going into default
Ca	CC		
C	C		
	D	DDD	
		DD	
		D	

departments and pension funds. The second main reason for seeking a high bond rating is that the higher rating saves the firm interest expense, as coupon rates on highly rated bonds are lower than those on lower-rated bonds because of the risk – expected return trade-off.

The growth of the high-yield sector of the bond market has attracted investors and issuers. Some firms prefer to issue debt rather than dividend-paying common stock as interest payments are tax deductible to the issuer. Others, as part of the firm's financial strategy, have issued bonds and used the funds to repurchase shares of common stock. Investors have noted that having junk bonds in a portfolio offers potential return enhancements and may diversify risk.

Over time, the stigma attached to junk bonds has diminished. Issuers and investors are more amenable to these securities. For example, in 1980, less than a third of S&P-rated bonds were not investment quality and many of those were "fallen angels"; that is, bonds that were originally issued with an investment-grade rating but then fell into the junk category because the issuing firm ran into financial difficulty.

By the late 1980s, more than half of rated debt was in the high-yield category, and by 2007 over 70% of S&P-rated firms had junk bonds outstanding. The number of AAA-rated and AA-rated companies fell from 17% of issuers in 1980 to 2% in 2007; B-rated bonds, on the other hand, have grown from 7% of issues in 1980 to over 40% of issues in 2007. Only two nonfinancial firms had an AAA rating in 2019: Johnson & Johnson, and Microsoft.[5] ExxonMobil was a third firm with an AAA bond rating, but it was downgraded in early 2016 because of the implications of falling oil prices and the firm's commitment to large capital expenditures and dividends to shareholders.

[5] Lucinda Shen, "Now There Are Only Two U.S. Companies with the Highest Credit Rating," *Fortune*, April 26, 2016, (https://fortune.com/2016/04/26/exxonmobil-sp-downgrade-aaa/ accessed May 28, 2016); Reuters, Vipal Monga, and Mike Cherney, "Lose Your Triple-A Rating? Who Cares?" *The Wall Street Journal* (April 29, 2014), pp. B1, B6; "S&P strips Pfizer's AAA rating on Wyeth acquisition" (October 16, 2009) https://www.reuters.com/article/companyNews/idUKN1636373320091016 (accessed October 17, 2009); Sereno Ng, "Junk Turns Golden, but May Be Laced With Tinsel," *The Wall Street Journal* (January 4, 2007), pp. C1, C2; Nicholas Riccio, "The Rise Of 'B' Rated Companies And Their Staying Power As An Asset Class," S&P's *CreditWeek* (January 3, 2007).

10.2.4 GLOBAL BOND MARKET

GLOBAL Many U.S. corporations have issued Eurodollar bonds. Eurodollar bonds are dollar-denominated bonds that are sold outside the United States. Because of this, they escape review by the SEC, somewhat reducing the expense of issuing the bonds. Eurodollar bonds usually have fixed coupons with annual coupon payments. Most mature in five to ten years, so they are not attractive for firms that want to issue long-term debt. Most Eurodollar bonds are debentures. This is not a major concern to investors, as only the largest, financially strongest firms have access to the Eurobond market. Investors *do* care that the bonds are sold in bearer form because investors can remain anonymous and evade taxes on coupon income. Some researchers believe this is the main reason Eurodollar bond interest rates are low relative to U.S. rates.[6]

Eurodollar bonds dollar-denominated bonds sold outside the United States

U.S. firms aren't the only issuers of securities outside their national borders. For example, foreign firms can issue securities in the United States if they follow U.S. security registration procedures. Yankee bonds are U.S. dollar denominated bonds that are issued in the United States by a foreign issuer. Some issuers find the longer maturities of Yankees attractive to meet long-term financing needs. While Eurodollar bonds typically mature in five to ten years, Yankees may have maturities as long as 30 years. Nonetheless, the euro (€) is becoming a strong competitor to the U.S. dollar for firms that want to raise funds in a currency that has broad appeal to many investors.[7]

Yankee bonds dollar-denominated bonds issued in the United States by a foreign issuer

Increasingly, the international bond market is ignoring national boundaries. A growing number of debt issues are being sold globally. The World Bank issued the first global bonds in 1989. Global bonds

global bonds bonds that are generally denominated in U.S. dollars and marketed globally

PERSONAL FINANCIAL PLANNING

Investing in Ladders and Barbells

As an introduction to stocks and bonds, this chapter is filled with applications to personal finance. From knowledge about the different types of stocks and bonds to how to read the stock and bond listings in the paper to basic valuation principles, all these tools and concepts can be used by individual investors as well as professionals.

Let's look at one application for a bond investor. Because of the "seesaw effect," lower interest rates cause bond prices to rise, and higher interest rates result in lower bond prices. But the yield curve doesn't just shift up and down over time; sometimes it twists. This means that short-term rates rise while long-term rates are

stable or falling, or that long-term rates rise while short-term rates are stable or falling. To avoid having their holdings hit by sudden moves in short-term or long-term rates, some investors employ a "ladder" strategy.

This strategy calls for investing equal amounts of money in bonds over a range of maturities so that interest rate cycles will average out over the business cycle to reduce the bond investor's risk. Alternatively, using a "barbell" approach, approximately equal amounts of short-term bonds and long-term bonds are purchased. By clumping holdings at either end of the maturity spectrum, investors hope to smooth out the effect of interest rate fluctuations on their bond portfolio.

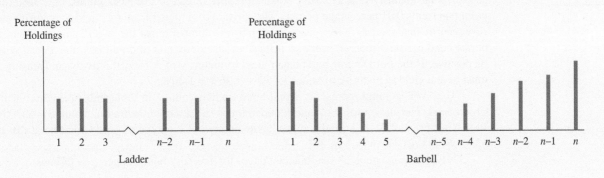

[6] W. Marr and J. Trimble, "The Persistent Borrowing Advantage of Eurodollar Bonds: A Plausible Explanation," *Journal of Applied Corporate Finance* (Summer 1988), pp. 65–70.

[7] Aline van Duyn, "Euro Corporate Bonds Give the Dollar a Run for its Money," *Financial Times* (June 29, 2001), p. 16.

usually are denominated in U.S. dollars. As they are marketed globally, their offering sizes typically exceed $1 billion. In addition to the World Bank, issuers now include the governments of Brazil, Finland, and Italy, and corporations such as Deutsche Telekom ($14.5 billion raised), Ford Motor Credit ($8.6 billion), Tecnost International Finance (Netherlands) ($8.3 billion), AT&T ($8 billion), Glitnir Bank (Iceland) ($1.25 billion), and Walmart ($5.8 billion).

DISCUSSION QUESTION 1

Which characteristics of bonds make some bonds more risky than others? Why do you think those characteristics affect a bond's risk?

10.2.5 READING BOND QUOTES

Figure 10.2 shows some of the bond quotation information available in the financial press or on websites such as https://finance.yahoo.com and https://markets.wsj.com/usoverview. The exhibit highlights a bond quote for a hypothetical bond issued by Ford Motor Credit (Ford Credit), the subsidiary of Ford Motor Company that raises funds to finance car loans and leases.

The ticker symbol "F" refers to Ford's common stock. In stock trading, ticker symbols are used as a shorthand notation rather than full company names. The Ford Credit bond has a coupon rate of 7.000%. If its par value is $1,000, as are most corporate bonds, then Ford Credit pays interest of 7% of $1,000, or $0.0700 \times 1,000 = 70.00 per year, or $35.00 every six months. The bond matures (that is, the principal repayment comes due) on 2027. The "Last Price" reports the closing price of the bond expressed as a percentage of par value. Since its par value is $1,000, a closing price 117.26% of par gives a value for the bond of $1,172.60.

FIGURE 10.2 Sample bond quotation

Company (Ticker)	Coupon	Maturity	Last Price	Last Yield	Spread	UST	Est. $ Vol (000S)
Ford Motor Credit (F)	7.000	2027	117.26	3.76	236	5	230,068

A commonly used term that is simple to compute is the current yield of a bond. We calculate current yield by dividing the annual coupon interest by the current price. The Ford Credit bond's current yield is $70.00/$1,172.60 = 5.97%. The current yield does not adequately represent the return on a bond investment as it considers income return only and ignores price changes.

The yield to maturity (YTM) is a better measure of investor return on a bond and is shown by the "Last Yield" in Figure 10.2. Yield to maturity represents an estimate of the investor's return on the bond if it was purchased today and held to maturity. We calculate the YTM using the bond's coupon, par value, last price, and time to maturity. Later, we will learn to compute a bond's yield to maturity. Here, the yield is presented to us as 3.76%.

The "Estimated Spread" is the difference between the yield to maturity on the Ford Credit bond and a similar maturity U.S. Treasury bond. Here, the spread is 236 basis points, or 2.36% (one basis point represents 0.01 percentage points). The spread is computed from the yield to maturity on a Treasury security that matures in five years, as seen by the number under the "UST" column. Since any corporate bond is riskier than Treasury securities because of default or credit risk, the spread will always be positive. If the Ford Credit bond has a yield to maturity of 3.76%, the five-year Treasury security must have a yield to maturity of about 3.76% − 2.36% = 1.40%.

The "Vol" column represents actual bond trading volume in thousands of dollars for this Ford Credit bond. The market value (quantity traded times last price) of the trading volume is $230,068,000. With a last price of $1,172.60, the approximate number of this type of Ford Credit bond that traded is $230,068,000/$1,172.60 = 196,203.

A typical price quote in the financial pages for Treasury bonds appears as follows:

Rate	Maturity Mo/Yr	Bid	Asked	Chg.	Asked Yld
4.000	Feb 27	100:27	100:28	−1	1.95

The coupon rate for the bond is 4.000% of par value, meaning that a $1,000 par value bond will pay $40 of interest annually, in two semi-annual payments of $20. The bond matures in February of 2027.

Treasury bond prices are expressed as percentages of par value and in 32nds of a point. The bid price, which is the price offered by investors wanting to buy the bonds, is 100 27/32% of par, or $1,008.4375. The ask price, which is the price requested by investors selling their bonds, is 100 28/32 of par, or $1,008.75. The bid–ask spread represents dealer profit, or $0.3125 per $1,000 par value bond. Spreads are often an indicator of a security's liquidity; the narrower the bid–ask spread, the greater the liquidity (and, usually, the greater the trading volume). The change in price from the previous day was −1/32 of a percentage point. The yield to maturity based on the asked price is 1.95%.[8]

LEARNING ACTIVITY

1. Learn more about these financing options by visiting https://www.treasurydirect.gov, https://www.ally.com/about/investor/term-notes/, and https://www.incapital.com.
2. Learn about the rating agencies and their processes at the following websites: https://www.standardandpoors.com, https://www.moodys.com, and http://www.fitchratings.com.
3. Learn more about the bond market and prices at https://learnbonds.com/ and www.investinginbonds.com.

10.3 DIFFERENT TYPES OF BONDS

An important attribute of a bond issue that affects its rating is the security, collateral, or assets that are pledged to back the bond issue. In the event the bond issuer defaults and misses a payment of coupon interest or principal, the collateral can be sold and distributed to the bond investors. It makes their investment in the issue more secure. There are a number of different types of bonds, each offering different levels of security to their investors.

Mortgage bonds, despite their name, are not secured by home mortgages. Rather, they are backed, or secured, by specifically pledged property of a firm. As a rule, the mortgage applies only to real estate, buildings, and other assets classified as real property. For a corporation that issues bonds to expand its plant facilities, the mortgage usually includes a lien, or legal claim, on the facilities to be constructed.

When a parcel of real estate has more than one mortgage lien against it, the first mortgage filed for recording at the appropriate government office – generally, the county recorder's office – has priority. The bonds outstanding against the mortgage are known as first mortgage bonds. The bonds outstanding against all mortgages subsequently recorded are known by the order in which they are filed, such as second or third mortgage bonds. Because first mortgage bonds have priority with respect to asset distribution if the business fails, they generally provide a lower yield to investors than the later liens.

An **equipment trust certificate** is a type of mortgage bond that gives the bondholder a claim to specific "rolling stock" (movable assets), such as railroad cars or airplanes. The serial numbers of the specific items of rolling stock are listed in the bond indenture and the collateral is periodically examined by the trustee to ensure its proper maintenance and repair.

There are two basic types of mortgage bonds. A **closed-end mortgage bond** does not permit future bond issues to be secured by any of the assets pledged as security under the closed-end issue. Alternatively, an **open-end mortgage bond** is one that allows the same assets to be used as security in future issues. As a rule, open-end mortgages usually stipulate that any additional real property acquired by the company automatically becomes a part of the property secured under the mortgage. This provides added protection to the lender.

Debenture bonds are unsecured obligations and depend on the general credit strength of the corporation for their security. They represent no specific pledge of property; their holders are classed as general creditors of the corporation equal with the holders of promissory notes and trade creditors. Debenture bonds are used by governmental bodies and by many industrial and utility corporations. The riskiest type of bond is a **subordinated debenture**. As the name implies, the claims of these

mortgage bonds backed, or secured, by specifically pledged property of a firm (real estate, buildings, and other assets classified as real property)

equipment trust certificate a type of mortgage bond that gives the bondholder a claim to specific "rolling stock" (movable assets), such as railroad cars or airplanes

closed-end mortgage bond does not permit future bond issues to be secured by any of the assets pledged as security under the closed-end issue

open-end mortgage bond allows the same assets to be used as security in future issues

debenture bonds unsecured obligations that depend on the general credit strength of the corporation for their security

subordinated debenture claims of these bonds are subordinate, or junior, to the claims of the debenture holders

---

[8] A fine point: the asked yield in the Treasury security quote will slightly understate the true yield to maturity (YTM). It is determined by computing the semi-annual yield given the coupon payments, ask price, and par value and then doubling it. To be exact, we would compound the semi-annual yield over two one-half-year periods. That is, if the reported Asked Yield is 1.95%, the computed semi-annual yield is 1.95/2, or 0.975%. Compounding this over two semi-annual periods gives a truer estimate of the YTM, $(1 + 0.00975)^2 − 1$, which equals 1.96%.

bondholders are subordinate, or junior, to the claims of debenture holders. Most junk bonds or high-yield bonds, which we discussed earlier, are subordinated debentures.

Another bond market innovation is "asset securitization." Securitization involves issuing bonds whose coupon and principal payments arise from another existing cash flow stream. Suppose a mortgage lender, by virtue of previously issued mortgages, has a steady cash flow stream coming into the firm from lenders making their mortgage payments. By selling bonds which use that cash flow stream as collateral, the mortgage banker can receive funds today rather than waiting for the mortgages to be paid off over time.[9] Principal and interest on the newly issued bonds will be paid by homeowners' mortgage payments. In essence, the mortgage payments will "pass through" the original mortgage lender to the investor who purchased the mortgage-backed securities. However, not all the interest payments are passed on; the mortgage lender will be paid a servicing fee from these cash flows to compensate them for collecting the mortgage payments and distributing them to the bondholders.

ETHICAL Securitization allows the original lender to reduce the risk exposure, as any homeowner defaults are a risk borne by the investor. In addition, the lender receives new funds, which can, in turn, form the basis for new loans and new issues of mortgage-backed securities. In 2007–2008, the agency issues of this arrangement became clearly known. It led to efforts to encourage loans of questionable quality ("subprime" mortgage loans), as the loans would be packaged and sold to others and the originator would reap a commission while selling these poor-quality loans.

Many other cash flow streams are amenable to securitization. Payment streams based on credit card receivables and auto loans have been packaged as bonds and sold to investors. Music artists who collect royalties from past recordings have taken advantage of securitization. In 1997, British rock star David Bowie initiated this trend by his involvement in a $55 million bond deal in which royalty rights from his past recordings were pooled and sold to investors. Interest on the bonds is paid by the royalty cash flow generated by compact disc, radio playtime and music, and ringtone downloads.[10] Other innovations include offering bonds backed by pools of insurance contracts. Interest on such bonds is paid from the policy premiums of the contract holders. Many times, however, these bonds have provisions for future payoffs that are affected by the occurrence of catastrophes such as hurricanes or earthquakes.[11] In 2018 Tesla sold $837 million in bonds that are use lease payments on Tesla's cars as security. The sale of these cars, when the leases expire, are another source of cash flow to repay bond investors.[12]

10.3.1 TIME TO MATURITY

A straight bond will have a set time to maturity. That is, it will pay coupon interest every six months until the bond matures, at which time the final interest payment is made and the bond's par value is paid to investors. But a variety of features can affect the bond's final maturity.

GLOBAL Geography can play a role. U.S. firms routinely issue bonds with 10 to 30-year maturities (and even longer in some instances). Bonds in the European market rarely extend their maturity past the seven to ten-year range, but this may change as European firms are accessing the capital markets more and rely on bank debt less for their longer-term financing needs.[13] Indeed, as interest rates have been quite low, some firms and governments are issuing very long-term bonds to "lock in" low interest rates. Norfork Southern (railroad), Électricité de France (a utility firm in France),

---

[9] Collateralized bonds pledge securities to protect bondholders against loss in case of default. An example of collateralized bonds is collateralized mortgage obligations (CMOs) sold by firms and agencies involved in the housing market. The CMO is backed by a pool of mortgages. Frank J. Fabozzi, *Fixed Income Analysis* (New Hope, PA; Frank J. Fabozzi Associates, 2000) and Frank J. Fabozzi with Steven V. Mann, ed., *The Handbook of Fixed-Income Securities*, 7th edition, (Chicago, IL: McGraw-Hill, 2005).

[10] Karen Richardson, "Bankers Hope For a Reprise of 'Bowie Bonds'" *The Wall Street Journal* (August 23, 2005), pp. C1, C3; anonymous, "Iron Maiden Bank Finishes $30 Million Sale of Bonds," *The Wall Street Journal* (February 9, 1999), p. C23. I.S.; "Bowie Ch-Ch-Changes the Market," *CFO* (April 1997); see also Patrick McGeehan, "Rock 'n' Roll Bonds Tap Investors' Faith in Future Royalties," *The Wall Street Journal* (February 10, 1998), p. C21.

[11] Patrick McGeehan, "Investment Banks Are Moving Fast to Offer Securities Backed by Pools of Insurance Policies," *The Wall Street Journal* (June 15, 1998), p. C4.

[12] Sam Goldfarb, "Tesla Wraps $837 Million Deal," *The Wall Street Journal* (December 15, 2018), page B2.

[13] Aline van Duyn, "Euro Corporate Bonds Give the Dollar a Run for its Money," *Financial Times* (June 29, 2001), p. 16.

Petrobras (Brazilian state oil company), and the government of Mexico have issued 100-year bonds in recent years.[14]

A convertible bond can be changed or converted, at the investor's option, into a specified number of shares of the issuer's common stock (defined as the bond's conversion ratio). The conversion ratio is set initially to make conversion unattractive. If the firm meets with success, however, its stock price will rise and the bond's price will be affected by its conversion value (the stock price times the conversion ratio) rather than its value as a straight bond. For example, suppose a firm has issued a $1,000 par value convertible bond. Its conversion ratio is 30 and the stock currently sells for $25 a share. The conversion value of the bond is 30 × $25/share or $750. It makes sense to hold onto the bond rather than convert a bond with a purchase price of about $1,000 into stock that is worth only $750. Should the stock's price rise to $40, the bond's conversion value will be 30 × $40/share or $1,200. Now it may be appropriate for investors to convert their bond into the more valuable shares. Why would a firm issue convertible bonds? Some may do so as way to raise equity at a time when the firm's stock or the overall stock market is out of favor. By selling convertible bonds, they can raise capital and erase the debt from their books when the bonds are converted after the stock price rises.

Callable bonds can be redeemed prior to maturity by the firm. Such bonds will be called and redeemed if, for example, a decline in interest rates makes it attractive for the firm to issue lower coupon debt to replace high coupon debt. A firm with cash from successful marketing efforts or a recent stock issue also may decide to retire its callable debt.

Most indentures state that, if called, a callable bond must be redeemed at its call price; typically, par value plus a call premium of one year's interest. Thus, to call a 12% coupon, $1,000 par value bond, an issuer must pay the bondholder $1,120.

Investors in callable bonds are said to be subject to call risk. Despite receiving the call price, investors are usually displeased when their bonds are called away. As bonds are typically called after a substantial decline in interest rates, the call eliminates their high coupon payments; investors will have to reinvest the proceeds in bonds that offer lower yields.

To attract investors, callable bonds must offer higher coupons or yields than noncallable bonds of similar credit quality and maturity. Many indentures specify a call deferment period immediately after the bond issue during which the bonds cannot be called.

Putable bonds (sometimes called retractable bonds) allow investors to force the issuer to redeem them prior to maturity. Indenture terms differ as to the circumstances when an investor can "put" the bond to the issuer prior to the maturity date and receive its par value. Some bond issues can be put only on certain dates. Others can be put to the issuer in case of a bond rating downgrade.[15] The put option allows the investor to receive the full face value of the bond, plus accrued interest. Since this protection is valuable, investors "pay" for it in the form of a lower coupon rate.

Extendable notes have their coupons reset every two or three years to reflect the current interest rate environment and any changes in the firm's credit quality. At each reset, the investor may accept the new coupon rate (and effectively extend the maturity of the investment) or put the bonds back to the firm.

An indenture may require the firm to retire the bond issue over time through payments to a sinking fund. A sinking fund requires the issuer to retire specified portions of the bond issue over time. This provides for an orderly and steady retirement of debt over time. Sinking funds are more common in bonds issued by firms with lower credit ratings. A higher-quality issuer may have only a small annual sinking fund obligation due to a perceived ability to repay investor's principal at maturity.

10.3.2 INCOME FROM BONDS

A typical bond will pay a fixed amount of interest each year over the bond's life. As we noted above, U.S. bonds pay interest semi-annually while Eurobonds pay interest annually.

convertible bond can be changed or converted, at the investor's option, into a specific number of shares of the issuer's common stock

conversion ratio number of shares into which a convertible bond can be converted

conversion value stock price times the conversion ratio

callable bond can be redeemed prior to maturity by the issuing firm

call price price paid to the investor for redemption prior to maturity, typically par value plus a call premium of one year's interest

call risk risk of having a bond called away and having to reinvest the proceeds at a lower interest rate

call deferment period specified period of time after the bond issue during which the bonds cannot be called

putable bonds (retractable bonds) allow the investor to force the issuer to redeem the bonds prior to maturity

extendable notes have their coupons reset every two or three years to reflect the current interest rate environment and any changes in the firm's credit quality; the investor can accept the new coupon rate or put the bonds back to the firm

sinking fund requirement that the issuer retire specified portions of the bond issue over time

---

[14] "PIMCO, Fidelity Stung by Collapse of Petrobras' 100-Year Bond," https://www.bloomberg.com/news/articles/2015-09-14/pimco-fidelity-stung-by-collapse-of-petrobras-s-100-year-bond (accessed July 15, 2019); Ralph Atkins, "Why Investors will make 100-year loans," *Financial Times* (June 4, 2015), https://www.ft.com/intl/cms/s/0/9d794036-09cd-11e5-a6a8-00144feabdc0.html#axzz3pVVxlLCF (accessed October 24, 2015); Mike Cherney, "Electricite de France Sells 100-Year Bonds," *The Wall Street Journal*, (January 14, 2014) https://www.wsj.com/articles/SB10001424052702303819704579319030410253894 (accessed October 24, 2015).

[15] Another way to offer protection in the face of a ratings downgrade is for the issue's coupon rate to rise to compensate for the higher credit risk.

Although most bonds pay a fixed coupon rate, some bonds have coupon payments that vary over time. The bond's indenture may tie coupon payments to an underlying market interest rate so that the interest payment will always be a certain level above, or will be a specified percentage of a market interest rate, such as the ten-year Treasury note rate. As of 2014, the U.S. Treasury has offered floating rate notes (or FRNs) to investors. The FRNs mature in two years and offer an interest rate that is tied to the three-month Treasury bill rate.[16] Others, such as the Deutsche Telekom bond issue mentioned above, will have a coupon rate that will increase if the bond's rating falls.

zero-coupon bond has no coupon payments; its only cash return to the investor is payment of the bond's principal, or par value, at maturity

Zero-coupon bonds pay no interest over the life of the bond. The investor buys the bond at a steep discount from its par value; the return to the investor over time is the difference between the purchase price and the bond's par value when it matures. A drawback to taxable investors is that the Internal Revenue Service (IRS) assumes interest is paid over the life of the bond so investors must pay tax on interest they don't receive. Because of these tax implications, zero-coupon bonds are best suited for tax-deferred investment accounts, such as individual retirement accounts (IRAs) or tax-exempt investment organizations, such as pension funds.

Why would an investor purchase a zero-coupon bond? Many bond investors have long-term time horizons before the invested funds are needed (to pay for a child's college education, personal retirement, or other financial goals). Such investors will not spend the bond's coupon interest when it is received; they will reinvest it in other securities. When these investors purchase regular bonds, they face the risk of not knowing what the return will be on the reinvested coupons over the life of the bond. Interest rates may rise, fall, or cycle up and down over the life of the investment. Zero-coupon bonds eliminate this uncertainty by, in essence, locking in the return (the difference between the price paid and the par value) when the bond is purchased.

Treasury Inflation Protected Securities U.S. Treasury debt with par value (and annual coupons) that rise with the official inflation rate each year

A large risk faced by bond investors is an unexpected change in inflation. An unexpected increase in inflation can cause lower real returns to an investor as the bond's fixed interest rate does not adjust to varying inflation. In 1997, the U.S. Treasury offered an innovation to investors in U.S. debt: **Treasury Inflation Protected Securities**.[17] They are issued in $1,000 minimum denominations and the principal value of the notes changes in accordance with changes in the consumer price index (CPI).[18]

Here's how Treasury Inflation Protected Securities (TIPS) work. Interest payments are computed based upon the inflation-adjusted principal value. In times of rising consumer prices, the principal value and interest payments rise in line with inflation. Should the CPI fall, the principal amount is reduced accordingly. As an example, suppose an inflation-indexed note with a $1,000 par value is sold at a 3% interest rate. If inflation over the next year is 4%, the principal value rises to $1,000 plus 4%, or $1,040. The annual interest payment will be 3% of $1,040; that is, $0.03 \times \$1,040$, or $31.20. With 4% inflation, the principal rises by 4% (from $1,000 to $1,040) as does the interest (from $30 to $31.20).

Although the principal is not paid until the note matures, the IRS considers the year-by-year change in principal as taxable income in the year in which the change in value is made. In the above example, the investor will pay taxes on $71.20, which is the sum of the $31.20 in interest received and the $40 increase in principal value. Because of this, these bonds will be most attractive to tax-exempt or tax-deferred investors, such as pension funds and individual IRA accounts.[19] To make the inflation protection more affordable to smaller investors, the U.S. Treasury now offers inflation-protected U.S. savings bonds.[20]

---

[16] Jason Zweig, "Floating a Few Cents to Investors," *The Wall Street Journal* (April 19, 2014), pp. B1, B7.

[17] Inflation-adjusted bonds have been offered by other countries for some time. For example, Israel first offered these securities in 1955, the UK in 1981, Australia in 1985, Canada in 1991, and Sweden in 1994.

[18] Because of the initial popularity of the inflation-adjusted T-notes, some federal agencies (Federal Home Loan Bank Board, Tennessee Valley Authority) have issued inflation-indexed notes as well.

[19] Gregory Zuckerman, "Inflation-Indexed Bonds Attract Fans," *The Wall Street Journal* (May 20, 1999), p. C1; Pu Shen, "Features and Risks of Treasury Inflation Protection Securities," *Federal Reserve Bank of Kansas City Economic Review* (first quarter, 1998), pp. 23–38.

[20] In addition, several corporations, such as Merrill Lynch, Morgan Stanley, Household International, Fannie Mae, and Sallie Mae, have issued inflation-protected bonds. Several banks, such as LaSalle Bank and Standard Federal Bank, have inflation-protected certificates of deposit. See Aaron Lucchetti, "Inflation Rears its Head . . . If Only on New Bond Issues," *The Wall Street Journal* (January 28, 2004), pp. C1, C4; Christine Richard, "Corporations, Banks Issue Debt With an Inflation-Wary Hook," *The Wall Street Journal* (September 24, 2003), p. C5.

Why are there so many variations in bondholder security, maturity, and income payouts among bond issues? For the same reason, there are different computers, carbonated beverages, and pizza; namely, to meet different needs in the market or, in the case of bonds, to meet the needs of different types of borrowers and lenders. Some borrowers reduce borrowing costs by offering lenders better collateral. Others want to maintain flexibility (or they have no collateral to offer), so they issue debentures and pay higher interest rates. From the lenders' perspective, zero-coupon bonds may be attractive as they eliminate reinvestment risk (the risk of reinvesting coupon income at lower interest rates). Similarly, sinking funds or call, put, or convertibility provisions are attractive to different investors in ever-changing market environments.

DISCUSSION QUESTION 2

If you were going to buy a bond, what characteristics would you want? Explain why.

10.4 CORPORATE EQUITY CAPITAL

Corporate equity capital is the financial capital supplied by the owners of a corporation. This ownership claim can be represented by a paper **stock certificate**, such as the one shown in Figure 10.3, although today most record keeping is done electronically. Shares are usually traded 100 shares at a time (called a "round lot") or multiples thereof. An "odd lot" is a trade involving less than 100 shares.

When stockholders sell their shares, the broker forwards the assigned stock certificate to the company and the secretary of the corporation destroys it. A new certificate is issued to the new owner, whose name will then be carried on the stock record. For larger corporations an official transfer agent, generally a trust company or a bank, is appointed for this task. The larger corporations may have an independent stock registrar to supervise the transfer of securities. When an investor sells stock, the stock certificate must be delivered to the stockbroker within two business days (called T + 2). When stock is purchased, adequate funds must be brought to the broker within three business days. As technology advances, so do regulations. In past years, the requirement was T + 5. It is now T + 2. Instantaneous settlement, called straight through processing (STP), will occur when all systems are electronically tied together.

corporate equity capital financial capital supplied by the owners of a corporation

stock certificate certificate showing an ownership claim of a specific company

FIGURE 10.3 Common stock certificate

street name allows stock to be held in the name of the brokerage house

Stock certificates can be kept in the owner's name and in his or her possession. Many investors find it convenient, however, to keep their stock holdings in street name. Stock held in street name is kept in the name of the brokerage house, but the broker's accounting system keeps track of dividends, proxy voting, and so on. Some investors find it convenient to keep shares in street name as there is then no need for the investor to safeguard the certificates, and delivery of the certificates within the T + 2 time frame is automatic.

Equity securities of the corporation may be grouped broadly into two classes: common stock and preferred stock. We discuss each below.

10.4.1 COMMON STOCK

common stock represents ownership shares in a corporation

Common stock (see Table 10.3) represents ownership shares in a corporation. Ownership gives common stockholders certain rights and privileges that bondholders do not have. Common shareholders can vote to select the corporation's board of directors. The board of directors, in turn, exercises general control over the firm. In addition to voting for the board, common shareholders may vote on major issues facing the firm, such as corporate charter changes and mergers.

The common shareholders have a claim on all business profits that remain after the holders of all other classes of debt and equity securities have received their coupon payments or returns. But the firm may wish to retain some of those profits to reinvest in the firm to finance modernization, expansion, and growth. When so declared by the board of directors, owners of a firm's common stock receive dividend payments. The dividend is typically a cash payment that allows shareholders to receive some income from their investment. To many investors, an attractive characteristic of common stock dividends is their potential to increase over time. As a firm achieves success, its profits should grow and the shareholders can expect to see the dollar amount of their dividends rise. Of course, success and growth are not guaranteed. A firm may experience poor earnings or losses, in which case shareholders bear the risk of smaller dividends or the elimination of dividend payments until the firm's financial situation improves.

The common stockholders have the lowest standing when a business venture is liquidated or fails. All creditors, bondholders, and preferred stockholders must, as a rule, be paid in full before common stockholders receive proceeds from liquidation. As with dividends, all bankruptcy or liquidation proceeds remaining after prior obligations are settled accrue to the common stockholders, but it is rare when the proceeds of an asset sale from a bankrupt corporation fulfill the claims of creditors and preferred stockholders. Common stockholders generally receive little, if anything, from liquidation proceedings. The common stockholders, therefore, are affected hardest by business failure just as they enjoy the primary benefits of business success.

par value (equity) stated value in the certificate of incorporation; for common stock, generally bears little relationship to the current price or book value of the share

The common stock of a corporation may be assigned a par value (equity), or stated value, in the certificate of incorporation. Unlike bonds, the par value of common stock usually bears little

TABLE 10.3   Elements of Common Stock

- **Represents an ownership claim**
- **Board of directors (board) oversees the firm on behalf of the shareholders and enforces the corporate charter**
- **Voting rights for board members and other important issues allowed by the corporate charter**
- **Lowest claim on assets and cash flow**
- **Par value is meaningless, and many firms have low or no-par stock**
- **Dividends:** Received only if declared by the firm's board

  Paid out from after-tax earnings and cash flow; not tax deductible

  Dividends are taxable when received by the shareholder

  Can vary over time
- **Maturity:** Never; stock remains in existence until firm goes bankrupt, merges with another firm, or is acquired by another firm

relationship to the current price or book value of the stock. It is used mainly for accounting purposes and some legal needs.[21]

Common stock may be divided into special groups, generally Class A and Class B, to permit the acquisition of additional capital without diluting the control of the business. When a corporation issues two classes of common stock, it will often give voting rights to only one class, generally Class B. Except for voting, owners of Class A stock will usually have most or all of the other rights and privileges of common stockholders. Issuing nonvoting equity securities is opposed by some government agencies, including the Securities and Exchange Commission (SEC) because it permits the concentration of ownership control. The New York Stock Exchange (NYSE) refuses to list the common stock of corporations that issue nonvoting classes of common stock.

At times, different stock classes are created following an acquisition of one corporation by another. For example, General Motors' Class E shares and Class H shares were issued in the past to help finance GM's acquisition of Electronic Data Systems (EDS) and Hughes Aircraft, respectively. The dividends on GM's Class E and H shares were related to the earnings of their respective subsidiary.

American depository receipts (ADRs) represent shares of common stock that trade on a foreign stock exchange. The receipts can be traded on U.S. exchanges. We'll learn more about ADRs in Chapter 11, Securities and Markets.

10.4.2 PREFERRED STOCK

Preferred stock (see Table 10.4) is an equity security that has a preference, or senior claim, to the firm's earnings and assets over common stock. Preferred shareholders must receive their fixed dividend before common shareholders can receive a dividend. In liquidation, the claims of the preferred shareholders are to be satisfied before common shareholders receive any proceeds. In contrast with common stock, preferred stock generally carries a stated fixed dividend. The dividend is specified as a percentage of par value or as a fixed number of dollars per year. For example, a preferred stock may be a 9% preferred, meaning that its annual dividend is 9% of its par or stated value. In such cases, unlike common stock, a preferred stock's par value does have important meaning, much like par value for a bond. The dividend for no-par preferred stock is stated in terms of a dollar amount, for example, preferred as to dividends in the amount of $9 annually. The holder of preferred stock accepts the limitation on the amount of dividends as a fair exchange for the priority held in the earnings and assets of the company.

Thus, unlike with common stock, the par value of a preferred stock is important. Dividends often are expressed as a percentage of par, and the par value represents the holder's claim on corporate assets

preferred stock equity security that has preference, or a senior claim, to the firm's earnings and assets over common stock

TABLE 10.4 Elements of Preferred Stock

- **Does not represent an ownership claim**
- **No voting rights unless dividends are missed**
- **Claim on assets and cash flow lies between those of bondholders (specifically, subordinated debenture holders) and common shareholders**
- **Par value is meaningful as it can determine the fixed annual dividend**
- **Dividends:** Annual dividends are stated as a dollar amount or as a percentage of par value

  Received only if declared by the firm's board

  Are paid out from after-tax earnings and cash flow; not tax deductible

  Taxable when received by the shareholder

  May be cumulative
- **Maturity:** Unless it has a callable or convertible feature, the stock never matures; it remains in existence until firm goes bankrupt, merges with another firm, or is acquired by another firm

---

[21] To show further that par value has little significance, consider that most states permit corporations to issue no-par stock.

in case of liquidation. Additionally, when shares of preferred stock are first issued, the initial selling price is frequently close to the share's par value.[22]

Because preferred stocks are frequently nonvoting, many corporations issue them as a means of obtaining equity capital without diluting the control of the current stockholders. Unlike coupon interest on bonds, the fixed preferred stock dividend is not a tax-deductible expense. A major source of preferred stock issues are regulated public utilities, such as gas and electric companies. For regulated firms, the nondeductibility of dividends is not as much of a concern as for other firms because the utilities' tax payments affect the rates they are allowed to charge.

For foreign firms to issue preferred stock, they must do so in the United States. The U.S. security markets are the only public financial markets in which preferred stock is sold.

Preferred stock may have special features. For example, it may be cumulative or noncumulative. **Cumulative preferred stock** requires that before dividends on common stock are paid, preferred dividends must be paid for the current period and for all previous periods in which preferred dividends were missed. Unlike debt holders, the preferred stockholders cannot force the payment of their dividends. They may have to wait until earnings are adequate to pay dividends. Cumulative preferred stock offers some protection for periods during which dividends are not declared.

Callable preferred stock gives the corporation the right to retire the preferred stock at its option. **Convertible preferred stock** has a special provision that makes it possible to convert it to common stock of the corporation, generally at the stockholder's option. This, like many of the special features that preferred stock may have, exists primarily to attract investors to buy securities at times when distribution would otherwise be difficult. Preferred stock that is cumulative and convertible is a popular financing choice for investors purchasing shares of stock in small firms with high growth potential.

Participating preferred stock allows preferred shareholders to participate with common shareholders when larger dividend payouts are available. Holders get a larger dividend, if sufficient earnings exist and if common shareholders will be getting a dividend larger than the preferred shareholders. It is a rarely used feature except in some private equity and venture capital investments.

The one tax advantage of preferred stock goes to corporate investors who purchase another firm's preferred. When one corporation buys stock of another firm, 70% of the dividend income received by the corporation is exempt from taxes. Thus, for every $100 of dividend income, only $30 is taxable to an investing corporation.

cumulative preferred stock requires that before dividends on common stock are paid, preferred dividends must be paid for the current period and for all previous periods in which preferred dividends were missed

callable preferred stock gives the corporation the right to retire the preferred stock at its option

convertible preferred stock has a special provision that makes it possible to convert it to common stock of the corporation, generally at the stockholder's option

participating preferred stock allows preferred shareholders to receive a larger dividend under certain conditions when common shareholder dividends increase

---

DISCUSSION QUESTION 3

Knowing what we know so far about bonds, common stock, and preferred stock, which characteristics do you like about each? Which type of security would you want to invest in today?

10.4.3 READING STOCK QUOTES

Information on stock prices is available from a number of print resources (such as *The Wall Street Journal* and other newspapers with financial sections) and the Internet. Figure 10.4 illustrates the stock quotation information that is available on these print and online resources.

The information from print sources reflects trading that occurred on the previous business day; online information can reflect current trading information but with a 15–20-minute delay in reporting. Information, such as that presented in Figure 10.4, is available on stock prices, recent trends or volatility in prices, the dividend paid by the company, and its earnings per share.

For example, Figure 10.4 shows an example using Microsoft's ticker symbol, MSFT. Tickers are shorthand notation for a stock. Rather than keying in a firm's full name many times, only the ticker needs be entered to obtain information. Microsoft's stock is traded on the National Association of Securities Dealers Automated Quotation (NASDAQ), an over-the-counter (OTC) exchange we'll discuss in Chapter 11. In the example shown, the most recent trade for Microsoft stock was for $52.87 a share. If

---

[22] A recent innovation is *hybrid capital*, a security that is considered equity for accounting purposes but whose payments to security holders are tax-deductible to the firm. Thus, it appears to be a perfect combination of the advantages of equity and debt. The details of issuing such capital can be difficult and involve aspects of accounting treatment, securities law, and bank regulation and are, therefore, beyond the scope of our discussion.

Firm Name: Microsoft	Ticker: MSFT
Market: NASDAQ	52 week range: $39.72 – 54.07
Last Trade: $52.87	Volume (1000s): 135,227
Change: 1.15	P/E: 35.72
	Dividend: $1.44
	Dividend Yield: 2.72%

FIGURE 10.4   Sample stock quotation information

a round lot (100 shares) was purchased at this price the cost of purchasing the shares would be $52.87 × 100 shares = $5,287 plus any commissions. The price of Microsoft stock rose $1.15 cents from the end of the previous trading day; that means the closing, or final, price of the previous trading day was $1.15 lower; namely, $52.87 − 1.15 = $51.72. If only the price of the final trade of the day is reported (as may be the case for newspaper listings), it will appear under the label of "close" to represent the day's closing price for the stock.

Looking at the information in the second column, we see that Microsoft's stock price has varied over the past 52 weeks from a low price of $39.72 to a high of $54.07. This wide range (about 36% of the low price) is common. Review for yourself the 52-week ranges of different stocks from a current issue of *The Wall Street Journal*. Many stocks may have 52-week ranges where the high price is double that of the low price.

The previous trading day, approximately 135,227,000 shares of Microsoft stock were traded. Many times in print media the volume is printed in terms of 1,000s (135227) or 100s (1352270) to save space.

The row labeled "P/E" gives the price/earnings ratio of the stock. It represents how many dollars investors are willing to pay for every one dollar of per-share earnings. Sometimes the P/E ratio is called the "earnings multiple" ratio because of this. The P/E ratio is computed by dividing the firm's latest annual earnings per share into its current stock price. Newspaper stock listings report only integer values of P/E ratios, so they would list Microsoft's P/E ratio as 36. Using the stock's price and the P/E ratio, we can compute an estimate Microsoft's earnings per share (EPS):

Price/EPS = 35.72 = ($52.87)/EPS; so our approximation for annual EPS is $1.48.

Next, the table lists the 12-month dividend paid by the firm; in this sample listing, Microsoft pays dividends at an annual rate of $1.44 per share to its owners. The final piece of information in the table is the dividend yield of the stock. The dividend yield is calculated as the stock's annual dividend divided by its current price. Since the current price is $52.87, the dividend yield is $1.44/$52.87, or 2.72%. In most listings this may be rounded to 2.7%.

Dots (. . .) or "NA" will appear as the dividend or dividend yield for some stocks. This indicates that the firm did not pay dividends in the previous 12 months. Similarly, lack of a number for the firm's P/E ratio indicates a firm with a negative net income.

As we saw earlier in this chapter, bonds have different characteristics with respect to time to maturity, coupon income payouts, callable, put options, and so forth. With only a few exceptions, equity has fewer variations. Except for some variations across preferred equity issues (callable, participating, or convertible) or different voting rights and dividend rights for common stock, there are not many variations of publicly traded equity issues.

LEARNING ACTIVITY

Get stock price quotes online and learn more about stock investing at https://www.fool.com, https://www.finance.yahoo.com, https://www.marketwatch.com.

The process of paying coupon interest on bonds is rather straightforward; it is a legally required payment under the terms of the bond's indenture. Only when a firm contacts the trustee that it will be unable to pay the required interest because of financial difficulty does the process become complex and legalistic.

10.5 DIVIDENDS AND STOCK REPURCHASES

Dividends, as we've learned, are not a legal obligation of the firm and may be skipped, decreased, increased, stopped, and started according to the collective wisdom of the corporation's board of directors. When they are paid, they are typically paid on a quarterly basis, four times over the course of a year.

Many firms offer shareholders the choice to receive a check for the amount of their dividends or to reinvest the dividends in the firm's stock. Dividend reinvestment plans (DRIPs) allow shareholders to purchase additional shares automatically with all or part of the investor's dividends. Fractional shares can be purchased and DRIP purchases have no or low commissions.

Suppose an investor owns sufficient shares to receive $10 in dividends on a stock from its quarterly declared dividend. If the stock price is $25, the DRIP program allows the investor to purchase $10/$25, or a 0.40 share of the firm's stock. If the stock price is $8, the investor's reinvested dividends will purchase $10/$8 or 1.25 shares of the stock.

If the investor favors the stock and wants to continue holding it, participating in a DRIP is an easy way of purchasing additional shares over time without any direct cash outlay. It allows income returns to be reinvested to facilitate compounding returns over time. However, as with all dividends, the declared dividend is taxable as income. Whether the dividends are received as cash or reinvested, the investor must pay taxes on them.

dividend reinvestment plans (DRIPs) allow shareholders to purchase additional shares automatically with all or part of the investor's dividends

10.5.1 HOW DO FIRMS DECIDE ON THE DOLLAR AMOUNT OF DIVIDENDS?

dividend payout ratio dividends per share divided by earnings per share (EPS)

Most firms that issue dividends try to maintain a consistent dividend payout ratio, which is dividends per share divided by earnings per share (EPS). The dividend payout ratio for our example, Microsoft, using the information from Figure 10.4 and our calculations, is its dividend of $1.44 per share divided by our calculation of earnings per share, $1.48:

$$\text{Dividend payout ratio} = \$1.44/\$1.48 = 0.97 \text{ or } 97\%$$

This is quite high. If this were the case, Microsoft likely expects its earnings to rise in the coming year. Rare is the firm that wants to continually return all of its earnings to shareholders as dividends; typically, funds are retained to finance growth and expansion.

How about the case of a firm that wants to start paying dividends? Microsoft's decision to start paying dividends in 2003 was prompted by its cash balance of $48 billion. Its decision to pay a special dividend totaling $30 billion to shareholders in 2004 arose as its cash balance had grown to $60 billion. Suffice it to say, most firms that initiate dividends do not generate as much cash as does Microsoft. Several firms raised dividends or accelerated dividend payments in late 2012 because they feared an increase in dividend tax rates due to the expiration of the Bush tax cuts.[23]

A key component of the "how much?" decision is what level of dividends is sustainable over time? A firm does not want to announce it will begin paying dividends and then have to reduce or eliminate the dividend at a later time due to the need to conserve cash. Dividends are thought to send a signal to investors about management's view of the future cash-generating ability of the firm. Managers and the board of directors have private information about the strategies, competitive responses, and opportunities facing the firm that are not known to the investing public. Thus, if the firm increases dividends, that is a positive signal or indicator to the financial markets that management believes the future looks stable, or improving, for the firm. A reduction in dividends is taken to be a pessimistic indicator of the firm's future, so firms set dividend levels so future reductions are unlikely given their current perspective on the firm's future. Studies have indicated that U.S. firms are increasing their dividends to their shareholders and reducing spending on new assets and research. This may be a danger sign for future profitability as future profits (and dividends) will be created from new products and innovation.[24]

---

[23] Dana Mattioli and Alexandra Berzon, "Dividends Come Early To Avoid Fiscal Cliff," *The Wall Street Journal* (November 27, 2012), page B1.
[24] Vipal Monga, David Benoit, and Theo Francis, "Companies Send More Cash Back to Shareholders," *The Wall Street Journal* (May 27, 2015), pp. A1, A10.

Most firms that start paying dividends will do so at a rather low level, perhaps just a penny a share. The fact that management and the board are sufficiently confident to issue a dividend is a positive signal to the financial markets. As the firm generates more cash, the firm will increase its dollar amount of dividends per share as well as its dividend payout ratio. After a while, the firm will determine a "target" dividend payout ratio that it seeks to maintain over time. However, dividends will not automatically rise along with earnings. If future earnings rise, dividends will not increase until the board feels the higher level of earnings are sustainable. (Remember, firms do not want to ever cut the dollar amount of the dividends per share if they can avoid it.) If the higher earnings appear to be sustainable, the firm will adjust the dividends per share accordingly toward the "target" dividend payout ratio.[25] Some call this the **target dividend payout policy**.

Some firms follow a different dividend strategy of consistently paying a low regular dividend but declaring a **special dividend** when times are particularly good. For a firm in a cyclical industry, with highly variable sales and earnings, this may be a strategy to conserve cash during industry recessions while maintaining the low but stable regular dividend. Shareholders are rewarded when rising earnings allow the company to declare an extra or special dividend. While such a dividend policy may help management control their cash balance, investors, who generally prefer certainty to uncertainty, do not favor such a strategy.

Other dividend payment strategies suffer from the same drawback of creating investor uncertainly due to variable dividend levels. The **residual dividend policy** states that dividends will vary based upon how much excess funds the firm has from year to year. Under a **constant payout ratio** strategy, the firm pays a constant percentage of earnings as dividends; as earnings rise and fall, so does the dollar amount of dividends. Please note that this is not the same as the target payout policy. The firm adjusts dividends around the target over time, depending on earnings sustainability; during some years, the actual payout ratio will exceed the target, and during others, it will be under it in order to have stable, predictable changes in dividends. The constant payout ratio maintains the payout ratio at the expense of a varying dollar amount of dividends per share.

The board of directors and management will consider several factors as they examine the level of dividend payout. Some of these factors are the following:

- Ability of the firm to generate cash to sustain the level of dividends. Recall that investors react badly to reductions in dividends. If a dividend level is thought to be unsustainable, the firm's stock price will fall as investors sell the stock.

- Legal and contractual considerations. Dividends, when they are paid, reduce a firm's equity. A firm cannot pay dividends if doing so will reduce the firm's equity below the par value of the common stock. In addition, a bond's indenture (or loan agreement with a bank) may restrict the dollar amount of dividends to ensure adequate cash is available to pay loan interest and principal.

- Growth opportunities. Growing firms require capital, and they will likely want to reinvest all profits into the company to finance expansion and move into new products or markets. Growing firms may seek additional funds from loans, bond issues, and new issues of stock. It is unlikely firms facing growth opportunities will want to initiate or significantly increase their dividends.

- Cost of other financing sources. Dividends are paid, for the most part, from internally generated funds, meaning cash that remains after the firm's bills, interest, and taxes are paid. If a firm has the ability to easily raise low-cost external financing sources, it will be better able to maintain a higher level of dividends. Firms that can raise outside financing by paying high interest rates or by issuing new shares of stock will likely have lower levels of dividends.

- Tax rates. Prior to 2003, dividend income was viewed as unattractive by some investors. Why? Because dividend income was taxed as income, at the investors' marginal income tax rate, which

target dividend payout policy a policy of adjusting the dividend payout ratio toward the target dividend payout ratio if the higher earnings appear to be sustainable

special dividend an extra dividend declared by the firm over and above its regular dividend payout

residual dividend policy a policy that states that dividends will vary based upon how much excess funds the firm has from year to year

constant payout ratio a strategy in which the firm pays a constant percentage of earnings as dividends; as earnings rise and fall, so does the dollar amount of dividends

---

[25] Discussions of dividend policy theories and practice are available in Julio Brandon and David L. Ikenberry, "Reappearing Dividends," *Journal of Applied Corporate Finance* (Fall 2004), 16 (4), pp. 89–100 and Alon Brav, John R. Graham, Campbell R. Harvey, and Roni Michaely, "Payout Policy in the 21st Century" (April 2003). NBER Working Paper No. W9657. Available at SSRN: http://ssrn.com/abstract=398560.

exceeded 30% (combined federal and state tax rates) for many. But the Jobs and Growth Tax Relief Reconciliation Act of 2003 reduced the top federal tax rate on dividends from 38 to 15%, the same as the top rate on long-term capital gains. Although surveys of financial officers indicate that tax rates are not a first-order concern when setting dividends, on the aggregate, firms markedly increased dividends after the law was passed. As noted above, President Obama's desire for the top dividend tax rate of 15% to rise to 39.6% caused some firms to accelerate their early 2013 dividend payments into late 2012.

In addition to giving cash dividends to shareholders, the firm's board of directors can announce other decisions, such as a stock dividend or stock split, that, at first glance, appear to give extra shares and wealth to shareholders. In reality, as we shall see in the next section, their effect on the value of a firm's stock and the wealth of shareholders is zero. But the board can make one other decision with respect to the firm's shares that will positively affects shareholders: a stock buyback or share repurchase program. We'll examine stock dividends, splits, and repurchases next.

10.5.2 STOCK DIVIDENDS AND STOCK SPLITS

stock dividend a dividend in which investors receive shares of stock rather than cash

A stock dividend is what it sounds like: a dividend paid with shares of stock rather than cash. Rather than mention a dollar figure, the announcement will state that the firm is distributing a 5% (or "X" per-cent) stock dividend. But a stock dividend has no net effect on the wealth of the shareholders. To see why, consider the following.

Suppose CUL8R Incorporated stock is currently priced at $10 a share, and there are 100,000 shares outstanding; the total market value of the firm is $10 × 100,000 or $1 million. Suppose you own 1,000 shares, meaning you own 1% of the shares outstanding and the value of your holdings is $10 × 1,000 shares or $10,000. CUL8R's board has declared a 10% stock dividend, so now you own 1,100 shares.

Are you any richer? The answer is no; you still own 1% of the shares outstanding, and the value of your CUL8R holdings is still $10,000. You own 1,100 shares, but the number of shares outstanding is 10% larger, too. There are 110,000 total shares, and you own 1% of this total. Nothing has happened to the value or the earnings ability of the firm with this paper transaction, so the firm's stock price will fall and will equal $1 million/110,000 shares, or approximately $9.09. There are some accounting entries that will affect the firm's equity account, but the total amount of equity in the accounting statements will remain the same.[26] The bottom line is a stock dividend distributes nothing to shareholders and removes nothing from the firm. No value is transferred.

stock split a process in which the firms distributes additional shares for every share owned

A stock split has a similar effect. The firm distributes extra shares for every share owned in a stock split. For example, a firm may announce a two-for-one stock split; this has the effect of doubling the number of shares outstanding and doubling the holdings of each investor, but as in the case of a stock dividend, the net effect on investor wealth is zero. You may own twice as many shares, but the stock price will be cut in half, leaving your ownership stake (both in terms of value and percentage owned) the same as it was before the stock split. Occasionally, a firm will announce a "reverse split" in which multiple shares are combined to form one new share. For example, a one-for-four reverse split means four old shares are equal to one new share. When this happens, the stock price will change so again the investor's wealth remains the same.

You may have noted that there is not much of a difference between a stock split and a stock dividend. They involve paper transactions in which the number of shares is increased but prices adjust downward to maintain investor wealth at a constant level. In terms of accounting, a distribution of five shares for four (a 25% stock dividend) is considered to be a stock split; a distribution of less than five for four (less than a 25% stock dividend) is considered to be a stock dividend.[27]

---

[26] The firm's combined value of its par value and additional paid-in capital accounts will rise by the market value of the stock dividend but the firm's retained earnings account will decline by this account, so the firm's equity account remains constant.

[27] There is a distinction in what happens to the equity account in the case of a stock split. For a stock split, the only change is to the number of shares outstanding and to the stock's par value (if any). None of the dollar amounts in the equity accounts change. So, if a firm has 100,000 shares outstanding of $1 par value stock and it announces a two-for-one stock split, the number of share outstanding becomes 200,000 and the par value becomes $0.50.

10.5.3 SHARE REPURCHASES

Rather than distribute funds to shareholders in the form of earnings, a firm can repurchase its shares. Why would a firm repurchase its shares of stock? A firm doing a small purchase (relative to the total amount of shares outstanding) can acquire shares used in management stock option incentive programs, in which managers can purchase shares of stock at pre-specified prices (more will be said about this Chapter 13, Business Organization and Financial Data). Other firms purchase shares of their own stock to use in stock-based acquisitions of other firms. That is, they repurchase shares from current shareholders and then distribute them to owners of a newly acquired firm.

A major reason for doing this is to reward longer-term shareholders by enhancing the value of the firm's shares. Increases in stock prices are not taxed until the shares are sold, and if the shares have been held longer than one year, the maximum tax on the increase in value (called a capital gain) is 15% for most investors. This tax savings is thought to be a major reason by some researchers for the increase in stock repurchases in recent years.

Another reason for stock repurchases is that the firm has the cash and sees its own stock as one of its most attractive investment alternatives. Rather than investing in expanding the business to new markets, the firm's board of directors and top managers believe the firm's stock is undervalued and offers potential returns. The stock can be purchased at what is perceived to be a low price and re-issued later, after the stock price rises. This is a firm "putting its money where its mouth is." This was a popular reason given for stock repurchases during the 2000–2002 stock market decline. On the other hand, it is an indicator that management is doing a poor job in identifying new corporate strategies for increasing the stock's value.

The following section applies the Chapter 9 time-value-of-money principles to expected cash flows from bond and equity investments. The process of valuation is important to business managers considering ways to issue securities as well as to investors who must make security buy and sell decisions.

DISCUSSION QUESTION 4

As a stock investor, what dividend policy would you like your investment firms to follow? Or would you prefer share repurchases? Explain your preference.

In Chapter 9, we learned how to find the present value (PV) of a series of future cash flows. The present value represents the current worth of the future cash flows. In other words, it represents the price someone would be willing to pay today to receive the expected future cash flows. For example, we saw an investor would be willing to pay $2,577 to receive a three-year annuity of $1,000 at an 8% discount rate.	**10.6 VALUATION PRINCIPLES**

All securities are valued on the basis of the cash inflows that they are expected to provide to their owners or investors. Thus, mathematically, we have two equations:

$$\text{price} = \frac{CF_1}{(1+r)^1} + \frac{CF_2}{(1+r)^2} + \frac{CF_3}{(1+r)^3} + \cdots + \frac{CF_n}{(1+r)^n} \tag{10.1}$$

or

$$\text{price} = \sum_{t=1}^{n} \frac{CF_t}{(1+r)^t} \tag{10.1a}$$

The maximum price we should be willing to pay equals the present value of expected cash flows. Recall from Chapters 8 and 9 that the r represents the appropriate discount rate or the rate of return required by investors. For securities with no default risk (such as Treasury bonds), the r reflects the combination of the real risk-free rate and expected inflation as measured by the nominal risk-free interest rate. For securities with default risk, such as the bonds and stocks issued by corporations, the r represents a nominal risk-free rate (that is, the Treasury bill rate) plus a premium to reflect default risk.

For illustration purposes, let's assume that a security is expected to pay its owner $100 per year for five years. Let's also assume that investors expect a 10% annual compound rate of return on this investment. The 10% rate is based on a risk-free rate of 6% plus a 4% default risk premium. What should be the security's current or present value?

The answer can be determined by using present value (PV) tables, a financial calculator, or a computer software program. For example, using Table 2 (Present Value of $1) in the book's Appendix, we can identify the appropriate present value interest factors (PVIF) at 10% as follows:

Year	Cash flow	×	PVIF @ 10%	=	Present value
1	$100		0.909		$90.90
2	100		0.826		82.60
3	100		0.751		75.10
4	100		0.683		68.30
5	100		0.621		62.10
					price = $379.00

Thus, the current or present value of the security at a 10% discount rate should be $379.

Notice how the table above resembles a spreadsheet. Indeed, spreadsheets are powerful tools for developing models to evaluate bonds and stocks. Using Excel, we can create a table to do this calculation:

	A	B	C	D
1				
2	Interest rate:	10%		
3	Number of years:	5		
4				
5	Year	Cash Flow	PVIF	Present Value
6	1	$100	0.909	$90.91
7	2	$100	0.826	$82.64
8	3	$100	0.751	$75.13
9	4	$100	0.683	$68.30
10	5	$100	0.621	$62.09
11				$379.08

The PVIF formula in cell C6 is = 1/(1+B2)^A6. In cell C6, the PVIF is computed as $1/(1 + 0.10)^1$, or 0.909 (to three decimal places). In cell C7, the interest rate remains the same, but the exponent changes to reflect the fact that the cash flow (CF) is discounted back two years: = 1/(1 + B2)^A7. The spreadsheet calculates this as $1/(1 + 0.10)^2$, or 0.826. We use the SUM function to add the numbers in cell D11: = SUM(D6:D10).

Of course, since the security's cash flow reflects a $100 five-year annuity, we could have used Table 4 (Present Value of a $1 Ordinary Annuity) in the book's Appendix to determine the security's present value as follows:

$$\text{price} = \text{cash flow annuity} \times \text{PVIFA} @ 10\%$$
$$= \$100 \times 3.791$$
$$= \$379.10$$

PVIFA refers to the present value interest factor of an annuity. Notice that there is a slight rounding error due to the use of three-digit tables.

The security's present value of cash flow can also be determined by using a financial calculator as follows. First, clear the calculator's memory. Next, enter 100 (or −100 depending on the calculator) using the annuity or payments (PMT) key. Enter 10 and press the %i key (some calculators use a key labeled as I/Y). Enter 5 and press the N key. Finally, press the compute (CPT) key followed by the present value (PV) key to calculate the security's current value of $379.08. (Note: some calculators will compute the PV just by pressing the PV key – you'll want to refer to your specific financial calculator's instructions for details).

Financial Calculator Solution:

Inputs: 5   10   −100

          [N]   [%i]   [PMT]

Press: [CPT]   [PV]

Solution: 379.08

Excel's PV function can compute the present value of an annuity, too. Recall the PV function has the following form: PV (periodic interest rate, number of periods, payment, future value, type). To solve for this five-year annuity, we can use the Excel spreadsheet:

Microsoft Excel

File Edit View Insert Format Tool

A10

	A	B	C
1	Interest rate:	10%	
2	Number of years:	5	
3	Cash flow	$100	
4			
5	Present value of the annuity:	-$379.08	
6			
7			
8			
9			
10			
11			

The Excel function in cell B5 will be = PV(B1,B2,B3,0,0). Cell B1 contains the interest rate; the number of years in the annuity, "5," is found in cell B2; and the periodic annuity payment, $100, is in cell B3. The desired future savings (future value) is zero for the current problem. Since we are computing a regular annuity, we can omit the final item or enter "0" in the final position. The Excel PV function returns a negative number. Recalling the cash flow (CF) diagrams from Chapter 9, if the $100 annuity represents cash inflows to an investor, the present value (PV) must represent an outflow; namely, the price an investor is willing to pay to receive a five-year annuity of $100. By convention, cash outflows are negative numbers and inflows are positive. Should you prefer not to have a negative PV number, simply insert a negative sign before the PV command, = -PV(B1,B2,B3,0,0), so the spreadsheet returns a positive present value:

Microsoft Excel

File Edit View Insert Format Too

B6

	A	B	C
1	Interest rate:	10%	
2	Number of years:	5	
3	Cash flow	$100	
4			
5	Present value of the annuity:	$379.08	
6			
7			

Now we can determine the values of bonds. Conceptually, bond valuation is similar to many of the PV examples covered in Chapter 9.

10.7 VALUATION OF BONDS	Corporate and government bonds usually provide for periodic payments of interest plus the return of the amount borrowed or par value when the bond matures. Equation 10.1 can be modified to incorporate these bond cash flows.

10.7.1 DETERMINING A BOND'S PRESENT VALUE

The value of a bond with annual coupon payments can be expressed as follows:

$$\text{Price} = \text{PV (expected future cash flows)} \quad \text{or}$$

$$\text{price} = \frac{c_1}{(1+r_b)^1} + \frac{c_2}{(1+r_b)^2} + \frac{c_3}{(1+r_b)^3} + \ldots + \frac{c_n}{(1+r_b)^n} + \frac{Par_n}{(1+r_b)^n} \tag{10.2}$$

Which is equal to,

$$\text{price} = \sum_{t=1}^{n} \frac{c_t}{(1+r_b)^t} + \frac{Par_n}{(1+r_b)^n} \tag{10.2a}$$

Or, in words,

$$\text{price} = \text{PV (coupons)} + \text{PV (principal or par value)}$$

where

Price = the bond's value now or in period zero,

C = the coupon payment,

Par = the bond's principal amount,

r_b = the rate of return required by investors on this quality or risk-class of bonds, given its bond rating; if coupons are paid semi-annually, this is the semi-annual required rate of return.

In words, we use both equation 9.7 (present value of an annuity) and equation 9.3 (present value of a single amount) to compute a bond's price. We first find the present value of the bond's expected coupon payments. Note that if the coupon payments are the same over time, this means we need to find the present value of an annuity. Second, we compute the present value of the bond's principal payment. Third, we add these two present values together to find the bond's price. The result is the bond's **intrinsic value** – that is, the maximum price we should be willing to pay for an asset. The intrinsic value represents our best estimate of the true economic value of an asset based upon a forecast of future cash flows and an estimate of the appropriate discount rate.

A point to watch for is the type of bond we are dealing with; Eurobonds pay coupon interest once a year, whereas American bonds pay interest twice a year, delivering one-half of the annual coupon to bondholders every six months. Thus, for American bonds, we need to adjust the calculation of equation (10.2a) for semi-annual cash flows. In this circumstance, n, the number of periods, equals

> **intrinsic value** the maximum price we should be willing to pay for an asset; the best estimate of the true economic value of an asset based upon a forecast of future cash flows and an estimate of the appropriate discount rate

$$n = 2 \times \text{the number of years until maturity}$$

And the required rate of return, r_b, is the semi-annual return. If the market interest rate is given as an annual percentage rate (APR), the semi-annual return is

$$\text{semi-annual interest rate} = \text{market rate}/2$$

Sometimes the APR is also called a stated annual rate.

If the market rate is given as 10%, stated as the APR, the semi-annual rate is 10%/2 or 5%.

If the semi-annual interest rate is known, the annual rate is found by doubling it:

$$\text{Annual percentage rate (APR)} = \text{semi-annual rate} \times 2$$

As an example, if we compute or are told that a bond's periodic semi-annual return is 3%, the APR on the bond is 3% × 2, or 6%.[28]

Most corporate bonds are issued in $1,000 denominations. To illustrate how a corporate bond's value is calculated, let's assume that a bond with $1,000 face value has a coupon rate of 8% and a ten-year life before maturity. Thus an investor will receive $80 ($1,000 × 0.08) annually; for U.S. corporate bonds, one-half of this annual amount, $40, will be paid every six months with the $1,000 paid at the end of ten years. We determine the bond's present value based on the interest rate required by investors on similar quality bonds. Let's assume investors require an 8% rate of return on bonds of similar quality.

With semi-annual coupons, the number of periods is 20 (2 × 10 years) and the periodic (in this case, semi-annual) interest rate is

$$\text{semi-annual interest rate} = \text{market rate} / 2 = 8\% / 2 = 4.0\%, \text{or } 0.04$$

We need to discount the $40 coupon annuity portion of the bond at the PVIFA at 4% for 20 periods, which is 13.590 (see Table 4 in the book's Appendix). Since the $1,000 principal will be received only at the end of 20 periods, we use 0.456, the PVIF at 4% for 20 years from Table 2 in the Appendix.[29]

Taking these together, we have

$$\$40 \times 13.590 = \$543.60$$
$$\$1,000 \times 0.456 = \underline{456.00}$$
$$\text{Bond value} = \$999.60$$

Note that an exact answer for the bond's value is $1,000; the calculation above is off slightly due to rounding error as the tables use only three decimal places. Had we used four or five decimal places for the interest factor, the final answer would be closer to $1,000. The value of the bond is based upon investors' requirement of a stated annual rate of 8% on bonds of this maturity and risk.

Rather than use tables, we can compute bond prices using a financial calculator's functions or spreadsheets. The spreadsheet format below shows the price of the above bond is $1,000.00:

	A	B	C	D	E
1					
2	Computing Bond Price using APR (annual percentage rate)				
3	Coupon rate	8.00%			
4	Number of years until maturity	10.00			
5	Number of coupon payments per year	2.00			
6	Par value	$1,000.00			
7	Market rate	8.00%	(APR)		
8					
9	Compute periodic interest rate:	4.00%	equals B7 / 2		
10	Compute number of periods:	20.00	equals B4 * B5		
11	Compute coupon cash flow:	$40.00	equals (B3 *B6)/B5		
12					
13	Bond price		$1,000.00	equals -PV(B9, B10, B11, B6, 0)	
14					
15					

---

[28] Do you have a credit card? By law, credit card interest rates are quoted on an annual percentage rate (APR) basis. Next time you get your credit card statement, read it over to see the monthly interest rate and the APR. If your monthly interest rate is 1.5%, the APR on the credit card is 18% (1.5% × 12 months). In general, APR = periodic rate × number of periods in a year.

For U.S. bonds, the periodic rate is a semi-annual rate, and the number of periods in a year is two. For a credit card, the periodic rate is a monthly rate and the number of periods in a year is 12.

If you were being charged interest on a weekly basis of 0.5%, the APR would be (0.5% × 52) which equals 26% as we multiply the weekly interest rate by the number of weeks in a year.

[29] For bonds paying semi-annual coupons, we must not think in terms of the number of years but rather the number of periods. Because the 4% periodic rate of return is a semi-annual rate, we use 20 semi-annual periods of time in both the coupon and par value present value calculations.

Suppose that investors required a 10% return, or yield, on bonds of similar quality and maturity. The 8% coupon bond must then fall in price to compensate for the fact that only $80 in annual interest is received by the investor. A market return of 10 percent corresponds to a semi-annual return of 10%/2 = 5%, or 0.05. The appropriate discount factors at 5% for 20 years from Tables 2 and 4 in the Appendix would be

$$40 \times 12.462 = \$498.48$$
$$\$1,000 \times 0.377 = \underline{377.00}$$
$$\text{Bond value} = \$875.48$$

Using the above spreadsheet and changing the market rate value of cell B7 from 8% to 10%, we easily find the new price of the bond, $875.38. The spreadsheet's price is more accurate as interest factors from the financial tables are rounded to only three decimal places. The benefit of this calculation with spreadsheets is clear; once we appropriately design the spreadsheet, we can change our inputs or assumptions and see the effect on the bond's price.

	A	B	C	D	E
1					
2	Computing Bond Price using APR (annual percentage rate)				
3	Coupon rate	8.00%			
4	Number of years until maturity	10.00			
5	Number of coupon payments per year	2.00			
6	Par value	$1,000.00			
7	Market rate	10.00%	(APR)		
8					
9	Compute periodic interest rate:	5.00%	equals B7 / 2		
10	Compute number of periods:	20.00	equals B4 * B5		
11	Compute coupon cash flow:	$40.00	equals (B3 *B6)/B5		
12					
13	Bond price	$875.38	equals -PV(B9, B10, B11, B6, 0)		
14					
15					

Thus, an investor would be willing to pay about $875 (rounded) for the bond. Although annual coupon payment remains at $80, a new investor would earn a 10% return because she or he would pay only $875.38 now and get back $1,000 at the end of ten years. A bond that sells below par value, such as this one, is said to be selling at a *discount* and is called a discount bond. Someone who purchases this discount bond today and holds it to maturity will receive, in addition to the stream of coupon interest payments, a gain of about $125, the difference between the bond's price ($875.38) and its principal repayment ($1,000).

discount bond bond that is selling below par value

A bond's price will reflect changes in market conditions while it remains outstanding. With its fixed 8% coupon rate, this bond will no longer be attractive to investors when alternative investments are yielding 10%. The bond's market price will have to fall in order to offer buyers a combined return of 10% from the coupon payments and the par value. This is an illustration that bond prices fall as interest rates rise.

If investors required less than an 8% (for example, 6%) return for bonds of this quality, then the above-described bond would have a value greater than $1,000; investors would find the bond's 8% coupon attractive when other bonds are offering closer to 6%. If it was selling to yield a return of 6% to investors, the bond's price will rise to $1,149.08 (check this on your own using the tables; the exact answer from a spreadsheet or financial calculator is $1,148.77). When a bond's price exceeds its par value, it is selling at a *premium*, and it is called a premium bond. The investor who holds the bond until maturity will receive the above-market coupon payments of 8% per year, offset by a loss of about $149 (the difference between its purchase price and par value). In most cases where the bond sells at a premium, interest rates have fallen after the bond's issue. This bond's 8% coupon rate makes it very attractive to investors; buying pressure increases its price until its overall yield matches the market rate of 6%.

premium bond bond that is selling in excess of its par value

10.7.2 CALCULATING THE YIELD TO MATURITY[30]

Many times, rather than compute price, investors want to estimate the return on a bond investment if they hold it until it matures (this is called the yield to maturity or YTM). Financial calculators and computer spreadsheet packages, such as Excel, can be used to find the exact return. An approximate answer for the yield to maturity can be obtained by using the following formula:

yield to maturity (YTM) return on a bond if it is held to maturity

$$\text{Approximate yield to maturity} = \frac{\text{Annual interest} + \dfrac{\text{par} - \text{price}}{\text{No. of years until maturity}}}{\dfrac{\text{par} + \text{price}}{2}} \quad (10.3)$$

The numerator of equation 10.3 equals the annual coupon interest plus a straight-line amortization of the difference between the current price and par value. It represents an approximation of the annual dollar return the bondholder expects to receive, as over time the bond's value will rise or fall so it equals its par value at maturity. This estimated annual return is divided by the average of the bond's par value and its current price to give us an approximate yield or percentage return if the bond is held until maturity.

From the example above, we know that if the bond can be purchased for $875, it offers investors a 10% return. Let's use equation 10.3 to estimate the approximate yield to maturity if we know the price is $875.48, annual coupons are $80, and the bond matures in ten years with a par value of $1,000:

$$\text{Approximate yield to maturity} = \frac{\$80 + \dfrac{\$1000 - \$875.48}{10}}{\dfrac{\$1000 + \$875.48}{2}}$$

$$= 0.0986 \text{ or } 9.86\%$$

The approximate answer of 9.86% is somewhat close to the exact yield to maturity of 10 percent but certainly shows the approximate nature of the formula.

Of course, the use of a financial calculator will give us a precise answer for the yield to maturity. We illustrate the calculation process for a ten-year (or, rather, 20-period) bond paying interest of $40 per period and a $1,000 principal repayment at maturity. First, we assume the bond is currently trading at $1,000. Second, we assume the price to be $875.48.

Financial Calculator Solution: $1,000 Current Price
(remember to "clear" the time-value-of-money memory before starting any time-value calculation!)

Inputs:	20	−1,000	40	1,000
	N	PV	PMT	FV
Press:	CPT	%i		
Solution:	4.00			

---

[30] The yield-to-maturity calculation assumes that all coupon cash flows are reinvested at the YTM throughout the bond's life. The realized compound yield (RCY) calculation allows the investor to compute the expected return on a bond using another, perhaps more realistic, return for how the bond's coupons are reinvested. The RCY calculation is done in two steps. First, the future value of all the bond's cash flows is computed using the assumed reinvestment rate. Second, the rate that equates the bond's current price and the future value of cash flows is calculated; this rate is the RCY.

For example, a bond investor may expect interest rates to fall so the reinvestment rate is expected to fall to 6% on ten-year bonds. That means the $40 semi-annual coupons are likely to be reinvested at a semi-annual rate of only 3%. After ten years (or 20 periods), the future value of the $40 coupons will be $40 × 26.870 (FVIFA factor for 3% and 20 years from Table 3 in the Appendix) or $1,074.80. Adding the $1,000 par value we'll receive at that time, the future value of all the bond's cash inflows is $2,074.80. If the current price of the bond is $1,000, the annual RCY is found by solving the future value equation for r: $FV = PV(1 + r)^n = \$2,074.80 = 1,000(1 + r)^{10}$. Solving for r, the realized compound yield is 7.57%.

Multiply this periodic return of 4% by two to get the annual percentage rate of 8%. Now, let's see the yield to maturity when the bond is trading at $875.48:

Financial Calculator Solution: $875.48 Current Price

Inputs:	20	−875.48	40	1,000
	N	PV	PMT	FV
Press:	CPT	%i		
Solution:	5.00			

This corresponds to an annual percentage rate of 10%.[31]

Given what we know about bonds and our time-value-of-money techniques, the following will be true, if all other influences are kept constant:

- The larger the coupon interest, the higher the bond's price. We've already seen that with a yield to maturity of 8%, a ten-year bond that pays annual interest of $80 will have a present value or price of $1,000. A bond that is identical except it has a 10% coupon rate will have a price of $50 × 13.590 + $1,000 × 0.456 = $1,135.50.

- The higher the yield to maturity, the lower the price of the bond; the lower the yield to maturity, the higher the bond's price. We have already seen this. When a ten-year bond with an 8% coupon sells at an 8% yield to maturity, its price is $1,000. When it sells at a 10% yield to maturity, its price is about $875. Its price is about $1,149 when the yield to maturity falls to 6%. Higher risk bonds (those with lower bond ratings) will have higher required yields and will sell at lower prices or with higher coupon rates.

10.7.3 RISK IN BOND VALUATION

Investors in domestic bonds face three types of risk: credit risk, interest rate risk, and reinvestment rate risk. Investors in foreign bonds are subject to two additional risks: political risk and exchange rate risk.

10.7.3.1 Credit Risk

credit risk (default risk)
the chance of nonpayment or delayed payment of interest or principal

The cash flows to be received by bond market investors are uncertain; like individuals, corporate debtors may make interest payments late or not at all. They may fail to repay principal at maturity. To compensate investors for this credit risk or default risk, rates of return on corporate bonds are higher than those on government securities with the same terms to maturity.

Government securities are presumed to be free of credit risk. In general, as investors perceive a higher likelihood of default, they demand higher default risk premiums (DRPs). Since perceptions of a bond's default risk may change over its term, the bond's yield to maturity (YTM) may also change even if all else remains constant. Firms, such as Moody's, Standard & Poor's, and Fitch, provide information on the riskiness of individual bond issues through their bond ratings. The bond rating is a measure of a bond's default risk.

The DRP is measured by the difference in the YTM, or spread, of two bonds of equal time to maturity. If a ten-year Treasury note has a yield of 5.4% and a ten-year Baa-rated corporate bond has a yield of 7.4%, the Baa-Treasury spread of 2.0 percentage points represents the DRP earned by investors who are willing to carry the extra risk of a Baa-rated bond.

Credit risk spreads fluctuate, based upon credit conditions and investors' willingness to take on risk. In good economic times when investors are optimistic, spreads generally narrow; in uncertain times or in a recession, there is a "flight to quality" as investors prefer safer securities and credit spreads widen. Figure 10.5 shows the behavior of spreads between Baa-rated bonds and Treasuries and between Aaa-rated bonds and Treasuries over time. During the 2007–2009 financial crisis, credit

---

[31] We can design a spreadsheet to incorporate the inputs and calculation of equation 10.3. We can also use several Excel functions (IRR, YIELD, YIELDMAT) to compute the exact yield to maturity, but their application is too advanced for the current discussion.

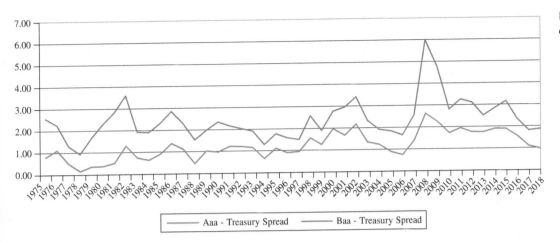

FIGURE 10.5 Annual credit risk spreads

spreads widened to near-record levels. During this time, particularly in Fall 2008, investors fled from risky securities and sought safety in Treasury securities. The credit spread has fallen and returned to more "normal" levels since then.

ETHICAL Ethics plays a role in determining a bond's rating. If management, through fraud or accounting gimmickry, make a firm appear more profitable or financially stable, the firm's bonds may have higher bond ratings than they should. After accounting irregularities were discovered at Enron, which at the time was one of the largest energy firms in the United States, its bond rating dropped to "junk" levels and its bank loans came due as a result of failing to meet its loan covenants.

10.7.4 INTEREST RATE RISK

As we introduced in the discussion of premium and discount bonds, bond prices change in response to changes in interest rates. We know the general level of interest rates in an economy fluctuates. For example, interest rates will change in response to changes in investors' expectations about future inflation rates. In Figure 10.6, we can see that the "seesaw effect" means that a rise in interest rates renders the fixed coupon interest payments on a bond less attractive, lowering its price. Therefore, bondholders are subject to the risk of capital loss from such interest rate changes should the bonds have to be sold prior to maturity.

A longer term to maturity, all else equal, increases the sensitivity of a bond's price to a given change in interest rates as the discount rate change compounds over a longer time period. Similarly, a lower coupon rate increases the sensitivity of the bond's price to market interest rate changes. This occurs because lower coupon bonds have most of their cash flow occurring further into the future when the par value is paid.

Because of **interest rate risk**, investors will demand a larger risk premium for bonds whose price is especially sensitive to market interest rate changes. Hence, we would expect higher yields to maturity (YTMs) for long-term bonds with low coupon rates rather than for short-term bonds with high coupon rates. The **horizon risk premium**, or **horizon spread**, is the difference in return earned by investing in a longer-term bond that has the same credit risk as a shorter-term bond. For example, suppose a five-year Treasury note has a yield of 4.7% and a ten-year Treasury note has a yield of 5.4%. The difference of 0.7 percentage points is the horizon spread, representing the extra return expected to be earned by investors in the longer-term notes for their exposure to higher levels of interest rate risk. Figure 10.7

interest rate risk fluctuating interest rates lead to varying asset prices; in the context of bonds, rising (falling) interest rates result in falling (rising) bond prices

horizon risk premium or horizon spread difference in return earned by investing in a longer-term bond that has the same credit risk as a shorter-term bond

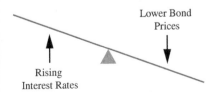
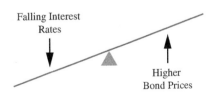

FIGURE 10.6 Relationship between current interest rates and bond prices: the seesaw effect

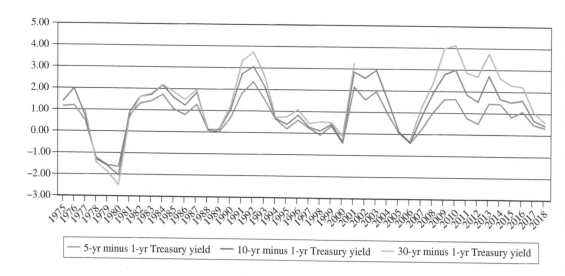

shows horizon spreads for five-year, ten-year, and 30-year Treasury securities, compared with one-year Treasury bills.[32]

The negative horizon spreads around 1979, 2001, and 2006 occurred when the yield curve was inverted and short-term rates exceeded long-term rates. An inverted yield curve typically happens before a recession begins, when short-term rates are rising because of inflationary pressures at the time. In 1983–1985, 1992, and 2009, the yield curve steepened, meaning rates on longer-term Treasury securities rose far above those of short-term Treasury securities. In the cases such as 2008–2009, the financial crisis created a flight to quality even within Treasuries as institutional and corporate funds poured into T-bills, the safest U.S. investment.

10.7.4.1 Reinvestment Rate Risk

The return an investor receives from a bond investment equals the bond's yield to maturity only if the coupon payments can be reinvested at a rate equal to the bond's yield to maturity. Recall the form of the interest factor in bond price (equation 10.2): $(1 + r_b)^n$. This assumes that all the cash flows are reinvested at the periodic rate r_b. If the coupons are reinvested at a lower rate, the investor's actual yield over time will be less than the bond's yield to maturity. Thus, **reinvestment rate risk**, or **rollover risk**, occurs when fluctuating interest rates cause coupon payments to be reinvested at different interest rates. Another illustration of reinvestment rate risk occurs when maturing bank CDs are rolled over into new CDs. The risk benefits the investor when the new CD rate is higher than the maturing CD rate; it works against the investor when the new CD rate is lower. Reinvestment rate risk is eliminated in zero-coupon securities, as they have no intermediate cash flows requiring reinvestment. For zero-coupon bonds, their yield to maturity is the compounded rate of return between the market price and the par value. Since, for a zero-coupon bond,

**reinvestment rate risk
(rollover risk)** fluctuating
interest rates cause coupon
or interest payments to be
reinvested at different interest
rates over time

$$\text{price} = \frac{Par_n}{(1 + r_b)^n}$$

the annual return or annual yield to maturity is $r_b = \sqrt[n]{\dfrac{Par_n}{\text{price}}} - 1$

If a zero-coupon bond has a time to maturity of ten years, a par value of $1000, and a current market price of $555, its yield to maturity is

$$\sqrt[10]{\frac{\$1000}{\$555}} - 1 = 0.0606 \text{ or } 6.06\%$$

[32] The U.S. Treasury did not issue 30-year securities from 2002 to 2005.

10.7.4.2 Risks of Nondomestic Bonds

GLOBAL Investors in nondomestic securities face a number of risks beyond those of domestic securities. Among these are political risk and exchange rate risk. **Political risk** can affect a bond investor in a number of ways. A foreign government may block currency exchanges, preventing the investor from repatriating coupon income. Social unrest may lead a foreign corporation to default on its bonds. Of course, exchange rate changes will cause fluctuations in the values of cash flows in terms of U.S. dollars, and this is called **exchange rate risk**.

> **DISCUSSION QUESTION 5**
>
> **What do you think will happen to interest rates and credit spreads over the next few months? Explain why you believe this and how would you invest given these expectations.**

political risk actions by a sovereign nation to interrupt or change the value of cash flows accruing to foreign investments

exchange rate risk fluctuating exchange rates lead to varying levels of U.S. dollar-denominated cash flows

---

10.8 VALUATION OF STOCKS

All securities are valued on the basis of the cash inflows that they are expected to provide to their owners or investors. As we saw in the above bond discussion,

$$\text{price} = \frac{CF_1}{(1+r)^1} + \frac{CF_2}{(1+r)^2} + \frac{CF_3}{(1+r)^3} + \cdots + \frac{CF_n}{(1+r)^n} \tag{10.1}$$

or

$$\text{price} = \sum_{t=1}^{n} \frac{CF_t}{(1+r)^t} \tag{10.1a}$$

Value or current price should equal the present value (PV) of expected future cash flows, which, represents the intrinsic value of the asset.

We have applied this general formula to the case of bond pricing. The cash flows from a typical bond are straightforward: the bond has a known and definite life, has fixed coupon payments paid on a regular basis, pays a known par value or principal when the bond matures, and should have a discount rate (yield to maturity) close to that of bonds with similar credit ratings.

Although the principle for determining an appropriate stock price is the same as that for determining a bond price, equity does not offer the certainty of bond cash flows. Common and preferred stocks are generally assumed to have infinite lives. For common stock, relevant cash flows (dividend payments) will likely vary over time. Finally, determining an appropriate rate at which to discount future dividends is difficult. Despite these difficulties, in this section we will see that the present value of all future dividends should equal a stock's intrinsic value, and that some simplifying assumptions can make the task of determining stock value easier. Our discussion in this section focuses on common stock. As we will see, the method for valuing preferred stock is a special case of common stock valuation.

It may seem rather strange to treat the stock price as nothing more than the present value of all future dividends. Who buys stock with no intention of ever selling it, even after retirement? Investors generally buy stock with the intention of selling it at some future time ranging from a few hours to 30 years later, or longer. Despite the length of any one investor's time horizon, the value of any dividend-paying common stock should equal the present value of all future dividends[33]:

$$\text{price} = \sum_{t=1}^{n} \frac{D_t}{(1+r_s)^t} \tag{10.4}$$

where n presumably becomes increasingly large – approaching infinity!

---

[33] Here is the intuition behind this statement. A stock is purchased today, in year T, with the plan of selling it in year T + 1. What should its current price be? The current price should equal the present value of dividends over year T and the selling price in year T + 1.

What will be the price of the stock in year T + 1? Suppose another investor plans on buying the stock at the beginning of year T + 1 and selling it a year later, in year T + 2. As before, the price of the stock at the beginning of year T + 1 should be the present value of the dividends paid in year T + 1 plus the selling price in year T + 2.

Through substitution, today's price will be the present value of the dividends in year T and T + 1 plus the expected selling price in year T + 2. We can continue extending this exercise through many years: year T + 3, T + 4, and so on. The result is that today's stock price will be the sum of the present value of future dividends.

What if a corporation currently pays no dividends and has no plans to pay dividends in the foreseeable future? The value of this company's stock will not be zero. Here's why. First, because the firm has no plans to pay dividends does not mean that it never will. To finance rapid growth, young firms often retain all their earnings; when they mature, they often pay a portion of earnings as dividends. Second, although the firm may not pay dividends to shareholders, it may be generating cash (or have the potential to do so). Someone buying the entire firm can claim the cash or profits, so its current price should reflect this value. Third, the firm's stock should be worth, at the least, the per-share liquidation value of its assets. But for a going concern, which is our focus in this chapter, the firm is worth the discounted cash flow value that can be captured by an acquirer.

Estimating all future dividend payments is impractical. Matters can be simplified considerably if we assume that the firm's dividends will remain constant or will grow at a constant rate over time.

10.8.1 VALUING STOCKS WITH CONSTANT DIVIDENDS

If the firm's dividends are expected to remain constant, so that $D_0 = D_1 = D_2 \ldots$, we can treat its stock as a perpetuity.

perpetuity A security that pays a constant periodic cash flow as long as the issuer exists. It can be considered to be an "infinite annuity."

A **perpetuity** is an annuity that never ends! It keeps going and going, paying cash flows on a regular basis throughout time.

That is, if you purchase a perpetuity, you are buying a cash flow stream that you will receive for the rest of your life. . . . which can be passed on to your children, your grandchildren, and so forth as long as the payer is in business and financially able to make the payments.

Is such a concept practical? Do perpetuities exist? In the past, some governments (for example, those in the UK) have issued perpetuity bonds that will pay interest as long as the government stands.[34] Preferred stock pays a fixed annual dividend forever (that is, as long as the firm exists and can pay the dividend), another example of a perpetuity.

The present value of a perpetuity is the cash flow divided by the discount rate. For stocks with constant dividends, this means equation 10.4 becomes the following:

$$P_0 = \frac{D_0}{r_s} \tag{10.5}$$

Many preferred stocks are valued using equation 10.5, since preferred stocks typically pay a constant dollar dividend and do not usually have finite lives or maturities. For example, if the FY Corporation's preferred stock currently pays a $2.00 dividend and investors require a 10 percent rate of return on preferred stocks of similar risk, the preferred stock's present value is the following:

$$P_0 = \frac{D_0}{r_s} = \frac{\$2.00}{0.10} = \$20.00$$

For a preferred stock with no stated maturity and a constant dividend, changes in price will occur only if the rate of return expected by investors changes.

10.8.2 VALUING STOCKS WITH CONSTANT DIVIDEND GROWTH RATES

Many firms have sales and earnings that increase over time; their dividends may rise, as well. If we assume that a firm's dividends grow at an annual rate of g percent, next year's dividend, D_1, will be $D_0(1 + g)$; the dividend in two years' time will be $D_0(1 + g)^2$. Generalizing, we have the following:

$$D_t = D_0(1 + g)^t$$

---

[34] And occasionally the government chooses to redeem or pay off the perpetuity bonds (called consols in the U.K.). See, for example, the *Financial Times* article, "UK to repay part of perpetual WWI loans," no author (October 31, 2014), https://www.ft.com/intl/fastft/229142/uk-repay-loans-from-wwi-south-sea-bubble (accessed October 29, 2015).

Equation 10.4 can be shown in expanded form in this way:

$$P_0 = \frac{D_0(1+g)}{(1+r_s)} + \frac{D_0(1+g)^2}{(1+r_s)^2} + \frac{D_0(1+g)^3}{(1+r_s)^3} + \ldots$$

As long as the dividend growth rate g is less than the discount rate r_s, each future term will be smaller than the preceding term. Although, technically, there are an infinite number of terms, the present value (PV) of dividends received farther into the future will move closer to zero. By accepting that the sum of all these terms is finite, equation 10.4 becomes the following:

$$P_0 = \frac{D_1}{(r_s - g)} \tag{10.6}$$

With D_1 equal to next year's dividend, namely, $D_0(1 + g)$, the current dividend increased by the g percent constant growth rate.

This result is known as the Gordon model, or the constant dividend growth model. The model assumes that a dividend is currently being paid, and this dividend will grow or increase at a constant rate over time. Of course, the assumption of constant growth in dividends may be unrealistic for a firm that is experiencing a period of high growth (or negative growth; that is, declining revenues). Neither will constant dividend growth be a workable assumption for a firm whose dividends rise and fall over the business cycle.

Gordon model (constant dividend growth model) a means of estimating common stock prices by assuming constant dividend growth over time

Let's assume the cash dividend per share for XYZ Company for last year was $1.89 and is expected to be $2.05 at the end of this year. This represents a percentage increase of 8.5% [($2.05 − $1.89)/$1.89]. If investors expect a 12% rate of return, then the estimated current stock value (P_0) would be the following:

$$P_0 = \$1.89(1.085)/(0.12 - 0.085) = (\$2.05/0.035) = \$58.59$$

Thus, if investors believed that the cash dividends would grow at an 8.5% rate indefinitely into the future and expected a 12% rate of return, they would pay $58.59 for the stock.

A simple spreadsheet can compute stock price using the constant growth assumption:

From this discussion, we can see there are four major influences on a stock's price. First is the firm's earnings per share, and second is the firm's dividend payout ratio; together, they determine a firm's dollar amount of dividends as:

Annual dividend (in dollars) = dividend payout ratio × earnings per share.

The third influence is the firm's expected growth rate in dividends, which will be affected by a number of firm, industry, and economic influences. The fourth is the shareholders' required return. From Chapter 8, we know this return is affected by the real interest rate in the economy, the expected inflation rate, and a risk premium to compensate investors for purchasing risky equities.

We can use the Gordon model to solve for any of the four unknown variables (price, dividends, required return, and growth) as long as we know the other three. For example, rearranging equation 10.4, we can use the market price of the stock to calculate the market's required return for the stock:

$$r_s = \frac{D_1}{P_0} + g$$

This equals the dividend yield (D_1/P_0) plus the expected growth rate. Similarly, using an estimate for the required return, we can estimate the market's consensus estimate for future dividend growth:

$$g = \frac{(P_0 \times r - D_0)}{(P_0 + D_0)}$$

This is especially valuable as a check against over-optimism on the part of investors when valuing a growth stock; that is, a stock whose earnings are expected to continue growing at a fast rate over time. At the height of the Internet stock bubble in 1999–2000, stocks of technology firms were priced assuming that 20 to 30% growth or higher was expected indefinitely. Such growth is impossible for long periods of time, so it was only a matter of time before their stock prices tumbled after slower sales growth resulted in slower earnings and cash flow growth for these firms.

10.8.3 RISK IN STOCK VALUATION

Investors in common stocks face a number of risks that bondholders do not. This additional risk leads them to require a higher rate of return on a firm's stock than on its debt securities. For example, in the event of corporate failure, the claims of stockholders have lower priority than those of bondholders. So, stockholders face a greater risk of loss than bondholders. Dividends can be variable and omitted, whereas bond cash flows have a legal obligation to be met.

ETHICAL Poor ethical decisions and poor management are another source of risk for stock investors in that such decisions can lower future cash flows and raise the required rate of return demanded by future investors. Accounting gimmickry and decisions by self-serving managers (more will be said about this in Chapter 11) can hurt stock prices, as happened with Enron, WorldCom, and Tyco. Poor customer or supplier relations, allegations of poor-quality products, and poor communications, as occurred between Ford Motor Company and one of its tire suppliers, Firestone, which hurt both companies and their shareholders. Volkswagen's admission of "fixing" emissions tests on its diesel car engines led to declines of over 35% in its stock price in a matter of a few days.

If the general level of interest rates rises, investors will demand a higher rate of return on stocks to maintain their risk premium differential over debt securities. This will force stock prices downward. Therefore, stockholders risk losses from any general upward movement of market interest rates, all else the same.

Also, future dividends, or dividend growth rates, are not known with certainty at the time stock is purchased. If poor corporate performance or adverse general economic conditions lead investors to lower their expectations about future dividend payments, this will lower the present value of shares of the stock, leaving the stockholder with the risk of capital loss. Stock analysts systematically review economic, industry, and firm conditions in great detail to gain insight into corporate growth prospects and the appropriate level of return that an investor should require of a stock.

10.8.4 VALUATION AND THE FINANCIAL ENVIRONMENT

The price of an asset is the present value of future cash flows; the discount rate used in the present value calculation is the required rate of return on the investment. Future cash flows of firms and the required returns of investors are affected by the global and domestic economic environments and the competition faced by firms. Slower sales or higher expenses can harm a firm's ability to pay its bond interest or dividends or to reinvest in its future growth. Besides affecting cash flows, these can affect investors' required rates of return by increasing risk premiums or credit spreads. Inflation pressures and capital market changes influence the level of interest rates and required returns.

10.8.5 GLOBAL ECONOMIC INFLUENCES

GLOBAL Two main overseas influences will affect firms.[35] The first is the condition of overseas economies. Growth in foreign economies will increase the demand for U.S. exports. Similarly, sluggish foreign demand will harm overseas sales and hurt the financial position of firms doing business overseas. The rate of economic growth overseas can affect the conditions faced by domestic firms, too, as growing demand globally may make it easier to raise prices and sluggish demand overseas may lead to intense competition in the U.S. market.

The second influence is the behavior of exchange rates, the price of a currency in terms of another currency. A change in exchange rates over time has two effects on the firm. Changing exchange rates lead to higher or lower U.S. dollar cash flows from overseas sales, more competitively priced import goods, or changing input costs. Thus, changing exchange rates affect profitability by influencing sales, price competition, and expenses. Changing exchange rates also affect the level of domestic interest rates. Expectations of a weaker U.S. dollar can lead to higher U.S. interest rates; to attract capital, U.S. rates will have to rise to compensate foreign investors for expected currency losses because of the weaker dollar.[36] Conversely, a stronger dollar can result in lower U.S. interest rates.

10.8.6 DOMESTIC ECONOMIC INFLUENCES

Individuals can spend only what they have (income and savings) or what their future earning capacity will allow them to borrow. Consumption spending (spending by individuals for items such as food, cars, clothes, computers, and so forth) comprises about two-thirds of gross domestic product (GDP) in the United States. Generally, higher disposable incomes (that is, income after taxes) lead to higher levels of consumption spending. Higher levels of spending mean inventories are reduced and companies need to produce more and hire additional workers to meet sales demand. Corporations will spend to obtain supplies and workers based upon expectations of future demand. Similarly, they will invest in additional plant and equipment based upon expected future sales and income. Economic growth results in higher levels of consumer spending and corporate investment, which in turn stimulates job growth and additional demand. Slow or negative growth can lead to layoffs, pessimistic expectations, and reduced consumer and corporate spending. These effects will directly influence company profits and cash flows.

Economic conditions affect required returns, too. Investors will be more optimistic in good economic times and more willing to accept lower-risk premiums on bond and stock investments. In poor economic times, credit spreads will rise as investors want to place their funds in safer investments.

Governments shape the domestic economy by fiscal policy (government spending and taxation decisions) and monetary policy. These decisions may affect consumer disposable income (fiscal policy) and the level of interest rates as well as inflation expectations (monetary policy) and, therefore, affect the valuation of the bond and stock markets.

Some industry sectors are sensitive to changes in consumer spending. Sales by auto manufacturers, computer firms, and other manufacturers of high-priced items will rise and fall by greater amounts over the business cycle than will food or pharmaceutical firms. Changes in interest rates affect some industries more than others, too; banks and the housing industry (and sellers of large household appliances) are sensitive to changes in interest rates more than, say, book and music publishers or restaurants.

---

[35] By "overseas," we refer to events outside of the domestic economy, whether water separates the countries or not. Thus, although we share land borders, to a U.S. firm, the economies of Canada and Mexico are overseas economies.

[36] To understand this effect, suppose initially the exchange rate between the U.S. dollar and euro is $1 = €1. Analysts anticipate the dollar will weaken over the year to $1 = €0.95. The European investor who invests €1 for every $1 of investment now expects to receive only €0.95 next year. The investor will require a higher expected return on his U.S. investment to compensate for the effects of the weakening dollar. This is similar to a U.S. investor seeking protection from anticipated inflation by increasing the required rate of return to reflect inflationary expectations.

10.8.7 INDUSTRY AND COMPETITION

A firm's profits are determined by its sales revenues, expenses, and taxes. We have mentioned taxes and some influences on sales and expenses in our discussion of global and domestic economies, but industry competition and the firm's position within the industry will have a large impact on its ability to generate profits over time. Tight competition means it will be difficult to raise prices to increase sales revenue or profitability. Nonprice forms of competition, such as customer service, product innovation, and the use of technology to the fullest extent in the manufacturing and sales processes may hurt profits by increasing expenses if the features do not generate sufficient sales. Competition may not come only from similar firms; for example, a variety of "entertainment" firms, from music to theater to movies to sports teams, vie for consumers' dollars. Trucking firms and railroads compete for freight transportation. Cable and satellite firms compete in the home television markets (and for Internet service, along with telephone service providers). Changes in the cost and availability of raw materials, labor, and energy can adversely affect a firm's competitive place in the market.

The influences of competition and supply ultimately affect a firm's profitability and investors' perceptions of the firm's risk. This, in turn, will affect its bond and stock prices. The most attractive firms for investing in will be those with a competitive advantage over their rivals. They may offer a high-quality product, be the low-cost producer, be innovators in the use of technology, or offer the best customer support. Whatever the source of the firm's advantage is, if it can build and maintain this advantage over time it will reap above-normal profits and be an attractive investment.

> **LEARNING ACTIVITY**
>
> 1. Examine estimates on the future earnings of firms at https://www.zacks.com and http://www.whispernumber.com. Another great resource of stock analysis is http://www.fool.com.
> 2. Read analysis and expectations of economic activity from websites such as http://www.morganstanley.com (click on "Ideas" or search for "Global Economic" on the website) and download exchange rate data from websites such as https://www.federalreserve.gov/releases/h10/current/.
> 3. The Economic Report of the President is available on the Internet; you can find the latest version by doing a web search for this title. Other good sources of domestic economic analysis and data include the Federal Reserve's website, https://www.federalreserve.gov; see especially the Beige Book analysis of economic conditions across the regions of the country. The St. Louis Federal Reserve's website, https://www.stlouisfed.org, has links to the FRED database and to education and analysis sites.
> 4. Some industry analyses and information is available on websites such as https://www.finance.yahoo.com and www.hoovers.com. Other helpful information on industries is available from trade groups. Use of a Web search engine can help you find these sources.

APPLYING FINANCE TO...

- **Institutions and Markets**   Bond and stock trading occurs in capital markets. Some institutions, such as investment banks, facilitate trading of these securities and develop different variations (for example, callable, putable) to meet the needs of different kinds of issuers and investors. For other institutions, bonds and stocks are another means of supplying capital in addition to bank loans, private placements, mortgages, and so forth to those needing access to funds.

- **Investments**   Bonds and stocks are tools used by investors; they are purchased in an attempt to meet an investor's goals and risk preferences over the investor's time horizon.

- **Financial Management**   These securities are a source of long-term financing for asset acquisition, implementing long-term strategies, and acquiring other firms.

SUMMARY

LO 10.1 Stock and debt offerings are major sources of long-term funds for businesses. Because of stock repurchases and because bonds have limited life, over time the amount of net bond issues exceeds that of stocks. Internal financing is a major source of financing, too, as the firm keeps some of its profits to reinvest in the firm's growth. Many firms raise funds overseas to finance overseas expansion, take advantage of lower financing rates and less regulation, or tap into a new and large source of investors.

LO 10.2 Bonds offer investors a fixed-income flow and priority in terms of liquidation. Bond covenants, which are found in the indenture, list some of the obligations of the issuer toward the bondholders. Bond ratings assess the collateral underlying the bonds as well as the ability of the issuers to make timely payments of interest and principal. Bonds can be sold overseas by U.S. issuers; non-U.S. firms can issue bonds in the United States, as long as Securities and Exchange Commission (SEC) requirements are fulfilled.

LO 10.3 Bonds can be secured by corporate assets or be unsecured; unsecured bonds are called debentures. Although bonds many times have a stated time to maturity, the bond may contain features or options to shorten or lengthen time to maturity, such as convertible bonds, callable or putable bonds, or extendable notes. A typical bond pays a fixed coupon on a regular basis, but some bonds offer floating interest rates or coupon payments that rise with inflation.

LO 10.4 Most equity offerings are sales of common stock. Preferred stock gives holders preference over common shareholders with respect to dividends and liquidation, but unlike the common shareholders, the (usually) fixed dividend received by preferred shareholders does not allow them to enjoy the benefits of future profit growth. Many investors buy common shares expecting dividends to rise over time.

LO 10.5 Many investors purchase shares of stock expecting to receive cash dividends. Dividends are paid quarterly when they are declared by the firm's board of directors. There are several strategies that can guide the board's decision regarding the level of dividends, including target payout, constant payout, and residual dividend. Some firms return funds to shareholders via share repurchases. Other firms may offer stock dividends or a stock split, which give the illusion of receiving value when none is transmitted.

LO 10.6 We can determine intrinsic value by applying time-value-of-money techniques to the cash flows that investors receive from bond and stock investments. The current price of an asset should equal the present value of future expected cash flows. If a security's price is known, these techniques can be used to estimate anticipated investment returns.

LO 10.7 When an investor purchases a bond, there is a contractual relationship. The issue is obligated to pay interest (called coupons) and to pay the bond's principal, or par value, when the bond matures. The intrinsic value of a bond is the present value of its coupon cash flows and its par value. We can use a bond's current market price and known cash flows (coupons and par value) to determine its yield to maturity – that is, what return an investor may receive from purchasing the bond today. Although its cash flows are known, bonds do present several risks to investors, including credit risk, interest rate risk, reinvestment rate risk, and additional risks if a nondomestic bond is purchased.

LO 10.8 The most we should be willing to pay for a share of stock is its intrinsic value. For a stock, this equals the present value of future dividends. We saw how to value preferred stock as a perpetuity. Common stock can be difficult to value given its indefinite life and varying dividends. We used the constant dividend growth model to simplify the estimation of intrinsic value. We discussed that the financial system and the economic environment are inseparable inputs to analyzing stocks and bonds. Firms' cash flows, and the outlook for their stock and bond issues, are affected by the global economy and domestic economy as growth overseas and at home will affect demand for the firm's products and its costs, too. Industry competition and technological change can make last year's "sure thing" become this year's bankruptcy filing. Changing demand for and supply of funds, fluctuating exchange rates, and monetary policy will influence inflationary expectations and required returns on securities. Much of what was learned in economics and in Part 1 of this book has implications for the behavior of the bond and stock market over time.

KEY TERMS

bearer bonds	callable preferred stock	closed-end mortgage bond	conversion value
bond rating	call deferment periods	common stock	convertible bond
bonds	call price	constant payout ratio	convertible
callable bond	call risk	conversion ratio	preferred stock

corporate equity capital	financial assets	par value (debt); face value	stock certificate
coupon payments	global bonds	par value (equity)	stock dividend
covenants	Gordon model (constant	perpetuity	stock split
credit risk (default risk)	dividend growth model)	political risk	street name
cumulative preferred stock	horizon risk premium or	preferred stock	subordinated debenture
debenture bonds	horizon risk spread	premium bond	target dividend
discount bond	interest rate risk	putable bonds	payout policy
dividend payout ratio	intrinsic value	registered bonds	Treasury Inflation
dividend reinvestment	junk bonds or	reinvestment rate risk	Protected Securities
plans (DRIPs)	high-yield bonds	residual dividend policy	trustee
equipment trust certificate	mortgage bonds	retractable bonds	trust indenture
Eurodollar bonds	open-end mortgage bond	rollover risk	Yankee bonds
exchange rate risk	participating	sinking fund	yield to maturity (YTM)
extendable notes	preferred stock	special dividend	zero-coupon bond

---

REVIEW QUESTIONS

1. **(LO 10.1)** Describe the relationship between internal and external financing in meeting the long-term financial needs of a firm.

2. **(LO 10.1)** What are the major sources of long-term funds available to business corporations? Indicate their relative importance.

3. **(LO 10.1)** Why would firms raise capital in markets other than their domestic or home market?

4. **(LO 10.2)** Can only large institutional investors purchase bonds? Explain.

5. **(LO 10.2)** Describe what is meant by bond covenants.

6. **(LO 10.2)** What are bond ratings?

7. **(LO 10.2)** What is meant by the following terms: convertible bonds, callable bonds, putable bonds, and Eurodollar bonds?

8. **(LO 10.2)** Why are investment-grade bonds given that name? Why are junk bonds known as high-yield bonds?

9. **(LO 10.2)** Why might a firm want to maintain a high bond rating? What has been happening to bond ratings in recent years?

10. **(LO 10.3)** How does a Treasury Inflation Protected Security (TIPS) bond differ from the typical U.S. Treasury security?

11. **(LO 10.3)** Briefly describe the types of bonds that can be issued to provide bondholder security.

12. **(LO 10.3)** Why might an investor find a zero-coupon bond an attractive investment?

13. **(LO 10.4)** What is a round lot of common stock?

14. **(LO 10.4)** Describe some of the characteristics of common stock.

15. **(LO 10.4)** List and briefly explain the special features usually associated with preferred stock.

16. **(LOS 10.4)** Why study stocks if the net amount of stock issues is negative?

17. **(LOS 10.4)** Why should investors consider common stock as an investment vehicle if they have a long-term time horizon?

18. **(LOS 10.5)** Why does dividend income growth exceed that of bond income growth over a period of time?

19. **(LOS 10.5)** How do firms decide how much of their earnings to distribute as dividends?

20. **(LOS 10.5)** Explain how an investor may view a stock dividend, a stock split, and a stock repurchase plan with regards to the value of his stock holdings.

21. **(LOS 10.6)** Briefly describe how securities are valued.

22. **(LOS 10.7)** Describe the process for valuing a bond.

23. **(LOS 10.7)** What is meant by the yield to maturity (YTM) on a bond?

24. **(LOS 10.7)** Briefly describe the types of risk faced by investors in domestic bonds. Indicate the additional risks associated with nondomestic bonds.

25. **(LOS 10.7)** What risk does a zero-coupon bond address?

26. **(LOS 10.7)** According to the behavior of interest rates in Figure 10.5, were investors more concerned or less concerned about risk over the 2002–2006 time period? Explain.

27. **(LOS 10.7)** What does it mean when the horizon spreads in Figure 10.7 dip below the X-axis?

28. **(LOS 10.7)** How do you think credit spreads behave over the course of the economic cycle?

29. **(LOS 10.7)** What is a "flight to quality?" Under what economic conditions might we see this?

30. **(LOS 10.8)** What is a capital gain? Is it taxed the same way as dividends?

31. **(LOS 10.8)** "Taxes on capital gains can be deferred." Explain what this statement means.

32. **(LOS 10.8)** Explain how a capital loss on the sale of a firm's stock can affect an investor's taxes.

33. **(LOS 10.8)** Describe the process for valuing a preferred stock.

34. **(LOS 10.8)** Describe the process for valuing a common stock when the cash dividend is expected to grow at a constant rate.

35. **(LOS 10.8)** Discuss the risks faced by common shareholders that are not related to the general level of interest rates.

36. **(LOS 10.8)** Under what economic forecast would you believe an auto manufacturer would be a good investment? A computer manufacturer?

37. **(LOS 10.8)** Discuss how changes in exchange rates can affect the outlook for both global and domestic firms.

38. **(LOS 10.8)** What can looking at data on inventories tell us about the condition of the economy? Data on business expansion or investment plans?

39. **(LOS 10.8)** Is industry competition good or bad if you are looking for attractive stock investments?

40. **(LOS 10.8)** Give examples of firms you believe have been successful over time because they are industry leaders in quality; they are the low-cost producer; they are innovative; they offer superior customer service.

41. **(LOS 10.8)** Let's assume energy prices are forecast to go higher. How would this affect your decision to purchase each of these stocks?
    a. ExxonMobil
    b. American Airlines
    c. Ford Motor Company
    d. Archer Daniels Midland, a food processor

PROBLEMS

1. Compute the annual interest payments and principal amount for a Treasury Inflation Protected Security (TIPS) with a par value of $1,000 and a 3 percent interest rate if inflation is 4 percent in year one, 5 percent in year two, and 6 percent in year three.

2. Judy Johnson is choosing between investing in two Treasury securities that mature in five years and have par values of $1,000. One is a Treasury note paying an annual coupon of 5.06 percent. The other is a TIPS that pays 3 percent interest annually.
    a. If inflation remains constant at 2 percent annually over the next five years, what will be Judy's annual interest income from the TIPS bond? From the Treasury note?
    b. How much interest will Judy receive over the five years from the Treasury note? From the TIPS?
    c. When each bond matures, what par value will Judy receive from the Treasury note? From the TIPS?
    d. After five years, what is Judy's total income (interest + par) from each bond? Should she use this total as a way of deciding which bond to purchase?

3. Using the regular Treasury note of Problem 2:
    a. What is its price if investors' required rate of return is 6.0 percent on similar bonds? Treasury notes pay interest semi-annually.

    b. Erron Corporation wants to issue five-year notes but investors require a credit risk spread of 3 percentage points. What is the anticipated coupon rate on the Erron notes?

4. Assume a $1,000 face value bond has a coupon rate of 8.5 percent, pays interest semi-annually, and has an eight-year life. If investors are willing to accept a 10 percent rate of return on bonds of similar quality, what is the present value or worth of this bond?

5. See Problem 4 to answer these two questions.
    a. By how much would the value of the bond in Problem 4 change if investors wanted an 8 percent rate of return?
    b. A bond with the same par value and coupon rate as the bond in Problem 4 has 14 years until maturity. If investors will use a 10 percent discount rate to value this bond, by how much should its price differ from the bond in Problem 4?

6. The Garcia Company's bonds have a face value of $1,000, will mature in ten years, and carry a coupon rate of 16 percent. Assume interest payments are made semi-annually.
    a. Determine the present value of the bond's cash flows if the required rate of return is 16 percent.
    b. How would your answer change if the required rate of return is 12 percent?

7. Judith Inc. bonds mature in eight years and pay a semi-annual coupon of $55. The bond's par value is $1,000.
   a. What is their current price if the market interest rate for bonds of similar quality is 9.2 percent?
   b. A change in Fed policy increases market interest rates 0.50 percentage points from their level in Part (a). What is the percentage change in the value of Judith Inc. bonds from their value in Part (a)?
   c. Better profits for Judith, Inc. reduces the market interest rate for its bonds to 9.0 percent. What is the percentage change in the value of Judith, Inc. bonds from the answer in Part (b)?

8. Kamins Corporation has two bond issues outstanding, each with a par value of $1,000. Information about each is listed below. Suppose market interest rates rise 1 percentage point across the yield curve. What will be the change in price for each of the bonds? Does this tell us anything about the relationship between time to maturity and interest rate risk?

   Bond A: 5 years to maturity, 8 percent coupon, market interest rate is 9 percent.

   Bond B: 12 years to maturity, 8 percent coupon, market interest rate is 9 percent.

9. Billon Corporation has two bond issues outstanding, each with a par value of $1,000. Information about each is listed below. Suppose market interest rates rise 1 percentage point across the yield curve. What will be the change in price for each of the bonds? Does this tell us anything about the relationship between coupon rate and interest rate risk?

   Bond A: ten years to maturity, 0 percent coupon, market interest rate is 9.62 percent.

   Bond B: ten years to maturity, 10 percent coupon, market interest rate is 9.62 percent.

10. Koppen Corporation has two bond issues outstanding, each with a par value of $1,000. Information about each is listed below. Suppose market interest rates rise 1 percentage point across the yield curve. What will be the change in price for each of the bonds? Does this tell us anything

about the relationship between frequency of cash flows and interest rate risk?

   Bond A: This bond is a Eurobond. It has ten years to maturity, pays a 7 percent coupon, and the market interest rate is 11.3 percent.

   Bond B: This is issued in the U.S. It has ten years to maturity, pays a 7 percent coupon, and the market interest rate is 11.3 percent.

11. BVA, Inc. has two bond issues outstanding, each with a par value of $1,000. Information about each is listed below. Suppose market interest rates rise 1 percentage point across the yield curve. What will be the change in price for each of the bonds? Does this tell us anything about the relationship between initial yield to maturity and interest rate risk?

   Bond A: 12 years to maturity, pays a 7 percent coupon, and the market interest rate on this BB-rated bond is 12.36 percent.

   Bond B: 12 years to maturity, pays a 7 percent coupon, and the market interest rate on this A-rated bond is 10.25 percent.

12. What is the approximate yield to maturity (use equation 10.3) and the exact yield to maturity (use a calculator) for the following bonds? Assume these are bonds issued in the United States.
   a. 10 years to maturity, 6 percent coupon rate, current price is $950.
   b. 16 years to maturity, 0 percent coupon rate, current price is $339.
   c. 25 years to maturity, 8.5 percent coupon rate, current price is $1030.

13. On Thursday, the following bond quotation appears in the newspaper. Interpret each item that appears in the quote and compute its current yield:

Company (Ticker)	Coupon	Mat.	Last Price	Last Yield	Est Spread	Est UST	$Vol (000S)
Wal-Mart Stores							
WMT	4.550	May 1, 2025	99.270	4.649	47	10	66,830

14. Perusing the corporate bond quotations, you write down some summary information:

Company (Ticker)	Coupon	Mat.	Last Price	Last Yield	Est Spread	Est UST	$Vol (000S)
Wal-Mart Stores							
WMT	4.550	10 years	99.270	4.649	47	10	66,830
Wal-Mart Stores							
WMT	4.125	8 years	99.554	4.200	2	10	50,320
Liberty Media							
L	5.700	10 years	102.750	5.314	112	10	26,045
Ford Motor Credit							
F	7.250	8 years	107.407	6.012	183	10	22,863

a. Which company is the riskiest? Why?

b. Which bond has the highest default risk? Why?

c. Why would Walmart have two bonds trading at different yields?

d. Compute the current yield for each of the four bonds.

e. Compute yield to maturity for each of the four bonds.

15. You run across the following bond quotation on a Friday.

Rate	Maturity Mo/Yr	BID	Asked	Chg.	Asked YLD
7.500	Nov 24	131:06	131:07	−9	5.04

a. What kind of security is it?

b. Interpret the information contained in the quote.

c. Suppose a corporate bond with the same time to maturity has a credit risk spread of 250 basis points. What should be the yield to maturity for the corporate bond?

16. **Challenge Problem** A $1,000 face value bond issued by the Dysane Company currently pays total annual interest of $79 per year and has a 13-year life.

a. What is the present value, or worth, of this bond if investors are willing to accept a 10 percent annual rate of return on bonds of similar quality if the bond is a Eurobond?

b. How would your answer in (a) change if the bond is a U.S. bond?

c. How would your answer in (b) change if, one year from now, investors only required a 6.5 percent annual rate of return on bond investments similar in quality to the Dysane bond?

d. Suppose the original bond can be purchased for $925. What is the bond's yield to maturity?

17. **Challenge Problem**

a. You own a two-bond portfolio. Each has a par value of $1,000. Bond A matures in five years, has a coupon rate of 8 percent, and has an annual yield to maturity (YTM) of 9.20 percent. Bond B matures in 15 years, has a coupon rate of 8 percent and has an annual YTM of 9.20 percent. Both bonds pay interest semi-annually. What is the value of your portfolio? What happens to the value of your portfolio if each YTM rises by one percentage point?

b. Rather than own a five-year bond and a 15-year bond, suppose you sell both of them and invest in two ten-year bonds. Each has a coupon rate of 8 percent (semi-annual coupons) and has a YTM of 9.20 percent. What is the value of your portfolio? What happens to the value of

your portfolio if the YTM on the bonds rises by one percentage point?

c. Based upon your answers to (a) and (b), evaluate the price changes between the two portfolios. Were the price changes the same? Why or why not?

18. **EXCEL** A bond with a par value of $1,000 has a coupon rate of 7 percent and matures in 15 years. Using a spreadsheet program, graph its price versus different yields to maturity, ranging from 1 percent to 20 percent. Is the relationship between price and yield linear? Why or why not?

19. Global Cycles (GC) offers investors a dividend reinvestment plan (DRIP) program. An investor purchases 100 shares of GC at a price of $20 per share on January 2. How many shares will the investor own on December 31 if the following dividends are paid and the investor participates in the DRIP program (assume the firm allows fractional shares and accounts for them up to three decimal places)? If the stock's price is $27.50 on December 31, what is the value of her investment in GC?

March 1: dividend paid of $0.50 per share; stock price is $21

June 1: dividend paid of $0.50 per share; stock price is $22.5

September 1: dividend paid of $0.55 per share; stock price is $19

December 1: dividend paid of $0.55 per share; stock price is $25

20. If a stock's earnings per share are $2.00, what will be the dividend per share if the payout ratio is 40 percent? If the following year's earnings per share are $2.10, what will the payout ratio be if the firm wants to maintain dividend growth of 8 percent?

21. You purchased 200 shares of H2O Corporation stock at a price of $20. Consider each of the following announcements separately. What will the price of the stock be after each change? How many shares will you own? What will be the total value of your holdings (value of stock plus any income)?

a. The firm announces a 10 percent stock dividend.

b. The firm announces a two-for-one stock split.

c. The firm announces a $0.50 per-share dividend (in your answer use the price of the stock on the ex-dividend date).

d. The firm announces it will repurchase 10 percent of its shares; you do not offer to sell any of your shares.

22. The Fridge-Air Company's preferred stock pays a dividend of $4.50 per share annually. If the required rate of return on comparable quality preferred stocks is 14 percent, calculate the value of Fridge-Air's preferred stock.

Learning Extension 10

Annualizing Rates of Return

LO 10.9 Calculate an investment's holding period return and compute the annualized rate of return when the holding period is less than or greater than one year.

An investment provides two sources of returns: income and price changes. Bonds pay coupon interest (income), and as we saw in Chapter 10, fluctuating market interest rates can lead to changing bond prices and capital gains or losses. Stocks may pay dividends (a source of investor income) and rise or fall in value over time, leading to capital gains or losses. Such is the case with other investment vehicles, such as real estate or mutual funds. In this learning extension, we'll learn how to compute the return over a period of time (holding period return) and how to annualize it (annualized return).

The dollar return on a single financial asset held for a specific time, or holding period, is given by the following:

$$\text{Dollar return} = \text{Income received} + \text{Price change} \qquad \text{(LE 10-1)}$$

We can call this a **holding period dollar return** as there is no time frame placed on the calculation. It can reflect dollar returns earned over two months or two years – or shorter or longer. The term "holding period" can refer to virtually any time frame. It can reflect the entire time period for which an investor has owned an asset or a smaller time frame.

holding period dollar return the sum of all income received during a time frame plus the change in the asset's price over the time frame

Suppose Amy held a share of stock, and she received dividends of $2 while the stock price rose from a purchase price of $25 to its current level of $30. Should Amy sell the stock today, her dollar return would be the following:

$$\text{Dollar return} = \text{Income received} + \text{price change}$$
$$= \$2 + (\$30 - \$25)$$
$$\$7 = \$2 + \$5$$

She received $2 in dividends and the value of her investment rose by $5 for a total dollar return of $7. To compare this investment return with others, it is best to measure the dollar return relative to the initial price paid for the stock. This **holding period return**, or HPR, is the dollar return divided by the initial price of the stock:

holding period return the percent return on an investment over any stated time frame

$$\text{Holding period return (HPR)} = \text{Dollar return/Initial price} \qquad \text{(LE 10-2)}$$

Amy's holding period return was:

$$\text{HPR} = (\text{Dollar return/Initial price}) = (\$7/\$25) = 0.28 \text{ or } 28 \text{ percent}$$

ANNUALIZED RATES OF RETURN

To compare the returns on one investment with another, they should be measured over equal time periods, such as a year, a month, or a day. By convention, most investors use annual returns as a means by which to compare investments. To *annualize a return* means to state it as the annual return that would result in the observed percentage return. Equation LE 10-3 gives us a formula for determining annualized returns:

$$\text{Annualized return} = (1 + \text{holding period return})^{1/n} - 1 \qquad \text{(LE 10-3)}$$

The n value is the number of years an investment was held. In this calculation, the holding period return must be expressed in decimal form. That is, 20 percent should be expressed as 0.20. A return of −8 percent would be noted as −0.08.

For a one-year example, Amy's annualized return is the same as her holding period return. This can be shown as follows:

$$\text{Annualized return} = (1+0.28)^{1/1} - 1$$
$$= (1.28)^{1} - 1 = 1.28 - 1 = 0.28 \text{ or } 28 \text{ percent}$$

The superscript fraction 1/1 indicates that Amy's investment was for one year. When investments are held for longer than one year, the fraction becomes less than one, indicating that the percentage return must be spread over a longer time period. For example, if Amy's investment was purchased two years ago, her annualized return would be the following:

$$\text{Annualized return} = (1+0.28)^{1/2} - 1$$
$$= (1.28)^{0.5} - 1 = 1.131 - 1 = 0.131 \text{ or } 13.1 \text{ percent}$$

Also notice that the annualized return is not just the 28 percent total return divided by two years, or 14 percent, which would be a simple average annual return. Rather, the annualized return measured by equation LE 10-3 captures the compounding or discounting effects of holding investments longer than one year.

It should now be apparent that as the investment holding period lengthens, the annualized return gets progressively smaller. For example, let's assume Amy earned her 28 percent total return over a period of four years. Her annualized return would be calculated as follows:

$$\text{Annualized return} = (1+0.28)^{1/4} - 1$$
$$= (1.28)^{0.25} - 1 = 1.064 - 1 = 0.064 \text{ or } 6.4 \text{ percent}$$

A financial calculator can be used to simplify the calculation effort as follows:

Financial Calculator Solution: 1-Year Investment

Exponent	$1/n = 1/1 = 1$
Input	1.28 $\boxed{Y^x}$ then 1 $\boxed{=}$ −1 $\boxed{=}$
Solution	0.28

Financial Calculator Solution: 2-Year Investment

Exponent	$1/n = 1/2 = 0.5$
Input	1.28 $\boxed{Y^x}$ then 0.5 $\boxed{=}$ −1 $\boxed{=}$
Solution	0.131

Financial Calculator Solution: 4-Year Investment

Exponent	$1/n = 1/4 = 0.25$
Input	1.28 $\boxed{Y^x}$ then 0.25 $\boxed{=}$ −1 $\boxed{=}$
Solution	0.064

Annualized returns can be calculated for investments held for less than one year. Let's assume Amy held her investment for nine months while earning a percentage return of 28 percent. What would be Amy's annualized return under this scenario?

$$\text{Annualized return} = (1 + 0.28)^{1/(9/12)} - 1$$
$$= (1.28)^{1/0.75} - 1 = (1.28)^{1.33} - 1 = 1.389 - 1 = 0.389 \text{ or } 38.9 \text{ percent}$$

Because most individual and institutional investors are interested in comparing annualized returns, you must know how to compute holding period returns and how to annualize them.

SUMMARY

LO 10.9 Investors hold investments for different time periods. Some for a few days, some for many decades. The holding period dollar return and holding period return are calculations used to determine the return over any given time frame of interest. Asset returns need to have the same time period frame of reference so we can compare their returns (and risks) over time. By convention, the annual return is a popular way to measure and compare returns across assets or investor performance. We can annualize any holding period return. The annualized return represents what annual rate of return would lead to the observed HPR over the time frame under review.

PROBLEMS

1. Given the information below, compute annualized returns:

Asset	Income	Price Change	Initial Price	Time Period
A	$ 2	$ 6	$29	15 months
B	0	10	40	11 months
C	50	70	30	7 years
D	3	−8	20	24 months

2. Given the information below, compute annualized returns:

Asset	Purchase Price	Current Price	Income Received	Time Period
A	$ 20	$ 26	$2	75 weeks
B	15	18	0.40	3 months
C	150	130	0	2 years
D	3.50	3.00	0.20	8 months

CHAPTER 11

Securities and Markets

LEARNING OBJECTIVES

After studying this chapter, you should be able to do the following:

LO 11.1 Describe the processes and institutions used by businesses to distribute new securities to the investing public in the primary market, including the use of underwriting and best efforts agreements.

LO 11.2 Summarize activities of a well-known public offering.

LO 11.3 Explain various ways that investment banks can assist security offerings in addition to traditional underwriting efforts.

LO 11.4 Describe the costs of "going public" when issuing securities in the primary market.

LO 11.5 Describe other functions of investment bankers, their recent attempts to innovate, and the regulations they follow.

LO 11.6 Explain the role of secondary markets in securities trading

and the structure of organized exchanges, such as the New York Stock Exchange.

LO 11.7 Summarize the types of orders used in securities trading and when they might be used by traders.

LO 11.8 Describe the various types of over-the-counter markets for securities trading.

LO 11.9 Explain factors that make for a good market for trading securities and the role of brokerage commissions in securities trading.

LO 11.10 Discuss issues of importance to investors, including how security market indexes are constructed and how to trade foreign securities.

LO 11.11 Recognize the role and importance of ethics in securities transactions and analysis.

Where we have been. . . For the savings process to work, funds must be routed from savings to the users of funds. Banks and other financial institutions assist with this process; so do securities markets. Chapter 10 introduced us to the characteristics of stocks and bonds, how they can be priced using time value concepts, and the risks that investors face when holding them. Supply and demand forces in financial markets set market prices for securities. Interest rates and asset prices rise and fall based upon investors' and issuers' desires to buy and sell securities.

Where we are going. . . The process of raising funds in securities markets is important for business firms. A firm's ability to raise funds will be the topic of future chapters: long-term fund raising is the focus of Chapter 18's capital structure discussion and short-term financing is discussed in Chapter 16.

How this chapter applies to me. . . Securities markets, typically the secondary markets such as the New York Stock Exchange, are in the news every day. Stock and bond indexes reflect the changing values of securities over time. Investors' decisions and reactions to news events lead to changes in interest rates, bond prices, and stock prices. Movements in market prices affect personal wealth. Many people make decisions through direct investment or through their decisions regarding where to place their 401(k) or Individual Retirement Account (IRA) investments that involve the securities markets. As a financial manager, the trend in your firm's stock price over time, relative to competitors and the overall market, is a reflection of how investors view your firm's prospects.

The goal of every investor is to *buy low and sell high*.

Will Rogers, the famous American humorist, gave his own thoughts in 1929 on how to succeed as an investor:

Buy a stock that will go up in value. If it doesn't go up, don't buy it!

Of course, the ability to buy securities at a low price and to sell them at a higher price is the goal of every investor, but it is difficult to do. In this chapter, we'll learn how securities are issued, about the different markets in which they are traded, and how investors can buy and sell securities.

Recall from Chapter 1 that newly created securities are sold in the primary market while existing securities are traded in the secondary market. The initial sale of newly issued debt or equity securities is called a flotation; the initial sale of equity to the public is called an initial public offering (IPO). To raise money, corporations usually use the services of firms called investment bankers (underwriters), whose main activity is marketing securities and dealing with the securities markets. Investment bankers act as intermediaries between corporations and the general public when corporations want to raise capital. Investment banks, for the most part, were separate, stand-alone firms. After the 2007–2009 financial crisis, most investment banks either failed (Bear Stearns, Lehman Brothers) or were purchased by stronger financial institutions (for example, Bank of America's acquisition of Merrill Lynch). Current investment banking firms include Bank of America (Bank of America Merrill Lynch), Barclays (Barclays Capital), Citigroup, Goldman Sachs, JPMorgan Chase & Co. (JPMorgan), and Morgan Stanley, among others.

11.1 ISSUING SECURITIES: PRIMARY SECURITIES MARKETS

primary markets original issue market in which securities are initially sold

secondary markets market in which existing securities are traded among investors

flotation initial sale of newly issued debt or equity securities

initial public offering (IPO) initial sale of equity to the public

investment bankers (underwriters) main activity is marketing securities and dealing with the securities markets

public offering sale of securities to the investing public

private placement sale of securities to a small group of private investors

due diligence detailed study of a corporation

prospectus highly regulated document that details the issuer's operations and finances and must be provided to each buyer of a newly issued security

11.1.1 PRIMARY MARKET FUNCTIONS OF INVESTMENT BANKERS

Although the specific activities of investment bankers differ depending upon their size and financial resources, the functions of investment bankers include originating, underwriting, and selling newly issued securities.

11.1.1.1 Originating

Most of the larger investment banking firms engage in originating securities. As an originator, the investment bank seeks to identify firms that may benefit from a public offering, which is a sale of securities to the investing public, or a private placement, which is a sale of securities to a small group of private investors. The Securities and Exchange Commission (SEC) regulates the public offering process. The private placement process has fewer regulations, but the securities can only be sold to investors who meet certain SEC-regulated guidelines for wealth and investment knowledge. Most of this section will focus on the role of an investment bank in a public offering.

Once the investment bank identifies a firm that may want to sell securities, the investment bank attempts to sell itself to the issuer as the best investment bank to handle the offering.[1] Once an agreement is reached, the investment bank makes a detailed study (called due diligence) of the corporation. The investment bank uses this information to determine the best means of raising the needed funds. The investment banker will recommend the types, terms, and offering price of securities that should be sold.[2] He or she aids the corporation in preparing the registration and informational materials required by the SEC.

One important and carefully regulated piece of information is the prospectus, which details the issuer's finances and must be provided to each buyer of the security. Some of the questions one chief financial officer (CFO) used to quiz prospective investment banking partners for his firm's IPOs are listed in Table 11.1. These questions cover several of the underwriting, selling, and aftermarket aspects of the going-public process, which we will discuss below.

---

[1] For one firm's process of selecting an investment banker, see Alix Nyberg, "The Tough Go Shopping," *CFO*, (January 2001), pp. 89–93; Orin C. Smith, "Wanted: The Right Investment Banker," *Financial Executive*, (November/December 1994), pp. 14–18. Mr. Smith describes his firm's experience of "going public" when he was chief financial officer of Starbucks Coffee Company.

[2] Chapter 18, Capital Structure and the Cost of Capital, will detail some of the items a firm and its investment bank will consider before deciding the securities type to be sold.

Table 11.1 Selections from One Firm's Quiz for Potential Investment Banking Firms Interested in Doing Its IPO

1. How would you position our company in relation to the market and its competition?
2. What companies would you choose as comparable companies from a valuation standpoint? How do you value our company and why?
3. Explain your pricing strategy for our firm's public offering and contrast it with at least four other recent IPOs that you have managed or co-managed.
4. How frequently will research reports be published during the two years following the offering? Present examples of frequency of your research for other IPOs in the last two years.
5. Under what circumstances would you stop research coverage of the company? Have you dropped coverage of any companies you have taken public in the last three years?
6. Please prepare a table that demonstrates your trading performance post-IPO for five or six high-profile IPOs that you have managed in the last 12 to 18 months.

Based upon Alix Nyberg, "The Tough Go Shopping," *CFO* (January 2001), p. 90.

Another piece of advice the investment bank gives firms who want to have an IPO is when to go public. At times, the investing public is particularly interested in firms operating in certain industries or that develop certain technologies. Firms that go public in "hot" IPO markets, meaning when investors are anxious to buy new issues and prices are bid up, sometimes, to twice or three times their initial offering price, are likely to receive better prices for their shares than if they go public in a "cold" market, when investors are less receptive to new stock issues.

11.1.1.2 Underwriting

Investment bankers not only help to sell securities to the investing public, they also sometimes assume the risk arising from the possibility that such securities may not be purchased by investors. This occurs when the investment banker enters into an **underwriting agreement** with the issuing corporation. As shown in Figure 11.1, with an underwriting agreement, securities are purchased at a predetermined or "firm commitment" price by the underwriters, who then sell them to investors at the **offer price**. The difference between the offer price and the price paid by the investment bank is called a **spread**. The spread is revenue to the investment bank, which is used to cover its expenses and to provide a profit from its underwriting activities.

When underwriting securities, the investment bank is carrying the risk of a failed offering. Once it purchases the securities from the issuers, the risk of any security price declines are carried solely by the investment banker. The spread represents a small cushion against a price decline as well as the potential profit the investment banker can earn from the risky underwriting activities.

The issuer has almost no price risk in a firm commitment offering once the offer price is set. The issuer receives the proceeds from the sale immediately, which it can spend on the purposes outlined in the prospectus. The investment bank carries, or underwrites, the risk of fluctuating stock prices. The investment bank carries the risk of loss, or at least the possibility of a smaller spread than expected, should the market's perception of the issuer change or an economic event (such as an unexpected attempt by the Fed to increase interest rates) result in a stock market decline before the investment bank can sell all the securities. But as we shall see in a later section, the phenomenon of "underpricing" or first-day price increases for IPOs is prevalent and reduces the possibility of an investment banker losing money on a firm commitment underwriting.

underwriting agreement contract in which the investment banker agrees to buy securities at a predetermined price and then resell them to investors

offer price price at which the security is sold to the investors

spread difference between the offer price and the price paid by the investment bank

FIGURE 11.1 Diagram of a firm commitment underwriting

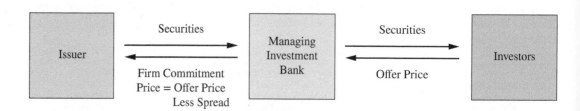

Another means of offering securities is called best-effort selling. Under a best-effort agreement, investment bankers try to sell the securities of the issuing corporation, but they assume no risk for a possible failure of the flotation. The investment bankers are paid a fee or commission for those securities they sell. The best-effort agreement is typically used when the investment bankers anticipate there may be some difficulty in selling the securities and they are unwilling to assume the underwriting risk. From the perspective of investors, an investment bank putting its money at risk with a firm commitment underwriting agreement would be preferable. Investors should view a best-effort offering with some concern. If the investment banker is not willing to support the firm's security sale, why should other investors?

best-effort agreement agreement which the investment bankers try to sell securities of the issuing corporation; but they assume no risk for the possible failure of the flotation

11.1.1.3 Selling

The amount of securities sold in public offerings is large. In 2003, over $5.3 trillion of equity and debt was raised; in 2006, over $7.6 trillion worth of debt and equity securities were sold in the primary market. This fell to about 4.4 trillion in the recessionary market of 2008 and rose to over $6.7 trillion in 2015 and over $6.8 trillion in 2018.[3] To assist the underwriting and best-effort process, the majority of large investment banking houses maintain "retail" outlets throughout the nation. Retail selling is selling to individual investors. There are also many independent retail brokerage outlets not large or financially strong enough to engage in major originating and underwriting functions. These independents may be able to assist the major investment banks in selling new issues. Like the underwriters, they depend upon the resale of securities at a price above their cost to cover expenses and provide profit from operations. A few of the large investment banking houses do not sell to individuals. Rather, they confine their activities entirely to originating, underwriting, and selling securities to institutional investors. Institutional investors are large investors, such as insurance companies, pension funds, investment companies, and other large financial institutions.

Regulatory authorities permit announcements of security offerings to be placed in newspapers and other publications. These announcements, called tombstones, are very restricted in wording and must not seem to be soliciting sales. An announcement is shown in Figure 11.2. This tombstone is careful to point out that "This is neither an offer to sell nor a solicitation of an offer to buy any of these securities." The word "tombstone" apparently derives from the small amount of information it provides and the large amount of white space it features. Boston Chicken was seeking to sell 10.35 million shares of common stock at an offer price of $34.50 a share. The underwriters are shown on the bottom of the announcement.

tombstones announcements of securities offerings placed in newspapers and other publications

The investment bank or banks chosen to originate and handle a flotation are called the lead bankers. In the issue shown in Figure 11.2, the two firms listed at the top, Merrill Lynch and Alex. Brown, are the lead bankers. These lead bankers formed a syndicate of several investment banking firms to participate in the underwriting and distribution of the issue. Syndicate members are listed under the lead bankers, in alphabetical order, in the tombstone ad. For large issues, many firms may be part of the syndicate. For an $8 billion Kraft Foods IPO in 2001, about 75 firms, including the lead bankers, were part of the syndicate. Visa's IPO, the largest ever at the time ($17 billion offering in 2008) had 15 firms in its syndicate. Alibaba's IPO, the largest so far at $25 billion in 2014 had six lead underwriters and a total syndicate of 35 firms.

syndicate group of several investment banking firms that participate in the underwriting and distributing of a security issue

The period after a new issue is initially sold to the public is called the aftermarket. This period may vary from a few hours to several weeks. During this period, the members of the syndicate may not sell the securities for less than the offering price. Investors who decide to sell their newly purchased securities may depress the market price temporarily, so the syndicate steps in to buy back the securities to prevent a larger price drop. This is called market stabilization. Although the Securities Exchange Act of 1934 prohibits manipulation of this sort by all others, underwriters are permitted to buy shares if the market price falls below the offering price. If market stabilization is allowed for a particular issue, it must be stipulated in the prospectus. If part of an issue remains unsold after a period of time, for example 30 days, members may leave the syndicate and sell their securities at whatever price the

aftermarket the period after a new issue is initially sold to the public; during this period, members of the syndicate may not sell the securities for less than the offering price

market stabilization intervention of the syndicate to buy back securities to prevent a larger price drop

---

[3] The first issue of *The Wall Street Journal* each year contains a summary of the prior year's largest IPOs and leading underwriting firms.

This announcement is under no circumstances to be construed as an offer to sell or as a solicitation of an offer to buy any of these securities. The offering is made only by the Prospectus.

New Issue   December 5, 1995

10,350,000 Shares

Boston Chicken, Inc.

Common Stock

Price $34.50 Per Share

Copies of the Prospectus may be obtained from any State or jurisdiction in which this announcement is circulated from only such of the undersigned or other dealers or brokers as may lawfully offer these securities in such State or jurisdiction.

Merrill Lynch & Co.		Alex. Brown & Sons Incorporated
Dean Witter Reynolds Inc.	A.G. Edwards & Sons, Inc.	Goldman, Sachs & Co.
Montgomery Securities	Morgan Stanley & Co. Incorporated	Oppenheimer & Co., Inc.
Piper Jaffray Inc.	Prudential Securities Incorporated	Schroder Wertheim & Co.
Smith Barney Inc.		Nesbitt Burns Securities Inc.
Arnhold and S. Bleichroeder, Inc.	J. C. Bradford & Co.	Equitable Securities Corporation
EVEREN Securities, Inc.	Hanifen, Imhoff Inc.	Interstate/Johnson Lane Corporation
Janney Montgomery Scott Inc.	Edward D. Jones & Co.	Ladenburg, Thalmann & Co. Inc.
Legg Mason Wood Walker Incorporated	Principal Financial Securities, Inc.	Pryor, McClendon, Counts & Co., Inc.
Rauscher Pierce Refsnes, Inc.	Wessels, Arnold & Henderson, L.L.C.	Wheat First Butcher Singer

market will allow. The lead underwriter decides when the syndicate is to break up, freeing members to sell at the prevailing market price.

As an example of underwriting risk, at times the lead banker is left holding many more shares of an offering than it would like.[4] Merrill Lynch and its investment funds once owned over one-half of outstanding shares of First USA Inc., a credit card company, more than three months after its initial public offering (IPO). Bond offerings can turn sour because of unexpected interest rate increases in the economy or credit deterioration by the firm. Convertible bonds are bonds that can be converted to shares of common stock at predetermined prices, and they are sometimes shunned by investors if the conversion and other features are not to their liking. Rumors were that JPMorgan was left owning

---

[4] Alexandra Peers and Craig Torres, "Underwriters Hold Huge Stakes in IPOs," *The Wall Street Journal* (August 12, 1992), p. C1.

80% of a convertible bond offering in 2000 for LSI Logic, a semiconductor firm; this was at the peak of the technology bull market. As the bear market continued into 2001, other firms (including CFSB, Salomon Smith Barney, and Merrill Lynch) were holding large stakes of convertible bond issues.[5] But underwriting is a lucrative business, earning firms billions of dollars in fees.

LEARNING ACTIVITY

Review recent offerings and position openings at investment banking firms such as Merrill Lynch (https://www.ml.com) and Morgan Stanley (https://www.morganstanley.com).

11.2 THE FACEBOOK IPO[6]

Few IPOs caught the attention of so many of a firm's customers as the Facebook IPO on May 18, 2012. At its IPO, Facebook's offer price was $38, valuing the social network at $104 billion, the largest ever by a U.S. firm at its initial offering. The IPO was slated to sell $18.4 billion of common stock. The reason for the difference between Facebook's market capitalization, or market value, at the IPO ($104 billion) and the value of the stock sold ($18.4 billion) is that some private investors and insiders (such as CEO Mark Zuckerberg) did not want to sell all their shares at the IPO or were prevented from doing it. After all, it would look poorly if all the insiders wanted to sell their shares at the IPO. Outside investors would wonder why they were selling and not keeping their shares, unless they were pessimistic about the firm's future.

With such a large offering, competition was fierce among investment bankers for who would get to take Facebook public – thereby earning publicity and large fees for the banker. The syndicate had 33 members; Morgan Stanley was selected as the primary or managing underwriter. Other major syndicate members included JPMorgan Chase & Co. and Goldman Sachs. Fees for taking Facebook public totaled $176 million.

During its "road show" when investment bankers were discussing the firm's risk and return potential, the preliminary price range for Facebook's IPO was between $28 and $35 per share. Such a wide range is common; pricing a new issue is full of uncertainty and assumptions, one of which is how potential buyers are pricing the shares and how eager they are to buy the IPO shares. The apparently high demand for Facebook's IPO caused the firm's management and its lead investment banker to increase the offering price range from $34 to $38 per share shortly before the initial public offering (IPO).

Still, demand for the IPO was high as Facebook was a profitable firm. If all of its users, about 900 million at the time of its IPO, lived in the same country, it would be the third most-populated nation in the world – not a bad start for a firm that didn't exist until 2004.

Despite its popularity, there was a flurry of worrisome news prior to the IPO. Facebook's financial news raised concerns. Prior to its May 2012 IPO, Facebook announced the latest quarter's sales revenues were down 6% from the prior quarter, and profits fell 32% over the same time frame. A major supplier of Facebook ads, General Motors (GM), decided to stop placing ads on Facebook as GM determined the ads weren't generating enough new car purchases.

In addition to the underwriters' decision to raise the IPO offering price, two days prior to the IPO they increased the number of shares to be sold by 25%. Typically in an IPO, investors request to

[5] Suzanne McGee, "First Boston's 'Son of Tyco' Deal Goes Sour," *The Wall Street Journal*, (February 15, 2001), pp. C1, C16; Gregory Zuckerman, "Stalled Convertible: J. P. Morgan Is Left Holding $400 Million of LSI Bond Issue," *The Wall Street Journal*, (March 2, 2000), pp. C1, C19.
[6] The section is based on a number of articles, including, S. Raice, A. Das, and J. Letzing, "Facebook Prices IPO at Record Value," *The Wall Street Journal*, (May 17, 2012); S. Raice, R. Dezember, and J. Bunge, "Facebook's IPO Sputters," *The Wall Street Journal*, (May 18, 2012); J. Strasburg, J. Bunge, and G. Chon, "Nasdaq's Facebook Problem," *The Wall Street Journal*, (May 21, 2012); J. Bunge, A. Lucchetti, and G. Chon, "Investors Pummel Facebook," *The Wall Street Journal*, (May 22, 2012); S. Raice, A. Das, and G. Chon, "Inside Fumbled Facebook Offering," *The Wall Street Journal*, (May 23, 2012); B. Philbin, "Morgan Stanley Chief Defends Facebook Handling," *The Wall Street Journal*, (May 30, 2012); D. Weidner, "Facebook IPO Facts, Fiction, and Flops," *The Wall Street Journal*, (May 30, 2012); M. Langley, A. Das, and A. Lucchetti, "Morgan Stanley Was 'Driver' on Facebook's Wild IPO Ride," *The Wall Street Journal*, (May 30, 2012); A. Lucchetti, "Facebook's Next Fight: Suits and More Suits," *The Wall Street Journal*, (September 26, 2012); T. Demos and A. Lucchetti, "Facebook's IPO Suits to be Handled in New York," *The Wall Street Journal*, (October 5, 2012); R. Winkler, "Facebook's Halloween Trick," *The Wall Street Journal*, (October 31, 2012); J. Light, "Facebook's Friends Left Early," *The Wall Street Journal*, (November 5, 2012).

purchase more shares than they expect to receive, hoping to receive about 50% of their order. When the smaller allotment is received, some investors enter the market to purchase additional shares, helping to create the first-trading day price rise. But the late decision to increase the offering by 25% caught some institutional (for example, hedge funds, pension funds, mutual funds) and some retail (individual) investors by surprise. They received more shares at the IPO than they expected to receive. One hedge fund manager received a half-million more shares than he expected. Some retail investors who didn't expect to receive any shares did receive some. All this helped to reduce demand at the opening of Facebook trading and led to an oversupply of shares that some wanted to sell.

Facebook's IPO on Friday May 18 started well as the price "popped" over 10% from the $38 offering price to over $42. The opening suffered from a 30-minute delay from National Association of Securities Dealers Automated Quotation (NASDAQ) computer and trading problems due, in part, to heavy trading volume: 571 million shares were traded by the end of the first day, which is a lot, considering 421 million shares were sold in the IPO. Facebook's price fell back to its $38 offering price, rose to the $41 range, but fell again before the end of the trading day, closing at $38.23, barely above the $38 offering price.

Morgan Stanley, the lead underwriter, had to enter the market to help stabilize the price as the lack of a sustained "pop," computer issues, and delayed trade confirmations (leading to confusion as to whether some investors' orders were executed) resulted in increased selling pressure on the stock.

On the next trading day, Monday May 21, selling pressure continued as investors had the weekend to consider the problems on the first day of trading, and many decided to sell some or all of their holdings. Facebook ended its first full day of trading down $4 from its offering price, closing at $34 per share. On the second full trading day, Tuesday May 22, the stock fell to $31. The stock would gyrate, closing below $18 per share in early September before rising back to the mid-20s by the end of 2012, 30% under its offering price.

What happened to Facebook's anticipated IPO? As we noted above, some disappointing news came out shortly before the IPO. In spite of this, the offering price and the number of shares to be offered were increased, something which occurs in a small fraction of initial public offerings. Personnel at the investment banks were having second thoughts, too. Stock analysts at some of the underwriters were informing selected clients they were going to reduce their estimates of Facebook's future earnings.

Another reason for the price decline is basic economics of supply and demand. Although the total number of Facebook shares hasn't changed, the number eligible to be sold and traded increased in the first few months after the IPO. The IPO's "lock up" provisions expired, allowing early investors (when Facebook was a private firm) to sell shares. After its 421 million share IPO, another 271 million shares were eligible to be sold and traded three months after the IPO (in August) and another 229 million shares in October. Another 800 million shares became eligible for trading in mid-November. Thus, the public "float," or publicly available shares, quadrupled during Facebook's first six months of trading. No doubt, some of these early investors opted to sell some of their shares, increasing supply and putting further downward pressure on Facebook's stock price.

In the four months following Facebook's IPO, about 50 lawsuits were filed. Some investors filed lawsuits against Facebook and its underwriters, claiming the analysts' forecast changes should have been shared with the entire marketplace prior to the IPO. Lawsuits were filed against NASDAQ, too, alleging losses due to the computer and trading malfunctions at the beginning of Facebook's public trading.

Although we've focused on the Facebook IPO in this section, Figure 11.3 panel A shows the time frame from late 2011 through 2012 was not kind to most high-tech IPOs. Facebook, Groupon, Yelp, and Zynga finished 2012 below their offering prices. During this time frame, the Standard & Poor's 500 (S&P500) rose over 10%. So, while the market was rising, these high-tech IPOs fell in value, in part because of disappointing news about the firms, their sales, and profits. Figure 11.3 Panel B shows several more recent high-tech IPOs – Alibaba, Twitter, King Digital Entertainment, Snapchat, and Spotify – and the pattern of poor stock price performance in the months following the IPO continued for these firms, too. Even with the rising stock market through 2018, buying shares of an IPO is not a consistent

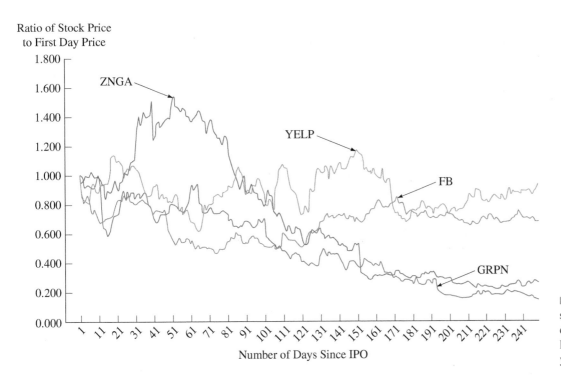

Ratio of Stock Price to First Day Price

Number of Days Since IPO

FIGURE 11.3 Panel A: share price performance of selected 2011 and 2012 IPOs from IPO date to one year later

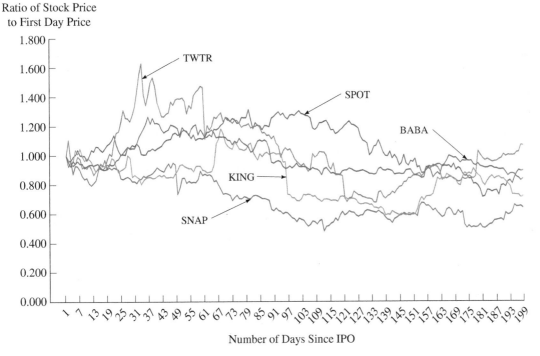

Ratio of Stock Price to First Day Price

Number of Days Since IPO

Panel B: Share Price Performance of More Recent High-tech IPOs from their IPO Date

way to earn profits. For example, of the ten largest initial public offerings in 2015, only four were selling above their offering price by the end of 2016 (and 2016 was a bull market year, with the S&P 500 index rising about 10 percent). Large IPOs in 2017 didn't fare much better with four of them losing money for their first-day investors and one breaking even. The investing principle of diversifying your holdings is true, even for "hot" IPO stocks, as evidence shows many of them flame out – in terms of stock price – not that long after the initial offering.

11.3 OTHER WAYS TO ASSIST ISSUING FIRMS

Firms that are already public and wish to raise additional funds have several choices. They can sell additional securities by using the underwriting process as discussed above. They can also choose to use shelf registration, sell securities to a private party, have a rights offering, or seek competitive bids. We discuss each of these below.

11.3.1 SHELF REGISTRATION

The SEC's Rule 415 allows firms to register security issues (debt and equity) and "put them on the shelf" for sale any time over the succeeding two years. Once registered, the securities can be offered for sale by submitting a short statement to the SEC whenever the firm needs the funds or market conditions are attractive. The **shelf registration** process saves issuers time and money. There is no cost or penalty for registering shelf securities and not issuing them. Filing fees are low, and the firm can take some securities from the shelf, sell them immediately through one underwriter, and later sell more with another underwriter. Not every firm can use shelf registration. Firms must meet four size, credit quality, and ethics requirements:

shelf registration allows firms to register security issues (both debt and equity) with the SEC and have them available to sell for two years

1. The market value of the firm's common stock must be at least $150 million.

2. It must have made no defaults on its debt in the previous three years.

3. The firm's debt must be investment grade (rated BBB or better).

4. The firm must not have been found guilty of violating the Securities Exchange Act of 1934 in the previous three years.

11.3.2 SELL SECURITIES TO A PRIVATE PARTY

ETHICAL A publicly held firm can choose to sell securities in a private placement. To keep current shareholders from suspecting any "sweetheart deals," privately placed equity is, typically, sold at a slight premium to the stock's current market price.

Private equity sales may occur if the firm is the rumored or actual target of a hostile takeover. Management may try to stall the takeover or stop it by selling a large block of voting stock to an investor or syndicate that seems friendlier. Occasionally, news stories contain articles of rumored deals involving firms in financial difficulty that are seeking equity infusions to keep them afloat.

Private placements of equity may fulfill a need for an emergency infusion of equity. Since the shares are not being sold in a public offering, the private placement avoids SEC registration and subsequent publicity. The private sale must follow other SEC regulations, however; the firm must disclose the sale after it occurs, and the private investors must meet SEC requirements as "accredited investors." Basically, accredited investors are those who are considered knowledgeable enough or sufficiently strong financially to invest without the protection provided by the SEC's registration process. Accredited investors can include wealthy individuals with investment experience as well as financial institutions, such as insurance companies and pension funds.

11.3.3 RIGHTS OFFERINGS

pre-emptive rights Right of existing shareholders to purchase new offerings of common stock or securities that can be converted to shares of common stock.

Under the charters of some corporations, if additional shares of common stock (or any security that may be converted to common stock) are to be issued, the securities must be offered for sale first to the existing common stockholders. That is, the existing shareholders have **pre-emptive rights** to purchase newly issued securities. The purpose of this regulation is to permit existing stockholders to maintain their proportional share of ownership. Once popular in the United States, rights offerings among public corporations became infrequent during the 1980s and 1990s, although they are still used among privately held firms. On the other hand, rights offerings remain popular among public firms in Europe.

11.3.4 COMPETITIVE BIDDING

State, local, and federal government bond issues, as well as those of governmental agencies, usually require competitive bidding by investment bankers before awarding underwriting agreements. This is the case for debt and equity securities issued by some public utilities. Large, financially strong firms will occasionally announce they are seeking competitive bids on a new security offering. Under these circumstances, there may be little initial negotiation between the investment houses and the issuer. In these cases, the issuer decides upon the size of issue and the type of security that it wishes to sell. Then, it invites the investment banking houses to offer bids for handling the securities. The investment banking group offering the highest price for the securities, and also providing information showing it will be able to carry through a successful flotation, will usually be awarded the contract.

A great deal of disagreement has existed about the relative advantages and disadvantages of competitive bidding by investment banking houses. Investment bankers strongly contend that the continuing advice they give is essential to an economical and efficient distribution of an issuer's primary market securities. Others contend that competitive bidding enables corporations to sell their securities at higher prices than would otherwise be the case.

A variation of competitive bidding, usually occurring when issuers seek bids solely from investment banking firms, is the **Dutch auction** bidding process, which allows smaller firms and individual investors to purchase securities. The U.S. Treasury uses a Dutch auction, and some IPOs use the Dutch auction mechanism. Most notable was the 2004 Google stock public offering. The process begins when the issuer and its investment banks determine a price range for the stock. After setting up an account with one of the underwriters, investors place bid prices for the number of shares they want to purchase via Internet, fax, or telephone. Bidders can place bids outside the price range if they believe demand will be high (higher bid price) or weak (lower bid price) than expected by underwriters. At the close of the bidding period, the underwriters determine the highest bid, or clearing price, at which all the offered shares are sold.

Dutch auction a bidding process that allows smaller firms and individual investors to purchase securities. Final selling price is determined by bidders' prices and the number of shares they are willing to buy.

For example, suppose a firm, Yoogle, wants to issue 100 million shares in a Dutch auction IPO. Assume only five bids are made:

Bidder	Price	Number of shares
A	$20.50	25 million
B	$20.47	25 million
C	$20.45	25 million
D	$20.43	25 million
E	$20.40	25 million

The clearing price is $20.43; the number of shares to be purchased at that price or higher allows all the offered shares to be sold. Investors A, B, C, and D will be able to purchase their desired number of shares, and investor E will receive no shares in the IPO.

If two or more investors place bids at the clearing price, the offering firm can make one of three choices. First, it can increase the offering size to absorb the extra demand; second, it can sell shares on a pro rata basis to the lowest bidders; and third, it can sell shares on a pro rata basis to all successful bidders. To illustrate, here is what would happen if investors D and E had each placed a bid of $20.43 for 25 million shares. At the clearing price of $20.43, there are orders for 125 million shares, but only 100 million shares are offered. Under the first option, Yoogle can decide (if the prospectus gives Yoogle permission to do so) to increase the offering size to 125 million shares and sell the desired amounts to each investor. With the second option, Yoogle allocates 75 million shares to bidders A, B, and C, and splits the remaining 25 million shares between bidders D and E in proportion to the size of their bids. Since they wanted the same number of shares, the remaining shares are divided evenly, with bidders D and E each receiving 12.5 million shares. Under the third option, with 100 million shares to sell and clearing price demand for 125 million, each investor receives 100/125, or 80%, of their desired number of shares. That is, bidders A, B, C, D, and E will receive 25 million × 0.80 shares, or 20 million shares, each.

11.4 COST OF GOING PUBLIC

One of the drawbacks of going public is its cost. The issuing firm faces direct out-of-pocket costs for accountants' and lawyers' fees, printing expenses, and filing fees.

In addition, the firm faces two additional costs, which together represent the difference between the market value of the firm's shares in the aftermarket and the actual proceeds the firm receives from the underwriters. The first of these costs is the spread, as discussed earlier. The second cost, **underpricing**, represents the difference between the aftermarket stock price and the offering price. Underpricing represents money left on the table or money the firm could have received had the offer price better approximated the aftermarket value of the stock. For example, suppose a firm raises $15 million by selling one million shares at an offer price of $15. By the close of trading on the first day, the firm's stock price is $20. The firm's market value rose (20 − 15) × 1 million shares, or $5 million. Had the securities originally been offered at $20, the firm might have received an additional $5 million for the stock. Some would argue that the firm left $5 million "on the table," financing it could have received had the stock been priced better. To view it another way, if the offer price had been $20, the firm could have raised $15 million by selling only 750,000 shares.

GLOBAL Studies of IPOs in the United States find that firms' IPOs are, on average, underpriced more if it is a smaller issue, if it is issued by a technology firm, if the firm has benefited from venture capital financing, and if the issue's underwriters are more prestigious.[7] Underpricing does not only occur in the United States. Table 11.2 shows that studies in many countries find large first-day returns to IPOs, indicating underpricing. Why underpricing occurs is a matter of debate among researchers; it evidently isn't dependent upon a country's security markets, regulations, or trading mechanisms since it occurs in so many different countries. Some theories include cases where some investors have better information (presumably via their own research) than others regarding the attractiveness of an IPO. To give incentive for the uninformed investors to continue to purchase primary market equity offerings, they on average must earn profits via underpricing. Other theories deal with irrational investor behavior: investors who want to purchase shares but are unable to in the public offering frantically bid up the prices of shares to purchase them from those who did purchase IPO shares.

Together, three costs (direct costs, the spread, and underpricing) make up an IPO's **flotation costs**. The flotation costs of an issue depend upon a number of factors, including the size of the offering, the issuing firm's earnings, its industry, and the condition of the stock market. The flotation costs, relative to the amount raised, are usually lower for a firm commitment offering than a best-effort offering. Best-effort offerings have higher costs for two reasons. First, it is typically higher-risk firms that utilize best-effort offerings, so the banker charges higher fees to compensate for his or her extra efforts. Second, on average, best-effort offerings raise smaller amounts of money, so the fixed costs of preparing the offering are spread over fewer shares sold. One study found that for U.S. corporations the average costs for IPOs of equity, not including underpricing, averaged 11.0% of the proceeds. For seasoned equity offerings (SEOs) – that is, follow-on equity offerings of firms that have public equity outstanding – these costs averaged 7.1%. For convertible bonds, the costs averaged 3.8%. For straight debt issues, issuing costs average 2.2%, although they were sensitive to the credit rating of the issue.[8]

Studies have shown that underpricing varies over time and with IPO volume. In addition, IPO volume is cyclical: periods of frantic IPO activity alternate with periods when few firms go public. There is a close relationship between IPO volume and underpricing. Periods of "hot IPO markets" have heavy IPO volume with more underpricing, and periods of low IPO volume or "cold IPO markets" show less underpricing. The data in Table 11.3 show these patterns since 1980. Note the hot IPO

underpricing represents the difference between the after-market stock price and the offering price

flotation costs composed of direct costs, the spread, and underpricing

---

[7] For reviews of these studies, see Jay R. Ritter, "Investment Bank and Securities Issuance," in George Constantinides, Milton Harris, and Rene Stulz, editors, *Handbook of the Economics of Finance*, (North-Holland, 2002).
[8] Inmoo Lee, Scott Lochhead, Jay Ritter, and Quanshui Zhao, "The Costs of Raising Capital," *Journal of Financial Research*, vol. 19, no. 1, (Spring 1996).

Table 11.2 Average initial returns for 52 countries

Country	Size	Time period	Average initial return
Argentina	26	1991–2013	4.2%
Australia	1,562	1976–2011	21.8%
Austria	103	1971–2013	6.4%
Belgium	154	1984–2017	11.0%
Brazil	303	1979–2018	30.3%
Bulgaria	9	2004–2007	36.5%
Canada	758	1971–2017	6.4%
Chile	86	1982–2018	6.94%
China	3,554	1990–2017	157.7%
Cyprus	73	1997–2012	20.3%
Denmark	164	1984–2011	7.4%
Egypt	62	1990–2017	9.4%
Finland	168	1971–2013	16.9%
France	834	1983–2017	9.7%
Germany	779	1978–2014	23.0%
Greece	373	1976–2013	50.8%
Hong Kong	2,042	1980–2017	44.5%
India	3,145	1990–2017	85.2%
Indonesia	531	1990–2017	26.4%
Iran	279	1991–2004	22.4%
Ireland	38	1991–2013	21.6%
Israel	348	1990–2006	13.8%
Italy	312	1985–2013	15.2%
Japan	3,488	1970–2016	44.7%
Jordan	53	1999–2008	149.0%
Korea	1,758	1980–2014	58.8%
Malaysia	562	1980–2018	51.0%
Mauritius	40	1989–2005	15.2%
Mexico	149	1987–2017	9.9%
Netherlands	212	1983–2017	13.3%
New Zealand	242	1979–2013	18.6%
Nigeria	125	1989–2017	12.8%
Norway	266	1984–2018	6.7%
Pakistan	80	2000–2013	22.1%
Philippines	173	1987–2018	17.3%
Poland	309	1991–2014	12.7%
Portugal	33	1992–2017	11.5%
Russia	64	1999–2013	3.3%
Saudi Arabia	80	2003–2011	239.8%
Singapore	687	1973–2017	25.8%
South Africa	316	1980–2013	17.4%
Spain	143	1986–2013	10.3%
Sri Lanka	105	1987–2008	33.5%

(Continued)

Table 11.2 (*Continued*)

Country	Size	Time period	Average initial return
Sweden	405	1980–2015	25.9%
Switzerland	164	1983–2013	27.3%
Taiwan	1,620	1980–2013	38.1%
Thailand	697	1987–2018	40.0%
Tunisia	38	2001–2014	21.7%
Turkey	404	1990–2014	9.6%
United Arab Emirates	24	2003–2010	270.1
United Kingdom	4,932	1959–2012	16.0%
United States	13,134	1960–2018	16.8%
Vietnam	69	2005–2012	49.1

Source: Tim Loughran, Jay R. Ritter, and Kristian Rydquist, "Initial Public Offerings: International Insights," *Pacific-Basin Finance Journal* (June 1994), vol. 2, pp. 165–199, updated December 20, 2018, https://site.warrington.ufl.edu/ritter/files/2019/01/Int.pdf.

Table 11.3   Number of Offerings and Average First-Day Returns (Underpricing) of Initial Public Offerings in 1980–2018

Year	Number of offerings	Average first-day return (%)
1980	75	13.9
1981	196	6.2
1982	80	10.5
1983	524	8.9
1984	218	2.8
1985	218	6.5
1986	477	6.1
1987	336	5.7
1988	129	5.4
1989	122	7.8
1990	116	10.4
1991	293	11.8
1992	416	10.2
1993	527	12.7
1994	411	9.8
1995	464	21.1
1996	690	17.3
1997	486	13.9
1998	316	20.3
1999	486	69.7
2000	382	56.2
2001	79	14.2
2002	70	8.6
2003	68	11.9
2004	183	12.3
2005	168	10.1
2006	162	11.9

Table 11.3 (*Continued*)

Year	Number of offerings	Average first-day return (%)
2007	160	14.0
2008	21	6.4
2009	43	10.6
2010	100	9.2
2011	82	13.2
2012	105	17.1
2013	162	20.9
2014	225	14.9
2015	122	18.7%
2016	78	14.2%
2017	119	12.5%
2018	143	17.8%

First-day returns are computed as the percentage return from the offering price to the first closing market price.
Source: Based on Table 8 Number of Offerings, Average First-day Returns, and Gross Proceeds of Initial Public Offerings in 1960–2018 of Jay R. Ritter, "Initial Public Offerings: Updated Statistics," unpublished (December 31, 2018), https://site.warrington.ufl.edu/ritter/files/2019/01/IPOs2018Statistics_Dec.pdf

markets in the late 1990s and the cooler markets in the early 1980s, late 1980s, and after the turn of the millennium.

LEARNING ACTIVITY

1. Jay Ritter of the University of Florida's Warrington College of Business is a leading academic researcher on IPOs. His website, https://site.warrington.ufl.edu/ritter/, offers data and recent research findings on IPOs.
2. Websites of firms involved in the Internet IPO market include W. R. Hambrecht & Co. (http://www.wrhambrecht.com). An information source on public offerings is https://www.investor.gov/additional-resources/news-alerts/alerts-bulletins/investor-bulletin-investing-ipo.

11.5 INVESTMENT BANKING FIRMS: OTHER FUNCTIONS, INNOVATIONS, REGULATIONS

Investment banking firms engage in many activities beyond their primary function of distributing long-term security instruments. For example, they have traditionally dominated the commercial paper market. Commercial paper is an important source of short-term financing for business that we will discuss in Chapter 16. Through buying and selling commercial paper, investment bankers assist with the short-term cash flow needs of many businesses. Three investment banking firms dominate commercial paper activities. They are Goldman Sachs, Merrill Lynch, and Credit Suisse.

In recent years, merger and acquisition (M&A) activities have increased in importance for many investment banking firms. Firms with strong M&A departments compete intensely for the highly profitable activity of corporate mergers or acquisitions. Investment banking firms act on behalf of corporate clients in identifying firms that may be suitable for merger. Large fees are charged for this service.

Other activities of investment bankers include the management of pension and endowment funds for businesses, colleges, churches, hospitals, and other institutions. In many cases, officers of investment banking firms are on the boards of directors of major corporations. In this capacity, they can offer financial advice and participate in the financial planning of the firm. Investment bankers also provide financial counseling on a fee basis.

Not all investment bankers engage in every one of these activities. The size of the firm largely dictates the various services it provides. Some firms, known as *boutiques*, specialize in a few activities, such as mergers or underwriting IPOs for high-tech firms.

11.5.1 INVESTMENT BANKING REGULATION

ETHICAL Federal regulation of investment banking is administered primarily under the provisions of the Securities Act of 1933. The chief purposes of the act are to provide full, fair, and accurate disclosure of the character of newly issued securities offered for sale, and to prevent fraud in the sale of such securities. The first purpose is achieved by requiring the issuer to file a registration statement with the Securities and Exchange Commission (SEC) and deliver a prospectus to potential investors. The SEC, however, does not pass judgment on the investment merit of any securities. It is illegal for a seller of securities to represent the SEC's approval of a registration statement as a recommendation of investment quality. The philosophy behind the Securities Act of 1933 is that the most effective regulatory device is the requirement that complete and accurate information be disclosed for securities on which investment decisions may be made. Although the SEC does not guarantee the accuracy of any statement made by an issuer of securities in a registration statement or prospectus, legal action may be taken against officers and other representatives of the issuing company for any false or incorrect statements. Full disclosure is, therefore, instrumental in accomplishing the second purpose, that of fraud prevention.

The Securities Exchange Act of 1934 established the SEC and gave it authority over the securities markets. In addition, attempts to manipulate securities prices were declared illegal. All brokers and dealers doing business in the organized markets must register with the SEC.

broker one who assists the trading process by buying or selling securities in the market for an investor

A **broker** assists the trading process by buying or selling securities in the market for an investor. They help to match buyers and sellers to facilitate trades at current market prices. They get paid a commission, typically a percentage of the value of the transaction or a flat fee for smaller trades. Most of the time, you will use a broker if you trade stocks. Names of wellknown brokers include Merrill Lynch, E-Trade, Charles Schwab, and Edward Jones.

dealer satisfies the investor's trades by buying and selling securities from his or her own inventory

A **dealer** satisfies investors' trades by buying and selling securities from his or her own inventory. Unlike a broker, a dealer is trading with their own capital, or money. They buy securities from those wishing to sell and they sell to those investors who want to buy. Rather than earning a commission, dealers make a profit on the spread – the difference between the price they pay and the price at which they sell securities.

SMALL BUSINESS PRACTICE

BUSINESS ANGELS: WHO ARE THEY?

Business angels are private investors who provide start-up capital for small businesses. Although they are wealthy individuals, angels seldom invest more than $100,000 in a firm. The annual investment in the angel market is estimated to be $20 billion. In addition to providing financing, angels provide valuable advice and sometimes help with the preparation of business plans. Robert Gaston completed a survey of over 400 angel investors for the Small Business Administration (SBA) and found the following: angels, typically, are entrepreneurs and over 80% are business owners or managers. Angels will consider small investments, are usually older than the individuals they are helping, and are the largest source of small business financial capital. Iris Lorenz-Fife in

Financing Your Business (Prentice-Hall) provides valuable advice on how to attract angels, how to react when angels respond, and a checklist for the small business person to examine in terms of deciding whether angels are right for you.

Angels usually identify small business investment opportunities through word-of-mouth referrals from bankers, accountants, lawyers, and business consultants. Angels are attracted to individuals who have the drive to succeed. When an angel responds to a business plan, ensure you spell out the amount, timing, and length of the investment. Also, the degree of involvement of the angel in the firm's operations should be spelled out in advance.

blue-sky laws protect the investor from fraudulent security offerings

In addition to federal regulation of investment banking, most states have **blue-sky laws** to protect investors from fraudulent security offerings. Blue-sky laws apparently get their name from the efforts of some unscrupulous operators who, if not restricted, would promise to sell investors pieces of the blue sky. Because state laws differ in their specific regulations, the federal government is the primary regulator of investment banking. The most common violation of state blue-sky laws is that of misrepresenting the financial condition and asset position of companies.

The Glass-Steagall Act of 1933 ended the ability of commercial banks to act as underwriters of newly issued securities. There were many commercial bank failures during the Great Depression, and there was thought to be evidence that some of the failures resulted from the underwriting activities and poor equity investments of banks. With the passage of the Gramm-Leach-Bliley Act of 1999, the walls between commercial banking and investment banking fell and the traditional boundaries among insurance, commercial banks, investment banks, and other financial institutions have blurred.

11.5.2 INNOVATIONS AMONG INVESTMENT BANKING FIRMS

As we saw in Chapter 10, investment banking firms have tried to meet the needs of issuers and investors by developing many variations of "debt" and "equity." As far as the process of underwriting is concerned, the Internet has had a relatively minor impact on public offerings. Some firms have tried using the Internet as a means to sell securities to small investors and to reduce the amount of underpricing of securities. Most investment banks are large, well-capitalized firms. Investors who receive IPO shares in an offering are typically large institutional clients of the investment banks and their favored retail customers (those with large brokerage accounts who do a lot of trading). The Internet has the potential to make investors more equal by allowing them to bid for shares in Dutch auctions. By selling shares to the highest bidders, all investors are treated equally; if small investors bid a higher price than an investment bank, they will receive their requested number of shares first. Second, by seeking bids, the hope is that the average price received by the issuing firm will exceed the price they would receive in a firm commitment underwriting. Bond offerings have been made available on the Internet, too. Internotes is a name given to bonds sold via the Internet. Corporations, government agencies, and municipalities have issued bonds using the Internet.[9]

Another means of going public for a private firm is to merge with or acquire a public firm. This is how the New York Stock Exchange (NYSE) "went public"; it purchased the publicly held electronic communications network (ECN) firm, Archipelago Holdings.

> **LEARNING ACTIVITY**
>
> 1. **An overview of various regulations and the Electronic Data Gathering and Retrieval (EDGAR) system for required SEC filings can be found at https://www.sec.gov.**
> 2. **Visit the site of a firm that facilitates Internet bond offerings: https://www.incapital.com/.**

The primary market, we have learned, is where securities are first issued; the issuer sells the securities in an offering to investors. Any trading of the securities, thereafter, occurs in the secondary market. The secondary markets provide liquidity to investors who wish to sell securities. It is safe to say that, were it not for secondary securities markets for trading between investors, there would be no primary market for the initial sale of securities. Selling securities to investors would be difficult if investors had no easy way to profit from their holdings or no way to sell them for cash. Secondary markets allow investors to shift their assets into different securities and different markets. These markets provide pricing information, thus providing a means to evaluate a firm's management and for management to determine how investors are interpreting its actions. The secondary market for securities has two components: organized security exchanges, which have physical trading floors, and the over-the-counter (OTC) market, a network of independent dealers and agents who communicate and trade electronically rather than on a trading floor. The NYSE is the prime example of an organized exchange while the NASDAQ is an OTC market.

A firm that fares poorly is penalized through pressure placed on its management by its stockholders as market prices of its securities fall in the secondary market. In addition, when such a firm seeks new capital, it will have to provide a higher expected return to investors. The position of a firm's

11.6 TRADING SECURITIES – SECONDARY SECURITIES MARKETS

---

[9] Rachel Koning, "Chicago Bonds Go Straight to Buyers," *The Wall Street Journal*, (September 15, 2005), page D2; Emily S. Plishner, "E-bonds: Will They Fly?" *CFO*, (March 2001), pp. 87–92; Terzah Ewing, "Too Hot an IPO? Andover.net's 252% Pop Raises Questions About Underwriter's 'Dutch Auction'," *The Wall Street Journal*, (December 9, 1999), pp. C1, C23; John Thackray, "A Kinder, Gentler IPO?" *CFO*, (October 1999), pp. 41–42; Silvia Ascarelli, "Investment Bank Niche Thrives for Online IPOs," *The Wall Street Journal*, (October 18, 1999), p. A431.

management becomes increasingly vulnerable as business deteriorates. Ultimately, the firm's directors may replace management, or the firm may be a target of a takeover attempt.

11.6.1 ORGANIZED SECURITY EXCHANGES

An organized securities exchange is a location with a trading floor where all trading takes place under rules created by the exchange. Organized exchanges in the United States include the New York Stock Exchange (NYSE; this is part of the NYSE Euronext group following a 2007 merger of a U.S. and a European stock exchange) as well as several regional exchanges, such as the Boston, Chicago, Cincinnati, Philadelphia, and Pacific Stock Exchanges. The regionals trade local and national issues, including *dual-listed* stocks, which are those traded on more than one exchange. Another national exchange, the American Stock Exchange (Amex), was merged into NYSE Euronext in 2008; it has become part of the larger stock exchange and, in 2009, was renamed NYSE Amex Equities. The "branding" function of marketing works in finance as well, as the NYSE Euronext firm seeks to take advantage of the stature and goodwill of the "NYSE" brand in such renaming.

In late 2013, the Intercontinental Exchange (ICE) made a bid, valued at the time at over $11 billion, to buy NYSE Euronext. The iconic "New York Stock Exchange" name, with its global recognition, remained after the acquisition. After the merger, the newly formed company, ICE Group, had two units: NYSE Euronext with a focus on stock trading, and the Intercontinental Exchange (ICE) with a focus on trading futures, options, and other such contracts.

The organized stock exchanges use the latest in electronic communications. This ensures an internally efficient trading mechanism where orders are tracked and processed quickly. It ensures that prices on the different exchanges are identical, so a trader cannot *arbitrage*, or purchase a security on one exchange at one price while selling it on another at a different price to lock in a riskless profit. The present methods of transmitting information within cities and between cities are in sharp contrast to the devices used before the introduction of the telegraph in 1844. Quotations were conveyed between New York and Philadelphia through signal flags in the daytime and light signals at night from high point to high point across New Jersey in as little as ten minutes.

Because of its relative importance and because in most respects its operations are typical of those of the other exchanges, the NYSE, sometimes called the "Big Board," will provide the basis for the following description of exchange organization and activities.

> **DISCUSSION QUESTION 1**
>
> **Would primary markets exist without the existence of secondary markets? Why or why not?**

11.6.2 STRUCTURE OF THE NEW YORK STOCK EXCHANGE

floor brokers independent brokers who handle the commission brokers' overflow

house brokers (commission brokers) act as agents to execute customers' orders for securities purchases and sales

independent brokers handle the commission brokers' overflow

registered traders individuals who purchase a seat on the exchange to buy and sell stocks for their own account

Like all the stock exchanges in the nation, the objective of the NYSE is to provide a convenient meeting place where buyers and sellers of securities, or their representatives, may conduct business. In addition, the NYSE provides facilities for transaction settlement, establishes rules for the trading processes and the activities of its members, provides publicity for the transactions, and establishes standards for the corporations whose securities are traded on the exchange. There are three basic types of members: designated market makers, floor brokers, and registered traders. In turn, there are two variations of floor brokers: house brokers and independent brokers.

The largest group of members on the New York Stock Exchange is the house brokers. The key function of house brokers, or commission brokers, is to act as agents to execute customers' orders for securities purchases and sales. In return, the broker receives a commission for the service. Merrill Lynch owns several seats used by their house brokers. Independent brokers handle the house brokers' overflow. When trading volume is particularly heavy, house brokers will ask an independent broker to help them in handling their orders. Registered traders are individuals who purchase a seat on the exchange to buy and sell stocks for their own account. Since they do their own trading, they do not pay any commissions. They may also be on retainer from a brokerage house, often a regional firm that does not want its own seat on the exchange.

Designated market markers (DMMs), or assigned dealers, have the responsibility of making a market in an assigned security. Each stock is assigned to a DMM,[10] who has a trading post on the exchange floor. DMMs select the opening price at the start of trading each day based upon the previous day's closing price and the backlog of buy and sell orders that exist. As market makers, DMMs maintain an inventory of the security in question and stand ready to buy or sell to maintain a fair and orderly market. That means they must be ready to purchase shares of their assigned stock when there are many sellers, and they must be willing to sell shares when traders want to buy. Exchange regulations require DMMs to maintain an orderly market, meaning that trading prices should not change by more than a few cents (stocks are traded in decimals, so the smallest difference in price can be one cent). DMMs maintain bid and ask prices for the security, and the margin between the two prices represents the DMMs' potential gross profit. The bid price is that price the buyer is willing to pay for the securities (thus, it represents the investor's selling price). The ask price is the price at which the owner is willing to sell securities (thus, it represents the investor's purchase price). If the current bid price from brokers is 50.00 and the current ask price is 50.05, DMMs may enter a bid of 50.02 or 50.03, or a lower ask price, to lower the spread and maintain market order.

A recent innovation to the NYSE is a new set of traders called **Supplemental Liquidity Providers (SLPs)**. Their purpose is to help add liquidity to the NYSE trading floor, meaning they supplement the work of DMMs by buying and selling shares throughout the day. To be an SLP, the firm must present the best bid, or offer, prices in their assigned securities at least 5% of the trading day. The NYSE pays the liquidity providers a rebate when they execute a trade. The goal is for the SLPs to generate more bid and ask prices, and to lead to tighter bid-ask spreads and greater liquidity in the stock market.

ETHICAL A penny may not seem like much, but an extra penny per share profit on the one billion shares traded each day on the NYSE can add up to a sizable sum. In the past, trading in listed stocks was supervised by "specialists" rather than DMMs or SLPs. Specialists, which did several of the functions of the current DMMs, had access to order flow information, meaning expected orders, and called limit orders that would be forthcoming should prices change (we will discuss limit orders in a few pages). Specialist firms were accused of placing their own interest above that of their customers by "front running." Front running occurred when a specialist traded to take advantage of information they had (but others did not) about large buy or sell orders that would soon be placed; for example, buying a stock for $23.27 knowing that in a few minutes a customer will place a large buy order which will likely push the price higher, to $23.30 or $23.32.

Another example of profiting from trades is "negative obligation"; that is, a specialist intervening in a trade when their assistance is unnecessary. It occurs when a specialist purchases shares from a seller and then immediately sells them to a buyer at a higher price. The two traders should have been allowed to trade between themselves without the specialist making a profit. In 2004, the NYSE and SEC fined five specialist firms $240 million for such tactics. The NYSE received sanctions, too, from the SEC and was forced to add staff and funds to increase its oversight of regulations and trading. The new DMM structure lessens the chance of such unfair trading activity.

Other exchanges face ethics issues, too. In the late 1990s, two dozen firms involved in NAS-DAQ trading were accused of setting unfairly high trading commissions and were fined a total of $900 million.

11.6.2.1 Listing Securities

All securities must be listed before they may be traded on the New York Stock Exchange (NYSE). To qualify for listing its security, a corporation must meet certain requirements regarding profitability, total value of outstanding stock, or stockholder's equity. Over time, the NYSE has revamped its listing standards in an attempt to attract more high-growth firms (which had been favoring the NASDAQ OTC market for listings) and more foreign companies.[11] The corporation also pays a fee for the privilege of

---

[10] The five designated market makers are Brendan E. Cryan & Co., Citadel Securities LLC, GTS Securities LLC, IMC Financial Markets and Virtu Americas LLC.

[11] The listing standards for U.S. firms can be found on the NYSE website, https://www.nyse.com/publicdocs/nyse/listing/NYSE_Initial_Listing_Standards_Summary.pdf

designated market makers (DMM) assigned dealers who have the responsibility of making a market in an assigned security

Supplemental Liquidity Providers (SLPs) help add liquidity to the NYSE trading floor, meaning they supplement the work of DMMs by buying and selling shares throughout the day

being listed. The original listing fee ranges from \$150,000 to \$250,000. Ongoing, annual fees range from \$35,000 to \$500,000, depending on the number of outstanding shares. The acceptance of the security by the exchange for listing on the Big Board does not constitute endorsement of its quality.

> **LEARNING ACTIVITY**
>
> 1. **Citadel Securities is a NYSE designated market maker; their website is https://www.citadelsecurities.com/. Names of other DMMs are available on the NYSE website, https://www.nyse.com/markets/nyse/trading-info.**
> 2. **Learn about the different exchanges and their listing requirements at http://www.nyse.com, and https://www.nasdaq.com. Many international exchanges are available on the Web, too. See, for example, the Toronto Stock Exchange, https://www.tsx.com; exchanges in the United Kingdom, https://www.londonstockexchange.com; the Tokyo Stock Exchange, https://www.jpx.co.jp/english/ and the Frankfort Stock Exchange, http://www.deutsche-boerse.com. Links to many more are available at www.world-exchanges.org (World Federation of Exchanges).**

11.7 SECURITY TRANSACTIONS

bid price offered by a potential buyer

ask price requested by the seller

spread difference between the bid and ask prices

Buying and selling securities is similar to buying and selling other items in a negotiated market. Whether you want to sell a house or a car, you have a price you are asking potential buyers to pay. Buyers of your house or car may not want to pay your price but will offer their own price, a bid, to see if you will agree to sell for a lower price. In security transactions, potential buyers place **bid** prices, as in an auction, and sellers have their **ask** prices. The difference between the lower bid and higher ask is the **spread**. The narrower the spread, the more liquid the market and the quicker a transaction can be made.

Internet sites inform us (with a time delay, unless you purchase access to real-time data) what the bid and ask prices are for a security throughout the day. For example, a quote from such a site for Microsoft stock may show the following:

$$\text{Bid: } 30.42 \times 50900$$

$$\text{Ask: } 30.43 \times 50800$$

This means there is demand for 50,900 shares by potential buyers at that point during the day and the highest bid price for Microsoft shares is \$30.42. There are 50,800 shares offered for sell at that time and the lowest asking price is \$30.43. With trading in pennies, this is the tightest spread possible, since only one cent separates the bid and ask prices. This shows that Microsoft stock, at least in this snapshot of time, is quite liquid.

Investors can place a number of different types of orders to buy or sell securities. To execute a trade, they need to contact a stock brokerage firm where they can set up an account. The investor can then specify the type of order to be placed as well as the number of shares to be traded in specific firms. Securities orders to buy and sell can be market, limit, or stop-loss orders.

11.7.1 MARKET ORDER

market order an order for immediate purchase or sale at the best possible price

An order for immediate purchase or sale at the best possible price is a **market order**. The brokerage firm that receives an order to trade shares of stock listed on the NYSE at the best price possible transmits the order to its New York office where the order is transmitted to its commission broker on the floor of the exchange.

11.7.2 LIMIT ORDER

limit order maximum buying price (limit buy) or the minimum selling price (limit sell) specified by the investor

In a **limit order**, the maximum buying price (limit buy) or the minimum selling price (limit sell) is specified by the investor. For example, if a commission broker has a limit buy order at 50 from an investor and other brokers have ask prices higher than 50, the order would not be filled at that moment. The broker will wait until a price of 50 or less becomes available. Of course, if the price of the stock progresses upward rather than downward, the order will not be completed. Limit orders may be placed to expire at the end of one day, one week, one month, or on a good-until-canceled basis.

11.7.3 STOP-LOSS ORDER

A **stop-loss order** is an order to sell stock at the market price when the price of the stock falls to a specified level. The stockholder may protect gains or limit losses due to a fall in the price of the stock by placing a stop-loss order at a price a few points below the current market price. For example, an investor paying $50 for shares of stock may place a stop-loss order at a price of $45. If the price does fall to $45, the commission broker sells the shares for as high a price as possible. This order does not guarantee a price of $45 to the seller since by the time the stock is actually sold a rapidly declining stock price may have fallen to well below $45. On the other hand, if the stock price does not reach the specified price, the order will not be executed.

These orders can be used to protect profits. If the stock increases in price after its purchase, the investor can cancel the old stop-loss order and issue a new one at a higher price.

There is risk in placing a stop order. At times, security prices can be very volatile, with sharp price declines followed by quick price increases, and vice versa. Sometimes, this occurs due to a software or other technical glitch in the exchange's trading system. If you hear about a quick price reversal, it may be referred to as a "flash crash." Volatility can enter the market because of a "fat finger syndrome," in which a trader punches the wrong order size into their computer. The danger in placing a stop order is that it may be executed following a quick price change. You may have entered a stop order to protect against a large loss – for instance, if a "flash crash" occurs, prices may quickly fall, and your order will be executed – but if prices quickly rise again, your stock will have been sold for no apparent economic reason. For this reason, the NYSE is no longer accepting stop orders after February 2016, although their use will continue on other exchanges.

stop-loss order order to sell stock at the market price when the price of the stock falls to a specified level

11.7.4 SHORT SALE

A **short sale** is a sale of securities that the seller does not own. An investor will want to short a stock if she or he feels the price will decline in the future. Shares of the stock are borrowed by the broker and sold in the stock market. In the event that a price decline does occur, the short seller covers the resulting short position by buying enough stock to repay the lender. If any dividends are paid during the time the stock is shorted, the short seller must pay the dividends owed on the borrowed shares.

short sale sale of securities that the seller does not own

As an example, suppose Amy thinks AT&T's stock price will fall in the future because of intense competition in the telecommunications industry. She contacts her broker – for example, Merrill Lynch – and gives instructions to sell 100 shares of AT&T short. The broker, in turn, arranges to borrow the necessary stock, probably from another Merrill Lynch investor who has their stock in **street name**, meaning they keep their stock certificates at the brokerage firm rather than taking personal possession of them. Having sold the borrowed stock, the brokerage house keeps the proceeds of the sale as collateral. In our example, if the securities were sold at $40, Merrill Lynch will keep the proceeds from the 100 shares, $4,000, in Amy's account. Let's say the stock drops to a price of $36 and Amy wants to cover her short position. She tells her broker to buy 100 shares, which costs her $3,600. Merrill Lynch returns the newly purchased shares to the account from which they were borrowed. Amy sold $4,000 worth of stock and purchased $3,600 worth of stock after it fell in price; the difference, $400, is Amy's profit, ignoring brokerage commissions. The person from whose account the shares were borrowed will never know that they were borrowed; Merrill Lynch's internal record keeping will keep track of all such transactions.

street name an investor's stock certificates are kept at the brokerage firm rather than taking personal possession of them

If the price of AT&T stock rises, the short seller must still cover her short position at some future time. If the price rises to $45 a share and the position is closed, Amy will pay $4,500 to purchase 100 shares to cover her position. Amy will suffer a loss of $500 ($4,000–$4,500) from her short sale.

Because short sales have an important effect on the market for securities, the SEC regulates them closely. Heavy short sale trades can place undue pressure on a firm's stock price. Among the restrictions on short sales is one related to selling only on an uptick. This means that a short sale can take place only when the last change in the market price of the stock, from transaction to transaction, was an increase. For example, if the most recent transaction prices were 39.95, 39.95, 40.00, 40.00, 40.00, the short sale would be allowed as the last price change was an increase. A short sale would not be allowed if the most recent transactions prices were, for example, 40.07, 40.01, 40.00 or 40.10, 40.00, 40.00, since the most recent price change was a decrease.

In addition, Federal Reserve System (Fed) and NYSE regulations require the short seller to maintain a margin, or deposit, of at least 50% of the price of the stock with the broker. Loans of stock are callable on 24 hours' notice.

11.7.5 BUYING ON MARGIN

buying on margin investors borrow money and invest it along with their own funds in securities

margin minimum percentage of the purchase price that investors must pay in cash; it is the ratio of the investor's equity (own money) to the market value of the security

Buying on margin means the investors borrow money and invest it along with their own funds in securities. The securities purchased in this way become collateral for the loan. The margin is the minimum percentage of the purchase price that investors must pay in cash. In other words, margin is the ratio of the investor's equity (own money) to the market value of the security. In order to buy on margin, the investor must have a margin account with the brokerage firm, which, in turn, arranges the necessary financing with banks.

Margin trading is risky; it magnifies the profits as well as the losses from investment positions. For example, suppose an investor borrows $20,000 and combines it with $30,000 of his own money to purchase $50,000 worth of stocks. His initial margin is 60% ($30,000 of his own money divided by the $50,000 value of the securities). Should the market value of his stock rise 10% to $55,000, the value of his equity rises to $35,000:

Market value of securities:	$55,000
Less: borrowed funds	$20,000
Value of investor's position:	$35,000

This increase in value to $35,000 represents a gain of 16.7% ($5,000/$30,000). A 10% rise in the stock's value increased the value of the investor's position by 16.7% because of the use of margin.

Margin also magnifies losses. If the value of the securities falls by 10% to $45,000, the value of the investor's equity would fall to $25,000:

Market value of securities:	$45,000
Less: borrowed funds	$20,000
Value of investor's position:	$25,000

This loss in value to $25,000 represents a loss of 16.7%. A 10% fall in the stock's value decreased the value of the investor's position by 16.7% because of the use of margin.

margin call the option of either closing out the position or investing additional cash to increase the position's equity or margin

initial margin initial equity percentage

maintenance margin minimum margin to which an investment may fall before a margin call will be placed

Should the value of the securities used as collateral in a margin trade begin to decline, the investor may receive a margin call from the brokerage firm. The investor will face a choice of either closing out the position or investing additional cash to increase the position's equity, or margin. If the market price of the pledged securities continues to decline and the investor fails to provide the new margin amount, the brokerage house will sell the securities. Under current Fed regulations, investors must have an initial margin of at least 50% when entering into a margined trade. The minimum maintenance margin to which the position can fall is 25% before the broker will have to close out the position. Depending upon the individual investor's creditworthiness, a brokerage firm can impose more stringent margin requirements.

The combination of falling prices, margin calls, and sales of securities can develop into a downward spiral for securities prices. This kind of spiral played an important role in the stock market crash of 1929. At that time, there was no regulatory restraint on margin sales and, in fact, margins of only 10% were common. An outcome of this was the Securities Act of 1933 and the Securities Exchange Act of 1934 to regulate short sales, margin trading, and the process of issuing and trading securities.

DISCUSSION QUESTION 2

Describe current situations where an investor might use a limit order, stop order, market order, trade on margin, or execute a short sale.

11.7.6 RECORD KEEPING

When a trade takes place, the information is sent to a central computer system, which, in turn, sends the information to display screens across the nation. This consolidated report includes all transactions on the New York Stock Exchange (NYSE) as well as those on the regional exchanges and other markets trading NYSE-listed stocks. Trades can be for a **round lot** of 100 shares or an **odd lot**, a trade of fewer than 100 shares.[12] The details of the purchase transaction are sent to the exchange's central office and then to the brokerage office where the order was placed. Trade information is also sent to the registrar of the company whose shares were traded. The company needs this information so new certificates can be issued in the name of the investor or the brokerage firm (if the shares are to be kept in street name). Likewise, records will be updated so dividends, annual reports, and shareholder voting material can be sent to the proper person.

round lot sale or purchase of 100 shares

odd lot sale or purchase of fewer than 100 shares

A security is bought in *street name* when the brokerage house buys the security in its own name on behalf of the investor. The advantage of this is the investor may sell the securities by phoning the broker without the necessity of signing and delivering the certificates. In the past, stock trades were settled in five days, and then three days, but regulations now require two days for settling trades. This two-day, or "T+2," requirement means that funds to purchase shares (or, if selling, stock certificates of the sold shares) must be presented to the stock broker within two days of the stock trade. This shorter settlement time should make street name accounts more appealing to investors. Plans are underway for a "T+1" (one day settlement requirement), and hopes exist for an all-electronic process that would make settlement immediate.

11.7.7 PROGRAM TRADING

Around 1975, stocks began to be traded in packages, or programs, as well as individually. **Program trading** is a technique for trading stocks as a group rather than individually. It is defined as the trading for a group of at least 15 different stocks with a value of at least $1 million. At first, program trades were simply trades of any portfolio of stocks held by an equity manager who wanted to change the portfolio's composition for any number of reasons. Today, the portfolios traded in package form are often made up of the stocks included in a stock index, such as the Standard & Poor's 500. In a typical week, 25% of all NYSE trades are program trades; in some weeks, the percentage has risen to over 40%. The most active program traders include Morgan Stanley, Merrill Lynch, UBS, Barclays Capital, and Goldman Sachs.

program trading technique for trading stocks as a group rather than individually; a minimum of 15 different stocks with a minimum value of $1 million are traded

A wide range of portfolio trading strategies is now described as program trading. The best-known form of program trading is *index arbitrage*, which is when traders buy and sell stocks with off-setting trades in futures and options to lock in profits from price differences between these different markets.[13] Program traders use computers to keep track of prices in the different markets and to give an execution signal when appropriate. At the moment the signal is given, the orders for the stocks are sent directly to the NYSE trading floor for execution by the proper designated market maker (DMM). The use of computers allows trades to be accomplished more quickly. This can cause problems if price movements trigger simultaneous sales orders by a number of large program traders, in which case a serious plunge in market prices may occur. As a result, efforts have been made to control some aspects of program trading by limiting its use on days when the Dow Jones Industrial Average (a well-known stock market index) rises or falls more than 10%.

LEARNING ACTIVITY

Examples of how trades are placed can be found on the websites of several exchanges, including https://www.nyse.com and https://www.nasdaq.com.

---

[12] For a few high-priced stocks listed on the New York Stock Exchange, a round lot is ten shares.
[13] Futures and options are discussed in this chapter's Learning Extension.

11.8 OVER-THE-COUNTER MARKET

In addition to the organized exchanges, the other major secondary market for securities trading is the over-the-counter (OTC) market. The largest OTC market is the NASDAQ system; NASDAQ stands for National Association of Securities Dealers Automated Quotation system. Although the OTC trades more than twice as many issues as the NYSE, it is composed mainly of stocks of smaller firms even though companies such as Intel, Microsoft, and Apple Computer are listed on it. Like the NYSE, both individual and institutional investors (mutual funds, pension funds, and so forth) place trades in the OTC market.

There are several differences between the organized exchanges and the OTC market. Organized exchanges have a central trading location, or floor, such as the NYSE trading floor on Wall Street in New York City. The OTC is a telecommunications network linking brokers and dealers that trade OTC stocks. The organized exchanges have DMMs that make markets and control trading in listed stocks; the OTC has no DMMs. Instead, OTC dealers buy from and sell for their own account to the public, other dealers, and commission brokers. In a sense, they operate in the manner of any merchant. They have an inventory, composed of the securities in which they specialize, that they hope to sell at a price enough above their purchase price to make a profit. The OTC markets argue that theirs is a competitive system, with multiple dealers making a market in a company's stock.

To trade in an OTC stock, investors contact their broker, who then checks a computer listing of dealers for that particular stock. After determining which dealer has the highest bid price or lowest ask price, the broker contacts the dealer to confirm the price and to execute the transaction.

ETHICAL The OTC market is regulated by the Maloney Act of 1938. This act amended the Securities Exchange Act of 1934 to extend SEC control to the OTC market. The law created the legal basis for OTC brokers and dealers to form national self-regulating trade associations. This was one instance where business requested government regulation. It stemmed from honest dealers in the investment field who had little protection against bad publicity resulting from the unscrupulous practices of a few OTC dealers. Under this provision, the Financial Industry Regulatory Authority (FINRA) was formed.[14] All rules adopted by FINRA must be reported to the SEC. The SEC has the authority to take away any powers of the FINRA.

The FINRA has established a lengthy set of rules and regulations intended to ensure fair practices and responsibility on the part of the association's members. Any broker or dealer engaged in OTC activities is eligible to become a member of the FINRA, as long as it can prove a record of responsible operation and the broker or dealer is willing to accept the FINRA code of ethics.

11.8.1 THIRD AND FOURTH SECURITY MARKETS

It should not be surprising that an activity as broad as the security market would give rise to special arrangements. Despite their names, the third and fourth markets are two additional types of secondary markets that have evolved over time.

third market market for large blocks of listed stocks that operates outside the confines of the organized exchanges

The **third market** is a market for large blocks of listed shares that operates outside the confines of the organized exchanges. In the third market, blocks of stock (units of 10,000 shares) are traded OTC. The participants are large institutions (such as mutual funds, insurance companies, and pension funds) that often need to trade large blocks of shares. Brokers assist the institutions in the third market by bringing buyers and sellers together and, in return, they receive a fee.

fourth market a market in which large institutional investors arrange the purchase and sale of securities among themselves without the benefit of broker or dealer

The **fourth market** is even further removed from the world of organized securities trading. Electronic communications networks (ECNs) are computerized trading systems that automatically match buy and sell orders at specified prices. Certain large institutional investors arrange purchases and sales of securities among themselves without the benefit of a broker or dealer. They subscribe to an electronic network in which offers to buy or sell are made known to other subscribers. The offers are made in code, and institutions wishing to accept a buy or sell offer know the identity of the other party only upon acceptance of the offer. A fee is paid to the network provider when the trade is completed. Those who support fourth market trading argue that transfers are often quicker and more economical, but confidentiality is an important feature to many firms.

---

[14] Prior to 2007, this organization was known as National Association of Security Dealers (NASD).

11.8.2 HIGH FREQUENCY TRADING

We've seen how computer programs are used in trading securities by the use of program trading. As trading becomes totally electronic, computer programmers, data analysts, and investors have a "need for speed" in order to analyze data and place orders more quickly than competitors. A penny profit by being the first to execute a trade may seem small, but multiplied by millions (or billions!) of shares each day and with about 250 trading days in a year – and a nearly 24-hour trading ability since computers don't have to eat or sleep – the total profit potential is quite large. **High frequency trading (HFT)** makes use of powerful computers and computer algorithms to analyze price patterns, both within and across different markets. Once a potentially profitable trade is found, the computer submits the order in microseconds.

In addition to profit-oriented trading, HFT provides liquidity to markets. In fact, many Supplemental Liquidity Providers on the NYSE are high frequency traders. HFTs are reimbursed by the NYSE for their willingness to provide liquidity – frequently by posting bid and ask prices just above and below the current market price to help facilitate the next trade. If a trade is executed (for example, the HFT buys shares offered to it at their posted bid price) the HFT will cancel their ask price and enter new bid and ask prices, again just above and below the market price. This gives the illusion of a large amount of canceled orders from HFTs. Although they do cancel orders in an attempt to test a market, they also cancel orders that were posted one or two transactions previously in order to update prices for a liquid market.

> **high frequency trading** uses powerful computers and computer algorithms to analyze price patterns, both within and across different markets, and to submit trades to exchanges in microseconds

> **LEARNING ACTIVITY**
>
> 1. The NASDAQ website is https://www.nasdaq.com.
> 2. Examples of ECNs are Instinet, https://www.instinet.com, and Bloomberg Tradebook, https://www.bloombergtradebook.com/.

11.9 WHAT MAKES A GOOD MARKET?

Consider the NYSE, NASDAQ, third market, and fourth market; what are the requirements for a good market? What makes one market better for trading than another, for a certain type of transaction?

Competition exists in our product markets. For example, the local Walmart store is a marketplace for buying and selling goods; the store is the seller and we, the consumers, are the buyers. Other stores nearby compete for the consumer dollar, wanting you to enter their store and to "trade" with them.

Competition exists among exchanges, too. The NYSE, NASDAQ, and others encourage firms to list their shares with them so that the exchange benefits from the trading volume. For example, the NYSE has been perceived as listing only quality firms that have many shareholders and a history of financial success. The NASDAQ has allowed smaller firms and firms without a financial track record to list with them. The NASDAQ's emphasis on technology (as, historically, trading occurs via market-making dealers and computers rather than in a physical location) has attracted many high-tech firms, such as Microsoft, Intel, Cisco Systems, and Apple, to list their shares on this exchange.

One exchange will boast of quicker execution of trades to encourage investors to trade securities on their exchange rather than with a competitor. For example, the NASDAQ has argued that its technology will allow faster trade execution than the NYSE's DMM system. Over time, the NYSE has responded by automating some trades that do not require interaction with a DMM.

A good market will have four characteristics: liquidity, quick and accurate trade execution, reasonable listing requirements, and low costs. Let's discuss each of these in turn.

First, a market is liquid if trades are executed quickly at a price close to fair market value. Generally, a market needs to have breadth and depth to be liquid. A market has depth if it can absorb large buy and sell orders without disrupting prices. This may mean there are investors with deep pockets willing to take the opposite side of a large trade or there are many traders, each of whom is willing to help execute the trade. A broad market, or one with breadth, attracts many traders. In general, having many traders makes a market more competitive; a few large traders may be able to set prices in their own favor rather than allow competitive forces determine price levels. Generally, trading is more liquid if the difference between the bidder's buy and the seller's ask price is small. Otherwise, large price jumps can occur, depending on how anxious a trader is to execute his buy or sell order.

The second characteristic, the quick and accurate execution of trades, is reasonably self-explanatory. The quicker the sale or purchase is executed, the quicker the investor can receive confirmation and know the transaction price. Studies have indicated that small stock transactions done electronically average one-tenth of a second to execute, whereas larger transactions can take up to ten seconds.[15] The size of the trade, the liquidity of the stock, and the venue affect the transaction time. Computer trading is quickest, NYSE DMM trading is the slowest, and NASDAQ dealers fall somewhere in between. But good recordkeeping is needed, too, to verify the price of the transactions. Accurate transactions records are necessary for portfolio managers (to measure the performance of their stock selections) and individual traders (for tax records).

Third, reasonable listing requirements allow investors to know the quality of the listed firm. The NYSE has the highest standards, in terms of stock ownership, earnings, and cash flow. But many firms that could meet the NYSE standards decide to list their shares elsewhere, believing costs may be cheaper and investor trade execution faster on another exchange. Nonetheless, the average size and profitability is lower for NASDAQ firms than for NYSE firms. The "pink sheet" (an OTC market, now computerized, that started trading speculative issues listed on pink sheets of paper)[16] has no listing fees and its quotes are provided only by dealers making a market in the stock. Its securities are fairly speculative.

Finally, a good market will offer reasonable listing fees to issuers (lest they price themselves out of the market for listings) and low cost to investors. Costs to investors include the commissions paid for stock or bond purchases but also "hidden" costs. Hidden costs include the lack of breadth (that is, few traders), so the buyer must pay the higher ask price of the security (or the seller must accept the lower bid price). Another hidden cost is price pressure, which is another indicator of a market that lacks good liquidity. Price pressure occurs when a large trade moves the market (that is, it causes the market price to change) before it can be fully executed. Professional traders learn to parcel out large trades into smaller trades and to work with several dealers or market makers to minimize price changes that occur because of the large size of the transaction. A market that can absorb such trades is a benefit to investors.

PERSONAL FINANCIAL PLANNING

Stock Market Indexes

"What did the market do today?" is an often heard question in financial circles. Although the subject of the question sounds ambiguous (which market is meant?), the speakers and their listener knows which market: the stock market; specifically, they are asking about the performance of the Dow Jones Industrial Average (DJIA), the well-known stock market index. Only 30 firms comprise the DJIA, but they are 30 large firms whose market capitalization (that is, the number of shares multiplied by the stock price) is large compared to those of other firms. There are dozens of stock market indexes, and even more examples of indexes abound for the bond markets.

Why are indexes so popular? First, they are a means of representing the movement of and returns to the overall market or a segment of the market. The DJIA 30, S&P500, and Wilshire 5000 are measures of stock market performance. The NYSE and NASDAQ indexes measure the performance of the New York and OTC stock markets.

Second, indexes are a useful comparison when you want to benchmark the performance of a portfolio. If your investment advisor recommends a portfolio of stocks that rose 10% in value while the S&P500 rose 20%, you may feel that his or her recommendations were not good. On the other hand, if his or her selections were all OTC stocks and the NASDAQ index rose only 5%, you may judge his or her performance more favorably.

Third, indexes are gaining popularity as investments themselves. Rather than investing to "beat the market," which is difficult to do (as we'll see in Chapter 12, with the discussion of efficient capital markets), more investors are coming to believe the saying, "if you can't beat them, join them." They are choosing to invest in the stocks and bonds that comprise an index in the hope of matching the index's performance over time. Many mutual funds exist so the small investor can do this quickly and easily by purchasing shares of the mutual fund.

[15] Gregory Crawford, "Inconsistency Haunts Investor Equity Trades, Report Says," *Pensions and Investments*, (January 9, 2006), p. 28.
[16] "Yellow sheets" refer to OTC bond market quotations for smaller and lower quality bond issues.

11.9.1 A WORD ON COMMISSIONS

It costs money to trade securities. About the only market participants who don't pay commissions are the exchange DMMs, Supplemental Liquidity Providers, and registered traders on the NYSE and dealers in OTC stocks.

Stock commissions vary from brokerage firm to brokerage firm. Some brokerage firms, called "full-service" brokerages, assist in your trades and have research staff that analyze firms and make recommendations on which stocks to buy or sell. Their analysts write research reports that are available to the firm's brokerage customers. Examples of full-service brokerages include Merrill Lynch, Wells Fargo, and Morgan Stanley.

"Discount" brokerages are for investors who want someone to do their stock transactions. Investors who do not desire or need the extra services of a full-service broker use discounters. Stereotypical discount investors make their own investment decisions and wish to trade at the lowest possible cost. Examples of discount brokerages include E*Trade, Charles Schwab, and TD Ameritrade. Internet-based brokerages with low overhead costs and basic services, offer stock trading that is inexpensive even when compared to discount brokers. Falling commissions and ease of access make online trading attractive to those who make their own investment decisions. Trading commissions for some online brokerages are under $7 a trade.

Commissions on security trades depend upon several additional factors. More-liquid securities (more actively traded securities or securities with a popular secondary market), generally, have lower commissions. On the other hand, commissions generally are higher, as a proportion of the market value of the securities purchased, for smaller trades that involve fewer shares or lower-priced shares. Many brokerages charge a minimum commission that may make small trades costly. They charge a transaction fee to cover their costs of processing the trade. Others assess fees if your account is inactive for a year; in other words, even if you don't trade, you still pay the broker some fees. As with so many other things in life, wise investors will shop around for the brokerage firm and broker that best meets their particular needs.

It is possible to buy shares of some companies without going through a stock broker. Some firms sell their shares directly to the public; this is called *direct investing*. Other firms allow shareholders to add to their stock holdings through dividend reinvestment plans; as the name implies, the shareholder's dividends are used to purchase shares (including partial or fractional shares) of the firm.

> **DISCUSSION QUESTION 3**
>
> **Merrill Lynch (https://www.ml.com) is a full-service broker; Charles Schwab (https://www.schwab.com) is a discount broker. E*TRADE (https://www.etrade.com) is an online broker. Visit their websites and compare and contrast their services. If you were going to trade stocks, which firm would you prefer to use as your broker? Why?**

> **LEARNING ACTIVITY**
>
> **Merrill Lynch (https://www.ml.com) is a full-service broker. Charles Schwab (https://www.schwab.com) is a premier discount broker that offers stock trading, some research, mutual funds, annuities, and life insurance. An example of an online broker is E*TRADE (https://www.etrade.com).**

In this section we'll review two topics of interest to many investors. The first is a highly publicized aspect of security markets – the use of market indexes. Second, we discuss ways for investors to purchase securities of non-U.S. firms.

11.10 SECURITY MARKET INDEXES AND TRADING FOREIGN SECURITIES

11.10.1 INDEXES

If one listens to the radio, watches television, or reads the newspaper, the phrases "Dow Jones Industrial Average" or "Standard & Poor's 500 Stock Index" will be encountered daily. The 30 stocks that are part of the Dow Jones Industrial Average (DJIA) are listed in Table 11.4. You are probably familiar with most of their names.

Table 11.4   Stocks in the Dow Jones Industrial Average (as of 2019)

American Express	Apple	Boeing
Caterpillar	Chevron	Cisco Systems
Coca-Cola	Disney	DowDuPont
ExxonMobil	Goldman Sachs	Home Depot
IBM	Intel	Johnson & Johnson
JPMorgan Chase	McDonalds	Merck
Microsoft	3M	Nike
Pfizer	Procter and Gamble	Travelers
UnitedHealth Group	United Technologies	Verizon
Visa	Walgreen	WalMart

Market indexes are useful for keeping track of trends in an overall market (such as the NYSE index, which tracks all stocks listed in the NYSE), a sector (the S&P400 industrials summarizes the movements in 400 stocks of industrial firms), or specific industries (Dow Jones' various industry indexes, such as those for banks, autos, chemicals, retail, and many others). Market indexes exist for many different countries' securities markets, including a variety of stock and bond market indexes.

There are many ways in which an index can be constructed. The previous paragraph indicated that indexes can cover various security market segments. Indexes also can be computed in different ways. For example, the Dow Jones Industrial Average of 30 large "blue chip" stocks is based upon a sum of their prices; it is an example of a price-weighted index. The S&P500 stock index, on the other hand, is computed partly by summing the market values (the stock price times the number of shares outstanding) of the 500 component stocks; it is an example of a value-weighted index. Still other indexes are based upon other computational schemes.

The 500 stocks comprising the S&P500 are not the largest 500 firms or the 500 stocks with the largest market values. The index committee of Standard & Poor's Corporation selects the stocks in the index. The committee tries to have each industry represented in the S&P500 index in proportion to its presence among all publicly traded stocks. Most of the changes that occur in the S&P500 index occur because of mergers, acquisitions, or bankruptcies among the firms. Because it is an index based upon market values, large market value firms, or "large capitalization" stocks as they are called, are the main influence on the index's movements over time. In most years, 25 to 30 stocks are replaced in the S&P 500 index.[17]

Bond indexes exist, too. Barclays (Treasury bonds) and Merrill Lynch (corporates) publish bond indexes that show trends in their respective markets. Other indexes will favor intermediate-term Treasury securities, longer-term agencies, and corporate bonds.

Indexes are popular methods for tracking a market. Although the 30 stocks in the Dow Jones Industrial Average, or even the 500 in the S&P index, don't comprise the entire U.S. stock market (which has about 4,000 to 5,000 publicly listed and actively traded firms on the NYSE or NASDAQ), their market values (stock price multiplied by number of shares) make up a large proportion of the U.S. stock market's value. Studies show the performance of the 30 stocks tends to track the overall U.S. stock market over time.

"Large capitalization" indexes include firms with large "market caps," or market capitalizations – that is, market value (price multiplied by number of shares) of $10 billion or more. Small capitalization indexes are made up of "small cap" firms, or those whose market values are less than $2 billion.[18] We can compare returns to large cap stocks and small cap stocks by comparing their respective indexes.

---

[17] David Blitzer, "Inside the S&P 500: Selecting Stocks," accessed December 11, 2015, https://www.indexologyblog.com/2013/07/09/inside-the-sp-500-selecting-stocks/.

[18] There is no official definition for large and small capitalization. Some sources use $10 billion as a minimum of a large cap stock and some sources use $2 billion as the maximum for a small cap stock. These dividing lines will be blurry as the level of stock prices (and market capitalizations) drift up and down over time.

The same is true for the bond market. For example, some bond indexes are made up of Treasury securities while others use junk bonds. Indexes can focus on the broad market (all stocks or all bonds) or on specific market sectors (indexes based only on consumer goods stocks, or only on small caps, or only on junk bonds).

Indexes are used to compare the performance of a portfolio over time. If a portfolio that is invested in large capitalization U.S. stocks consistently earns lower returns than a large cap index, it may be time to find a new investment advisor or portfolio manager.

Finally, indexes are used to create investable portfolios. Studies have shown it is difficult for most investors to consistently earn returns higher than the indexes, over time (more on this in Chapter 12). Thus, an investment option that is growing in popularity is to invest in an index fund – that is, a mutual fund that tries to replicate or copy a specific market index. For example, the Vanguard 500 Index Fund's goal is to replicate the performance of the S&P 500 index.

11.10.2 FOREIGN SECURITIES

`GLOBAL` The growth in the market value of foreign securities has occurred because of general economic expansion, deregulation of exchange rates, and liberalization of regulations of equity markets. The integration of the world's markets is emphasized by the fact that many securities are listed on several markets. The London Stock Exchange, for example, has over 600 foreign (that is, non-UK and non-European) listings, of which about 160 are U.S. firms. The major U.S. stock markets, the NYSE and NASDAQ, trade about 600 foreign stocks. Foreign stocks can be traded in the United States if they are registered with the Securities and Exchange Commission (SEC).

Why would foreign companies raise funds in the United States? The reason is similar to why U.S. firms will tap overseas markets: to gain access to new funding sources and to finance overseas assets with overseas financing. But another reason that foreign companies want a presence in the U.S. capital markets is the breadth and depth of those markets; companies can find an audience for their shares and raise huge amounts of capital. Some leading world economies have stock markets that are all but ignored by their citizens. Germans prefer the safety of savings accounts and bonds; only 13% own stocks.[19] Only 7% of Japanese own shares.[20] One reason for this is government pension systems, which diminish the need to invest long-term for one's retirement. Another reason is a culture that favors conservative investment strategies.

Investors and professional money managers have found it increasingly important to diversify their investments among the world's markets. Such diversification makes possible a broader search for investment values and can reduce the risk in investment portfolios.[21]

Investment in foreign shares by U.S. investors may be facilitated through the use of an **American depository receipt (ADR)**. These ADRs are traded on our exchanges and are as negotiable as other securities. They are created when a broker purchases shares of a foreign company's stock in its local stock market. The shares are delivered to a U.S. bank's local custodian bank in the foreign country. The bank then issues depository receipts. There is not necessarily a one-to-one relationship between shares and depository receipts; one depository receipt may represent five, ten, or more shares of the foreign company's stock. ADRs allow U.S. investors to invest in foreign firms without the problems of settling overseas trades or having to personally exchange currencies. ADRs are traded in dollars, and dividends are paid in dollars as well. A **global depository receipt (GDR)** is similar to an ADR, but it is listed on the London Stock Exchange. U.S. investors can buy GDRs through a broker in the United States.

As securities markets become more global, more and more foreign firms will seek to have their shares or ADRs listed on a U.S. exchange. There are nearly 2,200 ADRs from 90 countries, although

American depository receipt (ADR) receipt that represents foreign shares to U.S. investors

global depository receipt (GDR) listed on the London Stock Exchange; facilitates trading in foreign shares

---

[19] Chris Bryant, "Germans Miss Out on DAX Bonanza as Share Ownership Drops by Third," *Financial Times*, (March 20, 2015), accessed August 12, 2016, https://www.ft.com/cms/s/0/67b0de42-ce49-11e4-9712-00144feab7de.html#axzz4H89r1WjO

[20] Sara Calian and Silvia Ascorelli, "Europeans Lose Love for Stocks," *The Wall Street Journal*, (May 12, 2004), p. C1; Craig Karmin, "The Global Shareholder," *The Wall Street Journal*, (May 8, 2000), p. R4; Leo Lewis, "Japan Does Splits to Woo Mrs. Watanabe," *Financial Times*, (June 25, 2015), accessed August 12, 2016, https://www.ft.com/cms/s/0/796fc798-1b1e-11e5-8201-cbdb03d71480.html#axzz4H89r1WjO

[21] The topic of diversification and its effect on the risk of an investment portfolio will be discussed in Chapter 12.

CAREER OPPORTUNITIES IN FINANCE

FIELD: SECURITIES MARKETS

Opportunities

Individuals and institutions invest in stocks and bonds to finance assets and to create wealth. Many times, as with large corporations, these investments for any given day may be in the millions of dollars. Most investors, however, have neither the time nor the resources to properly plan these investments. Instead, investors turn to securities specialists to plan and execute investment decisions.

Jobs like these require that individuals have the ability to make sound decisions quickly under heavy pressure. For those who excel though, the opportunities are limitless. Brokerage firms, bank trust departments, and insurance companies typically hire professionals in this field.

Jobs

Account Executive, Securities Analyst

Responsibilities

An *account executive*, or securities broker, sells stocks and bonds to individual and institutional customers as well as manages client funds in a manner consistent with client risk-taking objectives. In addition, an account executive must actively pursue new clients and learn about new investment possibilities. Securities firms typically hire account executives to fill entry-level positions. Being a *securities analyst* may also mean being a securities trader for a brokerage firm. A securities analyst must evaluate the value of stocks and bonds and present this information to or act on this information for investors.

Education

A strong background in finance, economics, and marketing is necessary for these jobs. In addition, these jobs require the ability to communicate and negotiate effectively.

---

significant trading occurs in only a small portion of them.[22] Leading ADRs include telecom firms Nokia (Finland), Ericsson (Sweden), and Vodafone (UK), and oil firms British Petroleum (UK) and Royal Dutch Petroleum (Netherlands). Listing an ADR allows U.S. investors to trade a foreign firm's shares more easily. It also gives the foreign firm easier access to a large pool of U.S. investment capital. There is an ADR Index to track price trends.

> **LEARNING ACTIVITY**
>
> The Bank of New York developed the ADR Index. See it on the Internet at https://www.adrbnymellon.com.

11.11 INSIDE INFORMATION AND OTHER ETHICAL ISSUES

ETHICAL The capital markets are successful in allocating capital because of their integrity. Should investors lose confidence in the fairness of the capital markets, all will lose; investors lose an attractive means for investing funds, and issuers will lose access to low cost public capital.

Some individuals who deal in securities and have access to nonpublic, or private, information about mergers, new security offerings, or earnings announcements may be tempted to trade to take advantage of this information. Taking advantage of one's privileged access to information can lead to large profits from timely purchases or sales (or short sales) of securities. In the United States, taking advantage of private "inside" information is thought to be unfair to other investors. These factors, combined with the ease with which inside information can be used, explain why insider trading is not allowed under provisions of the Securities Exchange Act of 1934.

The most obvious opportunity for insider trading occurs for personnel of a corporation who, by virtue of their duties, have knowledge of developments that are destined to have an impact on the price of the corporation's stock. But such "insiders" are not limited to corporate personnel. Investment bankers, by virtue of their relationship with such corporations, may be aware of corporate difficulties, major officer changes, or merger possibilities. They, too, must take great care to avoid using such information illegally. Even blue-collar workers at printing firms that print prospectuses or merger offers have been found guilty of trading on private information based upon what they have read from their presses.

---

[22] Craig Karmin, "ADR Issuance Surges as Firms Abroad Tap Market for Capital," *The Wall Street Journal*, (December 8, 2000), p. C12.

Because the insider trading law is unclear, it is often difficult to tell when it is illegal to turn a tip into a profit. For example, a stock analyst may discover, through routine interviews with corporate officers, information destined to have an impact on the price of the company's stock. Such information conveyed to the analyst's clients may be, and has been considered to be, insider trading. The almost frantic efforts of large firms to control insider trading is understandable in light of the damage that can occur to their reputations. It is understandable, too, that the SEC has made strong efforts to resolve the question that continues to exist with respect to a meaningful and fair definition of insider information. After all, it is the investing public who, without access to this information, pays the price for insider information abuses. The SEC's Regulation Fair Disclosure (Regulation FD) mandates full, public disclosure of material nonpublic information that was otherwise sometimes disclosed to a select few, such as security analysts or large institutional investors. Insight into higher or lower earnings, for example, could result in trading profits (or reduced losses) for those receiving the information, and their clients, at the expense of others not privileged to have access to the information. Regulation FD mandates that if a company official discloses material nonpublic information to certain individuals, it must announce the information to all via public disclosure.

Another breach of investor confidence can occur via "churning." Churning occurs when a broker constantly buys and sells securities from a client's portfolio in an effort to generate commissions. Rather than making decisions that are in the client's best interest, frequent commission-generating trades may be made by brokers with selfish motives. There are times when frequent trading may be appropriate, but it should occur only within the clients' investing guidelines and with the client's interests at heart.

Unfortunately, the millions of dollars paid in investment banking fees result in occasional scandal among some who make poor choices. In 2003, several investment banking firms were fined $1.4 billion for ethical lapses. Through 2015, banks have paid over $150 billion in fines related to the housing crisis that helped precipitate the Great Recession.[23] Evidence showed stock analysts, whose stock recommendations should be unbiased, were sometimes rewarded for writing favorable reports to attract investment banking clients. Recall the first-day returns from IPOs in Table 11.3; in another ethical lapse, some banks allocated IPO shares to top officers of their client firms or to firms they wanted to attract as clients. Allocating shares that may enjoy a quick "pop" in price is a means of bribing clients. In addition to paying large fines, firms must separate stock research from investment banking practices and offer clients independent investment research written by analysts from other firms. Because ethics and integrity are at the center of fair and well-functioning securities markets, major professional certifications, such as the Chartered Financial Analyst (CFA®) and Certified Financial Planner (CFP™), have the topic of ethics as a central part of their certification programs.

> **DISCUSSION QUESTION 4**
>
> **Visit the website of the Certified Financial Planner (CFP) Board, https://www.cfp.net. Type the word "ethics" into the site's search function. Discuss some of the pages you see relating to how the CFP Board emphasizes ethics among its members.**

11.11.1 ETHICS AND JOB OPPORTUNITIES IN INVESTMENTS

Important components of the financial markets are the laws and regulations governing them. Without regulatory bodies and laws, the financial markets and securities trading would be hampered. Regulations dealing with deposit insurance in banks, the required discussion of risks in a new security prospectus, laws forbidding corporate "insiders" from using their privileged information for private gain, and requirements for fair dealings by brokers and dealers when trading for clients work to increase the public's sense of trust and confidence in the financial markets. Individuals who deal with clients must be registered in the state in which they work and must register with the Securities and Exchange Commission (SEC).

Regulations often arise from past abuses or problems. Many of the long-standing regulations in U.S. markets (the Securities Act of 1933 and the Securities Exchange Act of 1934) resulted from the

---

[23] John W. Schoen, "7 Years on From Crisis, $150 Billion in Bank Fines and Penalties," CNBC, April 30, 2015, accessed June 20, 2016, https://www.cnbc.com/2015/04/30/7-years-on-from-crisis-150-billion-in-bank-fines-and-penalties.html.

Table 11.5 Ethical Standards in Investment Professional Certifications

Chartered Financial Analyst (CFA®) Standards of Professional Conduct	Certified Financial Planner (CFP™) Code of Ethics and Professional Responsibility

Standard I: Professionalism
Standard II: Integrity of Capital Markets
Standard III: Duties to Clients
Standard IV: Duties to Employers
Standard V: Investment Analysis,
    Recommendations, and Actions
Standard VI: Conflicts of Interest
Standard VII: Responsibilities as a CFA Institute
    Member or CFA Candidate
For additional details, see www.cfainstitute.org.
	These Principles of the Code express the professional recognition of its responsibilities to the public, to clients, to colleagues, and to employers. They apply to all CFP designees and provide guidance to them in the performance of their professional services.
	Principle 1: Integrity
	Principle 2: Objectivity
	Principle 3: Competence
	Principle 4: Fairness
	Principle 5: Confidentiality
	Principle 6: Professionalism
	Principle 7: Diligence
	For additional details, see www.cfp.net

situation surrounding the stock market crash of 1929. More recently, the Sarbanes-Oxley Act of 2002 arose from corporate accounting scandals. The oversight provided by corporate boards and external auditors failed in some companies, and as a result, false financial statements hid the true condition of those companies. Once uncovered, corporate failure, bankruptcy, job losses, pension losses, and criminal charges involved companies such as Enron, Worldcom, Tyco, Arthur Andersen, HealthSouth Corporation, Olympus, and Toshiba.

Unfortunately, some others entrusted with people's savings have been found less than worthy as well. Several mutual fund firms and investment banks have been accused of wrongdoing in recent years. Stock analysts who worked at investment banking firms wrote false and optimistic research reports, hoping to attract or to keep clients using the firm's lucrative, high fee investment banking business. Others allocated shares of "hot," or popular, initial public offerings (IPOs) to top executives of firms that used the firm's investment banking business. Individuals and firms involved in such unethical dealings include Jack Grubman of Salomon Smith Barney and Henry Blodgett of Merrill Lynch. Of more-recent note is the Ponzi scheme (collecting funds from later investors to pay off earlier investors with what appears to be attractive returns) orchestrated by Bernie Madoff Investment Securities LLC and the firm's owner, Bernie Madoff.

To maintain the professionalism and ethical behavior within the investment field, professional designations have been developed. Few persons with the Chartered Financial Analyst (CFA®) or Certified Financial Planner (CFP™) designations were involved in these scandals because of the ethics training that is part of these programs. Individuals who receive the designations, by passing exams and having a requisite amount of work experience, show they have a certain level of expertise in their field and agree to abide by a code of ethics and professional standards in their dealings with clients and their employer. An overview of expected behaviors for holders of these two investment professional certifications is given in Table 11.5.

Ethics is an important concern within investment-related professions since practitioners advise clients and invest or handle large sums of money. Nearly any career path within the investments field has federal or state regulations on behavior in addition to those required from an earned professional designation.

<table>
<tr><td>APPLYING
FINANCE TO. . .</td><td>

• **Institutions and Markets** One can easily argue that securities markets exist because of the development of financial institutions and intermediaries over time to collect and allocate capital. In particular, investment banks and brokerage houses help firms and governments raise funds in the public and private markets. They assist investors who want to trade securities, and help to provide liquidity to the financial system.

</td><td>

• **Investments** Investors and analysts need to know the different ways to trade (long, short, margin) in securities markets and the risks of each. It is their desire to trade that creates a need for the securities markets and the institutions which facilitate their trading. New information is quickly evaluated by investors as a whole and reflected in changing market prices.

</td></tr>
</table>

• **Financial Management** Firms raise capital in the primary markets. Initial public offerings (IPOs) and secondary offerings are an important undertaking for financial managers who take their firms public. Others in private firms will arrange private placements or loans from banks, insurance companies, and other institutions. Securities markets set the interest rates and security prices for the firm; these are a reflection of the quality of the firm, risk, and investors' expectations of future cash flows.

SUMMARY

LO 11.1 Investment banks help to originate, underwrite, and sell new offerings of securities to the public. When they underwrite, or carry, the risk of a new offering, the investment bank purchases the securities from the issuer – so the issuer gets their funds immediately – and the investment bank sells the securities to the public. They make a profit on the spread, or difference between the firm commitment price they pay the issuer and the offer price for which they hope to sell the securities. In a best efforts offering, the investment bank does not have their own capital at risk. The issuer contracts with the investment bank to sell the new securities on a commission basis. The issuer does not receive funds until the securities are sold.

LO 11.2 The overview of the Facebook IPO shows what can go wrong, even when a well-known firm is going public with large Wall Street investment banks doing the underwriting. Some troubling news about possible future revenue occurred shortly before the IPO, but seemingly high demand for the shares resulted in an offer price and offering size that was larger than expected. But computer problems during the first day of trading and investor nervousness resulted in price volatility and the stock price falling well below the initial offer price in the days following the IPO.

LO 11.3 In addition to assisting with initial public offerings, investment banks can help firms raise funds through selling shelf-registered securities, rights offerings, competitive bids, Dutch auctions, and private placements.

LO 11.4 Flotation costs are made up of direct costs (out-of-pocket expenses, such as accountant and lawyer fees, printing expenses, filing fees), the spread between the firm commitment price the issuer receives and the offer price paid by public investors, and the underpricing. Underpricing represents the difference between the offer price and the market price of the securities after the first day's trading. Underpricing occurs in all national markets and the amount of underpricing rises in "hot" IPO markets and falls in "cold" IPO markets.

LO 11.5 Investment banks are involved in a variety of financial market activities besides helping firms raise money by issuing bonds and shares of stock. They play a role in helping firm's short-term financing needs by helping them sell commercial paper, assisting in merger and acquisition activities, and in managing the large portfolios of pension funds and endowment funds. When dealing with large sums of money, regulations are sure to follow – the Securities Act of 1933 and the Securities Exchange Act of 1934, for example. Rules regarding the behavior of brokers and dealers, as well as other laws, make financial markets one of the more heavily regulated sectors of the economy.

LO 11.6 The secondary markets allow for trading of existing securities. After the primary market offering, investors trade among themselves in secondary markets. The most well-known of the secondary markets for stocks is the New York Stock Exchange. Trading of securities is assisted on the NYSE by a variety of brokers, dealers, and designated market makers.

LO 11.7 Investors can place a market order to buy or sell a security at the current market price. For those who believe the current price is a bit too high (to buy) or low (for selling), stop orders and limit orders can be placed to specify the desired trading price. If the specified price is hit, the stop order will become a market order and will be executed. A limit order may not be executed if the price changes and moves away from the specified price before it can be executed. Investors who are pessimistic about a stock's prospects can borrow shares and do a short sale. Investors willing to take on extra risk can borrow funds when buying shares in order to do a margin trade.

LO 11.8 NASDAQ is the largest OTC, or over-the-counter market. Unlike the NYSE, which has a physical location, OTC markets are telecommunications networks designed to facilitate trading and sharing of dealer bid-ask prices. Specialized types of secondary markets have developed over time. The third market facilitates trading of 10,000 share blocks of stock among institutional investors. The fourth market allows institutional investors to trade anonymously with other institutional investors without benefit of a broker or dealer. High frequency trading (HFT) has impacted secondary markets, as HFT firms use computer algorithms and high-speed computers to identify potentially profitable trades and to supply liquidity to markets.

LO 11.9 A good market is one that allows for fast trades and has prices that don't fluctuate much between trades. Such a market will have liquidity with breadth (many traders) and depth (the ability to absorb large trades without large price changes). Trades will be quickly and accurately executed so investors will soon find out if their buy or sell order occurred and its price. Quality companies will want to have their securities listed on the exchange and the fees for listing will be reasonable and not draw away potential business from the exchange. Brokers typically assist investors in the trading process; as such, they earn commissions. Commissions are typically based on the quantity and quality of brokerage services provided (for example, stock research and company reports, portfolio updates), the size of the trade, and whether the security is widely traded or not (that is, its liquidity). Some brokers may charge additional fees for smaller accounts or for an account with little trading activity over the year.

LO 11.10 A great many stock and bond market indexes exist to measure returns and trends in the overall market and to service various segments or sectors of the market. Such indexes show trends, allow investors to estimate returns in a market, and compare performance over time with other market segments and with their own portfolios. Mutual funds have developed "index funds," which allow investors to purchase a pool of securities that represent an entire index. For investors who want to invest in individual firms, particularly overseas firms, American depository receipts are available for U.S.-based traders wanting to trade foreign stock on U.S. stock exchanges. Global depository receipts allowing trading in foreign shares that are not listed on U.S. exchanges.

LO 11.11 To efficiently allocate capital in an economy, financial markets must operate fairly. One set of investors can't be seen as having an advantage over others – unless that advantage is truly based on skill! Thus, insider trading – the use of private information from a company to trade its shares – is illegal in the United States. A variety of laws regulate exchanges, securities trading, and actions of brokers, dealers, and investors. Those who work on behalf of investors, such as security and financial analysts and financial planners, can study and take exams to earn professional designations such as the CFA charter (Chartered Financial Analyst) and CFP (Certified Financial Planner). Such designations indicate expertise in the field as well as knowledge of the ethical standards and practices of these disciplines. These professional designations can be revoked if the holder has been found to violate the law or the ethical standards of the designation.

KEY TERMS

aftermarket	flotation	maintenance margin	secondary markets
American depository receipt (ADR)	flotation costs	margin	shelf registration
ask	fourth market	margin call	short sale
best-effort agreement	global depository receipt (GDR)	market order	spread
bid	high frequency trading	market stabilization	stop-loss order
blue-sky laws	house brokers (commission brokers)	odd lot	street name
broker		offer price	supplemental liquidity providers (SLPs)
buying on margin	independent brokers	pre-emptive rights	syndicate
dealer	initial margin	primary markets	third market
designated market makers (DMM)	initial public offering (IPO)	private placement	tombstones
due diligence	investment bankers (underwriters)	program trading	underpricing
Dutch auction		prospectus	underwriting agreement
floor brokers	limit order	public offering	
		registered traders	
		round lot	

1. **(LO 11.1)** Why do corporations employ investment bankers?

2. **(LO 11.1)** Identify the primary market functions of investment bankers.

3. **(LO 11.1)** Discuss how investment bankers assume risk in the process of marketing securities of corporations. How do investment bankers try to minimize these risks?

4. **(LO 11.1)** Explain market stabilization.

5. **(LO 11.2)** What were some of the reasons for the decline in Facebook's stock price after its IPO?

6. **(LO 11.3)** Briefly describe the process of competitive bidding and discuss its relative advantages and disadvantages.

7. **(LO 11.4)** Identify the costs associated with going public.

8. **(LO 11.5)** Briefly describe how investment banking is regulated.

9. **(LO 11.5)** Describe the inroads into investment banking being made by commercial banks.

10. **(LO 11.6)** What are some of the characteristics of an organized securities exchange?

11. **(LO 11.6)** Describe the types of members of the New York Stock Exchange (NYSE).

12. **(LO 11.7)** Why is there a difference between bid and ask prices at some point in time for a specific security?

13. **(LO 11.7)** Describe the differences among the following three types of orders: market, limit, and stop loss.

14. **(LO 11.7)** What is a short sale?

15. **(LO 11.7)** Describe buying on margin.

16. **(LO 11.7)** What is program trading?

17. **(LO 11.8)** Describe several differences between the organized exchanges and the over-the-counter (OTC) market.

18. **(LO 11.8)** How do the third and fourth markets differ from other secondary markets?

19. **(LO 11.9)** What factors differentiate a good market from a poor market?

20. **(LO 11.9)** A security's liquidity is affected by what influences?

21. **(LO 11.9)** Why may a stock trade that takes one second to execute be preferable to a trade that takes nine seconds to execute?

22. **(LO 11.9)** What are some factors that influence the commission on a stock trade with a broker?

23. **(LO 11.10)** Give some examples of market indexes. Why are there so many different indexes?

24. **(LO 11.10)** What are American depository receipts (ADRs)?

25. **(LO 11.11)** Why is it illegal to trade on insider information?

26. **(LO 11.11)** What is Regulation FD, and how does it affect security trading?

27. **(LO 11.11)** Between 2007 and 2014, the costs of unethical behavior in investment banks (fines, lawyer costs, trading losses) were estimated at over $100 billion, about 6.6% of industry revenue. Will this be a deterrent?

1. You are the president and CEO of a family-owned manufacturing firm with assets of $45 million. The company articles of incorporation and state laws place no restrictions on the sale of stock to outsiders. An unexpected opportunity to expand arises that will require an additional investment of $14 million. A commitment must be made quickly if this opportunity is to be taken. Existing stockholders are not in a position to provide the additional investment. You wish to maintain family control of the firm regardless of which form of financing you might undertake. As a first step, you decide to contact an investment banking firm.

   a. What considerations might be important in the selection of an investment banking firm?

   b. A member of your board has asked if you have considered competitive bids for the distribution of your securities compared with a negotiated contract with a particular firm. What factors are involved in this decision?

   c. Assuming that you have decided upon a negotiated contract, what are the first questions that you would ask of the firm chosen to represent you?

   d. As the investment banker, what would be your first actions before offering advice?

e. Assuming the investment banking firm is willing to distribute your securities, describe the alternative plans that might be included in a contract with the banking firm.

f. How does the investment banking firm establish a selling strategy?

g. How might the investment banking firm protect itself against a drop in the price of the security during the selling process?

h. What follow-up services will be provided by the banking firm following a successful distribution of the securities?

i. Three years later, as an individual investor, you decide to add to your own holding of the security but only at a price that you consider appropriate. What form of order might you place with your broker?

2. In late 2014, you purchased the common stock of a company that has reported significant earnings increases in nearly every quarter since your purchase. The price of the stock increased from $12 a share at the time of the purchase to a current level of $45. Notwithstanding the success of the company, competitors are gaining much strength. Further, your analysis indicates that the stock may be over-priced based on your projection of future earnings growth. Your analysis, however, was the same one year ago and the earnings have continued to increase. Actions that you might take range from an outright sale of the stock (and the payment of capital gains tax) to doing nothing and continuing to hold the shares. You reflect on these choices as well as other actions that could be taken. Describe the various actions that you might take and their implications.

3. Which of the following securities is likely to be the most liquid according to these data? Explain.

Stock	Bid	Ask
R	$39.43	$39.55
S	13.67	13.77
T	116.02	116.25

4. You purchased shares of Broussard Company using 50% margin; you invested a total of $20,000 (buying 1,000 shares at a price of $20 per share) by using $10,000 of your own funds and borrowing $10,000. Determine your percentage profit or loss under the following situations (ignore borrowing costs, dividends, and taxes). In addition, what would the percentage profit and loss be in these scenarios if margin were not used?

a. the stock price rises to $23 a share

b. the stock price rises to $30 a share

c. the stock price falls to $16 a share

d. the stock price falls to $10 a share

5. Currently, the price of Mattco stock is $30 a share. You have $30,000 of your own funds to invest. Using the maximum margin allowed, what is your percentage profit or loss under the following situations (ignore dividends and taxes)? What would the percentage profit or loss be in each situation if margin were not used?

a. you purchase the stock and it rises to $33 a share

b. you purchase the stock and it rises to $35 a share

c. you purchase the stock and it falls to $25 a share

d. you purchase the stock and it falls to $20 a share

6. The Trio Index includes three stocks, Eins, Zwei, and Tri. Their current prices are listed below.

Stock	Price at time (t)
Eins	$10
Zwei	$20
Tri	$40

a. Between now and the next time period, the stock prices of Eins and Zwei increase 10% while Tri increases 20%. What is the percentage change in the price-weighted Trio Index?

b. Suppose, instead, that the price of Eins increases 20% while Zwei and Tri rise 10%. What is the percentage change in the price-weighted Trio Index? Why does it differ from the answer to part a?

7. The four stocks below are part of an index. Use the information below:

a. Compute a price-weighted index by adding their prices at time t and time $t + 1$. What is the percentage change in the index?

b. Compute a value-weighted index by adding their market values at time t and time $t + 1$. What is the percentage change in the index?

c. Why is there a difference between your answers to (a) and (b)?

Stock	# Of shares outstanding	Price at time (t)	Price at time ($t + 1$)
Eeny	100	10	15
Meeny	50	20	22
Miney	50	30	28
Moe	20	40	42

8. The Quad Index is comprised of four stocks: Uno, Dos, Tres, and Fore.

a. Given the data below on the number of shares outstanding and their share prices at time (t)

and time $(t + 1)$, what is the percentage change in the Quad Index if it is calculated as a price-weighted index? As a value-weighted index?

Stock	# Of shares outstanding	Price at time (t)	Price at time ($t + 1$)
Uno	1000	$10	$11
Dos	500	20	21
Tres	250	40	42
Fore	100	50	60

b. Instead of the prices shown above, suppose we switch the prices for Uno and Fore. That is, Uno's stock price is $50 at time ($t$) and it rises to $60 by time ($t + 1$), and Fore's stock price rises from $10 to $11 over the same time frame. What is the percentage change in the Quad Index if it is computed as a price-weighted index? As a value-weighted index?

c. Explain similarities or differences in your answers to Parts (a) and (b).

9. A U.S. firm wants to raise $10 million of capital so it can invest in new technology. How much will it need to raise to net $10 million using the average costs of raising funds in the chapter?

10. A U.S. firm wants to raise $15 million by selling 1 million shares at a net price of $15. We know that some say that firms "leave money on the table" because of the phenomenon of underpricing.

a. Using the average amount of underpricing in U.S. IPOs, how many fewer shares could it sell to raise these funds if the firm received a net price per share equal to the value of the shares at the end of the first day's trading?

b. How many less shares could it sell if the IPO was occurring in Germany?

c. How many less shares could it sell if the IPO was occurring in Korea?

d. How many less shares could it sell if the IPO was occurring in Canada?

11. Below are the results of a Dutch auction for an IPO of Bagel's Bagels, a trendy bagel and coffee shop chain. Bagel's is offering 50 million shares.

Bidder	Bid price	Number of shares
Matthew	$50.25	15 million
Kevin	49.75	20 million
Amy	49.45	20 million
Megan	49.00	10 million

a. What will be the clearing price?

b. How many shares will each bidder receive if Bagel's allocates shares on a pro rata basis to all the successful bidders?

12. Boneyard Biscuits' Dutch auction for an IPO was a great success. The firm offered 100 million shares. Bids appear below.

Bidder	Bid price	Number of shares
Manahan	$25.25	25 million
Campbell	24.95	30 million
Maloney	24.75	25 million
Touma	24.40	10 million
Clark	24.40	30 million
Fry	24.25	15 million

a. What is the clearing price?

b. What options do Boneyard and its underwriters have for allocating shares? How many shares will each bidder receive under each option?

13. EXCEL Problem: Develop a spreadsheet to do the dollar amount and percentage profit and loss calculations in Questions 4 and 5. Use as inputs to the spreadsheet the amount of your funds you are investing, the initial margin percentage, the maintenance margin percentage, and the stock's price. In addition, have the spreadsheet calculate the stock price at which you'll receive a margin call.

14. EXCEL Problem: Expand the spreadsheet of Problem 13 to consider one extra source of return and one extra cost to using margin. Specifically, modify the spreadsheet to include expected dividends per share and the cost of the margin loan (stated in APR format).

Assume that Broussard Corporation pays a dividend of $0.50 per share, Mattco pays an annual dividend of $0.80 per share, and the margin loan rate is 6%.

15. EXCEL Problem: Adjust the spreadsheet and its calculations in Problem 13 for one more complication, that being to have the length of the holding period (in quarters) be one of the spreadsheet's inputs. Compute the annualized return if the holding period for Mattco stock were (a) three months and (b) six months.

16. Challenge Problem: Get stock price data from https://finance.yahoo.com/ for ten stocks in the Dow Jones Industrial Average (DJIA) for the prior ten days and use these prices to compute a price-weighted index for each of these ten days. Chart the performance of your index versus the DJIA over this time period. How closely do they track one another? What is the total percentage change in each index? Comment on the differences in performance over this time frame.

Learning Extension 11

Introduction to Futures and Options

LO 11.12 Explain what a derivative security is and the role that futures and options contracts play in financial markets.

In addition to stocks and bonds, the financial system has developed other investment vehicles to meet the needs of various market participants. A type of instrument that is gaining widespread use among institutional investors and corporate financial managers is derivative securities. A **derivative security** has its value determined by, or derived from, the value of another investment vehicle. They go by a variety of names, such as forwards, futures, options, and swaps. In this Learning Extension we will focus on two types of derivatives: futures and options.

derivative security a security whose value is determined by, or derived from, the value of another investment vehicle

---

11.12 WHY DO DERIVATIVES EXIST?

spot market the cash market for trading securities; where securities are bought and sold

hedge an action which reduces risk; similar to the concept of insurance

Most assets that you are probably familiar with, such as stocks, bonds, gold, or real estate, are traded in the cash or spot market. The stock exchanges and the primary and secondary markets we examined earlier in the text are examples of **spot markets**. Trades occur in these markets, and cash, along with ownership of the asset, is transferred from buyer to seller.

At times, however, it may be advantageous to enter into a transaction with the promise that the exchange of asset and money will take place at a future time. Such an exchange allows a transaction price to be determined today for a trade that will not occur until a mutually agreed upon future date. Such is the case with a futures contract. As an example, in June, wheat farmers may desire to lock in the price at which they can sell their harvest in September. That way, their profits will not be affected by price swings in the wheat spot market between now and harvest.

For others, it may be desirable to enter into an agreement that allows for a future cash transaction but only if contract buyers find it in their best interest to do so. A derivative security called an *option contract* allows purchasers to decide whether or not to execute the trade in the future. For example, real estate developers may purchase an option for $10,000 to buy property at a fixed price of $500,000 sometime in the next year. Should the value of the property rise above $500,000 in the coming year, they will most likely choose to execute the option and purchase the land for $500,000. The wheat farmers may enter into an option contract to sell their harvest at a predetermined price; say, $3.00 a bushel. Should the spot market wheat price at harvest be $2.50/bushel, they will execute their option and receive the predetermined price of $3.00 a bushel. Should the spot wheat price be higher, say $4.00, they will choose to sell their wheat at the higher spot price and let the option contract expire. Similar option contracts exist for financial assets such as individual stocks, stock indexes, interest rates, and currencies.

Thus, derivatives such as futures and options have evolved to fulfill desirable economic purposes. They shift risk from those who don't like risk to those who are willing to bear it. They bring additional information into the market, and their trading mechanisms have evolved so it may be less costly, in terms of commissions and required investment, to invest in derivatives than in the cash market.

The prudent use of derivatives to **hedge**, or reduce risk, is similar to the concept of insurance. For example, auto insurance is used as a hedge against the large dollar expenses that could arise from a car accident. We pay an upfront price or premium to buy a certain level of protection for a limited amount of time. This is comparable to the concept of hedging with derivatives; hedging with derivatives can protect investors from large adverse price fluctuations in the value of an asset.

The growth in the volume of outstanding derivatives increased dramatically. In 1986, one estimate was that $2 trillion in value was traded; this rose to nearly $10 trillion in 1991, over $40 trillion on a worldwide basis by the end of 1995, $370 trillion in 2006, $512 trillion in 2009, $639 trillion in 2012, $500 trillion in 2015, and $600 trillion in 2018.[24]

---

[24] Fabio Fornari and Serge Jeanneau, "Derivatives Markets," *BIS Quarterly Review*, (March 2004), published by the Bank for International Settlements, Basle, Switzerland. Updated data are available at https://www.bis.org including https://stats.bis.org/statx/srs/table/d5.1. The value mentioned in this statistic is "notational" value, not the actual value of securities traded. Notional value is used to compute the size of the cash flow that is exchanged between market participants. Most futures contracts, for example, require a margin requirement of only 3 to 6% of the contract's notional value.

Speculation, or investing in derivatives in the anticipation of a favorable change in the cash market price, is a risky investment strategy. Speculators are not hedging an underlying investment. They hope for a price move that will bring them profits. The complexity of some derivatives has resulted in some investors undertaking risks they were not aware of, or so they say. In recent years, firms such as Barings PLC, Gibson Greetings, Metallgesellschaft, Procter and Gamble, several municipalities and colleges, and even well-respected Wall Street firms (Bear Stearns, Lehman Brothers) have suffered large losses and bankruptcy because of inappropriate speculation in the derivatives markets. In the following pages we describe several basic derivative securities.

FUTURES CONTRACTS

A futures contract obligates the owner to purchase or sell the underlying asset at a specified price on a specified day sometime in the future. Exchange traded futures contracts are traded on major futures exchanges. Exchange traded futures contracts are standardized as to terms and conditions, such as quality and quantity of the underlying asset and expiration dates (for example, corn delivered under a futures contract must meet certain moisture content standards, among others). This standardization allows futures to be bought and sold, just as common stocks are bought and sold in secondary markets. Someone purchasing (selling) a futures contract can negate their obligation by selling (purchasing) the identical type of contract. This is called a reversing trade.

Today, futures contracts are traded on agricultural goods, precious metals, oil, stock indexes, interest rates, and currencies. Some exchanges on which futures contracts are traded are listed in Table LE11.1.

A risk of entering a contract such as a futures contract is the creditworthiness of the entity on the other side of the transaction. Fortunately, exchange traded futures have little credit or default risk. Purchasers and sellers of futures are required to deposit funds, or initial margin, in a margin account with the exchange's clearing corporation or clearinghouse. The initial margin requirement is usually 3 to 6% of the price of the contract. Funds are added to or subtracted from the margin account daily, reflecting that day's price changes in the futures contract. At the end of each trading day, a special exchange committee determines an approximate closing price, called the settlement price. Thus, futures are cash-settled every day through this process, known as "marking to the market." As is the case with common stocks, should an investor's margin account become too low, the maintenance margin limit will be reached. Then, investors must place additional funds in the margin account or have their position closed.

Thus, rather than buying or selling futures from a specific investor, the futures exchange becomes the counterparty to all transactions. Should investors default, the exchange covers any losses rather than requiring any one investor to do so. But the daily settling of accounts through marking to the market and maintenance margin requirements can prevent investors' losses from growing indefinitely until contract maturity.

Figure LE11.1 presents an example of the futures quotation page from the Chicago Mercantile Exchange (CME or Merc) website. Suppose you were considering buying a futures contract on the S&P500 stock market index. Each contract has a value equal to $250 times the value of the S&P500 stock index. The value of the contract traded on the Merc will, over time, closely follow the variations

futures contract a contract obligating the owner to purchase or sell the underlying asset at a specified price on a specified day in the future

initial margin deposited funds necessary to purchase a derivatives contract

settlement price daily approximate closing price of a futures contract as decided by a special exchange committee

---

Table LE11.1   Selected U.S. Futures Exchanges

CME Group Inc., a CME/Chicago Board of Trade Company. Formerly two separate entities, the Chicago Board of Trade (CBOT) and the Chicago Mercantile Exchange (CME) merged in 2007. The New York Mercantile Exchange (NYMEX) was merged into the CME Group in late 2009. Items traded on the CME Group include futures contracts for agricultural commodities such as corn, wheat, and soybeans; financial futures contracts, especially those involving Treasury securities; futures contracts on stock indexes, interest rates, and foreign currencies; and metals and energy-related futures contracts including crude oil, gasoline, heating oil, natural gas, electricity, gold, silver, copper, aluminum, and platinum. Website: www.cmegroup.com.

Intercontinental Exchange (ICE) serves the global markets for agricultural, credit, currency, emissions, energy and equity index markets. ICE Futures Europe trades crude and refined oil futures. ICE Futures U.S. and ICE Futures Canada list agricultural, currency, and Russell Index markets. Among the commodity futures contracts traded on ICE are contracts for sugar, cotton, and coffee. Website: https://www.theice.com/.

Mth/Strike	Session							Prior Day		
	Open	High	Low	Last	Sett	Pt chge	Est vol	Sett	Vol	Int
MARXX	2,089.40	2,097.70	2,083.60	2,087.20	–	–0.90	4,456	2,088.10	2,256	94,209

FIGURE LE11.1 Sample listing of the S&P500 futures contract

See actual listings at https://www.cmegroup.com/trading/equity-index/us-index/sandp-500.html.

in the actual value of the S&P500 index in the cash or spot market. The March contract opened the day at 2,089.40 per contract (thus having a total contract value of 2,089.40 × $250, or $522,350), and so far during the day's trading had a high of 2,097.70 and a low of 2,083.60. The price of the last recorded transaction was 2,087.20, which is down 0.90 points from the previous day's close.

The settlement price, which is roughly the closing price, is the price at which contracts are marked to market; trading is still ongoing for the day when the data were downloaded so no settlement price is given. Trading volume thus far for the day was 4,456 contracts. Data from the previous trading day show a settlement price of 2,088.10, which is 0.90 higher than the current last price. The previous day's trading volume was 2,256 contracts. The open interest, which is the number of contracts currently outstanding, is 94,209.

OPTIONS

option financial contract that gives the owner the option of buying or selling a particular good at a specified price on or before a specified time or expiration date

strike price (exercise price) price at which the asset can be traded under an option contract

call option contract for the purchase of securities within a specific time period and at a specified price

put option contract for the sale of securities within a specific time period and at a specified price

option writer seller of an option contract

option premium price paid for the option

An **option** is a financial contract that gives the owner the option or choice of buying or selling a particular good at a specified price (called the **strike price** or **exercise price**) on or before a specified time or expiration date. Most of us are familiar with option arrangements of one sort or another.

In some ways a sports or theater ticket is an option. We can exercise it by attending the event at the appropriate time and place, or we can choose not to attend and let the ticket expire as worthless. As another example of an option, the owner of real estate may be paid a certain amount of money in return for a contract to purchase property within a certain time period at a specified price. If the option holder does not exercise the purchase privilege according to the terms of the contract, the option expires.

A contract for the purchase of securities is a **call option**. A **put option** is a contract for the sale of securities within a specific time period and at a specified price. Similar to futures trading, exchange traded options are standardized in terms of expiration dates, exercise prices, and the quantity and quality of the underlying asset upon which the contract is based. Thus, exchange traded options are liquid. A secondary market exists for trading in them. While the Chicago Board Options Exchange (CBOE) remains the main market, the New York, American, Pacific, and Philadelphia exchanges deal in option contracts. Today, options are traded on individual stocks, bonds, currencies, metal, and a wide variety of financial indexes. While most exchange traded options contracts expire in less than a year, the CBOE offers long-lived options on select stocks. Long-term Equity Anticipation Securities (LEAPS), have expiration dates up to three years in the future.

Through the organized exchanges, individual investors can sell or create the options. The seller of an option contract is the **option writer**. The price paid for the option is the **option premium**. It is what call buyers must pay for the right to acquire the asset at a given price at some time in the future, and what put buyers must pay for the right to sell the asset at a given price at some time in the future. The sellers, or writers, of the option receive the premium when they sell the option contract.

Figure LE11.2 presents an example of an option quotation. Suppose you were considering buying a call on XYZZ, and the current price of XYZZ's stock is $51.93. The website contains information on a variety of call and put options for XYZZ. The notation "20 April 50" refers to the contract's expiration date (April 2020) and strike price ($50). If you had done the last trade on the XYZZ 20 April 50 call, the price would have been $3.00 per option. Because each contract is for 100 calls, the total cost of buying the call option would have been $300. During the day, 161 contracts were traded. The number of outstanding 20 April 50 call option contracts is 36,539. The information on the other contracts is interpreted similarly.

How valuable is a call option? Suppose XYZZ's 2020 April 50 option is about to expire and the price of XYZZ's stock is $51.93. If the call option's price were $0.50, investors could buy the option for $0.50 and immediately choose to exercise it since they could buy the stock by paying only $50 a share.

XYZZ

Current Stock Price: $51.93

	Call			Put		
	Last	Vol	Open int.	Last	Vol	Open int.
20 April 50	3.00	161	36,539	1.50	100	6,286
20 April 55	8.25	55	5,789	2.90	150	2,456
22 April 50	8.00	17	1,528	6.50	10	355

FIGURE LE11.2 Stock option quotations

They will sell these shares at XYZZ's market price of $51.93 and receive a profit of $1.43. (They paid a total of $0.50 [option] plus $50 [exercise price], or $50.50; selling the stock for $51.93 results in a $1.43 profit.) This is an example of an **arbitrage** operation in which mispricing between two different markets leads to risk-free opportunities to profit.

arbitrage Trading in two or more markets to take advantage of different prices for the same asset at the same point in time

We are ignoring the effects of commissions in this section. Including commissions would have the effect of increasing the net price paid for any asset and reducing the net proceeds from selling it.

Other investors would want to take advantage of this opportunity. The buying pressure in the options market and selling pressure in the stock market by arbitragers would cause the option and/or stock prices to change and eliminate the risk-free profit opportunity. Thus, if the XYZZ call option were about to expire, its price would have to be $1.93 to eliminate arbitrage opportunities. With a price of $1.93, investors would be indifferent between buying the stock for $51.93 or buying the call for $1.93 and exercising it (total cost, $1.93 + $50 = $51.93).

On the other hand, suppose there is an April 55 call option for XYZZ that was about to expire. With the price of XYZZ stock at $51.93, an investor who pays any price for the option is making a mistake; why pay for an option to purchase the stock at $55 per share when the stock can be purchased for $51.93 per share? The value of the April 55 call option, if it were about to expire, would be zero.

To summarize, the intrinsic value of a call option will be the asset's value minus the exercise price (if the asset's value exceeds the exercise price), or it will be zero (if the asset's value is less than the strike price). If we let V equal the market value of the underlying asset (say, the XYZZ stock price) and X denote the option's exercise price, the value of an option prior to expiration will be the maximum of $V - X$ or 0. This can be written Max $[0, V - X]$. Panel A in Figure LE11.3 illustrates a payoff diagram for a call option from the option buyer's perspective.

The payoff diagram for the seller or writer of the call option is shown in panel B of Figure LE11.3; it is the opposite of the payoff to the option buyer. For the option writer, increases in the asset's price above the exercise price are harmful, since the call option allows the buyer to purchase the higher-priced asset at the lower exercise price. In the case of the 2020 April 50 call option, the writer may be forced to sell XYZZ stock for only $50 a share when its market value is $51.93 per share. As the stock's value climbs, the call writer faces a larger loss.

Payoff diagrams for put option buyers and writers are shown in panels C and D in Figure LE11.3. The put option allows the owner to sell the underlying asset at the exercise price, so the put option becomes more valuable to the buyer as the value of the asset falls below the exercise price.

Suppose there is a XYZZ put option that expires in April with a strike price of $55. If the market price of XYZZ's stock is $51.93, arbitrage will ensure this put option's price will be at least $3.07. For example, should the put's price be $0.50, arbitragers will buy the put for $0.50 and buy the stock for $51.93; they will immediately exercise the put, forcing the put writer to purchase their stock at the exercise price of $55. The arbitragers will gain a risk-free profit of $2.57 on every share (they paid $0.50 [put option] + $51.93 [stock's market value], or $52.43; selling the stock by exercising the put gives them $55, for a profit of $55 − $52.43 = $2.57). Thus, if the put option is about to expire, its price should be $55 − $51.93, or $3.07 to prevent arbitrage.

If the 2020 April 50 put option in Figure LE11.2 was about to expire and the stock's price is $51.93, the value of the put option would be worthless. After all, how many people would want to buy a put option that gave them the right to sell XYZZ at $50 a share when they can sell the stock on the NASDAQ, where XYZZ is traded, for the current market price of $51.93?

FIGURE LE11.3
Diagram for call and
put options showing
intrinsic values

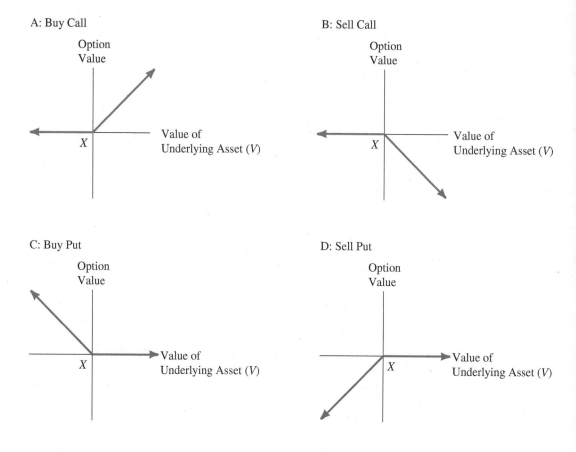

This example shows the intrinsic value of the put option at expiration is the maximum of $X - V$, or zero, or Max $[0, X - V]$. As the asset's value falls below the exercise price X, the value of the put option rises in correspondence with the fall of the asset's value, as seen in panel C.

The situation is reversed for the writer, or seller, of the put option. The payoff diagram for the writer of the put is shown in panel D of Figure LE11.3. As the asset's value falls below the exercise price, the put writer will be forced to purchase the asset for more than its current market value and will suffer a loss. For example, with the April 55 put option, the put writer may have to purchase the stock at the $55 exercise price, thereby paying $3.07 more than the stock's current market price of $51.93.

at-the-money exercise price equals the market price of the underlying asset

in-the-money option with a positive intrinsic value

out-of-the-money option with zero intrinsic value

Here's some more option terminology: an option is **at-the-money** if its exercise price equals the current market price of the underlying asset. An **in-the-money** option has a positive intrinsic value; that is, for a call (put) option, the underlying asset price exceeds (is below) the strike price, X. An **out-of-the-money** option has a zero intrinsic value; that is, for a call (put) option, the underlying asset price is below (exceeds) the strike price, X.

The option's value will equal its intrinsic value only at expiration. At all other times, the option's premium, or price, will exceed its intrinsic value. A major reason for this is time. The longer the option's time to expiration, the greater the chance of the option becoming in-the-money (if it was originally at-the-money or out-of-the-money) or becoming more in-the-money than it originally was. Another important influence on the option premium is the variability in the price of the underlying asset. The greater the asset's variability is over time, the greater is the chance of the option going in-the-money and increasing in value. Therefore, high volatility in the price of the underlying asset *increases* the option premium for both puts and calls.

time value or **speculative value of an option** difference between the option premium and its intrinsic value; it is larger the longer the time to expiration and the higher the underlying stock's price volatility

Note in Table LE11.2 that the premiums are higher for the 2022 option contracts with a $50 strike price than for the 2020 option contracts with a $50 strike price. This shows the **time value** or **speculative value of an options** contract. The time or speculative value is always positive as long as the contract isn't about to expire. Because of this, the option premium will always be greater than the option's intrinsic value.

OPTION PROFIT/LOSS DIAGRAMS

Futures carry an obligation to execute the contract (unless offset by another contract so the investor's net position is zero). An option contract is just that, meaning it gives the owner the option to purchase (call option) or sell (put option) an asset. Thus, if exercising the option will cause the owner to lose wealth, the option can expire unexercised and have a value of zero. While losses on futures can grow as a result of adverse moves in the value of the underlying asset, the owner of an option contract may be able to limit losses by merely choosing not to exercise the contract.

The profit or loss on an option contract depends upon if the option is exercised and on the premium paid (if buying the option) or received (if selling the option). The "payoff," or profit or loss, from an option position differs from the intrinsic value of the option at expiration. The intrinsic value diagrams in Figure LE11.3 will be shifted *down* by the size of the premium when buying a call or a put (since the option buyer pays the premium to the writer) and shifted *up* by the size of the premium when writing a call or put (as the option writer receives the premium).

Figure LE11.4a shows the payoff profile for the 2020 April 50 call option for the buyer of the option when the option expires. No matter how far the stock price falls, the call option's loss is limited to the $3 premium paid per share. But the call option buyer doesn't make a profit on the position until the underlying stock price rises above the strike price to compensate for $3 premium. The **break-even price** on this call option is the $50 strike price plus the $3 premium per share. The stock price must rise above $53 before the call option buyer makes a profit on this position. If, at expiration, the stock price is between $50 and $53, the loss per share will be less than $3 per share. For the call option buyer, the profit (or loss) per share at option expiration equals the intrinsic value minus the call option premium, that is, it will be Max $[(V - X), 0]$ – call premium.

For example, if the stock price at expiration is $55, the call option buyer's profit will be Max $(V - X, 0)$ – premium = Max $(\$55 - \$50, 0)$ – $3 = $5 – $3 = $2 per share. If the stock price at expiration is $45, the call buyer's loss (since the option finished out-of-the-money) will be Max $(V - X, 0)$ – premium = Max $(\$45 - \$50, 0)$ – $3 = $0 – $3 = $–3 per share.

For the call option writer, the payoff profile is flipped. The call writer's maximum profit is the call option premium of $3 per share and the call writer will profit until the stock price rises to $53. Any further increases in the stock's price will cause the call writer to have a loss – and the loss will continue

break-even price price such that the option position's profit is zero; for call option buyers it is the strike price plus the option premium; for put option buyers it is the strike price minus the option premium

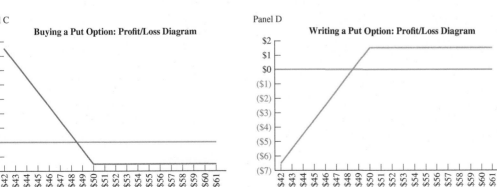

Panel A

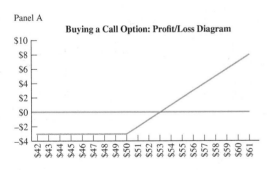

Panel B

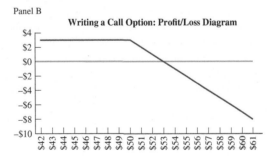

FIGURE LE11.4 Payoff profiles from buying/ writing a call and a put option

to grow as long as the stock price continues to rise. In such a case, the option writer may want to consider closing out his position by buying the identical call option to cancel out the written call position. For example, if the stock price rises to $57 and the option is exercised, the call writer must sell, for $50, a stock with a market price of $57. This $7 loss on the stock sale is reduced by the $3 call option premium paid to the writer, so the net loss is $4 per share.

Panels C and D in Figure LE11.4 show the payoff profiles for the put option buyer (Panel C) and put option writer (panel D). The premium for the 2020 April 50 put option is $1.50 per share. For the put option, the break-even price is $48.50 (the strike price of $50 minus the $1.50 premium). The profit or loss for the put buyer, at expiration, will be the put's intrinsic value minus the put premium; that is, it will be Max $[(X - V), 0]$ − put premium.

If the stock falls to $45 at expiration, the put buyer's profit will be Max ($50 − $45), 0) − $1.50 = $5 − $1.50 = $3.50. If the stock price at expiration is $55, the put option's intrinsic value is $0 and the put buyer's loss is the premium, $1.50.

The put writer's payoff profit mirrors the put buyer's. They face larger potential losses as the stock price falls, as the put obligates the put writer to pay $50 a share regardless of how low the price goes. Their loss is reduced by the $1.50 premium they received for writing the contract. The put writer's maximum profit is the $1.50 premium and they will make a profit if the stock price, at expiration, is $48.50 or higher. Once the stock price falls below $48.50, their losses will grow as the stock price falls. In such a case, the option writer may want to consider closing out his position by buying the identical put option to cancel out the written put position.

LEARNING ACTIVITY

The websites of futures and options exchanges offer visitors the chance to see time-delayed quotes. See, for example, the CME Group, https://www.cmegroup.com, and the Chicago Board Options Exchange, https://www.cboe.com.

SUMMARY

From recent headlines to investment seminars, derivatives are an investment vehicle that will become more prevalent. This Learning Extension has reviewed two types of derivatives: futures and options.

A futures contract represents an obligation to buy or sell the underlying asset at a specified price by a certain date. An options contract is similar, except the owner has the option not to exercise the contract.

Futures contracts can be used to "lock in" prices for a transaction that will not occur until later. They can be used to reduce the risk of price fluctuations. For example, the risk of changing prices in a long asset position (you own it) can be countered by a short position (sell) in an appropriate futures contract. The increases in the value of one position will offset the decreases in the value of the other.

Options are useful for hedging positions as well. Some options positions, such as buying a call option, have the added benefit of maintaining profit potential should the value of the underlying asset rise, while limiting the dollar losses should the underlying asset's value fall.

KEY TERMS

arbitrage	exercise price (strike price)	option	settlement price
at-the-money	futures contract	option premium	spot markets
break-even price	hedge	option writer	strike price (exercise price)
call option	initial margin	out-of-the-money	time value or speculative
derivative security	in-the-money	put option	value of an option

DISCUSSION QUESTIONS

1. Briefly describe a derivative security.

2. What is a futures contract?

3. What is an option contract?

4. Indicate the difference between a call option and a put option.

1. Determine the intrinsic values of the following call options when the stock is selling at $32 just prior to expiration of the options.
   a. $25 call price
   b. $30 call price
   c. $35 call price

2. Determine the intrinsic values of the following put options when the stock is selling at $63 just prior to expiration of the options.
   a. $55 put price
   b. $65 put price
   c. $75 put price

3. Determine the profit (or loss) to a call buyer and a call writer for the following call options when the stock is selling at $32 just prior to expiration of the options and the option premium is $2.50.
   a. $25 strike price
   b. $30 strike price
   c. $35 strike price

4. Determine the profit (or loss) to a put buyer and a put writer for the following put options when the stock is selling at $63 just prior to expiration of the options and the option premium is $3.
   a. $55 strike price
   b. $65 strike price
   c. $75 strike price

CHAPTER 12

Financial Return and Risk Concepts

LEARNING OBJECTIVES

After studying this chapter, you should be able to do the following:

LO 12.1 Compute the arithmetic average using return data for a single financial asset.

LO 12.2 Compute the variance and standard deviation using return data for a single financial asset.

LO 12.3 Describe sources of financial risk.

LO 12.4 Compute expected return and expected variance using scenario analysis.

LO 12.5 Summarize the historical rates of return and risk for different securities.

LO 12.6 Explain the concept of market efficiency and the three different types of efficient markets.

LO 12.7 Calculate the expected return on a portfolio of securities.

LO 12.8 Discuss how the combining of securities into portfolios reduces the overall or portfolio risk using the concept of correlation.

LO 12.9 Explain the difference between systematic and unsystematic risk.

LO 12.10 Describe the Capital Asset Pricing Model and explain the role of beta as a risk measure.

Where we have been. . . We know investors take their savings and direct them in various ways: some to bank accounts and some to stocks, bonds, or other investment vehicles. Investors direct their savings to various instruments by considering a number of factors: How safe is my money? Am I willing to risk a loss in hopes of achieving a large gain? What happens to my investment if security market prices rise or fall?

Where we are going. . . The concepts of risk and return presented in this chapter are important to investors and to the businesses that issue the bonds and stocks that investors purchase. Businesses use a variety of short- and long-term financing tools; the level of interest rates, expected return, and risk will guide firms as they make financing choices (Chapters 16 and 18) and their investment decisions (Chapter 17).

How this chapter applies to me. . . Perhaps no other chapter can affect your investing future more than this discussion of financial risk and return. When coupled with Chapter 10's discussion of bond and stock valuation, you will have a good working knowledge of investment fundamentals.

Peter Bernstein, a well-known financial consultant and researcher, gives us some insights into the word "risk":

> *The word "risk" derives from the early Italian risicare, which means "to dare." In this sense, risk is a choice rather than a fate. The actions we dare to take, which depend on how free we are to make choices, are what the story of risk is all about.*[1]

A closer look at financial risk will be the main topic of this chapter.

Investors place their funds in stocks, bonds, and other investments to attain their financial goals. But stock and bond market values rise and fall over time, based on what happens to interest rates, economic expectations, and other factors. Since no one can predict the future, the returns earned on

---

[1] Peter Bernstein, *Against the Gods: The Remarkable Story of Risk* (New York: John Wiley & Sons Inc. 1998).

investments are, for the most part, unknown. Some may look back and see how different investments performed in the past and predict future returns will be similar. Others do sophisticated economic and financial analyses to estimate future returns.

In this chapter, we will first learn how risk is measured relative to the average return for a single investment. We will review historical data showing the risk/return relationship. We will see that higher risk investments must compensate investors over time with higher expected returns. Our emphasis will shift to a discussion of the efficient markets hypothesis and its implications for investors. This leads to a discussion of the use and advantages of portfolio diversification, and we conclude the chapter with a discussion of systematic versus unsystematic risk.

Figure 12.1 shows monthly prices for the stocks of two firms, Walgreens and Microsoft. Microsoft stock trended upwards during this time frame. Walgreens also rose in value but then moved "sideways" over 2015–18. We can compute monthly returns on these stocks, taking their price changes and dividends into consideration. The monthly return is computed as the following:

> **12.1 HISTORICAL RETURN FOR A SINGLE FINANCIAL ASSET**

$$\text{Dollar return} = \text{Stock price at end of month} - \text{Stock price at beginning of month} + \text{Dividends}$$

To put things in terms of a percentage return, the month's percentage return is the following:

$$\text{Percentage return} = \text{Dollar return}/\text{Stock price at the beginning of the month}$$

For example, suppose in one month Walgreens' stock went from \$33.63 per share at the beginning of the month to \$34.31 at the end of the month. No dividends were paid that month. The dollar return is the following:

$$\text{Dollar return} = \$34.31 - \$33.63 = \$0.68$$

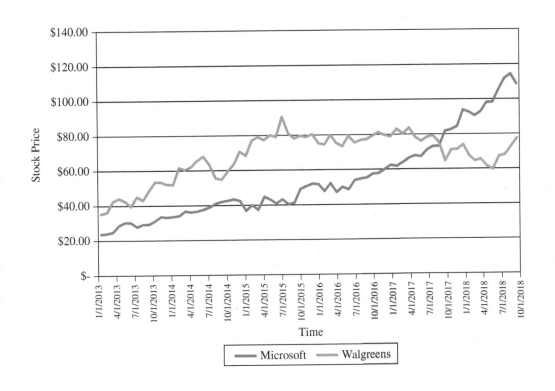

FIGURE 12.1 Microsoft and Walgreens stock prices, 2013–2018

The monthly percentage return is $0.68/33.63 = 0.02022, or 2.022%.

If a dividend were received, that amount would be added to the dollar return. For example, if a dividend of 4 cents had been received during the month, the dollar return would have been the following:

$$\text{Dollar return} = \$34.31 - \$33.63 + \$0.04 = \$0.72$$

The monthly percentage return is $0.72/33.63 + 0.02141, or 2.141%.

One way to measure the risk of an asset is to examine the variability of its returns. For comparison, an analyst may want to determine the level of return and the variability in returns for these two stocks to see whether investors in the higher risk stock earned a higher return over time to compensate or reward them for the higher risk.[2]

12.1.1 ARITHMETIC AVERAGE ANNUAL RATES OF RETURN

If historical, or ex post, data on a stock's returns are known, the analyst can compute historical average return and risk measures. If R_t represents the stock's return for period t, the *arithmetic average return*, $\bar{R}$, over n periods is given by the following formula:

$$\bar{R} = \frac{\sum_{t=1}^{n} R_t}{n} \tag{12.1}$$

The "Σ" symbol means to add or to sum the returns. We compute the arithmetic average return by adding the periodic returns and dividing the sum by n, the number of observations.

Let's assume that Padric held shares of Walgreens stocks over a six-year period. Furthermore, Serinca owned shares of Microsoft over the same six-year period. Following is a list of annual rates of returns over the six years for Walgreens and Microsoft stock:

Year	Percentage form		Decimal form	
	Microsoft	Walgreens	Microsoft	Walgreens
6	20.5%	13.3%	0.205	0.133
5	28.0%	34.9%	0.280	0.349
4	40.5%	57.4%	0.405	0.574
3	8.4%	15.7%	0.084	0.157
2	−4.6%	16.9%	−0.046	0.169
1	−6.6%	−19.4%	−0.066	−0.194
SUM	86.2%	118.8%	86.2%	118.8%
Average	14.4%	19.8%	0.144	0.198

Performing this calculation in Excel is straightforward. Placing the annual returns in columns B and C, we use the SUM function to add the Microsoft returns in cells B2 through B7 by typing = SUM (B2:B7) in cell B9. We divide this sum by six, the number of observations, to compute the average Microsoft return by typing = B9/6 in cell B10. Similar calculations for the Walgreens data are entered into column C.

---

[2] For simplicity, we will use stocks in our discussion here. The concepts are applicable to any asset.

	A	B	C	D
1	Year	Microsoft	Walgreens	
2	2016	0.205	0.133	
3	2015	0.280	0.349	
4	2014	0.405	0.574	
5	2013	0.084	0.157	
6	2012	-0.046	0.169	
7	2011	-0.066	-0.194	
8				
9	Sum	=SUM(B2:B7)	=SUM(C2:C7)	
10	Average = Sum/6	=B9/6	=C9/6	
11	Excel's AVERAGE function	=AVERAGE(B2:B7)	=AVERAGE(C2:C7)	
12				

We can compute the average return by using a special Excel function. If we entered = AVERAGE (B2:B7) in cell B11, we would obtain the same result of 14.4%.

Walgreens' stock has an arithmetic average annual rate of return over these six years of 19.8%, whereas the average annual return for Microsoft stock over the same six-year period was 14.4%. If we are willing to ignore risk as reflected in the variability of returns, an investment in the higher returning stock might be the preferred among the two. However, not all investors have the same tolerance for uncertainty or risk. Let's see how we might quantify this variability in past returns.

The historical risk of a stock can be measured by the variability of its returns in relation to this average. Some quantitative measures of this variability are the variance, standard deviation, and coefficient of variation. All these measures use **deviations** of periodic returns from the average return; that is, $R_t - \bar{R}$, where $\bar{R}$ denotes the average arithmetic return over some time frame.

Note that the sum of the deviations, $\Sigma(R_t - \bar{R})$, is *always* zero. When computing deviations, this is good way to check to see if a math error was made. If the sum of the deviations is not zero, an error was made, either in calculating the average return or in computing one or more deviations. Here's a quick example. Suppose we have three annual returns: 5%, 11%, and −4%. The average return is $[5\% + 11\% + (−4\%)] / 3$, which equals 4%. The three deviations are, as follows:

$$5\% - 4\% = 1\%$$
$$11\% - 4\% = 7\%$$
$$-4\% - 4\% = -8\%$$

The sum of the deviations, 1% + 7% + (−8%), equals zero, just as it should.

How can deviations be used to measure risk if they always add up to zero? By squaring them—that is, multiplying each deviation by itself. Squaring a number always results in a positive number: 7^2 is the same as 7×7 and equals 49. If we square a negative number: $(−8)^2$ we get a positive number—in this case, 64.

The **variance**, represented by the symbol σ^2, is computed by summing the squared deviations and dividing by $n − 1$. (You may recall from a prior course in statistics that when a sample is drawn from a population, dividing by $n − 1$ observations instead of n observations provides a more accurate estimate of the variance and standard deviation characteristics of the population.) In terms of a formula, variance is computed as

$$\sigma^2 = \frac{\sum_{t=1}^{n}(R_t - \bar{R})^2}{(n-1)} \tag{12.2}$$

12.2 HISTORICAL RISK MEASURES FOR A SINGLE FINANCIAL ASSET

deviations periodic return minus the average return; in general, it is any number in a data series minus the average value of the data series

variance computed by summing the squared deviations and dividing by $n − 1$

Stated in words, this formula requires several steps:

1. Find the average return, $\bar{R}$, over the time period being analyzed. If the returns aren't given to us, we will have to use the tools from Section 12.1 to compute periodic returns and their average.

2. Compute deviations by subtracting the average return from each individual return. Check to make sure the sum of the deviations is zero.

3. Square each deviation.

4. Add the squared deviations and divide this sum by $(n - 1)$, the number of observations minus 1, to finish calculating the variance.

In our three annual returns sample above, the deviations were 1%, 7%, and −8%. Squaring them, we have 1, 49, and 64. Summing them, we have $1 + 49 + 64 = 114$. Since we have three observations, we divide 114 by $(3 −1)$ to compute the variance: $114/2 = 57$.

We can find the historical variance in returns for Walgreens' and Microsoft's stocks over the six years as shown in Table 12.1. The results indicate an estimated variance of $649.9\%^2$ for Walgreens and $348.1\%^2$ for Microsoft. The units, percent squared ($\%^2$), may seem odd, but they are the result of the variance calculation in which the deviations are squared before they are added together and divided by $(n - 1)$.

Use of the SUM function and other Excel operators make these calculations less tedious. Of special note is the Excel function VAR. For example, if Walgreens' returns are in cells B2 through B7, typing = VAR (B2:B7) into another cell computes and displays the variance of Walgreens' returns.

12.2.1 STANDARD DEVIATION AS A MEASURE OF RISK

standard deviation the square root of the variance

Squaring the deviations can make variance difficult to interpret. What do units like percent squared or dollars squared tell an investor about a stock's risk? Because of this difficulty, analysts often prefer to use the **standard deviation**, σ, which is the square root of the variance:

$$\sigma = \sqrt{\sigma^2} \tag{12.3}$$

The standard deviation formula gives units of measurement that match those of the return data. Taking the square root of the variance of 649.9 for Walgreens stock gives a standard deviation of 25.5%. This compares to a standard deviation of 18.7% (i.e., the square root of 348.1) for Microsoft. Thus, Walgreens has a relatively higher average return (19.8% versus 14.4%) and a higher standard deviation (25.5% versus 18.7%) when compared to Walgreens for the time period we studied.

Table 12.1   Computing the Variance for the Returns on Microsoft and Walgreens

	Microsoft							Walgreens				
Year	Return	Minus	Average		Deviation	Deviation squared	Year	Return	Minus	Average		Deviation	Deviation squared
6	20.5%	−	14.4%	=	6.1%	37.11	2015	13.3%	−	19.8%	=	−6.5%	41.97
5	28.0%	−	14.4%	=	13.7%	186.46	2014	34.9%	−	19.8%	=	15.1%	228.83
4	40.5%	−	14.4%	=	26.1%	682.87	2013	57.4%	−	19.8%	=	37.6%	1414.23
3	8.4%	−	14.4%	=	−6.0%	35.63	2012	15.7%	−	19.8%	=	−4.1%	17.11
2	−4.6%	−	14.4%	=	−18.9%	357.84	2011	16.9%	−	19.8%	=	−2.9%	8.32
1	−6.6%	−	14.4%	=	−21.0%	440.73	2010	−19.4%	−	19.8%	=	−39.2%	1539.24
Sum =						$1740.63\%^2$	Sum =						$3249.71\%^2$
Variance = Sum/(6 − 1)				=		$348.1\%^2$	Variance = Sum/(6 − 1)				=		$649.9\%^2$
Standard deviation = SQRT (variance)				=		18.72%	Standard deviation = SQRT (variance)				=		25.5%

The square root can be found using a financial calculator with a square root key, as follows:

Financial Calculator Solution:		
	Walgreens stock	Microsoft stock
Inputs:	649.9	348.1
Press:	$\sqrt{}$	$\sqrt{}$
Solution:	25.5	18.7

Spreadsheets can be used, too. Since we know the standard deviation is the square root of the variance, Excel's SQRT function can be used by keying in = SQRT (cell containing the variance). To make the calculation simpler, we can use the STDEV function. If Microsoft's returns are in cells B2 through B7, using = STDEV (B2:B7) in another cell computes the standard deviation.

Sometimes calculations using real data may show that one firm had a higher return and a lower standard deviation than another firm. A result such as this for two firms, a small sample, is by no means a violation of the second principle of finance, that higher returns are expected for taking on more risk. It would indicate only what has happened in the recent past and is based on a limited number of data points. Over time, over many assets, we expect higher risk assets to have higher average returns.

Looking at historical annual returns on these stocks will tell us what their price range has been, namely how low and how high each stock price has been. If we have reason to believe the near future will be similar to the time period we have studied, we can use the standard deviation to help give an investor an intuitive feel for the possible range of returns that can occur. As shown in Figure 12.2, if the underlying distribution of returns is continuous and approximately normal (meaning bell-shaped), then we should expect 68% of actual periodic returns to fall within one standard deviation of the mean; that is, $\bar{R} \pm 1\sigma$. About 95% of observed returns will fall within two standard deviations of the average: $\bar{R} \pm 2\sigma$. Actual returns should fall within three standard deviations of the mean, $\bar{R} \pm 3\sigma$, about 99% of the time. Thus, if the mean and standard deviation are known, a rough range for expected returns over time can be estimated.

Applying this to our data for Walgreens and Microsoft, if returns over a long time period were approximately normally distributed and our six years of observations were a reasonable representation of returns over the long run, Table 12.2 should show the range of possible outcomes along with

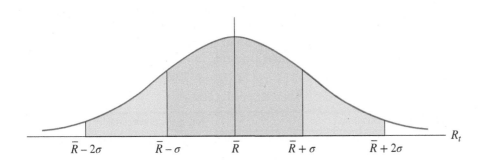

FIGURE 12.2
Normal distribution

Table 12.2 Distribution of Returns for WAG and MSFT

Stock	Percent of returns	Annual return estimates		
		Downside (%)	Average (%)	Upside (%)
Walgreens	68	−5.7	19.8	45.3
	95	−31.2	19.8	70.8
	99	−56.7	19.8	96.3
Microsoft	68	−4.3	14.4	33.0
	95	−23.0	14.4	51.7
	99	−41.6	14.4	70.3

approximate probabilities of occurrence. In words, we can say that 95% of the time the annual return on Walgreens' stock will fall between −31.2% and +70.8%, with an expected average annual return of 19.8%. For Microsoft, the annual return will fall within the range of −23.0% and +51.7% 95% of the time, and the expected average monthly return will be 14.4%. But with the overall stock market averaging about 10% annual return, it is unlikely that future return distributions for Walgreens and Microsoft will offer investors such high returns. The time period we used in these calculations was from 2010–2015, a period of generally rising stock prices.

One problem with using the standard deviation as a measure of risk is that we cannot tell which stock is riskier by looking at the standard deviation. For example, suppose stock A has an average annual return of 8% and an annual standard deviation of 16% while stock B has an average annual return of 12% annual standard deviation of 20% per year. Stock B has a higher standard deviation, but it also had a higher average annual return of 12%, versus 8% for stock A. Which stock is riskier?

The coefficient of variation allows us to make comparisons because it controls for the size of the average. The **coefficient of variation (CV)** is a measure of risk per unit of return; namely, the standard deviation of returns divided by average return. The coefficient of variation is computed as,

coefficient of variation (CV) a measure of risk per unit of return; namely, the standard deviation of returns divided by average return

$$CV = \frac{\sigma}{\overline{R}} \qquad (12.4)$$

A higher coefficient of variation (CV) indicates more risk per unit of return. A lower CV indicates less risk per unit of return. Stock A has a CV of 16/8, or 2.0, meaning that it offers 2.0 units of risk for every unit of return. Stock B has a CV of 20/12, or 1.67 units of risk per unit of return. Stock A is the riskier security based upon its CV, or units of risk for every one percentage point of return.

> **LEARNING ACTIVITY**
>
> **Stock price data are available at https://finance.yahoo.com. Daily, weekly, and monthly stock prices, adjusted for stock splits, can be downloaded into a spreadsheet. You can use the data to compute returns, average returns over a time period, and risk measures.**

12.3 WHERE DOES RISK COME FROM?

Being able to compute risk measures is important for a financial analyst, but perhaps more important is the ability to identify sources of risk and estimate their impact on different investments. For example, companies are affected by many risk sources. Table 12.3 shows a simple income statement for a firm. The income statement, as we will discuss in more detail in Chapter 13, shows the firm's sales revenues and expenses over a time period, such as a month, quarter, or year.

Table 12.3   A Firm's Income Statement Reflects Sources of Risk

Components of a firm's income statement	Potential sources of risk
Revenue	*Business Risk*: changes in quantity sold; varying price-cost margin
	Exchange Rate Risk: changes in U.S. dollars received from overseas sales
	Purchasing Power Risk: inability to raise prices at the same pace as expenses
Less: Expenses	*Business Risk*: amount of fixed costs
	Exchange Rate Risk: changes in U.S. dollars paid to overseas suppliers
	Purchasing Power Risk: inflation increases costs
Equals: Operating Income	*Financial Risk*: amount of fixed financial expenses
Less: Interest Expense	*Interest Rate Risk*: effect of changing interest rates on variable rate debt
Equals: Income Before Taxes	*Tax Risk*: changes in tax rates, laws, surcharges either at home or overseas
Less: Taxes	
Equals: Net Income	

The "top line" of the income statement is the firm's sales. From this, expenses are subtracted. We'll call this difference the firm's operating income. Next, interest paid on the firm's borrowings are subtracted, leaving pretax income, or income before taxes. Subtracting the taxes we owe, we are left with the "bottom line," net income or income after taxes.

Table 12.3 lists sources of risk that affect these components of the income statement. Business risk leads to variations in a firm's operating income over time. It is caused by changes in quantity sold, changes in the firm's markup on its sales (the price – cost margin), and its level of fixed costs.

> **business risk** variations in operating income over time because of variations in unit sales, price – cost margin, and/or fixed expenses

For example, when the cost of an input increases, such as rising labor costs, oil prices, or raw material costs, competitive pressures may not allow a firm to increase its selling prices to offset the increase expenses. This lowers the price-cost margin and, if all else is constant, will reduce the firm's operating profit. On the other hand, fixed costs can lead to variations in operating profit over time, too. Fixed costs are "fixed" in that they do not change in the face of higher or lower selling prices or quantity sold. When much of a firm's costs are fixed by contract (as in the case of labor union agreements, supply contracts, and lease agreements), a decline in sales revenues is not matched by a decline in expenses. Falling sales combined with stable expenses results in declining operating profits.

Other sources of profit variability include the following:

- **Exchange Rate Risk:** When a U.S. firm makes an overseas transaction, it may make or receive payment in a foreign currency. If it receives payment in a foreign currency, U.S. dollar sales revenues will fall and rise over time, depending upon if the dollar is strengthening (more units of foreign currency are needed to purchase one U.S. dollar) or weakening (fewer units of foreign currency are needed to purchase one U.S. dollar).

> **exchange rate risk** risk effect on revenues and expenses from variations in the value of the U.S. dollar in terms of other currencies

Conversely, if the U.S. firm needs to pay overseas suppliers in their home (nondollar) currency, such as the euro, the U.S. firm's dollar-based expenses will fall and rise, depending upon if the dollar strengthens or weakens. To summarize, if all else is held constant, then the following will occur:

	U.S. dollar revenues increase from overseas sales if:	U.S. dollar revenues decrease from overseas sales if:	U.S. dollar expenses increase to pay overseas suppliers if:	U.S. dollar expenses decrease to pay overseas suppliers if:
U.S. dollar strengthens		X		X
U.S. dollar weakens	X		X	

- **Purchasing power risk:** Inflation increases costs and can hurt the firm's profitability if it cannot raise prices to compensate for the increased expenses.

> **purchasing power risk** changes in inflation affect revenues, expenses, and profitability

SMALL BUSINESS PRACTICE

SHOULD YOU START YOUR OWN BUSINESS?

Most of us would agree that it is impossible for someone else to answer the question, "Should you start your own business?" However, an article by Joshua Hyatt titled "Should You Start a Business?" in *Small Business Success*, a supplement to *Inc.* magazine, provides a list of questions that you should ask yourself. First, "Is my idea good enough?" While it is unnecessary for your idea to be a revolutionary breakthrough, you must believe in it and be willing to commit the time and effort necessary to make it useful and exciting to others.

You should ask, "Do I have the management skills I'll need?" "How important is money to me?" "Can I live with the risk?" People who start companies don't necessarily do so because they thrive on risk. Rather, some entrepreneurs see starting a new business as being less risky than the alternative risk of working for a large company. Hyatt attributes the following quote to Paul Hawken of the firm Smith & Hawken: "The best entrepreneurs are risk avoiders. They identify the risk, and then they take actions to minimize the effects of it."

The final question Hyatt suggests you ask is "What do I tell my family?" It is important to talk with family members about the time, money, and energy commitment you will have to make if you decide to start your own business. Hyatt suggests the following: "Have a fallback plan. You can't make the boldest moves with your business if you feel you can't afford to be wrong."

financial risk variations in income before taxes over time because fixed interest expenses do not change when operating income rises or falls

- **Financial risk:** A firm with debt outstanding that requires fixed interest payments faces a situation similar to a firm with fixed operating expenses (see our business risk discussion, above). If sales decline and operating income falls, the fixed interest costs must be paid if the firm is to remain in operation, leading to declines in income before taxes. On the other hand, rising levels of operating profit do not cause the fixed financial cost to change, so more of the increased operating profit passes through to become an increase in income before taxes.

interest rate risk variations in interest expense unrelated to sales or operating income arising from changes in the level of interest rates in the economy

- **Interest rate risk:** Some of the firm's debt may have interest rates that vary according to the level of interest rates in the economy. Such changes in the cost of borrowing are usually unrelated to changes in the firm's sales or operating profits. Thus, variability in interest rates can increase or reduce income before taxes, irrespective of sales trends.

tax risk variations in a firm's tax rate and tax-related charges over time due to changing tax laws and regulations

- **Tax risk:** Changes in tax rates, laws, and surcharges, at home or overseas, add another layer of risk and potential variability to a firm's income.

> **DISCUSSION QUESTION 1**
>
> **The list in the book isn't all-inclusive, or for all types of firms—select a well-known firm and discuss what risks it faces. You may discuss risks mentioned in the previous section as well as other risks you believe it faces.**

12.4 EXPECTED MEASURES OF RETURN AND RISK

ex ante expected or fore-casted

The use of historical data to look backwards is valuable for examining returns and performance over time, but today's investment and business decisions must be made by looking forward, not backwards. Future returns will depend upon our decisions today and upon future events. We need to develop a way to estimate expected, or ex ante, measures of return and risk.

A popular method of forecasting future returns is to develop scenarios of future states of nature. A state of nature includes a set of economic trends and business conditions. The investor cannot control or predict what future states of nature will occur. One set of scenarios could be the following:

1. *Boom economy:* The domestic economy will grow at an above-average pace, inflation will increase slowly, and interest rate trends will be slightly upward. Company sales will be assisted by a healthy export environment.

2. *Normal conditions:* The domestic economy will grow at a pace close to its long-run average. Inflation rates and interest rates will be relatively stable. No major disruptions in our export markets are expected.

3. *Recession:* The domestic economy will grow slowly or maybe contract. Inflation will peak and start to decline, and short-term interest rates will fall. Slow export markets will lead to lower levels of foreign sales.

Each of the above three scenarios is a state of nature. The states of nature can be complicated or simple, few or many; but as a whole, they should include all reasonable (and maybe a few unreasonable) possible future environments. The above three scenarios assumed inflation, interest rates, and a firm's exports will follow the trends in the overall domestic economy. This, of course, does not have to be the case. A more complex set of states of nature may include separate scenarios for the domestic economy, inflation, interest rates, exports, and any other variables deemed important by the investment analyst.

Once the possible states of nature are projected, the analyst must assign a probability, or a chance of occurrence, to each one. For the above three scenarios, suppose the first scenario of a growing economy has a probability (p_1) of 0.30; the second scenario of normal conditions has a probability (p_2) of 0.40; the third, recession, scenario has a probability (p_3) of 0.30. In reality, these probabilities are developed from a combination of the analyst's experience or "gut feel," surveying other analysts on their beliefs, economic and industry forecasts, monetary policy, and a review of what has happened in the past under similar conditions. No formula can be used to determine probabilities for each state of nature. The only rules are that each state of nature needs a non-negative probability assigned to it and the probabilities of all the states of nature must sum to 1.00.

The analyst must forecast the stock's return for the year under each state of nature. If the above three states of nature are being used, analysts may forecast a 20% return under good economic conditions, 10% in normal times, and −5% in a recession. Thus, here's our states of nature or scenarios:

Name of scenario	Probability of the scenario	Expected return in the scenario
Boom economy	0.3	20%
Normal economy	0.4	10%
Recession	0.3	−5%

The expected return can now be found, using equation 12.5:

$$\text{Expected return } E(R) = \sum_{i=1}^{n} p_i R_i \tag{12.5}$$

p_i = probability of the ith scenario and R_i = the forecasted return in the ith scenario.

First, we multiply the probability of each state of nature by the return expected in it. Next, recalling that the Σ symbol means "sum" or "summation," we find the expected return by adding together these products.

The expected return, $E(R)$, is a weighted average of the different state of nature returns, where the weights are the probabilities of each state of nature occurring. Using the above probabilities and forecasted returns, the expected return using equation 12.5 is the following:

$$E(R) = (0.3)(20) + (0.4)(10) + (0.3)(-5) = 8.5\%$$

What does an expected return of 8.5% represent? It represents the average return if the scenarios could be replicated many times under identical conditions. In any one year, if the states-of-nature estimates are correct, the outcome will be either "boom" (a return of 20%), "normal" (10% return), or "recession" (return of −5%). If the cycle could be repeated many times, the average return over the cycles would be 8.5%.

Thus, the expected return does not refer to the expected outcome of a particular situation. It refers only to the *long-run* average outcome if the situation could be replicated many times. But this concept provides analysts with an intuitive measure of central tendency. And it also allows us to develop measures of return variability, or risk.[3]

Just as for historical data, measures of dispersion, or variance, can be computed once the average or expected value is found. The variance, σ^2, is found by using equation 12-6:

$$\sigma^2 = \sum_{i=1}^{n} p_i \left[R_i - E(R) \right]^2 \tag{12.6}$$

---

[3] The process of computing expected returns from scenarios is difficult to apply practically. Thus, some analysts prefer to estimate expected returns from historical return data and forecasts of future conditions by adding various asset risk premiums, such as a default risk or a liquidity risk premium, to the expected nominal interest rate. For example, an investor may believe a stock investment in AT&T deserves a risk premium of 5% over the nominal interest rate. If Treasury bills were currently offering a return of 4%, the expected return on an investment in AT&T stock would be 4% plus 5%, or 9%. When using this method, however, it becomes difficult to estimate measures of future risk.

This equation is similar in some respects to the formula for computing variance using historical data in Section 12.2:

First, the expected return, $E(R)$, takes the place of the average return, $\bar{R}$.

Second, the difference, $[R_i - E(R)]$, computed for each state of nature is similar to a deviation—"similar" in that this use of probabilities for each state of nature may make the sum of the deviations *differ* from zero in these *ex ante* return calculations.

Third, we square each "deviation": $[R_i - E(R)]^2$.

Fourth, since we are dealing with forecasts instead of dividing by a number based on the number of scenarios, we multiply each squared term by its corresponding probability: $p_i[R_i - E(R)]^2$.

Finally, we add these terms across the different states of nature to compute the expected variance.

As with historical, or ex post, measures, the standard deviation is the square root of the variance. The coefficient of variation is the standard deviation divided by the expected return. As with ex post or historical data, the coefficient of variation is easily interpreted: it represents the risk per unit of expected return.

Let's compute the variance, standard deviation, and coefficient of variation (CV) for the stock return using the three scenarios developed above. The expected return was computed to be 8.5%. Using equation 12-6, the variance of the forecast is the following:

$$\sigma^2 = (0.3)(20-8.5)^2 + (0.4)(10-8.5)^2 + (0.3)(-5-8.5)^2$$
$$= 39.675 + 0.90 + 54.675$$
$$= 95.25 \text{ percent squared}$$

The standard deviation will be the square root of this number, or 9.76%. The CV is the standard deviation divided by the expected return, or 9.76/8.5 = 1.15.

Is it practical to develop states of nature, determine their expected probabilities, and estimate expected return and risk? In other words, do investors do these calculations? There is evidence that scenario analysis does have practical implications. First, when the Federal Reserve Board (Fed) is expected to act to change short-term interest rates, market watchers and investors anticipate what the Fed may do. Periodicals, such as *The Wall Street Journal* and *USA Today*, survey practitioners on their expectations of Fed action. One news article presented this analysis prior to an expected interest rate cut by the Fed[4]:

Scenario	Probability	Likely market response[5]
No rate cut	Very unlikely	Stocks and bonds plunge
One-quarter point cut	Possible	Stocks and bonds fall
Half-point cut	Likely	Stocks and bonds could rise, at least initially
Three-quarter point cut, or more	Unlikely	Stocks and bonds surge

The market evidently anticipated the Fed's actions; that day the Fed announced it would attempt to reduce short-term rates by one-half point, which was the "likely" scenario. The stock

---

[4] E. S. Browning, "Investors Hold Breath, Awaiting Rate Cut," *The Wall Street Journal* (May 15, 2001), p. C1. For a corporate example, see Cari Tuna, "Pendulum is Swinging Back on 'Scenario Planning'," *The Wall Street Journal* (July 6, 2009), p. B6. For the Fed's off-again and on-again interest rate increase during 2015, see Craig Torres and Rich Miller, "How the Fed's Big Decision Next Week Could Play Out" (September 10, 2015), accessed December 23, 2015, https://www.bloomberg.com/news/articles/2015-09-10/how-the-fed-s-big-decision-next-week-could-play-out. The article shows a graphic with rising probabilities of the Fed increasing interest rates in September, October, or December 2015. The Fed did vote to raise interest rates 0.25% in December 2015.

[5] The likely market responses are based on the market expectations at the time regarding what the Fed might do. The market's responses will not always coincide with those listed here.

CAREER OPPORTUNITIES IN FINANCE

PERSONAL FINANCIAL PLANNING

Opportunities

Personal financial planning involves preparing for emergencies and protecting against catastrophes, such as premature death and the loss of real assets. Personal financial planning involves planning for the accumulation of wealth during an individual's working career to provide an adequate standard of living after retirement. Job opportunities include the fields of insurance (life, health, and property) and investments (money management, individual bonds and stocks, and mutual funds).

Jobs

Financial Planner
Financial Advisor

Responsibilities

A financial planner helps individuals develop personal financial plans that include establishing current and future financial goals, and assists individuals in setting up steps for carrying out the goals. Financial goals are set for cash reserves, insurance protection, and investing or saving to accumulate wealth over an individual's working lifetime.

A financial advisor focuses on maintaining and increasing the investment wealth of individuals. Investment advice is given in reference to the existing stage in the individual's "life cycle," as well as in terms of the individual's attitude toward investment risk. Advice is given on the target mix among cash reserves, bonds, and stocks. Specific investment recommendations may be provided.

Education

A bachelor's degree usually is a prerequisite. Additional education and training often are needed in the insurance and securities areas. Certification programs must be completed to sell securities. A Certified Financial Planner (CFP) designation also is available.

---

market closed nearly unchanged; the Dow Jones Industrial Average (DJIA) closed down that day 4.36 points (or 0.04% of the index's value) while the NASDAQ Composite Index closed up 3.66 points (0.18%).[6] As another example, several months later, the market anticipated a one-quarter point reduction, from 2.00% to 1.75%, in the federal funds rate. When the Fed did announce the rate cut to 1.75%, the DJIA and Standard & Poor's 500 (S&P 500) indexes moved less than 0.33%, reflecting that the market anticipated the move.[7] Other examples of scenario analysis exist in the print media and the blogosphere.[8] Websites exist which use market data on interest rate futures contracts to estimate the likelihood of an interest rate change by the Fed. See, for example, the site posted by the CME Group at https://www.cmegroup.com/trading/interest-rates/countdown-to-fomc.html.

The second insight is related to the first, in that although each individual investor may not compute a scenario analysis, the markets as a whole behave as if they do. Expected changes, news, or announcements will generally have little effect on security prices, so if an investor follows the consensus set of beliefs, he or she will find it difficult to earn above-average returns after adjusting for risk differences. To make above-average returns without undue risk, investors must do an analysis, determine if and where their forecasts differ from the market's consensus belief, and invest accordingly. If the investors' analysis is correct, their investments should benefit. Evidence of news "surprises" is many times seen in large stock price reactions following the news event. Following the re-election of President Obama in 2012, the U.S. stock market (as measured by the DJIA) fell 313 points, or 2.4%, the following trading day. Evidently, the market was expecting (or hoping) for another result. The election of Donald Trump was a surprise to many political pundits and market-watchers. The day after his 2016 election the Dow Jones Industrial Average rose 257 points or 1.1%, again indicating the market's surprise at the result.

---

[6] E. S. Browning, "Fed Delivers Expected Rate Cut, But Investors' Reaction is Muted," *The Wall Street Journal* (May 16, 2001), p. C1.

[7] E. S. Browning, "Stocks Fall Back Before Meeting of Fed on Rates," *The Wall Street Journal* (December 11, 2001), pp. C1, C17; E. S. Browning, "Fed Pessimism and Merck News Abet Late-Day Selloff," *The Wall Street Journal* (December 12, 2001), pp. C1, C19.

[8] See, for example, "Investment Outlook 2019, Credit Suisse," accessed January 22, 2019, https://www.credit-suisse.com/media/assets/microsite/docs/investment-outlook/investment-outlook-2019/cs-investment-outlook-2019-en.pdf. Students can google financial market scenario analysis to find others.

The third insight, a more complex form of decision analysis, is called *simulation*. Rather than use a limited number of states of nature with specific values for, say, inflation, economic growth, and so on, simulation allows many different combinations of the important variables that may determine stock returns. After running the analysis several thousand times, the computer can compute the average return from the simulation runs and the standard deviation of the returns. Businesses use this technique for a variety of decisions involving uncertain revenues or expenses.

LEARNING ACTIVITY

Try an Internet search of "scenario analysis" to see what examples you can find of this method. To learn more about simulation analysis, visit https://www.oracle.com/crystalball the website of a firm that markets simulation software.

12.5 HISTORICAL RETURNS AND RISK OF DIFFERENT ASSETS

In Chapter 9, we learned that the value of an asset is the present value (PV) of the expected cash flows that arise from owning the asset. To compute a PV, we need to know the size and timing of expected future cash flows from an asset. We must know the appropriate discount rate, or the required rate of return, at which to discount expected cash flows back to the present. Chapter 8 identified three components of the required rate of return: the real risk-free rate of return, inflation expectations, and a risk premium.

The first two components are the same for all investments. Their combined effect is approximated by the yield on a short-term Treasury bill. Expected returns differ as a result of different risk premiums. Thus, finance professionals say that *risk drives expected return* as does our second principle of finance. A low-risk investment will have a lower expected return than a high-risk investment. High-risk investments will have to offer investors higher expected returns to convince (typically) risk-averse people to place their savings at risk. Thus, longer-term Treasury bonds will have to offer investors higher expected returns than offered by Treasury bills. Common stock, by virtue of its equity claim and low priority on company cash flows and assets, will have to offer investors a larger expected return to compensate for its risk.

Evidence that high returns go hand in hand with high risk is seen in Table 12.4, which reports the average annual returns and standard deviations for different types of investments. The return distributions for common stocks have a large standard deviation, indicating more risk than the bond investments. However, investors who undertake such risk earn high rewards over the long haul, since stock returns reward investors more than conservative bond investments.

The return and risk measures for long-term government bonds show that less risk does result in less return. Treasury bills' average annual return is the lowest in the table, as is the standard deviation of their returns over time.

Although future returns and risk cannot be predicted precisely from past measures, Table 12.4 does present information that investors find useful when considering the relative risks and rewards of different investment strategies. Risk is a real factor for investors to consider. Just because large company stocks have an arithmetic average return of about 11% does not mean we should expect the stock market to rise by that amount each year. As the standard deviation of the annual returns indicates, 11% is the average return over a long time frame, during which there were substantial positive and negative deviations from the average. The recent behavior of the stock market during 2000–2002 (particularly the technology sector) and during 2007–2009 should remind us that market returns are not always positive. The S&P 500 stock market index lost over 9% in value during calendar year 2000, over 12% during 2001, and over 22% in 2002. The technology sector was hit hard during this time, as bankruptcies

Table 12.4 Historical Returns and Standard Deviation of Returns from Different Assets, 1928–2018

Asset	Treasury bills	Treasury bonds	Common stocks	Inflation rate
Average Annual Return	3.43%	5.10%	11.36%	3.06%
Standard Deviation	3.04%	7.70%	19.58%	3.81%

Source: http://pages.stern.nyu.edu/~adamodar/?_ga=2.134742769.1022468457.1563409022-1974826774.1563409022 and author calculations.

and oversupply resulted in some sectors losing 60% or more in value in 2000, with losses continuing through 2002. From October 2007 through March 2009, the DJIA lost over 52% of its value.

> **LEARNING ACTIVITY**
>
> **Data on asset returns can be found on the Internet, too. For example, visit Prof. Aswath Damodaran's website to see annual data on asset returns: https://pages.stern.nyu.edu/~adamodar/?_ga=2.134742769. 1022468457.1563409022-1974826774.1563409022.**

12.6 EFFICIENT CAPITAL MARKETS

Prices on securities change over the course of time. As we learned in Chapter 10, security prices are determined by the pattern of expected cash flows and a discount rate. Therefore, any change in price must reflect a change in expected cash flows, the discount rate, or both. Sometimes, identifiable news can cause assets' prices to change. Unexpected good news may cause investors to view an asset as less risky or to expect increases in future cash flows. Either reaction leads to an increase in an asset's price. Unexpected bad news can cause an opposite reaction: the asset may be viewed as more risky or its future cash flows may be expected to fall. Either reaction results in a falling asset price.

A market with systems that allow for quick execution of customers' trades is said to be operationally efficient. If a market adjusts prices quickly, and in an unbiased manner, after the arrival of important news surprises, it is said to be an *informationally efficient market*, or an efficient market. If the market for Microsoft stock is efficient, we should see a quick price change shortly after any announcement of an unexpected event that affects sales, earnings, or new products or after an unexpected announcement by a major competitor. A quick movement in the price of a stock, such as Microsoft, should take no longer than several minutes. After this price adjustment, future price changes should appear to be random. That is, the initial price reaction to the news should be *unbiased*—that is, on average, the initial price change will fully reflect the effects of the news. Put another way, we should not observe a consistent trend in a firm's stock price, on average, after the initial price reaction.

> **efficient market (informationally efficient market)** a market in which prices adjust quickly, and in an unbiased manner, after the arrival of important news surprises

In an efficient market, only unexpected news or surprises should cause prices to markedly rise or fall. Expected events should have no impact on asset prices, since investors' expectations would be reflected in their trading patterns and the asset's price.

For example, if investors expected Microsoft to announce that earnings for the past year rose 10%, Microsoft's current stock price should reflect that expectation. If Microsoft does announce a 10% earnings increase, no significant price change should occur as Microsoft's stock price reflected that information. If, however, Microsoft announced an earnings increase of 20% (a good surprise, given the market's expectation of a 10% increase) or an earnings decline of 5% (a bad surprise, given the market's expectation), the market would adjust Microsoft's price in reaction to the unexpected news.

Every time Microsoft's stock price changes in reaction to new information, it should show no continuing tendency to rise or fall after the price adjustment. Figure 12.3 illustrates this with the solid green line in the graph. After new, positive information hits the market and the price adjusts, no steady trend in either direction should persist. Ideally, the price reaction should resemble a stair-step pattern.

Any consistent trend in the same direction as the price change would be evidence of an *inefficient market* that does not quickly and correctly process new information to determine asset prices. This is shown by the solid blue line in Figure 12.3. This is an example of underreaction to good news; it takes a while for the news to be disseminated, for investors to recognize the value of the information, and for the stock price to rise to an appropriate level. If the market consistently behaved this way, investors who either receive information first and/or who can process it faster will have the opportunity to earn above-average profits as they can buy the stock after good news events (or sell it—or short sell it—after bad news events) and profit at the expense of other investors.

Likewise, evidence of price corrections or reversals after the immediate reaction to news implies an inefficient market that overreacts to news. This is shown in the dotted red line in Figure 12.3. Here, the market gets too optimistic or overvalues the impact of the good news event, and prices quickly rise above an appropriate level. Over time, investors realize the stock is overvalued and they sell. The price declines, over time, to the appropriate level. If the market consistently behaved this way, investors who recognized the pattern have the opportunity to earn above-average profits as they can short sell the stock after the price "pop" following good news events (or purchase after the price falls too far after bad news events) and profit at the expense of other investors as the price moves toward its proper level over time.

FIGURE 12.3 Price reaction in efficient and inefficient markets

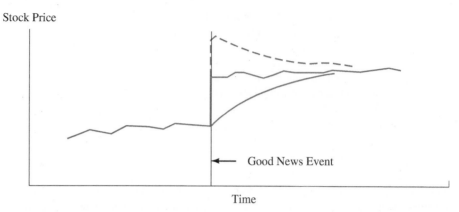

* Examples of price reaction in an efficient market (—) and inefficient markets following good news about a company. An inefficient market with an overreaction is indicated by (---); an inefficient market with an underreaction is indicated by (—).

In an efficient market, it is difficult to consistently find stocks whose prices do not fairly reflect the present values of future expected cash flows. Prices will change when the arrival of new information indicates that an upward or downward revision in this present value is appropriate. Occasionally overreactions and underreactions will occur; the difficulty is in correctly recognizing them often enough to earn higher returns, after adjusting for risk differences, than the overall market. Being right in recognizing, say, an overreaction may lead to a higher return on a stock trade; but being wrong can negate any previous profitable returns.

This means that in an efficient market, investors cannot consistently earn above-average profits (after controlling for risk differences among assets) from trades made after new information arrives at the market. The price adjustment occurs so rapidly that buy or sell orders placed after the announcement cannot, in the long run, result in risk-adjusted returns above the market's average return. An order to buy after the arrival of good news may result in large profits, but such a gain will occur only by chance, as will comparable losses. Stock price trends always return to their random ways after initially adjusting to the new information.[9]

Efficient markets result from interactions among many market participants, all analyzing available information in pursuit of advantage. Also, the information flows they analyze must be random in timing and content. (In an efficient market, no one can consistently predict tomorrow's news.) The profit motive leads investors to try to "buy low and sell high" on the basis of new information and their interpretation of it. Hordes of investors analyzing all available information about the economy and individual firms quickly identify incorrectly priced stocks. Resulting trading pushes those stocks to their correct levels. This causes prices in an efficient market to move in a random walk, meaning prices appear to fluctuate with no consistent or discernible pattern over time, in part due to the unpredictable nature of new information (news) entering the market. That is, a price increase in a securities trade has no predictable effect on the price change (up, down, or no change) of the next transaction. We expect security prices to behave as a random walk if new information—news—occurs in an unpredictable manner. That is, since no one can consistently predict tomorrow's headlines, or what may occur in the next hour, security prices will move randomly over time.[10]

Different assumptions about how much information is reflected in prices give rise to different types of market efficiency. A market in which prices reflect all knowledge, including past and current publicly known and private information, is a strong-form efficient market. In such an efficient market,

random walk prices appear to fluctuate with no consistent or discernible pattern over time, in part due to the unpredictable nature of new information (news) entering the market

strong-form efficient market a market in which prices reflect all knowledge, including past and current publicly known and private information

---

[9] Financial periodicals typically feature articles over time that comment on apparent inefficiencies or to provide evidence in favor of market efficiency. See, for example, Mark Gongloff, "Fed Move: Someone's Sure to Be Surprised," *The Wall Street Journal* (June 24, 2009), p. C1; and Tony Jackson, "Buffett and other blows to efficient market theory," *Financial Times* (June 29, 2009), p. 18.

[10] The insightful reader may be wondering how prices can demonstrate a random walk when evidence presented earlier in the chapter shows common stocks increasing in value by almost 11% per year on average over the past 80 years. Such a return seems to imply an upward trend, not random deviations. Market efficiency does not eliminate long-run upward and downward trends in the economy; it simply means investors cannot consistently predict which stocks will outperform or underperform the market averages on a risk-adjusted basis.

even corporate officers and other insiders cannot earn above-average, risk-adjusted profits from buying and selling stock. Even their detailed, exclusive information is reflected in current stock prices according to the strong-form hypothesis. Few markets can pass the test of strong-form efficiency, and insiders can profit from information not known by others. As discussed in the previous chapter, that is a reason why U.S. laws prohibit insider trading, or trading based on important, nonpublic information.

In a semistrong-form efficient market, all public information, both past and current, is reflected in asset prices. The U.S. stock market appears to be a fairly good example of a semistrong-form efficient market. News about the economy or individual companies appears to produce quick stock price changes without subsequent trends or price reversals.

A weak-form efficient market is a market in which prices reflect all past market information, such as past prices, price trends, and trading volume. Some investors, called chartists (technicians), examine graphs of past price movements, number of shares bought and sold, and other figures to predict future price movements. A weak-form efficient market implies that such investors are wasting their time; they cannot earn above-average, risk-adjusted profits by projecting past trends in market variables.

Market efficiency has several important practical implications. First, for investors, efficient markets make it difficult to invest to consistently "beat the market" by earning above-average returns after taking risk differences into account. Thus, over time, more individual and institutional investors have chosen to "index"; that is, to invest in securities that comprise the market indexes (such as the S&P500 index or Merrill Lynch's corporate bond index) rather than choose specific stocks or bonds. Indexers want to match the market's performance by placing funds in securities in the same proportion as their weight in the chosen index.[11] Over nearly any 10- to 15-year period, anywhere from two-thirds to three-quarters of professionally managed U.S. diversified stock mutual funds earned lower returns than a broad stock market index. Table 12.5 shows that professional mutual fund managers, except for three years (2005, 2007, and 2009) since 2001, have generally earned lower returns than the S&P500 stock market index. This is evidence in favor of the efficient market hypothesis. The bottom row of the table shows that over longer time frames (3, 5, 10, and 15 years), the general performance of the equity mutual funds tends to worsen. Over longer time periods, over 80% of large-capitalization funds earn returns lower than the S&P500 index.

Second, for corporate financial managers, stock price reactions to a firm's announcements of dividend changes, mergers, and strategies will present a fair view of how the marketplace feels about management's actions. Announcements followed by stock price declines indicate that the market believes the decision will hurt future cash flows or increase the riskiness of the firm. Announcements followed by stock price increases indicate that investors feel future cash flows will rise or risk will fall. By watching the market, managers can see how investors perceive their actions.

semistrong-form efficient market a market in which all public information, both past and current, is reflected in asset prices

weak-form efficient market market in which prices reflect all past market information, such as past prices, price trends, and trading volume

chartists (technicians) people who examine graphs of past price movements, number of shares bought and sold, and other figures to predict future price movements

Table 12.5 Percentage of Mutual Funds Underperforming the Benchmark Index, 2001–2018
A number of 50 or larger means most actively-managed mutual funds earned lower returns than the index

	Benchmark Index	Annual Performance																	
		2001	2002	2003	2004	2005	2006	2007	2008	2009	2010	2011	2012	2013	2014	2015	2016	2017	2018
All Large-Cap Funds	S&P 500	65.2	67.7	75.4	68.8	48.8	68.4	44.6	56.0	48.4	65.9	82.2	62.7	54.6	86.7	65.4	66.0	63.1	64.5

	Benchmark Index	Performance over Longer Time Frames			
		3-year 2016–2018	5-year 2014–2018	10-year 2009–2018	15-year 2004–2018
All Large-Cap Funds	S&P 500	79.0	82.1	85.1	91.6

Source: Aye Soe, CFA, Berlinda Liu, CFA, and Hamish Preston, *SPIVA® U.S. Scorecard, Year-End 2018*, S&P Dow Jones Indices https://us.spindices.com/documents/spiva/spiva-us-year-end-2018.pdf accessed March 21, 2019.

---

[11] In practice, it is difficult for index funds to exactly to match the performance of the chosen index because of the index funds' need to re-invest dividend or coupon income over time, as well as their need to handle cash coming in from new investors and to sell shares from investors who want to take their money out of the index fund.

Diversification for the Small Investor

Most people do not have the time and expertise needed to manage an asset portfolio. For many, acquiring the investment capital is difficult, too. Fortunately, such "small" investors, as they are called, have a way to obtain professional investment management and portfolio diversification. They can use investment companies.

An investment company is a corporation that invests the pooled funds of savers. Many investment companies purchase the stocks and bonds of corporations. Others specialize in holding short-term commercial paper, bank CDs, and U.S. Treasury bills and are known as money market mutual funds. The funds of many investors are pooled for the primary purpose of obtaining expert management and a wide diversity in security investments. The number and the size of investment companies have increased rapidly in the past decade.

Classification of Investment Companies

Investment companies are of two types: closed-end funds and mutual, or open-ended, funds, the latter of which are much more popular. Both types have the common objective of achieving intelligent diversification, or variety of investments, for the pooled funds of individuals.

Closed-End Funds

Ordinarily, money is initially raised to invest by selling stock or ownership shares in a closed-end fund. Owners of closed-end fund shares may sell their shares just as they would with any corporate security; that is, by selling them to other investors. The shares of closed-end funds are traded either on an organized securities exchange or in the over-the-counter market.

Mutual (Open-Ended) Funds

A mutual fund can invest in equity and debt securities, and it uses dividends and interest from these securities to pay dividends to shareholders. In contrast with closed-end funds, mutual funds continually sell shares to willing investors. Shareholders may sell their shares back to the mutual fund at any time. The purchase and selling price of mutual fund shares is related to the fund's net asset value (NAV). A fund's NAV is the per-share market value of the securities that the fund owns. Some large and well-known mutual fund companies are Fidelity, Vanguard, T. Rowe Price, and Scudder.

Securities and Exchange Commission (SEC) data indicate in 2018 that more than 9,000 mutual funds hold assets in the form of corporate and government securities in excess of $18 trillion, a popular method of investing indeed.

Now that we have discussed how difficult it is to earn rates of return higher than risk-adjusted "market" returns, what should investors do? First, investors can establish the amount of investment risk they are willing to accept and then find investments that have demonstrated comparable levels of risk. Second, investors can diversify away that portion of total risk that is said to be "unsystematic," or separate from movements in the economy and the overall market. In the next section, we take a closer look at the trade-off between expected return and risk and the role of systematic and unsystematic risk.

> **DISCUSSION QUESTION 2**
>
> **If the stock market is efficient, why do investors believe they can invest and earn higher returns than the overall market? Do you believe the stock market is efficient? Why or why not?**

> **LEARNING ACTIVITY**
>
> **Go to https://finance.yahoo.com and see who the day's biggest price gainers and losers in the stock market are. What news may have caused these price changes?**

12.7 PORTFOLIO RETURNS

Let's return to our earlier discussion of the stocks of Walgreens and Microsoft. Recall that Padric received a historical arithmetic average annual rate of return of 19.8% on Walgreens stock, with a standard deviation of 25.5% over six years. Serinca's historical average return and risk achieved by investing in Microsoft over the same six-year period were 14.4% and 18.7%, respectively.

Mary is considering an investment in common stocks and is considering purchasing shares in both Microsoft and Walgreens. This latter choice would be an example of building, or forming, a portfolio. A portfolio is any combination of assets or investments. Although many consider "investments" to be financial assets such as stocks, bonds, and CDs, they can also include real assets such as farmland, apartment buildings, gold, diamonds, and art work.

portfolio any combination of assets or investments

Mary realizes that future returns and risks for these two stocks may differ from the recent past. She estimates the following for Walgreens and Microsoft:

	Walgreens	Microsoft
Expected return	7%	12%
Standard deviation forecast	11%	20%

12.7.1 EXPECTED RETURN ON A PORTFOLIO

The expected rate of return on a portfolio, $E(R_p)$, is simply the weighted average of the expected returns, $E(R_i)$, of the individual assets in the portfolio:

$$E\left(R_p\right) = \sum_{i=1}^{n} w_i E\left(R_i\right) \tag{12.7}$$

The value w_i is the weight of the ith asset, or the proportion of the portfolio invested in that asset. The sum of these weights must equal 1.0.

Let's assume that Mary is willing to invest 50% of her available funds in Walgreens and 50% in Microsoft. We can use equation 12.7 to compute her expected portfolio return, assuming expected annual returns of 7.0% for Walgreens and 12.0% for Microsoft. Again, assuming these are expected returns, we have the following:

$$E\left(R_p\right) = 0.50\left(7.0\%\right) + 0.50\left(12.0\%\right) = 3.5\% + 6.0\% = 9.5\%$$

Now, let's assume that Ramon is willing to accept a little more variability in his portfolio returns relative to Mary, as a trade-off for a higher expected return. Consequently, Ramon has decided to invest 25% of his available funds in Walgreens and 75% in Microsoft. Using the expected annual returns for each stock, the expected average annual return on his portfolio would be the following:

$$E\left(R_p\right) = 0.25\left(7.0\%\right) + 0.75\left(12.0\%\right) = 1.75\% + 9.0\% = 10.75\%$$

The total risk of a portfolio can be measured by its variance or the standard deviation of its returns. Extending the concept of portfolio expected return, one might think that the variance of a portfolio is a weighted average of asset variances, or that the standard deviation of a portfolio is a weighted average of asset standard deviations. Unfortunately, this first guess is incorrect, and we cannot use an equation such as 12.7 to compute expected portfolio variance or standard deviation. To see why, look at the time series of returns illustrated in Figure 12.4.	**12.8 VARIANCE AND STANDARD DEVIATION OF RETURN ON A PORTFOLIO**

Consider the relationship between stocks and Treasury bonds. Stock prices are affected primarily by expectations of future economic growth, while Treasury bond prices are mainly affected by changes in the level of interest rates. At times, stock and bond returns will move together; at other times they will move in opposite directions.

Figure 12.4a indicates this general condition. It shows the returns of a stock index and a bond index. Bond returns were, generally, less volatile than stock returns over the 1990–2015 time period.

Suppose, however, investors place funds in stocks and bonds to form a portfolio of 50% stocks and 50% bonds. The portfolio's combined return in Figure 12.4b shows less risk. Why do the portfolio returns vary so much less?

Lower portfolio variability arises from the benefits of diversification. **Diversification** occurs when we invest in several different assets rather than just a single one. The benefits of diversification are greatest, as we see in Figure 12.4a, when asset returns have a **negative correlation**; that is, they tend to move in opposite directions, such as from about 1999 through 2004. Two sets of data are said to

diversification occurs when we invest in several different assets rather than just a single one

negative correlation when asset returns move in opposite directions

FIGURE 12.4A Stock and treasury bond returns 1990–2018

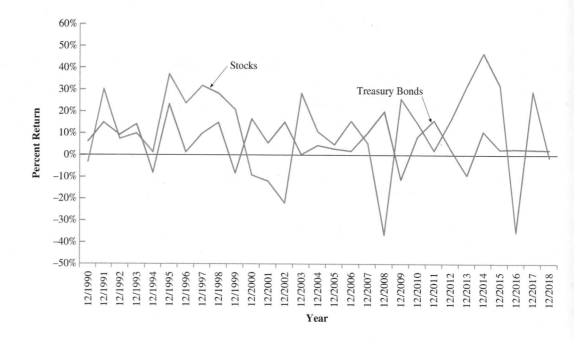

FIGURE 12.4B Stocks, treasury bond returns, and returns on a 50/50 stock/bond portfolio, 1990–2018

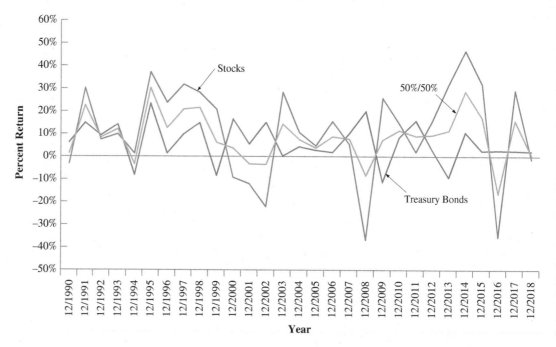

positive correlation when asset returns move together over time

correlation statistical concept that relates movements in one set of returns to movements in another set over time

have a **positive correlation** if their returns move together over time, as did the bond and stock returns during the 1991–1999 time frame.

Although the calculation of this measure is beyond the scope of this text,[12] **correlation** is a statistical concept that relates movements in one set of returns to movements in another set over time. Correlation ranges from −1 to +1. The more negative the correlation (i.e., a correlation closer to −1) the greater the risk reduction from combining the assets in a portfolio. The closer the closer to +1, the

---

[12] The development and calculation of correlations for portfolios can be found in most investments textbooks. See, for example, Frank K. Reilly and Edgar A. Norton, *Investments*, 7th ed. (Mason, OH: South-Western College Publishing, 2006), Chapter 8.

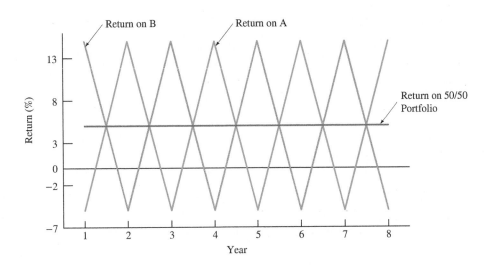

FIGURE 12.5 Potential impact of perfect negative correlation on portfolio risk

less the benefit from diversifying—that is, there won't be much risk reduction from combining the assets in a portfolio.

Part of many investors' strategy is to have investments in their portfolio that are not highly positively correlated with each other. In the real world of investing, it is difficult to find assets that are strongly negatively correlated. Over the 1990–2018 period, for example, the correlation between the stock and bond returns shown in Figure 12.4a and b was −0.19. The less positive or the more negative the correlation, the greater the risk reduction benefits from diversifying into different assets. This means that, although the individual assets may be risky, combining them in a portfolio may result in levels of portfolio risk below that of any of the constituent assets.

Here's an illustration of an extreme, and rather unrealistic, example. But it helps to show the effects of negative correlation on reducing risk in a portfolio. Figure 12.5 shows the return pattern for two asset's returns that are perfectly negatively correlated (i.e., the correlation is −1). When one return rises to 15%, the other falls to −5%, and vice versa. Over the eight years shows, the average return to both Assets A and B is 5%. Since the asset returns are an "opposite mirror image" of each other, their correlation is −1 and a 50/50 portfolio will have constant returns of 5%. Thus, combining two perfectly negatively correlation asset returns results in a zero-risk portfolio!

12.8.1 TO DIVERSIFY OR NOT TO DIVERSIFY?

The idea behind diversification is that, at times, some investments will do well while some perform poorly, and vice versa. Since it is difficult to forecast or "time" efficient markets, we should spread our funds across several different investments to prevent us from having a large exposure to any one investment. An example of the benefits of diversification is found in Table 12.6.

Our time frame is 25 years; $10,000 invested over this time frame at an average annual rate of 7% gives us $54,274.33 in our account. But what might happen if we divide our $10,000 initial investment into five subaccounts, investing $2,000 in each one? Suppose one of the investments turns out to be a total failure and we lose the entire $2,000 invested. The second investment earns no return at all; 25 years later we still have $2,000 in that account. The third subaccount earns a meager 5% annual average return over the 25 years. The fourth and fifth subaccounts perform better, one earning 10% and the other 12% on an average annual basis. Even though some accounts perform poorly, investing $2,000 in each of these five subaccounts will grow to become $64,442.25 over 25 years, a gain of more than $10,000 over our single-basket strategy, which earned 7%.

Investors should consider investing in a way that cuts across asset classes (such as stocks and bonds), industries, and country borders to benefit from the opportunities in a global investment marketplace. The "U.S. auto industry" used to be known as the Big Three: Ford Motor Company, General Motors, and Chrysler. But consider whether, after the merger between Chrysler and Germany's Daimler

Table 12.6 Diversification Illustration Invest $10,000 over 25 years

Investment strategy 1: All funds in one asset		Investment strategy 2: Invest equally in five different assets	
Number of assets =	1	Number of assets	5
Initial investment	$10,000	Amount invested per asset =	$2,000
Number of years =	25	Number of years =	25
		5 asset returns (annual)	
Annual asset return =	7%	Asset 1 return	−100%
		Asset 2 return	0%
		Asset 3 return	5%
		Asset 4 return	10%
		Asset 5 return	12%
Total accumulation at end of time frame:		Total accumulation at end of time frame:	
Total funds =	$54,274.33	Asset 1	$0.00
		Asset 2	$2,000.00
		Asset 3	$6,772.71
		Asset 4	$21,669.41
		Asset 5	$34,000.13
		Total funds =	$64,442.25

Benz to form Daimler Chrysler, is Daimler Chrysler a German or an American company?[13] Moreover, even though firms such as Ford or Coca-Cola may be headquartered in the United States, much of their product sales and revenue streams are outside the borders of the United States, and they compete globally. Investors need to look for good investments no matter where they may be in the global economy. Some studies have found that a firm's industry sector has more to do with its stock market performance than a "country" effect.[14]

12.9 PORTFOLIO RISK AND THE NUMBER OF INVESTMENTS IN THE PORTFOLIO	What happens to portfolio risk as more assets are added to a portfolio? Adding a second asset to a one-asset portfolio may reduce portfolio risk. Will portfolio risk continue to decline if we continue to diversify the portfolio by adding a third, a tenth, or a fiftieth asset to the portfolio?

The answer is no. The greatest reductions in portfolio risk come from combining assets with negative correlations. As each new asset reduces the variability of a portfolio's returns, it becomes more difficult to find additional assets with low correlations to the portfolio because all assets share a common environment. In U.S. markets, most assets' returns react in some way to the ups and downs of the business cycle. Once a portfolio includes a certain number of assets, the pervasive effects of national economic and financial market trends reduce the likelihood that further diversification can offer significant benefits.

We may look beyond our national borders and include non-U.S. assets in the portfolio to gain some additional reduction in portfolio risk, since the world's economies and financial markets do not move in lockstep. Even though the global product and financial markets are becoming more integrated, remaining differences suggest a well-diversified global asset portfolio will have a lower total risk than a well-diversified portfolio of U.S. assets. Even with a choice of global assets, however, diversification benefits are limited. The world's economies do not move in lockstep but neither do they have large negative correlations. Eventually, the benefits of further diversification will disappear.

---

[13] This question became moot in 2007 when Daimler spun off Chrysler, and it once again became U.S. owned.

[14] Craig Karmin, "Investing Overseas Reduces the Riskiness of a Portfolio," *The Wall Street Journal* (January 29, 2001), p. R15; Phyllis Feinberg, "Importance of Sectors Grows for International Investors," *Pensions and Investments* (November 27, 2000), p. 56.

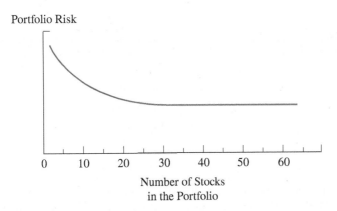

Portfolio Risk

Number of Stocks
in the Portfolio

FIGURE 12.6 Risk and
portfolio diversification

U.S. stock market data confirm this expected pattern.[15] By constructing a number of sample portfolios, with one stock, two stocks, three stocks, and so on, researchers have found that average portfolio risk declines as additional securities are added to the portfolio, as shown in Figure 12.6. After a portfolio includes 20 to 30 stocks, the risk reduction effect of adding more stocks is almost nil. The total risk of a well-diversified portfolio of U.S. stocks appears to be about one-half the risk of the average one-stock portfolio. In other words, constructing a well-diversified portfolio of about 20 stocks can reduce overall portfolio risk by one-half.

Further reductions in portfolio risk are documented when international securities are included in the analysis. It appears that only about 15 international stocks are needed to exhaust the risk-reducing benefits of diversification. The total risk of a well-diversified international portfolio of stocks is about one-third of the risk of an average one-stock portfolio; that is, up to two-thirds of portfolio risk can be eliminated in a well-diversified international portfolio!

12.9.1 SYSTEMATIC AND UNSYSTEMATIC RISK

Figure 12.6 can be used to show that two types of risk affect individual assets and portfolios of assets: risk that can be diversified away and risk that cannot be diversified away.

Figure 12.7 resembles Figure 12.6 with labels for these types of risks. The risk that is diversified away as assets are added to a portfolio is the firm-specific and industry-specific risk, or the "microeconomic" risk. This is known as **unsystematic risk**. Table 12.7 lists several sources of this risk.

Information that has negative implications for one firm may contain good news for another firm. For example, news of rising oil prices may be bad news for airlines but good news for oil companies.

unsystematic risk risk that can be diversified away as assets are added to a portfolio; also known as firm-specific or industry-specific risk

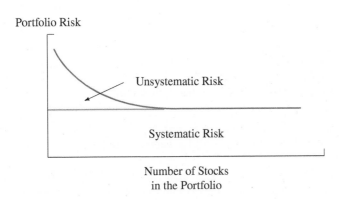

Portfolio Risk

Unsystematic Risk

Systematic Risk

Number of Stocks
in the Portfolio

FIGURE 12.7 Risk and
portfolio diversification

[15] J. Evans and S. H. Archer, "Diversification and the Reduction of Dispersion: An Empirical Analysis," *Journal of Finance* (December 1968), pp. 761–67.

Table 12.7 Examples of Risk

Diversifiable risk (also known as unsystematic risk or firm-specific risk, or micro risk)	Undiversifiable risk (also known as systematic risk, market risk, or macro risk)
Business Risk	Market Risk
Financial Risk	Interest Rate Risk
Event Risk	Purchasing Power Risk
Tax Risk	Exchange Rate Risk
Liquidity Risk	

The announcement of the resignation of a well-respected CEO may be bad for the company but good for competing firms. One firm's announcement of its intentions to build a technologically advanced plant may mean bad news for its competitors. In a well-diversified portfolio of firms from different industries, the effects of good news for one firm may cancel bad news for another firm. The overall impact of such news on the portfolio's returns should approach zero. In this way, diversification can effectively eliminate unsystematic risk. A well-diversified portfolio can reduce the effects on portfolio returns of firm- or industry-specific events—such as strikes, technological advances, and entry and exit of competitors—to zero.

Diversification cannot eliminate risk that is inherent in the macro economy. This undiversifiable risk is called **systematic risk** or **market risk**. General financial market trends affect most companies in similar ways. Macroeconomic events (e.g., changes in gross domestic product (GDP), war, major political events, rising optimism or pessimism among investors, tax increases or cuts, or a stronger or weaker dollar) have broad effects on product and financial markets. Even a well-diversified portfolio cannot escape these effects. Table 12.7 lists several sources of systematic risk.

Thus, the total risk of an asset has two components: unsystematic or firm-specific risk, and systematic or market risk:

$$\text{Total risk (portfolio variance)} = \text{systematic risk} + \text{unsystematic risk}$$

In practice and in theory, few investors have only one asset; rather, they own a portfolio of assets.[16] The unsystematic, microeconomic component of an asset's total risk disappears in a well-diversified portfolio. As we see in Figures 12.5 and 12.6, the level of unsystematic risk goes to zero as additional assets are added to a portfolio.

In a well-diversified portfolio, the only risk that remains is the systematic risk (i.e., the sensitivity of the asset's returns to macroeconomic events). This means the *only risk that should matter to financial markets is systematic risk*. When financial markets evaluate the trade-off between risk and expected return, they focus on the trade-off between systematic risk and expected return. We'll explore this key insight in the next section.

LEARNING ACTIVITY

Mutual fund companies offer investors a means of obtaining professional management in diversified portfolio of stocks and/or bonds for relatively modest investments. Many mutual fund websites have investor education links dealing with diversification. See, for example, https://www.vanguard.com and https://www.troweprice.com, as well as other mutual fund firms.

12.10 CAPITAL ASSET PRICING MODEL

If markets are efficient, is there still a trade-off between risk and expected return? If so, what will this trade-off look like?

From the previous section, we know systematic or market risk affects all stocks (and, more generally, all securities). The U.S. economy's economic trends, changes in interest rates, the U.S. dollar

---

systematic risk (market risk) risk that is inherent in the macro economy and cannot be eliminated through diversification

---

[16] Ownership by individual investors of shares of diversified mutual funds helps to achieve overall diversification for an investor.

exchange rate, Federal Reserve System (Fed) policy, and so on, are pervasive and affect returns and risk on most securities. All securities are affected by macroeconomic and other national events, so even a well-diversified portfolio will have some exposure to these systematic, or market-wide, sources of risk. Systematic risk cannot be diversified away.

Unsystematic risk is asset- or company-specific risk. What is good news for one company (e.g., a new product or patent announcement) may be bad news for another competitor. Or what is good news for one sector of the economy (rising oil prices for oil producers) is bad news for another (sectors dependent upon oil and gasoline, such as transportation industries). But as more securities are added to a portfolio, the effects of unsystematic risk are diversified away as the positive effects and negative effects on different companies and sectors cancel out leaving only the broad systematic risk exposure.

This has an important implication for the trade-off between expected return and risk. What is "risk"? As we have reviewed, only systematic risk should matter because prudent investors can and should diversify their portfolios to eliminate unsystematic risk. Thus only systematic risk should affect an asset's returns over time.

Regardless of their total risk (or standard deviation of returns), assets with higher levels of systematic risk should have higher expected returns; assets with lower levels of systematic risk should have lower levels of expected returns. From this perspective, we see that an asset's total risk is unimportant. What is important is how the asset affects the risk of the overall portfolio.

For example, what is the systematic risk of short-term Treasury bills (T-bills)? Purchasing a T-bill "locks in" a short-term return that is considered risk-free, as it is backed by the full faith and credit of the U.S. Government. While an investor owns that security, the return is not affected by economic events. In other words, the systematic risk of a T-bill investment is zero, or as close to zero as we can have in this world. If an investor adds T-bills to a portfolio, the effect on the overall portfolio will be to lower its systematic risk. Combining risky assets with a zero-risk asset will lower the overall systematic risk of the portfolio.

As another example, researchers have found is that, by itself, gold is a risky investment. It offers no income stream and its price fluctuates, sometimes with high volatility. But when it is put in a portfolio in combination with common stocks, an investment in gold can reduce a portfolio's total risk. The reason is that common stocks usually perform poorly when investors fear inflation, whereas gold prices rise when higher inflation is expected. So, including gold in a stock portfolio can have a negative effect on risk; that is, it can make the portfolio less risky. Gold, at times, may have *negative* systematic risk.

From the perspective of the financial markets, the **market portfolio** is the portfolio that contains all risky assets—all stocks, bonds, real estate, and so on. As it contains all risky assets, the market portfolio will have no unsystematic risk. The only risk contained in the market portfolio is systematic risk. That means that as the value of the market portfolio fluctuates over time, the pure effect of systematic risk is seen.[17]

market portfolio a portfolio that contains all risky assets

Since the market portfolio contains all risky assets, some assets that are sensitive to changes in macroeconomic variables, such as interest rates or GDP, will have higher exposures to systematic risk than the overall market portfolio. For examples, firms with sales that are heavily affected by the business cycle—such as auto manufacturers (Ford or GM) or heavy equipment firms (Caterpillar) might be expected to have above-average levels of systematic risk.

On the other hand, some assets' returns will be less sensitive to these influences and will have less systematic risk. In good economic times and bad, consumers still go to retail stores such as Walmart and buy breakfast cereal made by companies such as General Mills, so stocks of these firms might be expected to have below-average levels of systematic risk.

The way a stock's systematic risk is measured is to compare its returns over time to those of the market portfolio. Those assets whose returns generally rise and fall in line with the overall market will have the same systematic risk exposure as the market portfolio (see Figure 12.8a). Assets whose returns are more volatile (they typically rise higher and fall lower) than those of the market portfolio have systematic risk exposures that exceed those of the market portfolio (Figure12.8b). Assets whose

---

[17] It is only in the case of the market portfolio that the standard deviation (or variance) of returns shows the effect of systematic risk; for all other less-than-perfectly diversified portfolios, the portfolio's variance measures a combination of systematic and unsystematic risk influences.

FIGURE 12.8 Comparing asset returns and market portfolio returns over time

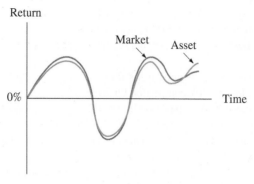

a: Same Systematic Risk as the Market Portfolio

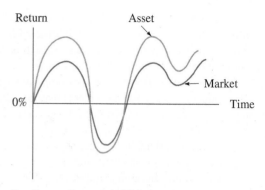

b: Greater Systematic Risk than the Market Portfolio

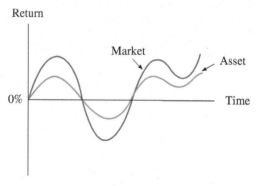

c: Less Systematic Risk than the Market Portfolio

returns are less volatile (their returns do not rise as high or fall as low as the market portfolio) have less systematic risk exposure than the market portfolio (Figure 12.8c).

An implication of this is for an asset's return expectations. Here are some examples:

- An asset with zero systematic risk. This means its returns do not change over time as the market rises and falls. Such an asset would have an expected return equal to the risk-free rate of return in the economy. For the United States, its expected return would be the Treasury bill return.

- An asset whose systematic risk matches the market portfolio, such as in Figure 12.8a. That is, if the market rises (falls) by, say, 5%, this asset's returns rise (fall) on average by 5%. Its expected return will equal that of the overall market since its systematic risk is the same as the overall market.

- An asset with greater systematic risk than the market, such as in Figure 12.8b. That is, if the market rises (falls) by, say, 5%, this asset's returns rise (fall) on average by *more* than 5%. Its expected return will be *greater* than that of the market's expected return since its systematic risk is *greater* than the overall market.

- An asset with less systematic risk than the market, such as in Figure 12.8c. That is, if the market rises (falls) by, say, 5%, this asset's returns rise (fall) on average by *less* than 5%. Its expected return will be *less* than that of the market's expected return since its systematic risk is *less* than the overall market.

From this "portfolio perspective," an asset's risk is measured not by total risk as measured by variance or standard deviation. The important measure of risk is its systematic risk, namely how it affects the risk of the overall market portfolio. Assets with higher systematic risk will tend to increase the systematic risk (and the expected return) of the portfolios in which they appear. Assets with low levels of systematic risk tend to lower the systematic risk (and the expected return) of the portfolios in which they appear.

These insights are the basis for the Capital Asset Pricing Model (CAPM). The CAPM states that the expected return of an asset depends upon its level of systematic risk. The asset's systematic risk

Capital Asset Pricing Model (CAPM) name given to a theory in finance that states the expected return of an asset depends upon its level of systematic risk

is measured relative to that of the market portfolio. In other words, the relative risk of an asset is that asset's contribution to the risk of a well-diversified portfolio.

Under the CAPM, **beta** (β) is the measure of an asset's systematic risk. It is important to note that beta is a measure of *relative* risk and is not an absolute or total risk measure such as standard deviation. A total risk measure allows a comparison between risk and the range of probable returns. Recall the normal distribution (Figure 12.2) and the return distributions shown in Table 12.2. If we know the average return and standard deviation, we can estimate the range of returns based on probabilities.

beta measure of an asset's systematic risk

Using beta, all we know is the asset's risk relative to the market; we can't measure the risk of the asset's returns in an absolute sense. A beta of, say, 0.8, doesn't give us the ability to generate a range of returns at different probability levels, as we did in Table 12.2.

Beta measures the volatility or variability of an asset's returns relative to the market portfolio. For example, if an asset's returns are one-half as volatile as those of the market portfolio, its beta will be 0.5. That means that if the market portfolio changes in value by 10%, on average the asset's value changes by 0.5, or 5%. If an asset's beta equals 1.4, then the asset's returns are 40% more volatile than the market. When the market changes in value by 10%, the asset's value changes, on average, by 1.4 times 10%, or 14%. With this definition of beta, the beta of the market portfolio, β_{MKT}, is 1.0. By definition, the market is exactly as volatile as itself.

Assets that are more volatile than the market, or equivalently, those that have greater systematic risk than the market, have betas greater than 1.0. What ever the market return, these assets' average returns are larger in absolute value. Assets that are less volatile than the market (i.e., those with less systematic risk) have betas less than 1.0. These assets' returns, on average, are less in absolute value than those of the market. Table 12.8 lists the historic betas for some stocks.

Table 12.8 Examples of Stock Betas

Firm name	Ticker symbol	Beta
Industrial Firms		
AT&T	T	0.61
Caterpillar	CAT	1.555
Coca-Cola	KO	0.42
Disney	DIS	0.67
DuPont	DWDP	1.43
General Electric	GE	0.32
Ford	F	0.67
McDonald's	MCD	0.38
Transportation Firms		
Alaska Air	ALK	1.40
CSX	CSX	1.49
Delta Airlines	DAL	1.39
FDX	FDX	1.93
J. B. Hunt	JBHT	1.03
Norfolk Southern	NSC	1.62
Utilities		
First Energy	FE	0.22
Ameren	AEE	0.19
American Electric Power	AEP	0.09
Consolidated Edison	ED	0.20
DTE Energy	DTE	0.24
Chesapeake Utilities	CPK	0.22

Source: https://finance.yahoo.com; accessed January 2019.

In practice, there is no true identifiable "market" portfolio since there are too many assets, including the value of natural resources and human capital (investments in training, educating, and developing) to attempt to measure returns on such a portfolio. What investment professionals use is a proxy, or substitute, for the true market portfolio. A popular measure of the market portfolio is a broad stock market index, such as the Standard & Poor's 500 (S&P500) index or the New York Stock Exchange (NYSE) index. Typically, when an asset's beta is estimated, it is measured relative to that of the S&P500 stock market index. How to estimate a stock's beta is the topic of this chapter's Learning Extension.

> **DISCUSSION QUESTION 3**
>
> **Do you think there might be a relationship between a stock's total risk and its systematic risk? Why or why not? Select two firms from Table 12.8 and explain why you believe there is a difference (or similarity) between their beta values.**

APPLYING FINANCE TO. . .

- **Institutions and Markets** Banks, brokerages, pension funds, insurance companies, and financial institutions of all types evaluate expected return, risk, and portfolios for their own and their clients' investments. Markets transmit perceived changes in asset risk and expected return through changes in security prices.

- **Investments** The trade-off between risk and expected return is a foundational concept in finance, cutting across markets, investments, and financial

management. Knowing how to compute and evaluate return and risk and knowing the important role that correlations play can help investors put together well-diversified portfolios.

- **Financial Management** Actions by investors affect a firm's stock price and the market interest rates on its bonds. Price changes relative to competing firms and the overall market inform management how investors view their actions.

SUMMARY

Financial risk and return concepts are among the most mathematical and confusing to the first-time finance student, but they are vital to understanding financial markets, institutions, and management. Much of modern investment analysis, portfolio management, and corporate finance is based upon the topics introduced in this chapter.

LO 12.1 Historical returns are computed from past income cash flows and price changes. We can use returns measured over periods of time to compute an average return.

LO 12.2 Once we have determined the average return we can compute measures of risk, such as variance, standard deviation, and the coefficient of variation.

LO 12.3 We used the components of a generic income statement to illustrate firm-specific sources of risk, including business risk, exchange rate risk, purchasing power risk, financial risk, interest rate risk, and tax risk.

LO 12.4 Scenario analysis is a widely used tool for estimating expected return and risk. Analysts can estimate the probability of each scenario, or state of nature, and its corresponding expected return to compute the expected return, variance, and standard deviation.

LO 12.5 Historical return data is useful in showing the risk/return trade-off over long periods of time. Stocks have earned higher average returns, with higher standard deviations, than Treasury bonds. In turn, Treasury bonds have earned higher average returns, with higher risk, than Treasury bills.

LO 12.6 Market efficiency is a key concept in finance. In efficient markets, prices adjust rapidly and in an unbiased manner (they do not consistently overshoot or undershoot) to new information. As such, it is difficult to earn returns higher than the overall market after controlling for risk differences. This section reviews three forms of market efficiency: weak-form (current prices reflect all past market information, including past prices and trading volume); semi-strong-form (current prices reflect all current and past publicly available information); strong-form (current prices reflect all information, public and private).

LO 12.7 A portfolio is a combination of financial assets or investments. The expected return of a portfolio is the weighted average of the expected returns from each asset in the portfolio.

LO 12.8 When assets are combined into portfolios, diversification effects may mitigate the effects of each individual asset's risk. When some assets' returns are poor, others may perform well. The correlation between asset returns is key to diversification. Correlation between two sets of returns always falls between −1 and +1. The risk-reducing effects of diversification are greater the lower the correlation is between returns.

LO 12.9 Adding assets to a portfolio may help reduce portfolio risk, but after a certain point, all unsystematic risk has been diversified away and only systematic (or market) risk remains.

LO 12.10 The Capital Asset Pricing Model explains the relationship between systematic risk and expected return. Systematic risk is measured by beta—the relative volatility of an asset's returns compared to the market portfolio's returns. In theory, the market portfolio contains all risky assets. In practice, as measuring returns on all risky assets (including investment in real assets as well as education and training investment in people) is not possible, a stock market proxy, or substitute, is used to measure market returns and to estimate beta.

KEY TERMS

beta	diversification	portfolio	systematic risk
business risk	efficient market	positive correlation	(market risk)
Capital Asset	(informationally effi-	purchasing	tax risk
Pricing	cient market)	power risk	unsystematic risk
Model (CAPM)	ex ante	random walk	variance
chartists (technicians)	exchange rate risk	semistrong-form	weak-form effi-
coefficient of	financial risk	efficient market	cient market
variation (CV)	interest rate risk	standard deviation	
correlation	market portfolio	strong-form efficient	
deviations	negative correlation	market	

REVIEW QUESTIONS

1. **(LO 12.1)** Explain how a percentage return is calculated, and describe the calculation of an arithmetic average return.

2. **(LO 12.2)** Describe how the variance and standard deviation are calculated, and indicate how they are used as measures of risk.

3. **(LO 12.2)** What is the coefficient of variation? How is it used as a measure of risk?

4. **(LO 12.3)** Business risk has three possible sources. What are they?

5. **(LO 12.3)** What sources of risk does a firm face, and which of those sources are reflected on the firm's income statement?

6. **(LO 12.3)** Suppose, in the preceding year, the U.S. dollar strengthens against other currencies. Explain its effect on U.S. dollar revenues and expenses for a global firm headquartered in the United States.

7. **(LO 12.4)** Describe the meaning of a *state of nature*, and explain how this concept is used to provide expected measures of return and risk.

8. **(LO 12.5)** Explain the historical relationships between return and risk for common stocks versus corporate bonds.

9. **(LO 12.6)** Explain market efficiency. What are the characteristics of an efficient market?

10. **(LO 12.6)** What are the differences among the weak, semi-strong, and strong forms of the efficient market hypothesis?

11. **(LO 12.6)** What type of market efficiency—none, weak, semi-strong, or strong—is reflected in each of the following statements?
    a. I know which stocks are going to rise in value by looking at their price changes over the past two weeks.
    b. Returns earned by company officers trading their own firm's stock are no higher than those of other investors.
    c. If a firm announces lower-than-expected earnings, you know the price will fall over a few days.
    d. By the time I heard the news about the dividend increase, the stock had already risen by a substantial amount.
    e. Whatever the stock market does in January, it will continue to move in that direction for the rest of the year.
    f. As soon as the chair of the Federal Reserve testified to Congress about future monetary policy, interest rates rose and stock prices dropped.

12. **(LO 12.6)** Explain if you agree or disagree with this statement: "After the merger announcement the stock price greatly increased. Then it fell for the next 1–2 days before becoming relatively stable. This is proof against the efficient market hypothesis."

13. **(LO 12.6)** How do mutual fund return data present evidence for or against efficient markets? Explain.

14. **(LO 12.7)** Define a portfolio, and describe how the expected return on a portfolio is computed.

15. **(LO 12.8)** Explain the terms *diversification* and *correlation* in the context of forming portfolios.

16. **(LO 12.8)** Explain the fallacy of this statement: "I'd rather put my money into a single, high-earning asset than in a portfolio of diversified investments; I'll earn more money with the single asset."

17. **(LO 12.9)** Describe what happens to portfolio risk as more and more assets are added to a portfolio. Are there advantages to international diversification?

18. **(LO 12.9)** How does systematic risk differ from unsystematic risk?

19. **(LO 12.9)** Classify each of the following as an example of systematic or unsystematic risk.
    a. The labor unions at Caterpillar Inc. declared a strike yesterday.
    b. Contrary to what polls stated, the president was re-elected.
    c. Disagreement about inflation policy leads to a fall in the euro relative to the dollar.
    d. The computer industry suffers lower profits because of aggressive pricing strategies on new desktop computers.
    e. Every Christmas selling season there is a "hot" toy that many parents try to purchase for their child.

20. **(LO 12.10)** What is the Capital Asset Pricing Model? Describe how it relates to expected return and risk.

21. **(LO 12.10)** Define the concept of beta, and describe what it measures.

22. **(LO 12.10)** What is the market portfolio? Can we invest in such a portfolio?

PROBLEMS

1. From the information below, compute the average annual return, the variance, standard deviation, and coefficient of variation for each asset.

Asset	Annual returns
A	5%, 10%, 15%, 4%
B	–6%, 20%, 2%, –5%, 10%
C	12%, 15%, 17%
D	10%, –10%, 20%, –15%, 8%, –7%

2. Based upon your answers to Question 1, which asset appears riskiest based on standard deviation? Based on coefficient of variation?

3. Recalling the definitions of risk premiums from Chapter 9 and using the Treasury bill return in Table 12.4 as an approximation to the nominal risk-free rate, what is the risk premium from investing in each of the other asset classes listed in Table 12.4?

4. What is the real, or after-inflation, return from each of the asset classes listed in Table 12.4?

5. RCMP Inc. shares rose 10% in value last year while the inflation rate was 3.5%. What was the real return on the stock? If an investor sold the stock after one year and paid taxes on the investment at a 15% tax rate, what is the real, after-tax return on the investment?

6. Find the real return on the following investments:

Stock	Nominal return	Inflation
A	10%	3%
B	15%	8%
C	–5%	2%

7. Find the real return, nominal after-tax return, and real after-tax return on the following:

Stock	Nominal return	Inflation	Tax rate
X	13.5%	5%	15%
Y	8.7%	4.7%	25%
Z	5.2%	2.5%	28%

8. The countries of Stabilato and Variato have the following average returns and standard deviations for their stocks, bond, and short-term government securities. What range of returns should you expect to earn 95% of the time for each asset class if you invested in Stabilato's securities? From investing in Variato's securities?

Stabilato asset	Average return	Standard deviation
Stocks	8%	3%
Bonds	5%	2%
Short-term government debt	3%	1%

Variato asset	Average return	Standard deviation
Stocks	15%	13%
Bonds	10%	8%
Short-term government debt	6%	3%

9. Using the information below, compute the percentage returns for the following securities:

Security	Price today	Price one year ago	Dividends received	Interest received
RoadRunner stock	$20.05	$18.67	$0.50	
Wiley Coyote stock	$33.42	$45.79	$1.10	
Acme long-term bonds	$1,015.38	$991.78		$100.00
Acme short-term bonds	$996.63	$991.78		$45.75
Xlingshot stock	$5.43	$3.45	$0.02	

10. Given her evaluation of current economic conditions, Ima Nutt believes there is a 20% probability of recession, a 50% chance of continued steady growth, and a 30% probability of inflationary growth. For each possibility, Ima has developed an interest rate forecast for long-term Treasury bond interest rates:

Economic forecast	Interest rate forecast (%)
Recession	6
Constant growth	9
Inflation	14

a. What is the expected interest rate under Ima's forecast?
b. What is the variance and standard deviation of Ima's interest rate forecast?
c. What is the coefficient of variation of Ima's interest rate forecast?
d. If the current long-term Treasury bond interest rate is 8 percent, should Ima consider purchasing a Treasury bond? Why or why not?

11. Ima is considering a purchase of Wallnut Company stock. Using the same scenarios and probabilities as in Problem 10, she estimates Wallnut's return is −5% in a recession, 20% in constant growth, and 10% in inflation.
a. What is Ima's expected return forecast for Wallnut stock?
b. What is the standard deviation of the forecast?
c. If Wallnut's current price is $20 per share and Wallnut is expected to pay a dividend of $0.80 per share next year, what price will Ima expect Wallnut to sell for in one year?

12. Ima's sister, Uma, has completed her own analysis of the economy and Wallnut's stock. Uma used recession, constant growth, and inflation scenarios, but with different probabilities and expected stock returns. Uma believes the probability of recession is 60%, and that in a recession Wallnut's stock return will be −20%. Uma believes the scenarios of constant growth and inflation are equally likely and that Wallnut's returns will be 15% in the constant growth scenario and 10% under the inflation scenario.
a. What is Uma's expected return forecast for Wallnut stock?
b. What is the standard deviation of the forecast?
c. If Wallnut's current price is $20.00 per share and is expected to pay a dividend of $0.80 per share next year, what price does Uma expect Wallnut to sell for in one year?

13. Scenario analysis has many practical applications in addition to being used to forecast security returns. In this problem, scenario analysis is used to forecast an exchange rate. Jim Danday's forecast for the euro/dollar exchange rate depends upon what the U.S. Federal Reserve and European central bankers do to their country's money supply. Jim is considering the following scenarios and exchange rate forecasts:

Central bank behavior	Probability of behavior forecast	Jim's forecast exchange rate
Euro banks increase MS growth; U.S. does not	.20	1.15 €/$
Euro banks, U.S. maintain constant MS growth	.30	1.05 €/$
U.S. increases MS growth; Euro banks do not	.35	0.95 €/$
U.S., Euro banks increase MS growth	.15	0.85 €/$

a. What is Jim's expected exchange rate forecast?

b. What is the variance of Jim's exchange rate forecast?

c. What is the coefficient of variation of Jim's exchange rate forecast?

14. Using the data in Table 12.4, calculate and interpret the coefficient of variation for each asset class.

15. Below is annual stock return data on Hollenbeck Corp. and Luzzi Edit Inc.

Year	Hollenbeck	Luzzi edit
1	10%	–3%
2	15%	0%
3	–10%	15%
4	5%	10%

a. What are the average return, variance, and standard deviation for each stock?

b. What is the expected portfolio return on a portfolio composed of
   i) 25% Hollenbeck and 75% Luzzi Edit?
   ii) 50% Hollenbeck and 50% Luzzi Edit?
   iii) 75% Hollenbeck and 25% Luzzi Edit?

c. Without doing any calculations, would you expect the correlation between the returns on Hollenbeck Corp. and Luzzi Edit's stock to be positive, negative, or zero? Why?

16. Reword is annual stock return data on AAB Company and YYZ Inc.

Year	AAB	YYZ
1	0%	5%
2	5%	10%
3	10%	15%
4	15%	20%
5	–10%	–20%

a. What is the average return, variance, and standard deviation for each stock?

b. If the conditions in the future are expected to be like those in the past few years, what is the expected portfolio return on a portfolio composed of?
   i) 25% AAB and 75% YYZ?
   ii) 50% AAB and 50% YYZ?
   iii) 75% AAB and 25% YYZ?

c. Without doing any calculations, would you expect the correlation between the returns on AAB and YYZ's stock to be positive, negative, or zero? Why?

17. Estimate the weights (w_i) for assets in the following portfolios given the following information about the portfolio holdings:

Portfolio		Price	Number of securities
A	Stock A	$25	200
	Stock B	$53	100
	Stock C	$119	100
B	Bond A	$975	10
	Bond B	$1,020	20
	Bond C	$888	10
	Bond D	$1,150	10
C	Stock A	$25	1,000
	Stock C	$119	500
	Bond D	$1,150	20
D	Stock B	$53	1,000
	Stock C	$119	100
	Bond A	$975	20
	Bond B	$1,020	10

18. Tim's portfolio contains two stocks, Lightco and Shineco. Last year his portfolio returned 14%. Lightco's return was 5% and Shineco returned 20%. What are the weights of each in Tim's portfolio?

19. The following year Tim adds a third stock, Brightco, and reallocates his funds among the three stocks. Lightco and Shineco have the same weight in the portfolio, and Brightco's weight is one-half of Lightco. During the year Lightco returns 10%, Shineco returns 12%, and Brightco loses 5%. What was the return on his portfolio?

20. **EXCEL** Spreadsheets are useful for computing statistics: averages, standard deviation, variance, and correlation are included as built-in functions. Below is recent monthly stock return data for ExxonMobil (XOM) and Microsoft (MSFT). Using a spreadsheet and its functions, compute the average, variance, standard deviation, and correlation between the returns for these stocks. What does the correlation between the returns imply for a portfolio containing both stocks?

Month	XOM return	MSFT return
November	–4.6%	10.4%
October	0.1%	13.6%
September	–1.9%	–10.3%
August	–3.3%	–13.8%
July	–4.4%	–9.3%
June	–1.6%	5.5%
May	0.7%	2.1%
April	9.4%	23.9%
March	–0.1%	–7.3%
February	–3.2%	–3.4%

21. **EXCEL** If the conditions in the future are expected to be like those in the past, what are the expected portfolio return and standard deviation of a portfolio composed of?
   a. 25% XOM and 75% MSFT?
   b. 50% XOM and 50% MSFT?
   c. 75% XOM and 25% MSFT?

22. **EXCEL** Construct a spreadsheet to replicate the analysis of Table 12.6. That is, assume $10,000 is invested in a single asset that returns 7% annually for 25 years and $2,000 is placed in five different investments, earning returns of –100%, 0%, 5%, 10%, and 12%, respectively, over the 20-year time frame. For each of the questions below, begin with the original scenario presented in Table 12.6.
   a. Experiment with the return on the fifth asset. How low can the return go and still have the diversified portfolio earn a higher return than the single-asset portfolio?
   b. What happens to the value of the diversified portfolio if the first two investments are a total loss?
   c. Suppose the single-asset portfolio earns a return of 8% annually. How does the return of the single-asset portfolio compare to that of the five-asset portfolio? How does it compare if the single-asset portfolio earns a 6% annual return?
   d. Assume that Asset 1 of the diversified portfolio remains a total loss (–100% return) and asset two earns no return. Make a table showing how sensitive the portfolio returns are to a 1 percentage point change in the return of each of the other three assets. That is, how is the diversified portfolio's value affected if the return on asset three is 4% or 6%? If the return on asset four is 9% or 11%? If the return on asset five is 11%? 13%? How does the total portfolio value change if each of the three asset's returns are one percentage point lower than in Table 12.6? If they are one percentage point higher?
   e. Using the sensitivity analysis of (c) and (d), explain how the two portfolios differ in their sensitivity to different returns on their assets. What are the implications of this for choosing between a single-asset portfolio and a diversified portfolio?

Learning Extension 12

Estimating Beta and Using the Security Market Line

LO 12.11 (Learning Extension) Estimate beta and compute expected return using the security market line.

LO 12.11A Demonstrate how to estimate a stock's beta.

LO 12.11B Compute expected return using the security market line.

12.11A ESTI-MATING BETA

We can estimate beta for a stock or portfolio of stocks relative to the overall stock market using simple linear regression analysis. The reader might recall the following equation from an earlier course in statistics. However, prior work in statistics is unnecessary to grasp the following concepts. In simple equation form, we have the following:

$$R_i = \alpha + \beta R_{MKT} + e_i \tag{LE12.1}$$

The value α = the alpha or intercept term β = the beta, or slope coefficient, that shows the size of the impact that market returns (R_{MKT}) have on stock returns (R_i), and e_i = an error term reflecting the fact that changes in market returns are not likely to fully explain changes in stock returns. This straight line is shown in Figure LE12.1.

Computer software programs and sophisticated financial calculators can perform the necessary calculations and find the beta coefficient with little effort. Spreadsheet software can perform this analysis, too. In addition, we can estimate beta the "long way" by using simple calculations done by hand or by using a simple calculator. We will demonstrate the long way of estimating beta so the reader can better understand the underlying process.

Let's begin by using the monthly returns over a recent six-month period between the market as measured by the S&P500 and Microsoft. In practice, beta is often computed using 60 months' worth of data, but we will use only six months for the purposes of this illustration:

FIGURE LE12.1
Graph of $R_i = \alpha + \beta R_{MKT} + e_i$

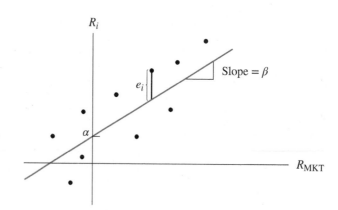

Month	MSFT return	S&P500 return
1	−2.0%	−1.7%
2	4.8%	−1.7%
3	−6.0%	−1.6%
4	−4.1%	1.2%
5	1.0%	1.7%
6	6.5%	5.1%

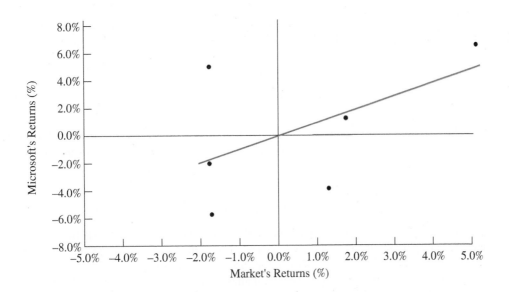

FIGURE LE12.2
Plot of returns
for Microsoft and
the S&P 500

We want to measure the systematic risk of Microsoft relative to the market. Let's first plot these returns on the graph in Figure LE12.2. The market's returns are plotted along the x (horizontal) axis because we are interested in examining how Microsoft's returns move with or respond to the market's returns. Microsoft's monthly returns are plotted along the y (vertical) axis. There is a positive (upward-sloping) relationship between the returns on the market and Microsoft's returns. We have inserted a line across the scatter plot of annual returns. In addition to having a positive relationship, the steepness of the slope of the line reflects how much Microsoft's returns respond to a change in the market's returns.

The beta coefficient is the slope of this line and indicates the sensitivity of Microsoft's returns to the market's returns. If beta is 0.93, that means if the market portfolio's returns are 10%, Microsoft's returns are, on average, 0.93 × 10%, or 9.3%. If the market's returns are expected to be 6% this year, Microsoft's returns are expected to be, on average, 0.93 × 6%, or 5.58%.

Let's calculate the slope, or beta, of the relationship between the returns on the market and returns on Microsoft. The calculations used to estimate beta are shown in Table LE12.1. A beta of 0.93 indicates that Microsoft was less risky than the market over this time frame. More specifically, we can say that, based on six months of past data, on average, a 1% increase (decrease) in the monthly return on the market was accompanied by a 0.93 percentage increase (decrease) in Microsoft's monthly returns. Our estimate was based on only six observations. Normally, betas are estimated using more data points.

Table LE12.1 How to Calculate a Beta Coefficient or Measure of Systematic Risk

Month	Rates of return S&P 500 X-axis	Microsoft Y-axis	Market's returns squared X^2	Product of the returns $X \times Y$
1	−1.70%	−2.00%	2.89%	3.40%
2	−1.70	4.8	2.89	−8.16
3	−1.60	−6.00	2.56	9.6
4	1.2	−4.10	1.44	−4.92
5	1.7	1	2.89	1.7
6	5.1	6.5	26.01	33.15
	Sum X = 3.00%	Sum Y = 0.20%	Sum X^2 = 38.68%	Sum XY = 34.77%

Estimating beta where $n = 6$ is the number of observations:

$$\beta = \frac{n\Sigma xy - (\Sigma x)(\Sigma y)}{n\Sigma x^2 - (\Sigma x)^2} = \frac{6(34.77) - (3.00)(0.20)}{6(38.68) - (3.0)(3.0)} = \frac{208.02}{223.08} = 0.93$$

The beta of a portfolio of assets can be estimated at least two ways. First, portfolio returns can be regressed on market returns using equation LE12-1. Second, the beta of a portfolio can be estimated by computing the weighted average of its component's betas:

$$Beta_p = \sum_{t=1}^{n} w_i beta_i \tag{LE12.2}$$

The value w_i is the weight of the ith asset in the portfolio. Unlike the portfolio variance risk measure, the systematic risk of a portfolio does equal the weighted average of its component's systematic risk.

12.11B SECURITY MARKET LINE

Once an asset's beta is estimated, it can be used to form the basis of return estimates or the required return that investors should expect from a security. Under the CAPM, the expected return/risk trade-off for an asset is given by the security market line (SML). The security market line represents the systematic risk/return trade-off for an asset. That is, it allows us to estimate the expected return on an asset if we know its beta, or amount of systematic risk. In equation form, the SML is, as follows:

$$E(R_i) = RFR + [E(R_{MKT}) - RFR]\beta_i \tag{LE12.3}$$

where

$E(R_i)$ is the expected rate of return for asset I;

RFR is the risk-free rate, usually measured by the rate of return on Treasury bills;

β_i is the measure of systematic risk (beta) for asset i; and

$E(R_{MKT}) =$ the expected return on the market portfolio.

The SML is shown graphically in Figure LE12.3. The dependent variable (the vertical axis) in this relationship is the expected return on the asset. The independent variable (the horizontal axis) is systematic risk, β_i.

The quantity $[E(R_{MKT}) - RFR]$ is the slope of the security market line. That is, for every one unit increase in beta, the expected return rises by $[E(R_{MKT}) - RFR]$. This quantity is called the **market risk premium**. It represents the extra expected return from investing in the risky market portfolio rather than the risk-free asset.

An asset's risk premium, or extra expected return, equals $[E(R_{MKT}) - RFR]\beta_i$; that is, the market risk premium multiplied by the asset's beta.

Note that these are all expected returns: expected market return, expected asset return. The CAPM and SML are based on expectations, although most of the testing and practical application of them use historical returns for the simple fact that it is difficult to measure market expectations.

market risk premium the slope of the security market line; represents the extra expected return from investing in the risky market portfolio rather than the risk-free asset

FIGURE LE12.3
Security market line

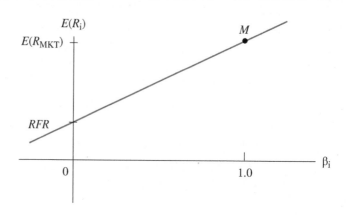

A confusing point for some is that it is the asset's risk that determines the asset's expected return, not the other way around. Thus, when doing our own investing, we first want to determine how much risk we are willing to have in our investment portfolio. That will determine the expected return of our investments. Some investors get this backwards—they focus, for example, on a return target such as "I want a return of 15%" and ignore that a high return will be affiliated with a high-risk portfolio. And the risk is this—the target return is NOT guaranteed! Because of risk, the actual return may be much lower than what was desired.

To illustrate the use of the SML, let's find the expected return on AT&T stock if the market is expected to rise 9%. We'll assume the Treasury bill rate is 4.0%. We'll need to use equation LE12-2, the security market line, to estimate AT&T's expected return under these conditions. We'll also need to use AT&T's beta listed in Table 12.8. Using its recent beta of 0.35, should the market rise 8%, AT&T's expected return is the following:

$$E\left(R_{AT\&T}\right) = 4 + \left[9 - 4\right] \times 0.359 = 5.75\%$$

With a beta of 0.35, AT&T's stock market return averages about one-third of the stock market's return in recent years. That is, if the stock market rose 10%, on average, AT&T stock will rise about 3.5%. If the market fell by 10%, on average AT&T stock will fall by about 3.5%.

SUMMARY

LO 12.11 A beta has several practical uses in finance. It is used to determine investors' required rate of return on an investment. Beta also is used to develop estimates of shareholders' required returns on their investments. Beta is estimated by a statistical technique that computes the slope of the line of best fit between the market portfolio's returns (vertical axis) and the asset's returns (horizontal axis). We can determine the beta of a portfolio similarly, or we can compute it the weighted average of its asset's betas.

LO 12.11B The security market line shows the trade-off between expected return and systematic risk (beta) for an asset. If we know an asset's beta and estimates of the capital market's risk-free rate and expected market return, we can estimate the asset's expected return.

PROBLEMS

1. Stock market forecasters are predicting the stock market will rise 5% next year. Given the beta of each stock below, what is the expected change in each stock's value?

Firm	Beta
BCD	1.25
NOP	0.70
WXY	1.10
ZYX	1.00

2. **EXCEL** Below is nine months' return data for Walgreens and the S&P 500.
   a. Estimate the intercept (alpha) and beta for Walgreens stock using spreadsheet functions.
   b. Interpret what the slope estimate means to a stock analyst.

c. Compute the R-squared of the regression using Excel's RSQ function. What does the R-squared tell us about the relationship between Walgreens' returns and those of the market?

Month	Walgreens Return	S&P500 Return
1	2.0%	7.5%
2	−5.9%	1.8%
3	0.2%	−8.2%
4	2.0%	−6.4%
5	−2.2%	−1.1%
6	−14.3%	−2.5%
7	−6.0%	0.5%
8	4.9%	7.7%
9	−7.9%	−6.4%

3. **EXCEL** As mentioned above, spreadsheets can do the work for us of computing beta. Use Excel's "slope" function to estimate the beta of Microsoft using the data in Table LE12.1. Use the "intercept" function to estimate the alpha or intercept term of the regression line.

4. You've collected data on the betas of various mutual funds. Each fund and its beta is listed below:

Mutual fund	Beta
Weak Fund	0.23
Fido Fund	0.77
Vanwatch	1.05
Temper	1.33

   a. Estimate the beta of your fund holdings if you held equal proportions of each of the above funds.

   b. Estimate the beta of your fund holdings if you had 20% of your investments in Weak Fund, 40% in Fido Fund, 15% in Vanwatch, and the remainder in Temper.

5. Using your answers to Problems a and b, estimate your portfolio's expected return if the security market line is estimated as $E(R_i) = 5.2 + 8.4(\beta_i)$.

6. Suppose the estimated security market line is $E(R_i) = 4.0 + 7(\beta_i)$.

   a. What is the current Treasury bill rate?

   b. What is the current market risk premium?

   c. What is the current expected market return?

   d. Explain what beta (β_i) measures.

7. Financial researchers at Smith Sharon, an investment bank, estimate the current security market line as $E(R_i) = 4.5 + 6.8(\beta_i)$.

   a. Explain what happens to expected return as beta increases from 1.0 to 2.0.

   b. Suppose an asset has a beta of −1.0. What is the expected return on this asset? Would anyone want to invest in it? Why or why not?

8. Stevens Incorporated's stock has a 14% return, a beta of 0.85, and the market return is 15%.

   a. What was the risk-free rate in the economy for the year?

   b. The stock market of another company had a return of 20%. What would you estimate its beta to be?

Financial Management

Part 3 deals with the applications of finance within a business firm. The practice of financial management requires businesspeople to work with financial institutions in the context of the financial market. If Walmart needs a short-term loan to help finance inventory for the Christmas selling season, it can go to a bank for the loan, but the interest rate that Walmart pays will be affected by the current level of interest rates in the economy, which is determined by a variety of economic conditions. If Walmart needs to raise millions of dollars to finance new expansion and construction, it can work with another type of financial institution, an investment bank, which will help Walmart sell bonds or shares of common stock to raise the needed funds. The interest rate on the bonds and the price of the stock are determined by the conditions of the financial markets.

Institutions and investors pay close attention to a firm's financial management policies. Market participants glean information from a firm's financial statements; namely, its balance sheet, income statement, and statement of cash flows. Changes in a firm's financial condition inform investors of a firm's strengthening or weakening position against its competitors. Investors and lending institutions may express concern if a firm's financing policy changes so that it begins to use more debt financing than it has in the past.

A firm's managers use information they obtain from the financial markets and institutions. They keep their eyes on the firm's stock price. Changes in the stock price may reflect investor happiness or dissatisfaction with the company and its management's decisions. Managers use interest rate and stock price information from the financial markets to evaluate the firm's own investments in its lines of business. The level and expected trend in short-term interest rates, long-term interest rates, and stock prices will influence management's decisions about how to raise funds to finance the firm's activities.

Chapter 13 introduces the various ways a business can be organized, and the financial implications of each organizational form. We discuss the financial goal of maximizing shareholder wealth as well as the three basic accounting statements: the balance sheet, income statement, and statement of cash flows. Chapter 14 continues the discussion of financial statements by showing how the information contained in them can be used to evaluate a firm's strengths and weaknesses. We review how managers use financial statement relationships to estimate the firm's future asset and financing needs.

Any firm will have short-term and long-term investment and financing needs. Chapter 15 discusses strategies and methods for managing a firm's short-term assets, such as cash, accounts receivable, and inventory. We show how a cash budget can be used to estimate a firm's future short-term financing needs. Chapter 16 reviews various sources of short-term financing for businesses, including bank loans, trade credit, and many other nonbank financing sources.

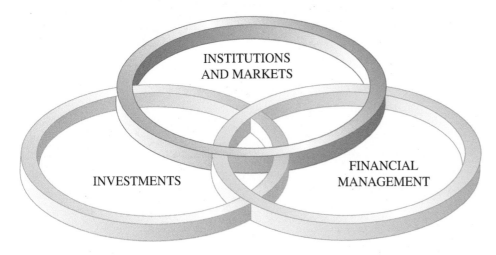

In Chapter 17, the focus changes to managing a firm's long-term assets. We introduce capital budgeting, which is a financial technique of deciding which assets a firm should invest in. Chapter 18 concludes Part 3 with a discussion of factors that influence firms' long-term financing choices. We bring the financial markets front and center in our discussion of how a firm uses financial information to determine its financing costs and how the financing costs affect its capital budgeting choices.

Business Organization and Financial Data

LEARNING OBJECTIVES

After studying this chapter, you should be able to do the following:

LO 13.1 Explain the role of mission statements with regard to business planning.

LO 13.2 Describe the three major forms of business organization.

LO 13.3 Distinguish between accounting and financial perspectives and the role of accounting principles in communicating information.

LO 13.4 Describe and summarize the information in the income statement.

LO 13.5 Describe and summarize the information in the balance sheet.

LO 13.6 Describe and summarize the information in the statement of cash flows.

LO 13.7 Describe applications of financial statement analysis to different situations.

LO 13.8 Identify the goal and functions of financial management.

LO 13.9 Describe the agency relationships in a business organization and their implications for financial management.

LO 13.10 Explain the role of finance in the firm's organizational chart.

Where we have been. . . We have seen how the financial system supports the flow of funds from saving units to those who need to borrow funds or raise equity by selling shares. Financial markets, interest rates, securities prices, risk, and return concerns help direct funds efficiently to their best purpose, to help the global economy run as smoothly as possible. One of the biggest users of capital in the financial markets are businesses, from the entrepreneur seeking start-up financing, to the firm issuing shares for the first time in an initial public offering (IPO), to an exporter arranging overseas financing for a purchase. No discussion of finance is complete without a look at financial management; meaning, how business uses the financial system and markets to raise funds and direct capital to keep their firms running and to meet customers' needs.

Where we are going. . . How a business is organized has implications on a manager's incentives. Financial statement information is valuable to investors and managers to help them make appropriate decisions. We'll see applications of these concepts in the next few chapters, including financial analysis (Chapter 14), managing working capital (Chapter 15), and capital budgeting analysis (Chapter 17).

How this chapter applies to me. . . Rather than accept the first job offered to you, try to work for a company with a mission and vision that relates to your personal values. Statistics show that, on average, people have five to seven different "careers" during their working lives as their employers and career paths change. You will probably not stay with the firm that hires you after graduation, but you want that first job and all successive positions to be a "fit" for your values and lifestyle. Annual reports are important sources of information about the firm to you as an investor and employee.

Successful businesses prepare financial plans. To make this point more clearly, we provide the following quotation from an unknown author:

Failure to plan is planning to fail.

An important part of planning is to do financial planning for a firm. All businesses require financing. Money is needed to finance plant and equipment and to support current operations. Some firms require little capital, and the industries in which these firms operate have a vast number of competitors. Any field of activity that requires little financial capital is open to a host of people who want to establish their own business, such as website designers or financial counselors. At the other extreme are businesses that require huge amounts of financial capital to operate even on a minimum scale. In the cement and steel industries, for example, because of capital requirements, only a few large firms dominate in national or regional markets.

We begin this chapter with a brief preview of some of the factors to consider when deciding to start a business. One of the decisions to be made is how the business will be organized. We discuss issues relating to a firm's goals, and problems that can arise if a firm's owners are not the same people as the firm's managers.

The remainder of the chapter focuses on the financial data provided by business firms. Those firms organized as corporations must provide a summary of their financial performance in an annual report to their shareholders. Included in annual reports are three basic financial statements that businesses need to prepare: the income statement, the balance sheet, and the statement of cash flows. Even individually owned, or closely held firms, need to prepare financial statements for tax purposes. Just as important, these financial statements contain much of the language of business, such as revenues, expenses, assets, liabilities, and equity. The financial statements are analyzed by the firm's managers, the firm's competitors, banks, and other financial market participants who are considering buying or selling the firm's securities. In this chapter's Learning Extension, we discuss taxation and depreciation concepts that business managers must understand if they are to be successful in managing their businesses.

13.1 STARTING A BUSINESS

In our market economy, individuals have the freedom to establish any legal business they choose. However, they must have adequate financial capital of their own or be able to arrange the necessary financing. The success of a business in raising funds for operations depends on its profit potential.

13.1.1 STRATEGIC PLAN WITH A VISION OR MISSION

mission statement statement of a firm's main reason for being; sometimes called a vision statement

A business should begin with a vision or **mission statement** that is consistent with the planned overall strategy. The vision or mission should indicate what the firm wants to produce, distribute, and sell or indicate what services it wants to provide. The statement helps declare what is the company's main reason for being; in times when new opportunities look attractive, the firm's managers should go back and read the mission statement to ensure their actions are consistent with it. Comments on quality objectives and customer and owner focus are, typically, found in vision and mission statements. Some statements are idealistic in their views.

Both small and large companies formulate strategic plans with visions and missions. Let's take a look at some of these statements.[1]

Wells Fargo, a nationwide diversified financial services company providing banking, insurance, investments, and other financial services, has the following vision:

We want to satisfy our customers' financial needs and help them succeed financially.

Merck & Company, Inc., one of the world's largest pharmaceutical companies, states its mission is the following:

To discover, develop and provide innovative products and services that save and improve lives around the world.

---

[1] The mission statements used in this chapter were found on each company's website.

SMALL BUSINESS PRACTICE

HABITS OF SUCCESSFUL SMALL COMPANIES

As we know, hundreds of thousands of firms start up each year. Many will fail or go out of business for various reasons. Some will struggle while a few will thrive. You probably are ready to ask, what are some of the characteristics or "habits" of firms that become successful? An article by Leslie Brokaw entitled "The Truth about Start-Ups" in *Small Business Success*, a supplement to *Inc.* magazine, has identified some of these habits. Each year *Inc.* identifies the 50 fastest-growing companies in the United States. These firms often are examined in an effort to identify common characteristics or habits. Following are some findings.

Successful small rapidly growing firms "often rely on team efforts." We often credit the success of a start-up to a single founder or chief executive officer (CEO). Rather, many successful firms are

started by team efforts in the form of founding partners. Successful firms generally are "headed by people who know their line of work." Past professional experience in their fields is a common characteristic of successful entrepreneurs. Brokaw also suggests that successful companies are founded and built by "people who have started other businesses." For example, many of the *Inc.* 500 CEOs had started at least one other business prior to their current business.

Brokaw also suggests that highly successful, rapidly growing firms are "disproportionately manufacturers and they're high tech." For example, nearly one-half of the *Inc.* 500 companies view themselves as being high-tech ventures. These rapidly growing firms also "are not owned by the founders alone." Many of the CEOs of *Inc.* 500 companies own less than 50% of the equity in their businesses.

Google, a division of Alphabet Inc., has a mission statement that is mainly focused on its search engine product:

Organize the world's information and make it universally accessible and useful.

Chick-fil-A, a fast-food restaurant best known for its chicken sandwiches and for being closed on Sundays, has a mission:

To glorify God by being a faithful steward of all that is entrusted to us and to have a positive influence on all who come into contact with Chick-fil-A.

13.1.2 BUSINESS AND FINANCIAL GOALS

A guiding force behind top management's decisions should be the mission statement. At the same time, the mission statement should not be carved in stone; it should be periodically reviewed to ensure it is current and reflects market needs in a dynamic, global economy. On the other hand, a business cannot chase every idea developed by its managers. Businesses need to stick to what they do best, or in the parlance of management, strategic goals should be related to the firm's core competencies.[2] Businesses must support their visions and missions with business and financial goals or plans, sometimes referred to as operating plans. Such plans may include specific numeric goals for customer satisfaction ratings, market share, and return to shareholders. Such plans allow managers to track their progress toward achieving the plan and mission of the firm.

Attracting and acquiring financing is necessary to obtain the factors of production necessary to conduct business operations. Allocation of these factors is largely automatic under the market system. Resources flow smoothly to those businesses that, through their past operations and the promise of profitable future operations, are able to pay for them. Investors, as providers of debt and equity capital, expect a return on their investment. As we saw in Chapter 12, actual returns usually differ from expected returns. This is the risk faced by investors, but the investor or the financial intermediary who assumes an unusually large risk does so with the full expectation that if things go well with the firm, the rewards for the investment will be great. Where the possible risk is small, the potential reward is small. As explained in Chapter 12, there is a trade-off between expected return and risk. Investment funds flow to risky firms and to safe firms, invested according to the intermediary's or the investors' risk preferences.

---

[2] C. K. Prahalad and G. Hamel, "The Core Competence of the Corporation," *Harvard Business Review* (May–June 1990), pp. 79–91.

LEARNING ACTIVITY

Most corporation's websites will have links to their mission or vision statements. Visit the home pages of firms you are familiar with and find their missions. The websites of the firms mentioned in this section are https://www.wellsfargo.com, https://www.merck.com, https://www.google.com, and https://www.chick-fil-a.com.

13.2 FORMS OF BUSINESS ORGANIZATION IN THE UNITED STATES

Three major forms of business ownership are used in the United States: proprietorships, partnerships, and corporations. Proprietorships are the most widely used form, although they are generally the smallest organizations in terms of assets. About 72% of U.S. firms are proprietorships, about 10% are partnerships, and the remaining 18% are corporations. In terms of revenues, 81% of sales are generated by corporations, about 15% by partnerships, and about 4% by proprietorships.[3]

The choice of a legal form of organization for a business is a strategic matter from many points of view. Managerial lines of authority and control, legal responsibility, and the allocation of income and risk are directly related to the form the organization takes. In this chapter, we look at the relationship between the legal form of organization and its sources and methods of financing, and its allocation of risk. Table 13.1 summarizes some of the points of this discussion.

13.2.1 PROPRIETORSHIP

proprietorship (sole proprietorship) a business venture owned by an individual who personally receives all profits and assumes all responsibility for the debts and losses of the business

The **proprietorship**, sometimes called a sole proprietorship, is a business venture owned by an individual who personally receives all profits and assumes all responsibility for the debts and losses of the business. Typically, the owner is the manager; he or she is in total control of the firm. Separating the

Table 13.1 Organizational Forms and Financial Characteristics

Organizational form	Number of owners	Owner's liability	Equity capital sources	Ease of start-up	Taxation	Liquidity of ownership	Life span
Proprietorship	1	Unlimited	Self, friends, relatives	Simple	Personal taxation	Difficult to sell	Linked to owner
Partnership (general)	>1	Unlimited, jointly and severally	Partners, friends, relatives	Not difficult	Personal taxation	Difficult to sell	Linked to owners
Limited partnership	At least 1 general, any number of limited partners	Limited partners' liability is limited to partners' investment	General and limited partners	More difficult	Personal taxation	Usually poor	Linked to general partner
Corporation	Unlimited	Limited to shareholders' investment	Common stock offerings	Difficult	Corporate taxation, but dividends are taxed twice, both as corporate earnings and personal income	Can be very liquid	Unlimited
Subchapter S corporation	<35	Limited to shareholders' investment	Sub S equity investors	Difficult	Income flows to shareholders for taxation at personal rates	Usually poor	Unlimited
Limited liability company (LLC)	Unlimited	Limited to owners' investment	Common stock offerings	Difficult	Income flows to shareholders for taxation at personal rates	Poor	Linked to current shareholders

[3] Data are taken from the 2012 *Statistical Abstract of the United States*; it can be found online at https://www.census.gov/library/publications/time-series/statistical_abstracts.html.

SMALL BUSINESS PRACTICE

THE FAMILY BUSINESS OR VENTURE

Family businesses continue to be very popular in the United States. With publicly held firms, corporate goals and the goals of managers may differ. For closely held firms that are nonfamily owned, the business goals and the personal goals of owner/managers are closely aligned. For family owned or family controlled firms, a third set of goals—family goals—also must be considered. When family goals are closely aligned with the business and manager goals, the business can benefit from family sharing and closeness. However, when family goals differ from business and/or manager goals, conflict and an argumentative environment may prevail. In such instances, these family controlled businesses often fail or the family is forced to sell.

Jeffry Timmons, in his book titled *New Venture Creation*, lists several problems that are unique to family businesses or ventures. First, problems of "control, fairness, and equity" often exist.

For example, family members may have different ideas on how the business should be run. Fairness and equity issues relate to the division of work and relative contributions to running the business. Second is the issue of "credibility," whereby founding parents find it difficult to believe that their children can perform in a manner comparable to their own. Third is a potential problem relating to "family dynamics." Since it often is difficult to separate business operations from family life, tensions in one area often spill over into the other area. Fourth is the problem of deciding succession. If succession is to involve a next-generation family member, the founder must disengage his or her ownership "rights" and delegate an increased level of responsibility to the new person in control. For successful succession to take place, the founder must be willing to assume the role of an advisor to the next-generation family member who was selected to run the firm in the future.

---

owner from the firm is difficult. Proprietorships outnumber all other forms of business organization in the United States. However, the economic power of these firms, as measured by number of employees and size of payroll, is less than that of the nation's corporations.

The financial capital of proprietorships is, many times, limited to the savings of the owner and funds that may be borrowed from friends, relatives, and banks. The investment made by the owner is called **equity capital**, or owner's equity. As the business grows and larger investments in capital are required, the owner may reach the point where additional funds cannot be borrowed without an increase in owner's equity. Lenders will generally insist on an increase in the owner's equity, because that equity provides a margin of safety for the lender.

equity capital investment made by the owner into the company

This point is where the proprietorship form of organization displays its basic weakness. In many cases, the owner's original investment exhausts his or her personal resources, and often those of friends and relatives. Unless profits from the venture are great enough to meet the increased equity needs, the firm is prevented from achieving its maximum growth. At this stage, it may be necessary to adopt a form of organization more appropriate for raising capital.

In addition, the life of the proprietorship is limited to that of the proprietor; when the proprietor dies, the business ends. Another weakness is the difficulty in transferring ownership (sometimes called ownership "liquidity") of the proprietorship. It can be difficult to sell a proprietorship. Among the complicating factors is that the firm is likely to sell at a discount, or for a percentage of its value, because of the difficulty in determining the business' past profitability, cash flows, risks, and future market potential. Much of what has made the proprietorship successful may be the proprietor or the information in the proprietor's mind.

Another weakness of proprietorship is that the owner's liability for debts of the firm is unlimited. Creditors may take the assets of the business to settle claims but they may take the personal assets of the proprietor as well. Thus, the proprietor may find his or her home and personal property under claim if the assets of the business are insufficient to meet the demands of creditors. The unlimited liability of the owner is, therefore, a serious disadvantage of the proprietorship.

On the positive side, a proprietorship business is easily started with minimal expense and, generally, has fewer government regulations to comply with than does a corporation. Profits from a proprietorship are taxed at personal, or individual, rates rather than at corporate income tax rates. Furthermore, converting a business that was established as a proprietorship into a corporation is easy when the need to finance growth warrants such a move.

13.2.2 PARTNERSHIP

partnership a form of business organization that exists when two or more persons own a business operated for profit

A **partnership** form of business organization exists when two or more persons own a business operated for profit. Although the partnership resembles the proprietorship, to some degree, there are important differences. See Table 13.1 for a summary.

Undoubtedly, one of the major reasons for the popularity of the partnership arrangement is that it allows individuals to pool their resources of money, property, equipment, knowledge, and business skills without the complications that often accompany incorporation. A partnership form may exist from the beginning of a business operation. In other cases, a firm that began as a proprietorship may reach the point where additional growth is impossible without increased equity capital. Bringing in new equity investors by converting to a partnership arrangement is one method of increasing the equity capital of a firm.

The number of partners that may be taken into a business venture is, theoretically, unlimited. However, the managerial difficulties and conflicts arising with many partners limit their number to a practical size. Thus, the partnership, like the proprietorship, eventually suffers from a lack of large amounts of equity capital. It is unusual to find more than a few partners in an industrial or commercial firm.

As is the case for a proprietorship, the life of a partnership is linked to that of its partners. Should a partner leave or die, the partnership officially dissolves unless a new partnership agreement is drafted. For purposes of taxation, the partnership's profits (and losses) are distributed to the partners and are taxable to the individual partner. Like proprietorships, partnerships typically have illiquid ownership stakes. The partners' shares of most small- to medium-sized business are often sold at a discount that reflects their lack of liquidity, their lack of majority control over the firm, and the need for the new partner to "fit" with the existing partners.

Like the proprietor, the members of a partnership team risk their personal assets as well as their investments in the business venture. In addition, if one of the partners negotiates a contract that results in substantial loss, each partner suffers a portion of the loss, based on a previously determined agreement on distribution of profits and losses. The other partners may, however, sue the offending partner if there is any violation of the articles of co-partnership.

More serious, perhaps, is a partner's liability for the actions of the business. In legal terms, each partner is jointly and severally liable for the partnership's debts. Under partnership law, each partner has unlimited liability for all the debts of the firm. This permits creditors to claim assets from one or more of the partners if the remaining partners are unable to cover their share of the loss.

limited partnership has at least one general partner who has unlimited liability; the liability of the limited partners is limited to their investment

limited partners face limited liability to their investments in the firm, meaning their personal assets cannot be attached to settle the firm's debt

These liability risks describe a general partnership. A **limited partnership** addresses the liability concern by identifying at least one general partner who has unlimited liability. The remaining **limited partners** face liability limited to their investments in the firm, meaning their personal assets cannot be attached to settle the firm's debts. They are "limited" as well in that they cannot participate in the operations of the firm. Operating decisions may be made only by the general partners. Some sports teams (such as the New York Yankees) are owned by limited partnerships. Broadway theater productions and real estate management and construction firms are other popular limited partnership vehicles.

13.2.3 CORPORATION

corporation legal entity created under state law in the United States with an unending life and limited financial liability to its owners

A **corporation** is a legal entity created under state law in the United States with an unending life and limited financial liability to its owners. In the case of *Dartmouth College vs. Woodward* in 1819, Chief Justice of the Supreme Court John Marshall described the status of the corporation as follows:

> *A corporation is an artificial being, invisible, intangible, and existing only in contemplation of law. Being the mere creature of law, it possesses only those properties which the charter of its creation confers upon it, either expressly, or as incidental to its very existence. . . . Among the most important are immortality and individuality, properties by which a perpetual succession of persons are considered as the same and may act as a single individual.*

In essence, the law has created an artificial being that has the rights, duties, and powers of a person. The definition includes the concept of many people united into one body that does not change its identity with changes in ownership. Advantages of being organized as a corporation include unlimited corporate life that is not tied to that of the owners, the ability to attract outside capital, limited financial liability for the owners, and the ease with which ownership can be transferred from investor to investor.

A corporation that has been in existence only a short time, like most new ventures, usually finds it difficult to attract investment funds from outsiders. The corporate form of organization does not ensure a flow of investment funds into the business. Rather, it removes several of the barriers to the flow of capital that exist in other forms of business organization. After a corporation becomes established and offers attractive returns for investors, these special features of the corporate form become significant. One of the important reasons corporations can accumulate large sums of capital is that they are allowed to sell capital stock. The stock may be offered to existing stockholders or to new investors in amounts suited to their purposes. As we discussed in Chapter 11, a firm can go public by first registering its shares with the Securities and Exchange Commission (SEC) and then selling them to the investing public. A corporation that has not gone through this process is a privately held corporation.

One of the advantages for corporate stockholders is the limitation on liability. Ordinarily, creditors and other claimants may look only to the assets of the corporation for satisfaction of their claims. They cannot take the personal assets of the owners (stockholders). This advantage is particularly appealing to the owner of a business who has built up considerable personal wealth and has other business interests. The limitation on liability may make it possible for promoters of new ventures to attract wealthy investors who would otherwise be unwilling to risk claims against their personal property.

On the other hand, the corporate form of organization may not always protect stockholders from personal risk beyond their investment when a business is relatively new or in a weak financial condition. Creditors may require that one or more of the stockholders add their signatures to the obligation of the corporation, making them personally liable for the obligation. After a corporation has established a good credit reputation, however, creditors and suppliers seldom insist on personal guarantees on the part of the stockholders.

Another important advantage of the corporation is the ease with which ownership may be transferred. Corporate stock may be transferred freely from one person to another. The purchaser of the stock then has all the rights and privileges formerly held by the seller. The corporation is not a party to the transfer of ownership and has no power to interfere with the sale or purchase of its stock. In contrast, there must be unanimous approval of the members of a partnership before a new partner can be brought into the business.

However, like proprietorships and partnerships, the corporate form of organization has its drawbacks. First, setting up a corporation is more time-consuming and costly because of legal requirements. Individuals who wish to incorporate must hire a lawyer to prepare a charter and a set of bylaws. The charter provides a corporate name, indicates the intended business activities, provides the names and addresses of directors, and indicates how the firm will be capitalized with stock. A corporation is chartered in a specific state by filing the charter with the secretary of that state. The bylaws are the rules established to govern the corporation and include how the firm will be managed, how directors will be elected, and the rights of stockholders. After beginning operation, the corporation must file financial and tax statements with state and federal government agencies.

A second drawback of the corporate form of organization is that corporate earnings distributed as shareholder dividends are subject to double taxation. That is, corporate earnings are taxed first at the appropriate corporate income tax rate. Then, if the corporation pays out a portion of its after-tax earnings in the form of dividends, the stockholders must pay personal income taxes on this income.

Two special forms of corporate organization in the United States allow dividends to escape double taxation. A subchapter S corporation (named for the section of the tax code that discusses this organization) must have fewer than 35 shareholders, none of whom is another corporation. Income from a subchapter S corporation flows untaxed to the shareholders. Thus, it is taxed only once, as personal income of the shareholders.

charter provides the corporate name, indicates the intended business activities, provides names and addresses of directors, and indicates how a firm will be capitalized with stock

bylaws the rules established to govern the corporation and include how the firm will be managed, how the directors will be elected, and the rights of the stockholders

subchapter S corporation has fewer than 35 shareholders, none of which is another corporation; its income flows untaxed to the shareholders and is taxed only once, as personal income of the shareholders

limited liability company (LLC) an organizational form, similar to a subchapter S corporation, that offers owners limited liability; its income is taxed only once, as personal income of the shareholders, and the firm can have an unlimited number of shareholders

A limited liability company (LLC) organizational form is similar to a subchapter S corporation. It offers owners limited liability, and its income is taxed only once, as personal income of the shareholders.[4] Unlike a subchapter S corporation, however, an LLC can have an unlimited number of shareholders, including other corporations. The LLC can sell shares without completing the costly and time-consuming process of registering them with the SEC, which is a requirement for standard corporations that sell their securities to the public. The LLC structure has drawbacks in that, should an owner leave, all others must formally agree to continue the firm. Also, all of the LLC's owners must take active roles in managing the company. To protect partners from unlimited liability, some large accounting firms formerly set up as partnerships, such as PricewaterhouseCoopers, have become LLCs. Other partnerships have decided to go the corporate route to limit the partners' liability and to gain access to the capital market; Goldman Sachs, an investment banking firm, has converted from partnership to corporate status.

Many countries' laws recognize the corporate form of organization. American corporations may use the suffixes Inc. or Corp. to designate themselves. British corporations use the suffix PLC, which stands for public limited company; limited refers to shareholders' liability in the firm. The suffix AG following the names of firms in Germany, Austria, Switzerland, or Liechtenstein is an abbreviation for Aktiengesellschaft, which means corporation.

It is up to the firm's owners to weigh the pros and cons and determine which organizational form suits the needs of their firm best. Each has its own implications for taxation, control by the owners, ability to trade ownership positions, limitations on liability, firm life, and raising capital.

DISCUSSION QUESTION 1

If you are going to start a business, what organizational form would you select? Why? What drawbacks might you face in organizing a business this way?

13.3 ACCOUNTING PRINCIPLES

generally accepted accounting principles (GAAP) set of guidelines as to the form and manner in which accounting information should be presented

Among the inputs used to construct the financial statements are generally accepted accounting principles (GAAP), which are formulated by the Financial Accounting Standards Board (FASB). The FASB recognizes that it would be improper for all companies to use identical and restrictive accounting principles. Some flexibility and choice are needed, as industries and firms within industries differ in their operating environments. On the negative side, this flexibility can result in firms that, at first glance, appear healthier than they are, and we'll see some examples of deceptive accounting in a future section. The financial analyst's task is to dig into the available financial information to separate those firms which only appear to be attractive from those which are in good financial shape.[5] Fortunately, FASB requires that financial statements include footnotes. These footnotes inform analysts of which accounting principles were used by the firm.

Accounting information is important for financial managers, investors, and financial institutions, but the focus of accounting information differs from the focus of finance personnel. Table 13.2 lists some important differences.

Much of accounting practice is based on the accrual concept. Under accrual accounting, revenues and their associated expenses are recognized when a sale occurs, regardless of when cash revenues or expenses occur. Let's use the example of a set of living room furniture sold in June. The sofa was constructed the previous November; the coffee table was manufactured in March; other pieces were

---

[4] LLCs are available in every state; state offices can provide details on how to establish an LLC (or any other organizational form). Some states allow LLPs, limited liability partnerships. An LLC can be established by a single person; LLPs require two or more persons. LLPs are similar in some states to limited partnerships except that the LLP structure gives limited liability to the general partner.

[5] Although the financial statements of U.S. firms must conform to GAAP, those of the U.S. government do not. In fact, a review of federal government accounting records found them to be woefully deficient. Fourteen of 24 departments and agencies flunked a corporate-style review of their books. Departments with accounting problems included the Treasury Department, Commerce Department, and the Departments of Agriculture, Health and Human Services, Transportation, and Defense. See Jacob M. Schlesinger, "U.S. Fails to Meet Standard Accounting Methods," *The Wall Street Journal*, (March 31, 1998), pp. A2, A6. In a more recent study of the 2008 federal budget deficit, if corporate-style accounting methods were used, the 2008 fiscal year deficit would have been $1 trillion rather than "only" $455 billion as reported by the U.S. government. See https://usatoday30.usatoday.com/news/washington/2008-12-15-deficit_N.htm (accessed June 1, 2013).

Table 13.2   Comparison of Accounting and Financial Perspectives

Accounting focus	Finance focus
Matching revenue and expenses (accrual concept)	Identifying cash inflows and outflows
Use of different accounting principles can lead to manipulation of financial statements	Track the cash flows to assess the "quality" of reported assets and earnings
Seek to measure firm profitability	Measure cash usage
Emphasis is historical	Looks forward
Attempts to track assets and depreciate them	Market value of assets

finished in the spring. Although the manufacturer's raw materials suppliers and the workers that made the furniture were paid a long time ago (last year, in the case of the sofa) the expenses will not appear on the firm's accounting books until the set is sold in June. At that time, the selling price of the living room set and its associated expenses are recorded using accrual accounting principles. The sales figure may be misleading, too. Although sales revenue may be "booked" in June when the furniture sells, the actual cash receipts from the sale may not come in until later if the store is financing the purchase for the buyer.

From the financial manager's perspective, cash is what matters most. He had to pay the firm's suppliers last year and the workers over the last several months. He knows, because customers will pay for their purchase under the monthly installment plan, that although revenue is recognized in June, the actual cash from the sale will come in over several months; the customers will not be finished paying for the furniture until the following year. The cash flows, or the cash expenses and cash revenues, occur over the space of many months and three calendar years; yet, under accrual accounting, the accounting revenues and expenses appear to have all occurred this year, in the month of June. Although the firm may appear profitable, it may be cash poor because of the lag between cash outflows and cash inflows. Whereas, from a historical perspective, the furniture store may be making a profit, what matters to the firm's treasurer (and the firm's lenders) is what cash inflows are expected in the near future so the firm can continue to stay in business and pay its bills in a timely manner.

Another difference between the perspectives of accountants and financial managers is in how they view assets. In the manufacturing economy, fixed assets are depreciated according to set schedules so their accounting value declines over time. However, for many firms, the most important assets are people, brand identity, technological innovation, and organizational knowledge rather than "hard" assets. Accountants are grappling with ways to value such "intangible" assets.[6]

As this example illustrates, an analyst may have to dig to obtain a true picture of the items featured in the firm's financial statements. In the following sections, we review the firm's major financial statements and their components.

GLOBAL An issue that managers and investors have had to grapple with is international accounting standards. Every nation has its own set of standards, some of which differ from U.S. GAAP. Table 13.3 presents several examples of the differences in profit that can arise depending on which country's accounting standards are followed. The International Accounting Standards Committee (IASC) has been working for over 40 years on a set of international accounting standards, so it will be easier to compare firm's financials across borders. It is hoped by many analysts that these standards will soon be acceptable alternatives in many countries, making intercountry firm comparisons and analyses easier than they are now.[7]

---

[6] Baruch Lev and Feng Gu, *The End of Accounting and the Path Forward for Investors and Managers*, (Wiley Finance, 2016); Thomas E. Weber, "Intangibles Are Tough To Value, but the Payoff Matters in Dot-Com Era," *The Wall Street Journal*, (May 14, 2001), p. B1; Jeffrey E. Garten, et al., *Strengthening Financial Markets: Do Investors Have the Information They Need?* (May 2001), https://www.fei.org/finrep/files/SEC-Taskforce-Final-6-6-2k1.pdf.

[7] Sarah Johnson, "Goodbye GAAP," *CFO*, (April 2009), pp. 49–54 available at https://www.cfo.com/article.cfm/10919122/c_10985924; Eric L. Reiner, "Fusing Together Financial Standards," *Treasury and Risk Management*, (March 2001), pp. 53–54; Elizabeth MacDonald, "The Outlook: Fixing Tower of Babel in Global Accounting," *The Wall Street Journal*, (May 11, 1998), p. A1; Ian Springsteel, "All For One, or None For All?" *CFO*, (April 1998), pp. 103–105.

Table 13.3 Comparing Profits: Home Country Accounting Standards versus U.S. GAAP

Firm	Year	Home country profit	U.S. GAAP profit
Daimler-Benz (Germany)	1992	$97 million	$–548 million
SmithKline Beecham (UK)	1993	$1.5 billion	$1.2 billion
British Airways (UK)	1993	$535 million	$353 million
Hoechst AG (Germany)	1995	$1.2 billion	$–40 million
Hoechst AG (Germany)	1996	$1.4 billion	$708 million
Aggregation of 17 Brazilian firms (NYSE listed ADRs)	2006	BRL18.286 billion	BRL 19.335 billion
SK Telecom Company Ltd	2009	KRW 1,056 billion	KRW 1,357 billion
Braskem SA	2009	BRL 767.8 million	BRL 232.7 million

Sources: Ilse Maria Beuren and Roberto Carlos Klann, "Divergences between the BR GAAP and US GAAP," *Journal of Accounting and Taxation*, vol. 2(2), (August 2010), pp. 031–041; Timothy Doupnik and Hector Perera, *International Accounting, 3rd Edition*, (McGraw Hill, 2012). Elizabeth MacDonald, "The Outlook: Fixing Tower of Babel in Global Accounting," *The Wall Street Journal*, (May 11, 1998), p. A1; Ian Springsteel, "All For One, or None For All?" *CFO*, (April 1998), pp. 103–105; Anita Raghaven and Michael R. Sesit, "Foreign Firms Raise More and More Money in the U.S. Markets," *The Wall Street Journal*, (October 5, 1993), p. A1.

The U.S. federal government, through the Securities and Exchange Commission (SEC), oversees the accuracy and truthfulness in public company financial statements. Company fines and jail time for corporate executives are punishments for public companies that purposefully deceive investors with fraudulent financial statements. Unfortunately, the U.S. government doesn't hold its own accounting to the same standards. For example, "savings" in a student loan program from 2015–2014 were reported as $135 billion; under standards that apply to corporations, the savings disappears and becomes an increased cost of $88 billion due to the unaccounted-for cost of government loan guarantees. Worse yet, the administrative costs of these (and other such programs) are counted elsewhere in the federal budget, so the costs are even higher.[8]

13.3.1 THE ANNUAL REPORT

An important component of manager – owner communication is the firm's financial statements. Firms organized as proprietorships or partnerships are not required to prepare financial reports or statements except for tax purposes. Of course, proprietors and partners must gather financial data so as to be able to evaluate their financial performance over time. Requests for bank loans need to be accompanied by recent financial statements, too.

In contrast, companies organized as corporations are required to prepare financial reports annually for the benefit of their shareholders. Public corporations are required to file annual reports with the SEC.

Annual report contains descriptive information on operating and financial performance during the past year, a discussion of current and future business opportunities, and financial statements that provide a numerical record of financial performance

An **annual report** contains descriptive information on operating and financial performance during the past year, a discussion of current and future business opportunities, and financial statements that provide a numerical record of financial performance. Usually, financial highlights are provided on the first page or two, followed by a letter to the stockholders by the firm's chairman of the board and chief executive officer (CEO). The CEO summarizes the financial results for the year and identifies the firm's strengths, such as employee talents and the size of its customer base. After the CEO's letter, most companies describe their current business areas, future opportunities, and financial goals, such as a target return on equity or earnings growth rate.

Three important financial statements are provided in the annual report: the statement of income (sometimes called the statement of operations), the balance sheet (sometimes called the statement

[8] Review and Outlook, "Fraudulent Government Accounting," *The Wall Street Journal*, (June 1, 2014), accessed December 29, 2015, at https://online.wsj.com/articles/fraudulent-government-accounting-1401662594.

of financial position), and the statement of cash flows. Management provides detailed notes to these financial statements. Annual reports, typically, provide a five- or ten-year summary of selected financial data for the firm.

> **LEARNING ACTIVITY**
>
> **The website of the Securities and Exchange Commission, https://www.sec.gov, gives users access to public corporation's financial filings through its electronic data gathering and retrieval (EDGAR) system.**

The income statement reports the revenues generated and expenses incurred by a firm over an accounting period, such as a quarter or year. The accrual concept is used to construct the income statement. Table 13.4 presents income statements for a firm, Walgreens, for 2017 and 2018. In 2018, Walgreens had net revenues of $131.5 billion (which is the same as the $131,537 million shown in the table—that is, $131,537,000,000) compared with $118.2 billion for 2017, which reflects an increase of over 11%. After deducting production costs and other expenses incurred in running the business, Walgreens' net income was $5,024 million in 2018, nearly 25% more than 2017's net income of $4,078 million.

In 2015, Walgreens completed a merger with a large European firm, Alliance Boots; the combined firm's official name is Walgreens Boots Alliance but we refer to it as "Walgreens" as that is shorter, and that is the name we see on drugstores across America. Prior to the merger, Alliance Boots was a pharmacy-led health and beauty products firm that was formed in 2006 after another merger, that of Boots Group and Alliance Unichem.

Let's look at some of the major income statement accounts in greater detail. The starting point of the income statement reflects the revenues or sales generated from the operations of the business. Often, gross revenues are larger than net revenues. This is due to sales returns and allowances that may occur over the time period reflected in the income statement. Sometimes, when customers make early payment on their bills, cash discounts are given by the firm. If customers buy in large quantities, trade discounts may be given. Thus, discounts will reduce gross revenues.

The costs of producing or manufacturing the products sold to earn revenues are grouped under cost of goods sold (COGS). These expenses reflect costs directly involved in production, such as raw materials, labor, and overhead and, thus, vary with the level of production output.

Selling, general and administrative expenses tend to be stable or fixed in nature and cover requirements such as record keeping and preparing financial and accounting statements. These expenses reflect the costs associated with selling the firm's products. This includes salaries and/or commissions generated by the sales force as well as promotional and advertising expenditures.

Depreciation is an estimate of the reduction in the economic value of the firm's plant and equipment caused by the creation of the firm's products or services. Each financial period's income statement shows the amount of depreciation expense specific to that period. Accumulated depreciation, or the

13.4 INCOME STATEMENT

income statement reports the revenues generated and expenses incurred by the firm over an accounting period, such as a quarter or a year

Table 13.4 Income Statement for Walgreens ($ millions)

	2018	2017
Revenue	131,537	118,214
Cost of goods sold	100,745	89,052
Sales, general, and administrative expenses	24,569	22,916
Operating income	6,223	6,246
Interest expense	−577	−643
Other income (expense)	+376	−742
Income before income taxes	6,022	4,861
Income taxes	998	783
Net income	5,024	4,078

sum of prior period depreciation expense, appears in the balance sheet. No cash outflow is associated with depreciation, so it is considered to be a noncash expense.

Operating income is a firm's income before interest and income taxes, and is sometimes referred to as earnings before interest and taxes (EBIT).

Interest expense is subtracted from operating income. When a portion of a firm's assets are financed with liabilities, interest charges usually result. This is true for bank loans and long-term corporate bonds. Operating income less interest expense gives the firm's pretax earnings, or earnings before taxes.

Businesses are required to pay federal income taxes on any profits. Most states tax business profits. Taxable earnings, or profit, are defined as income remaining after all other expenses have been deducted from revenues, except income taxes. Effective income tax rates can vary substantially depending on whether the firm is organized as a proprietorship, partnership, or corporation. More information on taxes appears in this chapter's Learning Extension.

The net income, or profits, remaining after income taxes are paid reflects the earnings available to the owners of the business. This income may be retained in the business to reduce existing liabilities, increase current assets, and/or acquire additional fixed assets. On the other hand, some or all of the income may be distributed to the owners of the business.

Because of accrual accounting, a firm's net income over some period may not be the same as its cash flow. The amount of cash flowing into the firm can be higher or lower than the net income figure.

For a corporation, a firm commonly shows its net income on a per-share basis. This is referred to as the earnings per share (EPS) and is calculated by dividing the net income by the number of shares of common stock that are outstanding. For Walgreens, EPS rose from $3.78 in 2017 to $5.07 in 2018. Although net income rose by 23%, EPS rose 34% in 2017–2018. The reason for this is the denominator of the EPS calculation: the number of shares outstanding fell between 2017 and 2018, so the EPS rose more than net income.

In some instances, corporations have both preferred and common stockholders. Dividends are paid to the "preferred" stockholders out of net income; the remaining earnings are called "income available to common stockholders." For example, if Walgreens had paid $200 million in preferred stock dividends in 2018, the remaining earnings available for common stockholders would have been $5,024 − $200 = $4,824 million.

Corporations frequently pay cash dividends to their common stockholders. The percentage of net income, or earnings, paid out as dividends is referred to as the dividend payout ratio. For example, in 2018 Walgreens paid common stock dividends of $1,739 million (this figure is given in Table 13.6); this represents a dividend payout ratio of about 35% ($1,739 million in dividends divided by net income of $5,024 million). The remaining earnings are retained in the business; for example, they can be used to repay debt, buy back shares of stock, or purchase new plant and equipment.

13.5 THE BALANCE SHEET

balance sheet statement of a company's financial position as of a particular date, usually at the end of a quarter or year

assets financial and physical items owned by a business

liabilities creditors' claims on a firm, which are the financial obligations of the business

equity funds supplied by the owners and represents their residual claim on the firm

The balance sheet is a statement of a company's financial position as of a particular date, usually at the end of a quarter or year. Whereas the income statement reflects the firm's operations over time, the balance sheet is a snapshot at a point in time. It reveals two broad categories of information: (1) the assets, or the financial and physical items owned by a business, and (2) the claims of creditors and owners in the business assets. The creditors' claims, which are the financial obligations of the business, are referred to as liabilities. The company's equity is the funds supplied by the owners and represents their residual claim on the firm.

In addition to providing a snapshot of a firm's financial condition, the balance sheet reveals much of the inner workings of the company's financial structure. The various types of assets indicate the results of recent business operations and the capacity for future operations. The creditors' claims and the owners' equity in the assets reveal the sources from which these assets have been derived. The term "balance sheet" indicates a relationship of equality between the assets of the business and the sources of funds used to obtain them that may be expressed as follows:

$$\text{Assets} = \text{Liabilities} + \text{Owners' equity}$$

Table 13.5   Balance Sheet for Walgreens ($ millions)

	2018	2017
Cash & Cash Equivalents	$785	$3,301
Accounts Receivable	$7,144	$6,528
Inventories	$10,976	$8,899
Other Current Assets	$1,178	$1,025
Total Current Assets	**$20,283**	**$19,753**
Net Fixed Assets	**$13,821**	**$13,642**
Other Long-Term Assets	$7,644	$6,826
Goodwill & Intangibles	$28,393	$25,788
Total Fixed Assets	$49,858	$46,256
TOTAL ASSETS	**$69,941**	**$66,009**
Accounts Payable	$14,660	$12,494
Short Term Debt	$1,999	$251
Other Current Liabilities	$8,440	$5,802
Total Current Liabilities	**$25,099**	**$18,547**
Long-Term Debt	$11,646	$12,684
Other Liabilities	$6,933	$6,504
TOTAL LIABILITIES	**$43,678**	**$37,735**
Preferred Equity	$0	$0
Common Equity		
Retained Earnings		
TOTAL STOCKHOLDERS' EQUITY	$26,263	$28,274
TOTAL LIABILITIES & EQUITY	**$69,941**	**$66,009**

This "balance sheet equation" or "accounting identity" shows that every dollar of a firm's assets must be financed by a dollar of liabilities (typically some type of credit or borrowing), a dollar of owner's equity, or some combination of the two. The firm's asset total shows what the firm owns; the total of liabilities and equity shows what the firm owes to its creditors and owners.

The balance sheet for Walgreens shown in Table 13.5 reveals this equality of assets and the financial interests in the assets. Total assets were $69,941 million in 2018, a 6% increase over 2017's asset level of $66,009 million.

Walgreens total liabilities increased from $37,735 million to $43,678 million, which is an increase of nearly 16%. Owner's equity, which for Walgreens is stockholders' equity, provided the balancing figure with $26,263 million in 2018 and $28,274 million in 2017. This was an increase of about 51%. This brief comparison shows the increase in assets was financed solely by an increase in debt (total liabilities) as equity fell over 7% during this time.

13.5.1 ASSETS

Assets that are most liquid are typically listed first. By liquidity, we mean the time it usually takes to convert the assets into cash. Two broad groups are identified on the balance sheet: current assets and fixed assets.

The current assets of a business include cash and other assets that are expected to be converted into cash within one year. Current assets thus represent the working capital needed to carry out the normal operations of the business. The principal current assets of a business are, typically, its cash and marketable securities, accounts receivable, and inventories.

current assets cash and all other assets that are expected to be converted into cash within one year

working capital assets needed to carry out the normal operations of the business

Cash and marketable securities include cash on hand and cash on deposit with banks; marketable securities, such as commercial paper issued by other firms; and U.S. government securities in the form of Treasury bills, notes, and bonds.

Accounts receivable, generally, arise from the sale of products, merchandise, or services on credit. The buyer's debts to the business are, generally, paid according to the credit terms of the sale. Some firms have notes receivable, which are written promises by a debtor of the business to pay a specified sum of money on or before a stated date. Notes receivable may come into existence in several ways. For example, overdue accounts receivable may be converted to notes receivable at the insistence of the seller or upon special request by the buyer. Notes receivable may also occur as a result of short-term loans made by the business to its employees or to other persons or businesses.

The materials and products that a manufacturing firm has on hand are shown as inventories on the balance sheet. Generally, a manufacturing firm categorizes its inventories in terms of raw materials, goods in the process of manufacture, and finished goods. Sometimes, the balance sheet will reveal the amount of inventory in each of these categories.

Fixed assets are the physical facilities used in the production, storage, display, and distribution of the products of a firm. These assets normally provide many years of service. The principal fixed assets are classified into two categories: (1) plant and equipment and (2) land. Intangible assets, which are assets you cannot see or feel, are accounted for on the balance sheet as they are created as the firm conducts business. An example of this is goodwill, which is an accounting concept as it represents the excess funds paid, when one firm merges with or purchases another, over and above the accounting value of the firm's net assets. For example, if a firm's net assets are worth $100 million but it has loyal customers, good workers, or a strong brand image, another firm may pay $125 million to purchase the firm. $25 million will appear on the balance sheet, after the merger, to reflect the value of the goodwill sold in the transaction.

In a manufacturing firm, a large investment in plant and equipment is usually required. As products are manufactured, some of the economic value of this plant and equipment lessens. This is called depreciation and accountants reflect this using up of real assets by charging off depreciation against the original cost of plant and equipment. Thus, the net plant and equipment information at any point in time is supposed to reflect their remaining useful lives. The net is calculated by subtracting the amount of depreciation that has accumulated over time from the gross plant and equipment. The topic of depreciation is discussed further in this chapter's Learning Extension.

Some firms own the land or real property on which their buildings or manufacturing plants are constructed. Other firms may own other land for expansion or investment purposes. The original cost of land owned is reflected on the firm's balance sheet. Under the tax code, land cannot be depreciated.

goodwill an intangible asset that represents the excess funds paid, when one firm merges with or purchases another, over and above the accounting value of the firm's net assets

depreciation devaluing a physical asset over the period of its expected life

13.5.2 LIABILITIES

Liabilities are the debts of a business. They come into existence through direct borrowing, purchases of goods and services on credit, and the accrual of obligations, such as wages and income taxes. Liabilities are classified as current and long-term.

The current liabilities of a business may be defined as those obligations that must be paid within one year. They include accounts payable, notes payable, and accrued liabilities that are to be met out of current funds and operations. Although the cash on hand plus marketable securities of the Walgreens is $785 million compared with current liabilities of $25,099, it is expected that normal business operations will convert receivables and inventory into cash in time to meet current liabilities as they become due.

Accounts payable are debts that arise primarily from the purchase of goods and supplies on credit terms. Accounts payable arising from the purchase of inventory on credit terms represent trade credit financing as opposed to direct short-term borrowing from banks and other lenders. An account payable shown on one firm's balance sheet appears as an account receivable on the balance sheet of the firm from which goods were purchased.

A note payable is a written promise to pay a specified amount of money to a creditor on or before a certain date. The most common occurrence of a note payable takes place when a business borrows money from a bank on a short-term basis to purchase materials or for other current operating requirements.

Current liabilities that reflect amounts owed but not due as of the date of the balance sheet are called accrued liabilities, or accruals. The most common forms of accruals are wages payable and taxes payable. These accounts exist because wages are, typically, paid weekly, biweekly, or monthly and income taxes are paid quarterly.

Business debts with maturities greater than one year are long-term liabilities. As we reviewed in Chapter 11, one of the common methods used by businesses for obtaining a long-term loan is to offer a mortgage to a lender as collateral for a corporate bond. In the event that the borrowing business fails to meet the obligations of the loan contract, the mortgage may be foreclosed; that is, the property may be seized through appropriate legal channels and sold to satisfy the indebtedness.

13.5.3 OWNERS' EQUITY

All businesses have owners' equity in one form or another. Owners' equity is the investment of the owners or owner in the business. It initially results from a cash outlay to purchase assets to operate the business. In some cases, the owners of a business may place their own assets, such as machinery, real estate, or equipment with the firm for its operation. In addition to contributing cash or property, owners' equity may be increased by allowing profits to remain with the business. On the balance sheet, the amount of owners' equity is always represented by the difference between total assets and total liabilities of the business. It reflects the owners' claims on the assets of the business as opposed to the creditors' claims.

In the case of a corporation, the owners' equity can be broken down into three different accounts. First, Walgreens has no preferred stock outstanding, so the preferred equity or stock account balance is zero. Second, the common stock, or common equity, account reflects the number of outstanding shares of common stock carried at a stated or par value and the capital paid in excess of par. The par value is an arbitrary value and, therefore, is not related to a firm's stock price or market value. Some firms have "no par" common stock, meaning the common stock has a par value of $0.

The third account is called the retained earnings account, and it shows the accumulated undistributed earnings (i.e., earnings *not* paid out as dividends) of the corporation over time. These retained earnings do not represent cash. They have been invested in the firm's current and/or fixed assets over the firm's lifetime. Together, these three accounts (preferred equity, common equity, and retained earnings) comprise the corporation's stockholders' equity. In the case of Walgreens, all of the stockholders equity belongs to common shareholders.

In addition to the income statement and balance sheet, corporate annual reports also want to measure changes in cash flows. All three of the previously described financial statements are prepared using an accrual accounting system whereby items are recorded as incurred but not necessarily when cash is received or disbursed. For example, a sale of $100 is recorded as a sale this year even though the cash is not expected to be collected until next year.

A **statement of cash flows** provides a summary of the cash inflows (sources) and cash outflows (uses) during a specified accounting period.[9] The statement consists of three sections: operating activities, investing activities, and financing activities.

The primary approach to constructing a statement of cash flows begins with the net income from the income statement as a cash inflow. We add back any noncash deductions, such as depreciation, which

13.6 STATEMENT OF CASH FLOWS

statement of cash flows provides a summary of the cash inflows (sources) and cash outflows (uses) during a specified accounting period

---

[9] For an overview of how to analyze a Statement of Cash Flows, see Anne Tergesen, "The Ins and Outs of Cash Flow," *Business Week*, (January 22, 2001), pp. 102–104.

were deducted by accounting principles although no cash outflow occurred. The other "cash flow" adjustments are made by examining the differences in the accounts from two consecutive balance sheets. More specifically, cash flows are determined as follows:

SOURCES

1. Amount of net income plus amount of depreciation

2. Decrease in an asset account

3. Increase in a liability account

4. Increase in an equity account

USES

1. Increase in an asset account

2. Decrease in a liability account

3. Decrease in an equity account

4. Amount of cash dividends

Changes in the cash account are excluded. In the statement of cash flows, all of the firm's sources and uses of cash are added together. Their sum equals the change in the firm's cash account. If the statement of cash flows is constructed correctly, the sum of the items should equal the difference in the cash account between the two balance sheets used to generate it.

Let's examine these more closely:

- Assets. The purchase of raw materials or an increase in the amount of finished goods held requires additional cash. Thus, it is a use and is, therefore, subtracted in the statement of cash flows. In contrast, collections of accounts receivable frees up cash; the reduction in accounts receivable is a source and is added in the statement of cash flows.

- Liabilities and equity. Borrowing money from a bank or receiving an added investment from a partner or stockholder represents a source of cash to the firm. In contrast, paying off a bank loan or repurchasing shares of stock is a use of cash.

Table 13.6 shows the statement of cash flows for Walgreens based on the 2018 income statement and the balance sheets as of fiscal year-end 2017 and 2018. Due to the accounting changes and firm consolidations over this time frame, some numbers may not match with differences in the 2017 and 2018 balance sheets. We will focus on the basic structure of the statement of cash flows in our discussion.

Notice that cash flows are grouped on the basis of operating activities, investing activities, and financing activities. Sources of funds from operations begin with net income of $5,024 million, adjustments to income of $-470, and depreciation of $1,516 million to reflect the fact that depreciation is a noncash charge against the firm's revenues. Including changes in other current accounts, the overall result was a net cash inflow from operations during 2018 of $8,265 million. The cash from operations is an important figure for businesses. It may be negative for growing firms, but generally, a firm cannot exist long if it continually creates net cash outflows from its operations.

Table 13.6 shows that Walgreens invested $1,367 million in plant and equipment in 2018. It also invested over $4,793 million in an investment in other firms. Overall, there was a net cash outflow of $5,501 million because of the firm's investing activities.

The net cash flow from financing activities amounted to a $5,295 million outflow during 2018. This net figure includes the payment of cash dividends of $1,739 million, a stock repurchase of $5,054 million, and proceeds from a sale of bonds of $1,596 million.

Table 13.6   Statement of Cash Flows, Walgreen 2018 ($ millions)

OPERATING ACTIVITIES	
Net Income	$5,024
Depreciation	$1,516
Adjustments to Net Income	–$470
Changes in Accounts Receivables	–$391
Changes in Liabilities	$1,323
Changes in Inventories	$331
Changes in Other Operating Activities	$932
Total Cash Flow From Operating Activities	**$8,265**
INVESTING ACTIVITIES	
Capital Expenditures	–$1,367
Investments	–$4,793
Other Cash Flows from Investing Activities	$659
Total Cash Flows from Investing Activities	**–$5,501**
FINANCING ACTIVITIES	
Dividends Paid	–$1,739
Sale Purchase of Stock	–$5,054
Net Borrowings	$1,596
Other Cash Flows from Financing Activities	–$98
Total Cash Flows From Financing Activities	**–$5,295**
Effect Of Exchange Rate Changes	$15
Net Change in Cash and Cash Equivalents	**–$2,516**

As the firm had global operations in 2018 following the merger of Alliance Boots in 2015, fluctuating exchange rates affected its dollar cash flows. The firm's cash flow was 15 million higher due to the effect of favorable exchange rate changes on the value of its cash flows.[10]

The overall result of operating, investing, and financing activities during 2018 was a $2,516 million decrease in the cash account. This is further verified by the fact that Table 13.4 shows the year-end 2018 cash balance of $785 million, that is $2,516 million lower than 2017's figure of $3,301 million.

> **LEARNING ACTIVITY**
>
> **See recent financial statements for any public company on the company's website, or on websites such as https://finance.yahoo.com; www.marketwatch.com; or https://quotes.wsj.com/company-list.**

Financial statements tell investors of differences in how companies operate. Across industries, the composition of firms' assets and liabilities will differ. Similarly, how firms generate earnings will depend upon the characteristics of the industry in which they compete and the products or service they offer to consumers. Directly comparing the financial statements of different firms is difficult. Because of size differences among firms, the dollar level of assets, liabilities, and expenses will be hard to compare.

13.7 FINANCIAL STATEMENTS OF DIFFERENT COMPANIES

---

[10] Readers interested in some of the accounting implications of exchange rate changes on financial statements can see S. L. Spencer and G. E. Richards, "Three Common Currency-Adjustment Pitfalls," *Journal of Accountancy*, (February 2012), accessed January 23, 2016, https://www.journalofaccountancy.com/issues/2012/feb/20113891.html.

13.7.1 COMMON-SIZE FINANCIAL STATEMENTS

common-size financial statements express balance sheet numbers as a percentage of total assets and income statement numbers as a percentage of total revenue to facilitate comparisons between different-sized firms

A means of addressing the size problem in performing firm comparisons is to use common-size financial statements. Common-size financial statements express balance sheet numbers as a percentage of total assets and income statement numbers as a percentage of revenue. In this way, comparison between firms is based on relative numbers rather than absolute dollar figures. Examining the percentages gives us insight into the competition within industries and the firms' methods of serving their markets.

Table 13.7 shows how common-size financial statements can aid the comparison of three different firms. Walgreens is a leading firm in the retail drug store industry, Microsoft is a major software and operating system provider, and ExxonMobil is a leading firm in the oil industry. The differences between the industries in which these firms operate are apparent when looking at their common-size financial statements.

Looking briefly at the balance sheets, we note the capital-intensive nature of oil exploration and refining as ExxonMobil only has 15% of its assets in current assets while the remainder are long-term assets; Walgreens and Microsoft have 29% and 64%, respectively, of their assets in the form of current assets. Further differences would be seen by examining the specific components of current assets.

ExxonMobil has more than half of its assets financed by equity while Microsoft and Walgreens have about two-thirds of their assets financed by debt. But the type of debt financing differs between these two firms: Walgreens has a higher percentage of short-term debt (current liabilities) while Microsoft uses more long-term debt financing.

Common-size income statements can be created, too, by dividing the various income statement categories by total revenues. Common-size statements are easily computed using spreadsheet software. Below, we place the 2018 income statement data for Walgreens in an Excel spreadsheet. Revenue is in cell B3, cost of goods sold in B4, and so on. To compute the common-size income statement, we merely divide these numbers by the revenue, cell B3. The formulas in column C show this. Using spreadsheets it is easy to convert balance sheet and income statement data into common-size format.

	A	B	C	D
1	**Income Statement**	**2018**	**Percent of**	**Percent of**
2		**$ millions**	**Revenue**	**Revenue**
3	Revenue	131537	100.0%	=B3/$B$3
4	Cost of Goods Sold	100745	76.6%	=B4/$B$3
5	**GROSS PROFIT**	**30792**	**23.4%**	=B5/$B$3
6	Selling, Gen'l & Admin.	24569	18.7%	=B6/$B$3
7	**OPERATING INCOME**	**6223**	**4.7%**	=B7/$B$3
8	Interest Expense	−577	−0.4%	=B8/$B$4
9	Other Expenses (Income)	($376)	−0.3%	=B9/$B$3
10	**INCOME BEFORE TAXES**	**$6,022**	**4.6%**	=B10/$B$3
11	Income Taxes	$998	0.8%	=B11/$B$3
12	**NET INCOME**	**$5,024**	**3.8%**	=B12/$B$3

Table 13.7   Common-Size Balance Sheets

ExxonMobil	% of assets	Microsoft	% of assets	Walgreens	% of assets
Current Assets	15.2	Current Assets	63.7	Current Assets	28.7
Fixed Assets	84.8	Fixed Assets	36.3	Fixed Assets	71.3
Total Assets	100.0	Total Assets	100.0	Total Assets	100.0
Current Liabilities	18.4	Current Liabilities	21.8	Current Liabilities	35.9
Long-term Debt	26.1	Long-term Debt	44.8	Long-term Debt	26.6
Stockholders' Equity	55.5	Stockholders' Equity	33.4	Stockholders' Equity	37.6
Total Liabilities + Equity	100.0	Total Liabilities + Equity	100.0	Total Liabilities + Equity	100.0

13.7.2 THE AUTO BAILOUT AND FINANCIAL STATEMENTS

In 2008, General Motors (GM) was teetering on the edge of bankruptcy due to decades of poor management, declining sales, and high costs, due in part to operating inefficiencies and high union wages and benefits. Table 13.8 indicates that in 2008 GM had negative equity, as total liabilities exceed total assets by $85 billion. It was running out of cash; it had $25 billion of cash in 2007 and had spent $10 billion of that in 2008. In 2008, GM's current assets were much less than its current liabilities: $44 billion compared to $76 billion.

Post-bankruptcy, due to a taxpayer infusion of dollars and running roughshod over borrower claims, total liabilities fell by over one-third, $68 billion, and equity rose $114 billion as the U.S. government become majority owner of the firm. In 2009, we saw total assets exceed total liabilities, the firm became solvent with positive equity, and the improved liquidity was seen in the comparison of current assets ($59 billion) to current liabilities ($52 billion). The increase in equity of $114 billion was due to the infusion of assets, especially liquid assets (total assets rose $46 billion and nearly one-half, or $22 billion, was cash), and to the reduction or dismissal of liability claims, as total liabilities fell $68 billion.

Such a turnaround was expected; the terms of the government ownership of GM made it much easier for GM to become profitable.[11] Long-term debt was reduced, bypassing the bankruptcy process meant to protect bondholders and placing other priorities ahead of bondholders' legal standing. The debt of GM was backed by the federal government, allowing GM to borrow at 2.2% in 2009 while Ford, a company not taking a government bailout, issued five-year bonds that year paying 8% interest.

The U.S. government invested about $65 billion of equity in GM and in 2009 owned 60% of the firm. The federal government's bailout used equity financing, as GM's precarious financial position could not be sustained with debt financing. By wiping debt off the balance sheet and injecting equity into the firm, the federal government made it easier for GM to become profitable, at least in the short-term, with taxpayers taking on the losses from the equity investment. In mid-2019, the market capitalization (value of all GM's common shares) was about $57 billion. With $65 billion invested in GM, the taxpayers have a long way to go before their investment breaks even. On a time-value-of-money basis, it will take even longer.[12]

Table 13.9 reviews Ford's financials. At the advent of the financial crisis, Ford was insolvent, with a negative equity as total liabilities exceeded total assets by $16 billion. But its current assets were greater than its current liabilities ($117 billion vs. $112 billion), and it had a larger cash cushion.

In 2009, after GM and Chrysler had received bailouts, Ford was still insolvent but by a lesser amount ($7 billion). Its current liabilities had fallen, leading to a better liquidity position of current assets ($111 billion) compared to current liabilities ($78 billion). In addition, there was modest improvement ($3 billion) in its cash position. Ford's management was able to reduce its assets by $19 billion, improve its liquidity, and reduce its indebtedness by $29 billion without government bailout, government ownership, or forced loss to debt holders. Ford did receive $5.9 billion in government loans in

Table 13.8   General Motors (GM) Balance Sheet ($ billions, rounded to nearest billion)

	2008	2009	Net change
Cash and marketable securities	15	37	+22
Current assets	44	59	+15
Total assets	91	137	+46
Current liabilities	76	52	−24
Total liabilities	176	108	−68
Equity	−85	29	+114

---

[11] Dennis K. Berman, "Magic Act: Conjuring Up a Profit at GM," *The Wall Street Journal*, (June 9, 2009), p. C1.

[12] For a review of government investments in the auto industry, see Steve Contorno, "Obama Says Automakers Have Paid Back all the Loans it Got from His Admin 'and more'," accessed January 31, 2019, https://www.politifact.com/truth-o-meter/statements/2015/jan/22/barack-obama/obama-says-automakers-have-paid-back-all-loans-it-/.

Table 13.9   Ford Balance Sheet ($ billions, rounded to nearest billion)

	2008	2009	Net change
Cash and marketable securities	40	43	+3
Current assets	117	111	−6
Total assets	223	204	−19
Current liabilities	112	78	−34
Total liabilities	239	210	−29
Equity	−16	−7	+9

2009 to retool its manufacturing plants to produce more fuel-efficient cars; but as we see in the above balance sheet, Ford's conservative financial management reduced its debt by $29 billion even after accepting this government loan.

Comparing the two firms, the secret to financial success is to build assets and take responsibility to pay debts; this allows the firm to build equity. Smart management is needed to ensure the firm succeeds responsibly. Business cycles come and go, but GM hit its market capitalization peak of $60 billion back in 1999, and it has been on a downward slide ever since, in both nominal and real (inflation-adjusted) terms. Management must take the long-term view in its decisions and not focus on short-term fixes in order to build sustainable growth in shareholder wealth.

> **DISCUSSION QUESTION 2**
>
> **Was it fair for the U.S. government to "rescue" some firms, such as GM, and not give assistance to better-managed firms who were also going through difficult times during the Great Recession? In late 2018 GM announced it was closing a number of plants in Michigan, Ohio, and Maryland and laying off 14,000 workers. Does this change your opinion of the 2008 rescue of GM?**

13.8 GOAL OF A FIRM

Although a firm may have a mission statement espousing goals of quality, customer service, quality products offered at fair prices, and so on, such qualitative statements are only a means to an end. The firm's managers need a definite, measurable benchmark against which to evaluate alternatives. The goal of any firm should be financial; namely, the maximization of the owners' (or the common shareholders') wealth.

Creditors have a fixed claim that usually doesn't change with variations in the value of the firm's assets over time. As we learned in Chapter 10, shareholders have a residual or junior claim on the firm's assets. Therefore, variations in a firm's value will be mainly reflected in the fluctuating value of the owners', or shareholders', wealth in the firm. Managers will want to select strategies that are expected to increase shareholders' wealth. Alternatives that harm shareholders' wealth should be rejected.[13]

This view is consistent with the process of attracting and acquiring capital and investing it to earn rates of return in excess of the investors' expected returns. If a firm is able to do this, the excess return will accrue to the firm's owners, the shareholders.

13.8.1 MEASURING SHAREHOLDER WEALTH

Shareholder wealth is measurable and it is observable daily in the financial sections of newspapers (at least for firms whose common stock is publicly traded). Shareholder wealth is nothing more than the market value of a firm's common stock. This market value of the shareholders' claim on a firm is equal to the following:

Shareholder wealth = Common stock price × Number of common shares outstanding

---

[13] Some mandatory projects, such as the need to retrofit factories due to regulation changes, may be costly and harm shareholder wealth. In this case, if several alternatives exist, the project that hurts shareholder wealth the least should be chosen. This may include the option of going out of business if the new regulations are too costly to obey.

This relationship allows analysts to keep track of changes in shareholder wealth on a regular basis to see which firms are most successful at returning value to shareholders. *As long as the number of common stock shares outstanding does not change appreciably, the market's perception of the firm and of its management's actions appears in the firm's stock price.*

For shareholder wealth maximization to be a realistic goal, the financial markets need to provide reasonably accurate information about the value of a firm. The stock market is sometimes criticized in the popular press as being shortsighted and unpredictable. Can it determine a fair value for the firm? The evidence on efficient markets from Chapter 12 suggests it can. Many studies show the market is oriented toward the long-run health and well-being of firms.[14] The weight of evidence favors the idea that the market generally does price stocks fairly. Stock price changes show the effect on firm value from the market's evaluation of the news.

ETHICAL Focusing on shareholder value does not mean other aspects of good management are ignored. Smart managers make decisions to service customers in a cost-efficient manner. Many studies have showed the value enhancement that occurs from maintaining the current customer base rather than having to continually find new customers to take the place of those who are dissatisfied. Similarly, smart managers treat and pay employees fairly. Table 13.10 shows the effect of unsatisfying jobs, employee turnover, and the cost impact of needing to hire and train replacement workers. Unmotivated and unhappy employees become unproductive employees who increase costs and prevent the firm from satisfying its goals. Research indicates that higher levels of employee satisfaction lead to higher stock prices.[15] Investment in capital (fixed asset) resources should lead to higher levels of production, efficiency, and profits as it is with human capital. Research indicates the value of employee and manager training programs in increasing shareholder wealth over time.[16] By focusing on firm value, managers work to maintain satisfactory relationships with financing sources so funds will be available to finance

Table 13.10   Happy and Productive Employees Help Increase Shareholder Wealth

A. Selected industry-wide costs of replacing employees	Annual turnover rate (%)	Industry-wide costs (direct replacement costs only) ($ Billions)	Costs as a percentage of industry earnings (%)
Specialty retail	97	23.2	50
Call centers	31	5.4	43
High tech	25	44.3	43
Fast food	123	3.4	16

Source: Sibson & Co.

B. Turnover rates and hiring costs	Annual turnover rate (%)	Cost per new hire
Banking	16.0	$6,110
Consumer products	23.0	$17,450
Insurance	13.1	$9,902
Manufacturing	17.8	$11,408
Pharmaceuticals	12.6	$13,632
Telecommunications	21.0	$7,176

Source: Saratoga℠ Institute.

---

[14] See the tables in Geoffrey Colvin, "America's Best and Worst Wealth Creators," *Fortune*, (December 18, 2000), pp. 207–216; and Alfred Rappaport, "CFOs and Strategists: Forging a Common Framework," *Harvard Business Review*, (May–June 1992), p. 87. Both of these articles have tables with estimates of the value of firm's future growth as reflected in current stock prices.

[15] Alex Edmans, University of Pennsylvania—The Wharton School working paper, "Does the Stock Market Fully Value Intangibles? Employee Satisfaction and Equity Prices," (August 12, 2009).

[16] David McCann, "Human Capital: Measured Response." *CFO Magazine*, (June 2011), pp. 21, 22, 25; Laurie Bassi, Paul Harrison, Jens Ludwig, and Daniel McMurrer, "The Impact of U.S. Firms' Investments in Human Capital on Stock Prices," working paper, (June 2004), accessed February 1, 2019, https://www.mtdiabloastd.org/Resources/Documents/Meetings/2010-07 Gina Jesse Impact on Stock 2004 research-Bassi.pdf.

future growth needs. Focusing on shareholder wealth is the best means of helping the long-term survival of the firm in a dynamic, global economy.

Spending funds on employee wellness programs appears to lead to increases in productivity, better performance, less sick days, and reductions in health care costs. Studies find a return of several dollars returned for each dollar spent on disease management and wellness programs—a low risk means of helping profitability and shareholder wealth.[17]

Shareholder wealth as a measure of firm performance is objective and forward looking, and it incorporates all influences on the firm and its stakeholders. No other measure of firm performance is so inclusive and practical for evaluating a firm's strategies.

A measure used in identifying successful firms, and that is growing in popularity, is **market value added (MVA)**. The MVA measures the value created by the firm's managers. It is equals to the market value of the firm's liabilities and equity, minus the amount of money investors paid to the firm (this is the "book value" found in the firm's financial statements) when these securities were first issued.

That is, market value added (MVA) equals the following:

$$MVA = \text{Market value of stock} + \text{Market value of debt} - \text{Book value of stock} - \text{Book value of debt}$$

Usually, a firm's market value of debt closely approximates its book value, so a close estimate of MVA is the market value of equity less the book value of equity. Stern Stewart & Company, a financial consulting firm, regularly reports firms' MVAs.

market value added (MVA) measures the value created by the firm's managers; is equal to the market value of the firm's liabilities and equity minus the amount of money investors paid to the firm when these securities were first issued

13.8.2 LINKING STRATEGY AND FINANCIAL PLANS

A firm's managers will want to pay close attention to movements in a company's stock price over time. These movements inform managers of how financial market participants view the risk and potential return from investing in the firm. If investors perceive the risk is too great relative to expected returns, they will sell the firm's stock and reinvest their money elsewhere.

To provide a link between a firm's strategy and its financial plans, managers can first review the firm's performance in the financial markets and then determine why the firm's stock price performed better or worse than its competitors, in the eyes of investors. Managers can take this information and examine the firm's internal operations. They need to examine financial measures to see how the firm has been generating cash, where this cash is being invested in the firm (new products, subsidiaries, etc.), and the return earned on these investments. Managers can then determine where poor returns are being earned and take corrective steps. Managers will want to evaluate the firm's operations and proposed new projects with an eye toward the firm's stock price. Projects that will add to shareholder wealth should be chosen for implementation. Projects that are expected to reduce shareholder wealth should be cast aside.

ETHICAL Executing a firm's financial strategy entails more than looking at numbers on a computer spreadsheet. It includes making necessary adjustments to the firm's use of debt, equity, and dividend policy to create more value to shareholders. It includes seeking new markets or customers for the firm's products, controlling costs or prudently raising prices, and efficiently using the firm's assets. In addition, to publicize its plans for creating value, management will want to communicate key components of its plan to shareholders and the financial markets. Other activities include ethically using accounting principles and the tax code to minimize the firm's taxes, increasing the efficiency of the firm's cash management, and managing the firm's risk exposures. Many of these topics are discussed in upcoming chapters.

---

[17] Jennifer Schaefer, "The Real ROI for Employee Wellness Programs," https://www.shrm.org/resourcesandtools/hr-topics/benefits/pages/real-roi-wellness.aspx accessed February 1, 2019; Stephen Miller, CEBS, "Employers See Wellness Link to Productivity, Performance," https://www.shrm.org/ResourcesAndTools/hr-topics/benefits/Pages/wellness-productivity-link-.aspx accessed February 1, 2019; Leonard L. Berry, Ann M. Mirabito, and William B. Baun, "What's the Hard Return on Employee Wellness Programs?," *Harvard Business Review*, December 2010, pp. 104–112.

DISCUSSION QUESTION 3

Review the business news from the past few days and looks for major stories about a business firm announcing new information or news that affect an industry. How did stock prices react to that new information? What was the market communicating to company management by the stock price reaction?

13.8.3 CRITERION FOR NONPUBLIC FIRMS

An obvious question to ask is which criterion to employ for organizations that have no observable market prices, such as a small closely held company or a not-for-profit organization. The answer lies in the factors that cause any productive asset to have value. From our discussion in Chapter 9 on the time value of money, we know assets have value because of the size, timing, and risk of their cash flows. Management needs to balance the risks, timing, and sizes of the cash flows of the organization to maximize what the decision maker believes would be the market value of owner's equity if it were traded in the financial markets.

Owners or managers of small firms face a different situation, however. Since they own their firms, they seek to maximize their own wealth, but this wealth may defy clear expression in dollar terms. Nonmonetary benefits may be personally important to the owner or manager, such as maintaining control of the firm, keeping the business in the family, or having adequate leisure time. From a purely monetary perspective, owners or managers may not be maximizing the financial wealth of the firm, but as the owners, they have to answer only to themselves as long as they make timely payments to their creditors and employees. Their decisions will attempt to maximize their total personal wealth, which includes monetary and nonmonetary components.

13.8.4 WHAT ABOUT ETHICS?

ETHICAL Critics frequently argue that emphasizing shareholder wealth may lead managers to focus on quick fixes to problems, even resorting to unethical behavior to maintain firm value. Some managers, unfortunately, do make decisions to ignore product quality or safety, worker safety, and the well-being of communities or to use deceitful selling practices. As long as these practices are not discovered or publicized, they may help keep shareholder value higher than it should be. But let's take a closer look at this type of behavior.

Unethical managers will make improper decisions regardless of the performance measure, so using shareholder value as a performance measure probably will not affect such abusive practices. By inflating firm revenues, keeping costs artificially low, or diverting scarce resources from needed to less-productive uses, unethical practices would improve nearly any performance measure, be it sales, costs, or market share. Thus, to blame ethical lapses on financial measures of firm performance is inappropriate.

Some would argue that all stakeholders (employees, customers, suppliers, bondholders, bankers, and shareholders) should be considerations in managers' decision making. They argue that focusing solely on shareholder wealth creates short-term thinking by managers. Holders of this perspective argue that managers focus on the current stock price and what will make it rise this year, with the result that managers resort to accounting tricks to increase short-term earnings reports, decide to conserve cash flow, or forgo undertaking long-term projects, so investment and innovation is discouraged.[18]

However, focusing on firm value may keep management's eyes on the longer-term consequences of its actions. Firms engaged in unethical or careless behavior run the danger of having this behavior exposed. Such revelations can harm the firm's reputation and shareholder value for extended periods as customers and employees feel their trust has been violated. Some evidence from a recent study suggests that firms with a social conscience may gain more financially in the marketplace.[19] An important aspect

---

[18] See, for example, the discussion in Russ Banham, "Whose Company Is It?" *CFO Magazine*, (December 2012), pp. 50–55; Lynn Stout, *The Shareholder Value Myth* (Berrett-Kohler Publishers, 2012).

[19] Justin Martin, "Good Citizenship Is Good Business," *Fortune*, (March 21, 1994), pp. 15–16. In addition, the cost to having your firm named in an unfavorable light in the financial and public press is high over time. An example is Daniel Fisher, "Shell Game: How Enron Concealed Losses, Inflated Earnings and Hid Secret Deals From the Authorities," *Forbes*, (January 7, 2002).

to corporate ethics is the control systems that a firm has in place to discourage such activity and to catch it if it occurs. As shareholders are many and dispersed, it is the role of the board and corporate governance to ensure managers are working for the shareholders' best interests rather than for a "quick fix" or their own selfish interests. Compensation systems that reward managers for longer-term company performance and share price performance can ensure that managers make appropriate decisions for the well-being of all stakeholders as well as shareholders. This quote by Richard Galanti, chief financial officer (CFO) of Costco, sums up the shareholder wealth perspective nicely:

> "Almost 30 years ago, our founders articulated our mission: provide the best quality products at the lowest price to our member customers," says Galanti. "Their plan for doing this was straightforward: obey the law and do not cut corners by taking a little butter out of the butter cookie; take care of customers, not just giving them quality products but also a return policy they could trust; take care of employees; respect but be fair with suppliers; and then take care of shareholders, in that order of priority."

> Why is the shareholder at the end of the list? *"Because if we're doing all these other things right, the shareholder will benefit,"* [emphasis added] Galanti replies. "That's what drives long-term value and ensures we'll be around for the next 20 years."[20]

13.9 CORPORATE GOVERNANCE

ETHICAL In most proprietorships and partnerships, the owners are the managers and they play an active role in managing their business. But in many firms, someone other than the owners makes business decisions; there is a separation of ownership and control. For example, professional managers run public corporations in the place of the shareholders. This arrangement may result in ethics problems. For example, dishonest managers can make decisions that increase expenses in order to benefit themselves (such company-owned vacation villas, corporate jets, high salaries) over shareholders. Or they can send stock prices higher by manipulating transactions and accounting rules so the firm appears more profitable than it is.

Unfortunately, the early 2000s brought a number of corporate scandals to light. Some stock analysts and their investment banking firms were accused of "hyping" stocks to attract lucrative investment banking fees. Firms such as Enron, Global Crossing, Parmalat, Rite-Aid, Tyco, WorldCom, and Xerox were accused of incorrect accounting practices and had to restate past years' financials; some executives were fined and sent to jail. Arthur Andersen, a venerable accounting firm, was restricted from doing further auditing work after employees shredded documents relating to Enron's accounting irregularities. Most of the scandals were caused by poor ethical decisions dealing with accounting practices that inflated earnings and stock prices.

CRISIS The 2007–2009 Great Recession brought to light other shortsighted corporate practices. Lack of oversight and proper risk management brought some Wall Street firms to the brink of bankruptcy, and some, such as Bear Stearns and Lehman Brothers, did fail. Panic created by concerns over the strength of the U.S. and global financial systems led to massive intervention by the Federal Reserve Board and central banks of other countries and massive increases in government spending as fiscal policy and monetary policy were jointly used to prevent a feared collapse. Workers' retirement plans were cut in half, and sometimes more, if they were heavily invested in the falling stock market during late 2007 to early 2009.

principals owners of the firm

agents managers hired by the principals to run the firm

principal–agent problem a problem in corporate governance in which conflict of interest occurs between the principals and agents

13.9.1 PRINCIPAL–AGENT PROBLEM

In legal parlance, the **principals**, or owners of the firm, hire managers (the **agents**) to run the firm. The agents should run the firm with the best interests of the principals in mind. However, ethical lapses, self-interest, or the principals' lack of trust in the agent can lead to conflicts of interest and suspicions between the two parties. This problem in corporate governance is called the **principal–agent problem**.

---

[20] Taken from Russ Banham, "Whose Company Is It?" *CFO Magazine*, (December 2012), p. 55.

FINANCE In a corporation, the common shareholders of a firm elect a board of directors. In theory, the board is to oversee managers and ensure they are working in the best interests of the shareholders. However, in practice, the board often has a closer relationship with management than with the shareholders. For example, top managers commonly sit on the firm's board of directors, and the firm's top managers often nominate candidates for board seats. For example, as recently as 1995, the board of Archer Daniels Midland (a grain processor) included the firm's CEO and three of his relatives. Other firms have had relatives of management as members of the board's audit committees, the important group that oversees the firm's financial controls.[21] These relationships can obscure loyalties and make the board a toothless watchdog for shareholders' interests. Of special concern are family-owned firms where a number of relatives may have senior management position or Board sets.

Managers, acting as agents, may seek their own interest by increasing their salaries, the size of their staffs, or their perquisites. Better known as "perks," the latter include club memberships, the use of company planes or luxurious company cars, gardening expenses, low-interest or no-interest loans, and lifetime benefits, such as paid long-term care insurance, the use of company cars and drivers, and access to company planes. Firms may also do business with other businesses in which the CEO has an ownership stake, blurring the distinction between doing what is best for shareholders and doing favors for the top officer.[22] And at times the firm's top managers make a bid to take the company private. Such situations can lead to conflicts of interest, as who knows better than the firm's top managers how to increase profits from their firm—and why don't they do so for the firm's current shareholders?[23]

Many managers like their jobs, their salaries, their perks, and their positions of power. Acting in their own interest, they would like to keep their jobs. This is always best seen when one firm tries to take over or merge with another target firm. Often, these takeovers include an offer to buy the firm's shares from its shareholders at a price above its current market price. There have been a number of situations when the target firm's management, in conjunction with its board, may seek to fight takeovers. They may try to pre-empt such merger or acquisition attempts by seeking changes in the corporate charter that would make such takeovers difficult to pursue.

Examples of such delaying tactics, or **poison pills**, include provisions that require super majorities (e.g., two-thirds) of existing shareholders to approve any takeover, provisions to allow the board to authorize and issue large quantities of stock in the event of a takeover attempt, or provisions to make expensive payouts to existing managers in the face of any successful buyout. Although managers may state that such actions are being taken with shareholders' best interests at heart, a possible consequence of their actions is to preserve their own jobs and income in the event of a takeover. However, in the face of investor unrest due to corporate scandals, fewer firms are adopting poison pills and some are taking steps to eliminate them or are allowing their provisions to expire. In recent years, Darden, Goodyear, First Energy, PG&E, and Raytheon have eliminated poison pills.[24]

poison pills provisions in a corporate charter that make a corporate takeover more unattractive

Because of these behaviors, the principal–agent problem imposes **agency costs** on shareholders. Agency costs are the tangible and intangible expenses borne by shareholders because of the actual or potential self-serving actions of managers. Agency costs include explicit, out-of-pocket expenses. Examples of these include the costs of auditing financial statements to verify their accuracy, purchasing liability insurance for board members and top managers, monitoring managers' actions by the board or by independent consultants, and paying inflated managerial salaries and perks.

agency costs tangible and intangible expenses borne by shareholders because of the actual or potential self-serving actions of managers

Implicit agency costs do not have a direct expense associated with them, but they harm shareholders anyway. Implicit agency costs include restrictions placed against managerial actions

---

[21] Joann S. Lublin and Elizabeth MacDonald, "More Independent Audit Committees Are Sought," *The Wall Street Journal*, (February 8, 1999), p. A2.

[22] Timothy D. Schellhardt and Joann S. Lublin, "All the Rage Among CEOs: Lifetime Perks," *The Wall Street Journal*, (July 6, 1999), p. A17, A24; Anonymous, "In a Cost-Cutting Era, Many CEOs Enjoy Imperial Perks," *The Wall Street Journal*, (March 7, 1995), pp. B1, B10.

[23] A recent example is Michael Dell's bid to take his firm, Dell Computer, private in a buyout financed by Michael Dell and an investment firm. The deal was completed in September 2013 and Sears chairman Eddie Lampert's offer to buy Sears out of bankruptcy in December 2018.

[24] Robin Sidel, "Where Are All the Poison Pills?" *The Wall Street Journal*, (March 2, 2004), pp. C1, C5.

(e.g., requiring shareholder votes for some major decisions) and covenants or restrictions placed on the firm by a lender.[25]

The end result of the principal–agent problem is a reduction in firm value. Investors will not pay as much for the firm's stock because they realize that the principal–agent problem and its attendant costs lower the firm's value. Agency costs will decline, and firm value will rise, as principals' trust and confidence in their agents rises. We will discuss some ways of reducing agency costs in the next section.

13.9.2 REDUCING AGENCY PROBLEMS

Two basic approaches can be used to reduce the consequences of managers making self-serving decisions. First, managers' incentives can be aligned to more-closely match those of shareholders.

stock options allow managers to purchase, at a future time, a stated number of the firm's shares at a specific price

A frequently used method for doing this in the past was to offer stock options to managers. The options allow managers to purchase, at a future time, a stated number of the firm's shares at a specific price. If the firm's stock price rises, the value of the shares, and therefore the managers' wealth, rises. Decisions that detract from the best interest of shareholders will affect management by making the stock options less valuable. But stock option plans are subject to several criticisms.[26] One is the past practice (since corrected by a revised accounting standard) of not reflecting the difference between market price and the (low) stock option price in the company's income statement; now it must be shown on the income statement as an expense.

ETHICAL Another problem with stock options is that managers are able to receive huge bonuses, because economic conditions create a rising stock market, regardless of their managerial skill. On the other hand, when the stock market falls, not all managers are financially harmed as some firms chose to revalue their stock options at lower prices.[27] Finally, stock options were blamed for some of the ethical lapses of managers in the late 1990s, when accounting decisions to push up a firm's earnings resulted in sharp stock price changes and a windfall for managers who cashed in their options.

CRISIS However, the goal of stock options is shared risk with shareholders. When executives execute the stock option and purchase stock, their wealth will have greater exposure to the firm's stock. A paper loss as options lose value is one thing; it is quite another to see a multimillion dollar real position shrink in the face of declining stock prices. Many executives lost large amounts of wealth as stock prices fell in 2007–2009. An article published near the bottom of the stock market's fall names many executives whose stock holdings in their firms plummeted in value.[28]

restricted stock shares of stock, awarded to managers, which vest, or become saleable, after a stated number of years, typically three to five

Use of restricted stock is gaining popularity as a way to align managers' interests with those of shareholders without the bad consequences of stock options. Restricted stock is given to employees but they cannot sell it until it vests, which typically occurs after three to five years. Employees who leave the firm before the stock vests lose their restricted shares. Under some company plans, top managers forfeit restricted shares if the firm has poor financial performance or they miss financial targets. Restricted stock's time to vest is typically longer than that of shorter-term stock options and it has less upside (large return) potential. But, whereas stock options can become worthless if the stock price does not rise sufficiently, restricted shares will retain some value as long as the firm doesn't go bankrupt. In addition, holders receive dividends of restricted shares even before they vest.

ETHICAL A second tool for controlling self-serving managers is to have closer oversight in order to make them more accountable. In the wake of corporate and accounting scandals, legislative mandate of controls is supplementing oversight by corporate boards. Some firms are increasing the number of

---

[25] Such covenants are placed on the firm to protect the lender's position and to ensure that available cash flow will be directed to repay the loan.

[26] Business periodicals and the press usually publicize the largest CEO salaries for the previous year. Such salaries can reach $80, $100, $120 million or more. The news reports fail to recognize much of this CEO income comes from exercising stock options. A CEO can make a lot of money on stock options if he or she performs the job well and raises the stock price.

[27] Ruth Simon and Ianthe Jeanne Dugan, "Options Overdose," *The Wall Street Journal*, (June 4, 2001), pp. C1, C17; Ken Brown, "Now, Some Hope for Their Stock to Tank," *The Wall Street Journal*, (June 4, 2001), pp. C1, C2.

[28] Alix Stuart, "Losing It: Holding a Personal Financial Stake in Their Companies Has Cost Many Managers a Bundle," *CFO*, (February 2009), pp. 75–78.

independent directors (i.e., individuals who are not part of the firm's management) on their boards. The Sarbanes-Oxley Act of 2002 was passed by the U.S. Congress in response to some of the previously cited corporate accounting and ethical scandals. Nicknamed "SOX" or "Sarbox," the act established the following standards:

- The Public Company Accounting Oversight Board (PCAOB), with five members, was created. The PCAOB, which reports to the SEC, registers firms that conduct corporate accounting audits; establishes auditing, quality control, ethical and independence standards for such firms; and audits the auditors in that the board can inspect their work and initiate disciplinary proceedings against firms that violate their standards and provisions of SOX.

- To eliminate conflicts of interest, accounting firms cannot perform other functions (bookkeeping, financial system consulting, etc.) in firms for which they perform audits. To maintain independence, the lead auditor must be changed at least every five years. The auditors must present their report to the board's audit committee. The audit committee must contain at least one "financial expert" as defined by the act. Only independent directors (i.e., directors who, except for their board service, do not work or do paid consulting for the firm) can sit on the audit committee.

- To enhance corporate responsibilities, the CEO and CFO of the firm must certify that the firm's financial reports conform to SOX requirements and good accounting practice. Jail (up to ten years) and/or fines (up to $1 million) await the officer who signs an incorrect statement. Corporations can no longer make loans to its officers and directors. In addition, firms must draft a code of ethics for its senior officers and have policies in place to protect "whistleblowers"; that is, persons who report alleged wrong-doing by the firm.

- Security analysts study corporations and write research reports regarding the prospects of a firm's stock, bonds, and other securities. Many times, an analyst works for an investment banking firm that can earn large fees by assisting corporations in their primary market offerings. SOX contains several provisions to ensure there are no conflicts of interest between the analysts' firm and possible investment banking clients. First, the research function must be separate from the investment banking function; research reports cannot be reviewed or approved by the investment banking arm of a Wall Street firm prior to the report's publication. Second, security analysts cannot be paid based upon the investment banking fees generated by favorable research reports written about the firm's clients. Third, reports must disclose if the security analyst owns any of the securities issued by the firm about which he is making a recommendation.

Sarbanes-Oxley and actions by the stock exchanges require more independent directors on corporate boards. Independent directors should be more inclined to analyze management's strategies and proposals and their effects on shareholder value. In addition, major institutional investors, such as pension funds and mutual funds, are becoming more vocal. Some are taking active roles in overseeing the performance of companies in which they hold stock by requesting meetings with management, criticizing management actions, and suggesting shareholder votes on issues of importance to the firm.

CRISIS Increased trust in the financial system and greater accounting transparency helps shareholder wealth. Several studies have shown that firms in countries with better corporate governance regulations have experienced higher stock returns.[29] Attempts to tighten corporate governance and reduce agency costs by regulation are gaining popularity overseas. A recent study by the Organization for Economic Cooperation and Development (OECD) recommends a number of so-called "U.S. management style" initiatives for its member countries. The report recommends that companies around the world adopt

---

[29] Phillip Day, "Corporate Governance Can be Strong Indicator of Stock Performance Within Emerging Markets," *The Wall Street Journal*, (May 1, 2001), p. C14; Craig Karmin, "Corporate-Governance Issues Hamper Emerging Markets," *The Wall Street Journal*, (November 8, 2000), pp. C1, C14; Robert L. Simison, "Firms World-Wide Should Adopt Ideas of U.S. Management, Panel Tells OECD," *The Wall Street Journal*, (April 2, 1998), p. A6.

practices such as shareholder wealth maximization, stronger shareholder rights to remove directors and to nominate and elect directors, independent boards to oversee managers, the avoidance of security analyst conflicts of interest, and independent auditors and whistleblower protection.[30] In the wake of the 2007–2009 financial crisis, the topic of executive compensation will likely be a controversial topic for many years. Companies seek to balance fairness to the taxpayer from government bailed-out firms, the need to attract and retain top-quality talent, and to mitigate risks from wrong incentives that compensation packages may create.[31]

DISCUSSION QUESTION 4

Do agency costs exist in government (federal, state, local) or nonprofit organizations? Explain.

LEARNING ACTIVITY

Two leading organizations that examine the corporate governance mechanisms of firms are Value Edge Advisors (https://valueedgeadvisors.com/) and Institutional Shareholder Services (https://www.issgovernance.com/).

13.10 FINANCE IN THE ORGANIZATION CHART

chief financial officer (CFO) responsible for the controller and the treasury functions of a firm

treasurer oversees the traditional functions of financial analysis, including capital budgeting, short- and long-term financing decisions, and current asset management

controller manages accounting, cost analysis, and tax planning

In all but the smallest of firms, a top manager with the title chief financial officer (CFO) or vice president of finance usually reports to the president. The firm's treasurer and its controller usually report to the CFO (Figure 13.1). The firm's treasurer oversees the traditional functions of financial analysis: capital budgeting, short- and long-term financing decisions, and current asset management. The controller traditionally manages accounting, cost analysis, and tax planning.

Compensation for financial officers at large public corporations is attractive, but hard work, long hours, and excellent skills in analytics, communication, and working with people are expected. The typical pay package includes salary, annual incentive pay, long-term incentive pay (which includes cash and restricted stock; that is, stock that cannot be sold for a specified number of years) and stock options. In 2017, the average CFO's pay package at corporations with over $1 billion in revenues totaled over $1.3 million. For smaller corporations the pay was less but still substantial; for firms with fewer than $1 billion in revenues, CFOs earned an average of $500,000–$700,000.[32] Becoming a CFO is a path to become a firm's CEO; estimates are that 62 of the Fortune 500 CEOs came from the CFO position.[33]

A firm's strategy for business success is plotted by its top officers and, in the case of a corporation, its board of directors. Often, this strategy will be reflected in the composition of the firm's balance sheet, as seen in Figure 13.2. Those involved in planning the firm's strategy follow the structure provided by the balance sheet in answering several basic questions:

1. *The capital budgeting question.* What fixed or long-term assets should the firm purchase to produce its product?

---

[30] Christopher Rhoads, "OECD Proposes Global Guidelines to Govern Firms," *The Wall Street Journal*, (January 12, 2004), and "OECD Countries Agree to New Corporate Governance Principles," (April 22, 2004), February 1, 2019, https://www.oecd.org/corporate/oecdcountriesagreenewcorporategovernanceprinciples.htm.

[31] Erin White, Joann S. Lublin, and Cari Tuna, "Range of Firms Alter Executive-Pay Policies," *The Wall Street Journal*, (October 24, 2009), p. A4; Jonathan Macey, "Washington's Plans May Result in Even Higher Executive Pay," *The Wall Street Journal*, (October 24, 2009), p. A15; Russ Banham, "Fray on Pay," *CFO*, (June 2009), pp. 38–45.

[32] For a more comprehensive review of corporate finance compensation, see Grant Thornton LLP, *Financial Executive Compensation Survey 2017*, Financial Executives Research Foundation, accessed February 1, 2019 at https://www.grantthornton.com/~/media/content-page-files/tax/pdfs/FEI-financial-exec-comp-survey-2017/FEI-survey-results-2017.ashx; Anne Field, "CFO Pay Package Survey Exclusive," *Treasury and Risk Magazine*, (May 1, 2012), https://www.treasuryandrisk.com/2012/05/01/cfo-pay-package-survey-exclusive; Steve Hargreaves, CNNMoney.com staff writer, "Morgan's Mack sees hefty pay raise," (February 26, 2007), accessed December 15, 2009, https://money.cnn.com/2007/02/23/news/companies/morgan_compensation/index.htm; John Labate, "Losing Altitude in a Stiff Wind," *Treasury and Risk Management*, (May 2004), p. 24; Jay Sherman, "Measuring Up," *Treasury and Risk Management*, (May 2001), pp. 31–34.

[33] Maxwell Murphy, "The Big Number Road to CEO Post Goes Through CFO at Some Big Firms," *The Wall Street Journal*, (September 18, 2012), p. B13.

2. *The capital structure question.* How should the firm finance these purchases?

3. *The operations or net working capital question.* How should the firm manage inventory, collect payments from customers, pay suppliers, and manage its cash account?

   The following chapters will delve into these topics, showing you the data financial managers need, how they analyze them, and how they use the shareholder wealth maximization goals to make decisions.

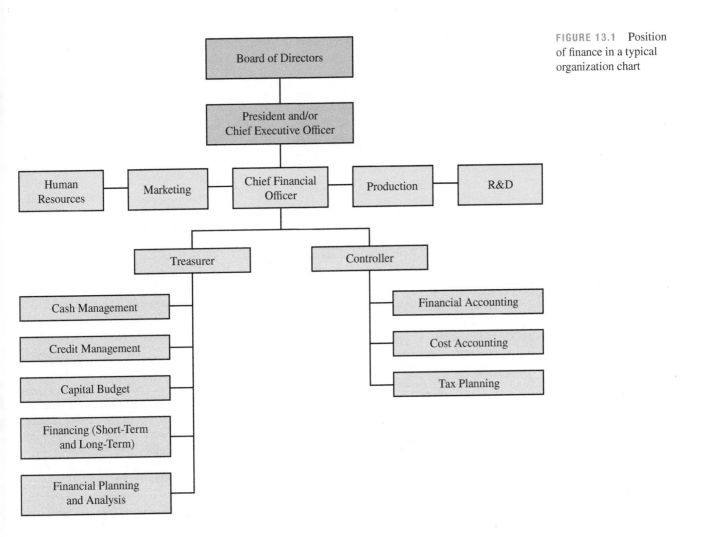

FIGURE 13.1 Position of finance in a typical organization chart

FIGURE 13.2 Balance sheet

- **Institutions and Markets** Lending decisions are made on the basis of who is responsible for repaying; in small firms, the proprietor or owner may have to guarantee any loans to the firm. Creditworthiness (ability to repay) and collateral are paramount to the lending decision. The markets and lending institutions will pay close attention to the firm's financial statements when making a loan and while the loan is outstanding.

- **Investments** Corporate governance and principal–agent problems are well-known to the financial markets and professional investors who work for mutual funds and pension funds. Firm values can rise or fall depending on whether the market perceives management's

actions as serving its shareholders or entrenching managers. All investors, including bond and stockholders, will be interested in the information contained in a firm's financial statements.

- **Financial Management** A firm's organizational form affects how its earnings are taxed and how easy it is to transfer ownership. A growing firm has to make decisions about how it may want to increase its equity base by going public and becoming a public corporation or growing more slowly if it wants to stay private as a nonpublic corporation, partnership, or proprietorship. Financial statements tell investors and competitors much about the performance of a public company.

SUMMARY

LO 13.1 By maintaining the firm's vision or mission when setting operating goals, managers should evaluate strategies and seek to increase shareholder wealth. Periodically, the mission statement should be reviewed and revised, if needed, to reflect changes in competition, technology, and other environmental factors.

LO 13.2 A firm can be organized in one of three basic ways: as a proprietorship, a partnership, or a corporation. Each has implications for capital-raising ability, ease of transferring ownership, and taxation.

LO 13.3 Finance makes much use of accounting statements in analysis and planning. Accounting, by its nature, is history focused, reporting on revenues and expenses over a past time period or reporting on a firm's assets, liabilities, and equity as of a point in time. Finance is forward looking, recognizing asset values in current markets, and is cash focused, not earnings focused. What matters to the finance professional is cash flows from and to the firm rather than accrual accounting concepts.

LO 13.4 The income statement shows the level of the firm's revenues and expenses, including taxes, over a specific period.

LO 13.5 The balance sheet indicates the firm's assets and how they were financed by various liabilities and equity as of a point in time. The balance sheet must always balance; that is, assets must always equal the sum of liabilities and equity.

LO 13.6 The statement of cash flows indicates the influences affecting the firm's cash account over time. It is an attempt to track cash

leaving the firm and cash coming into the firm due to firm operating activities, investing activities, and financial activities.

LO 13.7 Common-size financial statements can be used to compare different-sized firms or firms in different industries. A common-size balance sheet has all items expressed as a percent of total assets. A common-size income statement expresses items as a percent of total revenue. General categories of financial statement items (such as debt or current liability) can be used to determine company changes, as we did in a comparison of the financial fortunes of two U.S.-based car companies during the Great Recession.

LO 13.8 The goal of the financial manager is to maximize shareholder wealth. Shareholder wealth is the firm's common stock price multiplied by the number of common shares outstanding. If the number of shares is fairly constant, we can gauge, in an efficient market, the value of firm decisions or economic events by looking at the change in stock price. The use of a financial metric to measure firm progress does not create any more ethical conflicts than any other measure; devious, selfish, or dishonest managers will try to distort any measure (sales, costs, customer satisfaction, and so on) so that it favors their paycheck. The use of shareholder wealth is an impersonal, market-determined measure of firm success.

LO 13.9 Separation of firm ownership and control leads to the principal–agent problem. Agents (managers) may act in their own interest rather than in the owners' (principal's) interest. There are several means of reducing the effects of the agency problem, including linking the compensation of managers to the firm's stock price performance and increasing information about managers' decisions to the firm's owners.

LO 13.10 The top financial managers in a firm are likely to have titles such as chief financial officer (CFO), treasurer (deals primarily with cash and credit management, borrowing, capital budget spending) and controller (usually focuses on accounting issues, cost analysis, and tax issues). A firm's strategy can often be seen in the composition of its balance sheet as reflected in net working capital, capital budgeting decisions, and financing decisions.

agency costs
agents
annual report
assets
balance sheet
bylaws
charter
chief financial
   officer (CFO)
common-size financial
   statements

controller
corporation
current assets
depreciation
equity
equity capital
generally accepted
   accounting
   principles (GAAP)
goodwill
income statement

liabilities
limited liability
   company (LLC)
limited partners
limited partnership
market value
   added (MVA)
mission statement
partnership
poison pills
principal–agent problem

principals
proprietorship
restricted stock
statement of cash flows
stock options
subchapter S corporation
treasurer
working capital

REVIEW QUESTIONS

1. **(LO 13.1)** It has often been said that a business should begin with a vision or mission statement. Explain what this means.

2. **(LO 13.1)** How do the financial markets accommodate the needs of risky firms and safe firms?

3. **(LO 13.2)** Identify and briefly describe the three major forms of business ownership used in the United States.

4. **(LO 13.2)** What are the differences in owner liability within proprietorships and partnerships versus corporations?

5. **(LO 13.2)** Briefly describe the differences between a subchapter S corporation and a limited liability company.

6. **(LO 13.3)** What types of information are included in an annual report?

7. **(LO 13.3)** General accounting practice is based on the accrual concept. Explain what this means and briefly describe how this compares with the financial manager's focus on cash.

8. **(LO 13.4)** What is the purpose of the income statement? Briefly identify and describe the major types of expenses that are shown on the typical income statement.

9. **(LO 13.5)** What is the purpose of the balance sheet? Briefly identify and describe the major types of assets and the claims of creditors and owners shown on the typical balance sheet.

10. **(LO 13.5)** Describe the three different accounts that comprise the owners' equity section on a typical corporate balance sheet.

11. **(LO 13.6)** What is a statement of cash flows? What are the three standard sections contained in a statement of cash flows?

12. **(LO 13.7)** How can common-size financial statements be used?

13. **(LO 13.7)** How are industry operating differences reflected in firms' financial statements?

14. **(LO 13.7)** What was General Motors' financial position prior to its bailout in 2009? How did the bailout improve its financial position?

15. **(LO 13.7)** What steps did Ford Motor Company take from 2008 to 2009 as seen by its balance sheet?

16. **(LO 13.8)** Describe the financial goal espoused by business firms.

17. **(LO 13.8)** Briefly explain how shareholder wealth is measured.

18. **(LO 13.8)** What does it mean when a firm's market value added (MVA) is negative?

19. **(LO 13.8)** How are financial strategy and financial plans linked together?

20. **(LO 13.9)** What is meant by the principal–agent problem in the context of corporate governance?

21. **(LO 13.9)** Discuss some ways agents can make self-serving decisions.

22. **(LO 13.9)** What are the two main solutions for reducing the adverse effects of agency problems?

23. **(LO 13.9)** What is restricted stock? How does it improve managerial incentives compared to the use of stock options?

24. **(LO 13.10)** Describe four provisions of the Sarbanes-Oxley Act of 2002.

25. **(LO 13.10)** What are the responsibilities of a firm's controller?

26. **(LO 13.10)** Briefly describe the financial responsibilities undertaken by a firm's treasurer.

PROBLEMS

1. Use the "balance sheet equation" to determine owners' equity if liabilities are $5 million and assets are $10 million.

2. Use your knowledge of balance sheets to fill in the missing amounts:

Assets	
Cash	$10,000
Accounts receivable	100,000
Inventory	_____
Total current assets	220,000
Gross plant and equipment	500,000
Less: accumulated depreciation	_____
Net plant and equipment	375,000
Total assets	_____

Liabilities	
Accounts payable	$12,000
Notes payable	50,000
Total current liabilities	_____
Long-term debt	_____
Total liabilities	190,000
Common stock ($1 par, 100,000 shares)	_____
Paid-in capital	_____
Retained earnings	150,000
Total stockholders' equity	_____
Total liabilities and equity	_____

3. Use your knowledge of balance sheets to fill in the missing amounts:

Assets	
Cash	$50,000
Accounts receivable	80,000
Inventory	100,000

Assets	
Total current assets	_____
Gross plant and equipment	_____
Less: accumulated depreciation	130,000
Net plant and equipment	600,000
Total assets	_____

Liabilities	
Accounts payable	$12,000
Notes payable	50,000
Total current liabilities	_____
Long-term debt	_____
Total liabilities	_____
Common stock ($1 par, 100,000 shares)	_____
Paid-in capital	250,000
Retained earnings	200,000
Total stockholders' equity	_____
Total liabilities and equity	$830,000

4. Use your knowledge of balance sheets and common-size statements to fill in the missing dollar amounts:

Assets		
Cash	$25,000	3.4%
Accounts receivable	$125,000	_____
Inventory	_____	27.1%
Total current assets	$350,000	_____
Gross plant and equipment	_____	95.0%
Less: accumulated depreciation	$313,000	42.5%
Net plant and equipment	_____	_____
Total assets	$737,000	100.0%

Liabilities

Accounts payable	_____	15.7%
Notes payable	$29,000	3.9%
Total current liabilities	_____	_____
Long-term debt	$248,000	33.6%
Total liabilities	$393,000	_____
Common stock ($.01 par, 450,000 shares)	$4,500	0.6%
Paid-in capital	$220,500	29.9%
Retained earnings	_____	_____
Total stockholders' equity	$344,000	46.7%
Total liabilities and equity	_____	100.0%

5. Use your knowledge of income statements to fill in the missing items:

Sales	
Cost of goods sold	$575,000
Gross profit	1,600,000
General and administrative expense	200,000
Selling and marketing expense	_____
Depreciation	50,000
Operating income	_____
Interest	100,000
Income before taxes	_____
Income taxes (30%)	_____
Net income	$700,000

6. Use the following information to construct an income statement:

Interest	$25,000
Sales	$950,000
Income tax rate	25%
Selling and marketing expenses	$160,000
General and administrative expenses	$200,000
Gross profit	$550,000
Depreciation	$30,000
Cost of goods sold	$400,000

7. Use the following information to construct an income statement:

Cost of goods sold	$684,000
Gross profit	$546,000
General and administrative expense	$159,000

Selling and marketing expense	$134,000
Operating income	$228,000
Income before taxes	$87,000
Income tax rate	27%

8. Use your knowledge of income statements and common-size statements to fill in the missing dollar amounts:

Sales	$2,876,200	100.0%
Cost of goods sold	_____	74.7%
Gross profit	_____	25.3%
General and administrative expense	$250,000	8.7%
Selling and marketing expense	$140,000	4.9%
Depreciation	_____	3.8%
Operating income	$229,000	8.0%
Interest	_____	4.6%
Income before taxes	$97,000	3.4%
Income taxes (25%)	$24,250	0.8%
Net income	_____	2.5%

9. Challenge Problem Use a spreadsheet to construct a common-size balance sheet from the data in Problem 2 and a common-size income statement from the data in Problem 5.

10. Use the following income statement and balance sheet information to put together a statement of cash flows.

	2020
Sales	$1,230,000
Cost of goods sold	$684,000
Gross profit	$546,000
General and administrative expense	$159,000
Selling and marketing expense	$134,000
Depreciation	$25,000
Operating income	$228,000
Interest	$141,000
Income before taxes	$87,000
Income taxes (27%)	$23,490
Net income	$63,510
Dividends paid	$25,000

Assets	2020	2019
Cash	$25,000	$21,990
Accounts receivable	$125,000	$115,000
Inventory	$200,000	$215,000
Total current assets	$350,000	$351,990
Gross plant and equipment	$700,000	$475,000
Less: accumulated depreciation	$313,000	$288,000
Net plant and equipment	$387,000	$187,000
Total assets	$737,000	$538,990

Liabilities	2020	2019
Accounts payable	$116,000	$103,000
Notes payable	$29,000	$29,000
Total current liabilities	$145,000	$132,000
Long-term debt	$248,000	$152,000
Total liabilities	$393,000	$284,000
Common stock ($.01 par)	$4,500	$4,000
Paid-in capital	$220,500	$170,500
Retained earnings	$119,000	$80,490
Total stockholders' equity	$344,000	$254,990
Total liabilities and equity	$737,000	$538,990

11. **Challenge Problem** Using the financial statements below,
   a. Compute common-size financial statements.
   b. Put together a statement of cash flows of the firm. Where did the firm invest funds during the year? How did it finance these purchases?

Income Statements for EastNorth Manufacturing, Inc.

Years Ended December 31	2020	2019
Net revenues or sales	$700,000	$600,000
Cost of goods sold	450,000	375,000
Gross profit	250,000	225,000
Operating expenses:		
General and administrative	95,000	95,000
Selling and marketing	56,000	50,000
Depreciation	25,000	20,000
Operating income	74,000	60,000
Interest	14,000	10,000
Income before taxes	60,000	50,000
Income taxes (40%)	24,000	20,000
Net income	$36,000	$30,000
Number of shares outstanding	50,000	50,000
Earnings per share	$0.72	$0.60

Balance Sheets for Eastnorth Manufacturing, Inc.

Years Ended December 31 Assets	2020	2019
Cash and marketable securities	$25,000	$20,000
Accounts receivable	100,000	80,000
Inventories	125,000	100,000
Total current assets	250,000	200,000
Gross plant and equipment	300,000	225,000
Less: accumulated depreciation	−100,000	−75,000
Net plant and equipment	200,000	150,000
Land	50,000	50,000
Total fixed assets	250,000	200,000
Total assets	$500,000	$400,000
LIABILITIES AND EQUITY		
Accounts payable	$78,000	$65,000
Notes payable	34,000	10,000
Accrued liabilities	30,000	25,000
Total current liabilities	142,000	100,000
Long-term debt	140,000	100,000
Total liabilities	$282,000	$200,000
Common stock ($1 par, 50,000 shares)	$50,000	$50,000
Paid-in capital	100,000	100,000
Retained earnings	68,000	50,000
Total stockholders' equity	218,000	200,000
Total liabilities and equity	$500,000	$400,000

12. Compare and contrast the two common-size balance sheets below. Which one do you think may belong to an auto manufacturer? To a computer manufacturer?

Common-Size Balance Sheets

Assets	Firm A	Firm B
Cash	26.7%	10.6%
Accounts receivable	18.8%	0.9%
Inventory	1.7%	2.9%
Other current assets	7.9%	5.0%
Total current assets	55.1%	19.4%
Net plant and equipment	7.9%	13.3%
Other long-term assets	37.1%	67.3%
Total assets	100.0%	100.0%

Liabilities	Firm A	Firm B
Accounts payable	37.9%	6.5%
Notes payable	0.0%	0.6%
Other current liabilities	18.5%	19.0%
Total current liabilities	56.4%	26.0%
Long-term debt	2.6%	56.3%
Other liabilities	8.4%	13.9%
Total liabilities	67.5%	96.3%
Common equity	0.8%	1.0%
Retained earnings	31.7%	2.7%
Total stock-holders' equity	32.5%	3.7%
Total liabilities and equity	100.0%	100.0%

13. Compare and contrast the two common-size balance sheets below. Which one do you think may belong to a supermarket? To a jeweler?

Common-Size Balance Sheets

Assets	Firm A	Firm B
Cash	5.3%	2.7%
Accounts receivable	4.1%	0.0%
Inventory	37.5%	61.7%
Other current assets	5.9%	4.1%
Total current assets	52.8%	68.5%
Net plant and equipment	35.1%	20.6%
Other long-term assets	12.4%	11.0%
Total assets	100.0%	100.0%

Liabilities	Firm A	Firm B
Accounts payable	19.6%	23.8%
Notes payable	0.1%	0.0%
Other current liabilities	16.8%	3.6%
Total current liabilities	36.5%	27.4%
Long-term debt	11.9%	14.2%
Other liabilities	14.7%	8.0%
Total liabilities	63.1%	49.6%
Common equity	4.9%	4.9%
Retained earnings	32.0%	45.5%
Total stock-holders' equity	36.9%	50.4%
Total liabilities and equity	100.0%	100.0%

14. **Challenge Problem** Using the following financial statements:
    a. Compute common-size financial statements.
    b. Compute year-to-year percentage changes in the various accounts.
    c. What insights about the firm can you obtain from this analysis?

Balance Sheet—Yearly Data ($ in millions)

	2020	2019	2018	2017	2016
Cash & Cash Equivalents	16.9	12.8	141.8	144.0	73.0
Accounts Receivable	798.3	614.5	486.5	373.0	376.0
Inventories	3,482.4	2,830.8	2,462.6	2,027.0	1,733.0
Other Current Assets	96.3	92.0	130.8	79.0	144.0
Net Fixed Assets	4,345.3	3,428.2	2,593.9	2,144.0	1,754.0
Other Long-Term Assets	94.6	125.4	91.1	135.0	127.0
TOTAL ASSETS	8,833.8	7,103.7	5,906.7	4,902.0	4,207.0

	2020	2019	2018	2017	2016
Accounts Payable	1,546.8	1,364.0	1,130.3	907.0	813.0
Short-Term Debt	440.7	0.0	0.0	0.0	0.0
Other Current Liabilities	1,024.1	939.7	793.5	673.0	626.0
Long-Term Debt	0.0	0.0	0.0	0.0	0.0
Other Liabilities	615.0	566.0	498.6	473.0	395.0
TOTAL LIABILITIES	3,626.6	2,869.7	2,422.4	2,053.0	1,834.0
Preferred Equity	0.0	0.0	0.0	0.0	0.0
Common Equity	676.3	446.2	337.3	196.0	107.0
Retained Earnings	4,530.9	3,787.8	3,147.0	2,653.0	2,266.0
STOCKHOLDERS' EQUITY	5,207.2	4,234.0	3,484.3	2,849.0	2,373.0
TOTAL LIAB. & EQUITY	8,833.8	7,103.7	5,906.7	4,902.0	4,207.0

Income Statement—Yearly Data ($ in millions)

	2020	2019	2018	2017	2016
Revenue	24,623.0	21,206.9	17,838.8	15,307.0	13,363.0
Cost of Goods Sold	17,779.7	15,235.8	12,768.5	10,951.0	9,518.0
Selling, General and Admin.	5,175.8	4,516.9	3,844.8	3,332.0	2,973.0
Depreciation and Amort.	269.2	230.1	210.1	189.0	164.0
Research and Development	0.0	0.0	0.0	0.0	0.0
OPERATING INCOME	1,398.3	1,224.1	1,015.4	835.0	708.0
Interest Expense	3.1	0.4	0.4	1.0	2.0
Other Expenses (Income)	(27.5)	(39.6)	(12.3)	(43.0)	(6.0)
INCOME BEFORE TAXES	1,422.27	1,263.3	1,027.3	877.0	712.0
Income Taxes	537.1	486.4	403.2	340.0	276.0
INCOME AFTER TAXES	885.6	776.9	624.1	537.0	436.0
EPS (as reported)	0.86	0.76	0.62	0.54	0.44

Learning Extension 13

Federal Income Taxation

LO 13.11 (Learning Extension) Compute a person's and a firm's income tax liability and explain the role of depreciation as a way for firm's to reduce their taxes.

Taxes are a financial fact of life, both for individuals and for businesses. As we learned in Section 13.2, how taxes are handled depends on how the business is organized. For proprietorships and partnerships, a firm's income "flows through" to the individuals who own the business. The individuals pay personal income tax on their salaries and the firm's pre-tax profits. A corporation pays income tax on corporate income; the corporations owners—the shareholders—pay tax only on income they receive from their ownership claim (i.e., dividends) and on any difference between the price they paid for their shareholdings and the price they receive when they sell their personal shareholdings.

In addition to financing and risk factors, income tax liabilities may differ for each form of business organization selected. Income from partnerships and proprietorships is combined with other personal income for tax purposes. Below we show the sample tax rate schedules for a married couple filing jointly and for a single person.

13.11A INCOME TAX

LEARNING ACTIVITY
Get updated tax rate information and download forms from the IRS tax site, http://www.irs.gov.

Filing status	Taxable income	Marginal tax rate
Married Filing	$0–19,400	10%
Jointly	19,400–78,950	12
	78,950–168,400	22
	168,400–321,450	24
	321,450–408,200	32
	408,200–612,350	35
	Over 612,350	37
Single	$0–9,700	10%
	9,700–39,475	12
	39,475–84,200	22
	84,200–160,725	24
	160,725–204,100	32
	204,100–510,300	35
	Over 510,300	37

A cursory observation shows that personal income tax rates are *progressive tax rates* because the higher the income, the larger the percentage of income that must be paid in taxes. For example, let's assume the taxable income from a proprietorship (or from an employee) is $50,000 and the person has no additional income. If the person is married and filing a joint return and the spouse has no reportable income, the income will be taxed as follows:

$$0.10 \times \quad \$19,400 = \$1,940.00$$
$$0.12 \times (\$50,000 - 19,400) = \$3,672.00$$
$$\underline{}$$
$$\$50,000 \quad \$5,612.00$$

The *marginal tax rate* is the rate paid on the last dollar of income. In our example, it is 12% and applies to that portion of the taxable income between $19,400 and $78,950. The average tax rate is determined by dividing the tax amount of $5,612 by the $50,000 in taxable income; it equals 11.2%. The marginal tax rate is the most important rate when making business decisions. It shows the percentage of new income that will be paid to the government, or alternatively, that will be lost to the firm because of tax obligations.

A person with $50,000 in taxable income who is single would pay the following taxes:

$$
\begin{array}{lll}
0.10 \times \$9,700 & = & \$970.00 \\
0.12 \times (\$39,475 - 9,700) & = & \$3,573.00 \\
0.22 \times (\$50,000 - 39,475) & = & \$2,315.50 \\
\hline
\$50,000 & & \$6,858.50
\end{array}
$$

The single taxpayer has a 22% marginal tax rate. The average tax rate will be $6,858.50/$50,000 or 13.7%.

Personal taxable income as examined is *ordinary taxable income*. Gains or losses on capital assets such as real estate, bonds, and stocks are taxed differently if held for longer periods. Capital gains or losses arise from asset price changes. Income is taxed when it is received; capital gains or losses are taxed only when the asset is sold and the gain or loss is realized. *Unrealized capital gains* reflect the price appreciation of currently held assets; the tax liability on unrealized capital gains can be deferred indefinitely. Capital gains become only taxable after the asset has been sold for a price higher than its cost or *basis*. *Realized capital gains* occur when an appreciated asset has been sold; taxes are due on the realized capital gains only.

Capital gains taxes are paid on realized capital gains. The top capital gain tax rate is 20% for assets held longer than 12 months if income exceeds $488,850 (for married filing jointly). For joint filers, a 15% capital gains tax rate exist for income between $78,750 and $488,850; and the capital gains tax rate is zero—no capital gains taxes—if the joint income is under $78,750.

Higher income earners may face higher tax rates, too, under the requirements of the Affordable Care Act ("Obamacare"). The law requires a "net investment income tax" rate of 3.8% on investment income OR your adjusted income, depending on the situation. Two things are for certain: The changing tax laws will increase record-keeping requirements, and they will keep tax advisors busy.

Corporations, in contrast with proprietorships and partnerships, are taxed as separate entities. In 2019, the corporate tax rate was a flat tax rate of 21%. Regardless of the taxable income, a corporation faces only one tax bracket: 21%.

A corporation with taxable income of $50,000 pays $10,500 (a 21% marginal and average rate), compared with $5,612 for a person who is married and filing a joint return or $6,858.50 for a single taxpayer. However, income distributed from after-tax corporate profits to owners is taxed again in the form of personal ordinary income. Thus, deciding whether there would be an income tax advantage associated with being taxed as a corporation rather than a proprietorship or partnership is a complex undertaking.

A corporation with taxable income of $200,000 would have the following tax obligation: 21% × $200,000 = $42,000. The marginal tax rate would be 21% and the average tax rate would be 21% ($42,000/$200,000).

A corporation pays taxes on its taxable income. If cash from profits is distributed as dividends to stockholders, the stockholders must pay personal income taxes. This means that money paid out to the owners is taxed twice: once at the corporate level and once as personal income. Small businesses can sometimes qualify as S corporations under the Internal Revenue Code (IRC). These organizations receive the limited liability of a corporation but are taxed as proprietorships or partnerships. Thus, the S corporation avoids double taxation because the business is taxed as a proprietorship or partnership. Whether or not this taxation option is selected depends on the level of the owner's personal tax bracket.

Businesses also have the opportunity of carrying operating losses forward to offset taxable income. A new business corporation that loses, for example, $50,000 the first year can offset only taxable income earned in future years.

The United States had one of the higher corporate tax environments among developed nations.[34] However, the tax rate changes in the Tax Cut and Jobs Act of 2017 helped to substantially improve the tax environment of US corporations compared to their competitors in other countries. In 2018, the world-wide average corporate tax rate (weighted by GDP) was about 26.5%.[35]

<table>
<tr><td></td><td>**13.11B DEPRECIATION BASICS**</td></tr>
</table>

The 2017 Tax Cuts and Jobs Act (TCJA) modified some depreciation rules to allow for immediate expensing—that is, 100% first-year depreciation expense—in some circumstances and dollar limits. However, the law "sunsets" these provisions in five years; it will be up to a future Congress and President to allow the TCJA provisions to continue, revert to pre-TCJA rules, or be modified again.

Thus, rather than get lost in the trees of tax and depreciation details,[36] we focus on the "big picture" aspects of depreciation—those which remain in place, even after TJCA, and which will likely persist in some form in the future.

Depreciation write-offs are important to businesses because depreciation is deductible from income before taxes and, thus, reduces the firm's income tax liability. The following example illustrates the impact of deducting versus not deducting $20,000 in depreciation before computing income taxes liabilities.

	With depreciation	Without depreciation
Income before depreciation and income taxes	$100,000	$100,000
Less: Depreciation	20,000	0
Income before taxes	80,000	100,000
Less: Income taxes (@ 21%)	16,800	21,000
Net income	$63,200	$79,000

The depreciation deduction shields income from taxes. Notice that income before taxes is lower when depreciation is deducted, so the amount of income taxes paid is lower as well. This is an example of the *depreciation tax shield*. With depreciation, taxes are reduced by $4,200. The depreciation tax shield is equal to the tax rate multiplied by the depreciation expense. In this case, it is 0.21 × $20,000, or $4,200.

The effects of the depreciation tax shield are seen in the operating cash flow calculation as well. Ignoring any changes in the current asset and current liability accounts, operating cash flow is net income plus depreciation. With the depreciation deduction, the operating cash flow is $63,200 + $20,000 = $83,200. This is $4,200 higher than the operating cash flow without depreciation, $79,000 + $0 = $79,000.

The Tax Reform Act of 1986 modified the depreciation schedule for various types of assets. Examples of current modified accelerated cost recovery system (MACRS) guidelines are as follows:

	Percentage depreciation allowed by class of asset life	
Recovery year	3-Year	5-Year
1	33.00%	20.00%
2	45.00	32.00
3	15.00	19.20
4	7.00	11.52
5		11.52
6		5.76

[34] Chris Isidore, "U.S. corporate tax rate: No. 1 in the world," money.cnn.com, March 27, 2012; http://money.cnn.com/2012/03/27/pf/taxes/corporate-taxes/index.htm; Randy Myers, "Taxed to the Max," *CFO Magazine, March* 2009, pp. 69–72.

[35] Daniel Bunn, "Corporate Tax Rates Around the World, 2018," https://taxfoundation.org/corporate-tax-rates-around-world-2018/, accessed January 31, 2019.

[36] Those interested in depreciation specifics including Section 179 deductions, 50% special depreciation allowance, qualified real property, and other specifics of the TJCA can review IRS Publication 946 How to Depreciate Property (https://www.irs.gov/publications/p946).

Equipment in the three-year class is depreciated over a four-year period. Likewise automobiles, computers, and some manufacturing tools that qualify in the 5-year class life are depreciated over six years. Industrial equipment and buildings must be depreciated over longer time periods.

For example, let's assume that a business purchases a computer system for $10,000. The amount that could be written off or depreciated each year would be as follows:

Year	Purchase price		Depreciation percentage		Depreciation amount
1	$10,000	×	0.2000	=	$2,000
2	10,000	×	0.3200	=	3,200
3	10,000	×	0.1920	=	1,920
4	10,000	×	0.1152	=	1,152
5	10,000	×	0.1152	=	1,152
6	10,000	×	0.0576	=	576
				Total	$10,000

Thus, the computer system would be fully depreciated by the end of six years. The computer system may have an economic or useful life that is less than or more than its depreciable life.

13.11.1 A FEW WORDS ON DEPRECIATION METHODS

Internal Revenue Service (IRS) tax regulations allow two basic depreciation methods, straight-line depreciation and the modified accelerated cost recovery system (MACRS).

Annual straight-line depreciation expense is computed by dividing the asset's cost by an estimate of its useful life. The annual straight-line depreciation expense for an asset that costs $100,000 and is expected to be used for eight years is $100,000/8 = $12,500.

MACRS depreciates assets by an accelerated method. In essence, MACRS depreciates assets using the double-declining balance method until it becomes advantageous to use straight-line depreciation over the asset's remaining life.

To ensure uniformity, it assigns assets to depreciation classes:

3-year class	Designated tools and equipment used in research
5-year class	Cars, trucks, and some office equipment such as computers and copiers
7-year class	Other office equipment and industrial machinery
10-year class	Other long-lived equipment
27.5-year class	Residential real estate
31.5-year class	Commercial and industrial real estate

Assets in the 27.5- or 31.5-year classes must be depreciated with the straight-line method over the appropriate number of years. In addition, with some exceptions, MACRS follows a half-year convention. The asset receives a half-year's worth of depreciation in the year it is acquired, regardless of when it is purchased. Thus, assets in the three-year class are depreciated over four years. The owner writes off a half-year of depreciation in year 1, a full year of depreciation in each of years 2 and 3, and the remaining half-year of depreciation in year 4. That's why in the previous section the $10,000 computer system, which falls into the 5-year class, is depreciated over 6 years.

SUMMARY

LO 13.11A A fact of civilized life is that taxes are paid to government bodies. There are different tax schedules for persons, depending upon, for example, if they are single or married. Corporations pay income tax using another tax schedule. The tax rate paid on the next dollar of taxable income is the marginal tax rate; the average tax rate paid is the total taxes owed divided by taxable income.

LO 13.11B An asset such as a delivery truck needs to be periodically replaced. Its value five years after purchase will be much lower than its value when it was first purchased. Depreciation expense is an accounting method to track how fixed assets are "used up" in the course of business. It does not involve a cash outflow but depreciation expense is deducted from income. Thus, depreciation expense helps to lower a firm's taxable income and its tax bill. This is called the depreciation tax shield.

REVIEW QUESTIONS AND PROBLEMS

1. Why is it said that the personal income tax rate in the United States is progressive?

2. Corporate tax rates vary with the amount of taxable income. What is the range (lowest and highest) of corporate tax rates in the United States? Is this regressive, progressive, or neither?

3. What is meant by the statement that depreciation provides a tax shield? Explain how this works.

4. Determine the tax owed for corporations with the following amounts of taxable income:
   a. $60,000
   b. $150,000
   c. $500,000.

5. What would the tax obligation (ignore any Affordable Care Act tax implications) be for a married couple filing jointly with taxable earnings of:
   a. $60,000
   b. $150,000
   c. $500,000?
   d. What would be the personal tax obligation of a person filing her taxes under the "single" filing status if she had the above taxable income levels? Ignore any Affordable Care Act tax implications.

6. Find the annual depreciation expenses for the following items:
   a. Original cost is $35,000 for an asset in the three-year class.
   b. Original cost is $70,000 for an asset in the five-year class.

7. Assume a corporation earns $75,000 in net income.
   a. Determine the firm's income tax liability.
   b. Calculate the firm's average income tax rate.

8. Assume that a corporation purchases a new piece of equipment for $90,000. The equipment qualifies for a three-year class life for depreciation purposes.
   a. What is the dollar amount of depreciation that can be taken in the first year?
   b. Determine the depreciation for the remaining years.

CHAPTER 14

Financial Analysis and Long-Term Financial Planning

LEARNING OBJECTIVES

After studying this chapter, you should be able to do the following:

LO 14.1 Describe what is meant by financial statement analysis and ratio analysis.

LO 14.2 Explain, compute, and interpret liquidity ratios.

LO 14.3 Explain, compute, and interpret asset management ratios.

LO 14.4 Explain, compute, and interpret financial leverage ratios.

LO 14.5 Explain, compute, and interpret profitability ratios.

LO 14.6 Explain, compute, and interpret market value ratios and the quality of a firm's financial statements.

LO 14.7 Describe what is meant by DuPont analysis and explain its major components.

LO 14.8 Describe the link between asset investment requirements and sales growth, and compute a firm's external financing needs using the percentage of sales technique.

LO 14.9 Illustrate the cost–volume–profit analysis concept.

LO 14.10 Compute a firm's degree of operating leverage and explain how it is affected by fixed operating costs.

Where we have been. . . The previous chapter introduced the three basic financial statements and some basics of accounting, which is the language of business. Not only do financial market participants, such as bondholders, shareholders, and bankers analyze the financial statements, but the firm's managers also use them to analyze their own firms and their firm's competition, as well as plan for future strategies and financing needs.

Where we are going. . . A myriad of financial market participants will use and analyze financial statement information, particularly bankers, other lenders, suppliers, investors, and some of the firm's customers. We will see how and why they need this information in future chapters, especially Chapter 16 (Short-term Business Financing) and Chapter 18 (Capital Structure and the Cost of Capital).

How this chapter applies to me. . . Publicly available data can be analyzed to show workers and investors how well the firm is doing. For private firms, statement analysis and industry comparisons contain similar information for internal use. A few simple ratio calculations can tell you as an employee or investor how well a firm is doing and how it is making profits.

This chapter gives insight into how lenders make decisions about lending money to YOU. They will review your personal "balance sheet" (your assets and debts) and income statement (your monthly income and checking account information) when you apply for a car loan or mortgage.

Warren Buffet, CEO of Berkshire Hathaway Inc., is regarded as a financial genius and is appreciated for his insightful letters to his shareholders that appear in his firm's annual report. In 1987, he wrote the following:

> *Oftentimes in his shareholders' letter, a CEO will go on for pages detailing corporate performance that is woefully inadequate. He will nonetheless end with a warm paragraph describing his managerial comrades as "our most precious asset." Such comments sometimes make you wonder what the other assets can possibly be.*

Part of being a good manager is managing people and assets well. Successful financial analysis and planning require an understanding of a firm's external and internal environments. Prior chapters have discussed important external influences affecting firms, such as fluctuations in inflation, interest rates, exchange rates, and government policy. The firm's internal environment includes items that can be affected by management, such as organizational structure, worker motivation and productivity, cost control, and the firm's plant and operations.

Of course, a number of interrelationships exist between a firm's external and internal environment. Firm sales will be affected by the state of the economy, management's ability to handle growth, and the quality and marketing of the firm's product. Pricing decisions are influenced by the state of the economy, actions by competitors, and the firm's production costs.

The joint impact of the external and internal environments on a firm is best reflected in the firm's financial statements. These statements provide measures of the success or failure of the firm's strategies and policies, quantified in financial terms. Such information is valuable to the firm's managers, as well as to stock and bond analysts, bank loan officers, and competitors. The information found on the financial statements is invaluable for analyzing a firm's past as well as for planning for its future.

For investors, how we analyze financial statements will depend upon the economic environment, too. For example, a firm with high debt ratios may be an attractive investment at the end of a recession as economic growth begins. Rapidly expanding sales will generate cash to pay interest leaving high levels of profits. The same debt ratios at the end of a period of economic growth, with a recession growing near, may make the firm appear unattractive for investment purposes.

This chapter addresses how to analyze a firm's financial statements to identify a firm's strengths and weaknesses. We will discuss using financial statement information for financial planning and forecasting purposes, including estimating future asset needs and capital requirements.

14.1 FINANCIAL STATEMENT ANALYSIS

The financial statements discussed in Chapter 13 were designed to report a firm's financial position at a point in time, as well as the results of its operations over a period of time. The real usefulness of these statements comes from the help they provide in predicting the firm's future earnings and dividends along with the risks associated with these variables.

Financial statement analysis can affect nonfinance operations of a firm. For example, a salesperson could lose a new customer and a sales commission should a check of the customer's financial statements lead to the conclusion the customer is a bad credit risk. An analysis that indicates excessive levels of inventories could lead to a change in the firm's pricing and marketing strategies and could affect the firm's production plan, even leading to worker layoffs.

A firm's management reviews its financial statements to determine if progress is being made toward company goals. Internal documents based on this analysis inform division managers of the status of their divisions and product lines and how these results compare to the year's plan.

Many individuals and organizations analyze firms' financial statements. A firm that seeks credit, from a supplier firm or a bank, typically must submit financial statements for examination. Potential purchasers of a firm's bonds will analyze financial statements to gauge the firm's ability to make timely payments of interest and principal. Potential shareholders should examine financial statements as they are an excellent source of firm information. Present shareholders will want to examine financial statements to monitor firm performance.

14.1.1 RATIO ANALYSIS OF BALANCE SHEET AND INCOME STATEMENT

Ratio analysis is valuable method for gaining insights regarding a firm's strengths and weaknesses. Ratios are constructed by dividing various financial statement numbers into one another. The ratios can then be examined to more easily determine trends and reasons for changes in the financial statement quantities. Ratios are valuable tools, as they standardize balance sheet and income statement numbers. Thus, differences in firm size will not affect the analysis. A firm with $10 billion in sales can be easily compared to a firm with $1 billion or $200 million in sales.

ratio analysis financial technique that involves dividing various financial statement numbers into one another

trend analysis (time series analysis) used to evaluate a firm's performance over time

cross-sectional analysis different firms are compared at the same point in time

industry comparative analysis compares a firm's ratios against average ratios for other companies in the firm's industry

Three basic categories of ratio analysis are used. First, financial ratios can be used in trend analysis (also known as time series analysis) to evaluate a firm's performance over time. Second, ratios are used in cross-sectional analysis, in which different firms are compared at the same point in time. Third, industry comparative analysis is used to compare a firm's ratios against average ratios for other companies in the firm's industry. This allows the analyst to evaluate the firm's financial performance relative to industry norms.

Comparing a firm's ratios to average industry ratios requires caution. Some sources of industry data report the average for each ratio, others report the median, and others report the interquartile range for each ratio (i.e., the range for the middle 50% of ratio values reported by firms in the industry).

Five other difficulties can arise as well. First, by their nature, industry ratios are narrowly focused on a specific industry, but the operations of large firms such as AT&T, ExxonMobil, and IBM often cross many industry boundaries.

Second, accounting standards often differ among firms in an industry. This can create confusion, particularly when some firms in the industry adopt new accounting standards (set forth by the Financial Accounting Standards Board, or FASB) before others. Adopting standards early can affect a firm's ratios by making them appear unusually high or low as compared to the industry average.

Third, care must be taken when comparing different types of firms in the same industry. In one industry, there may be large and small firms, multinational and domestic firms, firms that operate nationally, and those which focus only on limited geographic markets. Some firms may use a year-end date of December 31 but others may choose another date for their end-of-year financial reporting.

Fourth, analysts and sources of public information on ratios may compute ratios differently. Some may use after-tax earnings, some pretax earnings; others may assume "debt" refers only to long-term debt while still others include all liabilities as debt. Some use year-end numbers from the most recent balance sheet while others may compute a financial ratio using an average value from the previous and the most recent balance sheet. Make sure you are aware of how a resource defines its ratios before using it for analysis.

Fifth, firms change over time, which may make it difficult to assess changes in financial ratios. A firm may merge with another firm or spin off (divest) a division. Such changes in the firm may affect the level of a financial ratio from earlier time periods. We'll see that first-hand in this chapter as we use Walgreens as our sample firm for computing financial ratios. In 2015, Walgreens completed a merger with a German retail drug store, Boots Alliance. Thus, recent financial statements and financial ratios will differ in some cases from prior years, as assets, liabilities, sales, and expenses of two firms are combined into one firm, Walgreens Boots Alliance, which we will simply refer to as "Walgreens."

A firm's financial statements are the best information source for time series or cross-sectional analysis. These materials appear in annual reports as well as 10-Q and 10-K filings with the Securities and Exchange Commission (SEC).

Data for industry average financial ratios are published by a number of organizations, such as Dun & Bradstreet, Risk Management Association, Standard & Poor's (S&P), and the Federal Trade Commission (FTC). These information sources are available at most libraries. In addition, analysts can create their own industry financial ratios by obtaining financial statement information on a firm and its competitors. The financial statement items can be added across the firms to give an "industry" balance sheet or income statement. These data can be used to compute ratios for comparison against the firm in question.

How an analyst interprets a ratio depends on for whom the analyst works. Whether a ratio appears favorable or unfavorable depends on the perspective of the user. For example, a short-term creditor, such as a bank loan officer, mostly wants to see a high degree of liquidity. This analyst is somewhat less concerned with a firm's profitability. An equity holder would rather see less liquidity and more profitability. Therefore, the analyst must keep in mind the perspective of the user in evaluating and interpreting the information contained in financial ratios.

14.1.2 TYPES OF FINANCIAL RATIOS

Many types of ratios can be calculated from financial statement data or stock market information. However, it is common practice to group ratios into five basic categories:

1. Liquidity ratios

2. Asset management ratios

3. Financial leverage ratios

4. Profitability ratios

5. Market value ratios

The first four categories are based on information taken from a firm's income statements and balance sheets. The fifth category relates stock market information to financial statement items. We will use the financial statements for Walgreens that were introduced in Chapter 13 to illustrate how financial statement analysis is conducted. Tables 14.1 and 14.2 contain Walgreens' balance sheets and income statements for several years. For comparative purposes, for each ratio group, we present graphs of Walgreens' ratios as well as ratios for a retail drug store industry competitor, CVS, over the 1997–2018 time period.

> **DISCUSSION QUESTION 1**
>
> **What kind of ratio analysis is more valuable to an analyst: time series, cross-sectional, or industry averages? Explain your choice.**

Table 14.1   Balance Sheets for Walgreens ($ millions)

	2015	2016	2017	2018
Cash & Cash Equivalents	$3,000	$9,807	$3,301	$785
Accounts Receivable	$6,849	$6,260	$6,528	$7,144
Inventories	$8,678	$8,956	$8,899	$10,976
Other Current Assets	$1,130	$860	$1,025	$1,178
Total Current Assets	$19,657	$25,883	$19,753	$20,083
Net Fixed Assets	$15,068	$14,335	$13,642	$13,821
Other Long Term Assets	$17,685	$6,641	$6,826	$7,644
Goodwill & Intangibles	$16,372	$25,829	$25,788	$28,393
TOTAL ASSETS	$68,782	$72,688	$66,009	$69,941
Accounts Payable	$10,088	$11,000	$12,494	$14,660
Short-Term Debt	$1,068	$63	$251	$1,999
Other Current Liabilities	$5,401	$4,292	$5,802	$8,440
Total Current Liabilities	$16,557	$17,013	$18,547	$25,099
Long-Term Debt	$13,315	$18,705	$12,684	$11,646
Other Liabilities	$8,049	$7,090	$6,504	$6,933
TOTAL LIABILITIES	$37,921	$42,407	$37,735	$43,678
Preferred Equity	$0	$0	$0	$0
Common Equity + Retained Earnings	$30,861	$30,281	$28,274	$26,263
TOTAL STOCKHOLDERS' EQUITY	$30,861	$30,281	$28,274	$26,263
TOTAL LIABILITIES & EQUITY	$68,782	$72,688	$66,009	$69,941

Table 14.2   Income Statements for Walgreens ($ millions)

	2015	2016	2017	2018
Revenue	$103,444	$117,351	$118,214	$131,537
Cost of Goods Sold	$76,520	$87,477	$89,052	$100,745
Selling, General, Administrative Expenses and Depreciation	$22,256	$23,425	$22,916	$24,569
Operating Income	$4,668	$6,449	$6,246	$6,223
Interest Expense	$471	$580	$643	$577
Other Expenses (Income)			$742	–$376
Income Before Taxes	$5,311	$5,188	$4,861	$6,022
Income Taxes	$1,056	$997	$760	$998
Net Income	$4,255	$4,173	$4,078	$5,024
Earnings Per Share	$4.05	$3.82	$3.78	$5.07

LEARNING ACTIVITY

1. Copies of Buffet's past chairman's letters are available at Berkshire Hathaway's website, https://www.berkshirehathaway.com.
2. Various industry ratios and industry analyses are available for different firms on websites such as https://finance.yahoo.com (enter a stock ticker symbol to get a price quote; then click on "profile"; once on the profile page, you can see the section and industry of the firm. Another site is http://www.hoovers.com/. Other websites also contain financial information, such as a corporation's home page and the SEC's EDGAR database of public firm filings, https://www.sec.gov/edgar.shtml).

14.2 LIQUIDITY RATIOS AND ANALYSIS

liquidity ratios indicate the ability of the firm to meet short-term obligations as they come due

net working capital dollar amount of a firm's current assets minus current liabilities; sometimes used as a measure of liquidity

The less liquid a firm is, the greater the risk of insolvency or default the firm has. Because debt obligations are paid with cash, the firm's cash flows ultimately determine solvency.

We can estimate the firm's liquidity position by examining specific balance sheet items. **Liquidity ratios** indicate the ability to meet short-term obligations to creditors as they mature, or come due. This form of liquidity analysis focuses on the relationship between current assets and current liabilities, and the rapidity with which receivables and inventory turn into cash during normal business operations. This means the immediate source of cash funds for paying bills must be cash on hand, proceeds from the sale of marketable securities, or the collection of accounts receivable. Additional liquidity comes from inventory that can be sold and, thus, converted into cash directly through cash sales or indirectly through credit sales (accounts receivable).

The dollar amount of a firm's **net working capital**, or its current assets minus current liabilities, is sometimes used as a measure of liquidity, but two popular ratios are also used to gauge a firm's liquidity position. The *current ratio* is a measure of a company's ability to pay off its short-term debt as it comes due. The current ratio is computed by dividing the current assets by the current liabilities. Typically, assets and liabilities with maturities of one year or less are considered to be current for financial statement purposes.

A low current ratio (low relative to, say, industry norms) may indicate a company may face difficulty in paying its bills. A high value for the current ratio, however, does not necessarily imply greater liquidity. It may suggest that funds are being inefficiently employed within the firm. Excessive amounts of inventory, accounts receivable, or idle cash balances could contribute to a high current ratio.

We can calculate the current ratio for 2018 and 2017 as follows:

CURRENT RATIO:
2018: (Current assets/Current liabilities) = ($20,083/$25,099) = 0.80 times
2017: ($19,753/$18,547) = 1.07 times

Walgreens' current ratio fell from 2017 to 2018. Table 14.1 shows Walgreens' current assets rose in 2018. Current liabilities rose in 2018, rising more than current assets (a 35% rise in current liabilities compared to a less than 2% rise in current assets). Although both quantities rose, the joint effect of the larger rise in current liabilities was a decline in the current ratio.

The *quick ratio*, or *acid test ratio*, is computed by dividing the sum of cash, marketable securities, and accounts receivable by the current liabilities. This comparison eliminates inventories from consideration since inventories are among the least liquid of the major current asset categories because they must first be converted to sales.

In general, a ratio of 1.0 indicates a reasonably liquid position in that an immediate liquidation of marketable securities at their current values and the collection of all accounts receivable, plus cash on hand, would be adequate to cover the firm's current liabilities. However, as this ratio declines, the firm must rely increasingly on converting inventories to sales to meet current liabilities as they come due. Walgreens' quick ratios for 2018 and 2017 are the following:

QUICK RATIO:

2018: (Cash + Marketable securities + Accounts receivable)/Current liabilities = ($785 + 7,144)/$16,557
= 0.32 times

2017: ($3,301 + 6,528)/$8,895 = 0.53 times

According to the financial statement data, Walgreens' quick ratio is well below 1.0. As we will see, this is not a major cause for concern in the retail drug store industry. In this industry, we expect lower quick ratios, as much of Walgreens' current assets consist of inventory that awaits sale on the company's store shelves and warehouses.

When assessing the firm's liquidity position, financial managers also are interested in how trade credit from suppliers, which we call accounts payable, is being used and paid for. This analysis requires taking data from a firm's income statement in addition to the balance sheet. The *average payment period* is computed by dividing the year-end accounts payable amount by the firm's average cost of goods sold (COGS) per day. We calculate the average daily COGS by dividing the income statement's COGS amount by 365 days in a year (366 in leap year).

AVERAGE PAYMENT PERIOD:

Accounts payable/(Cost of goods sold/365) = (Accounts payable/Cost of goods sold per day)

2018: [$14,660/($100,745/365)] = ($14,660/$276.01) = 53.1 days

2017: [$12,494/($89,052/365)] = ($12,494/$243.98) = 51.2 days

Walgreens slowed payments to its suppliers by nearly 2 days. Overall, the average payment period was fairly stable. Walgreens is able to delay payments to supplies by an average of almost two months.

Figure 14.1 illustrates the trend of Walgreens's liquidity ratios in comparison to those of a competitor, CVS. Walgreens' current ratio and quick ratio closely tracks the CVS ratios until 2012 when CVS's current and quick ratios rose sharply. Since both the current and quick ratio rose for CVS, we know inventory is not the reason as inventory doesn't appear in both ratios. Therefore, the increase in CVS's ratios is due to increases in its cash and receivables – or possibly declines in current liabilities. Walgreens' average payment period indicates that since 2003 the firm takes longer to pay suppliers than does CVS, with a marked increase in 2016 after its merger with Boots Alliance.

Overall, Walgreens' current and quick ratios have been relatively stable over this time frame, but analysis and asking questions of the firm's management may be needed due to the decline in these ratios in recent years. CVS's current and quick ratios have sharply risen in recent years while its average payment period has been stable in recent years until 2018. Walgreens' increase in average payment period may be the result of its larger global footprint after the merger with a German firm; no doubt suppliers will be watching Walgreens' payment behavior closely in the coming year. The increase in

FIGURE 14.1 Liquidity ratios for Walgreens versus CVS

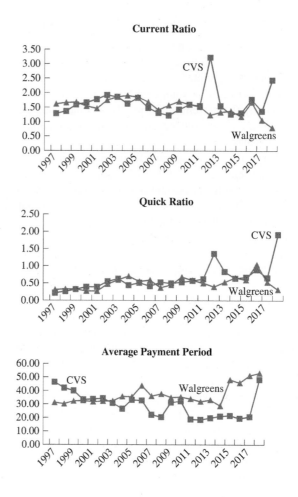

liquidity for CVS may not be a positive sign; it may indicate it has excess receivables and/or excess cash that it can better use by re-investing in the business. Or it could have been raising cash to finance its acquisition, at the end of 2018, of Aetna, a health insurance firm.

14.3 ASSET MANAGEMENT RATIOS AND ANALYSIS

asset management ratios indicate extent to which assets are turned over or used to support sales

Asset management ratios indicate the extent to which assets are turned over or used to support sales. These are sometimes referred to as *activity* or *utilization ratios* and each ratio in this category relates financial performance on the income statement with items on the balance sheet. Thus, we will be using information for Walgreens from Tables 14.1 and 14.2.

The *total assets turnover ratio* is computed by dividing net sales by the firm's total assets. It indicates how efficiently the firm is utilizing its total assets to produce revenues or sales. It is a measure of the dollars of sales generated by one dollar of the firm's assets. Generally, the more efficiently assets are used, the higher a firm's profits. The size of the ratio is influenced by characteristics of the industry within which the firm operates. Capital intensive electric utilities might have asset turnover ratios as low as 0.33, indicating they require $3 of investment in assets to produce $1 in revenues. In contrast, retail food chains with asset turnovers as high as 10 would require a $0.10 investment in assets to produce $1 in sales. A typical manufacturing firm has an asset turnover of about 1.5. Walgreens' 2017 and 2018 total assets turnover ratios are calculated as follows:

TOTAL ASSETS TURNOVER:
2018: (Net sales/Total assets) = ($131,537/$69,941) = 1.88 times
2017: ($118,214/$66,009) = 1.79 times

Asset utilization rose between 2017 and 2018 as sales revenue rose proportionately more (11%) than total assets (about 6%). Both components of the ratio rose – but since the percentage increase in the numerator (sales) was greater than the percentage change in the denominator (total assets), this asset efficiency ratio rose over 5% from its 2017 level. The ratio has been rising since Walgreens' 2015 merger with Boots Alliance, which is an indication all the "kinks" are worked out in this new global firm.

The *fixed assets turnover ratio* is computed by dividing net sales by the firm's net fixed assets and indicates the extent to which long-term assets are being used to produce sales. Similar to the interpretation given to the total asset turnover, the fixed assets turnover represents the dollars of sales generated by each dollar of fixed assets. Investment in plant and equipment is usually expensive. Consequently, unused or idle capacity is costly and often represents a major factor for a firm exhibiting poor operating performance. On the other hand, a high (compared to competitors or the industry average) fixed assets turnover ratio is not necessarily a favorable sign; it may occur because of efficient use of assets (good), or it may occur because of the firm's use of technologically obsolete equipment, which has small book value because of the effects of accumulated depreciation (poor). An astute analyst will do research to determine which is the case for the firm under analysis.

FIXED ASSETS TURNOVER:
2018: (Net sales/Net fixed assets) = ($131,537/$13,821) = 9.52 times
2017: ($118,214/$13,642) = 8.67 times

Walgreens' fixed assets turnover rose from 8.67 to 9.52, indicating that sales increased more rapidly than net fixed assets. In percentage terms, net fixed assets increased slightly more than 1% while sales rose over 11%. Since the 2015 merger, both the total asset turnover and fixed asset turnover ratios have been increasing. This could be a sign of increasing efficiency as a result of the merger. But the analyst will want to determine if spending to maintain and increase the asset base has slowed since the merger.

In reviewing Walgreens balance sheet, we note a large increase in "goodwill" between 2015 and 2016. Goodwill is an accounting concept to record the price paid in an acquisition that is over and above the book value of the target's assets. In other words, Walgreens paid much more than the book value of Boots Alliance's assets. This is typical for most mergers – as we've learned, the balance sheet records historical costs and historical values, whereas the finance – and business – view is forward-looking. Assets on the Boots Alliance balance sheet did not reflect their current market values, but the price paid for Walgreens to purchase Boots Alliance did incorporate expectations about their value and ability to generate cash flows. Like assets, the goodwill account balance will be reduced over time; assets are depreciated to show they are being "used up" over time. Similarly, the goodwill account is reduced (it is called amortization) over time.

The *average collection period* is calculated as the year-end accounts receivable divided by the average net sales per day, and thus, indicates the average number of days that sales are outstanding. In other words, it reports the number of days it takes, on average, to collect credit sales made to the firm's customers.[1] The average collection period measures the days of financing that a firm extends to its customers. Because of this, a shorter average collection period is usually preferred to a longer one. Another measure that can be used to provide this same information is the receivables turnover. The *receivables turnover* is computed by dividing annual sales, preferably credit sales, by the year-end accounts receivable. If the receivables turnover is six, this means that, on average, the average collection period is about two months (12 months divided by the turnover ratio of six). If the turnover is four times, the firm has an average collection period of about three months (12 months divided by the turnover ratio of four).

---

[1] In some ways, the average collection period is the "mirror image" of the average payment period, which is the average number of days the firm's suppliers extend credit to the firm.

Walgreens' average collection periods for 2018 and 2017 were the following:

AVERAGE COLLECTION PERIOD:

[Accounts receivable/(Net sales/365)] = (Accounts receivable/Net sales per day)
2018: [$7,144/($131,537/365)] = ($7,144/$360.38) = 19.8 days
2017: [$6,528/($118,214/365)] = ($6,528/$323.87) = 20.2 days

Walgreens' average collection period has been stable in recent years. This ratio rose following the merger with Boots Alliance in 2015. This may have been the result of the average of the "Walgreens" model of doing business with the "Boots Alliance" way of doing business – as well as the differences in past customers and customer payment practices of each firm. Since this sharp increase in 2015, the average collection period has fallen to about 20 days. Comparing the average collection and payment periods, Walgreens is in a positive situation, as it collects from its customers over 30 days faster than it pays its suppliers. This has positive implications for Walgreens' asset efficiency and for its liquidity.

As with other ratios, the average collection period may be too high or low. An unusually low number of days required to collect sales for a particular line of business may indicate an unnecessarily tight internal credit policy that could result in lost sales. The firm may be selecting only the best customers or may be insisting on unusually strict payment terms. On the other hand, a high average collection period may indicate the firm may have too lax a policy concerning customer quality and/or credit payment terms. Thus, in deciding on a proper credit policy, monitoring trends over time is important, as is comparing the firm's average collection period relative to industry norms. We will explore credit policies in greater detail in Chapter 15.

The *inventory turnover ratio* is computed by dividing the cost of goods sold by the year-end inventory.[2] Here we are seeking to determine how efficiently the amount of inventory is being managed,

CAREER OPPORTUNITIES IN FINANCE

BUSINESS FINANCIAL PLANNING

Opportunities

A business may be small, with a small budget and a straightforward market, or large, with budget well over $1 billion and a multinational market. In either case, analysts and planners play an important and necessary role in preserving the financial well-being of their firm. These jobs, therefore, are challenging, often unpredictable, and exciting. The risks are often high but so are the rewards.

Jobs

Financial Analyst
Financial Planner
Credit Analyst

Responsibilities

A financial analyst calculates a firm's past and ongoing financial performance relative to other firms in the same industry and/or a firm's own performance over time. Once this information is gathered,

a financial analyst evaluates the results and presents these findings to other departments of the firm.

A financial planner prepares short- and longer-term financial plans. A short-term financial plan, generally, involves estimating monthly cash needs for one year into the future. Business firms, typically, prepare five-year plans based on sales forecasts and estimates of capital expenditures needed to support the sales forecasts. A financial planner makes annual estimates of the external financing needed to support these sales targets over each five-year plan.

A credit analyst evaluates the creditworthiness of both a firm's potential customers and existing credit customers. Decisions whether to extend credit in the form of short-term financing are based on an assessment of the applicant's liquidity and ability to pay. In cases where credit has been extended, the credit analyst monitors credit customers for possible changes in the liquidity or the ability to pay in the short-run.

Education

These positions require at least a bachelor's degree along with a solid background in finance, economics, accounting, and computers.

---

[2] Cost of goods sold (COGS) often is used to compute this ratio instead of sales in order to remove the impact of profit margins on inventory turnover. Profit margins can vary over time, thus making interpreting the relationship between volume and inventory more difficult.

so, on the one hand, the firm does not have to finance excess inventory, and on the other hand, adequate inventory supplies exist to avoid being out of stock of an item and losing potential sales (and profits). Stated differently, the inventory turnover ratio indicates whether the inventory is out of line in relation to the volume of sales when compared against industry norms or when tracked over time for a specific firm.[3]

INVENTORY TURNOVER:
2018: (Cost of goods sold/Inventory) = ($100,745/$10,976) = 9.2 times
2017: ($89,052/$8,899) = 10.0 times

Walgreens' annual inventory turnover decreased slightly from 2017 to 2018. The ratio decreased as inventory rose more (about 23%) than the cost of goods sold (about 13%).

Inventory management requires a delicate balance between having too low an inventory turnover, which increases the likelihood of holding obsolete inventory, and too high an inventory turnover, which could lead to stock-outs and lost sales. These concepts will be discussed in greater detail in Chapter 15.

If a firm is growing rapidly (or shrinking rapidly), there may be distortions if year-end data is used for comparisons of ratios over time. To avoid such possible distortions, we can use the average inventory (beginning plus ending balances divided by two) to calculate inventory turnovers for comparison purposes.[4] Likewise, average data for other balance sheet accounts should be used when rapid growth or contraction is taking place for a specific firm.

Figure 14.2 illustrates Walgreens' asset management ratios in comparison to those of CVS between 1997 and 2018. Both firms have declining total asset turnover ratios over time. Although for many of these years Walgreens' total asset turnover was higher, both Walgreens and CVS have similar ratios in the mid-2010s. CVS's fixed asset turnover and average collection period have been higher than Walgreens', indicating possibly more efficient use of net fixed assets and an easier collection policy toward customer payments. Inventory turnover has been rising for both firms with CVS, generally, being slightly more efficient since 2007.

Financial leverage ratios indicate the extent to which borrowed, or debt, funds are used to finance assets, as well as the ability of the firm to meet its debt payment obligations.

The *total debt to total assets* ratio is computed by dividing the total debt, or total liabilities, of the business by the total assets. This ratio shows the portion of the total assets financed by all creditors and debtors. We obtain the relevant balance sheet information for Walgreens from Table 14.1.

TOTAL DEBT TO TOTAL ASSETS:
2018: (Total debt/Total assets) = ($43,678/$69,941) = 0.62 = 62%
2017: ($37,735/$66,009) = 0.57 = 57%

Walgreens' total debt ratio rose; its debts (liabilities) rose more quickly than its assets.

A total debt to asset ratio that is too high tells the financial manager the opportunities for securing additional borrowed funds are limited. Additional debt funds may be more costly in terms of the rate of interest that will have to be paid. Lenders will want higher expected returns to compensate for their risk of lending to a firm that has a high proportion of debt to assets. It is possible to have too low a ratio

> ## 14.4 FINANCIAL LEVERAGE RATIOS AND ANALYSIS
>
> Financial leverage ratios indicate the extent to which borrowed, or debt, funds are used to finance assets, as well as the ability of a firm to meet its debt payment obligations

---

[3] Economists view inventory levels as an indicator of future economic times. During the 2007–2009 Great Recession, firms trimmed inventories; at the then-current low levels, signs of increased consumer spending would require more production by firms and, possibly, increased hiring. The decline in fortunes for telecom firms during 2000–2001 was clearly evident in the behavior of their inventory turnover ratios. Rising inventories and falling sales led to plummeting profits, cash positions, and stock prices for many firms. See Ken Brown, "Some Tech Investors Shift Hopes to 2002," *The Wall Street Journal*, (February 21, 2001), pp. C1, C2.

[4] For firms with highly seasonal sales, the average of the inventory balance from the firm's quarterly balance sheets (which are distributed to shareholders of public firms) can be used.

FIGURE 14.2 Asset management ratios for Walgreens versus CVS

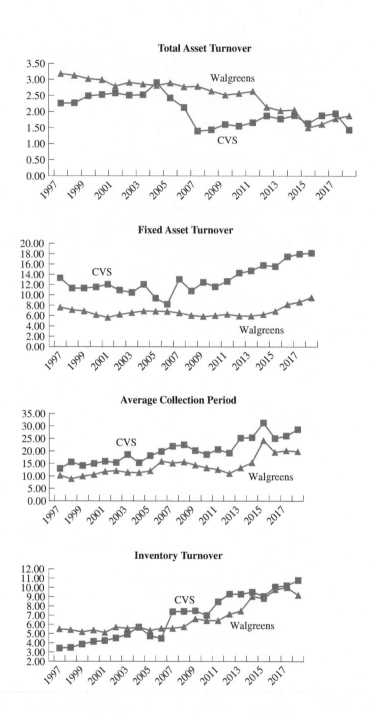

of total debt to total assets, which can be costly to the firm.[5] Since interest expenses are deductible for income tax purposes, the government, in effect, pays a portion of the debt financing costs. Furthermore, as we will see in Chapter 18, a firm's debt costs are lower than the effective costs of equity.

Sometimes, a debt ratio is calculated that shows the total debt in relation to the dollars the owners have put in the firm. This is referred to as the *total debt to equity ratio*. Walgreens' ratio for 2018 was 1.66 ($43,678/$26,263), versus 1.33 ($37,735/$28,274) in 2017. For every dollar of equity, the firm has borrowed about $1.33 cents in 2017; for every dollar of equity, it borrowed $1.66 in 2018. Walgreens debt ratios have been rising since it merged with Boots Alliance.

---

[5] A low debt ratio can arise from the continued profitability of a firm and its additions to retained earnings. These additions to retained earnings will increase the level of equity relative to debt, unless the firm issues additional debt.

The *equity multiplier ratio,* which provides another way of looking at the firm's debt burden, is calculated by dividing total assets by the firm's total equity.

EQUITY MULTIPLIER:
2018: (Total assets/Total equity) = ($69,941/$26,263) = 2.66
2017: ($66,009/$28,274) = 2.33

Similar to the total debt to total assets ratio, the equity multiplier rose between 2017 and 2018.

At first glance, the ratio appears to have little to do with leverage; it is total assets divided by stockholders' equity. But recall the accounting identity: Assets = Liabilities + Equity. A higher level of assets relative to equity suggests greater use of debt. Thus, larger values of the equity multiplier imply a greater use of leverage by the firm. This can be seen by using the accounting identity and dividing everything by equity:

$$\frac{\text{Total assets}}{\text{Equity}} = \frac{\text{Total liabilities}}{\text{Equity}} + \frac{\text{Equity}}{\text{Equity}}$$

$$\frac{\text{Total assets}}{\text{Equity}} = \frac{\text{Total liabilities}}{\text{Equity}} + 1$$

On the left, we have the equity multiplier; on the right, we have the total debt to equity ratio plus one. This shows that more reliance on debt in order to finance the firm results in a larger equity multiplier. While the equity multiplier does not add to the information derived from the other debt ratios, it is useful when financial analysis is conducted using certain financial models, as we will explain later in the chapter.

In addition to calculating debt ratios, the financial manager should be interested in the firm's ability to meet or service its interest and principal repayment obligations on the borrowed funds. This is accomplished through the calculation of interest coverage and fixed charge coverage ratios. These ratios make use of information directly from the income statement or from footnotes to a firm's financial statements.

The *interest coverage,* or *times-interest-earned ratio,* is calculated by dividing the firm's operating income, or earnings before interest and taxes (EBIT), by the annual interest expense.

INTEREST COVERAGE:
2018: (Earnings before interest & taxes/Interest expense) = ($6,223/$577) = 10.8
2017: ($6,246/$643) = 9.7

Walgreens' interest coverage ratios are large, which indicates that interest-bearing debt is a small portion of Walgreens' financial structure.

The interest coverage figure indicates the extent to which the operating income, or EBIT, level could decline before the ability to pay interest obligations would be impeded. With an interest coverage ratio of about 10, Walgreens' operating income can drop to 1/10 or 10% of its current level and interest payments still could be met. Suppose the interest coverage ratio was 5; in such a case, operating income could fall to 1/5 or 20% of its current level and the firm could still pay the interest coming due.

In addition to interest payments, there may be other fixed charges (such as rental or lease payments and periodic bond principal repayments, which are typically referred to as **sinking fund payments**). The *fixed charge coverage* ratio indicates the ability of a firm to meet its contractual obligations for interest, leases, and debt principal repayments out of its operating income.

sinking fund payments periodic bond principal repayments

Rental or lease payments are deductible on the income statement prior to the payment of income taxes, just as is the case with interest expenses. In contrast, a sinking fund payment is a repayment of debt and, thus, is *not* a deductible expense for income tax purposes. However, to be consistent with the other data, we must adjust the sinking fund payment to a before-tax basis. We do this by dividing the after-tax amount by one minus the effective tax rate.

While footnotes to Walgreens' balance sheets are not provided in Table 14.1, suppose Walgreens' annual reports shows property lease payments of $2,372 million in 2018 and $2,319 million in 2017, and no sinking fund obligations. We compute the fixed charge coverage ratio as follows. First, the numerator in the ratio must reflect earnings before interest, lease payments, and taxes, which we determine by adding the lease payment amount to the operating income, or EBIT, amount. Second, the denominator needs to show all relevant expenses on a before-tax basis. Sinking fund payments are made after-tax, so any sinking fund payments should be divided by (1 – firm's tax rate) to put them on a pretax basis. In the calculations below, we will assume no sinking fund payments, only the lease payments noted above.

FIXED CHARGE COVERAGE:

(Earnings before interest, lease payments, & taxes/{Interest + Lease payments + [(Sinking fund payment)/(1 – Tax rate)]})
2018: ($6,223 + 2,372)/($577 + 2,372 + 0) = 2.9
2017: ($6,246 + 2,319)/($643 + 2,319 + 0) = 2.9

This is a marked difference from the interest coverage ratio. Information in Walgreens' annual report to shareholders tells us that the firm usually leases its store space rather than purchasing it. These long-term leases are a substitute for debt financing for Walgreens.

The graphs of Walgreens' financial leverage ratios in Figure 14.3 show its debt ratios declining and then rising during the 1997–2018 time frame while CVS's ratios showed a similar pattern. Both

FIGURE 14.3 Financial leverage ratios for Walgreens versus CVS

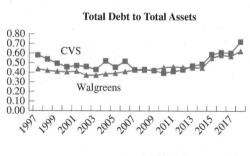

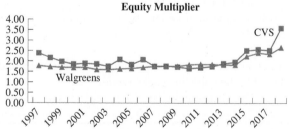

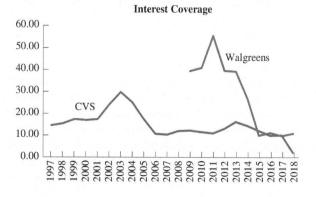

firms have little interest expense; the graph of the interest coverage ratio shows only CVS through 2009 has Walgreens had no interest-bearing longer-term debt until then. Walgreens' total debt ratios stayed below or fairly close to those of CVS over time.

From looking at Walgreens, we can make three important conclusions. First, not all liabilities are contractual debt. Walgreens has a debt to assets ratio of about 62% but until 2009 had little interest-bearing debt, either short-term (such as notes payable) or long-term on its balance sheet. Second, not all liabilities require interest to be paid. Again, Walgreens has a debt ratio of 62% but comparatively low interest payments. Third, to get a truer perspective of a firm's financial situation, all contractual fixed charges, including interest, lease payments, and sinking fund payments, should be examined. This requires some reading of the footnotes and other information in the firm's financial statements. Walgreens' high interest coverage ratio is reduced when fixed charges are considered and a fixed charge coverage ratio is computed.

Part of the reason for the behavior of Walgreens' ratios is that it acquired several firms in 2018. In the changing world of health care, size can be an advantage for negotiating with suppliers, corporate health care benefit providers, and government regulators; Walgreens, in recent years, has decided to grow by merger and acquisition. It acquired a 45% stake in European drugstore giant Alliance Boots GmbH for $6.7 billion, with an option to purchase the remainder of the firm by 2015, and it exercised this option and completed the transaction in 2015. Walgreens acquired online drug retailer drugstore.com in March 2014 for $429 million and Duane Reade in 2010 for $1.2 billion. To acquire these stakes, Walgreens used existing balance sheet cash as well as new debt issues. In 2016, Walgreens reversed course and shut down drugstore.com in order to build its own online brand.[6]

DISCUSSION QUESTION 2

Consider these three situations:
Situation 1: A firm's current ratio is rising over time while its quick ratio is stable.
Situation 2: A firm's total asset turnover ratio is rising but its fixed asset turnover ratio is falling.
Situation 3: A firm's equity multiplier is rising and its interest coverage ratio is falling.
Select one of these situations and discuss what may be occurring within the firm and whether the situation implies potential good news or potential bad news for the business.

Profitability ratios indicate the firm's ability to generate returns on its sales, assets, and equity. Two basic profit margin ratios are important to the financial manager. The *operating profit margin* is calculated as the firm's earnings before interest and taxes (EBIT) divided by net sales. This ratio indicates the firm's ability to control operating expenses relative to sales. Table 14.2 contains income statement information for the Walgreens Corporation and provides the necessary information for determining the operating profit margin.

14.5 PROFITABILITY RATIOS AND ANALYSIS

profitability ratios indicate the firm's ability to generate returns on its sales, assets, and equity

OPERATING PROFIT MARGIN:

2018: (Earnings before interest & taxes/Net sales) = ($6,223/$131,537) = 4.7%
2017: ($6,246/$118,214) = 5.3%

These results indicate that Walgreens' operating profitability fell from 2017 to 2018. Whether it was because of lower selling prices or higher costs, operating profit (EBIT) fell slightly from $6,246 to $6,223 while sales rose over 11% [($131,537 − $118,214)/$118,214)].[7]

---

[6] "Walgreen Hits The Gas On Growth With Another Acquisition," accessed August 23, 2016, https://www.forbes.com/sites/greatspeculations/2012/07/10/walgreen-hits-the-gas-on-growth-with-another-acquisition/#22f8de293ed8. For the closure of drugstore.com. see Taylor Soper, "Walgreens to shut down drugstore.com, 4 years after $429M acquisition", https://www.geekwire.com/2016/walgreens-shut-drugstore-com-4-years-429m-acquisition/ (accessed August 23, 2016).

[7] Some people get confused when computing a percentage return using time series data as we do here. They know to find the difference between two numbers – but which to divide it by? You should divide by the "older," or the earlier, number. That is, compute the percent change using the earlier number as the base: (newer number − older number)/older number. Or, in the case of our 2017 and 2018 data, compute [(2018 value − 2017 value)/2017 value].

The *net profit margin,* a widely used measure of firm profitability, is calculated as the firm's net income after taxes divided by net sales. In addition to considering operating expenses, this ratio indicates the ability to earn a return after meeting interest and tax obligations. Unlike its operating profit margin, Walgreens' net profit margin *rose* in 2018:

NET PROFIT MARGIN:
2018: (Net income/Net sales) = ($5,024/$103,444) = 3.82%
2017: ($4,078/$76,392) = 3.45%

Walgreens' net income rose more than 23% in the face of an 11% increase in sales, resulting in a higher net profit margin in 2018.

Three basic rate-of-return measures on assets and equity are important to the financial manager. The *operating return on assets* is computed as the earnings before interest and taxes (EBIT) divided by total assets. This ratio focuses on the firm's operating performance and ignores how the firm is financed and taxed. Relevant data for Walgreens must be taken from Tables 14.1 and 14.2.

OPERATING RETURN ON ASSETS:
2018: (Earnings before interest & taxes/Total assets) = ($6,223/$69,941) = 8.9%
2017: ($6,246/$66,009) = 9.5%

Walgreens' operating return on assets fell in 2018, consistent with the behavior of the operating profit margin, as the growth in assets was larger than the growth in operating income during the year.

The net return on total assets, commonly referred to as the *return on total assets,* is measured as the firm's net income divided by total assets. Here, we measure the return on investment in assets after a firm has covered its operating expenses, interest costs, and tax obligations. Similar to the net profit margin, Walgreens' return on total assets rose in 2018 as net income rose over 23% from its 2017 level while assets grew by about 6%:

RETURN ON TOTAL ASSETS:
2018: (Net income/Total assets) = ($5,024/$69,941) = 7.2%
2014: ($4,078/$66,009) = 6.2%

Recall how Walgreens leases many of its stores. This reduces its financing needs and reduces its level of fixed and total assets. In turn, this can help to increase asset-based profitability ratios, such as the return on total assets, if indeed the firm is profitable.

A final profitability ratio is the *return on equity* (ROE). It measures the return that shareholders earned on their equity invested in the firm. The ROE is measured as the firm's net income divided by stockholders' equity. This ratio reflects the fact that a portion of a firm's total assets is financed with borrowed funds. Walgreens' ROE rose in 2015:

RETURN ON EQUITY:
2015: (Net income/Common equity) = ($4,255/$30,861) = 19.1%
2017: ($2,031/$20,457) = 14.4%

Figure 14.4 presents several Walgreens, and CVS's profitability ratios. We see for the first half of the time frame, Walgreens' net profit margin was, generally, higher and more stable than that of CVS but since the Great Recession Walgreens' net profit margin has become more volatile and sometimes is lower than that of CVS until 2018, when CVS' profitability fell sharply. Return on assets (ROA) shows similar behavior. It appears to be on a downward trend since the beginning of the Great Recession until 2018. ROE shows similar variability in recent years. Overall, these profit ratio trends indicate, until 2018, that Walgreens is becoming more like CVS in terms of its level of profitability relative to sales, assets, and equity. CVS' acquisition of Aetna, a health insurer, in 2018 may have a short-term impact on its profitability.

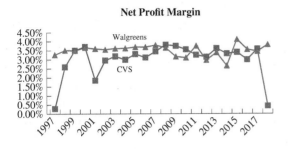

Net Profit Margin

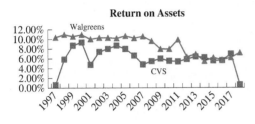

Return on Assets

Return on Equity

FIGURE 14.4 Profitability ratios for Walgreens versus CVS

14.6 MARKET VALUE RATIOS AND ANALYSIS

The **market value ratios** indicate the willingness of investors to value a firm in the marketplace relative to financial statement values. A firm's profitability, risk, quality of management, and many other factors are reflected in its stock and security prices by the efficient financial markets. Financial statements are historical in nature; the financial markets are forward-looking.[8] We know that stock prices seem to reflect much of the known information about a company and are fairly good indicators of a company's true value. Hence, market value ratios indicate the market's assessment of the value of the firm's securities.

The *price-earnings*, or *P/E*, *ratio* is the market price of the firm's common stock divided by its annual earnings per share (EPS). Sometimes called the *earnings multiple*, the P/E ratio shows how much investors are willing to pay for each dollar of the firm's EPS. Earnings per share come from the income statement, so it is sensitive to the many factors that affect net income. Although EPS cannot reflect the value of patents or assets, the firm's human resources, culture, quality of management, or risk, stock prices can and do reflect all these factors. A comparison of a firm's P/E ratio to that of the stock market as a whole, or to those of the firm's competitors, indicates the market's perception of the true value of the company.

The *price-to-book-value ratio* (or price/book ratio) measures the market's value of the firm relative to balance sheet equity. The book value of equity is the difference between the book values of assets and liabilities appearing on the balance sheet.[9] The price-to-book-value ratio is the market price per share divided by the book value of equity per share. A higher ratio suggests that investors are more optimistic about the market value of a firm's assets, its intangible assets, and its managers' abilities.

Figure 14.5 shows levels and trends in the P/E ratio and price/book ratio for Walgreens and CVS. The P/E for both firms generally declined from 2000 through the 2008–2009 Great Recession but then

market value ratios indicate the willingness of investors to value a firm in the marketplace relative to financial statement values

---

[8] Recall from Chapter 10 that stock prices are in part based upon investors' *expectations* of *future* dividend growth.

[9] Typically, it is equal to stockholders' equity.

FIGURE 14.5 Market value ratios for Walgreens versus CVS

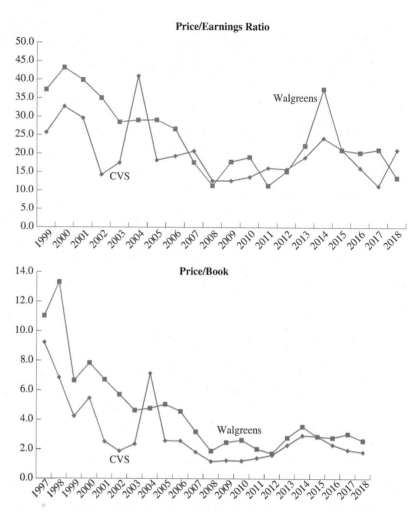

began to rise and stabilize a bit. At times the market gives a higher earnings multiple to Walgreens and at times a higher earnings multiple to CVS. The sharp rise in Walgreens' P/E in 2014 may have been due to optimism about the merger with Boots Alliance; its P/E decline in 2015 indicates the hoped-for synergies and profits may take longer to achieve than first expected. The price/book ratio shows a similar pattern but with Walgreens' ratio usually greater than CVS's ratio. The market appears to be less optimistic about both firms than it was fifteen or so years ago.

ETHICAL Financial managers and analysts often talk about the quality of a firm's earnings or the quality of its balance sheet. This has nothing to do with the size of a firm's earnings or assets or who audited the financial statements. Quality financial statements are those that reflect the firm's true economic condition. In other words, various accounting practices were not used to inflate the firm's earnings or assets to make the firm look stronger than it is. Thus, for a quality income statement, the firm's sales revenues are likely to be repeated in the future. Earnings are not affected by one-time charges. A quality balance sheet will represent inventory that is marketable and not out of fashion or technologically obsolete. It will represent limited debt, indicating the firm could easily borrow money should the need arise. The firm's assets will have market values that exceed the accounting book values; in other words, intangible assets (such as goodwill or patents) will not inflate the firm's assets. All else constant, a firm with higher quality financial statements will have higher market value ratios. This occurs as the market will recognize and reward the economic reality of a firm's earnings and assets that are not temporarily bloated by accounting gimmicks.

Attempts to play accounting tricks will affect the firm's ratios. Overstating existing inventory can have the effect of making the current cost of goods sold appear lower, thus inflating profits. Booking revenue in advance of true sales to customers will inflate sales and profits. The effect of such actions

SMALL BUSINESS PRACTICE

WHY DO BUSINESSES FAIL?

The Dun & Bradstreet Company (D&B) reports that, on average, over 60,000 businesses fail each year. The U.S. Department of Labor estimates that business terminations generally exceed 800,000 per year. Thus, many firms cease to exist for reasons other than bankruptcy. Businesses are merged with other firms, are sold to others, or have shut down their operations.

The U.S. Small Business Administration (SBA), in its annual report titled "The Facts about Small Business," finds that nearly one-fourth of all firms are dissolved in fewer than two years after starting operation. Over one-half of new businesses cease operating within four years of operation. Approximately 70% of all new businesses don't exist after eight years of operation.

A study of business failures by the SBA found that nearly one-half of the failures were associated with economic factors, such as inadequate sales or a lack of profits. Of the failures that do not cite economic factors, nearly 40% (or about 20% of total failures) are attributed to inadequate financial capital or too much debt. Other reasons include inadequate business or management experience, business or family conflicts, disasters, and fraud. From these findings, it is apparent that having adequate business, management, and financial education are important factors in determining whether a business venture will succeed.

---

will be to increase profitability and asset management ratios. Unfortunately, watching for accounting tricks or outright fraud is necessary for investors, as episodes have shown in recent years with companies in different industries, such as telecommunications equipment (Lucent), dot-com firms (many), and energy trading (Enron).[10]

14.6.1 SUMMARY OF RATIO ANALYSIS FOR WALGREENS

Let's review and summarize what we've learned about Walgreens by computing its ratios and comparing them to the industry averages. The liquidity ratios show consistency over time, but the gap between Walgreens and CVS has recently increased as CVS's liquidity ratios rose while Walgreens fell while Walgreens is taking longer to pay suppliers. But the asset management ratios show Walgreens' advantage in total asset turnover and collection period has declined over time while CVS has superior fixed asset turnover and typically has higher inventory turnover.

Should Walgreens need to raise money quickly, it should be able to issue debt, as Walgreens' debt ratios are similar to CVS and its interest coverage is large as it shuns interest-bearing debt. Walgreens used to have higher profitability ratios than CVS but these have declined until 2017.

The stock market has recognized Walgreens' trends, so now its market value ratios (price-earnings, market/book) are similar to those of CVS. Further analysis is needed to determine if Walgreens' fortunes will continue and how the CVS/Aetna merger will affect CVS' financials going forward. Will Walgreens' strategy lead to better success in the future than the CVS strategy? Stock analysts will need to make that determination before they recommend which company's stock that investors should purchase. Future financial statements and market value ratios will show who is right!

How does a supermarket generate profits? In general, supermarkets have low profit margins. Many of its goods are sold for pennies above cost. Profits are generated by rapid turnover. The shelves are restocked daily with new items to take the place of purchased items. Thus, supermarkets, generally, have high asset turnover ratios. Jewelry stores generate their profits differently. They typically have high profit margins but with low turnover. Jewelry items may sit on the shelf for months at a time until they are sold.

| 14.7 DUPONT METHOD OF RATIO ANALYSIS |

---

[10] Jonathan Weil, John Emshwiller, and Scot J. Paltrow, "Arthur Andersen Says it Disposed of Documents That Related to Enron," *The Wall Street Journal*, (January 11, 2002), pp. A1, A4; Dennis K. Berman and Rebecca Blumenstein, "Behind Lucent's Woes: All-Out Revenue Goal and Pressure to Meet It," *The Wall Street Journal*, (March 29, 2001), pp. A1, A8; Jonathan Weil, "'Going Concerns': Did Accountants Fail to Flag Problems at Dot-Com Casualties?" *The Wall Street Journal*, (February 9, 2001), pp. C1, C2.

This indicates that a firm can generate a return on its assets with two basic strategies: it can offer low prices and low profit margins, seeking high sales volumes on commodity products, as a supermarket does; or it can sell its quality or differentiated goods at high prices and rely on high profit margins to generate returns on low sales, the way a jewelry store does.

The return on total assets ratio can be used to examine this relationship and to determine how a given firm generates profits. The return on assets (ROA) can be broken into two components. It equals the product of the net profit margin and total asset turnover ratio:

$$\text{Return on total assets} = \text{Net profit margin} \times \text{Total asset turnover}$$
$$\left(\text{Net income} / \text{Assets}\right) = \left(\text{Net income} / \text{Sales}\right) \times \left(\text{Sales} / \text{Total assets}\right)$$

A supermarket's profit margin may be 1%, but its total asset turnover may be 10. This would give it a return on total assets of 1% × 10, or 10%. A jewelry store may have a 25% profit margin and have a total asset turnover of 0.40, also giving it a return on total assets of 10% (25% × 0.40). Yearly variations in a firm's return on total assets can be explained by changes in its profit margin, total asset turnover, or both.

Like the return on total assets, return on equity (ROE) can be broken down into component parts to tell us why the level of return changes from year to year or why the ROEs of two firms differ. The ROE is identical to return on assets multiplied by the equity multiplier:

$$\left(\text{Net income} / \text{Equity}\right) = \left(\text{Net income} / \text{Total assets}\right) \times \left(\text{Total assets} / \text{Equity}\right)$$

We saw how the return on total assets is made up of two other ratios, so ROE can be expanded to the following:

$$\text{Return on equity} = \text{Net profit margin} \times \text{Total asset turnover} \times \text{Equity multiplier}$$
$$\left(\text{Net income} / \text{Equity}\right) = \left(\text{Net income} / \text{Sales}\right) \times \left(\text{Sales} / \text{Total assets}\right) \times \left(\text{Total assets} / \text{Equity}\right)$$

Thus, a firm's ROE may differ from one year to the next or from a competitor's ROE as a result of differences in net profit margin, total asset turnover, or leverage. Unlike the other measures of profitability, ROE directly reflects a firm's use of leverage, or debt. If a firm uses relatively more liabilities to finance assets, the equity multiplier will rise, and, holding other factors constant, the firm's ROE will increase. This leveraging of a firm's ROE does not imply greater operating efficiency, only a greater use of debt financing.

DuPont analysis technique of breaking return on total assets and return on equity into their component parts

This technique of breaking return on assets and return on equity into their component parts is called **DuPont analysis**, named after the company that popularized it. Figure 14.6 illustrates how DuPont analysis can break down ROE and return on total assets into different components (profit margin, total asset turnover, and equity multiplier) and how these components can, in turn, be broken into their constituent parts for analysis. Thus, an indication that a firm's ROE has increased as a result of higher turnover can lead to study of the turnover ratio, using data from several years, to determine if the increase has resulted from higher sales volume, better management of assets, or some combination of the two.

Table 14.3 illustrates the use of DuPont analysis to explain the changes in Walgreens' return on equity (ROE) during the period 2015–2018. ROE was stable from 2015 to 2016 although the DuPont components changed: net profit margin declined, but this was offset by increases in asset turnover and leverage. ROE rose in 2017, because of an increase in total asset turnover (as profitability and leverage both fell). In 2018, all three components of ROE rose, resulting in an increase of over 30% in return on equity.

Managers and analysts prefer to see increases in the return on equity (ROE) arising from increased profitability or increased asset efficiency. Increases in ROE solely due to rising debt levels (i.e., a rising equity multiplier) are generally not viewed favorably.

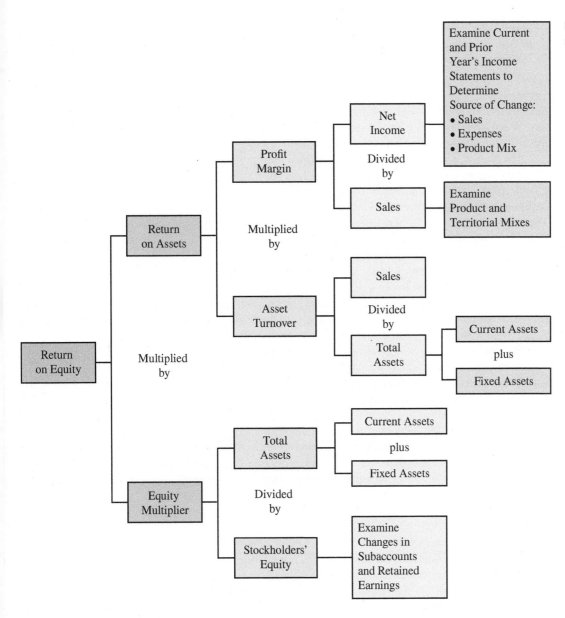

FIGURE 14.6 The DuPont system of financial analysis

Table 14.3 DuPont Analysis of Walgreens

	Net Profit Margin: Net Income / Sales	×	Total Asset Turnover: Sales / Total Assets	×	Equity Multiplier: Total Assets / Equity	=	Return On Equity: Net Income[*] / Equity
2015	4.11%	×	1.50	×	2.23	=	13.79%
2016	3.56%	×	1.61	×	2.40	=	13.78%
2017	3.45%	×	1.79	×	2.33	=	14.42%
2018	3.82%	×	1.88	×	2.66	=	19.13%

* Return on equity is as reported in the text by computing net income divided by stockholders' equity. The product of the three components may not equal this number exactly because of rounding.

> **DISCUSSION QUESTION 3**
>
> Besides profitability, can you develop a DuPont-type analysis that breaks a ratio into two or more components? Explain how your analysis can be used.

14.8 LONG-TERM FINANCIAL PLANNING

Financial ratios and financial statement relationships can be used to analyze firms and their competitors, as we have seen. They have a second important practical use; managers can use them to assist in the firm's financial planning process.

To plan, it is necessary to look forward. We have perfect hindsight, but foresight is what determines the success of a business. Long-range plans covering several years must be prepared to project growth in sales, assets, and employees. First, a sales forecast needs to be made that includes expected developments in the economy and that reflects possible competitive pressures from other businesses. The sales forecast must be supported by plans for an adequate investment in assets. For example, a manufacturing firm may need to invest in plant and equipment to produce an inventory that will fill forecasted sales orders. After determining the size of the necessary investment, plans must be made for estimating the amount of financing needed and for acquiring it. Adequate investment in human resources must be planned for as well.

In addition to long-range financial plans, or budgets, the financial manager is concerned with near-term cash inflows and outflows associated with the business. Cash flows are often monitored on a daily basis for large firms, while small firms may make only monthly cash budgets.

Financial analysis using ratios goes hand in hand with successful financial planning. An established firm should conduct a financial ratio analysis of past performance to aid in developing realistic future plans. The new firm should analyze the performance characteristics of other firms in the same industry before making plans.

In the remainder of this chapter, we focus on long-term financial planning techniques. The first, the percentage of sales technique, will illustrate how a sales forecast and knowledge of the firm's balance sheet and income statement can be used to estimate the firm's long-term asset and financing needs. The second, cost–volume–profit analysis, reviews a method a firm can use to determine the profitability of different sales levels and how many product units it needs to sell in order to turn a profit.

14.8.1 PERCENTAGE OF SALES TECHNIQUE

budgets financial plans indicating expected revenues, spending, and investment needs

Financial planning begins with a sales forecast for one or more years. These sales forecasts are the basis for written financial plans referred to as **budgets**. For established firms, sales forecasts are usually based on historical sales data that are used in statistical analyses to project into the future. Adjustments may be made to reflect possible changes in sales growth due to expected economic conditions, new products, and so forth. For example, a firm's sales may have been growing at a 10% average annual rate in the past. However, if a recession is anticipated, management might forecast a 0% growth rate for the next year. In contrast, a booming economic climate might be associated with a 15% annual growth rate. New firms without sales histories have to rely on information from the experiences of other firms in their industry. Accurate sales forecasting is an essential element of successful financial management. The percent-of-sales method uses the historical or anticipated relationship between sales revenue and balance sheet items to forecast additional asset investment requirements and how they will be financed. Suppose a firm has a total asset turnover ratio of 3.0 with sales of $60,000 and total assets of $20,000. By taking the inverse of this ratio, total assets divided by net sales, we can express assets as a percent of sales, which would be about 33% ($20,000/$60,000). This number can be used to help forecast future asset needs. For example, if our sample firm forecasts a 15% increase in sales ($60,000 × 15% = $9,000 sales increase), this would result in an anticipated new asset investment of about $3,000 (i.e., $9,000 × 33%) since additional assets will be required to produce, generate, and support the increase in sales.

Table 14.4 shows, for Walgreens, each major balance sheet item expressed as a percent of sales over the time period 2015–2018, as well as the average percentage during this time frame.[11] We will

---

[11] This is not the same as the common-size balance sheet from Chapter 13. The common-size balance sheet divides each item by total assets; the percent-of-sales balance sheet divides each item by sales.

Table 14.4 Percent-of-Sales Balance Sheets for Walgreens 2015–2018

Assets	2015	2016	2017	2018	Average
Cash & Cash Equivalents	2.9%	8.4%	2.8%	0.7%	3.7%
Accounts Receivable	6.6%	5.3%	5.5%	5.4%	5.7%
Inventories	8.4%	7.6%	7.5%	8.3%	8.0%
Other Current Assets	1.1%	0.7%	0.9%	0.7%	0.9%
Total Current Assets	19.0%	22.1%	16.7%	15.3%	18.3%
Net Fixed Assets	14.6%	12.2%	11.5%	10.5%	12.2%
Other Long-Term Assets	17.1%	5.7%	5.8%	5.8%	8.6%
Goodwill & Intangibles	15.8%	22.0%	21.8%	21.6%	20.3%
TOTAL ASSETS	66.5%	61.9%	55.8%	53.2%	59.4%
LIABILITIES AND EQUITY					
Accounts Payable	9.8%	9.4%	10.6%	11.1%	10.2%
Short-Term Debt	1.0%	0.1%	0.0%	1.5%	0.7%
Other Current Liabilities	5.2%	3.7%	0.3%	0.5%	2.4%
Total Current Liabilities	16.0%	14.5%	15.7%	19.1%	16.3%
Long-Term Debt	12.9%	15.9%	10.7%	8.9%	12.1%
Other Liabilities	7.8%	6.0%	6.2%	5.8%	6.4%
TOTAL LIABILITIES	36.7%	36.1%	31.9%	33.2%	34.5%
Preferred Equity	0.0%	0.0%	0.0%	0.0%	0.0%
Common equity	0.0%	0.0%	0.0%	0.0%	0.0%
Common equity & Retained Earnings	29.8%	25.8%	23.9%	20.0%	24.9%
STOCKHOLDERS' EQUITY	29.8%	25.8%	23.9%	20.0%	24.9%
TOTAL LIABILITIES & EQUITY	66.5%	61.9%	55.8%	53.2%	59.4%

use the average percentage relationship in the discussion that follows to illustrate the percent-of-sales technique for Walgreens.

14.8.2 ASSET INVESTMENT REQUIREMENTS

In 2018, Walgreens' sales were $131,537 (in millions). Suppose management believes sales will grow 15% next year. What is the anticipated increase in assets needed to support this higher sales level? We can use the average percentages in Table 14.4 to determine changes in various balance sheet accounts. A 15% increase in sales means sales will rise by 0.15 × $131,537, or $19,730.55. Over the past four years, Walgreens' ratio of total assets to sales has averaged about 59%. The increase in Walgreens' assets is forecast to be this average ratio times the increase in sales, or 0.59 × $19,730.55 = $11,641.02.

Since the balance sheet must balance, this increase in assets must be financed by some combination of new debt issues, new equity issues, or an increase in retained earnings resulting from the forecasted sales. This latter type of financing is called "internally generated funds," because it results from the firm's profits.

14.8.2.1 Internally Generated Financing

Internally generated funds for financing new asset investments come from profits. Let's assume that for Walgreens the $11,641.02 asset investment scenario will be what is needed next year. We are ready to plan how these assets will be financed from anticipated profits or external sources. The average profit margin during 2015–2018, for Walgreens, was about 3.7%. If net sales were expected to rise by 15% next year, the sales forecast is 1.15 × $131,537 = $151,267.55.[12] Assuming this average profit margin

---

[12] This can be found by taking sales of $131,537 and adding to it the 15% increase we computed above: $131,537 + $15,517 = $151,267.55.

continues, we would forecast next year's profits to be $5,596.90 ($151,267.55 × 3.7%). Examining the dividend record in Walgreens' annual report, we learn that the firm, over the course of the business cycle, pays about 35% of earnings to shareholders as dividends; this means it retains 65% of net income to help finance firm growth. Thus, after paying dividends, we expect Walgreens to have $3,637.98 (65% of $5,596.90) in internally generated funds to finance the expected $11,641.02 expansion in assets. The remaining $8,003.04 ($11,641.02 − $3,637.98) in assets will need to be financed with external funds. These can be short-term debt, long-term debt, or equity funds. Let's consider how the financial manager might plan the mix of short- and long-term funds from external sources.

14.8.2.2 External Financing Requirements

Walgreens can expect that a portion of its asset financing requirements will be met by almost automatic increases in certain current liability accounts, such as accounts payable and accrued liabilities. To meet planned sales increases, more credit purchases of inventory items will be necessary to support the higher sales level. Increases would be expected in accrued wages and taxes. These automatic liability accounts reduce the need for other external financing since they allow the firm to acquire additional inputs without an immediate cash outlay. As they usually rise and fall along with sales, these current liability accounts provide a spontaneous, or automatic, source of financing.

Table 14.4 shows that accounts payable and the other current liability accounts have averaged about 16% of sales for Walgreens. Based on a 15% expected increase in sales, current liabilities are expected to rise and provide about $3,156.89 ($19,730.55 × 16%) in spontaneous short-term funds. This would leave an external financing need for Walgreens of about $4,846.15 ($8,003.04 − $3,156.89) to cover the asset investment requirements. Management might choose to borrow the amount from a commercial bank, issue long-term debt, or request more equity funds from the owners.

To summarize briefly, the amount of new external funds needed to finance asset additions can be calculated as follows:

1. Forecast the dollar amount of the expected sales increase:
   Sales expected to grow 15%: new sales = 1.15 × $131,537 = $151,267.55
   Dollar amount of sales increase = 15% × $131,537 = $19,730.55 (or $151,267.55 − $131,537)

2. Determine the dollar amount of new asset investment necessary to support the sales increase.
   Additional assets = 59% × $19,730.55 = $11,641.02

3. Subtract the expected amount of retained profits from the planned asset investment.
   Expected profit = 3.7% × $151,267.55 = $5,596.90
   Expected addition to retained earnings = 0.65 × $5,596.90 = $3,637.98

4. Subtract the amount of spontaneous increases expected in accounts payable and the other current liabilities from the planned asset investment.
   Expected spontaneous financing = 16% × $19,730.55 = $3,156.89

5. The remaining dollar amount of asset investments determines the external financing needs
   External financing need = Change in assets − addition to retained earnings − spontaneous financing = $11,641.02 − $3,637.98 − $3,156.89 = $4,846.15

The actual asset investment required to support a specific sales increase could be altered if either of two developments occurs: (1) if the asset turnover ratio changes or (2) certain fixed assets do not have to be increased.

First, if Walgreens could improve its asset turnover ratio so assets are 45% of sales, a $19,730.55 increase in sales would require an asset investment of about $19,730.55 × 0.45, or $8,878.75, or roughly $2,762 less than the earlier calculation. (Remember that all numbers are in terms of millions of dollars, so this represents $2,762 million [or $2.762 billion] less in needed investment.)

Second, fixed assets, such as land or buildings, might not have to be increased each year along with an increase in sales. The deciding factor usually is whether the firm currently has excess production capacity. For example, according to Table 14.4, if only current assets (which average about 18% of sales) are expected to increase with sales next year, then the asset investment requirements would be about \$3,551.50 (i.e., \$19,730.55 × 18%). In this case, the expected increase in retained earnings of \$3,637.98 would be sufficient to finance the expected rise in assets.

Cost–volume–profit analysis represents another tool used by managers for financial planning purposes. It can be used to estimate the firm's operating profits at different levels of unit sales. A variation, called **break-even analysis**, can be used to estimate how many units of a product must be sold for the firm to "break even" or have a zero operating profit.

14.9 COST–VOLUME–PROFIT ANALYSIS

cost–volume–profit analysis used by managers for financial planning to estimate the firm's operating profits at different levels of unit sales

break-even analysis used to estimate how many units of a product must be sold for the firm to break even or have a zero operating profit

As an example of cost–volume–profit analysis, let's assume that Walgreens is considering adding a new product to its stores. It will be sold for \$10 per item. The variable costs, in this case, the cost of purchasing the item from its manufacturer, will be \$6. Fixed costs, mostly various administrative overhead expenses of tracking inventory and dealing with the supplier, are expected to be \$1,000 annually. Management is interested in knowing what level of operating profit will occur if unit sales are 2,000 per year.

From the format of an income statement (e.g., Table 14.2), we know that sales revenues minus various costs gives us operating profit, or earnings before interest and taxes (EBIT). Sales can be expressed as unit price (P) multiplied by quantity sold (Q), or $P \times Q$. The costs can be expressed by variable cost per unit (vc) and fixed costs (FC). The variable cost per unit (vc) times the quantity sold (Q) gives us total variable cost: $vc \times Q$. Total fixed costs, FC, are constant; they are called "fixed" because they do not change with increases or decreases in output. Thus, we can find operating income as follows:

$$\text{EBIT} = \text{Sales} - \text{Total variable costs} - \text{Fixed costs}$$

In terms of our symbols, this becomes the following:

$$\text{EBIT} = (P \times Q) - (vc \times Q) - FC \tag{14.1}$$

For our new product example, we have the following:

$$\begin{aligned}\text{EBIT} &= (\$10 \times 2,000) - (\$6 \times 2,000) - \$1,000 \\ &= \$20,000 - \$12,000 - \$1,000 \\ &= \$20,000 - \$13,000 \\ &= \$7,000\end{aligned}$$

If sales reach 2,000 units per year, the firm expects an increase in operating profit of \$7,000.

Management may want to know how many units of the product will have to be sold to break even. That is, what volume needs to be reached so the amount of total revenues equals total costs (variable costs plus fixed costs). At this point, operating income or EBIT is zero. The break-even point in units can be calculated by setting equation (14.1) equal to zero:

$$\text{EBIT} = (P \times Q) - (vc \times Q) - FC = 0$$

The quantity of unit sales that solves this equation is the break-even quantity; we'll call this Q_{BE}. Solving this equation for the break-even quantity, we have the following:

$$Q_{BE} = \left[FC / (P - vc) \right] \tag{14.2}$$

Using data from the new product example, we have the following:

$$Q_{BE} = \left[\$1,000 / (\$10 - \$6) \right] = (\$1,000 / \$4) = 250 \text{ units}$$

FIGURE 14.7 Cost–volume–profit relationships

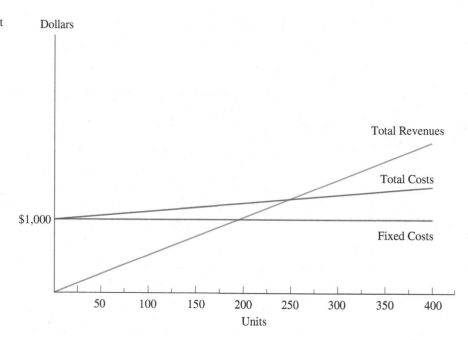

The firm must sell 250 units of the new product to break even.[13] This can be confirmed by substituting the relevant information in equation (14.1), as follows:

$$\text{EBIT} = \left(\$10 \times 250\right) - \left(\$6 \times 250\right) - \$1,000$$
$$= \$2,500 - \$1,500 - \$1,000$$
$$= \$2,500 - \$2,500$$
$$= 0$$

The break-even point in units, depicted graphically in Figure 14.7, occurs when total revenues equal total costs. The break-even point in sales dollars is equal to the selling price per unit times the break-even point in units. In our example, we have $10 times 250 units, or $2,500.

contribution margin contribution of each unit sold that goes toward paying fixed costs

The denominator of equation (14.2), $(P - vc)$, is called the contribution margin. It represents the contribution of each unit sold that goes toward paying the annual fixed costs. In our example, if $10 is the product's price, $6 of the revenue covers the unit's variable costs; the remainder, ($10 − $6) or $4, is the contribution toward paying the fixed costs. Since fixed costs are $1,000, the firm must sell $1,000/$4 units, or 250 units, before the fixed costs are covered.

14.10 DEGREE OF OPERATING LEVERAGE

A firm's sales revenues are rarely constant. The variability of sales, or revenues, over time indicates a basic operating business risk that must be considered when developing financial plans. In addition, changes in the amount of income shown on the income statement are affected by changes in sales and the use of fixed versus variable costs. As we'll see in this section, the greater the amount of fixed costs, the more variable will be operating profit.

The following portion of an income statement based on Walgreens data illustrates this point. Based on recent experience, we estimate variable costs, mainly Walgreens' cost of goods sold, to be about 77% of sales. Similarly, we assume Walgreens' selling, general, and administrative expenses are fixed as are depreciation expenses.

---

[13] As mentioned above, "break even" refers to zero operating profit. The firm may have negative net income if there are interest expenses. Recall that operating income, or EBIT, minus interest expense minus taxes equals net income.

	Current Situation
Net sales	$131,537
Less variable costs (about 77% of sales)	$100,745
Less fixed costs	$24,569
Earnings before interest and taxes	$6,223

Let's examine the impact of a 10% decrease and a 10% increase in next year's sales on the firm's operating income or earnings before interest and taxes (EBIT). The revised partial income statement would appear as follows:

	Percent Change in Sales		
	−10%	Base	10%
Net sales	$118,383.30	$131,537.00	$144,690.70
Less: variable costs (77% of sales)	$90,670.50	$100,745.00	$110,819.50
Less fixed costs	$24,569.00	$24,569.00	$24,569.00
Earnings before interest and taxes	$3,143.80	$6,223.00	$9,302.20
Percent change in operating income from the current level	−49.5%		49.5%

A 10% change in sales becomes magnified, or leveraged, into a 49.5% change in operating income. Operating income changes by such a large amount relative to the change in sales because some costs are fixed and do not change as revenues rise and fall. Increases in sales have a larger percentage impact on operating profit, as some costs do not change. Similarly, decreases in sales have a larger percentage reduction in operating profit as some costs are fixed and do not fall as sales fall.

The **degree of operating leverage (DOL)** measures the sensitivity of operating income to changes in the level of output:

> **degree of operating leverage (DOL)** measures the sensitivity of operating income to changes in the level of output

$$DOL = \text{percent change in EBIT} / \text{percent change in unit sales}$$

For Walgreens, the degree of operating leverage is the following:

$$DOL = \text{percent change in EBIT} / \text{percent change in unit sales} = 49.5\% / 10\% = 4.95$$

This is, if net sales increase by 10% next year, from $131,537 to $144,690.70, operating income is expected to rise from $6,223 to $9,302.20, a $3,079.20 or 49.5% increase. Thus, a 49.5% change in operating income divided by a 10% change in net sales produces a 4.95 magnification, or leverage effect. DOL also works in reverse and provides negative leverage when net sales decline. A 10% decline in sales volume becomes a 49.5% decline in operating income.

DOL can be represented by the following formula as well:

$$DOL = \frac{Q \times (P - vc)}{Q \times (P - vc) - FC} = \frac{\text{Sales} - \text{Total variable costs}}{\text{Sales} - \text{Total variable costs} - \text{Fixed costs}}$$

This relationship allows us to determine the degree of operating leverage with only one observation of sales, variable costs, and fixed costs. In the above example, the sales were $131,537 variable costs were $100,745; and fixed costs were $24,569. That means DOL equals the following:

$$DOL = \frac{\$131,537 - \$100,745}{\$131,537 - \$100,745 - \$24,569} = \frac{\$30,792}{\$6,223} = 4.95$$

This is the same result as when we used percentage changes in operating income and sales to estimate the DOL. A DOL of 4.95 means a 10% change in sales is expected to result in a 49.5% change in EBIT (i.e., 4.95 × 10%).

If we know a firm's DOL, we can estimate the effect of a change in sales on operating income. If the DOL is 4.95, a forecasted increase in sales of 5% is expected to increase operating income by (5% × 4.95) = 24.75%.

The operating leverage effect is solely due to the level of fixed costs. Suppose that Walgreens' fixed costs were lower; for example, $20,000. With sales of $131,537, variable costs of $100,745 and fixed costs of $20,000, EBIT will be $10,792:

	Current situation
Net sales	$131,537.00
Less: variable costs (77% of sales)	$100,745.00
Less fixed costs	$20,000.00
Earnings before interest and taxes	$10,792.00

The effect of this lower level of fixed costs and operating leverage on EBIT is, as follows:

	Percent change in sales		
	−10%	Base	10%
Net sales	$118,383.30	$131,537.00	$144,690.70
Less: variable costs (77% of sales)	$90,670.50	$100,745.00	$110,819.50
Less fixed costs	$20,000.00	$20,000.00	$20,000.00
Earnings before interest and taxes	$7,712.80	$10,792.00	$13,871.20
Percent change in operating income from the current level	−28.5%		28.5%

A 10% change in sales becomes magnified, or leveraged, into a 28.5% change in operating income. With the decrease to $20,000 in fixed costs, the degree of operating leverage (DOL) is 28.5%/10%, or 2.85%.

The magnification, or leverage, effect is solely due to the level of fixed costs. A higher level of fixed costs results in a higher level of operating leverage. This makes operating income more sensitive to changes in sales volume. Sophisticated financial planning models take into consideration the impact of operating leverage when projecting the next year's income.

APPLYING FINANCE TO. . .

• **Institutions and Markets** If a firm has strong financials, it is easier for it to sell securities through an investment bank or obtain loans from banks, insurance companies, and other lenders. Financial statement analysis is an important part of the capital allocation process to determine the likelihood of repayment of borrowed funds.

Several different types of ratios discussed in this chapter may appear in bond or loan covenants, particularly those dealing with liquidity and debt.

• **Investments** The economy, characteristics of the firm's industry, and competitive influences on the firm are reflected in financial statements and how analysts examine them. A firm's strategy and its success or failure, as well as the firm's strengths and weaknesses, will become evident in financial statement analysis. This information will help you determine if you should invest, not invest, or sell your investment in a firm's securities. Shareholders (owners) and bondholders (lenders) each have different concerns and focuses when examining financial ratios.

• **Financial Management** Financial statements show managers how the firm is progressing toward its goals. Some managers may want to "manage earnings" to reduce earnings variability and to hit earnings targets to satisfy investor expectations.

Managers know investors and other market participants will closely examine and analyze the firm's financials.

Managers' discussions of new strategies and initiatives need to be reflected in a better financial ratio compared to the firm's competitors. Micro data, not available to the public, on specific product and market performance, will assist managerial decision making.

LO 14.1 Financial statements, introduced in Chapter 13, are useful only if managers and financial analysts know how to use them. The focus of this chapter has been on the practical application of financial statements for analysis and financial forecasting. The information in financial statements can be examined by using various financial ratios. The ratios control for size differences between firms or for firm growth over time. By examining one firm's ratios over time, or in conjunction with an industry average, managers and analysts can pinpoint areas of strength and weakness in their firm and in their competitors.

LO 14.2 Liquidity ratios are useful in determining the ability of a firm to pay its short-term obligations. Liquidity ratios include the current ratio, quick ratio, and average payment period. Generally, higher liquidity ratios are better than lower, but excessive liquidity levels (or long payment periods) can be harmful for future profitability as current assets must be financed and lengthy payment periods can harm relations with suppliers.

LO 14.3 Asset management ratios measure how efficiently the firm's assets are used. Asset management ratios include the total asset turnover, fixed asset turnover, average collection period, and inventory turnover. Generally, higher turnover ratios (and lower collection periods) are positive signs but, as with most ratios, a value that is "too good" may indicate a problem. For example, fixed asset turnover ratios can rise simply from not replacing depreciating assets over time. As net fixed assets shrink because of depreciation, fixed asset turnover can rise.

LO 14.4 Financial leverage ratios provide information on the firm's use of debt to finance its assets. Excessive debt is not wanted due to high interest costs and the potential for bankruptcy if debts are not paid in a timely manner. But as we'll see in a later chapter (Chapter 18), low debt ratios indicate the firm's overall financing costs (debt and equity) may be higher than necessary. So once again, we look for "Goldilocks" ratios – not too high, which may indicate a problem, and not too low, which may indicate other issues.

LO 14.5 Profitability ratios measure the ability of a firm to earn a return on its sales, assets, and equity. Some analysts prefer to use operating profits (EBIT) as they are not affected by a firm's financing decisions and tax situation. Others prefer ratios that use the firm's "bottom line," its net income, to measure profitability. Using net income, the net profit margin measures how many pennies are earned on each dollar of revenue. Other popular measures include return on assets and return on equity.

LO 14.6 Analysts and managers also use market-based ratios to see how the financial marketplace evaluates the firm and its peers. Financial market values should be forward-looking, whereas accounting quantities are historical in nature, measuring what happened in the past. These ratios divide the stock market's price per share by a quantity such as earnings per share (P/E ratio or earnings multiple) or book value per share (price/book ratio).

LO 14.7 Changes in a ratio over time are caused by relative changes in the ratio's numerator and denominator and their components. Financial analysis does not stop with the calculation of a ratio. Changes in ratios over time or difference in ratios between firms should be explained. DuPont analysis is one tool for examining return on assets (ROA) or return on equity (ROE). Changes in the ROA occur because of changes in the profit margin and/or total asset turnover. Changes in ROE occur because of changes in the profit margin, total asset turnover, financial leverage, or some combination of these. DuPont analysis is valuable for helping to answer the question "Why?" a profitability measure rose or fell from one period to the next or relative to a competitor.

LO 14.8 Financial planning uses the financial statement relationships to estimate future asset and financing needs. The percent-of-sales methods use the relationship between balance sheet accounts and sales to estimate future asset needs. Combining a sales forecast, profit margin, and dividend policy, managers can estimate the increase in retained earnings that will provide internally generated financing. The difference between the forecasted increase in assets and the internally generated financing (such as additions to retained earnings and spontaneous current liability growth) equals the external financing the firm needs to plan to raise.

LO 14.9 Cost–volume–profit indicates how profits rise with quantity sold. Operating income equals sales revenue minus total variable costs minus fixed costs. Profits can be estimated given a sales forecast. In addition, the break-even quantity can be measured using product price, variable cost per unit, and fixed costs. As the name implies, the break-even quantity measures how much product must be sold before revenues are high enough to cover its production costs and fixed business costs.

LO 14.10 Operating income (EBIT) is affected by sales, variable costs, and fixed costs. If fixed costs change, the firm's break-even quantity will change. In addition, the firm's degree of operating leverage – computed using revenue, variable costs and fixed costs – shows the percentage change in operating income that is expected from a 1 percentage change in sales. For example, if DOL equals 5, a 1% increase (decrease) in sales is expected to result in a 5% increase (decrease) in EBIT. A firm's DOL will be higher if its fixed costs are higher (and, therefore, will have more volatile operating earnings if sales change). A lower level of fixed costs reduces a firm's degree of operating leverage, making earnings less volatile in the face of changes sales.

KEY TERMS

asset management ratios	cross-sectional analysis	industry comparative analysis	leverage ratio analysis
break-even analysis	ratio analysis	liquidity ratios	sinking fund payments
budgets	degree of operating leverage (DOL)	market value ratios	trend analysis (time series analysis)
contribution margin	DuPont analysis	net working capital	
cost–volume–profit analysis	financial leverage ratios	profitability ratios	

REVIEW QUESTIONS

1. **(LO14.1)** List some reasons why financial statement analysis is conducted. Identify some of the participants that analyze firms' financial statements.

2. **(LO14.1)** What is ratio analysis? Briefly describe the three basic categories or ways that ratio analysis is used.

3. **(LO14.1)** Identify the types of ratios that are used to analyze a firm's financial performance based on its income statements and balance sheets.

4. **(LO14.1)** Which type or category of ratios relates stock market information to financial statement items?

5. **(LO14.2)** What do liquidity ratios indicate? Identify some basic liquidity ratios.

6. **(LO14.3)** What do asset management ratios indicate? Identify some basic asset management ratios.

7. **(LO14.4)** What do financial leverage ratios indicate? Identify some measures of financial leverage.

8. **(LO14.5)** What do profitability ratios indicate? Identify some measures of profitability.

9. **(LO14.6)** What do market value ratios indicate? Identify some market value ratios.

10. **(LO14.7)** Describe the DuPont method, or system, of ratio analysis. What are the two major components of the system?

11. **(LO14.7)** How is the DuPont system related to both the balance sheet and the income statement?

12. **(LO14.8)** How is the process of financial planning used to estimate asset investment requirements?

13. **(LO14.8)** Explain how internally generated funds are used to reduce the need for external financing to fund asset investments.

14. **(LO14.8)** Explain how financial planning is used to determine a firm's external financing requirements.

15. **(LO14.9)** What is cost–volume–profit analysis? How can a firm use it?

16. **(LO14.9)** What is the purpose of knowing the break-even point?

17. **(LO14.9)** What will happen to the break-even point if the contribution margin rises (falls)?

18. **(LO14.10)** What does a firm's degree of operating leverage (DOL) indicate?

19. **(LO14.10)** Describe what would happen to the DOL if all costs were fixed? Variable?

1. The Robinson Company has the following current assets and current liabilities for these two years:

	2019	2020
Cash and marketable securities	$50,000	$50,000
Accounts receivable	300,000	350,000
Inventories	350,000	500,000
Total current assets	$700,000	$900,000
Accounts payable	$200,000	$250,000
Bank loan	0	$150,000
Accruals	$150,000	$200,000
Total current liabilities	$350,000	$600,000

a. Compare the current ratios between the two years.
b. Compare the acid test ratios between 2019 and 2020. Comment on your findings.

2. The Robinson Company had a cost of goods sold of $1,000,000 in 2019 and $1,200,000 in 2020.
a. Calculate the inventory turnover for each year. Comment on your findings.
b. What would have been the amount of inventories in 2020 if the 2019 turnover ratio had been maintained?

3. The Dayco Manufacturing Company had the following financial statement results for last year. Net sales were $1.2 million with net income of $90,000. Total assets at year-end amounted to $900,000.
a. Calculate Dayco's asset turnover ratio and its profit margin.
b. Show how the two ratios in Part (a) can be used to determine Dayco's rate of return on assets.
c. Dayco operation's industry average ratios are, as follows: Return on assets: 11%; Asset turnover: 2.5 times; Net profit margin: 3.6% Compare Dayco's performance against the industry averages.

4. Next year, Allgreens expects its sales to reach $33,000 with an investment in total assets of $10,750. Net income of $1,225 is anticipated. This year, sales were $30,000, total assets were $9,900, and net income was $1,000. Last year, these figures were $28,000, $9,000, and $750, respectively.
a. Use the DuPont system to compare Allgreens' anticipated performance against its prior year results. Comment on your findings.
b. How would Allgreens compare with the industry if it operates in the same industry as Dayco (see Problem 3) and if the industry average ratios remain the same over time?

5. Following are selected financial data in $ thousands for the Hunter Corporation:

	2020	2019
Current assets	$500	$400
Fixed assets, net	700	600
Total assets	1,200	1,000
Current liabilities	300	200
Long-term debt	200	200
Common equity	700	600
Total liabilities and equity	$1,200	$1,000
Net sales	$1,500	$1,200
Total expenses	−1,390	−1,100
Net income	110	100

a. Calculate Hunter's rate of return on total assets in 2020 and in 2019. Did the ratio improve or worsen?
b. Diagram the expanded DuPont system for Hunter for 2020. Insert the appropriate dollar amounts wherever possible.
c. Use the DuPont system to calculate the return on assets for the two years, and determine why they changed.

6. Following are financial statements for the Genatron Manufacturing Corporation for 2020 and 2019.

Genatron Manufacturing Corporation

Balance sheet	2020	2019
ASSETS		
Cash	$40,000	$50,000
Accts. receivable	260,000	200,000
Inventory	500,000	450,000
Total current assets	800,000	700,000
Fixed assets, net	400,000	300,000
Total assets	$1,200,000	$1,000,000
LIABILITIES AND EQUITY		
Accts. payable	$170,000	$130,000
Bank loan	90,000	90,000
Accruals	70,000	50,000
Total current liabilities	330,000	270,000
Long-term debt, 12%	400,000	300,000
Common stock, $10 par	300,000	300,000
Capital surplus	50,000	50,000
Retained earnings	120,000	80,000
Total liabilities & equity	$1,200,000	$1,000,000

Income statement	2020	2019
Net sales	$1,500,000	$1,300,000
Cost of goods sold	900,000	780,000
Gross profit	600,000	520,000
Expenses: general and administrative	150,000	150,000
Marketing	150,000	130,000
Depreciation	53,000	40,000
Interest	57,000	45,000
Earnings before taxes	190,000	155,000
Income taxes	76,000	62,000
Net income	$114,000	$93,000

a. Apply DuPont analysis to the 2020 and 2019 financial statements data.

b. Explain how financial performance differed between 2020 and 2019.

7. This problem uses the financial statements for the Genatron Manufacturing Corporation for the years 2020 and 2019 from Problem 6.

a. Calculate Genatron's dollar amount of net working capital in each year.

b. Calculate the current ratio and the acid test ratio in each year.

c. Calculate the average collection period and the inventory turnover ratio in each year.

d. What changes in the management of Genatron's current assets seem to have occurred between the two years?

8. Genatron Manufacturing expects its sales to increase by 10% in 2021. Estimate the firm's external financing needs by using the percent-of-sales method for the 2020 data. Assume that no excess capacity exists and that one-half of the 2021 net income will be retained in the business.

9. Rework Problem 8 assuming that Genatron Manufacturing expects its sales to increase by 20% in 2021. What is the amount of external financing needed?

10. Genatron wants to estimate what will happen to its income before interest and taxes if its net sales change from the 2020 level of $1,500,000. Refer to Genatron's 2020 income statement, shown in Problem 6, where the income before interest and taxes is $247,000 (EBT of $190,000 plus interest of $57,000). Assume that the cost of goods sold are variable expenses and that the other operating expenses are fixed.

a. Calculate the expected amount of income before interest and taxes for a 10% decrease and for a 10% increase in net sales for next year.

b. Determine the percentage change in income before interest and taxes given your calculations in Part a, and determine the degree of operating leverage.

11. **Challenge Problem.** Using the information in Tables 14.1 and 14.2, compute the financial ratios we discussed in this chapter for Walgreens using the 2015 and 2016 data.

12. **Challenge Problem.** Below are financial statements for Eastnorth Manufacturing. After computing the ratios we discussed in this chapter, discuss strong and weak points of Eastnorth's performance.

December 31	2020	2019	2018
ASSETS			
Cash and marketable securities	$25,000	$20,000	$16,000
Accounts receivable	100,000	80,000	56,000
Inventories	125,000	100,000	80,000
Total current assets	250,000	200,000	152,000
Gross plant and equipment	300,000	225,000	200,000
Less: accumulated depreciation	−100,000	−75,000	−50,000
Net plant and equipment	200,000	150,000	150,000
Land	50,000	50,000	50,000
Total fixed assets	250,000	200,000	200,000
Total assets	$500,000	$400,000	$352,000
LIABILITIES AND EQUITY			
Accounts payable	$78,000	$65,000	$58,000
Notes payable	34,000	10,000	10,000

December 31	2020	2019	2018
Accrued liabilities	30,000	25,000	25,000
Total current liabilities	142,000	100,000	93,000
Long-term debt	140,000	100,000	71,000
Total liabilities	$282,000	$200,000	$164,000
Common stock ($1 par, 50,000 shares)	$50,000	$50,000	$50,000
Paid-in capital	100,000	100,000	100,000
Retained earnings	68,000	50,000	38,000
Total stockholders' equity	218,000	200,000	188,000
Total liabilities and equity	$500,000	$400,000	$352,000

Years ended December 31	2020	2019	2018
Net revenues or sales	$700,000	$600,000	$540,000
Cost of goods sold	450,000	375,000	338,000
Gross profit	250,000	225,000	202,000
Operating expenses:			
General and administrative	95,000	95,000	95,000
Selling and marketing	56,000	50,000	45,000
Depreciation	25,000	20,000	15,000
Operating income	74,000	60,000	47,000
Interest	14,000	10,000	7,000
Income before taxes	60,000	50,000	40,000
Income taxes (40%)	24,000	20,000	16,000
Net income	$36,000	$30,000	$24,000
Number of shares outstanding	50,000	50,000	50,000
Earnings per share	$0.72	$0.60	$0.48

13. Following are the consolidated financial statements for Eastnorth Manufacturing's industry. Use DuPont analysis on the industry financial statements to determine why industry return on equity (ROE) changed from year to year.
Balance Sheets for INDUSTRY:

December 31	2020	2019	2018
ASSETS			
Cash and marketable securities	$30,000	$25,000	$20,000
Accounts receivable	110,000	90,000	60,000
Inventories	100,000	80,000	80,000
Total current assets	240,000	195,000	160,000
Gross plant and equipment	250,000	220,000	200,000
Less: accumulated depreciation	−100,000	−65,000	−50,000
Net plant and equipment	150,000	155,000	150,000
Land	50,000	50,000	50,000
Total fixed assets	200,000	205,000	200,000
Total assets	$440,000	$400,000	$360,000
LIABILITIES AND EQUITY			
Accounts payable	$58,000	$50,000	$45,000
Notes payable	50,000	50,000	50,000

December 31	2020	2019	2018
Accrued liabilities	0	0	0
Total current liabilities	108,000	100,000	95,000
Long-term debt	32,000	20,000	15,000
Total liabilities	$140,000	$120,000	$110,000
Total stockholders' equity	300,000	280,000	250,000
Total liabilities and equity	$440,000	$400,000	$360,000

Income Statements for INDUSTRY:

Years ended December 31	2020	2019	2018
Net revenues or sales	$1,100,000	$1,000,000	$900,000
Cost of goods sold	700,000	650,000	600,000
Gross profit	$400,000	$350,000	$300,000
Operating expenses:			
General and administrative	143,000	135,000	130,000
Selling and marketing	88,000	80,000	70,000
Depreciation	44,000	40,000	36,000
Operating income	125,000	95,000	64,000
Interest	15,000	15,000	14,000
Income before taxes	110,000	80,000	50,000
Income taxes (40%)	44,000	32,000	20,000
Net income	$66,000	$48,000	$30,000

14. Compare the reasons for the changes in return on equity for Eastnorth Manufacturing and its industry.

15. **Challenge Problem.** Compute the financial ratios for Eastnorth Manufacturing's industry. Using Eastnorth's ratios from Problem 12, graph the firm's and industry ratios as we have done in this chapter. Analyze Eastnorth's performance in comparison to its industry.

16. **Challenge Problem.** Evaluate the performance of Johnson & Johnson in comparison to its industry.

Ratio	Johnson & Johnson		Industry	
	Year 1	Year 2	Year 1	Year 2
Current Ratio	1.62	1.57	1.54	1.68
Quick Ratio	0.80	0.78	1.01	1.01
Total Asset Turnover	1.15	1.00	0.86	0.90
Fixed Asset Turnover	2.01	1.75	2.59	3.27
Average Collection Period	53.65	60.33	67.13	75.62
Inventory Turnover	2.79	2.45	2.16	2.05
Total Debt to Total Assets	0.55	0.55	0.53	0.51
Equity Multiplier	2.20	2.20	2.13	2.02
Interest Coverage	19.51	14.86	16.90	14.40
Net Profit Margin	12.6%	12.7%	14.2%	14.2%
Return on Assets	14.6%	12.8%	12.2%	11.7%
Return on Equity	32.1%	28.2%	26.1%	25.8%
Price/Earnings	16.38	17.55	21.45	22.03
Price/Book	5.18	4.94	3.93	3.78

17. Associated Containers Company is planning to manufacture and sell plastic pencil holders. Direct labor and raw materials will be $2.28 per unit. Fixed costs are $15,300 and the expected selling price is $3.49 per unit.
    a. Determine the break-even point (where operating profit is zero) in units and dollars.
    b. How much profit or loss before interest and taxes will there be if 10,825 units are sold?
    c. What will the selling price per unit have to be if 13,650 units are sold in order to break even?
    d. How much will variable costs per unit have to be to break even if only 9,500 units are expected to be sold and the selling price is $3.49?

18. **Challenge Problem.** Graph the revenue and cost lines to estimate the break-even point for the following data. Compute the break-even point mathematically.
    a. price = $12.95; variable cost/unit = $6.89; fixed costs = $10,000
    b. price = $23, 995; variable cost/unit = $16,545; fixed costs = $40 million
    c. price = $249; variable cost/unit = $50; fixed costs = $800,000

19. This problem uses the two years of financial statements data provided in Problem 6 for the Genatron Manufacturing Corporation.
    a. Calculate and compare each current assets account as a percentage of total assets for that year.
    b. Calculate and compare each current liabilities account as a percentage of total liabilities and equities for that year.
    c. Calculate the current ratio and the acid test ratio for each year. Describe the changes in liquidity, if any, that occurred between the two years.

20. The Jackman Company had sales of $1,000,000 and net income of $50,000 last year. Sales are expected to increase by 20% next year. Selected year-end balance sheet items were the following:

Current assets	$400,000
Fixed assets	$500,000
Total assets	$900,000
Current liabilities	$200,000
Long-term debt	$200,000
Owners' equity	$500,000
Total liabilities and equity	$900,000

a. Express each balance sheet item as a percent of this year's sales.
b. Estimate the new asset investment requirement for next year, assuming no excess production capacity.
c. Estimate the amount of internally generated funds for next year, assuming all profits will be retained in the firm.
d. If all current liabilities are expected to change spontaneously with sales, what will be their dollar increase next year?
e. Estimate Jackman's external financing requirements for next year.

21. Using the data in the chapter, estimate Walgreens' external financing needs if a 20% growth rate is expected.

22. Using Eastnorth Manufacturing's financial statements in Problem 12, estimate its external financing needs if a 10% growth in sales is expected and the firm pays out one-half of its earnings as dividends.

23. Using the financial statements presented in Problem 12, determine Eastnorth Manufacturing's degree of operating leverage in each of the years presented. Assume the cost of goods sold is variable and all other costs are fixed.

24. Using your estimate for the degree of operating leverage for Eastnorth in 2020, estimate the level of operating income if the following year's sales rise by 5%, or if the following year's sales fall by 12%.

25. Using the financial statements presented in Problem 6, determine Genatron's degree of operating leverage in each of the years presented. Assume the cost of goods sold and marketing expenses are variable costs and all other costs are fixed.

26. Using your estimate for the degree of operating leverage for Genatron in 2020 from Problem 25, estimate the level of operating income if the following year's sales rise by 5% or the following year's sales fall by 12%.

CHAPTER 15

Managing Working Capital

LEARNING OBJECTIVES

After studying this chapter, you should be able to do the following:

LO 15.1 Summarize the importance of working capital to the firm.

LO 15.2 Explain what is meant by a firm's operating cycle and its cash conversion cycle.

LO 15.3 Describe the impact of the operating cycle and cash conversion cycle on the size of investment in accounts receivable and inventories and payables financing.

LO 15.4 Explain how a cash budget is developed and how a treasurer will use it.

LO 15.5 Describe the motives underlying the management of cash and marketable securities.

LO 15.6 Illustrate methods firms can use to quicken cash collections and slow cash disbursements.

LO 15.7 Describe methods of accounts receivable management and calculate the profit implications of a credit policy change.

LO 15.8 Describe inventory management from the standpoint of the financial manager.

LO 15.9 Explain how technology is affecting working capital management.

Where we have been. . . The previous chapters have introduced us to financial statements and some ways they can help managers and investors. Financial statements contain data that are used to do ratio analysis and long-term financial planning. In addition to helping users identify trends, ratio analysis can help users analyze a firm's operating condition and can help with short-term financial planning.

Where we are going. . . A firm's short-term financing needs will be affected by near-term sales growth and how efficiently the firm manages its working capital accounts. Chapter 16 (Short-term Business Financing) reviews fund sources to help a firm finance its short-term needs. Ongoing short-term financing needs may reflect a need for permanent long-term financing; factors affecting long-term financing decisions were reviewed in Chapter 10's discussion of bonds and stocks. A related discussion, including the appropriate mix and use of debt and equity, will occur in Chapter 18 (Capital Structure and the Cost of Capital).

How this chapter applies to me. . . Business practices of managing short-term assets, such as cash, apply directly to personal issues. First, cash flow is important. We can create a personal cash budget, showing when cash inflows are expected to occur (paychecks, stock dividends, cash birthday gifts) and when expected outflows will occur (bills to be paid). Second, just as a business faces expected return/risk choices when wanting to invest extra cash, so do we. How soon will we need to use our extra cash? How much do we want to hold for transaction, precautionary, and speculative purposes? Do we want a safe place to put our excess funds with high liquidity but low return (such as a bank checking account), should we invest in Treasury bills (T-bills) via the TreasuryDirect program, or should we buy a longer-term certificate of deposit (CD), which offers higher expected returns but lower liquidity?

We begin this chapter with a frequently cited quote from an unknown author:

Happiness is a positive cash flow.

Inventory (representing future hoped-for sales) and accounts receivable (representing past sales and a future promise to pay cash) are important items for a firm. Investments such as these in working capital must be converted to cash at some future time. A positive cash flow occurs when the cash coming into the firm exceeds the cash leaving the firm.

A firm can invest in working capital and fixed capital. Working capital is a firm's current assets and consists of cash, marketable securities, accounts receivable, and inventories. Fixed capital is a firm's fixed assets, which include plant, equipment, and property. In this chapter, we focus on managing a firm's working capital. The financial manager must decide how much to invest in working capital, or current assets, and how to finance these current assets.

How important are working capital issues? In a word, very. Firms that cannot obtain needed short-term financing are candidates for bankruptcy. Supplies and raw materials are converted to inventory. When sold, inventory may become an account receivable and, ultimately, cash. Unexpected increases in inventory or receivables can harm a firm's best-laid long-term plans. If poor planning causes a mismatch between assets and financing sources or between cash inflows and cash outflows, bankruptcy is a real possibility.

Better management of working capital has great benefits to firms. Recall the balance sheet equation (Total assets = Total liabilities + Equity) that each dollar of assets must be financed by a combination of a dollar of liabilities and equity. Less investment in current assets means less financing is needed, so the costs of financing will be lower, too. Lower financial costs go straight to the "bottom line" in the form of higher profits.

CRISIS In a recessionary economy, as we had during 2007–2009, it is paramount to free up cash and reduce financing needs. It is not unusual, as reported annually in *CFO* magazine's working capital scorecard issue, for the most improved firms to reduce their working capital needs by $1 billion or more. If a medium-size company (one with $10 billion in sales) could improve its working capital practices to the level of the most efficient firm, the firm could reduce noncash current assets by $1.4 billion.[1] When financing is difficult to obtain, that can help build a nice cash cushion.

The management consulting firm McKinsey estimates firms can reduce the cash needed to run a business by 20–30%. After the Great Recession, Alcoa reduced its cash conversion cycle by 23 days and freed up $1.4 billion in cash for other corporate purposes.

Efforts to reduce a working capital have firm-wide benefits that go beyond the numbers on the balance sheet and income statement. A firm with good working capital management practices will likely have good processes in marketing and manufacturing; good communication and sharing of metrics between sales, finance, and production; and good discipline in plant operations. Improvements in forecasting product demand will result in better inventory management, lower inventory costs, better cash flow forecasts, and less need for a financing buffer. Regular meetings to remind division heads and plant managers about the status of the firm's working capital can help create an atmosphere where people are concerned about efficiency and cutting waste.[2]

ETHICAL "Window dressing" occurs when firms take actions at the end of their fiscal year (or sometimes toward the end of a quarter) to make themselves appear to be more profitable or financially healthy. At times, firms discount prices to help move inventory, give customers incentives to pay bills early, and implement more aggressive collection efforts for late payers while seeking to slow payments to their own vendors.[3] These have the effect of increasing sales, reducing inventory, and increasing balance sheet cash. However, the consequences are clear: first, they put themselves in a hole for the next period, and second, they know they can hurt customer and vendor relations as well as add stress to

[1] Sean Brown and Matt Stone, "Making Working Capital Work Harder for You,: McKinsey & Company, December 2018, https://www.mckinsey.com/business-functions/strategy-and-corporate-finance/our-insights/make-working-capital-work-harder-for-you; accessed February 4, 2019; Ryan Davies and David Merin, "Uncovering Cash and Insights from Working Capital," *Corporate Finance Practice, McKinsey & Company*, July 2014; Randy Myers, "Tight Makes Right," *CFO* (December 2008), pp. 64–70; Randy Myers, "No Time to Lose," *CFO* (September 2008), pp. 81–86; Randy Myers, "Cleaner (Balance) Sheet," *CFO* (June 2008), pp. 47–53. The June issue of *CFO* magazine typically includes their "Working Capital Scorecard" in which they review firms' performance in managing working capital and highlight the methods of firms that reduced working capital by the most in the past year.

[2] Michael Hunstad, "Fresh Forecast," *AFP Exchange* (November 2008), pp. 46–49; Bob Douglas, "Money Movement," *AFP Exchange* (November 2008), pp. 50–51; Gary Silha, "Tenneco Cash Management," *AFP Exchange* (November 2008), pp. 52–57.

[3] Karen M. Kroll, "Let the Games Continue," *CFO* (May 2008), pp. 77–79.

FIGURE 15.1 Current assets divided by total assets, various firms

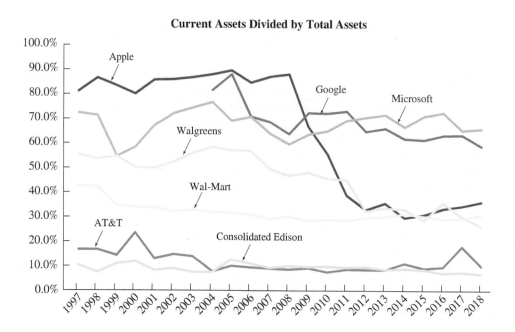

the firm's personnel over time. And sophisticated investors know to watch for changes in the working capital accounts, such as these, as they review a firm's financial statements.

Current assets, typically, comprise from one-third to one-half of a firm's total assets. They are affected by the firm's day-to-day marketing, production, and human resource issues. A survey of financial managers found they spend nearly 70% of their time dealing with financial planning, budgeting, and working capital issues.[4] Figure 15.1 shows the level and variability over time of the ratio of current assets to total assets for several firms. Consolidated Edison (an electric utility) and AT&T have lower proportions of current assets to total assets, whereas technology firms, such as Microsoft and Google, have relatively higher levels of current assets to total assets. Apple Computer's ratio has fallen in recent years; although its level of current assets has been rising, its growth in fixed assets and long-term investments has increased total assets at a faster rate so the ratio of current assets to total assets has fallen. For example, in 2008 Apple Computer's current assets and total assets (in millions of dollars) were $34,690 and $39,572, respectively, so the ratio of current to total assets was 87.7%. In 2018, Apple Computer's current assets were $131,339 million while its total assets were $365,725 million. The ratio of current to total assets fell to 36% because, while current assets nearly tripled during this period, its total assets ballooned over 800%.

The first part of this chapter describes how a firm's operating cycle affects the amount of working capital it carries. Next, we will review how to prepare and use a cash budget. Our final emphasis is on methods used to manage cash and marketable securities, accounts receivable, and inventories.

15.2 OPERATING AND CASH CONVERSION CYCLES

Two important concepts in managing short-term finances are the operating cycle and cash conversion cycle.

15.2.1 OPERATING CYCLE

operating cycle measures the time between receiving raw materials and collecting cash from receivables

The **operating cycle** measures the time between receiving raw materials and collecting cash from receivables. Figure 15.2 graphically depicts the operating cycle for a manufacturing firm. Raw materials are purchased and products are manufactured from them to become finished goods. Effort then is

---

[4] Lawrence J. Gitman and Charles E. Maxwell, "Financial Activities of Major U.S. Firms: Survey and Analysis of Fortune's 1000," *Financial Management* (Winter 1985), pp. 57–65.

FIGURE 15.2   The operating cycle

made to sell the finished goods. If the goods are sold on credit, then the receivables must be collected. A service firm would have a similar cycle except for the manufacturing stage. That is, finished goods would be purchased and then consumed in the process of providing a service, and receivables would be collected. Of course, the operating cycles of service and manufacturing firms would be shortened if sales are made for cash and not on credit.

Figure 15.3 depicts a timeline reflecting the operating cycle for a manufacturing firm. The cycle begins with the receipt of raw materials. The inventory period involves producing or processing the materials into final products or finished goods and ends when the finished goods are sold. If the finished goods are sold on credit, the second major period of interest is the accounts receivable period or average collection period. It covers the time from when the goods are sold until the receivables are collected in the form of cash. The inventory period and the accounts receivable period together constitute the firm's operating cycle.

A firm's operating cycle is expressed, in equation form, as:

Operating cycle = Inventory period + Accounts receivable period

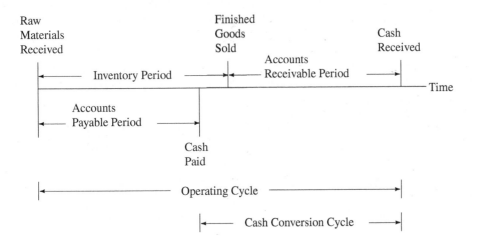

FIGURE 15.3   The operating cycle and cash conversion cycle

15.2.2 CASH CONVERSION CYCLE

In many instances, the initial purchase of raw materials or finished goods for resale is on credit. Thus, suppliers can provide financing in the form of accounts payable. The accounts payable period covers the time between when the order for raw materials is invoiced and when the resulting payable is paid. The accounts payable period is subtracted from the length of the operating cycle to get the **cash conversion cycle**.

cash conversion cycle time between a firm's paying its suppliers for inventory and collecting cash from customers on a sale of the finished product

The cash conversion cycle measures a firm's financing gap in terms of time. In other words, it is the time between when the firm pays its suppliers and when it collects money from its customers. It is the time between when materials are ordered and receivables are collected, less the time over which payables are outstanding. Of course, if no credit is extended by suppliers, then the operating cycle and the cash conversion cycle will be the same. The cash conversion cycle is shown in Figure 15.3.

A firm's cash conversion cycle is expressed, in equation form, as:

$$\text{Cash conversion cycle} = \text{Operating cycle} - \text{Accounts payable period}$$

which is the same as:

$$\text{Cash conversion cycle} = \text{Inventory period} + \text{Accounts receivable period} - \text{Accounts payable period}$$

Increases in the cash conversion cycle mean the firm must finance itself for a longer time. This will increase the firm's short-term financing needs and financing costs. Financial managers will want to monitor the cash conversion cycle and take action should it begin to lengthen. Shorter cash conversion cycles mean the firm will reduce its short-term financing needs and financing costs.

Two items determine the length of the operating cycle: inventory period and accounts receivable period. Three items affect the cash conversion cycle: inventory period, accounts receivable period, and accounts payable period.

15.2.3 DETERMINING THE LENGTH OF THE OPERATING CYCLE AND CASH CONVERSION CYCLE

We can estimate the length of a firm's operating and cash conversion cycles using information from a firm's income statement and balance sheet. All that needs to be done is to calculate three ratios that will tell us the firm's inventory, accounts receivable, and accounts payable periods. Table 15.1 contains selected balance sheets and income statement items for Walgreens.

15.2.3.1 Inventory Period

First, we would like to know how many days items were in inventory during 2018; that is, the time between when raw materials were received and the corresponding finished goods were sold. To determine the length of this period, we can use the inventory turnover ratio (cost of goods sold divided by inventories) from Chapter 14. As we saw in that chapter, the inventory turnover (rounded to two decimal places) for Walgreens is 9.18 times ($100,745/$10,976), meaning Walgreens turns over, or transforms, its inventory into finished products and sells them 9.18 times a year. To determine the inventory conversion period, we divide the 365 days in a year by this inventory turnover ratio (365/9.18) to get 39.8 days.

Table 15.1   Selected Financial Data for Walgreens ($ millions)

	2018
Revenue	$131,537
Cost of goods sold	$100,745
Accounts receivable	$7,144
Inventories	$10,976
Accounts payable	$14,660

As an alternative calculation, we can divide the 2018 year-end inventories amount by the 2018 cost of goods sold (COGS) per day. In ratio form, we have the following:

$$\text{Inventory conversion period} = \frac{\text{Inventory}}{\text{COGS}/365} = \frac{\text{Inventory}}{\text{COGS per day}}$$

$$= \frac{\$10,976}{\$100,745/365} = \frac{\$10,976}{\$276.01} = 39.8 \text{ days}$$

It took about 39.8 days in 2018 for Walgreens to complete the inventory conversion period.

15.2.3.2 Accounts Receivable Period

The second step is to determine the average collection period in 2018 for Walgreens. We saw this ratio in Chapter 14. It measures the average time between when a product is sold on credit and cash is received from the buyer. It is calculated as follows:

$$\text{Average collection period} = \frac{\text{Accounts receivable}}{\text{Net sales}/365}$$

$$= \frac{\$7,144}{\$131,537/365} = \frac{\$7,144}{\$360.38} = 19.8 \text{ days}$$

During 2018, Walgreens needed an average of 19.8 days from the time finished goods were sold on credit to when the resulting receivables were collected.

The operating cycle is determined as follows:

$$\text{Operating cycle} = \text{Inventory conversion period} + \text{Average collection period}$$

Walgreens' average 2018 operating cycle was 39.8 days to process and sell its inventory plus 19.8 days to collect its receivables for a total of 59.6 days.

15.2.3.3 Average Payment Period

The average payment period represents the time it takes Walgreens to pay its suppliers. We were first introduced to this ratio in Chapter 14. The average payment period is calculated by dividing a firm's accounts payable by its cost of goods sold per day. Using the information from Table 15.1, the average payment period is calculated as follows:

$$\text{Average payment period} = \frac{\text{Accounts payable}}{\text{Cost of goods sold}/365}$$

$$= \frac{\$14,660}{\$100,745/365} = \frac{\$14,660}{\$276.01} = 53.1 \text{ days}$$

Thus, Walgreens was able to get, on average, about 53.1 days of credit from its suppliers in 2018.

The cash conversion cycle is the operating cycle less the average payment period:

$$\text{Cash conversion cycle} = \text{Operating cycle} - \text{Average payment period}$$

For Walgreens, we start with an operating cycle of 59.6 days and subtract the average payment period of 53.1 days to arrive at a cash conversion cycle of 6.5 days for 2018. The average time between when Walgreens paid for materials and when it received payment from its customers after their final sale was 6–7 days. Managing the cash conversion cycle is a major task of a firm's financial manager. The shorter the cash conversion cycle, the smaller will be the firm's investment in inventory and receivables, and, consequently, the less will be its financing needs.

DISCUSSION QUESTION 1

We usually think of risk and return in the context of long-term investments or assets such as stocks and bonds. How might a firm's working capital choices and management of its operating and cash conversion cycles have risk/return implications?

15.3 INVESTMENTS IN RECEIVABLES, INVENTORY, AND PAYABLE FINANCING

Let's take a closer look at how the length of the operating cycle affects the amount of funds invested in accounts receivable and inventories. Using Walgreens' 2018 sales of $131,537,[5] average sales per day were $360.38 ($131,537/365). We know that, in 2018, it took Walgreens an average of 19.8 days to collect its accounts receivable. We can use this information to find Walgreens' average investment in accounts receivable. We multiply the net sales per day of $360.38 by the average collection period:

$$\text{Receivables investment amount} = \text{Net sales per day} \times \text{Average collection period}$$
$$\text{Receivables investment amount} = \$360.38 \times 19.8 \text{ days} = \$7,135.52$$

This should be no surprise to us since we used Walgreens' $7,144 accounts receivable balance to determine the average collection period; the slight difference in numbers is due to rounding the net sales per day to the nearest penny and the average collection period to the nearest tenth.

What will the investment be next year in accounts receivable if sales increase by 10% to $144,690.70 and the average collection period remains at 19.8 days? Intuitively, if there is a constant relationship between sales and receivables, a 10% increase in sales should lead to a 10% increase in receivables. An estimate of the new receivables balance would be $7,144 (2018 level) plus 10%, for a total of $7,858.40.

We can also find the new accounts receivable balance by finding the new sales per day and multiplying it by the collection period. Dividing $144,690.70 by 365, we get $396.41 sales per day; multiplying it by 19.8 days gives us the following:

$$\text{Receivables investment amount} = \$396.41 \times 19.8 \text{ days} = \$7,848.90$$

In this case, our initial estimate of $7,858.40 was correct (within rounding of the inputs) because the collection period remained the same. Walgreens' investment in accounts receivable will have to increase by $714 (i.e., $7,858 − $7,144) to support a sales increase of $13,154 (i.e., $144,690.70 − $131,537) as long as the average collection period remains at 19.8 days.

What will happen if the relationship between sales and accounts receivable does not remain constant? For example, as sales rise or fall over time, the accounts receivable period may change. If the economy goes into a recession, the accounts receivable period may rise as customers take longer to pay their bills. Alternatively, focusing the firm's marketing efforts on better credit-quality customers may allow the firm to increase sales and reduce its receivables balance if more customers pay early. Now, what will be the necessary investment in accounts receivable if sales increase to $144,690.70 but Walgreens is able to decrease its average collection period to 18 days? We find the answer to be the following:

$$\text{Receivables investment amount} = \$396.41 \times 18 \text{ days} = \$7,135.38$$

Thus, a reduction of almost two days in the average collection period would mean the amount of investment required in accounts receivable to support a 10% increase in sales would decline $8.62 million ($7,135.38 − $7,144).

A similar analysis can be conducted in terms of inventories. The 2018 COGS was $100,745 for the year, or 276.01 on a per-day basis ($100,745/365). We know that in 2018 it took Walgreens on average 39.8 days between the time raw materials were received and the time the finished goods were

---

[5] Recall that Walgreens' income statement and balance sheet numbers are in terms of millions of dollars.

sold. By multiplying the average cost of goods per day times the inventory conversion period, we can determine the investment required in inventories:

$$\text{Inventories investment amount} = \text{Average cost of goods sold per day} \times \text{Inventory conversion period}$$

For Walgreens in 2018, we have the following:

$$\text{Inventories investment amount} = 276.01 \times 39.8 \text{ days} = \$10,985$$

This, of course, is the same amount, within rounding error, shown for the inventories account in Table 15.1 for Walgreens.

This required investment will change if the COGS, the inventory conversion period, or both change. For example, let's assume that the firm's COGS increases by 10% to $110,819.50 because of an increase in sales. This would be a new COGS per day of $303.62 ($110,819.50/365). If the inventory conversion period remains at 39.8 days, the new investment in inventories should be about 10% higher, too:

$$\text{Inventories investment amount} = \$303.62 \times 39.8 \text{ days} = \$12,084, \text{ which is an increase of } \$1,108$$

($12,084 − $10,976), or about 10% (difference due to rounding).

If Walgreens could find a way to lower its inventory conversion period to, say, 35 days, the net impact on the investment in inventories of a 10% sales rise would be the following:

$$\text{Inventories investment amount} = \$303.62 \times 35 \text{ days} = \$10,626.70$$

Thus, even though sales and COGS increase next year, a decline in the inventory conversion period to 35 days results in a decrease in the investment in inventories by $349.30 ($10,626.70 − $10,976). Walgreens may achieve a reduction in its inventory conversion period by managing inventories more efficiently. Some strategies for doing this are discussed in the last section of this chapter.

The size of the accounts payable account is affected by two basic factors: the level of the firm's cost of goods sold and the average payment period. Table 15.1 indicates that the COGS for Walgreens was $100,745 in 2018. On a per-day basis, the COGS was 276.01 ($100,745/365). We previously calculated the 2018 average payment period at 53.1 days. Given this information, we can determine the required amount of accounts payable as follows:

$$\text{Accounts payable} = \text{Cost of goods sold per day} \times \text{Average payment period}$$

For Walgreens, in 2018, we have the following:

$$\text{Accounts payable} = 276.01 \times 53.1 \text{ days} = \$14,656.13$$

This amount, of course, is the same, within rounding error, as the accounts payable amount shown in Table 15.1 for Walgreens at the end of 2018.

Of course, as a firm's cost of goods sold increases, its credit purchases and its accounts payable should increase. For example, if Walgreens' COGS increases by 10% to $110,819.50 next year, we expect accounts payable, currently $14,660, to rise by 10% as well, if the payment period does not change. A COGS of $110,819.50 gives a daily average COGS of $110,819.50/365 days, or $303.62. If the average payment period remains at 53.1 days, the projected amount in the accounts payable account is the following:

$$\text{Accounts payable} = \$303.62 \times 53.1 \text{ days} = \$16,121.16$$

This represents, approximately, a 10% increase in payables. It should be recognized that while an increase in sales and COGS should result in an increase in the investment in accounts receivable and inventories, these increases will be partially offset by an increase in accounts payable, other things being equal. If the accounts payable period rises to 55 days, the new accounts payable balance will be the following:

$$\text{Accounts payable} = \$303.62 \times 55 \text{ days} = \$16,699.10$$

Table 15.2 Effect of a 10% Increase in Sales and Cost of Goods Sold on Receivables, Inventory, and Payables

Account	2018 Results for Walgreens	10% Increase in sales and cost of goods sold	
Investment			
Accounts receivable	$7,144	$7,848.90	
Inventories	$10,976	$12,084	Change in investment
Total	$18,120	$19,933	$1,813
Financing			Change in AP financing
Accounts payable	$14,660	$16,121	$1,461
Net Investment			Change in Net Investment
Investment – Financing	$3,460	$3,812	$352

Assumptions: Average collection period = 19.8 days; inventory period = 39.8 days; average payment period = 53.1 days.

Our estimates of the effects on receivables, inventory, and payables are shown in summary form in Table 15.2, under the assumption that sales and cost of goods sold both rise by 10% – but that no changes occur in the operating and cash conversion cycles.

Thus, while investment in accounts receivable and inventories would be expected to increase by $1,813, from $18,120 to $19,933, the expected increase in accounts payable of $1,461, from $14,660 to $16,121, causes the net impact to be a $352 increase in needed financing. The financial manager will have to plan ahead to obtain the necessary funds to support this expected increase in net working capital. He or she can obtain funds from short-term financing sources, as discussed in Chapter 16, or he or she may decide to tap long-term sources, such as stocks and bonds.

Table 15.3 summarizes our estimates of receivables, inventory, and payables if sales and COGS rise by 10% and changes occur in the operating and cash conversion cycles. Specifically, Table 15.3 shows the effects of an average collection period of 18 days, inventory period of 35 days, and a payables period of 55 days, along with a 10% rise in sales and cost of goods sold. The effect of these minor changes in cash conversion cycle components is remarkable. The firm's net investment in these working capital accounts will fall to $1,063, nearly $2,400 less than the current (2018) situation and nearly $2,750 less than the scenario in Table 15.2.

In a later section, we discuss another important topic: the management of working capital assets. From our discussion, it should be clear that more efficient management of working capital assets and faster cash collection will lessen the firm's needs for financing. Small working capital account balances mean less debt and external equity financing is needed, saving the firm extra financing expenses. Activities that decrease the cash conversion cycle will reduce the firm's need to obtain financing.

Table 15.3 Effect of 10% Increase in Sales and Cost of Goods Sold on Receivables, Inventory, and Payables

Account	2018 Results for Walgreens	10% Increase in sales and cost of goods sold	Difference
Investment			
Accounts Receivable	$7,144	$7,135.38	($8.62)
Inventories	$10,976	$10,626.70	($349.30)
Total	$18,120	$17,762.08	($357.92)
Financing			
Accounts Payable	$14,660	$16,699.10	$2,039.10
Net Investment			
Investment – Financing	$3,460	$1,062.98	($2,397.02)

Assumptions: Average collection period = 18 days; inventory period = 35 days; average payment period = 55 days.

We have seen how financial ratios can be used to estimate the firm's total financing needs over the course of a year. As we learned in Chapter 14, expected sales growth may require the firm to acquire additional current assets and fixed assets to support higher sales levels. By combining the sales forecast and the firm's total asset turnover ratio, we can estimate the amount of assets needed to support the sales forecast. The projected increase in assets less the estimated increase in current liabilities and retained earnings will give the financial analyst an estimate of the firm's needs for external financing.

The previous section illustrated a quick means of estimating working capital financing needs by comparing expected changes in current assets and current liabilities. The estimated change in current assets minus the expected change in current liabilities measures the change in working capital. This growth (or decline) in working capital must be financed, via short-term financing or long-term financing.

Such methods are appropriate as a first approximation toward estimating a firm's yearly financing needs, but a firm needs more precise information than this. Over the course of a year, large bills may need to be paid before subsequent cash inflows occur. Dividend checks will be mailed to shareholders, workers and suppliers will need to be paid, and interest on debt and perhaps even the principal that was borrowed will have to be repaid. During any one week or month, the firm's need for cash may exceed the above annual estimates. A firm's treasurer will need to closely track and forecast daily and weekly cash inflows and outflows to ensure cash is available to pay necessary expenses. Should the firm's cash balance become low, the treasurer will need to plan to acquire the needed funds by borrowing money or selling marketable securities. A cash budget is a tool the treasurer uses to forecast future cash flows and to estimate future short-term borrowing needs.

cash budget a tool the treasurer uses to forecast future cash flows and estimate future short-term borrowing needs

A budget is a financial forecast of spending, income, or both. A cash budget details the periodic cash inflows and cash outflows of a firm over some time frame. Small- and medium-size firms may prepare monthly cash budgets, whereas larger firms will forecast cash flows weekly or daily. If cash surpluses are forecast, the treasurer can plan how the firm's excess cash can be invested to earn interest.[6] If a cash deficit is forecast, the treasurer can plan how to best raise the necessary funds. We'll construct a cash budget for a manufacturing firm, Eastnorth Manufacturing, in this section. Eastnorth Manufacturing's sales pattern is seasonal, with sales typically rising at the end of the calendar year, followed by a sharp sales decline at the beginning of the calendar year. We'll see how the decision for the firm to have level production during the year rather than seasonal production will affect its cash needs throughout the year.

To construct a cash budget, three sets of information are needed: the firm's minimum desired cash balance, estimated cash inflows, and estimated cash outflows. We discuss each of these below.

15.4.1 MINIMUM DESIRED CASH BALANCE

Most firms have a minimum desired cash balance. Some cash will be needed to pay the month's bills, but extra cash may be desired because the forecasts of cash inflows and outflows will be imperfect. To protect against lower-than-expected cash inflows (or higher-than-expected cash outflows), a *cash buffer* is needed. The size of the cash buffer depends on several influences, including the firm's ability to acquire financing easily on short notice, the predictability of cash inflows and outflows, and management's preferences.

15.4.2 ESTIMATED CASH INFLOWS

The estimates of cash inflows are driven by two main factors: the sales forecast and customer payment patterns. Over any period, the main sources of cash inflows for the firm will be cash sales and collections of receivables. If we know the proportion of cash sales and the percentage of customers who pay their bills every month, we can use sales forecasts to estimate future cash inflows.

---

[6] The treasurer may want to invest any cash above the firm's immediate needs to earn a return on the excess funds, depending on liquidity needs, return expectations, and risk of any investment.

FIGURE 15.4 Sales data, 2017–2019, Eastnorth Manufacturing Inc.

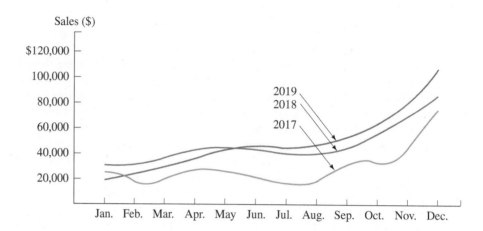

Sales forecasts will be affected by seasonal patterns. Monthly sales figures will differ for swimsuit makers and snow blower manufacturers. Managers can determine seasonal patterns by plotting monthly or quarterly sales figures, as in Figure 15.4.

For example, Table 15.4 presents Eastnorth Manufacturing's actual November and December 2019 sales and forecasted sales for January, February, March, and April 2020. From Figure 15.4, Eastnorth Manufacturing (Eastnorth) knows that its sales volume is highly seasonal, with a large proportion of sales occurring in the last few months of the year. All of Eastnorth's sales are credit sales and become accounts receivable. From reviewing past payment patterns, Eastnorth knows that receivables representing 50% of a month's sales are paid one month after purchase while the remaining 50% are paid two months later. Thus, for January – April, each month's cash inflows have two sources: cash comes into the firm equal to 50% of the sales volume from the previous month and cash comes into the firm equal to 50% of the sales volume from two months prior. Thus, for January, cash inflows reflect 50% of December's sales (50% of December's sales equals $50,000) plus 50% of November's sales (50% of November's sales equals $40,000), for a total expected inflow of $90,000.

15.4.3 ESTIMATED CASH OUTFLOWS

Every month Eastnorth will have bills to pay, and these cash outflows need to appear in the cash budget. Suppliers of raw materials must be paid, as well as the firm's payroll. Rental or lease payments, utility bills, and so forth are other examples of regular outflows that should be listed in the budget. Interest on borrowing may be due at specific times, as will dividends and tax payments. Any anticipated purchases of plant and equipment must be listed in the budget. Over the course of the year production can be seasonal, rising and falling along with the sales forecast, or it can be level, producing a constant amount of product every month. Here, we assume Eastnorth uses seasonal production. Later, we will see the effect of a level production schedule on Eastnorth's cash budget.

Table 15.5 shows Eastnorth's expected cash disbursements. Raw materials and supplies equal to 50% of each month's sales are purchased each month. Eastnorth pays its suppliers two months after the goods are purchased. Each month's estimated salary and overhead expenses are $20,000. Interest

Table 15.4 Monthly Cash Inflows, Eastnorth Manufacturing Inc.

	Nov.	Dec.	Jan.	Feb.	Mar.	Apr.
Sales	$80,000	$100,000	$30,000	$40,000	$50,000	$60,000
Collections						
50% of sales of the previous month		40,000	50,000	15,000	20,000	25,000
50% of sales of the second previous month			40,000	50,000	15,000	20,000
Total cash receipts			$90,000	$65,000	$35,000	$45,000

Table 15.5 Monthly Cash Outflows, Eastnorth Manufacturing, Inc.

	Nov.	Dec.	Jan.	Feb.	Mar.	Apr.
Sales	$80,000	$100,000	$30,000	$40,000	$50,000	$60,000
Materials and supplies purchases (50% of monthly sales)	40,000	50,000	15,000	20,000	25,000	30,000
Payments 100% of purchases of the second previous month				40,000	50,000	15,000	20,000
Salaries and overhead				20,000	20,000	20,000	20,000
Interest				7,000		
Dividends					6,000	
Taxes					3,000	
Capital expenditures				50,000		
Total cash payments			$60,000	$127,000	$44,000	$40,000

payments of $7,000 are due in February, and a quarterly dividend, expected to be $6,000, is to be paid in March. Quarterly taxes of $3,000 need to be paid in March. In anticipation of growing sales, Eastnorth is planning to purchase $50,000 worth of capital equipment in February.

15.4.4 CONSTRUCTING THE CASH BUDGET

After listing all the estimated cash inflows and cash outflows for each month, we can estimate the monthly net cash flow. As shown in Table 15.6, this is the difference between Eastnorth's cash receipts and cash payments from Tables 15.4 and 15.5.

From Table 15.6, we see that January will be a month with a large positive net cash flow, but February and March are expected to have larger cash outflows than cash inflows. April is expected to have more cash coming into the firm than going out from it. To help Eastnorth determine its short-term financing needs, we need to put together a cash budget that indicates Eastnorth's minimum desired cash balance as well as its monthly loan (or loan repayment) needs. We'll assume Eastnorth's minimum desired cash balance is $25,000. Should the cash position in any month fall below $25,000, Eastnorth's treasurer will need to borrow sufficient funds so the cash balance is restored to the $25,000 level. Table 15.7 illustrates Eastnorth's monthly cash budget.

Table 15.6 Net Monthly Cash Flows, Seasonal Production, Eastnorth Manufacturing Inc.

	Jan.	Feb.	Mar.	Apr.
Total cash receipts	$90,000	$65,000	$35,000	$45,000
Less: Total cash payments	$60,000	127,000	$44,000	$40,000
Net cash flow	$30,000	($62,000)	($9,000)	$5,000

Table 15.7 Monthly Cash Budget, Seasonal Production, Eastnorth Manufacturing Inc.

	Jan.	Feb.	Mar.	Apr.
Net cash flow	$30,000	($62,000)	($9,000)	$5,000
Beginning cash balance	25,000	55,000	25,000	25,000
Cumulative cash balance	55,000	(7,000)	16,000	30,000
Monthly loan (or repayment)	0	32,000	9,000	(5,000)
Cumulative loan balance	0	32,000	41,000	36,000
Ending cash balance	$55,000	$25,000	$25,000	$25,000

From Table 15.6, we see that January's net cash flow is $30,000. Adding this to Eastnorth's cash balance of $25,000 at the beginning of January gives Eastnorth a cumulative cash balance of $55,000. Eastnorth's treasurer may want to make plans to invest some of this excess cash in marketable securities to earn extra interest income.

The cash balance at the end of January becomes the cash balance at the beginning of February. Adding the $55,000 cash balance to February's net cash flow of −$62,000 means that Eastnorth is forecasted to spend $7,000 more in cash than it is expected to have available. To meet the expected payments and raise the cash balance to its minimum desired level of $25,000, Eastnorth's treasurer will need to borrow $7,000 + $25,000, or $32,000, during the month of February. After so doing, the ending cash balance of February will be $25,000.

When March's net cash flow of −$9,000 is added to March's beginning cash balance of $25,000, Eastnorth's available cash will be $16,000. To maintain the minimum desired cash balance of $25,000, Eastnorth should plan to borrow $9,000. When this is added to the outstanding loans from February, Eastnorth's total loan balance at the end of March will be $32,000 + $9,000, or $41,000. The ending cash balance in March will be $25,000.

April's positive net cash flow, when added to the beginning cash balance, will give Eastnorth a positive cash balance of $30,000. This exceeds Eastnorth's minimum desired cash balance of $25,000, so the excess cash of $5,000 will likely be used to repay some of Eastnorth's recently acquired debt. By so doing, Eastnorth's cumulative loan balance will fall to $36,000.

This example illustrates the usefulness of cash budgeting. Forecasted sales are used to estimate future cash inflows and cash outflows based on expected payment patterns. The treasurer can plan to invest excess cash or to borrow needed funds. In addition to its value as a planning tool, the cash budget will be a necessary component of any short-term loan request from a bank. The bank will not only want to see when and how much the firm may need to borrow, but also when the firm can repay the loan.

15.4.5 SEASONAL VERSUS LEVEL PRODUCTION

The example assumes that Eastnorth uses seasonal production to meet its seasonal sales forecast. Raw materials purchases will rise or fall in anticipation of higher or lower sales. Such a strategy can minimize the effect of seasonal sales on inventory. Goods are manufactured before they are sold, but seasonal production can lead to other problems, such as an idle plant and laid-off workers during slow sales months, and production bottlenecks during busy times. Consequently, for better production efficiency, some firms with seasonal sales use a level production plan. Under a level production plan, the same amount of raw material is purchased and the same amount of finished product is manufactured every month. Inventory builds up in anticipation of the higher seasonal sales while cash and accounts receivable are low. When the selling season begins, inventories fall and receivables rise. After a time, inventories are nearly exhausted and the firm is collecting cash from its customers. The changing composition of current assets for a firm with a seasonal sales pattern is illustrated in Figure 15.5.

Now let's see how Eastnorth's cash budget will be affected if it switches to a level production plan. In Table 15.4, the schedule of cash inflows will not be affected, but in Table 15.5, the schedule

FIGURE 15.5 Changing composition of current assets with seasonal sales and level production

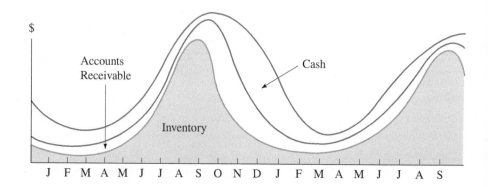

Table 15.8   Monthly Cash Outflows, Level Production

	Nov.	Dec.	Jan.	Feb.	Mar.	Apr.
Sales	$80,000	$100,000	$30,000	$40,000	$50,000	$60,000
Materials and supplies purchases (50% of average monthly sales)	29,200	29,200	29,200	29,200	29,200	29,200
Payments (100% of purchases of the second previous month)			29,200	29,200	29,200	29,200
Salaries and overhead			20,000	20,000	20,000	20,000
Interest				7,000		
Dividends					6,000	
Taxes					3,000	
Capital expenditures				50,000		
Total cash payments			$49,200	$106,200	$58,200	$49,200

Table 15.9   Net Monthly Cash Flows, Level Production

	Jan.	Feb.	Mar.	Apr.
Total cash receipts	$90,000	$65,000	$35,000	$45,000
Less: Total cash payments	49,200	106,200	58,200	49,200
Net cash flow	$40,800	($41,200)	($23,200)	($4,200)

Table 15.10   Monthly Cash Budget, Level Production

	Jan.	Feb.	Mar.	Apr.
Net cash flow	$40,800	($41,200)	($23,200)	($4,200)
Beginning cash balance	25,000	65,800	25,000	25,000
Cumulative cash balance	65,800	24,600	1,800	20,800
Monthly loan (or repayment)	0	400	23,200	4,200
Cumulative loan balance	0	400	23,600	27,800
Ending cash balance	$65,800	$25,000	$25,000	$25,000

will be changed to reflect a level pattern of materials purchases. We will assume that the amount of materials and supplies over the course of a year is one-half of estimated sales. If forecasted sales are $700,000, this means Eastnorth purchases $350,000 of materials over the course of a year, or approximately $29,200 each month. Table 15.8 shows the revised cash outflow schedule assuming purchases, and subsequent payments, of a constant $29,200 each month.

With these new cash payments, Table 15.9 shows the monthly net cash flows and Table 15.10 shows the new cash budget. In January, the level production plan leads to a higher cash balance than under the seasonal plan, but sustained production levels during Eastnorth's slow sales months lead to monthly cash deficits in February, March, and April. Under seasonal production, net cash flow returned to positive in April and some loans could be repaid. With level production, the cumulative loan balance continues to grow through April.

The projections on the cash budget will reflect the firm's marketing efforts as well as its credit policies, how it manages its receivables, and how it decides to manage its production and inventories. In general, firms with larger receivables balances and easier credit terms will have slower cash receipt inflows, but this must be balanced against the competitive impact of tightening its receivables management policies. Firms with larger inventories will face large accounts payable balances and larger cash payments than firms operating on leaner inventories and tighter production schedules. Thus, how a firm manages its working capital accounts will be a concern to the company's treasurer. We examine these topics in the next section.

DISCUSSION QUESTION 2

What influences might affect the size of a firm's cash buffer?

15.5
MANAGEMENT OF CURRENT ASSETS

Management of current assets involves the administration of cash and marketable securities, accounts receivable, and inventories. On the one hand, the financial manager should strive to minimize the investment in current assets because of the cost of financing them. On the other hand, adequate cash and marketable securities are necessary for liquidity purposes, acceptable credit terms are necessary to maintain sales, and appropriate inventory levels must be kept to avoid running out of stock and losing sales. Therefore, successful management requires a continual balancing of the costs and benefits associated with investment in current assets.

15.5.1 CASH MANAGEMENT

Some large firms exist with almost no cash balances, although others hold billions of dollars in cash and marketable securities.[7] For firms that operate with little or no cash, whatever funds they need, they obtain from short-term bank loans or overdrafts that are repaid the next day from cash inflows or from selling marketable securities.

Typically, business firms should strive to minimize their cash holdings, since until 2011 firms could not earn interest on checking accounts. But given the low interest rates they now can receive, corporate treasurers still seek ways to earn higher returns with very low risk on their excess cash. But still, businesses receive some compensation if they keep excess cash in demand deposits (checking accounts) at commercial banks through "earnings credits." The earnings credits are used to offset or reduce bank service charges paid by the firm (such as for collecting checks, processing payments, and taking deposits). In late 2009 and early 2010, when three-month T-bill rates were under 0.10%, the earnings credit allowance at some banks was 0.50% or higher. This made keeping cash in the bank an attractive alternative in such low-rate environments. It should be noted, however, that if a firm's earnings credits exceed its bank service charges, the excess credits cannot be paid out to the firm, nor can the excess roll over to the next period.[8]

The greater the ability of a firm to tap short-term sources of financing (discussed in Chapter 16), the less the need to hold cash and marketable securities balances. Firms that do hold cash generally do so for three motives, which we discuss below.[9]

Some cash is necessary to carry on day-to-day operations. This is the **transactions motive**, or demand for holding cash. If cash inflows and outflows could be projected with virtual certainty, the transactions demand for cash could, theoretically, be reduced to zero. Most businesses prepare cash flow forecasts, or budgets, wanting to predict the amount of cash holdings they will need. However, most firms are forced to hold some cash because of cash flow uncertainties, and because minimum cash balances often are required on loans from commercial banks.

precautionary motives holding funds to meet unexpected demands

Marketable securities are held primarily for **precautionary motives**. These are demands for funds that may be caused by unpredictable events, such as delays in production or in the collection of receivables. Marketable securities can be sold to satisfy such liquidity problems. In the event of strong seasonal sales patterns, marketable securities can be used to reduce wide fluctuations in short-term

---

[7] In the late 1990s, Ford Motor Company's balance sheet showed over $25 billion in cash and marketable securities; it argued the cash was need to help the firm invest for the future and weather economic downturns. This was true as its cash balance fell to under $5 billion in 2001 before rising to nearly $34 billion at the end of 2006. In March 2009, at the trough of the recession, it still held $21 billion in cash without having received government bailout funds. By 2009, Microsoft had over $36 billion in cash and marketable securities on its balance sheet because of its highly profitable products. By mid-2018, Microsoft's cash and marketable securities balance was over $133 billion.

[8] Vincent Ryan, "More Than Zero—with short-term Treasury yields at rock bottom, companies are seeking higher returns for their cash," *CFO* (April 2009), pp. 33–35.

[9] For a detailed discussion of an empirical study of some of these motives, see T. Opler, L. Pinkowitz, R. Stulz, and R. Williamson, "Corporate Cash Holdings," *Journal of Applied Corporate Finance*, vol. 14, no. 1 (Spring 2001), pp. 55–66; and T. Opler, L. Pinkowitz, R. Stulz, and R. Williamson, "Determinants and Implications of Corporate Cash Holdings," *Journal of Financial Economics*, vol. 52 (1999), pp. 3–46.

financing requirements. Funds may be held for precautionary purposes so the firm can continue to invest in assets (plant, equipment, and technology) even if future sales and cash flows fall.

Marketable securities may be held for **speculative motives**. In certain instances, a firm might be able to take advantage of unusual cash discounts or price bargains on materials if it can pay quickly with cash. Marketable securities are easily converted into cash for such purposes.

> **speculative motives** holding marketable securities to take advantage of unusual cash discounts or price bargains on materials if it can pay quickly with cash

But a fourth motive for holding cash is evident. A curiosity in recent years is the decision by U.S. firms to hold large amounts of cash, amounts which far exceed those needed for transactions, precautionary, or speculative motives. For example, in 2011, one estimate was that the firms making up Standard & Poor's 500 (S&P500) stock index held almost $1 trillion in cash.[10] By 2015, the amount exceeded $1.45 trillion.[11] To put this in perspective, this potential for buying goods and services, hiring workers, investing in plant and equipment, or paying dividends exceeded the U.S. government's 2009 stimulus spending package of nearly $800 billion by nearly 50%.

GLOBAL Massive amounts of cash are being held by individual firms, including Apple Computer ($85 billion), Cisco Systems ($42 billion), Microsoft ($133 billion), and Alphabet (Google) ($72.8 billion).[12] Until recently, much of this cash is being held outside of the United States.

The reason for holding all this cash outside of the United States is the high cost of bringing cash from overseas business into the United States. That is, there are **tax motives** for holding cash outside of the United States. The U.S. corporate tax rates were among the highest in the world as of 2016, at 35%. Although credits are given for taxes paid overseas, the high U.S. tax rate makes it costly to bring funds into the United States to reinvest here. Some firms found it cheaper to borrow money than to bring cash they have into the United States and pay taxes on it. Taxes do matter when firms want to preserve their cash, and as they seek ways to maximize shareholder wealth over time. The Tax Cuts and Jobs Act, passed in 2017, should help reduce this tax motive for holding cash overseas. The U.S. corporate tax rate was reduced to 21%, reducing the penalty faced by firms who transferred their overseas profits back to the United States for reinvestment.

> **tax motives** holding cash outside of the United States to avoid high U.S. corporate tax rates for bringing cash from overseas profits into the country

15.5.2 MARKETABLE SECURITIES

To qualify as a marketable security, an investment must be highly liquid; that is, it must be readily convertible to cash without a large loss of value. This requires that it have a short maturity and that an active secondary market exist so it can be sold prior to maturity if necessary. The security must be of high quality, with little chance that the borrower will default. U.S. Treasury bills (T-bills) offer the highest quality, liquidity, and marketability. Other investments that serve well as marketable securities include negotiable certificates of deposit (CDs) and commercial paper, both of which offer higher rates but are more risky and less liquid than T-bills. Business firms can hold excess funds in money market accounts, or they can purchase banker's acceptances or short-term notes of U.S. government agencies. We discuss the characteristics of several financial instruments used as marketable securities.

15.5.2.1 U.S. Treasury Bills

Treasury bills are sold at a discount through competitive bidding in a weekly auction. These bills are offered in all parts of the country but sell mostly in New York City. Treasury bills are actively traded in secondary money markets, mostly those in New York City.

Figure 15.6 shows the levels and volatility, or tendency to change rapidly, of three-month. Treasury bill yields between 1997 and 2019. The yields were around 5% in 1997 and peaked during this time frame at about 6% in 2000. They declined with the beginning of the 2001 recession

---

[10] Jason Zweig, "What Will It Take for Companies to Unlock Their Cash Hoards?" *The Wall Street Journal* (May 28, 2011), pp. B1, B2.

[11] Clayton Brown, "Led by Apple, S&P 500 Firms Pile Up Cash in Third Quarter," accessed January 29, 2016, at http://www.valuewalk.com/2015/12/third-quarter-sp-500/.

[12] Clayton Brown, "Led by Apple, S&P 500 Firms Pile Up Cash in Third Quarter," accessed January 29, 2016, at http://www.valuewalk.com/2015/12/third-quarter-sp-500/. Other articles dealing with cash-rich firms include Kate Linebaugh, "Top U.S. Firms Are Cash-Rich Abroad, Cash-Poor at Home," *The Wall Street Journal* (December 4, 2012), pp. B1, B6; Joseph Harry, "Overseas Cash Hoards: Look But Don't Touch," accessed January 26, 2013, at http://seekingalpha.com/article/989901-overseas-cash-hoards-look-but-don-t-touch.

SMALL BUSINESS PRACTICE

IMPORTANCE OF WORKING CAPITAL MANAGEMENT FOR SMALL BUSINESSES

For U.S. manufacturing firms, current assets represent about 40% of total assets and current liabilities are about 25% of total financing. A financial manager may spend over one-half of his or her time on the management of working capital, and the first job after graduation for many finance students will be in the area of working capital.

The management of working capital is important to the entrepreneurial or venture firm. The need for all types of financial capital is important as the firm moves from a start-up situation to rapid growth in revenues. To reduce financing needs, the small firm must keep only a necessary level of inventories on hand. Too much inventory causes unnecessary financing costs and increases the likelihood of having obsolete, unsaleable products. Of course, too little inventory could result in "stock-outs" and the loss of potential sales.

To be competitive, businesses often must offer credit to their customers, which results in the need to finance accounts receivable.

However, the entrepreneurial or venture firm should not overlook the possibility that customers, in some cases, can provide financing help in the form of advance payments. For example, if you produce and sell an important component essential to a customer's own product that it markets and sells, your customer may be willing to provide partial payments in advance to you to ensure you will continue to manufacture the products on time, and that you will maintain quality.

A venture, or entrepreneurial, firm may find it advantageous to seek longer repayment terms from suppliers to help finance growth in sales. In fact, sometimes suppliers will negotiate the conversion of accounts payables to notes payable. Such a conversion usually costs the small business money. Rather, to convert an accounts payable with 30-day terms to a notes payable due in 90 days usually requires the payment of interest on the amount of the notes payable in addition to the amount owed when the accounts payable comes due.

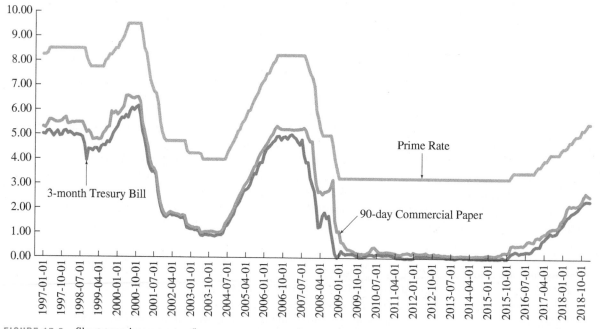

FIGURE 15.6 Short-term interest rates (bars represent economic recessions)

Source: St. Louis Federal Reserve District Bank, FRED Economic Data, https://research.stlouisfed.org/fred2/, accessed February 7, 2019.

following attempts by the Federal Reserve System to stimulate the economy. Rates rose in 2004–2007 as the Fed increased its discount rate and federal funds rate as economic growth increased demand for loanable funds before easing in late 2007. With the Great Recession, interest rates declined sharply in late 2007 and T-bills stayed near 0% until the Fed started to raise interest rates again in December 2015.

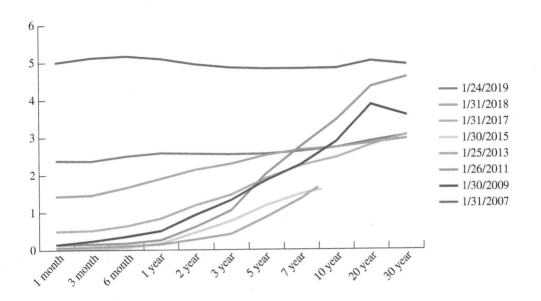

FIGURE 15.7   Examples of the yield curve

Source: U.S. Department of the Treasury, Daily Treasury Yield Curve Rates, https://www.treasury.gov/resource-center/data-chart-center/interest-rates/Pages/TextView.aspx?data=yield, accessed February 7, 2019.

U.S. T-bills are considered to be risk-free in that there is nearly no risk of default. Consequently, interest rates are, as expected, higher for other money market instruments of similar maturity at the same point in time. Figure 15.6 shows the prime rate on bank loans and the 90-day commercial paper rate (for short-term corporate borrowing) are both higher than T-bill rates but tend to follow the T-bill rate's movements over time.

Figure 15.7 shows recent examples of the yield curve. Some corporate financial managers attempt to "ride the yield curve" when the yield curve is upward sloping by buying longer-term securities rather than short-term ones with their excess cash. To understand why they do this, recall what happens as we purchase longer-term securities (by "longer-term" in this context, we mean securities that mature in, say, one year, rather than one month). First, longer maturities mean (if the yield curve is upward sloping) higher interest income. Second, as the security nears maturity, and if the yield curve is upward sloping, its market yield will fall; we know from Chapter 10 that a falling interest rate results in higher prices for fixed-income securities. Thus, aggressive financial managers ride the curve to try to get higher returns on their investments of excess cash.

It is interesting to note the behavior of the yield curve before (2007), during (2008 and 2009), and after (2010-on) the Great Recession. Interest rates rose from 2005 to 2007 and the yield curve shifted upward as the economy grew and the yield curve flattened out. In 2008, shortly after the Great Recession officially began in December 2007, the yield curve started to shift downward due to worsening economic and financial market conditions, and the Federal Reserve began to reduce interest rates. Rates continued to fall during 2008 and 2009 – and even after the recession, due to sluggish economic growth and the Fed's zero interest rate policy coupled with its "quantitative easing" bond-buying activities. The Fed started to raise interest rates in December 2015 and the yield curve has been drifting upward since. You can check the website below to see how Treasury interest rates compare with those in Figure 15.7.

15.5.2.2 Federal Funds

Federal funds are not an investment alternative for excess cash, except in the case of financial institutions. At times, a commercial bank or other depository institution may find its reserves are temporarily greater than their required reserves. These temporary excess reserves, federal funds as they are called when loaned, are lent on a day-to-day basis to other depository institutions temporarily short of reserves.

The lending for a one-day period is generally done by an electronic funds transfer and can be illustrated with an example involving two commercial banks. The deal may be made by one or more messages from the bank wanting to borrow funds, or it may be arranged through a federal funds broker. Funds are electronically transferred from the lending bank's reserve account to the borrowing bank's reserve account at the Federal Reserve Bank. Repayment of the loan plus interest occurs the next day.

FIGURE 15.8 Federal funds and three-month T-bill rates

Source: St. Louis Federal Reserve District Bank, FRED Economic Data, https://research.stlouisfed.org/fred2/, accessed February 7, 2019.

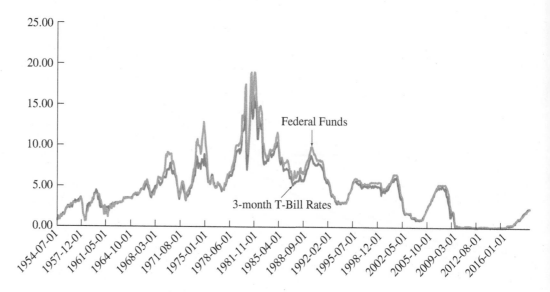

Many of these transactions are between New York City banks, but banks in other cities enter the New York money market, usually as lenders. The most common trading unit for federal funds is $1 million, but this is often exceeded.

Federal funds rates usually parallel U.S. T-bill rates, as is shown in Figure 15.8, and they have mainly remained above the three-month T-bill rate since 1995. Normally, the spread, or difference, between the two rates is narrow. During periods of tight money and credit, however, federal funds can be bid up to high levels. Banks and other depository institutions choose, within limits, between borrowing at the discount rate from the Fed and borrowing federal funds to meet reserve requirements. If they could be freely be substituted for each other, the discount rate set in accordance with monetary policy objectives would set an upper limit for the federal funds rate, since banks would borrow at the lower of the two rates. In practice, however, banks prefer to borrow federal funds even at the high rates that occur when money is tight, rather than borrow too frequently from the Fed, which discourages continued use of this alternative. The sharp decline in both interest rates is evident starting with the Great Recession; they both stayed at historic lows as the Federal Reserve kept interest rates near zero for much of the 2009–2015 period. The rates in Figure 15.8 have increased since 2015, becuase that is when the Fed started to raise interest rates.

15.5.2.3 Commercial Paper

Commercial paper is the short-term, unsecured notes of well-known business firms, such as IBM or General Electric (GE). Financially strong firms, such as these, are able to raise short-term funds almost at will by selling "IOUs" to financial market participants who seek short-term investments for their funds. Major finance companies and nonfinancial corporations have sold commercial paper through dealers or commercial paper houses for many years. More recently, many issuers, particularly finance companies, have issued or sold their own commercial paper.

Interest rates on commercial paper tend to closely follow T-bill rates over time, as can be seen in Figure 15.6. Because of somewhat greater default risk, commercial paper rates for similar maturities are higher than T-bill rates at any point in time. Since commercial paper rates are typically below bank prime rates, they are a valuable short-term financing source for high quality business firms.

15.5.2.4 Negotiable Certificates of Deposit

A certificate of deposit (CD) is, in essence, a receipt issued by a bank in exchange for a deposit of funds. The bank agrees to pay the amount deposited plus interest to the bearer of the receipt on the date specified on the certificate. Many banks had issued such certificates as early as the turn of the century, but before 1960 they were rarely issued in negotiable form. Negotiable CDs can be traded in the secondary market before maturity.

The volume of negotiable CDs (usually issued in denominations of $100,000 or more) has increased dramatically. Interest rates on these CDs usually parallel rates on other money market instruments, such as commercial paper and banker's acceptances, and are above the less risky T-bill rates.

15.5.2.5 Banker's Acceptances

GLOBAL This form of business paper primarily finances exports and imports and, since it is the unconditional obligation of the accepting bank rather than a firm, it generally has a high quality rating. Yields on banker's acceptances closely follow yields on commercial paper.

15.5.2.6 Eurodollars

GLOBAL Eurodollars are deposits placed in foreign banks that remain denominated in U.S. dollars. A demand deposit in a U.S. bank becomes a Eurodollar when the holder of such a deposit transfers it to a foreign bank or an overseas branch of an American bank. After the transfer, the foreign bank holds a claim against the U.S. bank while the original deposit holder (usually a business firm) holds a Eurodollar deposit. It is called a Eurodollar deposit because it is denominated in U.S. dollars rather than in the currency of the country in which the foreign bank operates.

Large commercial banks have raised money by borrowing from the Eurodollar market through their overseas branches. Overseas branches of U.S. banks and banks outside the United States get funds in the Eurodollar market by accepting dollars in interest-bearing time deposit accounts. These dollar deposits are lent anywhere in the world, usually on a short-term basis. Banks, generally, transfer funds by telephone or electronically, lending large sums without collateral between banks. Banks that handle Eurodollars are located in Europe, with London as the center, and in other financial centers throughout the world, including such places as Singapore and the Bahamas.

Eurodollar deposit liabilities have arisen because the dollar is used as an international currency, and because foreigners are holding more dollars as a result of the ongoing U.S. balance of payment problems. Eurodollars are supplied by national and international corporations, banks, insurance companies, wealthy individuals, and some foreign governments and agencies. Eurodollar loan recipients are a diverse group, but commercial banks, multinational corporations, and national corporations are heavy users.

U.S. banks have entered the Eurodollar market through their overseas branches for three reasons: to finance business activity abroad, to switch Eurodollars into other currencies, and to lend to other Eurodollar banks. The most important reason, and the one that has received the most publicity in the United States, is for banking offices in the United States to borrow Eurodollars from their overseas branches. In this way, they get funds at lower costs and during periods of tight money.

15.5.2.7 Municipal Securities

Securities issued by municipalities, such as cities, towns, states, and school districts, pay interest that, under law, is exempt from federal income taxes. For this reason, some companies like to invest some of their excess cash in short-term municipal securities. For a corporation with a 30% marginal tax rate, earning an annual rate of 4% on municipal securities is equivalent to earning $4/(1 - 0.30)$ or 5.71% on taxable securities.

Where do firms invest their short-term cash holdings? U.S. government securities (mainly Treasury bills) are the most popular place to "park" cash, followed by CDs (time deposits), commercial paper, and other short-term investments, such as banker's acceptances and Eurodollars.

15.5.2.8 Short-term Investment Policy Statement

When the firm invests excess cash, it does not want to take undue risks. The funds will be needed in the future to pay bills or dividends, invest in capital budget projects, or repurchase outstanding bonds or shares of stock. A firm will seek the safety of principal (the amount invested) as the first priority when investing excess cash. A second important consideration is liquidity, which is the ability to sell the security and raise cash quickly, easily, and at a price close to fair market value. A third consideration, ranked last among these three, is return. The risk/expected return trade-off for investing excess cash is traditionally decided in terms of safe, low risk securities like those we've reviewed in this section.

Table 15.11   Sample Short-Term Investment Policy Guidelines

Investment	Maximum investment	Rating	Maximum maturity
Commercial Paper	$15 million/issuer	A1/P1	180 days
Certificates of Deposit	$25 million/institution	A1/P1 Bank Rating	270 days
U.S. Treasuries	None	Not applicable	18 months
Municipal securities	$10 million/issuer	A1/MIG1	15 months
Banker's Acceptances	$15 million/issuer	A1/P1	120 days

short-term investment policy statement guidelines that detail the type of securities the treasurer can invest in, their safety or default rating, maximum amounts that can be invested in each, and the maximum maturity of the securities purchased

A firm's treasurer will develop guidelines to use when investing the firm's excess cash. These guidelines, called a **short-term investment policy statement**, will detail the type of securities the treasurer can invest in, their safety or default rating, maximum amounts that can be invested in each, and the maximum maturity of the securities purchased. Except for possibly U.S. Treasury securities, most short-term investment policy statements will require some degree of diversification. Diversification will keep the firm's cash from being invested in one or a small number of issuers to protect against undue risk and potential loss in case an issuer gets into financial trouble. Table 15.11 shows a summary of one firm's short-term investment policy statement. It allows investment in five different short-term securities and limits exposure to any one issuer (except in the case of U.S. Treasuries) by specifying the maximum amount of securities from any one issuer that the portfolio can hold at any point in time.

Unlike bond ratings, the credit ratings on short-term obligations can be rated A-1, A-2, and A-3 or P-1, P-2, and P-3. Short-term municipal obligations can have "MIG" ratings to designate that they are issued by a municipality. Typically, only top-rated securities are allowed to be used when investing excess cash.

Some firms, rather than invest in individual securities, invest in money market mutual funds that are designed especially for use by corporate investors. Such funds will invest in a diversified pool of short-term securities and will face their own self-imposed limits on diversification, ratings, and maximum maturity.

The firm's financial managers will review the investment policy on a periodic basis to determine whether they should raise or lower limits, and whether they should expand or reduce the list of permissible securities. But they will always keep the focus on safety, liquidity, with return being in third place as a consideration.

FINANCE In times of low interest rates – which has been the case since the Great Recession – corporate treasurers have had difficulty in earning interest from their excess cash holdings. According to one source, in the early 2010s, a $100 million investment would earn only $30,000 – about 0.03% when invested in a money market fund that invested in safe and liquid securities. Investing in longer-term securities, such as two-year Treasury securities, could have earned the firm about $250,000 a year. Investing funds in short-term corporate bonds would have earned even more. But the finance principle of the trade-off between risk and return is still true! It is possible to earn higher expected returns by taking on more risk – but that may not be a wise strategy given the purpose of the firm's liquidity reserves. That said, some corporate treasurers are "laddering" their marketable security portfolios by having some invested in very-short-term securities and others spread among longer maturities to try to earn higher yields in a low interest rate environment.[13]

15.5.2.9 The Financial Crisis and its Impact on Short-Term Firm Financing

CRISIS The financial crisis and Great Recession of 2007–2009 had strong effects on the ability of borrower firms to obtain short-term financing, and on firms with surplus funds to invest in short-term instruments. Figure 15.9 illustrates the daily difference in interest rates between one-month AA-rated commercial paper and one-month (four-week) Treasury bills from mid-2001 until 2019, and how the cost of short-term corporate borrowing has settled down since the depths of the crisis.

---

[13] Jerry Klien and Brenden Joues, "Managing the High Cost of Liquidity," *Treasury and Risk* (September 15, 2015), accessed February 7, 2019, at http://www.treasuryandrisk.com/2015/09/15/managing-the-high-cost-of-liquidity.

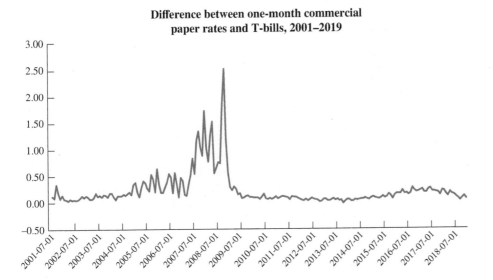

Difference between one-month commercial paper rates and T-bills, 2001–2019

FIGURE 15.9 Difference between one-month commercial paper rates and T-bills, 2001–2019

Source: St. Louis Federal Reserve District Bank, FRED Economic Data, https://research.stlouis-fed.org/fred2/, accessed February 7, 2019.

Major spikes in the risk premium between commercial paper and T-bills indicate great stresses to the financial system for issuers and investors. The initial spike to the left of the graph occurred around September 11, 2001, when the terrorist attack closed U.S. financial markets for several days. The largest spikes, around August 2007 and the fall of 2008, were related to the subprime crisis and the September/October 2008 turmoil in the financial markets as Lehman Brothers, a long-standing investment bank, went bankrupt and the U.S. financial system was teetering on the edge. As shown by the graph, spreads had become more normal and less volatile by the end of 2009. By the end of 2015, when the Federal Reserve started to raise interest rates, the spread, or difference between commercial paper and T-bill rates, was around 0.13 percentage points.

The sharp increases, or spikes, in the risk premium indicate periods of investors fleeing investments of perceived risk (commercial paper) and placing funds in the safest assets (T-bills). They represent times when liquidity "dried up" and firms that were desperate to obtain short-term financing (the topic of our next chapter) were forced to offer high risk premiums to find willing investors and lenders.

These episodes show why liquidity, marketability, and high quality are paramount in seeking places to invest excess cash. Risk and expected return go together in the stock and bond markets (Chapter 10) and in the marketable securities market.[14]

LEARNING ACTIVITY

1. **Visit the website of the St. Louis Fed to download current data on interest rates: https://research. stlouisfed.org/fred2/. Also, search for "living yield curve" using a Web search engine or go to https://stockcharts.com/freecharts/yieldcurve.php, clicking the "animate" button shows over 30 years of changing yield curve history.**
2. **What are the current levels of interest rates on short-term and long-term U.S. Treasury securities? Look at current rates, and historical ones, at the Treasury website: https://www.treasury. gov/resource-center/data-chart-center/interest-rates/Pages/TextView.aspx?data=yield.**

---

[14] Another casualty of the 2007–2009 financial crisis was auction rate (or adjustable rate) preferred stock. These were special preferred stock issues that had their dividend rate "reset," or adjusted, in weekly or monthly auctions run by sponsoring investment banks. In theory, investors could earn higher weekly returns on what was considered to be a short-term investment; short-term as, at any auction, the securities could be sold to other investors or back to the issuing firm. The regular adjustments to the dividend rate would keep the price of the preferred shares close to their par value, so there was thought to be little price risk. The nearly $330 billion market collapsed in early 2008 as the credit squeeze found an excess of investors wanting to sell their securities and the sponsoring firms and their investment banks having insufficient liquidity to repurchase the shares. In early 2010, billions of dollars were still held by firms waiting to redeem the shares, including $230 million owned by retailer Abercrombie and Fitch. In some cases, holders for auction-rate securities may have to hold them 20 years or more until they mature, which is a bad time frame for "short-term" investments. See, e.g., Liz Rappaport, "$20 Billion Fight Over Auction Notes, *The Wall Street Journal* (January 2, 2010), pp. A1, A4; Vincent Ryan, "Buyer's Remorse," *CFO* (July/August 2009), pp. 26–28; Terence R. Foster, "The Lure of Incremental Yield: When Will it Return?" *AFP Exchange* (May 2008), pp. 12–14.

15.6 GETTING – AND KEEPING – THE CASH

float the delay between when funds are sent by a payer to a payee

ETHICAL In addition to prudent investment of excess cash, there is another aspect of cash management: managing the cash conversion cycle by speeding up cash collections to receive cash as quickly as possible from customers (reducing the accounts receivable period) and keeping cash as long as possible (lengthening the accounts payable period). Ethically, there are concerns with lengthening the payables period by paying bills late; it is also bad business. But firms use several tools to speed up collections and slow down disbursements. Most of them use the concept of float. *Float* is the delay that occurs when funds are sent by a payer to a payee. *Collection float* is the time between when a payer sends payment and the funds are credited to the payee's bank account. *Disbursement float* is the time between when a payer sends payment and when the funds are deducted from the payer's bank account. Individuals can appreciate the concept of float just by comparing their checkbook balance to the bank's record of their checking account balance. The difference between the two amounts arises because of float.

By taking steps to reduce collection float or to increase disbursement float, the firm's treasurer can reduce the cash conversion cycle. Reducing the cash conversion cycle benefits the firm in two ways. First, as we've seen earlier in the chapter, it reduces the need for external financing. All else equal, a firm with a cash conversion cycle of 30 days uses less outside financing than one with a cycle of 32 days. The second benefit is increased profitability. Extra cash can be invested in securities, used to reduce interest-bearing loans, invested productively in the firm, or distributed to shareholders.

delivery or transmission float the delay in transferring the means of payment from the payer (customer) to the payee (the provider of the goods or services)

Float, whether we are dealing with collections or disbursements, has three components. First is *delivery or transmission float*. This is the delay in transferring the means of payment from the payer (customer) to the payee (the provider of the goods or services). A payment placed in the mail may take several days before it reaches its destination; payments via couriers such as Federal Express or DHL may be presented overnight and electronic transmission of payments occur with virtually no delivery float.

processing float delays in processing incoming payments from customers by the receiving firm

The second component is *processing float*, which are delays in processing incoming payments from customers by the receiving firm. Once a payment reaches its destination, "in-house" delays can arise since an envelope must be opened by the firm's accounts receivable staff (or banking partner) and its contents processed, deposited, and entered into the firm's financial processing system. Electronic payments do not come in an envelope, but they must be routed correctly and any differences corrected between invoices and payments.

clearing float the delay in transferring funds between payer and payee because of the banking system check-clearing processes

The third component is *clearing float*. This is the delay in transferring funds between payer and payee because of the banking system check-clearing processes. You have probably seen this in your bank statements or in your bank's check availability policy; funds from a check deposited in your account may be unavailable to you for one to three days. This is the time needed for the check to be routed back to the payer's bank and for the payer's bank to transfer funds to your bank.

lockbox system a system in which payments are sent to a P.O. Box and processed by a bank to reduce collection float

Seeking ways to reduce the components of collection float is one of the practical issues facing a firm's treasurer. To speed up cash collections from customers, firms can use a *lockbox system*. If you pay your phone bill, utility bill, or credit card bill to a "P.O. Box number" address, the firm receiving your payment is probably using a lockbox. Most lockboxes are managed by banks.[15] Several times a day, bank personnel will empty the postal box and immediately begin processing and depositing payments from customers. A firm will consider mail delivery times, average number of pieces of mail received, and the average size of the receipts from customers before deciding where the lockboxes should be geographically located.

pre-authorized checks regular (typically, monthly) deductions by a vendor from a customer's checking account

Pre-authorized checks are a means of reducing delivery and processing delays. If you have monthly expenses automatically deducted from your checking account, that is an example of a pre-authorized check; the checks allow firms to regularly deduct payments from customers' bank accounts. They are a means to pay utility, cable, and insurance bills. Pre-authorized checks are initiated by the company to deduct funds from customers' accounts. Much of the process is automated, reducing delivery and processing delays.

---

[15] Lockbox systems are complex for large firms. General Electric uses over 150 lockboxes managed by three banks for collecting receipts from its various global divisions. Richard Gamble, "More Than Just a Pretty Image," *Treasury and Risk Management* (May 2004), pp. 41–44.

Processing delays, as well as some delivery delays, are reduced by the use of technology. Large incoming payments (say, over $1 million) can be automatically flagged by the lockbox bank and alerts sent to the firm's treasurer. Electronic check images and electronic payments (rather than the use of paper checks) reduce mail and processing delays. Forms recognition technology allows incoming payments and data to be read electronically, and for data to be stored in a form usable to the vendor. Use of the Internet and other electronic means for making payments eliminates delivery float and speeds processing. Lockboxes and pre-authorized checks reduce processing delays, as processing is handled by banks, speeding deposit of incoming receipts.

Clearing float is reduced by the Fed and the banking system. Under Check 21, a law that went into effect in late 2004, payee banks can present electronic or digital images of checks to payer banks, rather than having to physically deliver paper checks, for payment. As this technology is adopted, clearing delays will be reduced since this law eliminates the need to physically transport, record, and reconcile billions of paper checks per year.

ETHICAL Fewer options are available for slowing disbursements. A customer who is slow in their disbursements might be considered a poor customer at best or unethical at worst. When credit gets tight, the slow-paying customers are the first to be terminated. Most disbursement systems involve selected banks where funds to be disbursed are deposited to maximize float. Many firms use a **zero-balance account** in which just enough funds are transferred into an account to cover that day's checks presented for payment.

zero-balance account an account in which just enough funds are transferred into an account to cover that day's checks presented for payment

It may be only a matter of time before float disappears on most business-to-business (B2B) and person-to-business (P2B) transactions. The growth of communications systems has resulted in firms using **electronic data interchange** as a means to send invoices and electronic payment for goods and services. Internet trading exchanges and Web-based funds transfer are the next steps in eliminating float.[16]

electronic data interchange the use of communications and computer systems to convey ordering, invoice, and payment information between suppliers and customers

Another method that is growing in popularity is **remote capture**. Remote capture allows the company receiving a check to scan it through a device that records the relevant bank, account, and other payment information. Once scanned, the information can be sent digitally to the firm's bank. Such electronic processing eliminates paper handling and the need to complete a deposit slip listing each of the day's checks. It reduces the potential keying errors and reduces float, as electronic images are transmitted from the recipient, the recipient's bank, the payer's bank, and the payer's bank account. After scanning, the paper check can be destroyed or returned to the customer. Some stores have the scanners located by cash registers; the check is returned to the customer after it has been run through the scanner, thus helping customers to keep track of their spending and use of checks.

remote capture scanning of paper checks to electronically gather and transmit the payment information

Another payment mechanism is the use of debit cards; use of the debit card speeds the process of deducting funds from the customer's checking account and adding it to the firm's cash balances.

Many people today use "online bill pay" as a way to pay bills and manage their accounts without having to write a paper check. For businesses, it is also less expensive and less time-consuming to do business electronically rather by paper check. That is why many businesses pay regular bills, such as payroll, electronically through direct deposit. One study found that a small business paying 100 employees twice a month can save almost $5,800 a year by using direct deposit rather than paper checks. For large businesses, the savings adds up to over $1 million per year.[17] The U.S. government now uses direct deposit for Social Security checks, eliminating paper and postage costs.

ETHICAL In addition to lower costs, use of an electronic payment mechanism reduces the possibility of fraud and identity theft. Anywhere from three to ten people will handle a paper check before it is returned in a monthly bank statement. Paper checks can be "washed" of the original payee's information and another name inserted for payment. Using a desktop scanner, a person can scan in a check, make changes, and print out a new version of the check to be paid to a different person or with a different amount. Unlike paper checks, electronic payments are made and processed under the tight

---

[16] Kenneth N. Kuttner and James J. McAndrews, "Personal On-Line Payments," *Economic Policy Review*, Federal Reserve Bank of New York (December 2001), pp. 35–50; Edward Teach, "Going Virtual," *CFO* (May 2000), pp. 81–88.

[17] NACHA – the Electronic Payments Association, *Direct Deposit/Direct Payment General Information*, 2nd ed., (Herndon, VA; June 2003). Original calculations for 1st edition made by Joseph D. Tinucci, Tinucci and Associates Inc., March 2001.

Table 15.12   Methods to Reduce the Components of Collection and Disbursement Float

Components of Float	Types of Float	
	Collection Float	**Disbursement Float**
Delivery	Lockboxes	Selection of disbursement banks to maximize delivery float, clearing float, and to maximize prudent returns on corporate cash (such as using zero-balance accounts)
	Pre-authorized checks	
	Electronic payments	
Processing	Lockboxes	
	Pre-authorized checks	
	Electronic payments	
	Use of technology	
	Digital imaging	
Clearing	Banking system improvements to allow electronic images rather than paper checks	

computer and network security that exists in banks and in transmissions between banks. You may have seen the benefits of personal payment systems and their security if you have used systems such as Apple Pay and Google Pay to purchase items. The transactions are secure and act as either a debit card or a credit card transaction.

Table 15.12 summarizes various ways to address float so the firm can hold onto its cash for as long as is ethically possible.

DISCUSSION QUESTION 3

Are there any ethical implications of firms' attempts to speed up cash collections or to slow down cash disbursements? What might happen if we move to a paperless (no cash, no paper checks) money transfer system?

LEARNING ACTIVITY

1. Visit https://www.afponline.org, the website of the Treasury Management Association. The site is specifically oriented toward those working in cash collection, disbursement, management, and investment. Learn about the Certified Treasury Professional (CTP) professional designation while visiting this site.
2. Visit https://www.nacha.org, the website of the National Automated Clearinghouse Association – the Electronic Payments Association, to learn more about electronic payment processing.

15.7 ACCOUNTS RECEIVABLE MANAGEMENT

The management of receivables involves conducting credit analysis, setting credit terms, and carrying out collection efforts. Taken together, these decision areas determine the level of investment in accounts receivable. The selling of goods on credit is, generally, driven by industry norms and competitive pressures. The time it takes to collect accounts receivable depends on industry norms for credit terms, as well as the firm's policies for setting credit standards and carrying out collection efforts.

15.7.1 CREDIT ANALYSIS

ETHICAL Credit analysis involves appraising the creditworthiness, or quality, of a potential customer. It determines whether credit should be granted to the borrower, and if so, how much. The decision is made on the basis of the applicant's character, capacity, capital, collateral, and conditions, known as the five Cs of credit analysis.

Some of these involve an analysis of a potential buyer's financial statements using the ratios we saw in Chapter 14. Character is the ethical quality of the applicant on which one can base a judgment

character ethical quality of the applicant on which one can base a judgment about his or her willingness to pay bills and is best judged by reviewing past credit history for long overdue or unpaid obligations

about his or her willingness to pay bills and is best judged by reviewing past credit history for long overdue or unpaid obligations. **Capacity** is the ability to pay bills and often involves an examination of liquidity ratios. **Capital** indicates the adequacy of owners' equity relative to existing liabilities as the underlying support for creditworthiness. **Collateral** reflects whether assets are available to provide security for the potential credit. **Conditions** refer to the current economic climate and state of the business cycle. They are an important consideration in assessing whether the applicant can meet credit obligations.

Once a firm has established its credit quality standards, credit analysis is used to determine whether an applicant is granted credit or rejected, or whether the applicant falls into a marginal category. Whether credit should be extended to marginal applicants depends on such factors as the prevailing economic conditions and the extent to which the selling firm has excess production capacity. During periods of economic downturn and excess capacity, a firm may need to sell to lower quality applicants who may be slow to pay but are unlikely to default.

An example of this is comes from your local car dealership. To entice buyers when sales are sluggish, auto manufacturers may offer below-market financing rates, attractive refunds, and/or low (or no) down payment requirements. Sales can rise sharply as a result of aggressive marketing via credit terms, but an unfortunate result, as Mitsubishi found in 2003–2004, is that some buyers found themselves unable to repay the loans with the result of large losses accruing to the firm. When Mitsubishi tightened its credit standards, sales fell sharply. The success of a firm requires a product offering good value to customers more so than attractive credit terms.

15.7.2 CREDIT-REPORTING AGENCIES

Several sources of credit information are available to help a firm decide whether to extend credit. **Credit bureaus** exist to obtain credit information about business firms and individuals. They are not-for-profit institutions, established and supported by the businesses they serve.

The local mercantile, or business, credit bureau provides a central record for credit information on firms in the community. Bureau members submit lists of their customers to the bureau. The bureau determines the credit standing of these customers by contacting other bureau members who have extended credit to them. Thus, a member firm need only contact its credit bureau for information on prospective customers rather than deal with many individual firms.

The exchange of mercantile credit information from bureau to bureau is accomplished through the National Credit Interchange System. Credit bureau reports are factual rather than analytical, and it is up to each credit analyst to interpret the facts.

Local retail credit bureaus have been established to consolidate and distribute credit information on individuals in the community. These organizations are generally owned and operated by participating members on a nonprofit basis. A central organization known as the Associated Credit Bureaus of America enables local retail credit bureaus in the United States to transmit credit information from bureau to bureau.

GLOBAL American businesses selling to foreign customers encounter all the problems involved in a domestic sale, such as credit checking, plus several others. Among these are increased distance, language differences, complicated shipping and government regulations, differences in legal systems, and political instability. To help exporters with these problems, the National Association of Credit Management established the Foreign Credit Interchange Bureau (FCIB). Local credit bureaus increase their information on business credit risks by pooling credit and collection experience; FCIB members have established a central file of information covering several decades of credit experience. The FCIB is located in New York to serve the numerous export and financial organizations there that do business overseas.

Some private firms operate as credit-reporting agencies. The best known is Dun & Bradstreet (D&B), which has been in operation for over a century and provides credit information on businesses of all kinds. The information is brought into the company through many channels. The company employs full- and part-time employees for direct investigation, communicates directly with business establishments by mail to supplement information files, and obtains the financial statements of companies

capacity the ability to pay bills and often involves an examination of liquidity ratios

capital indicates the adequacy of owners' equity relative to existing liabilities as the underlying support for creditworthiness

collateral reflects whether assets are available to provide security for the potential credit

conditions refer to the current economic climate and state of the business cycle

credit bureaus not-for-profit institutions that obtain credit information about business firms and individuals being evaluated. All information filed with public authorities and financial and trade papers is gathered and analyzed to produce a credit analysis. The basic service supplied to the manufacturers, wholesalers, banks, and insurance companies who subscribe to D&B is rendered in two ways: through written reports on individual businesses and through a reference book.

A D&B report is, typically, divided into five sections: rating and summary, trade payments, financial information, operation and location, and history. In addition, they publish a composite reference book of ratings on thousands of manufacturers, wholesalers, retailers, and other businesses six times per year.

When many customers want to apply for credit, in-depth credit analysis focusing on the five Cs is impractical. Companies that offer credit cards use a sophisticated statistical tool called credit scoring. Credit scoring takes information about thousands of customers and, through computer number crunching, develops a formula that tries to predict who is a good credit risk (someone who will likely pay their bill in a timely manner) and who is a poor credit risk. To make this determination, credit scoring models use quantitative items: a person's income, past mortgage or credit card payment history, marital status, homeowner/renter status, and current debts.

However, such models will make errors. One person applied for a credit card and was rejected despite having a clean credit record. He earned $123,100 in salary at age 41 in a job with excellent security. The person was Lawrence B. Lindsey, who at the time was on the board of governors of the Federal Reserve System. Ben Bernanke, formerly chair of the Federal Reserve, was turned down for a mortgage refinance in last 2014 as the computer model flagged his application that he had recently changed jobs – true, as his term as Fed chair was over and he was now beginning a lucrative career writing a book and giving speeches at $100,000 or more a speech. A man who helps set interest rate and bank policy was rejected because the computer models could not handle the qualitative data that explained why his credit report appeared as it did – or foresee that his earnings potential is far greater than while in his former Federal Reserve position. Ironically, in an earlier speech, Mr. Lindsey predicted the following about credit scoring: "We will obtain the fairness of the machine, but lose the judgment, talents, and sense of justice that only humans can bring to decision making."[18]

15.7.3 CREDIT TERMS AND COLLECTION EFFORTS

trade credit credit extended on purchases to a firm's customers

Credit extended on purchases to a firm's customers is called **trade credit** and is discussed more fully in Chapter 16. This credit appears as accounts payable on the balance sheet of the customer and as receivables to the seller. The seller sets the terms of the credit. For example, the firm might require full payment in 60 days, expressed as net 60. If all customers pay promptly in 60 days, this would result in a receivables turnover of 365/60, or about six times a year.[19] Thus, annual net sales of $720,000 would require an average receivables investment of about $120,000. A change in credit terms or in the enforcement of the terms through the collection effort will alter the average investment in receivables. The imposition of net 50-day terms would lead to an increase in the receivables turnover to 7.3 (365/50) times and the average investment in receivables would decline to about $100,000 ($720,000/7.3). If it costs, say, 15% to finance assets,[20] then the $20,000 reduction in receivables would result in a savings of $3,000 ($20,000 × 15%).

We are assuming that a reduction in the credit period and in the receivables portion of the short-term operating cycle will not cause lost sales. The financial manager must not impose credit terms that will lower sales and cause lost profits that would more than offset any financing cost savings.

---

[18] David Wessel, "A Man Who Governs Credit is Denied a Toys 'R' Us Card," *The Wall Street Journal* (December 14, 1995), p. B1. For the story about Ben Bernanke, see Neil Irwin, "Why Ben Bernanke Can't Refinance His Mortgage," (October 2, 2014), accessed January 30.2016, at http://www.nytimes.com/2014/10/03/upshot/why-ben-bernanke-cant-refinance-his-mortgage.html.

[19] The turnover of current asset accounts such as receivables and inventories, like total assets turnover, is an asset utilization ratio. A higher ratio implies better usage of assets.

[20] The 15% figure represents the cost of financing assets through the firm's liabilities and equity, which is the right-hand side of the balance sheet. Any change in assets must be financed by a change in liabilities and equity. The 15% figure does not represent the cost of managing accounts receivable from a human or technology perspective.

GLOBAL In global business, a concern in managing overseas accounts is the effect of changing exchange rates on the funds received by the firm. For example, suppose a firm sells an item for $50 to customers in the United States and for €57 to customers in France, based upon an exchange rate of about $1 = 1.14 euros. Over the next 60 days when payment is due, should the dollar strengthen to, say, $1 = 1.20 euros, the firm will receive only a €57/1.20 euros per dollar, or $47.5, which will hurt its profitability.

A firm can handle this issue in one of two ways. First, the firm can invoice customers in the firm's home currency. That is, a U.S. firm can request payment from a customer in France in terms of the U.S. dollar instead of the euro. This shifts the risk of changing exchange rates to the payer. Second, if a U.S. firm allows customers to pay in their own currencies rather than in U.S. dollars, the firm can hedge, or reduce, the risk of changing exchange rates by using currency futures or options contracts. General information about futures and options contracts is in the Learning Extension to Chapter 11.

The collection effort also involves administering past due accounts. Techniques include sending letters, making telephone calls, and even making personal visits for large customers with past due bills. One credit card company sent Hallmark greeting cards to its delinquent customers to encourage them to contact the firm to arrange payment schedules. If a customer continues to fail to pay a bill, then the account may be turned over to a commercial collection firm. If this fails, the last resort is to take legal action.[21] The use of email payment requests is gaining popularity as a means to quickly and cheaply contact customers who are behind in their payments.

A lax collection policy may result in the average collection period for receivables being longer than the credit period as stated in the terms. As seen, the average collection period is the ratio of accounts receivable to the average sales per day. For example, a firm might sell on credit terms of net 60 days and have net sales of $720,000 and an accounts receivable balance of $150,000. For this firm, the average collection period is the following:

$$\frac{\text{Accounts receivable}}{\text{Net sales} / 365} = \frac{\$150,000}{\$720,000 / 365} = \frac{\$150,000}{\$1,973} = 76 \text{ days}$$

This shows the accounts receivable are outstanding an average of 76 days instead of the stated 60-day credit period. Increasing credit standards or improving the collection effort might reduce the average collection period to 60 days and the accounts receivable balance to $120,000. Lowering either a firm's credit standards or the customer credit quality will cause the average collection period to lengthen, as poorer-quality customers are, generally, slower payers. Thus, the financial manager must balance the advantages of increased sales from more customers against the cost of financing higher receivable investments and increased collection costs.

For example, suppose a firm is considering lowering its credit standards to increase sales. Table 15.13 summarizes the analysis to determine if the credit change makes financial sense. The estimated sales will rise by $100,000. Additional bad debt expense from poor credit risks is expected to be 5%, leaving a net revenue increase of $95,000. With a profit margin of 10%, the incremental benefit of lowering standards is $9,500.

The costs of lowering credit standards will be the cost of financing higher receivables and inventory balances. If sales rise by $100,000, the firm expects its average receivables balance will rise by $14,000 and its average inventory balance will rise by $18,000, for an increase of $32,000 in current assets. If the cost of financing these assets is 15%, the cost of the looser credit policy is $32,000 × 0.15, or $4,800. The incremental benefit of $9,500 is larger than the incremental cost, $4,800, so the firm should go ahead with its plan. This analysis requires that the additional risks of the looser credit policy are reflected in the 15% cost of financing. This may differ from the firm's cost of financing its other assets. Recall from Chapter 12 that expected return and risk are linked; should the added accounts be more risky than the firm's assets as a whole because of their greater risk of nonpayment, the cost of financing the risky assets may need to be adjusted.

---

[21] See Brenda L. Moore, "Dunning Debtors," *The Wall Street Journal* (May 4, 2001), pp. R9, R11 for insights into the process of collecting past-due accounts.

Table 15.13 Analysis of a Change in Credit Policy

Marginal or Additional Benefits:

Increased sales (estimate): $100,000.

Additional bad debt expense from change in sales: 5%

0.05 × $100,000 = $5,000 in losses

Net estimated increase in sales: $95,000

Expected profit margin: 10%

Net increase in profits = 0.10 × $95,000 = $9,500

Marginal or Additional Costs:

Increases in asset accounts:

Accounts receivables average increase: $14,000

Inventory average increase: $18,000

Total: $32,000 increase in current assets to be financed

Cost of financing: 15%

Net increase in financing costs = 0.15 × $32,000 = $4,800

DISCUSSION QUESTION 4

Select one of the Cs of credit analysis and explain how you would attempt to measure it.

LEARNING ACTIVITY

1. A source of credit information for business customers is Dun & Bradstreet, https://www.dnb.com. Your own personal credit information can be obtained from credit bureau firms such as Equifax (https://www.equifax.com), Experian (https://www.experian.com), and Trans Union Corporation (https://www.transunion.com). Through https://www.annualcreditreport.com, a government-sponsored website, you may obtain a free copy of your credit report from each of the three personal credit bureaus.

2. For more information on credit scoring, see https://www.myfico.com and https://www.vantagescore.com.

3. Learn more about current issues in short-term finance at https://www.cfo.com and https://www.treasuryandrisk.com.

15.8 INVENTORY MANAGEMENT

Inventory administration is primarily a production management function. The length of the production process and the production manager's willingness to accept delays will influence the amount invested in raw materials and work in process. The amount of finished goods on hand may vary, depending on the firm's willingness to accept stock-outs and lost sales.

Costs of owning raw materials, such as financing, storage, and insurance, need to be balanced against the costs of ordering the materials. Production managers attempt to balance these costs by determining the optimal number of units to order that will minimize inventory costs of total raw materials.

Let's assume that a firm's cost of goods sold is $600,000 and it has inventories on hand of $100,000. Recall that the inventory turnover is computed as follows:

$$\frac{\text{Cost of goods sold}}{\text{Inventories}} = \frac{\$600,000}{\$100,000} = 6 \text{ times}$$

If the firm is able to increase its inventory turnover to, say, eight times, then the investment in inventories could be reduced to $75,000 ($600,000/8) and some financing costs would be saved. However, if a tight inventory policy is imposed, lost sales due to stock-outs could result in lost profits that more than offset financing cost savings. Thus, the financial manager must balance possible savings against potential added costs when managing investments in inventories.

The just-in-time (JIT) inventory control system aims to reduce the amount of inventories they must carry. Under this system, substantial coordination is required between the manufacturer and its suppliers so that materials needed in the manufacturing process are delivered just in time to avoid halts in production. For example, automobile manufacturers who used to keep a two-week supply of certain parts now place orders on a daily basis and expect daily shipment and delivery. As we will mention in Chapter 17, higher fuel costs can cause firms to reconsider the wisdom of daily deliveries in fuel-inefficient trucks.

Corporate fads may come and go, but one that is sure to stay is the attempt by corporations to reduce their net working capital by reducing their current asset account balances. Some firms have a goal of operating with zero working capital. Although they may not attain it, striving for this goal creates opportunities to discover efficiencies, improve production processes and customer relations, and free up cash. At a time when firms need cash to invest in overseas facilities and markets, invest in new technology, and service debt, the uncovering of cash by reducing working capital is similar to finding a treasure chest.

The average Fortune 500 firm has 20 cents of working capital for every $1 of sales; a grand total of over $500 billion for all the firms on the list. A small increase in working capital efficiency can have a significant impact on cash flow. A report by PwC (formerly PriceWaterhouseCoopers) estimates that firms can improve their cash flow by 1.3 trillion euros by managing their working capital more efficiently.[22] It is no accident that Amazon's first year of profitability, 2001, was accompanied by an increase in inventory turnover from 9 to 13; the extra asset efficiency helped to deliver savings and profits to its bottom line.[23]

Cutting working capital generates cash and can increase company earnings. Financing costs should decline as less financing is needed to support large receivables and inventory balances. Costs of warehousing and handling inventory will fall as inventory levels are pared. Slimmed down current asset balances will lead to reductions in firms' total assets. The results of cost savings and smaller asset bases will mean higher returns on assets and, in all likelihood, increases in shareholder wealth.

Another innovation in inventory management is JIT II. JIT II moves the JIT relationship between vendor and purchaser a step tighter. The position of buyer's purchaser or materials planner is eliminated and replaced by a supplier representative. This person works closely with the buyer to, at times, manage inventories and issue purchase orders to supply additional materials. The advantages of this system are increased efficiency by reducing inventory, eliminated duplicate positions, and planning assistance. For JIT II to work effectively, the buyer must trust the supplier along two dimensions: the supplier's products will continue to meet the buyer's needs, and the proprietary information to which the vendor's representative has access will remain private and not be shared outside this specific buyer – vendor relationship.

Technology is fast improving the ability of firms to manage cash and receivables, to control inventory, and to communicate with customers and suppliers more efficiently. Firms in industries such as auto manufacturing, oil and gas, and retailing, are initiating Internet-based systems (portals) for ordering items from suppliers. Portals are specialized and secure websites through which clients can access order and account information. Business-to-business (B2B) portals have the promise of lowering procurement and supply chain costs. They also provide a way for firms to sell excess inventory or assets.

> **15.9 TECH-NOLOGY AND WORKING CAPITAL MANAGEMENT**

15.9.1 CASH MANAGEMENT

The Internet (and corporate intranets) allows treasurers and other finance personnel to closely track the firm's cash flows and needs. Information on bank balances, incoming checks, and the status of disbursements are available online through bank portals. The use of the Web allows the transfer of funds

---

[22] D. Windaus, et al. Navigating Uncertainty: PwC's Annual Global Working Capital Study 2018–2019, https://www.pwc.com/gx/en/working-capital-management-services/assets/pwc-working-capital-survey-2018-2019.pdf, accessed February 8, 2019.

[23] Ronald Fink, "Forget the Float?" *CFO* (July 2001), pp. 54–62; Randy Myers, "Cash Crop," *CFO* (August 2000), pp. 59–82; S. L. Mintz, "Lean Green Machines," *CFO* (July 2000), pp. 76–94; Shawn Tully, "Raiding a Company's Hidden Cash," *Fortune* (August 22, 1994), pp. 82–87.

between corporate accounts and the initiation of electronic payments and pre-authorized check transactions. Traveling executives can access treasury information online, from the firm's main bank and from all of its banking relationships. Access to such information allows the treasurer to forecast and estimate the firm's needs for cash on a day-to-day basis and, thus, reduce the level of excess cash and keep short-term borrowing at the minimum level needed.

15.9.2 PROCESSING INVOICES AND FLOAT

Technology has revolutionized order processing. Imagine collecting orders by hand, keying them into a computer (sometimes twice as a check against keying errors), printing bills, stuffing envelopes, mailing bills, waiting for customers to pay their bills, processing incoming payments and reconciling differences, handling the collection process, and writing off bad debts, which are all labor-intensive and time-intensive.

Electronic data interchange (EDI) systems helped to computerize some of the payment and collection process. EDI allows a limited amount of invoice information to accompany an electronic bill payment. However, the expanding use of extensible markup language (XML) in business applications is automating much of this process. Many of you are aware of hypertext markup language (HTML), the language that Web browsers use to read, interpret, and display Web pages. XML goes a step beyond HTML. XML tells computer systems what kind of information is being transmitted (e.g., financial, invoice, ordering, pictures), so different computer systems can recognize data and communicate with each other. XML systems will help firms process orders more efficiently and reduce, if not nearly eliminate, processing float.

A variation to XML is electronic invoice presentment and payments (EIPP) systems. Working through an Internet portal, vendors and customers can more efficiently process and pay for orders. Consider this example. A client orders ten computers online from a vendor. The automated system collects the order, approves it, and prepares the computers for shipping. When they are delivered, the client realizes one of the computers does not work. The client goes online, pulls up the invoice, and marks the disputed item. This starts an automated process that adjusts the invoice to bill the client for the working computers for online payment (perhaps via XML). Others are notified electronically, too, and by way of email the dispute is resolved; either a shipping label is sent so the bad machine can be returned to the vendor or a technician is sent to fix it or a replacement computer is sent to the client and the invoice adjusted. EIPP systems speed ordering, dispute resolution, and payment collection.

15.9.3 TRACKING INVENTORY

The movement toward JIT, better supplier – buyer communications, and information technology (IT) has improved sales forecasting and production processes. You are familiar with product scanners at store checkout lines; many times, the scanned information is sent directly to suppliers detailing the necessary size of the next morning's product shipment.

Tracking inventory allows firms to reduce the inventory conversion period (and, thus, the cash conversion cycle), reduce costs, and track shipments more effectively. Bar codes on boxes are scanned to track inventory in transit between vendor, warehouse, retail store, and checkout counter. Radio frequency identification (RFID) tags take inventory tracking one step further. The RFID tag sends out a radio signal to electronic readers that allow companies to know the location of inventory on a minute-by-minute basis. RFID tags for cargo containers can send alarms when a break-in has occurred; when it has been sitting in one location for too long; or if any preset condition relating to temperature, air pressure, motion, and so on inside the container is violated. Tracking with such detail can reduce theft and spoilage as well as inventory levels and the costs of carrying inventory.

LEARNING ACTIVITY

Examples of B2B websites include https://b2b.statefarm.com/b2b/index.html (insurance repairs and other services) and https://www.itex.com (bartering website for B2B trading)

• **Institutions and Markets**   The market determines short-term interest rates, based partly on Fed policy, on expectations of future Fed policy and inflation, and on the supply and demand of short-term funds. Banks and other financial services firms are eager to attract firm's excess short-term funds so they, in turn, can lend them to entities that desire short-term financing.

• **Investments**   We usually think that investing involves long-term assets (bonds, stocks, buildings, corporate strategies), but it involves short-term assets, too. Investing excess cash can be a means of increasing profits. The expected return/risk trade-off holds true for short-term investments as well as long-term investments.

• **Financial Management**   A firm's long-term goal is to maximize shareholder wealth, but it needs to survive the short-term first. To do so, the firm needs to maintain its liquidity and manage its cash, receivables, and inventory to satisfy its creditors, suppliers, and customers. A firm with poor cash, credit, and inventory management will have unhappy customers, lenders, and suppliers and may not be in business much longer.

LO 15.1   Working capital is another term for current assets. Inventories are produced and sold (or services are rendered) to clients, and if not paid for immediately in cash by the customer, an account receivable is created that is paid by the customer on mutually agreed upon terms. This "flow" from product/service sale to receivable to cash allows the firm to maintain a cash balance to pay its bills and its workers and to continue to operate in the short run. It is cash, not earnings, that keeps a firm in business.

LO 15.2   A firm's operating cycle measures the time it takes from when raw materials are received, processed into finished goods, and sold to when cash is collected from the sale of the finished products. The cash conversion cycle is similar to the operating cycle except that it measures the time between when the firm pays for its materials purchases and when cash is collected from their sale. Firms with faster inventory turnovers, faster receivables turnovers, and slower average payment periods will have shorter cash conversion cycles.

LO 15.3   In general, the longer the operating cycle, the greater the balance of a firm's inventory and accounts receivable will be. As assets, they must be financed by firm borrowing or owners' equity. Thus, the longer the cycle is, the greater the firm's financing needs and accompanying financing costs. One offset is if the firm obtains short-term finance through accounts payable – money it owes to its suppliers. Both the operating and cash conversion cycle and its components will be affected by seasonal sales patterns and business cycles.

LO 15.4   Company treasurers are interested in watching a firm's cash flows and forecasting future cash flows to ensure adequate cash is available to pay the firm's obligations when they are due. A cash budget provides a treasurer with some detail on expected cash inflows and cash outflows. Specifically, it shows the amounts and the sources of expected cash inflows (from sales forecasts and customers paying their credit obligations) and outflows (such as payments to suppliers, utilities, workers, interest on debt, and dividends to shareholders). By using the cash budget, the treasurer can plan how best to invest cash surpluses and borrow to cover cash deficits.

LO 15.5   The four motives for a firm to hold cash and marketable securities are (a) the transactions motive, for financing day-to-day operations; (b) the precautionary motive, to hedge against random events such as production delays due to mechanical breakdowns or extreme weather; (c) the speculative motive, to take advantage of "great deals" offered by suppliers on materials or asset needs; and (d) the tax motives, where funds are kept outside of the United States due to high U.S. corporate tax rates. Investing excess cash in marketable securities is a process in which the treasurer balances the need for safety and liquidity of the invested funds with the desire to earn returns on the investment. Popular marketable securities investments include Treasury bills (T-bills), negotiable certificates of deposit (CDs), commercial paper, and Eurodollar deposits.

LO 15.6   Firms wish to collect cash as quickly and efficiently as possible while holding on to cash as long as law and ethics allow. Ways to "play the bank float" or speed up collections from customers can include electronic funds payment or having customers send checks by courier for next-day delivery. Lockboxes (to speed up the mail delivery to banks in various locations) and pre-authorized checks (so the firm can obtain funds without waiting for a customer to send a check) are some ways to reduce types of float. Remote capture of a mailed-in check (or cash offered at a store's cash register) and online bill pay can speed collections, as can encouraging the use of debit cards by cash register customers. If customer – supplier relations will not be harmed, and if ethical considerations are properly observed, disbursement float can be increased by mailing paper checks, either from remote processing centers (thus increasing delivery float and clearing float) or by drawing checks on banks located in smaller cities or towns.

LO 15.7 Marketing concerns are a major determinant of accounts receivable policies as tighter credit may cause lost sales. Credit departments need to review the five Cs of a potential customer's credit background: character, capacity, capital, collateral, and conditions. Credit reports may be "pulled" from credit bureaus to judge a potential client's bill-paying history. A change in credit policy considers the impact on sales, bad debt expense, accounts receivable and inventory management expenses, and financing cost implications.

LO 15.8 Production and purchasing issues may dominate the inventory decision. Nonetheless, financial managers need to be part of these strategic discussions and aware of the factors that affect these decisions. More firms have realized that significant amounts of cash are tied up in working capital. Ways to increase inventory "turns" and improve supplier relationships with respect to inventory purchases and payments can save the firm money, both in storage and in financing excess inventory.

LO 15.9 Attempts to speed up cash collections, slow disbursements, and reduce receivables and inventories can free up cash, lead to more efficient operations, and increase firm profitability and shareholder wealth.

KEY TERMS

capacity	conditions	operating cycle	short-term investment
capital	delivery or transmission	precautionary	policy statement
cash budget	float	motives	speculative motives
cash conversion cycle	electronic data	pre-authorized	trade credit
character	interchange	checks	transactions motive
clearing float	float	processing float	zero-balance account
collateral	lockbox system	remote capture	

REVIEW QUESTIONS

1. **(LO 15.1)** What is working capital?

2. **(LO 15.2)** Briefly describe a manufacturing firm's operating cycle.

3. **(LO 15.2)** Explain how the cash conversion cycle differs from the operating cycle.

4. **(LO 15.2)** Describe how the length of the cash conversion cycle is determined.

5. **(LO 15.2)** Explain how the length of the operating cycle affects the amount of funds invested in accounts receivable and inventories.

6. **(LO 15.3)** What affects the amount of financing provided by accounts payable as viewed in terms of the cash conversion cycle?

7. **(LO 15.4)** What is a cash budget? How does the treasurer use forecasts of cash surpluses and cash deficits?

8. **(LO 15.4)** Three sets of information are needed to construct a cash budget. Explain what they are.

9. **(LO 15.4)** Why might firms want to maintain minimum cash balances?

10. **(LO 15.4)** What are the sources of cash inflows to a firm over any time frame?

11. **(LO 15.4)** What are the sources of cash outflows from a firm over any time frame?

12. **(LO 15.4)** How does the choice of level or seasonal production affect a firm's cash over the course of a year?

13. **(LO 15.4)** Describe what happens to a firm's current asset accounts if the firm has seasonal sales and uses (a) level production or (b) seasonal production.

14. **(LO 15.5)** Describe the four motives or reasons for holding cash.

15. **(LO 15.5)** What characteristics should an investment have to qualify as an acceptable marketable security?

16. **(LO 15.5)** Identify and briefly describe several financial instruments used as marketable securities.

17. **(LO 15.5)** Why would a corporation want to invest excess cash in securities issued by a municipality?

18. **(LO 15.5)** What are the three main concerns of a treasurer when investing a firm's excess cash?

19. **(LO 15.5)** Why is a short-term investment policy statement necessary?

20. **(LO 15.6)** What is float? Why is it important to cash management?

21. **(LO 15.6)** What are the three components of float? Which are under the control of the firm seeking to reduce collection float?

22. **(LO 15.6)** What are some strategies a firm can use to speed up its collections by reducing float?

23. **(LO 15.6)** How can processing float be reduced?

24. **(LO 15.6)** How can a firm use float to slow down its disbursements?

25. **(LO 15.6)** Why can't a firm that wants to increase disbursement float make payments after the stated due date?

26. **(LO 15.6)** How does remote capture reduce float?

27. **(LO 15.6)** Besides lower expenses, explain another advantage of using electronic payments rather than paper checks.

28. **(LO 15.7)** What is credit analysis? Identify the five Cs of credit analysis.

29. **(LO 15.7)** Describe various credit-reporting agencies that provide information on business credit applicants.

30. **(LO 15.7)** How can a firm control the risk of changing exchange rates when billing an overseas customer?

31. **(LO 15.7)** What risks arise when a firm lowers its credit standards to try to increase sales volume?

32. **(LO 15.7)** How do credit terms and collection efforts affect the investment in accounts receivable?

33. **(LO 15.8)** How is the financial manager involved in the management of inventories?

34. **(LO 15.8)** What are the benefits to a firm of reducing its working capital?

35. **(LO 15.8)** What is JIT II?

36. **(LO 15.9)** How is technology affecting cash management? Order processing?

37. **(LO 15.9)** How is technology changing inventory management?

PROBLEMS

1. Pretty Lady Cosmetic Products has an average production process time of 40 days. Finished goods are kept on hanvd for an average of 15 days before they are sold. Accounts receivable are outstanding an average of 35 days, and the firm receives 40 days of credit on its purchases from suppliers.
   a. Estimate the average length of the firm's short-term operating cycle. How often would the cycle turn over in a year?
   b. Assume net sales of $1,200,000 and cost of goods sold of $900,000. Determine the average investment in accounts receivable, inventories, and accounts payable. What would be the net financing need considering only these three accounts?

2. The Robinson Company has the following current assets and current liabilities for these two years:

	2019	2020
Cash and marketable securities	$50,000	$50,000
Accounts receivable	300,000	350,000
Inventories	350,000	500,000
Total current assets	$700,000	$900,000

	2019	2020
Accounts payable	$200,000	$250,000
Bank loan	0	150,000
Accruals	150,000	200,000
Total current liabilities	$350,000	$600,000

If sales in 2019 were $1.2 million, sales in 2020 were $1.3 million, and cost of goods sold was 70% of sales, how long were Robinson's operating cycles and cash conversion cycles in each of these years? What caused them to change during this time?

3. The Robinson Company from Problem 2 had net sales of $1,200,000 in 2019 and $1,300,000 in 2020.
   a. Determine the receivables turnover in each year.
   b. Calculate the average collection period for each year.
   c. Based on the receivables turnover for 2019, estimate the investment in receivables if net sales were $1,300,000 in 2020. How much of a change in the 2020 receivables occurred?

4. Suppose the Robinson Company had a cost of goods sold of $1,000,000 in 2019 and $1,200,000 in 2020.
   a. Calculate the inventory turnover for each year. Comment on your findings.
   b. What would have been the amount of inventories in 2020 if the 2019 turnover ratio had been maintained?

5. Given Robinson's 2019 and 2020 financial information presented in Problems 2 and 4,
   a. Compute its operating and cash conversion cycle in each year.
   b. What was Robinson's net investment in working capital each year?

6. Robinson expects its 2021 sales and cost of goods sold to grow by 5% over their 2020 levels.
   a. What will be the effect on its levels of receivables, inventories, and payments if the components of its cash conversion cycle remain at their 2020 levels? What will be its net investment in working capital?
   b. What will be the impact on its net investment in working capital in 2021 if Robinson is able to reduce its collection period by five days, reduce its inventory period by six days, and increase its payment period by two days?

7. Robinson expects its 2021 sales and cost of goods sold to grow by 20% over their 2020 levels.
   a. What will be the effect on its levels of receivables, inventories, and payments if the components of its cash conversion cycle remain at their 2020 levels? What will be its net investment in working capital?
   b. What will be the impact on its net investment in working capital in 2021 if Robinson can reduce its inventory period by ten days?

8. The following are financial statements for the Genatron Manufacturing Corporation for the years 2019 and 2020:

Selected Balance Sheet Information

	2019	2020
Cash	$50,000	$40,000
Accounts receivable	200,000	260,000
Inventory	450,000	500,000
Total current assets	$700,000	$800,000
Bank loan, 10%	$90,000	$90,000
Accounts payable	130,000	170,000
Accruals	50,000	70,000
Total current liabilities	$270,000	$330,000
Long-term debt, 12%	300,000	400,000

Selected Income Statement Information

	2019	2020
Net sales	$1,300,000	$1,500,000
Cost of goods sold	780,000	900,000
Gross profit	$520,000	$600,000
Net income	$93,000	$114,000

Calculate Genatron's operating cycle and cash conversion cycle for 2019 and 2020. Why did they change between these years?

9. Genatron Manufacturing expects its sales to increase by 10% in 2021. Estimate the firm's investment in accounts receivable, inventory, and accounts payable in 2021.

10. With concerns of increased competition, Genatron is planning in case its 2021 sales fall by 5% from their 2020 levels. If cost of goods sold and the current asset and liability accounts decrease proportionately, calculate the following:
    a. The 2021 cash conversion cycle.
    b. The 2021 net investment in working capital.

11. In Problem 15.10, we assumed the current asset and liability accounts decrease proportionately with Genatron's sales. This is probably unrealistic following a decline in sales. What will be the impact on the working capital accounts if its collection period lengthens by five days, its inventory period lengthens by seven days, and its payment period lengthens by three days, if Genatron's sales and COGS fall 5% from their 2020 levels?

12. Suppose Eastnorth Manufacturing is planning to change its credit policies next year. It anticipates that 10% of each month's sales will be for cash, two-thirds of each month's receivables will be collected in the following month, and one-third will be collected two months following their sale. Assuming that Eastnorth's sales forecast in Table 15.4 remains the same and the expected cash outflows in Table 15.5 remain the same, determine Eastnorth's revised cash budget.

13. Eastnorth's suppliers are upset that Eastnorth takes two months to pay its accounts payable; they demand that in the following year Eastnorth pay its bills within 30 days, or one month after purchase.
    a. Using this new information, update Eastnorth's cash outflow forecast shown in Table 15.5.
    b. Using the cash inflows given in Table 15.4, construct a revised cash budget for Eastnorth.

14. Of its monthly sales, The Kingsman Company historically has had 25% cash sales with the remainder paid within one month. Each month's purchases are equal to 75% of the next month's sales forecast; suppliers are paid one month after the purchase. Salary expenses are $50,000 a month, except in January, when bonuses equal to 1% of the previous year's sales are paid out. Interest on a bond issue of $10,000 is due in March. Overhead and utilities are expected to be $25,000 monthly. Dividends of $45,000 are to be paid in March. Kingsman's 2020 sales totaled $2 million; December sales were $200,000. Kingsman's estimated sales are as follows: January, $100,000; February, $200,000; March, $250,000; and April, $300,000.

    a. What are Kingsman's expected monthly cash inflows during January through April?
    b. What are Kingsman's expected monthly cash outflows during January through April?
    c. Determine Kingsman's monthly cash budget for January through April. Assume a minimum desired cash balance of $40,000 and an ending December cash balance of $50,000.

15. Redo Problem 15.14, using the following monthly sales estimates:

January	$300,000
February	$250,000
March	$200,000
April	$100,000

16. **Challenge Problem** Using the information provided in Problem 15.14, construct cash budgets from each of the following scenarios. Use the data from Problem 15.14 as the "base case." What insights do we obtain from a cash budget scenario analysis?

    a. Best case: Sales are 10% higher than the base; purchases are 5% lower than the base; and cash sales are 30% of sales.
    b. Worst case: Sales are 10% lower than the base; purchases are 5% higher than the base; and cash sales are 15% of sales.

17. **Challenge Problem** CDLater's projected sales for the first four months of 201X are the following:

January	$60,000
February	$55,000
March	$65,000
April	$70,000

The firm expects to collect 10% of sales in cash, 60% in one month, and 25% in two months, with 5% in uncollectible bad debts. Sales for the previous November and December were $55,000 and $80,000, respectively.

The firm buys raw materials 30 days prior to expected sales; that is, the materials for January are bought by the beginning of December, with payment made by the end of December. Materials costs are 58% of sales.

Wages for the months of January, February, and March are expected to be $6,000 per month. Other monthly expenses amount to $5,000 a month and are paid in cash each month. Taxes due for an earlier quarter are paid in the second month of the succeeding quarter. The taxes due for the prior quarter were $9,000.

The firm plans to buy a new car in January for $18,000. An old vehicle will be sold for a net amount of $2,000. A note of $10,000 will be due for payment in February. A quarterly loan installment payment of $7,500 is due in March.

The beginning cash balance in January is $8,000. The company policy is to maintain a minimum cash balance of $5,000. It has an outstanding loan balance of $10,000 in December. Should the firm need to borrow to meet expected monthly shortfalls, the interest cost is 1.5% per month and is paid each month on the total amount of borrowed funds outstanding at the end of the previous month.

Prepare a monthly cash budget for January, February, and March.

18. Mattam Corporation's yearly sales are $5 million, and its average collection period is 32 days. Only 10% of sales are for cash and the remainder is credit sales.

    a. What is Mattam's investment in accounts receivable?
    b. If Mattam extends its credit period, it estimates that the average collection period will rise to 40 days and credit sales will increase by 20% from current levels. What is the expected increase in Mattam's accounts receivable balance if it extends its credit period?
    c. If Mattam's net profit margin is 12%, the expected increase in bad debt expense is 10% of the new sales, and the cost of financing the increase in receivables is 18%, should Mattam extend the credit period?

19. Pa Bell Inc. wants to increase its credit standards. They expect sales will fall by $50,000, and that bad debt expense will fall by 10% of this amount.

The firm has a 15% profit margin on its sales. The tougher credit standards will lower the firm's average receivables balance by $10,000 and the average inventory balance by $8,000. The cost of financing current assets is estimated to be 12%. Should Pa Bell adopt the tighter credit standards? Why or why not?

20. Robinson Company (recall their data from Problems 2–4) has a 2020 profit margin of 5%. It is examining the possibility of loosening its credit policy. Analysis shows that sales may rise 10% while bad debts on the change in sales will be 2%. The cost of financing the increase in current assets is 10%.
    a. Should Robinson change its credit policy?
    b. Using the information stated in the problem, at what profit margin is Robinson indifferent between changing the policy or maintaining its current standard?
    c. Using the information stated in the problem, at what financing cost is Robinson indifferent between changing or maintaining the credit policy?

d. Using the information stated in the problem, by what amount can the current assets change so that Robinson is indifferent between changing or maintaining their credit policy?

21. Genatron Manufacturing (from Problem 8) is considering changing its credit standards. Analysis shows that sales may fall 5% from 2020 levels, with no bad debts from the change in sales. The cost of financing the increase in current assets is 8%.
    a. Should Genatron change its credit policy?
    b. Using the information stated in the problem, at what profit margin is Genatron indifferent between changing its policy or maintaining its current standard?
    c. Using the information stated in the problem, at what financing cost is Genatron indifferent between changing or maintaining the credit policy?
    d. Using the information stated in the problem, by what amount can the current assets change so that Genatron is indifferent between changing or maintaining its credit policy?

Short-Term Business Financing

CHAPTER 16

Assets ($)

LEARNING OBJECTIVES

After studying this chapter, you should be able to do the following:

LO 16.1 Identify and describe strategies for financing working capital.

LO 16.2 Identify and explain the influences that affect short-term financing requirements.

LO 16.3 Identify the types of unsecured loans made by commercial banks to business borrowers.

LO 16.4 Describe nonbank sources of financing, such as trade credit, commercial finance, and commercial paper.

LO 16.5 Describe what "pledging" is and how factors function as a source of short-term business financing.

LO 16.6 Describe the use of inventory and other sources of security for bank loans.

LO 16.7 Calculate the cost of a short-term financing arrangement.

Thus, seasonal varia
as inventory and acc

The level of
porary, or fluctuatir
sales fluctuations m
accounts receivable
and inventory items
some minimum leve

A firm can us
rary current assets.

16.1.1 MATURIT

Panel A of Figure 1
and permanent cur
owners. The tempo
is also called the r
the maturities of th
permanent current
sources. Temporary
An example would
sales. After the inv
the amount of curr
be positive, as in F
greater than 1.0.

Figure 16.4 F
from maturity matc
long-term financing

16.1.2 AGGRES!

Panel B in Figure 1
all current assets, t
assets are financed

Where we have been. . . The balance sheet identity is the following: total assets equals liabilities plus stockholders' equity. In other words, a firm's assets must be financed from one or a combination of two basic sources: debt and owner's equity. Among the assets that need to be financed are short-term or current assets; that is, cash, marketable securities, accounts receivable, and inventory. The previous chapter examined some issues relating to managing current assets, including forecasting their level and forecasting short-term borrowing needs (the cash budget). This chapter will discuss basic financing strategies for the firm and review popular short-term financing sources.

Where we are going. . . Access to short-term financing and sources of liquidity are the lubricant that keeps a firm's business engine running well. If sources of liquidity and access to credit disappear, chances are the firm will not survive long.

How this chapter applies to me. . . A firm facing liquidity problems may not be a prudent choice as a future employer; its lack of cash and difficulty in attracting financing may make it a candidate for merger or bankruptcy, both of which can disrupt one's business career. But just as businesses need a liquidity buffer and access to liquidity, so do individuals. Personal financial planning experts suggest keeping three to six months of living expenses in a liquid savings account for emergencies or personal crises, such as a short-term disability situation or job loss/layoff. For most people, access to short-term credit occurs via credit cards, and as for businesses, over-reliance on short-term credit can lead to future financial crises unless the high interest credit card debt is promptly paid.

Willie Sutton, a famous bank robber from years gone by, was once asked in a jail interview why he robbed so many banks. Willie replied this way:

Because that's where the money is.

Not a good life philosophy! Fortunately, better ways exist for obtaining needed financing; and businesses are not limited only to bank financing.

Many times companies use long-term financing sources, such as the stocks and bonds discussed in Chapter 10, to acquire fixed assets. But the firm's current assets need to be financed. Sometimes, firms primarily use short-term financing sources to finance current assets, sometimes they rely mainly on long-term sources, and other times, they use both.

In this chapter, we review several strategies for financing current assets. As we shall see, management must strategically decide on the relative amounts of short- and long-term financing the

---

[2] For example, in Chapter
component of the perman

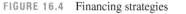

FIGURE 16.4   Financing strategies

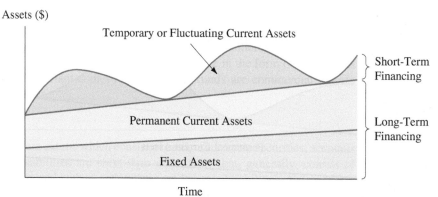

Panel A: Maturity Matching

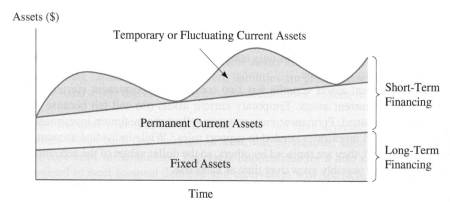

Panel B: Aggressive Financing

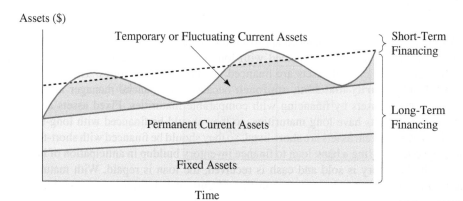

Panel C: Conservative Financing

Such an approach could result in liquidity problems should sales decline in the future. Since all current assets are financed with current liabilities, the current ratio would be equal to 1.0 under this aggressive scenario, and net working capital will be zero as the dollar amount of current assets equals the dollar amount of current liabilities. An even more aggressive approach would be for the firm to rely on short-term funds to finance all the current assets as well as some of the fixed assets. In such a case, the structure of the firm's balance sheet would resemble Figure 16.2. Its net working capital would be negative and its current ratio would be less than 1.0.

16.1.3 CONSERVATIVE APPROACH

Panel C in Figure 16.4 depicts a conservative approach to the financing of a firm's assets. In this case, except for automatic or "spontaneous" financing provided by accounts payable and accrued liabilities, all the financing is done through long-term debt and equity funds. At times, the firm will have excess liquidity when available funds exceed necessary current asset levels. During these periods the firm will have large cash balances and will probably seek to invest the excess cash in marketable securities. As the amount of current assets is much greater than that of current liabilities, net working capital will be positive and the current ratio will comfortably exceed 1.0.

Like many other aspects of finance, deciding how much short-term financing the firm should use relative to long-term financing has risk/return implications. In Chapter 8, we discussed the yield curve and know that short-term securities generally have lower yields than long-term securities. From the borrower's perspective, that means the cost of paying short-term financing charges (short-term interest rates) will be less than the cost of paying long-term financing charges (long-term interest rates and equity holders' required rates of return).[3]

CRISIS Compared with a *conservative* plan that relies more on long-term financing, an *aggressive* financing plan using more short-term financing will have lower financing costs and will, all else being equal, be more profitable. As it comes due, short-term debt is replaced by new short-term debt. This replacement process is called "rolling over the debt." But with the expectation of higher return comes higher risk. Short-term interest rates are more volatile than long-term rates, and in periods of tight money, as during 2007–2009 or when inflation is a concern, short-term rates can rise quickly, as seen in Figure 15.9 graph of the commercial paper premium over Treasury bills (T-bills), sharply increasing the cost of using short-term money. Sources of short-term credit may disappear as they did during the financial crisis in 2007–2009, requiring unprecedented action by the Federal Reserve to pump liquidity into the banking sector. In such a credit crunch, banks may not have enough funds to satisfy borrowing demand and investors may be unwilling to purchase the firm's short-term debt. A conservative financing plan has a higher financing cost, but lower risk of not being able to borrow when short-term funds are needed.

Figure 16.5 illustrates fluctuations and trends over time of net working capital at several firms. Some firms had strategies to reduce net working capital; we see the largest declines in net working capital in Apple (from almost 60% of total assets to almost 0%) and Google. Apple sought to reduce inventories and receivables to free up precious cash that was locked into current assets. With the exception of Microsoft in recent years, most other firms in Figure 16.5 have reduced net working capital relative to assets – or, if already low (such as AT&T and Con Ed), have held it relatively steady.

Some firms use an aggressive financing approach, such as can be seen in AT&T's and Wal-Mart's negative net working capital figures. Other firms follow a maturity-matching approach as net working capital, relative to total assets, fluctuates close to or around 0%, such as Con Ed.

Whether the firm uses an aggressive approach, a conservative approach, or maturity matching depends on an evaluation of many factors. The company's operating characteristics will affect a firm's financing strategy. Other factors having an impact include cost, flexibility, the ease of future financing, and other qualitative influences. A firm's cash budget, as discussed in Chapter 15, can indicate when short-term financing needs may rise – and when they can be repaid.

16.2 FACTORS AFFECTING SHORT-TERM FINANCING

16.2.1 OPERATING CHARACTERISTICS

The nature of the demand for funds depends partly on the industry in which a business operates and on the characteristics of the business. The demand for funds is influenced by seasonal variations in sales and company growth. The need for funds also depends on business cycle fluctuations.

---

[3] We discussed security holders' rates of return in Chapters 10 and 12 and will review the cost of financing a firm with long-term debt and equity in Chapter 18.

FIGURE 16.5 Net working capital divided by total assets

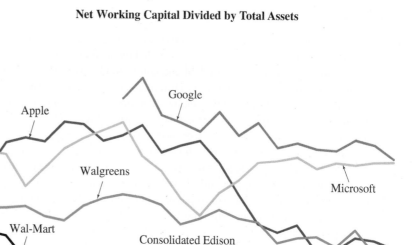

16.2.1.1 Mix of Current and Fixed Assets

Some industries, such as utilities and oil refineries, have larger proportions of fixed assets to current assets and will prefer to use long-term financing. Others, such as service industries, have larger proportions of current assets to fixed assets and will prefer short-term financing. Within each industry, some firms will choose different operating structures with different levels of operating leverage, a topic we discussed in Chapter 14.

While manufacturing companies often require substantial investments in fixed assets for manufacturing purposes, they have significant investments in inventories and receivables. Manufacturers, generally, have a more-equal balance between current and fixed assets than do electric utility and telephone companies and will use more short-term financing than utilities. The same is true for large retail stores. They often lease their quarters and hold substantial assets in the form of inventories and receivables. They are characterized by high current assets to fixed assets ratios and will have a greater tendency than utilities to use short-term debt. An industry that needs large amounts of fixed capital can do more long-term financing than one with a small investment in fixed assets.

16.2.1.2 Size and Age of the Firm

A company's size and age and its stage in the financial life cycle may influence management's short-/long-term financing mix decisions. A new company's only source of funds may be the owner and, possibly, his or her friends. Some long-term funds may be raised by mortgaging real estate and buying equipment on installment, and some current borrowing may be possible to meet seasonal needs. As a business grows, it has more access to short-term capital from finance companies and banks. Further along, its growth and good record of profitability may enable a business to arrange longer-term financing with banks or other financial agencies, such as insurance companies. At this stage in its financial development, it may expand its group of owners by issuing stock to people other than the owner and a few friends.

16.2.1.3 Growth and Profitability

A company's growth prospects affect financing decisions. If a company is growing faster than it can generate funds from internal sources, it must consider a plan for long-term financing. Even if it can finance its needs in the current situation from short-term sources, it may be unwise to do so. Sound

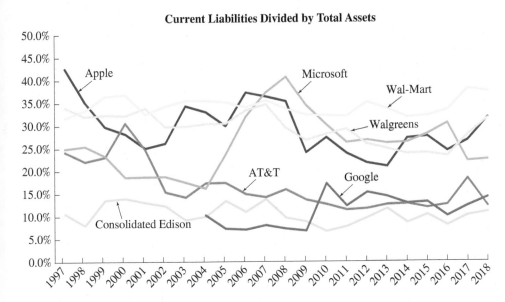

Current Liabilities Divided by Total Assets

FIGURE 16.6 Current liabilities divided by total assets for selected firms

financial planning calls for raising long-term funds at appropriate times. A firm that is generating cash profits will need less outside financing than one that is less profitable. The internally generated cash flows can help pay bills in a timely manner, thus requiring less short-term financing.

Some examples of ratios of current liabilities to total assets are presented in Figure 16.6. Google has a low amount of short-term financing as it is flush with cash from recent stock offerings from its profits. Con Ed, a regulated utility, has an asset base that is mainly fixed so it uses little short-term financing. Wal-mart and Walgreens rely on long-term facility leases for financing their stores, have moderate amounts of current liabilities. Both firms are well-known for a focus on just-in-time (JIT) inventory and product delivery environment. It has little long-term debt financing as it relies mainly on short-term financing for its large amount of current assets. Sears' ratio of short-term financing to total assets (not pictured in Figure 16.6) was rising over time; stock market analysts warned about Sears' debt load, and as of late 2015 its bond credit rating (by Fitch), stood at CC; it filed for bankruptcy in 2018.[4] The rise in short-term financing could be an indication of financial duress by the firm.

16.2.1.4 Seasonal Variation

Our earlier discussion of Figure 16.3 pointed out that seasonal variations in sales affect the demand for current assets. Inventories are built up to meet seasonal needs, and receivables rise as sales increase. The peak of receivables will come after the peak in sales, the amount of intervening time depending on the credit terms and payment practices of customers. Accounts payable will increase as inventories are purchased. The difference between the increase in current assets and accounts payable should be financed by short-term borrowing, because the need for funds will disappear as inventories are sold and accounts receivable are collected. When a need for additional funds is financed by a short-term loan, such a loan is said to be self-liquidating since funds are made available to repay it as inventories and receivables are reduced.

16.2.1.5 Sales Trend

A firm's sales trend affects the financing mix. As sales grow, fixed assets and current assets must grow to support the sales growth as depicted in Figure 16.3. This need for funds is ongoing unless the upward trend of sales is reversed.

---

[4] See https://www.businesswire.com/news/home/20151118006386/en/Fitch-Affirms-Sears-Holdings-CC, accessed February 5, 2016.

FIGURE 16.7 Patterns of short- and long-term financing needs over time for a growing firm

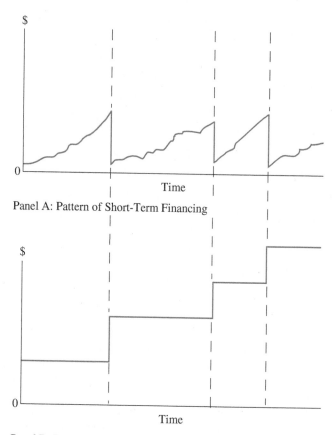

Panel A: Pattern of Short-Term Financing

Panel B: Pattern of Long-Term Financing

If asset growth is initially financed by short-term borrowing, the outstanding borrowings will continue to rise as sales rise. The amount of debt may rise year by year as the growth trend continues upward. After a while, the current ratio will drop to such a level that no financing institution will provide additional funds. The only alternative is long-term financing. Long-term financing often rises to reduce excess levels of short-term financing.

As we will learn later in this chapter, short-term financing can be increased over time in small increments, if needed, by applying for loans and negotiating with borrowers, as seen in Panel A of Figure 16.7. Long-term external financing, however, is "lumpy." Because of the time and cost of floating a bond or stock issue or negotiating a long-term loan or private placement, long-term securities are usually issued only in large quantities, as seen in Panel B of Figure 16.7.

16.2.1.6 Cyclical Variations

The need for current funds increases when the business cycle or the sales cycle of an industry experiences an upswing. Since the cycle is not regular in timing or degree, it is hard to predict exactly how much, or for how long, added funds will be needed. The need should be estimated for a year ahead in the budget and checked quarterly. When the sales volume of business decreases, the need for funds to finance accounts receivable and inventory will decrease as well. The need for financing may increase temporarily during the downturn. This will occur if the cash conversion cycle lengthens, as receivables are collected more slowly and inventories move more slowly and drop in value.

If cyclical needs for funds are met by current borrowing, the loan may not be self-liquidating in a year. There are hazards in financing these needs on a short-term basis. The lending institution may demand payment of all or part of the loan as business turns down. Funds may be needed more than ever at this stage of the cycle, and the need may last until receivables can be collected and inventory can be reduced. Firms in cyclical industries should use a more conservative approach that makes use of long-term financing. Major U.S. automobile firms, in their highly cyclical business, prepare for the next recession by building cash reserves. Ford Motor Company, for example, went through $10 billion in cash during the 1990–1991 recession and $8.5 billion during 1999–2001.

CRISIS At the beginning of 2006, before the 2007–2009 Great Recession and credit crisis hit, Ford and its car financing subsidiary had over $39 billion in cash and short-term marketable securities as a cushion. General Motors had over $50 billion and DaimlerChrysler had $7.1 billion in cash and marketable securities. For these latter two firms, the cash was insufficient, as GM filed for bankruptcy and received a U.S. government rescue financing package. DaimlerChrysler was sold by its German parent firm, received government bailout funds, and is now known as FCA US LLC, better known as Fiat Chrysler.

16.2.2 OTHER INFLUENCES IN SHORT-TERM FINANCING

Using short-term borrowing rather than other forms of financing has other advantages. Short-term borrowing offers more flexibility than long-term financing since a business can borrow only those sums needed and can pay them off if the need for financing diminishes. Long-term financing cannot be retired easily, and it may include a prepayment penalty, as is the case with the call premium for callable bonds. If an enterprise finances its growing current asset requirements entirely through long-term financing during a period of general business expansion, it may be burdened with excess funds and financing costs during a subsequent period of general business contraction. Using short-term financing along with long-term financing creates a financial flexibility that is not possible with long-term financing alone.

Short-term financing has advantages that result from continuing relationships with a bank or other financial institution. The firm that depends almost entirely on long-term financing for its needs will not enjoy the close relationship with its bank that it might otherwise. A record of frequent borrowing and prompt repayment to a bank is important in sound financial management. A bank will make every effort to accommodate regular business customers who do this. The enterprise that has not established this working relationship with its bank will scarcely be in a position to seek special loans when it has emergency needs. The credit experience of a business with short-term financing may be the only basis with which its potential long-term lenders will be able to judge it. Hence, the business that intends to seek long-term loans may wish to establish a good credit reputation based on its short-term financing.

Offsetting these advantages of short-term financing is the need for frequent renewals. Even though short-term credit is usually easy to obtain, time and effort must be spent at frequent intervals because of the short duration of these loans, and when sales revenues decline, a great deal of negotiation may be required to receive needed credit.

Frequent maturities create an added risk. The bank or finance company can call the loan whenever it is due, and the bank, may not want to roll over the loan. Borrowing costs may rise if short-term interest rates increase. A company in a temporary slump due to the business cycle or some internal problem could work out its problems in time with adequate financing. If the company had acquired funds on a long-term basis, it might have a better chance of resolving its problems. On the other hand, if it relies heavily on short-term financing, its loans may be reduced or not renewed, which may make it impossible to recover and might lead to liquidation.

Now that we have an understanding of short-term versus long-term financing strategies and factors that affect the relative use of short-term financing, we turn our attention toward various sources of short-term financing. Short-term financing sources include bank loans, trade credit or accounts payable, and commercial paper, among others. Financial managers should recall the five C's discussed in the Chapter 15 section on accounts receivable management; the ability to obtain short-term financing is made easier for firms with acknowledged character (ethics), the capacity to pay bills, a strong capital base, collateral to act as security for loans, and with favorable conditions in the economy and the firm's industry.

DISCUSSION QUESTION 1

Select one of the firms from Figure 16.5 or Figure 16.6 and discuss how the issues reviewed in this section apply to the firm's choice of short-term financing strategy.

16.3 PROVIDERS OF SHORT-TERM FINANCING

Businesses can attempt to obtain short-term financing from a number of different providers and by a number of methods. Some sources are financial institutions, such as banks, which lend to firms for working capital and long-term purposes (such as equipment loans). When a small business is deemed too risky for a bank loan, it may be able to obtain financing with a government loan guarantee through the U.S. Small Business Administration (SBA). With respect to small business equity funding, the JOBS Act makes it easier for small businesses to raise equity.

Although many banks require a pledge of specific assets, the unsecured loan remains the primary type of loan arrangement. The stated rate on such loans is based on the bank's **prime rate**, or the interest rate a bank charges its most creditworthy customers. Interest rates on loans are typically stated in terms of the prime rate plus a risk differential, such as prime + 2%. Loan papers will call this "prime plus 2" (or simply $P + 2$). Higher-risk borrowers will have higher differentials in order to compensate the bank for lending to riskier customers.

prime rate interest rate the bank charges its most credit-worthy customers

16.3.1 BANK LINES OF CREDIT

A business and a bank often have an agreement regarding the amount of credit the business will have at its disposal. The loan limit the bank establishes for each of its business customers is called a **line of credit**. The cost for a line of credit is the interest rate for the period during which money is borrowed.

line of credit loan limit the bank establishes for each of its business customers

Under a line of credit, the business does not wait until money is needed to negotiate the loan. Rather, it files the necessary financial statements and other evidences of financial condition with the bank prior to the need for credit. The banker is interested in how well the business has fared in the past and its probable future because the line of credit is, typically, extended for a year at a time. The banker may require that other debts of the business be subordinated to, or come after, the bank claim. Banks usually require their business customers to "clean up" their lines of credit for a specified period of time each year, meaning that they have no outstanding borrowing against the line of credit, usually for a minimum of two weeks. This ensures the line of credit is being used for short-term financing purposes rather than for long-term needs.

Continued access to a line of credit may be subject to the bank's approval if the business operation has major changes. A major shift or change in management personnel or in the manufacture or sale of particular products can influence a company's future success. Hence, the bank, having contributed substantially to the business's financial resources, is interested in these activities. The bank may seek information on the business through organized credit bureaus, through contact with other businesses having dealings with the firm, and through other banks.

If the business needs more money than anticipated at the time the line of credit was set up, it may request the bank to increase the limit on its line of credit. It must be prepared, however, to offer sound evidence of the need for additional funds and the ability to repay the increased loan from business operations. A request for an increased line of credit frequently occurs when a business is growing and needs more capital to make its growth possible. Banks, following the principle of maturity matching discussed previously, generally insist expansion be financed with long-term funds, but they may assist growth by temporarily providing a part of the increased needs. The business that is unable to obtain additional unsecured credit from its bank may seek a loan secured with collateral from the bank or from other lenders. These other forms of borrowing are discussed later in this chapter.

Bank mergers have affected the ability of firms to obtain lines of credit. Table 16.1 lists large banks that were in existence, in one form or another, from 1990 to 2019; by 2019, they had merged into three banks. That doesn't mean, however, the larger banks are eager participants in meeting the line of credit needs of larger firms; fewer banks have meant tighter credit and higher fees.[5] A survey of corporate financial officers found that 78% believed the mergers reduced the number of loans and 72% had fears of monopolistic pricing by merged banks. Fortunately, as the field of banking changes to one of financial services, other entities, such as commercial finance companies, insurance

---

[5] Jathon Sapsford and Paul Sherer, "Fewer Banks Means Costlier Credit Lines," *The Wall Street Journal* (March 14, 2001), pp. C1, C16.

Table 16.1   Merging Banks

Banks and financial services firms in existence sometime during 1990–2019	Surviving banks in 2019 after merger
JPMorgan	JPMorgan Chase & Co.
Manufacturers Hanover Trust	
Chemical Bank	
Chase Manhattan Bank	
Banc One	
First Chicago	
NBD Bancorp	
Washington Mutual	
Bear Stearns	
Bank of America	Bank of America
Continental Bank	
Security Pacific	
Nations Bank	
Barnett	
Bank Boston	
Bay Bank	
Fleet	
Shawmut	
Fleet Boston	
LaSalle Bank	
Countrywide Financial	
Merrill Lynch	
Wells Fargo	Wells Fargo
First Union	
Signet	
CoreStates	
Norwest Corporation	
Greater Bay Bancorp	
Wachovia Bank	

companies, and even some mutual funds are lending to firms and taking the place of the traditional banking relationship.

Although the practice is diminishing, some banks require a **compensating balance** of 10–20% of outstanding unsecured loans be kept on deposit by some borrowers. The most frequently cited justification for this requirement is that, because banks cannot lend without deposits, bank borrowers should be required to be depositors. But compensating balances are a means of increasing the effective cost of borrowing by increasing the amount on which interest is computed.

compensating balance requirement that 10–20% of a loan be kept on deposit at the bank

16.3.2 COMPUTING INTEREST RATES

Chapter 9 illustrated how to use time value of money concepts to calculate interest rates. The same concepts can be used to calculate the true cost of borrowing funds from a bank. If, for example, Eastnorth Manufacturing can borrow $10,000 for six months at 8% annual percentage rate (APR), the six-month interest cost will be 8%/2 × $10,000, or $400. Eastnorth will repay the $10,000 principal and $400 in interest after six months. As we learned in Chapter 5, the true, or effective, interest rate on this loan is the following:

$$EAR = (1 + APR / m)^m - 1 \qquad (16.1)$$

or

$$(1 + 0.08 / 2)^2 - 1 = 0.0816, \text{ or } 8.16\%$$

discounted loan borrower receives the principal less the interest at the time the loan is made; the principal is repaid at maturity

At times banks will discount a loan. A **discounted loan** is one in which the borrower receives the principal less the interest at the time the loan is made. The principal is repaid at maturity. Discounting has the effect of reducing the available funds received by the borrower while raising the effective interest rate. If Eastnorth's loan is discounted, Eastnorth will receive $9,600 ($10,000 less $400) and will repay $10,000; in essence, paying $400 interest on the $9,600 funds received. This is a periodic rate of $400/$9,600, or 4.17%.[6] The effective annual rate is $(1 + 0.0417)^2 - 1$, or 8.51%, an increase of 0.35 percentage points over the undiscounted loan.

When a loan is discounted, a firm has to borrow more money than the amount it needs. To counteract the effect of discounting when acquiring $10,000 in usable funds, they will have to borrow $10,000/(1 − 0.04), or $10,416.67. When a loan of $10,416.67 is discounted at a six-month rate of 4%, the net proceeds to Eastnorth will be $10,000 (i.e., $10,416.67 − [0.04][10,416.67] = $10,000). In general, to receive the desired usable funds, the loan request must equal the following:

$$\text{Loan request} = \text{Desired usable funds} / (1 - \text{discount}) \qquad (16.2)$$

A loan with a compensating balance is similar to a discounted loan in terms of its effect on the effective interest rate and usable funds. Compensating balances are equivalent to discounting when the firm currently has no money on deposit at the bank. The firm's loan request should be large enough so that after funds are placed in the compensating balance it will have the usable funds it desires. For compensating balance loans, equation 16.2 becomes the following:

$$\text{Loan request} = \frac{\text{Desired usable funds}}{(1 - \text{Compensating balance requirement})} \qquad (16.3)$$

This is identical to equation 16.2, except the discount percent is replaced by the compensating balance percentage.

16.3.3 REVOLVING CREDIT AGREEMENTS

The officers of a business may feel certain that an agreed-upon line of credit will provide the necessary capital requirements for the coming year, but the bank is not obligated to continue to offer the line of credit if the firm's financial condition worsens. Line of credit agreements usually allow the bank to reduce or withdraw its credit extension to the firm.

revolving credit agreement a commitment in the form of a standby agreement for a guaranteed line of credit; a legal obligation of the bank to provide up to the agreed-upon borrowing limit during the time the agreement is in effect

A well-established business with an excellent credit rating may be able to obtain a **revolving credit agreement**. A revolving credit agreement (also called a revolver) is a commitment in the form of a standby agreement for a guaranteed line of credit. Unlike a line of credit, a revolving credit agreement is a legal obligation of the bank to provide funds up to the agreed-upon borrowing limit during the time the agreement is in effect. In addition to paying interest on borrowed funds for the loan period, the business must pay a commission, or fee, to the bank based on the unused portion of the credit line, or the money it has "on call" during the agreement period. This fee is usually between 0.25% and 0.50% of the unused amount of the line.[7]

---

[6] This periodic rate can be computed using our Chapter 9 concepts. We know that $FV = PV (1 + r)^n$. Since FV equals $10,000 (the amount to be repaid), PV equals $9,600 (the usable funds received after discounting), and n is 1 for our six-month time frame, we have the following: $10,000 = $9,600 (1 + r)^1$. Solving for r, we see the periodic interest rate is 4.17%.

[7] Banks are a major participant in the commercial paper market (discussed later in this chapter) as they frequently support this market by offering paper issuers a line of credit, or an arrangement similar to the revolving credit agreement described above, to act as a secondary source of funds for repaying its commercial paper loans.

To compute the effective cost of a revolver, the joint effect of interest on borrowed funds and the commitment fee on the un-borrowed portion of the agreement must be considered. Suppose Eastnorth has a one-year $1 million revolver with a local bank. The annual interest rate on the agreement is 9% with a commitment fee of 0.40% on the un-borrowed portion. Eastnorth expects to have average outstanding borrowings against the revolver of $300,000. Over the year, the interest cost on the average amount borrowed is $0.09 \times \$300,000$, or $27,000. The commitment fee on the average un-borrowed portion is $0.0040 \times \$700,000$, or $2,800. With total interest and fees of $29,800 ($27,000 + $2,800) on average borrowings of $300,000, the expected annual cost of the revolver is $29,800/$300,000, or 9.93%.

16.3.4 SMALL BUSINESS ADMINISTRATION

The U.S. Small Business Administration (SBA) was established by the federal government to provide financial assistance to small firms unable to obtain loans through private channels on reasonable terms. Created in 1953, the SBA provides a variety of services in addition to loan guarantees through its more than 100 field offices.

The reason businesses use SBA loan guarantees is explained by the stated objectives of the SBA: to enable deserving small businesses to obtain financial assistance otherwise unavailable through private channels on reasonable terms. When the SBA was established, it was recognized that the nation's economic development depended largely on the freedom of new business ventures to enter into active operation. Yet, the increased concentration of investable funds with large institutional investors, such as life insurance companies, investment companies, and others, made it increasingly difficult for new and small business ventures to attract investment capital. The lack of a track record made loans hard to obtain from traditional bank sources.

The SBA does not make loans; instead, it guarantees them. Under their 7(a) loan program, the SBA will guarantee up to 85% of the loan amount for loans of $150,000 or less. For loans larger than $150,000 up to $5 million, a small business can obtain a guarantee of up to 75%. The loan guarantee means a bank can lend a sum to a small business owner and only have a small portion of the funds at risk. In case of default, the SBA will repay the loan. For example, a bank lending $100,000 under the SBA loan guarantee program has 85% of the loan guaranteed by the SBA. This means that 15%, or $15,000, of their funds is at risk. In the event that the borrower cannot repay the loan, the SBA will reimburse the bank for up to $85,000.

If a firm is able to obtain financing elsewhere, its loan application to the SBA is rejected. An applicant for a loan must prove that funds needed are unavailable from any bank, that no other private lending sources are available, that issuing securities is impracticable, that financing cannot be arranged by disposing of business assets, and that the personal credit of the owners cannot be used. These loans may not be used for paying existing creditors or for speculative purposes.

In addition to its business lending activities, the SBA is responsible for several related financial activities. These include development company loans, disaster loans, lease guarantees, surety bond support, minority enterprise programs, procurement assistance, and support for investment companies that service small businesses.

SBA working capital loans are limited to seven years, while regular business loans have a maximum maturity of 25 years. It sets a maximum allowable rate that banks can charge on guaranteed loans. These rates are adjusted periodically by the SBA to reflect changes in market conditions.

16.3.4.1 JOBS Act

To assist small firms, the Jumpstart Our Business Startups (JOBS) Act became law in 2012. It allows firms to achieve equity financing more easily than in the past. Although this discussion could be included in the section on a firm's capital structure (see Chapter 18), a firm may use the JOBS Act to raise modest amounts of equity to help finance growth, similarly to the other vehicles mentioned in this chapter. The main difference is that the other vehicles involve debt financing while the JOBS Act allows for equity to be invested by new shareholders without going through the costly and time-consuming use of investment banks and the SEC registration process (as discussed in Chapter 11).

SMALL BUSINESS PRACTICE

BANK FINANCING FOR SMALL BUSINESSES

Getting a small business bank loan is much harder than it was in the 1980s. Bankers are making greater demands on entrepreneurial or venture firms. More comprehensive financial statements must be provided and more collateral, such as equipment or working capital in the form of inventories or receivables, pledged. Banks lend at the "prime rate," which is their best rate, to larger businesses. In contrast, small businesses are asked to pay two or more points above prime. For example, if the prime rate is 8%, small businesses will have to pay interest rates of 10% or more to obtain bank loans.

Iris Lorenz-Fife, in her book *Financing Your Business* (Prentice Hall, 1997), lists the five most common reasons given by bankers when they decide not to make loans to small businesses. The first reason is the "owner's equity is too low relative to the size of the loan that is requested." The second reason relates to the "value of the collateral being offered is too low or unreliable." A third reason is that the "firm is a one-person business with no adequate managerial backup." A fourth reason centers on the belief that the business "will need more time to repay the loan than the bank's usual terms." The fifth reason for rejecting a loan application from a small business is that the banker believes the small business owner/manager "has inadequate managerial experience or ability."

If you have a small business loan application rejected by a bank, you should ask the banker why it was rejected and ask what changes in the application would be necessary to successfully obtaining a bank loan.

The JOBS Act allows firms (called emerging growth companies) with under $1 billion in sales to advertise a need for equity capital more easily and to find investors. Called "crowdfunding," such appeals for capital can occur via the Internet, Web portals, and advertising. Prior to the JOBS Act, investors had to have $1 million in net worth before they could invest in such firms; now the firm's limit is $100,000 in net worth, provided the individual invests no more than $2,000 in a firm. Emerging growth companies can raise up to $1 million a year this way from individual investors. For an emerging growth company seeking to do an initial public offering (IPO), the need to provide up to five years of selected financial data is reduced to two years. Other regulatory burdens for going public are relaxed as well.[8]

LEARNING ACTIVITY

1. **Examine bank websites and learn about their offerings to small and medium businesses and large corporations. Include in your search, the websites of local banks as well as large banks, such as https://www.jpmorganchase.com and https://www.bankofamerica.com.**
2. **Learn about financing opportunities for small businesses through the U.S. Small Business Administration at www.sba.gov.**
3. **https://www.crowdsourcing.org, https://cfpa.org/, and https://www.cfira.org are industry sites dealing with crowdfunding news and events.**

16.4 NONBANK SHORT-TERM FINANCING SOURCES

In addition to banks, businesses have several other sources they may be able to use to raise short-term financing. In this section, we review accounts payable, commercial finance companies, and a financing source for large businesses with good credit: commercial paper.

16.4.1 TRADE CREDIT FROM SUPPLIERS

The most important single form of short-term business financing is the credit extended by one business organization to another. Accounts receivable together with longer-term notes receivable taken by manufacturers, wholesalers, jobbers, and other businesses that sell products or services to businesses are known as trade credit.

---

[8] Vincent Ryan, "Advertise but Verify," *CFO Magazine* (November 2012), p. 21; Jamie Farrell; "The JOBS Act: What Startups and Small Businesses Need to Know," accessed January 29, 2013, at https://www.forbes.com/sites/work-in-progress/2012/09/21/the-jobs-act-what-startups-and-small-businesses-need-to-know-infographic/; McGladrey LLP, "An overview of the JOBS Act" (May 1, 2012), https://mcgladrey.com/pdf/jobs_act_overview.pdf, accessed January 29, 2013.

The establishment of trade credit is the least formal of all forms of financing. It involves an order for goods or services by one business and the delivery of goods or performance of service by the selling business. The purchasing business receives an invoice stating the terms of the transaction and the time period within which payment is to be made. The purchaser adds the liability to accounts payable. The seller adds the claim to accounts receivable. In some situations, the seller may insist on written evidence of liability from the purchaser. Such written evidence is usually in the form of a note payable by the purchaser; the seller considers it a note receivable. Before a business organization delivers goods or performs a service for another business, it must determine the purchaser's ability and willingness to pay for the order.[9] The responsibility of such credit analysis in most businesses belongs to the credit manager.

16.4.1.1 Terms for Trade Credit

Sales may be made on terms such as cash, end of month (E.O.M.), middle of month (M.O.M.), or receipt of goods (R.O.G.). Or such terms as 2/10, net 30 may be offered, which means the purchaser may deduct 2% from the purchase price if payment is made within ten days of shipment; if not paid within ten days, the net amount is due within 30 days. Such **trade discounts** to purchasers for early payment are common and are designed to provide incentive for prompt payment of bills. Occasionally, sellers offer only net terms such as net 30 or net 60.

trade discounts provided to purchasers as an incentive for prompt payment of bills

A cash sale, contrary to its implication, usually involves credit because the purchaser is often permitted a certain number of days within which to make payment. For example, a sale of merchandise in which the purchaser is permitted up to ten days to pay may be considered a cash transaction, but credit is outstanding to the purchaser for that time. Even for the firm that purchases products entirely on a cash basis, the volume of accounts payable outstanding on its books at any one time may be large.

16.4.1.2 Cost of Trade Credit

When trade credit terms do not provide a discount for early payment of obligations, there is no cost to the buyer for such financing. Even when discounts are available, it may seem that no cost for trade credit exists, since failing to take the early payment discount requires the purchaser to pay the net price. A cost is involved, however, when a discount is not taken. For example, with terms of 2/10, net 30, the cost is the loss of the 2% discount that could have been taken if payment were made within the ten-day period.

To compare the cost of trade credit and bank credit, the cost of the trade credit must be placed on an annual interest rate basis. For example, if the terms of sale are 2/10, net 30, the cost of trade credit is the loss of the 2% discount that the purchaser fails to take if she or he extends the payment period from ten days up to 30 days. The lost 2% is the cost of trade credit for those 20 days. If we consider that it is the discounted price (invoice price minus the percentage discount) that is being financed, the approximate effective cost (EC) is the following:

$$EC = \frac{\% \text{ discount}}{100\% - \% \text{ discount}} \times \frac{365 \text{ days}}{\text{Credit period} - \text{discount days}} \qquad (16.4)$$

For our 2/10, net 30 example, we have, as follows:

$$EC = \frac{2\%}{100\% - 2\%} \times \frac{365}{30 - 10} = 2.04\% \times 18.25 = 37.2\%$$

---

[9] We discussed the process of credit evaluation in Chapter 15.

This shows that the cost of trade credit typically exceeds the cost of bank loan rates. Thus, it is usually worthwhile to borrow funds to take advantage of cash discounts on trade credit. Failure to take advantage of the trade discount is the same as borrowing from the vendor at the effective cost.[10]

The cost of trade credit in most lines of business activity is high when discounts are missed. However, it should not be assumed that high cost necessarily makes trade credit an undesirable source of short-term financing. It can be the most important form of financing for small and growing businesses unable to qualify for short-term credit through customary financial channels.

The firm in a weak financial condition will find trade credit more available than bank credit. The bank stands to gain only the interest on the loan if repayment is made, but it will lose the entire sum loaned if the borrower's obligation is unmet. The manufacturer or merchant, on the other hand, has a profit margin on the goods sold. If the purchaser fails to meet the obligation, the maximum the seller will lose is the cost of the goods (COGS) delivered to the purchaser.

16.4.2 COMMERCIAL FINANCE COMPANIES

The first commercial finance company in the United States was chartered about 100 years ago. Since that time, the number of these institutions has increased to more than 500. Some of these organizations are small, offering limited financial services to their customers, while others have vast resources and engage in broadly diversified programs of business lending.

A **commercial finance company** is an organization without a bank charter that advances funds to businesses by discounting accounts receivable, making loans secured by chattel mortgages on machinery or liens on inventory, or financing deferred-payment sales of commercial and industrial equipment. Some also do lease financing to assist businesses needing machinery, trucks, or other heavy equipment in their line of business. These companies also are known as commercial credit companies, commercial receivables companies, and discount companies.

Commercial finance companies, such as CIT Group, Celtic Capital, and GE Capital, offer many of the same services as commercial banks for financing accounts receivable and inventory. Lending funds based upon the amount of a firm's accounts receivable balances was originated by commercial finance companies and later was adopted by commercial banks. Consumer and business financing can be obtained from firms such as General Electric Capital and Ford Motor Credit.

Commercial finance companies grew to their present number because they were free to experiment with new and highly specialized types of credit arrangements. State laws concerning lending on the basis of accounts receivable were, generally, more favorable to these nonbanking organizations. In addition, they were able to charge high enough rates to make a profitable return on high-risk loans. Frequently, these rates were far above rates bankers were permitted to charge.

In addition to financing accounts receivable and inventories, commercial finance companies provide a vast amount of credit for businesses by financing commercial vehicles, industrial and farm equipment, and other types of business credit. The Secured Finance Network estimates the total volume of business credit outstanding by the commercial finance companies to be almost $215 billion.[11]

commercial finance company organization without a bank charter that advances funds to businesses by discounting accounts receivable, making loans secured by chattel mortgages on machinery or liens on inventory, or financing deferred-payment sales of commercial and industrial equipment

[10] Astute readers will note that these popular formulas do not take period-by-period compounding into account. The true effective cost can be determined as follows:

$$\text{Effective Cost} = \left(1 + \frac{\% \text{ discount}}{100\% - \% \text{ discount}}\right)^{365/(\text{Credit period} - \text{discount days})} - 1$$

In the text example, we have the following:

$$\text{True effective cost} = \left(1 + \frac{2\%}{100\% - 2\%}\right)^{365/(30-10)} - 1$$
$$= (1.0204)^{365/20} - 1$$
$$= 1.446 - 1 = 0.446, \text{ or } 44.6\%$$

[11] R. S. Carmichael & Co. Inc. and Commercial Finance Association, *Annual Asset-Based Lending and Factoring Surveys, 2014*, issued March 31, 2015, accessed July 2, 2016, at https://www.cfa.com/eweb/DynamicPage.aspx?Site=cfa&WebKey=2f388eee-12cc-441b-9584-986d6261fc51. The Commercial Finance Association is now known as Secured Finance Network.

The equity position of commercial finance companies is greater than that of banks. However, these organizations do not operate on equity capital alone. Additional long-term capital is acquired by selling debenture, or unsecured, bonds. In addition, commercial banks lend a large volume of money at wholesale rates to commercial finance companies, which, in turn, lend it to business borrowers at retail rates. Nonbank financial intermediaries, commercial firms, and industrial firms often find it advantageous to invest their temporary surplus funds in the commercial paper of commercial finance companies. These sources of short-term funds permit the commercial finance companies to meet their peak loan demands without having too much long-term debt, only part of which would be used during slack lending periods.

When viewing the high interest rates (sometimes as high as 15–20%) for commercial finance company loans, the question may arise: why would a borrower use these companies? A business with ample current assets and a highly liquid position may be advised to rely on other short-term financing sources. When business is most brisk and growth possibilities most favorable, the need for additional short-term funds becomes pressing, as it is when customers are slow in paying their bills and the company needs cash.

A business will, typically, first request an increase in its bank line of credit. Failing this, an additional loan from a bank may be secured by pledging inventory or receivables as collateral. However, not all banks actively engage in this financial arrangement. Thus, a business may have to deal with a commercial finance company. Commercial finance companies can operate through a system of branches on a regional or national basis, unhampered by restrictions placed on bank branch operations. Therefore, they can acquire the business volume necessary to cover overhead and provide the needed diversification of risks for high-risk financing. Several bank holding companies have purchased or established commercial finance companies to take advantage of their special operating characteristics.

16.4.3 COMMERCIAL PAPER

CRISIS A final source of short-term financing is not a specific type of lender but the financial market-place itself. Large U.S. corporations of high credit quality can issue or sell **commercial paper**, which is a short-term promissory note. This means the notes are backed by the issuer's credit quality; there is no security or collateral behind them. Commercial paper may be sold directly by the issuer to financial institutions or other investors. Alternatively, it can be sold to commercial paper houses or dealers who purchase the promissory notes to resell them to individuals or businesses. A fee based on the amount of notes purchased, charged to the issuer of the notes, provides the basic income of commercial paper dealers. With about $1.1 trillion outstanding in early 2019, trading in this short maturity form of debt is at about one-half of the level that it was before the financial crisis began in late 2007. Fears of financial uncertainty can send shockwaves through the commercial paper market, as we saw in 2007–2009. The commercial paper market all but dried up as investors fled to the safety of U.S. Treasury securities in the fear of possible financial system meltdown. Many firms could access commercial paper financing only after the Fed stepped in to provide liquidity and backing to the market.[12]

commercial paper short-term promissory note sold by high-credit-quality corporations; notes are backed by the issuer's credit quality

A firm that wishes to obtain funds from a commercial paper house must have an unquestioned reputation for sound operation. First the commercial paper house makes a thorough investigation of the firm's financial position. If the firm's notes can be sold easily, an agreement is made for the outright sale of a block of the firm's promissory notes to the commercial paper house. The house will resell these notes as quickly as possible to banks, pension fund managers, business corporations with surplus funds, or other investors. The notes are usually prepared in denominations of $100,000 or more, with maturities ranging from a few days to 270 days.[13] The size of the notes and the maturities can be adjusted to suit individual investor requirements.

Commercial paper is sold on a discount basis. Dealers will pay the borrower the face amount of the notes minus the interest charge and a fee, usually between 0.02% and 0.05%. The interest charge

---

[12] The Commercial Paper Funding Facility is described at https://www.federalreserve.gov/monetarypolicy/cpff.htm.

[13] Commercial paper has a maximum maturity of 270 days, as Securities and Exchange Commission (SEC) regulations require that securities with maturities exceeding 270 days must go though the costly and time-consuming SEC registration process.

is determined by the general level of prevailing rates in the money market and the strength of the borrowing company. When these notes are resold to banks and other lenders, the prevailing interest charge is deducted from the face value of the notes. Hence, the commercial paper dealer receives the fee as compensation for the negotiation and intermediation.

Commercial paper is no longer sold only through dealers or brokers. Investors can buy commercial paper online through an electronic trading system. The first firm to offer its paper online was Ford Motor Company on a commercial paper trading system designed by CS First Boston. Since then, others have developed online commercial paper systems to facilitate the direct issue of paper to investors. In recent years, the most successful of them has been offered by Fidelity National Information Services (FIS). Online issuance of paper allows issuers to cut in half the fees usually collected by dealers.

Commercial paper is issued by large, well-known, and financially stable firms; they have the ability to raise large sums of short-term financing quickly and with a bank's backing.[14] Many of the borrowers of commercial paper are financial firms, such as commercial finance companies; they seek to finance their own lending and leasing operations by raising short-term funds through commercial paper. They will borrow at the commercial paper rate and lend the funds to others at higher interest rates.

Suppose Eastnorth Manufacturing wants to issue $100,000 of commercial paper that will mature in nine months (270 days). The placement fee is 0.10% and the interest charge will be 7.5% over the nine-month period. To compute Eastnorth's effective financing cost, we must determine the net proceeds, or usable funds, Eastnorth will obtain from the sale as well as the total interest charges it will pay. The net proceeds will be the $100,000 raised, minus the interest, less the placement fee:

$$\text{Net proceeds} = \$100,000 - [(0.075)(\$100,000)] - [(0.0010)(\$100,000)]$$
$$= \$100,000 - \$7,500 - \$100$$
$$= \$92,400$$

The interest charge is $0.075 \times \$100,000$, or $7,500, and the placement fee is $100, for total expenses of $7,600. The nine-month financing cost for the commercial paper issue is the following:

$$\text{9-month cost} = \$7,600 / \$92,400 = 0.0823, \text{ or } 8.23\%$$

The annualized cost of the commercial paper issue will be the following:

$$(1 + 0.0823)^{12/9} - 1 = 0.1111 \text{ or } 11.11\%$$

The most important reason to a firm for issuing commercial paper is that the cost of borrowing is generally less than regular bank rates. The reason for the lower rates is that only the largest, most financially stable firms can issue commercial paper. Unlike banks, which typically service a geographic region, commercial paper is sold by dealers to investors worldwide, so international short-term rates rather than bank loan committees help determine commercial paper rates. The need for compensating bank balances that increase interest costs on short-term bank loans is avoided. Loan restrictions on the amount that can be borrowed from a single bank may favor the issuance of commercial paper by large corporations.

Like bonds, commercial paper is rated. The rating is important to the issuer because the higher the rating, the lower the interest expense. Industrial firms and other nonbank lenders often purchase commercial paper as a more profitable alternative to Treasury bills (T-bills) for investing excess cash.

Commercial paper provides a yield slightly above that of short-term government securities, as we saw in Figure 15.6. Although commercial banks were historically the main purchasers of commercial paper, it is held by industrial corporations, money market mutual funds, and other lenders.

---

[14] Banks are a major player in the commercial paper market as they offer issuers a line of credit equal to their amount of paper outstanding. Up until 1999, Standard & Poor's (S&P) required this to award its top A-1 rating to a firm issuing paper. S&P now considers all sources of liquidity that can be used to redeem the paper.

Many top-rated U.S. commercial paper issuers can issue paper overseas. The European commercial paper (Euro CP) market offers advantages to commercial paper issuers just as the Eurodollar bond market offers advantages over the U.S. bond market. There is no SEC regulation of the Euro CP market, so commercial paper maturities are generally a little longer and interest costs lower. In addition, Euro CP is available only to the "cream" of the commercial paper issuers, so no ratings are needed. Investors know the safest issuers. So, not having to pay for a rating makes the Euro CP market attractive to those firms able to use it.

LEARNING ACTIVITY

1. **The Secured Finance Network is a trade association for commercial finance companies. Learn more about the industry at https://www.sfnet.com/.**
2. **For a variety of financial market information, see the Bloomberg website at https://www.bloomberg.com.**

We have reviewed several types of short-term financing in our discussion of financing providers. For example, in our prior discussion of banks, we discussed lines of credit, revolving credit agreements, and SBA loan guarantees. Suppliers offer trade credit. The financial markets offer the ability to sell commercial paper. In this section, we will discuss other varieties of short-term financing. For the most part, these financing arrangements are available from banks and commercial finance companies and are forms of secured financing. Secured lending (also called asset-based lending) means that there is some collateral or security backing the loan that can be claimed or sold by the lender if the borrower defaults. We have seen this type of lending before in the Chapter 10 discussion of mortgage bonds. In this section, we examine the use of asset-based lending for short-term financing purposes.

> ### 16.5 ADDITIONAL VARIETIES OF SHORT-TERM FINANCING

> **secured lending or asset-based lending** collateral or security backing the loan that can be claimed or sold by the lender if the borrower defaults

16.5.1 ACCOUNTS RECEIVABLE FINANCING

The business that does not qualify for an unsecured bank loan or that has emergency needs for funds in excess of its line of credit may decide to use its accounts receivable as a way to raise needed funds. Two methods exist for using accounts receivable as a form of asset-based lending. First, the firm can borrow using its accounts receivable balances as a pledge. This is called pledging accounts receivable. Second, the firm can sell its accounts receivable to a factor; thus, selling accounts receivable balances is called *factoring*.

These two methods of using accounts receivable to raise funds differ in many ways. We'll discuss the general process of each before reviewing the differences between them.

> **pledge** obtain a short-term loan by using accounts receivable as collateral

> **factor** a firm that engages in accounts receivable financing by purchasing accounts and assuming all credit risks

16.5.1.1 Pledging Accounts Receivable

Rather than wait until its customers pay on each of their accounts, a firm can pledge its accounts and get a loan. By so doing, the firm obtains funds sooner, albeit at a cost. The word "accounts" in accounts receivable is plural. When a firm pledges its accounts receivable, each customer's account is reviewed to see if it is creditworthy to become security, or collateral, for a loan. The lender, usually a bank or finance company, gives close attention to the borrower's collection experience on its receivables and to certain characteristics of its accounts receivable.

The bank may spot-check the receivables of the firm and may, in some cases, analyze each account to determine how quickly the firm's customers make payments. The bank must know something about these customers; it will probably check on their credit ratings from a source such as Dun & Bradstreet (D&B). Their ability to pay their debts will strongly influence how well the business applying for the loan can collect payment.

In addition, the bank studies the type and quality of goods sold. If the merchandise is inferior, the customers may have objections and have slower payment of bills or sales returns. Accounts receivable are of little value as security for a loan if large quantities of merchandise are returned and the amount of accounts receivable is reduced accordingly.

A loan based on accounts receivable is usually no more than 80% of the gross receivables. This amount should be reduced by any discounts allowed to customers for quick payment, and by the normal percentage of merchandise returns. If the bank believes many of the loan applicant's customers are unsuitable risks or if adequate credit ratings are unavailable, it will lend a lower percentage of the face value of the receivables. Additionally, if a single customer is a large proportion of the firm's credit sales, the percentage lent against that account may be less than usual; this protects the bank in case a large customer of the firm experiences financial difficulties, which may create subsequent cash flow problems for the supplying firm.

Pledging accounts receivable is not a simple process. The firm's accounts receivable are reviewed by the bank to determine their level and if they are acceptable to form the basis for a loan. At the time the loan is made, individual accounts on the ledger of the business are designated clearly as having been pledged for the bank loan. Only those accounts suitable for collateral purposes for the bank are designated. When these accounts are paid in full or become unsatisfactory, they are replaced by other accounts.

Pledging accounts receivable involves sending invoices and funds (electronically or by paper) back and forth among the firm, its customers, and the bank offering the loan. For example, the bank receives copies of all shipping invoices to show the goods have been shipped and the account receivable is valid. Thus, invoice material is transferred from firm to customer and from firm to bank. Similarly, several transfers of funds exist. First, the bank lends funds to the firm. Second, the firm's customers make payments on the pledged receivables. Third, the firm sends such payments to the bank to repay the loan.

ETHICAL It is usually more expensive to pledge receivables than to borrow funds from a bank. Under a pledged receivables arrangement, the firm pays interest on the loan (namely, the funds advanced to it) and a separate fee to cover the extra work needed for the loan. The bank must periodically check or audit the books of the business to see that it is living up to the terms of the agreement and sending customer payments to it in a timely basis. As customers pay their bills on the pledged account assigned for the loan, the proceeds must be turned over to the bank. The bank reserves the right to audit the business's books and to have an outside accounting firm examine the books periodically.

In what is referred to as "supply chain financing," some banks in the United States are helping the cash flow of smaller businesses by offering pledging (or factoring, discussed in the next section) services to small businesses that sell goods to larger businesses – but charges interest at a rate based on the larger firm's credit rating.[15] With supply chain financing, the bank, in order to keep the large firm's supply of inventory at appropriate levels, will offer a small business that supplies goods to a large business the chance to pledge its receivables from its customers. Due to the consistent relation with the larger firm, the bank offers the small business supplier a lending interest rate commensurate with the large firm's credit rating. In this way, the small business has predictable cash flow and the large business has a more stable supply relationship – as now there is less of a chance of the small business going bankrupt if its customers are slow to pay their bills. And the bank that finances the small firm's receivables has a new client and new sources of income from the interest it receives from the financing it provides – all parties "win" with supply chain financing.

16.5.1.2 Factoring Accounts Receivable

Pledging involves borrowing against receivables balances; factoring involves selling the accounts. A financing firm, or factor, purchases the accounts receivable outright and assumes all credit risks. Under **maturity factoring**, the firm selling its accounts receivable is paid on the normal collection date, or net due date, of the account. Under **advance factoring**, the factor pays the firm for its receivables before the account due date.

Under a factoring arrangement, customers whose accounts are sold are notified that their bills are payable to the factor. The task of collecting on the accounts is, therefore, shifted from the seller of the accounts to the factor. Some factors include GE Capital, Platinum Funding, and units of several large banks.

Factoring can be done *with recourse* or *without recourse*. With recourse, the factor can return an unpaid account to the firm and any funds advanced for that account must be returned to the factor.

maturity factoring firm selling its receivables is paid on the normal collection date, or net due date, of the account

advance factoring factor pays the firm for its receivables before the account due date

---

[15] Vipal Monga and Ruth Simon, "Banks Offer Smaller Companies an Indirect Route to Raising Cash," *The Wall Street Journal* (October 27, 2015), accessed on February 5, 2016 at https://www.wsj.com/articles/banks-offer-smaller-companies-an-indirect-route-to-raising-cash-1445903854.

Without recourse, the accounts are sold to the factor and any bad or slow-paying accounts are the factor's responsibility.

Rather than occasionally selling accounts to the factor, many times the factor becomes the firm's partner. A typical arrangement has the factor become the firm's credit department. That is, all requests to sell goods on credit to new and existing customers are routed to the factor for approval, saving the firm time and expense in hiring, training, staffing, and running its own credit department. The factor's credit department members must be prompt and accurate in their credit analyses and, because they work closely with the firm's clients, must retain the goodwill of the companies that use its services.

Should the factor reject a credit request from a new customer of the firm or reject a request to increase an existing credit limit on an existing customer of the firm, the firm can always choose to extend the credit itself. In such cases, the firm will keep those accounts on its books and will have to service the accounts; meaning, to send bills, collect payments, and deal with any slow or nonpayers.

To use a factor, a contract is drawn establishing the duties and obligations of the seller and the factor. The contract provides that the accepted accounts be assigned to the factor for payment and that sales invoices to these customers, together with the original shipping documents, be delivered daily to the factor along with information on all credits, allowances, and returns of merchandise.

The contract includes the conditions under which accounts may be sold to the factor, such as type of firm, the customer's geographic area, and acceptable credit ratings. Another important part of the contract is the collection procedures to be followed in case a customer is slow in paying its bill. As we saw in Chapter 15, collecting accounts receivable can be a costly process, especially when a customer is alienated by aggressive collection efforts. A firm will want to know what collection process the factor follows, as future sales may be lost if the factor is too aggressive.

The charge for factoring has two components. First, interest is charged on the money advanced. Second, a factoring commission, or service charge, is figured as a percentage of the face amount of the receivables. This charge typically ranges from 1.5% to 3% of the face amount of the accounts financed. Factors will typically lend 80% of the remainder, although they may reduce the loan amount from 5% to 15% of the total amount of receivables factored to make adjustments, such as for merchandise that is returned to the seller. This portion of the receivables is returned to the seller if it is not needed for adjustment purposes.

For example, suppose a firm is owed $70,000 by a customer that rarely pays its bills any sooner than 60 days after the invoice. Assuming the customer meets the factor's credit standards, the firm will receive 80% of the $70,000, or $56,000, within a day or two of accepting the account. If the interest rate for a 60-day account is 2% and the factoring fee is 3%, the cost of the factoring arrangement will be $3,500 (5% of $70,000). Assuming the customer pays its bill in full on day 60, the firm will receive an additional $10,500, which is the amount of the invoice ($70,000) less the advance ($56,000), less the combined factoring and interest costs ($3,500). Thus, the firm collects $66,500 of the original $70,000 invoice; $56,000 was received after a one- or two-day delay and the remainder was received at around day 60.

Although a factor's services may be used by a firm unable to secure financing through customary channels, financially strong companies may use these services to good advantage. In fact, factors are of greatest benefit to companies enjoying strong sales and growth. During such periods, companies experience shortages of working capital. The sale of receivables without recourse (i.e., sellers do not have to repay any funds received from the factor in the case of a bad debt) has the effect of substituting cash for accounts receivable. This may make greater growth and profitability possible.

GLOBAL Some firms factor their receivables for other reasons. First, the cost of doing business through credit sales is definite and can be determined in advance because the factor assumes all risks of collection. This is a form of credit insurance. Second, factoring eliminates expenses, including bookkeeping costs, the maintenance of a credit department, and the collection of delinquent accounts. A further advantage, but of a less tangible nature, is that factoring frees the management of a business from concern with financial matters and permits it to concentrate on production and distribution. Factoring has become increasingly important in supporting export sales. A firm that is unfamiliar with the problems of financing international shipments of goods is relieved of such details by factoring foreign receivables.

Although factoring services are regarded highly by some businesses, others object to their use. The two reasons cited most frequently are the cost and the implication of financial weakness. The cost of factoring is higher than the cost of borrowing from a bank under the terms of an unsecured loan. However, concluding that the net cost of factoring is higher is difficult. The elimination of overhead costs that would otherwise be necessary plus the reality that management need not concern itself with financial matters may offset the additional cost involved in factoring.

Few industries are affected by factors as much as retailing. Factors guarantee payment to suppliers of many large retail firms. With such guarantees, suppliers ship goods to the retailers, confident they will get paid. Should factors refuse to guarantee payments to suppliers because the factors believe a retailer to be on shaky financial ground, a retailing firm can find it has no merchandise to sell. Thus, predictions about poor finances can become a self-fulfilling prophecy. Once one factor hesitates to stand behind a retailer's credit, they all turn their backs on the retailer since no factor wants to be alone supporting a financially troubled firm. Factors act as an early warning signal of a retailer's real or imagined financial deterioration. In 1995, Bradlees, a discount retailer, filed for Chapter 11 bankruptcy protection after factors refused to guarantee Bradlees' receivables to its suppliers. A few months later Caldor, another discount retailer, filed for bankruptcy protection for the same reason: the factors would not support it. When factors refuse to accept a retailer's credit, the retailer's suppliers must decide whether to continue shipping and take the risk of nonpayment by the financially troubled retailer or to stop shipping and possibly lose a client. With the bankruptcy filings, over time, of retail stores such as Federated Department Stores, Allied Stores, Macy's, Jamesway, Bradlees, Caldor, and Sears, the suppliers may be listening to the factors.[16]

It is not always retail outlets that close due to the inability to obtain factor financing. In the Great Recession of 2007–2009, a lender and a factor were the victim of the slow economy; CIT Group filed for bankruptcy protection in 2009. Prior to that, it was a large factor to many small businesses, franchisees, and participated in SBA lending.[17] Fortunately, the firm did recover from its bankruptcy filing and continues to finance businesses with loans and factoring services.

Pledging and factoring have many similarities. To help differentiate them, Table 16.2 summarizes some of their differences.

16.5.2 ACCEPTANCES

Another type of receivable instrument that arises from sales transactions is an acceptance. An acceptance is a receivable from the sale of merchandise on the basis of a draft or bill of exchange drawn against the buyer or the buyer's bank. The bank "accepts" the draft, indicating that payment will be made on a specified future date by the bank if the debtor cannot pay the bill on time.

The accepted draft or bill of exchange is returned to the seller of the merchandise where it may be held until the date payment is due. During this period, the business may discount, or sell, such acceptances to another bank in order to get cash – or can use the acceptance as a form of payment to others.

The use of the banker's acceptance is discussed in detail in Chapter 6 in connection with an international shipment of goods. But they can be used for financing with one's home country, too. In some countries, acceptances are used as a secondary currency. That is, a firm receives an acceptance from a customer's bank; in turn, the firm uses the acceptance paper to pay one of its suppliers – who in turn uses the acceptance to pay its bills. As long as the initial amount owed is "accepted" by a bank with a good credit rating, the paper can be used until cash is finally transmitted on the acceptances by either the original debtor or the accepting bank.[18]

---

[16] Joseph Pereira, "Bradlees Seeks Bankruptcy Protection, But Denies it is Facing Liquidity Crisis," *The Wall Street Journal* (June 26, 1995), p. A10; Susan Pulliam and Laura Bird, "Concern Rises about Retailer Caldor's Ability to Deal with Cutthroat Rivalry; Stock Sinks," *The Wall Street Journal* (August 24, 1995), p. C2; Laura Bird, "Caldor Files for Bankruptcy Protection in Face of Weak Sales, Jittery Suppliers," *The Wall Street Journal* (September 19, 1995), p. A3; Roger Lowenstein, "Lenders' Stampede Tramples Caldor," *The Wall Street Journal* (October 26, 1995), p. C1.

[17] See, e.g., Catherine Clifford, "CIT's Long Goodbye," accessed January 29, 2013, at https://money.cnn.com/2009/11/03/smallbusiness/cit_bankruptcy_ripple_effects/.

[18] For an example of this in the Chinese economy, see Dinny McMahon, "China Cash Shortage Brings IOUs to Fore; Use of Acceptance Drafts Grows as Economy Slows, Banks Hesitate to Lend," *The Wall Street Journal* (April 4, 2014), pp. C1, C2.

Table 16.2   Comparison of Pledging and Factoring Accounts Receivable

Pledging accounts receivable	Factoring accounts receivable
It is a loan against accounts receivable	It is a sale of accounts receivable
Accounts receivable balances remain on the balance sheet	Accounts receivable balances are removed from the balance sheet
Customer pays the firm, which submits the payment to the bank	Customer pays the factor
Firm makes each credit decision	Factor makes the credit decision; firm can choose to extend credit on its own
Charges:	Charges:
• interest rate on loan	• interest rate on funds advanced
• audit fees for periodic review of accounts, payments	• service charge
Additional cost: paper and funds flow between firm and bank	

DISCUSSION QUESTION 2

How will receivables financing methods – from either banks or other sources – affect how accounts receivable are managed, as we learned in the Chapter 15 Learning Objective?

LEARNING ACTIVITY

Learn about factors and other asset-based lenders by visiting websites such as https://www.gecapital.com, https://www.textronfinancial.com, and https://www.celticcapital.com.

Accounts receivable financing is a method of financing a creditor's promise to pay for goods already obtained. On the other hand, inventory represents goods that are "on the premises," which provides additional security in case of borrower default. Other forms of security for business loans can include financial securities, such as stocks and bonds, that are owned by the business or its owners. For smaller businesses, an owner's cash value of a life insurance policy can be used as loan security, or the financing source may want the owner to personally guarantee the loan.

16.6 INVENTORY FINANCING AND OTHER SECURED LOANS

16.6.1 INVENTORY LOANS

A business may use its inventory as collateral for a loan in much the same manner that it may borrow on its receivables. The bank evaluates the physical condition of the firm's inventory and the inventory's general composition. Staple items that are in constant demand serve well as collateral for loans. Style and fashion items, such as designer clothes, are less acceptable as collateral, except for brief periods. Firms that use inventory as collateral usually do so because they are not in a position to obtain further funds on an unsecured basis.

The bank may protect itself when lending to a business by having a **blanket inventory lien**, or a claim against inventory when individual items are indistinguishable, as may be the case with grain or with clothing items. For such loans, a borrower may receive only 60–80% of the inventory's value in a loan. A manufacturer's work-in-process inventory may receive only 20–30% of its value.

blanket inventory lien claim against inventory when individual items are indistinguishable

In other cases, when goods can be identified, a **trust receipt** may be used. Money is borrowed against specific items in inventory. This method of financing, sometimes called floor plan financing, is used by car dealerships and appliance stores where inventory items financed by trust receipts can be identified by serial number. Under a trust receipt arrangement, the bank retains ownership of the goods until they are sold in the regular course of business. Audits are a matter of checking serial numbers of inventory items to determine if items held against a trust receipt have been sold.

trust receipt lien against specific identifiable items in inventory; with this arrangement, the bank retains ownership of the goods until they are sold in the regular course of business

warehouse receipt issued by the warehouse, indicating inventory is placed in a bonded warehouse for safekeeping; items are removed as they are paid for

field warehouse a warehouse on the grounds of the borrowing business establishment

In some cases, when inventory is used as collateral, the bank may insist the inventory be placed in a bonded and licensed warehouse. The **warehouse receipt** issued by the warehouse is turned over to the bank, which holds it until the loan is repaid.

For a business to deliver large, bulky items of inventory to a warehouse for storage can be inconvenient. Using a **field warehouse** solves this problem. A field warehousing enterprise has the power to establish a field warehouse on the grounds of the borrowing business establishment. Field warehouses differ from the typical public warehouse in that they serve a single customer on whose property the field warehouse is established and they exist only until the loan is repaid.

In setting up a field warehouse, the warehouse operator usually must obtain a lease on that portion of the property to be used for warehousing purposes. Then he or she must establish fences, barriers, walks, and other postings to indicate clear possession of the property. This is done to avoid accidental or deliberate removal of stored items during business operations. A guard may be posted to check on the safety of the warehoused goods or a room may be sealed and the seal inspected periodically to ensure the company is honoring its agreement.

There must be a complete statement of the commodities or items to be warehoused, and agreements must be made about the property's maintenance, proper fire precautions, insurance, and other necessary physical requirements. Under certain circumstances, the warehouse operator is authorized to release some of goods by the day, week, or month to make a rotation of merchandise possible. Under this arrangement, physical inventories must be taken occasionally.

Field warehouses are in operation throughout the United States but are concentrated in the Central and Pacific Coast regions. Canned goods, miscellaneous groceries, lumber, timber, and building supplies fill about two-fifths of all field warehouses in this country. Those banks that make loans involving commodities will generally accept field warehouse receipts as collateral.

Inventory loans are somewhat more expensive than unsecured loans to business borrowers. The higher cost is due in part to the cost of warehousing operations and because the borrower's credit rating may be low. Bank interest rates for warehouse loans ordinarily are somewhat higher than for unsecured loans.[19] In addition, a warehouse fee of 1–2% of the loan, depending on size and other factors, must be paid.

Technology can assist the valuing of inventory, especially if the inventory is equipment.[20] Digital writing and recording devices, such as digital cameras, allow items to be photographed and the information saved electronically for later recall. Business-to-business (B2B) auction sites and even eBay auction prices have been used to estimate an item's value.[21]

16.6.2 LOANS SECURED BY STOCKS AND BONDS

Stocks and bonds are often used as collateral for short-term loans. These securities are welcomed as collateral primarily because of their marketability and their value. If the securities are highly marketable and if their value is high enough to cover the amount of the loan requested even if the stock's price goes down somewhat, a banker will extend a loan. Securities listed on one of the national exchanges are preferred because frequent price quotations are available. Banks will usually loan from 60% to 70% of the market value of listed stocks and from 70% to 80% of the market value of high-grade bonds.

Only assignable stocks and bonds are eligible for this type of collateral financing with the exception of nonassignable U.S. savings bonds. When assignable securities are placed with a bank, a stock or bond power is executed that authorizes the bank to sell or dispose of the securities should it become necessary to do so to protect the loan.

---

[19] Inventory loans, like receivable loans, are made by commercial finance companies. Their interest rates usually are higher than those charged by banks.

[20] Firms can obtain loans against the firm's equipment used in its operations as well as what might be manufactured or sold from inventory.

[21] Hilary Rosenberg, "Mining the Balance Sheet," *CFO* (May 2001), pp. 103–108; Robert S. MacDonald, "Technology Tools Used in the Equipment Appraisal Process," *The Secured Lender* (August 2001), p. 8.

16.6.3 OTHER FORMS OF SECURITY FOR LOANS

Security for short-term bank loans may include the cash surrender value of life insurance policies and guarantee of a loan by a party other than the borrower.

16.6.3.1 Life Insurance Loans

Whole life insurance – sometimes called permanent life insurance – provides a death benefit to a beneficiary when the policyholder passes away. But during the person's life, they pay life insurance premiums on a regular basis to keep the policy in force (similar to the case of a car insurance policy). But with permanent life insurance, part of the premium goes into a "savings" account and is invested over time; should the person live into retirement this cash value of the policy can be used to help pay their living expenses. During one's life, this cash value can be tapped for making loans or for security on a loan.[22]

Small businesses frequently obtain needed short-term bank loans by pledging the cash surrender value, or the amount they will receive on cancellation, of the owner's life insurance policies. The policies must be assignable, and many insurance companies insist their own assignment forms be used for such purposes. Because of the safety afforded the bank by the cash surrender values, these loans usually carry a lower interest rate than loans on other types of business collateral. Another reason for the favorable rates is the borrower could borrow directly from the insurance company. Even so, bank interest rates are many times higher than those of insurance companies to their policyholders. As a result, the number of these loans made by insurance companies has increased.

16.6.3.2 Co-maker Loans

Many small businesses must provide the bank with a guarantor, in the form of a cosigner, to their notes. The cosigner is expected to have a credit rating at least as satisfactory as, and usually far better than, the firm requesting the loan.

> **LEARNING ACTIVITY**
>
> Have you visited https://www.ebay.com to look for items of interest? Do a search for items that may comprise excess inventory. Another business oriented site is https://www.salvagesale.com.

For most asset-based and unsecured loans, a simple method can be used to combine the interest expenses and fees to determine the true interest cost of a short-term loan. Fortunately, we discussed this earlier in this chapter when we examined commercial paper. Here, we break it into steps and present an example.

| 16.7 THE COST OF SHORT-TERM FINANCING |

First, determine the amount to be borrowed. Discounted loans or bank loans with compensating balances will need to use equations 16.2 and 16.3 to determine the amount.

Second, determine the interest expense on the borrowed funds. This is the interest rate multiplied by the amount borrowed.

Third, determine the fees and other expenses associated with using the financing source. We know, for example, that factors charge a service fee, inventory loans may carry warehouse charges, and pledged loans usually carry extra fees because of the extra analysis done by the lender.

Fourth, estimate the net proceeds. This may be the same as the amount borrowed, but in the case of discounted loans (such as commercial paper) the net proceeds will be less than the amount borrowed.

Fifth, to estimate the financing cost, divide the sum of the interest expenses and fees (steps 2 and 3) by the net proceeds (step 4). Annualize this rate, if necessary.

---

[22] The movie, "It's a Wonderful Life" is shown several times on television during the Christmas holiday season. If you've seen this movie, you may recall the scene where a distraught George Bailey goes to his banker nemesis, Henry Potter, to ask for a loan as the Bailey Building and Loan is short of cash. Potter asks Bailey what security he can offer on a loan and George pulls out a life insurance policy from his pocket – but Potter scoffs when he learns of its the low cash value (he calls it "equity" in the movie).

Here's an example. Fluoridated Manufacturing (FM) is considering short-term financing choices. A factor is willing to advance 80% of its receivables and charge it a 2% fee as compensation for analyzing the receivables and determining which it will purchase. FM estimates it will pay 12% APR to receive cash an average of 45 days earlier. The current receivables balance is $10,000.

Let's do the analysis step-by-step:

1. Determine the amount to be received. With receivables of $10,000 and an advance rate of 80%, FM will receive $10,000 × 0.80 = $8,000.

2. Determine the interest expense. With a 12% APR, the daily interest charge is 0.12/365. Factoring allows FM to receive its funds an average of 45 days sooner, so the interest expense is $8,000 × (0.12/365) × 45 = $118.36.

3. Determine the fees and other expenses. The factor's fee is 2% for basing a loan on a receivables balance of $10,000. The fees are 0.02 × $10,000 = $200.

4. Estimate the net proceeds. There is no discounting, so the net proceeds will be $8,000. We assume FM will pay the fees out of pocket. The net proceeds will be smaller if the $200 in fees is deducted by the factor from the loan amount.

5. The financing cost is $118.36 + $200 = $318.36, with net proceeds of $8,000. The percentage cost is $318.36/$8,000 = 0.0398, or 3.98% for 45 days of financing. The annualized rate is $(1 + 0.0398)^{365/45} - 1 = 0.3724$, or 37.24%.

The above process should help determine the financing cost of almost any lending arrangement, whether by a bank, commercial finance company, factor, or other short-term finance source.

DISCUSSION QUESTION 3

If you were CEO of a private company – so no public offering of stocks or bonds have occurred and there are no plans for public offerings – what would be your preferences for your top three sources of financing? Explain why you choose these three sources.

APPLYING FINANCE TO...

- **Institutions and Markets** We have seen in earlier chapters how the financial markets determine financing rates. Interest rates facing borrowers depend on the risk-free rate and a risk premium. Financial institutions have developed many ways to meet the short-term financing needs of firms, including instruments offering different maturities, security (collateral) requirements, and control, meaning who "supervises" the collateral arrangements.

- **Investments** Just as a capital market investor reviews a bond issuer's creditworthiness and a company's share price appreciation potential, similar care must be taken when analyzing a firm seeking a short-term loan or other financing arrangement. The primary concern will be the firm's ability to generate cash to repay the short-term loan. Cash generation, not sales or accounting profits, will be paramount.

- **Financial Management** Managers must balance the opportunity cost of excess cash with the costs of paying short-term financing rates, and consider the dangers of a credit crunch when short-term financing dries up. A firm's treasurer wants to maintain liquidity, which includes the firm's access to short-term financing sources, at all times.

SUMMARY

LO 16.1 Working capital, it has been said, is the grease that keeps the wheels turning in a company. Inventories are needed to meet customer demand for the firm's products. When they are sold, accounts receivable are created that will one day be converted into cash. This cash is used to pay suppliers, workers, creditors, taxes, and shareholder dividends. A firm without working capital is a firm unlikely to remain in business.

Two classes of working capital exist: permanent, the minimum necessary for smooth company operations, and temporary, which occurs because of seasonal or cyclical fluctuations in sales demand. A company financing strategy that uses long-term sources to finance its working capital is a conservative strategy that reduces profits but increases liquidity. An aggressive strategy that uses more short-term financing has less liquidity but may increase company profits.

LO 16.2 Management decisions on how the firm should be financed are affected by several influences, including the characteristics of the firm's industry, its asset base, seasonality, sales cycles, and sales trends.

LO 16.3 A line of credit allows a business to borrow up to a stated amount during the year for short-term financing needs. To help ensure the funds are for short-term purposes, the bank may require a clean-up period during which the firm has no line of credit balances outstanding. Whereas a line of credit can be withdrawn by the bank, a revolving credit agreement is a guarantee the bank will make funds available over a stated time frame. If a business is deemed to be too risky for a conventional bank loan, the firm can seek a loan guarantee for a bank loan from the Small Business Administration. In case of default, the SBA will repay the part of the loan defaulted upon.

LO 16.4 One firm's account receivable is another firm's account payable. Trade credit is nothing more than a firm's accounts payable. As a liability, it is a source of financing to a firm, as the firm receives and can use supplies (goods and/or services) and does not have to pay for them immediately. As such, the trade credit helps to finance inventory or whatever asset was purchased with the account payable. Commercial finance companies can lend funds (secured or unsecured) as do banks, but they are not banks as they don't accept deposits. They help finance receivables, inventory, and equipment purchases, such as trucks and other industrial equipment. Commercial paper is basically an "IOU" sold by the most creditworthy firms to raise short-term funds. Given the high credit rating of the issuers, they can finance some short-term needs more cheaply with commercial paper than from bank borrowing.

LO 16.5 Asset-backed financing, such as pledging and factoring receivables are usually higher-cost financing sources, primarily because smaller, less creditworthy firms rely on them for financing. In pledging, a firm uses its accounts receivable as collateral for a loan. The loan, plus interest, is repaid as the receivables are collected from customers. When receivables are factored, they are sold to the factor and customer payments are directed to the factor. In most cases, the factor takes on the risk of customer nonpayment – thus, the factor will review the customer payment records and credit standing before committing funds. In some cases, a business may outsource its credit department to a factor, who in turn makes all the credit decisions and sets the firm's credit policy.

LO 16.6 The main considerations with inventory financing are the marketability of the items and how secure they are against theft and spoilage. Inventory financing ranges from trust receipts, where inventory – such as cars and large home appliances – remains under the borrower's control, to warehouse receipts and field warehouses, where the lender takes control over inventory. In the latter case, inventory isn't released unless evidence is provided that it has been sold. For smaller businesses, assets of the owner(s) may be required, in some circumstances, as collateral or security for a loan. These assets can include liquid securities, such as common stocks and bonds, or assignment of life insurance policy cash value or the owner's personal guarantee (as co-maker) on the business loan.

LO 16.7 Firms have many possible sources of short-term financing, from bank loans (including lines of credit and revolving credit), to commercial paper, to trade credit. The treasurer should use care to evaluate the cost of each financing source by calculating its effective annual cost, by incorporating all interest charges and fees into the analysis, and by comparing the principal of the loan with the usable funds received.

advance factoring	discounted loan	net working capital	trust receipt	**KEY TERMS**
blanket inventory lien	factor	pledge	warehouse receipt	
commercial finance company	field warehouse	prime rate	working capital	
commercial paper	line of credit	revolving credit agreement		
compensating balance	maturity factoring	secured lending		
	maturity-matching approach	trade discounts		

1. **(LO 16.1)** What is net working capital? Briefly describe the financing implications when net working capital is positive.

2. **(LO 16.1)** What are "permanent" current assets? How do "temporary" current assets differ from permanent current assets?

3. **(LO 16.1)** Explain the strategies businesses can use to finance their assets with short-term funds and with long-term funds.

4. **(LO 16.1)** Explain how a conservative approach to financing a firm's assets is a low-risk/low-expected return strategy whereas an aggressive approach to financing is a high-risk/high-expected return strategy.

5. **(LO 16.2)** What influences affect the nature of the demand for short-term versus long-term funds?

6. **(LO 16.3)** Prepare a list of advantages and disadvantages of short-term bank borrowing over other short-term financing sources.

7. **(LO 16.3)** What is meant by an unsecured loan? Are these loans an important form of bank lending?

8. **(LO 16.3)** Explain what a bank line of credit is.

9. **(LO 16.3)** Explain how discounting and compensating balances affect the effective cost of bank financing.

10. **(LO 16.3)** Describe the revolving credit agreement and compare it with the bank line of credit.

11. **(LO 16.3)** How does the U.S. Small Business Administration provide financing to businesses?

12. **(LO 16.3)** What is the JOBS Act and what is its purpose?

13. **(LO 16.4)** What is trade credit? Briefly describe some of the possible terms for trade credit.

14. **(LO 16.4)** What are the primary reasons for using trade credit for short-term financing?

15. **(LO 16.4)** Under what circumstances would a business secure its financing through a commercial finance company?

16. **(LO 16.4)** What is commercial paper, and how important is it as a source of financing?

17. **(LO 16.4)** Is commercial paper a reliable source of financing? Why or why not?

18. **(LO 16.5)** When might a business seek accounts receivable financing?

19. **(LO 16.5)** What safeguards may a bank establish to protect itself when it lends on the basis of a customer's receivables pledged as collateral for a loan?

20. **(LO 16.5)** Describe how a factor differs from a commercial finance company in terms of accounts receivable financing.

21. **(LO 16.5)** Why would a business use a factor's services?

22. **(LO 16.6)** When a business firm uses its inventory as collateral for a bank loan, how is the problem of storing and guarding the inventory handled for the bank?

1. A supplier is offering your firm a cash discount of 2% if purchases are paid for within ten days; otherwise, the bill is due at the end of 60 days. Would you recommend borrowing from a bank at an 18% annual interest rate to take advantage of the cash discount offer? Explain your answer.

2. Assume you have been offered cash discounts on merchandise that can be purchased from either of two suppliers. Supplier A offers trade credit terms of 3/20, net 70, and supplier B offers 4/15, net 80. What is the approximate effective cost of missing the cash discounts from each supplier? If you could not take advantage of either cash discount offer, which supplier would you select?

3. Obtain a current issue of the Federal Reserve Bulletin, or review a copy from the Fed website (https://www.federalreserve.gov) or the St. Louis Fed website (https://www.stlouisfed.org), and determine the changes in the prime rate that have

occurred since the end of 2000. Comment on any trends in the data.

4. Compute the effective cost of not taking the cash discount under the following trade credit terms:
   a. 2/10 net 40
   b. 2/10 net 50
   c. 3/10 net 50
   d. 2/20 net 40

5. What conclusions can you make about credit terms from reviewing your answers to Problem 16.4?

6. Your firm needs to raise funds for inventory expansion.
   a. What is the effective annual rate on a loan of $150,000 if it is discounted at a 12% stated annual rate and it matures in five months?
   b. How much must you borrow to obtain usable funds of $150,000?
   c. What is the effective annual rate if you borrow the funds computed in (b)?

7. Bank A offers loans with a 10% stated annual rate and a 10% compensating balance. You wish to obtain $250,000 in a six-month loan.
   a. How much must you borrow to obtain $250,000 in usable funds? Assume you do not have any funds on deposit at the bank. What is the effective annual rate on a six-month loan?
   b. How much must you borrow to obtain $250,000 in usable funds if you currently have $10,000 on deposit at the bank? What is the effective annual rate on a six-month loan?
   c. How much must you borrow to obtain $250,000 in usable funds if you have $30,000 deposited at the bank?

   What is the effective annual rate on a six-month loan?

8. Compute the effective annual rates of the following:
   a. $1 million maturing in 90 days with a stated annual rate of 6%. Fees are 0.02% of the principal.
   b. $15 million maturing in 60 days with a stated annual rate of 7.6%. Fees are 0.05% of the principal.
   c. $500,000 maturing in 180 days with a stated annual rate of 8.25%. Fees are 0.03% of the principal.
   d. $50 million maturing in 210 days with a stated annual rate of 6.5%. Fees are 0.10% of the principal.

9. Construct a spreadsheet that computes the effective annual rates on the commercial paper offerings. Inputs to the spreadsheet should include the dollar amount of paper to be issued, the number of days the paper is outstanding, the stated annual rate, and fees. All paper is sold on a discount basis. Use it to find the effective annual rates in Problem 16.8.

10. Wonder Dog Leash Company is examining their accounts receivable patterns. Wonder's customers are offered terms of 1/10 net 30. Of their receivables, $150,000 is current, $75,000 is one month overdue, $30,000 is two months overdue, and $20,000 is over two months overdue.
    a. What proportion of Wonder's customers pay their bills on time?
    b. What is the effective cost of Wonder's terms of trade credit?
    c. What might happen to their receivables balance if they changed their terms to 1/15 net 30? To 2/10 net 30?

11. Wonder Dog Leash Company is seeking to raise cash and is in negotiation with Big Bucks finance company (BB) to pledge their receivables.
    BB is willing to loan funds against 75% of current (i.e., not overdue) receivables at a 15%

annual percentage rate (see the aging of receivables in Problem 16.10). To pay for its evaluation of Wonder's receivables, BB charges a 2.5% fee on the total balance of current receivables.
   a. If a loan's average term is 30 days, what is the effective interest rate if Wonder pledges its receivables?
   b. What is the effective rate if Wonder negotiates a loan of 45 days with no other changes in the loan's terms?

12. Michael's Computers is evaluating proposals from two different factors that will provide receivables financing. Big Fee Factoring will finance the receivables at an annual percentage rate (APR) of 8%, discounted, and charges a fee of 4%. High Rate Factoring offers an APR of 14% (nondiscounted) with fees of 2%. The average term of either loan is expected to be 35 days. With an average receivables balance of $250,000, which proposal should Michael's accept?

13. Michael's Computers' local bank offers the firm a 12-month revolving credit agreement (revolver) of $500,000. The revolver's APR is 12% with a commitment fee of 0.5% on the unused portion.
    Over the course of a year, Michael's chief financial officer (CFO) believes it will have an average balance of $280,000 on the revolver, with a low of $50,000 and a high of $450,000. What is the annual effective cost of this proposed agreement?

14. Banc Two wants to attract Michael's Computers Inc. to become a customer. Their sales force contacts Michael's and offers them line of credit financing. The line of credit will be for $500,000 with a one month clean-up period. The APR on borrowed funds is 11%. Banc Two will offer the line of credit if Michael's opens an account and maintains an average balance of $100,000 over the next 12 months. As in Problem 16.13, ignoring compensating balances, Michael's CFO believes its financing needs will average $280,000 monthly over the next year, with a low monthly need of $50,000 and a high need forecast of $450,000.
    a. Will the line of credit satisfy Michael's needs for short-term funds?
    b. How much money will Michael's draw down from the line of credit during a low-use month?
    c. How much will Michael's need to borrow in a month before it maximizes its use of the line of credit?
    d. What is the average cost to Michael's of using the line of credit for a year?

15. Montcalm Enterprises is seeking bids on short-term loans with area banks. It expects its average outstanding borrowings to equal $320,000. Which of

the following terms offers Montcalm the lowest effective rate?

a. Town Bank: revolving credit agreement for $500,000 with a 15% APR, 0.5% commitment fee on the unused portion.

b. Village Bank: revolving credit agreement for $400,000 with a 12% APR, 1.0% commitment fee on the unused portion and a 10% compensating balance requirement based on the size of the bank's commitment.

16. Beckheart is seeking financing for its inventory. Safe-Proof Warehouses offers space in their facility for Beckheart's inventory. They offer loans with a 15% APR equal to 60% of the inventory. Monthly fees for the usage of the warehouse are $500 plus 0.5% of the inventory's value. If Beckheart has saleable inventory of $2 million, answer the following:

a. How much money can the firm borrow?

b. What is the interest cost of the loan in dollars over a year?

c. What is the total amount of fees to be paid in a year?

d. What is the effective annual rate of using Safe-Proof to finance Beckheart's inventory?

17. CDRW is evaluating an inventory financing arrangement with DVD Banks. CDRW estimates an average monthly inventory balance of $800,000. DVD Bank is offering a 12% APR loan on 75% of the value of the inventory. DVD's inventory storage and evaluation fees will be 1% a month on the total value of the inventory. What is the annual effective rate of the inventory loan?

18. Which of the following offer the lowest effective rate for Wolf Howl jackets? Assume Wolf Howl will need to borrow $800,000 for 180 days.

a. A 14% APR bank loan

b. A 13% APR, discounted bank loan

c. 12.5% APR with fees of 1% for receivables financing

d. A $2 million revolving credit agreement with an APR of 12%, a commitment fee of 0.5% on the unused balance, and a 10% compensating balance requirement

19. **Challenge Problem** Visit a firm's website and obtain historical quarterly balance sheet information from it or from its SEC EDGAR filings (https://www.walmart.com and https://www.walgreens.com may be two good sites to use). Record quarterly balance sheet data for several years in a spreadsheet. Compute and graph the firm's financing mix (e.g., by computing the ratio of current liabilities to total assets) and asset mix (by computing the ratio of current assets to total assets). What happens to the firm's financing mix and asset mix over time? Do the financing and asset mix ratios move together? Are any seasonal effects in the firm's working capital position and financing evident? What conclusions can you draw about the firm's use of short-term financing?

20. **Challenge Problem** Use the information below for this problem. Comfin Company has estimates on its level of current and total assets for the next two years:

a. Estimate the permanent and temporary current asset levels for Comfin over these months. Find the average amount for fixed assets, permanent current assets, and temporary current assets in year 201X and year 201X + 1.

b. What average amounts of short- and long-term financing should Comfin have during each year if it wants to follow a maturity-matching financing strategy?

c. What average amounts of short- and long-term financing should Comfin have during each year if it wants to follow an aggressive financing strategy?

d. Suppose Comfin's cost of short-term funds is 8% and its cost of long-term funds is 15%. Use your answers in (b) and (c) to compute the cost of each strategy.

e. What are the pro and con arguments toward each strategy in terms of profitability, risk, and company liquidity?

Comfin Company data for Problem 16.20.

Year 201X	Jan	Feb	Mar	Apr	May	June	July	Aug	Sept	Oct	Nov	Dec
Total Assets	$500,000	$475,000	$460,000	$470,000	$475,000	$485,000	$495,000	$555,000	$600,000	$650,000	$700,000	$750,000
Current Assets	$250,000	$220,000	$199,900	$204,698	$204,392	$208,980	$213,459	$262,829	$307,085	$351,227	$395,251	$439,156

Year 201X + 1	Jan	Feb	Mar	Apr	May	June	July	Aug	Sept	Oct	Nov	Dec
Total Assets	$600,000	$570,000	$552,000	$564,000	$570,000	$582,000	$594,000	$660,000	$720,000	$780,000	$840,000	$900,000
Current Assets	$350,000	$350,000	$352,100	$359,302	$365,608	$373,020	$380,541	$397,171	$412,915	$428,773	$444,749	$460,844

Capital Budgeting Analysis

LEARNING OBJECTIVES

After studying this chapter, you should be able to do the following:

LO 17.1 Explain how the capital budgeting process should be related to a firm's mission and strategies.

LO 17.2 Identify and describe the five steps in the capital budgeting process.

LO 17.3 Calculate net present value, describe what it measures, and explain how it is used in capital budgeting analysis.

LO 17.4 Calculate internal rate of return, describe what it measures, and explain how it is used in capital budgeting analysis.

LO 17.5 Calculate modified internal rate of return, describe what it measures, and explain how it is used in capital budgeting analysis.

LO 17.6 Calculate profitability index, describe what it measures, and explain how it is used in capital budgeting analysis.

LO 17.7 Calculate payback, describe what it measures, and explain how it is used in capital budgeting analysis.

LO 17.8 Explain the conflicts that arise between project rankings determined by the various capital budgeting methods, and describe the practical issues that arise between theory and practice when using the capital budgeting methods.

LO 17.9 Explain how relevant cash flows are determined for capital budgeting decision purposes.

LO 17.10 Describe how managers can be held accountable for their project's cash flow estimates.

LO 17.11 Discuss how a project's risk can be incorporated into capital budgeting analysis.

Where we have been. . . In Chapter 13, at the beginning of the financial management section of this book, we considered how firms will have a mission or vision statement; that is, a reason for being. This chapter will examine how firms can "put feet to their words" and make decisions to purchase fixed assets and pursue strategies to help them fulfill their mission. The previous two chapters examined how a firm should manage and finance its current assets. Now our focus will shift to fixed assets.

Where we are going. . . Once a firm decides which fixed assets and corporate strategies to pursue, it must finance them. This will be the focus of Chapter 18, "Capital Structure and the Cost of Capital."

How this chapter applies to me. . . Capital budgeting analysis is a framework for evaluating all business decisions; it is not only a tool for the "financial" types. Proper analysis will identify relevant cash flows and an appropriate discount rate to reflect the strategy's risk and will compare the project's benefits and costs by considering the time value of money. It causes managers to consider more than a "feel good" or "sounds right" criterion for investing in projects. Whether the investment is one in a business strategy, building a new warehouse, seeking fuel-efficient methods of doing business, upgrading information technology systems, or investing in human resources, we should try to quantify the benefits and cost of these choices in order to evaluate them properly.

To achieve success over time, a firm's managers must identify and invest in the following:

Projects that provide positive net present values to maximize shareholder wealth.

Good ideas become good strategies when the numbers, such as cash flow forecasts, show the likelihood of shareholder wealth increasing because of the project. The firm's value will rise when a capital investment provides the firm with positive cash flows after the investment has been recovered, the cost of obtaining the necessary financing has been paid, and the timing of the project's cash flows has been taken into consideration.

17.1 MISSION, VISION, AND CAPITAL BUDGETING

As first discussed in Chapter 13, every firm should have a vision or mission – meaning, a reason for being. To implement its mission, a firm needs to have a competitive advantage. A competitive advantage is the reason why a firm's customers are willing to purchase its products or services rather than those of another firm. Large corporations spend millions on researching their customers and competitors to gather information they can use to maintain or expand their competitive advantage. Integral to the process of maintaining or expanding a firm's competitive advantage are its decisions concerning what products to offer and what markets or market segments to serve.

capital budgeting process of identifying, evaluating, and implementing a firm's investment opportunities

Capital budgeting is the process of identifying, evaluating, and implementing a firm's investment opportunities. Capital budgeting seeks to identify projects that will enhance a firm's competitive advantage and, by so doing, will increase shareholders' wealth. By its nature, capital budgeting involves long-term projects, although capital budgeting techniques can be applied to working capital decisions.[1] Capital budgeting projects usually require large initial investments and may involve acquiring or constructing plant and equipment. A project's expected time frame may be as short as a year or as long as 20 or 30 years. Projects may include implementing new production technologies, products, markets, or mergers. Given their size and duration, the projects undertaken by the firm should reflect its overall strategy for meeting future goals. Given the length of most projects, time value of money concepts should be used to evaluate them.

The typical capital budgeting project involves a large up-front cash outlay, followed by a series of smaller cash inflows and outflows, but the project's cash flows, including the total up-front cost of the project, are not known with certainty before the project starts. The firm must evaluate the size, timing, and risk of the project's cash flows to determine if it enhances shareholder wealth.

The profitability of a firm is affected to the greatest extent by its management's success in making capital budget investment decisions. A fixed-asset decision will be sound only if it produces a stream of future cash inflows that earns the firm an acceptable rate of return on its invested capital.

Fixed-asset management requires financial managers to compare capital expenditures for plant and equipment against the cash flow benefits received from these investments over several years. When properly adjusted benefits exceed expenditures, these projects will help increase the firm's value.

Investment in assets provides the basis for a firm's earning power or profitability. Plant, equipment, training, and infrastructure are employed to manufacture inventories or provide services that will be sold for profit, produce cash inflows, and enhance the firm's value. The financial manager must make appropriate capital budgeting decisions for these to occur. The types of decisions include whether to replace existing equipment with new equipment, expand existing product lines by adding more plant and equipment similar to that in use, or expand into new product areas requiring new types of assets.

mutually exclusive projects a project that, when selected, precludes others from being undertaken

independent projects projects not in direct competition with one another

Capital budgeting decisions can involve mutually exclusive or independent projects. As an example of **mutually exclusive projects**, two or more machines that perform the same function may be available from competing suppliers, possibly at different costs and with different expected cash benefits. The financial manager is responsible for choosing the best of these alternatives since only one can be chosen. Selecting one project precludes the other from being undertaken. **Independent projects** do not compete with one another. They are to be evaluated based on their expected effect on shareholder wealth. All such projects that enhance shareholder wealth should be included in the firm's capital budget.

---

[1] See John Zietlow, Matthew Hill, and Terry Maness, *Short-Term Financial Management* (San Diego, CA: Cognella, 2017); Ned C. Hill and William Sartoris, *Short-Term Financial Management*, 3rd ed. (Englewood Cliffs, NJ: Prentice-Hall, 1995).

In this chapter, we focus on only a small part of what is a complex topic. We present an overview of the capital budgeting process and some techniques used to evaluate potential investments. Then, we briefly discuss the process of estimating the cash flows expected from a capital budgeting project. We then cover how a project's risk can affect the evaluation process.

17.1.1 IDENTIFYING POTENTIAL CAPITAL BUDGET PROJECTS

From Chapter 10, we know that the market value of an investment is the present value of future cash flows to be received from the investment. The net benefit, or **net present value (NPV)**, of an investment is the present value of a project's cash flows minus its cost:

> **net present value (NPV)** present value of a project's cash flows minus its cost

$$\text{Net present value} = \text{Present value of cash flows} - \text{Cost of the project} \qquad (17.1)$$

Should the net present value be positive (the investor pays less than the market value of the investment), the owner's wealth increases by the amount of the net present value. If, for example, the present value of an asset's cash flows is $100 and we can purchase it for only $80, our wealth will rise by $20. If, instead, we were foolish enough to pay $130 for the investment, our wealth will fall by $30. To maximize shareholder wealth, we need to find assets or capital budgeting projects that have positive net present values.

Where do businesses find attractive capital budgeting projects? Business managers need to search for projects related to the firm's present lines of business or future plans. It would be foolish, for example, for a computer manufacturer to consider investing in land and mining equipment to prospect for gold. Despite management beliefs about future trends in gold prices and despite their confidence in their ability to find gold, such a project is far afield from the firm's current markets, products, and expertise.

Businesses should seek guidance to focus their search for capital budgeting projects. One popular corporate planning tool, known as **Mission, Objectives, Goals, and Strategies (MOGS)** develops project plans that fit well with a firm's plans. Under this strategy, the firm's managers first develop the firm's mission – its reason for being. Once developed, objectives can be formed (for example, to have the highest rating for product quality in its industry). Then, goals based upon the objectives are stated (for example, to receive industry association innovation awards by 2022 and earn the highest industry ranking in quality by 2025). Finally, managers develop strategies to try to achieve the goals, such as new product features or innovative technology offerings. A firm should have a MOGS plan, or something similar to it, in place to give direction to company planning and to help the firm's officers identify potential capital budgeting projects.

> **mission, objectives, goals, and strategies (MOGS)** corporate planning tool that aids in developing project plans that fit well with a firm's plans

Managers define and redefine the firm's mission, objectives, goals, and strategies over time, as part of the long-term plan. This long-term plan provides a foundation for the next five to ten years of operating plans for the firm. The long-term plan is operationalized, or implemented, in the annual capital budget. To develop the capital budget, managers must find investment opportunities that are suitable to the overall strategic objectives of the firm; its position within the various markets it serves; the government fiscal, monetary, and tax policies; and the leadership of the firm's management. Attractive capital budgeting projects take the firm from its present position to a desired future market position and, as a consequence, maintain or increase its shareholders' wealth.[2]

SWOT analysis examines a firm's *s*trengths, *w*eaknesses, *o*pportunities, and *t*hreats. With it, managers can identify capital budgeting projects that allow the firm to exploit its competitive advantages or prevent others from exploiting its weaknesses.

> **SWOT analysis** review of a firm's internal strengths and weaknesses, and its external opportunities and threats

Strengths and weaknesses come from the firm's internal abilities, or lack thereof. Strengths give the firm a comparative advantage in the marketplace. Perceived strengths can include good customer service, high-quality products, strong brand image and customer loyalty, innovative research and development (R&D) efforts, market leadership, or strong financial resources. Once identified, strengths can be used to correct or mitigate a firm's weaknesses. Weaknesses give competitors opportunities to gain

---

[2] For a seminal piece on the role of value maximization in a firm versus stakeholder theory or the "balanced scorecard," see Michael C. Jensen, "Value Maximization, Stakeholder Theory, and the Corporate Objective Function," *Journal of Applied Corporate Finance*, Fall 2001, vol. 14, no. 5, pp. 8–21.

advantages over the firm. The firm can select capital investments to mitigate or correct weaknesses that have been identified. For example, a single-country producer who finds it difficult to compete in a global market can achieve global economies of scale (that is, achieve "global scale") by making investments that will allow it to export or produce its product overseas.

CRISIS Opportunities and threats represent external conditions that affect the firm, such as competitive forces, new technologies, government regulations, and domestic and international economic trends. The 2007–2009 Great Recession affected economies and firms around the globe. Those firms with strong brands and adequate liquidity survived; others, such as General Motors, Chrysler, and AIG, needed government bailouts or they went bankrupt, as did Bear Stearns. As another example of this effect, in recent years consumers have tended to favor "green" technology and have been willing to pay a premium price for it. Changing environmental regulation and government-sponsored regulations have been opportunities to some (wind energy firms) and threats to others (coal-fired utility plants).

Where do positive NPV projects come from? From economics, we learn that economic profits in a competitive market are zero (recall that zero economic profit implies that the firm is earning a fair accounting return on its invested capital). In a competitive marketplace, we should be suspicious of any capital budgeting project that appears to have a positive net present value. Any positive economic profit or positive NPV must arise from one or two sources. One source is a market imperfection or inefficiency (such as an entry barrier or monopoly situation) that prevents competition from driving the NPV to zero. The second source of a positive NPV might involve cost-saving projects that allow the firm to reduce costs below their current level. Events that could cause such a situation to exist for a project include the following:

1. *Economies of scale and high capital requirements* typically go together. High sales volumes are sometimes needed to cover large fixed costs of plant and equipment. Scale economies occur as average production cost declines with rising output per period. Any new entrant must have available financing to construct a large-scale factory and be able to sell in sufficient quantity to be cost competitive – requirements that can prevent entry and promote positive net present values for investments by existing firms.

2. *Product differentiation* can generate positive net present values. Differentiation comes from consumers' belief in there being a difference between firms' products, whether or not a real difference exists. Differentiation leads to an imperfect market where one firm can set higher prices. Potential sources of differentiation include "branding" created through advertising and promotion expenditures, R&D, and quality differences.

3. *Absolute cost advantages* can place competitors at a cost disadvantage. A firm that enters a market early can learn about the production and distribution process first, making its use of assets, technology, raw inputs, and personnel more efficient than that of competitors. The firm can cut costs and prices, and can maintain market leadership. Similar advantages can result from possessing proprietary technology protected by patents. Early entry into foreign markets can allow the firm to gain experience over its competitors as it can more effectively make inroads into new markets and start to build customer loyalty.

4. *Differences in access to distribution channels* may result in unique advantages by reducing competitors' access to consumers. Shelf space is limited at retail outlets, and store owners hesitate to take space from a current supplier and give it to a new entrant. A motivated and well-trained sales force may keep competitors from chipping away at a firm's market share. The next time you are at the grocery store, take a look at the varieties of breakfast cereal produced by the large firms in the industry!

5. *Government policy* can hinder new and potential entrants, and give existing competitors unique advantages. An increasing regulatory burden on an industry may discourage entry by increasing the complexity and costs of entry. Domestic industries can seek import quotas to limit the extent of foreign entry and competition. Of course, similar quotas by other countries, perhaps raised in retaliation to the domestic quotas, will hurt the firm that initially sought protection. The policy of a foreign government toward nondomestic producers, as well as the stability of the government, can contribute to the political risk of investing or doing business overseas.

The capital budgeting process involves the preparation and analysis of a business case request for funding and usually consists of the following five stages:

17.2 CAPITAL BUDGETING PROCESS

1. Identification

2. Development

3. Selection

4. Implementation

5. Follow-up

The identification stage involves finding potential capital investment opportunities and identifying if each project involves a replacement decision and/or revenue expansion. The development stage requires estimating relevant cash inflows and outflows. It also involves discussing the pros and cons of each project. Development sometimes requires asking what the strategic impact will be of *not* doing the project.

The selection stage involves applying the appropriate capital budgeting techniques to make a final accept or reject decision. In the implementation stage, accepted projects must be executed in a timely fashion. Finally, decisions need to be reviewed periodically, with a follow-up stage analysis to determine if projects are meeting expectations. If disappointing results occur, it is sometimes necessary to terminate or abandon previous decisions.

GLOBAL The multinational corporation (MNC) must go through the same capital budgeting process for projects. In addition, however, MNCs need to consider possible added political and economic risks when making their decisions. Risk adjustments may be necessary because of the possibility of seizure of assets, unstable currencies, and weak foreign economies. In addition, MNCs must analyze the impact of foreign exchange controls and foreign tax regulations on a project's cash flows in relation to the final amounts that may be paid to the parent firm.

In Chapter 13, we stated how a company's mission should guide management in making investment decisions as they strive to meet goals and maximize shareholder wealth. We looked at mission statements for several firms also. Here, let's review some of the capital projects in which these firms are investing.

Wells Fargo: This financial institution is implementing a number of strategies to cross-sell products, with a special emphasis on home equity loans. It has acquired a number of financial institutions, including Wachovia and banks located in various states. Technology investments have improved its online financial services capabilities and improve customer service. Wells Fargo's strategy is to increase customer loyalty and to increase customer satisfaction with bank visits.

Merck: As a pharmaceutical company, its future relies on investing in research and developing a portfolio of products to meet the health needs of consumers. It initiates, curtails, expands, and shepherds a variety of formulations through the FDA drug approval process to maintain and grow its future cash flows. In late 2009, it completed its acquisition of Schering-Plough.

Google: Now a division of Alphabet Inc., Google continues to refine its search capabilities and, via the parent firm, play a part in email (Gmail), video (YouTube), driverless cars, and other cutting edge technologies.

Chick-fil-A: Growth in sales and earnings in the restaurant industry comes mainly via innovative new products, new outlet openings, and acquisitions. Its award-winning ad campaigns, featuring cows encouraging us to "Eat Mor Chikin," have increased sales.

Capital budgeting decisions require a great deal of analysis. Information generation develops three types of data: internal financial data, external economic and political data, and nonfinancial data. These data are combined to estimate a project's cash flows.

Table 17.1 lists data items that may need to be gathered in the information generation stage, depending on the project's size and scope. Many economic influences can directly impact a project's success by affecting sales revenues, costs, exchange rates, and overall project cash flows. Regulatory trends and political environment factors, in the domestic and foreign economies, may help or hinder the success of proposed projects.

---

identification stage finds potential capital investment opportunities and identifying if a project involves a replacement decision and/or revenue expansion

development stage requires estimating relevant cash inflows and outflows

selection stage applying appropriate capital budgeting techniques to make a final accept or reject decision

implementation stage accepted projects are executed in a timely fashion; cash outflows occur as the firm invests in the capital budgeting project

follow-up stage determining through analysis if a project is meeting expectations

Table 17.1 Examples of Data Needed in Project Analysis

External economic and political data
Business cycle stages
Inflation trends
Interest rates trends
Exchange rate trends
Freedom of cross-border currency flows
Political stability and environment
Regulations
Taxes

Internal financial data	Nonfinancial data
Investment costs (fixed assets and working capital)	Distribution channels
Market studies and estimates of revenues, costs, cash flows	Quantity, quality of labor force in different global locations
Financing costs (cost of capital)	Labor – management relations
Transportation costs	Status of technological change in the industry
Publicly available information on competitor's plans, operating results	Competitive analysis of the industry, potential reaction of competitors

Financial data relevant to the project are developed from sources such as marketing research, production analysis, and economic analysis. Using the firm's research and internal data, analysts estimate the cost of the investment, working capital needs, projected cash flows, and financing costs. If public information is available on competitors' lines of business, this should be incorporated into the analysis to estimate potential cash flows and to determine the effects of the project on the competition.

Nonfinancial information relevant to the cash flow estimation process includes data on the means used to distribute products to consumers, quality and quantity of the labor force, dynamics of technological change in the targeted market, and information from a strategic analysis of competitors. Analysts should assess the strengths and weaknesses of competitors and how they will react if the firm undertakes its own project.

To illustrate, in mid-1998, a strike against General Motors (GM) caused its management to reexamine its capital budgeting plan. GM had been planning to invest $21 billion in its U.S. plants between 1998 and 2002. The prospect of poor labor relations and inefficient union work rules was giving GM leaders second thoughts about its planned U.S. capital investment.[3] Political risks, on the other hand, can affect overseas projects. Delays have occurred in developing oil fields in Kazakhstan and Turkmenistan because the projects involved building an oil pipeline across politically unstable or unfriendly countries in order to get the oil to waterways and oil tankers.[4] In another example, the surprise introduction of a seven-seat model in the European compact minivan market by competitors caused Ford to abandon its plans to introduce a five-seat model, after several years and many millions had already been spent on design efforts.[5] Also, the push for "green" products is driving many firms, from auto manufacturers to manufacturers of household products, to develop more environmentally friendly products, or to at least proclaim the green benefits on their product packaging.[6]

---

[3] Micheline Maynard, "GM May Rethink Plant Investments," *USA Today*, (June 18, 1998), p. 1B.

[4] Hugh Pope, "Scramble for Oil in Central Asia Hits Roadblocks," *The Wall Street Journal*, (March 13, 1998), p. A12.

[5] Scott Miller, "Ford Scraps Plans for Compact Minivan, Years in Planning, in Cost-Cutting Effort," *The Wall Street Journal*, (February 14, 2000), p. A18.

[6] Author unknown, "Toyota Prius Dominates Green Vehicle List," *Environmental Leader*, (January 17, 2013), accessed February 8, 2019, https://www.environmentalleader.com/2013/01/toyota-prius-dominates-green-vehicle-list/; Author unknown, "Walmart Prescribes Green Packaging, Concentrated Clorox," *Environmental Leader*, (January 29, 2013), accessed February 8, 2019, https://www.environmentalleader.com/2013/01/walmart-prescribes-green-packaging-concentrated-clorox/.

Table 17.1 lists some of the information that firms may use to evaluate capital spending projects. For a specific industry example, oil and gas companies ranked seven items, from most important to least important, for their effect on capital spending decisions:

1. Forecasts of natural gas prices

2. Forecasts of crude oil prices

3. Forecasted demand for natural gas

4. Forecasted demand for crude oil

5. Availability and cost of outside funds to finance projects

6. Regulatory requirements or constraints on projects

7. Tax considerations

Natural gas prices, crude oil prices, and their demand determine company revenues. Higher prices (demand) will result in higher sales revenues and, all else being constant, higher profits. Moreover, since oil and gas are substitute products, oil producers will be interested in natural gas price and demand trends, and vice versa. With large oil companies allocating billions of dollars each year to capital spending, the ability to raise external funds is a consideration, should additions to retained earnings be insufficient to finance all of the attractive projects. Because of environmental concerns, oil and gas production is heavily regulated. The intricacies of the tax code affect oil and gas investment decisions also. U.S. income taxes affect these companies, as do depreciation and oil and gas depletion allowances, tax codes of the different countries in which they drill, credits for taxes paid to different jurisdictions, and so on. Firms sometimes plan for growing capital budgets when oil and gas prices are low to take advantage of future price upswings, and trim spending when prices are high since they do not want to overextend themselves before over supply occurs and prices fall.[7]

In recent years, energy prices, and oil prices in particular have become more volatile, rising through 2008, falling sharply in Great Recession, rising again through 2014 before falling again during 2014–2016. This trend of volatility has led many companies in energy-intensive sectors to design new ways of operating and to initiate capital budgeting projects that will lower energy costs. Indeed, many sectors of the economy are becoming more green and incorporating sustainability as a major focus of their business strategies.[8] In this context, "sustainability" refers less to keeping the business operating into the future and more about the use of materials for indefinite periods without causing environmental damage or depleting resources. The focus of such projects is to reduce waste and conserve natural resources. Sustainable strategies will seek to use renewable resources. Whereas some fear we may someday deplete oil reserves, there is less concern over naturally renewable (and potentially carbon-reducing) energy sources, such as wind, wave, solar, and nuclear energy and biofuels from corn, soybeans, and algae.

Such concerns are large for transportation-related industries, such as trucking, railroad, and airline carriers and for those who use the services of the retail and capital goods sectors. When fuel costs are low, just-in-time (JIT) inventory systems with daily shipments make sense in order to keep inventory costs down. But higher energy prices will be passed on by shippers and suppliers, so inventory storage and warehouse decisions take prominence over JIT efficiency. Some estimate that corporate supply chain transportation costs consume about 7% of energy in developed economies. As a result, firms are looking at ways to lower costs and dependence on oil by upgrading truck fleets with auxiliary power systems, tire inflation sensors, and better aerodynamics. They are considering projects to replace large trucks with smaller, more fuel-efficient vehicles for deliveries into congested areas. Smaller warehouses

[7] Thaddeus Herrick, "Big Oil Firms Trim Exploration Spending," *The Wall Street Journal*, (September 26, 2000), p. A2; Anne Reifenberg, "Big Oil Opens Capital-Spending Spigot for Overseas Projects Amid Price Slump," *The Wall Street Journal*, (January 3, 1996), p. A2.

[8] Vincent Ryan, "Sucking It Up," *CFO*, (April 2008), pp. 66–73; S. L. Mintz, "What Goes Down Will Come Up," *CFO*, (December 2008), pp. 51–55.

closer together rather than mega warehouses miles from the product's final destination may help lower transportation costs, too. Even loading a truck becomes a science, in an effort to use the available space as efficiently as possible and reduce trips and energy costs.

Energy price trends may also affect exports and imports. High fuel bills will lead to lower corporate profits, and some costs will pass through to consumers. Industries that rely heavily on imported goods from overseas may want to consider the energy benefits for producing those goods at home rather than paying higher shipping costs.

DISCUSSION QUESTION 1

Name a company and suggest a capital budgeting project it should consider doing. Explain why you believe the project is appropriate and good idea for the company to pursue.

LEARNING ACTIVITY

1. Details of investments can be seen in annual reports and news releases, both of which can be accessed via the firms' websites, https://www.wellsfargo.com, https://www.merck.com, https://www.abc.xyz, and https://www.chick-fil-a.com.
2. Visit the Environmental Protection Agency's SmartWay program to see what options exist to help businesses lower transportation costs: https://www.epa.gov/smartway/.

17.3 CAPITAL BUDGETING TECHNIQUES – NET PRESENT VALUE

FINANCE Appropriate methods or techniques are required to evaluate capital budgeting projects so that wealth-maximizing decisions can be made. The techniques used should reflect the time value of money, since cash outlays for plant and equipment occur now while the benefits occur in the future. Five methods are widely utilized: net present value (NPV), internal rate of return (IRR), modified internal rate of return (MIRR), profitability index (PI), and the payback period. Of these five methods, the payback period is the *least* preferable because it does not account for the time value of money.

The net present value (NPV) method is arguably the best method to evaluate capital budgeting projects. A project's NPV is calculated as the present value (PV) of all cash flows for the life of the project less the initial investment or outlay as we saw in equation 17.1. It considers the time value of money and includes all of the project's cash flows in the analysis. In addition, its value measures the project's dollar impact on shareholder wealth. The NPV measures the expected dollar change in shareholder wealth from doing the project. That is, a project with an NPV of $1 million is expected to increase shareholder wealth by $1 million. Thus, projects with positive NPVs are expected to add to shareholder wealth while projects with negative NPVs should be shunned.

To apply the NPV method, we need to know the project's estimated cash flows and the required rate of return in order to discount the cash flow. We discuss methods of estimating cash flows in the next chapter. The required rate of return should reflect the cost of long-term debt and equity capital funds for projects with the same risk as the one under consideration. In the following example, we'll assume that the required rate of return, or cost of capital, is 10%. In Chapter 18, we will cover the process of determining the cost of capital.

cost of capital project's required rate of return

We apply the NPV technique to projects A and B. Their cash flows are shown in Table 17.2. Assuming a 10% cost of capital, the cash flows are multiplied by the 10% present value interest factor

Table 17.2 Cash Flow Data for Projects A and B

Year	Project A	Project B
0	$–20,000	$–25,000
1	5,800	4,000
2	5,800	4,000
3	5,800	8,000
4	5,800	10,000
5	5,800	10,000

Table 17.3   Net Present Value Calculations for Projects A and B

Year	Project A Cash flow	x	10% PVIF	=	Present value	Project B Cash flow	x	10% PVIF	=	Present value
0	−$20,000		1.000		−$20,000	−$25,000		1.000		−$25,000
1	5,800		0.909		5,272	4,000		0.909		3,636
2	5,800		0.826		4,791	4,000		0.826		3,304
3	5,800		0.751		4,356	8,000		0.751		6,008
4	5,800		0.683		3,961	10,000		0.683		6,830
5	5,800		0.621		3,602	10,000		0.621		6,210
				Net present value = $1,982					Net present value = $988	

(PVIF) (from Table 2 in the Appendix) to get the PVs shown in Table 17.3. There is no discount factor for the initial outlays because they occur before any time has passed (i.e., in year zero). Positive NPVs are shown for both projects. This means an investment in either project will add to shareholder wealth. However, project A, with the higher NPV of $1,982, is preferable to project B, which has a NPV of $988.

A positive NPV means the project's cash inflows are sufficient to repay the initial, up-front (time zero) costs as well as the financing cost of 10% over the project's life. Since their NPVs are greater than zero, each project's return is greater than the 10% cost of capital.

Financial calculators can compute NPV. For example, for project A, we can enter the following:

For HP 10 B II Financial Calculator:

$-20,000$ CF$_j$

5800 CF$_j$

5800 CF$_j$

5800 CF$_j$

5800 CF$_j$

5800 CF$_j$

$10\ i$ (interest rate key)

Pushing the NPV key next, we have an exact answer for the NPV: $1,986.56.

For the TI BA II Plus Financial Calculator, we do the following calculations:

To	Press	Display
Select Cash Flow worksheet.	CF	CFo = 0.00
Enter initial cash flow.	20000 +/− **ENTER**	CFo = −20,000
Enter cash flow for first year.	↓ **5800** ENTER	C01 = 5,800
	↓	F01 = 1.00
Enter cash flows for the second year	↓ **5800** ENTER	C01 = 5,800
	↓	F01 = 1.00
Enter cash flows for the third year	↓ **5800** ENTER	C01 = 5,800
	↓	F01 = 1.00
Enter cash flows for the fourth year	↓ **5800** ENTER	C01 = 5,800
	↓	F01 = 1.00
Enter cash flows for the fifth year	↓ **5800** ENTER	C01 = 5,800
	↓	F01 = 1.00

Computing NPV

To	Press	Display
Prepare to compute NPV	NPV	I = 0.00
Enter interest rate per period	10 ENTER	I = 10.00
Compute NPV	↓ CPT	NPV = 1,986.56

Doing this calculation for project B, we find its NPV is $992.01.

A shortcut method can be used to calculate the NPV for project A. Since the cash inflows form an annuity, we could have used the present value interest factor of an annuity (PVIFA) at 10% for five years from Table 4 in the Appendix, which is 3.791. The NPV can be calculated, as follows:

$$\$5,800 \times 3.791 = \$21,988 \text{ PV cash inflows}$$

$$\underline{-20,000 \text{ Initial outlay}}$$

$$\$1,988 \text{ Net present value}$$

The $1,988 NPV figure using PVIFA differs slightly from the $1,982 using PVIF because of rounding the PVIFs in the Appendix tables. When cash inflows are not in the form of an annuity, as in the case of project B, the longer calculation process shown in Table 17.3 must be used to find the net present value.

Projects with negative NPVs are unacceptable to a firm. They provide returns lower than the cost of capital and would cause the firm's value to fall. In our example, projects A and B have positive NPVs and are acceptable. If they are mutually exclusive projects, managers should chose project A as its NPV of $1,986.56 is higher than project B's NPV of $992.01. Clearly, the financial manager must make capital budgeting decisions on the basis of their expected impact on the firm's value.

17.3.1 USING SPREADSHEET FUNCTIONS

In addition to multiplying with factors found in a PV table or using a financial calculator, electronic spreadsheet packages, such as Excel, make the task of computing a NPV simple, too. Suppose, we have the cash flows for project A in column B, rows 2 through 7 of an Excel spreadsheet:

To compute the NPV, we can use Excel's NPV function, with modification. We need to modify its use because Excel's NPV does not calculate NPV as we do in this chapter. Excel's NPV function computes the sum of PVs assuming the value in the first cell listed is to be discounted back one period, the value in the second cell is to be discounted back two periods, and so on. But most capital budgeting problems have a "time zero," or "current," investment that is not discounted; in our example, the investment of $20,000 at time zero is expressed in PV terms.

To get around this problem, we use Excel's NPV function to find the sum of the PVs in periods one through the end of the project (cells B3 through B7 in our case) and then add the initial negative investment cash outflow of $20,000 in cell B2. In the above example, in cell B8, we typed = NPV (10%, B3:B7) + B2, and the spreadsheet computes an exact value of the NPV: $1,986.56.

The NPV function has the following form:

$$= \text{NPV} \left(\text{discount rate, cell of time one cash flow : cell of last cash flow} \right)$$

The discount rate can be typed as a percentage (10%) or as a decimal equivalent (0.1). If you type in the "%" symbol, Excel assumes the number is a percentage; otherwise, the decimal equivalent is assumed. Be careful: if you key in "10" rather than "10%," the spreadsheet will use a discount rate of 1000%.

17.4 CAPITAL BUDGETING TECHNIQUES – INTERNAL RATE OF RETURN

We know from our discussion of bonds in Chapter 10 that an inverse relationship, or "seesaw effect," exists between bond prices and interest rates. As investors' required rates of return rise, bond prices fall; as investors' required rates of return fall, bond prices rise. A similar relationship exists between NPV and a firm's required rate of return, or a project's cost of capital. For a given set of cash flows, a higher cost of capital will lead to a lower NPV; a lower cost of capital, however, will increase a project's NPV. Figure 17.1 shows this relationship, called the **NPV profile**, between NPV and the cost of capital. As the cost of capital on a project rises, the NPV changes from positive, to zero, to negative. The cost of capital at which the NPV is zero deserves special attention.

While the NPV method tells us that projects A and B provide expected returns greater than 10%, we do not know the actual rates of return. The **internal rate of return (IRR) method** finds the return that causes the NPV to be zero; namely, the point where the NPV profile crosses the 0 axis in Figure 17.1. Net present value will equal zero when the PV of the cash flows equals the project's initial investment, as seen in equation 17.2[9]:

$$\text{NPV} = \sum_{t=1}^{n} [\text{CF}_t / (1 + \text{IRR})^t - \text{Initial Investment}] = 0 \qquad (17.2)$$

NPV profile the graphical relationship between a project's NPV and cost of capital

internal rate of return (IRR) method return that causes the net present value to be zero

A trial-and-error process can be used to find the internal rate of return (IRR), but financial calculators and computer spreadsheets (such as Excel's IRR function) provide a much quicker means of estimating internal rates of return.

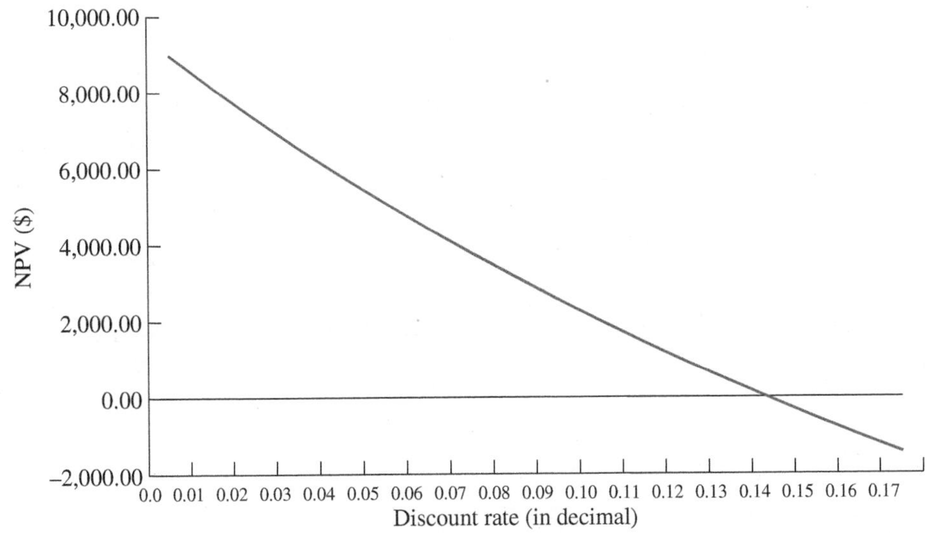

FIGURE 17.1 Relationship between NPV and discount rates

---

[9] This method is also used to find the yield to maturity on bonds in Chapter 10.

Let's illustrate the IRR process first for project A. Because the cash inflows form an annuity, the IRR is easy to find. From Chapter 9, we know the following:

Present value of an annuity = PVIFA × annuity cash flow

Rearranging, we divide the initial capital budgeting outlay (PV annuity) by the cash inflow annuity amount to find the present value interest factor (PVIF) for an ordinary annuity:

PVIFA = PV annuity / Annual receipt

For project A, the PVIFA is 3.448 ($20,000/5,800). We know this PVIFA of 3.448 is for five years. By turning to Table 4 in the Appendix, "Present Value of a $1 Ordinary Annuity," we can read across the five-year row until we find a PVIFA close to 3.448. It falls between 3.605 (12%) and 3.433 (14%) but is closer to the PVIFA at 14%. Thus, the IRR for project A is slightly less than 14%.

Of course, with financial calculators and computer spreadsheets, there are other, more precise, ways to find the internal rate of return. As an example, we will use a financial calculator and project A's cash flows:

For HP 10 B II Financial Calculator, enter the following data:

$$-20{,}000 \ CF_j$$
$$5800 \ CF_j$$
$$5800 \ CF_j$$
$$5800 \ CF_j$$
$$5800 \ CF_j$$
$$5800 \ CF_j$$

Pushing the IRR key (for some calculators, you may need to push a shift, or "2nd," key before pushing the IRR key). Doing so, we find the IRR is 13.82%.

For the TI BA II Plus Financial Calculator, enter the following data:

To	Press	Display
Select Cash Flow worksheet.	CF	CFo = 0.00
Enter initial cash flow.	20000 +/− ENTER	CFo = −20,000
Enter cash flow for first year.	↓ **5800** ENTER	C01 = 5,800
	↓	F01 = 1.00
Enter cash flows for the second year	↓ **5800** ENTER	C01 = 5,800
	↓	F01 = 1.00
Enter cash flows for the third year	↓ **5800** ENTER	C01 = 5,800
	↓	F01 = 1.00
Enter cash flows for the fourth year	↓ **5800** ENTER	C01 = 5,800
	↓	F01 = 1.00
Enter cash flows for the fifth year	↓ **5800** ENTER	C01 = 5,800
	↓	F01 = 1.00

Computing NPV

To	Press	Display
Prepare to compute IRR	IRR	IRR = 0.00
Compute internal rate of return	↓ CPT	IRR = 13.82

Using spreadsheets, we can illustrate two ways to determine the internal rate of return. We will use project A, with its annuity cash flows, in these examples. First, we can successively compute values of NPV using different discount rates:

Discount Rate (%)	Project A's NPV	
0	$9,000.00	
1	$8,149.90	
2	$7,338.07	
3	$6,562.30	
4	$5,820.57	
5	$5,110.96	
6	$4,431.71	
7	$3,781.15	
8	$3,157.72	
9	$2,559.98	
10	$1,986.56	
11	$1,436.20	
12	$907.70	
13	$399.94	
14	–$88.13	The NPV goes from
15	–$557.50	positive to negative here, so the IRR
16	–$1,009.10	must lie between
17	–$1,443.79	13% and 14%.

This shows the IRR is between 13% and 14%. This information can be used as input into Excel's graphing capabilities and the NPV profile can be graphed, which is how we constructed Figure 17.1. The NPV profile gives us a visual perspective of how sensitive the NPV is to a change in the project's cost of capital, or discount rate.

The second way to use the spreadsheet is to compute the IRR by using Excel's IRR function. Let's assume the time 0 through time 5 cash flows for project A are in cells B2 through B7, as below. By keying = IRR(B2:B7) into a cell (B9, in this case), the spreadsheet will compute an exact value of the internal rate of return for project A:

In our example, the initial (time zero) cash flow is found in cell B2. Cell B7 contains the final cash inflow for time period five. Using the IRR function, we obtain an exact value for project A's IRR, 13.82%, the same as we found using a financial calculator.

The IRR function has the form = IRR(cell of time zero cash flow : cell of last cash flow, initial estimate for the IRR). The last item, the initial estimate for the IRR, is optional and we did not use it in the above example for project A. To input an initial guess, we can use percentages (10%) or decimal

Table 17.4 Net Present Value Calculation for Project B Using a 12% Discount Rate

Year	Cash flow	×	12% PVIF	=	Present value
0	–$25,000		1.000		–$25,000
1	4,000		0.893		3,572
2	4,000		0.797		3,188
3	8,000		0.712		5,696
4	10,000		0.636		6,360
5	10,000		0.567		5,670
					Net present value = –$514

equivalents (0.10). Many times, we can omit this initial guess and the IRR function will compute the IRR with ease.

For project B, with its unequal cash flows, a financial calculator or spreadsheet program are the most useful. But a trial-and-error process can also be used to find the IRR for project B. Discounting the cash flows at a 10% rate results in a positive NPV of $988, as calculated in Table 17.3. A positive NPV indicates that we need to try a higher discount rate, such as 12%, to find the discount rate that results in a zero net present value. The 12% PVIFs are taken from Table 2 in the Appendix, "Present Value of $1."[10] In Table 17.4, we calculate that when the cash flows are discounted at a 12% rate, the NPV becomes minus $514.

This indicates that the IRR falls between 10% and 12%. Since minus $514 is closer to zero than $988 is, you might guess that the IRR is a little above 11%. But to obtain an exact answer, we need to use a financial calculator or electronic spreadsheet. Doing so, we learn that project B's IRR is 11.3%.

Projects A and B are acceptable because they provide returns higher than the 10% cost of capital. However, if the projects are mutually exclusive, we would select project A over project B because A's NPV is higher.[11]

17.4.1 NPV AND IRR

The NPV and IRR methods will always agree as to whether a project enhances or harms shareholder wealth. If a project returns more than its cost of capital, the NPV is positive. If a project returns less than its cost of capital, the NPV is negative. An issue with the use of IRR is that it may rank projects differently than the NPV. If that occurs, what decision should be made?

If the projects are independent, there is no real issue; the firm should do all projects with positive NPVs. To state this similarly but in another way, the firm should do all projects with IRRs greater than their required returns.

If the projects are mutually exclusive, however, the decision should be made to follow the rankings created by the NPV method. The NPV measures the change in shareholder wealth that is expected to be generated by the project. As managers should maximize shareholder wealth, they should prefer the project with the higher NPV, *not* the higher IRR.

A second issue that can occur with IRR is that the cash flows of a project may alternate in sign; meaning, some cash flows are positive and some negative. In such a case, it is mathematically possible to have two or more IRRs. For example, consider the case of a project with an initial outlay of $100, a positive cash flow of $300 in year one, and a cash outflow of –$200 in year two because of shut-down costs. Such a project has two IRRs: 0% and 100%:

$$\text{NPV at } 0\%: -100 + 300/(1+0)^1 + -200/(1+0)^2 = -100 + 300 - 200 = 0$$
$$\text{NPV at } 100\%: -100 + 300/(1+1.00)^1 + -200/(1+1.00)^2 = -100 + 150 - 50 = 0$$

---

[10] Similar to the "seesaw effect" in bond pricing, a higher discount rate results in a lower NPV, as seen in Figure 17.1.

[11] For several reasons, a project with an NPV below that of another project may have a higher IRR than the competing project. That is why it is best to calculate each project's NPV in addition to the IRR. The project with the highest NPV is the one that is expected to add the most to shareholder wealth.

It is easy to think of a real-world project that may require substantial renovations or maintenance over time, or one that may have large end-of-life decommissioning or shut-down costs. Thus, for this reason NPV is the preferred approach rather than internal rate of return.

A common misconception is that the IRR represents the compounded return on the funds originally invested in the project. What IRR measures is the return earned on the funds that remain internally invested in the project (hence the name, *internal* rate of return). Some cash flows from a project are a return of the principal (original investment), while some pay a return on the remaining balance of funds invested in the project.

To show that the IRR measures the return earned on the funds that remain internally invested in a project, we present the following example. Martin and Barbara have decided to upgrade their business computer system to improve the quality and efficiency of their work. The initial investment is $5,000 and the project will save them $2,010.57 each year for three years. They have determined the IRR on the project to be 10%. We show how the IRR represents the return on the year-by-year unrecovered costs of the project.

Below is the cash flow schedule constructed for Martin and Barbara's computer upgrade project.

(1) Year	(2) Beginning investment value	(3) Cash inflow (Savings)	(4) 10% Return on the invested funds (2) × 0.10	(5) Reduction in the invested funds (3) − (4)	(6) Ending value of invested funds (2) − (5)
1	$5,000.00	$2,010.57	$500.00	$1,510.57	$3,489.43
2	3,489.43	2,010.57	348.94	1,661.63	1,827.80
3	1,827.80	2,010.57	182.78	1,827.79	0.01*

*Value is not 0.00 due to rounding.

This table shows that the yearly cash saving of $2,010.57 from the computer upgrade project represents a return on the funds that remain invested (Column 4) and a reduction in the funds that remain invested in the project (Column 5). The project does not earn a 10% return, or $500 annually, on the initial $5,000 investment for all three years. The 10% IRR represents the return on the funds that remain invested in the project over its lifetime rather than each year's return on the original investment.

17.5 CAPITAL BUDGETING TECHNIQUES – MODIFIED INTERNAL RATE OF RETURN

Modified internal rate of return (MIRR) solves some of the problems presented by IRR. MIRR rankings of mutually exclusive projects with comparably sized initial investments will agree with the NPV rankings of those projects. Additionally, the MIRR calculation always gives a single answer. It will not give us multiple answers as the IRR approach sometimes does.

MIRR is calculated in a three-step process:

1. Using the required rate of return as the discount rate, find the present value (PV) of all cash outflows. (For a conventional project, this will be just the initial cost of the project.) This step converts all the cash outflows into a lump-sum PV at time 0.

2. Using the required return as the re-investment or compounding rate, compute the *future* value (FV) of each cash inflow as of the end of the project's life, time N, and add them together. This sum is sometimes called the *terminal value*. This step converts all inflows into a lump-sum future value at time N.

3. Find the discount rate that equates the PV of the outflows and the terminal value; this discount rate is the modified internal rate of return.

modified internal rate of return (MIRR) method a technique that solves some of the problems presented by IRR; MIRR rankings of mutually exclusive projects with comparably sized initial investments will agree with the NPV rankings of those projects

Figure 17.2 illustrates this process using the cash flow data from project A and a required return of 10%.

In the first step, the PV of the project's outflows is its initial investment, $20,000.

Second, we find the FV of each of the project's inflows as of the end of the fifth and final year of the project. The year one cash inflow of $5,800 is compounded over four years to the end of year five; its FV at the end of year five is $8,491.78. The year-two cash flow is compounded for three years to the end of year five; its FV at the end of year five is $7,719.80. Similarly, we compute the FVs for the

FIGURE 17.2
MIRR for project A

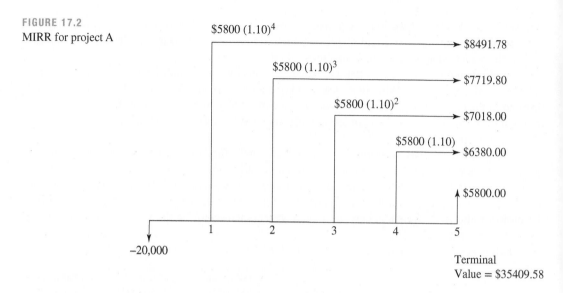

$$\$5800\,(1.10)^4 \longrightarrow \$8491.78$$
$$\$5800\,(1.10)^3 \longrightarrow \$7719.80$$
$$\$5800\,(1.10)^2 \longrightarrow \$7018.00$$
$$\$5800\,(1.10) \longrightarrow \$6380.00$$
$$\$5800.00$$

$$-20{,}000$$

Terminal
Value = \$35409.58

year three, four, and five cash inflows. The year five cash inflow needs no compounding as it occurs at the end of year five. Adding the FVs yields the sum \$35,409.58; this is the project's terminal value.

Third, we find the discount rate that sets the PV of the outflows equal to the terminal value:

$$FV = PV(1+r)^n = \$35{,}409.58 = \$20{,}000(1+r)^5$$

Solving, we find that the MIRR is 12.10%.

Using a spreadsheet, Excel has a function, MIRR, to do this calculation:

	A	B	C	D	E	F	G
1	Time	Cash Flow					
2	0	-$20,000					
3	1	$5,800					
4	2	$5,800					
5	3	$5,800					
6	4	$5,800					
7	5	$5,800					
8	NPV =	$1,986.56	=NPV(10%,B3:B7) + B2				
9	IRR =	13.82%	=IRR(B2:B7)				
10	MIRR =	12.10%	=MIRR(B2:B7,10%,10%)				
11							

The MIRR function has the form, =MIRR(cell of time zero cash flow : cell of last cash flow, finance rate, re-investment rate). The finance rate is the interest rate paid on borrowing to finance the cash out-flows. The re-investment rate is the rate used to compound or find the FV of the cash inflows. We used the firm's required rate of return of 10% for both of these in this example.

Similar calculations show the MIRR for project B is 10.86%. MIRR ranks project A (12.10%) higher than project B (10.86%); this is the same ranking as NPV gave the projects.

The decision rule for MIRR is similar to that for IRR – a project is acceptable if its MIRR exceeds the project's minimum required return. A drawback to the MIRR is that it is a relative measure of attractiveness; it does not indicate the dollar amount by which projects change shareholder wealth.[12]

---

[12] The reason the MIRR ranks projects in the same order as the NPV method is because the MIRR is a transformation of the NPV calculation. The terminal value calculation in the MIRR method is equal to the FV of the PV of the inflows. For example, for project A, the PV of the inflows is \$21,986.56. At the 10% required return, the FV of this amount in year five is $\$21{,}986.56(1.10)^5 = \$35{,}409.57$, which, with some rounding error, is the terminal value we computed above.

Another discounted cash flow technique for evaluating capital budgeting projects is the profitability index (PI), also called the benefit/cost ratio. The PI method computes the ratio between the present values of the inflows and outflows:

$$PI = \frac{\text{Present value of future cash flows}}{\text{Initial cost}} = \frac{\sum_{t=1}^{n} \frac{CF_t}{(1+r)^t}}{CF_0} \qquad (17.3)$$

profitability index (PI) or benefit/cost ratio ratio between the present values of the inflows and the outflows

The PI measures the relative benefits of undertaking a project; namely, the PV of benefits received for each dollar invested. A PI of 2, for example, means that the project returns a PV of $2 for every $1 invested. Since it would be foolish to invest in a project that returns less than a dollar for every dollar invested, the profitability index has a natural decision rule: accept a project that has a PI greater than 1.0, and reject a project that has a PI less than 1.0.

Using the data in Table 17.3, we calculate the PV of project A's inflows to be $21,982. Since its initial cost is $20,000, project A has a PI of $21,982/$20,000, or 1.099. Project B's cash inflows have a PV of $25,988, so its PI is $25,988/$25,000, or 1.040.

The relationship between PI and NPV should be clear. Whenever NPV is positive, PI exceeds 1.0. Likewise, whenever NPV is negative, PI is less than 1.0. Thus, the NPV, IRR, and PI always agree on which projects would enhance shareholder wealth and which would diminish it.

The payback period method does not consider the time value of money so it is a nondiscounted cash flow technique. So, why discuss it? We discuss it because it is simple to compute and still used by some firms. You need to know this technique and be able to explain why it should be avoided to make investment decisions.

The payback period method determines the time in years it will take to recover, or "pay back," the initial investment in fixed assets. Management will choose the projects whose paybacks are less than a management-specified period.

In cases where the cash benefits form an annuity, the payback period is easily calculated:

payback period method determines the time in years it will take to recover, or pay back, the initial investment in fixed assets

Payback period = Initial outlay / Annual cash inflow

For project A, we have payback period = $20,000/$5,800 = 3.4 years.

The initial investment outflow for project B is $25,000. Cash inflows for project B will total $16,000 ($4,000 + $4,000 + $8,000) for the first three years. This leaves $9,000 ($25,000 − $16,000) unrecovered. With a $10,000 cash flow expected in year four, it will take an additional 0.9 of a year ($9,000/$10,000) before the investment is recovered. Thus, the payback period for project B is 3.9 years. Based solely on the payback period technique, project A would be chosen over project B because it recoups its investment more quickly.

However, the payback period evaluation method suffers from two drawbacks. First, the technique does not consider the time value of money. The second limitation is that all cash flows beyond the payback period are ignored. Project B will return $10,000 in cash inflow in year five, which is more than project A's fifth-year cash inflow. The possible significance of this difference is overlooked by the payback period method.

A large accounting firm conducted a study of store remodeling and renovations. Their findings are disturbing for some retailers: these investments may never pay for themselves. The study found that large discounters, such as K-Mart and Target, have payback periods that average 20 years for renovation projects. The IRRs on such projects range from 1% to 6%. For family apparel specialty stores (such as Eddie Bauer), it was a different story. Their remodeling IRRs were as high as 67% with payback periods that averaged 19 months. (The participants in the study were not revealed; the store names used above are only examples of stores in the different retail categories.)

SMALL BUSINESS PRACTICE

A SMALL BUSINESS RESOURCE CENTER

Bloomberg Business has established a small business resource center. Access is available at http://www.bloomberg.com/small-business. The center is interactive and provides a variety of information on such topics as market research, managing a workforce, finance, and technology. In addition, the center provides services in the form of access to a variety of *Business Week* articles on technology, franchises, and other small business related topics, including daily reports and breaking business stories.

Information relating to operating and financing a business at various life cycle stages is provided at https://www.sba.gov/managing-business/forms%20. For example, if you wish to start a new business, you can examine the necessary forms to begin operation. Information on financing and growing a business is provided, as is information for owner/managers who are seeking to sell their firms or find other ways to exit their businesses.

The study concludes that having a good market position is more important to success than a renovation project. Poor returns on some stores' renovations apparently occurred because stores were trying to modernize in the face of new competition rather than realigning company strategy to respond to a successful competitor.[13]

> **DISCUSSION QUESTION 2**
>
> **The book describes why NPV is the best technique to evaluate capital budgeting projects. Besides NPV, which technique do you think is "best"? Explain why.**

17.8 CONFLICTS BETWEEN DISCOUNTED CASH FLOW TECHNIQUES

NPV, IRR, MIRR, and PI will *always* agree on whether a project should be accepted or rejected. So, if the firm is considering only independent projects, it makes little practical difference which method is used. All of them always give consistent indicators as to whether a given project would increase or decrease shareholder wealth.

When mutually exclusive projects are ranked from most attractive to least attractive, NPV may rate them differently from the other techniques. The main reason for this is that NPV measures one aspect of the project, whereas IRR and PI measure another. NPV measures the dollar change in shareholder wealth that arises from undertaking the project. As relative measures of project attractiveness, IRR and PI indicate the rate of profitability a project adds to shareholder wealth but not the dollar amount. A project with a lower IRR or PI may add more to shareholder value than another mutually exclusive project if the projects have different cash flow patterns, time horizons, or sizes.

17.8.1 DIFFERENT CASH FLOW PATTERNS

Projects that provide larger cash flows in their early stages can seem to provide more funds than a project with more even cash flows. If the IRR exceeds the firm's required rate of return, the effects of compounding larger cash flows at a rate exceeding the required return may result in the project receiving a higher ranking by the IRR method than by the NPV method. Thus, projects with larger earlier cash flows may have higher IRR rankings than those with larger later cash flows.

17.8.2 DIFFERENT TIME HORIZONS

A shorter project may free up invested funds sooner and, consequently, offer a higher IRR. A long-term project's cash flows will remain internally invested in the project for a longer period. Unless those future cash flows are large, the discounting process may reduce their perceived present value, eroding

---

[13] Christina Duff, "Discount Retailers Get No Quick Fix from Remodeling Stores, Study Says," *The Wall Street Journal*, (March 27, 1995), p. A15C.

the IRR of the longer-term project. The IRR of a desirable project must exceed the project's required return; the NPV formula uses a lower discount rate, so it values later cash flows more favorably than does the IRR calculation.

Suppose projects Short and Long each require an initial investment of $100. In two years, project Short returns a lump sum of $200. Project Long lasts ten times longer and returns ten times more than Short; that is, Long will return a lump sum of $2,000 in 20 years. A quick calculation will confirm that Short has an IRR of 41.42%; Long has an IRR of 16.16%, but, at a 10% cost of capital, Long's NPV of $197.29 exceeds the $65.29 NPV of Short.

17.8.3 DIFFERENT SIZES

Projects with smaller initial investments may have higher PIs and IRRs, but their small size may appear to make them less attractive from an NPV perspective. For example, consider projects Small and Large:

Project	Initial outlay	PV of cash flows	NPV	PI
Small	$100.00	$150.00	$50	1.5
Large	1,000.00	1,100.00	$100	1.1

The NPV method ranks project Large first because of its larger NPV, but PI ranks project Small first.

Thus, rankings among capital budgeting projects may differ for the three reasons above. The discounted cash flow methods each provide a different perspective on project attractiveness. Since the goal of the decision process is to maximize shareholder wealth, the NPV approach remains preferred among the others.

17.8.4 DIFFERENCE BETWEEN THEORY AND PRACTICE

Thus far, this chapter has presented the basic concepts and techniques of capital budgeting. The capital budgeting process wants to identify projects that will maximize shareholder value. Using the firm's mission and objectives as a guide, managers seek to identify market or product segments in which the firm can build, maintain, or expand a competitive advantage.

We have reviewed five capital budgeting techniques: net present value (NPV), internal rate of return (IRR), modified internal rate of return (MIRR), profitability index (PI), and the payback method. The first four each use discounted cash flows to incorporate the time value of money into the analysis. The final method ignores time value considerations. Financial managers favor the use of discounted cash flow (DCF) techniques.

Theory suggests analysts should evaluate capital budgeting projects using DCF techniques that incorporate all relevant cash flows, base decisions on clear and objective criteria, and indicate projects' impacts on shareholder wealth. The NPV method satisfies these conditions better than other methods. Surveys of practitioners find, however, that while NPV is widely used, there is a surprising continued popularity of nondiscounted cash flow techniques as primary or secondary evaluation methods.

Over time, studies have found that use of DCF techniques have become more prevalent among practitioners. Surveys indicate IRR is the most favored capital budgeting analysis techniques. The payback is especially popular as a secondary or supplementary method of analysis. One survey found that about 75% of chief financial officers (CFOs) use NPV, IRR, or both to evaluate capital budgeting projects. Surprisingly, over half of the firms computed the payback period, too, to evaluate projects.[14] A survey of techniques used by multinational firms confirms these results.[15]

Why might real-world decision makers favor IRR and payback over NPV? One reason could be ignorance. Over time, surveys have shown that the use of DCF techniques has become more prevalent, perhaps because business schools have taught students the virtues of time value of money and NPV.

---

[14] John R. Graham and Campbell R. Harvey, "The Theory and Practice of Corporate Finance: Evidence from the Field," *Journal of Financial Economics*, 2001, vol. 60, no. 1, pp. 187–243.

[15] M. Stanley and S. Block, "A Survey of Multinational Capital Budgeting," *Financial Review*, (March 1984), pp. 36–54.

The apparent sustaining power of IRR and payback techniques, however, suggests the possibility of other reasons. Let's examine several of them.

17.8.4.1 Safety Margin

Suppose an analyst tells you that the NPV of project Big is $100,000 while a competing project, project Small, has an NPV of $60,000. From our earlier discussion, it would appear that you should select Big because of its larger NPV. But what if Big requires a $5 million investment while Small requires only a $600,000 investment? If the PV estimates of project Big's cash flows are off by only 2%, the forecasted positive NPV becomes negative. The PV of Small's cash flows can deviate from plan by 10% before the project turns into a loser.

Suppose, instead, the analyst tells you that Big's IRR is 10.5%, Small's IRR is 15%, and the required return is 10.0%. Would you feel confident that Big is the more attractive project despite its higher NPV? Perhaps not, as a small change in cash flows could push Big's IRR below 10%.

This rather contrived example illustrates why managers in the real world may prefer to use relative DCF measures, such as the IRR or the profitability index. IRR and PI give the decision maker an intuitive feel for a project's "safety margin." The decision maker will sleep better at night after deciding to undertake a smaller project with a larger safety margin and reject a large project with a small safety margin. Most managers have seen reality defy forecasts, and they know that an inadequate safety margin can make taking big investment risks unwise. Post-project audits can give the firm a better perspective on the accuracy or inaccuracy of its cash flow forecasting techniques. This information can help improve management's perspective on the safety cushion needed for a typical project.

17.8.4.2 Managerial Flexibility and Options

The popularity of NPV and DCF techniques also suffers because they are difficult to apply to projects that entail future investment opportunities or options. These techniques do not suit some situations in which managerial flexibility can be valuable. For example, if a project involves a joint venture, an R&D effort, or a move into new markets, management may face several choices once the project is underway. After seeing the initial results, management may decide to continue the project as planned, to expand its scope in the face of success, to decrease the scope of the project, to defer further investment, or to abandon the project. These kinds of decisions can improve a project's potential for upside return while limiting its loss potential. Such flexibility is hard to model in terms of cash flows and discount rates. Payback periods, for example, may be useful as a means to give managers a general feel for how much time a project needs to at least break even and recover its costs.

Conflicts may arise when a firm wants to coordinate strategy analysis and shareholder value analysis. The numbers on the analyst's spreadsheet may fail to justify the actions the corporate planner strongly feels will lead to competitive advantage and future investment opportunities. But strategic analysis and financial analysis, if properly applied, are compatible. More often than not, conflicts between these two sets of tools result from inadequate estimates of the cash flows from implementing a strategy. Unless the cash flows that result from a strategic plan are estimated correctly, good projects can be rejected on the basis of inaccurate NPVs or IRRs. The process of estimating a project's cash flows is the next topic of the section and is examined in more depth in this chapter's Learning Extension.

17.9 ESTIMATING PROJECT CASH FLOWS

This section reviews methods of developing cash flow forecasts based on input from engineering, economic, and market analyses, as well as from examination of the firm's competitive advantages.

17.9.1 ISOLATING PROJECT CASH FLOWS

stand-alone principle analysis focuses on the project's own cash flows, uncontaminated by cash flows from the firm's other activities

To estimate the cash flows of a proposed capital budgeting project, the project must be viewed separately from the rest of the firm. This stand-alone principle ensures that analysts focus on the project's own cash flows, uncontaminated by cash flows from the firm's other activities. We should treat the project as its own mini-firm and create financial statements specific to the project.

17.9.1.1 Relevant Project Cash Flows

A project's relevant cash flows include its incremental after-tax cash flows, any cannibalization or enhancement effects, and opportunity costs.

17.9.1.1.1 Incremental After-Tax Cash Flows. The stand-alone principle requires the analyst to examine the future after-tax cash flows that occur only as a result of the project. These are the project's **incremental cash flows**. The cash flows are incremental as they represent the difference between the firm's after-tax cash flows with the project and its **base case**, or the after-tax cash flows without the project. To calculate this difference, analysts must identify all cash flows that will rise or fall as a consequence of pursuing the future project. This includes any expected changes in revenues, expenses, and depreciation, as well as investments in fixed assets and net working capital.

> **incremental cash flows** represent the difference between the firm's after-tax cash flows with the project and the firm's after-tax cash flows without the project

> **base case** firm's after-tax cash flows without the project

ETHICAL Managerial estimates need to be checked and verified as part of the capital budget review process. Ethical lapses, such as inflating revenues and decreasing expenses to make a project look more attractive, may result in harm to the firm and reductions in shareholder wealth.

Estimating incremental after-tax cash flows for a project requires a more thorough analysis than does determining the expected change in cash flows from the firm's current condition. If future strategic moves by competitors are expected to damage or eliminate a firm's competitive advantage, the firm's base case cash flow forecast should reflect this situation. A project's incremental cash flows would then reflect expected changes from this declining trend.

For example, a firm such as Intel must consider competitors' responses when it invests in R&D to develop new computer chips. Intel's base case must include the impact on its sales if it does not develop the next generation of computer chips first. In the fast-moving technology market, being second to market could mean billions of dollars' worth of lost sales.

Intel has poured billions of dollars into factory improvement and expansion projects in order to increase its production capacity. The goal is to maintain and increase Intel's competitive advantage over other chip manufacturers and to sustain cash flow growth. Greater capacity means greater economies of scale, lower costs, and better competitive position in the computer chip market. With forecasted chip demand experiencing double-digit growth rates each year, Intel needs additional capacity to maintain its current market share of the chip market.

17.9.1.1.2 Cannibalization or Enhancement. **Cannibalization** occurs when a project robs cash flow from the firm's existing lines of business. When a soft drink firm is thinking about introducing a new flavor or a new diet product, the project's incremental cash flows should consider how much the new offering will erode the sales and cash flows of the firm's other products. Corporate strategists reportedly considered how the introduction of Pepsi One, a new low-calorie cola soft drink product, would affect sales of Diet Pepsi and Pepsi-Cola.[16] Similarly, Intel engineers and strategists agonized for months before deciding it needed to design a new computer chip to advance the technology of one of its highly successful computer chips.[17] On the other hand, Microsoft was slow to develop and introduce other products, which may have detracted from the success of its personal computer-based operating system software. Products that didn't see the light day – or not until much later – include a tablet computer, a web-based Office product (in 2001), software for cars that allowed drivers to play digital music and hear email, and Office products that were compatible with Apple's iPhone. The CEO at the time, Steven Ballmer, thought these projects cannibalized Microsoft's main products and would have taken resources away from Office and Windows developments.[18]

> **cannibalization** this occurs when a project robs cash flow from the firm's existing lines of business

Enhancement is less common than cannibalization; it is the increase in the cash flows of the firm's other products that occur because of a new project. For example, adding a delicatessen to a grocery store may increase cash flows more than the deli sales alone if new deli customers also purchase grocery items.

> **enhancement** increase in the cash flows of the firm's other products that occur because of a new project

[16] Nikhil Deogun, "Pepsi Takes Aim at Coke With New One-Calorie Drink," *The Wall Street Journal*, (October 5, 1998), p. B4.

[17] David P. Hamilton, "Circuit Break: Gambling It Can Move Beyond PC, Intel Offers a New Microprocessor," *The Wall Street Journal*, (May 29, 2001), pp. A1, A8.

[18] Shira Ovide, "Next CEO's Job: Fix Microsoft Culture," *The Wall Street Journal*, (August 26, 2013), p. B1, accessed February 8, 2019, at http://www.wsj.com/articles/SB10001424127887324906304579035141246779898.

17.9.1.1.3 Opportunity Costs. From economics, we know that an opportunity cost is the cost of passing up the next best alternative. For example, the opportunity cost of a building is its market value. By deciding to continue to own it, the firm is foregoing the cash it could receive from selling it. Economics teaches the TINSTAAFL principle: "there is no such thing as a free lunch." Capital budgeting analysis frequently applies this principle to existing assets.

If a firm is thinking about placing a new manufacturing plant in a building it owns, the firm cannot assume the building is free and assign it to the project at zero cost. The project's cash flow estimates should include the market value of the building as a cost of investing since this represents cash flows the firm cannot receive from selling the building.

17.9.1.2 Irrelevant Cash Flows

Now that we've examined some factors that influence cash flow estimates and should be included, let's look at some factors that should be excluded from the calculation.

17.9.1.2.1 Sunk Costs. A sunk cost is a project-related expense that does not depend on whether or not the project is undertaken. For example, assume a firm commissioned and paid for a feasibility study for a project last year. The funds for the study have been committed and spent. The study's cost is not an incremental cash flow as it is not affected by the firm's future decision to pursue or abandon the project. Therefore, the cost must be excluded from the project's cash flow estimates.

17.9.1.2.2 Financing Costs. It may seem important to account for financing cash flows such as interest and loan repayments, but a good reason exists for excluding them from cash flow estimates. When cash flows are discounted – as in the NPV, IRR, MIRR, and PI methods – the project's cost of financing is reflected in the choice of the discount rate. As we shall discuss in more detail in Chapter 18, a project's minimum required rate of return, or cost of capital, incorporates a project's financing costs. Including financing costs in the cash flows and discounting them at the project's cost of capital would result in a double counting of the financing costs.

17.9.2 APPROACHES TO ESTIMATING PROJECT CASH FLOWS

As an initial step of the financial analysis of a capital budgeting proposal, we should construct year-by-year projected balance sheets and income statements for the project. Analysis of these forecasted statements tell us what the expected cash flows from the project will be. Changes over time in the project's working capital requirements or investment needs will represent the project's cash inflows or outflows. Similarly, the net income and noncash expenses from the project are part of the project's periodic cash flows.

As was discussed in Chapter 13, one of the financial statements that must be issued by public firms is the statement of cash flows. Here, we use the format of the statement of cash flows to identify the periodic cash flows of a capital budgeting project.

Recall that a firm's statement of cash flows has three sections. The first section, cash flows from operations, reports on cash generated by the firm's day-to-day manufacturing and marketing activities. The second section, cash flows from investments, usually involves data for investments in subsidiaries or the firm's plant and equipment. The third section lists the firm's financing cash flows, including sales and purchases of debt as well as dividend payments.

Using this format for a capital budgeting project, cash flows from operations summarizes the sources of a project's operating cash flows. Cash flows from investing activities report a firm's fixed-asset investments in the capital budgeting project. As explained earlier, cash flows from financing activities are excluded from a project's cash flow analysis since their impact is measured in the discount rate or cost of capital used to discount a project's cash flow.

Table 17.5 summarizes the similarities between company and project cash flow statements. The following sections explore these relationships in more detail.

Table 17.5   Firm versus Project Statement of Cash Flows

Firm versus project Statement of cash flows	
The firm's cash flow statement	**A project's cash flow statement**
Cash Flow from Operations	**Cash Flow from Operations**
Net Income	Net Income
+Depreciation	+Depreciation
+Current sources	+Current sources
−Current uses	−Current uses
Cash Flow from Investment Activities	**Cash Flow from Investment Activities**
−Change in gross fixed assets	−Funds invested in the project's fixed assets
−Change in investments	
Cash Flow from Financing Activities	**Cash Flow from Financing Activities**
−Dividends paid	Not applicable
+Net new bond issues	
+Net new stock issues	

17.9.2.1 Cash Flow from Operations

Cash flow from operations is a measure of the cash entering and leaving the firm as a result of the firm's business. Cash flow from operations equals net income plus depreciation plus funds from sources arising from changes in current asset and liability accounts, minus uses from changes in current asset and liability accounts for a given period of time. A period-by-period project income statement can estimate the net income from a project as in Table 17.6.

All sales revenues may not be cash inflows. For example, if customers buy the firm's products with credit, some of the increase in sales revenue may increase accounts receivable rather than cash. Similarly, not all costs reflect cash outflows. Such is the case if the firm buys supplies or raw materials on credit. Some expenses may be paid in cash and others may create changes in accounts payable. For these reasons, to compute cash flow, we need to include an adjustment, the change in net working capital, to reflect such situations.

Depreciation is a noncash expense. Accounting rules allow us to compute taxable income by deducting depreciation expense from revenues, although no cash leaves the firm. Since it is a noncash expense, when we compute operating cash flows, we add depreciation back after we have computed net income.

Thus, a project's operating cash flows are computed in the following way:

$$\text{Cash flow from operations} = \text{Net income} + \text{Depreciation} - \text{Change in net working capital} \quad (17.4)$$

Net income, as seen in Table 17.6, equals (Sales − Costs − Depreciation − Taxes); if T represents the firm's tax rate, this relationship for net income will become [(Sales − Costs − Depreciation)$(1 − T)$].

Table 17.6   A Project Income Statement

Project sales	(generally a cash inflow)
−Project costs	(generally a cash outflow)
−Depreciation	(a noncash expense)
EBIT = EBT	(earnings before interest and taxes, which also equals earnings before taxes as financing costs are ignored in cash flow analysis)
−Taxes	(a cash outflow)
Net income	

In most cases of capital budgeting analysis, operating cash flow is calculated in part by using the traditional net working capital measure of current assets minus current liabilities. *This occurs since, typically, a project's cash flows are immediately returned to the firm. The project's balance sheet cash account always will be zero.* Thus, current sources and current uses can be summarized in the period-by-period change in a project's net working capital.[19]

Some might wonder, or be confused by, why we subtract the change in net working capital when computing operating cash flow. To illustrate the reasoning for this, suppose current assets are $700 and current liabilities are $400; this means net working capital is $300. Cash comes into the firm if customers pay $200 of their accounts receivable. This reduces accounts receivable and current assets to $500 ($700 – $200 payment) and net working capital to $100 ($500 current assets – $400 current liabilities).[20] Thus, net working capital decreases when there is a source, or inflow, of operating cash to the firm. When we *subtract* this *negative* change in net working capital, it becomes a *positive* addition to operating cash flow:

$$-(-\$200 \text{ change in net working capital}) = +\$200 \text{ change in operating cash flow}$$

Conversely, suppose with $700 in current assets and $400 in current liabilities (and a net working capital of $700 – $400 = $300) we pay $150 in bills we owe to suppliers. As a result, cash flows out of the firm and accounts payable falls by $150, as does current liabilities. The new value of current liabilities is $250 ($400 – $150), and the new value for net working capital is $700 – $250 = $450. Net working capital has risen $150, from $300 to $450. Thus, net working capital increases when there is a use, or outflow, of operating cash from the firm. When we subtract this increase in net working capital it becomes a *reduction* to operating cash flow:

$$-(+\$150 \text{ change in net working capital}) = -\$150 \text{ change in operating cash flow}$$

17.9.2.2 Cash Flow from Investment Activities

Cash flow from investment activities will record the firm's period-by-period fixed-asset investments in the capital project; namely, the plant and equipment necessary to pursue the project. Cash flow from investments is usually negative at the beginning of a project as the firm spends cash to acquire, build, modify, or replace assets. The cash flow from investments may be positive at the end of a project if it sells assets for salvage value.

17.9.2.3 Cash Flow from Financing Activities

Capital budgeting analysis excludes cash flows from financing activities. As discussed earlier, relevant after-tax financing costs are incorporated into the discount rate used to discount estimated cash flows to the present.

17.9.2.4 An Example

Now let's look at an example. Suppose you are considering opening a campus ice cream shop. Your initial investment in depreciating assets will be $10,000, and your initial investment in net working capital (which will include such inventory items as cones, ice cream, and toppings) will be $3,500. You forecast no future changes in net working capital. You will depreciate fixed assets on a straight-line basis over four years.[21]

---

[19] An exception to this rule is overseas projects. For internal financing purposes or because of currency restraints, some cash may remain with the overseas subsidiary. In this case, an overseas project's cash flows should include only the cash that is returned to the parent firm.

[20] As noted in the prior paragraph, a capital budgeting project's balance sheet will typically have a zero cash balance as all cash inflows are claimed by the firm and all cash outflows are paid by the firm.

[21] Current income tax laws specify allowable methods for depreciating business assets. Accelerated depreciation methods are popular but they add unnecessary complexity to the discussion. Straight-line depreciation is a permitted method, so we assume it in most of our discussions.

The shop's forecasted net income is $0, $1,500, $2,500, and $4,000 over each of the next four years. At the end of four years, you expect to graduate with a bachelor's degree and some entrepreneurial work experience, and you will sell your enterprise to another student. You hope you can sell your business for $12,000. For simplicity, ignore any tax implications from the sale. What are the cash flows from this project?

It is sometimes easier to estimate cash flows if you construct a table, or use a spreadsheet, such as the one shown below. It summarizes the project's incremental after-tax cash flows by year and by cash flow category. For example, at the current time (year zero), the only expected cash flows are a $10,000 investment in fixed assets and a $3,500 outflow for net working capital. Depreciating the $10,000 in fixed assets on a straight-line basis over four years gives a yearly depreciation expense of $10,000/4, or $2,500.

Year one net income is expected to be $0; along with the $2,500 depreciation expense and no change in net working capital, year one's operating cash flow is estimated at $2,500. Since you anticipate no investing cash flows, year one's total cash flow is estimated to be $2,500.

The cash flows for years two, three, and four are computed similarly. In year four, the operating cash flows are supplemented by an investing cash flow of $12,000 from the sale of the business. Thus, year four's total cash flows equal $18,500: $4,000 from net income, $2,500 from depreciation, and $12,000 from the sale of the business.

| Year | Operating cash flows | | | | Investing cash flows | | |
	Net income	+	Depreciation	− Change in NWC	Change in fixed assets	=	Total cash flow
0	$0		$0	$−3,500	$−10,000		$−13,500
1	0		2,500	0	0		2,500
2	1,500		2,500	0	0		4,000
3	2,500		2,500	0	0		5,000
4	4,000		2,500	0	12,000		18,500

If 12% is your required rate of return, the NPV of this endeavor is $7,236.90, so your personal wealth should rise from opening the ice cream shop.

17.9.2.5 Depreciation as a Tax Shield

Depreciation plays an important role in determining operating cash flow. As discussed above, it is a noncash expense. By deducting depreciation expenses, a firm lowers its pretax income (earnings before taxes, or EBT), its tax bill, and its net income, and it increases its operating cash flow. A short example will show how this deduction *lowers* net income but *raises* operating cash flow.

Suppose JohnnyJim Products has $1,000 in sales and expenses for wages and supplies of $300. Let's see how a depreciation expense of $100 affects its profitability and its net income. Table 17.7 shows two income statements: one without depreciation expense and another with depreciation expense. To simplify the example, we will assume the change in net working capital is zero and that JohnnyJim's tax rate is 40%.

Table 17.7 JohnnyJim Products Income Statements, With and Without Depreciation Expense

	With depreciation expense	Without depreciation expense
Sales	$1000	$1000
−Costs	−300	−300
−Depreciation	−100	0
EBT	$600	$700
−Taxes (40%)	240	280
Net Income	$360	$420

Using equation 17.4, JohnnyJim's operating cash flow with depreciation is the following:

Cash flow from operations = Net income + Depreciation − Change in net working capital

$$= \$360 \qquad + \$100 \qquad - \$0 = \$460$$

Its operating cash flow without depreciation is the following:

Cash flow from operations = Net income + Depreciation − Change in net working capital

$$= \$420 \qquad + \$0 \qquad - \$0 = \$420$$

Although depreciation lowers its net income, JohnnyJim's operating cash flow is $40 higher with depreciation expense than without depreciation expense. The reason the operating cash flow with depreciation is $40 higher is because JohnnyJim's tax bill is $40 lower. By lowering earnings before taxes, noncash depreciation expense lowers a cash expense; that is, taxes, are lower by $40. This $40 reduction leads to an operating cash flow that is $40 higher than the example using no depreciation.

The $40 savings in taxes arises from a combination of the tax rate, T, and the depreciation expense. With a 40% tax rate, a depreciation expense of $100 increases expenses and lowers taxes by $(0.40)(\$100)$, or $40.

This term, (T)(Depreciation), the tax rate multiplied by the depreciation expense, is called the **depreciation tax shield**. It represents the tax savings the firm receives from its noncash depreciation expense. With a 40% tax rate, a depreciation expense of $100 reduces a firm's tax bill by $40.

Despite political claims that tax incentives are needed to boost capital spending and investment, a healthy economy can do more for capital investment than the most generous politicians. The United States enjoyed a capital spending boom in the 1990s despite doing without favorable tax law changes, investment tax credits, or changes in depreciation rules. A good economy with sustained growth and low inflation is the best combination for corporate investment. As one corporate executive said, "We're not sitting on our hands waiting for government tax policy to change. If you want to protect and extend your market position, you invest the money. We would do that no matter what."

Economists do favor incentives, such as a capital gains tax cut, that would increase savings in the economy. Greater savings, all else being constant, would mean lower interest rates, higher stock prices, and lower financing costs for firms buying plant and equipment.[22]

> **depreciation tax shield** tax reduction due to depreciation of fixed assets; equals the amount of the depreciation expense multiplied by the firm's tax rate, shown as (T) (Depreciation)

17.10 KEEPING MANAGERS HONEST

ETHICAL We now discuss the fifth stage of the capital budgeting process – the follow-up, sometimes called the audit or control phase. In this stage, a firm's financial analysts track the spending and results of the firm's current capital budgeting projects.

Many firms review spending during the implementation stage of approved projects. Quarterly reports are often required in which the manager overseeing the project summarizes spending to date, compares it to budgeted amounts, and explains differences between the two. Such oversight during the implementation stage allows top managers to foresee cost overruns. Some firms require projects that are expected to exceed their budgets by a certain dollar amount or percentage to file new appropriation requests to secure the additional funds. Implementation audits allow managers to learn about potential trouble areas so future proposals can account for them in their initial analysis; implementation audits also give top management information on which managers generally provide the best estimates of project costs.

Besides implementation control, firms should compare forecasted cash flows to performance after the project has been completed. This provides data regarding the accuracy over time of cash flow forecasts, thus, permitting the firm to discover what went right with the project, what went wrong, and why. Audits force management to discover and justify any major deviations of actual performance from forecasted performance. Specific reasons for deviations from a budget are needed for the experience to be helpful to all involved.

---

[22] Joseph Spiers, "The Most Important Economic Event of the Decade," *Fortune*, (April 3, 1995), pp. 33–40.

An effective control system will record the names of the persons who make the estimates so top management can evaluate business units and managers on the accuracy of their estimates. Such a system pinpoints personal responsibility. If, for example, a department head estimates a proposed expenditure would allow the department to reduce personnel by 10%, the department head can be questioned if the proposed cuts do not come to pass. Such a system will control intra-firm agency problems by reducing "padding"; that is, overestimating the benefits of favorite or convenient project proposals. This increases the incentives for department heads to manage in ways that help the firm achieve its goals. Despite this, some research indicates psychological factors that led to biases which overestimate cash flows and underestimate completion times – even in the face of past experience. Better and more complete data, from different sources, is needed to get more objective and fair estimates.[23]

The control or post-audit phase sometimes requires the firm to consider terminating or abandoning an approved project. The possibility of abandoning an investment prior to the end of its estimated useful or economic life expands the options available to management and reduces the risk associated with a poor decision. This form of contingency planning gives decision makers a second chance when dealing with the economic and political uncertainties of the future.

In a survey, researchers found that three-fourths of responding Fortune 500 firms audited their cash flow estimates.[24] Nearly all of the firms that performed audits compared initial investment outlay estimates with actual costs. All evaluated operating cash flow estimates, and two-thirds audited salvage value estimates.

About two-thirds of firms that performed audits claimed that initial investment outlay estimates usually were within 10% of forecasts. Only 43% of firms that performed audits could make the same claim with respect to operating cash flows. Over 30% of the firms confessed that operating cash flow estimates differed from performance by 16% or more.[25]

To be successful, the cash flow estimation process requires a commitment by the corporation and its top policy-setting managers; this commitment includes a management information system the firm uses to support the estimation process. Past experience in estimating cash flows, requiring cash flow estimates for all projects, and maintaining systematic approaches to cash flow estimation appear to help firms achieve success in forecasting cash flows.

In volatile economic environments, such as the first decade of the 21st century, business professional know that historical averages and point estimates are likely to be incorrect. The business environment is complex and is affected, as we saw in 2007–2009, by factors beyond a manager's control.

Chapter 12 introduced the concept of scenario analysis as a means of gauging outcomes in an uncertain future. More professionals at all levels of business have realized the value of playing "what if" scenarios and creating plans for what should be done if certain economic and business events occur.[26]

DISCUSSION QUESTION 3

What are your ideas for how to keep managers "honest" when they estimate cash flows and the risk associated with a capital budgeting project they favor?

17.11 RISK-RELATED CONSIDERATIONS

The degree of risk associated with expected cash inflows may vary among different investments. For example, a decision about whether to replace an existing machine with a new, more efficient machine would not involve substantial cash inflow uncertainty, because the firm has some operating experience with the existing machine. Likewise, expansion in existing product lines allows the firm to base cash flow expectations on past operating results and marketing data. These capital budgeting decisions can

---

[23] Bent Flyvbjerg, Massimo Garbuio, and Dan Lovallo, "Better Forecasting for Large Capital Projects," McKinsey & Company, (December 2014), accessed February 8, 2019, at http://www.mckinsey.com/business-functions/strategy-and-corporate-finance/our-insights/better-forecasting-for-large-capital-projects.

[24] R. Pohlman, E. Santiago, and F. Markel, "Cash Flow Estimation Practices at Large Firms," *Financial Management*, Summer 1988, pp. 71–78.

[25] In the last chapter, we argued that safety margin concerns may lead managers to prefer selection methods such as IRR and PI over NPV. With error rates such as these, you can see why safety margins would concern analysts and decision makers.

[26] Vincent Ryan, "Future Tense," *CFO*, (December 2008), p. 37–42.

be made by discounting cash flows at the firm's cost of capital, or required rate of return, because they are comparable in risk to the firm's other assets.

Expansion projects involving new areas, new product lines, and overseas expansion are usually associated with greater cash inflow uncertainty. To compensate for this greater risk, financial managers often use concepts based upon the trade-off between risk and expected return. A higher-risk project needs to be evaluated using a higher required rate of return. To use a financial markets analogy, given the current return offered on safe short-term Treasury bills, investors will not want to invest in risky common stocks unless the expected returns are commensurate with the higher risk of stocks. Similarly, managers should not choose higher-risk capital budgeting projects unless the projects' expected returns are in line with their risks.

The **risk-adjusted discount rate (RADR)** approach does this, adjusting the required rate of return at which the analyst discounts a project's cash flows. Projects with higher (or lower) risk levels demand higher (or lower) discount rates. A project is expected to enhance shareholder wealth only if its NPV based on a risk-adjusted discount rate is positive.

One way to determine project RADRs is for the firm's managers to use past experience to create risk classes, or categories, for different types of capital budgeting projects. Each risk category can be given a generic description to indicate the project types it should include, and a required rate of return or "hurdle rate" to assign those projects.[27]

An example is shown in Table 17.8, which assigns projects of average risk (or those whose risk is about the same as the firm's overall risk) a discount rate equal to the firm's cost of capital. That is, projects of average risk must earn an average return, as defined by the firm's cost of financing. Projects with below-average risk levels are discounted at a rate below the cost of capital. Projects of above-average risk must earn premiums over the firm's cost of capital to be acceptable. Subjectivity enters this process as management must decide the number of categories, the description of each risk category, and the required rate of return to assign to each category. Differences of opinion or internal firm politics may lead to controversy in classifying a project. Clearly defined category descriptions can minimize such problems.

> **risk-adjusted discount rate (RADR)** adjusts the required rate of return at which the analyst discounts a project's cash flows based on the project's risk

Table 17.8 Risk Categories, RMEN Corporation

Below-average risk:

Replacement decisions that require no change, or only a minor change, in technology; no change in plant layout required

Discount rate = Cost of capital – 2%

Average risk:

Replacement decisions involving significant changes in technology or plant layout; all cost-saving decisions; expansions and improvements in the firm's main product lines

Discount rate = Cost of capital

Above-average risk:

Applied research and development; introduction of new products not related to major product lines; expansion of production or marketing efforts into developed economies in Europe and Asia

Discount rate = Cost of capital + 2%

High risk:

Expansion of production or marketing efforts into less-developed and emerging economies; introduction of products not related to any of the firm's current product lines

Discount rate = Cost of capital + 5%

---

[27] Another, more complicated, technique is to use the capital asset pricing model (CAPM). A beta is calculated for each project based on analysis of firms in lines of business similar to that of the proposed project. The security market line (SML) is used with the beta estimate to approximate the project's required return.

For example, let's use the previously presented data for projects A and B to illustrate the use of risk-adjusted discount rates. Let's assume that projects A and B are independent projects. Project A involves expansion in an existing product line, whereas project B is for a new product. The firm's cost of capital, 10%, would be the appropriate discount rate for project A. Recall that this would result in a net present value of $1,982.

In contrast, a higher discount rate, say 12%, for project B (that is, is the 10% cost of capital plus a 2 percentage point risk premium), might be judged appropriate by the financial manager. This would result in an NPV of –$514. Thus, on a risk-adjusted basis, project A would still be acceptable to the firm, but project B would be rejected. Making adjustments for risk differences is a difficult but necessary task if the financial manager is to make capital budgeting decisions that will increase the firm's value.

DISCUSSION QUESTION 4

At times, the field of finance is criticized for being short-term oriented – managers are accused of making decisions based upon the near-time impact on stock price rather than the long-term good of the company. Some argue that financial techniques lead to nonsustainable and environmentally unfriendly decisions by a firm's chief officers. Based upon what you've learned thus far in this and other chapters, are these criticisms fair and appropriate? If they are, what tools should managers use to make decisions?

APPLYING FINANCE TO. . .

- **Institutions and Markets** Financial institutions and markets play an indirect role in the capital budgeting process. The participants in the markets use the flow of information from the firm and its competitors, as well as economic and industry conditions, to evaluate firms. Their analysis and reactions are seen in the firm's stock price changes and bond rating changes. In turn, market return expectations are used to determine the discount rate in the NPV calculation. This process will be covered in Chapter 18.

- **Investments** Investors, security analysts, and portfolio managers are continually evaluating a firm's performance. Investment in projects likely to return a positive NPV is a sign of forward-thinking managers who have shareholder interests at heart. Stock price and bond ratings respond favorably to a firm's wealth-maximizing capital budgeting and resource allocation decisions.

- **Financial Management** A way to operationalize shareholder wealth maximization is to identify and select projects expected to have positive net present values. Managers must use capital budgeting evaluation techniques, adjust project evaluation for risk, and seek to invest in projects that enhance shareholder value.

SUMMARY

LO 17.1 A firm's long-term success depends on its strategy and its competitors' actions. The capital budget allocates funds to different projects, usually long-term, that are primarily used to purchase fixed assets to help a firm build or maintain a competitive advantage. Potential projects can arise from a review of the firm's mission, objectives, goals, and strategies (MOGS) or a SWOT (strengths, weaknesses, opportunities, threats) analysis by management. Attractive capital budgeting projects usually arise from one or more of the following sources of a firm's competitive advantage: economies of scale, product differentiation, absolute cost advantages, differences in access to distribution channels, or government policy that favors one group of firms over another (or over new entrants).

LO 17.2 The capital budgeting process is composed of five stages: identification, development, selection, implementation, and follow-up.

LO 17.3 Since the capital budgeting process involves the analysis of cash flows over time, it is best to examine projects using a selection technique that considers the time value of money. The net present value, internal rate of return, modified internal rate of return, and profitability index are four such methods. A fifth method, the payback period, measures how quickly a project will pay for itself but ignores time value concerns. Of these selection methods, the net present value is the best since it measures the dollar amount by which a project will change shareholder wealth. It is equal to the present value of a project's cash flows minus its initial outlay or cost.

LO 17.4 The internal rate of return is the discount rate such that the present value of the cash flows equals the initial cost of a capital budgeting project. A project is acceptable if its IRR exceeds the firm's cost of capital. The IRR measures the return earned on the funds that remained invested in a project over time. A drawback of the IRR measure is there may be more than one IRR if the project's cash flows alternate between positive and negative over the project's life.

LO 17.5 The modified internal rate of return (MIRR) tries to address the "multiple answer" issue of the IRR. There is only one MIRR for a given set of cash flow estimates. It is computed by first finding the present value of all cash outflows of a project, using the cost of capital as the discount rate. Second, compute the terminal value – the sum of the future values – of a project's cash flows, compounding the cash flows at the firm's cost of capital. Third, find the discount rate that equates the present value of the outflows and the terminal value. This discount rate is the MIRR. The project is acceptable if the MIRR exceeds the firm's cost of capital.

LO 17.6 The profitability index is the present value of a project's cash flows divided by the project's initial cost. The present value is computed using the firm's cost of capital. It shows the dollars of benefit from doing a project compared to each dollar of cost. If the PI is greater than one, the project is acceptable as it will add to shareholder wealth.

LO 17.7 The payback period is the time it takes for a project to pay for itself – that is, for the cash inflows to equal the cost of the project. Shorter paybacks are preferred to longer paybacks. The main drawbacks to using the payback method are, first, that it ignores the time value of money and, second, all cash flows after the payback period are ignored. The only thing that matters is the length of time it takes for the cumulative cash flows to equal the project's cost.

LO 17.8 All discounted cash flow methods of evaluating capital budgeting projects – NPV, IRR, MIRR, and PI – will agree on the decision to accept or reject a project. But when mutually exclusive projects are under consideration, these methods may rank projects differently. We learned that some causes of differences in ranking include different cash flow patterns, different time horizons, and different sizes of the projects. Although, in theory, NPV is the best way to evaluate projects – it is estimates the dollar impact on shareholder wealth – managers may prefer measures that give then an intuitive feel for a project's safety margin, knowing that cash flow estimates may be incorrect.

LO 17.9 Estimating cash flows is a difficult part of evaluating capital budgeting projects. Projected earnings must be converted into cash flows by using the methods discussed in this chapter. Depreciation expense acts as a tax shield because it reduces a project's tax bill and works to increase a project's after-tax cash flows. By focusing solely on numbers, financial analysts of capital budgeting projects can lose sight of the strategic importance behind the analysis. On the other hand, strategists need to be aware of the need for shareholder value-enhancing projects. Analysts must be sure the financial analysis includes the correct base case, cannibalization and competitor retaliation effects, and proper risk adjustments.

LO 17.10 The fifth step of the capital budgeting process is the follow-up, or audit stage. Here, management estimates of cash flows are compared to the project's actual cash flows. The firm should have processes in place to track projected and actual cash flows, determine causes of variations between them, and learn from their forecasting errors in an effort to improve the capital budgeting process. Managers should be held responsible if their estimates prove to be consistently inflated, project after project. A project whose cash flows are well under budget should be considered for termination – better to stop future underperformance than allow it to continue to drain the firm's resources.

LO 17.11 As with financial market investments, corporate investments should include risk/expected return considerations. Higher-risk projects should be evaluated using higher discount rates. One means of doing so is to use risk-adjusted discount rates where products in different risk categories are assigned a discount rate based upon the firm's cost of capital and the risk of the project.

The next chapter will examine how firms can estimate their cost of capital. This is important, as the cost of financing the firm will be used as the discount rate for evaluating average risk capital budgeting projects.

KEY TERMS

base case	identification stage	modified internal rate of	risk-adjusted discount
benefit/cost ratio	implementation stage	return (MIRR)	rate (RADR)
cannibalization	incremental cash flows	mutually exclusive	selection stage
capital budgeting	independent projects	projects	stand-alone
cost of capital	internal rate of return	net present value (NPV)	principle
depreciation tax shield	(IRR) method	NPV profile	SWOT analysis
development stage	mission, objectives,	opportunity cost	sunk cost
enhancement	goals, and strat-	payback period method	
follow-up stage	egies (MOGS)	profitability index (PI)	

REVIEW QUESTIONS

1. **(LO 17.1)** What is capital budgeting? Briefly describe some characteristics of capital budgeting.

2. **(LO 17.1)** Why is proper management of fixed assets crucial to the success of a firm?

3. **(LO 17.1)** How do mutually exclusive projects and independent projects differ?

4. **(LO 17.1)** Where do businesses find attractive capital budgeting projects?

5. **(LO 17.2)** Briefly describe the five stages in the capital budgeting process.

6. **(LO 17.2)** Identify some capital budgeting considerations unique to multinational corporations.

7. **(LO 17.2)** What kinds of financial data are needed to conduct project analysis?

8. **(LO 17.2)** What kinds of nonfinancial information are needed to conduct project analysis?

9. **(LO 17.3)** What is meant by a project's net present value? How is it used for choosing among projects?

10. **(LO 17.4)** Identify the internal rate of return method and describe how it is used in making capital budgeting decisions.

11. **(LO 17.5)** How does the modified internal rate of return measure improve upon the IRR measure?

12. **(LO 17.6)** Describe the term "profitability index (PI)," and explain how it is used to compare projects.

13. **(LO 17.7)** Describe the payback period method for making capital budgeting decisions.

14. **(LO 17.8)** Why do the NPV, IRR, and PI technique sometimes rank projects differently?

15. **(LO 17.8)** Why might managers want to use other techniques besides NPV to make capital budgeting decisions?

16. **(LO 17.9)** How is the stand-alone principle applied when evaluating whether to invest in projects?

17. **(LO 17.9)** What are the three types of relevant cash flows to be considered in analyzing a project?

18. **(LO 17.9)** Label each of the following as a cannibalization effect, enhancement effect, or neither. Explain your answers.
   a. A computer manufacturer seeks to produce a high-quality engineering work station, thinking that consumers will believe the firm's standard PC products will also be of higher quality.
   b. An airline offers taxicab service to and from the airport.
   c. A gas station adds service bays and a small convenience store.
   d. A mainframe computer manufacturer sells personal computers.
   e. A snack food manufacturer starts marketing a new line of fat-free snacks.
   f. A firm seeks to export its products to foreign countries.

19. **(LO 17.9)** What types of cash flows are considered irrelevant when analyzing a project?

20. **(LO 17.9)** "Our firm owns property around Chicago that would be an ideal location for the new warehouse, and since we own the land, there isn't any cash flow needed to purchase it." Do you agree or disagree with this statement? Explain.

21. **(LO 17.9)** "Our bank will finance the product expansion project with at a loan interest rate of 10%. Make sure the project's cash flow estimates include this interest expense." Do you agree or disagree? Explain.

22. **(LO 17.9)** Classify each of the following as a sunk cost, an opportunity cost, or neither.
   a. The firm has spent $1 million to develop the next-generation robotic arm; it is examining whether the project should continue.
   b. A piece of ground owned by the firm can be used as the site for a new facility.
   c. Another $200,000 of R&D spending will probably be needed to work out the bugs of a new software package.

23. **(LO 17.9)** How is a project's cash flow statement similar to that of a firm? How is it different?

24. **(LO 17.9)** Why is the change in net working capital included in operating cash flow estimates?

25. **(LO 17.9)** Why is depreciation considered a tax shield?

26. **(LO 17.10)** What is a way to keep managers accountable for their capital budgeting forecasts and estimates?

27. **(LO 17.11)** What is a risk-adjusted discount rate (RADR)? How are RADRs determined for individual projects?

PROBLEMS

1. Find the net present value (NPV) and profitability index (PI) of a project that costs $1,500 and returns $800 in year one and $850 in year two. Assume the project's cost of capital is 8%.

2. Find the NPV and PI of an annuity that pays $500 per year for eight years and costs $2,500. Assume a discount rate of 6%.

3. Find a project's IRR that returns $17,000 three years from now if it costs $12,000.

4. Find a project's IRR and MIRR if it has estimated cash flows of $5,500 annually for seven years, if its year-zero investment is $25,000, and the firm's minimum required rate of return on the project is 10%.

5. For the following projects, compute NPV, IRR, MIRR, PI, and payback. If these projects are mutually exclusive, which one(s) should be done? If they are independent, which one(s) should be undertaken?

	A	B	C	D
Year 0	−1,000	−1,500	−500	−2,000
Year 1	400	500	100	600
Year 2	400	500	300	800
Year 3	400	700	250	200
Year 4	400	200	200	300
Discount rate	10%	12%	15%	8%

6. The Sanders Electric Company is evaluating two projects for possible inclusion in the firm's capital budget. Project M will require a $37,000 investment while project O's investment will be $46,000. After-tax cash inflows are estimated as follows for the two projects:

Year	Project M	Project O
1	$12,000	$10,000
2	12,000	10,000
3	12,000	15,000
4	12,000	15,000
5		15,000

a. Determine the payback period for each project.
b. Calculate the NPV and PI for each project based on a 10% cost of capital. Which, if either, of the projects is acceptable?
c. Determine the IRR and MIRR for projects M and O.

7. AA Auto Parts Company has a corporate tax rate of 34% and depreciation of $19,180. Compute its depreciation tax shield.

8. A project is estimated to generate sales revenue of $10 million with expenses of $9 million. No change in net working capital is expected. Marginal profits will be taxed at a 35% rate. If the project's operating cash flow is $1 million, what is the project's depreciation expense? Its net income?

9. Compute operating cash flows for the following:
a. A project that is expected to have sales of $10,000, expenses of $5,000, depreciation of $200, an investment of $50 in net working capital, and a 20% tax rate.
b. A project has the simplified project income statement below. In addition, assume the project will require a $75 investment in net working capital.

Sales	$925.00
−Costs	−315.00
−Depreciation	−100.00
EBIT = EBT	510.00
−Taxes (at 34%)	−173.40
Net Income	336.60

c. For a capital budgeting proposal, assume this year's cash sales are forecast to be $220, cash expenses $130, and depreciation $80. Assume the firm is in the 30% tax bracket.

10. A machine can be purchased for $10,500, including transportation charges, but installation costs will require $1,500 more. The machine is expected to last four years and produce annual cash revenues of $6,000. Annual cash operating expenses are expected to be $2,000, with depreciation of $3,000 per year. The firm has a 30% tax rate. Determine the relevant after-tax cash flows and prepare a cash flow schedule.

11. Use the information in Problem 17.10 to do the following:
    a. Calculate the payback period for the machine.
    b. If the project's cost of capital is 10%, would you recommend buying the machine?
    c. Estimate the IRR for the machine.

12. The Brassy Fin Pet Shop is considering an expansion. Construction will cost $90,000 and will be depreciated to zero, using straight-line depreciation, over five years. Earnings before depreciation are expected to be $20,000 in each of the next five years. The firm's tax rate is 34%.
    a. What are the project's cash flows?
    b. Should the project be undertaken if the firm's cost of capital is 11%?

13. The following is a simplified project annual income statement for Ma & Pa Incorporated for each year of an eight-year project. Its up-front cost is $2,000. Its cost of capital is 12%.

Sales	$925.00
less cash expenses	310.00
less depreciation	250.00
Earnings before taxes	$365.00
Less taxes (at 35%)	127.75
Net income	$237.25

    a. Compute the project's after-tax cash flow.
    b. Compute and interpret the project's NPV, IRR, profitability index, and payback period.

14. **Challenge Problem** Annual savings from project X include a reduction of ten clerical employees with annual salaries of $15,000 each, $8,000 from reduced production delays, $12,000 from lost sales due to inventory stock-outs, and $3,000 in reduced utility costs. Project X costs $250,000 and will be depreciated over a five-year period using straight-line depreciation. Incremental expenses of the system include two new operators with annual salaries of $40,000 each and operating expenses of $12,000 per year. The firm's tax rate is 34%.
    a. Find project X's initial cash outlay.
    b. Find the project's operating cash flows over the five-year period.
    c. If the project's required return is 12%, should it be implemented?

15. **Challenge Problem** You are considering becoming a franchisee with the Kopy-Kopy Copy and Pizza Delivery Service. For $50,000, they give you training and exclusive territorial rights.

    Equipment can be purchased through the home office for an additional $50,000, all of which will be straight-line depreciated. The home office

estimates your territory can generate $100,000 in sales volume in the first year and sales will grow 10% in each of the following four years, at which time you plan on selling the business for $50,000, after taxes. From reading their brochures and talking to several other franchisees, you believe costs, excluding depreciation, are about 60% of sales. You also know the home office requires you to pay a 15% royalty on your gross sales revenue.

    Using a 30% tax rate and a 10% return requirement, how will this opportunity affect your personal wealth?

16. **Challenge Problem** The ice cream shop described in the text has been a smash success. Customers from the next college town are pleading with you to open one closer to them. Based on your operating experience and knowledge of local real estate, you believe opening a new ice cream shop will require an investment of $20,000 in fixed assets and $3,000 in working capital. Fixed assets will be straight-line depreciated over five years. Preliminary market research indicates sales revenue in the first year should be about $50,000 and variable costs, excluding depreciation, will be about 80% of sales. To be on the safe side, you assume sales revenue will not change over the next five years. At the end of five years, you estimate you can sell your business, after taxes, for $25,000. Using a 28% tax rate and a 12% required return, should you expand?

17. **Challenge Problem** Sensitivity analysis involves changing one variable at a time in a capital budgeting situation and seeing how NPV changes. Perform sensitivity analysis on the each of the following variables in Problem 17.16 to determine its effect on NPV.
    a. Sales can be 10% higher or lower than expected each year.
    b. Expenses may be 10% higher or lower than expected each year.
    c. Your initial investment in fixed assets and working capital may be 50% higher than originally estimated.

18. Project R requires an investment of $45,000 and is expected to produce after-tax cash inflows of $15,000 per year for five years. The cost of capital is 10%.
    a. Determine the payback period, the NPV, and the PI for project R. Is the project acceptable?
    b. Assume the risk-adjusted discount rate is 14%. Calculate the risk-adjusted net present value. Is the project acceptable after adjusting for its greater risk?
    c. Calculate the internal rate of return.

19. Assume the financial manager of the Sanders Electric Company in Problem 17.6 believes that project M is comparable in risk to the firm's other assets. In contrast, project O's after-tax cash inflows has greater uncertainty. Sanders Electric uses a 4 percentage point risk premium for riskier projects. The firm's cost of capital is 10%.
    a. Determine the risk-adjusted NPVs for project M and project O, using RADRs where appropriate.
    b. Are both projects acceptable investments? Which one would you choose?

20. The BioTek Corporation has a basic cost of capital of 15% and is considering investing in one or both of the following projects. Project HiTek will require an investment of $453,000, while project LoTek's investment will be $276,000. The following after-tax cash flows (including the investment outflows in year zero) are estimated for each project.

Year	Project Hitek	Project Lotek
0	$–453,000	$–276,000
1	132,000	74,000
2	169,500	83,400
3	193,000	121,000

Year	Project Hitek	Project Lotek
4	150,700	54,900
5	102,000	101,000
6	0	29,500
7	0	18,000

a. Determine the PV of the cash inflows for each project and then calculate their NPVs by subtracting the appropriate dollar amount of capital investment. Which, if either, of the projects is acceptable?
b. Calculate the IRRs for project HiTek and project LoTek. Which project would be preferred?
c. Assume that BioTek uses RADRs to adjust for differences in risk among different investment opportunities. BioTek projects are discounted at the firm's cost of capital of 15%. A risk premium of three percentage points is assigned to LoTek-type projects, while a 6 percentage point risk premium is used for projects similar to HiTek. Determine the risk-adjusted PV of the cash inflows for LoTek and HiTek and calculate their risk-adjusted net present values. Should BioTek invest in either, both, or neither project?

Learning Extension 17

Estimating Project Cash Flows

LO 17.12 (Learning Extension) Apply cash flow estimation and capital budgeting methods to different types of projects.

LO 17.13 (Learning Extension) Apply cash flow estimation and NPV analysis to a revenue expanding project, a cost-saving project, and to a need to determine a minimum bid price.

How are cash flow estimates developed? In this section, we give you a practical overview of how an analyst develops the data to estimate cash flows.

As we noted in Chapter 13's Learning Extension, The 2017 Tax Cuts and Jobs Act (TCJA) modified some depreciation rules to allow for immediate expensing – that is, 100% first-year depreciation expense – in some circumstances and dollar limits. However, the law "sunsets" these provisions in five years (2022); it will be up to a future Congress and President to allow the TCJA provisions to continue, revert to pre-TCJA rules, or be modified again.

Thus, rather than get lost in the trees of tax and depreciation details, we focus on the "big picture" aspects of depreciation – those which remain in place, even after TJCA, and which will likely persist in some form in the future.

A typical project encompasses three stages. First is the initial outlay or investment. Second is the operating life of the project, be it market expansion, a building, or technology. The final stage is at the end of the project's useful life. For projects involving fixed assets or business lines, this can involve selling assets and reclaiming working capital. But for projects that have an indefinite life, such as business expansion, a few years of careful cash flow estimations may give way in the third stage to an estimate of terminal value – that is, what the present value of project cash flows might be far into the future. We'll examine each of the three stages below.

> **17.12 PROJECT STAGES AND CASH FLOW ESTIMATION**

INITIAL OUTLAY

The first cash flow estimate is the initial investment in the project. Engineering estimates may be available for projects that require designing or modifying equipment and buildings. Engineers will examine preliminary designs or architectural sketches and estimate the quantities of materials needed. Estimates of purchases, transportation costs, and construction expenses can be developed based on current market prices.

Another way to estimate a project's acquisition or construction cost is to solicit bids from construction or equipment manufacturers based upon preliminary design specifications. An approximate cost can be determined through discussions with bidding firms. If the firm is large enough that it has an in-house engineering or real estate acquisition staff, this expertise can be tapped to estimate relevant costs.

The expense of developing cost estimates is a sunk cost. That money is spent and gone whether or not the proposed project is accepted; it should be excluded from the project's cash flow estimates. However, the initial outlay estimate must consider opportunity costs if the project will use property or equipment presently owned by the firm.

The investment cost estimate may have to be adjusted if the project involves replacing an asset with another, presumably newer and more cost-efficient model. If the old asset is going to be sold, the investment outlay must be reduced by the after-tax proceeds from the sale of the old asset. We will shortly discuss some of the specifics of adjusting for salvage value.

Finally, even though a project's initial outlay may involve property and equipment (investing cash flows), it may have implications for net working capital (operating cash flows). For example, if a project affects the firm's production process, inventory levels may change. New raw materials needs may affect accounts payable. These kinds of expected changes in net working capital must be included as part of the initial outlay.

CASH FLOWS DURING THE PROJECT'S OPERATING LIFE

Operating cash flows can be estimated using equation 17.4. The difficulty is determining the amounts for sales, costs, depreciation, taxes, and net working capital changes in order to enter these into the calculations.

A project with the main purpose of reducing costs should have a presumed impact on sales of zero. Expected cost savings can be derived from engineering estimates or production management techniques. Suppliers can often estimate the potential cost savings from new machines or processes, but these sales claims may be untrustworthy; the careful manager runs independent tests and trial runs, preferably at the plant that will house the new project, to verify any claims.

One asset often replaces another in cost-saving projects. This can involve a difference in depreciation schedules between the old and new asset (not to mention salvage value differences), which the analyst must incorporate into the analysis. More will be said about this point later in the chapter when we review an example.

Revenue enhancing or revenue sustaining projects build or protect a firm's competitive advantage or extend its market penetration. Market researchers can provide detailed data about new products or features and the costs to develop them in order to help the financial analyst construct cash flow estimates. Such research may include sales forecasts or information on price, quantity, and quality trends in the market segment. If the project concerns one of the firm's current products, the production staff can often provide data to estimate the cost implications of greater sales. If the project involves a new product offering, engineers or the production staff should be able to provide production cost estimates. Depreciation expense can be estimated from the estimated initial investment outlay for the property or equipment needed for the project.

Net working capital may change over the course of the project's life. Operating cash flow estimates must reflect these changes in net working capital.

SALVAGE VALUE AND NWC RECOVERY AT PROJECT TERMINATION

If the project is expected to have a definite life span, the analysis must consider the salvage value of the project's assets. Any increases in net working capital in the course of a project are generally assumed to be recovered by the firm and converted to cash at the project's end.

Any property or equipment that is expected to be sold, either for use by someone else or for scrap, will generate inflows. The cash flow for the sale will have to be adjusted to account for tax implications if the asset's selling price differs from its book value. Book value (BV) represents an asset's original cost less accumulated depreciation. At the end of a project, if the selling price of an asset equals its book value there is no need for tax adjustments; the after-tax cash flow equals the selling price. If the asset's selling price exceeds its book value, then the asset was depreciated too quickly on the firm's books. The amount of the recovered depreciation (Price − BV) is taxed at the firm's marginal tax rate for ordinary income. Thus, the tax owed the government is T(Price − BV). The total after-tax proceeds will be Price − T(Price − BV); that is, the selling price less the tax obligation. If the selling price is less than the asset's book value, the firm suffers a loss. This loss reflects failure to depreciate the asset's book value quickly enough. The firm's taxable income is reduced by the amount of the loss, and taxes will be reduced by T(Price − BV).

If T(Price − BV) is positive, the firm owes taxes, reducing the after-tax proceeds of the asset sale; if T(Price − BV) is negative, the firm reduces its tax bill, increasing the after-tax sale proceeds. When T(Price − BV) is zero, the transaction causes is no tax adjustment to be made. Thus, a general relationship for the after-tax salvage value is the following:

$$\text{After-tax salvage value} = \text{Price} - T\left(\text{Price} - \text{BV}\right) \tag{LE17.1}$$

Let's look at an example. Assume an asset originally cost $100, had an expected life of ten years, and was depreciated on a straight-line basis. Seven years later, the firm must determine the after-tax cash flow from selling the asset if the selling price is (a) $50, (b) $30, or (c) $15. Assume the marginal tax rate for ordinary income is 34%.

First, we must determine the asset's book value, and then equation LE17.1 can be used to compute cash flows for three situations. With an original cost of $100 and straight-line depreciation over ten years, its yearly depreciation expense is $100/10 = $10. As seven years have passed, accumulated depreciation is now $70 (7 × $10/year), so the asset's book value is $100 minus $70, or $30.

If the asset's sale price is $50, the firm has recovered some past depreciation and it must reduce the salvage value cash flow by the resulting tax liability. The after-tax salvage value is the following:

$$\text{Price} - T(\text{Price} - \text{BV}) = \$50 - 0.34(\$50 - \$30) = \$43.20$$

If the asset's sale price is $30, this price equals the book value. According to equation LE17.1, the after-tax salvage value is $30: Price − T(Price − BV) = $30 − 0.34($30 − $30) = $30.

If the asset's sale price is $15, the firm suffers a loss, as the price is below book value. This means the salvage value cash flow will rise above $15 by the amount of the subsequent tax savings. The after-tax cash flow equals the following:

$$\text{Price} - T(\text{Price} - \text{BV}) = \$15 - 0.34(\$15 - \$30) = \$20.10.$$

By their nature, after-tax salvage values are difficult to estimate since the salvage value and expected future tax rate are uncertain. As a practical matter, if the project termination is many years in the future, the present value of the salvage proceeds will be small and inconsequential to the analysis. If necessary, however, the analyst can develop a salvage value forecast in two ways. First, one could tap the expertise of those involved in secondary market uses of the asset. Second, one could forecast future scrap material prices for the asset. Typically, the after-tax salvage cash flow is calculated using the firm's current tax rate as an estimate for the future tax rate.

The problems of estimating values in the distant future are difficult when the project involves a major strategic investment that the firm expects to maintain over a long period of time. In such a situation, the firm may estimate annual cash flows for a number of years (say, ten years) and attempt to estimate the project's value as a going concern at the end of this time horizon. One method the firm can use to estimate the project's going-concern value is the constant dividend growth model discussed in Chapter 10:

$$\text{Price}_{\text{horizon}} = \frac{\text{Dividend}_{\text{horizon}+1}}{r - g} \qquad \text{(LE17.2)}$$

The "salvage value" of the project is its going-concern value at the end of the time horizon; the dividend is its expected operating cash flow one year past the horizon. The required rate of return, r, is the project's required return. The expected growth rate, g, is the analyst's estimate of the constant growth rate for operating cash flows after the horizon.

LEARNING ACTIVITY

Some firms sell old equipment on auction sites, such as http://www.ebay.com, to recover final or "salvage" cash flows at the end of a project's term. Another more business-oriented site is http://www.salvagesale.com.

In this section, we review practical applications of cash flow estimation for a revenue expanding project, for a cost-saving project, and in setting a bid price.

> **17.13 APPLICATIONS**

CASH FLOW ESTIMATION FOR A REVENUE EXPANDING PROJECT

Let's examine a firm's decision to build an addition to a present plant in response to a forecast showing rising sales. For simplicity, we'll assume construction for the addition occurs in year zero. The plant has an expected useful life of five years and can be sold for $1 million at the end of the project. We need to

Table LE17.1   Initial Outlays for Plant Addition Project ($ Millions)

	$t = 0$
Depreciable outlays	−$4.5
Expensed cash outlays, after tax	−0.4
	−$4.9

determine the initial outlay, the incremental after-tax operating cash flow, and the salvage value for the project. We will assume the project's minimum required return is 10% and its tax rate is 40%.

Initial Outlay   The up-front expenses include those that are depreciable for tax purposes and those that are not depreciable. Depreciable outlays include construction labor, materials, preparation and transportation of materials, and equipment in the plant addition. For this example, we'll assume depreciable outlays are $4.5 million in year zero. Other expenses include costs for additional workers to operate the new plant and expenses associated with hiring, relocating, and training the workers. As with other expenses, this cost is deducted from the project's year-zero taxable income. The plant managers estimate that these costs will total $0.4 million after tax.

As seen in Table LE17.1, the initial after-tax outlays are $4.9 million in year zero. Of this cost, $4.5 million is depreciable while the remaining $0.4 million is expensed in year zero.

Incremental After-tax Operating Cash Flows   For simplicity, assume that the incremental sales and costs arising from the plant addition project will be constant over the five-year life of the addition. Sales are expected to rise by $3.0 million and costs will increase by $0.635 million. Using straight-line depreciation, the depreciable outlays of $4.5 million will increase the firm's depreciation expense by $4.5 million/5 years, or $0.90 million per year.

The expected increase in sales volume and production will require more working capital. Net working capital is expected to rise by $0.1 million in year one as the plant goes online. In year five, the plant addition will cease operations and the firm will recover the $0.1 million.[28]

Table LE17.2 presents these data in income statement format and calculates the operating cash flows using equation 17.4.

Salvage Value   In year five, the project will generate a cash inflow as the firm receives the after-tax salvage value of the plant addition and the resale value of equipment from the addition. These items will be fully depreciated by the end of year five, that is, their book values will be zero. Their collective market value was given as $1.0 million, so the after-tax salvage value cash flow is the following:

$$\text{Price} - t(\text{Price} - \text{BV}) = \$1.0 \text{ million} - 0.4(\$1.0 \text{ million} - 0) = \$0.600 \text{ million}$$

Table LE17.2   Project Income Statement, for Years 1 through 5 ($ millions)

Sales	$3.000
−Costs	−0.635
−Depreciation	−0.900
EBT	$1.465
−Taxes (40%)	−0.586
Net income	$0.879

---

[28] The funds will be recovered as inventory is sold, accounts receivable are collected, and raw material accounts payable are paid in full.

Operating Cash Flow Estimates Using Equation 17-4, spreadsheet format:

	Year 1	Years 2–4	Year 5
Tax rate: 40%			
Sales	$3.000	$3.000	$3.000
–Cost	–$0.635	–$0.635	–$0.635
–Depreciation	–$0.900	–$0.900	–$0.900
SUM = EBT	$1.465	$1.465	$1.465
After-tax: EBT × (1 – t)	$0.879	$0.879	$0.879
+Depreciation	$0.900	$0.900	$0.900
–change NWC	–$0.100	$0.000	$0.100
Operating CF	$1.679	$1.779	$1.879

Calculating the project's operating cash flow through direct application of equation 17.4, we have the following:

$$(\text{Sales} - \text{Costs} - \text{Depreciation})(1 - t) + \text{Depreciation} - \text{change in net working capital}$$
$$= (\$3.000 - 0.635 - \$0.900)(1 - 0.40) + \$0.900 - \$0.100 = \$1.679 \text{ for year one}$$

With no further changes in net working capital, the operating cash flow for years two through four is the following:

$$\text{OCF} = (\$3.000 - 0.635 - \$0.900)(1 - 0.40) + \$0.900 - \$0 = \$1.779$$

With the net working capital recovery, operating cash flow in year five is the following:

$$\text{OCF} = (\$3.000 - 0.635 - \$0.900)(1 - 0.40) + \$0.900 - (-\$0.1) = \$1.879$$

Table LE17.3 Cash Flow Summary and NPV Calculation ($ millions)

Year	Initial outlay	Operating cash flows	Salvage value	Total incremental cash flows	PVIF (10%)	PV of cash flows
0	$–4.9	$ 0.000	$ 0.0	$–4.90	1.0000	$–4.90
1	0.0	1.679	0.0	1.679	0.9091	1.53
2	0.0	1.779	0.0	1.779	0.8264	1.47
3	0.0	1.779	0.0	1.779	0.7513	1.34
4	0.0	1.779	0.0	1.779	0.6830	1.22
5	0.0	1.879	0.6	2.479	0.6209	1.54
						NPV = $ 2.20

Is the Project Beneficial to Shareholders? Table LE17.3 summarizes the expansion project's incremental cash flows. The net initial outlay, after-tax operating cash flows, and salvage value determine if the project will increase shareholder wealth. Table LE17.3 uses this information to compute the PVs of the cash flows, using a 10% required return, for the NPV calculation. Since the project's NPV is positive, the plant expansion project should be undertaken; shareholders will benefit from it.

CASH FLOW ESTIMATION FOR A COST-SAVING PROJECT

For a cost-saving project, the incremental cash flows are usually the difference between the cash flows of two mutually exclusive investments: keeping the existing capital equipment and purchasing new equipment. Suppose a firm is considering a project to replace an older computer system with a more

Table LE17.4   Total Outlays

Cash Outflows on the New Computer	
Purchase price	$7,700
Transportation	1,800
Hookup cost	200
Office modification	2,300
Total depreciable outlays	$12,000
Cash Inflows from Disposal of Old Computer	
After-tax salvage value	$3,600
Initial Investment Outlay	
Cash outflows for new computer	$12,000
Cash inflow from disposal of old computer	–$3,600
Initial investment outlay	$8,400

cost-efficient model. The decision depends on the difference between the cash flows from the initial investment in the new equipment, the operating cash flows, and the salvage values.

Initial Investment Outlay The total cost of the investment consists of the total outlay required to purchase and prepare the new computer for operation, less the after-tax salvage value of the older model. For simplicity, let's assume the new computer's expected useful life, three years, equals the expected remaining useful life of the old system.

Table LE17.4 lists the depreciable cash outlays. Added to the purchase price of $7,700 are transportation, hookup, and modification costs, which result in a total depreciable cost of $12,000. Table LE17.4 also shows the after-tax salvage cash flow of the old system of $3,600. This brings the initial total cash outlay for this project to $12,000 minus $3,600, or $8,400.

Incremental After-Tax Operating Cash Flows For a cost-saving project, it is safe to assume the incremental sale revenues are zero; so, if the firm's revenues are $500,000, they will not change after the project is done. Suppose the estimated costs of operating the old system and the new system are as follows:

	$t = 1$	$t = 2$	$t = 3$
Old computer system	$3,000	$3,500	$4,000
New computer system	$500	$2,000	$3,000

The incremental depreciation charge is the difference between depreciation charges on the new computer and those on the old one. Using straight-line depreciation, the new computer's depreciation will be its cost of $12,000 divided by three years, or $4,000 per year. The future depreciation of the old computer depends on the firm's depreciation method selected at the time of purchase. Assuming the firm acquired the old computer two years earlier at a cost of $10,000, expecting a life of five years, its straight-line annual depreciation charges are $2,000 per year.

We will assume that replacing one computer system with another will have no impact on the firm's current assets and current liabilities. Thus, changes in net working capital will be zero.

Using a 40% tax rate and the above information on sales, costs, depreciation, and net working capital, Table LE17.5 applies equation 17.4 to estimate operating cash flows.

In Table LE17.5, we apply equation 17.4 to each year. For example, for the first year, we list the operating cash flow components for the old system: costs of $3,000, depreciation of $2,000, and no change in net working capital. We do the same for the new system: costs of $500, depreciation of $4,000, and no change in net working capital. The incremental operating cash flow of replacing computer systems in the first year is $2,300. Similarly, we find the incremental operating cash flows for year two is $1,700 and year three is $1,400.

Table LE17.5 Incremental After-Tax Operating Cash Flows

Year 1 tax rate: 40%	Old system	New system	Incremental cash flows (new – old)
Sales	$500,000	$500,000	$0
–Cost	–$3,000	–$500	$2,500
–Depreciation	–$2,000	–$4,000	–$2,000
SUM	$495,000	$495,500	$500
×(1 – T)	$297,000	$297,300	$300
+Depreciation	$2,000	$4,000	$2,000
–Change NWC	$0	$0	$0
Operating CF	$299,000	$301,300	$2,300

Year 2 tax rate: 40%	Old system	New system	Incremental cash flows (new – old)
Sales	$500,000	$500,000	$0
Cost	–$3,500	–$2,000	$1,500
Depreciation	–$2,000	–$4,000	–$2,000
SUM	$494,500	$494,000	–$500
×(1 – T)	$296,700	$296,400	–$300
+Depreciation	$2,000	$4,000	$2,000
–Change NWC	$0	$0	$0
Operating CF	$298,700	$300,400	$1,700

Year 3 tax rate: 40%	Old system	New system	Incremental cash flows (new – old)
Sales	$500,000	$500,000	$0
Cost	–$4,000	–$3,000	$1,000
Depreciation	–$2,000	–$4,000	–$2,000
SUM	$494,000	$493,000	–$1,000
×(1 – T)	$296,400	$295,800	–$600
+Depreciation	$2,000	$4,000	$2,000
–Change NWC	$0	$0	$0
Operating CF	$298,400	$299,800	$1,400
Summary:	$t = 1$	$t = 2$	$t = 3$
Incremental after-tax OCF	$2,300	$1,700	$1,400

Salvage Value At the end of the third year, we will assume the new computer will have a market value of $1,000 whereas the old computer, if kept, will be worthless. Since the old computer system will have a book value and a market value of $0, its after-tax salvage value is $0.

The new computer's book value will be zero after three years. Its after-tax salvage value will be the selling price of $1,000 less the tax obligation of $400 [0.4($1,000 – $0)], or $600. The incremental salvage value cash flow will be $600 (new computer) – $0 (old computer), or $600.

Is the Project Beneficial to Shareholders? Table LE17.6 summarizes the incremental cash flows: the net initial outlay, the after-tax operating cash flows, and the salvage value. Assuming a 10% minimum required rate of return, the NPV is –$3,401. The computer replacement project is unacceptable because the negative NPV indicates that the project would decrease shareholder wealth by $3,401.

Table LE17.6   Cash Flow Summary and NPV Calculation

Year	Initial outlay	Operating cash flows	Salvage value	Total incremental cash flows	PVIF (10%)	PV of cash flows
0	–$8,400	$0	$0	$8,400	1.0000	–$8,400
1	0	2,300	0	2,300	0.9091	2,091
2	0	1,700	0	1,700	0.8264	1,405
3	0	1,400	600	2,000	0.7513	1,503
						NPV = –$3,401

SETTING A BID PRICE

Often a corporation or government that needs a fixed asset or service will solicit bids for its manufacture. The firm's request for proposals (RFPs) will list the desired attributes and specifications of the item. Firms will respond to the RFP with the hope of winning the solicitor's approval by verifying that it can produce the item at the lowest cost. The firm that makes the lowest bid will most likely win the contract.

Before placing a bid in response to an RFP, a firm's financial analysts must determine the price that will allow the firm to cover its costs and earn a sufficient return so its shareholders are not harmed. Put another way, the bidding firm must determine the minimum price at which the project will have a zero net present value. Any bid below this price would result in a negative NPV and hurt the firm's shareholders. To determine the minimum bid price, the analyst must work backward to develop cash flow estimates consistent with a zero NPV and then convert the cash flow estimates into a unit price.

Suppose you are the chief financial officer for You-go Inc., a manufacturer of high-quality motorized bicycles. An RFP from a large city is seeking bids for motorized bicycles for use by police officers on patrol. Your firm's motorized bicycles will require special modifications to make them suitable for police work. Among other requirements, the RFP notes that 100 bicycles will have to be delivered each year for the next three years. Assume You-go's required return on such projects is 20% and the firm's tax rate is 40%.

Initial Investment Outlay To increase production to meet the city's request and to modify the cycles for police use, the firm's plant and equipment will need to be expanded at a cost of $120,000 this year. It will cost about $10,000, after taxes, to hire and train new workers. Net working capital needs are expected to increase $40,000 this year. The firm will recover this increase in net working capital in the third year as it fills the production requirement.

This brings the total investment to $170,000, including $120,000 in depreciable assets. These assets will be straight-line depreciated over the three years of the project's life; thus, depreciation expense is expected to be $120,000/3, or $40,000 per year.

If the firm wins the bid, labor costs are expected to rise by $50,000 per year. Raw materials expenses will rise by $20,000 per year. Thus, expenses will increase by $70,000 annually as a result of this project.

Salvage Value The salvage value of the specialized equipment needed for this project is expected to be only $20,000 after three years. Since the assets will be fully depreciated to a book value of $0 at the end of three years, the after-tax proceeds from their sale will be $20,000 – 0.4($20,000 – $0) = $12,000.

Estimating Yearly Operating Cash Flows Table LE17.7 summarizes the information known thus far. The initial outlay totals $170,000 in year zero, and salvage value is $12,000 in year three. The operating cash flows are unknown, but they will increase by $40,000 in year three due to the recovery of net working capital.

Table LE17.7   Cash Flow Summary

Year	Initial outlay	Operating cash flows	Salvage value	Total incremental cash flows
0	–$170,000	$0	$0	–$170,000
1	0	X	0	X
2	0	X	0	X
3	0	X + $40,000	$12,000	X + $52,000

To make this information easier to work with, let's simplify the information presented in the table. Let's add the *present value* of the year three cash inflow of $52,000 to the initial cash outflow of $170,000. This gives a present value of the known cash flows of the following:

$$-\$170,000 + \$52,000(1/1.20)^3 = -\$139,907.41$$

This removes the effects of the salvage value and the recovery of net working capital from the project's annual cash flows. The cash flows in years one through three are now a three-year annuity, with a net year zero investment of $139,907.41 in present value terms:

Year	Cash flow
0	–$139,907.41
1	X
2	X
3	X

The NPV of this series of cash flows is the PV of the three-year $X annuity, less $139,907.41. To determine the minimum operating cash flow that will leave shareholder wealth unharmed, we set NPV to zero and solve for X:

$$\text{NPV} = 0 = (\$X)(\text{PVIFA for 3 years}, 20\%) - \$139,907.41$$

Using interest factor table or a financial calculator, the present value interest factor of an annuity (PVIFA) for three years and 20% is 2.1065. Solving for $X, we find the operating cash flow annuity is $66,417.58.

Using this minimum operating cash flow, we can work backward to determine the minimum sales revenue consistent with a zero-NPV bid. Recall the project's annual costs are $70,000, its annual depreciation expense is $40,000, and the firm's tax rate is 40%. We can ignore the change in net working capital as we incorporated that in the analysis in Table LE17.7 and the cash flow estimate of $66,417.58. Using equation 17.4 and simplifying, we have the following:

$$\text{Operating cash flow} = (\text{Sales} - \text{Costs} - \text{Depreciation})(1-T)$$
$$+ \text{Depreciation} - \text{change in net working capital}$$

$$\$66,417.58 = (\text{Sales} - \$70,000 - \$40,000) \ (1-0.40) + \$40,000 - 0$$
$$\$66,417.58 = (\text{Sales} - \$110,000) \ (0.60) + \$40,000$$
$$\$66,417.58 = (\text{Sales}) \ (0.60) - \$66,000 + \$40,000$$
$$\$66,417.58 = (\text{Sales}) \ (0.60) - \$26,000$$
$$\$92,417.58 = (\text{Sales}) \ (0.60)$$

Solving for sales to find the minimum total sales revenue, we see sales equals $92,417.58/0.60 = $154,029.30 per year. Dividing total annual sales by 100 cycles gives us the minimum bid per cycle, $1,540.29. This unit price represents the lowest price the firm can bid without adversely affecting shareholder wealth.

We see from these applications that to approach a cash flow estimation problem, we should first estimate initial cash outlay, including property and equipment expenditures, necessary changes in net working capital, and other start-up expenses, such as hiring new workers. Second, we estimate the periodic operating cash flows using equation 17.4, making sure to include any changes in net working capital over the lifetime of the project. Third, we estimate after-tax salvage value cash flows. Once we have these three estimates we can use the techniques discussed in Chapter 17 to estimate NPV, IRR, MIRR, PI, or payback period.

SUMMARY

LO 17.12 Estimating cash flows is a difficult part of evaluating capital budgeting projects. Projected earnings, expenses, and fixed-asset investments must be converted into cash flows by using the methods discussed in this chapter. We reviewed practical ways – including the use of market research, past experience, and engineering estimates to estimate the three main cash flows in capital budgeting analysis: initial investment outlay, incremental after-tax operating cash flows, and salvage value

LO 17.13 We reviewed the process of estimating the initial investment outlay, incremental after-tax operating cash flows, and salvage value and applied to NPV criterion to three types of capital budgeting projects: revenue expending; cost saving; and determining a bid price that covers all costs, including the cost of capital.

REVIEW QUESTIONS

1. **(LO 17.12)** What information sources are used to develop estimates for these project components:
   a. Initial outlays?
   b. Operating life?
   c. Salvage value?

2. **(LO 17.12)** Why might there be tax implications when an asset is sold at the termination of a capital budgeting project?

3. **(LO 17.13)** Explain the process to estimating cash flows for a revenue enhancing project.

4. **(LO 17.13)** Explain the process to estimating cash flows for a cost-saving project.

5. **(LO 17.13)** Explain the process to estimating a bid price by estimating zero NPV cash flow needs.

PROBLEMS

1. Suppose the Quick Towing Company purchases a new tow truck. The old truck had a book value of $1,000 and was sold for $1,420. If Quick Towing is in the 34% marginal tax bracket, what is the tax liability on the sale of the truck? What is the after-tax cash flow on the sale?

2. Hammond's Fish Market purchased a $30,000 fork lift truck. It has a five-year useful life. The firm's tax rate is 25%.
   a. If the fork lift is straight-line depreciated, what is the firm's tax savings from depreciation?
   b. What will be its book value (BV) at the end of year three?
   c. Suppose the fork lift can be sold for $10,000 at the end of three years. What is its after-tax salvage value?

3. Lisowski Laptops (LL) is examining the possibility of manufacturing and selling a notebook computer that is compatible with PC and Macintosh systems and that can receive television signals. Its estimated selling price is $2,500. Variable costs (supplies and labor) will equal $1,500 per unit, and

fixed costs per year would approximate $200,000. Up-front investments in plant and equipment will total $270,000, which will be straight-line depreciated over three years. The initial working capital investment will be $100,000 and will rise proportionately with sales. Bill, the CEO, forecasts laptop sales will be 50,000 units the first year, 60,000 units the second, and 45,000 units the third year, at which time product life cycles would require closing down production of the model. At that time, the market value of the project's assets will be about $70,000. LL's tax rate is 40% and its required return on projects such as this one is 17%. Should Lisowski Laptops offer the new computer?

4. Preston Industries' current sales volume is $100 million a year. Preston is examining the advantages of electronic data interchange (EDI). The technology will allow Preston to electronically communicate with suppliers and customers and send and receive purchase orders, invoices, and cash. It will save Preston money by lowering costs in the purchasing, customer service, accounts

payable, and accounting departments. Initial estimates are that savings will equal $100,000 a year. Investment in EDI technology will include $500,000 in depreciable expenses and $100,000 in nondepreciable expenses. Assets will be depreciated on a straight-line basis for four years. Implementation of EDI is expected to reduce Preston's net working capital by $200,000. Because of changing technology, Preston's president, Carol, wants to estimate the effect of switching to EDI on shareholder wealth over a four-year time horizon assuming that advances in technology will make the equipment worthless at the end of four years. At a 30% tax rate and 13% required rate of return, should Preston Industries switch to EDI?

5. Bart and Morticia, owners of the prestigious Gomez-Addams Office Towers, are concerned about high heating and cooling costs and client complaints of temperature variation within the building. They commissioned an engineering study by Frasco-Prew Associates to identify the cause of the problems and suggest corrective action. Frasco-Prew's basic recommendation is to install a new heating, ventilation, and air conditioning (HVAC) system, featuring electronic climate control, in the Towers. Over the next four years, the engineers estimate a new system will reduce heating and cooling costs by $125,000 a year. Cost of the new system will be $500,000 and can be depreciated over four years. Using a 25%

tax rate and a 14% required return, should Bart and Morticia change the HVAC system? Use a four-year time horizon.

6. Casey's Baseball Bats is planning to export their product to the Asian market. They estimate up-front expenses of $1 million this year (year 0) and $3 million next year (year 1). Operating cash flows in years two, three, and four will be (in dollars) $100,000, $200,000, and $400,000, respectively. After year four, they expect operating cash flows to grow at 10% a year indefinitely. If 15% is the required return on the project, what is its NPV?

7. The No-Shoplift Security Company is interested in bidding on a contract to provide a new security system for a large department store chain. The new security system would be phased into ten stores per year for five years. No-Shoplift can purchase the hardware for $50,000 per installation. The labor and material cost per installation is approximately $15,000. In addition, No-Shoplift will need to purchase $100,000 in new equipment for the installation, which will be depreciated to zero using the straight-line method over five years. This equipment will be sold in five years for $25,000. Finally, an investment of $50,000 in net working capital will be needed. Assume that the relevant tax rate is 34%. If the No-Shoplift Security Company requires a 10% return on its investments, what price should it bid?

CHAPTER 18

Capital Structure and the Cost of Capital

LEARNING OBJECTIVES

After studying this chapter, you should be able to do the following:

LO 18.1 Explain how capital structure affects a firm's capital budgeting discount rate.

LO 18.2 Describe the relationship between required return and cost of capital.

LO 18.3 Calculate a firm's cost of debt financing and cost of equity financing.

LO 18.4 Explain how a firm can estimate its cost of capital.

LO 18.5 Explain how a firm's growth potential, dividend policy, and capital structure are related.

LO 18.6 Explain how EBIT/eps analysis can assist management in choosing a capital structure.

LO 18.7 Describe how a firm's business risk and financial risk together can affect the relationship between sales and earnings per share.

LO 18.8 Describe the factors that affect a firm's capital structure.

Where we have been. . . We have seen how a firm can choose a short- or long-term financing strategy (Chapter 16) and familiarize itself with the workings of the financial markets, security pricing, and IPOs (Chapters 10 and 11). Part of the financing decision depends on the firm's asset needs. New asset purchases, restructurings, or corporate strategies may lead to the need for new financing or a new financing strategy for the firm. Likewise, changes in financial market conditions (due to fluctuations in interest rates, stock price, or exchange rates) may make new financial strategies look appealing.

Where we are going. . . We've gone full circle now. Part 1 of this text, "Institutions and Markets," discussed the purpose, evolution, and working of financial institutions. Part 2, "Investments," showed how these institutions and the financial markets work to bring together suppliers and users of capital, how interest rates are determined on a variety of financial instruments, how securities markets work, how securities are priced, and how risk and return influence investor decisions and security prices. Part 3, "Financial Management," has reviewed financial statements and financial decisions in the context of businesses. And what inputs do firms use to help guide their long-term financing decisions and corporate strategies? As we will see in this chapter, the inputs are none other than information from the financial system and financial markets.

How this chapter applies to me. . . High levels of consumer debt are used as a harbinger of tough economic times ahead. Similar to a firm, individuals have a capital structure, too. Add up your assets, subtract any debts, and the balance is your net worth, or "equity." Your own personal capital structure is your mixture of debt and equity that is used to finance what you own and your lifestyle. Like a firm, use of debt without the ability to make interest payments and to reduce the principal can lead to financial distress. The best use of debt for individuals is similar to that of firms: use in moderation and only to help purchase assets with the potential to grow in value, such as a house. At the current time, you may be using student loans to finance an investment in yourself, namely your education. Because of your education, your future earnings potential is expected to be greater than it otherwise would be and gives you the ability to repay the loan.

In Shakespeare's play *Hamlet,* the elder Polonius counsels his son Laertes,

Neither a borrower nor a lender be.

We can tell that Polonius did not study modern-day finance! Lending money, in the form of buying bonds or putting money in a bank account, can be an attractive investment strategy for some, and businesses often find themselves needing to borrow or raise funds for short periods (which was the topic of Chapter 16) or longer periods. This chapter looks at the analysis a firm should do when funds are needed for longer periods.

The previous chapters described the capital budgeting process. We learned how to estimate a project's cash flows and how to use techniques, such as net present value (NPV) and internal rate of return (IRR), for evaluating projects. In Chapter 17 we assumed that the project's discount rate, or its cost of capital, was given. In this chapter, we will explain how managers can estimate their firm's cost of capital for "average risk" projects. This discount rate is adjusted up or down, as we learned in Chapter 17, depending on the project's risk.

Before managers can estimate the cost of capital, two inputs are needed. First, the cost of each financing source needs to be determined. Second, managers must determine the appropriate financing mix to use to fund the firm. Once these are known, managers can estimate the firm's weighted average cost of capital (WACC).

18.1 WHY CHOOSE A CAPITAL STRUCTURE?

A firm's mix of debt and equity used to finance its assets defines the firm's **capital structure** as seen in Figure 18.1. In this chapter, we will first review the importance of a firm's capital structure and how the capital structure and the costs of each financing source can be combined to provide an estimate of the WACC. We'll examine the interrelationship among a firm's growth rate, dividend policy, and capital structure decisions. Then we'll review the influences that affect a firm's choice of a capital structure over time.

Obviously, a target capital structure is important as it determines the proportion of debt and equity used to estimate a firm's cost of capital. There is, however, a second, more important reason. The firm's **optimum debt/equity mix** minimizes the firm's **cost of capital**, which, in turn helps, the firm to maximize shareholder wealth.

For example, suppose a firm expects cash flows of $20 million annually in perpetuity. Each of the three capital structures shown in Table 18.1 has a different weighted average cost of capital. Following the perpetuity valuation rule from Chapter 9, firm value is computed by dividing the expected cash flow by the firm's cost of capital under each capital structure. Capital Structure 2 in the following table minimizes the cost of capital at 8%, which, in turn, maximizes the value of the firm at $250 million.

A nonoptimal capital structure with too much or little debt leads to higher financing costs, and the firm will likely reject some capital budgeting projects that could have increased shareholder wealth with an optimal financing mix. For example, suppose a firm has a minimum cost of capital of 8%, but poor analysis leads management to choose a capital structure that results in a 10% cost of capital. It would then reject an average risk project that costs $100,000 and returns cash flows of $26,000 in years one through five at a 10% cost of capital (NPV = −$1,434). This project would be acceptable at the minimum possible cost of capital of 8% (NPV = $3,818).

capital structure firm's mix of debt and equity used to finance a firm's assets

optimum debt/equity mix proportionate use of debt and equity that minimizes the firm's cost of capital

cost of capital minimum acceptable rate of return to a firm on a project

FIGURE 18.1   The balance sheet

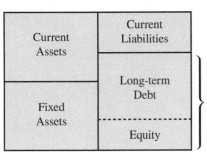

Table 18.1   Capital Structure Options

	Capital structure 1	Capital structure 2	Capital structure 3
Debt	25.0%	40.0%	70.0%
Equity	75.0%	60.0%	30.0%
Weighted average cost of capital	10.0%	8.0%	12.5%
Firm value under			
Capital Structure 1: $20 million/0.10 = $200 million			
Capital Structure 2: $20 million/0.08 = $250 million			
Capital Structure 3: $20 million/0.125 = $160 million			

There is another, more intuitive way to see the importance of finding the optimal capital structure. A project's NPV represents the increase in shareholders' wealth from undertaking a project. From Chapter 10, we know there is an inverse relationship between value and discount rates (the "seesaw effect"). Thus, a lower weighted average cost of capital gives higher project NPVs, and results in higher levels of shareholder wealth.

18.1.1 TRENDS IN CORPORATE USE OF DEBT

The ratio of long-term debt to gross domestic product (GDP) for U.S. corporations grew during the 1960s until, as seen in Figure 18.2, the mid-1970s, exceeding 35% only for limited occasions. But the relative use of debt rose until 1989, peaking at a nearly 45% of GDP. Many firms restructured

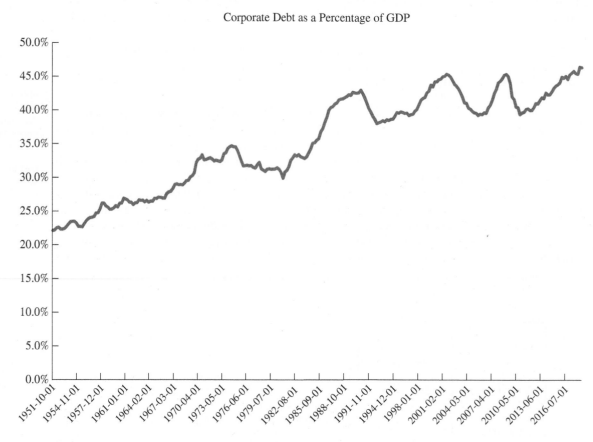

FIGURE 18.2   Corporate debt as a percentage of GDP, 1951–2018

Source: Author calculations from FRED data, St. Louis Federal Reserve Bank.

themselves financially during the 1980s. Some did so in attempts to lower their cost of capital by taking advantage of the tax deductibility of interest through issuing debt to repurchase common stock, thereby increasing their debt to equity ratios. Other firms went private in the 1980s, fought off takeovers, or acquired other firms, financing the transactions with large amounts of debt. The surge in bankruptcies at the beginning of the 1990s shows the folly of such excessive use of debt.

Into the early 1990s, the ratio of debt to economic activity fell as firms issued equity to strengthen their balance sheets and to reduce the probability of financial distress due to over-borrowing. But as the economy grew in the 1990s, so did the relative use of debt, until the economic slowdown in the early part of the new millennium started to reduce debt levels. From 2001 through the present, we have seen the same cycle – a recessionary economy causing firms to shed debt, only for the corporate economy to borrow again as the economy grew through 2008. Use of debt fell during the Great Recession, but it rose again through 2019 as the economy recovered and grew.

18.1.2 CASHING IN ON LOW INTEREST RATES

CRISIS The Federal Reserve System has pursued an active monetary policy to lower interest rates since the beginning of the 2007–2009 Great Recession. It did so through a number of "quantitative easing" events in which it purchased securities in an attempt to raise bond prices and lower interest rates. Overall, the attempt to lower interest rates has been successful through 2016. Ten-year Treasury bonds that yielded over 5% in 2007 yielded as low as 1.5% in 2012. After rising in 2013 to slightly over 3%, rates again dropped to well below 2% in 2016. Interest rates on 30-year Treasury bonds had similar declines, with yields falling from over 5% in 2007 to below 3% in 2012, and remaining there into 2019.[1]

The low interest rate environment was great news for borrowers. Home mortgage rates, which were nearly 7% in 2007, fell to 3.3% in 2012 and remained under 4% into 2019. Corporations noticed the trend in falling interest rates, too. Baa-rated corporate bond yields fell from over 9% in 2008 to around 4.5% in 2012 before rising to the lower 5% range in 2019. Corporate treasurers took advantage of this "cheap money" and increased their borrowing. Issuances of 30-year corporate bonds hit nearly 20-year highs and overall business borrowing (short- and long-term) rose from pre-recession levels. Total business debt issuance rose from 2007 to 2017, and in 2017 it was over $1.6 trillion, a record.[2] But lower interest rates hit savers hard, as interest rates on savings accounts fell to nearly zero, on average, and five-year certificates of deposit (CDs) offered, on average, interest rates below 1% in 2012 and have stayed below 1% until 2018. With the Fed's aggressive monetary policies, interest rates fell to near-record low levels on several fronts.

The U.S. debt rating downgrade by Standard & Poor's (S&P) from AAA to AA+ in August 2011 meant some corporate borrowers had higher credit ratings than the U.S. government. In late 2012, short-term debt of AAA-rated firms ExxonMobil and Johnson & Johnson had *lower* yields than comparable maturity U.S. debt.

Many companies took advantage of the low interest rates. Corporations issued debt to store funds for later use, or they opted to issue debt rather than equity since debt was so inexpensive. As one analyst said, "No treasurer or CFO wants to be the one treasurer or CFO who didn't get cheap long-term money when it was available."[3]

But what a windfall; that is, low-cost borrowing for some is a danger for others. Investor demand was high for securities that could offer higher yields than bank savings or Treasuries. Long-term investors (such as pension funds) were seeking long-term assets in which to invest. But investors seeking higher yields were making several investment decisions that over time may hurt their returns.

---

[1] Matt Wirz, "As Corporate Bond Yields Sink, Risks for Investors Rise, *The Wall Street Journal* (August 13, 2012), p. C1; Vipal Monga, "Companies Feast on Cheap Money," *The Wall Street Journal* (October 9, 2012), pp. B1, B7; Patrick McGee and Katy Burne. "The New Haven for Investors," *The Wall Street Journal* (November 7, 2012), p. C1; David Wessel, "Fed's Easing Yields a Hidden Benefit," *The Wall Street Journal* (November 29, 2012), p. A4.

[2] SIFMA, accessed February 9, 2019, https://www.sifma.org/resources/research/bond-chart/.

[3] Mark Gray, an analyst with Moody's, as quoted in Vipal Monga, "Companies Feast on Cheap Money," *The Wall Street Journal* (October 9, 2012), pp. B1, B7.

First, investors seeking higher bond returns started buying more "junk" or high-yield bonds (we discussed these below-investment-grade bonds in Chapter 10). Yields on bonds rated BB fell from over 16% in 2008 to under 5% in 2013; rates have risen slightly and fallen again since then, being slightly more than 5% in early 2019. Remember from Chapter 10, bond prices and bond yields move in opposite directions (the seesaw effect). So, as investor demand rose for riskier securities, the prices on junk bonds rose, lowering their yields. The danger for investors is to ignore risk at their own peril. Seeking higher yields can occur only at higher risk, and low-rated corporate bonds have higher default risk than investment-grade bonds.

Second, investors sought higher yields by buying longer maturity securities. The Fed's Operation Twist during 2011–2012 had the goal of buying longer-term bonds. This increase in demand raised bond prices and lowered yields on long-term bonds and mortgages. The operation was successful, since 30-year Treasury yields fell below 3% in late 2012. The danger for investors, however, is interest rate risk. Long-term bond prices are more sensitive to changes in interest rates than are short-term bond prices. A small rise in long-term interest rates could lead to falling bond prices and lower returns.

Third, related to the above risk, is the risk of rising inflation and interest rates. Should the economy begin to recover more strongly than it has, inflation may rise and interest rates may rise as well. Rising interest rates lead to falling bond prices and losses to bond investors who sell their bonds prior to maturity. Even if investors hold a bond to maturity, they may face declines in purchasing power as the inflation rate may exceed the low coupon rate on the bond.

Recall from Table 12.4, the long-term average inflation rate in the U.S. economy is about 3%. Should inflation average 3% in the future, investors buying long-term bonds with yields below this will lose money on a real, or after-inflation, basis. And if investors have to pay taxes on their coupon income, the after-tax return will likely fall below the inflation rate as well, giving investors a negative real return.

18.2 REQUIRED RATE OF RETURN AND THE COST OF CAPITAL

Investors in a project expect to earn a return on their investment. This expected return depends on current capital market conditions (e.g., levels of stock prices and interest rates) and the project risk. The minimum acceptable rate of return of a project is the return that generates sufficient cash flow to pay investors their expected return.

To illustrate, suppose a firm wants to spend $1,000 on an average risk capital budgeting project, financing the investment by borrowing $600 and selling $400 worth of common stock. The firm must pay interest on the debt at a rate of 9% while shareholders expect a 15% return on their investment. To compensate the firm's investors adequately, the project should generate an annual pretax expected cash flow equal to the following:

$$\text{Lender's interest} + \text{Shareholders' return} = \text{Annual expected cash flow}$$
$$= (0.09)(\$600) + (0.15)(\$400)$$
$$= \$54 + \$60 = \$114$$

The project's pre-tax minimum rate of return must then equal the following:

$$\text{Minimum cash flow}/\text{Investment} = \text{Minimum rate of return}$$
$$= \$114/\$1,000 = 11.4\%$$

As another means to determine this, the expected return of each financing source could be weighted by its relative use. The firm is raising 60% of the project's funds from debt and 40% from equity. This results in a minimum pretax required return of the following:

$$(0.60)(9\%) + (0.40)(15\%) = 11.4\%$$

Thus, the required rate of return on a project represents a weighted average of lenders' and owners' return expectations. Since a cash flow, or return, to an investor represents a cash outflow, or a cost, to the firm, the minimum required rate of return is a weighted average of the firm's costs of various sources

SMALL BUSINESS PRACTICE

VENTURE CAPITAL AS A SOURCE OF FINANCING FOR THE SMALL BUSINESS

Venture capitalists are usually members of partnerships that consist of a few general partners. The typical venture capital partnership manages between $50 million and $100 million in assets. The general approach for raising investment funds for a venture capital firm is to set up a "venture capital fund" and seek financial commitments from investors to fund the "fund." It is common to organize a venture capital fund as a limited partnership in which the venture capitalist is the general partner and the other investors are limited investors. The general partner might invest 1% of the funds and the limited partners the remainder. Investors make an initial contribution and commit to provide additional funds up to some stated maximum during the fund's life, which is usually ten years. Often an option exists to extend the fund for two or three more years. At the end of a fund's life, cash and securities are distributed to the investors.

What are the sources of venture capital? According to *Venture Capital Journal*, pension funds provide over one-third of annual venture capital funds. Second in importance as suppliers of venture capital are foundations and endowments, with 22% of the funds raised. Endowment contributions come largely from university endowments. Investments by insurance firms and bank portfolios play a major role, as do investments by high net worth individuals and families.

---

of capital. Thus, the required rate of return on a project is equivalent to the project's cost of capital. It is this number that should be used as a discount rate when evaluating a project's NPV. *Required rate of return, cost of capital,* and *discount rate* are different terms for the same concept.

It is fair to ask, why is the minimum required return equal to a *weighted* average of financing costs? If a firm can finance a project using all debt at an interest cost of 8%, shouldn't the project be accepted if it has a positive NPV using an 8% discount rate or if its IRR exceeds 8%? The answer is, not necessarily. Suppose this week, a project of average risk is financed by borrowing at 8% and has an IRR of 9%, so the board of directors votes to accept the project. Next quarter, because the firm's debt ratios are high, the firm's board decides to finance all new projects with equity. If the cost of equity is 15% and a potential project with average risk has an IRR of 12%, it will be turned down. It is hard to envision a board maximizing the firm's value by accepting projects with 9% expected returns while rejecting projects with the same risk that have expected returns of 12%. That is why the WACC is used, so project acceptance is not affected by how it is specifically financed.

Relevant cash flows are incremental after-tax cash flows. To be consistent, these cash flows must be discounted using an incremental after-tax cost of capital. The firm's relevant cost of capital is computed from after-tax financing costs. Firms pay preferred and common stock dividends out of net income, so these expenses represent after-tax costs to the firm. Because debt interest is paid from pretax income, the cost of debt requires adjustment to an after-tax basis before computing the cost of capital.

| **18.3 COST OF CAPITAL** |

A project's incremental cash flows must be discounted at a cost of capital that represents the incremental or marginal cost to the firm for financing the project; that is, the cost of raising one additional dollar of capital. Thus, the cost of debt and equity that determines the cost of capital must not come from historical averages or past costs but must come from projections of future costs. The firm's analysts must evaluate investors' expected returns under likely market conditions and use these expected returns to compute the firm's marginal future cost of raising funds by each method.

Conceptually, investors' required returns equal the firm's financing costs. The following sections use the valuation concepts for bonds and stocks from Chapter 10 to find investors' required returns on bonds, preferred stock, and common stock. We then adjust these required returns to reflect the firm's after-tax cost of financing.

18.3.1 COST OF DEBT

The firm's unadjusted cost of debt financing equals the yield to maturity (YTM) on new debt issues, either a long-term bank loan or a bond issue. The YTM represents the cost to the firm of borrowing funds in the current market environment. The firm's current financing costs determine its current cost of capital.

A firm can determine its cost of debt by several methods. If the firm targets an "A" rating (or any other bond rating), a review of the yields to maturity on A-rated bonds in Standard & Poor's Bond Guide can provide an estimate of the firm's current borrowing costs. Several additional factors will affect the firm's specific borrowing costs, including covenants and features of the proposed bond issue as well as the number of years until the bond or loan matures, or comes due. It is important to examine bonds whose ratings and characteristics resemble those the firm wants to match.

In addition, the firm can solicit the advice of investment bankers on the cost of issuing new debt. Or if the firm has debt currently trading, it can use public market prices and yields to estimate its current cost of debt. The publicly traded bond's yield to maturity can be found using the techniques for determining the internal rate of return on an investment discussed in Chapters 9 and 10. Finally, a firm can seek long-term debt financing from a bank or a consortium of banks. Preliminary discussions with the bankers will indicate a ballpark interest rate the firm can expect to pay on its borrowing.

The yield estimate, however derived, is an estimate of the coupon rate on newly issued bonds (as bonds are usually issued with prices close to their par value) or the interest rate on a loan. Interest is a pretax expense, so the interest estimate should be adjusted to reflect the tax shield provided by debt financing. If the YTM is the pretax interest cost estimate, the after-tax estimate is YTM times $(1 - T)$, where T is the firm's marginal tax rate.[4] Thus the after-tax cost of debt, k_d, is the following:

$$k_d = \text{YTM} \left(1 - T\right) \tag{18.1}$$

Suppose Eastnorth Manufacturing has a 40% marginal tax rate and it can issue debt with a 10% yield to maturity. Its after-tax cost of debt will be 10% (1 − 0.40) = 6%.

18.3.2 COST OF PREFERRED STOCK

Chapter 9 explained how to model preferred stock as a perpetuity. The investor pays a price, P, for a share of preferred stock and, in return, expects to receive D_p of dividends every year, forever. Valuing the stock as perpetuity, the maximum price an investor will pay for a share is D_p/r_p, where r_p represents the rate of return required by investors in the firm's preferred stock. Rearranging the valuation equation to solve for r_p yields the following equation:

$$r_p = D_p / P$$

When issuing preferred stock, the firm will not receive the full price, P, per share; instead, there will be a flotation cost of F_p per share.[5] Thus, the cost to the firm of preferred stock financing, k_p, is the following result:

$$k_p = D_p / \left(P - F_p\right) \tag{18.2}$$

Suppose a firm wants to issue preferred stock that pays an annual dividend of $5 a share. The price of the stock is $55, and the cost of floating a new issue will be $3 a share. The cost of preferred stock to this firm is will be $k_p = D_p/(P - F_p) = \$5/(\$55 - \$3) = 0.0962$, or 9.62%.

18.3.3 COST OF COMMON EQUITY

Unlike debt and preferred stock, cash flows from common equity are not fixed or known beforehand, and their risk is harder to evaluate. In addition, firms have two sources of common equity, retained earnings and new stock issues, which are two costs of common equity. It may be clear that an explicit

---

[4] In reality, this is an approximation. We know from Chapter 10 that the YTM reflects interest paid and the difference between market price and par value. Only the interest is tax deductible to the firm. For coupon-paying bond issues, the coupon rate many times is set so the bonds' market or offering price is close to par. In these cases, equation 18.1 is a close approximation to the cost of debt.

[5] Flotation costs were discussed in Chapter 11.

cost (dividends) is associated with issuing new common equity, but although the firm pays no extra dividends to use retained earnings, they are not a free source of financing. We must consider the opportunity cost of using funds the shareholders could have received as dividends.

Retained earnings are the portion of net income the firm does not distribute as dividends. As owners of the firm, common shareholders have a claim on all of its net income, but they receive only the amount the firm's board declares as dividends.

From the shareholders' perspective, the opportunity cost of retained earnings is the return the shareholders could earn by investing the funds in assets whose risk is similar to that of the firm. Suppose, for example, that shareholders expect a 15% return on their investment in a firm's common stock. If the firm could not invest its retained earnings to achieve a risk-adjusted 15% expected return, shareholders would be better off receiving all of its net income as dividends. That way, they can re-invest the funds in similar-risk assets that can provide a 15% expected return.

To maximize shareholder wealth, management must recognize that retained earnings have a cost. That cost, k_{re}, is the return that shareholders expect from their investment in the firm. We will review two methods of estimating the cost of retained earnings. One method uses the security market line (SML); the other uses the assumption of constant dividend growth.

18.3.3.1 Cost of Retained Earnings: Security Market Line (SML) Approach

Learning Extension from Chapter 12 developed the security market line (SML), which can provide an estimate of shareholder required return based on a stock's systematic risk. The security market line equation is, as follows:

$$E(R_i) = \text{RFR} + \beta_i (R_{\text{MKT}} - \text{RFR})$$

It gives the required return as a combination of the risk-free return (RFR) and a risk premium that is the product of a stock's systematic risk, measured by β_i, and the market risk premium ($R_{\text{MKT}} - \text{RFR}$). The required shareholder return is the opportunity cost the firm must earn on its retained earnings. Thus, this is an estimate for the cost of retained earnings:

$$k_{re} = E(R_i) = \text{RFR} + \beta_i (R_{\text{MKT}} - \text{RFR}) \tag{18.3}$$

For example, assume the current T-bill rate is 4.5% and analysts estimate the current market risk premium is above its historical average at 9.0%. Suppose also that analysts estimate Eastnorth Manufacturing's β to be 1.30. What is Eastnorth Manufacturing's cost of retained earnings, using the SML approach?

All the information we need in order to apply equation 18.3 was presented above:

$$k_{re} = E(R_i) = \text{RFR} + \beta_i (R_{\text{MKT}} - \text{RFR}) = 4.5\% + \left[(1.3)(9\%)\right] = 16.2\%$$

Using the SML, Eastnorth Manufacturing's cost of retained earnings is 16.2%.

18.3.3.2 Cost of Retained Earnings: Constant Dividend Growth Model

Chapter 10 presented the constant dividend growth model to estimate a firm's stock price:

$$p = \frac{D_1}{r_{cs} - g} \tag{18.4}$$

where

   P = the stock's price

   g = the expected (constant) dividend growth rate

   D_1 = next year's expected dividend (equal to the current dividend increased by $g\%$)

   r_{cs} = the shareholders' required return on the stock

Rather than use the model to determine a price, however, we can substitute today's stock price for P and solve for the shareholders' required rate of return, r_{cs}:

$$k_{re} = r_{cs} = \frac{D_1}{P} + g \qquad (18.5)$$

The shareholders' required return represents the firm's cost of retained earnings, k_{re}. The ratio D_1/P represents the current income yield to shareholders from their investment of P. From the firm's perspective, this ratio represents the ratio of dividends it pays to its current market value. The growth rate, g, represents shareholders' expected capital gain, arising from dividend growth. From the firm's perspective, g can be viewed as an opportunity cost of raising equity today. It is expected to be able to sell equity at a g percent higher price next year.

18.3.4 COST OF NEW COMMON STOCK

flotation costs costs of issuing stock; includes accounting, legal, and printing costs of offering shares to the public, as well as the commission or fees earned by the investment bankers who market the new securities to investors

To estimate the cost of new equity, we must modify equation 18.5 to reflect the extra cost to the firm of issuing securities in the primary market. The costs of issuing stock, or **flotation costs**, include the accounting, legal, and printing costs of offering shares to the public, as well as the commission or fees earned by the investment bankers who market the new securities to investors.

If the flotation cost is F per share, the cost of issuing new common stock, or k_n, is given by equation 18.6:

$$k_n = \frac{D_1}{P - F} + g \qquad (18.6)$$

Suppose a firm has just paid a dividend of $2.50 a share. Its stock price is $50 a share, and the expected growth rate of dividends is 6%. The current dividend of $2.50 must be multiplied by a factor to reflect the expected 6% growth for D_1, next year's dividend. Using equation 18.5, the cost of using retained earnings as a financing source is the following:

$$k_{cs} = \frac{2.50(1+0.06)}{\$50} + 0.06 = \frac{\$2.65}{\$50} + 0.06$$
$$= 0.053 + 0.06 = 0.113, \text{ or } 11.3\%$$

If new common stock is to be issued to finance the project, and flotation costs are expected to be $4 per share, we need to use equation 18.6 to estimate the cost of new common equity:

$$k_{cs} = \frac{2.50(1+0.06)}{\$50 - \$4} + 0.06 = \frac{\$2.65}{\$46} + 0.06$$
$$= 0.058 + 0.06 = 0.118, \text{ or } 11.8\%$$

The cost of using new common stock is 11.8%.

We learned about the concept of efficient markets in Chapter 12; namely, that current market prices and interest rates reflect all known information and the market's expectations about the future. Financial managers can do little to "fight the market." If managers feel their financing costs are too high, then the market usually perceives risk the managers are ignoring. The efficient market ensures financing costs are in line with the market's perception of firms' risks and expected returns.

> **DISCUSSION QUESTION 1**
>
> **With interest rates at or near historic lows since the end of the Great Recession, why didn't business firms borrow as much as possible? Why didn't individuals borrow as much as they could to buy a house or newer cars?**

We have seen how to compute the costs of the firm's basic capital structure components. Now we will combine the components to find the weighted average of the firm's financing costs.

The firm's **weighted average cost of capital (WACC)** represents the minimum required rate of return on its capital budgeting projects.

WACC is found by multiplying the marginal cost of each capital structure component by its appropriate weight and summing the terms:

$$\text{WACC} = w_d k_d + w_p k_p + w_e k_e \tag{18.7}$$

The weights of debt, preferred equity, and common equity in the firm's capital structure are given by w_d, w_p, and w_e, respectively. As the WACC covers all of the firm's capital financing sources, the weights must sum to 1.0.

The firm's cost of common equity, k_e, can reflect the cost of retained earnings, k_{re}, or the cost of new common stock, k_n, whichever is appropriate. Most firms rely on retained earnings to raise the common equity portion of their financial needs. If retained earnings are insufficient, they can issue common stock to meet the shortfall. In this case, k_n is substituted for the cost of common equity.

18.4 WEIGHTED AVERAGE COST OF CAPITAL

weighted average cost of capital (WACC) represents the minimum required rate of return on a capital budgeting project; it is found by multiplying the marginal cost of each capital structure component by its appropriate weight and summing the terms

18.4.1 CAPITAL STRUCTURE WEIGHTS

The weights in equation 18.7 represent a specific intended financing mix. These target weights represent a mix of debt and equity the firm will want to achieve or maintain over the planning horizon. As much as possible, the target weights should reflect the combination of debt and equity that management believes will minimize the firm's weighted average cost of capital. The firm should make an effort, over time, to move toward and maintain its target capital structure mix of debt and equity.

18.4.2 MEASURING THE TARGET WEIGHTS

As the firm moves toward a target capital structure, how will it know when it arrives? There are two ways to measure the debt and equity mix in the firm's capital structure.

One method uses target weights based on the firm's book values, or balance sheet amounts, of debt and equity. The weight of debt in the firm's capital structure equals the book value of its debt divided by the book value of its assets. Similarly, the equity weight is the book value of its stockholders' equity divided by total assets. Once the target weights are determined, the firm can issue or repurchase appropriate quantities of debt and equity over time to move the balance sheet numbers toward the target weights.

A second method uses the market values of the firm's debt and equity to compare target and actual weights. The actual weight of debt in the firm's capital structure equals the market value of its debt divided by the market value of its assets. Similarly, the equity weight is the market value of the firm's stockholders' equity divided by the market value of its assets. Calculated this way, bond and stock market price fluctuations, as well as new issues and security repurchases, can move the firm toward or away from its target.

Financial theory favors the second method as most appropriate. Current *market* values are used to compute the various costs of financing, so it is intuitive that *market*-based costs should be weighted by *market*-based weights.

The basic capital structure of a firm may include debt, preferred equity, and common equity. In practice, calculating the cost of these components is sometimes complicated by the existence of hybrid financing structures (e.g., convertible debt) and other variations on straight debt, preferred equity, or common equity.[6] A discussion of this advanced topic is beyond the scope of this book.

---

[6] For insights into how to handle these more complex financing structures, see McKinsey & Company Inc., Tim Koller, Marc Goedhart, and David Wessels, *Valuation: Measuring and Managing the Value of Companies*, 6th ed. (Hoboken, NJ: Wiley, 2015), or most intermediate-level corporate finance textbooks.

As an example, let's compute the WACC for Eastnorth Manufacturing. Assume that Eastnorth Manufacturing has determined that its target capital structure should include one-third debt and two-thirds common equity. Eastnorth Manufacturing's current after-tax cost of debt is 6.0%, and its current cost of retained earnings is 15.0%. What is Eastnorth Manufacturing's WACC, assuming that last year's operations generated sufficient retained earnings to finance this year's capital budget?

Since sufficient new retained earnings exist, Eastnorth Manufacturing will not need to issue shares to implement its capital budget. Thus, the cost of retained earnings will be used to estimate its weighted average cost of capital. The target capital structure is one-third debt and two-thirds common equity. Using equation 18.7, Eastnorth Manufacturing's WACC is the following:

$$\text{WACC} = (1/3)\ (6.0\%) + (2/3)\ (15.0\%)$$
$$= 12.0\%$$

Given current market conditions and Eastnorth Manufacturing's target capital structure weights, the firm should use a discount rate of 12.0% when computing the NPV for average risk projects.[7]

To compare Eastnorth Manufacturing's current capital structure with its target capital structure, let's assume that Eastnorth Manufacturing has two bond issues outstanding. One is rated AA and has a YTM of 8.8%; the other is rated A and yields 9.5%. The firm also has preferred stock and common stock outstanding. The table below shows the current market prices and the number of shares or bonds outstanding. How does Eastnorth Manufacturing's current capital structure compare to its target?

Security	Current price	Number outstanding
AA bonds	$1,050	10,000 bonds
A bonds	1,025	20,000 bonds
Preferred stock	40	250,000 shares
Common stock	50	700,000 shares

To begin, Eastnorth Manufacturing's target capital structure of one-third debt and two-thirds common equity leaves no room for preferred stock. Eastnorth Manufacturing's management has decided not to raise funds with new preferred stock issues. Using the given information, let's compute the market values of Eastnorth Manufacturing's securities and their current market value weights and compare these figures to Eastnorth Manufacturing's target capital structure. A security's market value is found by multiplying its market price by the number of bonds or shares outstanding. The figures in the previous table give these market values and weights:

Security	Market value ($ millions)	Market weight
AA bonds	$10.50	0.138
A bonds	20.50	0.270
Preferred stock	10.00	0.132
Common stock	35.00	0.460
Total	$76.00	1.000

Presently, Eastnorth Manufacturing's capital structure is made up of 41% debt, about 46% common equity, and about 13% preferred equity. To move toward its target capital structure, Eastnorth Manufacturing may want to issue common stock and use the proceeds to purchase outstanding preferred stock and bonds. Eastnorth Manufacturing does not need to restructure its finances immediately. The flotation costs and administrative fees of such a program would be prohibitive. Some movement toward the target capital structure would occur if Eastnorth Manufacturing could identify several positive-NPV projects. Barring a market downtrend, these projects would increase its market value of equity. Also, it could use future additions to retained earnings to repurchase some outstanding debt or preferred equity.

---

[7] For a good case study of estimating the cost of capital for firms in the food processing industry, see Samuel C. Weaver, "Using Value Line to Estimate the Cost of Capital and Industry Capital Structure," *Journal of Financial Education*, Fall 2003, vol. 29, pp. 55–71.

18.4.3 WHAT DO BUSINESSES USE AS THEIR COST OF CAPITAL?

Surveys of U.S. firms find that most firms use after-tax WACC as their required rate of return for projects. Other methods include management-determined target returns or the cost of some specific source of funds. A survey of U.S.-based multinationals found, surprisingly, that one-half of them use a single firm-wide discount rate to evaluate projects regardless of risk differences. The most popular method for estimating the cost of equity is the SML approach; surveys have shown that up to 85% of firms use this method. Because of its assumption regarding growth, few firms use the constant dividend growth model; about 4% of firms in a 2013 survey used this method, compared to 15% of firms in a 1999 survey and about 30% in a 1982 survey. It may take a while, but business managers do learn about financial theory and concepts.[8]

The student who has been watching the financial markets throughout the course, or possibly the past several years, may notice a potential problem with the formulas in this section. The cost of debt relies on current interest rates for a firm's debt. Similarly, the cost of equity relies on current estimates of beta (SML approach) or stock price. These values are always changing. Figure 18.3 shows an nearly 100-year history of investment-grade bond yields, and Figure 18.4 presents a history of stock prices for one of the world's largest firms, ExxonMobil and a firm that just went public in 2012, Facebook. It is obvious changing stock prices make cost of equity estimates problematic.

Although periods occur when corporate bond yields are stable, the effects of the business cycle, Fed policy, and financial market risk premiums have resulted in more variability than stability with respect to interest rates in general and corporate bond yields in particular.

Similarly, stock prices and annual returns show little stability. This is expected, since we learned in Chapter 12 that risk levels determine expected returns; if stock prices were stable, that would not reward investors over time with higher expected returns. Table 12.4 shows historical variability in stocks and other financial assets. In Chapter 12, we reviewed the historical returns and risk of Walgreens and Microsoft stock. In Figure 18.4, we see a similar story: ExxonMobil's and Facebook's stock price are volatile and constantly changing.

As we learned in Chapter 12's discussion of efficient markets, some variability is expected as news (about the global or national economy, a firm's industry, and a specific firm) will be quickly reflected in stock prices. Over the period shown in Figure 18.4, ExxonMobil's stock price ranged from about $56 (mid-2010) to $104 (mid-2014). Facebook hit a low price of about $18 in 2012 and a high of over $200 a share in 2018.

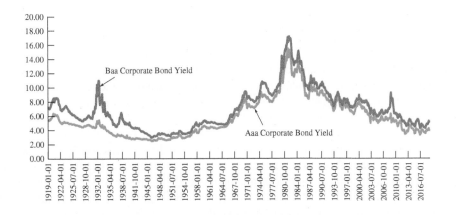

FIGURE 18.3 Corporate bond yields, 1919–2019

Source: FRED data, St. Louis Federal Reserve Bank.

[8] M. Castedello and Schoniger, *Cost of Capital Study 2017*, KPMG; https://assets.kpmg/content/dam/kpmg/ch/pdf/cost-of-capital-study-2017-en.pdf; accessed February 9, 2019. Association for Financial Professionals, *2013 AFP Estimating and Applying Cost of Capital* (October 2013), accessed September 1, 2016, at http://www.afponline.org/docs/default-source/default-document-library/pub/2013-cost-of-capital-survey-highlights. John R. Graham and Campbell R. Harvey, "The Theory and Practice of Corporate Finance: Evidence from the Field," *Journal of Financial Economics*, Vol. 60, No. 1, 2001, pp. 187–243; Lawrence J. Gitman and Pieter A. Vandenberg, "Cost of Capital Techniques Used by Major US Firms: 1997 vs. 1980," *Financial Practice and Education*, Fall 2000, pp. 53–68; Lawrence J. Gitman and Vincent Mercurio, "Cost of Capital Techniques Used by Major U.S. Firms: Survey and Analysis of Fortune's 1000," *Financial Management*, Vol. 14, 1982, pp. 21–29.

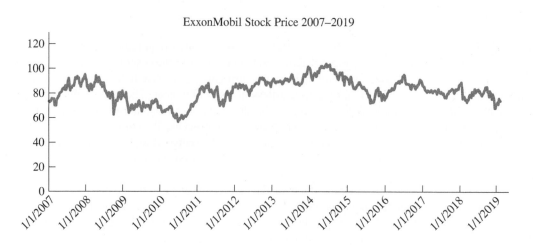

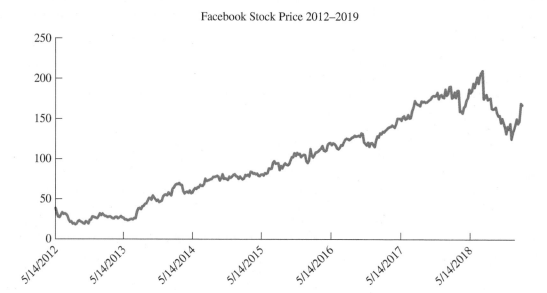

FIGURE 18.4   ExxonMobil and Facebook stock prices

What should a financial manager to do? The answer is to focus on the longer-term, not on day-to-day market fluctuations.[9] Business cycles and financial market cycles come and go, and cost of capital calculations should account for these variations over time, but not with daily revisions.

Rather than focus on the current day's interest rate or stock price, a longer-term perspective is needed. This is appropriate, as the capital investment under consideration is likely long-term as well. Today's costs matter most only if the firm needs to raise capital by getting bank loans, issuing bonds, or issuing shares of stock. If internal funds (accumulated cash and retained earnings) can be used, the firm can use a longer-term average cost of capital that should better reflect the firm's history and prospects rather than current conditions. Some subjective adjustments may be appropriate because of risk perceptions in the financial markets (much like the cost of capital adjustments of project risk in Chapter 17). The firm will have historic information on the difference, or spread, between its costs of debt and equity. Perhaps that spread is 4%. One way to check the reasonableness of a recent cost of capital calculation is to compare the costs of debt and equity; does the new spread differ markedly from 4%? Financial managers can adjust the cost of capital used to evaluate projects based on current

---

[9] Randy Myers, "A Losing Formula," *CFO* (May 2009), pp. 17–18.

financing costs and known, reasonable, historical relationships between financial sources in light of current financial market concerns, or "jitters."

CRISIS Without such adjustments, the cost of capital may appear large during market panics when interest rates spike and/or stock prices fall, such as during the 2007–2009 Great Recession. Financial market history has shown that during a recession is the best time to invest in financial assets if you are an individual, or in your business and product if you are a manager. When others are pessimistic and slashing capital budgets, this is a great time to prepare for the coming business cycle upturn. Cost of capital calculations using current data may appear to rule out any such investing, as the cost of capital will skyrocket as stock prices plunge. But keeping a longer-term value and using current and historical stock/bond premium relationships may lead to financial and strategic decisions to invest in capital budgeting projects.

18.4.4 DIFFICULTY OF MAKING CAPITAL STRUCTURE DECISIONS

Examining the various influences that affect a firm's capital structure is difficult. Unlike NPV or operating cash flow, we have no formula to determine the proportions of debt and equity a firm should use to finance its assets.

But we are not totally lost. Financial theory and research on firm behavior have given us a set of guidelines or principles by which to evaluate a firm's proper mix of debt and equity. We can simplify the discussion by referring only to debt and equity, with little distinction between the various types of debt and equity. We discuss some of the variations in debt and equity later in the chapter.

In the following sections, we'll examine a number of interrelationships affecting a firm's capital structure decisions. First is the firm's growth rate. All else equal, a firm with higher growth levels will need to tap the capital markets more frequently than a slow- or no-growth firm. Second, given a firm's growth rate, the need for outside capital depends upon its return on assets (ROA) and dividend policy. Again, all else equal, a firm with a larger ROA can rely more on retained earnings as a source of financing and will favor equity over debt financing. A firm with a large dividend payout will need more outside capital to finance growth. Next, we will examine some analytical tools and theories advanced and tested to explain firms' capital structures.

Figure 18.5 shows the ratio of long-term debt to total assets for several firms. The graph shows a wide variation in capital structures. Google (now with the corporate name of Alphabet), which went public in 2004 and had a secondary equity offering in 2005, has little debt. Apple and Microsoft, whose true assets are software, ideas, and knowledge rather than bricks and mortar, had low debt ratios but they are rising as they issued debt to take advantage of low interest rates since the Great Recession. Walgreens has a low ratio of long-term debt to assets but that is because it leases, rather than owns, many of its stores to conserve capital. Over most of the time frame, the firms with the highest level

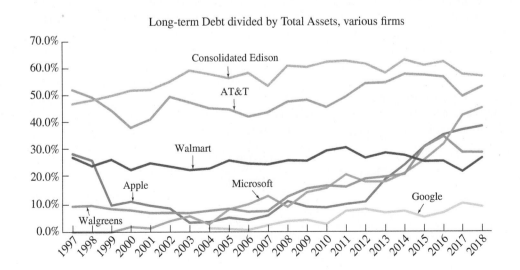

FIGURE 18.5 Long-term debt divided by total assets, various firms, 1997–2018

of debt relative to assets are Consolidated Edison (Con Ed) and AT&T. This is no surprise, since as a utility most of its asset base are fixed assets, which are more amenable to borrowing than ideas or software. In addition, Con Ed, since it is regulated, should be able to charge electric rates sufficient to service the debt interest.

LEARNING ACTIVITY

1. A firm may have only one class of common stock but many bonds outstanding. Data on bonds outstanding for a specific firm can be found in the financial reports on firms' websites and in Mergent's Bond Record, found in your library or on the Internet at https://www.mergent.com.
2. Cost of capital is included in the calculation of economic value added, a measure of firm performance developed by Stern Stewart & Company. Stern Stewart's website, https://www.sternstewart.com, contains information on the importance of the cost of capital as well as practitioner-oriented research reports.

18.5 PLANNING GROWTH RATES

A firm's growth is partly determined by management's strategy to acquire or maintain market share in a growing or stable market. But management's plans for future sales, asset, and financing growth may not happen because of the competitive struggle in the marketplace. Growth that is faster or slower than expected may occur. A simple financial planning tool, the internal growth rate model, is available to determine how quickly a firm can grow without running short of cash.

18.5.1 INTERNAL GROWTH RATE

internal growth rate a measure of how quickly a firm can increase its asset base over the next year without raising outside funds

The **internal growth rate** measures how quickly a firm can increase its asset base over the next year without raising outside funds. It does not measure divisional growth or break down total growth into domestic or international components. The internal growth rate gives a general, company-wide value.

It is equal to the ratio of the expected increase in retained earnings over the next year to the current asset base, as follows:

$$\frac{\text{Expected change in retained earnings}}{\text{Total assets}}$$

This can also be calculated in the following way:

$$\text{Internal growth rate } (g) = \frac{(RR)(ROA)}{1-(RR)(ROA)} \tag{18.8}$$

retention rate the proportion of each dollar of earnings per share that is retained by the firm

dividend payout ratio the proportion of each dollar of earnings that is paid to shareholders as a dividend; equals one minus the retention rate

RR is the firm's retention rate, and ROA is its return on assets. The internal growth rate divides the product of these values by one minus this product.[10] The **retention rate** represents the proportion of every dollar of earnings per share that is retained by the firm; in other words, it is equal to one minus the **dividend payout ratio**.

Suppose a firm pays out 40% of its earnings as dividends and has averaged a 15% ROA for the past several years; how quickly can the firm grow without needing to tap outside financing sources? A 40% dividend payout ratio means the firm's retention rate is $1.00 - 0.40 = 0.60$. Of every dollar of net income, the firm distributes $0.40 as dividends and retains $0.60. With a 15% ROA, equation 18.8 tells us the internal growth rate for the firm is the following:

$$\text{Internal growth rate} = \frac{(0.60)(0.15)}{1-(0.60)(0.15)} = 0.099 \text{ or } 9.9\%$$

---

[10] An end-of-chapter problem (Problem 13) invites you to derive this relationship.

If it relies only on new additions to retained earnings to finance asset acquisition and maintains its past profitability and dividend payout, the firm can increase its asset base by a little less than 10% next year.[11]

The internal growth rate makes the restrictive assumption that the firm will pursue no outside financing sources. Should the firm grow at its internal growth rate, its retained earnings account will continually rise (assuming profitable sales) while its dollar amount of debt outstanding will remain constant. *Thus, the relative amount of debt in its capital structure declines over time and the debt level will likely fall below its proportion in management's ideal financing mix.*

18.5.2 SUSTAINABLE GROWTH RATE

Perhaps a more realistic assumption would be to allow management to borrow funds over time to maintain steady capital structure ratios. As the stockholder's equity account rises from new additions to retained earnings, the firm issues new debt to keep its debt to equity ratio constant over time.

This rate of growth is the sustainable growth rate. It measures how quickly the firm can grow when it uses internal equity and debt financing to keep its capital structure constant over time.

sustainable growth rate the estimate of how quickly a firm can grow when it uses internal equity and debt financing to keep its capital structure constant over time

The sustainable growth rate is computed as follows:

$$\text{Sustainable growth rate} = \frac{(\text{RR})(\text{ROE})}{1-(\text{RR})(\text{ROE})}$$

The firm's retention rate (RR) is multiplied by its return on equity (ROE), divided by one minus this product.[12]

Suppose the firm in the prior example maintains a debt to equity ratio of 1.0 (which is equivalent to an equity multiplier of 2.0) to minimize its financing costs. What would be the firm's sustainable growth rate? From the discussion in Chapter 14 analyzing DuPont, we know that ROE = ROA × equity multiplier.

Since the firm has an ROA of 15%, its ROE equals 15% × 2 = 30%; with an RR of 0.60, the sustainable growth rate equals the following:

$$\text{Sustainable growth rate} = \frac{(0.60)(0.30)}{1-(0.60)(0.30)} = 0.2195 \text{ or } 21.95\%$$

Thus, without outside financing, the firm can increase sales and assets by less than 10%; by maintaining a constant capital structure, the firm can grow by nearly 22% if it can maintain its levels of profitability and earnings retention.

---

[11] Most managers plan and think in terms of sales dollars rather than size, so it may help to relate the internal growth rate to sales growth. If the firm's total asset turnover ratio is expected to remain constant into the foreseeable future, the growth in sales will equal the internal growth rate computed above. For example, suppose the total asset turnover ratio of 2.0 is expected to remain constant over the next few years:

$$\frac{\text{Sales}}{\text{TA}} = 2.0$$

Sales and assets will rise at their respective growth rates:

$$\frac{\text{Sales}\,(1+g_s)}{\text{TA}\,(1+g_a)} = 2.0$$

Then

$$2.0 = \frac{(\text{Sales})(1+g_s)}{(\text{TA})(1+g_a)} = 2.0\frac{(1+g_s)}{(1+g_a)}$$

This implies that $1 + g_s = 1 + g_a$, or that sales growth will equal asset growth.

[12] You have a chance to derive this relationship in one of the end-of-chapter problems (Problem 14).

18.5.3 EFFECTS OF UNEXPECTEDLY HIGHER (OR LOWER) GROWTH

The internal and sustainable growth rates are planning tools. These formulas cannot make a firm grow by a certain prescribed amount. Changing global competition and political and credit market conditions can cause growth to deviate from planned growth.

The internal and sustainable growth rate relationships suggest three measurable influences impacting growth: dividend policy (as reflected in the retention rate), profitability (as measured by ROA), and the firm's capital structure (as measured by the equity multiplier). A fourth influence that is harder to measure is management's preferences and beliefs about using external financing rather than relying solely on changes in retained earnings. Should actual growth differ from planned growth, one or more of these factors will have to be adjusted to prevent financial difficulty or to absorb excess funds.

18.5.3.1 Dividend Policy

A reduction in the dividend payout ratio implies a higher retention rate and the ability for the firm to grow more quickly if all else remains constant. Thus, a quickly growing firm may decide to maintain a low dividend payout (thereby increasing its addition to retained earnings) in an effort to finance its growth. More mature, more-slowly growing firms usually increase their dividend payout (and have smaller relative additions to retained earnings) as growth opportunities diminish.

18.5.3.2 Profitability

Higher ROAs generate more net income, larger additions to retained earnings, and faster growth, when all else is held constant. Recall the equation used in the DuPont analysis in Chapter 14:

$$ROA = Profit\ margin \times Total\ asset\ turnover$$

Management can attempt to change ROAs by influencing these factors should growth outpace or fall short of the planned rate.

18.5.3.3 Capital Structure

The equity multiplier is determined by the firm's financing policy. A firm that uses a larger amount of debt can support a higher sustainable growth rate when all else remains constant. If growth exceeds the sustainable growth rate, a firm can finance the difference by taking on additional debt.

One or more of these variables must deviate from planned levels to accommodate a difference between planned and actual growth. If a firm's growth exceeds the planned rate, management will have to reduce its dividend payout, increase profitability, use more debt, or use a combination of these options. If growth slows, the firm will need to increase its dividend payout, reduce profitability, reduce its use of debt, or choose a combination of these alternatives. If outside financing is needed, the external financing needs calculation from Chapter 14 can help estimate the amount of funds needed.

The firm's ability to grow is affected by management's strategy, by competitive conditions, and by the firm's access to capital and levels of additions to retained earnings. These influences of growth, dividend payout, and the amount of retained earnings determine the firm's need for outside capital. We first learned this in Chapter 14, when estimating a firm's external financing requirements.

As we saw then, a firm's external financing needs can come from short-term financing sources, such as notes payable and reductions in lines of credit as well as spontaneous financing sources, such as accounts payable. We reviewed influences on a firm's short-term/long-term financing mix in Chapter 16. In the next section, we'll examine influences on a firm's long-term financing strategy.

18.6 EBIT/eps ANALYSIS

EBIT/eps analysis allows managers to see how different capital structures affect the earnings and risk levels of their firms

As a first step in capital structure analysis, let's examine how different capital structures affect the earnings and risk of a firm in a simple world with no corporate income taxes. We use a tool of financial analysis called EBIT/eps analysis. EBIT/eps analysis allows managers to see how different capital structures affect the earnings and risk levels of their firms. Specifically, it shows the graphical relationship between a firm's operating earnings, or earnings before interest and taxes (EBIT), and earnings per share (eps). If we ignore taxes, these two quantities differ only by the firm's interest expense and by the fact that eps is net income stated on a per-share basis. Examining scenarios with different EBIT levels can help managers to see the effects of different capital structures on the firm's earnings per share.

Table 18.2   Current and Proposed Capital Structures for the Bennett Corporation

	Current	Proposed
Total assets	$100 million	$100 million
Debt	0 million	50 million
Equity	100 million	50 million
Common stock price	$25	$25
Number of shares	4,000,000	2,000,000
Interest rate	10%	10%

Table 18.3   Scenario Analysis with Current and Proposed Capital Structures

Current – No debt, 4 million shares (millions omitted)		
EBIT 50% below expectations	**Expected**	**EBIT 50% above expectations**
EBIT	$6.00	$12.00	$18.00
– I	0.00	0.00	0.00
NI	$6.00	$12.00	$18.00
eps	$1.50	$3.00	$4.50

Proposed-50% debt (10% coupon), 2 million shares (millions omitted)		
EBIT 50% below expectations	**Expected**	**EBIT 50% above expectations**
EBIT	$6.00	$12.00	$18.00
– I	5.00	5.00	5.00
NI	$1.00	$7.00	$13.00
eps	$0.50	$3.50	$6.50

Let's assume the Bennett Corporation is considering whether it should restructure its financing. As seen in Table 18.2, Bennett currently finances its $100 million in assets entirely with equity. Under the proposed change, Bennett will issue $50 million in bonds and use this money to repurchase $50 million of its stock. If the stock's price is $25 a share, Bennett will repurchase 2 million shares of stock. Bennett expects to pay 10% interest on the new bonds, for an annual interest expense of $5 million.

Assuming that Bennett's expected EBIT for next year is $12 million, let's see how the proposed restructuring may affect earnings per share. For simplicity, we will ignore taxes, so earnings per share (eps) will be computed as (EBIT – interest expense) divided by the number of shares. As shown in Table 18.3, the scenario analysis assumes that Bennett's EBIT will be either $12 million, 50% lower ($6 million), or 50% higher ($18 million). Figure 18.6 graphs the EBIT/eps combinations that result from the scenario analysis of the current and proposed capital structures. For lower EBIT levels, the current all-equity capital structure leads to higher earnings per share. At higher levels of EBIT, the proposed 50% equity 50% debt capital structure results in higher eps levels.

18.6.1 INDIFFERENCE LEVEL

Figure 18.6 shows that the EBIT/eps lines cross. This means that, at some EBIT level, Bennett will be indifferent between the two capital structures, inasmuch as they result in the same earnings per share.

Under Bennett's current capital structure, eps is computed as (EBIT – $0 interest)/4 million shares. Under the proposed structure, eps is calculated as (EBIT – $5 million interest)/2 million shares. To find the level of EBIT where the lines cross – that is, where the combination of eps and EBIT are

FIGURE 18.6 EBIT/
eps analysis, bennett
corporation

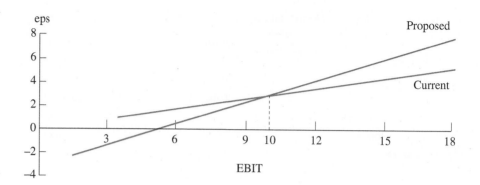

the same under each capital structure – we set these two earnings per-share values equal to each other and solve for EBIT:

$$\frac{EBIT - 0}{4} = \frac{EBIT - 5}{2}$$

Doing so, we learn that the earnings per share under the two plans are the same when EBIT equals $10 million.[13] When EBIT exceeds $10 million, the proposed, more-highly leveraged capital structure will have the higher earnings per share. When EBIT is less than $10 million, the current, less-leveraged capital structure will have the higher earnings per share.

The indifference level of $10 million in EBIT did not occur by chance. It equals the firm's interest cost of 10% multiplied by its total assets ($100 million). In other words, if the firm can earn an operating return on assets (EBIT/TA) greater than its interest cost, leverage is beneficial in that it results in higher earnings per share. If the firm's operating return on assets is less than its 10% interest cost, leverage is expensive relative to the firm's earning ability and results in lower earnings per share. If Bennett believes EBIT will meet expectations at $12 million, the proposed capital structure change is attractive.

18.6.2 IMPLICATIONS OF EBIT/eps ANALYSIS

EBIT/eps analysis has several practical implications. First, as seen, it shows the EBIT ranges where a firm may prefer one capital structure over another. The firm may decide to increase or decrease its financial leverage, depending on whether its expected EBIT is above or below the indifference EBIT level.

Second, EBIT fluctuates over time, depending on sales growth, industry competitive conditions, and the firm's operating leverage. Variations in EBIT will produce changes in earnings per share. Should the firm's expected EBIT lie above the indifference EBIT level, the firm's managers will need to consider potential variation of earnings in their EBIT forecast. Depending on its uncertainty, management may decide to use a more conservative financing strategy with less debt.

This shows the drawback of using EBIT/eps analysis. It inadequately captures the risk facing investors and how it affects shareholder wealth. We seek a capital structure that maximizes the firm's value, not earnings per share. Although eps may rise with financial leverage under certain EBIT values, the eps value that maximizes firm value will likely be less than the maximum earnings per value. The firm's investors, both lenders and shareholders, consider the risk of cash flows when valuing investments. A relationship among debt, eps, and firm value appears in Figure 18.7. Because of the risk of excessive debt, the maximum firm value occurs at a lower debt ratio compared to maximum earnings per share.

---

[13] By cross-multiplying, 2 EBIT = 4 EBIT − 20. Solving for EBIT, we obtain EBIT = 10.

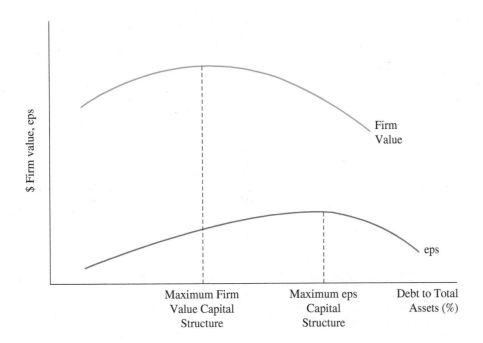

FIGURE 18.7   Firm value, earnings per share, and debt ratios

A firm's **business risk** is measured by its variability in EBIT over time. Business risk is affected by several factors, including the business cycle, competitive pressures, and the firm's operating leverage or its level of fixed operating costs. The following section reviews business risk and the combined effects of business and financial risk on management's choice of a capital structure.

business risk measured by variability in EBIT over time and is determined by the products the firm sells and the production processes it uses

---

DISCUSSION QUESTION 2

EBIT/eps analysis is a simple tool financial managers can use. How good of a tool do you believe it is? Does it make any assumptions that should be considered as part of the decision process to change a firm's capital structure?

Business risk is determined by the products the firm sells and the production processes it uses. The effects of business risk are seen in the variability of operating income or EBIT over time. In fact, one popular measure of a firm's business risk is the standard deviation of EBIT.[14]

Table 18.4 shows a simplified income statement. Because business risk is measured by variability in EBIT or operating income, line items that affect business risk appear on the top half of the income statement between sales revenue and EBIT. This suggests that a firm's business risk is affected by three major influences: unit volume or quantity sold, the relationship between selling price and variable costs, and the firm's fixed costs.

18.7 COMBINED OPERATING AND FINANCIAL LEVERAGE EFFECTS

18.7.1 UNIT VOLUME VARIABILITY

Variability in the quantity sold of the firm's products or services will cause variation in sales revenue, variable costs, and operating income. Fluctuating sales volumes can arise from factors such as pricing strategy from competitive products, new technologies or products, customer impressions of product or service quality, and other factors affecting customer brand loyalty.

---

[14] To control for the effects of firm size when comparing different firms, some use the standard deviation of operating return on assets; that is, the standard deviation of EBIT/Total assets.

Table 18.4   Effects of Business Risk and Financial Risk on a Simplified Income Statement

Impact of Business Risk (Top Half of Income Statement)	Sales revenue (equals price × quantity sold) Less variable costs (such as labor and materials; equals variable cost per unit × quantity) Less fixed costs (such as rent and depreciation expenses) Earnings before interest and taxes (operating income)
Impact of Financial Risk (Bottom Half of Income Statement)	Less interest expense (bank loans, bonds, other debt; a fixed expense as it is not dependent on sales) EBT (earnings before taxes) Less taxes (a variable expense, dependent on EBT) Net Income
	eps = Net Income/Number of Shares

18.7.2 PRICE–VARIABLE COST MARGIN

A second factor affecting business risk is the firm's ability to maintain a constant, positive difference between price and per-unit variable costs. If the margin between price and cost fluctuates, the firm's operating income will fluctuate, too. Competitive pricing pressures, input supply shocks, labor union contracts, and other cost influences can cause the price – variable cost margin to vary over time, thus contributing to business risk.

18.7.3 FIXED COSTS

The variability of sales or revenues over time is a basic operating risk. Furthermore, when fixed operating costs, such as rental payments, lease payments, contractual employee salaries, and general and administrative overhead expenses exist, they create operating leverage and increase business risk. Since fixed costs do not rise and fall along with sales revenues, fluctuating revenues lead to variability in operating income or earnings before income and taxes (EBIT). As we learned in Chapter 14, the effect of operating leverage is that a given percentage change in net sales will result in a greater percentage change in operating income, or EBIT.

Operating leverage affects the top portion of a firm's income statement, as shown in Table 18.4. It relates changes in sales to changes in EBIT, or operating income. We saw in Chapter 14 that the effect of fixed operating costs on a firm's business risk can be measured by the degree of operating leverage (DOL). Equation 18.9 repeats these relationships from Chapter 14:

$$\text{DOL} = \frac{\text{Percentage change in EBIT}}{\text{Percentage change in sales}} = \frac{\text{Sales} - \text{Variable cost}}{\text{Sales} - \text{Variable cost} - \text{Fixed cost}} \qquad (18.9)$$

In a similar fashion, when money is borrowed, financial leverage will be created as the firm will have a fixed financial obligation, or interest, to pay. Financial leverage affects the bottom half of a firm's income statement. A given percentage change in the firm's EBIT will produce a larger percentage change in the firm's net income, or eps. A small percentage change in EBIT may be levered or magnified into a larger percentage change in net income.

18.7.4 DEGREE OF FINANCIAL LEVERAGE

degree of financial leverage (DFL) measures the sensitivity of eps to changes in EBIT

A firm's financial risk reflects its interest expense, or in financial jargon, its financial leverage. A quick way to determine a firm's exposure to financial risk is to compute its degree of financial leverage. The **degree of financial leverage (DFL)** measures the sensitivity of earnings per share to changes in EBIT:

The equation is as follows:

$$\text{DFL} = \frac{\text{Percentage change in eps}}{\text{Percentage change in EBIT}} \qquad (18.10)$$

This definition means that DFL represents the percentage change in earnings per share arising from a 1% change in earnings before interest and taxes. For example, a DFL of 1.25 means the firm's eps will rise (or fall) by 1.25% for every 1% increase (or decrease) in EBIT; a 1% change in EBIT becomes magnified to a 1.25% change in earnings per share.

There is a more straightforward way to compute a firm's DFL that avoids handling percentage changes in variables. This formula is given in equation 18.11:

$$DFL = \frac{EBIT}{EBIT - I} = \frac{EBIT}{EBT} \qquad (18.11)$$

DFL equals the firm's earnings before interest and taxes divided by EBIT minus interest expense, or earnings before taxes (EBT).

Let's use equation 18.11 to find the degree of financial leverage when EBIT equals \$50 and interest expense equals \$10, \$20, and \$0. When EBIT equals \$50 and interest expense equals \$10, DFL equals \$50/(\$50 − \$10) = 1.25. When interest expense is \$20, DFL equals \$50/(\$50 − \$20) = 1.67. Higher interest expense leads to greater financial risk and greater eps sensitivity to changes in EBIT.

When the interest expense is zero, the DFL is \$50/(\$50 − \$0) = 1.00. That is, the percentage change in eps will be the same as the percentage change in EBIT. Without any fixed financial cost, no financial leverage and no magnification effect occur.

18.7.5 TOTAL RISK

Total earnings risk, or total variability in earnings per share, is the result of combining the effects of business risk and financial risk. As shown in Table 18.4, operating leverage and financial leverage combine to magnify a given percentage change in sales to a potentially much greater percentage change in earnings.

Together, operating and financial leverage produce an effect called **combined leverage**. A firm's **degree of combined leverage (DCL)** is the percentage change in eps that results from a 1% change in sales volume.

The equation is as follows:

$$DCL = \frac{\text{Percentage change in eps}}{\text{Percentage change in sales}} \qquad (18.12)$$

A straightforward relationship exists among the degree of operating leverage, the degree of financial leverage, and the degree of combined leverage. A firm's DCL is the product of its degree of operating leverage and its degree of financial leverage[15]:

$$DCL = DOL \times DFL \qquad (18.13)$$

The DCL represents the impact on eps of the effects of operating leverage and financial leverage on a given change in sales revenue.

combined leverage effect on earnings produced by the operating and financial leverage

degree of combined leverage percentage change in eps that results from a 1% change in sales volume

---

[15] Recall that the DOL is the percentage change in EBIT divided by the percentage change in sales; the DFL is the percentage change in eps divided by the percentage change in EBIT. Multiplying these two formulas gives the definition of DCL in equation 18.12:

$$\frac{\text{Percentage change in EBIT}}{\text{Percentage change in sales}} \times \frac{\text{Percentage change in eps}}{\text{Percentage change in EBIT}}$$

$$= DOL \times DFL = \frac{\text{Percentage change in eps}}{\text{Percentage change in sales}} = DCL$$

Table 18.5 Effects of Leverage on the Income Statement

| | | Next year | |
	This year	10% Sales decrease	10% Sales increase
Net sales	$700,000	$630,000	$770,000
Less: variable costs (60% of sales)	420,000	378,000	462,000
Less: fixed costs	200,000	200,000	200,000
Earnings before interest and taxes	80,000	52,000	108,000
Less: interest expenses	20,000	20,000	20,000
Income before taxes	60,000	32,000	88,000
Less: income taxes (30%)	18,000	9,600	26,400
Net income	$42,000	$22,400	$61,600
Percent change in operating income (EBIT)		−35.0%	+35.0%
Percent change in net income		−46.7%	+46.7%

Let's illustrate this concept with a full income statement for this year and a 10% decrease and a 10% increase in net sales for next year, as seen in Table 18.5.

We can estimate, directly, the individual effects of operating and financial leverage and their combined effects. First, from Chapter 14, the DOL is estimated in this way:

$$\text{DOL} = \frac{\text{Sales} - \text{Variable cost}}{\text{Sales} - \text{Variable cost} - \text{Fixed cost}}$$

$$= \frac{\$700,000 - \$420,000}{\$700,000 - \$420,000 - \$200,000} = \frac{\$280,000}{80,000} = 3.50$$

This is the same as the percentage change in EBIT (35%) divided by the percentage change in sales (10%) in Table 18.5:

$$\text{DOL} = \frac{35\%}{10\%} = 3.50$$

The DFL measures the impact of fixed financial expenses and is estimated in the following way:

$$\text{DFL} = \frac{\text{EBIT}}{\text{EBIT} - \text{I}}$$

Thus, DFL is equal to the following:

$$\text{DFL} = \frac{\$80,000}{\$80,000 - \$20,000} = \frac{\$80,000}{\$60,000} = 1.33$$

This is the same as the percentage change in eps (46.7%) divided by the percentage change in EBIT (35%) in Table 18.5:

$$\text{DFL} = \frac{46.7\%}{35.0\%} = 1.33$$

Finally, the DCL can be estimated by finding the product of the DOL and the DFL as follows:

$$DCL = DOL \times DFL$$
$$= 3.5 \times 1.33$$
$$= 4.66$$

Except for rounding, this is the same as the percentage change in eps (46.7%) divided by the percentage change in sales (10%): 46.7%/10% = 4.67.

By knowing the DCL factor, we can estimate next year's change in net income (assuming no major change occurs in the income tax rate) by multiplying the expected percentage change in net sales by the DCL of 4.67. For example, a 10% increase in net sales will increase net income by 46.7% (10% times the combined leverage factor of 4.67). Combined leverage works in both directions, and a decline in net sales might place the firm in a difficult financial position. A 10% decline in sales will be expected to reduce net income and eps by 46.7%.

Using operating and financial leverage produces a compound impact when a change in net sales occurs. Thus, from a risk perspective, the financial manager must use operating and financial leverage to form an acceptable combined leverage effect.

For example, if a firm's stockholders do not like large amounts of risk, a firm with a high DOL may attempt to keep financial leverage low. In other words, it will use relatively less debt and more equity to finance its assets. Likewise, a firm with low business risk (that is, steady sales and low fixed operating expenses), such as an electric utility, can support a higher DFL and use relatively more debt financing. There is no evidence that firms adjust their DOLs and DFLs to match some standard degree of combined leverage, but their relationship does imply a potential trade-off between a firm's business and financial risk.

An insight from our discussion of combined leverage is that a firm with greater business risk may be inclined to use less debt in its capital structure, while a firm with less business risk may use more debt in its capital structure. Theories of financial researchers have shed light on additional influences on the capital structure decision.

18.8 INSIGHTS FROM THEORY AND PRACTICE

18.8.1 TAXES AND NONDEBT TAX SHIELDS

Interest on debt is a tax-deductible expense whereas stock dividends are not; dividends are paid from after-tax dollars. This gives firms a tax incentive to use debt financing.

In reality, the benefits of tax-deductible debt have limits. Business risk leads to EBIT variations over time, which can lead to uncertainty about the firm's ability to fully use future interest deductions. For example, if a firm has a negative or zero operating income, an interest deduction will provide little help; it just makes the pretax losses larger. Firms in lower tax brackets have less tax incentive to borrow than those in higher tax brackets.

In addition, firms have other tax-deductible expenses besides interest. Various cash and noncash expenses, such as depreciation, R&D, and advertising expenses, can reduce operating income. Thus, the tax deductibility of debt becomes less important to firms with large nondebt tax shields. Foreign tax credits, granted by the U.S. government to firms that pay taxes to foreign governments, also diminish the impact of the interest deduction.

18.8.2 BANKRUPTCY COSTS

The major drawback to debt in the capital structure is its legal requirement for timely payment of interest and principal. As the debt/total asset ratio rises, or as earnings become more volatile, the firm will face higher borrowing costs, driven upward by bond investors requiring higher yields to compensate for additional risk.

FIGURE 18.8 The static trade-off hypothesis: weighted average cost of capital versus debt ratio

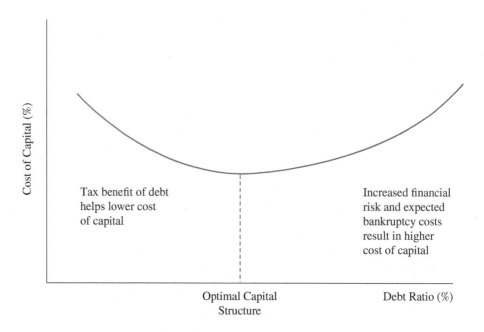

bankruptcy costs explicit expenses, such as legal and accounting fees and court costs, along with implicit costs, such as the use of management time and skills in preventing and escaping bankruptcy

A rational marketplace will evaluate the probability and associated costs of bankruptcy for a levered firm. **Bankruptcy costs** include explicit expenses, such as legal and accounting fees and court costs, along with implicit costs, such as the use of management time and skills in preventing and escaping bankruptcy. Marketing the firm's products and keeping good people on staff is difficult when the firm is nearing bankruptcy.[16] An efficient market will evaluate the present value of the expected bankruptcy costs and reduce its estimate of the firm's value accordingly.

static trade-off hypothesis a theory that states firms will balance the advantages of debt with its disadvantages

The **static trade-off hypothesis** states that firms will balance the advantages of debt (its lower cost and tax deductibility of interest) with its disadvantages (greater possibility of bankruptcy and the value of explicit and implicit bankruptcy costs). This is illustrated in Figure 18.8. At low debt levels, using debt more is beneficial because debt's lower cost lowers the weighted average cost of capital (WACC) and increases the firm's value. But further increases in debt beyond the optimal capital structure level reduce the firm's value, as investors' perceptions of the increased cost of bankruptcy outweigh the tax benefits of additional debt.

Bond ratings, discussed in Chapter 10, guide investors and managers in evaluating the risk of increasing debt to the capital structure. Studies have shown the probability of financial distress and bankruptcy rises as a firm's bond ratings decline. Some firms use their bond rating as a guide for their capital structure decision; for example, maintaining debt at a level consistent with an "A" bond rating. To preserve some financing flexibility, firms may keep their debt ratios lower than necessary to maintain their target debt rating. So, should they need to raise additional debt, they can do so and still be able to maintain their desired rating.

Table 18.6 shows the decline in senior debt ratings among U.S. firms. In 1980, 50% of firms with rated senior debt had a rating of A or higher. In 1999, in good economic times, only 18% of firms had an A rating or better; by 2006, the proportion had sunk lower to 11%. This has the opposite effect on low-rated issues; the percentage of junk bonds (rated BB or lower) has swelled from 32% in 1980 to 71% in 2006. Several factors may account for this decline in credit quality, including more risk-tolerant investors, more risk-taking corporate managers, and perceptions of lower bankruptcy costs. In 2019, only two U.S. corporations were AAA rated: Johnson & Johnson and Microsoft.[17]

---

[16] Potential customers shy away from a financially troubled firm fearing it may not survive to provide warranty service or spare parts for their products. Customers may also fear financial distress may lead management to reduce customer service or product maintenance, such as the decline in ridership for an airline when it declares bankruptcy. Good employees with marketable skills may decide to change jobs rather than risk unemployment due to business failure.

[17] In April 2016, due to declining oil prices and steady capital spending plans, S&P downgraded ExxonMobil from AAA to AA+. See Ciara Linnane, "ExxonMobil's downgrade leaves just two AAA-rated companies in the U.S.," accessed July 14, 2016, http://www. marketwatch.com/story/exxon-mobils-downgrade-leaves-just-two-aaa-rated-companies-in-the-us-2016-04-26. In April 2014, ADP (Automatic Data Processing) was downgraded from AAA following the spin-off of a subsidiary, with plans to use the proceeds to repurchase stock. A fifth firm, Pfizer, downgraded to AA due to the debt and cash flow aspects of its 2009 acquisition of Wyeth Labs.

Table 18.6   Distribution of U.S. Industrial Senior Debt Ratings

Rating	Percentage of firms with rating in 1980	Percentage of firms with rating in 1999	Percentage of firms with rating in 2006
AAA/AA	17	5	2
A	33	13	9
BBB	18	20	18
BB	22	24	25
B	7	32	42
CCC/D	3	6	4

Sources: Serena Ng, "Junk Turns Golden, but May Be Laced With Tinsel," *The Wall Street Journal* (January 4, 2007), pp. C1, C2; David Lindorff, "Who Needs a Triple A?" *Treasury and Risk Management* (May/June 2000), pp. 47–48.

18.8.3 AGENCY COSTS

From Chapter 13, we know that agency costs are restrictions placed on corporate managers to limit their discretion. They measure the cost of distrust between investors and management. To protect bondholders, covenants may require the firm to maintain a minimum liquidity level or they may restrict future debt issues, future dividend payments, or certain forms of financial restructuring. Agency costs may take the form of explicit expenses, such as a requirement that the firm's finances be periodically audited.

The cost to the firm's shareholders of excessive covenants and interference with management discretion will likely cause firms to avoid excessive debt in the United States. In other words, the relationship between the level of agency costs and firm debt will look similar to that of bankruptcy costs and firm debt in Figure 18.8. The joint effect of bankruptcy and agency costs will reduce the optimal debt financing level for a firm below the level that would be appropriate if agency costs were zero.

GLOBAL The situation may be different for non-U.S. companies. Agency costs may differ across national borders as a result of different accounting principles, banking structures, and securities laws and regulations. U.S. and UK firms use more equity financing than firms in France, Germany, and Japan, which use relatively more debt financing. Some argue these apparent differences can be explained by differences in equity and debt agency costs across the countries.[18] For example, agency costs of equity seem to be lower in the United States and the United Kingdom. These countries have more accurate systems of accounting than the other countries, with higher auditing standards. Dividends and financial statements are distributed to shareholders more frequently, as well, which allows shareholders to monitor management more easily.

Germany, France, and Japan, on the other hand, all have systems of debt finance that may reduce the agency costs of lending. In these countries, a bank can hold an equity stake in a corporation, meet the bulk of the corporation's borrowing needs, and have representation on the corporate board of directors. Corporations can own stock in other companies and have representatives on other companies' boards. Companies frequently get financial advice from groups of banks and other large corporations with which they have interlocking directorates. These institutional arrangements reduce the monitoring and agency costs of debt; thus, debt ratios are higher in France, Germany, and Japan.[19]

18.8.4 A FIRM'S ASSETS AND ITS FINANCING POLICY

Firms' asset structures and capital structures are related because of agency and bankruptcy costs. Evidence shows that firms with fungible, tangible assets (i.e., assets in place that can be easily sold and used by another firm, such as railroad cars or automobiles) use more debt financing than firms with

---

[18] See J. Rutherford, "An International Perspective on the Capital Structure Puzzle," *Midland Corporate Finance Journal*, Fall 1985, pp. 60–72. For a perspective on several countries in the Asia Pacific region, see Rataporn Deesomsak, Krishna Paudyal, and Gioia Pescetto, "The Determinants of Capital Structure: Evidence from the Asia Pacific Region," *Journal of Multinational Financial Management*, vol. 14, issue 4–5, 2004, pp. 387–405.

[19] Higher debt ratios exist in these countries, after allowing for differences in accounting principles.

many intangible assets. Examples of intangible assets include growth opportunities, the value of the firm's R&D efforts, and customer loyalty built and maintained through large advertising expenditures.

Agency costs and bankruptcy costs impose lighter burdens on financing for investments in tangible assets. A lender can more easily monitor the use of tangible assets, such as physical plant and equipment. Well-developed accounting rules govern methods for tracking such asset values. Also, tangible assets can be sold and reused, and they will not lose all of their value following a period of financial distress. Such may not be the case for intangible assets whose value mainly resides within the firm.

18.8.5 THE PECKING ORDER HYPOTHESIS

One perspective on firms' capital structure decisions is based on repeated observations of how corporations seem to raise funds over time. The theory behind this perspective is based on the belief that management knows more about the firm and its opportunities than does the financial marketplace, and it is based on the belief that management does not want to be forced to issue equity when stock prices are depressed.

Evidence shows that corporations rely mainly on additions to retained earnings to finance growth and capital budgeting projects. If they need outside financing, firms typically issue debt first, as it imposes lower risk on the investor than equity and it costs less to the corporation. Should a firm approach its debt capacity, it may well favor hybrid securities, such as convertible bonds, over common stock. As a last resort, the firm will issue common equity. Thus, the firm has a financing "pecking order" rather than a goal to maintain a specific target debt/equity ratio over time.

pecking order hypothesis a theory that managers prefer to use additions to retained earnings to finance the firm, then debt, and as a final resort, new equity

Under this pecking order hypothesis, financial theory implies that firms have no optimal debt/equity ratios.[20] Instead, they follow the pecking order, exhausting internal equity (retained earnings) first and resorting to external equity (new issues of common stock) as a last resort. Observed debt ratios represent the cumulative result of a firm's need to use external financing over time and reflect the joint effects of growth, attractive investment opportunities, and dividend policy.

Under the pecking order hypothesis, firms with higher profitability should have lower debt ratios, as these firms' additions to retained earnings reduce their need to borrow. Under the static trade-off hypothesis, a firm with higher profitability should have a lower probability of bankruptcy and a higher tax rate, thus leading to *higher* debt ratios. Most empirical evidence resolves this conflict in favor of the pecking order hypothesis; studies show more-profitable firms tend to have lower debt ratios.

18.8.6 MARKET TIMING

market timing hypothesis firms time the market by issuing stock when their stock prices are high and repurchasing shares when their stock values are low

Like the pecking order hypothesis, this perspective is based upon observations of how firms raise funds in practice. The market timing hypothesis states that firms time the equity market by issuing stock when their stock prices are high and repurchasing shares when their stock values are low.[21] Research studies have found that firms prefer to issue stock when earnings expectations by the market are overly optimistic. Managers have admitted that overvaluation and undervaluation of their stock is an important consideration in issuing equity.[22] Researchers argue that firms, after issuing or repurchasing equity in attempts to time the equity market, do not move the firm back to its former capital structure. Rather, low-leverage firms are those that were, on balance, successful in raising funds when their equity market values were high; high-leverage firms, on average, are those that raised funds when their equity market values were low.

As noted earlier in this chapter, firms can time interest rates by increasing their relative use of debt when interest rates are perceived to be low, as was the case in 2012–2016.

---

[20] Stewart C. Myers and Nicholas S. Majluf, "Corporate Financing and Investment Decisions When Firms Have Information That Investors Do Not Have," *Journal of Financial Economics*, vol. 13, 1984, pp. 187–221; Stewart C. Myers, "The Capital Structure Puzzle," *Journal of Finance*, vol. 39, 1984, pp. 575–592.

[21] Malcolm Baker and Jeffrey Wurgler, "Market Timing and Capital Structure," *Journal of Finance*, vol. 57, no. 1, (February 2002), pp. 1–32.

[22] John R. Graham and Campbell R. Harvey, "The Theory and Practice of Corporate Finance: Evidence from the Field," *Journal of Financial Economics*, vol. 60, 2001, pp. 187–243.

An apparent implication of the pecking order and market timing hypotheses is that the firm has no optimal capital structure. What implication does this have for computing a cost of capital and using it to evaluate capital budgeting projects? The answer: hardly any. Recall that the WACC represents the minimum required return on a firm's average risk capital budgeting projects. The target capital structure weights reflect *management's* impression of a capital structure that is *sustainable* in the long run, and that allows financing flexibility over time. Using the target structure and current financing costs, management can compute the weighted average cost of capital. The cost of capital calculation is paramount; should a firm fail to earn an appropriate return on its capital budgeting projects, shareholder wealth and firm value will decline.

Part of the uncertainty over which theoretical perspective may be correct arises from capital structure choices that depart from "plain vanilla" debt and equity. Firms have devised a myriad of financing flavors, as we discuss next.

18.8.7 BEYOND DEBT AND EQUITY

Bright Wall Street investment bankers have introduced many variations on these two themes in attempts to market new and different instruments to meet the needs of many kinds of issuers and investors.[23] Today, firms can choose among various security issues, as we saw in Chapter 10. Consequently, many firms have several debt and equity layers on their balance sheets.

Debt can be made convertible to equity. Its maturity can be extended or shortened at the firm's option. Debt issues can be made senior or subordinate to other debt issues. Coupon interest rates can be fixed, float up or down along with other interest rates, or be indexed to a commodity price.[24] Some bond issues do not pay interest. Corporations can issue bonds in the United States or overseas. Bonds can be sold alone or with warrants attached that allow the bond investor to purchase shares of common stock at predetermined prices over time.

Likewise, equity variations exist. Preferred stock has a claim on the firm that is junior to the bondholder claim but senior to the common shareholder claim. Preferred stock can pay dividends at a fixed or a variable rate.

Even types of common stock can differ. Firms can have different classes of common equity. Some classes can provide holders with higher levels of dividend income. Some classes may have superior voting rights. Examples of such firms include Google, Facebook, Ford Motor Company, and Visa. Firms have issued separate classes of equity to finance acquisitions, distributing part of the acquired firm's earnings as dividends to holders of that particular class of stock. Such was the case with General Motors. It issued its Class E stock to finance its acquisition of EDS in the 1980s; dividends on the Class E shares were determined by the earnings of the EDS subsidiary.

All these variations of debt and equity give the firm valuable flexibility. Corporate financial managers' decisions about the structure of a security issue may be more difficult now, but these choices also can allow them to lower the cost of capital and increase firm value.[25]

18.8.8 GUIDELINES FOR FINANCING STRATEGY

We have covered a lot of ground and a lot of controversy. Let's summarize the practical implications of these discussions and list the influences of theory and real-world evidence on a firm's capital structure decisions.

---

[23] Finance is not just finance; it sometimes involves marketing research and analysis. Wall Street firms serve two customers: issuers and investors. By designing innovative securities to better meet their customers' needs, investment bankers can exploit market niches by being the first mover into a new product area. Such innovation will attract business, enhance income, and increase the firm's reputation among market players.

[24] For example, a silver mining firm whose profits and cash flow are sensitive to silver's market price can reduce its financial leverage by issuing bonds that pay interest at a rate related to silver price fluctuations.

[25] An accessible review of issues related to capital structure and cost of capital is available in Zander's 8-part series "WACC: Practical Guide for Strategic Decision-Making" found on http://zanders.eu/en/latest-insights/wacc-practical-guide-for-strategic-decision-making-part-1 with subsequent parts ending in 2, 3, and so on. Zanders, Treasury and Finance Solutions, is a European-based consulting firm. Their series on WACC was featured on the gtnews website, March 2006–March 2007.

18.8.8.1 Business Risk

Firms in the same industry will generally face the same business risks. Many financial managers confess they examine their competitors' capital structures to determine if their own financial strategies are appropriate. A firm's DOL affects the amount of debt it can issue. Firms with highly variable EBIT cannot afford to issue large amounts of debt, as the combined effects of high business and financial risk may imperil the firm's future. In general, greater EBIT variability reduces the firm's reliance on debt.[26]

18.8.8.2 Taxes and Nondebt Tax Shields

Under current tax regulations, the debt interest deduction is a strong influence in favor of debt. The tax incentive for debt financing can diminish as a firm accumulates nondebt tax shields, such as depreciation expense, R&D, and large advertising outlays.

18.8.8.3 Mix of Tangible and Intangible Assets

Agency costs and bankruptcy costs can make debt less attractive as a financing alternative for firms with large amounts of intangible assets, such as goodwill, customer loyalty, R&D, and growth opportunities.

18.8.8.4 Financial Flexibility

Among the greatest concern of financial managers is maintaining access to capital. Without the ability to raise financing, a firm may have to pass up attractive investment opportunities, or a temporary cash crunch may push it to the edge of default. Loss of financial flexibility can disrupt the firm more than the strictest bond covenants. Some firms seek financial flexibility by maintaining financial slack or unused debt capacity. One way to do this is to maintain an investment-grade bond rating or to maintain large lines of credit.

It may be good to have financing that can be eliminated if it is unnecessary. The firm can arrange for debt financing with a maturity matching the expected period of need. For maturity matching, debt holds an important advantage over preferred stock or common stock financing, because equity securities do not have a stated maturity, which makes it possible to retire them conveniently. A lease arrangement for fixed assets is advantageous, because the lease term may be set to coincide with the duration of the need for the assets.

18.8.8.5 Control of the Firm

Common shareholders receive dividends and have voting control of the firm. Additional equity issues will likely reduce per-share dividends and dilute control. If shareholders worry about control, they may force a firm to use more debt financing and less external equity financing.

18.8.8.6 Profitability

Firms with above-average profitability can reduce flotation costs and restrictive debt covenants by relying on internal equity to finance capital budgeting projects. More-profitable firms tend to use less debt financing.

18.8.8.7 Financial Market Conditions

A firm can minimize its financing costs by issuing debt when interest rates are near cyclical lows, especially if economists forecast rising rates in the future. Likewise, it is advantageous to issue stock when stock prices are high rather than depressed.

18.8.8.8 Management's Attitude Toward Debt and Risk

When push comes to shove, it is people, meaning the management team, who decide about financing policy. Some management teams may be more conservative and hesitant to issue debt; others may be more aggressive and willing to increase the firm's financial leverage. Their judgment and expectations for the firm's financial future will affect the firm's capital structure.

---

[26] Securities can reduce the adverse effects of price swings that might contribute to business risk. Bonds with coupons that rise and fall with changes in commodity prices, market interest rates, or foreign currencies can mitigate the effects of EBIT variations on net income. Firms can reduce political risk exposure from their foreign operations by financing foreign assets with host country bank loans or debt issues.

DISCUSSION QUESTION 3

Since its founding, Facebook has had very little long-term debt on its balance sheet. You've been hired as a consultant to Facebook's board. Explain if you would recommend a change in Facebook's capital structure policy – and why.

LEARNING ACTIVITY

1. Learn about bond default rates and financial distress in discussions of S&P ratings such as the one at https://www.spratings.com/documents/20184/774196/2018AnnualGlobalCorporateDefaultAndRat ingTransitionStudy.pdf.

2. Cutting-edge research on capital structure issues and many other finance topics can be found from the links on https://www.ssrn.com/en/index.cfm/fen/, the home page of the Financial Economics Network. Another site, https://www.cfo.com, contains items of interest on financing and other corporate finance topics.

- **Institutions and Markets** A firm's capital structure is affected by the costs it faces from raising capital. Depository institutions and investment banks funnel savings to those wanting to raise funds. They do so in a way that lowers flotation and other transactions costs associated with raising funds, thereby making it easier for firms to raise capital. Security analysts and bond rating agencies convey opinions to investors regarding the attractiveness of a firm's securities.

- **Investments** Dividends and the price appreciation potential in equity are attractive to many investors. Investors examine a firm's prospects and "vote with their dollars" by deciding which investments look most attractive from a risk/expected return trade-off. The market prices of a firm's securities and the ratings (given the firm's bonds) are used as inputs into the firm's decision-making process, because they determine the cost of financing the firm's assets. Therefore, they are a cost the firm must consider in its capital budgeting decisions.

- **Financial Management** Financial managers need to listen to the market. Trends in interest rates will affect the firm's choice of short-term and long-term borrowing. Changes in stock prices that differ from those of the overall market or the firm's industry group send positive or negative messages to managers about how investors evaluate the firm's future prospects. Financial capital is expensive; the cost of financing assets, whether in the form of higher inventory or equipment, must be part of the firm's investment decisions.

SUMMARY

LO 18.1 The capital structure decision is a difficult but important one for managers to make. An inappropriate mix of debt and equity can lead to higher financing costs, which will hurt shareholders' wealth. It can affect capital budgeting actions, too; as we learned in this chapter, the after-tax cost of capital is the required return on average risk capital budgeting projects. The cost of capital will be higher than it should be if management selects a target capital structure that has too little debt compared to equity – or too much.

LO 18.2 The required return on a capital budget project is the return needed to pay for its appropriate financing sources. A firm's target capital structure and financing costs determine the overall cost of capital (also called the weighted average cost of capital). This weighted average cost of capital is the required return for an average risk project. In line with the expected return/risk trade-off, safer projects should have lower costs of capital (required returns) and higher risk projects should have higher costs of capital (required returns). In finance, we have three different terms for the same concept: cost of capital, required return, and discount rate all refer to the same concept. From the financing side, it is the cost of capital; from the capital budgeting perspective it is the required return and required return is used as the discount rate to find a project's NPV.

LO 18.3 We reviewed how to estimate the cost of debt, which must be the firm's after-tax cost of debt, as interest is tax-deductible. The after-tax cost of debt is used for consistency, as all other costs (preferred stock, common stock, retained earnings) are already after-tax. The costs of preferred and common equity are "after tax" as dividends are paid out from net income. In addition, as we learned in Chapter 17, capital budget cash flows are after-tax cash flows. We want to discount after-tax cash flows with after-tax cost of capital.

LO 18.4 Once a target capital structure is selected, the cost of each financing source is weighted by its target weight to find the weighted average cost of capital (WACC). The WACC will be the required return when doing capital budgeting analysis of an average risk project.

LO 18.5 A firm with higher sales and asset growth, all else the same, will need more outside financing. If the firm has adequate profits, annual additions to retained earnings can internally finance much of the growth; if the firm does not have adequate profits, the firm will need to access the capital markets to either raise debt or equity financing – or both. And if a profitable firm decides to change its dividend policy, this will affect future additions to retained earnings and the ability of the firm to rely on internal equity financing for future capital budgeting projects. To summarize: all else equal,

- Faster growth leads to greater financing needs.
- Higher profits allow the firm to rely more on internal equity (additions to retained earnings) to finance growth.
- Higher dividend payouts lead to lower additions to retained earnings, less ability to rely on internal equity as a source of financing, and greater reliance on capital markets to raise debt and equity. Since it is less costly to issue debt (and debt does not dilute the current stockholders' ownership of the firm), firms tend to issue debt as external financing source – something we first saw back in Figure 10.1.

LO 18.6 This chapter reviews EBIT/eps analysis. EBIT/eps analysis is used to compare two capital structures (usually a firm's current capital structure and a proposed change). EBIT/eps analysis is a visual tool to help management see how sensitive eps is to changes in EBIT. EBIT/eps analysis graphs combinations of EBIT and eps for each capital structure. Most of the time, there will be an "indifference point" where the two EBIT/eps lines cross. If management believes EBIT will fall below this indifference level, the lower debt capital structure will likely result in a higher earnings per share. If EBIT is likely to be greater than the indifference level, the more-highly leveraged capital structure will likely have higher earnings per share.

LO 18.7 This chapter reviews several tools used to examine a firm's capital structure, including business risk, financial risk, and combined leverage. Business risk is the variability of EBIT (operating income) over time. Items such as unit sales variability, variability in price-cost margins, and the level of fixed operating costs affect a firm's business risk. The higher the business risk, the less willing one may think that management would be to take on financial risk. Financial risk occurs when there are fixed financing costs – that is, interest expense – in the firm's capital structure. We can compute the degree of operating leverage (DOL) to estimate the effect of fixed operating costs; DOL measures the effect on EBIT of a 1% change in sales revenue. The degree of financial leverage (DFL) measures the impact of fixed financing costs; it equals the percentage change in earnings per share for each 1% change in EBIT. Taken together, if we multiply the DOL and DFL, we have the degree of combined leverage (DCL). The DCL measures the percent change in earnings per share of a 1% change in sales.

LO 18.8 Several findings of theoretical and empirical studies indicate a broad number of influences on a firm's capital structure decision. These include management's desire to balance the benefits and drawbacks of debt, financing pecking orders (to finance firm expansion, managers prefer to use additions to retained earnings, then to issue debt, and finally to issue new shares of stock), market timing (issue stock when share prices are high), and agency cost issues, among others.

KEY TERMS

bankruptcy costs	degree of financial leverage (DFL)	market timing hypothesis	static trade-off hypothesis
business risk	dividend payout ratio	optimum debt/equity mix	sustainable growth rate
capital structure	EBIT/eps analysis	pecking order hypothesis	weighted average cost of
combined leverage	flotation costs	retention rate	capital (WACC)
cost of capital	internal growth rate		
degree of combined leverage (DCL)			

1. **(LO 18.1)** What is a firm's capital structure?

2. **(LO 18.1)** Explain why determining a firm's optimum debt/equity mix is important.

3. **(LO 18.1)** Briefly describe the trends that have occurred in the corporate use of debt.

4. **(LO 18.1)** How have the Fed's policies since the 2007–2009 Great Recession affected corporate financing decisions?

5. **(LO 18.1)** How did the Fed's loose money policies after the 2007–2009 Great Recession affect investors?

6. **(LO 18.1)** Following the Fed's efforts to lower interest rates, what actions by investors increased their potential exposure to risk?

7. **(LO 18.2)** What is the relationship between a firm's cost of capital and investor required rates of return?

8. **(LO 18.3)** How can a firm estimate its cost of debt financing?

9. **(LO 18.3)** Describe how the cost of preferred stock is determined.

10. **(LO 18.3)** Describe two methods for estimating the cost of retained earnings.

11. **(LO 18.3)** How does the cost of new common stock differ from the cost of retained earnings?

12. **(LO 18.4)** What is the weighted average cost of capital (WACC)? Describe how it is calculated.

13. **(LO 18.4)** Should book value weights or market value weights be used to evaluate a firm's current capital structure weights? Why?

14. **(LO 18.5)** The management of Albar Incorporated has decided to increase the firm's use of debt from 30% to 45% of assets. How will this affect its internal growth rate in the future? Its sustainable growth rate?

15. **(LO 18.5)** A booming economy creates an unexpectedly high sales growth rate for a firm with a low internal growth rate. How can the firm respond to this unplanned sales increase?

16. **(LO 18.5)** How does management's strategy toward corporate growth and dividends affect its capital structure policy?

17. **(LO 18.6)** What is EBIT/eps analysis? What information does it provide managers?

18. **(LO 18.6)** Describe the term "indifference level" in conjunction with EBIT/eps analysis.

19. **(LO 18.7)** Describe how a firm's business risk can be measured, and indicate how operating leverage impacts business risk.

20. **(LO 18.7)** How is financial leverage created? Describe how the degree of financial leverage is calculated.

21. **(LO 18.7)** Briefly explain the concepts of business risk, operating leverage, and financial leverage in terms of an income statement.

22. **(LO 18.7)** How might the following influences affect a firm's business risk? Consider each separately.
    a. Imports increase the level of competition.
    b. Labor costs decline.
    c. Healthcare costs (provided for all employees) increase.
    d. The firm's proportion of social security and unemployment insurance taxes rises.
    e. Adoption of new technology allows the firm to produce the same output with fewer employees.

23. **(LO 18.7)** How might the following influences affect a firm's financial risk? Consider each separately.
    a. Interest rates on the firm's short-term bank loans are reduced.
    b. The firm refinances a mortgage on one of its buildings at a lower interest rate.
    c. Tax rates decline.
    d. The firm's stock price rises.
    e. The firm suffers a sales and operating income decline.

24. **(LO 18.7)** What is meant by the degree of combined leverage?

25. **(LO 18.7)** Describe how the degree of combined leverage (DCL) can be determined by the degree of operating leverage (DOL) and the degree of financial leverage (DFL).

26. **(LO 18.8)** Briefly explain how the factors of flexibility and timing affect the mix between debt and equity capital.

27. **(LO 18.8)** How do corporate control concerns affect a firm's capital structure?

28. **(LO 18.8)** If a firm is eligible to receive tax credits, how might that affect its debt use?

29. **(LO 18.8)** Describe the reasoning behind the static trade-off hypothesis.

30. **(LO 18.8)** How do agency costs affect a firm's optimal capital structure? How can differences in agency costs explain capital structure differences across countries?

31. **(LO 18.8)** How do you expect the capital structures of two firms to differ if one is involved in steel production and the other designs software to solve business problems?

32. **(LO 18.8)** What implications might the pecking order and market timing hypotheses have for an optimal capital structure? Is the WACC an important concept under these hypotheses?

PROBLEMS

1. AQ&Q has EBIT of $2 million, total assets of $10 million, stockholders' equity of $4 million, and pretax interest expense of 10%.
   a. What is AQ&Q's indifference level of EBIT?
   b. Given its current situation, might it benefit from increasing or decreasing its use of debt? Explain.
   c. Suppose AQ&Q's average tax rate is 40%. How does this affect your answers to (a) and (b)?

2. URA Incorporated has an operating income of $5 million, total assets of $45 million, outstanding debt of $20 million, and annual interest expense of $3 million.
   a. What is URA's indifference level of EBIT?
   b. Given its current situation, might URA benefit from increasing or decreasing its use of debt? Explain.
   c. Suppose forecasted net income is $4 million next year. If it has a 40% average tax rate, what will be its expected level of earnings before interest and taxes (EBIT)? Will this forecast change your answer to (b)? Why?

3. Stern's Stews Inc. is considering a new capital structure. Its current and proposed capital structures are the following:

	Current	Proposed
Total assets	$150 million	$150 million
Debt	25 million	100 million
Equity	125 million	50 million
Common stock price	$50	$50
Number of shares	2,500,000	1,000,000
Interest rate	12%	12%

Stern's Stews' president expects next year's EBIT to be $20 million, but it may be 25% higher or lower. Ignoring taxes, perform an EBIT/eps analysis. What is the indifference level of earnings before interest and taxes? Should Stern's Stews change its capital structure? Why?

4. Faulkner's Fine Fries Inc. (FFF) is thinking about reducing its debt burden. Given the following capital structure information and an expected EBIT of $50 million (plus or minus 10%) next year, should FFF change their capital structure?

	Current	Proposed
Total assets	$750 million	$750 million
Debt	450 million	300 million
Equity	300 million	450 million
Common stock price	$30	$30
Number of shares	10,000,000	15,000,000
Interest rate	12%	12%

5. Redo Problem 4, assuming the less-leveraged capital structure will result in a borrowing cost of 10% and a common stock price of $40.

6. A firm has sales of $10 million, variable costs of $4 million, fixed expenses of $1.5 million, interest costs of $2 million, and a 30% average tax rate.
   a. Compute its DOL, DFL, and DCL.
   b. What will be the expected level of EBIT and net income if next year's sales rise 10%?
   c. What will be the expected level of EBIT and net income if next year's sales fall 20%?

7. Here are the income statements for Genatron Manufacturing Corporation for 2019 and 2020

Income Statement	2019	2020
Net sales	$1,300,000	$1,500,000
Cost of goods sold	780,000	900,000
Gross profit	$520,000	$600,000
General and administrative	150,000	150,000
Marketing expenses	130,000	150,000
Depreciation	40,000	53,000
Interest	45,000	57,000
Earnings before taxes	$155,000	$190,000
Income taxes	62,000	76,000
Net income	$93,000	$114,000

Assuming one-half of the general and administrative expenses are fixed costs, estimate Genatron's DOL, DFL, and DCL in 2019 and 2020.

8. The Nutrex Corporation wants to calculate its WACC. Its target capital structure weights are 40% long-term debt and 60% common equity. The before-tax cost of debt is estimated to be 10% and the company is in the 40% tax bracket. The current risk-free interest rate is 8% on Treasury bills. The expected return on the market is 13% and the firm's stock beta is 1.8.
   a. What is Nutrex's cost of debt?
   b. Estimate Nutrex's expected return on common equity using the security market line (SML).
   c. Calculate the after-tax WACC.

9. The following are balance sheets for the Genatron Manufacturing Corporation for the years 2019 and 2020:

Balance Sheet	2019	2020
Cash	$50,000	$40,000
Accounts receivable	200,000	260,000
Inventory	450,000	500,000
Total current assets	700,000	800,000
Fixed assets (net)	300,000	400,000
Total assets	$1,000,000	$1,200,000
Bank loan, 10%	$90,000	$90,000
Accounts payable	130,000	170,000
Accruals	50,000	70,000
Total current liabilities	$270,000	$330,000
Long-term debt, 12%	300,000	400,000
Common stock, $10 par	300,000	300,000
Capital surplus	50,000	50,000
Retained earnings	80,000	120,000
Total liabilities and equity	$1,000,000	$1,200,000

   a. Calculate the WACC based on book value weights. Assume an after-tax cost of new debt of 8.63% and a cost of common equity of 16.5%.
   b. The current market value of Genatron's long-term debt is $350,000. The common stock price is $20 per share and 30,000 shares are outstanding. Calculate the WACC using market value weights and the component capital costs in (a).
   c. Recalculate the WACC based on book value and market value weights assuming the before-tax cost of debt will be 18%, the company is in the 40% income tax bracket, and the after-tax cost of common equity capital is 21%.

10. The Basic Biotech Corporation wants to determine its WACC. Its target capital structure weights

are 50% long-term debt and 50% common equity. The before-tax cost of debt is estimated to be 10%, and the company is in the 30% tax bracket. The current risk-free interest rate is 8% on Treasury bills (T-bills). The after-tax cost of common equity capital is 14.5%. Calculate the after-tax weighted average cost of capital.

11. **Challenge Problem** Use various Internet resources and information contained in this text to estimate the cost of debt, cost of retained earnings, the cost of new equity, and the WACC for the following firms: Walgreens, Microsoft, and ExxonMobil. As an approximation, use current book value ratios as estimates of their target capital structure weights.

12. **Challenge Problem** Through library or Internet resources, find information regarding the sources of long-term financing for AT&T. What are the current market prices for its outstanding bonds and stock? Estimate its current market value weights. Estimate the cost of each financing source and, assuming the current market value weights equal AT&T's target capital structure, estimate its weighted average cost of capital.

13. Derive equation 18.8 for the internal growth rate. Let S = last year's sales revenue; A = last year's total assets; D = last year's total liabilities; E = last year's stockholder's equity; NI/S = the firm's (presumably constant) profit margin, the ratio of net income to sales; g = the firm's expected sales growth rate; and RR = the firm's (presumably constant) retention ratio.
   Using these symbols and relationships you are familiar with, find the following:
   a. What will this year's net income equal?
   b. How much will be added to stockholder's equity this year?
   c. What is this year's level of assets?
   d. What is the change in assets between last year and this year?
   e. The change in assets computed in (d) has to be financed.

Assuming only internal financing is available; compute the firm's internal growth rate. (Hint: Set your answers to (b) and (d) equal to each other, and solve for g, the growth rate.)

14. Using the same notation used in the previous problem, assume the firm will raise some funds externally to keep the firm's debt/equity (D/E) ratio constant.
   a. What will this year's net income equal?
   b. How much will be added to stockholder's equity this year?

c. If the D/E ratio remains constant, how much external debt can the firm raise this year?

d. What is this year's level of assets?

e. What is the change in assets between this year and the last?

f. The change in assets computed in (e) has to be financed. Assuming a constant D/E ratio, compute the firm's sustainable growth rate. (Hint: Add your answers to (b) and (c), set them equal to the solution to (e), and solve for g.)

15. Below are items from recent financial statements from Moss and Mole Manufacturing:

Current Balance Sheet (all numbers are in thousands)	
Total assets	$192,000
Stockholder's equity	$44,000
Total liabilities	$148,000
Current Income Statement	
Sales	$260,000
Net income	$37,500
Dividends paid	$18,750

a. Find M&MM's internal growth rate.

b. Find their sustainable growth rate.

16. The following information is from the financial statements of Bagle's Biscuits:

Current Balance Sheet (all numbers are in millions)	
Total assets	$134.9
Stockholder's equity	$51.7
Total liabilities	$83.2
Current Income Statement	
Sales	$137.5
Net income	$8.0
Dividends paid	$3.2

a. Find Bagle's internal growth rate.

b. Compute Bagle's sustainable growth rate.

17. Income statements for Mount Lewis Copy Centers for 2019 and 2020 appear below. Data are in thousands of dollars.

	2019	2020
Sales	$20,000	$21,000
Cost of goods sold	10,000	10,500
Leases	2,500	3,000
Depreciation	2,000	2,100
EBIT	$5,500	$5,400

	2019	2020
Interest	3,000	3,200
EBT	$2,500	$2,200
Taxes (30%)	750	660
Net income	$1,750	$1,540

a. Compute and interpret the DOL, DFL, and DCL in 2019. Assume the components of the costs of goods sold (COGS) are all variable costs.

b. Compute and interpret the DOL, DFL, and DCL in 2020. Assume the components of the COGS are all variable costs.

c. Why did these numbers change between 2019 and 2020?

18. Using the income statements from the Mount Lewis Copy Centers for 2019 and 2020 in Problem 17, find the percentage change in sales, EBIT, and net income. Use them to compute the DOL, DFL, and degree of combined leverage (DCL).

19. Here's a recent income statement from TC1 Telecommunications Services Inc. (TC1). Numbers are in millions of dollars:

Sales	$53.7
Costs of goods sold	20.2
Depreciation	13.9
EBIT	$19.6
Interest expense	12.4
EBT	$7.2
Taxes (25%)	1.8
Net Income	$5.4

a. Compute TC1's DFL, DOL, and DCL if one-half of the costs of good sold are variable costs and one-half are fixed costs.

b. Assume during the current year TC1's sales rise to $59.5 million. What is your estimate of TC1's net income this year?

c. Assume during the current year TC1's sales fall to $49.3 million. What is your revised estimate for TC1's net income?

20. **Challenge Problem** Company A1 intends to raise $3 million by either of two financing plans:

Plan A: Sell 100,000 shares of stock at $30 net to firm

Plan B: Issue $3 million in long-term bonds with a 10% coupon

The firm expects an EBIT of $1 million. Currently A1 has 50,000 shares outstanding and no debt in its capital structure. Its tax rate is 34%.

a. What EBIT indifference level is associated with these two proposals?

b. Draw an EBIT/eps graph showing the various levels of eps and EBIT including the expected EBIT. What should A1 do in this case?

21. **Challenge Problem** Big 10 + 1 Corp. intends to raise $5 million by one of two financing plans:

Plan A: Sell 1,250,000 shares at $4 per share net to the firm

Plan B: Issue $5 million in ten-year debentures with a 9% coupon rate

The firm expects an EBIT level of $800,000. Currently Big 10 + 1 has 100,000 shares outstanding and $2 million of debt with a 5% coupon in its capital structure. The tax rate is 34%.

a. Draw an EBIT/eps graph showing the various levels of eps and EBIT.

b. What is the EBIT indifference point?

c. When will eps be zero under either alternative?

d. What type of financing should the firm choose?

e. Suppose under the equity financing option at an EBIT level of $800,000, the firm's price-earnings (P/E) ratio is 10; for the debt financing option, the P/E ratio is 7. What should the firm do?

22. **Challenge Problem** Champion Telecommunications is restructuring. Currently Champion has no debt outstanding. After it restructures, debt will be $5 million. The rate offered to bondholders is 10%. Champion currently has 700,000 shares outstanding at a market price of $40/share. Earnings per share are expected to rise.

a. What minimum level of EBIT is Champion expecting? Ignore the consequences of taxes.

b. Calculate the minimum level of EBIT that Champion's managers are expecting if the interest rate on debt is 5%.

c. Assume that Champion had EBIT of $2 million; was the leverage beneficial in (a) or in (b)?

Appendix

TABLE 1

Future Value of $1 (FVIF)

TABLE 2

Present Value of $1 (PVIF)

TABLE 3

Future Value of a $1 Ordinary Annuity (FVIFA)

TABLE 4

Present Value of a $1 Ordinary Annuity (PVIFA)

Table 1 Future Value of $1 (FVIF)

YEAR	1%	2%	3%	4%	5%	6%	7%	8%	9%
1	1.010	1.020	1.030	1.040	1.050	1.060	1.070	1.080	1.090
2	1.020	1.040	1.061	1.082	1.102	1.124	1.145	1.166	1.188
3	1.030	1.061	1.093	1.125	1.158	1.191	1.225	1.260	1.295
4	1.041	1.082	1.126	1.170	1.216	1.262	1.311	1.360	1.412
5	1.051	1.104	1.159	1.217	1.276	1.338	1.403	1.469	1.539
6	1.062	1.126	1.194	1.265	1.340	1.419	1.501	1.587	1.677
7	1.072	1.149	1.230	1.316	1.407	1.504	1.606	1.714	1.828
8	1.083	1.172	1.267	1.369	1.477	1.594	1.718	1.851	1.993
9	1.094	1.195	1.305	1.423	1.551	1.689	1.838	1.999	2.172
10	1.105	1.219	1.344	1.480	1.629	1.791	1.967	2.159	2.367
11	1.116	1.243	1.384	1.539	1.710	1.898	2.105	2.332	2.580
12	1.127	1.268	1.426	1.601	1.796	2.012	2.252	2.518	2.813
13	1.138	1.294	1.469	1.665	1.886	2.113	2.410	2.720	3.066
14	1.149	1.319	1.513	1.732	1.980	2.261	2.579	2.937	3.342
15	1.161	1.346	1.558	1.801	2.079	2.397	2.759	3.172	3.642
16	1.173	1.373	1.605	1.873	2.183	2.540	2.952	3.426	3.970
17	1.184	1.400	1.653	1.948	2.292	2.693	3.159	3.700	4.328
18	1.196	1.428	1.702	2.026	2.407	2.854	3.380	3.996	4.717
19	1.208	1.457	1.754	2.107	2.527	3.026	3.617	4.316	5.142
20	1.220	1.486	1.806	2.191	2.653	3.207	3.870	4.661	5.604
25	1.282	1.641	2.094	2.666	3.386	4.292	5.427	6.848	8.623
30	1.348	1.811	2.427	3.243	4.322	5.743	7.612	10.063	13.268

(*continues*)

Note: The basic equation for finding the future value interest factor (FVIF) is:

$$FVIF_{r,n} = (1 + r)^n$$

where r is the interest rate and n is the number of periods in years.

Table 1   Future Value of $1 (FVIF) (*Continued*)

10%	12%	14%	15%	16%	18%	20%	25%	30%
1.100	1.120	1.140	1.150	1.160	1.180	1.200	1.250	1.300
1.210	1.254	1.300	1.322	1.346	1.392	1.440	1.563	1.690
1.331	1.405	1.482	1.521	1.561	1.643	1.728	1.953	2.197
1.464	1.574	1.689	1.749	1.811	1.939	2.074	2.441	2.856
1.611	1.762	1.925	2.011	2.100	2.288	2.488	3.052	3.713
1.772	1.974	2.195	2.313	2.436	2.700	2.986	3.815	4.827
1.949	2.211	2.502	2.660	2.826	3.185	3.583	4.768	6.276
2.144	2.476	2.853	3.059	3.278	3.759	4.300	5.960	8.157
2.358	2.773	3.252	3.518	3.803	4.435	5.160	7.451	10.604
2.594	3.106	3.707	4.046	4.411	5.234	6.192	9.313	13.786
2.853	3.479	4.226	4.652	5.117	6.176	7.430	11.642	17.922
3.138	3.896	4.818	5.350	5.936	7.288	8.916	14.552	23.298
3.452	4.363	5.492	6.153	6.886	8.599	10.699	18.190	30.288
3.797	4.887	6.261	7.076	7.988	10.147	12.839	22.737	39.374
4.177	5.474	7.138	8.137	9.266	11.974	15.407	28.422	51.186
4.595	6.130	8.137	9.358	10.748	14.129	18.488	35.527	66.542
5.054	6.866	9.276	10.761	12.468	16.672	22.186	44.409	86.504
5.560	7.690	10.575	12.375	14.463	19.673	26.623	55.511	112.460
6.116	8.613	12.056	14.232	16.777	23.214	31.948	69.389	146.190
6.728	9.646	13.743	16.367	19.461	27.393	38.338	86.736	190.050
10.835	17.000	26.462	32.919	40.874	62.669	95.396	264.700	705.640
17.449	29.960	50.950	66.212	85.850	143.371	237.376	807.790	2,620.000

Table 2 Present Value of $1 (PVIF)

YEAR	1%	2%	3%	4%	5%	6%	7%	8%	9%	10%
1	0.990	0.980	0.971	0.962	0.952	0.943	0.935	0.926	0.917	0.909
2	0.980	0.961	0.943	0.925	0.907	0.890	0.873	0.857	0.842	0.826
3	0.971	0.942	0.915	0.889	0.864	0.840	0.816	0.794	0.772	0.751
4	0.961	0.924	0.888	0.855	0.823	0.792	0.763	0.735	0.708	0.683
5	0.951	0.906	0.863	0.822	0.784	0.747	0.713	0.681	0.650	0.621
6	0.942	0.888	0.837	0.790	0.746	0.705	0.666	0.630	0.596	0.564
7	0.933	0.871	0.813	0.760	0.711	0.665	0.623	0.583	0.547	0.513
8	0.923	0.853	0.789	0.731	0.677	0.627	0.582	0.540	0.502	0.467
9	0.914	0.837	0.766	0.703	0.645	0.592	0.544	0.500	0.460	0.424
10	0.905	0.820	0.744	0.676	0.614	0.558	0.508	0.463	0.422	0.386
11	0.896	0.804	0.722	0.650	0.585	0.527	0.475	0.429	0.388	0.350
12	0.887	0.788	0.701	0.625	0.557	0.497	0.444	0.397	0.356	0.319
13	0.879	0.773	0.681	0.601	0.530	0.469	0.415	0.368	0.326	0.290
14	0.870	0.758	0.661	0.577	0.505	0.442	0.388	0.340	0.299	0.263
15	0.861	0.743	0.642	0.555	0.481	0.417	0.362	0.315	0.275	0.239
16	0.853	0.728	0.623	0.534	0.458	0.394	0.339	0.292	0.252	0.218
17	0.844	0.714	0.605	0.513	0.436	0.391	0.317	0.270	0.231	0.198
18	0.836	0.700	0.587	0.494	0.416	0.350	0.296	0.250	0.212	0.180
19	0.828	0.686	0.570	0.475	0.396	0.331	0.276	0.232	0.194	0.164
20	0.820	0.673	0.554	0.456	0.377	0.312	0.258	0.215	0.178	0.149
25	0.780	0.610	0.478	0.375	0.295	0.233	0.184	0.146	0.116	0.092
30	0.742	0.552	0.412	0.308	0.231	0.174	0.131	0.099	0.075	0.057

(*continues*)

Note: The basic equation for finding the present value interest factor (PVIF) is:

$$PVIF_{r,n} = \frac{1}{(1+r)^n}$$

where r is the interest or discount rate and n is the number of periods in years.

Table 2   Present Value of $1 (PVIF) (*Continued*)

12%	14%	15%	16%	18%	20%	25%	30%
0.893	0.877	0.870	0.862	0.847	0.833	0.800	0.769
0.797	0.769	0.756	0.743	0.718	0.694	0.640	0.592
0.712	0.675	0.658	0.641	0.609	0.579	0.512	0.455
0.636	0.592	0.572	0.552	0.516	0.482	0.410	0.350
0.567	0.519	0.497	0.476	0.437	0.402	0.328	0.269
0.507	0.456	0.432	0.410	0.370	0.335	0.262	0.207
0.452	0.400	0.376	0.354	0.314	0.279	0.210	0.159
0.404	0.351	0.327	0.305	0.266	0.233	0.168	0.123
0.361	0.308	0.284	0.263	0.225	0.194	0.134	0.094
0.322	0.270	0.247	0.227	0.191	0.162	0.107	0.073
0.287	0.237	0.215	0.195	0.162	0.135	0.086	0.056
0.257	0.208	0.187	0.168	0.137	0.112	0.069	0.043
0.229	0.182	0.163	0.145	0.116	0.093	0.055	0.033
0.205	0.160	0.141	0.125	0.099	0.078	0.044	0.025
0.183	0.140	0.123	0.108	0.084	0.065	0.035	0.020
0.163	0.123	0.107	0.093	0.071	0.054	0.028	0.015
0.146	0.108	0.093	0.080	0.060	0.045	0.023	0.012
0.130	0.095	0.081	0.069	0.051	0.038	0.018	0.009
0.116	0.083	0.070	0.060	0.043	0.031	0.014	0.007
0.104	0.073	0.061	0.051	0.037	0.026	0.012	0.005
0.059	0.038	0.030	0.024	0.016	0.010	0.004	0.001
0.033	0.020	0.015	0.012	0.007	0.004	0.001	0.000

Table 3 Future Value of a $1 Ordinary Annuity (FVIFA)

YEAR	1%	2%	3%	4%	5%	6%	7%	8%
1	1.000	1.000	1.000	1.000	1.000	1.000	1.000	1.000
2	2.010	2.020	2.030	2.040	2.050	2.060	2.070	2.080
3	3.030	3.060	3.091	3.122	3.152	3.184	3.215	3.246
4	4.060	4.122	4.184	4.246	4.310	4.375	4.440	4.506
5	5.101	5.204	5.309	5.416	5.526	5.637	5.751	5.867
6	6.152	6.308	6.468	6.633	6.802	6.975	7.153	7.336
7	7.214	7.434	7.662	7.898	8.142	8.394	8.654	8.923
8	8.286	8.583	8.892	9.214	9.549	9.897	10.260	10.637
9	9.369	9.755	10.159	10.583	11.027	11.491	11.978	12.488
10	10.462	10.950	11.464	12.006	12.578	13.181	13.816	14.487
11	11.567	12.169	12.808	13.486	14.207	14.972	15.784	16.645
12	12.683	13.412	14.192	15.026	15.917	16.870	17.888	18.977
13	13.809	14.680	15.618	16.627	17.713	18.882	20.141	21.495
14	14.947	15.974	17.086	18.292	19.599	21.015	22.550	24.215
15	16.097	17.293	18.599	20.024	21.579	23.276	25.129	27.152
16	17.258	18.639	20.157	21.825	23.657	25.673	27.888	30.324
17	18.430	20.012	21.762	23.698	25.840	28.213	30.840	33.750
18	19.615	21.412	23.414	25.645	28.132	30.906	33.999	37.450
19	20.811	22.841	25.117	27.671	30.539	33.760	37.379	41.466
20	22.019	24.297	26.870	29.778	33.066	36.786	40.995	45.762
25	28.243	32.030	36.459	41.646	47.727	54.865	63.249	73.106
30	34.785	40.568	47.575	56.805	66.439	79.058	94.461	113.283

(*continues*)

Note: The basic equation for finding the future value interest factor of an ordinary annuity (FVIFA) is:

$$FVIFA_{r,n} = \sum_{t=1}^{n}(1+r)^{n-t} = \frac{(1+r)^n - 1}{r}$$

where r is the interest rate and n is the number of periods in years.

Future Value of a $1 Annuity Due (FVIFAD)
The future value interest factor of an annuity due (FVIFAD) may be found by using the following formula to convert FVIFA values found in Table 3:

$$FVIFAD_{r,n} = FVIFA_{r,n}(1+r)$$

where r is the interest rate and n is the number of periods in years.

Table 3 Future Value of a $1 Ordinary Annuity (FVIFA) (*Continued*)

9%	10%	12%	14%	16%	18%	20%	25%	30%
1.000	1.000	1.000	1.000	1.000	1.000	1.000	1.000	1.000
2.090	2.100	2.120	2.140	2.160	2.180	2.200	2.250	2.300
3.278	3.310	3.374	3.440	3.506	3.572	3.640	3.813	3.990
4.573	4.641	4.779	4.921	5.066	5.215	5.368	5.766	6.187
5.985	6.105	6.353	6.610	6.877	7.154	7.442	8.207	9.043
7.523	7.716	8.115	8.536	8.977	9.442	9.930	11.259	12.756
9.200	9.487	10.089	10.730	11.414	12.142	12.916	15.073	17.583
11.028	11.436	12.300	13.233	14.240	15.327	16.499	19.842	23.858
13.021	13.579	14.776	16.085	17.518	19.086	20.799	25.802	32.015
15.193	15.937	17.549	19.337	21.321	23.521	25.959	33.253	42.619
17.560	18.531	20.655	23.044	25.733	28.755	32.150	42.566	56.405
20.141	21.384	24.133	27.271	30.850	34.931	39.580	54.208	74.327
22.953	24.523	28.029	32.089	36.786	42.219	48.497	68.760	97.625
26.019	27.975	32.393	37.581	43.672	50.818	59.196	86.949	127.910
29.361	31.772	37.280	43.842	51.660	60.965	72.035	109.690	167.290
33.003	35.950	42.753	50.980	60.925	72.939	87.442	138.110	218.470
36.974	40.545	48.884	59.118	71.673	87.068	105.931	173.640	285.010
41.301	45.599	55.750	68.394	84.141	103.740	128.117	218.050	371.520
46.018	51.159	63.440	78.969	98.603	123.414	154.740	273.560	483.970
51.160	57.275	72.052	91.025	115.380	146.628	186.688	342.950	630.170
84.701	98.347	133.334	181.871	249.214	342.603	471.981	1,054.800	2,348.800
136.308	164.494	241.333	356.787	530.312	790.948	1,181.882	3,227.200	8,730.000

Table 4   Present Value of a $1 Ordinary Annuity (PVIFA)

YEAR	1%	2%	3%	4%	5%	6%	7%	8%	9%	10%
1	0.990	0.980	0.971	0.962	0.952	0.943	0.935	0.926	0.917	0.909
2	1.970	1.942	1.913	1.886	1.859	1.833	1.808	1.783	1.759	1.736
3	2.941	2.884	2.829	2.775	2.723	2.673	2.624	2.577	2.531	2.487
4	3.902	3.808	3.717	3.630	3.546	3.465	3.387	3.312	3.240	3.170
5	4.853	4.713	4.580	4.452	4.329	4.212	4.100	3.993	3.890	3.791
6	5.795	5.601	5.417	5.242	5.076	4.917	4.767	4.623	4.486	4.355
7	6.728	6.472	6.230	6.002	5.786	5.582	5.389	5.206	5.033	4.868
8	7.652	7.325	7.020	6.733	6.463	6.210	5.971	5.747	5.535	5.335
9	8.566	8.162	7.786	7.435	7.108	6.802	6.515	6.247	5.995	5.759
10	9.471	8.983	8.530	8.111	7.722	7.360	7.024	6.710	6.418	6.145
11	10.368	9.787	9.253	8.760	8.306	7.887	7.499	7.139	6.805	6.495
12	11.255	10.575	9.954	9.385	8.863	8.384	7.943	7.536	7.161	6.814
13	12.134	11.348	10.635	9.986	9.394	8.853	8.358	7.904	7.487	7.103
14	13.004	12.106	11.296	10.563	9.899	9.295	8.745	8.244	7.786	7.367
15	13.865	12.849	11.938	11.118	10.380	9.712	9.108	8.559	8.061	7.606
16	14.718	13.578	12.561	11.652	10.838	10.106	9.447	8.851	8.313	7.824
17	15.562	14.292	13.166	12.166	11.274	10.477	9.763	9.122	8.544	8.022
18	16.398	14.992	13.754	12.659	11.690	10.828	10.059	9.372	8.756	8.201
19	17.226	15.678	14.324	13.134	12.085	11.158	10.336	9.604	8.950	8.365
20	18.046	16.351	14.877	13.590	12.462	11.470	10.594	9.818	9.129	8.514
25	22.023	19.523	17.413	15.622	14.094	12.783	11.654	10.675	9.823	9.077
30	25.808	22.397	19.600	17.292	15.372	13.765	12.409	11.258	10.274	9.427

(continues)

Note: The basic equation for finding the present value interest factor of an ordinary annuity (PVIFA) is:

$$\text{PVIFA}_{r,n} = \sum_{t=1}^{n} \frac{1}{(1+r)^t} = \frac{1 - \frac{1}{(1+r)^n}}{r}$$

where r is the interest or discount rate and n is the number of periods in years.

Present Value of a $1 Annuity Due (PVIFAD)

The present value interest factor of an annuity due (PVIFAD) may be found by using the following formula to convert PVIFA values found in Table 4:

$$\text{PVIFAD}_{r,n} = \text{PVIFA}_{r,n}(1+r)$$

where r is the interest or discount rate and n is the number of periods in years.

Table 4   Present Value of a $1 Ordinary Annuity (PVIFA) (*Continued*)

12%	14%	16%	18%	20%	25%	30%
0.893	0.877	0.862	0.847	0.833	0.800	0.769
1.690	1.647	1.605	1.566	1.528	1.440	1.361
2.402	2.322	2.246	2.174	2.106	1.952	1.816
3.037	2.914	2.798	2.690	2.589	2.362	2.166
3.605	3.433	3.274	3.127	2.991	2.689	2.436
4.111	3.889	3.685	3.498	3.326	2.951	2.643
4.564	4.288	4.039	3.812	3.605	3.161	2.802
4.968	4.639	4.344	4.078	3.837	3.329	2.925
5.328	4.946	4.607	4.303	4.031	3.463	3.019
5.650	5.216	4.833	4.494	4.193	3.571	3.092
5.938	5.453	5.029	4.656	4.327	3.656	3.147
6.194	5.660	5.197	4.793	4.439	3.725	3.190
6.424	5.842	5.342	4.910	4.533	3.780	3.223
6.628	6.002	5.468	5.008	4.611	3.824	3.249
6.811	6.142	5.575	5.092	4.675	3.859	3.268
6.974	6.265	5.668	5.162	4.730	3.887	3.283
7.120	5.373	5.749	4.222	4.775	3.910	3.295
7.250	6.467	5.818	5.273	4.812	3.928	3.304
7.366	6.550	5.877	5.316	4.843	3.942	3.311
7.469	6.623	5.929	5.353	4.870	3.954	3.316
7.843	6.873	6.097	5.467	4.948	3.985	3.329
8.055	7.003	6.177	5.517	4.979	3.995	3.332

Glossary

Accommodative function Fed efforts to meet credit needs of individuals and institutions, clearing checks, and supporting depository institutions

Adjustable-rate mortgage (ARM) Has an interest rate that changes or varies over time with market determined interest rates on a U.S. Treasury bill or other debt security

Administrative inflation The tendency of prices, aided by union-corporation contracts, to rise during economic expansion and to resist declines during recessions

Advance factoring Factor pays the firm for its receivables before the account due date

Aftermarket The period after a new issue is initially sold to the public; during this period, members of the syndicate may not sell the securities for less than the offering price

Agency costs Tangible and intangible expenses borne by shareholders because of the actual or potential self-serving actions of managers

Agents The managers hired by the principals to run the firm

Aggregate demand Total demand for final goods and services in the economy at a point in time

American depository receipt (ADR) Receipt that represents foreign shares to U.S. investors

Amortized loan A loan repaid in equal payments over a specified time period

Annual percentage rate (APR) Determined by multiplying the interest rate charged per period by the number of periods in a year

Annual report Contains descriptive information on operating and financial performance during the past year, a discussion of current and future business opportunities, and financial statements that provide a numerical record of financial performance

Annuity A series of equal payments (receipts) that occur over a number of time periods

Annuity due Exists when equal periodic payments start at time period zero or, in other words, the beginning of each time period

Arbitrage The simultaneous, or nearly simultaneous, purchasing of commodities, securities, or bills of exchange in one market and selling them in another where the price is higher

Ask Price requested by the seller

Asset-based lending Collateral or security backing the loan that can be claimed or sold by the lender if the borrower defaults

Asset management ratios Indicate extent to which assets are turned over or used to support sales

Assets Financial and physical items owned by a business

At-the-money Exercise price equals the market price of the underlying asset

Autocratic capitalism Country or state organized as an autocratic political system that uses elements of a markets-based economic system

Automatic stabilizers Federal government programs that act on a continuing basis to stabilize disposable income and economic activity in general

Automatic transfer service (ATS) accounts Used to make direct deposits to, and payments from, checkable deposit accounts

Balance of payments Involves all of a country's international transactions, including foreign investment, private and government grants, military spending overseas, and many other items besides the buying and selling of goods and services

Balance of trade The net balance of exports and imports of goods and services

Balance sheet Statement of a company's financial position as of a particular date, usually at the end of a quarter or year

Bank liquidity Reflects the ability to meet depositor withdrawals and to pay off other liabilities when they come due

Bank Holding Company Act of 1956 Defined bank holding companies, established control over MBHC expansions, and required divestment of their existing non-banking interests

Bank reserves A depository institution's vault cash and funds held at its regional Federal Reserve Bank

Bank solvency Reflects the ability to keep the value of a bank's assets greater than its liabilities

Banker's acceptance Promise of future payment issued by a firm and guaranteed by a bank

Banking system Commercial banks, S&Ls, savings banks, and credit unions

Bankruptcy costs Explicit expenses, such as legal and accounting fees and court costs, along with implicit costs, such as the use of management time and skills in preventing and escaping bankruptcy

Barter Exchange of goods or services without using money

Base case For project analysis, the firm's after-tax cash flows without the project

Bearer bonds Have coupons that are "clipped" and presented, like a check, to the bank for payment; the bond issuer does not know who is receiving the interest payments

Best-effort agreement Agreement which the investment bankers try to sell securities of the issuing corporation, but they assume no risk for the possible failure of the flotation

Beta Measure of an asset's systematic risk

Bid Price offered by a potential buyer

Bimetallic standard Monetary standard based on two metals, usually silver and gold

Bitcoin Specific type of cryptocurrency that uses a ledger system technology called blockchain to record, maintain, and secure payment transactions

Blanket inventory lien Claim against an inventory when individual items are indistinguishable

Blue-sky laws Protect the investor from fraudulent security offerings

Bond Agreement or contract between investor (lender) and a debtor (borrower), typically a business firm or government body

Bond markets Where debt securities with longer-term maturities are originated and traded

Bond ratings Assess both the collateral underlying the bonds as well as the ability of the issuer to make timely payments of interest and principal

Break-even analysis Used to estimate how many units of a product must be sold for the firm to break even or have a zero profit

Break-even price Price such that the option position's profit is zero; for call option buyers it is the strike price plus the option premium; for put option buyers it is the strike price minus the option premium

Bretton woods system A system in which individual currencies would be tied to gold through the U.S. dollar via fixed or pegged exchange rates

Brexit The plan for the withdrawal of the United Kingdom from the European Union

Broker One who assists the trading process by buying or selling securities in the market for an investor

Brokerage firms Assist individuals who want to purchase new or existing securities issues or who want to sell previously purchased securities

Budget deficit Occurs when tax revenues (receipts) are less than expenditures (outlays)

Budget surplus Occurs when tax revenues (receipts) are more than expenditures (outlays)

Budgets Financial plans indicating expected revenues, spending, and investment needs

Business risk (1) variations in operating income over time because of variations in unit sales, price–cost margin, and/or fixed expenses; (2) measured by variability in EBIT over time and is determined by the products the firm sells and the production processes it uses

Buying on margin Investors borrow money and invest it along with their own funds in securities

Bylaws The rules established to govern the corporation and include how the firm will be managed, how the directors will be elected, and the rights of the stockholders

Call deferment period Specified period of time after the bond issue during which the bonds cannot be called

Call option A contract for the purchase of securities

Call price Price paid to the investor for redemption prior to maturity, typically par value plus a call premium of one year's interest

Call risk Risk of having a bond called away and re-investing the proceeds at a lower interest rate

Callable bonds Can be redeemed prior to maturity by the issuing firm

Callable preferred stock Gives the corporation the right to retire the preferred stock at its option

Cannibalization This occurs when a project robs cash flow from the firm's existing lines of business

Capacity The ability to pay bills and often involves an examination of liquidity ratios

Capital Indicates the adequacy of owners' equity relative to existing liabilities as the underlying support for creditworthiness

Capitalism Economic system with private ownership of assets, production of goods and services for profit, a price mechanism for allocating resources, and financial markets

Capital account Summary of the flow of funds between one country and all other countries involving the transfer of financial assets across country borders during a specified time period

Capital budgeting Process of identifying, evaluating, and implementing a firm's investment opportunities

Capital consumption adjustment (depreciation) The estimate of the "using up" of plant and equipment assets for business purposes

Capital formation Creation of capital goods including residential and commercial buildings, equipment and machinery, and business inventories

Capital markets Where debt instruments or securities with maturities longer than one year and corporate stocks or equity securities are issued and traded

Capital structure Firm's mix of debt and equity used to finance a firm's assets

Cash budget A tool the treasurer uses to forecast future cash flows and estimate future short-term borrowing needs

Cash conversion cycle Time between a firm's paying its suppliers for inventory and collecting cash from customers on a sale of the finished product

Central bank Federal government agency that facilitates the operation of the financial system and regulates money supply growth

Certificates of deposit (CDs) Time deposits with a stated maturity, which pay a fixed rate of interest or are sold at a discount

Character Ethical quality of the applicant on which one can base a judgment about his or her willingness to pay bills and is best judged by reviewing his past credit history for long overdue or unpaid obligations

Charter Provides the corporate name, indicates the intended business activities, provides names and addresses of directors, and indicates how a firm will be capitalized with stock

Chartists (technicians) People who examine graphs of past price movements, number of shares bought and sold, and other figures to predict future price movements

Chief financial officer (CFO) Responsible for the controller and the treasury functions of a firm

Clean draft A draft that is not accompanied by any special documents and is generally used when the exporter has confidence in the importer's ability to meet the draft when presented

Clearing float The delay in transferring funds between payer and payee because of the banking system check-clearing processes

Closed-end mortgage bond Does not permit future bond issues to be secured by any of the assets pledged as security under the closed-end issue

Coefficient of variation (CV) A measure of risk per unit of return

Collateral Reflects whether assets are available to provide security for the potential credit

Combined leverage Effect on earnings produced by the operating and financial leverage

Commercial banks Depository institutions that accept deposits, issue check-writing accounts, and make loans to businesses and individuals

Commercial finance company Organization without a bank charter that advances funds to businesses by discounting accounts receivable, making loans secured by chattel mortgages on machinery or liens on inventory, or financing deferred-payment sales of commercial and industrial equipment

Commercial letter of credit A bank's written statement to an individual or firm guaranteeing acceptance and payment of a draft up to a specified sum if the draft is presented according to the terms of the letter

Commercial paper Short-term unsecured promissory note issued by a high-credit-quality corporation

Common stock Ownership shares in a corporation

Common-size financial statements Expresses balance sheet numbers as a percentage of total assets and income statement numbers as a percentage of total revenue to facilitate comparisons between different-sized firms

Compensating balance Requirement that 10–20% of a loan be kept on deposit at the bank

Compound interest Involves earning interest on interest in addition to interest on the principal or initial investment

Compounding Arithmetic process whereby an initial value increases or grows at a compound interest rate over time to reach a value in the future

Conditions Current economic climate and state of the business cycle

Constant payout ratio A strategy in which the firm pays a constant percentage of earnings as dividends; as earnings rise and fall, so does the dollar amount of dividends

Consumer Credit Protection Act Requires the clear explanation of consumer credit costs and garnishment procedures (taking wages or property by legal means) and prohibiting overly high-priced credit transactions

Contractual savings Savings accumulated on a regular schedule for a specified length of time by prior agreement

Contractual savings organizations Collect premiums on insurance policies and employee/employer contributions from participants and provide retirement benefits and insurance against major financial losses

Contribution margin Contribution of each unit sold that goes toward paying fixed costs

Controller Manages accounting, cost analysis, and tax planning

Conversion ratio Number of shares into which a convertible bond can be converted

Conversion value Stock price times the conversion ratio

Convertible bond Can be changed or converted, at the investor's option, into a specific number of shares of the issuer's common stock

Convertible preferred stock Has a special provision that makes it possible to convert it to common stock of the corporation, generally at the stockholder's option

Corporate bond Debt instrument issued by a corporation to raise long-term funds

Corporate equity capital Financial capital supplied by the owners of a corporation

Corporate retention rate Calculated as undistributed profits divided by profits after taxes

Corporation Legal entity created under state law in the United States with an unending life and limited financial liability to its owners

Correlation Statistical concept that relates movements in one set of returns to movements in another set over time

Cost of capital (1) Minimum acceptable rate of return to a firm on a project; (2) the project's required rate of return

Cost-push inflation Occurs when prices are raised to cover rising production costs, such as wages

Cost–volume–profit analysis Used by managers for financial planning to estimate the firm's operating profits at different levels of unit sales

Covenants Impose restrictions or extra duties on the firm

Credit bureaus Not-for-profit institutions that obtain credit information about business firms and individuals

Credit cards Provide predetermined credit limits to consumers at the time the cards are issued

Credit money Money backed by the creditworthiness of the issuer

Credit rating Indicates the expected likelihood that a borrower will miss interest or principal payments and possibly default

on the debt obligation in the form of a loan, mortgage, or bond

Credit risk (default risk) The chance of nonpayment or delayed payment of interest or principal

Credit score A number that indicates an individual's creditworthiness or likelihood that a debt will be paid according to the terms that were initially agreed to

Credit unions Cooperative nonprofit organizations that exist primarily to provide member depositors with consumer credit

Cross-sectional analysis Different firms are compared at the same point in time

Crowding out Lack of funds for private borrowing caused by the sale of government obligations to cover large federal deficits

Cryptocurrency Decentralized and unregulated digital money that uses cryptography to record, maintain, and secure electronic payments

Cumulative preferred stock Requires that before dividends on common stock are paid, preferred dividends must be paid for the current period and for all previous periods in which preferred dividends were missed

Currency appreciation Occurs when there is an increase in a currency's value

Currency depreciation Occurs when there is a decrease in a currency's value

Currency exchange markets (foreign exchange markets) Electronic markets where banks and institutional traders buy and sell currencies on behalf of businesses, other clients, and themselves

Currency exchange rate Value of one currency relative to another currency

Currency exchange rate risk The price risk associated with fluctuating exchange rates over time

Current account Shows the flow of income into and out of the United States during a specified period

Current assets Cash and all other assets that are expected to be converted into cash within one year

Dealer Satisfies the investor's trades by buying and selling securities from his or her own inventory

Dealer system Composed of a closely linked network of dealers and brokers in government securities with an effective marketing network throughout the United States

Debenture bonds Unsecured obligations that depend on the general credit strength of the corporation for their security

Debit cards Provide for the immediate direct transfer of deposit amounts

Debt management Includes determining the types of refunding to carry out, the types of securities to sell, the interest rate patterns to use, and decisions to make on callable issues

Debt securities Obligations to repay borrowed funds

Debt securities markets Where money market securities, bonds (corporate, financial institution, and government), and mortgages are originated and traded

Default risk Risk that a borrower will not pay interest and/or repay the principal on a loan or other debt instrument according to the agreed contractual terms

Default risk premium Indicates compensation for the possibility that the borrower will not pay interest and/or will not repay principal according to the financial instrument's contractual arrangements

Defensive activities Fed activities that contribute to the smooth, everyday functioning of the economy

Deficit economic unit Spends more money than it brings in and must balance its money receipts with money expenditures by obtaining money from surplus units

Deficit financing Affects the monetary and banking system when the spending rate is faster than the collection of taxes and other funds

Deficit reserves Amount by which a depository institution's bank reserves are less than required reserves

Degree of combined leverage (DCL) Percentage change in eps that results from a 1% change in sales volume

Degree of financial leverage (DFL) Measures the sensitivity of eps to changes in EBIT

Degree of operating leverage (DOL) Measures the sensitivity of operating income to changes in the level of output

Delivery or transmission float The delay in transferring the means of payment from the payer (customer) to the payee (the provider of the goods or services)

Demand-pull inflation An excessive demand for goods and services during periods of economic expansion relative to supply

Democracy System of government where limited authority and power are granted by law to its people who participate by voting on government goals and actions

Democratic capitalism Country or state organized as a democracy that uses or adopts a capitalistic economic system

Deposit money Money backed by the creditworthiness of the depository institution that issued the deposit

Depository institutions Accept deposits from individuals and then lend these pooled savings to businesses, governments, and individuals

Depreciation Devaluing a physical asset over the period of its expected life

Depreciation tax shield Tax reduction due to depreciation of fixed assets; equals the amount of the depreciation expense multiplied by the firm's tax rate

Derivative deposit Occurs when reserves created from a primary deposit are made available to borrowers through bank loans

Derivative securities markets Where financial contracts or instruments that derive their values from underlying debt and equity securities are originated and traded

Derivative security Financial contract that derives its value from the value of another asset, such as a bond or stock

Designated market makers (DMM) Assigned dealers who have the responsibility of making a market in an assigned security

Development stage Requires estimating relevant cash inflows and outflows

Deviations Computed as a periodic return minus the average return

Digital currency Electronic money that serves as a medium of exchange for making payments

Direct quotation method Indicates the value of one unit of a foreign currency in terms of a home country's currency

Discount bond Bond that is selling below par value

Discounted loan Borrower receives the principal less the interest at the time the loan is made; the principal is repaid at maturity

Discounting Arithmetic process whereby a future value (FV) decreases at a compound interest rate over time to reach a present value (PV)

Discretionary spending Government spending provided by passage of appropriations bills that set aside funds for specific federal agencies and programs

Dissave Spend accumulated savings rather than further reduce consumption spending

Diversification Occurs when we invest in several different assets rather than just a single one

Dividend payout ratio (1) Dividends per share divided by earnings per share (eps); (2) the proportion of each dollar of earnings that is paid to shareholders as a dividend; equals one minus the retention rate

Dividend reinvestment plans (DRIPS) Allow shareholders to purchase additional shares automatically with all or part of the investor's dividends

Documentary draft Draft that is accompanied by an order bill of lading along with other papers, such as insurance receipts, certificates of sanitation, and consular invoices

Dodd–Frank Wall Street Reform and Consumer Protection Act of 2010 Promotes financial stability in the financial system by improving accountability and transparency, and provides increased consumer protection

Draft (bill of exchange) An unconditional written order, signed by the party drawing it, requiring the party to whom it is addressed to pay a certain sum of money to order or to bearer

Dual banking system Allows commercial banks to obtain charters from the federal government or a state government

Due diligence Detailed study of a corporation

DuPont analysis Technique of breaking return on total assets and return on equity into their component parts

Dutch auction A bidding process, which allows smaller firms and individual investors to purchase securities

Dynamic actions Fed actions that stimulate or repress the level of prices or economic activity

EBIT/eps analysis Allows managers to see how different capital structures affect the earnings and risk levels of their firms

Economic risk Risk associated with possible slow or negative economic growth, as well as variability in economic growth

Effective annual rate (EAR) Measures the true interest rate when compounding occurs more frequently than once a year

Efficient market (informationally efficient market) A market in which prices adjust quickly after the arrival of important news surprises

Electronic data interchange The use of communications and computer systems to convey ordering, invoice, and payment information between suppliers and customers

Enhancement Increase in the cash flows of the firm's other products that occur because of a new project

Entrepreneurial finance Study of how growth-driven, performance-focused, early-stage firms raise financial capital and manage their operations and assets

Equilibrium exchange rate Currency exchange rate where the supply and demand for a currency are in balance

Equilibrium interest rate Price that equates the demand for and supply of loanable funds

Equipment trust certificate A type of mortgage bond that gives the bondholder a claim to specific "rolling stock" (movable assets), such as railroad cars or airplanes

Equity Funds supplied by the owners and represents their residual claim on the firm

Equity securities Ownership shares, called common stocks, in corporations

Equity securities markets Where ownership rights in corporations are initially sold and traded

Ethical behavior How an individual or organization treats others legally, fairly, and honestly

Euro A single currency that has replaced the individual currencies of the eurozone member countries

Eurodollar bonds Dollar-denominated bonds sold outside the United States

European Central Bank (ECB) Conducts monetary policy for the 12 European countries that joined the European monetary union and adopted the euro as their common currency

European Union (EU) Organization established to promote trade and economic development among European countries

Eurozone members Countries that have adopted the euro as their common currency

Ex ante Expected or forecasted

Excess reserves Amount by which a depository institution's bank reserves are greater than required reserves

Exchange rate risk (1) Effect on revenues and expenses from variations in the value of the U.S. dollar in terms of other currencies; (2) fluctuating exchange rates lead to varying levels of U.S. dollar-denominated cash flows

Exercise price (strike price) Price at which the asset can be traded under a futures or option contract

Expectations theory States that the shape of the yield curve reflects investor expectations about future inflation rates

Export Import bank Bank established to help finance and facilitate exports and imports between the United States and other countries

Extendable notes Have their coupons reset every two or three years to reflect the current interest rate environment and any changes in the firm's credit quality; the investor can accept the new coupon rate or put the bonds back to the firm

Factor A firm that engages in accounts receivable financing by purchasing accounts and assuming all credit risks

Fed discount rate Interest rate that a bank must pay to borrow from its regional reserve bank

Fed's board of governors Seven-member board of the federal reserve that sets monetary policy

Federal budget Annual revenue and expenditure plans that reflect fiscal policy objectives concerning government influence on economic activity

Federal funds Short-term loans, usually with maturities of one day to one week, made between depository institutions

Federal funds rate rate on overnight loans from banks with excess reserves to banks that have deficit reserves

Federal Home Loan Mortgage Corporation (Freddie Mac) Formed to aid mortgage markets by purchasing and holding mortgage loans

Federal National Mortgage Association (Fannie Mae) Created to support the financial markets by purchasing home mortgages from banks and, thus, freeing the proceeds, which could be lent to other borrowers

Federal Reserve float Temporary increase in bank reserves that results when checks are credited to the reserve account of the depositing bank before they are debited from the account of the banks on which they are drawn

Federal Reserve System (FED) U.S. Central bank that sets monetary policy and regulates banking system

Federal statutory debt limits Limits on the federal debt set by congress

Fiat money Legal tender proclaimed to be money by law

Field warehouse A warehouse on the grounds of the borrowing business establishment

Finance Study of how individuals, institutions, governments, and businesses acquire, spend, and manage money and other financial assets

Finance companies Provide loans directly to consumers and businesses or aid individuals in obtaining financing

Financial account Summary of the flow of funds between one country and all other countries involving foreign investments in fixed assets and financial assets during a specified time period

Financial assets (1) Claims against the income or assets of individuals, businesses, and governments; (2) money, debt instruments, equity securities, and other financial contracts that are backed by real assets and the earning abilities of issuers

Financial environment Financial system, institutions or intermediaries, financial markets, business firms, individuals, and global interactions that contribute to an efficiently operating economy

Financial institutions Organizations or intermediaries that help the financial system operate efficiently and transfer funds from savers and investors to individuals, businesses, and governments that seek to spend or invest the funds in physical assets

Financial intermediation Process by which individual savings are accumulated in depository institutions and, in turn, lent or invested

Financial leverage ratios Indicate the extent to which borrowed or debt funds are used to finance assets, as well as the ability of a firm to meet its debt payment obligations

Financial management Involves financial planning, asset management, and fund-raising decisions to enhance the value of businesses

Financial markets Physical locations or electronic forums that facilitate the flow of funds among investors, businesses, and governments

Financial risk Variations in income before taxes over time because fixed interest expenses do not change when operating income rises or falls

Financial system A complex mix of financial intermediaries, markets, instruments, policy makers, and regulations that interact to expedite the flow of financial capital from savings into investments

Financial systemic risk Possibility that the collapse of one or several financial institutions could lead to the collapse of an entire financial system or market

First mortgage bonds Backed or secured by specifically pledged property of a firm (real estate, buildings, and other assets classified as real property)

Fiscal policy Involves setting the annual national budget and reflects government influence on economic activity through taxation and expenditure plans

Fixed-rate mortgage Fixed interest rate with constant monthly payments over the life of the loan, which is typically 15 or 30 years

Flexible exchange rates A system in which currency exchange rates are determined by supply and demand

Float The delay between when funds are sent by a payer to a payee

Flotation Initial sale of newly issued debt or equity securities

Flotation costs (1) Composed of direct costs, the spread, and underpricing; (2) costs of issuing stock; includes accounting, legal, and printing costs of offering shares to the public as well as the commission or fees earned by the investment bankers who market the new securities to investors

Follow-up stage Determines, through analysis, if a company is meeting expectations

Foreign exchange markets Electronic markets in which banks and institutional traders buy and sell various currencies on behalf of businesses and other clients

Forward contract Specifies the currencies to be exchanged, an exchange rate, and a future date when the transaction will be completed

Forward exchange rate Negotiated exchange rate for the purchase or sale of a currency where delivery will take place at a future date

Forward rate Exchange rate specified in the forward contract

Fourth market A market in which large institutional investors arrange the purchase and sale of securities among themselves without the benefit of broker or dealer

Fractional reserve system A system in which banks are required by the Fed to hold reserves equal to a specified percentage of their deposits

Full-bodied money Coins that contain the same value in metal as their face value

Future value Value of a savings amount or an investment at a specified time or date in the future

Futures contract A contract obligating the owner to purchase or sell the underlying asset at a specified price on a specified day

Generally accepted accounting principles (GAAP) Set of guidelines as to the form and manner in which accounting information should be presented

Glass–Steagall Act of 1933 Provided for separation of commercial banking and investment banking activities in the United States

Global bonds Bonds that are generally denominated in U.S. dollars and marketed globally

Global depository receipt (GDR) Listed on the London stock exchange; facilitates trading in foreign shares

Gold standard A standard in which currencies of major countries are convertible into gold at fixed exchange rates

Goodwill An intangible asset that represents the excess funds paid when one firm merges with or purchases another over and above the accounting value of the firm's net assets

Gordon model (constant dividend growth model) A means of estimating common stock prices by assuming constant dividend growth over time

Government expenditures (GE) Expenditures for goods and services plus gross investments by federal, state, and local governments

Government National Mortgage Association (Ginnie Mae) created to issue its own debt securities to obtain funds that are invested in mortgages made to low-income to moderate-income home purchasers

Gramm–Leach–Bliley Act of 1999 Repealed the separation of commercial banking and investment banking provided for in the Glass–Steagall Act of 1933

Gross domestic product (GDP) Measure of the output of goods and services in an economy

Gross private domestic investment (GPDI) Measures fixed investment in residential and nonresidential structures, producers' durable equipment, and changes in business inventories

Hedge An action which reduces risk; similar to the concept of insurance

Hedging Action taken to reduce risk or insure against a possible negative outcome

High frequency trading (HFT) Uses powerful computers and computer algorithms to analyze price patterns, both within and across different markets, and to submit trades to exchanges in microseconds

High-yield bonds (junk bonds) With ratings lower than Baa, bonds that have a substantial probability of default

Holding period dollar return The sum of all income received during a time frame plus the change in the asset's price over the time frame

Holding period return The percent return on an investment over any stated time frame

Horizon risk premium or horizon spread Difference in return earned by investing in a longer-term bond that has the same credit risk as a shorter-term bond

House brokers (commission brokers) Act as agents to execute customers' orders for securities purchases and sales

Identification stage Finding potential capital investment opportunities and identifying if a project involves a replacement decision and/or revenue expansion

Implementation stage Accepted projects are executed in a timely fashion; cash outflows occur as the firm invests in the capital budgeting project

In-the-money An option with a positive intrinsic value

Income statement Reports the revenues generated and expenses incurred by the firm over an accounting period, such as a quarter or a year

Incremental cash flows Represent the difference between the firm's after-tax cash flows with the project and the firm's after-tax cash flows without the project

Independent brokers Handle the commission brokers' overflow

Independent projects Projects not in direct competition with one another

Indirect quotation method Indicates the number of units of a foreign currency needed to purchase one unit of the home country's currency

Individual net worth Sum of an individual's money, real assets, and financial assets or claims against others, less the individual's debt obligations

Industry comparative analysis Compares a firm's ratios against average ratios for other companies in the firm's industry

Inflation An increase in the prices of goods or services that is not offset by an increase in their quality

Inflation-adjusted interest rate Interest rate earned after adjusting for the change in purchasing power

Inflation premium Average inflation rate expected over the life of the instrument

Initial margin (1) Deposited funds necessary to purchase a derivatives contract; (2) initial equity percentage

Initial public offering (IPO) Initial sale of equity to the public

Insurance companies Provide financial protection to individuals and businesses for life, property, liability, and health uncertainties

Interest rate Basic price that equates the demand for and supply of loanable funds in the financial markets

Interest rate risk (1) Reflects the possibility of changes or fluctuations in market values of fixed-rate debt instruments as market interest rates change over time; (2) variations in interest expense unrelated to sales or operating income arising from changes in the level of interest rates in the economy

Internal growth rate A measure of how quickly a firm can increase its asset base over the next year without raising outside funds

Internal rate of return (IRR) method Return that causes the net present value to be zero

International banking When banks operate in more than one country

International Fisher effect (IFE) Currency of a country with a relatively lower nominal interest rate (due to a lower expected inflation rate) will have its currency appreciate relative to a country with a relatively higher interest rate

International Monetary Fund (IMF) Created to promote world trade through monitoring and maintaining fixed exchange rates and by making loans to countries facing balance of trade and payments problems

International monetary system A system of institutions and mechanisms to foster international trade, manage the flow of financial capital, and determine currency exchange rates

Intrinsic value The maximum price we should be willing to pay for an asset; the best estimate of the true economic value of an asset based upon a forecast of future cash flows and an estimate of the appropriate discount rate

Investment bank Helps businesses sell their new debt and equity securities to raise financial capital

Investment bankers (underwriters) Main activity is marketing securities and dealing with the securities markets

Investment banking firms Sell or market new securities issued by businesses to individual and institutional investors

Investment companies Sell shares in their firms to individuals and others and invest the pooled proceeds in corporate and government securities

Investment grade bonds Ratings of Baa or higher that meet financial institution investment standards

Investments Involve the sale or marketing of securities, the analysis of securities, and the management of investment risk through portfolio diversification

Junk bonds (high-yield bonds) Bonds with ratings that are below investment grade; that is Ba1, BB+, or lower

Liabilities Creditors' claims on a firm, which are the financial obligations of the business

Limit order Maximum buying price (limit buy) or the minimum selling price (limit sell) specified by the investor

Limited branch banking Allows additional banking offices within a geographically defined distance of a bank's main office

Limited liability company (LLC) An organizational form, similar to a subchapter S corporation, that offers owners limited liability; its income is taxed only once, as personal income of the shareholders, and the firm can have an unlimited number of shareholders

Limited partners Face limited liability to their investments in the firm, meaning their personal assets cannot be attached to settle the firm's debt

Limited partnership Has at least one general partner who has unlimited liability; the liability of the limited partners is limited to their investment

Line of credit Loan limit the bank establishes for each of its business customers

Liquidity The ease with which an asset can be exchanged for money or other assets

Liquidity preference theory Holds that investors or debt instrument holders prefer to invest short term so they have greater liquidity and less maturity or interest rate risk

Liquidity premium Compensation for those financial debt instruments that cannot easily be converted to cash at prices close to their estimated fair market values

Liquidity ratios Indicate the ability of the firm to meet short-term obligations as they come due

Liquidity risk Likelihood that a bank will be unable to meet its depositor withdrawal demands and/or other liabilities when they are due

Loan amortization schedule A schedule of the breakdown of each payment between interest and principal as well as the remaining balance after each payment

Loanable funds theory Holds that interest rates are a function of the supply of and demand for loanable funds

Lockbox system A system in which payments are sent to a P.O. Box and processed by a bank to reduce collection float

M1 money supply Consists of currency, travelers' checks, demand deposits, and other checkable deposits at depository institutions

M2 money supply M1 plus highly liquid financial assets, including savings accounts, small time deposits, and retail money market mutual funds (mmmfs)

Maintenance margin Minimum margin to which an investment may fall before a margin call will be placed

Mandatory spending Government spending on entitlement programs that must be funded according to existing law

Margin The ratio of the investor's equity (own money) to the market value of the security

Margin call The option of either closing out the position or investing additional cash to increase the position's equity or margin

Market interest rate Interest rate observed in the marketplace for a debt instrument

Market order An order for immediate purchase or sale at the best possible price

Market portfolio A portfolio that contains all risky assets

Market risk premium The slope of the security market line; represents the extra expected return from investing in the risky market portfolio rather than the risk-free asset

Market segmentation theory Holds that securities of different maturities are not perfect substitutes for one another

Market stabilization Intervention of the syndicate to buy back securities to prevent a larger price drop

Market timing hypothesis Firms time the market by issuing stock when their stock prices are high and repurchasing shares when their stock values are low

Market value added (MVA) Measures the value created by the firm's managers and equals the market value of the firm's liabilities and equity minus the amount of money investors paid to the firm when these securities were first issued

Market value ratios Indicate the willingness of investors to value a firm in the marketplace relative to financial statement values

Marketable government securities Securities that can be purchased and sold through customary market channels

Maturity factoring Firm selling its receivables is paid on the normal collection date or net due date of the account

Maturity risk premium The added return expected by lenders or investors because of interest rate risk on instruments with longer maturities

Maturity-matching approach Financing strategy that attempts to match the maturities of assets with the maturities of the liabilities with which they are financed

Medium of exchange The basic function of money

Merchandise trade balance The net difference between a country's import and export of goods

Mission statement Statement of a firm's main reason for being; sometimes called a vision statement

Mission, objectives, goals, and strategies (MOGS) A corporate planning tool that aids in developing project plans that fit well with a firm's plans

Modified internal rate of return (MIRR) method A technique that solves some of the problems presented by IRR. MIRR rankings of mutually exclusive projects with comparably sized initial investments will agree with the npv rankings of those projects

Monetary base (MB) Banking system reserves plus currency held by the public

Monetary policy Involves regulating the growth of the money supply and regulating its cost and availability

Monetizing the debt The Fed buys government securities, financing some of the deficit and providing additional reserves to the banking system, thus increasing the money supply

Money Physical or electronic asset accepted as payment for goods, services, and debts

Money market mutual funds (MMMFs) Issue shares to customers and invest the proceeds in highly liquid, short maturity, interest-bearing debt instruments called money market investments

Money market securities Debt instruments or securities with maturities of one year or less

Money markets Where debt securities with maturities of one year or less are issued and traded

Money multiplier (m) Number of times the monetary base can be expanded or magnified to produce a given money supply level

Mortgage Loan backed by real property in the form of buildings and houses

Mortgage banking firms Help individuals obtain mortgage loans by bringing together borrowers and institutional investors

Mortgage markets Where loans to purchase real estate (buildings and houses) are originated in primary markets and traded in secondary markets

Mortgage-backed security A debt security created by pooling together a group of mortgage loans whose periodic payments belong to the holders of the security

Multibank holding companies (MBHCs) Permits a firm to own and control two or more banks

Multinational corporation A firm that engages in international business activities such as the selling, or purchasing, of goods and services involving foreign countries

Municipal bond Debt instrument issued by a state or local government

Mutual funds Open-end investment companies that can issue an unlimited number of their shares to their investors and use the pooled proceeds to purchase corporate and government securities

Mutually exclusive projects A project that, when selected, precludes others from being undertaken

National debt   Total debt owed by a government

Negative correlation   When asset returns move in opposite directions

Negative interest rate   Occurs when a financial institution or government charges an amount greater than the interest it pays to depositors or debt security holders

Negotiable certificate of deposit (negotiable CD)   Short-term debt instrument issued by depository institutions to individual or institutional depositors

Net exports (NE)   Exports of goods and services minus imports

Net present value (NPV)   Present value of a project's cash flows minus its cost

Net working capital   Dollar amount of a firm's current assets minus current liabilities; sometimes used as a measure of liquidity

Nominal interest rate   Interest rate that is observed in the marketplace and that includes a premium for expected inflation

Noncumulative preferred stock   Makes no provision for the accumulation of past missed dividends

Nonmarketable government securities   Securities that cannot be transferred to other persons or institutions and can be redeemed only by being turned in to the U.S. government

NPV profile   The graphical relationship between a project's NPV and cost of capital

Odd lot   Sale or purchase of fewer than 100 shares

Offer price   Price at which the security is sold to the investors

One-bank holding companies (OBHCs)   Permits a firm to own and control one bank

Open-end mortgage bond   Allows the same assets to be used as security in future issues

Open-market operations   Buying and selling of securities in the open market by the Fed through its FOMC to alter bank reserves

Operating cycle   Measures the time between receiving raw materials and collecting cash from receivables

Opportunity cost   Cost of passing up the next best alternative

Optimum debt/equity mix   Proportionate use of debt and equity that minimizes the firm's cost of capital

Option   Financial contract that gives the owner the option of buying or selling a particular good at a specified price on or before a specified time or expiration date

Option premium   The price paid for the option

Option writer   Seller of an option contract

Order bill of lading   Represents the written acceptance of goods for shipment by a transportation company and the terms under which the goods are to be transported to their destination

Ordinary annuity   Equal payments (receipts) occur at the end of each time period

Out-of-the-money   An option with zero intrinsic value

Par value (face value)   Principal amount of a loan or bond that the issuer is obligated to repay at maturity

Participating preferred stock   Allows preferred shareholders to receive a larger dividend under certain conditions when common shareholder dividends increase

Partnership   A form of business organization that exists when two or more persons own a business operated for profit

Payback period method   Determines the time in years it will take to recover, or pay back, the initial investment in fixed assets

Pecking order hypothesis   A theory that states managers prefer to use additions to retained earnings to finance the firm, then debt, and (as a final resort) new equity

Pension funds   Receive contributions from employees and/or their employers and invest the proceeds on behalf of the employees

Personal consumption expenditures (PCE)   Expenditures by individuals for durable goods, nondurable goods, and services

Personal finance   Study of how individuals prepare for financial emergencies, protect against premature death and the loss of property, and accumulate wealth over time

Personal saving   Savings of individuals equal to personal income less personal current taxes less personal outlays

Pledging (pledge)   Obtain a short-term loan by using accounts receivable as collateral

Poison pills   Provisions in a corporate charter that make a corporate takeover more unattractive

Political risk   The risk associated with the possibility that a national government might confiscate or expropriate assets held by foreigners

Portfolio   Any combination of financial assets or investments

Positive correlation   When asset returns move together over time

Pre-authorized checks   Regular (typically monthly) deductions by a vendor from a customer's checking account

Precautionary motives   Holding funds to meet unexpected demands

Preferred stock   Equity security that has preference, or a senior claim, to the firm's earnings and assets over common stock

Premium bond   Bond that is selling in excess of its par value

Present value   Amount or value today of a savings or an investment

Primary deposit   The deposit of a check drawn on the Fed; it adds new reserves to the bank where deposited and to the banking system

Primary markets   Where the initial offering or origination of debt and equity securities takes place

Primary reserves   Vault cash and deposits held at other depository institutions and at Federal Reserve banks

Prime mortgage   A home loan to a borrower with relatively high creditworthiness indicating a relatively high likelihood that mortgage payments will be made when due

Prime rate   Interest rate charged by banks for short-term unsecured loans to a bank's highest-quality (most creditworthy) business customers

Principal-agent problem   A problem in corporate governance in which conflict of interest occurs between the principals and agents

Principals   Owners of the firm

Private placement   Sale of securities to a small group of private investors

Processing float   Delays in processing incoming payments from customers by the receiving firm

Profitability index (PI) (benefit/cost ratio)   Ratio between the present values of the inflows and the outflows

Profitability ratios Indicate the firm's ability to generate returns on its sales, assets, and equity

Program trading Technique for trading stocks as a group rather than individually; a minimum of 15 different stocks with a minimum value of $1 million are traded

Proprietorship (sole proprietorship) A business venture owned by an individual who personally receives all profits and assumes all responsibility for the debts and losses of the business

Prospectus Highly regulated document that details the issuer's operations and finances and must be provided to each buyer of a newly issued security

Public offering Sale of securities to the investing public

Purchasing power Amount of goods and services that can be purchased with a unit of money

Purchasing power parity (PPP) States that a country with a relatively higher expected inflation rate will have its currency depreciate relative to a country (or group of countries using a single currency) with a relatively lower inflation rate

Purchasing power risk Changes in inflation affect revenues, expenses, and profitability

Put option Contract for the sale of securities within a specific time period and at a specified price

Putable bonds (retractable bonds) Allow the investor to force the issuer to redeem the bonds prior to maturity

Quantitative easing (QE) A nontraditional monetary policy designed to stimulate economic activity when conventional monetary policy methods are ineffective

Random walk Prices appear to fluctuate randomly over time, driven by the random arrival of new information

Ratio analysis Financial technique that involves dividing various financial statement numbers into one another

Real assets Include the direct ownership of land, buildings or homes, equipment, inventories, durable goods, and precious metals

Real rate of interest Interest rate on a risk-free debt instrument when no inflation is expected

Registered bonds Bonds issued in the United States and for which the issuer knows the names of the bondholders, and the interest payments are sent directly to the bondholder

Registered traders Individuals who purchase a seat on the exchange to buy and sell stocks for their own account

Regulation Z Enacts the truth in lending section of the Consumer Credit Protection Act with the intent to make consumers aware of and able to compare costs of alternate forms of credit

Reinvestment rate risk (rollover risk) Fluctuating interest rates cause coupon or interest payments to be reinvested at different interest rates over time

Remote capture Scanning of paper checks to electronically gather and transmit the payment information

Representative full-bodied money Paper money that is backed by an amount of precious metal equal in value to the face amount of the paper money

Repurchase agreement Short-term debt security sold by a business firm or financial institution to another business or institution where the seller agrees to repurchase the security at a specified price and date

Required reserves Minimum amount of reserves that a depository institution must hold against its deposit liabilities

Required reserves ratio Percentage of deposits that must be held as reserves by a depository institution

Residual dividend policy A policy that states that dividends will vary based upon how much excess funds the firm has from year to year

Restricted stock Shares of stock, awarded to managers, which vest, or become saleable, after a stated number of years, typically three to five

Retention rate The proportion of each dollar of earnings per share that is retained by the firm

Revolving credit agreement (revolver) A commitment in the form of a standby agreement for a guaranteed line of credit; a legal obligation of the bank to provide up to the agreed-upon borrowing limit during the time the agreement is in effect

Risk-adjusted discount rate (RADR) Adjusts the required rate of return at which the analyst discounts a project's cash flows based on the project's risk

Risk-free rate of interest The combination of real rate of interest and the inflation premium, which in the United States is represented by U.S. Treasury debt instruments or securities

Round lot Sale or purchase of 100 shares

Rule of 72 A shortcut method used to approximate the time required for an investment to double in value

Savings Occur when all of an economic unit's income is not consumed and are represented by the accumulation of cash and other financial assets

Savings and loan associations (S&Ls) Accept individual savings and lend pooled savings to individuals, primarily in the form of mortgage loans, and to businesses

Savings banks Accept the savings of individuals and lend pooled savings to individuals, primarily in the form of mortgage loans

Savings deficit Occurs when an economic unit's direct investment in real assets exceeds current income

Savings surplus Occurs when an economic unit, such as individuals taken as a group, has current income that exceeds its direct investment in real assets

Savings-investment process Involves the direct or indirect transfer of individual savings to business firms in exchange for their debt or stock securities

Secondary markets Physical locations or electronic forums where debt (bonds and mortgages) and equity securities are traded

Secondary reserves Short-term securities held by banks that are quickly converted into cash at little cost to the banks

Secured lending (asset-based lending) Collateral or security backing the loan that can be claimed or sold by the lender if the borrower defaults

Secured loan Loan backed by collateral

Securities firms Accept and invest individual savings and also facilitate the sale and transfer of securities between investors

Securitization Process of pooling and packaging mortgage loans into debt securities

Selection stage Applies appropriate capital budgeting techniques to make a final accept or reject decision

Semistrong-form efficient market A market in which all public information, past and current, is reflected in asset prices

Settlement price Daily approximate closing price of a futures contract as decided by a special exchange committee

Shelf registration Allows firms to register security issues (both debt and equity) with the SEC and have them available to sell for two years

Short sale Sale of securities that the seller does not own

Short-term investment policy statement Guidelines that detail the type of securities the treasurer can invest in, their safety or default rating, maximum amounts that can be invested in each, and the maximum maturity of the securities purchased

Sight draft An instrument requiring immediate payment

Simple interest Interest earned only on the investment's principal

Sinking fund Requirement that the issuer retire specified portions of the bond issue over time

Sinking fund payments Periodic bond principal repayments

Special dividend An extra dividend declared by the firm over and above its regular dividend payout

Special drawing rights (SDRs) Reserve assets created by the IMF and consisting of a basket or portfolio of currencies that could be used to make international payments

Speculative inflation Caused by the expectation that prices will continue to rise, resulting in increased buying to avoid even higher future prices

Speculative motives Holding marketable securities to take advantage of unusual cash discounts or price bargains on materials if it can pay quickly with cash

Speculative value or time value of an option Difference between the option premium and its intrinsic value; it is larger the longer the time to expiration and the higher the underlying stock's price volatility

Spot exchange rate Current rate being quoted for delivery of the currency on the spot

Spot market The cash market for trading securities; where securities are bought and sold

Spread (1) Difference between the bid and ask prices; (2) difference between the offer price and the price paid by the investment bank

Stand-alone principle Analysis focuses on the project's own cash flows, uncontaminated by cash flows from the firm's other activities

Standard deviation The square root of the variance

Standard of value Prices and contracts for deferred payments are expressed in terms of the monetary unit

Statement of cash flows Provides a summary of the cash inflows (sources) and cash outflows (uses) during a specified accounting period

Statewide branch banking Allows banks to operate offices throughout a state

Static trade-off hypothesis A theory that states firms will balance the advantages of debt with its disadvantages

Stock certificate Certificate showing an ownership claim of a specific company

Stock dividend A dividend in which investors receive shares of stock rather than cash

Stock options Allow managers to purchase, at a future time, a stated number of the firm's shares at a specific price

Stock split A process in which the firms distributes additional shares for every share owned

Stop-loss order Order to sell stock at the market price when the price of the stock falls to a specified level

Store of value Money held for some period of time before it is spent

Street name An investor's stock certificates are kept electronically at the brokerage firm rather than investor taking personal possession of them

Strike price (exercise price) Price at which the asset can be traded under an option contract

SWOT analysis A review of a firm's internal strengths and weaknesses and its external opportunities and threats

Strong-form efficient market A market in which prices reflect all knowledge, including past and current publicly known and private information

Subchapter S corporation Has 100 or fewer shareholders, none of which is another corporation; its income flows untaxed to the shareholders and is taxed only once, as personal income of the shareholders

Subordinate debenture Claims of these bonds are subordinate or junior to the claims of the debenture holders

Subprime mortgage Home loan made to a borrower with a relatively poor credit score indicating a higher likelihood that the borrower will miss mortgage payments when due

Sunk cost Project-related expense not dependent upon whether or not the project is undertaken

Supplemental Liquidity Providers (SLPs) Help add liquidity to the NYSE trading floor, meaning they supplement the work of DMMs by buying and selling shares throughout the day

Surplus economic unit Generates more money than it spends, and thus, it has excess money to save or invest

Sustainable growth rate The estimate of how quickly a firm can grow when it uses internal equity and debt financing to keep its capital structure constant over time

Syndicate Group of several investment banking firms that participate in the underwriting and distributing a security issue

Systematic risk (market risk) Risk that is inherent in the macro economy and cannot be eliminated through diversification

Target dividend payout policy A policy of adjusting the dividend payout dollar amount toward the target dividend payout ratio

Tax motives The motive to hold cash outside of the United States due to high U.S. corporate tax rates for bringing cash from overseas profits back into the United States

Tax policy Sets the level and structure of taxes to affect the economy

Tax risk Variations in a firm's tax rate and tax-related charges over time due to changing tax laws and regulations

Term structure Indicates the relationship between interest rates or yields and the maturity of comparable quality debt instruments

Third market Market for large blocks of listed stocks that operates outside the confines of the organized exchanges

Thrift institutions Noncommercial bank depository institutions referred to as savings and loan associations, savings banks, and credit unions that accumulate individual savings and lend primarily to other individuals

Time draft An instrument requiring payment at a later date

Time value or speculative value of an option Difference between the option premium and its intrinsic value; it is larger the longer the time to expiration and the higher the underlying stock's price volatility

Time value of money Math of finance whereby a financial return is earned over time by saving or investing money

Token coins Coins with face values higher than the value of their metal content

Tombstones Announcements of securities offerings to be placed in newspapers and other publications

Trade credit Credit extended on purchases to a firm's customers

Trade discounts Provided to purchasers as an incentive for prompt payment of bills

Trade tariff Tax on imports of goods and services

Transactions motive Demand for holding cash needed to conduct day-to-day operations

Transfer payments Government payments for which no current productive services is rendered

Traveler's letter of credit Issued by a bank in one country and addressed to a list of foreign banks, which have agreed to purchase sight drafts presented to them by persons with appropriate letters of credit

Treasurer Oversees the traditional functions of financial analysis, including capital budgeting, short-term and long-term financing decisions, and current asset management

Treasury bills Federal debt obligations issued with maturities up to one year

Treasury bonds Federal obligations issued with original maturities in excess of 10 years, often issued for 20 and sometimes even 30 years

Treasury notes Federal obligations usually issued for maturities of 2 to 10 years

Trend analysis (time series analysis) Used to evaluate a firm's performance over time

Trust indenture An extensive document and details the various provisions and covenants of the loan arrangement

Trust receipt (1) An instrument through which a bank retains title to goods until they are paid for; (2) lien against specific identifiable items in inventory; whereby the bank retains ownership of the goods until they are sold in the regular course of business

Trustee Represents the bondholders to ensure the bond issuer respects the indenture's provisions

Underpricing Represents the difference between the aftermarket stock price and the offering price

Underwriting agreement Contract in which the investment banker agrees to buy securities at a predetermined price and then resell them to investors

Undistributed profits (earnings retained in the business) Profits remaining after taxes and, in the case of corporations, after the cash dividends are paid to stockholders

Unit banking Exists when a bank can have only one full-service office

Universal bank Bank that engages in commercial banking and investment banking

Unsecured loan Loan that is a general claim against the assets of the borrower

Unsystematic risk Risk that can be diversified away as assets are added to a portfolio. Also known as firm-specific risk or industry-specific risk

Usury The act of lending money at an excessively high interest rate

Variance Derived by summing the squared deviations and dividing by $n - 1$

Velocity of money Measures the rate of circulation of the money supply; the average number of times each dollar is spent on purchases of goods and services and is calculated as nominal GDP (GDP in current dollars) divided by M1

Virtual currency Unregulated digital money issued, and often controlled, by its decentralized developers and used to make electronic payments

Voluntary savings Savings in the form of financial assets held or set aside for use in the future

Warehouse receipt A receipt issued by the warehouse indicating inventory is placed in a bonded warehouse for safekeeping; items are removed as they are paid for

Weak-form efficient market Market in which prices reflect all past information, such as information in last year's annual report, previous earnings announcements, and other past news

Weighted average cost of capital (WACC) Represents the minimum required rate of return on a capital-budgeting project; it is found by multiplying the marginal cost of each capital structure component by its appropriate weight and summing the terms

Working capital A firm's current assets, which consist of cash, marketable securities, accounts receivable, and inventories

World Bank Created to help economic growth in developing countries (also called the International Bank for Reconstruction and Development)

Yankee bonds Dollar-denominated bonds issued in the United States by a foreign issuer

Yield curve Graphic presentation of the term structure of interest rates at a given point in time

Yield to maturity (YTM) Return on a bond investment if it is held to maturity

Zero-balance account An account in which just enough funds are transferred into an account to cover that day's checks presented for payment

Zero-coupon bond Has no coupon payments; its only cash return to the investor is payment of the bond's principal, or par value, at maturity

Index